The Oxford Handbook of Multimethod
and Mixed Methods Research Inquiry

OXFORD LIBRARY OF PSYCHOLOGY

OXFORD LIBRARY OF PSYCHOLOGY

Editor in Chief **PETER E. NATHAN**

The Oxford Handbook of Multimethod and Mixed Methods Research Inquiry

Edited by

Sharlene Hesse-Biber

R. Burke Johnson

march, 2019

Kayla —
what a pleasure to have
you in our class — &
appreciate you ideas &
insights into mixed
methods research!
My best wishes,
Sharlene

OXFORD
UNIVERSITY PRESS

OXFORD
UNIVERSITY PRESS

Oxford University Press is a department of the University of
Oxford. It furthers the University's objective of excellence in research,
scholarship, and education by publishing worldwide.

Oxford   New York
Auckland   Cape Town   Dar es Salaam   Hong Kong   Karachi
Kuala Lumpur   Madrid   Melbourne   Mexico City   Nairobi
New Delhi   Shanghai   Taipei   Toronto

With offices in
Argentina   Austria   Brazil   Chile   Czech Republic   France   Greece
Guatemala   Hungary   Italy   Japan   Poland   Portugal   Singapore
South Korea   Switzerland   Thailand   Turkey   Ukraine   Vietnam

Oxford is a registered trademark of Oxford University Press
in the UK and certain other countries.

Published in the United States of America by
Oxford University Press
198 Madison Avenue, New York, NY 10016

Library of Congress Cataloging-in-Publication Data
The Oxford handbook of multimethod and mixed methods research inquiry / edited by Sharlene Hesse-Biber and R. Burke
Johnson.
    pages cm.—(Oxford library of psychology)
Includes index.
ISBN 978–0–19–993362–4
1. Social sciences—Research—Methodology.   I. Hesse-Biber, Sharlene Nagy.   II. Johnson, Burke.
H62.O947 2015
001.4′2—dc23
2014035160

9 8 7 6 5 4 3 2 1
Printed in the United States of America
on acid-free paper

I dedicate this *Handbook* to the multimethod and mixed methods community in hopes that this work will promote dialogue respectively across the range of MMMR divides seeking to learn from one another. The *Handbook* is also dedicated to my dearest sister, Janet Green Fisher, whose youthful life was cut short by breast cancer.

Sharlene Hesse-Biber

To my mom, Hilda Faith Shelton Johnson (1915–2012), and my father, Thomas Butt Johnson (1907–1986), for giving me the values that will always drive my life and work.

R. Burke Johnson

SHORT CONTENTS

OXFORD LIBRARY OF PSYCHOLOGY

The *Oxford Library of Psychology,* a landmark series of handbooks, is published by Oxford University Press, one of the world's oldest and most highly respected publishers, with a tradition of publishing significant books in psychology. The ambitious goal of the *Oxford Library of Psychology* is nothing less than to span a vibrant, wide-ranging field and, in so doing, to fill a clear market need.

Encompassing a comprehensive set of handbooks, organized hierarchically, the *Library* incorporates volumes at different levels, each designed to meet a distinct need. At one level are a set of handbooks designed broadly to survey the major subfields of psychology; at another are numerous handbooks that cover important current focal research and scholarly areas of psychology in depth and detail. Planned as a reflection of the dynamism of psychology, the *Library* will grow and expand as psychology itself develops, thereby highlighting significant new research that will impact on the field. Adding to its accessibility and ease of use, the *Library* will be published in print and, later on, electronically.

The *Library* surveys psychology's principal subfields with a set of handbooks that capture the current status and future prospects of those major subdisciplines. This initial set includes handbooks of social and personality psychology, clinical psychology, counseling psychology, school psychology, educational psychology, industrial and organizational psychology, cognitive psychology, cognitive neuroscience, methods and measurements, history, neuropsychology, personality assessment, developmental psychology, and more. Each handbook undertakes to review one of psychology's major subdisciplines with breadth, comprehensiveness, and exemplary scholarship. In addition to these broadly conceived volumes, the *Library* also includes a large number of handbooks designed to explore in depth more specialized areas of scholarship and research, such as stress, health and coping, anxiety and related disorders, cognitive development, or child and adolescent assessment. In contrast to the broad coverage of the subfield handbooks, each of these latter volumes focuses on an especially productive, more highly focused line of scholarship and research. Whether at the broadest or most specific level, however, all of the *Library* handbooks offer synthetic coverage that reviews and evaluates the relevant past and present research and anticipates research in the future. Each handbook in the *Library* includes introductory and concluding chapters written by its editor to provide a roadmap to the handbook's table of contents and to offer informed anticipations of significant future developments in that field.

An undertaking of this scope calls for handbook editors and chapter authors who are established scholars in the areas about which they write. Many of the nation's and world's most productive and best-respected psychologists have agreed to edit *Library* handbooks or write authoritative chapters in their areas of expertise.

For whom has the *Oxford Library of Psychology* been written? Because of its breadth, depth, and accessibility, the *Library* serves a diverse audience, including graduate students in psychology and their faculty mentors, scholars, researchers, and practitioners in psychology and related fields. Each will find in the *Library* the information they seek on the subfield or focal area of psychology in which they work or are interested.

Befitting its commitment to accessibility, each handbook includes a comprehensive index, as well as extensive references to help guide research. And because the *Library* was designed from its inception as an online as well as a print resource, its structure and contents will be readily and rationally searchable online. Further, once the *Library* is released online, the handbooks will be regularly and thoroughly updated.

In summary, the *Oxford Library of Psychology* will grow organically to provide a thoroughly informed perspective on the field of psychology, one that reflects both psychology's dynamism and its increasing interdisciplinarity. Once published electronically, the *Library* is also destined to become a uniquely valuable interactive tool, with extended search and browsing capabilities. As you begin to consult this handbook, we sincerely hope you will share our enthusiasm for the more than 500-year tradition of Oxford University Press for excellence, innovation, and quality, as exemplified by the *Oxford Library of Psychology*.

Peter E. Nathan
Editor-in-Chief
Oxford Library of Psychology

ABOUT THE EDITORS

Sharlene Hesse-Biber

Sharlene Janice Nagy Hesse-Biber is professor of sociology and the director of the Women's and Gender Studies Program at Boston College in Chestnut Hill, Massachusetts. She has published widely on the impact of sociocultural factors on women's body image, including her book *Am I Thin Enough Yet? The Cult of Thinness and the Commercialization of Identity* (Oxford, 1996), which was selected as one of *Choice* magazine's best academic books for 1996. She recently published *The Cult of Thinness* (Oxford, 2007). She is the coauthor of *Working Women in America: Split Dreams* (Oxford, 2000, 2005). She is coeditor of *Feminist Approaches to Theory and Methodology: An Interdisciplinary Reader* (Oxford, 1999), *Approaches to Qualitative Research: A Reader on Theory and Practice* (Oxford, 2004), and *Emergent Methods in Social Research* (SAGE, 2006). She is coauthor of *The Practice of Qualitative Research* (SAGE, 2006; second edition, 2010). She is editor of the *Handbook of Feminist Research: Theory and Praxis* (SAGE, 2007, 2012), which was selected as one of the Critics' Choice Award winners by the American Education Studies Association and was also chosen as one of *Choice* Magazine's Outstanding Academic titles for 2007. She is editor of *Feminist Research Practice: A Primer* (SAGE, 2014). She is coeditor of the *Handbook of Emergent Methods* (Guilford, 2008). She is a contributor to the *Handbook of Grounded Theory* (SAGE, 2008) as well the *SAGE Handbook of Mixed Methods Research* (SAGE, 2nd edition, 2010). She is author of *Mixed Methods Research: Merging Theory with Practice* (Guilford, 2010). She has recently published a monograph, *Waiting for Cancer to Come: Genetic Testing and Women's Medical Decision Making for Breast and Ovarian Cancer* (University of Michigan Press, 2014). She is codeveloper of the software program HyperRESEARCH, a computer-assisted program for analyzing qualitative data, and the new transcription tool HyperTRANSCRIBE. A fully functional free demo of these programs is available at www.researchware.com. This website provides links to a free teaching edition for both programs.

R. Burke Johnson

R. Burke Johnson is a professor in the Department of Professional Studies at the University of South Alabama. He earned his PhD from the Research, Evaluation, Measurement, and Statistics Program at the University of Georgia. He also has master's degrees in psychology, sociology, and public administration/public policy, providing him a multidisciplinary perspective on theory and research methodology. He is coauthor or coeditor of six books (including the present handbook). He was guest editor for two special issues on mixed methods research, one for the *American Behavioral Scientist* and the other for *Research in the Schools* (http://www.msera.org/rits_131.htm). He was on the editorial board of the *Educational Researcher* and was an associate editor of the *Journal of Mixed Methods Research* in its early years. Burke is interested in all areas of methodology, including its history and the philosophy of social science.

The Handbook's Vision: Casting a Wide Net

The Oxford Handbook Multimethod and Mixed Methods Research Inquiry will focus its lens on the part of the research landscape where multimethod and mixed methods research (MMMR) resides. The *Handbook* is designed to offer a range of knowledge-building perspectives and tools to the research community who wish to traverse this landscape. The *Handbook* is not prescriptive but rather aims to "cast a wide net" with the goals of enhancing new ways of asking complex questions and providing valuable and innovative perspectives and tools to get at these questions. The goal is to promote a multiple theoretical and interdisciplinary vision and praxis by covering a range of theoretical approaches to mixed methods research (MMR) from qualitative-interpretative paradigms to quantitative-postpositivist perspectives. While the *Handbook* suggests strategies for navigating the MMMR landscape, it resists dogmatism by insisting there is no single "right answer" to any of the challenges and questions posed by the landscape.

The theoretical and practice framework stresses the importance of maintaining a tight linkage between theory and method. This linkage will avoid a methods-centric approach to MMMR and encourage researchers to begin by concentrating on the research problem and its foundational substructure. All research is rooted in a point of view, and being conscious of this focus is critical to understanding how to use any research methods tools, including MMMR designs.

This project is a place for acknowledging points of disagreement, convergence, and sometimes contention as well as conciliatory views that exist within and between diverse multimethod and mixed methods communities. The *Handbook* provides a space for voices at both the center and the margins of discourse on multimethod and mixed methods knowledge-building. To gain legitimacy for knowledge-building, it is critical to remain open to new ideas and be willing to dialogue across differences. For example, to what extent is our community of knowledge-builders responsive to others' versions of reality? Dialoguing across differences serves to draw on the strengths of diversity—not to divide but to help multimethod and mixed methods researchers combine their quests to uncover complex issues. In doing so, we may produce more authentic and trustworthy research that can lead to the betterment of society. The *Handbook* is a resource for supporting these research goals.

The *Handbook* is thus positioned to offer the research community a range of critical and emerging perspectives and insights on all parts of the research process without privileging any one type of knowledge-building. It also provides a set of *cautionary tales* that are not often discussed among those who already inhabit the MMMR landscape. It offers strategies for communication and knowledge-building in this landscape, especially regarding how to communicate across a range of differences (disciplinary, paradigmatic, methods, analytical, interpretative).

The Handbook Structure

Before proceeding with a brief walk-through of the *Handbook* contents, we want to stress that each chapter is intended to reach out to a range of readers: (a) researchers who come from a wide range of disciplines and practitioners within and outside the academy who seek to use "cutting-edge" MMMR approaches that can provide them with insights into the overall research process; this group also includes policymakers and activists who are interested in *how* to conduct research for social change; (b) academics seeking new perspectives on their teaching of research methods in their upper-level undergraduate and graduate-level research methods courses; (c) graduate students and upper-division undergraduates who wish to find out more about the field of MMMR and the range of new, cutting-edge perspectives and critiques. The variety of uses of this *Handbook* required careful consideration by the authors in chapter organization and writing style. The following were the goals we strove to achieve. For practitioners and policymakers, the *Handbook* chapters are written in as much "nontechnical" language as possible. The chapters wherever possible seek to address ongoing debates in the field, practical applications, and relevant issues for research that impacts social policy and social change.

For academics, the *Handbook* reflects the most current thinking about MMMR emerging within and across the disciplines. Each chapter is structured to include research examples that cross a range of disciplines, as well as interdisciplinary research settings. For faculty and students using the *Handbook* in their courses, chapter content (concepts/ideas) is grounded with specific examples from the literature. The chapter content also stresses the diversity of research scholarship in a given area, and some chapters take on a specific global focus. For social activists, some chapters specifically address the ongoing power relationships in which research is practiced and used and also provide methods and strategies for social change. The book is organized into five parts, each of which has a specific focus.

Part One: Linking Theory and Method in Multimethod and Mixed Methods Research

The chapters in Part One provide explanations of some important foundational issues and perspectives in the field of MMMR. The authors discuss the critical linkage between theoretical approaches and methods practices. Each chapter emphasizes the importance of considering the philosophical substructure of MMMR projects and provides some concrete case-study examples across the disciplines with regard to the application of a given theoretical perspective in the praxis of MMMR research.

In Chapter 1, Sharlene Hesse-Biber, Deborah Rodriguez, and Nollaig A. Frost discuss the range of meanings regarding " A Qualitatively Driven Approach to

Multimethod and Mixed Methods Research." Their objective is to look at the types of reasons researchers might deploy in their work and what specific questions interface well with this approach. They provide in-depth case studies of the applications of a qualitatively driven MMMR approach across a range of research and disciplinary and interdisciplinary perspectives.

In Chapter 2, Melvin M. Mark looks at quantitatively driven mixed methods designs. Melvin M. Mark clarifies distinctions between mixed methods and multimethod research and then explains the many different ways in which MMMR can be employed in a quantitatively driven study. The chapter points out that there is a long history of mixing methods, prior to mixed methods literature, and this literature can be useful. There is judgment required to decide which aspects of a study to mix or make multiple, and it is important to put the research question as the forefront of the study rather than the methods.

In Chapter 3, "Thinking Outside the Q Boxes," Lisa D. Pearce argues that social inquiry need not be tightly bound and limited by placing inquiry into two conceptual boxes labeled "qualitative" and "quantitative." Multimethod and mixed methods research is often seen as combining or integrating things from each box. Pearce argues that there are many ways researchers can reach across these conceptual divides through a range of dialogical processes that can open up space for innovation and creativity in research inquiry that is "holistic" in character. She advocates for a "mixed research" model for breaking out of the qualitative/quantitative binary and viewing these two modes of inquiry lying along a continuum.

In Chapter 4, John W. Creswell revisits his long history in designing and conducting mixed methods with the goal of advancing scientific practices. He presents 10 scientific practices that have emerged in the past decade that signal the arrival of mixed methods as a "science." His central thesis is that to best reach a practical audience that seeks to conduct this form of inquiry, a focus on scientific practices needs to occur. This chapter identifies these practices, explains the recent literature on each, and highlights significant articles that illustrate these practices.

In Chapter 5, "Feminist Approaches to Multimethod and Mixed Methods Research: Theory and Praxis," authors Sharlene Hesse-Biber and Amy J. Griffin explore the evolution of feminist perspectives across the decades. They first introduce the specific goals of feminist praxis and how feminist researchers aim to unearth subjugated knowledge and empower marginalized populations. They go on to examine the different methods, both quantitative and qualitative, feminist researchers employ and how they mix methods to develop a nuanced understanding of lived experience of women and other oppressed groups. They provide in-depth examples and case studies that use a feminist approach to multimethod and mixed methods that specifically link theory with methods.

In Chapter 6, "Transformative and Indigenous Frameworks for Multimethod and Mixed Methods Research," Fiona Cram and Donna M. Mertens critically examine the philosophical and theoretical stances that are associated with addressing issues of social transformation and Indigenous rights through the use of MMMR. They identify the application of transformative principles and Indigenous approaches in the design of MMMR studies from a variety of sectors and countries. They evaluate arguments related to the role of MMMR with regard to facilitating issues of human rights and social justice.

In Chapter 7, Olena Hankivisky and Daniel Grace analyze and emphasize difference and intersectionality in "Understanding and Emphasizing Difference and Intersectionality in Multimethod and Mixed Methods Research." They provide an overview of intersectionality, specifically looking at its research questions and principles, and they analyze both quantitative and qualitative intersectionality informed approaches. The authors use HIV and education research as case studies to show how researchers use intersectionality in mixed methods projects.

In Chapter 8, "Interdisciplinary and Transdisciplinary Multimethod and Mixed Methods Research," Rick Szostak encourages collaboration between interdisciplinary and MMMR researchers. He compares and contrasts the insights of interdisciplinarity and transdisciplinarity and then draws insights from these literatures for MMMR approaches.

In Chapter 9, "Putting Ethics on the Mixed Methods Map," Judith Preissle, Rebecca M. Glover-Kudon, Elizabeth A. Rohan, Jennifer E. Boehm, and Amy DeGroff examine ethics in MMR by assessing the current literature. They also discuss and provide examples of ethical challenges and issues that arise in all phases of MMR. Last, the chapter explores how MMR may help provide flexibility to make ethical and moral decisions.

Part Two: Conducting Exploratory, Confirmatory, and Interactive Multimethod and Mixed Methods Research

The second part of the *Handbook* focuses on the variety of issues and problems researchers confront in their practice of mixing theoretical approaches across the research process. How does adding a new method change the nature of research praxis? We highlight some of the most important of these general "praxis" issues, as researchers hailing from a range of different theoretical perspectives begin to apply MMMR designs in the service of answering their research questions.

In Chapter 10, Jennifer Leeman, Corrine I. Voils, and Margarete Sandelowski look at mixed methods literature reviews and how they can be synthesized and used as evidence to contribute to complex social and health interventions. The authors illustrate and give examples of how mixed methods literature reviews have been applied to complex interventions. Some of the challenges that arise, as well as suggestions for overcoming them, are also discussed.

Albert Hunter and John Brewer focus on "Designing Multimethod Research" in Chapter 11. The chapter first gives a historical timeline of quantitative, qualitative, and multimethod research approaches. The authors describe the many different ways multimethod research can be carried out, such as combinations of quantitative approaches, qualitative approaches, or a mixture of quantitative and qualitative approaches. By the end of the chapter, the reader should also understand the "enacted" and "emergent" aspects of research design and understand the difference between contextual and structural effects in research.

In Chapter 12, Janice M. Morse provides a detailed analytical frame for looking at "Issues in Qualitatively Driven Mixed-Method Designs: Walking Through a Mixed-Method Project." Morse takes the reader through a qualitatively driven mixed method design from idea to completion. Using a hypothetical project, she illustrates the process and discusses strategies for maintaining rigor in mixed methods designs, such as theoretical drive, pacing, and diagramming. The chapter also helps the reader navigate pitfalls and issues that may arise when using qualitative methods and discusses how to surmount the difficulties.

Chapter 13, "Designing Integration in Multimethod and Mixed Methods Research," explores the research design in a mixed or multimethod study. Authors Joseph Maxwell, Margaret Chmiel, and Sylvia E. Rogers want the reader to understand how to integrate multiple models in their work, as well as how to draw conclusions and test interpretations from integrating qualitative and quantitative data. Because there is still some lack of understanding about integrating approaches and methods, the authors suggest researchers should consider writing about their experiences more.

Chapter 14, "Validity in Multimethod and Mixed Research," Kathleen M. T. Collins explores the understanding of integration as a defining characteristic of MMMR. She also emphasizes the importance of clarity of language when discussing this methodology. The chapter looks at the key attributes of defining validity across the different research paradigms, and determining the combination of validity types relevant for each research study.

Julia Brannen and Rebecca O'Connell identify the ways in which data from mixed methods research can be integrated in Chapter 15, "Data Analysis I: Overview of Data Analysis Strategies." The chapter enables the reader to consider issues that are likely to affect the analysis of mixed methods research, and it identifies ways MMMR can be integrated to give examples of different strategies. Using a particular type of MMMR in which national survey data are analyzed along with a qualitative study, the authors examine the complexities of analyzing data when integrating qualitative and quantitative data.

In Chapter 16, Tony J. Onwuegbuzie and John H. Hitchcock take another look at data analysis in mixed methods research. Their chapter, "Advanced Mixed Analysis Approaches," outlines advanced mixed analysis approaches and introduces a conceptual framework called *crossover mixed analysis*. The authors discuss this framework and how it can be used for many different research philosophies.

In Chapter 17, Pat Bazeley discusses how to write up a MMMR project. She encourages researchers to integrate the mixed and multimethod results in the presentation rather than separating results. She uses examples and gives strategies for researchers to do this throughout her chapter, "Writing Up Multimethod and Mixed Methods Research for Diverse Audiences."

In Chapter 18, Jennifer P. Wisdom and Michael D. Fetters discuss specific strategies and proposals for funding mixed methods research. "Funding for Mixed Methods Research: Sources and Strategies" describes how to interpret sponsors' funding opportunities in order to prepare a strong MMR project proposal that has a high probability of being funded. The chapter also provides insights for how applications are evaluated and how to interpret reviewers' feedback to strengthen proposals.

The last chapter in this section, Chapter 19, is "Mentoring the Next Generation in Mixed Methods Research." Rebecca K. Frels, Isadore Newman, and Carole Newman's chapter identifies some key considerations in mentoring practices. Through the use of first-person mentoring accounts, they demonstrate how mentoring praxis in MMR involves a humanistic process. They provide a specific framework for how to supervise and mentor the next generation of mixed methods researchers from a humanistic standpoint.

Part Three: Contextualizing Multimethod and Mixed Methods Research Within and Across Disciplines and Applied Settings

In Part Three, we address how mixed and multimethod designs are practiced across the disciplines and in applied research settings. What types of research issues and problems are addressed within these disciplinary borders? With what results? What are some of the particular issues that researchers in applied settings confront as they integrate MMMR into their research? What are some of the specific techniques used in these specific disciplines and settings?

Chapter 20 starts off Part Three with "Multimethod and Mixed Methods Research in the Fields of Education and Anthropology" by Jori N. Hall and Judith Preissle. The authors consider the differences and similarities of research in education and anthropology and how mixed methods approaches in these fields can contribute to social services. After looking at the evolution of research in these fields, the authors talk about ways that mixed and multimethod approaches can be applied to the fields of education and anthropology, and they identify key challenges of conducting this type of research in the specified fields. Last, the chapter explores the future of how MMMR will be reconstructed and applied in education and anthropology research.

In Chapter 21, "Evolving Mixed and Multimethod Approaches in Psychology," Nollaig A. Frost and Rachel L. Shaw first identify why method has become so important for psychology. They proceed to help the reader understand how and why psychology has demanded more complex and nuanced insights into human behavior, requiring both qualitative and quantitative approaches. They also consider the emergence of mixed methods such as Q methodology and pragmatism in psychology.

Bradley D. Olson and Leonard A. Jason describe participatory MMR in Chapter 22, "Participatory Mixed Methods Research." They illustrate how this approach is used with a community-based network of resident-run recovery homes for substance abuse. University researchers paired up with a self-help organization for over 20 years to investigate what occurs in the recovery homes. The mixed quantitative and qualitative methods gave both the community members and the researchers a richer understanding of what was going on in these recovery homes. The chapter points out advantages of mixed-group methods and the future directions for this type of a participatory framework.

Chapter 23, "Moving from Randomized Controlled Trials to Mixed Methods Intervention Evaluations," explores why mixed methods intervention evaluations are needed and the different ways they can be carried out. Sarah J. Drabble and

Alicia O'Cathain also note some of the challenges and solutions when undertaking mixed methods intervention evaluations.

Donna M. Mertens and Michelle Tarsilla describe the history of mixed methods evaluation and why mixed methods are important in evaluation in Chapter 24, "Mixed Methods Evaluation." The authors define MMR in evaluation, provide examples of evaluations that have been conducted, and discuss issues that might arise from using mixed or multimethod approaches in evaluations. The chapter concludes with a discussion about directions for the future.

Multimethod and mixed methods are well suited to prevention research in global health, even though their application has not been thoroughly discussed at this point, according to Stevan Weine in Chapter 25, "Applying Multimethod and Mixed Methods to Prevention Research in Global Health." Weine illustrates the key opportunities and challenges of using multimethod and mixed methods for undergoing prevention research. He uses an example of a study about HIV risk and protection among Tajik labor migrants, and he talks about using strategic triangulation as a key preventive intervention.

The main objectives of Chapter 26, "History and Emergent Practices of Multimethod and Mixed Methods in Business Research," are to provide a historical overview of business scholars who pioneered MMMR and examine the recent works about multimethod and mixed methods in the business field. The authors, José F. Molina-Azorin and Roslyn A. Cameron, provide exemplars to show the reader how the research works, and they end the chapter by providing a future agenda for mixed methods in the business research community.

Chapter 27 rounds out this section by engaging with traditional international development evaluation approaches and asks the question: "How Does Mixed Methods Research Add Value to Our Understanding of Development?" Nicola A. Jones, Paola Pereznieto, and Elizabeth Presler-Marshall first discuss the overall challenges evaluators face in undertaking research in a developing country context. They explore the issues of traditional standard "one-size-fits-all" development models that often did not address the issues and needs of diverse local cultural contexts. They advocate taking a mixed methods approach that can add more complex, localized understanding of the efficacy and value of any given intervention. They explore these ideas using in-depth case studies that deploy a MMR design.

Part Four: Incorporating New Technologies into Multimethod and Mixed Methods Research

Part Four begins with an exploration of the varied ways in which qualitative and quantitative methods have been combined using new technologies. In Chapter 28, "Mixed Methods and Multimodal Research and Internet Technologies," Christine M. Hine explores the motivations of mixing methods in Internet research and gives examples of how this can be done. She also points out the methodological advantages, as well as the challenges, of using mixed modal approaches in Internet research.

Chapter 29, "Conducting Multimethod and Mixed Methods Research Online," examines conducting research online using MMMR approaches.

Janet E. Salmons uses selected exemplars to show that researchers can use a wide range of information and communications technologies, such as e-mail, social media, mapping tools, videoconferencing, and more. She analyzes a set of exemplars to look at how the different technologies influence the experiences of the researchers, participants, and the phenomena being investigated.

In Chapter 30, "Emergent Technologies in Multimethod and Mixed Methods Research: Incorporating Mobile Technologies," Leo Remijn, Nathalie Stembert, Ingrid J. Mulder, and Sunil Choenni analyze how mobile technologies can be used in MMMR. Smartphones today are increasing in functionality and can measure ambient light, GPS, accelerometer, and temperature. Emergent technologies such as this can offer a lot to MMMR. First the authors give an overview of the mobile devices that are emerging, and then they explain how the technologies create new possibilities to gather, process, and interpret data.

In Chapter 31 Jane L. Fielding and Nigel G. Fielding also look at emergent technologies in MMMR, but they focus on GIS and CAQDAS. The objectives of the chapter, "Emergent Technologies in Multimethod and Mixed Methods Research: Incorporating GIS and CAQDAS," are to introduce spatial analysis in MMMR and explain the use of technologies for data collection and analysis in MMMR through examples and strategies.

Part Five: Commentaries: Dialoguing About Future Directions of Multimethod and Mixed Methods Research

This is a section in the *Handbook* where divergent perspectives are highlighted. There are many points of disagreement, convergence, and sometimes contention as well as conciliatory outcomes. Part Five adds to the many voices at the center and margins of discourse on knowledge-building in the area of MMMR. To gain legitimacy for knowledge-building, it is critical to remain open to new ideas and be willing to dialogue across differences. For example, to what extent is our community of knowledge-builders responsive to each other's versions of reality? Dialoguing across our differences serves to draw on the strengths of its diversity—not to divide but to help mixed and multimethod researchers combine their quests to uncover complex issues, and it is hoped in doing so we can produce more authentic and trustworthy research that can lead to the betterment of society.

Chapter 32 titled, "What Problem Are We Trying to Solve? Practical and Innovative Uses of Multimethod and Mixed Methods Research," aims to understand how MMMR can be justified on the basis of its practical utility and its potential to facilitate innovation. The authors, Thomas A. Schwandt and Lauren Lichty, emphasize that MMMR can contribute new ideas and solutions to complex social problems.

Udo Kelle adds to this section with his chapter, "Mixed Methods and the Problems of Theory Building and Theory Testing in the Social Sciences." Chapter 33 aims to distinguish between the application, the testing, and the building of theories that can be used in qualitative and quantitative research. Kelle wants the reader to recognize how theory is used and how problems of theory are solved in different mixed methods designs.

In Chapter 34, "Preserving Distinctions Within the Multimethod and Mixed Methods Research Merger," Jennifer C. Greene argues against a multimethod and mixed methods merger. She analyzes in detail two evaluation designs of the same obesity prevention program. One design uses a multimethod approach and the other uses a mixed methods approach. Greene discusses these two different designs and in doing so provides a strong argument for preserving this methods distinction.

Albert Hunter and John Brewer's Chapter 35, "Conundrums of Multimethod Research," examines three types of conundrums that continue to blur researchers' understanding of just what multimethod research is about and how to differentiate its contribution from other methods approaches such as mixed methods. One conundrum they consider is the relation of multimethod to the social sciences, the second concerns how mulitmethod relates to social theory (methods strive to initiate, reformulate, refocus, and clarify theory), and the third conundrum raises issues about the very definition of what multimethod research is (it can be multiple quantitative or qualitative methods and it can also include a mix of qualitative and quantitative methods). Multimethod approaches are particularly good at getting at multilevel analyses that examine both structural effects and individual properties.

Guidelines for MMR projects centers around the degree to which guidelines for best practices should be institutionalized. This prompts questions such as: How much guidance is helpful, in what, and from where? What roles do and should forms of guidelines for best practice in MMR play in the development of these research approaches? Julianne Cheek, in Chapter 36, looks at the impacts of moving the field of mixed methods toward best practice guidelines. If this move happens, it might impact what can be called MMR and how it can be carried out. Cheek notes that such a move could compromise the "mixed methods way of thinking" and move to new forms of methods-centric thinking. This is discussed in her chapter, "It Depends: Possible Impacts of Moving the Field of Mixed Methods Research Toward Best Practice Guidelines."

How can we harness MMR for social justice in the short and long run? Sharon Crasnow's Chapter 37, "Feminism, Causation, and Mixed Method Research," explores methodological, epistemological, and ontological implications of causality and how feminist research might combine methods in support of feminist social justice goals.

In Chapter 38, "Causality, Generalizability, and the Future of Mixed Methods Research," Robert K. Yin also considers causation in the context of generalizability in MMR. In addition he looks at the future contributions of MMR and how the mixing of methods can augment preexisting qualities of qualitative and quantitative methods.

In Chapter 39, "Mixed Methods: Dissonance and Values in Research With Marginalized Groups," co-authors, Dawn Freshwater and Pamela Fisher addresses the preoccupation with integration of data and how this can undermine social justice–related aspirations by erasing marginalized perspectives. They identify this as a particular feature of MMR undertaken in medicine and health sciences. They look at the value of research conducted in transformative-emancipatory paradigms.

Chapter 40, "Harnessing Global Social Justice and Social Change with Multimethod and Mixed Methods Research," looks at the context of inequities and the need to understand the problems before solutions are sought. Fiona Cram discusses tools that can be used to enable researchers to privilege the voices of the marginalized. She also looks at how MMMR can evaluate the initiatives that seek to redress inequities.

We hope that this *Handbook* will foster dialogue across methodological and methods divides. We urge our readers to engage with their own set of values onto the social world and engage reflexively regarding how their values may enter into their research practice at all stages of the research process—from the choice of a research question to their selection of a set of methods, designs, analyses, and interpretations. We strongly believe that engagement with these issues has the potential to lead to a set of rich new questions that can foster a deep and complex understanding of our social world.

Our best wishes to all,

Sharlene Hesse-Biber and R. Burke Johnson

ACKNOWLEDGMENTS

Sharlene Hesse-Biber's Acknowledgments:

The Oxford Handbook of Multimethod and Mixed Methods Research Inquiry would not be possible without the assistance and support of many members of my academic community. First, I want to express a heartfelt thank you to all the authors of the *Handbook* for providing stellar, state-of-the-art *Handbook* chapters on a range of multimethod and mixed methods perspectives. I also want to express my gratitude to my coeditor, Dr. R. Burke Johnson, for his expertise and thoughtful feedback throughout the *Handbook* project.

I want to express my heartfelt gratitude to the Boston College Undergraduate Research Fellowship Committee, especially the support I have received from Dean William Petri in my research endeavors throughout my years at Boston College.

I want to especially send my appreciation and thanks to Jessica Stevens (Boston College, class of 2014) and Boston College undergraduate Hilary Flowers (Boston College, class of 2010) for their leadership in keeping this *Handbook* project organized and also for providing in-depth, stellar editorial assistance and outstanding general academic support. In addition, I want to express my special appreciation to Boston College undergraduates Lauren Simao, Brittany Duncan, Chiara Heintz, and Darby Sullivan for their research assistance and copyediting expertise on the *Handbook* chapters.

I want to express my deep respect and admiration to Dr. Julianne Cheek and Dr. Judith Preissle for their invaluable comments on the Introduction to the *Handbook* chapter.

The *Handbook* would not be possible without the vision, wisdom, and support of the Oxford *Handbook* editor, Abby Gross. Her editorial expertise and guidance were invaluable.

I want to express my love and deepest appreciation to my family, in particular my daughters, Julia Ariel and Sarah Alexandra, for their patience, love, and forbearance. In addition, I want to thank my extended family—my mother, Helene Stockert, as well as my sister, Georgia Geraghty, and brother, Charles Nagy.

Last, I want to thank my wonderful Portuguese water dogs, Zoli and his brother Max. They both remind me of the importance of play in our lives, and they keep me connected to the things that matter to me outside of my work life.

R. Burke Johnson's Acknowledgments:

Of most importance, I offer my acknowledgment to all of the authors of this handbook. This is their handbook. Sincere thanks go to my co-editor Sharlene Hesse-Biber for interacting, listening, understanding, and making this truly a joint project from beginning to end. Our idea was born several years ago, and it is great to see it come to fruition. My thanks go to our Oxford editor, Abby Gross, for suggesting that Sharlene and I edit this handbook and then making it possible. I also send my thanks to Abbas Tashakkori and Charles Teddlie for showing me the way to make social science and society better and to Jennifer C. Greene for reminding us of the importance of dialogue with difference. Special thanks go to my wife, Dr. Lisa Turner, for helping me in every possible way.

CONTRIBUTORS

Pat Bazeley
Research Support P/L
Bowral NSW Australia
University of New South Wales
Centre for Primary Health Care
and Equity
Kensington, Australia

Jennifer E. Boehm
Centers for Disease Control and Prevention
Atlanta, GA, USA

Julia Brannen
UCL Institute of Education
Thomas Coram Research Unit
London, UK

John Brewer
Department of Sociology
Trinity College
Hartford, CT, USA

Roslyn A. Cameron
Curtin University, Bentley Campus
Curtin Business School, School of
Management
Perth, WA, Australia

Julianne Cheek
Østfold University College
Department of Business, Languages and
Social Sciences
Halden, Norway

Margaret Chmiel
Smithsonian Science Education Center
Smithsonian Institution
Washington DC, USA

Sunil Choenni
Rotterdam University of Applied Sciences,
Creating 010
Rotterdam, The Netherlands
and
Ministry of Security and Justice
Research and Documentation Centre, The
Hague, The Netherlands

Fiona Cram
Katoa Ltd
Auckland, New Zealand

Sharon Crasnow
Norco College
Department of Arts, Humanities, and
World Languages
Norco, CA, USA

Kathleen M. T. Collins
University of Arkansas—College of
Education and Health Professions
Department of Curriculum and
Instruction
Fayetteville, AR, USA

John W. Creswell
Professor of Educational Psychology
University of Nebraska–Lincoln
Lincoln, NE, USA

Amy DeGroff
Division of Cancer Prevention and Control
Centers for Disease Control and Prevention
Atlanta, GA, USA

Sarah J. Drabble
University of Sheffield
School of Health and Related Research
Sheffield, South Yorkshire, UK

Michael D. Fetters
Professor of Family Medicine
University of Michigan Medical School
Ann Arbor, MI, USA

Jane L. Fielding
University of Surrey
Faculty of Arts & Human Sciences
Sociology Department
Guildford, Surrey, UK

Nigel G. Fielding
University of Surrey
Faculty of Arts & Human Sciences
Sociology Department
Guildford, Surrey, UK

Pamela Fisher
University of Leeds School of Healthcare
Faculty of Medicine and Health
Leeds, UK

Rebecca K. Frels
Lamar University
Education and Human Development
Department of Counseling and Special
　Populations
Beaumont, TX, USA

Dawn Freshwater
University of Leeds, UK
and
Senior Deputy Vice-Chancellor
University of Western Australia
Perth, Australia

Nollaig A. Frost
Middlesex University
Department of Psychology
School of Science and Technology
London, UK

Rebecca M. Glover-Kudon
Centers for Disease Control and
　Prevention
Division of Cancer Prevention and
　Control
Atlanta, GA, USA

Daniel Grace
Institute for Intersectionality Research
　and Policy
Simon Fraser University
Vancouver, BC, Canada
and
Dalla Lana School of Public Health
University of Toronto
Toronto, Canada

Jennifer C. Greene
University of Illinois at
　Urbana-Champaign
College of Education
Department of Educational Psychology
Champaign, IL, USA

Amy J. Griffin
Boston College
Graduate School of Social Work
Cambridge, MA, USA

Jori N. Hall
University of Georgia College of Education
Department of Lifelong Education,
　Administration, and Policy
Athens, GA, USA

Olena Hankivsky
London School of Hygiene and Tropical
　Medicine
London, UK
and
School of Public Policy
Institute for Intersectionality Research
　and Policy
Simon Fraser University
Vancouver, BC, Canada

Sharlene Hesse-Biber
Boston College
Department of Sociology
Chestnut Hill, MA, USA

Christine M. Hine
University of Surrey
Faculty of Arts & Human Sciences
Sociology Department
Guildford, Surrey, UK

John H. Hitchcock
Indiana University
School of Education
Bloomington, IN, USA

Albert Hunter
Northwestern University
Department of Sociology
Evanston, IL, USA

Leonard A. Jason
DePaul University College of Science
　and Health
Center for Community Research
Chicago, IL, USA

R. Burke Johnson
University of South Alabama
College of Education
Department of Professional Studies
Mobile, AL, USA

Nicola A. Jones
Social Development Programme
Overseas Development Institute
London, UK

Udo Kelle
Helmut Schmidt University
University of the Federal Armed Forces
School for Humanities and Social sciences
Hamburg, Germany

Jennifer Leeman
University of North Carolina at
Chapel Hill
School of Nursing
Chapel Hill, NC, USA

Lauren Lichty
University of Washington -Bothell
School of Interdisciplinary Arts and
Sciences
Bothell, WA, USA

Melvin M. Mark
Pennsylvania State University
Department of Psychology
University Park, PA, USA

Joseph Maxwell
College of Education and Human
Development
George Mason University
Fairfax, VA, USA

Donna M. Mertens
Gallaudet University, Retired
Beltsville, MD, USA

José F. Molina-Azorín
University of Alicante, Faculty of
Economics and Business Management
Department of Management
Alicante, Spain

Janice M. Morse
College of Nursing
University of Utah
Salt Lake City, UT, USA

Ingrid J. Mulder
Rotterdam University of Applied Sciences,
Creating 010
Rotterdam, The Netherlands
and
Faculty of Industrial Design Engineering
Delft University of Technology
Delft, The Netherlands

Carole Newman
Florida International University
Leadership and Professional Studies
Miami, FL USA

Isadore Newman
Florida International University, College
of Education
Department of Human and Molecular
Genetics, College of Medicine, Florida
International University

Alicia O'Cathain
University of Sheffield
School of Health and Related Research
Sheffield, South Yorkshire, UK

Rebecca O'Connell
UCL Institute of Education
Thomas Coram Research Unit
London, UK

Bradley D. Olson
National Louis University
Psychology Department
Chicago, IL, USA

Anthony J. Onwuegbuzie
Sam Houston State University
Department of Educational Leadership
and Counseling
Conroe, TX, USA

Lisa D. Pearce
University of North Carolina at Chapel Hill
Department of Sociology
Chapel Hill, NC, USA

Paola Pereznieto
Overseas Development Institute
Social Development Programme
London, UK

Judith Preissle
University of Georgia College of Education
Department of Lifelong Education,
Administration, and Policy
Athens, GA, USA

Elizabeth Presler-Marshall
Independent Consultant
Chapel Hill, NC, USA

Leo Remijn
Rotterdam University of Applied Sciences,
Creating 010
Rotterdam, The Netherlands
and
Rotterdam University of Applied Sciences,
School of Communication, Media, and
Information Technology
Rotterdam, The Netherlands

Sylvia E. Rogers
College of Education
Department of Professional Studies
University of South Alabama
Mobile, AL, USA

Elizabeth A. Rohan
Centers for Disease Control and Prevention
Division of Cancer Prevention and Control
Atlanta, GA, USA

Deborah Rodriguez
Middlesex University London
Psychology Department
School of Health and Education
London, UK

Janet E. Salmons
Capella University
School of Business and Technology
Boulder, CO, USA

Margarete Sandelowski
University of North Carolina at Chapel Hill
School of Nursing
Chapel Hill, NC, USA

Thomas A. Schwandt
University of Illinois at Urbana–Champaign
Department of Educational Psychology
Champaign, IL, USA

Rachel L. Shaw
Aston University
School of Live and Health Sciences
Leamington Spa, Warwickshire, UK

Nathalie Stembert
Rotterdam University of Applied Sciences,
    Creating 010
Rotterdam, The Netherlands
and
Rotterdam University of Applied Sciences,
    School of Communication, Media, and
    Information Technology
Rotterdam, The Netherlands

Rick Szostak
University of Alberta
Department of Economics
Edmonton, Alberta, Canada

Michele Tarsilla
Western Michigan University
Evaluation Center
Kalamazoo, MI, USA

Corrine I. Voils
Duke University Medical Center
Health Science Specialist
Durham Veterans Affairs
    Medical Center
Durham, NC, USA

Stevan Weine
University of Illinois at Chicago
College of Medicine
Chicago, IL, USA

Jennifer P. Wisdom
Associate Vice President
    for Research
George Washington University
Washington, DC, USA

Robert K. Yin
COSMOS Corporation
Bethesda, MD, USA

CONTENTS

Part Three • Contextualizing Multimethod and Mixed Methods Research Within and Across Disciplines and Applied Settings

Introduction: Navigating a Turbulent Research Landscape: Working the Boundaries, Tensions, Diversity, and Contradictions of Multimethod and Mixed Methods Inquiry

Sharlene Hesse-Biber

Abstract

The metaphorical concept of *border work* provides an introductory starting point for this *Handbook*'s overall vision. To engage in multimethod and mixed methods research (MMMR) requires working at the borders of disciplines and navigating across a turbulent MMMR landscape characterized by deep epistemic, theoretical, and methods divides. This chapter introduces the research challenges multimethod and mixed methods researchers confront in doing border work. Multimethod and mixed methods researchers are given a wealth of research strategies that provide "ways forward" for incorporating ethics, diversity, social justice, and social policy into the MMMR praxis. This chapter also tackles the range of new technologies, theoretical perspectives, and MMMR designs for bridging qualitative and quantitative divides. The chapter ends with the collective research wisdom gathered from our *Handbook* authors who shared their research insights and the items they would place in their MMMR backpack for their journey.

Key Words: multimethods, mixed methods, border work, new technologies, diversity, ethics, social justice, social policy

The concept of a border provides a metaphor for imagining the journey this *Oxford Handbook of Multimethod and Mixed Methods Research Inquiry* will take you on. The concept of a border informs the *Handbook*'s very organization and the underlying themes contained within its different parts. Each part of the *Handbook* can be considered to be a type of border. As readers move between these chapters and from one part of the *Handbook* to another, they engage in crossing borders. Navigating borders and crossing borders is the act of doing border work. Let's explore these concepts in more detail.

Paula Gunn Allen (1992) used the term *border studies* to refer to those researchers crossing the borders of multiple disciplines. Higonett (1994) employs the anthropological term *contact zone* to depict the interactions and engagements of scholars working at disciplinary borders that are not "static lines of demarcation" but "improvisational and interactive." A border "localizes what it strives to contain or release. It is rarely a smooth seam." Borders are sites of innovation, "of rupture, connection, transmission," and those working at the borders begin to "move beyond one-way questions" (Higonett, 1994, pp. 2–3; See also Hesse-Biber & Leckenby, 2003).

Traditional academic disciplines set up borders. Residing within them are the specific methods practices and theoretical perspectives that are often influenced by departmental cultures. They provide research courses training students in specific disciplinary methods and encourage publications in targeted disciplinary journals. Academic disciplinary borders can and do pose barriers to those researchers who engage with mixed methods research.

Mixed methods research projects, in contrast, seek to forge a diffuse and open set of interdisciplinary and transdisciplinary research relationship structures—a process known as "de-disciplining" (see Richardson, 2000). Transgressing disciplinary boundaries can provide new ground for mixed methods researchers from different disciplines to collaborate and engage with new questions, thus offering a space to brainstorm about their ideas and research praxis, as well as a place for forging new pathways toward interdisciplinary work. Crossing disciplinary borders may require mixed methods researchers to become flexible, patient, resilient, sensitive to difference, and willing to take risks in applying theory and praxis.

The fields of multimethod and mixed methods research (MMMR) hold a prominent place in the de-disciplining process given their potential to provide the flexibility to tackle complex analytical and interpretative issues that arise when bringing diverse ways of thinking and different types of data to bear in seeking answers to multifaceted questions (See Part Three: Contextualizing Multimethod and Mixed Methods Research Within and Across Disciplines and in Applied Settings, in this volume).

To engage in border work means that you, the researcher, will begin to see yourself *working the tensions* that lie within and between these borders. This type of work will often remove you from your methods and theoretical comfort zones. Practicing MMMR entails crossing a range of different borders. For example, a research sociologist who uses economic theory and quantitative data to understand the rates of violence against women may thereby create an innovative theory of violence not found within his or her own discipline.

While crossing borders can provide some unique opportunities, such crossing of borders also contains a set of cautionary tales. Patai and Koertge (1994) call attention to "interdisciplinary opportunism"—a situation where scholars who appropriate work from another field do so in a random and uncritical manner. While they apply this idea to scholars working within women's studies,

their concerns apply to all scholars who work at the borders of multiple disciplines. Crossing borders also implies crossing important epistemological, methodological, and pedagogical divisions within and between these spaces. Working across these different divides, then, requires caution when borrowing concepts and ideas from other disciplines: Are you using ideas/concepts from other disciplines uncritically? Is your definition syncing with another's? Have you gained enough expertise in a range of disciplines to know you are doing so? Do you have the research methods and analytical interpretive and writing skills you will need to traverse and engage with these borders?

Working at the borders and reaching across lines of demarcation also allows the researcher to engage with a range of differences, and in doing so, act to change the world. To engage in border work is to engage in some way with "the other(s)." Living in the contradictions and tensions serve to illuminate what may often be invisible (see chapters in this volume by Cram & Mertens; Szostak; and Hankivsky & Grace). Border work often requires creativity and risk taking as researchers negotiate a balance between being "at home" and being "in exile"—a place Teresa de Lauretis (1988) notes, where one is giving up a "place that is safe."

The MMMR landscape also contains a set of research actors whose goals are multiple and diverse, with some seeking new knowledge frames and understandings with the goal of social justice and social transformation (Mertens, 2007, 2009; Cram, this volume; Freshwater & Fisher, this volume); others seek to generate new paradigmatic frames of knowledge-building that can facilitate new research designs and modes of inquiry whose goal seeks a common ground among different perspectives onto the social world (see Morse; Maxwell, Chmiel, & Roger, this volume). Still others seek to tame this new territory by reinstitutionalizing knowledge borders through promoting MMMR guidelines that, while initially offering support to novice researchers may, for example, have the unintended consequence of impeding the innovation and openness of exploration within and between the mixed methods and other research communities (see Cheek, this volume). Like any new knowledge-building terrain, the history of research methods already bears witness to the tendency of researchers to colonize new ground; there is a precedential pattern of "taming" the turbulence through research structure formalization in order to legitimate specific brands of methodologies and methods for extracting knowledge (see Platt, 1996).

Further transforming the MMMR landscape is the advent of a *new set of research actors* who bring with them a range of funding resources tied to carrying out very specific research agendas. These actors comprise a range of policymakers and government funding agencies whose focus and mandate are very applied and problem specific. Some of these highly practitioner-based agendas often deemphasize theoretical frameworks, favoring instead an empirically oriented results-based management modeling approach that measures a program's performance against a set of quantitative indicators that ask the question: Did the intervention work or not work? These new actors often privilege evidence-based practices and a quantitatively driven logic model of research design that others in the MMMR community believe undermines the legitimacy and role that other less "measurement-oriented" perspectives and outcomes support (for a critique, see, e.g., Giddings, 2006; Natsios, 2010; Best, 2014, pp. 164-208).

There are, however, additional challenges that those crossing the MMMR terrain may likely encounter that come out of my lived experiences in coediting this *Handbook* that engaged me with the wide range of MMMR scholarship contained within the *Handbook*. Some of these challenges also come from reflecting on my own values/attitudes and engaging in dialogue with a diverse range of members within and outside the MMMR community. I draw these ideas as well from the range of MMMR projects and experiences I have intensely engaged with, as well the insights I have gained in writing a mixed methods textbook (Hesse-Biber, 2010a), editing mixed methods special issues and articles (e.g., Hesse-Biber, 2010b, 2013; Hesse-Biber & Johnson, 2013; Mertens & Hesse-Biber, 2013). I also draw on my experience as a teacher of MMMR and listening deeply to my research methods students' experiences in learning about MMMR. In addition, I am cognizant of the fact that there is much I do not know, and I am mindful of the importance of those whose voices in the MMMR still remain silent and subjugated. So the challenges listed in this chapter are to be viewed as a working list that can be added to and revised. These challenges are not the only ones you may encounter on your MMMR journey, and they are not meant to be untempered assertions but points of dialoguing around the collective MMMR journey experience.

Challenge 1: Negotiating Multimethod and Mixed Methods Research Chasms
Epistemic Tensions at the Border

The past few decades have witnessed the beginnings of an emergent discussion of the role of theory in MMMR, but much of the early discussion centered on whether or not various theoretical perspectives/paradigms or ways of thinking could in fact be mixed. Could a quantitative researcher practice mixed methods? Could a qualitative researcher? How? These were the early presuppositional tensions often depicted as "paradigm wars" (see Tashakkori & Teddlie, 1998, 2003, 2010) that arose among mixed methods practitioners.

Some researchers, termed *purists*, found it difficult or impossible to cross these philosophical and methods boundaries, seeing these two methods as independent and unmixable philosophically (Guba, 1987; Guba & Lincoln, 1989; Smith & Heshusius, 1986). A purist approach to mixing methods might stress the need for researchers to choose either qualitative or quantitative methodologies. The purists are entirely skeptical of attempts to cross the divide between the two methodologies and see mixed methods as incompatible with a strongly formulated sense of epistemological perspective.

For the purist, a researcher mixing the two would be avoiding questioning the nature of knowledge claims and the way humans can come to know the world around them. Purist researchers privilege one side of the divide or the other but do not perceive the utility or logic of an untheorized study that freely combines different research approaches. Purists are not adverse to MMR but, in its praxis, are fully aware of the tight link between methodology and method. For example, a qualitatively driven approach to MMR will be clear on the dominance of the qualitative framework and, while open to incorporating a quantitative method, the goal of this method is to enhance the understanding of what is essentially a qualitatively driven mixed methods project.

Unlike a purist, a *pragmatic approach* would ask, "What is needed to answer the research question?" In answering this question, a pragmatist does not look to his or her epistemological perspective for guidance but instead seeks the best method or methods for answering the question. A pragmatist engages the subject of inquiry from all possible angles while using all available tools to fully answer the question. The original "philosophical perspective" of "pragmatism" derived from the work of Charles

S. Peirce, William James, George H. Mead, and John Dewey. *Philosophical pragmatism* centers on the research question and advocates using a range of methods that best meet its needs and research purpose. David Morgan's (2013) work on "pragmatic inquiry" saw its praxis as one of *taking actions* and experiencing their results. He notes: "Inquiry occurs when you confront situations that fall outside your existing knowledge and then take action to extend your knowledge so you know how to proceed when you encounter similar situations" (p. 7). What is produced in this type of knowledge-building model are "warranted beliefs" about specific actions and their consequences (Morgan, 2013, p. 7). Such a philosophical pragmatic approach was seen for some mixed methods scholars as an important "middle ground" perspective (see Biesta, 2010; Johnson & Onwuegbuzie, 2004).

The *dialectical approach* (Greene & Caracelli, 1997; Greene & Hall, 2010; Greene, this volume; Johnson, & Stefurak, 2013) creates a spiraling conversation between the epistemological paradigms and the methods themselves. Within these spirals, researchers interrogate both sides of their research design in order to articulate and explore the gains and losses that result in deploying both methods and the outcome of their mixing. The research design builds in moments when the two methods speak to one another, traversing but not breaking down epistemological perspectives that hold qualitative and quantitative methodologies apart from one another.

These epistemic border crossing conundrums arose early on in the MMR field during which the tension between the methods and the processes of mixing them came to the surface. Those within the mixed methods community could begin to envision how interpretive and constructionist frameworks that inform qualitative research might also inform the types of quantitative measures used. The positivist and postpositivist perspectives that relied on quantitative methodologies that aim to draw out generalizations could see the importance of qualitative designs that often served to inform the context of their quantitative results by grounding them in lived experience.

These early foundational concerns and tensions seemed to soften to the extent that some in the MMMR community even declared that the paradigm wars were over (see Bryman, 2006b; Morgan, 2007; Tashakkori & Teddlie, 2003). This declaration encouraged some researchers within the MMMR community to envision, for example, how interpretive and constructionist frameworks that inform qualitative research might also inform the types of quantitative measures they were currently using in their own research. Some positivist and postpositivist methodologists began to acknowledge the importance of qualitative designs in informing the context of their quantitative results by grounding them in lived experience.

However, over time, some multimethod and mixed methods researchers (e.g., Freshwater & Fisher, this volume) started to raise serious concerns about these types of epistemic border crossings. Pragmatism has grown into a leading theoretical framework for mixed methods researchers (see Creswell & Plano-Clark, 2011; Johnson & Gray, 2010). Some scholars felt that the current, more popular version of pragmatism had turned into *a practical pragmatism* that boiled down to a "what works" approach able to sidestep these hard "epistemological issues" in the "philosophical pragmatic" approach Dewey and colleagues were engaged with early on (see Mutch, 2009). This delinking of pragmatism from its philosophical roots, then, freed up and encouraged a type of "methodological eclecticism" (Mutch, 2009; see also Yanchar & Williams, 2006, p. 3).

Making the decision to follow a practical pragmatism framework provided an opportunity for those researchers not versed in a range of theoretical perspectives to engage with a mixed methods praxis without worrying about the concerns of the arguments launched by those taking a purist approach, However, such a framing of pragmatism, notes Clarke (2012), *misrepresents* its early foundational meaning. Clarke notes:

> In the US there has long been what I see as a misuse of the term pragmatic largely to equal expedience based in the logics of homo economicus, with some form of capitalism as the only reasonable path. In sharp contrast, pragmatist a la Dewey and others referred to what would work, be feasible given the conditions of the situation. As such it is more closely akin to Foucault's "conditions of possibility" (Foucault, 1975), elucidating what needs to be taken into account to answer his question, "What is to be done?" (Foucault, 1991, 84). (p. 405)

Jennifer C. Greene (2008) has also voiced important theoretical issues with regard to what she perceived as the unreflective theorizing and practices stemming from using a more practical pragmatic approach. She urged those researchers specifically deploying pragmatism to consider a series of specific questions in their praxis:

> How do the assumptions and stances of pragmatism influence inquiry decisions? For example, where do the consequentialist, actionable assumptions about social knowledge that are advanced in most pragmatic philosophies show up in practice? What does knowledge that integrates knowing and acting look like and how is it validated? (p. 13).

Crossing Disciplinary Borders

The very architecture of research inquiry is morphing. Research projects once housed in "disciplines" are now breaking out of their disciplinary borders. The fields of MMMR have a prominent place in the de-disciplining process given their potential to address complex analytical and interpretative issues, multiple methodologies, and a range of data to bear in answering complex questions (see Part Three, Contextualizing Multimethod and Mixed Methods Research Within and Across Disciplines in Applied Settings, in this volume)

This de-disciplining process in turn impacts how MMMR is practiced. Increasingly "team-based" projects involving several researchers from across disciplines may become the norm. Several chapters in this *Handbook* underscore the importance of looking beyond our own disciplines so that we might expand our disciplinary visions in order to re-revision (see Szostak, this volume). As the chapters in our *Handbook* attest, engaging in MMMR inquiry often means working at disciplinary margins, collaborating between disciplines, and bridging the qualitative–quantitative divide.

Engaging with a MMMR approach also means crossing *communications chasms,* and doing so may raise a number of new research challenges: How do researchers from different praxis and theoretical spaces converse across conceptual divides? How do the results of different research components communicate with one another? How is meaning created across these at times deep divides? (see, e.g., O'Cathain, Murphy, & Nicholl, 2008). Some project members may include the stakeholders funding the project and raises yet another set of conundrums: Do policymakers funding the project support the research design, conceptualization, and goals? (For an analysis of funding for mixed methods, see Wisdom & Fetters, this volume.)

To what extent do team members entering a turbulent MMMR landscape come with the range of tools they might need for their journey? There may

also exists a "tool chasm," as well as "skills chasm." So, for example, researchers may need to decide on the extent to which they need to re-skill and learn how to use a different set of tools and/or bring along a diverse research team equipped to handle highly specialized tools that certain research may require (see Hesse-Biber & Leavy, 2008). Beyond tools and new skills sets, do researchers have a set of methodological lenses they can call on to assess a given situation from a range of angles? What in fact is the "proper mix" of lenses across the variety of considerations that go into a project that is needed—both for a given researcher and the team they comprise? (See Sandelowski, 2014.)

One important overall consideration in planning an expedition across the MMMR landscape (and it may also play a significant role in determining the composition of any given research team) is the extent to which a researcher advocates for a specialized set of team members who spend many years honing a given set of theoretical lenses, methods, and analytical skills. There may be a need for team members who are specialists and those who excel at building and crossing bridges between specialties.

This conundrum around desirable skill sets raises important pedagogical issues and writing dilemmas that may have profound implications for how to train the next generation of researchers who will traverse this terrain (see, e.g., Frels, Newman, & Newman, this volume; Bazeley, this volume). To what extent should MMMR courses and workshops move toward integration or specialization? Perhaps what is needed is MMMR training that runs along a continuum of knowledge-production skills and theoretical lenses. Some researchers may reside at either one end or the other, while many will seek to move toward a position that begins to address both a range of skills and a variety of lenses. This means, then, a pedagogy of learning that is open in its praxis and not limited to narrow definitions and skill sets.

Several other considerations are worth knowing about before leaving this specific challenge. One insight that merits consideration is that not all research questions require a MMMR design—a monomethod and lens may be all that is required (Ahmed & Sil, 2012). There is a truism running around in the mixed methods literature that centers on the idea that two different methods can add value to a MMR project. In addition, any weaknesses resulting from using one method is said to be offset by using another method. Sandelowski

(2012) tackles this "weakness" logic and suggests that it is "hardly ever questioned" (p. 235). Ahmed and Sil assert that buying into this type of methods logic misses an important opportunity for researchers to focus on the issue regarding how different monomethods brought into the same empirical inquiry space offer potential for a dialogic process to take hold, thereby expanding the capacity of MMR for "cross-cultural communication" (p. 948).

The authors of this *Handbook* are cognizant about centering on the dialogic process in MMMR praxis, one that focuses on *the mixing process* and advocates finding strategies for listening across differences in methods practices and definitional concepts, as well as being open to actively communicating with the goal of understanding possibilities of joint contributions toward a more complex understanding. These are the skills that need to be developed within the MMMR community that just a reliance on the positive of two negatives can provide (see especially all chapters in Part Three, this volume).

The following are some strategies that might be useful for MMMR that entail working at the borders of multiple disciplines and whose work requires negotiating innovative ideas from multiple disciplinary sites. Klein's (1990) research into the personality characteristics associated with interdisciplinary perspectives suggests that they are high on "reliability, flexibility, patience, resilience, sensitivity to others, risk-taking, a thick skin, and a preference for diversity and new social roles" (p. 182). Becoming an interdisciplinarian requires good communication skills and teamwork among colleagues from different disciplines and, within the classroom setting, between faculty and students. Klein notes that the wider the gap between disciplines and the number of disciplines involved may create wider communication gaps (p. 183).

Challenge 2: Navigating the Definitional Terrain Borders of Multimethod and Mixed Methods Research

The practice of MMMR is not new. Multimethod and mixed methods was used starting with the earliest of social research inquiries. Early on, studies of poverty within families dates back to the 1800s in Europe by Frederic Le Play (1855), Charles Booth (1892–1897), as well as Bohm Rowntree (1901). Hall and Preissle (this volume) note that the discipline of anthropology is one where "methods and methodologies have always been mixed and multiple." They note that "collecting, surveying, and a variety of analytical examinations of material thus acquired—qualitative, quantitative, and mixed—have. . . been integral to what fieldworkers and ethnographers do. Recording in photograph and film and counting linguistic and material items date to the 19th-century practices" (Hall & Preissle, this volume).

While not labeled as "mixed methods," then, researchers across disciplines used both qualitative and quantitative approaches and techniques that included demographic analysis of survey data, participant observations, and social mapping techniques and also deployed multiple perspectives—a positivist as well as an interpretative approach. For example, the Chicago School of Sociology, founded in the 1920s, while focusing on urban ethnography, also collected quantitative data from a positivist approach. Robert Park, a core member of the Chicago School, together with R. D. McKenzie and Ernest Burgess (1925), used mixed methods designs to the study of inner-city urban life. Thomas and Znaniecki's (1918–1920) research on *The Polish Peasant in Europe and America* examined the lived experiences of migrants to America (especially the city of Chicago) and Europe during industrialization. These researchers used a variety of MMMR from interviews, diaries, and letters, as well as official documents. However, what is new in the movement is the formalization of the definition and practices of MMR.

The MMR landscape has undergone a dramatic transformation within the past three decades. The early 1990s saw the rise of a formalizing of mixing methods research moving its praxis toward that of a "bounded" entity—a formalized separate research practice. The formalized naming of what was once a subjugated practice among most researchers was now heralded as a "third methodological movement" (Tashakkori & Teddlie, 2003). In fact, this movement toward formalization has been well underway in mixed methods research as a field over the past few decades and serves to solidify specific theoretical and research design practices whose goals are to enhance scientific knowledge (see, e.g., Creswell & Plano Clark, 2007; Johnson & Onwuegbuzie, 2004; Leech & Onwuegbuzie, 2006; Tashakkori & Teddlie, 1998, 2003). Others seek to promote mixed methods scientific practice through identifying specific mixed methods designs that promote rigor and can move the field closer to that of a scientific enterprise (see chapters in this volume by Creswell; Morse; Collins; Crasnow; and Yin).

The definitional and praxis borders of MMR continues to be contested (see Guest, 2013) within and outside the community, but what most approaches to mixed methods have in common is the mixing of at least one qualitative and one quantitative method in the same research project or set of related projects (e.g., in a longitudinal study). Some definitions of mixed methods expand to include the intentional mixing of approaches or methodological traditions as well as analytical techniques. In addition, some definitions of mixed methods go on to state that such a mixing can provide a "fuller," more "synergistic," "better" understanding than using just one approach/ method. Some researchers employ a variety of terms, like *integrating, linking, connecting* and *dialoguing* (for a comparison of definitions, see, e.g., Creswell & Plano Clark, 2011, p. 5; Greene, 2007; Johnson & Onwuegbuzie, 2004; Johnson, Onwuegbuzie, & Turner, 2007). Creswell and Plano Clark (2007, 2011), for example, differentiate multimethod studies from mixed methods studies by noting that the former are studies in which multiple types of qualitative or quantitative data are collected in a single research project. Johnson and Onwuegbuzie argue for extending this definition and assert that MMR should comprise not only the combining qualitative and quantitative methods but also its approaches, concepts, as well as a specific language of praxis into one research study.

The MMMR landscape also contains a set of research actors whose goals are multiple and diverse, with some seeking new knowledge and understanding with the goal of social justice and social change (Cram; Freshwater, & Fisher, this volume; Mertens, 2007); others seek to generate new paradigmatic frames of knowledge-building that can facilitate new research designs and modes of inquiry (see Denscombe, 2008; Hunter & Brewer, this volume; Maxwell, Chmiel, & Roger, this volume; Morse, this volume). Still others seek to tame this new territory by reinstitutionalizing knowledge borders through promoting MMR guidelines that, while initially offering support to novice researchers may, for example, have the unintended consequence of impeding the innovation and openness of exploration within and between the mixed methods and other research communities (see Cheek, this volume).

Multimethod research differentiates itself from mixed methods in that its definitional borders do not require having at least one quantitative/qualitative method in any given research project. A multimethod strategy does not necessarily require the mixing or integration of methods. Brewer and Hunter (1989, 2006, this volume) note that multimethod research is deployed "to attack a research problem with an arsenal of methods that have non overlapping weaknesses in addition to their complementary strengths" (1989, p. 17). An early example of a multimethod approach can be found in Campbell and Fiske's (1959) work on measurement validation of psychological traits using a multitrait-multimethod matrix approach. An assumption contained in a multimethod approach is that more methods are better. For example, Hunter and Brewer (2006) go on to note in their monograph on multimethod: "each new set of data increases our confidence that the research results reflect reality rather than methodological error" (p. 4). Hunter and Brewer (2006) suggest that using multimethod can also assist in sorting out "divergent findings" by noting: "They signal the need to analyze a research problem further and to be cautious in interpreting the significance of any one set of data" (p. 4).

Following these moves to solidify the definitional boundaries of MMMR, there was a similar movement within the field to formalize MMR practice by suggesting a specific set of research designs with their own notation systems and accompanying sets of template design practices. This action ushered in textbooks and articles on the "how-to's" of mixed methods praxis for novice researchers wanting to learn the specific guidelines for good practices (see, e.g., Creswell & Plano Clark, 2007, 2011; Leech & Onwuegbuzie, 2006; Teddlie & Tashakkori, 2006).

Fueling the movement toward institutionalizing MMR practice was a set of newly formed "best practices" guidelines. The document, published and sanctioned by a major government funding agency, the Office of Behavioural and Social Sciences Research of the National Institutes of Health (2011), was titled *Best Practices for Mixed Methods Research in the Health Sciences* and sought to formally identify a set of best practices for doing mixed methods (see other such standards: Bryman, Becker, & Sempik, 2008; Heyvaert, Hannes, Maes, & Onghena, 2013).

Why Are Definitions and Frameworks Important for the Mixed Methods Research Inquiry Process?

How we define and frame MMR practice has implications for the overall legitimacy and acceptance of what one is doing and how it is received by others within a given research community. Those who possess the power to define concepts within a community of practice can control and socially construct what becomes "real." The creation of borders—both symbolic and material—is critical for the survival, nurturing, and maintaining of any community.

However, if these borders promote strict border divisions that become too tightly controlled, they can begin to contain and exclude different ways of knowing. For example, in their review of the state of MMMR in the field of education, Hall and Preissle (this volume) caution against the use of preconceived mixed methods designs that take into account the "complexities of education policy and local educational contexts," one that promotes a process they term "reflective integration" (Hall & Preissle, this volume).

The editors and authors of this handbook are cognizant of the importance of pushing against borderlines, as Trinh T. Minh-ha notes, in order to seek a place "where one never stops, wailing on the edges, incurring constantly the risk of falling off one side or the other side of the limit while undoing, redoing, modifying this limit" (Minh-ha, 1991, p. 218). Julianne Cheek, in her chapter in this volume notes, "Without dialogue across. . . differences, any move of the field of mixed methods research toward best practice guidelines may well be premature and have the effect, intended or otherwise, of homogenizing or even shutting down dialogue about what "best" is in relation to mixed methods research." Pushing borders is a critical part of navigating the MMR terrain.

As we leave this challenge, it is also important to recognize those other MMR scholars and researchers within the MMMR contemporary community that do not especially agree with framing mixed methods research as a *new* form of research inquiry. Instead, they see MMR as "less as a new mode of inquiry than as a new way of recognizing and speaking about the methodological and design mixes constituting all empirical inquiry" (Sandelowski, 2014, pp. 6–7).

Challenge 3: Negotiating Data Collection, Analysis, and Interpretative Borders

A challenge that continues to plague the field of MMR for many decades is the thorny issue of what to do with data gathered across qualitative and quantitative divides. How can a qualitative researcher, for example, assess the importance and meaning of the quantitative data collected? What should be the overall goal in the analysis of different data types? Should they be integrated? How? Should they be separate analyses? Why? (See Brannen & O'Connell, this volume; Onwuegbuzie & Hitchcock, this volume; see also Bazeley, 2006, 2009.)

One important factor in the analysis and interpretation stage in a mixed methods design is an awareness of a researcher's own standpoint or methodological positioning. Giddings and Grant (2007), for example, have noted that without this type of reflexivity, one of the two methods may be included in a superficial way (p. 58). This is especially important when those conducting the research come from different disciplines that are often rooted in particular research methodologies, which each have their particular assumptions about the social world, their favored methods, and analytical techniques.

What is clear from the research into barriers to integration is that there is a skills gap among those conducting MMR that may require the addition of new analytical options for assessing how different data forms can connect to one another. These analytical options are still emerging among those members who are traversing this landscape.

It behooves researchers who are traversing this landscape, then, to think about deploying emerging new analytical tools and perspectives and to also perhaps reflect on how their analytical lenses will or will not be applicable once these data have been collected and represented (see, e.g., Leeman, Voils, & Sandelowski, this volume; Pearce, this volume). Emergent technologies can also play an integral part in our analytical understandings of these diverse data forms.

The good news is that there is an emergence of new paths along the MMR analytical terrain as demonstrated by the development of a range of emergent analytical MMR frameworks for integrating both qualitative and quantitative data (see Brannen & O'Connell, this volume; Onwuegbuzie & Hitchcock, this volume). These analytical developments open up new analytical ground for moving MMR beyond a parallel analytical approach (Zhang & Creswell, 2013). One such example is that of data transformation (i.e., the process of qualitizing and quantitizing; see, e.g., Sandelowski, Volis, & Knafi, 2009). In addition, computer-assisted data analysis programs now include a mixed methods component to facilitate complex analyses of mixed methods data (Bazeley, 2003; Fielding & Fielding, this volume).

Important in fostering a robust mixed methods analytical and interpretative process as well is the development of a profound appreciation for the potential contributions a given methodological perspective can bring to a mixed methods project. A respect for methodological, methods, analytical, and interpretative difference is a critical ingredient to mixed methods praxis. As is all too well known within the mixed methods community, many mixed methods projects still remain "unmixed," with little interaction between the two methods (Bryman, 2006b, 2007; Yin, 2006). In effect, we are still witnessing the publication of parallel quantitative and quantitative components. (For a discussion of these issues, see Bazeley, 2006; Bryman, 2006a, 2007; O'Cathain & Drabble, this volume; O'Cathain, Murphy, & Nicholl, 2007, 2009).

Engaging with this type of MMR thinking will also require researchers to come out of their methods and theoretical comfort zones. This is often a process in which the research becomes both an insider and an outsider, taking on multiple standpoints and negotiating different researcher identities simultaneously. This is aptly expressed and worth repeating here, Trinh T. Minh-ha's (1992) concept of "multiple subjectivities," in which researchers are encouraged to push on their own specific disciplinary "borderline."

The next and perhaps most hidden of challenges is power related: Who will decide the research methods procedures for traversing this new analytical and interpretive terrain? Who decides what the best practices for application of our new tools/technologies will be? Who decides what works? What is credible knowledge building?

Challenge 4: Acquiring Deep Awareness of the Politics of Knowledge
Dealing with Border Patrols: Securing the Terrain of Knowledge-Building and its Politics

Border work involves both acquiring new knowledge and action, and therefore a characteristic of this work is that it is a process that contains the flow of power and privilege. Foucault (1976) notes that making knowledge claims goes hand in hand with power claims. Working at and across a range of research borders also raises important questions concerning the epistemological basis of knowledge-building. Under what conditions are boundaries of knowledge constructed? Linda Tuhiwai Smith (1999) in her work, *Decolonizing Methodologies*, suggests that "research is not an innocent or distant academic exercise but an activity that has something at stake and that occurs in a set of political and social conditions" (p. 5).

There is a political dimension to knowledge-building. In his classic work, *The Structure of Scientific Revolutions*, Kuhn (1960) suggests scientific practice at any given moment is marked by particular paradigm, or way of knowing. He posits that our knowledge-building capacity is filtered through the particular model or paradigm(s) currently housed in a particular field. These paradigmatic ways of knowing are theoretically derived worldviews, and they provide the conceptual frameworks by which we construct and understand social reality. A paradigm allows us to observe only certain aspects of the MMMR landscape (what is there and what is not) and what it is we should be focusing on. Kuhn argues that "facts" are paradigm specific, meaning that those "facts" differ according to the lens we live and work within. One critical factor in sustaining any given paradigm is how successful it competes for followers and its ability to continue to solve complex puzzles.

However, paradigms are embedded in the substructure of a given scientific community and its social institutions. These scientific practices become "normalized" over time, and are often sustained by nonrational factors and subjective phenomena. Those whose work resides inside the dominant paradigm also receive institutional supports that recognize their scholarship, and their work appears in those prestigious journals and grant agencies within their respective fields that often support the dominant paradigm's approach. So the power to ask questions that matter is often held by those powerful reigning paradigmatic groups who hold the power to define what passes as knowledge, what questions are formulated, and ultimately those models or paradigms that serve to formulate explanations of reality.

Freshwater and Fisher (this volume) argue that the MMR community is also impacted by the politics of knowledge-building that Kuhn addresses. They stress that MMR's social justice mission may be at risk given the growing "reconfiguration "of how knowledge has been built." More specifically, they focus on what they see as a pulling back on "independent scholarship in the face of growing demands for the production of knowledge suited to market-driven economies." They note the growing movement of neoliberal economic and political structures leading a "decline of the collegial system based on academic and intellectual authority toward management hierarchies." As evidence, they point to the growing power of the "regulatory audit" as reflected in the UK government's mandate to apply quantitative impact measures of accountability within universities. They go on to note: "This constitutes a move from an era of *Mode 1 knowledge production* (knowledge that is disciplined -based and instigated by the researcher) to one of *Mode 2 knowledge production* (problem based and interdisciplinary)" (Freshwater & Fisher, this volume; see also Denzin, 2009; Nowotny, Scott, & Gibbons, 2001).

The early 2000s witnessed the beginnings of a discussion of theoretical bias in MMR. There was a concern among some mixed methods researchers that the current practice of mixed methods leaned toward a "postpositivist" theoretical stance especially in those disciplines that favored evidence-based practices, with qualitatively driven approaches absent and the use/misuse of qualitative methods without their theoretical underpinnings (Denzin, 2010; Denzin & Lincoln, 2005; Giddings, 2006; Howe, 2004). For example, Giddings voiced concern that much of the MMR up to that point stemmed from positivistic methodology—what she calls, "positivism dressed in drag," with the qualitative component of the mixed methods project placed in a very secondary role. She notes:

> A design is set in place, a protocol followed. In the main, the questions are descriptive, traditional positivist research language is used with a dusting of words from other paradigms, and the designs come up with structured descriptive results. Integration is at a descriptive level. A qualitative aspect of the study is often "fitted in." The thinking is clearly positivist and pragmatic. The message often received by a naïve researcher, however, is that mixed methods combines and shares "thinking" at the paradigm level. (p. 200)

According to Giddings (2006), the idea that mixed methods now combines the best of both qualitative and quantitative approaches is a "new guise," for what is primarily positivism (p. 200). Giddings expressed her uneasiness with what

she saw as an "add and stir" qualitative component into a general positivistic mixed methods approach (p. 202). Giddings' article launched a heated debate about the role of qualitative methods and approaches in MMR that continues into the contemporary period. Other mixed methods scholars (see, e.g., Creswell, Shope, Plano Clark, & Greene, 2006; Mason, 2006) took specific issue with this viewpoint, citing the empirical MMR, especially in the health sciences, that gave specific priority to qualitative research in mixed methods designs.

Yet the debate on the dominance of specific MMR designs continues today with a focus on examining the extent to which specific disciplinary locations and funding preferences can shape the specific contours of a given MMR design (see: Freshwater & Fisher, this volume). In addition, the increasing shift to an "audit model" of accountability in knowledge-building and the growth of MMR whose goal is to perhaps "tame" the turbulence of mixed methods praxis keeps the importance of examining the sociopolitical context of MMR knowledge-building a challenge that will remain and one that is critical to continue to address.

The crossing of borders in MMR potentially offers a powerful antidote to dominant paradigmatic viewpoints. To interface with an interdisciplinary perspective is transformative and acknowledges, as Namaste (1992) notes regarding the political dimension of knowledge-building:

> To engage in interdisciplinary work is a practice that seeks to recognize and transform the current (un)reality of disciplinary boundaries. It understands the ways in which knowledge is currently carved up within academe, yet seeks to deconstruct the production of truths, the operations of power, and the assumptions about knowledge which are implicit in that apparatus. It implicitly—and sometimes explicitly—asks 'Who's doing the carving?' and ' In whose interest?'. . . In this context, interdisciplinary work can be understood as a politics of intervention, and as theoretically and politically necessary. (p. 58)

As evidenced by this handbook and the expanding horizon of MMR literature overall, many researchers are staking their claims to new forms of knowledge-building. In addition, new and future claims to, and ways of claiming, power are emerging that promise to increase the turbulence within and across the MMR landscape as a whole.

Challenge 5: Practicing Reflexivity

Conducting research across disciplinary borders also highlights how important it is researchers to reflect on their own *standpoint* within the research process. Hesse-Biber and Piatelli (2012) note the importance of "holistic reflexivity" (2012) by noting, "Reflexivity is a holistic process that takes place along all stages of the research process—from the formulation of the research problem, to the shifting standpoint of the researcher and participants, through interpretation and writing" (p. 560).

Reay (2012) notes that as one traverses this turbulent landscape, notes there will been a need for "continuous interrogation" of self and other as reflexivity consists of "complex and constantly shifting processes which require constant monitoring and re-evaluation" (p. 637). A researchers' values and attitudes are important parts of the reflection process—what values do researchers bring to their work? In addition, reflexivity is a process that moves beyond individual reflection and is also

> a communal process that requires attentiveness to how the structural, political, and cultural environments of the researcher, the participants, and the nature of the study affect the research process and product. Reflexivity at this level fosters sharing, engaged relationships and participatory knowledge building practices, hence, producing less hierarchical and more ethical, socially relevant research. (Hesse-Biber & Piatelli, 2012, p. 560)

The practice of reflexivity holds promise of bringing subjugated knowledges to the surface and thus can awareness that "all knowledge is affected by the social conditions under which it is produced and that it is grounded in both the social location and the social biography of the observer and the observed" (Mann & Kelley, 1997, p. 392). A methodology that incorporates reflexivity can, if done well, lead to the "development of critical consciousness of both researcher and participants, improvement of the lives of those involved in the research process, and transformation of fundamental societal structures and relationships" (Maguire, 1987, p. 29; see also Hertz, 1997).

Reflexivity then, helps to break down the idea that research is the "view from nowhere." Reflecting on the many ways our own agendas impact the research process at all points in our research—from the selection of the research problem to the selection of method and the ways in which we analyze and interpret our findings—is crucial for creating authenticity in the research process.

Challenge 6: Border Tensions of Differences: Difference Matters, Social Justice Matters, and Axiology Matters

MMMR is not *just* about mixing and combining methods. Tools must be clearly linked to epistemologies, political stances, methodologies, theoretical perspectives, and axiologies/values engagement. Difference itself is contextual and undergoing change; some differences are highlighted or rendered invisible depending on the social context. Hesse-Biber and Yaiser's (2004) work on difference notes, for example, that status characteristics such as social class, age, ethnicity, and sexuality can be prominent in some interactions and rendered unimportant in others. Gorelick (1996) suggests that in studying difference it is critical to consider the relational qualities of difference that allow the researcher to move beyond describing difference to "an analysis of the forces producing those differences and relationships and the dynamic structure of which they are a changing part (p. 41). Here the epiphany is simply the revelation that difference operates differently in various contexts.

A further epiphany on difference is that until the community of scholars working the turbulent landscape has a range of scholars who hail from a range of differences—more Black, Asian, and Latino minority faculty, women from working-class and poor backgrounds, disabled and lesbian, transgendered and gay researchers—the conundrum of how to represent the "other" may continue to be stifled. Even when there is a growing recognition that difference matters, one needs to ponder the implications of "speaking for the other" (see Alcoff, 1991–1992; Spivak, 1988) when those individuals doing the researching are predominantly White, middle class, able bodied, heterosexual, and hailing from the developed world. So an important difference epiphany is the need to advocate for the inclusion of difference within and among those who conduct research on this turbulent terrain and the inclusion of difference in our research endeavors (see, e.g., chapters in this volume by Cram & Mertens; Hankivksy & Grace; and Hesse-Biber & Griffin).

Challenge 7: Navigating Technological Borders

The MMMR terrain is increasingly mediated by emergent technologies (see Hesse-Biber, 2011). The rise of emergent technologies—including multimedia Web 2.0, mobile and geospatial technologies, and the rise of multiplatform software—is transforming how MMMR researchers use and deploy traditional tools and is also expanding the range of knowledge-building tools (see: Horrigna 2007; Internet World Statistics, 2010).

These new technologies also change the medium through which communications are sent and received. This *Handbook* recognizes that technology is a medium (technology "delivers" information) of communication that has an independent impact on its users in its own right regardless of its content. It is important to consider how new technologies and modes of communication (such as online surveys and ethnographies) impact MMMR praxis (see Hesse-Biber & Griffin, 2013; James & Busher, 2010; Salmons, this volume).

Some research about how technology is deployed in MMMR demonstrates that by varying modes in timing (synchronous/asynchronous), direction (unidirectional/bidirectional), and public/private forums it can impact the meaning and interpretations of the message being delivered. These new technologies "are a transformative force that will challenge received knowledge, generate original empirical insights, and catalyze new theories" (Hackett, 2011, p. 26).

Technological tools are constantly evolving and pushing the boundaries with regard to the organization of the research process in that they introduce new modes of data collection and provide the researcher with new ways to mine data and generate new data forms. They also bring new challenges into the research arena by adding different levels of communication, such as the digital and virtual (see chapters in this volume by Salmons; Hine; Remijn, Stembert, Mulder, & Choenni; and Fielding & Fielding).

New borders are crossed between the "real" and "virtual" with attendant obstacles (the research teams may be scattered at distant physical locations and come together virtually only as, in effect, disembodied beings). These new technologies are forming their own research structures, often outside of traditional academic settings and funded by for-profit entities. The MMMR community is witnessing a shift from a "one data set" study structure toward multiple data sets aggregated from a range of structural levels (micro/meso/macro) emanating from a variety of sources (online/offline/mobile/hybrid). Adding to the complexity of these new data forms, the increasing streaming of these data in real time means that they are more and more characterized by their longitudinal quality. When so many methods for data collection and analysis are required, one of the challenges for mixed

methods researchers is to reconceptualize the very definition of MMR as something more than just the use of one qualitative and one quantitative data collection method.

We know that varying modes in timing (synchronous/asynchronous), direction (unidirectional/bidirectional), and public/private forums can impact meaning and interpretations of the message being delivered. These new technologies "are a transformative force that will challenge received knowledge, generate original empirical insights, and catalyze new theories" (Hackett, 2011, p. 26; see also Eagle, 2011).

However, there is a downside to the introduction of new technologies into MMMR practice. For example, ethical boundaries can become uncertain as private and public information becomes blurred, such as when highly personal information available publicly over the Internet is collected and deployed in a MMMR study. What are the ethical procedures surrounding the issues in securing "informed consent" when a research project goes online? Some basic concepts that form the bedrock of ethics practices such as insuring the confidentiality of research participants can easily be comprised in a cyber-world (Gunkel, 2011; Hesse-Biber, 2011; Hesse-Biber & Griffin, 2013, also see Salmons, this volume)?

The exponential growth of "big data," arising from the collection of large volumes of user-generated and streaming digital data from networking sites such as Twitter and Facebook, may also place pressures on mixed methods researchers to transform traditional modes of collecting and analyzing data generated from these sites. These technological developments may also morph MMMR practices as these emergent mixed and multimethods data and analytical forms challenge researchers to reconceptualize their basic methods concepts and even methodological perspectives. In turn, multimethod and mixed methods researchers can offer insights to big data analytical techniques by providing ways to integrate big data at multiple levels of inquiry and bring a range of qualitatively driven insights to big data through the asking of complex questions and the potential for providing a more in-depth complex understanding of the social worlds of the digital and real (see Hesse-Biber & Johnson, 2013).

These are only some of the major regions of turbulence in the MMMR research landscape. There are others researchers will experience on their journey across the MMMR landscape as well as many factors that may determine the type of experience they have. The experience will depend in large part on researcher standpoint—the values and attitudes that make up one's view of the social research landscape,; the skills, research experience, and tools one brings; who, if anyone, comes along; and what they bring with them.

Navigating Multimethod and Mixed Methods Research Tensions Together: Getting Ready the Journey

Mapping the multimethod and mixed methods terrain (see Creswell, 2010) can serve to provide some important preliminary guidance especially for novice researchers seeking to conduct MMMR. However, I do not necessarily recommend becoming too reliant on any specific MMMR map as a guide. While maps may seem innocuous, says cartographer D. Dorling (1997), they need to be used with caution:

> For all the power they contain, maps are just pieces of paper or merely ephemeral pixels on a computer screen. It is people who order, draw, purchase, use, and learn from maps. And it is people who will improve them—not necessarily by making them more accurate or objective but, for a start, by being more honest about how and why they are made and by teaching more carefully about how to read them. We can all be more open about why we make particular choices to map certain things, certain people, and certain places. We can all think more carefully than we have done in the past about these things. We can also all look at other maps with a slightly more open and inquisitive mind and ask why the map shows what it shows, rather than try merely to understand how best the relationship between land and people can be painted onto paper. (p. 279)

How much one relies on any map is also dependent on the type of research questions (explanatory and/or exploratory) addressed. Wagner's (1993) distinction with regard to types of research questions is a useful heuristic idea in gauging the degree of reliance on any specific map. He notes that some research questions have the goal of filling in the "blank spots" in a field of inquiry that is already mapped, such that the question relies on the nuances of already mapped out questions and significant findings. These mapped inquiry terrains, however, still need to be interrogated, but the degrees of freedom in inquiry are more constrained. However, if we all stick to this type of inquiry (the trails mapped by others), we may never uncover those blind spots along the way—those

areas of inquiry we fail to see or address or even know that we do not know about (Wagner, 1993).

In addition, it might be important to consider that by sticking too closely to a map that already contains precarved inquiry trails that lie on often shifting terrain may significantly prevent one from seeking out new ground and insights that may lie within MMR landscape but remain subjugated. Before using any inquiry map, it might be important to ask some questions, such as: Whose viewpoint was taken into account in the mapping process? What does the map exclude? Will following a specific map and its research trails reproduce someone else's reality, research experience, interests, and agenda? Who benefits from following a specific trail or set of trails? What are the ethical conundrums in any mapping design? (See Preissle, Glover-Kudon, Rohan, Boehm, & DeGroff, this volume.) How can we unearth the ethical substructure of the MMMR terrain that still remains subjugated?

So if not a given map, then what? One might begin by making the decision to not be overly reliant on any one map but also taking what one thinks is critical information from a given set of mappings of the terrain by those who have journeyed before, but also making the commitment to being open to charting new ground.

By privileging the charting of your own journey, you empower yourself to venture out of your own theoretical and methods routines as you venture onto the MMMR landscape, with the wisdom and skills you have already garnered but bent also on blazing a new set of trails as well. Your final mapping post-journey can be recorded for you and other future travelers to compare and contrast. You can think of mapping as an iterative process, something not fixed but morphing, by being open to the collective wisdom of the whole. Thus mapping as a collective and interactive process can be of value to the MMMR community; it can be continually open to innovation and can serve to encourage others to forge new trails and even revisit more established trails with a critical perspective, committed to recording their mapping results for others to compare and learn from.

You might also think about bringing a backpack along on your journey, one that allows mobility and agility while also providing storage space for the range of technological tools, as well as material and nonmaterial resources they many deem essential to their MMMR journey. These are insights that can serve to guide, empower, and sustain a MMMR journey as a decision-making guide as you traverse the MMMR terrain. There exists a range and type of backpacks that can also be tailored to a given researcher's specific needs. Some backpacks allow for attaching customized accessories—those specialized tools and items—those one may require in an emergency or to use to tackle unexpected turbulence along the way.

The border challenges I have thus far elaborated in this Introduction were the insights I found useful to have in my own backpack. Some of the border challenges I present are analytical epiphanies while others are more skills based; still some others are more researcher identity-based epiphanies. I also had to discard some things on my journey as a way to shed the weight of my backpack that was slowing me down. Some of these things included former ways of doing things—those ideas and skills that kept me from stepping out of my own theory-methods comfort zone.

I end this *Handbook* Introduction with a range of insights gathered from some of our *Handbook* authors who agreed to share with all of you the range of things and insights they might take with them on their MMMR journey. I asked *Handbook* authors to dialogue with me around the following question: What would you put in your MMMR backpack as you traversed the MMMR terrain? *Handbook* authors' insights, ideas, and extraordinary wisdom are something you might also want to also consider as you begin your own MMMR journey. The voices of *Handbook* authors reveal a range of lived experiences as fellow travelers along the MMMR terrain. I invite you to visit our *Handbook* website for each authors' entire comments.

The type of entry an author or coauthor contributed was variable—from one sentence to many paragraphs. In looking over the entries I have received, thus far, several themes emerged. Some advice was practical and material, focusing on very specific material resources they would bring with them on their journey; still others provided a range of cognitive and socioemotional insights and cautionary tales from their prior experiences along the trail. Still others provided uplifting words of wisdom they felt might sustain and uplift a weary MMMR traveler.

Handbook Authors' Thematic Backpack Insights
Developing Open-Mindedness

Having an open mind was a theme that resonated with our authors. The overall meanings of this theme centered on being open to allow for the

possibility of dialogue. Jennifer C. Greene sought to promote a "renewed respectful listening" to the range of voices and perspectives within the MMMR community. Sylvia E. Rogers wholeheartedly endorses this idea by noting,

> As a new scholar, one of the most important things that I pull out of my backpack frequently is patience and listening. Insights do not always pop up immediately in front of me, it takes patience and listening skills to engage with the data and understand what the data are telling me.

Amy Griffin suggests two important elements that facilitate being open-minded, namely "patience and compromise." She notes further,

> Research and policy both take time, especially when conversing across disciplines and potential areas of focus. This can be a long and sometimes frustrating process; however, by continuing to listen, reflect, ask questions, and [have a] willingness to work together, one's research will be more meaningful and beneficial to the greater community.

Listening to one's data is another aspect of being open-minded. Leonard A. Jason and Isadore Newman both stress this point in different ways. Leonard A. Jason notes that "linear thinking," based on statistics and methods, must "catch up with what we see and hear, but which are still rarely documented by our research." Isadore Newman notes that all research requires "phenomenological judgment." He goes on to note that even when a researcher relies on statistical significance testing, qualitative judgment enters into just what this means.

Being open to differences in perspective is also dimension of open-mindedness. Rachel L. Shaw suggests inviting those holding different perspectives along on our MMMR journey such that "Together we can make the journey across the choppy seas of epistemological and technical challenges to reach our destination and become a world leading mixed methods research team!" Roslyn A. Cameron in fact argues for a "methodological melting pot" and specifically advocates for the inclusion of multidisciplinary team-based research. She further suggests that the characteristics of a multidisciplinary team-based research are critical to harnessing the potential for open-mindedness required in a MMR project by noting.

> There is something interesting about those who actively seek engagement in multidisciplinary teams

and the level of openness in considering a mixed methods approach. This is very much like the level of openness to travel abroad, to leave comfort zones, take risks and to see and experience other traditions and cultural practices and to begin to see everyday activities through the perspectives of others.

Nigel G. Fielding and Jane L. Fielding also remind us that communicating across MMR divides also includes cultural divides and point to the importance of taking along a perspective on mixed methods that also includes alternative meanings, by noting:

> The message here, perhaps, is that equivalence of meaning is important, and cultural translation is not trivial, even in things that seem straightforward. Mixing methods intrinsically involves working across cultures, notably the differing cultures of quantitative and qualitative research, but increasingly drawing in ideas, concepts and techniques from other fields altogether. Taking a mixed methods approach seriously forces researchers to be more explicit. That is a virtue.

Acquiring Collaboration, Balance and Team-based Research Environments

Another important ingredient to obtain "dialogue" among MMMR communities is the concept of "balancing" and being in "collaboration" with different points of view that may often require working within a team-based environment.

Julianne Cheek notes that "In every debate or discussion about any aspect of mixed method research, it is important that all points of view and facets of that discussion are able to be heard and balanced against each other in order to be evaluated on their merits." Creating a level discourse field is critical to dialoguing across different MMMR perspective. Pat Bazeley notes that collaboration with other MMMR in and of itself has the potential to foster "insights and stimulation."

These sentiments are echoed by Janet E. Salmons, who notes the importance of "balance and scope" in any MMMR project. Using her own experience as a qualitative researcher she appreciates the importance of learning "how to integrate quantitative methods and findings to balance the results of qualitative inquiry and to increase the scope of the study. Rick Szostak is in support of the importance of honoring different perspectives and notes, "We are trained as scholars to argue for one theoretical position but should appreciate that there is usually value in multiple perspectives. We should seek to integrate the best of differing insights rather than seeking all-out victory for one."

Taking these multiple insights together suggests that the road to dialogue does not lie with a framing of our research goals to mean that of "winning" or defending our research position but rather taking the route toward maximizing the potential of discovering a range of ideas and thinking collectively to discover new possibilities and alternatives.

Yet the ingredients needed to promote dialogue across divergent communities may require additional strategies. Donna M. Mertens suggests that we need to explore the range of sites for dialogue beyond coming together across the qualitative–quantitative divide. She notes, "We are not limited to quant and qual, but we can look at the variety of ways of knowing and gathering and making visible knowledge that comes in many different forms—dance, music, poetry, art, and statistics"

Yes, you may say, but wait, there are those important socioemotional factors, those that cannot easily be measured, but nonetheless are also critical to the dialogic process. Judith Preissle reminds us of the importance of fostering the qualities of friendship, trust, and companionship that she herself has learned in her "other" job that entails the rescuing of animals in her community. It is these qualities that are also critical in building on "the quality of commitment among partners." By the way, if you have an RV, even better, suggests Amy DeGroff, who states, "I like to think of my having an RV with all of you traveling along with me on our MMMR journey."

Nigel G. Fielding and Jane L. Fielding note that at its heart "doing mixed methods research is an endeavor that tends toward teamwork" by nothing that "while there are gifted people who combine a quantitative and a qualitative instinct in the same head" this does not always happen. Elizabeth A. Rohan suggests that one important key ingredient in effective team-based research is to create a vibrant research climate that makes dialogue possible." While taking a team-based approach to mixed methods research is important, she notes, there is the work that needs to take place in the selection of the particular makeup of one's MMR team. She notes,

> I pay particular attention to choosing my colleagues for the journey. While they don't fit inside my backpack, my teammates help me carry a large backpack, filled with the skills we each bring to the research endeavor. Each of us carries the backpack

for a while, depending on whose skills are most needed for a particular task, but, in the end, the load is ours to bear together. Side by side, we share the exertion and the sense of purpose needed to reach the destination.

Stevan Weine's insights regarding balance and collaboration take us beyond the research community context; he notes, "Researchers conducting MMMR should engage collaboratively with families, communities, and organizations through participatory research and capacity building. The process of working with communities is as or more important than the outcomes."

The next set of insights center on the question regarding: What are the traits that are crucial for dialoguing? Our *Handbook* authors also weighed in on this issue, and a number of our authors were quick to point out the importance of taking a flexible approach to knowledge-building across the MMMR terrain.

Nurturing Flexibility That Allows for Innovation and Creativity

Rebecca O'Connell and Julia Brannen, for example, note the importance of flexibility as an important trait to nurture as they cross the MMR turbulent landscape. They note how important it is for researchers to acquire "plenty of ingenuity, creativity, and flexibility. In our backpack we would carry the proviso that there is no one successful method for integrating mixed method research, given the different means by which different types of data are produced."

Fiona Cram suggests that the keys to successfully dialoguing with others is to cultivate "a 'relaxed and responsive flexibility.' By this I mean that we have enough skills and tools/methods and relaxed attitude in our backpack to be responsive to the feedback and requests of our participant communities." Cram goes on to note,

> It's interesting that we're always looking for the mix of methods that will let our communities "hold the pen" and so we have to be relaxed, responsive, and flexible when they chose to hold that pen in a different way than we initially intended. Our communities also want to know how we see mixed methods being mixed, and for what purpose.

Nollaig A. Frost wants to gain expertise in a wide range of "methods and designs as possible so that I am prepared to take the research in directions it calls for rather than those I had planned

for, if necessary." But for Frost, one key ingredient in doing so is to acquire humility. She expands on this by stating, "In my quest to know more about topics I recognize that my toolbox can include the skills of others as well as my own."

Yet developing some socioemotional and cognitive skills may not be enough to engage with the qualitative–quantitative divide. Rebecca M. Glover-Kudon brings us back to the issue of also being prepared with the necessary level of methods skills required for the journey across the MMMR turbulent terrain. She notes,

> Serious expeditions need to be well-equipped. I came to mixed-methods as an evaluation practitioner, tasked with informing a wide range of programmatic and/or policy decisions in a public health context. Armed with both sets of tools, quantitative and qualitative, I feel I can respond more nimbly to the research questions at hand, rather than be limited to a particular toolbox.

In order to engage in this type of cognitive thinking, John H. Hitchcock notes the need to foster a question-driven approach to MMR:

> It may be better to think of research as a singular enterprise that is driven by questions rather than a compendium of methodologies that can appear to be incompatible. More often than not, I think a mixed methods approach will help me find the fullest answers, but I let the questions (and too often a budget) dictate design.

Uncovering the Hidden Philosophical, Ethical, and Social Justice and Social Change Dimensions of MMMR Inquiry Frameworks

One of the most ephemeral of issues with regard to MMMR is a consideration of the foundational substructure within which MMMR is housed. While this may appear to be a very esoteric issue for some MMMR members, I would argue that it is a critical issue to engage with and a critical element in our journey toward dialoguing with the range of differences that comprise the MMMR turbulent landscape.

The remarks of Sharon Crasnow highlight the importance of bringing attention to the assumptions any researcher is buying into with regard to such questions as the nature of the social world by noting, "Philosophical tools need something to be applied to and without looking at how methods are actually used in particular research projects in the social sciences; there is no philosophy of social science." Robert K. Yin questions some basic issues regarding MMMR generalizations:

I am not even aware that anyone is working on filling these lacunae, which call for codifying how to fairly and effectively operationalize key procedures central to all of quantitative and qualitative research—that is: how to test rival explanations, or how to establish that triangulation has occurred, or how to claim relevant generalizations when not following the statistical sample-to-population generalization procedure. My contribution to the *Handbook* suggests that these are truly lacunae that MMMR needs to exercise leadership in filling.

Margarete Sandelowski's comments speak to the importance of fostering a social justice/social change framework (along with others who address this issue in the *Handbook* such as Donna M. Mertens, Fiona Cram, and others) in the work that MMR engages with. In doing so, Sandelowski's remarks remind us of the importance of reflecting on our own set of values and biases that we bring the MMR enterprise.: "Keep your eye on the prize; we conduct mixed-methods research not for the sake merely of conducting it but rather for the knowledge we produce to have positive impact in the world. Substance should never be sacrificed for methodolatry."

Jori N. Hall follows up by stressing the importance of MMR engagement with ethical practices. She asserts,

Although there are many items in my backpack, I consistently find myself searching for one: "an ethical mindset.". . . In practice, an ethical mindset is imperative particularly as it relates to researchers examining how mixed methods designs interact with the local context and the participants therein.

Acquiring an Understanding of the Importance of Reflexivity

A number of our *Handbook* authors mentioned the importance of bringing a reflexive perspective onto MMMR research. Judith Preissle notes, "My knapsack, of course, has whatever is conducive to napping; rest and reflection are crucial for problem solving." Albert Hunter advises researchers to bring a "multimethod backpack [that] when unpacked is seen to contain the defining diverse elements that make up science itself. And, these should be applied reflexively to 'multimethods' as well."

Udo Kelle suggests that

What is needed in my opinion is a methodological debate which is a continuous and ongoing reflection

of concrete research practice. The other point refers to the relation between research topic, research question, method, and (substantive) theory. We should always remind ourselves and our research and doctoral students that the choice of the right method (whether qualitative or quantitative) is influenced by theoretical ideas about the field under investigation. That influence is always present, albeit it is often left implicit (and in that case it should be made explicit).

Sarah J. Drabble remarks on how reflexivity centers "on the deeper methodological issues." Melvin M. Mark suggests using a compass that includes "maintaining perspective about why one cares about MMMR, which for most people presumably involved the questions they're asking." John Creswell's remarks remind us about the importance of reflexivity in a global context, by noting that the actions, images, and symbols of MMMR are important in promoting a "growing global interest in adapting mixed methods for those around the world."

One last, but not by any means final, insight from our *Handbook* authors is reflective of just what it takes for you, the researcher, to engage with a MMMR project, namely, the importance of considering the level of professional research commitment and time to completion of a given MMMR project.

Commitment and Engagement

Several of our *Handbook* authors raised some cautionary points regarding just what it would take for those within and outside the MMMR community to engage with a MMMR project.

Nicola A. Jones and Paola Pereznieto were emphatic about the importance of researchers, especially those engaged with international development MMMR, to dedicate "the time, resources and commitment to provide thorough and hands-on training and mentoring to local research partners who are often more familiar with doing research using structured surveys for quantitative data collection than using qualitative and participatory methods." Jennifer P. Wisdom's backpack insights provide an important follow-up to Jones and Pereznieto's concerns by noting the importance of having a project manager to oversee the range of demands required of any MMR project that also seeks external funding. Wisdom shares her wealth of experience in seeking funding for MMR projects. She provides information for those who seek to venture into the world of competitive research funding and offers some important advice: She notes that it is

> imperative to have a plan for completing the required products within the timelines set by funders or others. Project management techniques have provided to me with a way to structure study activities to maximize both time spent in the joy of absorption while ensuring completion of activities in a timely manner.

As you start your MMMR journey, I hope that you might think about what symbolic or material things you might want to take along with you.

Some Closing Thoughts as You Begin Your Journey

Handbook authors push on the boundaries of traditional knowledge-building by venturing out of their methods routine and utiliing their creativity and intellect in the service of answering complex questions that arise from a range of newly emerging theoretical perspectives, as well as responding to immediate problems within their research environments.

Moving across the many borders and challenges that are discussed in this Handbook introduction and elaborated on in the Handbook as a whole may also require that multimethod and mixed methods researchers reframe their approach and methods practices. So, for example, monomethods and single disciplinary research may give way to "team-based" interdisciplinary projects. Such crossing of research approaches, methods, and disciplinary divides may provide the potential new synergy for imagining a cacophony of visions in conversation with the goal of addressing complex questions with multifaceted challenges. Having a backpack and not being too reliant on a particular premapped research trail may promote flexibility for multimethod and mixed methods researchers to change their course along their MMMR journey.

It is my personal hope that this *Handbook* will encourage other researchers to begin to create accounts of their own MMMR practices and histories. These accounts can help build on the range of MMMR perspectives and practices that reside within and across the disciplines and beyond. Engaging in a deep dialogic process that is ongoing and open toward the inclusion of a diverse and multiple perspectives onto the MMMR landscape may hold the promise of unleashing the synergistic potential of MMMR endeavors.

References

Ahmed, A., & Sil, R. (2012). When multi-method research subverts methodological pluralism—or, why we still need single-method research? *Perspectives on Politics, 10*(4), 935–953. doi:10.1017/S1537592712002836

Alcoff, L. (1991–1992). The problem of speaking for others. *Cultural Critique, 20*, 5–32. Retrieved from http://www.jstor.org/stable/1354221

Allen, P. G. (1992). Border studies: The intersections of gender and color. In J. Gibaldi (Ed.), *Introduction to scholarship in modern languages and literatures* (2nd ed.; pp. 303–319): New York: Modern Language Association of America.

Bazeley, P. (2003). Computerized data analysis for mixed methods research. In A. Tashakkori & C. Teddlie (Eds.), *Handbook of mixed methods in social & behavioral research* (pp. 385–422). Thousand Oaks, CA: SAGE.

Bazeley, P. (2006). The contribution of computer software to integrating qualitative and quantitative data and analyses, *Research in the Schools, 13*(1), 64–74.

Bazeley P. (2009). Editorial: Integrating data analyses in mixed method research. *Journal of Mixed Methods Research, 3*(3), 203–207.

Best, J. (2014). *Governing failure: Provisional expertise and the transformation of global development finance.* New York. Cambridge University Press.

Biesta, G. (2010). Pragmatism and the philosophical foundations of mixed methods research. In A. Tashakkori & C. Teddlie (Eds.), *SAGE Handbook of mixed methods in social & behavioral research* (2nd ed., pp. 95–118). Thousand Oaks, CA: SAGE.

Booth, C. (1886–1903). *Life and labour of the people of London.* London: Macmillan.

Brewer, J., & Hunter, A. (1989). *Multimethods research: A synthesis of styles.* Newbury Park, CA: SAGE.

Bryman, A. (2006a). Integrating quantitative and qualitative research: How is it done? *Qualitative Research, 6*, 97–113.

Bryman, A. (2006b). Paradigm peace and the implication for quality. *International Journal of Social Research Methodology, 9*(3), 111–126.

Bryman, A. (2007). Barriers to integrating quantitative and research. *Journal of Mixed Methods Research, 1*(8), 8–22.

Bryman, A., Becker, S., & Sempik, J. (2008). Quality criteria for quantitative, qualitative, and mixed methods research: A view from social policy. *International Journal of Social Research Methodology, 11*, 261–276. doi:10.1080/13645570701401644

Campbell, D. T., & Fiske, D. W. (1959). Convergent and discriminant validation by the multitrait-multimethod matrix. *Psychological Bulletin, 56*, 81–105.

Creswell, J. W. (2010). Mapping the developing landscape of mixed methods research. In A. Tashakkori & C. Teddlie (Eds.), *SAGE Handbook of mixed methods in social & behavioral research* (2nd ed., pp. 45–68).Thousand Oaks, CA: SAGE.

Creswell, J. W., & Plano Clark, V. L. (2007). *Designing and conducting mixed methods research.* Thousand Oaks, CA: SAGE.

Creswell, J. W., & Plano Clark, V. L. (2011). *Designing and conducting mixed methods research* (2nd ed.). Thousand Oak, CA: SAGE.

Creswell, J. W., Shope, R., Plano Clark, V. L., & Green, D. O. (2006). How interpretive qualitative research extends mixed methods research. *Research in the Schools, 13*, 1–11.

De Lauretis, T. (1988). Displacing hegemonic discourses: Reflections on feminist theory in the 1980s. *Inscriptions*, 3(4), 127–145.

Denscombe, M. (2008). Communities of practice: A research paradigm for the mixed methods approach. *Journal of Mixed Methods Research*, 2(3), 270–283.

Denzin, N. (2009). The elephant in the living room: Or extending the conversation about the politics of evidence. *Qualitative Research*, 9(2), 139–160.

Denzin, N. K. (2010). Moments, mixed methods, and paradigm dialogs. *Qualitative Inquiry*, 16, 419–427.

Denzin, N. K., & Lincoln, Y. S. (Eds.). (2005). *The SAGE handbook of qualitative research* (3rd ed.). Thousand Oaks, CA: SAGE.

Dewey, J. (2009). *Democracy and education*. Radford, VA: Wilder. (Original work published 1916)

Dorling, D. (1997). Human cartography: When is it good to map? *Environment and Planning*, 30, 277–288.

Eagle, N. (2011). Mobile phones as sensors for social research. In S. N. Hesse-Biber (Ed.), *The handbook of emergent technologies in social research* (pp. 492–521). New York: Oxford University Press.

Foucault, M. (1975). *The birth of the clinic: An archeology of medical perception*. New York: Vintage/Random House.

Foucault, M. (1991). Questions of methods. In G. Burchell, C. Gordon, & P. Miller (Eds.), *The Foucault effect: Studies in governmentality* (pp. 73–86). Chicago: University of Chicago Press.

Giddings, L. S. (2006). Mixed methods research: Positivism dressed in drag? *Journal of Research in Nursing*, 11(3), 195–203.

Giddings, L. S., & Grant, B. M. (2007). A Trojan horse for positivism? *Advances in Nursing Science*, 30, 52–60.

Gorelick, S. (1996). Contradictions of feminist methodology. In E. Ngan-Ling Chow, D. Wilkinson, & M. B. Zinn (Eds.), *Race, class & gender: Common bonds, different voices*. Thousand Oaks, CA: SAGE.

Greene, J. C. (2006). Toward a methodology of mixed methods social inquiry. *Research in the Schools*, 13(1), 93–98.

Greene, J. C. (2007). *Mixed methods in social inquiry*. San Francisco, CA: Jossey-Bass.

Greene, J. C. (2008). Is mixed methods social inquiry a distinctive methodology? *Journal of Mixed Methods Research*, 2(1), 7–22.

Greene, J., & Caracelli, V. (1997). Defining and describing the paradigm issue in mixed-method evaluation. *New Directions for Evaluation*, 74, 5–17. doi:10.1002/ev.1068

Greene, J. C., & Hall, J. N. (2010). Dialectics and pragmatism: Being of consequence. In A. Tashakkori & C. Teddlie (Eds.), *SAGE handbook of mixed methods in social & behavioral research* (pp. 119–144). Thousand Oaks, CA: SAGE.

Guba, E. G. (1987). What have we learned about naturalistic evaluation? *Evaluation Practice*, 8(1), 23–43. doi:http://dx.doi.org/10.1016/S0886-1633(87)80037-5

Guba, E. G. (1989). In Lincoln Y. S. (Ed.), *Fourth generation evaluation*. Newbury Park, CA: SAGE. Retrieved from http://search.lib.unc.edu?R=UNCb2306971

Guest, G. (2013). Describing mixed methods research: An alternative to typologies. *Journal of Mixed Methods Research*, 7, 141–151. doi:10.1177/1558689812461179

Gunkel, D. J. (2011). To tell the truth: The internet and emergent epistemological challenges in social research. In S. N. Hesse-Biber (Ed.), *The handbook of emergent technologies in social research* (pp. 47–64). New York: Oxford University Press.

Hackett, E. J. (2011). Possible dreams: Research technologies and the transformation of the human sciences. In S. N. Hesse-Biber's (Ed.). *The handbook of emergent technologies in social research* (pp. 25–46). New York: Oxford University Press.

Hertz, R. (Ed.). (1997). *Reflexivity & voice*. Thousand Oaks, CA: SAGE.

Hesse-Biber, S. (2010a). *Mixed methods research: Merging theory with practice*. New York: Guilford Press.

Hesse-Biber, S. N. (2010b). Qualitative approaches to mixed methods practice. *Qualitative Inquiry*, 16(6), 455–468.

Hesse-Biber, S. (2013). Thinking outside the randomized control trials experimental box for enhancing credibility and social justice. In D. M. Mertens & S. Hesse-Biber (Eds.), *Mixed methods and credibility of evidence in evaluation* (pp. 49–60). (New Directions for Evaluation 138). New York: Wiley/Jossey-Bass.

Hesse-Biber, S. (2014). *Waiting for cancer to come: Genetic testing and women's medical decision making for breast and ovarian cancer*. Ann Arbor: University of Michigan Press

Hesse-Biber, S. (Ed.). (2011). *The handbook of emergent technologies in social research*. New York: Oxford University Press.

Hesse-Biber, S., & Griffin, A. (2013). Internet-mediated technologies and mixed methods research: Problems and prospects. *Journal of Mixed Methods Research*, 7(1), 43–61.

Hesse-Biber, S., & Johnson, R. B. (2013). Coming at things differently: Future directions of possible engagement with mixed methods research. *Journal of Mixed Methods Research*, 7(2), 103–109.

Hesse-Biber, S. N., & Leckenby, D. (Eds.). (2003). *Women in catholic higher education: Border work, living experiences and social justice*. Lanham, MD: Lexington Books.

Hesse-Biber, S. N., & Leavy, P. L. (Eds.). (2008). *Handbook of Emergent methods in social research*. New York: Guilford Press.

Hesse-Biber, S. N., & Piatelli, D. (2012). The feminist practice of holistic reflexivity. In S. N. Hesse-Biber (Ed.), *The handbook of feminist research: Theory and praxis* (2nd ed., pp.28–45). Thousand Oaks, CA: SAGE.

Hesse-Biber, S. N., & Yaiser, M. L. (2004). *Feminist perspectives on social research*. New York: Oxford University Press.

Heyvaert, M., Hannes, K., Maes, B., & Onghena, P. (2013). Critical appraisal of mixed methods studies. *Journal of Mixed Methods Research*, 7, 302–307. doi:10.1177/1558689813479449

Higonett, M. R. (1994). *Borderwork*. Ithaca, NY: Cornell University Press.

Horrigan, J. (2007). Wireless internet access. Pew Internet and American Life Project. Retrieved from http://apo.org.au/?q=node/16732

Howe, K. R. (2004). A critique of experimentalism. *Qualitative Inquiry*, 10, 42–61.

Hunter, A., & Brewer, J. (2006). *Foundations of multimethod research*. Thousand Oaks, CA: SAGE.

Internet World Statistics. (2010). U.S. Internet usage statistics. Retrieved from http://www.internetworldstats.com/am/us.htm

James, N., & Busher, H. (2010). *Online interviewing*. London: SAGE.

Johnson, R. B., & Onwuegbuzie, A. J. (2004). Mixed methods research: A research paradigm whose time has come. *Educational Researcher*, 33(7), 14–26.

Johnson, R. B., Onwuegbuzie, A. J., & Turner, L. A. (2007). Towards a definition of mixed methods research: A research paradigm whose time has come, *Journal of Mixed Methods Research, 1*(2), 112–133.

Johnson, R. B., & Stefurak, T. (2013). Considering the evidence-and-credibility discussion in evaluation through the lens of dialectical pluralism. In D. M. Mertens & S. Hesse-Biber (Eds.), *Mixed methods and credibility of evidence in evaluation* (pp. 37–48) (New Directions for Evaluation 138). New York: Wiley/Jossey-Bass

Johnson, R., & Gray, R. (2010). A history of philosophical and theoretical issues for mixed methods research. In A. Tashakkori & C. Teddlie (Eds.), *SAGE handbook of mixed methods in social & behavioral research* (2nd ed., pp. 69–94). Thousand Oaks, CA: SAGE.

Klein, J. T. (1990). *Interdisciplinarity: History, theory, and practice.* Detroit, MI: Wayne State University Press.

Kuhn, T. S. (1960). *The structure of scientific revolutions.* Chicago: University of Chicago Press.

Le Play, F. (1855). European workers. In C. B. Silver (Ed.), *Frederick Le Play on family, work, and social change.* Chicago: University of Chicago Press.

Leech, N. L., & Onwuegbuzie A. J. (2006). A typology of mixed methods research designs. *Quality & Quantity, 42*(2), 265–275.

Maguire, P. (1987). *Doing participatory research: A feminist approach.* Amherst, MA: Center for International Education

Mann, S. A., & Kelley, L. R. (1997). Standing at the crossroads of modernist thought: Collins, Smith, and the new feminist epistemologies. *Gender and Society, 11*(4), 391–408.

Mason J. (2006). Mixing methods in a qualitatively driven way. *Qualitative Research, 6*(1), 9–25. doi:10.1177/1468794106058866

Mertens, D. M. (2007). Transformative paradigm: Mixed methods and social justice. *Journal of Mixed Methods Research, 1*, 212–225. doi:10.1177/1558689807302811

Mertens, D. M. (2009). *Transformative research and evaluation.* New York: Guilford Press.

Mertens, D. M., & Hesse-Biber, S. (Eds.). (2013). *Mixed methods and credibility of evidence in evaluation* (New Directions for Evaluation 138). New York: Wiley/Jossey-Bass.

Minh-ha, T. (1991) *Framer framed.* New York: Routledge.

Morgan, D. L. (2007). Paradigms lost and pragmatism regained: Methodological implications of combining qualitative and quantitative methods. *Journal of Mixed Methods Research 1*(1), 48–76.

Morgan, D. L. (2013). *Integrating qualitative and quantitative methods: A pragmatic approach.* Thousand Oaks, CA: SAGE.

Mutch, C. (2009). Mixed method research: Methodological eclecticism or muddled thinking? *Journal of Educational Leadership, Policy and Practice, 24*(2), 18–30. Retrieved from http://search.informit.com.au/documentSummary;dn=942182859009376

Namaste, K. (1993). Deconstruction, lesbian and gay studies, and interdisciplinary work: Theoretical, political and institutional strategies. *Journal of Homosexuality,* 24(1–2), 49–64. doi:10.1300/J082v24n01_04

Natsios, A. (2010). *The clash of the counter-bureaucracy and development.* Washington, DC: Center for Global Development.

National Institutes of Health, Office of Behavioral and Social Sciences Research. (2011). *Best practices for mixed methods research in the health sciences.* Retrieved from http://obssr.od.nih.gov/mixed_methods_research

Nowotny, H., Scott, P., & Gibbons, M. (2001). *Re-thinking science: Knowledge and the public in an age of uncertainty.* New York: Wiley.

O'Cathain, A., Murphy, E., & Nicholl, J. (2007). Integration and publications as indicators of "yield" from mixed methods studies. *Journal of Mixed Methods Research, 1*(2), 147–163.

O'Cathain, A., Murphy, E., & Nicholl, J. (2008). Multidisciplinary, interdisciplinary, or dysfunctional? Team working in mixed-methods research. *Qualitative Health Research, 18*(11), 1574–1585.

O'Cathain, A., Nicholl, J., & Murphy, E. (2009). Structural issues affecting mixed methods studies in health research: A qualitative study. *BMC Medical Research Methodology, 9*, 82. Retrieved from http://www.biomedcentral.com/1471-2288/9/82

Onwuegbuzie, A. J. (2012). Introduction: Putting the mixed back into quantitative and qualitative research in educational research and beyond: Moving toward the radical middle. *International Journal of Multiple Research Approaches, 6*, 192–219.

Park, R., McKenzie, R. D., & Burgess, E. (1925). *The city: Suggestions for the study of human nature in the urban environment.* Chicago: University of Chicago Press.

Patai, D., & Koertge, N. (1994). *Professing feminism: Cautionary tales from the strange world of women's studies.* New York: Basic Books.

Platt, J. (1996). *A history of sociological research methods in America 1920–1960.* Cambridge, UK: Cambridge University Press

Reay, D. (2012). Future directions in difference research: Recognizing and responding to difference in the research process. In S. N. Hesse-Biber (Ed.), *The handbook of feminist research: Theory and praxis* (2nd ed., pp. 627–640). Thousand Oaks, CA: SAGE.

Richardson, L. (2000) Skirting a pleated text de-disciplining and academic life. In E. St. Pierre & W. Pillow (Eds.), *Working the ruins* (pp. 153–163). New York: Routledge/ Taylor & Francis.

Rowntree, B. S. (1901). *Poverty: A study of town life.* London: Macmillan.

Sandelowski, M. (2012). The weakness of the strong/weak comparison of modes of inquiry (Editorial). *Research in Nursing & Health, 35*, 325–327.

Sandelowski, M. (2014). Unmixing mixed-methods research. *Research in Nursing & Health, 37*, 3–8. doi:10.1002/nur.21570

Sandelowski, M., Voils, C. I., & Knafl, G. (2009). On quantitizing. *Journal of Mixed Methods Research, 3*, 208–222. doi:10.1002/nur.21475

Smith, J. K., & Heshusius, L. (1986). Closing down the conversation: The end of the quantitative-qualitative among educational inquiries. *Educational Researcher, 15*, 4–12.

Smith, L. T. (1999). *Decolonizing methodologies: Research and indigenous people.* London: Zed Books.

Spivak, G. C. (1988). Can the subaltern speak? In C. Nelson & L. Grossberg (Eds.), *Marxism and the interpretation of culture* (pp. 271–313). Urbana: University of Illinois Press.

Tashakkori, A., & Teddlie, C. (1998). *Mixed methodology: Combining qualitative and quantitative approaches.* Thousand Oaks, CA: SAGE.

Tashakkori, A., & Teddlie, C. (Eds.). (2003). *Handbook of mixed methods in social & behavioral research.* Thousand Oaks, CA: SAGE.

Tashakkori, A., & Teddlie, C. (Eds.). (2010). *SAGE handbook of mixed methods in social & behavioral research* (2nd ed.). Thousand Oaks, CA: SAGE.

Teddlie, C., & Tashakkori, A. (2006). A general typology in research designs featuring mixed methods. *Research in the Schools, 13,* 12–28.

Thomas, W. I., & Znaniecki, F. (1918). *The Polish peasant in America.* Boston: Gorham Press.

Trinh, Minh-ha, T. (1991) *Framer framed.* New York: Routledge.

Wagner, J. (1993). Ignorance in educational research: or, how can you *not* know that? *Educational Researcher, 22*(5), 15–23.

Yanchar, S. C., & Williams, D. D. (2006). Reconsidering the compatibility thesis and eclecticism: Five proposed guidelines for method use. *Educational Researcher, 35*(9), 3–12.

Yin, R. K. (2006). Mixed methods research: Are the methods genuinely integrated or merely parallel? *Research in the Schools, 13*(1), 41–47.

Zhang, W., & Creswell, J. (2013). The use of mixing procedure of mixed methods in healthcare research. *Medical Care, 51*(8). doi:10.1097/MLR.0b013e31824642fd

PART 1

Linking Theory and Method in Multimethod and Mixed Methods Research

1

A Qualitatively Driven Approach to Multimethod and Mixed Methods Research

Sharlene Hesse-Biber, Deborah Rodriguez, *and* Nollaig A. Frost

Abstract

This chapter addresses the meaning of qualitatively driven inquiry and what this implies in the context of multimethod and mixed methods research. This chapter distinguishes between qualitatively driven mixed and multimethods approaches and considers why and how methods may be mixed using a qualitatively driven approach. The chapter identifies some key reasons for using qualitatively driven multimethod and mixed methods approaches to inquiry. In-depth empirical case studies illustrate the insights gained from deploying a qualitatively driven approach. The chapter concludes with an in-depth discussion of the value of these approaches and considers their contribution more widely to the field of multimethod and mixed methods research.

Key Words: mixed methods, multimethods, qualitatively driven mixed methods research, qualitatively driven multimethod research

I love listening to people. It is labor-intensive work. It's not the easiest work to do in terms of time, but I consider the stories that I hear from people gifts that I get from them. . . . I think one of the really important mandates of sociology, for me, is the idea of giving voice to the experiences of people whose voices and experiences might otherwise not be heard, marginalized, or shunted off to the side. And I'm trying to bring their voices and experiences to center stage, you might say. . . . It's an instance of what, I think, C. W. Mills meant when he talked about "translating private troubles into public issues."

—*David Karp, Ph.D. Sociologist (private communication)*

Sociologist David Karp's work on depression and mental illness (Karp, 1996) captures the essence of this chapter. Karp's research approach seeks to fully engage with his participants via in-depth interviews. His goal is to understand their lived experiences regarding what it is like to live with depression and mental illness. He aims to give voice to what is subjective and varied. There is not one "truth" out there but multiple stories of the depression and mental illness experience. Karp carefully listens and also reflects on what his participants are saying to him. In doing so, he takes a qualitatively driven approach to his work, one that privileges the exploration of the process of human meaning-making.

In Karp's work on depression, he uses quantitative research as an auxiliary component to his primary qualitative methodology as a means of both understanding the broader "objective" context of depression (rates of depression in the wider population, wider sociological variables that have been known to correlate with depression statistically) and contextualizing his qualitative research on people's "experiences" of depression. After surveying the almost exclusively "positivist" or "clinical" research literature on depression, Karp came to the conclusion that a qualitatively driven approach was vitally needed.

What Is Qualitatively Driven Inquiry?

A "qualitatively driven approach" is used here as an umbrella term that encompasses several theoretical traditions. All of these approaches have the common core assumption that social reality is constructed and that subjective meaning is a critical component of knowledge-building. A qualitative tradition recognizes the importance of the subjective human creation of meaning but does not always reject outright some aspect of objectivity. As Crabtree and Miller (1999) state: "Pluralism, not relativism, is stressed, with focus on the circular dynamic tension of subject and object" (p. 10).

There are theoretical variations among qualitatively driven approaches, and various theorists have categorized these variations in somewhat different ways. This chapter deploys Denzin and Lincoln's (1998) three-category cluster of variations in qualitative research approaches. The first variation is a *constructivist* or *interpretative* approach. This approach assumes social reality is subjective, consisting of narratives or meanings constructed/co-constructed by individuals and others within a specific social context.

A second qualitatively driven variation, *critical theory,* is especially focused on how power, control, and ideology create dominant understandings of social reality. Critical theorists center on the power dynamics generated by a set of meanings (ideologies) about individuals' social reality and lived experiences. An example of this approach comes from postmodernist research, which questions the very foundation of "social reality." A postmodern perspective focuses on the how social life is produced and privileged by those in power with the goal of "emancipating" and uncovering social injustice.[1] Reality for the postmodernist, then, is "representational" rather than "real" or "true."

A third variation are *feminist perspectives* that center knowledge-building by focusing on the lived experiences of women and other marginalized groups with the goal of accessing and highlighting subjugated knowledges. Feminist perspectives, such as *feminist standpoint theory*, are aware of the hegemonic biases of traditional positivistic concerns, especially as they pertain to issues of "objectivity" within the research process whereby individuals must place their own values and concerns outside the research endeavor. For the feminist researcher, there is no knowledge that is without bias. There is no view from "nowhere" as knowledge itself is imbued with the power and authority of those who seek it. They point to the longstanding androcentric (male) bias of early knowledge-building, especially as practiced by early positivists, which often left out the concerns and issues of women, as well as issues of difference in terms of race, class, ethnicity, and sexual preference in their research problems and analyses. The issues of those whose lives have been "subjugated" by traditional research is now foregrounded in feminist perspectives. There is, then, a push to address and reorient androcentric bias in the research process.

Table 1.1 captures some of the general differences between a qualitatively driven and a quantitatively driven approach. It's important to note that these differences lie along a continuum. We have avoided the creation of a binary between these two types of methodological approaches. As we move toward the center of the continuum, we may in fact witness how these perspectives can share a standpoint on some of the major dimensions that are said to differentiate both approaches. For example, while we have listed that the overall type of analysis plan for a qualitatively driven project is to generate theory, qualitative approaches to research can also test ideas generated from the ongoing collection of qualitative data. In this example, there is an interdependent relationship between data collection and data analysis, such that qualitatively driven researchers seek to "test out" new ideas generated from their data throughout the entire qualitatively driven analytical process.

It was not until the early 2000s that the field of mixed methods saw the beginnings of a discussion of theoretical bias in mixed methods research (MMR). Some mixed methods researchers were concerned that the current practice of mixed methods leaned toward a "post-positivist" theoretical stance, with qualitatively driven approaches absent and the use/misuse of qualitative methods without their theoretical underpinnings (Howe, 2004; Denzin & Lincoln, 2005; Giddings, 2006; Holmes, 2007). For example, Giddings (2006) argued that the practice of MMR up to that point stemmed from positivistic methodology—what she calls, "positivism dressed in drag," with the qualitative component of the mixed methods project placed in a very secondary role. Giddings' article launched a contentious debate concerning the role of qualitatively driven approaches in MMR that continues into the contemporary period. Prior to Giddings', concern was also expressed by Sandelowski (1996) who also provided an important framework whereby experimental researchers might benefit from incorporating a qualitative

Table 1.1 Qualitatively Driven and Quantitatively Driven Approaches Compared on Several Key Research Dimensions Along a Subjective–Objective Continuum

	Subjective ◄─────────────► Objective	
	Qualitatively Driven	Quantitatively Driven
Ontology: What is the nature of the reality?	Social reality is multiple.	There is a concrete social world "out there."
Epistemology: What can we know and who can know?	Goal is to understand multiple subjectivities. Individuals are the "experts." Through intersubjectivity we understand human behaviors. There is no definitive subject–object split in knowledge-building.	Goal is to ascertain "the truth" in order to predict and even uncover "laws" of human behavior through objective social inquiry. Scientists are the experts.
Types of questions	The purpose of this research is to understand (the what, how, and why).	Statement of relationship between independent and dependent variable. Question phrased in terms of a hypothesis.
Type of data collected	Naturalistic settings: Participant observation (fieldwork) In-depth interviews Focus groups Unobtrusive data: Documents	Surveys, Experiments: Randomized controlled trials Systematic reviews/meta-analyses
Type of analysis	Inductive: Goal is to generate theory. Looks for general themes/patterns in the data. Uses "thick description." Compares and contrasts thematic data. Specific types of analyses examples: Grounded theory, narrative analysis	Deductive: Test out hypothesis. Explain variation in the independent variables by controlling the dependent variables. Stress is on statistical measurement.
Goal	Understand a "process."	Generalize, predict, and control research outcomes.

component into clinical trials (see also, Sandelowski, 2000). Later on, Mason (2006) and others (Creswell, Shope, Plano Clark, & Green, 2006) took specific issue with those who argued that qualitative approaches only played a secondary role in MMR, by citing the empirical mixed methods research designs, especially in the health sciences, that gave specific priority to the qualitative component.

What Is a Qualitatively Driven Approach to Mixed Methods Research?

An important dimension that characterizes a qualitatively driven mixed methods project is a commitment to privileging a *qualitative approach* (in the form of a qualitatively driven epistemology and methodology) that forms the core of the overall MMR project with the quantitative approach and method taking on a secondary role in the mixed methods design. The role of the secondary

or auxiliary method is to *ask a subquestion or set of subquestions that assist in the elaboration or clarification of overall core qualitatively driven research question(s)*. Within a qualitatively driven mixed methods study, the core method is always qualitative and is depicted in all caps (QUAL), and the quantitative component is depicted in lowercase letters (quan). Within a qualitatively driven mixed methods approach, there remain contested areas with regard to whether or not the secondary component in fact can form a separate study by itself. Some mixed methods researchers note that to engage in a qualitatively driven design means that the secondary component *cannot* stand on its own as a separate study (see Morse, 2003, 2010, this volume; Morse & Niehaus, 2009).

Qualitatively driven approaches with regard to mixed methods offer a range of insights into the ongoing discussion of MMR, especially as it relates to arguments concerning the mixing of research paradigms, issues of power, and authority inside and outside the research process. There is a transformative quality to many of these perspectives in that they speak to social justice and social change as primary research objectives. Qualitatively driven praxis promotes a deep listening between the researcher and the researched in order to obtain "deeper and more genuine expressions of beliefs and values that emerge through dialogue [and] foster a more accurate description of views held" (Howe, 2004, p. 54). Additionally, qualitatively driven approaches tend to be more open to exploratory research and theory generation and less with regard to confirmatory results (hypothesis testing). In fact, the process of qualitatively building knowledge is *iterative*, meaning the researchers test out (in a much less formal manner) their analytical ideas as they continue to analyze, memo about, and collect more data in a process known in grounded theory as *analytical induction* (see Charmaz, 2006).

In this chapter we do not necessarily draw a sharp boundary around the ultimate contribution of the secondary component's role in a qualitatively driven MMR design. Rather it is seen as lying along a continuum where at one end the secondary study cannot stand on its own and at the other it borders on making a contribution to the core qualitative component but may also be complete in itself. The results from the secondary component may be useful in specific research contexts and while being secondary in one qualitatively driven study may also be published separately as an independent study. The results may also be used and linked to yet another type of multimethod or mixed methods design where they play a more primary role and so on.

Reasons for Selecting Mixing Methods from a Qualitatively Driven Approach

There are a range of different reasons why a researcher might want to deploy a qualitatively driven multimethod and mixed methods research (MMMR) design that directly stems from the type of theoretical perspective (methodology) that links a qualitatively driven research problem with a particular method or set of methods. It's important to note that methods are tools; a researcher's methodology determines the way in which a tool will be utilized. The rationale for mixing methods must be tightly linked to one's methodology and the questions that emanate

from this perspective. Also, when working with a qualitatively driven set of methodologies, it may be difficult for researchers to state upfront the exact MMMR design they will ultimately utilize, as it is often the case with a qualitatively driven design that the overall research process is iterative, which means it is ongoing and the researcher is led by the data to ask yet another set of questions that call for a particular type of method and so on. Locking one's MMMR project into a particular MMMR design template a priori may be difficult when doing research from a qualitatively driven standpoint.

In a multimethod research design a qualitatively driven project may call on a *second qualitative method as its auxiliary component*: the second qualitative method would take on a secondary role (qual) in the service of a primary QUAL method. The addition of a second qualitative method would serve a supplementary function in that it answers a different question, but its primary aim is to support the core qualitatively driven approach and question. This qualitatively driven design would be called a *multimethod design* by its use of *two* different qualitative methods.

Some argue that qualitatively driven multimethod research differs from pluralism in qualitative research, in which qualitative methods are combined as they are in multimethod designs but there is more flexibility about the status of the methods used (see, e.g., Frost et al., 2010, 2011). Depending on the reason for their introduction to the study and the stage in the research process at which the decision is made to use additional qualitative methods, each qualitative method may be afforded equal, adjunct, or greater status in its use to address a research question or evolving set of research questions.

If a qualitatively driven project design is being used, it means researchers have reasons to utilize a MMR design; these are considered in the next section.

Reasons for Selecting a Qualitatively Driven Multimethod and Mixed Methods Design

There are a number of reasons why a qualitatively driven researcher would utilize a MMMR project.[2] These always relate to researchers' qualitatively driven approaches to the social world and the set of questions that specifically emanate from these perspectives.

To Obtain a Representative Qualitative Sample for the Purpose of Enhancing Qualitative Findings

Conducting a quantitative demographic survey on a random sample of the researcher's target population first (quan), followed by a qualitative study (QUAL), enables the researcher to select a qualitative subsample from this population that is representative of the target population.

To Enhance the Generalizability of a Qualitative Study

The researcher uses findings from the quantitative study to select a qualitative sample that is reflective of the wider population in order to more readily generalize from in-depth research findings. This is especially the case when the researcher samples directly from the quantitative sample—in this way both studies are directly linked.

To Cast a Wider Net

By casting a wider net, the researcher can identify a specific population of interest that may be hard to locate (purposive sampling). For example, if a researcher is interested in the lived experiences of BRCA positive mutation males but finds it difficult to secure a large enough sample to interview. By first conducting a general quantitative health survey, a researcher might be able to locate a subsample for a follow-up set of intensive qualitative interviews, which in fact is the main motivation for conducting the survey itself.

To Assist in Defining a Population of Interest

Based on specific research findings gather from their quantitative survey, researchers can locate a sub-sample of interest. For example, suppose researchers are interested in conducting a survey of employers' attitudes toward female workers. As a result of the findings from the quantitative study, they note the high degree of stereotyping of the female workers, especially with regard to issues of race. On the basis of these findings they may decide to subsequently conduct an in-depth study to explore employers' stereotypical attitudes by focusing specifically on employers working in male-dominated occupations. The focus of qualitative inquiry is sparked directly from the surveys findings.

To Provide Options for Enhancing the Validity and Reliability of Qualitative Findings

A qualitatively driven mixed methods design can also aid in exploring contradictory results found between the quantitative and qualitative studies. By linking the qualitative with the quantitative at the data gathering stage (i.e., the researcher draws a qualitative sample directly from the quantitative sample first collected), the researcher is provided with the possibility of assessing the validity and reliability of the qualitative findings. For example, those qualitative researchers who ask similar questions in both the quantitative and qualitative study are provided with an opportunity to grapple with issues of reliability, validity, and contradiction of research findings by ascertaining (a) the extent to which research findings from similar questions yield similar responses (reliability) and (b) the extent to which their responses appear to address the same underlying issues, such that there is general agreement in their responses (triangulation with the goal of increasing the validity of a study).

To Conduct a Concurrent Study With the Quantitative Embedded/Nested in the Qualitative

This research design holds the potential to assist the researcher in developing a more robust understanding of the qualitative results by integrating quantitative findings from a set of closed-ended questions (quan) embedded in the QUAL. Quantitative data that are gathered may answer a different question, but the findings are in service of the core qualitatively driven approach. At the analysis stage, the findings from both these studies are in conversation with one another, with the quantitative component adding richness/understanding to the core, qualitatively driven component. So, for example, qualitatively driven researchers may juxtapose the findings from the quantitative component to help understand the core (qualitatively driven) findings from the QUAL component. The quan component's findings are used to explore the range of disparate findings they may discover in their QUAL component in order to generate new questions and explore these differences and thus gain a more complex understanding of their research problem.

For Serendipitous Use of Quantitative Findings in Case of Outliers

A quantitative study may reveal the presence of a subpopulation of "outliers" in the initial quan study, which provides an opportunity to expand knowledge regarding the overall research problem and generates new problem questions that require exploration in a QUAL approach follow-up research project.

For Purposeful Use of Quantitative Findings

In this case, the qualitatively driven researcher deliberately uses a quantitative component as a way to potentially generate new qualitative research questions. Mixed methods can assist researchers in acquiring specific topical issues and concerns they wish to explore. Here, the quantitative component serves to initiate or spark new hypotheses or research questions that researchers can pursue in-depth.

For Serendipitous Use of Juxtaposing Quantitative and Qualitative Findings

An originally parallel mixed methods design (one quan and one QUAL study conducted simultaneously) is expanded to include a follow-up qualitative study that can potentially explore disparate findings between the qualitative and quantitative findings with the aim of generating new questions that can be explored qualitatively, thereby permitting a more complex understanding of a research problem.

For Qualitative Theory Testing

Following up with a quantitative study is done in order to test the validity of qualitative findings on a wider population. The researcher conducts a qualitative study first, followed by a quantitative study in order to "test out" the theoretical ideas generated from the qualitative study. In this case, researchers are interested in ascertaining whether their theoretical ideas and findings are generalized to a larger population.

To Obtain a More Comprehensive Understanding of a Phenomenon From Differing Perspectives

The researcher uses a QUAL core component and supplements this by gathering secondary qual datasets regarding particular aspects of the phenomenon from the differing perspectives of people who are involved with the same experience. The findings from the auxiliary qual component cannot be understood outside of the context of the core QUAL component (QUAL-qual).

For example, students may recall differently what a teacher says about the positives and negatives of their coursework when receiving verbal feedback. The researcher could record the verbal feedback session between the teacher and the student and analyze the content of what the teacher said. The researcher could then interview the students later on in the day, asking them what was said/what happened in the feedback session. These interviews seek to gather particular aspects of information and are interpretable only in the context of the core component.

To Develop a More Rounded Understanding/Theoretical Framework

This is achieved through comparing and contrasting two independent datasets. The researcher starts with a QUAL component whereby through the analysis process issues specific to each independent group are identified. The researcher then develops secondary qual components to address and further explore these issues, proceeding to compare and contrast them.

For example, suppose a researcher wants to understand how single men and single women, respectively, experience the adoption process. The researcher could conduct semistructured interviews (QUAL) and, through the analysis, identify issues that are specific to the single men group and issues that are specific to the single women group. The researcher could then conduct a few semistructured interviews (qual) with each group with the specific view to compare and contrast these datasets.

To Explore Changes in Participants Sooner

Changes can be explored after participants experience a certain phenomenon without having to wait for a long time while the experience takes place. The researcher would use a before and after design with different participants who share a similar experience. The researcher could conduct the secondary qual component with the "before" participants and the primary QUAL component with the "after" participants.

For example, suppose a researcher wants to understand how undergoing a year-long job placement may change students' views of potential careers in their chosen subject area. The researcher may conduct a few semistructured interviews (qual) to understand students' perspectives on potential careers before going on to the placement ("before" group). The researcher may also conduct a larger number of semistructured interviews (QUAL) with students who have completed their year-long job placement to explore their views of potential careers ("after" group), without having to wait for a year until the "before" group has undergone this experience.

For Serendipitous Use of Qualitative Findings

A QUAL-qual design may not always be the intention of the researcher at the start of the project but may be implemented iteratively to complete a project when unexpected findings leave an important point unanswered in relation to the main research question.

The researcher may have started the project with the intention of conducting a single-method qualitative study but then comes across unexpected findings in the analysis that need further exploration to answer the main research question. She may supplement her qualitative study with a secondary qualitative method that is specifically designed to address the unanswered point. The design of the project then becomes QUAL-qual, and the findings of the secondary component are interpreted in the context of the core component.

Similarly, the initial intention of the researcher may be to conduct a single-method qualitative study but they may decide later on to supplement this as a result of unexpected interesting findings that may warrant further exploration. The supplementary method specifically focuses on these unexpectedly interesting findings and feeds back into the main research question.

To Gain Insight into the Multiple Layers of the Experience of a Phenomenon

Researchers use several qualitative methods, and they all may play an equal role or one may play a greater role than the other. This would depend on the research question, the reason for their inclusion, and the stage at which they are included in the project.

For example, a researcher may want to explore how mothers make the transition to second-time motherhood, where the second child has been labelled with a disability, by conducting semistructured interviews. These interviews may be analyzed using structural narrative analysis, which seeks to give understanding on how a story is told.

The researcher may then analyze the same interview data by using a thematic narrative analysis, which seeks to provide insight into narratives that do not follow the conventional story form and permits deeper inspection by exploring what is said.

Overall, multimethod designs may also particularly suit when there is a lack of clarity of the theoretical framework and when exploring areas that have not received much attention or have not received any attention thus far.

A Qualitatively Driven Approach to MMMR Design

We inductively derived a set of mixed methods design "templates" that are based on the reasons qualitatively driven researchers might want to mix methods. These templates, however, do not cover all the variety of reasons or the range of mixed methods designs a qualitatively driven researcher might select from. These templates should be thought of as working models of MMMR designs that can and should be tweaked or added to, and some components may need to be deleted, depending on the particular research problem or set of problems that emerge during the course of the research project. We advocate this iterative approach to MMMR design, given that the nature of a qualitative approach to research is often subject to change as the research project proceeds and alters its course in response to new research findings, which in turn may prompt new research questions along the way.

Suggested Qualitatively Driven Mixed Methods Templates

In the following section, we describe examples of MMR designs that qualitatively driven researchers might find useful, given their specific research goals. All of these designs are meant to answer core, qualitatively driven research questions, with the quantitative component (quan) taking on a secondary role in mixed methods designs assisting the qualitatively driven component's research goals.

NESTED/EMBEDDED MIXED METHODS DESIGNS

A qualitatively driven mixed methods nested/embedded design consists of the concurrent mixing of qualitative and quantitative methods carried out as separate studies within the same research project, with the qualitative component taking a core/dominant role. Qualitatively driven

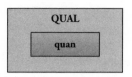

Fig. 1.1 Qualitatively driven nested/embedded mixed methods design

researchers may be motivated to make use of this type of design to gather some descriptive quantitative information, such as demographic statistics of the population they study, in order to place the findings from their qualitative study into a larger context (see Figure 1.1).

This design can offer researchers some opportunities reflexivity regarding how their quantitative findings may raise new questions that are connected in some substantive way to their research problem, rather than using the quantitative data only for descriptive purposes. For instance, researchers might seek out points of connection, guided by their original research question, at both the data analysis and data interpretation stages, by consciously comparing and contrasting the research findings from both data sets.

QUALITATIVELY DRIVEN SEQUENTIAL MIXED METHOD DESIGNS

There are several types of qualitatively driven sequential mixed methods designs, but their overall commonality is that the quantitative study (quan) is in the service of the dominant qualitative (QUAL) component. The studies are sequential in that one study follows and builds on the next. The first of these sequential designs is as follows:

QUAL → quan → Findings and Interpretation

The qualitatively driven sequential design sees the qualitative component first in the study followed by the quantitative component second and taking on a secondary or assisting role. A number of scenarios can emanate from this type of design. In one scenario, the quantitative results assist in the interpretation of the major qualitative findings. A secondary function of the quantitative component would be to "test out" some of the theories generated by the

dominant qualitative findings. The quantitative component might also be utilized as a way to generalize results from the qualitative study to a wider population. What is common to all of these reasons is the centering of the qualitative component's findings with the quantitative component used to enhance and elaborate these findings to a wider population.

QUALITATIVELY DRIVEN SEQUENTIAL ITERATIVE DESIGN

We might take this first qualitatively driven sequential model depicted in Figure 1.2 and extend it through time, given the iterative nature of qualitatively driven research. Picking up on the idea that a quantitative component is used in the service of the qualitative in that it tests out ideas generated from the qualitative component, we can then extend the qualitatively driven sequential model through time, generating a more qualitatively driven sequential iterative design whereby theory generated from the qualitative component is tested out on a representative population and findings are compared. Then, if needed, the theory is revised and tested out again in an ongoing process of theory generation and testing in a series of "wave" studies (see Figure 1.2).

QUALITATIVELY DRIVEN SEQUENTIAL MIXED METHODS DESIGNS THAT REVEAL SUBJUGATED KNOWLEDGES

Sometimes researchers taking a qualitative approach use a sequential design in order to find out more about their target sample or to obtain a more representative sample for further in-depth investigation of the research problem. In this case, starting the sequential study with the quantitative component is done with the goal of generalizing and validating the dominant qualitative study, by obtaining a more representative sample or getting at a hard-to-find sample as input for the dominant qualitative study that follows.

Researchers can also integrate the data from both studies in this explanatory mixed methods design at the data interpretation stage by allowing for the comparison of research findings, especially if the two studies have utilized similar questions of interest to the research question. This would serve

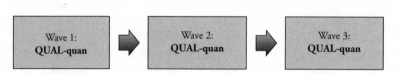

Fig. 1.2 Qualitatively driven sequential iterative mixed methods design

to increase the validity of the qualitative results and potentially provide a more complex understanding of qualitative results where there is an apparent contradiction. Findings from each study may interact at the data analysis and interpretation stage by comparing and contrasting findings with the goal of perhaps generalizing qualitative findings to different samples and/or validating QUAL findings by comparing findings from similar questions asked in quan and QUAL study.

Quan→ QUAL→ Findings and Interpretation

Suggested Qualitatively Driven Multimethods Templates

In this section we describe examples of multimethod designs that may be of use to researchers depending on their research questions. Similarly to qualitatively driven mixed method designs, multimethod designs consist of a primary QUAL component, which is served by a secondary qualitative (qual) component in order to address the research goals.

MULTIMETHOD CONCURRENT DESIGN

A qualitatively driven multimethod concurrent design is comprised of two components that occur more or less at the same time. The supplementary qual component takes place at the same time as the primary QUAL component as follows:

QUAL + qual → Findings and Interpretation

This design usually consists of two separate data sets, which may or may not originate from two separate groups of participants, depending on the research question and the availability of participants. The data also tend to be analyzed separately, with the results from the auxiliary secondary component supplementing the results from the primary component.

This type of multimethod design might be used for a variety of reasons. One particular reason may be that the secondary qual component provides a second and different perspective to that offered through the sole use of the primary QUAL component. Another particular reason may be that the secondary qual component can be analyzed at a different level (e.g., micro level) than the level at which the primary QUAL component is analyzed (e.g., macro level).

MULTIMETHOD SEQUENTIAL DESIGN

A qualitatively driven multimethod sequential design consists of two separate studies in which the subsequent secondary qual component ensues and develops from the primary QUAL component as follows:

QUAL → qual → Findings and Interpretation

This design is usually composed of two separate data sets, although this is not always the case as we will see in one of the multimethod case studies presented in the next section. It also normally consists of different participants and different methods of data collection. The core QUAL component of the overall study is carried out first, including data collection and analysis. This then serves the secondary qual component, which builds on the findings of the primary component in its method of data collection and analysis.

Again, there are several reasons why this type of multimethod design may be used. It may be to obtain different perspectives or to obtain a more detailed and comprehensive perspective of a particular phenomenon. The secondary qual component may also be used to test the findings from the primary QUAL component.

Qualitatively Driven Multimethods and Mixed Methods Case Studies

We present several examples of qualitatively driven MMMR studies.[3] In the analysis of each study, we are guided by several sensitizing questions one might ask when contemplating a mixed methods/multimethods study from a qualitatively driven perspective and that one might think about when utilizing these MMMR designs.

• How does the mixed methods research design or multimethod design further the goals of a qualitatively driven approach to understanding social reality? How can a mixed methods or multimethod design further the goals of a qualitative approach to understanding social reality?
• Why and how do qualitative researchers employ mixed methods and/or multimethods across the research process at (a) the data-gathering stage, (b) the data analysis stage, and (c) the interpretative stage?
• What are some of the challenges MMMR researchers confront during each of these stages?
• What are the missed opportunities to further knowledge-building and why?
• What are the particular strengths of combining methods with respect to a qualitatively driven perspective?

Mixed Method Case Study 1: Understanding Rape Culture

Sarah McMahon (2007) explored the subculture of college student athletes and sought to understand the meaning, role, and salience of rape myths that exist within college cultures. She utilized a qualitatively driven mixed methods design that allowed her to access the subjugated knowledge contained within rape cultures. Prior research into this topic tended toward an overreliance on quantitative measures to the detriment of gaining insight on students' lived understandings of rape myths. McMahon reasoned that a qualitatively driven design would allow her to more fully "capture the essence of rape myths that may not materialize through the use of quantitative surveys" (p. 358). Her end goal was to give voice to students' concerns and views about rape. A secondary aim tied to and dependent on the first study goal was to compare what students said on a survey versus what they talked about in a more open-ended conversation with their peers and one on one with an interviewer. Toward the beginning of her project, McMahon sought confirmation of the quantitative (survey) results and qualitative (focus groups and individual interviews) findings. However, once her study was underway, she became increasingly skeptical of this aim, doubting whether her quantitative and qualitative findings would ever triangulate with one another.

McMahon's sequential qualitatively driven mixed methods design (see Figure 1.3) started out with a survey (quan) consisting of 205 sophomore and junior student athletes at one northeast public university. The survey asked participants to fill out a number of quantitative attitudinal scales, including the Identification of Acquaintance Rape Attitudes Scale, which identifies acquaintance rape attitudes and the Marlowe-Crowne Social Desirability Scale, which indicated participant response bias. The statistical findings from the survey revealed a very low acceptance of rape myths among the student survey population. However, the survey data also showed a higher acceptance of violence among men and individuals who did not know a survivor of sexual assault.

The QUAL phase of her study consisted of focus groups followed by semistructured interviews. Data collection was facilitated by someone of the same gender as the participants (p. 360). Focus group questions were developed by McMahon in conjunction with student athletes in the campus peer-education program and university staff who served victims of sexual violence. Individual interviews were conducted to elaborate on themes McMahon discovered in the focus groups and to determine any differences in students' responses between situations (i.e., group setting vs. individual). The interview guide was designed specifically to address focus-group topics that needed "more in-depth exploration" or clarification (p. 361).

The qualitative findings from the focus groups and individual qualitative interviews revealed "subtle yet pervasive rape myths" that fell into four major themes: "the misunderstanding of consent, the belief in 'accidental' and fabricated rape, the contention that some women provoke rape, and the invulnerability of female athletes" (p. 363). McMahon found that the survey findings contradicted what she found via the focus group and individual interview data. The survey's findings revealed a "low acceptance of rape myths . . . was contradicted by the findings of the focus groups and individual interviews, which indicated the presence of subtle rape myths" (p. 362).

McMahon explained this by affirming the quality of qualitative data with regard to the answers provided in the qualitative components of her research project. She wrote: "further exploration revealed myriad subtle, yet powerful, beliefs that there are certain situations in which violence is acceptable, unintentional, or the fault of the victim. The simple statement that 'no means no' disguises a range of more subtle rape-supportive beliefs" (p. 366). The qualitative components of her MMR design revealed the subtle nuances of each individual answer, thereby allowing for rape-supportive beliefs to be exposed in her research.

Fig. 1.3 McMahon's (2007) qualitatively driven sequential mixed methods design

McMahon's use of qualitatively driven mixed methods design reveals that the opinions of respondents may shift based on the type of research methods deployed. The survey data consisted of closed-ended questions, which limited the breadth of participants' answers. Her qualitative component allowed space for participants to not only answer the specific questions they were asked during the focus group and interview component but also to elaborate on their feelings more comprehensively. For example, many of the participants answered the survey in such a way that the researcher concluded the majority of respondents felt that sexual coercion was wrong under all circumstances. During the interviews, however, many of the participants expressed that they generally believed that rape was wrong but that the victim was also partly to blame, thereby leading to a partial contradiction of the quantitative findings. McMahon elaborates on this point further by noting

> The skewed results of the survey indicate that most of the participants believed that sexual violence is wrong, and they largely disagreed with many of the victim-blaming statements. However, once the same types of questions were posed in a group setting where the student athletes interacted with their teammates, a different set of responses were provided that included more rape-supportive attitudes and victim-blaming beliefs. (p. 366)

Thus McMahon's qualitatively driven research design allowed her to expose subjugated knowledge that was buried beneath the dominant college discourse on rape culture.

Mixed Method Case Study 2: Enhancing the Validity of Clinical Trials by Uncovering Subjugated Knowledges

Paterniti et al. (2005) designed a qualitatively driven sequential mixed methods study with an overarching goal of gaining knowledge concerning Asian Americans' and their caretakers' lived experiences with cancer clinical trials.

The impetus for their study was the overall low accrual rates in clinical trials, particularly among minority populations that stemmed from "the history of both research atrocities and clinical atrocities, as well as general disparities in healthcare" (p. 3016). These factors were found to lower access among minority populations to novel and potentially life-saving cancer therapies. Paterniti et al.'s goal was to obtain a broad base of data that would especially capture the experiences of a diverse

population while also going deeper into the experiences of Asian-American participants in clinical trials through extensive qualitative field observations.

The researchers, in an effort to expand the diversity of their research study, partnered with a number of organizations in California to access and increase the overall diversity of their target population of clinical trial users. In their data collection the researchers started off with an informal qualitative component (QUAL) that consisted of members from the organizational partnerships they had created with several oncology and cancer information associations, with the goal of enhancing the survey design, as well as working on a plan for distributing surveys to a more diverse group of cancer patients and their caretakers in oncology-based clinical settings. The purpose of this design was to strengthen the face validity of the survey instrument. The data gathered from these organizational members consisted of "monthly steering committee meetings to direct the course of survey design and distribution, as well as to give direction regarding the face validity and feasibility of the instrument" (p. 3016). In addition, data was collected (QUAL) from 10 cancer patients recruited from the target population who provided feedback on a pilot version of the survey instrument. Thus the first component consisted of the following qualitatively driven design:

QUAL + QUAL→ quan → Interpretation and Findings

The second part of the study consisted of using the validated survey and administering it to the target population through the partnership networks created during patient visits to the oncology clinic. The quantitative (quan) survey aimed to assess cancer patients' and their caretakers' lived experiences with clinical trials and trial reimbursement ($n = 1,187$). A QUAL observational study was also added to the design, and its purpose was to carefully examine the clinical trial recruitment process itself. The observation study consisted of a purposive sampling of cancer patients who were said to be eligible for a cancer clinical trial and their caretakers. This sampling procedure allowed the researchers to obtain a diverse sample of clinical trial participants. The sample ranged in age from 19 to 85 years with a mean age of 63 years. The gender distribution was skewed with 75% of the sample male. Racial/ethnic difference sample breakdown showed that 59% were White; 5% were Asian; 5% were African, Latino, or Native America; and 22%

were not identified for race/ethnicity. The design for this phase of the study consisted of the following concurrent design:

QUAN + QUAL→ Findings and Interpretation

The researchers immersed themselves in the recruitment process and took detailed field notes of the interactions they observed in the clinical trial accrual process. They noted the ethnic identity and other personal information they could garner such as the gender age and occupation of patients, based on medical reports from physicians (not medical records). They used a grounded theory to analyze their field observations, which covered a total of 56 hours over nine months.

Through an analysis of both the quantitative and qualitative data, Paterniti et al. found a number of disparities among Asian American respondents. Asian American respondents were less likely to have heard the term "clinical trial" and less likely to have participated in or known someone who had participated in a trial but were more likely to understand trial reimbursement factors (pp. 3018–3019). Non-White respondents overall were much less likely to report being willing to participate in a clinical trial. These quantitative findings helped to place the dominant qualitative findings into a wider clinical perspective on clinical trials with regard to minority participation.

The grounded theory analysis of the qualitative data resulted in the identification of five stages in patient recruitment: (1) presentation of potential participants, among whom Asian Americans tended to be younger and have made direct requests for participation; (2) information about trial and therapies; (3) identifying criteria for participation, both among doctors and between doctors, patients, and caregivers, which often presented a challenge for those who were old enough but whose stage of disease progression was too far for trial consideration; (4) specifying parameters for the trial, which none of the Asian patients met in order to advance to the stage of (5) administering cancer therapies.

Using a qualitatively driven mixed methods approach allowed Paterniti et al. to gather a broad base sample from their quantitative survey that then allowed them to place their in-depth observations from minority and nonminority experiences focusing in particular, on the experiences of Asian participants into a broader demographic context. Although the data only represents a geographically and otherwise restricted sample that is not generalizable to different/larger

populations, this study was unique in its mixed methods approach and provides an important look at patient recruitment in clinical trials. Paterniti et al. recommend more education campaigns at the community level to raise awareness about clinical trials and recruitment campaigns to increase trial diversity.

Mixed Method Case Study 3: Fostering Social Change for Women: Studying Gender Inequality in the Workplace

Louise Marie Roth's research, *Selling Women Short: Gender and Money on Wall Street* (2006), addresses the issue of gender inequality in the workplace. Roth wanted to understand the "structural factors" within the workplace setting that may contribute to the gender–wage gap and its persistence over time. She studied successful female Wall Street MBAs, whose credentials make them on par with their male counterparts. These women had equivalent "human capital"[4] qualifications and, like their male counterparts, were hired at high-ranking Wall Street securities firms as their first jobs.

Roth deployed a mixed methods embedded design that nested her quantitative closed-ended questions into primarily qualitative in-depth interviews (see Figure 1.4). Her cohort convenience sample consisted of 76 men and women who had completed their MBAs in 1991, 1992, or 1993 and subsequently worked on Wall Street (however, some of her participants may or may not have been still working on Wall Street at the time of their interview). Roth conducted her interviews between 1998 and 1999, asking questions that addressed women's "career history from before the MBA until the time of the interview" (p. 203).

Roth's qualitative component was a semi-structured interview that asked male and female participants about their everyday lived experiences in their workplace. Her questions were designed to give

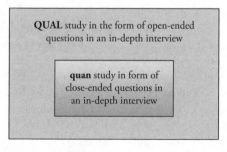

Fig. 1.4 Roth's (2006) qualitatively driven nested/embedded mixed methods design

Roth a broader understanding of the potential ways in which the workplace environment worked to generate gendered inequities (see Benokraitis & Feagin, 1995; Hesse-Biber & Carter, 2005). The quantitative component was embedded in the qualitative consisting of closed-ended and semi-structured questions that allowed Roth to track respondents' wages over time, along with other specific career conditions, such as job changes, salary information (including bonuses), and reports on their performance evaluations carried out by their employers.

A quantitative and qualitative analyses of her data were carried out. The statistical analysis of the quantitative data that allowed Roth to take into account all those factors that might legitimately explain gendered differences in wages such as number of hours worked, any human capital differences, and so on. Her quantitative analysis revealed the presence of a significant gender gap in wages that remained unexplained even when controlling for any legitimate factors that might otherwise make a legitimate difference.

While her quantitative findings revealed the extent of the wage gap and provided a numerical understanding of the gap, it was only when the qualitative data was brought into dialogue with her quantitative findings that Roth was able to gain a fuller and more complex understanding of the specific processes within the workplace that might have contributed to the gender gap in wages. A grounded theory analysis of participants' stories regarding their lived experiences at work allowed Roth to access subjugated knowledge of the inner workings of the workplace environment. Performing a grounded theory analysis also allowed Roth to explain the gendered wage gap's persistence over time despite the general climate on Wall Street in the early 1990s being one of growing opportunities for women's advancement.

By listening to men and women's voices, Roth was able to provide a picture of structural discrimination in the workplace. These are the unarticulated and even unconscious practices and actions of employers that insure and perpetuate the gender gap in wages. Roth notes

> On Wall Street, these interpersonal and
> organizational dynamics occur through a bonus
> system where pay supposedly reflects performance.
> Despite a supposed basis in individual merit, this
> variable pay system not only coexists with gender
> inequality between workers in the same jobs, it can
> even help reproduce this inequality. (p. 10)

Roth's qualitatively driven approach allowed her to unearth her participants' lived experiences over time to reveal the hidden inner structures of the workplace that consist of discriminatory organizational practices with regard to decision-making in performance evaluations that are tightly tied to wage increases and promotion.

It is through dialoguing with her findings from her mixed methods nested design that allowed Roth to pinpoint how macro differences among men and women's wages are connected to specific organizational practices. Roth's qualitative data exposed the hidden aspects of the organizational climate that promoted employers' "taste for discrimination." Just as some women may choose certain jobs that fit a traditional image of appropriate work for women, employers are also influenced by these cultural images. Employers choose male or female workers because they seek traits believed to be masculine or feminine, regardless of whether specific women or men possess such traits. So, to some extent, women's labor-market situation is a result of employers' "irrational preferences" (Becker, 1957). Roth's qualitatively driven approach also helped her truly delve underneath the surface and explore the experiences of her participants. Roth's aim was not to ask for a convergence of results but rather to be comfortable residing on multiple levels and in multiple realities that inform one another. By focusing on the policies and practices of Wall Street securities firms, Roth helped us better understand the macro processes that tend to confine women to jobs characterized by low wages, little mobility, and limited prestige. This approach blames the structure instead of the victim and suggests a different strategy for improving women's labor-force status.

Mixed Method Case Study 4: Unwritten Rules of Talking to Doctors About Depression: Integrating Qualitative and Quantitative Methods

Wittink, Barg, and Gallo (2006) wanted to assess whether there were discrepancies between doctors' and their patients' perspectives on depression by exploring the patients' views about interactions with their doctor. They focused on older patients who identified as being depressed. Wittink et al. deployed a qualitatively driven sequential mixed methods design so that they could "link the themes regarding how patients talk to their physicians with personal characteristics and standard measures of distress" (p. 303), thus allowing them to both test and generate hypotheses.

A quantitative survey (qual) collected data on older primary care patients and their physicians concerning regarding how older primary care patients report depression comprised the first component of their mixed methods study. The quantitative component allowed the researchers to draw a subsample from this larger study—those participants who identified themselves as depressed and also had physician ratings of depression—for further research. The QUAL component consisted of semistructured interviews (QUAL) carried out with the patients to explore their views about interactions with their doctor.

The quantitative study then allowed the researchers to purposively recruit from this larger study. Forty eight participants were selected because they had identified as being depressed, and their doctors had also rated them for depression on the quantitative survey (see Figure 1.5). It was qualitatively driven as the emphasis was in exploring and seeking to understand the patients' views about how they interact with their doctor and whether this influences how they communicate about depression.

The researchers gathered quantitative assessment data from the parent quantitative study and participants scores on these measures were also tied to the semi structured interview data at the analysis stage of the study. The authors gathered a variety of quantitative measures: the Center for Epidemiologic Studies Depression scales, which looks at depression in community samples; the Beck Anxiety Inventory, which measures the severity of anxiety symptoms; the Beck Hopelessness Scale, which assesses factors related to suicidal thoughts; the Medical Outcomes Study, which is assesses health; and the Mini-Mental State Examination scales, which measure cognition and global functioning, as well as personal characteristics.

These quantitative measures served "to examine selected objective assessment measures that have been associated with recognition of depression in primary care settings" (p. 303) and were administered to the patient participants. Further, the patients' doctors were also given the Physician Evaluation of the Patient at the Index Visit, which rated the patients' levels of depression and how well the doctor knew the patient.

The overall data analysis for this study was conducted in two separate quantitative and qualitative phases. In the first phase, using the quantitative data gathered on the subsample, Wittink et al. identified two groups—those who identified as being depressed while their doctors did not rate them as being depressed (discordant group) and those who identified as being depressed while their doctors did rate them as being depressed (concordant group). The personal quantitative characteristics of both groups were compared and tested for significance using t-tests. In the second qualitative analysis phase, researchers iteratively coded and developed themes with regard to patients' communication with their doctors. During this stage of the analytical process, the researchers did not have access to the quantitative data or results.

The quantitative analysis showed that there were no significant differences in personal characteristics apart from age between the discordant group and the concordant group. The qualitative analysis, however, revealed four major themes that "relate to the patients' perception of the relationship with their physician" (p. 305): "My doctor just picked it up," "I'm a good patient," "They just check out your heart and things," and "They'll just send you to a psychiatrist." Wittink et al. then compared the themes generated from the qualitative analysis across the computed quantitative scores and found that patients who discussed the "My doctor just picks it up" theme and the "They'll just send you to a psychiatrist" theme were rated as being depressed by the doctor. These quantitative and qualitative analysis findings

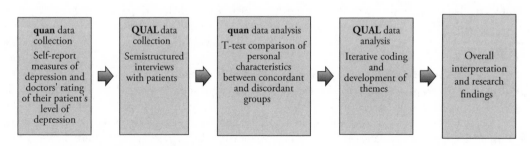

Fig. 1.5 Wittink, Barg, and Gallo's (2006) qualitatively driven sequential mixed methods design

revealed that patients identified as being depressed are influenced in their interactions with their doctors by the manner in which doctors indicate how emotional issues will be addressed.

Using a qualitatively driven sequential mixed methods design permitted both hypothesis testing and hypothesis generating in a single study. This is a good example of how the secondary quantitative component enhances the primary qualitative findings: by identifying patients who are depressed and whether or not their doctors also rate them as being depressed provides context for understanding how depressed patients are influenced by their perception of their interaction with their doctors. These findings are of importance and have clinical implications with regard to "the ability of doctors to recognise depression and negotiate a treatment plan" (p. 308). Conversely, had Wittink et al. conducted a solely quantitative study, they would have missed the patients' perspectives, which was the part of the study that contributed to the understanding of the interactions around depression between the patients and their doctors.

Multimethod Analytic Design. Case Study 5: Draw-and-Tell Conversations With Children About Fear

Martha Driessnack (2006) set out to introduce a child-centered approach to conducting research with children focusing on children's experiences of fear. Driessnack highlighted that children have typically been researched using measures that are adult-centered, such as through traditional measures like questionnaires, surveys, and so on. However, these measures may not necessarily be appropriate when the focus shifts from research about children to research on the children themselves. Therefore Driessnack chose a qualitatively driven multimethod analytic design with the intention of empowering the children she was researching with regard to the researcher and the research context. She did so by choosing the child-centered approach of draw-and-tell conversation as it is a part of everyday life for children—children are

offered the opportunity to draw and this then facilitates a conversation where narratives are elicited. Children construct stories of personal events in a manner that empowers them rather than the researcher.

Purposively and criterion based, Driessnack recruited 22 child participants through a school where there was a broad demographic range, so as to have access to children who were in their typical daily environment. Participants were between 7 and 8 years of age—an age where although their grasp of verbal skills is still limited, children are still capable of constructing stories of personal events. Driessnack provided a range of drawing materials from which the children could choose and asked each child to "think about a time when he or she was most afraid, draw it, and, when finished with the drawing, tell me all about it" (p. 1419).

Driessnack employed a qualitatively driven multimethod analytic design (see Figure 1.6). She used a linguistic approach to narrative analysis (QUAL) for analysis of narrative structure to consider how children shared their experiences of fear. Once this was complete within and across all 22 conversations, she returned to the children's narratives to examine what the children had shared about their experiences of fear by using thematic analysis (qual).

The qualitative (QUAL) linguistic narrative structural analysis (QUAL) revealed that the children's stories about fear were told in a manner that provided a lot of orienting detail about who was present in the story, locations, time, and ongoing/looming events but where the children rarely notably featured themselves. The children also provided evaluations of their stories by emphasizing what did not take place and what did not seem right. The analysis also revealed a notable lack of resolution, or ending, to the children's narratives and that these were mostly told in the present tense as opposed to the past tense. This qualitative analysis highlighted that the fear may still be present and unresolved and that, as an emotion,

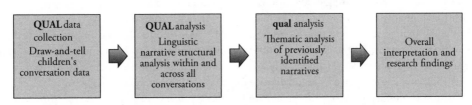

Fig. 1.6 Driessnack's (2006) Qualitatively driven multimethod analytic design

fear is "known or experienced only as it remains unresolved" (p. 1428).

The qualitative thematic analysis (qual) was then applied to the identified narratives and revealed five themes "that emerged and united the stories around feelings of being alone and taken off guard or by surprise, being unable to help themselves or obtain help from others, and the experience or sense of impending doom" (p. 1428). This qualitative analysis highlighted the necessary circumstances for an experience to be considered as fearful by children.

Driessnack's study is a good example of how a qualitatively driven multi analytic QUAL-qual multimethod analytic design increased the depth and extent of the analysis—the secondary qual analysis component added to the primary QUAL analytic component. While the core analytic component identified certain structures in how the children told stories about their experiences of fear, the auxiliary qualitative (qual) analytic component revealed what the children said in their narratives about how their fear was experienced.

Closing Thoughts and Future Directions

Qualitatively driven mixed methods designs offer the MMR community a set of methodological approaches that center on the importance of a qualitative perspective, one that seeks to understand lived experience and often subjugated knowledge with the goal of also working toward issues of social justice and social transformation. Such a view does not seek to upend or diminish the benefits of a more quantitatively driven approach but is meant to push against earlier MMR practices that leaned toward a more positivist mixed methods orientation, without reflecting on the broader role that a qualitative approach might bring to a variety of research questions.

These earlier mixed methods designs primarily viewed the qualitative component in the role of "handmaiden" or "second best" to the more dominant quantitative component. This praxis led some in the mixed methods community to critique such practices as tending toward reducing qualitative research to a set of auxiliary techniques for variously supplementing, humanizing, or illustrating a primarily "expert" quantitative research design (Giddings, 2006; Giddings & Grant, 2007). Brannen (2005) noted that the most frequent design among sequential mixed methods studies placed the qualitative component in a secondary role, "where qualitative pilot work is likely to precede and be subservient to

a larger survey" (p. 15). Bryman's (2006, 2007) content analysis study of MMR articles and interviews with mixed methods researchers noted the dominance of the quantitative component in most mixed methods designs, as well as a lack of integrating research findings using different methods.

Qualitatively driven approaches to MMMR enable researchers to focus on questions that seek access to unique perspectives on lived experience. They foreground questions and methods that seek to highlight the dynamism and complexity of experience and hold the promise of offering a set of research designs that are structured to explore a topic of inquiry that may require greater depth than one approach or traditional mixed methods research alone do.

While we have pointed out the important contributions a quantitative component can bring to a qualitatively driven MMMR project, it is critical that researchers be clear on the reasons for the inclusion of a quantitative component. This is also the case for the addition of a secondary qualitative component. As with all MMMR designs, qualitatively driven MMMR designs must clearly show the aims that these approaches are addressing. These may be in addition to aims met by uniparadigmatic quantitative or qualitative components of the study.

We should also note that several of the case study examples also focus on the use of *multiple analytical designs* that can reveal different and complex interpretations and findings interrogating the same data set. These qualitatively driven multiple analytical lenses can be placed in dialogue with each other to produce a richer and more complex understanding of the data gathered from a single analytical lens.

It is also important to provide a cautionary note regarding the potential of qualitatively driven MMMR. It may be the case that adding an additional qualitative or quantitative method to a qualitatively driven project does *not* move our theoretical understanding of a given issue forward. The researcher must be willing to be reflective and ask whether adding another method to a primarily qualitatively driven project will serve to enhance qualitative understanding.

In addition, pursuing a qualitatively driven MMMR design also requires new research skills and resources, and here it behooves researchers to begin to question the extent to which they may need to *retool their research skills or approach their project with a team of differently skilled researchers.* The team route to mixed methods does not come without its own set of issues in terms of coordinating how the findings are integrated, if at all (Bryman, 2007, 2008; Leech, 2010). Bringing together researchers who view data with different worldviews may mean that some are drawn only to their preferred approach, having less faith in other approaches and biasing the reporting of findings accordingly. Others may simply not have training or understanding in other approaches and may struggle to see the value of them. Clearly setting out the design and the status of each method to be used at the outset of the study and allowing for the introduction of new methods as the research evolves may be particularly important in qualitatively driven MMMR. One of the advantages of placing qualitative methods to the fore is the creativity in exploring information for which it allows. As with uniparadigmatic qualitative research, the qualitatively driven MMR approach flexes with the unfolding of the data and its findings, thus recognizing more deeply the complexity of experience and understanding.

Qualitative methods are often brought to MMMR to "repopulate" it, that is, to reflect the relationships between researcher and researched so as to allow for issues such as race, class, and gender to be illuminated rather than obscured in universalizing understandings.

Qualitatively driven MMMR holds the potential to capitalize on the reflexive aspect of conducting research by explicitly attending to and making prominent these relationships. This, combined with clear, theoretically informed qualitatively driven research designs, can foster outcomes that are transparent across the research process and that are credible in their status. The value of the quantitative component in qualitatively driven mixed methods designs also provides an opportunity for qualitative findings to be considered in different contexts and for their wider implications to be evaluated.

The range of qualitatively driven MMMR designs that this chapter has discussed illustrates not only the myriad of ways in which MMMR has evolved but also the variety of applications to which it can be put. The field of research has opened up so that human experience is valued and recognized while the scientific approach that they bring makes this approach credible and trustworthy. The approaches share a common premise that places the research question central to the inquiry while also recognizing the need for rigorous choice of methodology and employment of methods. The potential for qualitatively driven MMMR to advance our understanding of human experience, support, relationships, and interaction is huge and invokes responsibility among researchers to consider carefully not only what they are researching but how they are doing so and their role in the process.

Discussion Questions

1. How does qualitatively driven MMMR differ from traditional MMR?

2. What differences are there between qualitatively driven multimethods and mixed methods approach designs?

3. What reasons are there for using qualitatively driven multimethods or mixed methods approach designs?

4. Why might you choose a qualitatively driven MMMR approach?

Suggested Websites
Glossary of Mixed Methods Terms/Concepts
http://www.fiu.edu/~bridges/glossary.htm

A list of terms and definitions adopted from Tashakkori and Teddlie's (2003) *Handbook of Mixed Methods in Social and Behavioral Research* (Thousand Oaks, CA: SAGE).

Issues in Mixing Qualitative and Quantitative Approaches to Research
http://www.researchsupport.com.au/MMIssues.pdf

This article examines the use of mixed methods and the resulting issues, including demands, paradigmatic problems, and lack of increased validity.

Network for Pluralism in Qualitative Research Blog
http://npqr.wordpress.com

This website provides interactive support, resources, and information to researchers interested in combining qualitative methods with each other. It has a worldwide membership of over 200 researchers and offers a page for questions and answers from network members.

Notes

1. Some variations on this paradigm are said to include Marxist, feminist, ethnic, cultural, and queer studies. Denzin and Lincoln (2000) pose a separate paradigm for these variations they term "materialist-realist ontology" (p. 21).

2. Some of these reasons are adapted from Hesse-Biber (2010a) and Morse (2010).

3. Case studies 1 and 3 are adapted from: Hesse-Biber (2010b).

4. The term *human capital* refers to those dimensions that affect one's ability to produce on the job factors such as educational level, number of years worked, job training, absenteeism, and turnover.

References

Becker, H. A. (1957). How families meet the costs of hospitalization and medical care. *Marriage and Family Living, 19*(2), 166–171.

Benokraitis, N. V., & Feagin, J. R. (1995). *Modern sexism: Blatant, subtle, and covert discrimination.* New York, NY: Prentice Hall.

Brannen, J. (2005, December). Mixed methods research: A discussion. NCRM Methods Review Papers. Swindon, UK: ESRC National Centre for Research Methods.

Bryman, A. (2006). Integrating quantitative and qualitative research: How is it done? *Qualitative Research, 6*(1), 97–113.

Bryman, A. (2007). Barriers to integrating quantitative and qualitative research. *Journal of Mixed Methods Research, 1*(1), 8–22.

Bryman, A. (2008). Why do researchers integrate/combine/mesh/blend/mix/merge/fuse quantitative and qualitative research? In M. M. Bergman (Ed.), *Advances in mixed methods research* (pp. 89–100). London: SAGE.

Charmaz, K. (2006). *Constructing grounded theory.* London, England: Sage.

Crabtree, B. F., & Miller, W. L. (1999). Using codes and code manuals: A template organizing style of interpretation. In B. F. Crabtree & W. L. Miller (Eds.), *Doing qualitative research* (pp. 163–177). Thousand Oaks, CA: Sage.

Creswell, J. W., Shope, R., Plano Clark, V. L., & Green, D. O. (2006). How interpretive qualitative research extends mixed methods research. *Research in the Schools, 13*(1), 1–11.

Denzin, N., & Lincoln, Y. (Eds.). (1998). *Collecting and interpreting qualitative materials.* Thousand Oaks, CA: Sage.

Denzin, N., & Lincoln, Y. (Eds.). (2000). *The SAGE handbook of qualitative research.* Thousand Oaks, CA: Sage.

Denzin, N. K., & Lincoln, Y. S. (2005). Introduction: The discipline and practice of qualitative research. In N. K. Denzin & Y. S. Lincoln (Eds.), *The SAGE handbook of qualitative research* (pp. 1–32). Thousand Oaks, CA: Sage.

Driessnack, M. (2006). Draw-and-tell conversations with children about fear. *Qualitative Health Research, 16*(10), 1414–1435.

Frost, N. A., Esin, C., Holt, A., Mehdizadeh, L., Brooks-Gordon, B., & Shinebourne, P. (2011). Pluralism in qualitative research: Consensual findings individual interpretations. *Qualitative Research in Psychology 8*(1), 93–113.

Frost, N. A., Nolas, S.-M., Brooks-Gordon, B., Esin, C., Holt, A., Mehdizadeh, L., & Shinebourne, P. (2010). Pluralism in qualitative research: The impact of different researchers and qualitative approaches on the analysis of qualitative data. *Qualitative Research, 10*(4), 441–461.

Giddings, L. S. (2006). Mixed methods research: Positivism dressed in drag? *Journal of Research in Nursing, 11*(3), 195–203.

Giddings, L., & Grant, B. (2007). A Trojan horse for positivism? A critique of mixed methods research. *Advances in Nursing Science, 30*(1), 52–60.

Hesse-Biber, S. N. (1995). Unleashing Frankenstein's monster: The use of computers in qualitative research. In R. G. Burgess (Ed.), *Studies in qualitative methodology* (Vol. 5, pp. 549–593). London, England: JAI Press.

Hesse-Biber, S. N. (2010a). *Mixed methods research: Merging theory with practice.* New York, NY: Guilford Press.

Hesse-Biber, S. N. (2010b). Qualitative approaches to mixed methods practice. *Qualitative Inquiry, 16*(6), 455–468.

Hesse-Biber, S. N., & Carter, G. (2005). *Working women in America: Split dreams* (2nd ed.). New York, NY: Oxford University Press.

Holmes, C. A. (July, 2006). *Mixed (up) methods, methodology and interpretive frameworks.* Paper presented at the Mixed Methods Conference, Cambridge, UK.

Howe, K. R. (2004). A critique of experimentalism. *Qualitative Inquiry, 10*(1), 42–61.

Karp, D. (1996). *Speaking of sadness: Disconnection and the meanings of illness.* New York, NY: Oxford University Press.

Leech, N. (2010). Interviews with the early developers of mixed methods research. In A. Tashakkori & C. Teddlie (Eds.), *Mixed methodology: Combining qualitative and quantitative approaches* (2nd ed., pp. 253–272). Thousand Oaks, CA: Sage.

Mason, J. (2006). Mixing methods in a qualitatively driven way. *Qualitative Research, 6*(1), 9–25. doi: 10.1177/1468794106058866

McMahon, S. (2007). Understanding community-specific rape myths exploring student athlete culture. *Affilia, 22*(4), 357–370.

Morse, J. M. (2003). Principles of mixed and multi-method research design. In A. Tashakkori & C. Teddlie (Eds.), *Handbook of mixed methods in social & behavioural research* (pp. 189–208). Thousand Oaks, CA: Sage.

Morse, J. M. (2010). Simultaneous and sequential qualitative mixed method designs. *Qualitative Inquiry, 16*(6), 483–491.

Morse, J. M., & Niehaus, L. (2009). *Mixed method design: Principles and procedures.* Walnut Creek, CA: Left Coast Press.

Paterniti, D. A., Chen, M. S., Chiechi, C., Beckett, L. A., Horan, N., Turrell, C., . . . Lara, P. N. (2005). Asian Americans and cancer clinical trials: A mixed methods approach to understanding awareness and experience. *Cancer, 104*(12 Suppl.), 3015–3024.

Roth, L. M. (2006). *Selling women short: Gender and money on Wall Street.* Princeton, NJ: Princeton University Press.

Sandelowski, M. (1996). Using qualitative methods in intervention studies. *Research in Nursing & Health, 19*(4), 359–364.

Sandelowski, M. (2000). Focus on research methods: Whatever happened to qualitative description? *Research in Nursing and Health, 23*(4), 334–340.

Tashakkori, A., & Teddlie, C. (1998). *Mixed methodology: Combining qualitative and quantitative approaches.* Thousand Oaks, CA: Sage.

Wittink, M. N., Barg, F. K., & Gallo, J. J. (2006). Unwritten rule of talking to doctors about depression: Integrating qualitative and quantitative methods. *Annals of Family Medicine, 4*(4), 302–309.

Mixed and Multimethods in Predominantly Quantitative Studies, Especially Experiments and Quasi-Experiments

Melvin M. Mark

Abstract

This chapter addresses mixed and multimethods research from the perspective of a quantitative researcher. The chapter illustrates how qualitative data have long informed and contributed to predominantly quantitative studies; emphasizes the importance of the research question driving study design, rather than an allegiance to quantitative, qualitative, or mixed methods; describes several models of alternative purposes for mixing methods; briefly reviews caveats about the possible downsides of using such models, including the potential for a study to be lauded because of its design despite its flaws in addressing the research question; and illustrates a wide variety of ways in which mixed and multimethods can contribute to experimental and quasi-experimental research, which includes (especially for quasi-experiments) assessing the plausibility of and attempting to rule out classic validity threats.

Key Words: mixed methods, multimethods, quasi-experiment, research question, experimental and quasi-experimental research

Readers of some papers about mixed methods might infer that the mixing of qualitative and quantitative methods is a relatively new innovation. If so, that is an unintended consequence of authors concentrating on previous literature that focuses on the mixing of methods, rather than on examples of mixing that predate such literature. Although frameworks to characterize the mixing of methods tend to be of more recent vintage, combining qualitative and quantitative methods within a single study or research program has a long and distinguished history in practice.

Earlier instances exist, but consider three examples from a single discipline, social psychology.

• Attitude measurement is a widely used quantitative procedure in psychology and elsewhere in much of the social and behavioral sciences. Typically, study participants are asked to respond to multiple items, perhaps by indicating their degree of agreement or disagreement. The researcher conducts a statistical procedure, such as a simple averaging across items, so that each respondent's attitude is represented by a single number, often on a 5- or 7-point scale. Although the result is quantitative, the breakthrough articles on attitude scale development indicated that, in the process of developing the multiple items that are given to respondents, the investigator should start with more qualitative methods. Most commonly, pioneers of attitude measurement emphasized reviewing written materials relevant to the general topic, such as newspaper articles, magazines, books, and speeches. Interviewing people was suggested as another possibility. Although early attitude theorists did not use the term, effectively what they suggest was a kind of content analysis to identify the specific topics to represent in the individual items in a multiple item scale (e.g., Likert, 1932, p. 12; Thurstone, 1928, p. 544). As an aside, the very fact that multiple-item scales, rather than single items, were advocated is a relatively early example of the logic of multimethods. The idea was that no single item was perfect or even adequate and that with multiple-item scales one could better converge on the respondent's "real" attitude.

• The conformity studies conducted by Solomon Asch (1956) are a classic in social psychology. In the original study, Asch repeatedly asked participants to look at a "target" line and, when it was their turn, to report out loud which one of three other "comparison" lines was the same length. Unknown to the actual study participants, the other people in the room were not, as it appeared, also students who had just arrived for the study. In fact, the others were confederates working with the experimenter. On a set of "critical trials," the confederates each selected a line that did not in fact match the target line. Among the quantitative findings that Asch reported was the percentage of critical trials on which participants conformed to the group or, put differently, made an error. Across participants, errors took place on 37% of the critical trials; in contrast, errors occurred in less than 1% of the trials in a control condition without confederates making errors. Decades later, textbooks still commonly report this finding, sometimes with additional findings from one or more of the variations Asch examined in subsequent studies. For example, he subsequently examined the effect on conformity rates of having fewer versus more confederates, or of including among the confederates a dissenter who gave the correct answer on critical trials. What readers of textbook summaries are not likely to know is that roughly half of the pages Asch used in reporting the original study findings consisted of qualitative results from interviews of study participants and from direct observation. Asch reported on participants' internal reactions and their stated reasons for complying or not complying with the confederates. He also classified participants into different subgroups (e.g., those who showed "independence without confidence") and presented the interview responses from a typical member of each subgroup. Asch's descriptions of his study participants' internal struggles make for compelling reading.

• The Robbers Cave experiment of Sherif, Harvey, White, Hood, and Sherif (1961) is another classic in social psychology, though not as often recounted in textbooks today. The researchers obtained the use of a Boy Scouts camp in the Robbers Cave State Park in southeastern Oklahoma. They recruited campers who were healthy, "normal" boys who did not know each other. Camper selection was guided by a review of school records as well as interviews with teachers and parents. At the start of the study, the researchers created two separate groups of boys, with each group unaware of the other's existence. The researchers were initially interested in the development of in-group status. Subsequently, the two groups were brought together, and the researchers monitored intergroup conflict. In a later phase, the researchers staged problems that could only be solved if the two groups of boys worked together. The related research question involved whether the presence of these "superordinate goals" would overcome the previously observed intergroup conflict and hostility. Data collection involved multimethods, both quantitative and qualitative. At a couple of key time points, the boys were asked to report on their liking of the other campers, as well as to complete items assessing the extent to which they stereotyped the other group. The liking data were used to compute sociometrics, an early form of network analysis. The quantitative data were compared over time, for example to show changes following the superordinate goals phase. Researchers acting as camp staff collected observational data and at times interviewed boys about events the staff had not seen directly. In addition, an estimated 1,200 pictures were taken (staff members initially introduced themselves as "shutterbugs"). The qualitative data shaped the narrative presentation of the study. The report described events such as when one of the groups stole and burned the other's flag, with the latter group then reciprocating by vandalizing the first group's cabin. More than 40 pictures were included in the monograph-length report. However, the quantitative data received a good deal of attention in the assessment of the effects of superordinate goals.

Several inferences can be drawn from these three examples:

1. Skilled researchers have long been mixing qualitative and quantitative methods. Many

examples other than the three here exist. Moreover, there would be a much longer list of examples to select from if studies with multimethods, both quantitative or both qualitative, were also considered.

2. The mixing of methods can occur in a wide variety of ways. For instance, in the attitude measurement example, qualitative methods were used in the preparation of a quantitative method that is the researcher's primary focus. In contrast, in the Asch study, qualitative and quantitative measures were both implemented at about the same time in a single overall research design. Findings were presented in a complementary fashion, with the qualitative findings elaborating on and helping explain the quantitative findings. Mixing took place in multiple ways in the Robbers Cave study. As one example, qualitative interviews played an important role in the selection of the boys who would participate. Most notably, multiple forms of measures were employed within the study, with the qualitative findings largely shaping the narrative that the researchers presented.

3. Sherif and his colleagues (1961) explicitly discussed their combining of methods as a strength of the Robbers Cave study. Nevertheless, across the three examples, what stands out about the combining of methods, qualitative and quantitative, is that in a certain way it seemed unremarkable. No special theory or model of mixed or multimethods had to be invoked. To the contrary, the choice of methods, including the mixing of qualitative and quantitative, was secondary to and followed from the research questions under investigation. Put differently, the researchers were simply trying to use the best possible methods, and in the case of the attitude measurement specialists, to develop the best method, to address the research questions at hand.

This chapter appears in a *Handbook of Mixed and Multimethod Research*. From the vantage of most quantitatively oriented researchers, the double M, mixed *and* multimethod, is important. To explain why, brief definitional and historical notes are needed, duplicative as they may be of material in chapter 1 and elsewhere in this handbook. The term *mixed methods* generally is used to refer to the combining of qualitative and quantitative methods in a single study or linked series of studies. *Multimethods*, in contrast, refers more broadly to the combining of two or more methods, with no suggestion that *both* qualitative

and quantitative methods are involved. For readers who are not fans of the term "multimethods" or who find it awkward in places, please simply translate it as "multiple methods."

Although historical exceptions might be cited, it appears that for the most part explicit consideration of multimethods preceded comparable attention to mixed methods. For example, key publications that provide a conceptual foundation for multimethods appeared in the late 1950s and 1960s (e.g., Campbell & Fiske, 1959; Webb, Campbell, Schwartz, & Sechrest, 1966), while comparable publications on mixed methods came later (e.g., Jick, 1979; Greene, Caracelli, & Graham, 1989; Greene & McClintock, 1985). Quantitatively oriented researchers tend to have been influenced more by the earlier work on multimethods than by the more recent work on mixed methods.

In addition, quantitatively oriented social science researchers tend not to be aligned with paradigms that lead either to drawing a firm line between qualitative and quantitative methods or to a prioritization of mixed methods rather than multimethods. Quantitatively oriented researchers are likely to be post-positivists (e.g., Cook, 1985), though they may also refer to themselves paradigmatically in other ways, such as evolutionary critical realists (e.g., Cook & Campbell, 1979, p. 28). A good number of quantitatively oriented researchers would probably qualify as paradigmatic agnostics, being deeply concerned with their particular research area and minimally if at all concerned with the perceived abstractions of paradigms. (For readers interested in further discussion of alternative paradigms and their linkages to research approaches, this handbook is a rich resource, especially Part I.)

From the vantage point of most quantitatively oriented researchers, then, the broader notion of multimethods probably makes more sense than the narrower idea of mixed methods. (Note that "narrower" here refers to the expectation that mixing methods requires the combining of qualitative and quantitative, while using multimethods does not imply that constraint.) The quantitatively oriented researcher might ask: Why prioritize the adding of a qualitative method over adding a quantitative one, if adding a second quantitative method would better address the research questions at hand? For instance, imagine a researcher planning a randomized experiment in a field setting to test the effectiveness of a preschool program. Imagine further that the researcher also wants to complement the experiment with methods that will help describe the participants and context. Should the researcher start with a preference for a qualitative method, such as direct observation, so that the study will be a mixed methods study? Or should the researcher instead simply try to figure out which ancillary method(s), whether qualitative or quantitative, make(s) the most sense for describing clients and context in the situation at hand, given available resources and other constraints? I believe most quantitatively oriented researchers would opt for the latter approach. That is, quantitatively oriented researchers probably do not give a priority to mixed methods over multimethods.

Even if quantitatively oriented researchers tend to relate better to the more general idea of multimethods than to the narrower idea of mixed methods, there are reasons that these researchers should be familiar with the growing literature on mixed methods. One simple reason arises from the fact that at times using qualitative and quantitative methods together will be the best choice for a study, which means that the researcher may face issues that have been addressed in the mixed methods literature (e.g., alternative approaches to integrating qualitative and quantitative data). In addition, the mixed methods literature is the primary home to a set of frameworks or models that can be used to guide thinking about the combining of methods, whether all quantitative, all quantitative, or mixed.

Before turning to these models, four background matters deserve comment. First, at various points in the chapter, I refer to some practice or another as being relatively common or fairly infrequent. These claims are not the result of a formal survey of a sample of studies that mix or might mix methods. Rather they are impressionistic judgments, based on my reading, observation, conversations, and beliefs. Second, the chapter contains numerous statements about how quantitatively oriented social science researchers are likely to think or act. Again, these statements are impressionistic. Third, the chapter sometimes refers explicitly to mixed methods (i.e., quantitative and qualitative together) or to multimethods (at least two methods, of any combination, including the possibility of two quantitative and no qualitative methods). In addition, the phrase "combining methods" is sometimes used to allow for either mixed or multimethods. Fourth, the term *method* is used here in a relatively general and flexible way, encompassing measures, designs, design features and components, and procedures linked closely over time.

Related to the latter point, Cook (1985), in an influential paper on "post-positivist critical multiplism," indicated that

> a study that is truly multiplist requires the capacity not only to answer multiple research questions but also to uncover novel questions and issues. It also requires multiple constructs; multiple measures of each construct; and multiple populations of persons, settings, and times. Also needed are multiple mechanisms for triangulating on inferences about cause; multiple data analyses for every important substantive question; and commentary by many people who have unique values and method preferences that relate to research questions and procedures. (p. 54)

Going beyond the methods of a single study, Cook also generated a longer list of characteristics that can be made multiple:

> Among other things, multiplism is associated with the call for (1) multiple operationalism. . .; (2) multimethod research. . .; (3) planned research programs based on multiple interconnected studies. . .; (4) the synthesis of multiple studies related to each other in haphazard fashion. . .; (5) the construction of complex multivariate causal models instead of simple univariate ones. . .; (6) the competitive testing of multiple rival hypotheses rather than testing a single hypothesis. . .; (7) the use of multiple stakeholders to interpret research questions. . .; (8) the use of multiple theoretical and value frameworks to interpret research questions and findings. . .; (9) the advocacy that multiple analysts examine important data sets; and (10) the desirability of multitargeted research that seeks to probe many different types of issues within a single study. (pp. 21–22, italics and references omitted)

The focus of the present chapter is more on those aspects of multiplism to which Cook refers that fall within a single study, or in a closely interlinked set of studies, rather than in an ongoing research program.

Models for Mixed and Multimethods

Starting for the most part in the mid-1980s, the literature on multimethod and especially mixed methods has seen a notable development: the creation of various frameworks or models that characterize studies with mixed or multimethods. The first of these models attempted to characterize the alternative purposes to which mixed or multimethods could be put. Other frameworks attempted to lay out alternative designs, or forms of analysis, or attributes of mixed or multimethod studies' quality. Of these different kinds of frameworks, the focus here is on those that describe the different purposes or ends to which mixed or multimethods can be put.

Rossman and Wilson (1985) provided one of the first such models, and the influence of their work persists. In short, Rossman and Wilson described three alternative purposes for mixing qualitative and quantitative methods: (a) *corroboration*, that is, a search for triangulation or convergence on an answer; (b) *elaboration*, that is, the enhancement or enrichment of a finding across methods; and (c) *initiation*, that is, the generation of new questions or interpretations.

Mark and Shotland (1987) focused on multimethod rather than mixed methods. They described three primary "models" of multimethods. It might be better to refer to this work as comprising a single model, or framework, describing three alternative primary purposes or intended uses of multimethods. One of Mark and Shotland's purposes is *triangulation*, equivalent to Rossman and Wilson's (1985) corroboration. The concept of triangulation has a long history in quantitative social science method, largely associated with Campbell and his associates (e.g., Webb et al., 1966). The term is also used in qualitative research, stemming largely from an influential text by Denzin (1978, and later editions). The metaphor probably originated in surveying, where a point of interest can be located by finding the point of convergence from two known surveying points. Indeed, convergence is a common synonym for triangulation.

Drawing on Reichardt and Gollob (1987), Mark and Shotland's (1987) second purpose for multimethods is *bracketing*, which is a kind of counterpoint to triangulation. Triangulation suggests that the goal of using different methods is to converge on a single answer to a research question, such as finding a single estimate of the effect of a social program on an outcome of interest. (Note, however, that the term is used in varying ways throughout the literature.) The idea of bracketing, in contrast, is that two or more methods can provide a range of alternative answers or estimates. Rather than the triangulation of surveying, a metaphor for bracketing is the confidence interval associated with a statistical test. However, in bracketing the interval or range arises not from a single statistical procedure but from the observed discrepancies in the findings from the two (or more) methods.

Both triangulation and bracketing involve trying to answer a single research question, such as what if any effect an educational program has on student achievement. Triangulation combines the findings from two or more methods to get the best possible single answer, while bracketing focuses on the range of answers across the methods. In contrast, Mark and Shotland's (1987) third purpose for multimethods is to address *complementary purposes*, whereby the different methods are employed to address different ends. Mark and Shotland describe give four kinds of complementary purposes. One, *enhancing interpretability*, is similar to Rossman and Wilson's (1985) elaboration. Under this form of complementary purposes, one method is used as the primary means of answering the research question, and the other method clarifies or puts the metaphoric flesh on the bone. Another form of complementary purposes involves *alternative tasks*, where the two methods do not address the same research question but rather focus on distinct but conceptually related questions. For instance, one method might estimate the effect of an educational program, while a different method examines the process by which the program has its effects. A third form of complementary purposes involves investigating *alternative levels of analysis*. For example, one method might examine behavioral effects while another focuses on physiological ones. The final form of complementary purposes given by Mark and Shotland occurs when a secondary method is used to *assess the plausibility of threats* to validity. For example, a researcher might conduct interviews to try to identify possible examples of history as a threat in an interrupted time-series study (for an example see Steiner & Mark, 1985). In retrospect, alternative levels of analysis and assessing the plausibility of threats could be seen as more specific instances of using multimethods for alternative tasks. As we shall see later, the possible list of alternative tasks for complementary methods is quite long.

Greene et al. (1989), in what has been the most influential of these models, identified five possible purposes for mixed methods. Three of these—*triangulation, complementarity*, and *initiation*—correspond respectively to Rossman and Wilson's (1985) corroboration, elaboration, and initiation. A fourth of Greene et al.'s purposes, *expansion*, refers to the use of different methods for different components of a study. Thus expansion is similar to Mark and Shotland's (1987) alternative tasks form of complementary purposes. Greene et al.'s fifth purpose is *development*. Development occurs when one method is used to help create (i.e., develop) another method. As an example, focus groups are sometimes carried out to help a researcher create survey items.

Table 2.1 provides a comparison and tentative integration across the three models. The first three columns list the purposes from Rossman and Wilson (1985), Mark and Shotland (1987), and Greene et al. (1989), respectively. Purposes listed in the same row are the same or at least largely overlap. As the table shows, the three models all include triangulation (or convergence). All three also include the idea of one method being used to provide clearer, more detailed, or more meaningful exposition of the results from another method. Across models this purpose was variously labeled as elaboration, complementary purposes for interpretability, and complementarity. In a common example, quotes from interviews are often used to enhance and illustrate findings from a survey. Greene et al. include the purpose of expansion, which corresponds to Mark and Shotland's alternative tasks, at least when the alternative tasks involve different components of a study. Greene et al. also list development, whereby one method contributes to the construction or refinement of another. Logically this could be put under the umbrella of Mark and Shotland's complementary purposes.

However, development may be distinct and notable enough as a purpose to warrant a separate label, especially given that development typically implies that the two methods are carried out sequentially, while (other) complementary purposes may be addressed simultaneously.

Both Rossman and Wilson (1985) and Greene et al. (1989) list initiation, while Mark and Shotland (1987) do not. Rossman and Wilson state that initiation "prompts new interpretations, suggests area for further exploration, or recasts the entire research question" (p. 637). They further indicate that when initiation is the purpose, "rather than seeking confirmatory evidence," the mixed methods study "searches for the provocative." Mark and Shotland may not have included initiation or its equivalent as a purpose, thinking in part that findings of this provocative sort may at times emerge but are not willed into being when one designs a study. (Of course, as many researchers have learned, the same is true of triangulation!) A companion paper by Shotland and Mark (1987) suggests another possible reason they did not include initiation as a purpose.

Shotland and Mark (1987) deal with inferential problems that can arise when multimethods are used. One of these problems occurs when, contrary to the researcher's expectations, the two methods actually address different questions. Returning

Table 2.1 Summary and Integration of Three Models of Alternative Purposes for (and Consequences of) Combining Methods

Rossman & Wilson (1985)	Mark & Shotland (1985, 1987)	Greene et al. (1989)	Integrated
Convergence	Triangulation	Triangulation	Triangulation
	Bracketing		Bracketing
Elaboration	CP: Interpretability	Complementary	Elaboration of findings
	CP: Alternative tasks	Expansion	Component-specific methods
		Development	Development
Initiation		Initiation	Initiation
	CP: Alternative levels of analysis		Other CP
	CP: Assess plausibility of validity threats		Other CP
			Complementing validity strengths and weaknesses

Note. CP = complementary purposes.

to the metaphor from which the notion of triangulation may have come, imagine two surveyors, a known distance apart, but who are looking in opposite directions. Their observations will not converge, and, because they are not looking toward the same thing, it will be hard to learn anything useful from their discrepant observations (other than, perhaps, that the two surveyors were not looking in the same direction). When a researcher is seeking initiation, he or she might elect to use relatively different and independent methods (Greene, 2007). For instance, in a randomized trial estimating the effect of a welfare reform initiative, the mixed methods researcher seeking initiation might employ a relatively disparate method, such as inviting self-directed ethnographers to examine the lived experience of treatment and comparison group members. Informal reports from researchers who have used such disparate methods indicate that the two methods may simply not inform each other. The enthographic work might focus on shared patterns of challenge and triumph across individuals with limited resources, while the randomized experiments focuses on whether there are improved outcomes associated with the novel welfare approach, even if these may be modest or small in size (assuming statistical power). This kind of discrepancy across methods' focus is not inevitable, of course. However, the possibility would seem to increase as methods become more disparate and are kept relatively independent of each other. The possibility of such discrepancies may be more concerning to quantitatively than qualitatively oriented researchers.

All of this is not to say that researchers who seek initiation are condemned to never to find it, nor is it to say that quantitatively oriented researchers are blind to the possibility of discrepant findings that prompt new interpretations, raise new questions, or challenge old understandings. Indeed, in his 1985 paper on critical multiplism, Cook referred to the possibility that multimethods may result in empirical puzzles that call for resolution. If Cook and other quantitatively oriented researchers recognize the possibility of such empirical puzzles—and further, if they see such puzzles as a potentially important source of new and better ideas—do they in any way differ from the more qualitatively oriented theorists of mixed methods who put initiation forward as an attractive purpose (Greene et al., 1989; Rossman & Wilson, 1985)? The answer may be that quantitatively oriented researchers are less likely to see discrepant results as a *goal to be sought*

when designing research. Instead, their thinking may be as follows: If one is seeking triangulation and a discrepancy arises, then wrestling with the unexpected empirical puzzle may well be productive. In contrast, quantitatively oriented researchers may think: If methods are selected because they seem likely to give discrepant results and they indeed do so, the discrepancy may be neither all that informative nor enlightening. The discrepancy may leave open so many alternatives as to be hard to follow up on. These alternative questions, in general terms, are: Do the intentionally diverse methods give different results because (a) one method is technically sound and the other is not (e.g., one form of measurement is valid and reliable, and the other is not), (b) the two address related questions with differing answers (e.g., student performance shows change as a result of a treatment but teacher views of students change more slowly due to the persistence of person perception), or (c) the two address unrelated questions?

Fans of initiation as a purpose of multimethods may also have less commitment to answering a specific question and more to general understanding of a general phenomenon. Quantitatively oriented researchers may be more likely to want to obtain the best available answer regarding the hypothesis or research question being addressed in a study. This may be especially true for more applied research, such as program and policy evaluation, where relevant stakeholders' concerns may have generated the research question. Quantitatively oriented, multimethod evaluators may be as concerned about specious uncertainty as about specious certainty. They may want to use multiple measures, for example, to avoid specious certainty about the existence and size of a treatment effect but not want to use purposely divergent methods that could be informative but might initiate a dead-end puzzle that could have real costs in terms of deferring the use of findings. Initiation-oriented mixed methods researchers may instead emphasize the value not of a single question such as the size of a treatment effect but rather of a more general understanding of, say, a program and its participants in context.

Returning to Table 2.1, although Mark and Shotland (1987) did not include initiation as a possible purpose of multimethods, theirs is the only framework to list bracketing. Recall that with bracketing the idea is to focus on the range of findings across methods, rather than to emphasize convergence as in triangulation. In a sense, bracketing might be seen as a more quantitatively oriented cousin of initiation. (Recall that for bracketing the metaphor is that of a confidence interval, with the interval arising not from a single statistical procedure but from the observed discrepancies in the findings from the multimethods.)

The other listings in Table 2.1 are additional forms of the general complementary purposes category put forward by Mark and Shotland. These include studying alternative levels of analysis and assessing the plausibility of threats to validity (especially, but not only, threats to internal validity).

The final column of Table 2.1 provides an attempt to integrate the three models. Triangulation, bracketing, development, and initiation are familiar both in concept and terminology. The inclusion of all of these is justified in part by a minor shift in the focus of the integrated model. That is, the final column is now intended as a model of alternative purposes *or consequences* of combining methods. This allows for the possibility that one researcher might set out with the purpose of triangulation or bracketing, while another sets out with the purpose of initiation. It also allows for a shift between the initially intended purpose and the eventual consequence of mixing methods. In particular, a mixed or multipmethods researcher might set out with the intended purpose of triangulation, but if an empirical puzzle occurs and the researcher wrestles with it, initiation would be the actual consequence. The framing of the final column as purposes or consequences also allows for what one hopes is a less frequent occurrence. That is, the researcher might combine methods without a clear purpose (other than, perhaps, getting the approval of a funder or adviser), but one or more of the alternatives in Table 2.1 emerges as a consequence.

The final column of Table 2.1 provides two familiar purposes but with modified names. The term *elaboration of findings* harkens back to Rossman and Wilson's (1985) elaboration. However, given that the simpler term *elaboration* could be interpreted in other ways, the longer term is meant to clarify that the findings from one method are elaborated upon using the results from another method. *Component-specific methods* corresponds to Mark and Shotland's alternative tasks and Greene et al.'s (1989) expansion. The idea, as the new term indicates, is that different methods are used for different components of the research (whether concurrently or sequentially).

In addition to models that identify alternative purposes (or consequences) of mixed and

multimethods, frameworks have been put forward to classify different kinds of mixed methods designs. Leaders in this work include Tashakkori and Teddlie (1998, 2003), Greene (2007; Greene et al., 1989), and Creswell (2010; Creswell, Plano Clark, Gutmann, & Hanson, 2003). The present chapter does not include a detailed review or synthesis of the alternative frameworks/models that have been proposed to characterize mixed methods designs (though several chapters in this handbook do). Instead, following Greene (2007), a limited number of dimensions are presented that appear to capture at least some of the key characteristics along which mixed and multimethod studies differ. In addition to *purpose*, these dimensions include *timing*, that is, whether the methods are conducted at the same time or instead one method is sequenced before the other; *status*, or dominance, referring to whether one method is primary and the other secondary versus the different methods being equal in standing; *(in)dependence*, that is, whether the two methods are carried out without one informing the other versus having one method and its results inform the other; and the *methods themselves*, for example, whether one is using one self-report measure and a peer-report measure of the same outcome versus using a randomized experiment and ethnography to assess the effects of a social program.

These four dimensions can be illustrated with the three examples from the beginning of the chapter. In the case of classic attitude measurement, qualitative methods such as content analysis were used to guide the creation of attitude items. This mixing of methods involves development as a purpose, sequential timing, with the first method (content analysis) secondary to the subsequent method, and with the methods dependent in that the results of the first feed directly into the development of the second. In the Asch example, the qualitative and quantitative methods largely represent component-specific methods, with the quantitative the key measure of conformity, and with the qualitative measures allowing classification of participants into subgroups and analysis of the processes involved. Elaboration of findings also took place in the Asch study, with qualitative reports adding detail to the quantitative results. The quantitative methods may be seen as primary, but relative method status is not as clear as in the attitude measurement example. The different types of measures were independent (prior to their integration in the results). In the Robbers Cave example, methods were mixed in multiple ways. Camper selection, prior to the primary study, relied on interviews. This then involved development as the purpose, with sequential timing, dependence, and secondary status for the interviews relative to the primary study that followed. In addition, during the primary study, qualitative and quantitative data collection took place (more or less) simultaneously. Multiple purposes were served, including triangulation (with both qualitative and quantitative findings showing a reduction in outgroup hostility following the superordinate goals), elaboration (with qualitative observations providing a richer account of quantitative findings), and component-specific methods (with qualitative methods giving information about underlying processes that the quantitative data did not address).

As the interpretation of these three classic studies illustrates, applications of frameworks such as those summarized in Table 2.1 can become ambiguous in practice. Whether the qualitative component of the Asch study is seen as secondary to or equal to the quantitative in status is a matter of judgment. The mixed measures of the Robbers Cave study serve multiple purposes, not only one. Frameworks often simplify relative to the complexities of actual practice.

Consider again the idea that the alternatives in the integrated model, shown in the final column of Table 2.1, could be either intended purposes or actual consequences of combining methods. In part, this is a recognition of the way purpose can change over the course of a study, perhaps because of the specific findings that emerge. This is one kind of messiness that arises in actual practice as opposed to the tidiness of conceptual frameworks. Future users (and teachers) of frameworks such as those in Table 2.1 might be well served not to treat the alternatives they contain as clean distinctions to be followed in practice. Instead, they might be seen as orienting concepts, as alternative possibilities that can help researchers make thoughtful choices at various points in the research process.

Beyond the frameworks summarized in this section, other frameworks exist that describe alternative ways of *combining data* from the qualitative and quantitative components of a mixed methods study. Yet other models describe multiple ways to *characterize the quality* of a mixed method study. See elsewhere in this handbook for reviews of this work.

Caveats Regarding the Use of Methods-Related Frameworks

Scholars develop models of research methods and related matters (e.g., validity types, validity threats) largely out of the hope that such models will contribute to the training of new researchers, help guide researchers as they design studies, and aid in the evaluation and synthesis of the literature. As with most conceptual aids, however, there are possible downsides. In particular, they can serve as heuristics, or cognitive shortcuts, that substitute for more effortful thought. A researcher may not think creatively about possible options in the specific circumstances of an upcoming study, assuming instead that a model of mixed methods lays out the possible options.

This concern applies not only to relative novices but also to experts. Reichardt (1985) and Mark (1986) pointed to different examples from the classic Cook and Campbell (1979) volume on quasi-experiments in which regression to the mean was a plausible validity threat but was ignored. In both cases, the possible regression to the mean artifact did not look like the usual examples, nor did the study designs look like that of the studies in which regression to the mean has usually been discussed. Presumably as a result, even world-class content experts like Cook and Campbell failed to see the potential threat. Vigilance and deliberate effort may be required to ensure that models of mixed methods designs serve as an aid to thoughtful judgment rather than as a dispensation from such judgment.

Yet another potential dysfunction can arise from less than optimal use of models such as those describing alternative mixed methods designs. Again, there is an analog from the literature on quasi-experimentation. Campbell occasionally rued the fact that weak studies were celebrated as quasi-experiments by their authors. Even worse, the quasi-experiment label may have increased the attractiveness of the studies to reviewers and editors, at least for a time. Campbell half-jokingly suggested that such studies should instead be called queasy-experiments rather than quasi-experiments. Similar to this concern of Campbell's, advocates of mixed and multimethods should be mindful of the possibility of weak studies that are wrapped in the flag of mixed or multimethods. Situating a study in relation to contemporary frameworks of mixed methods does not in and of itself make a study notable or meritorious. To take a specific example, some contemporary authors contend that a study is notable in large part because qualitative data are transformed into quantitative data within the broader design of a randomized experiment. Many quantitatively oriented researchers may not be impressed: There are probably thousands of experiments and quasi-experiments in various substantive literatures in which qualitative data are collected, coded, and analyzed quantitatively (e.g., studies of parent–child interaction that include taped interactions that are then coded into categories for analysis). For these researchers, what would make the study notable is the extent to which it does a good job of addressing an important research question. Frameworks and, more generally, methodological concepts can be helpful, but they are not ends in themselves. Nevertheless, if used judiciously, they can be a valuable aid, especially in highlighting alternatives for those planning research.

From Frameworks to Methods, Multiple and Mixed

Frameworks that delineate alternative purposes and consequences of combining methods can help clarify *why* methods should be combined. But they do not directly describe the lay of the land in terms of specific combinations of methods that might fruitfully be combined. The next section addresses possible combinations of methods in conjunction with two general quantitative methods that serve important roles in some research areas, that is, randomized experiments and quasi-experiments. Of course, many other quantitative methods exist that can be part of a mixed or multimethod investigation, and it would be possible to describe and illustrate ways of combining methods in association with almost any quantitative method. Nevertheless, consideration of randomized experiments and quasi-experiments gives a reasonable, even if partial, overview of the many ways methods can be combined.

Randomized Experiments

In some areas of research, randomized experiments are used with considerable frequency. Cook and Groom (2008) indicate that randomized experiments dominate contemporary mainstream social psychology, for example. In the applied area of program evaluation, the last decade has seen advocacy from some quarters for the increased use of randomized experiments, under the label of randomized controlled trials (RCTs). The advocacy of RCTs in evaluation, which has occurred in areas from education in the United States to

international development, is not without controversy (e.g., Shaffer, 2011). Nevertheless, randomized experiments appear to be increasingly used in at least some program and policy areas.

Randomized experiments are designed to address a causal question. More specifically, they provide a general technology for assessing whether, and to what extent, a potential causal variable makes a difference in a possible effect variable. Note that this can be distinguished from the task of identifying the cause of some known effect, as when epidemiologists search for the cause of an outbreak of salmonella. Note also that well-conducted experiments are strong in terms of what Campbell (e.g., Campbell & Stanley, 1966) labeled internal validity, that is, estimating the effect of a potential causal variable for the persons, settings, and times examined in the study As an example, a randomized experiment might be used to estimate the effect of a new online teaching program. In this example, two groups or "conditions" are created (more conditions can be created if the research question requires it). Some students, in the treatment condition, would have access to the online program after school, in addition to the traditional textbook and in-class instruction. Other students, in the comparison group, would receive only traditional instruction (this is sometimes called a treatment-as-usual comparison group). The potential causal variable (e.g., the treatment vs. control conditions) is often called the independent variable, with the potential effect (e.g., student performance) labeled the dependent variable. Alternatively, these are sometimes called the treatment and outcome, respectively.

The basic logic of the randomized experiment is simple. The idea is to (a) create two (or more) comparable groups, (b) expose them to the different conditions of the independent variable, and subsequently (c) see whether the groups differ on average in terms of the dependent variable. For the first of these tasks, that is, the creation of comparable groups, random assignment is strongly favored by many quantitatively oriented researchers. The fundamental reason is that, in the absence of random assignment, the two groups could well vary for a variety of reasons. For example, if students or schools were able to choose whether to use the add-on online math program, students with the greatest interest in math, or schools with more concern about math test scores, might be more likely to elect to be in the treatment condition. In contrast, if students (or classrooms or schools) are randomly assigned, within certain statistical limits the resulting groups are comparable. In addition, statistical tests can take into account the random error associated with random assignment.

Mixed and Multimethods in the Randomized Experiment

A premise of this chapter is that a researcher can mix and make multiple almost any aspect of quantitative methods. The randomized experiment, which can be viewed as a single, integrated method, can alternatively be seen as a combination of numerous conceptual steps and research procedures. At a minimum, these include the following:

(**1**) the creation, and possibly revision, of the research question(s) to be addressed;

(**2**) the selection or creation of the means of

(a) manipulating the independent variable and
(b) measuring the dependent variable;

(3) the preparation of other necessary procedures, such as those involving site selection, participant recruitment, and research staff training;

(4) the actual conduct of the study, including random assignment, implementation of the independent variable, and measurement of the dependent variable(s);

(**5**) data analysis; and

(**6**) interpretation of findings and subsequent reporting.

The preceding steps are more or less necessary for a randomized experiment to occur. Other possible steps are optional but occur with enough frequency to warrant consideration. A few of these steps do not add any substantive research questions beyond that of the treatment–outcome relation. Rather, these optional ancillaries can assess or contribute to the (internal and construct) validity of the experiment (Cook & Campbell, 1979). These include

(**7**) validation of the independent variable manipulation;

(**8**) validation of the outcome measure(s); and

(**9**) the assessment of compliance with random assignment, including noncompliance due to attrition.

Another set of ancillaries adds an additional research question to that of the treatment–outcome relation. Among such ancillaries that are added relatively frequently in practice are

(**10**) investigating mediation, that is, trying to identify the mechanisms by which the independent variable brings about its effects in the dependent variable;

(**11**) the study of moderation, that is, assessing whether the treatment's effects vary across participant subgroups or settings;

(12) describing the participants and context of the study; and

(**13**) otherwise probing the external limits of the findings, that is, considering whether the finding are likely to hold or to vary across different circumstances.

For those items in the preceding list that are bolded, discussion follows of ways in which methods can be combined for that aspect of an experiment, whether mixed or multiple. A complementary and largely overlapping list is presented in Exhibit 18.1 of Johnson and Christensen (2014, p. 487).

ISSUE (1): GENERATION OF RESEARCH QUESTIONS

Although the generation of a research question(s) generally receives less attention than more concrete research operations in discussions of mixed and multimethods, this is an important aspect of critical multiplism. If methods are added to help formulate the research question, this can be viewed in terms of the frameworks presented earlier. Formulating a research question necessarily precedes the actual conduct of a randomized experiment, so this kind of combining methods is sequential, with the initial method secondary in status to the primary study and with the purpose of development (Greene, 2007). As a general example, in so-called basic research, previous studies commonly inform the design of a new study. This influence is often noted in the introduction of articles and in the discussion and introduction that bridges studies in a multistudy report; however, researchers rarely appear to consider this as an instance of a development-focused, sequential, multimethod design or research program.

Development, in the Greene et al. (2007) sense, can also occur when qualitative observation inspires research hypotheses that are subsequently tested in experiments. For example, Bob Cialdini is an expert in social influence who has derived hypotheses from a wide range of observations.

He has done so by spending time at a car dealership, by listening to the nature of requests made by charitable solicitors, and by observing the behavior of fans after Ohio State either won or lost football games (Cialdini, 2001). Cialdini has noted the role of his everyday observations in the development of hypotheses he has tested. However, he does not appear to claim to be a mixed methods researcher. (As an aside, a question can be raised about whether the kind of everyday observations Cialdini has made should be taken as part of a mixed methods design. Or is a more formally designed study required? Especially given Cialdini's skills as an observer of human behavior, I am inclined to be inclusive—but others may disagree.)

The idea of using qualitative methods for hypothesis generation and quantitative methods for hypothesis testing has been suggested repeatedly. If such statements are intended to imply that qualitative methods are restricted to hypothesis generation and quantitative methods to hypothesis testing, they are simply wrong (e.g., Ragin, 1987). If, however, the intention is to specify this sequence as a relatively common one, at least among some quantitatively oriented researchers, then the idea conveys an important example of mixing methods for the purpose of development.

Another general approach to combining methods for the development of an experiment's research question(s) has received increased though still limited attention in recent years. In program and policy evaluation, as well as in other areas of applied research, stakeholder input has been suggested for decades as a way to generate the key research questions (e.g., Bryk, 1983; Mark & Shotland, 1985). More recently, evaluation scholars have gone further, in that they have suggested more explicit research methods for capturing stakeholder views. One rationale for stakeholder input derives from the idea that evaluations require value-laden decisions, such as choosing from among the many possible outcomes in an experimental evaluation, and that stakeholders should be making these decisions (Shaffer, 2013). House and Howe (1999) advocate "deliberative democratic evaluation," in which members of relevant stakeholder groups first receive background information and then take part in facilitated group meetings, with the goal of reaching agreement on the research questions to be addressed. (In deliberative democratic evaluation, the stakeholders meet repeatedly over time, including after results are in, so that the stakeholders can discuss the interpretation of the eventual findings.)

In a related approach that uses multimethod rather than mixed methods, Henry (2002) conducted sample surveys of relevant stakeholder groups (e.g., teachers, school administrators, parents, and the public) and used these to inform decisions about which of a large potential set of outcomes would be measured in an evaluation of a universal preschool program in Georgia. In both cases, the stakeholder input can be reported systematically. And, in both cases, the mixing (House & Howe, 1999) or making multiple (Henry, 2002) of methods serves the purpose of development, with the earlier method being employed to help formulate the subsequent study's research question.

ISSUE (2): CONCEPTUALIZATION AND OPERATIONALIZATION OF INDEPENDENT AND DEPENDENT VARIABLES

Beyond the choice of research questions, mixed or multimethods can also be used in service of developing the particular way in which the independent variable will be manipulated or the dependent variable(s) will be measured. One can surmise that quantitatively oriented social science researchers often engage in combining methods for development in this way, even though they commonly do not report such mixing in any great detail. They may not even consider it as an instance of mixed or multimethods. If they did, they would characterize the purpose as development, the methods sequential, the initial method secondary to the later one, and the methods dependent. The use of qualitative procedures in service of the development of an attitude scale, described at the beginning of this chapter, is one general example of mixing for the purpose of development.

In planning an experiment, this could occur as the researcher develops the specific procedures to use in measuring the dependent variable. Pilot testing is a general process that is common in some experimental traditions (e.g., Aronson, Wilson, & Brewer, 1998). In pilot testing, a portion of a forthcoming study is implemented, and pilot participants are interviewed to probe their interpretations of the procedures. Pilot testing has a long history in laboratory social psychology and elsewhere. Often pilot testing is designed to ensure that the research procedures are in fact manipulating the independent variable construct of interest and not inadvertently manipulating other constructs. One approach involves interviews with pilot participants after they take part in the relevant portion of the experiment. In at least some cases, the pilot testing phase can be time consuming, involving repeated iterations after problems are found and procedures revised. Nevertheless, the pilot testing may not be reported in formal research reports, and, if any mention of the piloting occurs, it is probably cursory. Again, the sequence of methods seems clearly to fit the notion of mixed methods for development as articulated by Greene et al. (1989), but the quantitatively oriented researcher may not even realize that he or she has engaged in sequential mixed methods (unless he or she has read this chapter, perhaps!).

Turning to the dependent variable, methods can also be combined in terms of having more than one measure of a single outcome variable in an experiment. Any combination is possible, though in many research areas at least one is likely to be quantitative. For quantitatively oriented researchers, the intended purpose will often be triangulation, but bracketing or initiation could result. When a qualitative measure co-occurs with a quantitative one, the qualitative may be used for elaboration of the quantitative findings. The Asch and Robbers Cave studies illustrate. Multiple or mixed measures can also be used to measure two or more distinct outcomes. This would be an instance of a component-specific method.

Methods can be combined in another way that involves measurement of an experiment's dependent measure. That is, a qualitative procedure can be used to measure the outcome of interest within the framework of a randomized experiment. Robinson and Mendelson (2012) have named the resulting design a "qualitative experiment." They illustrate this with a study in which focus groups and in-depth interviews were embedded within a multigroup design. Despite the potential value of such a design, many other earlier examples exist. For instance, studies of human development and of interpersonal relationships often use an experimental design and capture real-time interactions (between child and parent or between spouses) on videotape. These qualitative observations are typically coded into quantitative data. For earlier examples, consider the inclusion of qualitative data, reported as such, in both the Asch and Robbers Cave experiment. Such studies are commonplace in certain research areas, despite more recent attention to them in the mixed methods literature.

ISSUE (5): DATA ANALYSIS

Data analysis is also an aspect of experiments for which Cook's (1985) critical multiplism is possible. This could involve traditional quantitatively focused analyses being conducted, along with independent combining of findings across methods from a more qualitative tradition (Smith, 1997). Several other relevant suggestions were made by Donald Campbell (1984), in a paper titled "Can We Be Scientific in applied Social Science?" Campbell noted several challenges to applied social research, such as program evaluation, and in response offered several recommendations for practice. One of the challenges Campbell pointed to is that the social processes that help regulate most scientific processes, such as expectations for replication and criticism across scholars with different positions, tend not to play the same role in program evaluation. Instead, a single evaluation team is usually selected for a single large-scale evaluation, and there are no opportunities for others to analyze the data prior to the release of findings—and prior to any potential use of the results. Among Campbell's suggestions are (a) splitting large evaluation projects into at least two experiments with separate researcher teams, so that various decisions, including decisions about data analyses, are made independently; (b) enabling competitive reanalyses of data from large studies (even better would be competitive analyses prior to the release of findings); and (c) legitimizing minority-opinion reports from any members of the research team who have dissenting views.

Campbell's suggestions are consistent with a more recent concern raised, among others, by House (2011) about the possible consequences of researcher motivations. House focuses on the possible consequences of conflicts of interest and draws on cases of medical research in which selective reporting of results and other decisions that investigators make can result in misleading findings.

Similar concerns can be raised in the context of program evaluations. One possibility is that, even if a program is ineffective, some significant positive result may be reported if multiple analyses are conducted. When multiple analyses are conducted, care must be taken to avoid capitalizing on chance by conducting a large number of analyses. Recall that statistical significance refers simply to a finding being unlikely to have arisen by chance. Thus, if numerous analyses are conducted and no adjustments are made, the odds of "significance" arising by chance increase. As Stigler (1987) put it, "Beware the problem of testing too many hypotheses; the more you torture the data, the more likely they are to confess, but confession obtained under duress may not be admissible in the court of scientific opinion" (p. 148). Consider then the possible implications of conducting analyses for each of several subgroups, separately for each of several items (e.g., in a substance use prevention program separate items about beer, wine, hard liquor, cigarettes, other tobacco products, marijuana, etc.). Imagine further that multiple response options exist and that, for each item about various substances, the researcher dichotomizes the multiple response options every possible way (e.g., the researcher conducts one analysis contrasting those who have never used the substance with all others, then conducts another analysis contrasting those who have not used in the last month with all others, then conducts a second analysis contrasting those who either have not used or only used once or twice in the last month with all others, and so on for the other response options). An excessive multiplicity of analyses can be a problem, not a blessing! (Data exploration can be added to hypothesis testing, as Mark, Henry, and Julnes [2001] suggest under the umbrella of "principled discovery," but care is required.)

ISSUE (6): INTERPRETATION AND REPORTING

It appears that quantitatively oriented researchers use mixed or multimethods less often for the interpretation of findings and subsequent reporting than for many other components of a study. Still, a few approaches exist that at least conform with Cook's (1985) idea of critical multiplism, even if they may not feature a clear integration of more than one method. First, multiple perspectives are incorporated in the interpretation of some large studies through mechanisms such as an advisory board. The advisory board may be constructed to represent diverse perspectives (Campbell, 1984; Cook, 1985) and can offer views on the meaning and implications of findings. Second, if House (2011) and Howe's (2005) democratic deliberative approach to evaluation, described previously, works as intended (Howe, 2005), it will allow for interpretations and judgments (e.g., "the program was a success") that are based on the collective view of the multiple stakeholder groups who are represented. Third, "member checks" can be integrated in experiments or other quantitative studies, even though the concept comes from and is usually employed in qualitative research (Lincoln & Guba, 1985). In a member check, the researcher shares the interpretation of findings with members of the group who provided the data and seeks their agreement or reinterpretations. Fourth, researchers can

adopt a standard practice of the US Government Accountability Office (GAO) that is related to member checks. When the GAO evaluates a program, they provide a draft, including recommendations, to the agency involved. The agency can provide comments, and these are published with the final report. In these and other ways, researchers who work in areas in which replication by others is unlikely, such as portions of program evaluation, can approximate the "disputatious community" to which Campbell (1984) refers.

Combining Methods for Ancillaries to an Experiment

As noted previously, there are several ancillaries that are not necessary for a randomized experiment but are relatively common additions. In a sense, these require the combining of methods. That is, a method beyond the basic experiment must be conducted for the ancillary to exist. Experiments with any of these ancillaries have component-specific methods as the purpose of combining of methods. For instance, an experiment would be used to estimate the average effect of the treatment on the outcome, while another method would be used to study mediation. Relative status would be case-specific for several ancillaries. For example, in one study the mediational component may be secondary to the experiment, while in another study the experiment could be conducted to enable the mediational test. Generally the two methods would be dependent, with one informing the other. In most instances, the methods would be carried out simultaneously, but exceptions exist, such as when a measure used in an experiment is validated either before or after the experiment is conducted.

Mixed or multimethods can also occur in the sense of using two (or more) methods to carry out a single ancillary. As an example, quantitative and qualitative methods could be combined to study mediation.

ISSUE (7): VALIDATION OF THE INDEPENDENT VARIABLE MANIPULATION

Mixed or multimethods could be employed in order to validate an independent variable manipulation that is being used in an experiment. This could involve adding methods to assess whether a treatment was implemented with quality, as when observers note the degree of compliance with a curriculum by the teachers who are implementing it; checking on whether participants actually received the treatment to which they were randomly assigned; conducting a manipulation check to see if an independent measure actually manipulated the causal construct of interest; and searching for confounds, that is, trying to assess whether the independent variable inadvertently manipulated constructs other than the intended one (e.g., Aronson et al., 1998; Boruch, 1997; Shadish, Cook, & Campbell, 2002).

Shaffer (2013) gives several examples from international development in which qualitative observation helped explain the observed findings from experimental and quasi-experimental evaluation. In one, information from ethnographies helped explain why an iron supplement intervention did not reduce anemia. Despite earlier respondent claims, most households were not giving children the supplements, due to their bad taste and possible side effects (including vomiting and diarrhea).

ISSUE (9): ASSESSING COMPLIANCE WITH RANDOM ASSIGNMENT

One of the most common problems for randomized evaluations in field settings is attrition, that is, participants who drop out over the life of the study. Attrition reduces one's ability to generalize to the kind of participants who tend to drop out. Attrition that is differential across groups can create spurious effects. Attrition also reduces statistical power and, with attrition rates of 40% to 50% common in some kinds of studies (Ribisl et al., 1996), the loss of power can be considerable.

The best way to deal with attrition is to try to minimize it, such as building in processes for tracking participants and pilot testing to avoid obstacles to continued participation (Ribisl et al., 1996; also see Boruch, 1997; Shadish et al., 2002). In essence, methods may be mixed sequentially for a development purpose. Again, this is a combining of methods that most quantitatively oriented researchers probably would not see as such.

Despite the use of preventative steps, attrition may occur. Suffice it to say here that there are alternative approaches to analysis for dealing with attrition (including intent-to-treat analysis, multiple imputation, and others; see e.g., Graham, 2012). Researchers may use two or more different forms of analyses to deal with missing data to ensure that the conclusion from the research does not depend on the specific analysis chosen. In the language of Table 2.1, the multiple analyses are used for triangulation or, lacking that, bracketing.

ISSUE (10): MEDIATION

The study of mediation is among the ancillary tasks that appear to be most often piggybacked on a randomized experiment. Recall that the randomized experiment, in its basic form, provides an estimate of the average effect of the independent variable on the dependent variable. For mediation, as for the other ancillary tasks discussed later, the researcher combines methods to answer both the average effect question and a related but distinct question. Mixed or multimethods will typically be required to carry out these additional tasks. In each case, these would be specific instances of the more general category of the component-specific research purpose from the integrated model in Table 2.1.

The study of mediation involves trying to test the mechanisms by which the independent variable brings about its effects on the dependent variable. For instance, if a media campaign results in increased recycling, presumably this is not because of magic. Rather, the media campaign may have influenced residents' perceptions of the environmental benefits of recycling, or affected social norms by making recycling seem more socially desirable, or increased people's sense of self-efficacy regarding their ability to sort recyclables properly. Or perhaps some combination of these and other intermediate factors were generated by the media campaign, and these intermediate changes in turn led to the increased recycling. The study of mediators is alternatively referred to as the search for mechanisms, the study of causal pathways, or the testing of program theory.

For many quantitatively oriented researchers, studying mediation will entail multimethod rather than mixed methods, with the addition of another quantitative method. That is, the researcher will include measures not only of the outcome(s) of interest but also of the possible mediators. And additional analyses will be conducted to test mediation. A range of quantitative techniques exists, from a multistep regression procedure suggested by Baron and Kenny (1986), to structural equation models and related variants, to methods employing bootstrapping (see Preacher & Hayes, 2008, for a review). The analyses typically result in coefficients indicating the strength of the relationship between the independent variable and the mediator(s) and between the mediator(s) and outcome, as well as a test of significance of the mediational pathway connecting all three. Donaldson, Graham, Piccinin, and Hansen (1995) present an example, showing why resistance skill only programs such as DARE are generally not effective.

Qualitative methods can also be employed to test mediation. A range of qualitative methods can be employed, including interviews, observation, and content analyses (e.g., of media coverage). The aim is to identify whether changes take place in the sequence suggested by a mediational model and whether the evidence is consistent with the assertion that the relationship is causal. Weitzman, Mijanovich, Silver, and Brecher (2009) provide an example of mixed methods to test a (mediational) program theory while also estimating the effects of a community-based intervention. Qualitative methods may be relatively more attractive to quantitatively oriented researchers when there is not an explicit mediational model before the study begins. (In principle, qualitative mediational tests can be conducted before, during, or after an experimental or quasi-experimental test of treatment effects. It appears that most often in practice, these two components will be implemented concurrently for the sake of efficiency.)

Although the study of mediation is not the most visible use of mixed methods in the Robbers Cave and Asch studies, to some extent it took place in both. In the Robbers Cave study, the researchers pointed to qualitative observations indicating that while the campers encountered multiple instances of superordinate goals, certain changes were taking place. Campers began to see members of the out-group as individuals and to be concerned about just allocations of resources between the two groups. This kind of individuation and perception of the outgroup as within the scope of justice may mediate the reduction in intergroup hostility. In the conformity study, Asch (1956) identified different subgroups of participants and noted alternative pathways that led them to conform. (Thus, Asch studied "moderated mediation" before the term was invented.)

ISSUE (11): MODERATION

Another research task that can be added to an RCT is the study of moderation. Moderation refers to the possibility that a treatment's effects vary across participant subgroups or settings. A prevention program may be more effective for boys than for girls, for example. In this instance, gender would be said to moderate the treatment effect. In the language of the analysis of variance, moderation involves the study of statistical interaction effects. Quantitatively oriented researchers are likely to study moderation by testing for interaction effects in an analysis of variance, or conducting an analogous moderated regression, or the comparable version of other statistical procedures. With this approach, care must be taken to avoid capitalizing on chance by conducting a large number of subgroup analyses. Recall Stigler's (1987) warning about torturing the data too much.

Qualitative methods can also be used to study moderation. For instance, the "extreme groups" qualitative technique can be adapted to focus on subgroups or individuals who appear to benefit most and least from an intervention (Fenzel & Blyth, 1986). Comparative case study analysis can be employed in multisite studies (Ragin, 1987). However, the study of moderation, in conjunction with a randomized experiment, appears to be substantially less likely to involve mixedmethods than multimethods.

ISSUE (13): PROBING GENERALIZABILITY

Experimentalists may also want to add methods that will aid in probing the external validity limits of the findings. That is, the goal would be to assess whether the findings are likely to hold or to vary across different circumstances. The study of moderators would contribute to this effort, in the sense of revealing whether the treatment effect varies as a function of the moderator(s) studied. Description of the participants and context can also be helpful in terms of providing information to those who are considering implementing the program elsewhere. For instance, a superintendent and school board thinking of purchasing online math software can take into account whether the kind of students and schools involved in an experimental program evaluation are like those in their own school district. This could involve quantitative approaches such as brief surveys of student and teachers and analyses of data from archives about the schools or communities. Qualitative methods are also an option, for example, to characterize the culture of the schools in which an intervention is implemented, to capture the way in which the intervention fit or failed to fit with school's ongoing routines and, more generally, to provide thick description (Geertz, 1973).

Quasi-Experiments

Quasi-experiments are approximations of randomized experiments, that is, studies with some of the characteristics of experiments but lacking random assignment. Quasi-experiments may be used when the effect of a treatment on an outcome is of interest but random assignment is infeasible or unethical. Several different quasi-experimental designs exist, ranging in how susceptible they are to internal validity threats. That is, the designs differ with regard to the general plausibility of alternative explanations of their results.

A Primer on Alternative Quasi-Experimental Designs and Associated Internal Validity Threats

Among the simplest quasi-experimental designs is the *pretest–posttest one-group design*. For example, a researcher might measure students' math performance, then offer online instruction, and subsequently measure math performance again. Several internal validity threats are generally plausible in studies such as this. "History," for instance, refers to the possibility that a specific event, other than the treatment on interest, also occurred between the pretest and posttest, and this other event caused a change in the outcome. Perhaps students received classroom math instruction on the same topics. "Maturation" refers to the possibility that outcome scores change simply because participants are older at the time of the posttest than at the pretest (maturation also includes a variety of processes that can occur over time within research participants, such as growing older, hungrier, more fatigued, wiser, and the like). The simple pretest–posttest design is subject to several internal validity threats in addition to history and maturation. These include threats known as instrumentation, regression to the mean, testing, and attrition (see Cook & Campbell, 1979, and Shadish et al., 2002, for descriptions and examples).

A better quasi-experiment is the *interrupted time-series* (ITS) *design*. ITS designs use "time-series data," that is, repeated measurement of an outcome variable (e.g., weekly math tests) to estimate the effect of a treatment. In a *simple interrupted time-series design*, a series of pretest observations is collected, a treatment is abruptly introduced, and the series of (posttest) observations continues. If the treatment is effective, the posttest scores should be better relative to the trend in the pretest scores. Moreover, the simple ITS design helps rule out some internal validity threats, including the maturation threat that is often plausible with the pretest–posttest one-group design. If the pattern of maturation is relatively steady over time, then the ITS design allows the researcher to estimate the pattern of maturation from the trend in the pretreatment observations. That is, the pretest time-series observations could show the maturational pattern before the treatment is implemented. To conclude that a treatment effect has occurred in the simple ITS design, the researcher would have to see an elevation in scores relative to the pretreatment trend (see additional discussion in Shadish et al., 2002, including consideration of the possibility of nonlinear maturation).

The simple ITS design does not, however, rule out all internal validity threats. History remains a potential threat, if some event other than the treatment occurred at about the same time and could have effects scores on the outcome variable. The plausibility of history (and other validity threats) can be reduced by shifting from the simple ITS to more complex ITS designs, such as when an untreated control group is added (Shadish et al., 2002). Alternatively, other methods can be combined with the simple ITS design. That is, mixed or multmethods can be used to help probe the plausibility of validity threats, as discussed later.

Other quasi-experimental designs use comparison groups without time-series data. When assignment to conditions is not random, designs of this sort may be called nonequivalent group designs. In these quasi-experiments, individuals either self-select into the different groups (e.g., individuals may choose to participate in an afterschool online math program or not), or are assigned in some nonrandom fashion into the groups by others such as program administrators (e.g., teachers are allowed to assign some students to the program), or group assignment is determined nonrandomly by one's location (e.g., the program is implemented in one school district but not another one).

In the simplest nonequivalent groups design, the *posttest only nonequivalent groups design*, conditions are formed other than at random, there is no pretest, and a posttest measure of the outcome is taken in an effort to estimate the treatment effect. In most cases this design is seriously flawed, as it is susceptible to the validity threat known as "selection." Selection occurs when the posttest difference between the treatment and comparison group results from *pre-existing differences* between the groups, rather than from the effect of the program. In general, in most cases without random assignment, unless there is other convincing information to the contrary, it is quite plausible that the groups would have differed even in the absence of a treatment effect.

A pretest can be added to the nonequivalent groups design, resulting in the *pretest–posttest non-equivalent groups design*. The pretest is used to try to take account of initial between-group differences. In essence, the researcher is asking whether the posttest difference is greater than the pretest difference. The potential problem is that the gap between groups might have been growing, even in the absence of a treatment effect. The old saying "the rich get richer" is sometimes true. This possibility is captured by the validity threat called "selection by maturation," which refers to the possibility that one of the groups would change at a different rate than the other group, even if there actually were no treatment effect.

One way to try to avoid selection and selection by maturation threats is to implement a stronger quasi-experimental design, such as the so-called regression-discontinuity design. Another approach is to use statistical procedures in an attempt to control for selection bias. Various alternatives exist, including difference in differences, regression analyses, structural equation modeling, and the use of propensity scores (Morgan & Winship, 2007; Rubin, 2006).

Mixed and Multimethods in Quasi-Experiments

The previous examples of various ways in which methods can be combined in randomized experiments generally apply to quasi-experiments as well. Thus, among numerous other options, a quasi-experiment might include dialogic procedures that help develop the research question(s), pilot testing that helps develop the specific way the independent variable is manipulated, qualitative interviews and observations that are used to clarify the meaning of quantitative results, a second set of analyses by an independent team; another dialogic process so as to interpret findings through the lens of multiple values perspectives, and tests of both mediation and moderation.

In terms of combining methods, the primary distinction between experiments and quasi-experiments is as follows. In quasi-experiments, there is a far more important potential role for additional methods to play in probing the plausibility of internal validity threats. The results of such efforts can either help confirm that a threat applies or help render it implausible as an explanation for the study findings. For example, Steiner and Mark (1985) conducted an ITS study to assess the effectiveness of a community action group. A grassroots group had developed to protest the actions of a local bank. Among other actions, the group mobilized a mass withdrawal, asking customers to move money out of the bank.

Quantitative analyses showed a large and statistically significant decline in the bank's holdings soon after. Could this be a result of the internal validity threat of history rather than of the community action group's efforts? To see, Steiner and Mark conducted interviews with bank personnel and community members asking about other factors that could have affected the bank's holdings. They also reviewed the local newspaper. No historical events were found that could have caused the decline, thus supporting the interpretation that the quantitative decline shown in the ITS design was indeed attributable to the community group's actions.

Mixed and multimethods, in conjunction with a quasi-experimental design, can directly or indirectly aid in dealing with a variety of internal validity threats. In addition to the threat of history, selection and selection by maturation threats can be addressed in several ways: (a) Local stakeholders may have implicit theories about group differences and maturational patterns that can be revealed in interviews. The observed data can then be compared with the stakeholder theories of selection and maturation to see if the observed results can be explained away by those validity threats. (b) Historical data may be available that can provide evidence about selection and maturational patterns in the recent past. (c) The purpose of development can be served, if qualitative procedures precede the quasi-experiment and are used to identify background features and possible confounds that should be included as control variables in analyses intended to control for selection bias. (d) Alternative forms of quantitative analyses exist that are intended to deal with selection-related bias. Often it will be advisable to conduct multiple analyses of a quasi-experiment. If the results converge, the triangulation across analyses will increase confidence. If the results diverge, then bracketing presumably applies.

These suggestions are consistent with the view of Donald Campbell, widely remembered as an advocate for randomized experiments and strong quasi-experiments and developer of the original framework identifying internal and other validity threats. Campbell (1978, 1994) was explicit about the importance of qualitative knowing. For instance, Campbell (1994) pointed to "the *mistaken belief that quantitative measures replace qualitative knowing.*" Instead, he said, "qualitative knowing is absolutely essential as a prerequisite foundation for quantification in any science" (p. 32). Regarding validity threats, Campbell further indicated that

"To rule out plausible rival hypotheses we need situation-specific wisdom. The lack of this knowledge (whether it be called ethnography, or program history, or gossip) makes us incompetent estimators of program impacts" (p. 323).

Consistent with Campbell's general view, researchers should remember that, just because a validity threat can apply to a specific design *in general*, this does not mean it is operating in a *particular study* using that design (more accurately, it does not mean that the threat is potent enough to obscure the true treatment effect). Eckert (2000) illustrated this lesson in the context of World Bank training programs. Eckert showed that various theoretical threats to his simple one-group pretest–posttest quasi-experimental design did not apply, given the specifics of his studies. For example, Eckert argued it is implausible for maturation to lead spontaneously to increased knowledge of the kind being trained. As this example illustrates, even in cases where no formal mixing of methods occurs, quasi-experiments and other quantitative studies are likely to involve a mix of qualitative and quantitative, with the qualitative coming from practitioner wisdom, general background knowledge, informal observation, and the like.

Conclusions

A premise of this chapter is that, for researchers who are primarily quantitative in their orientation, mixed and multimethods occur fairly commonly. However, many instances of combining methods, such as pilot testing to develop the manipulation of an independent variable, may not be viewed as combining methods or seen as worth remarking upon (especially in journal articles with page constraints). In addition, as noted in this chapter, many steps in an experiment or quasi-experiment can involve the combining of methods.

That being the case, an important question arises: Which aspects *should* be made multiple, either in a given study or in a series of studies? Cook (1985) noted the absence of an algorithm for deciding what to make multiple. In a sense, the answer is simple: Mix or make methods multiple in whatever way optimizes the quality of one's research, the strength of inference it allows, and the likelihood of informing and influencing the relevant audiences. And do this while taking into account the state of relevant knowledge, the practical constraints (including resources, time, and capacity), as well as the audience for one's research. Thus the process of deciding about mixed and multimethods

is no different than the other judgments required to design, carry out, analyze, and interpret research.

At the same time, different aspects of methodological theory may be helpful in making such judgments than are usually offered when training quantitative researchers. For example, a framework describing alternative purposes or, better conceptualized, alternative possible consequences of combining methods can, if used wisely, aid in judgments about when and which methods to combine. The present chapter and, more generally, this handbook are intended to be of assistance in such efforts.

Discussion Questions

1. Look at the alternative purposes or consequences of combining methods in the final column of Table 2.1. For each purpose, sketch out a study in which that purpose might be given priority.

2. Review Cook's list of ways research can be multiplist and this chapter's list of ways in which an experiment or quasi-experiment can use mixed or multimethods. Thinking of a study you know about, discuss which aspects of the study are most important to make multiple and why.

3. Many discussions of mixed and multimethods give scant if any attention to using methods for determining research questions. Could systematic methods be used to help specify research questions in your area of research or to related, applied areas?

4. This chapter suggests that most quantitatively oriented researchers are likely to prefer the idea of multimethods to that of mixed methods. Do you agree? Why or why not?

Suggested Websites

http://onlinelibrary.wiley.com/doi/10.1002/ev.v1986:31/issuetoc

1986 issue of *New Directions for Program Evaluation*. Includes discussion of quasi-experimentation and critical multiplism.

http://onlinelibrary.wiley.com/doi/10.1002/ev.1660/abstract

1993 issue of *New Directions for Program Evaluation*. Includes discussion of critical multiplism.

References

Aronson, E., Wilson, T. D., & Brewer, M. B. (1998). Experimentation in social psychology. In D. T. Gilbert, S. T. Fiske, & G. Lindzey (Eds.), *The handbook of social psychology* (Vol. 1, 4th ed., pp. 99–142). New York, NY: McGraw-Hill.

Asch, S. E. (1956). Studies of independence and conformity: A minority of one against a unanimous majority. *Psychological Monographs*, *70*(9), 1–70.

Baron, R. M., & Kenny, D. A. (1986). The moderator–mediator distinction in social psychological research: Conceptual, strategic, and statistical considerations. *Journal of Personality and Social Psychology*, *51*(6), 1173–1182.

Boruch, R. F. (1997). *Randomized experiments for planning and evaluation: A practical guide*. Thousand Oaks, CA: Sage.

Bryk, A. S. (Ed.). (1983). *Stakeholder-based evaluation*. San Francisco, CA: Jossey-Bass.

Campbell, D. T. (1978). Qualitative knowing in action research. In M. Brenner, P. Marsh, & M. Brenner (Eds.), *The social context of methods*. (pp. 184–209). London, England: Croom Helm.

Campbell, D. T. (1984). Can we be scientific in applied social science? In R. F. Conner et al. (Eds.), *Evaluation studies review annual* (Vol. 9) (pp. 26–48). Beverly Hills, CA: Sage.

Campbell, D. T., & Fiske, D. W. (1959). Convergent and discriminant validation by the multitrait–multimethod matrix. *Psychological Bulletin*, *56*(2), 81–105.

Campbell, D. T., & Stanley, J. C. (1966). *Experimental and quasi-experimental designs for research*. Boston, MA: Houghton Mifflin.

Cialdini, R. B. (2001). *Influence: Science and practice* (4th ed.). Boston, MA: Allyn & Bacon.

Cook, T. (1985). Postpositivist critical multiplism. In R. L. Shotland & M. M. Mark (Eds.), *Social science and social policy* (pp. 21–62). Beverly Hills, CA: Sage.

Cook T. D., & Campbell, D. T. (1979). *Quasi-experimentation: Design and analysis issues for field settings*. Chicago, IL: Rand McNally.

Cook, T., & Groom, C. (2008). The methodological assumptions of social psychology: The mutual dependence of substantive theory and method choice. In C. Sansone, C. Morf, & A. Panter (Eds.), *The SAGE handbook of methods in social psychology* (pp. 19–45). Thousand Oaks, CA: Sage. doi: http://dx.doi.org/10.4135/9781412976190.n2

Cook, T. D., & Reichardt, C. S. (Eds.). (1979). *Qualitative and quantitative methods in evaluation research*. Beverly Hills, CA: Sage.

Creswell J. W. (2010). Mapping the developing landscape of mixed methods research. In A. Tashakkori & C. Teddlie (Eds.), *SAGE handbook of mixed methods in social & behavioral research* (2nd ed., pp. 45–68). Thousand Oaks, CA: Sage.

Creswell, J. W., Plano Clark, V. L., Gutmann, M. L., & Hanson, W. E. (2003). Advanced mixed methods research designs. In A. Tashakkori & C. Teddlie (Eds.), *Handbook of mixed methods in social & behavioral research*. (pp. 209–240) Thousand Oaks, CA: Sage.

Denzin, N. K. (1978). *The research act: A theoretical introduction to sociological methods*. New York, NY: McGraw-Hill.

Donaldson, S. I., Graham, J. W., Piccinin, A. M., & Hansen, W. B. (1995). Resistance-skills training and onset of alcohol use: Evidence for beneficial and potentially harmful effects in public schools and in private Catholic schools. *Health Psychology*, *14*(4): 291–300.

Eckert, W. A. (2000). Situational enhancement of design validity: The case of training evaluation at the World Bank Institute. *American Journal of Evaluation*, *21*(2), 185–193.

Fenzel, L. M., & Blyth, D. A. (1986). Individual adjustments to school transitions: An exploration of the role of supportive peer relations. *Journal of Early Adolescence*, *6*(4), 315–328.

Geertz, C. (1973). Thick description: Toward an interpretive theory of culture. In *The interpretation of cultures: Selected essays* (pp. 3–32). New York, NY: Basic Books.

Graham, J. W. (2012) *Missing data: Analysis and design*. New York, NY: Springer.

Greene, J. C. (2007). *Mixed methods in social inquiry*. San Francisco, CA: Wiley.

Greene, J. C., Caracelli, V. J., & Graham, W. F. (1989). Toward a conceptual framework for mixed-method evaluation design. *Educational Evaluation and Policy Analysis*, *11*(3), 255–274.

Greene, J.C., & McClintock, C. (1985). Triangulation in evaluation: Design and analysis issues. *Evaluation Review*, *9*(5), 523–545.

Henry, G. T. (2002). Choosing criteria to judge program success: A values inquiry. *Evaluation*, *8*(2), 182–204.

Howe, K. R. (2005). Deliberative democratic evaluation: Successes and limitations of an evaluation of school choice. *Teachers College Record*, *7*(10), 2274–2297.

House, E. R. (2011). Conflict of interest and Campbellian validity. In H. T. Chen, S. I. Donaldson, & M. M. Mark (Eds.), *Advancing validity in outcome evaluation: Theory and practice* (Vol. 130, pp. 69–80). San Francisco, CA: Jossey Bass.

House, E., & Howe, K. (1999). *Values in evaluation and social research*. Thousand Oaks, CA: Sage.

Jick, T. D. (1979). Mixing qualitative and quantitative methods: Triangulation in action. *Administrative Science Quarterly*, *24*(4), 602–611.

Johnson, R. B., & Christensen, L. B. (2014). *Educational research methods: Quantitative, qualitative, and mixed approaches* (5th ed.). Los Angeles, CA: Sage.

Likert, R. (1932). A Technique for the Measurement of Attitudes. *Archives of Psychology*, *140*, 1–55.

Lincoln, Y., & Guba, E. (1985). *Naturalistic inquiry*. Newbury Park, CA: Sage.

Mark, M. M. (1986). Validity typologies and the logic and practice of quasi-experimentation. In W. M. K. Trochim (Ed.), *Advances in quasi-experimental design and analysis* (pp. 47–66). San Francisco, CA: Jossey-Bass.

Mark, M. M., & Shotland, R. L. (1985). Stakeholder-based evaluation and value judgments. *Evaluation Review*, *9*(5), 605–626.

Mark, M. M., & Shotland, R. L. (1987). Alternative models for the use of multiple methods. In M. M. Mark & R. L. Shotland (Eds.), *Multiple methods in program evaluation* (pp. 95–100). San Francisco, CA: Jossey-Bass.

Morgan, S. L., & Winship, C. (2007). *Counterfactuals and causal inference: Methods and principles for social research*. Cambridge, UK: Cambridge University Press.

Preacher, K. J., & Hayes, A. F. (2008). Contemporary approaches to assessing mediation in communication research. In A. F. Hayes, M. D. Slater, & L. B. Snyder (Eds.), *The SAGE sourcebook of advanced data analysis methods for communication research* (pp. 13–54). Thousand Oaks, CA: Sage.

Ragin, C. C. (1987). *The comparative method: Moving beyond qualitative and quantitative strategies*. Berkeley: University of California Press.

Reichardt, C. S. (1985). Reinterpreting Seaver's study of teacher expectancies as a regression artifact. *Journal of Educational Psychology*, *77*(2), 231–236.

Reichardt, C. S., & Gollob, H. F. (1987). Taking uncertainty into account when estimating effects. In M. M. Mark & R. L. Shotland (Eds.), *Multiple methods in program evaluation*. (pp. 7–22). San Francisco, CA: Jossey-Bass.

Ribisl, K. M., Walton, M., Mowbray, C. T., Luke, D. A., Davidson, W. S. II, & Bootsmiller, B. J. (1996). Minimizing participant attrition in panel studies through the use of effective retention and tracking strategies: Review and recommendations. *Evaluation and Program Planning, 19*(1), 1–25.

Rubin, D.B. (2006). *Matched sampling for causal effects.* Cambridge, UK: Cambridge University Press.

Robinson, S., & Mendelson, A. (2012). A qualitative experiment: Research on mediated meaning construction using a hybrid approach. *Journal of Mixed Methods Research, 6*(4), 332–347.

Rossman, G. B., & Wilson, B. L. (1985). Numbers and words: Combining quantitative and qualitative methods in a single large-scale evaluation study. *Evaluation Review, 9*(5), 627–643.

Shadish, W., Cook, T., & Campbell, D. (2002). *Experimental and quasi-experimental designs for generalized causal inference.* Boston, MA: Houghton Mifflin.

Shaffer, P. (2011). Against excessive rhetoric in impact assessment: Overstating the case for randomised controlled experiments. *Journal of Development Studies, 47*(11), 1619–1635.

Shaffer, P. (2013). *Q-squared: Combining qualitative and quantitative approaches in poverty analysis.* Oxford, UK: Oxford University Press.

Sherif, M., Harvey, O. J., White, B. J., Hood, W., & Sherif, C. W. (1961). *Intergroup conflict and cooperation: The Robbers Cave experiment.* Norman, OK: University Book Exchange.

Shotland, R. L., & Mark, M. M. (1987). Improving inferences from multiple methods. In M. M. Mark & R. L. Shotland (Eds.), *Multiple methods in program evaluation* (pp. 77–94). San Francisco, CA: Jossey-Bass.

Smith, M. L. (1997). Mixing and matching: Methods and models. In J. C. Greene & V. J. Caracelli (Eds.), *Advances in mixed-method evaluation: The challenges and benefits of integrating diverse paradigms* (pp. 73–86). San Francisco, CA: Jossey-Bass.

Steiner, D., & Mark, M. M. (1985). The impact of a community action group: An illustration of the potential of time series analysis for the study of community groups. *American Journal of Community Psychology, 13*(1), 13–30.

Stigler, S. M. (1987). Testing hypotheses or fitting models: Another look at mass extinction. In M. H. Nitecki & A. Hoffman (Eds.), *Neutral models in biology* (pp. 145–149). Oxford, UK: Oxford University Press.

Tashakkori, A., & Teddlie, C. (1998). Mixed methodology: Combining qualitative and quantitative approaches. Thousand Oaks, CA: Sage.

Tashakkori, A., & Teddlie, C. (2003). The past and the future of mixed model research: From "methodological triangulation" to "mixed model designs." In A. Tashakkori & C. Teddlie (Eds.), *Handbook of mixed methods in social & behavioral research* (pp. 671–702). Thousand Oaks, CA: Sage.

Thurstone, L. L. (1928). Attitudes can be measured. *American Journal of Sociology, 33*, 529–554.

Webb, E. J., Campbell, D. T., Schwartz, R. D., & Sechrest, L. (1966). *Unobtrusive measures: Nonreactive research in the social sciences.* Chicago, IL: Rand McNally.

Weitzman, B. C., Mijanovich, T., Silver, D., & Brecher, C. (2009). Finding the impact in a messy intervention: Using an integrated design to evaluate a comprehensive community initiative. *American Journal of Evaluation, 30*(4), 495–514.

Thinking Outside the Q Boxes: Further Motivating a Mixed Research Perspective

Lisa D. Pearce

Abstract

This chapter highlights the limitations of defining research logic as generally "qualitative," "quantitative," or even a mix of the two. Key philosophical and practical "positions of research" on "axes of inquiry" are outlined in a way that allows researchers and their projects to either line positions up in standard ways, such as deductive quantitative data analysis or reflexive qualitative data analysis, or to enact synergistic mixes of positions on the axes. Mixed positions might result in reflexive quantitative data analysis or deductive qualitative data analysis. This mixed research perspective aims to invigorate the quality, reach, and contribution of all rigorous research (mono-method or mixed methods), no matter how its philosophical foundations or practical positions align.

Key Words: research logic, mixed methods, mixed research, mono-method, positions of research

Most current discussions of mixed methods or multimethod research operate within a frame that assumes two distinct research paradigms—the qualitative and the quantitative—and assumes that mixed method or multimethod research is social inquiry that combines the two in some way. Therefore, the general view is that we can put all things "qualitative" in one conceptual box and all things "quantitative" in another conceptual box, and mixing involves drawing from each Q box in an iterative or integrated fashion. A complicating factor is that each Q box or approach is assumed to encompass several facets of social inquiry—including ontology, epistemology, axiology, and methodology—and all facets are generally assumed to be tightly interlocked for any given approach (Elliott, 2005). The approach for one facet is regularly assumed to be dictated by the approaches chosen within the other facets. For example, rigorous "quantitative" research is assumed to be value-neutral, deductive, and generalizable, and exceptional "qualitative" research is expected to be interpretive,

inductive, and context-specific. This narrow way of thinking limits social science by marginalizing research that operates outside of the Q boxes—research that unexpectedly mixes facets of social inquiry like feminist approaches to statistical data analyses, exploratory analyses of quantitative data, or confirmatory analyses using qualitative data (Biesta, 2010; Lieber & Weisner, 2010; Tukey, 1980). In this chapter, I argue that a thorough understanding of the social world requires a view of social inquiry that acknowledges the value in a variety of philosophical and practical research positions and expects creative, synergistic mixes of these positions, in addition to more standard combinations, within and across empirical projects.

Social Inquiry and Its Facets

Social inquiry is any endeavor to explore, describe, understand, or explain an aspect of the social world. A variety of thinkers from a range of disciplines and backgrounds have described social inquiry as diametric, or comprised of two oppositional perspectives or approaches. Some present divergent approaches as antithetical, and thus researchers are advised to choose one or the other in which to train and conduct their work (Guba, 1987; Guba & Lincoln, 1989). Others view the diametric approaches as two parts of a mutually reinforcing whole—a constant exchange between "rigor" and "imagination" (Abbott, 2004, p. 3) or a combined effort to "measure carefully" and "listen hard" (Bernard, 2000, p. 18). In other words, there is a yin and a yang of social inquiry, each with its own strengths and weaknesses for teaching us about the social phenomena we study, and valuing only one approach is limiting (Johnson, 2012; Johnson & Stefurak, 2013). For example, rigor and measurement give us ways to confirm theory, but we must have imagination and listen and watch carefully to identify important questions and discover theoretical ideas that advance our understandings of the social world. Likewise, if we only had ideas about how the social world worked and no empirical tests to increase or decrease our confidence in the ideas, our knowledge of social processes would be severely limited.

Even if the world of social science was entirely comprised of mono-method studies, each field would need a variety of researchers and studies to ensure a diversity of perspectives. As Page (2007) notes, "most scientific breakthroughs and business innovations involve a person seeing a problem or situation differently" (p. 25). Often the new view is the result of a unique researcher, theory, or method being applied to the research problem. Thus one cannot overstate the value of appreciating the contributions that a wide variety of research approaches have to offer, whether approaches are mixed within research projects, across a researcher's career, or within a field's history.

I and others refer to this general model of research—in which a diversity of approaches dialogue to advance science—as "mixed research" (Johnson, 2012; Johnson & Onwuegbuzie, 2004). Mixed research is a holistic perspective on research that recognizes a set of diametric stances, or what I refer to from here on as *axes of inquiry*, from which research operates (e.g., inductive-to-deductive, subjective-to-objective, specific-to-general, etc.) and explicitly values research engaging both ends of the various axes to advance science (Greene, 2006; Morgan, 2007). This approach also allows positions on the multiple axes of inquiry to be independent from one another so that, for example, studies that are inductive need not be restricted to small or purposive samples (Axinn & Pearce, 2006).

There are a variety of these yin/yang-like axes of inquiry that every research project is situated along, either consciously or not, and science could benefit from a more careful consideration of where each piece of research is truly located. Several scholars have begun to identify these axes of inquiry, including Morgan's (2007) discussion of abduction, intersubjectivity, and transferability; Teddlie and Tashakkori's (2009, p. 95) presentation of a "multidimensional continuum of research projects"; and Johnson and Christensen's (2014) multiple-dimension process approach to mixed design. Niglas (2010) proposes a way to integrate some of these axes and to identify where in the resulting multidimensional space various projects are situated. Maxwell and Loomis (2003) also call for less emphasis on the "uniform" qualitative or quantitative paradigms and argue that "While the connections among [the components of these paradigms] are crucial to the overall coherence of a particular research design, the possible legitimate ways of putting together these components are multiple rather than singular" (p. 251). They use this approach to reveal the "logic in use" of a set of projects after the fact, revealing how research design and conduct is much more complicated than a one-dimensional view of the qualitative–quantitative continuum would suggest.

My goal here is to step back and draw on the work of many to develop an overarching model of the various "positions" social inquiry takes and to consider how various positions can be mixed and matched to produce the evidence needed to advance social theory. Any approach to social inquiry is characterized by what Greene (2006) refers to as "domains" of methodology. She highlights four domains, and, synthesizing her categories along with other proposals for holistic views of social inquiry, I propose two larger domains of social inquiry—*philosophical positions* and *practical positions*—each containing a set of subdomains. The two domains are often related but are not necessarily determined by or dependent on each other (Maxwell & Mittapalli, 2010). Figure 3.1 graphically presents the domains, described in the following sections.

First Domain: Philosophical Positions

One of the two larger domains of social inquiry is that which includes the philosophical positions from which researchers operate. Three of the most commonly discussed philosophical positions are epistemology, ontology, and axiology. Epistemology

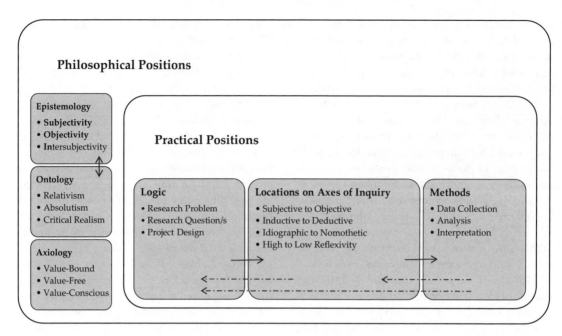

Fig. 3.1 Facets of social inquiry.

is a philosophical branch concerned with what knowledge is, how we know what we know, and the standards required to justify our beliefs. This often means decisions about the relationship between researchers and their cases or participants or how well we can come to know the social dynamics we study (Guba & Lincoln, 1994). In terms of a continuum, epistemology is presented as running from a subjective point of view to an objective point of view. The ontological continuum encompasses beliefs about the nature of reality ranging from the idea that there are multiple constructed realities to the idea that there is an objective, external reality that can be comprehended (Biesta, 2010; Mertens, 2003). The axiological continuum represents the degree to which values are or are not a part of social inquiry and which ones are used (Teddlie & Tashakkori, 2009).

Positions that social inquiry take along these three philosophical continua are undoubtedly interrelated. For example, Teddlie and Tashakkori (2009, p. 88) provide summaries of a few research paradigms and the types of epistemology, ontology, and axiology associated with each. It stands to reason there are especially close linkages between what we can know (ontology) and how we can justify that we know it (epistemology). If there is not one objective truth, then a researcher will need to take a subjective point of view in observing and listening to participants. However, there

is certainly room for mixing different variants of epistemology and ontology. Researchers operating in the pragmatic tradition (Peirce, 1877) often alternate between more subjective and more objective positions in an effort to summarize what they call an imperfectly or probabilistically defined external reality (Teddlie & Tashakkori, 2009). This approach is labeled "intersubjectivity" by Morgan (2007). Intersubjective approaches are often motivated by a critical realist ontology—that intransitive aspects of reality (persistent structures and processes) provide a point of reference for testing theories (Bhaskar, 1978; McEvoy & Richards, 2006). So, when it comes to epistemology and ontology, researchers usually take one of three general approaches to their research as a whole: (a) striving to be both subjective and relativistic, (b) aiming to be objective and absolutist, or (c) taking an intersubjective, mixed, or perhaps critical realist standpoint. When operating from one of the first two approaches, one's practical work will then always align in the same place on the subjective-to-objective axis of inquiry (discussed further later), but operating within the third approach means that a researcher's projects might occur at different locations on the axis, depending on the questions being asked and the methods being used. Therefore, one's philosophical position can be treated as separate from a researcher's choice of method or data (Biesta, 2010).

Axiology, the third subdomain of the philosophical positions, is often assumed to tightly correspond with epistemology and ontology. We are accustomed to research that is subjective and relative being more value-infused and research that is more objective being value-free, but this does not have to be the case. In fact, there are analyses of quantitative data that strive for objectivity in their use of data that are motivated by strong feminist values or conflict theory (DeVault, 1996; Risman, 1993; Stewart, 2008). One approach to mixed methods research that requires a commitment to marginalized communities is the Transformative Framework (Mertens, 2009). As Risman (1993) puts it, "One can take a feminist perspective and epistemological concerns and incorporate them into any methodological technique. And one can ignore feminist insights and agendas in any methodological tradition" (p. 24).

The three philosophical positions outlined here are properties of researchers, whether explicit or implicit, and undoubtedly influence choices of the practical positions described here. However, just as there are not fixed combinations among the philosophical positions, there are also no fixed links between certain philosophical positions and practical positions (Maxwell & Mittapalli, 2010). It often seems this way, because certain research communities have developed common cultures or shared meanings (Morgan, 2007), but it is possible to combine positions in creative ways.

Second Domain: Practical Positions

The second of the two larger domains of social inquiry is that of practical positions or choices made in the application of a specific project. I propose three highly interrelated subdomains making up the domain of practical positions: *logic, locations on the axes of inquiry*, and *methods*. In Figure 3.1, the solid arrows connecting these three subdomains indicate what is assumed to be the most typical ordering of decisions across these parts of the research process, but, as the dashed lines indicate, it may also be the case that a choice of method(s) drives a location on the axes of inquiry or the precise logic of a research project. I discuss how these three subdomains commonly unfold and influence each other.

LOGIC

The first subdomain of practical positions taken up in research is the logic of a given inquiry, and this subdomain involves at least three components of

its own—the research problem, the research questions, and the project design. The research problem outlines a content area, which can be driven by a desire to revise or develop theory or extend a body of empirical evidence.

Research questions are more specific. Good research questions clearly point up to theories or concepts and down to empirical data available to speak to the question (Alford, 1998). Many argue that good questions make obvious the methods a project utilizes, and researchers should carefully consider what tools are best to answer a given question. This is why the solid arrows move from the logic subdomain to the other two subdomains in Figure 3.1.

The next component of logic is project design, or the plan for research. Research design translates the research problem and resulting question(s) into concrete steps of empirical research, which operate from fruitful positions on the axes of inquiry (described later) through specific methods (Gorard, 2010). The research design lays out a defensible plan for the method or methods to be conducted and the case selection or sampling procedure to be followed (Axinn & Pearce, 2006; Greene, 2006).

LOCATIONS ON THE AXES OF INQUIRY

Locations on the axes of inquiry are practical aspects of inquiry that overlap to some degree with epistemological or ontological assumptions from the philosophical domain of research. In fact, Greene (2006) defines them together as one domain. However, whereas the philosophical positions are for one's approach to research at large, locations on the various axes of inquiry are determined at the level of a research project rather than researcher. Researchers who consistently prioritize either subjectivity or objectivity with participants will hold a similar position when it comes to a specific project, but researchers whose epistemology is intersubjective will position themselves on the practical objective–subjective axis of inquiry according to the "logic" of the project (discussed earlier). For this reason, I have separated the philosophical and practical subjective-to-objective axes in my conceptual model of social inquiry.

In this practical subdomain, I provide four axes of inquiry as examples. First, there is the continuum from subjective to objective. It is impossible to be purely one or the other as human researchers, but there are reasons to strive for one end or to use the two in dialogue with each other (Hammersley, 1992; Morgan, 2007). Although we learn a great deal from unique cases and the perspectives of those being studied, to advance theory, it is important to look for cross-cutting similarities that could be intersubjectively defined.

A second axis of inquiry is that from inductive to deductive. This is one of the most commonly discussed dichotomies of research (Abbot, 2004). At times we aim to explore and discover, and at other times we aim to test and confirm. Always operating from an inductive standpoint runs the risk of continually suggesting new and creative theory with no systematic assessment of when and where theory holds beyond the local setting. Using only deductive procedures severely limits the possibility that new discoveries are made or previously unconsidered explanations for social behavior are obtained.

Third, there is the axis of inquiry that runs from an idiographic approach, in which research drills deep to understand a particular case or context in its own right, to the nomothetic approach, where the goal is to generalize beyond the particular cases under examination (Johnson & Stefurak, 2014). Some sort of transferability of ideas must be achieved to be an important contribution to science, regardless of where a study is positioned on the axis. This is likely to be in the form of statistical inference toward the nomothetic end of the axis and logical inference toward the idiographic end (Mitchell, 1983; Small, 2009; Yin, 2014).

A fourth axis of inquiry involves the level of reflexivity used in an inquiry. This is the degree to which a researcher considers his or her influence in a given project, or awareness of how one's own experiences and values shape the research. Although reflexive thoughts are usually publicly shared only by researchers presenting qualitative data and analyzed in mainly subjective, inductive, and idiographic manners, that should not keep other researchers from using high levels of reflexivity in their work (Finlay, 1998; Risman, 1993). Revisions may or may not result from reflexivity, but the process of reflection will likely be instructive to the researcher and improve the quality of the research.

METHODS

The methods subdomain is similar to what Greene (2006) defines as "guidelines for practice" (p. 94). It is in this subdomain that procedures for each method of data collection and/or data analysis are selected. The methods are closely tied to the logic in use, because they must be selected and conducted in a way that provides solid evidence pertaining to the research question(s). Not every project involves primary data collection, but when it does, this is the domain in which state-of-the-art procedures for a given method should be identified and followed. Although methods of data collection and analysis are concrete tools that involve the collection and/or analysis of data, they also have epistemological qualities; hence, the term *qualitative method* implies a method that is applied in subjective, inductive, idiographic, and reflexive manners. However, a method is not necessarily bound up with a fixed set of epistemological bases. For example, the extended case method is a form of ethnography, but Burawoy (1998) argues that it can be used for making generalizations to larger society from single cases.

Due to method specialization, many researchers choose questions of inquiry that lend themselves to the methods they know best (Clark & Badiee, 2010). Similarly, researchers may prefer or become more comfortable with approaches that operate from various points on the axes of inquiry, so those positions may drive the form a research question takes. This assumes that where a study should be situated on multiple axes of inquiry is innate to the question. For example, Clark and Badiee (2010) note that among other defining characteristics "quantitative" questions tend to involve variables (as opposed to considering the whole person/group/etc.) and "qualitative" questions work from an inductive perspective and focus on the local and particular (Johnson & Christensen, 2014). These processes are indicated by the dashed arrows from the locations and methods subdomains back to the logic subdomain in Figure 3.1. There is no one pathway to choosing the practical features of a research project. In the best studies, choices regarding research logic, positions on the axes of inquiry, and methods are made in dialogue with each other, fine-tuning the research plan to achieve a solid fit across them.

On the one hand it is useful to reflect on which types of research questions fit best with which types of methods. On the other hand, it is important to remember that some excellent research challenges longstanding assumptions for what counts as "qualitative" or "quantitative" research. For example, there are qualitative data and analyses that focus on variables, and there are quantitative data and analyses that are inductive, such as cluster or latent class analysis (LCA) or quantitative associational measures used in content analysis. Thus it may be limiting to talk of "qualitative" and "quantitative" research questions. Instead, there should be an interactive dialogue between all the practical components of a research project until an appropriate fit between them is achieved.

Mixing Positions

With this model of social inquiry laid out, it is now possible to think about how mixing philosophical and practical positions can be more complicated, creative, and productive than when we envision mono-method projects or components of mixed methods projects as coming entirely out of one Q box or the other. For some research, it is possible and desirable to design a hybrid method or multimethod project that capitalizes on an atypical mix of research positions, meaning the Q boxes fail as an organizing design framework. These are examples of using the mixed research approach defined earlier. I prefer the term *mixed research*, because it limits the confusion that results from the phrase *mixed methods research* containing the word *methods* (Creswell, 2010). For some it implies that methods (whether we are talking research methods, methods of data collection, sampling methods, or methods of data analysis) are either qualitative or quantitative, and I contend we should resist the urge to assume methods fit one Q box or the other (Biesta, 2010; Onwuegbuzie & Leech, 2005).

All research would be better understood and evaluated if it were described in terms of its philosophical and practical positions rather than assuming it is (or should be) consistent with all things "qualitative" or all things "quantitative." When we review others' research, we should focus on the philosophical and practical positions from which they operate rather than assume a uniform set of choices. For example, a cluster analysis of quantitative data is not deductive, and an analysis of qualitative data is not necessarily inductive. It is in these cases that a clear description of positionality would go a long way toward better understanding the aims and quality of research marginalized with descriptors like qualitatively driven quantitative research or qualitative research in the service of quantitative research (see Giddings & Grant, 2007).

I am not arguing that one cannot or should not conduct research that might match the assumptions of a cohesive paradigm of qualitative or quantitative research. Mono-method research located squarely in one Q box or the other can be of exceptionally high quality, innovative, and groundbreaking. Also, mixed research that pairs one

subjective–inductive–idiographic–reflexive endeavor with an objective–deductive–nomothetic–nonreflexive endeavor can be a completely justifiable design. However, researchers often design and employ applications of one or more methods that involve more complicated mixes of positions, and rather than avoid or marginalize that type of approach, we should recognize its value. In the following I provide several concrete applications that demonstrate the concepts and arguments laid out here.

Mixed Research Exemplified
OBJECTIVE APPROACHES TO QUALITATIVE DATA ANALYSIS

A relatively recently published mixed methods study by Schmutz and Faupel (2010) serves as a useful example of a project in which the qualitative data are analyzed from more of an objective than subjective position and more of a deductive than inductive position on the axes of inquiry. This research is about the gendered nature of the conference of cultural legitimacy and consecration, or iconic prestige, in popular music. The first phase of the project was to analyze a set of quantitative data compiled for 1,503 music albums that were recognized at the time of their release (1955–2003) through such accolades as a top spot on the *Billboard* album charts, being nominated for a Grammy, or receiving recognition from the *Village Voice* critics' lists. Regression analyses showed strong effects (direct and indirect) of gender on the likelihood of being recognized as one of *Rolling Stone*'s top 500 Greatest Albums of All Time in 2003. The gender effect was partially explained by male artists being more likely to be culturally legitimated through awards when an album is released. What the quantitative data could not shed light on is how critics' assessments of music quality and status unfold differently depending on the gender of an artist. To answer this related question, the authors turned to a set of qualitative data—the actual written reviews of each of *Rolling Stone*'s 500 Greatest Albums of All Time.

At this point, one might expect the "qualitative analysis" to be an inductive and subjective analysis of themes that *emerge* from how critics discuss female musicians differently than male musicians. That is because in a mixed methods or "qualitative" project, we seem to start with the assumption that researchers working with qualitative data will locate themselves along the "qualitative" positions on the axes of inquiry. However, these authors relied on theory and prior research to provide five coding categories before examining the data: historical importance, intellectualizing discourse and high art criteria, ideology of the autonomous artist, social networks, and authenticity. These five types of discourse were theorized in the front end of the article, suggesting the coding categories were determined in a theory-driven, or an etic rather than emic, fashion. Three coders initially worked on a small sample of all the reviews to refine a coding scheme. They reported an intercoder reliability score, suggesting they aimed to have as objective a coding exercise as possible.

There may have been an unreported inductive coding phase in which the five coding categories (or a subset of them) were discovered in the data. Often authors choose or editors or reviewers request a standard outline to an article that implies that we go into our data collection and/or analysis with a clear sense of the concepts and hypotheses that guide our research (i.e., the theory section comes first and then the methods and findings are reported). This makes writing and reading the research more straightforward, but it obscures the reality that research is complicated and usually requires refinements to research questions or hypotheses, as well as key concepts based on what is found in the data (qualitative *or* quantitative). It would be helpful if we more often acknowledged the actual unfolding of analysis and theorizing in footnotes or an appendix at the least.

It is not just the use of qualitative data that could benefit from this kind of transparency. Bentler (2007) argues for this kind of strategy in the use of structural equation modeling methods, recommending that authors provide reviewers with verification as to whether every parameter in the model is purely a priori and then explanations of any model modifications that were made. This is an example of being transparent when one's initial theoretical model is adapted in light of discoveries about the empirical data during analysis.

When reporting results from their qualitative data analysis, Schmutz and Faupel (2010) went through each of the five themes or coding categories, first giving a quantitative measure of how often the particular types of discourse were enacted and then quoting phrases as examples. At the end of the results section, the authors provided two extended examples of reviews to better contextualize and compare the discourse in situ. The authors provide convincing evidence that male artists tend to be lauded for their historical importance, artistic autonomy, and high art criteria, whereas

female artists are more often commended for their social networks and perceived emotional authenticity (Schmutz & Faupel, 2010). Knowing how reviewers talk about the artists provides very useful insight as to why gender differences are so clear in the quantitative data.

Regardless of how coding and analysis of the qualitative data actually unfolded, the part that is described is framed as near the objective and deductive ends of those two axes of inquiry. I argue this does nothing to compromise the quality of the research. There will be times when we need to work with data that come to us in the form of the actual words our participants use (rather than survey questions and response categories defined by researchers), but it may be that the contribution to be made is to take speculations based on prior results or theory and collect empirical evidence to confirm (or disconfirm) the ideas. Theory testing is an important part of science.

In the case of this research study, the analysis was conducted with a population of *Rolling Stone* reviews—all 500, so there is no concern about generalizing to the *Rolling Stone* procedures for choosing which albums to honor. The methods used here led to important insights, important enough to be published in a highly ranked sociology journal, *Social Forces*.

Ultimately, some may ask whether the second phase of this research (that using qualitative data) is "qualitative research." It doesn't exactly fit in that Q box. In fact, it is a prime example of the style of mixed methods research criticized for being "A Trojan Horse for Positivism" (Giddings & Grant, 2007) or being classified as "quantitatively driven mixed methods research" (Hesse-Biber, 2010). Perhaps one reason these classifications emerged is that, unfortunately, more subjective, inductive, idiographic, and reflexive social inquiry has been and continues to be marginalized in academia. I address this reality further in my concluding thoughts, but it must be acknowledged here. It is just as unfortunate that in efforts to address that marginalization, perfectly defendable research contributing important insights to social inquiry is often unnecessarily criticized for not conforming to absolutist criteria about what it means for research to be "qualitative." If we instead better acknowledge the "logic-in-use" (Maxwell & Loomis, 2003) behind our research in application and judge it on its own intentions, we would greatly expand the possibilities for mixed research.

ANALYSIS OF QUANTITATIVE DATA IN AN INDUCTIVE, PERSON-CENTERED MANNER

One way I have come to see the possibilities available through a mixed research perspective is by discovering the usefulness of inductive or exploratory analyses of quantitative data (Tukey, 1980), especially those that take a more person-centered and less variable-based approach to understanding human identity and behavior. Holistic, person-based approaches emphasize the individual as a whole (Bergman & Magnusson 1997; Magnusson, 1998). In other words, rather than focusing on isolated variables, a person-based approach considers the various ways in which individuals live out unique combinations of beliefs and/or practices (Dymnicki & Henry, 2012). These person-based methods, in fact, try to use quantitative data to do more of what ethnographic observation or very inductive analyses of qualitative data often do, which is to consider the case as a whole and to allow for unique seemingly inconsistent beliefs and behaviors.

A variety of statistical methods can be used as tools for inductive analysis of quantitative data. Some examples include cluster analysis, LCA, exploratory factor analysis, configural frequency analysis, data mining methods, comparative method, and symbolic data analysis. Other statistical methods can be used in a "person-oriented way," such as latent growth curve modeling and polynomial decomposition of repeated measures analysis of variance results (Bogat, Zarrett, Peck, & von Eye, 2012).

I use an example from my own work to highlight this type of approach to analyzing quantitative data. Following the second wave of data collection for the National Study of Youth and Religion, I set out to write a book (with Melinda Denton) that would describe how religiosity and spirituality changed in the first three years our nationally representative cohort of 13- to 17-year-olds was followed (2002–2005). Taking a variable by variable approach (e.g., belief in God, attendance at services, frequency of prayer, salience of religion, etc.) meant an overwhelming abundance of results that did little to tell us how these variables combine to define the religious/spiritual lives of these youth. Averaging multiple quantitative measures of religiosity to create an index or set of indices was unsatisfying, because we knew from our many in-person, semistructured interviews that some youth were active in religious institutions but religion did not mean much to them, whereas other youth had a strong sense of personal religiosity/spirituality but little institutional involvement. These two types of youth would have similar "average" scores of religiosity, but we knew that they were two very different kinds of youth, and their unique styles of religiosity/spirituality were interesting in their own right. Fortunately, a colleague of mine, E. Michael Foster, wisely suggested we look into latent class methods for a solution to our problem of matching our conceptualization of religiosity/spirituality with our survey data.

Latent class analysis is a data reduction technique similar to factor analysis or cluster analysis (Muthén & Muthén, 2000). The focus is on identifying subgroups of individuals in a population with different profiles or different mixes of responses to a set of selected indicators. For example, we were looking to identify a set of common ways (or latent classes) in which religious beliefs, practices, and salience were mixed and matched in different ways. Although we were relatively sure there would be a class of individuals who tended to have very high levels of belief, practice, and salience, as well as a group with very low levels across the board, we were most interested in the individuals who fell between these types. In other words, what were the common profiles of religiosity/spirituality when consistency across the different measures was not present?

With LCA, it is rare to hypothesize the number and types of classes that will result. Instead, the output suggests which number of classes provides the best fitting model, and, for that model, statistical results suggest the ways in which a member of any given class is likely to answer the questions used as indicators. These results suggest patterns in the data much like those that are inductively discovered through repeated reading and analysis of qualitative data. In fact, an alternate approach would have been for us to pour over our hundreds of interview transcripts to come up with a classification system based on our interpretation of the qualitative data. Either way, we would be imposing our interpretations of patterns that emerge from the data. From a critical realist perspective, both approaches take forms of empirical data and produce as rigorous a representation of the observable as possible, recognizing we always fall short of "objective truth" but that we aim for developing well-confirmed beliefs about the social world that capture the complexities and dynamics of human life as best as possible (Peirce, 1877).

In our case, the LCA suggested a model with five latent classes labeled the Abiders, the Adapters, the Assenters, the Avoiders, and the Atheists (Pearce & Denton, 2011; Pearce, Foster, & Hardie, 2013). The Atheist and Abider categories are the two consistently either low or high religiosity/spirituality classes we expected to find. The middle three classes, however, are not simply a group of respondents falling somewhere in between the irreligious and very religious but are a set of subgroups whose mixture of beliefs, experiences, and practices are complex and interesting. The Adapters have higher personal religiosity and spirituality but are less involved in religious institutions. The Assenters are more institutionally involved than Adapters, but religion is less salient for them than for Adapters or Abiders. The Avoiders resemble Atheists, finding little importance in religion and having virtually no religious practice in their life. However, they do believe in God and have little doubt about their beliefs.

In sum, LCA is a tool for suggesting new yet unobserved patterns in data representing social life. It does not follow the common assumption that statistical analysis is always confirmatory or deductive. This does not render it "bad" quantitative research, because we should not always require that the use of quantitative data be based on a hypothesis-testing model. Neither do I mean to suggest this method is perfectly comparable to the inductive analysis of qualitative data. One key difference is that variables in quantitative survey data involve responses that were designed by researchers and selected by respondents. In less structured interviews, responses are nearly always expressed in participants' own words, and, unlike in surveys, less structured interview participants can bring up topics or ideas unanticipated by the researcher. Therefore, there is still a limit to the kinds of discovery possible with a method like LCA. However, given the vast amount of survey data existing in the world, there is tremendous possibility for these types of inductive analyses to help us reenvision categories and classifications and to learn from a more person-centered analysis of quantitative survey data in addition to standard variable-centered approaches.

In addition, some weaknesses of person-centered quantitative data analysis can be compensated for by mixing qualitative data analysis with inductive forms of quantitative analysis. For our book, we supplemented the LCA results with careful analysis of the interview transcripts (qualitative data) belonging to those who were most likely to belong to each of the five classes. This was possible because we had a nested sample—our interview participants had also completed the National Study of Youth and Religion telephone survey, so we could use their quantitative results to see which class they were most likely to belong. This allowed us to check that the latent classes resonated with differences we saw in the qualitative data and allowed us to develop an even richer understanding of each class, through their own narratives and stories.

NOMOTHETIC USES OF QUALITATIVE DATA

In sociology and many other disciplines, there is a lively debate about the need for or usefulness of "representativeness" in case selection. Small (2009) lays out the issues clearly. The question should not be whether a nomothetic approach is a preferable goal in and of itself; the question should be, "What is your research design?" or "What positions on the axes of inquiry are you operating from in combination with which method(s)?" If the aim is to generalize theoretically or logically and not empirically or statistically, a purposeful selection of cases can work. And, when using a small number of cases (even if randomly selected), it is unlikely that a wide enough range of cases have been chosen to truly represent the population at large—especially in populations with any degree of heterogeneity (Small, 2009). On the other hand, an increasing number of research projects are selecting large numbers of cases for conducting semistructured interviews (see, e.g., Newman, 1999; Smith & Denton, 2005) or ethnographic observations (Burton, Purvin, & Garrett-Peters, 2009). A variety of ways of selecting cases are suggested by Johnson and Christensen (2014), including maximum variation, extreme case, typical case, critical case, or negative case sampling. These approaches make representative sampling possible, but some ask whether it is a desirable approach when collecting qualitative data. I argue it depends on one's preferred position on the idiographic-to-nomothetic axis of inquiry.

One high-quality study using a large number of representatively sampled semistructured interviews is Gerson's (2010) research on how the generation of young people who were raised in the final decades of the 20th century, experiencing vast amounts of family change, now view family life and their own preferences for family formation and organization. She analyzes interviews from a sample of 120 young adults (ages 18–32), including an equal number of native-born women and men from various economic backgrounds (poor or near poor, 16%; working class, 38%; and middle or upper middle class, 46%),different racial/ethnic groups (non-Hispanic White, 55%; African American, 22%; Latino/Latina, 17%; and Asian, 6%), and those having grown up in diverse forms of family organization and structure (homemaker–breadwinner, 33%; dual-earner, 27%; and single-parent, 40%). Two-thirds of her sample was obtained by recruiting members of a random digit dial sample who participated in the Study of the Immigrant Second Generation in Metropolitan New York. She recontacted native-born participants of that study and supplemented with a random sample of enrollees of a continuing education program in New York City. The latter group helped boost the proportion of the sample with a college degree. So, in the end, the sample was not perfectly, statistically representative in the sense that we know the probability that any given participant had in being selected, but the demographics of the sample suggest that at least in terms of race, class, and gender, this was a group of young adults fairly representative of native-born, young adults living in the New York Metropolitan area at the time of the study.

Gerson's (2010) sample has two strengths. First, she can use the group as a whole to generalize to this generation's views on issues of work, family, and gender. One example is that she convincingly demonstrates a strong sense from all participants regardless of gender, race, class, or family background that "family functioning trumps family form" (p. 208). Family life is conveyed by these participants as a process and a journey. These young people consistently recognize that it is "the *quality* of a family's bonds and the *flexibility* of its members" that render a family strong, not its form at any given moment in time (p. 209).

The second strength of her sample is that the demographic variability allows for a variety of subcategory comparisons. For example, she convincingly shows that across all other categories there is an important gender difference at play. Young women and men have reached different conclusions about strategies for dealing with the challenges of balancing two careers and a host of domestic responsibilities—in the event an egalitarian arrangement is too difficult to implement, women plan to be self-reliant and pursue their career and family life on their own. Men plan to revert to a neotraditional breadwinner–housewife model. The gulf between expectations is an unrecognized threat to the ability for heterosexual couples to negotiate an approach to work and family that is satisfying to both.

Back to a question frequently posed: Is a large and representative sample preferable for semistructured interview studies? In Gerson's (2010) case, a key aim was to represent the view of a particular generation, so she positioned herself more to the nomothetic end of that axis of inquiry. Some might then ask, why not conduct a survey and draw an even more representative sample of this age group across a variety of locations? I assume the answer would be that a survey would require a well-developed sense of what questions to ask and the language in which to frame response options.[1] Otherwise, we might not have seen the language of family flexibility, process, and journeys evolve. In fact, most surveys on family life focus on contemporaneous evaluation of family forms, relationship quality, and so on, so a cross-sectional survey would run the risk of reifying the notion that family forms are static and primary causes of youth and young adult outcomes. In other words, the reason to keep semistructured interviews as the method of choice in this design is to position the research more toward the inductive and subjective ends of two other axes of inquiry. Thus if the goal of a given research endeavor is to discover general and population-specific ways of understanding social processes, loosely structured interviews or observations of a relatively large and representative (therefore diverse) set of cases is an appropriate approach.[2] And, in general, there is a great deal of value in positioning a project on either end of the nomothetic–idiographic axis, especially in designing a project that involves both approaches, when the chosen position fits well with the aims of the research.

REFLEXIVITY IN USES OF QUANTITATIVE DATA

As discussed earlier, reflexivity is the process whereby a researcher is honest and open about all phases of data collection and analysis, including descriptions of the researcher's own relationship to the topic and participants (Creswell, 2013). This includes ways in which the researcher's own identity, values, and position in society might influence his or her interactions with participants and interpretations of the data (Hesse-Biber, 2010). Reflexivity is a practice almost entirely used by those collecting and analyzing qualitative data, although it is both possible and useful to be reflexive about one's collection and analysis of quantitative data (Hesse-Biber, 2012).

Two recent publications discuss the application of reflexivity in quantitative research endeavors—work by Walker, Read, and Priest (2013) and Ryan and Golden (2006). Susan Walker (Walker et al., 2013), kept a reflective journal throughout her retrospective audit of hospice case notes using quantitative data analysis. She collected these quantitative data from a hospice clinic where she used to work, so the act of reflexivity allowed her to document how her personal background influenced the data that were available and her interpretation of them. Being reflexive as the data are collected and analyzed also documents the researcher's reactions, thoughts, and feelings during the process, promoting self-awareness about the process. Walker and colleagues report strengths of the approach as (a) highlighting difficulties in data collection and how insider rapport and knowledge helped the researcher overcome these challenges, (b) recording important decisions in the process that will inform analysis and could benefit future researchers designing new studies, and (c) making transparent the fact that even with quantitative data, the analysis (or ideas about it) often begins during data collection, making it a much more abductive than deductive process.

Another application of reflexivity to so-called quantitative research is provided by Ryan and Golden (2006) and their study of depression among Irish immigrants living in London. The researchers themselves were immigrants from Ireland, and they describe how their own backgrounds helped them recruit and develop rapport with respondents but also became a burden when respondents were comfortable relaying lengthy stories that were not a part of data collection or when respondents expected reciprocation by the researchers in sharing their own experiences.

Both examples of reflexivity in the use of quantitative data make clear the possible benefits and challenges to (a) gaining access, (b) assessing data quality, and (c) brainstorming future research projects that active reflexivity produces. However, neither article is specific about how reflexivity in regard to forming research questions and interpreting data can benefit researchers using quantitative data. For example, Ryan and Golden (2006) mention that they use logistic regression, evaluate results with likelihood ratio tests, and present finding as odds ratios with 95% confidence intervals, but there is no discussion of how their own backgrounds or interactions with respondents may have influenced their hypotheses, coding of measures, decisions about analytical samples, or interpretations of findings. Although not the norm in journals where quantitative data analyses are most often reported, this type of reflexivity could be enormously useful to students looking for "behind-the-scenes" guidance in how research really unfolds.

Concluding Thoughts

For me, this chapter is a plea to social scientists that we continually work to avoid necessarily conflating facets of epistemology, ontology, axiology, and methodology into necessarily distinct types of research—"qualitative" or "quantitative." Even those who find the two types compatible in a mixed methods approach often reify the methodological types in drawing from one or the other to design a study. I argue instead that we take a mixed research perspective that recognizes the philosophical components of a researcher's identity but understands they do not necessarily dictate practical aspects of social inquiry. Specifically, researchers who operate from a sort of critical realist pragmatism are relatively free to design research that selects locations on the axes of inquiry (e.g., subjective-to-objective, inductive-to-deductive, idiographic-nomothetic, and low-to-high reflexivity) that fit the logic and methods in use (McEvoy & Richards, 2006). And, importantly, critiques of this research should focus on philosophical and practical positions of research (as well as their subdomains) rather than overly simplified assumptions about what defines good "qualitative" or "quantitative" research.

I do not mean to discount research or researchers that use approaches that perfectly match the outlines of a purely qualitative or quantitative style of research. Some of the greatest contributions to social science fit in these categories. What I find limiting is a worldview that expects *all* research to fit in one or the other Q box and/or finds one Q box to be more valuable than the other. As I laid out in the beginning of the chapter, social inquiry cannot advance without a mix of perspectives—the yin and the yang of research.

Importantly, critical realists and pragmatic researchers are relatively free to design research using methods outside of the Q boxes. The sociologist in me recognizes our choices are always constrained. We work in a world of peer review where our opportunities and rewards are tied to meeting expectations and achieving legitimacy. As Figure 3.2 illustrates, when we design and conduct research, our choice of method(s) is shaped by multiple factors of varying importance. Countless

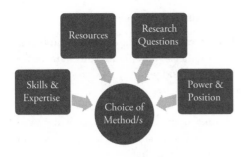

Fig. 3.2 Factors affecting method choice.

research methods textbooks proclaim that our research design should be driven by our research questions, but there is no denying there are other factors involved. For one, we rarely design research that requires a method or approach for which we have no training or experience. Instead, we are likely to alter our question in a way that fits better with the use of our methods of expertise, or we expand our team to include experts in those methods. Another constraining factor is resources. We can have the best research questions and a perfectly matched set of methods, but if the time or cost is beyond our resources, we have to rethink that plan. Finally, there are issues of power and position that shape our choice of methods. Dumitrica (2010) demonstrates the issues well for the extreme case of a graduate student considering an auto-ethnographic approach. Highlighting issues of power and knowledge, she shows that institutional contexts of power (committees, departments, colleges/universities, professional organizations, or disciplines) are both external to a scholar as well as internal, shaping one's own values and presentations of self within academe.

For these reasons, I argue it is important to take a critical perspective and question the overriding assumptions about facets of social inquiry. If we continue to slip into thinking of methods as either quantitative or qualitative, we run the risk of limiting creativity in social inquiry.

Another danger in being imprecise about labeling and evaluating our research in terms such as those laid out in this chapter is that we fuel the marginalization and thus understandable frustration of researchers who identify as qualitative researchers, or those who operate from primarily subjective, relative, value-bound philosophies and usually practice subjective, inductive, idiographic, and reflexive research. When a mixed research study such as Schmutz and Faupel's (2010) on gender and the consecration of popular music

(discussed previously) includes a confirmatory analysis of qualitative data and is labeled "qualitative research," those who identify as qualitative researchers may feel as if the style of research they conduct is being compromised. And, in fact, many published mixed methods research studies integrate uses of qualitative data that are not situated on the so-called qualitative ends of the axes of inquiry I presented (Hesse-Biber, 2010). Many of these studies claim to be operating from a mixed methods framework that integrates quantitative and qualitative paradigms of research, and this would include the philosophical features, as well as the practical features of each paradigm. This reinforces the marginalization of other forms of knowing (e.g., phenomenological research that generally starts without hypotheses or preconceptions and aims to describe rather than to explain), limiting the questions being asked and discoveries being made (Giddings & Grant, 2007). I agree that it is important to recognize this tendency in mixed methods research at large and to encourage (through training and funding) more projects that actively integrate truly subjective, relative, value-bound, inductive, idiographic, and reflexive features in their research. Quality social inquiry needs that diversity. If we described and discussed the philosophical and practical stances of research projects more explicitly, as outlined in this chapter, we would better recognize when one type of research is being confused with another. This could better prevent faulty assumptions about or unreasonable expectations of a particular form of inquiry and help avoid having scholars or their work misrepresented or devalued.

There are other misunderstanding and types of confusion that result from not clearly specifying positions in the philosophical or practical domains of research. One myth I regularly hear is, "Qualitative research takes longer than quantitative research." What is usually underlying this statement is the fact that primary data collection and analysis takes longer than secondary data analysis. Thus study duration is a practical issue of data and methods, not a characteristic of research philosophy.

A related myth is that "One can never be both a qualitative and a quantitative expert." First, there are so many data collection and analysis methods that no one person could actually specialize in all that pertain to either quantitative or qualitative approaches on his or her own, so I doubt one can truly be an expert in whatever it is people consider "qualitative" or "quantitative" research to be. Second, in the social sciences, we are better scholars, more able to contribute to social inquiry at large, if we develop expertise in a variety of approaches. Third, there are countless examples of researchers or teams who carefully identified and developed skills that reside in very different positions along the axes of inquiry that answer questions in a powerful way. If researchers worked to identify themselves and their work more in terms of their philosophical and practical positions on the axes of inquiry, we might avoid confusion over what training it takes to be fully competent for a particular research design.

Another course of action to reverse methodcentrism[3] would be to radically redesign the ways in which undergraduate methods courses and graduate training programs reify the qualitative–quantitative framework (McEvoy & Richards, 2006; Onwuegbuzie & Leech, 2005). Some textbooks have moved in this direction by including a third approach, mixed research (e.g., Johnson & Christensen, 2014), or organizing around types of data collection and analysis methods rather than having two distinct sections (e.g., Singleton & Straits, 2010). However, most training programs continue to offer separate "qualitative" and "quantitative" classes. Neither of which usually scratch the surface of what is possible with each type of data. I would argue students need a strong background in philosophical positions as well as axes of inquiry and logic or design, taught in an integrated manner, and then additional courses could focus in on particular methods (e.g., survey data collection, participant observation, structural equation modeling, grounded theory, etc.).

My goal in writing this chapter has been to challenge readers to think about how they envision, present, and discuss research. A new lexicon that takes us outside the boxes labeled "qualitative" and "quantitative" to explicitly as well as implicitly cross the boundaries insinuated will increase the possibilities for research and clarify our understanding and evaluation of various projects. It will hopefully also squelch the unproductive accusations of one type of research being better than another or one type of research being handmaiden to the other. We should want all parts of our research to strive and shine for what they are. Valuing this holistic view of social inquiry should improve the quality, reach, and contribution of all rigorous research, no matter what the philosophical foundations or practical positions.

Discussion Questions

1. With one research project in mind (your own or another's), how would you characterize the philosophical and practical positions from which it operates?

2. Do you agree or disagree that we should avoid thinking in terms of research being in a Q box or some combination of elements from both? Explain why or why not.

3. How might you design a project that takes place outside the Q boxes?

4. What changes in one's writing style or language could be made to avoid readers expecting a project to meet their particular expectations of "quantitative" or "qualitative" research?

5. Define a mixed research perspective.

Suggested Websites

http://mmira.wildapricot.org/
Mixed Methods International Research Association

Notes

1. Of course there is always the option of using open-ended survey instruments, but the advantages to this more structured approach should outweigh the challenge of coding the data after the fact.

2. Of course *observing* a large number of cases generally requires more time and money than is available. However, for one successful example, see the Three City Study (Burton et al. 2009).

3. Methodcentrism is the valuing of one type of method or approach over another.

References

Abbott, A. D. (2004). *Methods of discovery: Heuristics for the social sciences.* New York, NY: W.W. Norton & Co.

Alford, R. R. (1998). *The craft of inquiry: Theories, methods, evidence.* New York, NY: Oxford University Press.

Axinn, W. G., & Pearce, L. D. (2006). *Mixed method data collection strategies.* New York: Cambridge University Press.

Bentler, P. M. (2007). On tests and indices for evaluating structural models. *Personality and Individual Differences, 42*(5), 825–829.

Bergman, L. R., & Magnusson, D. (1997). A person-oriented approach in research on developmental psychopathology. *Development and Psychopathology, 9,* 291–319.

Bernard, H. R. (2000). *Social research methods: Qualitative and quantitative approaches.* Thousand Oaks, CA: Sage.

Bhaskar, R., (1978). *A realist theory of science.* Atlantic Highlands, NJ: Humanities Press.

Biesta, G. (2010). Pragmatism and the philosophical foundations of mixed methods research. In A. Tashakkori & C. Teddlie (Eds.), *SAGE handbook of mixed methods in social & behavioral research* (2nd ed., pp. 95–118). Los Angeles, CA: Sage.

Bogat, G. A., Zarrett, N., Peck, S. C., & von Eye, A. (2012). The person-oriented approach and community research. In L. A. Jason & D. S. Glenwick (Eds.), *Methodological* approaches to community-based research (pp. 89–109). Washington, DC: American Psychological Association.

Burawoy, M. (1998). The extended case method. Sociological Theory, 16(1), 4–33.

Burton, L. M., Purvin, D., & Garrett-Peters, R. (2009). Longitudinal ethnography: Uncovering domestic abuse in low-income women's lives. In G. H. Elder Jr. & J. Z. Giele (Eds.), The craft of life course research(pp. 70–92). New York, NY: Guilford Press.

Clark, V. L. P., & Badiee, M. (2010). Research questions in mixed methods research. In A. Tashakkori & C. Teddlie (Eds.), SAGE handbook of mixed methods in social & behavioral research (2nd ed., pp. 275–304). Los Angeles, CA: Sage.

Creswell, J. W. (2010). Mapping the developing landscape of mixed methods research. In A. Tashakkori & C. Teddlie (Eds.), SAGE handbook of mixed methods in social & behavioral research (2nd ed., pp. 45–68). Los Angeles, CA: Sage.

Creswell, J. W. (2013). Qualitative inquiry & research design: Choosing among five approaches. Los Angeles, CA: Sage.

DeVault, M. L. (1996). Talking back to sociology: Distinctive contributions of feminist methodology. Annual Review of Sociology, 22, 29–50.

Dumitrica, D. D. (2010). Choosing methods, negotiating legitimacy. A metalogue on autoethnography. Graduate Journal of Social Science, 7(1), 18–38.

Dymnicki, A. B., & Henry, D. B. (2012). Clustering and its applications in community research. In L. A. Jason & D. S. Glenwick (Eds.), Methodological approaches to community-based research.(pp. 71–88) Washington, DC: American Psychological Association.

Elliott, J. (2005). Using narrative in social research: Qualitative and quantitative approaches. Thousand Oaks, CA: Sage.

Finlay, L. (1998). 'Reflexivity: An essential component for all research? British Journal of Occupational Therapy, 61(10), 453–456.

Gerson, K. (2010). The unfinished revolution: How a new generation is reshaping family, work, and gender in America. New York, NY: Oxford University Press.

Giddings, L. S., & Grant, B. M. (2007). A Trojan horse for positivism? A critique of mixed methods research. Advances in Nursing Science, 30(1), 52–60.

Gorard, S. (2010). Research design, as independent of methods. In A. Tashakkori & C. Teddlie (Eds.), SAGE handbook of mixed methods in social & behavioral research (2nd ed., pp. 237–252). Los Angeles, CA: Sage.

Greene, J. C. (2006). Toward a methodology of mixed methods social inquiry. Research in the Schools, 13(1), 93–98.

Guba, E. G. (1987). What have we learned about naturalistic evaluation? Evaluation Practice, 8(1), 23–43.

Guba, E. G., & Lincoln Y. S. (1989). Fourth generation evaluation. Newbury Park, CA: Sage.

Guba, E. G., & Lincoln, Y. S. (1994). Competing paradigms in qualitative research. In N. K. Denzin & Y. Lincoln (Eds.), The SAGE handbook of qualitative research (pp. 105–117). Thousand Oaks, CA: Sage.

Hammersley, M. (1992). What's wrong with ethnography? Methodological explorations. London, England: Routledge.

Hesse-Biber, S. (2010). Mixed methods research: Merging theory with practice. New York, NY: Guilford Press.

Hesse-Biber, S. (2012). Weaving a multimethodology and mixed methods praxis into randomized control trials to enhance credibility. Qualitative Inquiry, 18(10), 876–889.

Johnson, R. B. (2012). Dialectical pluralism and mixed research. American Behavioral Scientist, 56(6), 751–754.

Johnson, R. B., & Christensen, L. (2014). Educational research methods: Quantitative, qualitative, and mixed approaches. Los Angeles, CA: Sage.

Johnson, R. B., & Onwuegbuzie, A. J. (2004). Mixed methods research: A research paradigm whose time has come. Educational Researcher, 33(7), 14–26.

Johnson, R. B., & Stefurak, T. (2013). Considering the evidence-and-credibility discussion in evaluation through the lens of dialectical pluralism. New Directions for Evaluation, 138, 37–48.

Lieber, E., & Weisner, T. S. (2010). Meeting the practical challenges of mixed methods research. In A. Tashakkori & C. Teddlie (Eds.), SAGE handbook of mixed methods in social & behavioral research (2nd ed., pp. 559–579). Los Angeles, CA: Sage.

Magnusson, D. (1998). The logic and implications of a person-oriented approach. In L. R. Bergman, R. B. Cairns, J. Kagan, & M. Radke-Yarrow (Eds.), Methods and models for studying the individual (pp. 33–62). London, England: Sage.

Maxwell, J. A., & Loomis, D. M. (2003). Mixed methods design: An alternative approach. In A. Tashakkori & C. Teddlie (Eds.), Handbook of mixed methods in social & behavioral research (1st ed., pp. 241–272). Thousand Oaks, CA: Sage.

Maxwell, J. A., & Mittapalli, K. (2010). Realism as a stance for mixed methods research. In A. Tashakkori & C. Teddlie (Eds.), SAGE handbook of mixed methods in social & behavioral research (2nd ed., pp. 145–168). Los Angeles, CA: Sage.

McEvoy, P., & Richards, D. (2006). A critical realist rationale for using a combination of quantitative and qualitative methods. Journal of Research in Nursing, 11(1), 66–78.

Mertens, D. M. (2003). Mixed methods and the politics of human research: The transformative-emancipatory perspective. In A. Tashakkori & C. Teddlie (Eds.), Handbook of mixed methods in social & behavioral research (1st ed., pp. 135–164). Thousand Oaks, CA: Sage.

Mertens, D. M. (2009). Transformative research and evaluation. New York, NY: Guilford Press.

Mitchell, J. C. (1983). Case and situation analysis. The Sociological Review, 31(2), 187–211.

Morgan, D. L. (2007). Paradigms lost and pragmatism regained: Methodological implications of combining qualitative and quantitative methods. Journal of Mixed Methods Research, 1(1), 48–76.

Muthén, B., & Muthén, L. K. (2000). Integrating person-centered and variable-centered analyses: Growth mixture modeling with latent trajectory classes. Alcoholism: Clinical and Experimental Research, 24(6), 882–891.

Newman, K. S. (1999). No shame in my game: The working poor in the inner city. New York, NY: Knopf and the Russell Sage Foundation.

Niglas, K. (2010). The multidimensional model of research methodology: An integrated set of continua. In A. Tashakkori & C. Teddlie (Eds.), SAGE handbook of mixed methods in social & behavioral research (2nd ed., pp. 215–236). Los Angeles, CA: Sage.

Onwuegbuzie, A. J., & Leech, N. L. (2005). Taking the "Q" out of research: Teaching research methodology courses without the divide between quantitative and qualitative paradigms. Quality and Quantity, 39(3), 267–295.

Page, S. E. (2007). *The difference: How the power of diversity creates better groups, firms, schools, and societies.* Princeton, NJ: Princeton University Press.

Pearce, L. D., & Denton, M. L. (2011). *A faith of their own: Stability and change in the religiosity of America's adolescents.* New York, NY: Oxford University Press.

Pearce, L. D., Foster, E. M., & Hardie, J. H. (2013). A person-centered examination of adolescent religiosity using latent class analysis. *Journal for the Scientific Study of Religion, 52*(1), 57–79.

Peirce, C. S. (1877). The fixation of belief. *Popular Science Monthly, 12*, 1–15.

Risman, B. J. (1993). Methodological implications of feminist scholarship. *The American Sociologist, 24*(3–4), 15–25.

Ryan, L., & Golden, A. (2006). "Tick the box please": A reflexive approach to doing quantitative social research. *Sociology, 40*(6), 1191–1200.

Schmutz, V., & Faupel, A. (2010). Gender and cultural consecration in popular music. *Social Forces, 89*(2), 685–707.

Singleton, R., & Straits, B. C. (2010). *Approaches to social research.* New York, NY: Oxford University Press.

Small, M. L. (2009). "How many cases do I need?": On science and the logic of case selection in field-based research. *Ethnography, 10*(1), 5–38.

Smith, C., & Denton, M. L. (2005). *Soul searching: The religious and spiritual lives of American teenagers.* New York, NY: Oxford University Press.

Stewart, Q. T. (2008). Swimming upstream: Theory and methodology in race research. In T. Z. Eduardo Bonilla-Silva (Ed.), *White logic, white methods: Racism and methodology* (pp. 111–126). Lanham, MD: Rowman & Littlefield.

Teddlie, C., & Tashakkori, A. (2009). *Foundations of mixed methods research: Integrating quantitative and qualitative approaches in the social and behavioral sciences.* Los Angeles, CA: Sage.

Tukey, J. W. (1980). We need both exploratory and confirmatory. *The American Statistician, 34*(1), 23–25.

Walker, S., Read, S., & Priest, H. (2013). Use of reflexivity in a mixed methods study. *Nurse Researcher, 20*(3), 38.

Yin, R. K. (2014). *Case study research: Design and methods.* Los Angeles, CA: Sage.

Revisiting Mixed Methods and Advancing Scientific Practices

John W. Creswell

Abstract

This chapter reviews the developments in mixed methods during the past few years. The chapter introduces 10 scientific developments to emerge in the mixed methods research field. These developments relate to the characteristics of mixed methods and the terms used within it, the value of mixed methods, incorporating philosophies and theory into a mixed methods study, mixed methods designs and procedures, recognizing threats to validity, research questions, displays of jointly presenting results, the writing structure of a study, and the criteria to evaluate the quality of a study. The chapter concludes with recommendations for the future conduct of mixed methods research based on these scientific developments.

Key Words: mixed methods, research, quantitative approaches, qualitative approaches, scientific practices,

Introduction

During the spring, 2013, when I served as a visiting professor of public health at Harvard, I had the opportunity to present to students and faculty at Harvard's Institute for the Social Sciences. This was more than a simple presentation—it was an awakening for me to the needs of scholars about mixed methods research. My topic was "Mixed Methods Research—The State of the Art." The audience was largely composed of social scientists from Harvard and nearby schools. Also in the audience was my host, a professor from the School of Public Health. My presentation was delivered in about 45 minutes, and I fielded some questions from individuals who seemed interested in mixed methods research. After the presentation ended, my host from public health asked me an intriguing question: "Are all of you social scientists so abstract?" With this question, he inferred that I skimmed the surface in a way that would not be appealing to practical researchers in the

health sciences. At that point I began rethinking mixed methods research to better emphasize that yes, it was a science, and yes, there have been many applied scientific developments in how to conduct mixed methods research in the past decade. I vowed to begin reporting these developments.

After this workshop experience, I now believe that conveying information to those new to mixed methods needs to start with commentary about its scientific developments. This moves it away from abstract ideas to practical use. It also calls for identifying the precise scientific developments that have occurred in the field, and, most important, branding them as "scientific developments" for academic audiences. Unquestionably, much has evolved in this area in mixed methods in the past few years. For example, we have specific designs for the procedures of research, ways to represent the complexity of quantitative and qualitative data together, and visualizations or models of the major features of our designs. It is precisely these technological advances, the scientific methods that have evolved, that need to be highlighted in our mixed methods presentations and writings.

Science is a good word to use because it resonates well with a health science audience (as well as a social and behavioral science audience). Granted not all scholars, especially some social scientists, think in terms of science and how it develops and proceeds forward. My premise is based on a core principle that science advances based on the accumulation of knowledge. I realize that this is only one way to conceptualize "research." But I believe that we have entered a new era in the development of mixed methods, one characterized by increasing complexities and technical features. Moreover, mixed methods might be seen as the first major social science research methodology in the 20th and now 21st century to fully utilize the digital capabilities to advance it. Mixed methods is emerging through digital flowcharts, the use of computer software for analysis, and the Internet for reaching individuals around the world who may not have access to current books, conference workshops, and mixed methods content specialists.

Thus as I surveyed the needs of the fields, both in social sciences and health, after my presentation at Harvard, I began speaking about distinct scientific developments in the field that, if used by empirical investigators, would considerably enhance their scholarly work. In this chapter, I hope to convey 10 different scientific developments in mixed methods. Many of these are reported in existing diverse chapters and books on mixed methods. For each one, I define the development, talk about current practices, and convey how the developments are continually being shaped as mixed methods becomes more and more refined into a science. I do not present the developments in any special order, but the 10 I include are (1) being able to identify the essential characteristics of mixed methods research (MMR); (2) using a distinct terminology that helps to communicate about the field and define it; (3) discussing the value-added of mixed methods over traditional quantitative and qualitative research; (4) incorporating philosophies and theories into mixed methods studies; (5) reassessing the types of mixed methods designs to focus on a parsimonious set of basic and advanced designs that simplify the task of choosing a design and conducting MMR; (6) recognizing methodological issues or threats to validity that reside in the types of mixed methods designs; (7) stating a new type of question, a mixed methods question, that is implied by investigators conducting a mixed methods study; (8) using representational models, called joint displays, to convey the quantitative and qualitative results together in a study; (9) structuring the writing of a study to mirror the specific type of designs used in the study; and (10) applying criteria to evaluate the quality of a mixed methods study. Although these 10 points are not meant to be exhaustive and have certainly appeared in different publications over the past few years (e.g., Creswell & Plano Clark, 2011), they have never been pulled together as a set and spoken of, as far as I know, as the scientific advancements in MMR. Their identification and labeling as part of the science enables the larger social science and health science communities to see them as distinct developments and to incorporate them into new studies. After I discuss each one, I then turn to specific recommendations for future work that will build on these developments in the ever-emerging field of mixed methods. I begin by recapping what has developed in mixed methods over the past few years as a benchmark for new scientific features.

The Expanding Field of Mixed Methods

These scientific developments I speak of did not exist five years ago. Partly this is due to writers presenting mixed methods in a clearer voice and a more concise way (e.g., Greene, 2007). It is also due to having more and more mixed methods empirical studies, journal articles, and funded projects reported in the literature (Onwuegbuzie, 2012). In response, writers such as myself are learning from published journal articles. We now have journals specifically devoted to MMR, such as the *Journal of Mixed Methods Research* (http://mmr.sagepub.com/), *Field Methods* (http://www.qualquant.net/FM/), and *International Journal of Multiple Research Approaches* (http://pubs.e-contentmanagement.com/loi/mra). As a field, it has also expanded considerably through methodological writings in different fields and in leading journals. It is quite popular in many fields in the health sciences (Creswell, Klassen, Plano Clark, & Smith, 2011; Ivankova & Kawamura, 2010). It has also expanded internationally with interests in many regions of the world, such as in the African countries, in Europe, and in the Southeast Asian countries. It might be seen by some as an Anglo-American methodology, especially in view of the international conference, first housed at Cambridge University and then at Leeds University in the UK, and recently coming back to the United States at Boston College in 2014 (https://www.facebook.com/MMIRA2014). Major books are being published on mixed methods, with a large number—estimated to be 24—coming from international authors (Onwuegbuzie, 2012). It has also expanded through interest by private foundations, through workshops, and the federal government (Plano Clark, 2010) and through websites of "best practices": advancing how to conduct rigorous mixed methods investigations (Creswell et al., 2011). We would add to this the new courses on MMR emerging on many large, distinguished campuses across the United States and in England. In the spring of 2014, Harvard hosted a mixed methods course in its Department of Global Health and Social Medicine in the School of Medicine. During the summer of 2013, an international, interdisciplinary professional association began—the Mixed Methods International Research Association (mmira.wildapricot.org/)—to draw together the world's mixed methods writers, investigators, and researchers.

Scientific Developments

I begin with the most basic development to emerge—the definition of mixed methods—and then proceed to identify additional developments that are more technical in nature.

A Science of Defined Boundaries

A science needs to have distinguishing features as well as ways of separating it from other approaches. In recent years it has been contested terrain as to what the boundaries of mixed methods might be. In 2007, more than 19 scholars provided their definitions for mixed methods (Johnson, Onwuegbuzie, & Turner, 2007). Some took a philosophical orientation, some a methodological approach of thinking across many phases of research, and some a methods orientation. I have personally taken a methods orientation because I believe that it is a concrete way to understand mixed methods, especially for those new to the idea. Beginning from the perspective of philosophy loses those who are not familiar with the epistemological and ontological issues of inquiry. Talking about the process of research that stretches from the philosophical to the implications creates many questions for those not specifically trained in a detailed understanding of the process such as drawing inferences or designing research questions. What is an important element of mixed methods—the methods—gets lost in all of the phases of research that may not be

understood in the same way by different investigators. In many fields, people can easily enter their research from a methods perspective. It is concrete, and it is a specific place to think about research. For example, in the health sciences, the idea of qualitative research often resides in conducting focus groups. Of course, there is much more to qualitative inquiry than that, but the methods become a framework for thinking about research. Also, when asked what kind of research they are doing, some newer researchers respond that they are conducting a survey or doing interviews. In short, the natural tendency to think about research often comes from viewing it as a "method." Thus my core characteristics of mixed methods, as I call them, builds on thinking about mixed methods as a "method" and "mixing" the methods:

> Mixed methods is an approach to research in which the investigator collects, analyzes, and interprets both quantitative and qualitative data (closed- and open-ended information), integrates or combines the two approaches in various ways, and frames the study within a specific type of design or procedure. Sometimes the researcher makes specific their philosophical assumptions, and more often than not, they include a theory that guides the quantitative or qualitative strand of their research or both. Also, both strands need to be conducted using rigorous methods of data collection and analysis.

So my definition works from a methods orientation. This allows me to clearly think about mixed methods as a "method" and to distinguish it from other types of methods being used in social, behavioral, and health research. For example, mixed methods is not simply collecting and analyzing both quantitative and qualitative data. This view, however, falls short because it does not incorporate a central feature of mixed methods—the integration or combining of the two types of data in which, I believe, something extra is added to both the quantitative and qualitative strand of a study. Also, mixed methods is not adding qualitative data to a quantitative design. Mixed methods can be employed in this way, but we can also add quantitative data to qualitative, and the "adding" component suggests a diminished stature for what is added. In mixed methods, both quantitative and qualitative approaches are highly and equally valued. Mixed methods further is not simply collecting multiple forms of qualitative data (e.g., interviews and observations) or collecting multiple types of quantitative data (e.g., surveys, experimental data), although some researchers will take this perspective. To me, taking this perspective diminishes the power of mixed methods, that something unique and creative will occur out of collecting two different types of data (e.g., the quantitative trends and the qualitative personal experiences). Thus I say that mixed methods involves collecting *both* quantitative and qualitative data. Historically, when investigators collected multiple forms of quantitative data, the term *multimethod* was used (Campbell & Fiske, 1959), not *mixed methods*. More recently, Johnson et al. (2007) found that major players in the mixed methods field tended to collect both qualitative and quantitative methods. Others disagree, such as Morse and Niehaus (2009) who state that "a mixed methods design may also mix two qualitative methods or two quantitative methods." (p. 20). Viewing mixed methods as mixing only qualitative methods or only quantitative methods does not seem to capture the richness that the two differing databases provide to understand research problems or questions. In addition, mixed methods is not simply an evaluation technique, such as formative and summative, although in employing this technique a researcher could collect and integrate both quantitative and qualitative data. Distinct from evaluation procedures, mixed methods is a systematic method, and it involves planning and consciously combining both quantitative and qualitative data. Mixed methods is not collecting qualitative data and analyzing it quantitatively. This is the approach of content analysis (Krippendorff, 2012). The full advantage of mixed methods follows from collecting *both* quantitative and qualitative data. Finally, MMR is not "mixed model" research. Mixed model research is a quantitative approach that involves including both random and fixed effects of errors in a statistical analysis (Raudenbush & Bryk, 2002).

A Language Science

All sciences have means of communication within their groups and to the world of research that includes people not familiar with their approach. A language has developed around mixed methods that researchers new to the approach must learn. At the back of most mixed methods books are glossary terms, and these terms often are similar from one text to another. A key term is the name *mixed methods* itself. Today, with the establishment of the *Handbook of Mixed Methods in Social & Behavioral Research* (Tashakkori & Teddlie, 2010), the *Journal of Mixed Methods Research*, and the Mixed Method

International Research Association, we have the term *mixed methods* as a common label for this form of research. It has been called other names—such as multimethod, integrated, or mixed research—but the label "mixed methods" seems to be popularly used in the field. Unquestionably, the terminology for mixed methods has evolved from the use of quantitative or qualitative terms (e.g., *triangulation*, a qualitative term, found its way into mixed methods in the early years; Tashakkori & Teddlie, 1998), to the perspective of separate terms from either quantitative or qualitative (e.g., *legitimation*; Onwuegbuzie & Johnson, 2006; Tashakkori & Teddlie, 2003). We now have moved toward more descriptive and less confusing terms for those learning mixed methods. For example, take the terms *priority* and *sequence* advanced by Morgan in 1998. In time, these terms have become confusing. What does it mean to give priority to the quantitative or qualitative phase of a study? Do we count the number of published pages given to each? Are the two approaches implemented sequentially when they are apart by minutes rather than days? A clearer term, I believe, is to talk about the *intent* of the design, such as to compare two databases or have one explain the other. This moves the language, I believe, onto much firmer grounds for understanding the nature of a mixed methods design. In addition, entirely new terms have entered the lexicon of mixed methods that were not present even a decade ago, such as joint displays, mixed methods questions, and data transformation approaches.

A Legitimate Science

New sciences must legitimate themselves and gain acceptance as a valued approach to research. Mixed methods is no exception, and it has been slowly building in this area. Around 2006, the president of SAGE Publishing first called to my attention the issue of whether mixed methods actually added any additional insight—or value—to a quantitative or qualitative approach. Unfortunately, the question of the value-added of mixed methods is still under scrutiny by many individuals in the research community, and mixed methods scholars have not seemed to pose any concrete solutions to the problem. Being able to advance its value is central to creating a legitimate science of mixed methods. In 2010 a student in my graduate program in mixed methods at the University of Nebraska–Lincoln actually put to an empirical test this question (Haines, 2010). Student participants were randomly assigned to one of three groups. Each group read a passage about results—quantitative, qualitative, and mixed methods—reported in the same study (the study was written specifically for this experiment). On a follow-up survey measuring the value of the results, students who read the mixed methods passage perceived it to be more valuable than the students who read the quantitative or qualitative passage. In a qualitative follow-up to this experiment, the students reported that the mixed methods article had rigorous methods and gave readers a deep meaning of the phenomenon under study.

An alternative way to examine value-added would be to analyze closely what authors of empirical mixed methods studies claim is the unique contribution of their approach. Farquhar, Ewing, and Booth (2011) provided an excellent illustration. This article included a table that specified how mixed methods added to the study, such as teasing out important elements of the intervention, providing limitations of the quantitative research, and using quantitative findings to compare with quantitative results. Finally, we can discuss value-added by reviewing the rationales for the use of MMR that have been stated by authors in the mixed methods literature over the years. The benefit might be that qualitative data helps explain the quantitative results, best explores the types of questions that need to be asked, helps to shape a program or a set of intervention activities that might actually work, or yields new variables that may not have occurred to researchers before the study began or variables that were apparent in the literature (Bryman, 2006; Creswell & Plano Clark, 2011).

In sum, we are still working on thinking and writing about the value-added of MMR, and the question can be approached through multiple perspectives. We do know that a mixed methods study typically involves collecting multiple forms of data that may be more than either gathered in only quantitative or qualitative research. We also know that its use has increased substantially in recent years (Onwuegbuzie, 2012), providing a subtext testimony to its value.

A Science with Philosophical and Theoretical Foundations

Science is often developed first by philosophers who seek to establish the foundation for the inquiry. Later the methodologists enter the picture and add the techniques for conducting the research. During the 1990s, the "paradigm debate" occupied the attention of mixed methods writers (Howe,

2004; Reichardt & Rallis, 1994). Now, I believe, the debate has subsided, and thoughtful scholars are discussing useful philosophical approaches that provide the foundation for mixed methods. This discussion has proceeded not based on establishing the one true philosophy but on allowing researchers to adopt the philosophy with which they are the most comfortable.

For example, in 2003 Tashakkori and Teddlie suggested that pragmatism formed the central philosophy advanced by 13 mixed methods scholars. More recently, Maxwell (2012) discussed the critical realist approach that equally applied to qualitative and MMR. Johnson (2012) suggested that dialectic pluralism is a good philosophy for MMR because it advances an approach for incorporating different paradigms, theories, and stakeholder views. New philosophies are emerging all the time, and a key question for a mixed methods investigator is whether they make explicit in their studies their philosophical assumption. In the health sciences, it seems that there is neither room in publications nor interest in making explicit the philosophy undergirding mixed methods. In the social sciences, the reverse is often true.

Theory, on the other hand, has found a central place in mixed methods for social, behavioral, and health scientists. I think about theory use in mixed methods as one of two forms: social/behavioral theories (e.g., theory of adaptation, theory of change, and so forth) or a theory that frames a social justice orientation or a transformative perspective (Mertens, 2009). In the health sciences, the use of behavioral/social science theory popularly frames mixed methods studies. Examples would be quality-of-life theories, behavioral change theories, and adoption and adaptation theories. For example, to study caregivers for family members affected by HIV and AIDS in South Africa, Petros (2011) used social exchange theory; Püschel and Thompson (2011) used the PRECEDE model of predisposing factors, enabling factors, and reinforcing change factors; Ivankova and Stick (2006) used a theory of student attrition in their investigation of study of student persistence in a distance education graduate program.

The social justice theoretical orientation may be one of transformation in which the intent is to address injustices in the world and help bring about an improved society for underrepresented groups (see Mertens, 2009, for the transformative perspective applied to MMR). For example, Sweetman, Badiee, and Creswell (2010) reported on 39 mixed methods studies that utilized a feminist lens, a racial orientation, and other frameworks. One theoretical transformative orientation helpful to stakeholders in communities is community-based participatory research. In community health, especially, researchers are incorporating mixed methods procedures using community-based participatory research. A good illustration of this approach would be the study of the transition of homeless individuals from a hospital to a shelter by Greysen, Allen, Lucas, Wang, and Rosenthal (2012). In this study, the authors not only gathered quantitative and qualitative data—they also involved the key stakeholders in both the shelters and the hospital in many phases of the research. In the article, the authors make explicit how these stakeholders participated in the phases of the research from the formation of the study and the implications of its results.

We are beginning to learn how to write a theory—social, behavioral, or transformative—into a mixed methods study (Mertens, 2003). This has resulted from a close inspection of many studies available, such as the feminist mixed methods project looking at gender equity by Hodgkin (2008). It might appear at the beginning as an overall framework for the study or it might be threaded throughout the study and inform many parts of the project. It might inform both the quantitative and qualitative strands of a mixed methods study, such as its use by Betancourt et al. (2011) in their study of family strengthening in Rwanda. In my writings with Plano Clark (Creswell & Plano Clark, 2011) we have discussed how a transformative or advocacy theory might be threaded throughout a mixed methods study, such as at the beginning in the literature review, in the advocacy/participatory wording of the research question, in the sensitivity to the population in data collection process, in the themes in the findings or results, and in the call to action at the end of a study.

Scientific Basic and Advanced Designs

Throughout the development of research methodologies, writers have focused on the types of procedures useful in conducting investigations. During the 1960s, Campbell and Stanley (1966) identified the types of experimental and quasi-experimental designs that are still prevalent today. In 1987, Jacob identified the primary types of designs available to qualitative researchers. Thus, following in this history of the evolution of different types of designs for procedures in conducting research, MMR has also proliferated into multiple designs. In fact, no topic has been more extensively discussed in the literature of mixed methods than research designs (Creswell & Plano Clark, 2011). Many types of designs have been introduced over the years, and they come with different names, different procedures, and diverse levels of complexity. We recorded 13 different classifications of designs in 2011 (Creswell & Plano Clark, 2011). With this proliferation has also come increasing complexity, and I feel that now the beginning inquirer ends up with a baffling array of designs that limit his or her ability to choose one or understand how to conduct the design. Researchers present too many mixed methods designs with a confusing array of arrows and boxes that inhibit their replication or use by another person. My approach has always been to think in terms of a parsimonious set of designs, to focus only on those designs popularly used, and to encourage researchers to seek out variants of them when needed. The use of simple, elegant, straightforward designs has another benefit: a design becomes an anchor in research for thinking about other aspects of the research process, such as how to phrase the title, how to think about combining or integrating quantitative and qualitative data, and how to consider issues such as validity and ethics.

The science of mixed methods can proceed by clarifying our designs and presenting them in an understandable way. Thus I suggest that at the heart of every mixed methods study resides a basic design, and figuring out that design is the first step for an investigator. Further, these basic designs are only three types, and they form the core of the intent of the mixed methods study. Sometimes we add on to these basic designs certain features that encase them in more complex features. I call these advanced designs.

Three basic designs and three advanced designs are illustrated in Figures 4.1 and 4.2. Parts of these designs are discussed elsewhere by different authors (e.g., Creswell, 2014a, 2014b; Morse & Niehaus, 2009; Teddlie & Tashakkori, 2009). They do not exhaust the possibilities of designs, but they provide core models of designs within which investigators can innovate.

There are three basic designs, as shown in Figure 4.1: the convergent design, the explanatory sequential design, and the exploratory sequential design. The procedures of a convergent design are to collect both quantitative and qualitative data, analyze both sets separately, and then compare the results. Thus the intent is to compare two different

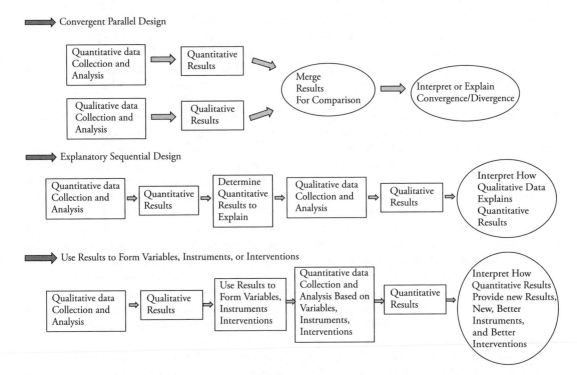

Fig. 4.1 Basic mixed methods designs. Creswell, 2014a. Used with permission from SAGE Publications.

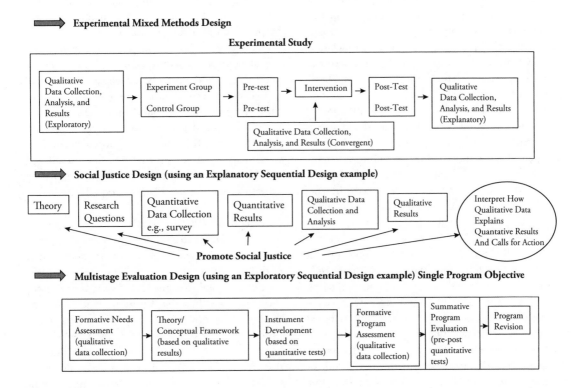

Fig. 4.2 Advanced mixed methods designs. Creswell, 2014a. Used with permission from SAGE Publications.

perspectives on a topic and see if the databases converge or are similar. The procedures for an explanatory sequential design are to start by collecting and analyzing quantitative data, look closely at the results, and then follow up on the results with qualitative data collection and analysis. The intent is to help explain the quantitative results with qualitative data. An exploratory sequential design takes just the opposite approach. The researcher begins by collecting and analyzing qualitative data. From this analysis, the researcher uses the results to develop something quantitative—such as an instrument or an intervention—and then in the final phase of the research the investigator applies or tests the quantitative instrument or intervention. The intent of this design is to explore first because there are no existing instruments or intervention activities to study a population, or the existing concepts or variables cannot be adapted to a particular setting. Most mixed methods studies fall into one of these three basic types or some variation of them.

Advanced designs, as shown in Figure 4.2, include a basic design plus something more added to the design. For example, an experimental framework, a social justice perspective, or a program evaluation dimension might be added to a basic design. The intent of adding qualitative data into an experimental trial is to first explore before the trial begins, to gather qualitative data about personal experiences during the trial, to follow up after the trials with qualitative data to better understand the outcome results, or to plan the next experiment (Creswell, Fetters, Plano Clark, & Morales, 2009). Alternatively, added into a basic design might be a social justice framework that surrounds the mixed methods procedures. The intent with this design is to advance a social justice agenda and include the theoretical orientation of a lens that informs many of the phases of the research. In the third advanced design, the program evaluation design, the investigator provides a longitudinal study involving many substudies, all connected to fulfill a common objective. These substudies may be a qualitative project, a quantitative project, or a mixed methods project involving both forms of data, and with one study building on the other. For example, in evaluating a program, the researcher might conduct a qualitative needs assessment, design a program based on theory, implement the program, and quantitatively test whether it works successfully. The intent is to use a basic design within the framework of a long-term program evaluation objective. This design is easily seen in program evaluation mixed methods studies, such as the one by Nastasi et al. (2007) in their multiyear study of a program implemented for youth in Sri Lanka.

It is difficult to say which designs are most popular, but in our analysis of mixed methods projects in the mental health trauma area (see Creswell & Zhang, 2009), many examples of the explanatory sequential design were found because the design starts with a quantitative phase, a phase easily accepted within the quantitatively oriented health sciences. In the health sciences, popular designs include the intervention design (because of the gold standard of randomized controlled trials), the community-based participatory research design (because of the need to provide health services to communities that they will accept), and the program evaluation design, in which new health services are tested out over time with patient and hospital populations. In the social and behavioral sciences, the popular designs will differ and likely reflect the scholarly communities' acceptance of qualitative research or quantitative research. This acceptance will direct, in turn, the design and what starts the introduction to the study and forms the basic feature of the design.

What is also interesting about the emergence of designs is that we have good diagrams of the procedures that researchers might use in their presentations or in their papers. These diagrams might be presented as a simple model of a few boxes or elaborated with boxes indicating the major elements, detailed procedures identified for each step, and specific products to be developed at each step. Moreover, we can identify a flow of activities for these designs, such as found in a useful book on visualizing social science research by Wheeldon and Ahlberg (2012). Researchers can also add into these diagrams notation that was first established by Morse in 1991 and has now been elaborated by others (see Creswell & Plano Clark, 2011).

Scientific Validity Threats

When Campbell and Stanley wrote their classic book on experimental and quasi-experimental research in 1966, they not only assessed the types of experimental designs that were being used; they also identified the threats to validity for the designs. I believe that we are now taking a cue from their work in the mixed methods field as we begin to identify the types of designs and pinpoint threats (or they might be called methodological issues) that arise when conducting a mixed methods design. Moreover, because we have some sense of the types of designs, we also can now look at them closely, inspect empirical investigations that use them, and make statements about the potential threats that researchers need to anticipate when conducting the designs.

What are some of these threats? As shown in Table 4.1, they differ for types of mixed methods designs. These differences can be seen in sampling and sample size, time and resources, skills of researchers, and combining or connecting data. For example, in a convergent design, the potential threats lie in sample size and not being cognizant of whether the sample sizes should be equal or unequal between the quantitative and qualitative strands and at the integration stage of not carefully weighing alternative approaches to integration. In an explanatory design, the issues reside in not clearly following up on the quantitative results to explain them further in the qualitative data collection. Further, this follow-up needs to consider both what types of questions to ask and which participants can best answer the questions. In an exploratory design, a challenge lies in how to translate the qualitative results into an instrument or into an intervention. Also, when instruments are developed, a rigorous procedure of scale development must occur, such as found in DeVellis (2006). In an intervention design, investigators need to not only identify a rationale for inclusion of qualitative data in certain stages in the experiment but also realize how this qualitative data collection might bias the outcome results. We can place these threats into designs and build on visual models of mixed methods designs such as Wheeldon and Ahlberg (2012). Using the convergent design as an illustration, as shown in Figure 4.3, I have placed the validity threats into a visual model of the procedures in the mixed methods design. These threats relate to not creating parallel questions, not addressing equal or unequal sample sizes, not treating results separately, not conveying the approach to merging the data, and not explaining discrepancies between the quantitative and qualitative data when they occur. In this way, by recognizing threats to validity, investigators can see where they may occur, anticipate them, and present strategies for addressing them.

Science of Linking Designs to Questions

Researchers know that the methods are intended to answer specific research questions or hypotheses. It is clear in quantitative research that the research questions focus on such factors as determining if a treatment works or what variables might influence an outcome. In qualitative research, the questions often have to do with exploring the meaning of a phenomenon, understanding how

Table 4.1 Threats to Validity in Six Mixed Methods Designs

Type of Design	Potential Threats
Convergent Design	• Use parallel quantitative and qualitative questions • Decide on sample size • Determine how to merge the data (side by side, data transformation, joint display) • Explain divergent results
Exploratory Sequential Design	• Determine how to go from qualitative results to quantitative instrument, variables, etc. • If developing an instrument, use good psychometric procedures
Explanatory Sequential Design	• Assess array of possible quantitative results to follow up • Determine who can best provide qualitative follow-up • Make sure that qualitative explains the quantitative results
Experimental, Intervention Design	• Decide where/why to put qualitative data into experiment • Make sure that qualitative does not bias outcomes • Consider challenges associated with basic designs
Social Justice/ Participatory Design	• Decide how social justice/community involvement will flow into study and how to negotiate this involvement • Consider challenges associated with basic designs
Program Evaluation Design	• Keep the focus on the long-term objective • Consider challenges associated with basic designs

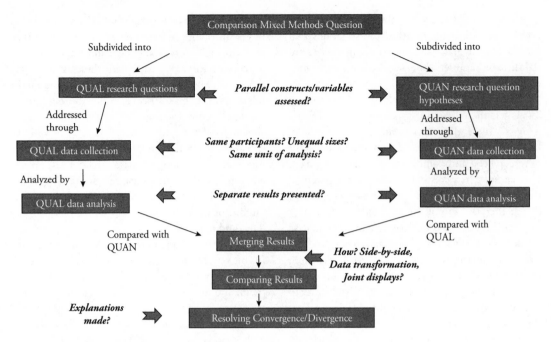

Fig. 4.3 Validity threats comparing quantitative and qualitative results (convergent design).

people experience something, or what theory can be generated that explains a broad process. The types of questions posed in quantitative and qualitative research can be easily identified. What types of questions are best answered with mixed methods? This question is typically not squarely addressed in the mixed methods literature. It was this thinking that led mixed methods researchers to suggest that in mixed methods, we have a new type of research question, one that does not appear in our research methods books: a mixed methods question. Discussions first appeared in the *Journal of Mixed Methods Research* through an editorial (Tashakkori & Creswell, 2007), and now we are beginning to see them in published studies and discussed in texts (e.g., Creswell & Plano Clark, 2011). The key to identifying this mixed methods question lies in relating it to a type of design. Thus there are different ways to phrase this question, such as writing it from a more methods orientation to a content focus or some combination (called "hybrids" in Tashakkori & Creswell, 2007). For example, Classen et al. (2007) provide this example: "From a qualitative meta-synthesis, how do the stakeholder perspectives, needs, and goals for safe and unsafe driving outcomes support or inform the salient factors found in the FARS dataset?" (pp. 679–680). In this example, the qualitative component is represented by the comment

about stakeholder perspectives, and the outcomes represent the quantitative component. We know that a convergent design is being used because it is reflected in the words "support" or "inform," which suggests that the researchers will compare two different databases. For an explanatory design, the question may be: How do the qualitative results help to explain the quantitative findings? For an exploratory design, the mixed methods question might be: How do the qualitative findings help to design an improved quantitative instrument (or intervention)? Or how are the qualitative findings from a small number of people generalized to a larger sample from a population? Of course there are variations for each design, but the central thought here is that the mixed methods question fits the design being used in a study, and it is presented to audiences in a way they can understand.

The Science of Representation

More and more attention today is being given to how to analyze both the qualitative and the quantitative data in tandem. This attention focuses on the question of integration (Bryman, 2006; Plano Clark, Garrett, & Leslie-Pelecky, 2009). How do we merge, for example, text data from qualitative research with numeric data from quantitative data? Ambiguity exists as to how to accomplish this integration, what forms it might take, and whether it relates to the type of design, the methods of data, or the interpretation (Fetters, Curry, & Creswell, 2014). One way to think about integration from a data standpoint is to consider joint displays, a procedure of arraying the qualitative results (e.g., themes) against the quantitative results (e.g., scores) in a table, graphs, or a discussion. The idea is that the two sources of data can be more easily compared if they reside in one place or side by side. They may more easily be seen as one database extending or explaining the other database. Li, Marquart, and Zercher (2000) provide a good visual of arraying quantitative and qualitative results together in which they identified common themes (or questions) and then positioned the quantitative and qualitative results in columns beside each other. What they might have done is added an additional column to illustrate points of divergence or convergence between the two databases for each of the themes. Such a joint display works well for a convergent design, but it can also be presented for other types of designs. In Table 4.2, I present a joint display that I developed for a hypothetical mixed methods study using an explanatory sequential design in an intervention trial in which the qualitative data helps to explain the quantitative data. In this table, I present data with results from the quantitative analysis and a column for the qualitative data that helps to explain the quantitative results. This table illustrates that the joint displays may not be complicated and difficult to understand. In a graph of geo-coded information the graph can illustrate both the quantitative density of a problem as well as pull-out quotes from individuals in each density area. Computer software has aided us in creating these joint displays. One qualitative software product, MAXQDA (Verbi

Software), for example, now has a pull-down menu for mixed methods, which can assist the researcher in creating joint displays of the data.

Scientific Writing Structures

Since many published empirical mixed methods studies are now available in the literature, we have good models for how to write and compose mixed methods studies and what mixed methods components to put into them. I often talk about the "architecture" of a research study (Creswell, 2014c). The science of mixed methods proceeds through learning the structural properties of writing studies for publication. For example, we now pay attention to the creation of good mixed methods titles, complete purpose statements, multiple research questions (quantitative, qualitative, and mixed methods), detailed discussions about mixed methods procedures, including the types of quantitative and qualitative data and how they are integrated, and mixed methods references. There have been some recommendations for how to publish mixed methods studies (Stange, Crabtree, & Miller, 2006), especially when the journal reviewers call for short articles—around 3,000 to 6,000 words). When we established the *Journal of Mixed Methods Research* in 2007, we allowed manuscripts of empirical investigations of 10,000 to 12,000 words, a luxury in today's journal environment. However, some ideas are developing as to how to write a short mixed methods article, despite the multiple forms of data being collected and the multiple analysis strategies. One approach is to review studies that use one type of design—say the convergent design—and see how the authors wrote the articles for publication. Another approach is to consider a mixed methods study as having

Table 4.2 Joint Display in an Explanatory Sequential Intervention Design

Quantitative Results	Qualitative Follow-Up Interviews Explaining Quantitative Results	How Qualitative Findings Helped to Explain Quantitative Results
No significant difference between the intervention and the control conditions on the five standardized measures	Follow-up interviews revealed that half of the caregivers felt that the intervention enhanced their competence, confidence, coping, and ability to handle caregiving responsibilities. Caregivers also highlighted the importance of their interactions with the peer helpers.	The qualitative interviews provided some positive impacts of the intervention, impacts that would not have been gained if only the statistical results were considered.

three parts—the quantitative study, the qualitative study, and the mixed methods study. Each could be published separately with cross-referencing from one article to the other so readers understand that all three articles are crafted from one mixed methods project. A good example comes from an international publication on the use of mammogram screening in Chile (Püschel & Thompson, 2011). This overall project was divided into three papers, with the quantitative paper published in one journal (Püschel, Coronado, et al., 2010), the qualitative paper printed in another one (Püschel, Thompson, et al., 2010), and the third mixed methods paper published in a third journal (Püschel & Thompson, 2011). By the dates of publication, we can see that the quantitative and qualitative articles were probably placed first in journals followed by the mixed methods article. Also, by inspecting these three articles closely, we can begin to understand how an overall mixed methods study might be abbreviated to fit a shorter word length. This was accomplished by Püschel and Thompson by abbreviating the methods discussion, not reporting both the quantitative and qualitative results but combining them, and casting both the quantitative and qualitative findings within one central theory.

Scientific Evaluation Criteria

Finally, standards for evaluating the quality of a mixed methods study are now being produced. There are certainly advantages and disadvantages to using guidelines for standards. They help beginning researchers navigate the terrain of mixed methods, whereas more experienced researchers may see them as creating boundaries on how they view and conduct mixed methods. Standards should not be seen as rigid templates but as general guidelines for use. In the mixed methods field, several authors have created useful guidelines (see O'Cathain, Murphy, & Nicholl, 2008), and, more recently, the federal government has issued some quality criteria. For example, the National Science Foundation has a document that provides guidelines for mixed methods evaluation research (Frechtling, 2002), and the medical community has the CONSORT guidelines (Ioannidis et al., 2004) for guidance for composing a randomized trial. The National Institutes of Health (Office of Behavioral and Social Science Research; Creswell et al., 2011) has provided recommendations on a website for the "best practices" of mixed methods in the health sciences ((http://obssr.od.nih.gov/mixed_methods_research/pdf/Best_Practices_for_Mixed_Methods_Research.

pdf). A checklist in the best practices recommendations addresses several scientific aspects of mixed methods that I have discussed, such as integration, a rationale of the use of mixed methods, and how it adds value to a study beyond that gained from either quantitative or qualitative research. Of special note in best practices would be the table of review criteria, useful for individuals preparing an application for the National Institutes of Health or individuals who are evaluating such applications. How rigidly we need to specify how mixed methods works is, of course, open to debate, and it seems to vary depending on whether the field is in the health sciences or the social sciences. However, I do find that beginning mixed methods researchers appreciate some quality guidelines as they develop graduate student proposals for theses and dissertations, conference presentations, journal article submissions, and applications for private and public funds. Application developers and reviewers on study panels also stand to profit from quality guidelines.

Discussion and Recommendations

It is helpful to talk about the "science" of mixed methods and to discuss how our knowledge has accumulated about the scientific developments to emerge over the past few years. Some will disagree with me that we need a science of mixed methods, or even that it is a scientific approach. For the health sciences in which I have been working, as my example of my presentation and comments that I received at Harvard illustrates, it makes good sense, and it enhances the credibility and legitimacy of the approach as well as highlights procedures for using the approach in a practical way (Stewart, Makwarimba, Barnfather, Letourneau, & Neufeld, 2008). Building on the 10 points of the science of mixed methods, my recommendations are as follows:

1. For individuals new to mixed methods, such as those flowing into the field from the health sciences today, we need a commonly accepted definition of mixed methods and one that clearly sets the boundaries between what is and what is not this form of research.

2. The terms in mixed methods continue to improve, and we need to clarify some misconceptions that arose during the early development of the methodology. Glossaries and terms used should reflect a language unique from quantitative or qualitative words and embrace new terms that are coming into frequent use such as a "joint display" or a "mixed methods question."

3. We need more empirical tests as well as clearer rationales presented in the empirical articles about how the mixed methods procedure actually added components to the study that might not have been present using only quantitative or qualitative research. We need to continue to provide evidence of the add-on value of mixed methods. This is more than simply conveying in our mixed methods studies the value of a particular study; it also includes stating how the use of mixed methods improves insights that might be obtained from either quantitative or qualitative approaches.

4. We need to continue to honor different philosophical stances in mixed methods and not pursue the single best philosophical position. We also need to recognize that philosophy will have no place in discussions in some fields because of the field's pragmatic thinking. We also need to recognize that theory often informs our research, whether it is a social, behavioral, or social justice theory. How it can inform both the quantitative and qualitative strands of a mixed methods study needs further exploration. With many studies now published in mixed methods that use theoretical orientations, we can carefully study their structure and better understand how to make explicit the theoretical orientation in the writing structure.

5. All writers in mixed methods do not recognize the centrality of design in thinking about the science of mixed methods. Out of recognizing a design comes many other features of procedures in mixed methods, from the wording of a title to the research questions to the writing structure of the report. When authors do not recognize this, their discussions of mixed methods become disjointed and do not relate to central features helpful in integrating all aspects of a design. Future discussions need to focus on the steps in conducting the designs, use databases to illustrate the procedures of designs, extend the discussion beyond the procedures and into validity and ethical issues, and continue to recognize the variants that exist within each of the six designs.

6. Challenges to using the designs—called here the scientific threats to validity—are not well understood by those engaging in MMR. It is safe to say that investigators are not clearly addressing them as potential limitations in empirical mixed methods studies. Understanding them requires knowing a design and being able to look into published empirical mixed methods articles to see what challenges emerged.

7. Mixed methods questions have not yet arrived in the mainstream mixed methods literature or thinking. Although investigators can easily determine what questions match quantitative approaches or qualitative approaches, their thinking has not been extended to mixed methods. So the first step is to recognize that a mixed methods question would be useful in a study and then to consider how to write them in a way that will be understandable to both content and method specialists.

8. Integration involves combining the quantitative and qualitative results. Joint displays have developed, but we need a categorization of types and how they relate to the different types of mixed methods designs. Armed with this knowledge, we can then begin to think about computer programs that will help us design the information that goes into these displays.

9. We do not have a good understanding of the architecture (Creswell, 2014c) of writing mixed methods empirical journal articles. This understanding, I believe, must proceed on relating the writing to the type of design and being able to write shorter mixed methods studies suitable especially for health science journals. Too few mixed methods authors have turned their attention to writing and publishing mixed methods studies.

10. Criteria for evaluating research is a topic always in flux and debatable. No one clearly owns the definitive criteria. However, it must be recognized that some fields require protocols and checklists of standards because they frequently use them or because they want to standardize a field of research. I believe that evaluation criteria is a given in our research communities, and we need some guidelines, especially for federal projects in the United States and abroad. Our discussion should proceed from whether we should have guidelines to what fields will require guidelines and what they should be.

The future holds more discussion about the science of mixed methods and new ways to make the field clearer and better understood. When I speak before an audience about mixed methods, I will bring in practical illustrations and tie these more closely to discrete scientific principles to have emerged in the last few years.

Discussion Questions

1. How would you define mixed methods research? What is essential to include in this definition?

2. Identify some of the advantages and disadvantages of thinking of mixed methods as a "scientific" field. How would this thinking relate to your particular specialization?

3. Define the following terms: exploratory sequential design, mixed methods question, joint display.

4. Should your field have standards of quality that are used to evaluate a mixed methods study? Advance pros and cons for the use of standards.

5. Are two methods better than one? Identify the value-added of two methods over a quantitative method or a qualitative method.

Suggested Websites

https://www.mmira.wildapricot.org/
Mixed Methods International Research Association. Contact for information about the association and how you can join.

https://www.facebook.com/MMIRA2014
Link for the International Mixed Methods Conference held at Boston College, June 27–29, 2014.

http://mmr.sagepub.com/
Website for the *Journal of Mixed Methods Research*, a journal dedicated to advancing interdisciplinary and international information on MMR.

http://obssr.od.nih.gov/scientific_areas/methodology/mixed_methods_research/section2.aspx
Main page for the Office of Behavioral and Social Science Research at the National Institutes of Health "best practices" recommendations for MMR in the health sciences.

http://www.methodspace.com/
Active online community for MMR and discussion.

References

Betancourt, T., Myers-Ohki, S. E., Stevenson, A., Ingabire, C., Kanyanganzi, F., Munyana, M., & Beardslee, W. R. (2011). Using mixed-methods research to adapt and evaluate a family strengthening intervention in Rwanda. *African Journal of Traumatic Stress, 2*(1), 32–45.

Bryman, A. (2006). Integrating quantitative and qualitative research: How is it done? *Qualitative Research, 6*(1), 97–113. doi:10.1177/1468794106058877

Campbell, D. T., & Fiske, D. W. (1959). Convergent and discriminant validation by the multitrait–multimethod matrix. *Psychological Bulletin, 56*, 81–105.

Campbell, D. T., & Stanley, J. C. (1966). Experimental and quasi-experimental designs for research. In N. L. Gage (Ed.), *Handbook of research on teaching* (pp. 1–76). Chicago, IL: Rand McNally.

Classen, S., Lopez, E. D. S., Winter, S., Awadzi, K. D., Ferree, N., & Garvan, C. W. (2007). Population-based health promotion perspective for older driver safety: Conceptual framework to intervention plan. *Clinical Interventions in Aging, 2*(4), 677–693.

Creswell, J. W. (2014a). *A concise introduction to mixed methods research.* Los Angeles, CA: Sage.

Creswell, J. W. (2014b). *Educational research: Planning, conducting, and evaluating quantitative and qualitative research* (5th ed.). Upper Saddle River, NJ: Pearson Education.

Creswell, J. W. (2014c). *Research design: Qualitative, quantitative, and mixed methods approaches.* Thousand Oaks, CA: Sage.

Creswell, J. W., Fetters, M. D., Plano Clark, V. L., & Morales, A. (2009). Mixed methods intervention trials. In S. Andrew & E. J. Halcomb (Eds.), *Mixed methods research for nursing and the health sciences* (pp. 161–180). Oxford, UK: Wiley.

Creswell, J. W., Klassen, A. C., Plano Clark, V. L., & Smith, K. C. (2011, August). *Best practices for mixed methods research in the health sciences.* Washington, DC: National Institutes of Health. Retrieved from http://obssr.od.nih.gov/mixed_methods_research

Creswell, J. W., & Plano Clark, V. L. (2011). *Designing and conducting mixed methods research* (2nd ed.). Thousand Oaks, CA: Sage.

Creswell, J. W., & Zhang, W. (2009). The application of mixed methods designs to trauma research. *Journal of Traumatic Stress, 22*(6), 612–621.

DeVellis, R. F. (2006). *Scale development: Theory and applications* (2nd ed.). Thousand Oaks, CA: Sage.

Fetters, M. D., Curry, L., & Creswell, J.W. (2014). Achieving integration in mixed methods designs—principles and practices. *Health Services Research, 48*(6 Pt 2), 2134–2156.

Farquhar, M. C., Ewing, G., & Booth, S. (2011). Using mixed methods to develop and evaluate complex interventions in palliative care research. *Palliative Medicine, 25*(8), 748–757. doi:10.1177/0269216311417919

Frechtling, J. (January, 2002). *The 2002 user friendly handbook for project evaluation.* Washington, DC: National Science Foundation. Retrieved from http://www.nsf.gov/pubs/2002/nsf02057/start.htm

Greysen, S. R., Allen, R., Lucas, G. I., Wang, E. A., & Rosenthal, M. S. (2012). Understanding transitions in care from hospital to homeless shelter: A mixed-methods, community-based participatory approach. *Journal of General Internal Medicine, 27*(11), 1484–1491. doi:10.1007/s11606-012-2117-2

Greene, J. C. (2007). *Mixed methods in social inquiry.* San Francisco, CA: Jossey-Bass.

Haines, C. (2010). *Value added by mixed methods research.* (Unpublished doctoral dissertation). University of Nebraska–Lincoln.

Hodgkin, S. (2008). Telling it all: A story of women's social capital using a mixed methods approach. *Journal of Mixed Methods Research, 2*(4), 296–316. doi:10.1177/1558689808321641

Howe, K. R. (2004). A critique of experimentalism. *Qualitative Inquiry, 10*(1), 42–61. doi:10.1177/107780040325949.

Ioannidis, J. P. A., Evans, S. J. W., Getzsche, P. C., O'Neill, R. T., Altman, D. G, Schulz, K., & Moher, D. (2004). Better reporting of harms in randomized trials: An Extension of the CONSORT statement. *Annals of Internal Medicine, 141*, 781–788.

Ivankova, N. V., & Kawamura, Y. (2010). Emerging trends in the utilization of integrated designs in the social, behavioral and health sciences. In A. Tashakkori & C. Teddlie (Eds.), *SAGE handbook of mixed methods in social & behavioral research* (2nd ed., pp. 581–611). Thousand Oaks, CA: Sage.

Ivankova, N. V., & Stick, S. L. (2006). Students' persistence in a distributed doctoral program in educational leadership in higher education: A mixed methods study. *Research in Higher Education, 48*(1), 93–135. doi:10.1007/s11162-006-9025-4

Jacob, E. (1987). Qualitative research traditions: A review. *Review of Educational Research, 57*, 1–50.

Johnson, R. B. (2012). Dialectical pluralism and mixed methods. *American Behavioral Scientist, 56*(6), 751–754.

Johnson, R. B., Onwuegbuzie, A. J., & Turner, L. A. (2007). Toward a definition of mixed methods research. *Journal of Mixed Methods Research 1*(2), 112–133.

Krippendorff, K. H. (2012). *Content analysis: Introduction to its methodology* (3rd ed.). Thousand Oaks, CA: Sage.

Li, S., Marquart, J. M., & Zercher, C. (2000). Conceptual issues and analytic strategies in mixed-method studies of preschool inclusion. *Journal of Early Intervention, 23*(2), 116–132. doi:10.1177/105381510002300206.

Maxwell, J. A. (2012). *A realist approach for qualitative research.* Los Angeles, CA: Sage.

Mertens, D. M. (2003). Mixed methods and the politics of human research: The transformative emancipatory perspective. In A. Tashakkori & C. Teddlie (Eds.), *Handbook of mixed methods in social & behavioral research* (pp. 135–164). Thousand Oaks, CA: Sage.

Mertens, D. M. (2009). *Transformative research and evaluation.* New York, NY: Guilford Press.

Morgan, D. L. (1998). Practical strategies for combining qualitative and quantitative methods: Applications to health research. *Qualitative Health Research, 8*(3), 362–376. doi:10.1177/104973239800800307

Morse, J. M. (1991). Approaches to qualitative–quantitative methodological triangulation. *Nursing Research, 40*(2), 120–123.

Morse, J. M., & Niehaus, L. (2009). *Mixed methods design: Principles and procedures.* Walnut Creek, CA: Left Coast Press.

Nastasi, B. K., Hitchcock, J., Sarkar, S., Burkholder, G., Varjas, K., & Jayasena, A. (2007). Mixed methods in intervention research: Theory to adaptation. *Journal of Mixed Methods Research, 1*(2), 164–182. doi:10.1177/1558689806298181.

O'Cathain, A., Murphy, E., & Nicholl, J. (2008). The quality of mixed methods studies in health services research. *Journal of Health Services Research Policy, 13*(2), 92–98.

Onwuegbuzie, A. J. (2012). Putting the MIXED back into quantitative and qualitative research in educational research and beyond: Moving toward the radical middle. *International Journal of Multiple Research Approaches, 6*(3), 192–219.

Onwuegbuzie, A. J., & Johnson, R. B. (2006). The validity issue in mixed research. *Research in the Schools, 13*(1), 48–63.

Petros, S. G. (2011). Use of a mixed methods approach to investigate the support needs of older caregivers to family members affected by HIV and AIDS in South Africa. *Journal of Mixed Methods Research, 6*(4), 275–293. doi:10.1177/1558689811425915

Plano Clark, V. L. (2010). The adoption and practice of mixed methods: U.S. trends in federally funded health-related research. *Qualitative Inquiry, 16*(6), 428–440. doi:10.1177/1077800410364609

Plano Clark, V. L., Garrett, A. L., & Leslie-Pelecky, D. L. (2009). Applying three strategies for integrating quantitative and qualitative databases in a mixed methods study of a nontraditional graduate education program. *Field Methods, 22*, 154–174.

Püschel, K., Coronado, G., Soto, G., Gonzalez, K., Martinez, J., Holte, S., & Thompson, B. (2010). Strategies for increasing mammography screening in primary care in Chile: Results of a randomized clinical trial. *Cancer Epidemiology, Biomarkers & Prevention, 19*(9), 2254–2261. doi:10.1158/1055-9965.EPI-10-0313

Püschel, K., & Thompson, B. (2011). Mammogram screening in Chile: Using mixed methods to implement health policy planning at the primary care level. *Breast, 20*(Suppl 2), S40–S45. doi:10.1016/j.breast.2011.02.002

Püschel, K., Thompson, B., Coronado, G., Gonzalez, K., Rain, C., & Rivera, S. (2010). "If I feel something wrong, then I will get a mammogram": Understanding barriers and facilitators for mammography screening among Chilean women. *Family Practice, 27*(1), 85–92. doi:10.1093/fampra/cmp080

Raudenbush, S. W., & Bryk, A. S. (2002). *Hierarchical linear models: Applications and data analysis methods* (2nd ed.). Thousand Oaks, CA: Sage.

Reichardt, C. S., & Rallis, S. F. (1994). *The qualitative–quantitative debate: New perspectives.* New Directions for Program Evaluation 61. San Francisco, CA: Jossey-Bass.

Stange, K. C., Crabtree, B. F., & Miller, W. L. (2006). Publishing multimethod research. *Annals of Family Medicine, 4*, 292–294.

Stewart, M., Makwarimba, E., Barnfather, A., Letourneau, N., & Neufeld, A. (2008). Researching reducing health disparities: Mixed-methods approaches. *Social Science & Medicine, 66*(6), 1406–1417. doi:10.1016/j.socscimed.2007.11.02

Sweetman, D., Badiee, M., & Creswell, J. W. (2010). Use of the transformative framework in mixed methods studies. *Qualitative Inquiry, 16*(6), 441–454. doi:10.1177/1077800410364610

Tashakkori, A., & Creswell, J. W. (2007). Exploring the nature of research questions in mixed methods research [Editorial]. *Journal of Mixed Methods Research, 1*(3), 207–211. doi:10.1177/1558689807302814

Tashakkori, A., & Teddlie, C. (1998). *Mixed methodology: Combining qualitative and quantitative approaches.* Thousand Oaks, CA: Sage.

Tashakkori, A., & Teddlie, C. (Eds.). (2003). *Handbook of mixed methods in social & behavioral research.* Thousand Oaks, CA: Sage.

Teddlie, C., & Tashakkori, A. (2009). *Foundations of mixed methods research: Integrating quantitative and qualitative approaches in the social and behavioral sciences.* Thousand Oaks, CA: Sage.

Tashakkori, A., & Teddlie, C. (Eds.) (2010). *SAGE handbook of mixed methods in social & behavioral research* (2nd ed.). Thousand Oaks, CA: Sage.

Wheeldon, J. P., & Ahlberg, M. K. (2012). *Visualizing social science research: Maps, methods, & meaning.* Thousand Oaks, CA: Sage.

Feminist Approaches to Multimethod and Mixed Methods Research: Theory and Praxis

Sharlene Hesse-Biber *and* Amy J. Griffin

Abstract

This chapter illuminates the evolution of feminist perspectives across the past several decades. We discuss the definition of feminist research and introduce the specific goals of feminist praxis, including how feminist researchers aim to unearth subjugated knowledge and empower underprivileged groups. We examine how feminist researchers employ multimethod and mixed methods research designs to address complex research questions that foster and develop a nuanced understanding of the diversity of lived experiences. The chapter provides in-depth case studies from a range of feminist perspectives that use multimethod and mixed methods feminist research designs.

Key Words: feminist theory, feminist research, subjugated knowledge, lived experience, mixed methods, multimethods, reflexivity, intersectionality

Introduction

Thus humanity is male and man defines woman not in herself but as relative to him; she is not regarded as an autonomous being.... For him she is sex—absolute sex, no less. She is defined and differentiated with reference to man and not he with reference to her; she is the incidental, the inessential as opposed to the essential. He is the Subject, he is the Absolute—she is the other.

—*de Beauvoir, 1953, pp. xviii, xxiii*

Women [were] largely excluded from the work of producing the forms of thought and the images and symbols in which thought is expressed and ordered.... The circle of men whose writing and talk was significant to each other extends backwards in time as far as our records reach. What men were doing was relevant to men, was written by men about men for men. Men listened to what one another said.

—*Smith, 1978, p. 281*

We begin with voices, visions, and experiences of feminist activists and scholars speaking to us across the decades starting from the mid-20th century. There lies within these voices, a feminist consciousness that opens up intellectual and emotional space for all women to articulate their relations to one another and the wider society—spaces where the personal transforms into the political. Feminist researcher and sociologist Dorothy Smith expresses women's deep feelings of exclusion from the dominant avenues of knowledge-building, seeing their own experiences, concerns, and worth diminished and invalidated by the dominant powers of their society. Feminist perspectives also carry messages of empowerment that challenge the encircling of knowledge claims by those who occupy privileged positions. Feminist thinking and practice requires taking steps from the "margins to the center" while eliminating boundaries that privilege dominant forms of knowledge-building, boundaries that mark who can be a knower and what can be known. For Simone de Beauvoir, it is the line between the "inessential" and the "essential"; for Dorothy

Smith, it is the path that encircles dominant knowledge, where women's lived experiences lie outside its circumference or huddled at the margins.

What Is Feminist Research?

Feminist perspectives are multiple and varied and draw on the insights and struggles articulated in these diverse historical quotes. Feminist empiricism, standpoint theories, postmodernism, and transnational feminist perspectives all recognize the importance of women's lived experiences to the goal of unearthing subjugated knowledge. Each of these feminist perspectives forges links between feminism and social activism (Hesse-Biber, Leavy, & Yaiser, 2004). Feminist perspectives also carry messages of empowerment that challenge the encircling of knowledge claims by those who occupy privileged positions.

To engage in feminist research means to challenge knowledge that excludes while seeing to include—assuming that what is true for dominant groups must also be true for women and other oppressed groups. Feminists ask "new" questions that place women's lives and those of "other" marginalized groups at the center of social inquiry. Feminist research *disrupts* traditional ways of knowing to create rich new meanings, a process the Trinh Minh-ha (1991) terms becoming "both/and"—insider and outsider—taking on a multitude of different standpoints and negotiating these identities simultaneously.

> Feminist praxis refers to the varied ways feminist research proceeds. A feminist praxis approach privileges listening to the experiences of the other(s) as legitimate knowledge. Feminist praxis is mindful of hierarchies of power and authority in the research process that are so well voiced by Linda Tuhiwai Smith (2005), including those power differentials that lie within research practices that can reinforce the status quo, creating divisions between colonizer and colonized.

This chapter aims to illuminate how feminist researchers use multimethod and mixed methods in the service of understanding the often hidden knowledge of the diversity of women's experiences and concerns. Feminist research inquiry centers women's experiences, mindful of the diversity of women's lives that are intersected by differences across race, class, ethnicity, and so on. Feminist research aims to promote social change and social justice for women and other underprivileged groups, such that the knowledge-building that is produced from any given feminist research project also has the goal of enabling women to "understand and change their situations" (Lather, 1991, p. 226).

Feminist Approaches Challenge Male Bias in the Research Process

Historically, most research on women took the form of an "add women and stir" model (Sapiro, 1995) that gave little credence to the uniqueness of the range of women's experiences or voices. Findings were based mainly on male research participants and were then generalized to both men and women. In the 1960s through the 1980s, feminist scholars and researchers called attention to examples of such male bias within the sciences and social sciences. These feminist scholars and researchers, known as *feminist empiricists* (Hundleby, 2012; Naples & Gurr, 2014), embarked on projects to "correct" these biases by adding women into research samples and asking new questions that enabled women's experiences and perspectives to gain a hearing (Chafetz, 1990; Campbell, 1994).

Margrit Eichler and Jeanne Lapointe's (1985) research primer, *On the Treatment of Sexes in Research*, provides a critique of empirical research as well as a checklist for inclusion of gender as a category of analysis in social research. Their work provides many important nuggets of advice concerning what *not* to do (p. 9). Some of these include

- Not treating Western sex roles as universal
- Not transforming statistical differences into innate differences
- Not translating differences as inferiority

Feminist empiricist researchers did much to "deconstruct" what they perceived as errors across a range of academic disciplines and professional fields. Feminist empiricists' insights into male bias and their goals of eradicating sexist research cascaded across the disciplines of psychology, philosophy, history and sociology, education, anthropology, and the fields of law, medicine, language, and communications. The 1970s and 1980s saw the publication of many different path-breaking anthologies critical of androcentric research. In 1975, Marcia Millman and Rosabeth Moss Kanter coedited the volume *Another Voice: Feminist Perspectives on Social Life and Social Science*. In their editorial introduction, they compare traditional knowledge-building with the story of the "The Emperor's New Clothes." They note,

> Everyone knows the story about the Emperor and his fine clothes; although the townspeople persuaded themselves that the Emperor was elegantly costumed, a child, possessing an unspoiled vision, showed the citizenry that the Emperor was

really naked. . . . The story also reminds us that collective delusions can be undone by introducing fresh perspectives. (p. vii)

Sociologists Millman and Kanter (1975) criticized the androcentric bias of sociology by noting how sociology uses certain "field-defining models" that prevent the asking of new questions. Many anthologies quickly followed, including Sandra Harding's (1987) *Feminism and Methodology*. In the preface to this volume, Harding raises a central issue, namely, "Is there a distinctive feminist method of inquiry?" She suggests that at the heart of feminist inquiry are the emergent questions and issues that feminists raise about the social reality and the practices of traditional research, and this becomes evident as we look inside Harding's edited volume. In doing so, we find feminist research that seeks, for example, to interrogate the relationship between gender and the social sciences. To name just a few of the contributions to this volume, Bonnie Thornton Dill's (1987) article in this volume points to the tendency of researchers, including some feminist researchers, to generalize women's social situation, leaving out differences of race, class, and cultural context. She uses the example of "femininity" and explains how the concept has been dominated by images of white middle- and upper middle class conceptions of womanhood. She provides alternative frameworks for analyzing the concept by taking women's race, class, and cultural context-bound differences into account. Joan Kelly-Gadol (1987) provides a critique of the androcentrism of historical method. Kelly-Gadol focuses on historians' use of field-defining concepts such as "periodization," a particular set of events historians chose to focus on (usually those activities men were engaged in, such as diplomatic and constitutional history, as well as political, economic, and cultural history). She troubles the concept of periodization by including gender as a category of analysis that opens the possibility of asking new questions: Was the period of *Renaissance* beneficial for women? While the Renaissance brought dramatic changes in social and cultural life that benefited many men, a growing division between the private and the public life meant that most women, even those of the upper class, experienced increasing segregation from men and a loss of power and freedom in the public sphere. Kelly-Gadol's vision of including women in history changes the fundamental way historians visualize historical periods.

In addition, our understanding of social change also shifts when we conceive of women as agents of historical change.

Feminist empiricists set out with the goal of eliminating sexist research through better defining samples, using measures that are not sexist or biased, and finally giving a voice to women (Morawski, 1994). The feminist perspective framework is fluid and ever changing to incorporate a range of new perspectives and a move toward inclusion of diverse women's lives transnationally (Naples & Desai, 2002; Mohanty, 2003; Swarr & Nagar, 2010).

Movement to Feminist Standpoint Perspectives on Knowledge Building

Feminist theorist Nancy Hartstock (1987) argued that because of women's location within the sexual division of labor and because of their experience of oppression, women would have greater insights as researchers into the lives of other women. Members of the dominant group, on the other hand, were thought to have only a partial viewpoint based on their privileged position. Standpoint is thus an achievement that is earned. (Hesse-Biber & Yaiser, 2004). Dorothy Smith (1987) was an early pioneer of a women's standpoint approach. She asserts that a way of knowing must start from women's lives, and she stresses the importance of women's own knowledge and experience in creating knowledge (p. 107).

Donna Haraway (1988) introduced the concept of "situated knowledge," whereby knowledge is thought to be "achieved" by acknowledging the specificity and unique aspects of women's experiences and not by denying the existence of values, biases, and politics in academia and research. Dorothy Smith first explored this theory by taking into account women's everyday experiences, especially by finding and analyzing the gaps that occur when women try to fit their lives into the dominant culture's way of conceptualizing women's situations. This way, the researcher is able to better understand the relationship between the oppressor and the oppressed.

Other feminists criticized early feminist standpoint theorists and feminist empiricists for promoting the universality of gendered experience and emphasized issues of difference, such as issues of race, class, ethnicity, and sexual preference (Collins, 1990). Black sociologist Patricia Hill Collins stressed the importance of black feminist thought: "the ideas produced by black women that clarify a standpoint of and for Black women" (p. 37). By listening to the experiences of the "other," one obtains a more complete understanding of knowledge. Black women have had to follow the rules of White privilege in order navigate their social world but at the same time need to be aware of their marginalized position in terms of their race and gender. Collins conceptualizes race, class, and gender as "interlocking systems of oppression" (see also Dill, 1983; King, 1988). Feminist scholars and researchers continue to engage issues of difference across gender, ethnicity, and class. As Bonnie Thornton Dill (1987) reminds us, "Our analysis must include critical accounts of women's situation in every race, class, and culture—we must work to provide resources so that every woman can define problematics, generate concepts and theories" (Dill, 1987, p. 97).

In the first decade of the 21st century, feminists are further expanding their focus on difference to include issues of sexual preference and disability, as well as nationality and geographical region. There is a growing awareness among feminist researchers of the importance of women's experiences in a global context with respect to issues of imperialism, colonialism, and national identity (Bhavnani, 2012; Dill & Kohlman, 2012). Historian Deniz Kandiyoti (1999) discusses the tendency of some Western feminist researchers to "universalize" disciplinary concepts, ignoring the ethnocentrism that lies deep within constructs such as patriarchy. Frequently, analyses that incorporate race, class, and gender differences ignore the diversity among women with regard to their particular geographical/cultural placement across the globe.

In order to combat this, global critical race feminists are working from a feminist perspective that centers difference by drawing on postmodern conceptualizations of power and knowledge in a global and increasingly interconnected context. Adrien Wing (1997) explains that feminists working in this new tradition must account for the context of global postmodern forms of power when considering the nature and impact of intersectionality, which is the standpoint created based on a combination of locations within the social structure (i.e., race, class, gender, sexuality, geography, etc.). Chela Sandoval (2000) urges feminists to become more reflexive in how they carry out their research projects and urges them to privilege projects whose goal is emancipation—especially those individuals who remain marginalized

by neo-colonial global societies. The goal is to decolonize old emergent structures of domination and subjugation. Postcolonial feminist Spivak (1994) notes

> On the other side of the international division of labor, the subject of exploitation cannot know and speak the text of female exploitation even if the absurdity of the nonrepresenting intellectual making space for them to speak is achieved. The woman is doubly in shadow. (p. 894)

What Are Feminist Approaches to Multimethod and Mixed Methods Praxis?

Feminist researchers employ a range of methods to answer their research questions. They use both qualitative data collection methods, such as interviews, and quantitative data collection methods, such as surveys. Feminist researchers' reasons for mixing methods is tightly linked to their research question or set of questions. Some feminists might choose mixed methods for the same reasons that nonfeminist researchers do. While qualitative methods and the use of multiple qualitative methods are an important part of feminist research praxis, mixed methods (qualitative and quantitative) research designs lend themselves to the following feminist research goals:

- Exploring women's subjugated knowledge by giving voice to women's experiences, in particular knowledge ignored by traditional research approaches that leave out gender as a category of inquiry.
- Exploring multiple understandings of the nature of social reality, as this particularly pertains to women's issues and standpoints.
- Studying across differences in terms of race, class, gender, and so on.
- Fostering social justice and social change on behalf of women and other oppressed groups.

There are often multiple objectives contained within any given feminist research project, and, as we shall see, feminists use a variety of mixed methods designs. This chapter explores how feminist researchers tackle some of the major dimensions of feminist research and specifically how mixed methods can serve to further feminist research problems and perspectives.

Multimethod and mixed methods are not inherently housed in any one theoretical tradition, such as feminism; instead, they are a set of techniques by which researchers are able to approach specific research questions. While qualitative methods have been more associated with feminist research than quantitative methods, there is ongoing discussion about the advantages and disadvantages of different methods within the feminist community (Roberts, 1981; Bowles & Duelli, & Klein, 1983). Some feminists believe that qualitative methods are generally "better" and "more feminist" than quantitative approaches because they see quantitative methods as methods that have been used to reinforce the "status quo" (Miner & Jayaratne, 2014, p. 300). From this perspective, quantitative methods are limited because they are patriarchal tools that undermine social change and the goals of feminist research (Reinharz, 1985); in the words of Black feminist scholar Audre Lorde (1984), "the master's tools will never dismantle the master's house" (p. 13). However, many feminist researchers view the combination of qualitative and quantitative methods as a productive way of conducting research; they understand that quantitative methods can be an important supplement, and, when practiced well, they have the ability to "dismantle the master's house."

Mixed methods research (MMR) provides the potential for deepening our knowledge around a particular topic. By conducting MMR, a researcher may be able to more efficiently pare out subjugated knowledge that one method may miss if conducted alone (Reinharz, 1992). The ability of quantitative methods and qualitative methods to uncover different types of knowledge may allow for an increased understanding of phenomena for subjugated populations for feminist researchers. The qualitative approach in particular may allow for validation of quantitative findings that may have typically excluded certain groups or testing theories through the lived experiences of the historically voiceless populations. MMR allows for the potential of new ways of forming knowledge and new ways of changing the way research is conducted.

Letting the research questions guide the process is important in any multimethod and mixed methods research project. The feminist praxis of MMMR takes into account the issue of power differentials (e.g., Hesse-Biber, 2007; Hesse-Biber, 2010), authority, ethics, issues of difference (e.g., Hesse-Biber & Leavy, 2006), and reflexivity throughout the entire process (DeVault, 1990; Reinharz, 1992). Being reflexive helps one to remain objective and is a central tenet to feminist research. A researcher must be able to self-reflect on

biases, social background, location, and assumptions in order "maximize" what Sandra Harding (1993) calls "strong objectivity" and earlier called "feminist objectivity" by Donna Haraway (1988) in order to assess and decipher how these social locations may play a role in the research process (Harding, 1993; Hesse-Biber & Piatelli, 2007). When researchers practice reflexivity, it also allows them to reflect on how their research agenda may affect all points in the research process, whether it is designing the model, selecting the participants, or interpreting the findings (Hesse-Biber & Piatelli, 2007). Through remaining reflexive and continuing to sharpen those skills, researchers will be conscious of themselves and their agenda through all aspects of their research projects.

The Praxis of Feminist Approaches to Multimethod and Mixed Methods Research

Mixed methods research designs can provide feminists with an important set of knowledge-excavation tools. Yet not all MMR that purports to study women's lives is feminist in its purpose, spirit, or design. We now move to explore how MMMR designs can serve to further feminist research perspectives and research goals. We present a series of case studies that exemplify how feminist researchers might harness the synergy contained in the promise of MMMR. These case studies are not exhaustive of the many other ways mixed methods can be successfully harnessed by feminist researchers. They do, however, illustrate how mixed methods can enhance the major principles of feminist research praxis and goals.

As you approach each of these case studies, there are several sensitizing questions you might apply to each, namely:

• What particular research problems do feminist researchers tackle using a mixed methods design?
• What specific MMMR designs are deployed by feminists and why?
• At what stage(s) in the process of a research project do feminists mix methods (e.g., data collection, data analysis, data interpretation)? What are the specific advantages and disadvantages of using a mixed methods approach?
• What makes the research case an example of a feminist approach to mixed methods?

Case Study Examples

Case Study 1: Using Triangulation to Assess the Validity of Social Science Measures: Understanding Girls' Attitudes toward Science

Buck, Cook, Quigley, Eastwood, and Lucas (2009) studied the attitudes toward science of African American girls of low socioeconomic status (SES) in urban areas. Applying what they term a "critical feminist perspective," they sought to challenge early cultural feminist ideas that tended to essentialize the category of woman by centering the concerns of "girls from non-White middle class populations" (p. 388). Their aim was to explore differences among women with regard to gender and its intersection with race and class. They were particularly interested in the within-group differences among low-SES African American girls in terms of their attitudes toward science and the experiences that shape those attitudes. By attending to difference in their research project, the authors were in a position to get at subjugated knowledge about a particular race, class, and gender group's lived experiences.

The authors employed a sequential explanatory mixed methods design to study a sample of African American girls in the fourth, fifth, and sixth grades at one all-girls elementary academy. The goal of using multimethod and mixed methods, data sources, and theoretical approaches was in the service of triangulating (converging) their results in order increase the overall validity (truthfulness) of their measures and overall findings. This use of the term *triangulation* is closer to its early mathematical definition. The practice of triangulation is used by surveyors in order to locate an object in space by relying on the position of two known objects to extrapolate a third unknown object. Social scientists used this mathematical concept to pursue the construct validity of psychometric attitudinal measures. They did this by using multiple data sources to hone in on a more "truthful" measurement process (Campbell & Fiske, 1959).

Buck et al. (2009) note the following concerning their more mathematical use of triangulation:

> Our study was triangulated through the use of multiple methods, data sources, and theoretical schemes. The use of different methodological approaches was obvious by the inclusion of both quantitative and qualitative approaches. In addition, we used multiple data sources through the use of numerous group interviews and a survey instrument. The individual perspectives of the research team members further strengthened our study by assuring that different theoretical constructs came together throughout the study. (p. 394)

Their first mixed methods component consisted of a survey given to a sample of 86 girls that contained a modified Attitudes Toward Science Inventory (mATSI) that was "designed to measure fifth-grade African American girls' and boys' attitudes toward science" (p. 392). The analysis of the quantitative data from the survey data revealed four profiles of girls' attitudes toward science using the mATSI-scaled items. The subsequent qualitative component consisted of a purposive sample of 30 girls across the fourth, fifth, and sixth grades at the same school, who comprised eight focus groups consisting of three to four girls each. The focus groups were asked both open and semistructured questions, some of which were based on the results of their quantitative profile findings. A primary goal of the focus groups were to experientially ground the quantitative profile categories. Their research design is depicted in Figure 5.1.

The overall goal of employing a sequential mixed methods explanatory design was "to use qualitative results to assist in explaining and interpreting quantitative findings" (p. 392). More specifically, the researchers utilized the findings from the focus group data to accomplish the goal of validating the four science profiles they extracted from the quantitative scores provided by the mATSI data in their quantitative component.

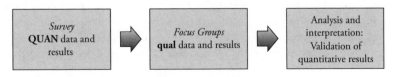

Fig. 5.1 Buck et al.'s (2009) sequential explanatory mixed methods design.

In what sense do the researchers integrate their qualitative and quantitative components? During the analysis and interpretation stage of their study, whose goal is validation of the quantitative findings, there appears to be little dialectical analysis and interpretation between the two data sets, especially with regard to interrogating the veracity of their quantitative profile findings. Instead, the analysis and interpretation consist of using their qualitative findings to bring a more contextual understanding of their quantitative profiles, using the girls' everyday experiences with science to provide a richer social context for understanding the meaning of the four quantitative science profiles.

The authors' use of a mixed methods explanatory approach with the goal of triangulation as a validation tool is an important development from the early feminist empiricist researchers who, while maintaining a positivistic framework, sought to advocate for the inclusion of women and upend the bias they perceived to be contained within social science research tools and measurements and make these measures more objective and truthful. In addition, the authors tie their research findings to the promotion of social change, noting, "these typologies enabled us to offer specific recommendations to educators to help navigate the complexity of individuals with whom they work in the science classroom" (p. 408). They advocate for changing the structure of the science classroom learning environment so that it reflects the importance of including the voices of minority girls' experiences in how social science is conducted and suggest a more problem-based learning approach to be incorporated into the science curriculum.

At this important *design decision point* in their project, positioning their mixed methods design as a *sequential explanatory mixed methods design* could have in fact limited the ability of the researchers to excavate new knowledge concerning girls' attitudes toward science beyond the four profile categories they extracted from their mATSI scale. Because the research began with a specific agenda—a survey using the mATSI—the girls entered the project not as knowers in their own right but as voices whose goal and purpose was determined a priori (the agenda was determined by the researchers) to validate a set of quantitative profiles.

The crucial question then, and one that a feminist lens might apply in assessing this study's findings, is whether or not their mixed methods study design adequately gave voice to young African American girls' attitudes, problems, and hopes as they expressed them in the focus groups. While the authors extracted qualitative themes from their data and quoted the voices of the girls speaking about what it means for them to be an African American female and their experiences with science, their stories were not placed in conversation with the quantitative component but instead were used to enhance and validate findings from their quantitative study. The goal of these voices is to buttress a pre-existing measure, not necessarily to listen to them with the goal of understanding their lived experiences. By employing a sequential explanatory mixed methods design, Buck and colleagues (2009) lost degrees of freedom that would have allowed them to reflect more deeply on the meaning of their qualitative results, outside of validating the quantitative.

They also missed an opportunity for more directly engaging in a dialectic between the survey profile findings and the qualitative themes contained in their data. By starting out with the preexisting mATSI instrument and stirring in difference, the authors failed to harness the strength of a qualitative approach in the service of excavating new knowledge beyond validation. For example: What new questions do their qualitative interviews raise that are not being addressed by the profiles? What is left out of the profiles? What is problematic about them? In fact, the authors a priori decided to keep one of the scale's measures that dealt with "perception of the teacher" from the analysis because, as they note, "we were interested in the girls' general perceptions of science, rather than their views of their teacher" (p. 393). Yet it is not clear why their teachers do not also impact students' general perceptions of science. Leaving out a dimension of a scale that has already been modified seems problematic and in fact may compromise the integrity of the original scaling procedure. This issue is especially important to consider when the entire qualitative component of their study was intended to validate the quantitative data.

Case Study 2: Using Triangulation to Explore Black and Minority Women Students' Science Classroom Experiences

The review of literature on women's experience in science by Osborne, Simon, and Collins (2003) notes that the lack of clarity in much of the research and suggest that the measures surrounding girls' and women's attitudes toward science are "bedeviled by a lack of clarity" (p. 1053). We saw that Buck et al. (2009) utilized a mixed methods sequential explanatory design that sought to get at subjugated knowledge behind a widely used scale on minority women's attitudes toward science, considering race in the context of class and gender. Yet, as we noted, there were downsides to using triangulation as a tool for validation when working within a research landscape that contains a great deal of subjugated knowledge already. Researchers may need to deploy triangulation as an excavation tool when dealing with this type of terrain, which would allow them to go beyond the narrow use of validation (Denzin, 1970).

Angela Johnson (2007) employed "methodological triangulation" with a sequential exploratory multimethod design in order to explore Black and minority women's experiences with science. Johnson started out her research project by conducting 16 intensive interviews with Black, Latina, and American Indian female science students recruited from a science enrichment program at a large predominately White university. The interviews focused on female students' choice of science as a major, their experiences in learning science, especially their classroom experiences, and how (if at all) their ethnicity might have impacted their feelings about science. To increase the validity of her study, Johnson employed "member checks" at different points throughout her research process, which consisted of asking her female participants for feedback on their interview transcript as well as the analysis of the data she had collected.

The second part of her study was an ethnographic participant observation of eight science classes (including laboratory classes) that her interviewees were enrolled in. She studied their individual in-classroom behaviors as well as the overall interaction within the classroom setting. She paid "particular attention to the institutional practices and recurrent personal interactions in common across the settings" (Johnson, 2007, p. 809). Figure 5.2 depicts the stages of her research design.

Johnson (2007) begins her article by talking about her own researcher standpoint as a White female and the specific attitudes and values she brings to her research project, which influence her point of view on the problem she is investigating. Being cognizant of one's research standpoint is an important characteristic of a feminist approach to research that includes attention to axiological practice. Axiology refers to an awareness of our values, attitudes, and biases and acknowledging how they might play a role in how we conduct our research in terms of (a) what questions are asked or not asked in our research; (b) what type of data is or is not collected; and (c) the type of methods, measurement, analysis, and interpretation shape our understanding of the research process. Johnson notes

> I was originally drawn to this study because of my rather unusual experiences as a physics instructor. I am a White woman but. . . I taught high school physics (including advanced placement physics) for 7 years in a school that was predominantly non-White; I then taught physics enrichment seminars in a university program for high-achieving students of color. Thus, for the past 20 years, I have been actively engaged in increasing the access of women of color to the sciences. (p. 808)

Given Johnson's firsthand experience in working with a diverse group of science students, she is cautious about any tendency she may harbor regarding her own observations about women's science experience as well as the culture of the science classroom environment. She questioned the usual explanations for women students' lack of participation in science based on their lack of interest and schooling. Instead

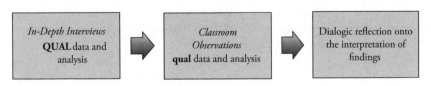

Fig. 5.2 Johnson's (2007) sequential exploratory multimethod design.

she examines other factors that appear more salient to her such as discrimination against women science students by professors and departments as a possible explanation.

We can see that one way in which Johnson (2007) dealt with issues of validity was not through triangulation in the mathematical sense of the term but rather through thinking about validity as increasing the trustworthiness of her data by practicing strong reflexivity. She is upfront with readers about her research biases and is conscious not to allow her initial attitudes and values to overshadow her research observations. In addition, as her research proceeded she brought in another validation tool: allowing participants to review the interview transcript and changing the transcript in response to their feedback.

Johnson (2007) did not utilize a narrow definition of triangulation or analyze the two data sets to confirm one another. Instead she analyzed both her qualitative data sets separately then placed them in conversation with each other by employing a dialectic triangulation approach that differs from Buck and colleagues' (2009) use of this term. Triangulation as used by Johnson is more of a "dialectical process" that enables the researcher to attain a more complex understanding of the research results by placing disparate findings in dialogue with one another. Johnson's dialectical dissonant analysis looked for the ways in which the findings for both methods components converged and diverged. This back-and-forth analysis and interpretation process brought her individual in-depth interviews into conversation with her classroom ethnographic observations that then allowed her to place young women's attitudes and experiences toward science in the wider context of the classroom environment. This allowed her to see how science practiced in the classroom setting often conflicts with young women's own values and attitudes expressed in interviews. In addition, the issues and concerns female students raised in the interviews—noting that while the girls were eager to enter into science, they expressed doubts about continuing with it—generated a new set of questions/hypotheses the author then pursued by using her ethnographic observations to reveal the wider structural barriers these young women face within the science classroom environment. Her study began to turn toward an identification of barriers minority women confront in the classroom that can upend their strong positive attitudes toward science.

Johnson's (2007) sequential multimethod study is in the tradition of *feminist standpoint theory* that starts off research from women's lives, in this case centering the voices of low-SES, minority science majors. Johnson was cognizant of how these female science students' experiences are connected to and shaped by the analytical intersections of their gender with their race and class backgrounds (see, e.g., Dill, 1987). Her goal was to gain an understanding of the complexity of women's experiences as science majors by using ethnographic observations of women's classroom experiences as the second component of her multimethod study. Johnson's research aimed to provide a structural understanding of the variety of roadblocks college science majors face that serve to impede their progression into the sciences by suggesting specific policy recommendations to educators that directly stem from her research finding, a cornerstone of feminist research. Her research explains the importance of supporting minority women's strong interest in the sciences in order to encourage future mobility in science-related careers

Case Study 3: Using Mixed Methods to Validate Scales Regarding Sexual Aggression

Past research suggests that rape often goes unreported (see, e.g., Koss, 1993, 1996; Fisher, Culen, & Turner, 2000), possibly because of the high degree of trauma, stigma and guilt rape victims often experience. Especially with regard to acquaintance rape, the offense of rape often hinges on the issue of consent and rape trials often come down to judgement, making it difficult for the victim to "prove" a rape took place. Additionally, quantitative questionnaires often use terms such as *rape* or *coercion*, terms that may not match the interpretation of what a woman believes happened to her. Thus there is a need to better understand the complexity rape itself and the experiences of rape victims in order to gain an accurate set of measurements to estimate the incidence and prevalence of rape in order to address ways to prevent sexual assaults and support and empower rape victims.

Testa, VanZile-Tamsen, Livingston, and Koss (2004) explored the ability of a measurement tool (the Sexual Experiences Survey) to accurately capture the experiences of sexual aggression among women. The Sexual Experiences Survey is an assessment tool used to measure women's experience of sexual assault. It is composed of 10 items that provide examples of sexually aggressive experiences as a way to spark recall for the respondent, yet it avoids terms such as *rape*, which, as noted, can be a stigmatizing term. The scale categorizes women into groupings of the sexual assault based on their responses, such as rape, attempted rape, verbally coerced intercourse, or sexual contact. The authors used a sequential explanatory mixed methods design in order to validate the sexual experiences survey using qualitative methods.

The first component of the study sampled women between the ages of 18 and 30 living in Buffalo, New York, and the immediate suburbs. Women completed computer-assisted self-interviews, which measured past sexual experience as well as aspects of the personality and drug and alcohol use. This technique was chosen because it is believed that the women would be more comfortable truthfully answering sensitive questions in private. Women who did not endorse any items on the Sexual Experiences Survey were asked, "Have you ever had an experience in which you were concerned that a man might be sexually aggressive toward you, or attempt to go further sexually than you were prepared to go, but for whatever reason no aggression occurred?" (Testa et al., 2004, p. 259). This question aimed to uncover any information that the Sexual Experiences Survey may not capture in regard to sexual aggressive incidents.

The authors invited the subsample of women who had had sexually aggressive experiences to participate in a follow-up in-depth, semistructured interview conducted by female interviewers. The semistructured interviews asked the women to describe their most recent sexual aggression incident, "when it occurred, her relationship to the perpetrator, the activities that preceded the incident, whether penetration had occurred, whether physical force or injury was involved, her responses or resistance to his actions, and the alcohol and drug use of the woman and the perpetrator at the time of the assault" (Testa et al., 2004, p. 259). At the conclusion of the semistructured interview, the respondents were asked to rate how traumatic the experience was for them on a 6-point Likert-type scale.

A subset of interview transcripts were then analyzed by three independent coders with no knowledge of which category the women were initially placed into. The transcripts from the interviews were subsequently given to independent observers to "endorse" whether the description of a women's experience, with regard to rape, also matched the interpretation of the coder as an incident of rape to validate the Sexual Experiences Survey items. The subset of women was selected based on the category they received on the survey (16 rape, 19 attempted rape, 21 coercions, 20 contact, and 61 "close call" incidents). The coders were allowed the freedom to code the incident as "a) not an incident of unwanted sex, b) an incident of unwanted sex but none of the items are adequate to describe it, or c) insufficient information to code" (Testa et al., 2004, p. 260) if they felt the survey categories did not capture the woman's experience (see Figure 5.3).

The results of the research suggest that of the 1,014 initial respondents, 37.8% (383) women endorsed at least one item on the Sexual Experiences Survey. Indicating that these women experienced some form of sexual victimization since 14 years of age. The type of incident that the women positively responded to on the Sexual Experiences Survey were independently confirmed by independent coders as a Sexual Experiences Survey category or some other type of unwanted sexual experience not captured on the scale. However, the results do suggest that the Sexual Experiences Survey may fail to capture what may actually be sexual aggression, resulting in false negatives. This interpretation is based off the 7% of women who responded negatively to all Sexual Experiences Survey item but answered to follow-up question that they feared they would be sexually assaulted, which coders believed represented contact or some other form of sexual aggression not represented on the Sexual Experiences Survey, representing "close-call" responses and a grey area of interpretation. Although there was accuracy by the coders in

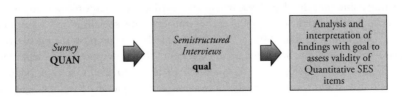

Fig. 5.3 Testa et al.'s (2004) sequential explanatory mixed methods design.

endorsing responses of rape and coercion, there was some discrepancy among coders when it came to "contact" and "attempted rape." The authors attribute the lack of agreement to the lack of probing during the interview or to the confusing wording on the Sexual Experiences Survey. The main reason is most likely from the subjective interpretation of the women on what "the line" is in terms of defining something as "attempted rape," a stronger allegation compared to "contact." A woman's response to positively endorsing the attempted rape question on the Sexual Experiences Survey "may depend on her perception of the perpetrator's intent, rather than the actual severity of the sex acts" (p. 263).

Although this article represents qualitative methods that are in service to the quantitative survey, the authors used feminist perspectives to explore whether the quantitative survey actually measures the traumatic sexual aggression experiences for women that are vastly underreported, through the validation techniques of qualitative interviews. This type of research is sorely needed, as all too often, we rely solely on scales to provide the only answer to a problem, but the sequential explanatory nature of this study allowed for such validation to occur. In making the "qual" in service to the "QUAN," the authors were able to develop a more thorough understanding of the nature of the scale and concepts that may be missing because they confirmed that the Sexual Experiences Survey completes its intended function as a "surveillance measure for sexual aggression," while the qualitative interviews provide deeper insight into further research that is needed on sexual aggression.

It appears, however, that the researchers missed an important opportunity to ground their qualitative interviews by listening more carefully to women's experiences. The researchers also comment on this issue by noting that their probing tactics needed to be better utilized, and the lack of probing leads one to question if the authors were really asking the "right" questions to this group of women. However, through giving the women a voice, the project aims to empower them and their stories in the hopes that they will not feel ashamed or have to hide their experience. This type of information would be useful in working with victims and aid in making assessments to accurately capture experiences of sexual aggression without placing a stigma on or re-traumatizing women.

Case Study 4: The Socialization of Gender Within Latino Families

Raffaelli and Ontai (2004) provide an example of the importance of moving toward culturally appropriate measures while capturing the voice of a typically invisible population. Their research deals with parenting and gender socialization among the Latino population. As the authors and other feminist researchers note, the majority of research on normative development has been based on European American samples (McDade, 1995; Ruble & Martin, 1998), and many times ethnicity is ignored during analysis (Lytton & Romney, 1991). Raffaelli and Ontai recognized this gap in the research and aimed to fill it through providing the voice of Latina women's experiences within a family unit and how they experienced parenting practices as a child. The research goals were as follows: "1) to examine parenting practices specifically linked to gender-related socialization; and 2) to identify factors linked to within-group differences in gender-related socialization" (p. 288).

The sample includes representatives from Mexican, Cuban, Puerto Rican, and other Central/South American families. Through prior research in the field, the authors worked off the premise that certain "Latino values" are recognized within empirical research: *familismo* (strong family relationships and the value of the feminine role of childbearing), *respeto* (respect and hierarchy within social relationship), and strong gender role divisions (men are dominant and independent whereas women are submissive, chaste, and dependent; Comas-Diaz, 1987; Flores, Eyre, & Millstein, 1998; Parke & Buriel, 1998). In using these values as a starting point, they developed research goals (noted earlier), while recognizing that these values may not capture all family socialization practices that impact gender socialization ("what it means to be a man or woman" (Raffaelli & Ontai, 2004, p. 288). In order to best accomplish their goals, the researchers conducted a two-phase study; the first was a small exploratory study composed of in-depth interviews, the findings of which led to the development of a quantitative survey provided to a larger population.

The first qualitative study was composed of a convenience sample of 22 women ages 20 to 45 years who grew up in Spanish-speaking households but lived in the United States for at least 8 years and were fluent in English, as interviews were conducted in English. The interviews were conducted using open-ended and structured questions that dealt with the themes and goals of the study: "sexual socialization within the family of origin; early romantic and sexual experiences; and sexuality-related beliefs, attitudes, and behaviors" (Raffaelli & Ontai, 2004, p. 289). At the beginning of each interview the authors expressed their goals and noted they hoped the participants would act as co-creators in this research, so they could ask the right questions and uncover subjugated knowledge, a key aspect of feminist praxis. In doing so, the authors treated the participants as co-researchers and "enlisted [them] as collaborators in making meaning of their experiences" (p. 289). This process also helped to break down the power dynamic between the researchers and the participants and empowered the participants.

The authors used a grounded theory approach to comb through the transcripts, allowing themes to emerge aside from the initial, empirically based hypothesis. The results from the retrospective interviews revealed differential treatment does exist between daughters and sons (even though men were not accounted for in the interviews).

The themes and codes that emerged from the qualitative component were used to create the structured measures in the quantitative survey in the second phase of this research. The authors then aimed to take the study a step further:

> because this was a small-scale exploratory study that included only women, it is impossible either to draw conclusions about how common these socialization patterns are or to examine correlates of different socialization patterns. Therefore, the qualitative findings were used to create structured measures of different aspects of family experiences that were included in a survey administered in a second study. (p. 291)

This sparked the start of the Study 2, the quantitative portion of this mixed methods study. This study recruited participants, 19 to 25 years of age, from four Midwestern universities. These enrolled students, men and women, self-identified at their respective university as Latino/Hispanic, resulting in a sample size of 166 participants. The decision to include men in the second part of the research was based on the authors' research goals to understand the socialization patterns and develop a better understanding of gender differences of children in Latino families. The scales in the quantitative portion resulted from the content analysis of the qualitative interviews; however, the parental gender roles attitudes scale was adapted from the established USCS Attitudes Toward Gender Scale (Leaper, 1993). The findings from Study 2 confirmed the findings from Study 1. This illustrates how the authors had the two portions of the study and methods "talk" to each other, as well as triangulating the results. The findings from Study 2 also provided more information to the researchers that was not initially gathered in Study 1, most likely a result of including men in the sample and having a larger sample size. By including men in the study, the difference between the experiences of sons and daughters was illuminated even further (see Figure 5.4).

This study allowed Raffaelli and Ontai (2004) to conduct a mixed methods analysis that takes the initial steps at breaking down the established empirical literature that uses European American families as normative in gender socialization patterns. In order to give voice to subjugated Latina women in this study, the authors asked the participants to be co-creators in the meaning-making by privileging their experiences. Through the qualitative portion of the study and collaboration with the participants, they were able to infuse difference into the survey questionnaire with regard to a larger population of Latinas. However, as always, this study is not without limitations. The authors recognize that the scales were developed solely from the experiences of women in the interviews, but men took the survey, so the items

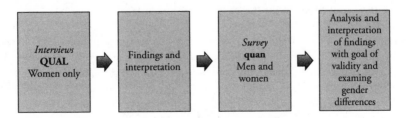

Fig. 5.4 Raffaelli and Ontai's (2004) sequential exploratory mixed methods design.

may not have encapsulated all experiences of both genders. Moving forward, it may also be useful to understand between-group differences. Do differences exist between Puerto Rican and Mexican families, South American and Central American families, and so on? Additionally, exploring how Latino parents actually define what it means to be a man or a woman may help to further illuminate these findings. The second phase of this study used Latino/a students at Midwestern universities. As such, future studies should explore those with a range of educational accomplishments, immigration status, and greater demographic representations (i.e., expanding outside the Midwest; urban vs. rural, etc.) in order to get at a representative sample of Latinos in this country. This knowledge is extremely important as the United States becomes increasingly heterogeneous, and researchers and practitioners need to be aware of the varying ways families interact and raise children, understanding different "norms."

The researchers missed several important opportunities within the qualitative portion of this research. The first was that their qualitative interviews may have been too structured in order to truly unearth subjugated knowledge. Although the researchers told the participants they wanted them to be co-participants in the research process, by providing all the open-ended and structured questions, they may have inadvertently established a power dynamic early on that may have impacted answers and the respondents comfort with "going off topic." The other main missed opportunity in the qualitative portion of the study was the use of professional transcription services by the authors. The process of transcription allows for researchers to become immersed in the data and begin to see themes emerge. The researchers did use research assistants to check the accuracy of the transcription, and it was during this process of (two independent coders) locating segments of the transcripts that dealt with focal domains of the research interests that emergent themes were also identified. Coders then compared notes and discussed possible discrepancies; however, how discrepancies were handled was not discussed.

Case Study 5: Sexual Education and Behaviors of Thai Teenagers

Vuttanont, Greenhalgh, Griffin, and Boynton's (2006) study of the sexual behavior of teenagers in Thailand illuminates a lack in research of how the rapid social and economic changes in Thailand is effecting the sexual behavior of teenagers. Currently in Thailand, teen pregnancy and sexually transmitted diseases are on the rise. However, traditions in Thai society call for girls to socialized as "docile, submissive, modest, and disinterested in sex until marriage" (p. 2069). These traditional sentiments are in conflict with the rapid Western modernization of Thailand and the desires of teenagers. In order to begin to understand these changing social norms, the authors aimed to understand the components and differences of sexual education at public schools, what teenagers know and understand about sex, and what parents, teachers, and policymakers value and think about this issue within a major province in Thailand.

In order to achieve this aim, the authors developed a sequential exploratory mixed methods design based in the largest province of Thailand (see Figure 5.5). The authors aimed for "maximum variation" (p. 2070) within selection the secondary schools, in terms of the socioeconomic make-up of pupils and "prevailing cultural norms, religion, religiosity, geographical location (urban or rural), and current approach to providing sex education" (p. 2070). The initial qualitative component of the mixed method study included a field study. This first component in their mixed methods design provided the researchers with an understanding of the current practices within Thailand. Preliminary field research to identify key stakeholders on

sexual health issues for teenagers in this province of Thailand included interviews with public health representatives, sex education policy makers, religious leaders, and teachers, regarding their work within sexual education. Additionally, national and local policy documents on sexual health and public health were analyzed. School resources on sex education and relationships as well as empirical literature on sexual health and sex education within Thailand were reviewed.

The next components in their mixed methods design included a survey followed by the inclusion of focus groups. The quantitative survey was a modification from surveys provided by the World Health Organization. The original instrument has

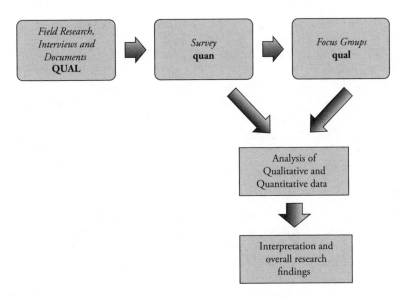

Fig. 5.5 Vuttanont et al.'s (2006) sequential exploratory mixed methods design.

the following aim: "This instrument is intended to be no more than a point of departure for investigators wishing to study the sexual and reproductive health of young people. It should always be adapted to local circumstances and priorities and, whenever possible, be used in conjunction with qualitative methods of investigation" (p. 2070).

The instrument was modified to a 73-item survey. Topics covered "knowledge of sexually transmitted infections (STIs), safer sex, condom use, awareness of sexual and reproductive health services, communicating about sex, and reproductive health knowledge" (p. 2070). Students (ages 12–21, N = 2301) had the option to complete the survey in a location of their choosing; most completed the instrument at school, but some students chose to complete the survey in private, such as home. Parents (N = 351) were asked to complete a 10-item survey that aimed to assess their sexual health knowledge, attitudes of teenagers and sexual behavior, and attitudes toward sex education. In contrast to the student survey, the researcher was present in the distribution and completion of the parent survey; however, participants sealed their responses in an envelope to preserve anonymity of responses.

The next component consisted of qualitative focus groups. Teachers were utilized to help identify students for focus groups that matched certain criteria such as "risk takers," "studious," or "sporty" for instance, additionally boys and girls were also separated. A subsample of parents volunteered for focus groups. Focus groups were composed of 20

groups of 8 to 12 pupils (N = 185) and two groups of parents (N = 23). Student focus groups asked questions regarding "sexual and reproductive heath knowledge, views about sex education and suggestions for improvements to their current sex education" (p. 2070). The student focus groups provided vignettes about two youth about the same age and sex as the group, which proved to be a successful way to spark discussion. An example of such a vignette is as follows: "Mali is the same age as you. Her parents are very strict and they tell her that she must not get a boyfriend until she has finished secondary school. . . How do you think Mali would feel? What do you think she should do?" (p. 2071). Focus groups with parents dealt with "their own memories of sex education, their views about the sex education their teenagers were receiving, and their suggestions for changes and improvements to current sex education" (p. 2071).

The quantitative and qualitative components were brought into conversation with each other during the analysis phase. The focus groups and narrative interviews were transcribed in Thai and then translated into English. Coding of a subsample of the qualitative data occurred by the three researchers and then brought into discussion with each to work through discrepancies and further interpretations. These discussions led to the development of coding matrices for further thematic analyses. Data were then entered from all transcripts into these established coded themes allowing the authors "to identify key themes, explore discourses, compare these across respondents, and generate hypotheses where appropriate" (p. 2071). As new hypotheses emerged, the authors would re-analyze data together and refine themes in order to accurately interpret the stories.

The following themes emerged in the data analysis: "role ambiguity and confused identity; awareness, curiosity, and desire; knowledge and skills gaps; limited parental input; and impulsivity, risk taking, and coercion" (p. 2072). The findings suggest competing values between modern society and traditional Thai values. Differences emerged in the type of sex education that is offered between schools, as teachers modified topics based on their own comfort levels and personal values (e.g., how to put on a condom and discussion HIV/AIDS). Basically no schools discussed emotional issues in relationships, how to negotiate dating and the physical components, or homosexuality.

Gender played a major role in the findings as girls tended to discuss the emotional connection and love as playing roles in sexual behavior and dating, whereas boys talked about "being men" and "playing it safe." Both student groups wanted to have "modern relationships" but in their discussions with the researchers still brought up traditional values, such as "modesty" and obeying parents (p. 2072). Religion, kin, and school culture pulled them towards traditional norms, whereas media and perception of peer pressure moved them toward more modern beliefs and desires. The majority of teenagers responded with a high degree of awareness and sex and sexuality, but continued to be curious and have many questions about it. Within focus groups, boys tended to ask questions regarding "what happens in the sexual act and how to perform sexually" whereas girls wanted to know how to "get and keep a boyfriend and how to manage a sexual situation" (p. 2074).

The focus groups with the students illuminated the "shortage of practical sessions, life skills training, or discussion about emotional issues in sex education" (p. 2074) in regards to STIs, how to use a condom, the importance of a condom, the likelihood of pregnancy, and how sex can emotionally impact a relationship.

Parental focus groups revealed concern over their children and the impact of the "rapid social change on their children's sexual awareness and behavior" (p. 2073). Parents were interested in how to better protect their children from the "moral and physical dangers of premature sex" (p. 2074). As somewhat common in the literature, there are differing opinions by parents on the appropriateness of their child's behavior based on gender. Parents noted that they "accepted" that boys might succumb to their "sexual impulses" more readily, however, they were less accepting of their daughters having such "impulses" or "encounters" (p. 2074). Parents understood that in the current society, dating is a "fact of life" but could not justify the conflict with family values and traditions of modesty and obeying parents, highlighting the juxtaposition of modern society and traditional values.

The quantitative survey allowed the researchers to get an overall understanding of whether the pupils learning about different topics within sexual education classes, such as condom use, STIs, HIV/AIDS, pregnancy, how to act within a relationship, etc. These results also suggested gender differences in recall of what is being taught. For example, girls recall more than boys in regards to menstrual cycles, sexuality, and abortions, but remembering what is taught in class verse what is picked up through the media and at home may play a role in recall. "Overall, Thai teenagers were enthusiastic about sex education and requested more of it, especially around managing relationships and negotiating in potentially sexual situations" (p. 2077).

Vuttanont and colleagues (2006) study contains many elements of feminist research praxis. It especially gives voice to the diversity of stakeholders involved in this issue. Through their focus groups with boys, girls, parents, and narrative interviews with public health workers, religious leaders, and teachers, they were able to get a thorough sense of a historically not talked about issue in the Thai society. Recent social changes and the influx of Western media have forced the Thai people to realize the need to address the issue of sexually transmitted diseases and teen pregnancies as they are on the rise. Battling the discord between wanting to embody traditional values and dating in a modern society adds confusion for all stakeholders in terms of best practices within sexual education and responsibly acting on "impulses" for teenagers.

One issue the authors might consider is that of the potential power dynamics between the researchers and their participants. The authors note that during the course of their research they would be called on to offer "informal advice" regarding sex education—some parents wanted to know what they should specifically be teaching their children, some young people sought their advice regarding some aspect of sex education they didn't know (Vuttanonet et al., 2006, p. 2077). Although the authors mentioned this issue, they did not use the practice of reflexivity to examine how giving such advice may have, in fact, widened the power differential more so than typically occurs between a researcher and a participant and how this in turn may have impacted their research findings.

The findings suggest that teenagers "have reasonable knowledge of biological issues from sex education but are confused and uncertain about how to obtain or use contraception, avoid pregnancy and transmission of STIs, negotiate personal and intimate relationships, and find sources of support and advice" (p. 2078). The authors in this study did an excellent job at concurrently analyzing the quantitative and qualitative data and have them "talk" to each other so one helps to further explain the other, without one of the methods taking precedence.

While the authors acknowledge that this is a purely exploratory study and do not make any recommendations in terms of policy changes, but through this study they are able to develop an understanding of a new conflict that is happening within the Thai community as teenagers are growing up in a vastly different society compared to a generation ago. This research has the potential to help those moving forward in making policy changes and appropriately addressing teenagers on public health and health relationships. Furthermore, the authors were able to empower many different groups of people through their stories, but perhaps most importantly they empowered a group of teenagers who are curious and want to learn more about sex education resources and dialoguing about their own relationships to significant others in their peer group.

Conclusion

Providing a variety of case studies with different goals and use of multimethod and mixed methods offers a window into how researchers utilize feminist principles of practice in their multimethod and mixed methods design. The studies range in design, goals, and research questions, but all have the common thread of getting at subjugated knowledge and focusing on issues of difference, empowerment, and social change. What is also important to note is that studies deploying feminist praxis goals do not shy away from using quantitative data in the service of answering complex research questions (Jayaratne & Stewart, 1991). Many of these case studies, in fact, reveal the integral role a quantitative component can play in enhancing our understanding of a complex social problem.

A feminist research praxis is mindful of the importance of deploying reflexivity across the research process. A reflectivity praxis allows the opportunity for researchers to analyze the biases and assumptions they bring into a given research project and provides them a strategy for scanning these biases not only during the data collection phase of a project but also during the analysis, interpretation, and writing up of their research findings. By being aware of power imbalances and their own stance within the research process, researchers are able to interpret the results within both a macro and a micro context; an example of this was exemplified in Johnson (2007).

The case studies also reveal those moments where there are missed opportunities for a researcher to reflect on, for example, issues of power and authority in the research process. Vuttanont et al.'s (2006) research, for instance, might have benefitted more from acknowledging the power differentials between the researcher and the researched and how this in turn might have impacted their research findings.

Within all the case studies there is a tight link between researchers' questions and methods. The selection of multimethod or mixed methods should not be conducted for the sake of conducting such design—two methods may not be better than one. Any selection of a method needs to be grounded in what it is the researcher wants to know. What is the research question? Additionally, the unfolding of multimethod and mixed methods project exemplified in these case studies reveals how important it is that the researchers have knowledge of and skills in practicing a range of qualitative and quantitative methods in order to adequately conduct a rigorous research study. Such knowledge and skills can go a long way in avoiding "sprinkling" tactics that one often observes when a researcher's skills are not honed—for instance when a quantitative researcher adds on a few qualitative interview quotes and calls the design "mixed methods," or when a qualitative researcher adds on a few descriptive survey items and calls the project a "mixed methods study." The application of any method needs to reflect the research questions and goals of the study. At the data analysis stage, methods findings need to "talk" to one another, as we have observed in these case studies.

Accomplishing these integration goals may require that researchers involved in a mixed methods project collaborate with researchers who are strong in the varying methods. Being well versed in both methods will also alleviate the challenge of what to do when disparate findings occur, as may happen within mixed methods studies, "[they] need not immediately assume that one should be refuted and the other accepted" (Sprague & Zimmerman, 2004, p. 53). Diving into the data and having findings inform each other will help deepen findings and potentially provide an understanding and context for why the disparate findings may occur.

As also seen in the case studies, feminist researchers who take up mixed and multimethods research can run into obstacles along the way. For example, they may inadvertently introduce androcentric biases to their projects. For example, Buck et al. (2009) utilized the mATSI to understand young girls' attitudes toward science but as we saw relying too heavily on this measure alone limited their ability to unearth new knowledge.

Additionally, some of the limitations of the case studies have shown how feminist researchers at times do not go far enough to connect their quantitative and qualitative components. A lack of synergy can occur when the tensions and ambiguities that arise between the two sets of separate data are not accounted for or explored. The possibilities for social change and transformation are narrowed when the quantitative and qualitative sets of data are not integrated to their fullest extent, as seen in Testa and colleagues' (2004) study. Their article focused on validation of the Sexual Experience Survey and in doing so, the authors missed an opportunity to take into account more fully those concerns and issues women in their interviews articulate that lied outside of what is currently captured by this widely used measure of sexual aggression.

By fully engaging with the mixture of quantitative and qualitative creates potential synergy in one's research but can also deepen our understanding on new topics and aid in moving a research project toward social change.

Further, feminist approaches to MMMR grounds the research question in the chosen method(s) used. MMMR designs are not in themselves "methods-centric," as the design usually unfolds as the process of data collection proceeds. The design takes shape as the researcher iteratively gathers data, analyzes and interprets it, and decides on the next steps. An example of this can be seen in the Raffaelli and Ontai (2004) study. The authors aimed to understand gender socialization

patterns for Latina children, especially differences that may exist for women. As the study progressed, the authors included men to further illuminate differences.

Feminist perspectives are not constrained by a single methodology (theoretical perspective); instead, they are applicable across a spectrum of views on reality, from positivism to postmodernism. A feminist approach to MMMR encourages researchers to push beyond triangulation mixed methods designs and accommodates the tensions and ambiguities that arise from the use of diverse methods. Such an approach does not suggest that researchers should discontinue inquiry with the emergence of ambiguous findings but instead suggests that new knowledge is discovered in ambiguities. Marginalized knowledge can be brought to the foreground in the course of allowing tensions to remain in the research data, such as the uncovering of "close calls" in Testa and colleagues' (2004) study.

Feminist approaches to MMMR allows, then, the possibility for researchers to reach many diverse populations whose knowledge lays buried, providing a range of tools that will assist in seeking out subjugated knowledge that dominant perspectives on knowledge-building often miss (Reinharz, 1992). Vuttanont et al.'s (2006) study is a good example of how a sequential exploratory mixed methods design and concurrent analysis of qualitative and quantitative data can bring a diverse set of stakeholders into conversation and resulting in a broader understanding of a complex and changing issue with regard to sexual education and behaviors of Thai teenagers.

The practice of multimethod and mixed methods research holds the possibility for increasing the layers of meaning that often remain hidden and undifferentiated by using a range of methods. The mixing of quantitative methods with qualitative provides a potential mechanism for legitimating women's knowledge-building by testing out new theories as well as placing women's lived experience in a broader sociopolitical context. This dual-methods approach as presented in the case studies is also an effective strategy to advance social policy and promote social change for women and underprivileged people.

Overall, a feminist approach and praxis onto multimethod and mixed methods studies, as we have observed in these case studies, can also generate the knowledge researchers need as well to pursue social justice goals for oppressed groups.

Discussion Questions

1. What are some of the most important goals of feminist research?

2. In what ways do feminist perspectives seek to unearth subjugated knowledge and explore the experiences of underprivileged groups?

3. What research problems do feminist researchers tend to explore?

4. How do feminist researchers utilize multimethod and mixed methods, and what do their research designs usually look like? How do they carry out a multimethod or mixed methods research project?

5. Select one of the case studies and explain what features made it an example of a feminist approach.

References

Bhavnani, K. (1993). Tracing the contours: Feminist research and feminist objectivity. *Women's Studies International Forum, 16*, 95–104.

Bowles, G., & Duelli-Klein, R. D. (Eds.). (1983). *Theories of women's studies.* London: Routledge & Kegan Paul.

Buck, G., Cook, K., Quigley, C., Eastwood, J., & Lucas, Y. (2009). Profiles of urban, low SES, African American girls' attitudes toward science: A sequential explanatory mixed methods study. *Journal of Mixed Methods Research, 3*(4), 386–410.

Campbell, D. T., & Fiske, D. W. (1959). Convergent and discriminant validation by the multitrait-multimethod matrix. *Psychological Bulletin, 56*(2), 81–105.

Campbell, R. (1994). The virtues of feminist empiricism. *Hypatia, 9*(1), 90–115.

Chafetz, J. S. (1990, August). *Some thoughts by an "unrepentant positivist" who considers herself a feminist nonetheless.* Paper presented at the 85th Annual Meeting of the American Sociological Association, Washington, DC.

Collins, P. H. (1990). *Black feminist thought: Knowledge, consciousness, and the politics of empowerment.* New York: Routledge.

Comas-Diaz, L. (1987). Feminist therapy with Hispanic/Latina women: Myth or reality? *Women and Therapy, 6*(4), 39–61.

De Beauvoir, S. (1953). *The second sex.* New York: Knopf.

Denzin, N. K. (1970). Strategies of multiple triangulation. In N. Denzin (Ed.), *The research act in sociology: A theoretical introduction to sociological method* (pp. 297–313). New York: McGraw-Hill.

DeVault, M. L. 1990. Talking and listening from women's standpoint: Feminist strategies for interviewing and analysis." *Social Problems* 37: 96–116.

Dill, B. T. (1983). Race, class, and gender: Prospects for an all-inclusive sisterhood. *Feminist Studies, 9*(Spring), 131–150.

Dill, B. T. (1987). The dialectics of black womanhood. In S. Harding (Ed.), *Feminism and methodology* (pp. 97–108). Bloomington: Indiana University Press.

Dill, B. T., & Kohlman, M. H. (2012). Intersectionality: A transformative paradigm in feminist theory and social justice. In S. Hesse-Biber (Ed.), *Handbook of feminist research: Theory and praxis* (pp. 154–174). Thousand Oaks, CA: SAGE.

Eichler, M., & Lapointe, J. (1985). *On the treatment of the sexes in research.* Ottawa, ON: Social Sciences and Humanities Council.

Fisher, B. S., Cullen, F. T., & Turner, M. G. (2000). *The sexual victimization of college women* (Rep. No. NCJ 182369). Washington, DC: U.S. Department of Justice.

Flores, E., Eyre, S., & Millstein, S. G. (1998). Sociocultural beliefs related to sex among Mexican American adolescents. *Hispanic Journal of Behavioral Sciences, 20*, 60–82.

Haraway, D. (1988). Situated knowledges: The science question in feminism and the privilege of partial perspective. *Feminist Studies, 14*, 575–599.

Harding, S. G. (1987). Is there a feminist method? In S. Harding (Ed.) *Feminism and methodology: Social science issues* (pp 1–14). Bloomington: Indiana University Press.

Harding, S. G. (1993). Rethinking standpoint epistemology: "What is strong objectivity?" In L. Alcoff & E. Potter (Eds.), *Feminist epistemologies* (pp. 49–82). New York: Routledge.

Hesse-Biber, S. N. (Ed.). (2007). *Handbook of feminist research: Theory and praxis.* Thousand Oaks, CA: SAGE.

Hesse-Biber, S. N. (2010). *Mixed method research: Merging theory with practice.* New York: Guilford Press.

Hesse-Biber, S. N., & Leavy, P. (Eds.). (2006). *Emergent methods in social research.* Thousand Oaks, CA: SAGE.

Hesse-Biber, S. N., Leavy, P., & Yaiser, M. L. (2004). Feminist approaches to research as a process: Reconceptualizing epistemology, methodology, and method. In S. N. Hesse-Biber & M. L. Yaiser (Eds.), *Feminist perspectives on social research* (pp. 3–26). New York: Oxford University Press.

Hesse-Biber, S. N., & Piatelli, D. (2007). From theory to method and back again: The synergistic praxis of theory and method. In S. Hesse-Biber (Ed.), *Handbook of feminist research: Theory and praxis* (pp. 143–153). Thousand Oaks, CA: SAGE.

Hesse-Biber, S. N., & Yaiser, M. L. (Eds.). (2004). *Feminist perspectives on social research.* New York: Oxford University Press.

Hundleby, C. E. (2012) Feminist empiricism. In S. Hesse-Biber (Ed.), *Handbook of feminist research: Theory and praxis* (pp. 28–45). Thousand Oaks, CA: SAGE.

Jayaratne, T. E., & Stewart, A. J. (1991). Quantitative and qualitative methods in the social sciences: Current feminist issues and practical strategies. In M. M. Fonow & J. A. Cook (Eds.), *Beyond methodology: Feminist scholarship as lived research* (pp. 85–106). Bloomington: Indiana University Press.

Johnson, A. C. (2007). Unintended consequences: How science professors discourage women of colour. *Science Education, 91*(5), 805–821.

Kandiyoti, D. (1999). Islam and patriarchy: A comparative perspective. In S. Hesse-Biber, C. Gilmartin, & R. Lydenberg (Eds.), *Feminist approaches to theory and methodology* (pp. 219–235). New York: Oxford University Press.

King, D. (1988). Multiple jeopardy, multiple consciousness: The cotext of a black feminist ideology. *Signs: Journal of Women in Culture and Society, 14*(1), 42–72.

Koss, M. P. (1993). Detecting the scope of rape: A review of prevalence research methods. *Journal of Interpersonal Violence, 8*, 198–222.

Koss, M. P. (1996). The measurement of rape victimization in crime surveys. *Criminal Justice and Behavior, 23*, 55–69.

Lather, P. (1991). *Getting smart: Feminist research and pedagogy with/in the postmodern.* New York: Routledge.

Leaper, C. (1993). *USCS Attitudes Toward Gender Scale.* Unpublished manuscript, University of California at Santa Cruz.

Lorde, A. (1984). *Sister outsider: Essays and speeches.* Berkeley, CA: Crossing Press.

Lytton, H., & Romney, D. M. (1991). Parents' differential socialization of boys and girls: A meta-analysis. *Psychological Bulletin, 109*, 267–296.

McDade, K. (1995). How we parent: Race and ethnic differences. In C. K. Jacobson, (Ed.), *American families: Issues in race and ethnicity* (pp. 283–300). New York: Garland.

Millman, M., & Kanter, R. M. (Eds.). (1975). *Another voice: Feminist perspectives on social life and social science.* New York: Anchor Press/Doubleday.

Miner, K., & Jayaratne, T. E. (2014). Feminist survey research. In S. Hesse-Biber (Ed.), *Feminist research practice: A primer* (2nd ed. pp. 296–329). Thousand Oaks, CA: SAGE.

Mohanty, C. T. (2003). *Feminism without borders: Decolonizing theory, practicing solidarity.* Durham, NC: Duke University Press.

Morawski, J. G. (1994). *Practicing feminisms, reconstructing psychology.* Ann Arbor: University of Michigan Press.

Naples, N. A., & Desai, M. *Women's activism and globalization: Linking local struggles and transnational politics.* New York: Routledge, 2002.

Naples, N. A., & Gurr, B. (2014). Feminist empiricism and standpoint theory: Approaches to understanding the social world. In. S. Hesse-Biber (Ed.), *Feminist research practice: A primer* (2nd ed., pp. 14–41). Thousand Oaks, CA: SAGE.

Osborne, J., Simon, S., & Collins, S. (2003) Attitudes towards science: A review of the literature and its implications. *International Journal of Science Education, 25*(9), 1049–1079.

Parke, R. D., & Buriel, R. (1998). Socialization in the family: Ethnic and ecological perspectives. In N. Eisenberg (Ed.), *Handbook of child psychology: Vol. 3. Social, emotional, and personality development* (5th ed., pp. 463–552). New York: Wiley.

Raffaelli, M., & Ontai, L. L. (2004). Gender socialization in Latino/a families: Results from two retrospective studies. *Sex Roles: A Journal of Research, 50*(5–6), 287–299.

Reinharz, S. (1985). Feminist distrust: Problems of context and content in sociological work. In D. Berg & K. Smith (Eds.), *Exploring clinical methods for social research* (pp. 63–84). New York: Wiley.

Reinharz, S. (1992). *Feminist methods in social research.* New York: Oxford University Press.

Roberts, H. (1981). *Doing feminist research.* Boston: Routledge & Kegan Paul.

Ruble, D. M., & Martin, C. L. (1998). Gender development. In N. Eisenberg (Ed.), *Handbook of child psychology: Vol. 3. Social, emotional, and personality development* (5th ed., pp. 933–1016). New York: Wiley.

Sandoval, Chela. (2000). *Methodology of the oppressed.* Minneapolis: University of Minnesota Press.

Sapiro, V. (1995). Feminist studies and political science—and vice versa. In D. Stanton & A. J. Stewart (Eds.), *Feminisms in the academy* (pp. 291–310). Ann Arbor: University of Michigan Press.

Smith, D. E. (1978). A peculiar eclipsing: Women's exclusion from man's culture. *Women's Studies International Quarterly, 1*(4), 281–296.

Smith, D. E. (1987). *The everyday world as problematic: A feminist sociology.* Toronto: University of Toronto Press.

Smith, L. T. (2005). *Decolonizing methodologies: Research and indigenous peoples* (2nd ed.). London: Zed Books.

Spivak, G. C. (1994). Can the subaltern speak? In P. Williams & L. Chrismen (Eds.), *Colonial discourse and post-colonial theory: A reader* (pp. 66–111). New York: Columbia University Press.

Sprague, J., & Zimmerman, M. K. (2004). Overcoming dualisms: A feminist agenda for sociological methodology. In S. N. Hesse-Biber & P. Leavy (Eds.), Approaches to qualitative research: A reader on theory and practice (pp. 39-61). New York: Oxford University Press.

Swarr, A. L., & Nagar, R. (Eds.). (2010). *Critical transnational feminist praxis.* Albany, NY: SUNY University Press.

Testa, M., VanZile-Tamsen, C., Livingston, J. A., & Koss, M. P. (2004). Assessing women's experiences of sexual aggression using the Sexual Experiences Survey: Evidence for validity and implications for research. *Psychology of Women Quarterly, 28*(3), 256–265.

Trinh, T. M. (1991). *Framer framed.* New York: Routledge.

Wing, A. K. (1997). Brief reflections toward a multiplicative theory and praxis of being. In A. K. Wing (Ed.), *Critical race feminism: A reader* (pp. 27–34). New York: New York University Press.

Transformative and Indigenous Frameworks for Multimethod and Mixed Methods Research

Fiona Cram *and* Donna M. Mertens

Abstract

The transformative paradigm brings together many philosophical strands where social justice operates as a first principle in research endeavors. Multimethod and mixed methods research (MMR) is an appropriate research response to understanding, explaining, and intervening for transformation. Incorporating Indigenous research within the transformative paradigm stretches understandings of social justice to acknowledge Indigenous aspirations for self-determination and decolonization. The commonalities and tensions that arise when transformative research takes into account both social justice and decolonization are explored across the philosophical assumptions of the transformative paradigm. The inclusion of Indigenous research within the transformative paradigm reinforces the importance of respectful research relationships that strengthen connectedness and knowledge. It is within this web of relationships that MMR helps examine, explain, and resolve complex problems and where discussion can happen about how transformation will be inclusive of all peoples.

Key Words: transformative paradigm, social justice, Indigenous research, decolonization, respectful relationships

Addressing inequalities is not a choice—it's a moral and practical necessity. A moral necessity that speaks directly to our conscience. . . our sense of fairness and justice. . . our conviction that all people must have a fair opportunity to live full, healthy lives, no matter where they live, no matter what barriers they face. That is their right. And a practical necessity, because a focus on equity in our work saves more lives.

—Lake, 2013, p. 1

Not only did the spirit beings give the world a shape, they imbued it with a moral structure—handing down eternal ceremonial and social laws whereby all contemporary humans have equal intrinsic value, and a share of goods. Because no distinction is made between material

and spiritual, ancestor, story, sacred site, song and singer are all, in essence, the same thing. Australia, then, is a narrative.

—Davidson, 1989, pp. 2, 6; cited in Howitt & Suchet-Pearson, 2003, p. 3

Integration Tensions and the Role of Mixed Methods

Researchers who agree with the positions expressed in the two quotations that open this chapter have articulated their assumptions and implemented their approaches to change in a number of ways. Two of these are the subjects of this chapter: transformative and Indigenous approaches to research. As authors of this chapter, we have struggled with the relationship between these topics. The essential connection between the two is starting research with the goal of social transformation, so on the surface it seems both logical and unproblematic to describe the connections between a transformative paradigm and Indigenous research. In our dive beneath this surface, we invite readers to think along with us about these connections, as well as the tensions and contradictions, that arise when a dialogue is opened between transformative and Indigenous research as frameworks for multimethod and mixed methods research (MMMR) designed to address issues of human rights and social justice.

Indigenous researchers sometimes describe their research frame as a paradigm (Chilisa, 2012; Cram & Phillips, 2012; Wilson, 2008) or methodology (Smith, 1999), while others describe it as a theoretical lens, an approach, or a perspective. The way Indigenous research is described probably reflects the many distinct Indigenous populations. A common theme is that Indigenous research is done by, with, and for Indigenous people. Some may ask: why the emphasis on Indigenous peoples and research in this chapter? George Sefa Dei (2006) writes that such anticolonial thought needs to be articulated because

> colonialism has not ended and we see around us today various examples of colonial and neo-colonial relations produced within our schools, colleges, universities, homes, families, workplaces and other institutional settings. It is often said that globalization is the new word for imperialism. (p. 1)

For Mertens (2009), the transformative paradigm is a "meta-physical umbrella" that brings together many philosophical strands where social justice operates as a first principle. Mertens and Wilson (2012) extend this umbrella to include Indigenous research and evaluation. In doing so, questions are raised about what social justice looks like when Indigenous first principles of self-determination and decolonization are incorporated into the transformative paradigm, and what tensions this may then spark with others' social justice aspirations.

While philosophic tensions are undoubtedly present among many of those sheltering under the transformative umbrella, these are arguably heightened by the history of colonization and betrayal of Indigenous peoples. The alliance between the transformative and Indigenous agenda is therefore not an entirely comfortable fit; however, we take the position, at this point in time, that the Indigenous voice can be brought into the transformative paradigm as a way of stretching and

enriching understandings of the meaning of conducting research for the purpose of social transformation. This is possible because the transformative paradigm has space within it for many worlds and tolerance of the complexity of subjectivities and identities of inhabitants.

If a paradigm is indeed a set of first principles about the nature of the world, as asserted by Guba and Lincoln (1989), then these first principles are readily evidenced in the values inherent in the many United Nations' international covenants and declarations that assert human rights around the globe. For example, the UN Convention on the Rights of People with Disabilities (United Nations, 2010) affirms "that discrimination against any person on the basis of disability is a violation of the inherent dignity and worth of the human person" (p. 2). The rights of Indigenous peoples to their identity and the maintenance of their beliefs, as well as their right to self-determination, are encapsulated in the United Nations Declaration on the Rights of Indigenous Peoples (United Nations, 2007). These first principles are necessary because they are about redressing the acts of violence that have been, and continue to be, perpetrated against marginalized, colonized, and minoritized peoples' epistemologies, ontologies, and cosmologies. For Indigenous peoples, these principles are about decolonization and sovereignty; for non-Indigenous peoples, they are about social justice.

Decolonization is not about improving those corners of society that seem to be broken for, and exclusionary of, Indigenous peoples—including research methodology. Rather, decolonization is about sovereignty, land, and resources and the freedom to live as Indigenous peoples (Tuck & Yang, 2012). This is partially what Indigenous peoples have to add to the discussion of paradigms, namely, a holding firm of the line that decolonization means the return of their lands and their lives. In addition, Chilisa (2012) describes social justice in Indigenous research as occurring when research changes from a deficit- to a strengths-based lens in its examination of research participants' lives.

If decolonization is the transformation sought by Indigenous peoples, it also poses a question for other marginalized peoples to contemplate: "What do you want?" For example, New Zealand research with people with intellectual disabilities found that topmost on their agenda for transformation is a world where they can live "ordinary" lives (National Health Committee, 2003). The same may well be true of many marginalized groups, that is, a desire for a day-to-day life that is unmarked by signs and signifiers of difference and the implications these have for the distribution of the resources of society (e.g., education, employment, housing). The United Nations declarations and conventions that make visible the dimensions of diversity associated with denial of human rights have been criticized as being too idealistic (Wronka, 2008), yet they represent aspirations for how things should be. As researchers, we have the opportunity to frame our work in support of how things should be by considering the transformative paradigm and Indigenous ways of approaching research and how the use of mixed methods can support this framing

Research Paradigms

Having established the background thinking for the solidarity between the transformative paradigm and Indigenous mixed method research,
we now move to how we are thinking about this solidarity through a description of the transformative paradigm. This paradigm emerged in response to the everyday realities, needs, and aspirations of those marginalized within societies to broader concerns about human rights and equity that speak to providing avenues for transformative change. Given that the concerns and dilemmas faced by marginalized peoples are complex and multilayered, aptly described by many as "wicked problems" (Brown, Deane, Harris, & Russell, 2010), we also showcase here how mixed method research is an appropriate research response to understanding, explaining, and intervening for transformation. The description of the transformative paradigm therefore draws on, and is followed by, examples of mixed method transformative research including, as seen in the following, research about plant closure and involuntary job loss presented in boxed sections throughout this chapter.

Plant Closure and Kaupapa Māori Mixed Methods Research

What happens when a major industry in a town closes its doors, making several hundred workers redundant? Involuntary job loss is a traumatic life experience, whether it is a shock or the anticipated consequence of an economic downturn. Unsurprisingly, the loss of income and support structures provided by paid employment can disrupt people's access to healthcare and the food, housing, and other consumables they require to maintain good health (Broom et al., 2006).

When the Whakatu Freezing Works (meat-processing plant) in Hawke's Bay New Zealand closed suddenly on October 10, 1986, 2,160 workers found themselves shut out of the Works and without jobs. The impact on the community was said to be devastating, with people moving away, couples splitting up, people losing their homes, and commerce slowing because of people's lack of disposable income. There was also talk about the health of Māori workers being hardest hit, with people being able to name Māori ex-workers who had died prematurely. A neighboring Works, Tomoana, remained open until August 1994 and then it too closed. This time, a resource center was established as a one-stop shop to assist those who had lost their jobs.

These events set the scene for mixed methods research that was ongoing from its beginnings in the early 1990s into the impact of the closure of the Works on workers and their families and the wider community. The research, titled "Mauri Mahi, Mauri Ora, Mauri Noho, Mauri Mate[1]: Health Effects of Unemployment," was led by Vera Keefe[2] and carried out by researchers at Te Rōpū Rangahau Hauora a Eru Pōmare (Eru Pomare Māori Health Research Centre) at the University of Otago, Wellington. Three main methods were used within a Kaupapa Māori (by Māori, for Māori) research methodology, namely, an epidemiology study of a retrospective cohort of employees; qualitative Memorywork groups, focus groups, and interviews with men, women, young people, and several key informants affected by the closure of the Whakatu Works; and a case study of the Tomoana Resource Centre, the key intervention following the closure of the Tomoana Freezing Works. The case study involved key informant interviews, document analysis, media analysis, and participant observation. This research is described in boxed sections throughout this chapter to illustrate the philosophical assumptions of the transformative paradigm and how these play out within Indigenous research.

The word *paradigm* became part of the common parlance in research communities with the publication of *The Structure of Scientific Revolutions* by Thomas Kuhn (1970). Kuhn used the term *paradigm* to describe a worldview that existed in science that determined which theories would be viewed as acceptable and which research methods were appropriate to investigate relevant phenomenon. Guba and Lincoln (1989, 2005) adapted Kuhn's concept of paradigms for characterizing shifts in thinking in social research. They accepted Kuhn's idea that worldviews (paradigms) are used to justify specific approaches to research and that new worldviews emerge when status quo approaches are no longer able to explain new phenomenon. However, Guba and Lincoln did not specifically accept that one paradigm will replace another in the social sciences when anomalies cannot be explained within an existing paradigm. Rather, Guba and Lincoln's concept of paradigm in the social sciences reflected fundamental differences in the assumptions that researchers make in their work. They included the following philosophical assumptions to define the various paradigms that are functioning in the social sciences: (a) axiological: nature of ethics; (b) ontological: nature of reality, (c) epistemological: nature of knowledge and the relationship between the researcher and the participants; and (d) methodological: nature of systematic inquiry (Guba & Lincoln, 1989, 2005).

The transformative paradigm is one of several worldviews that provide support for the use of mixed methods based on the logical connection between its philosophical assumptions and its methodological implications. The transformative paradigm emerged first as the emancipatory paradigm (Lather, 1992; Mertens, 1998), and then Mertens (1999) changed its name to *transformative* in order to shift the focus to the active agency of community members in change processes. The impetus for this reframing of philosophical assumptions arose from tensions created because a great deal of research has been done on marginalized populations, but little has changed in the quality of the lives of people who are poor and/or discriminated against based on race/ethnicity, disability, deafness, gender, Indigeneity, and other relevant dimensions of diversity (Castellano, 2004; Chilisa, 2012; Sullivan, 2009). For example, "the 'bad name' that research has within Indigenous communities is not about the notion of research itself; rather it is about how that research has been practiced, by whom, and for what purpose that has

created ill-feeling" (Cram, Chilisa, & Mertens, 2013, p. 11; see also LaFrance & Crazy Bull, 2009).

Members of marginalized communities, such as First Nations in Canada (Wilson, 2008), Māori in New Zealand (Smith, 2012), and deaf people in the United States (Harris, Holmes,& Mertens, 2009), have called for changes in thinking about and conducting research so that it more accurately reflects their cultures and can serve as a mechanism for social change. Thus the transformative paradigm represents a shift from paradigms of research that yield results that are not seen as useful, valuable, and/or accurate by members of marginalized communities and their advocates to a worldview that places priority on addressing "issues of power inequities, the impact of privilege and the consequences of these for achieving social justice" (Mertens & Wilson, 2012, p. 163).

The use of mixed methods within the transformative paradigm lays a foundation for change for at least four reasons. First, different methods can capture different aspects of people's lived reality, and together mixed methods can provide insight into the complexities of people's lives. Second, use of multimethod and mixed methods provides the flexibility needed to use culturally appropriate strategies for data collection, a critical part of transformative research. Third, different people in decision-making positions value different research methods. Some may value ethnographies, others may require population enumeration, and yet others may be compelled by disaggregated data and disparities analyses. Using mixed methods increases the likelihood that portions of the research findings will speak to a broad range of audiences. Fourth, the combined analytical strength of an integrated mixed methods analysis is a compelling combination of numbers and voices. For change-inducing research findings to enter into the channels stakeholders (including communities) can open, researchers need to build relationships with stakeholders. They then need to strengthen the capability of stakeholders to understand and advocate for research findings, especially why these findings should facilitate something transformative.

The transformative paradigm is commensurate with a number of theoretical frameworks, such as feminist theory, Indigenous theory, disability rights theory, critical theory, critical race theory, queer theory, human rights theory, and deafness rights theory. For example, Hesse-Biber (2012) discusses how a feminist theoretical lens contributes to the conduct of research "on behalf of women and other oppressed groups with the goal of uncovering subjugated knowledge—oppressed groups' voices and ways of thinking that have been devalued by dominant, patriarchal, forms of knowledge—and promoting social change and social justice" (p. 138). Nightingale's (2003) study on forest land usage in Nepal is an example of how a feminist lens in a mixed methods study yielded insights that were used as a basis for the transformation of social policy. Through the use of oral histories, participant observation, and in-depth interviews combined with traditional quantitative geographic techniques of aerial photos the research identified important and valued changes in the forest and the necessity for developing mechanisms for women to be part of the decision-making process.

Transformative Philosophical Assumptions

The transformative philosophical assumptions are described in this section. Figure 6.1 provides a summary of these assumptions. Transformative axiological assumptions speak to the need for a research ethic that is cognizant of and responsive to history, culture, (in)equity, and the importance of relationships and reciprocity. The ontological assumptions recognize the multifaceted nature of reality, including versions of reality that do and do not uphold human rights. The ontological assumption that reality is relationships is included here

from Indigenous theorists. The transformative epistemological assumptions recognize that knowledge is constructed within the context of power and privilege, that knowledge is relational, and that relationships of trust are needed to conduct responsive research. The methodological assumptions embed the importance of research privileging the voice of the oppressed, authentically representing people's lives, acknowledging complexity and contradiction, and having a structural analysis. Each of these assumptions is described more fully in the following.

Transformative Axiological Assumption

The transformative axiological assumption makes explicit that the nature of ethics is connected to the use of research as a mechanism for addressing issues of human rights and social justice. As part of this assumption, the researcher needs to be culturally respectful and prepared to address inequities in alignment with the UN Conventions and Declarations described earlier in this chapter. A precursor to being culturally respectful is the need to know about the community's history, cultural norms, beliefs, values, behaviors, and practices, the variations of those cultural aspects within communities, and how cultural aspects either support the pursuit of human rights or sustain an oppressive status quo. Thus, methodologically, the

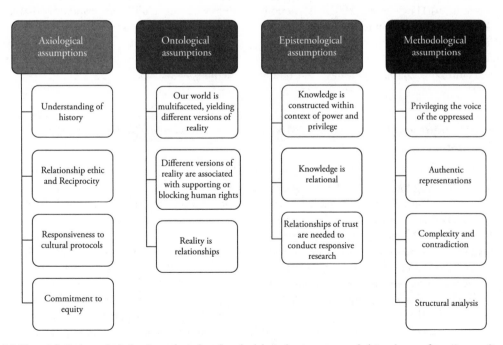

Fig. 6.1 The axiological, ontological, epistemological, and methodological assumptions underlying the transformative paradigm. Adapted from Mertens and Wilson, 2012, p. 171, Figure 6.1.

door is open to the use of mixed methods as a way of coming to an understanding of the complexity of cultural issues in a research study.

The transformative axiological assumption is made richer by inclusion of Indigenous scholars' viewpoints on the nature of ethics. Smith (1999) describes the colonization agenda as a way to make Indigenous people less than human. In reaction to this, Indigenous people's research ethic is based on decolonization and incorporates Indigenous struggles for humanity, the reclamation of their histories, and the restoration of hope (Smith, 2012). Through the assertion of humanity, Indigenous peoples will re-emerge from the margins of the "often fetishized historical memory of settler colonialism" (Sium, Desai, & Ritskes, 2012, p. 3). The maintenance of and the sustenance Indigenous peoples draw from the connections they have with one another is part of this struggle. Weber-Pillwax (2001) writes that in order to be healthy, these relationships must be based on the three *R*s of respect, reciprocity, and responsibility. These terms are culturally embedded and so need to be defined by those who participate in research, that is, what practices for them are respectful, reciprocal, and responsible. Similar demands for good research practices also arise within other cultures. Why, for example, would the deaf community open up to a researcher without first some reassurances that they meet the 3R criteria, as these criteria are conceptualized within the community (Harris et al., 2009)? A relationship ethic can help communities and researchers understand one another and work together. Russell Bishop (1996) describes this as "identifying, through culturally appropriate means, your bodily linkage, your engagement, your connectedness, and therefore unspoken but implicit connectedness to other people" (p. 152).

Chilisa (2012) describes a relational aspect to axiology that emanates from the African concept of Ubuntu, meaning that every action that we take needs to be taken with respect for all living and nonliving things, as well as respect for all who came before us and who are here now. Similar concepts are found in other Indigenous communities. For example S. Wilson (2008), a member of the Opaskwayak Cree Nation of northern Canada, describes research as ceremony—a ceremony that includes spiritual connections between persons and higher beings, humanity, or the environment. The researcher is then tasked to understand social phenomenon by interconnections between the sacred and the practical aspects of research. Research and researchers are accountable to these relationships. Thus relational axiology is commensurate with and adds richness to the transformative axiological assumption.

How would research methodologies change if we started our work with the premise that we are all connected and that we have a responsibility for ethical work that is respectful of all who came before us, who are here with us (living and nonliving), and who will come after us? Such a stance supports the use of multimethod and mixed methods to provide the knowledge base and interactive opportunities needed to develop ethical relationships that can result in understanding that is both factual and spiritual. The next boxed description of the plant closing study illustrates how transformative and Indigenous values guided the use of mixed methods.

Plant Closure and Kaupapa Māori Mixed Methods Research: The Axiological Assumption

Central to the Te Rōpū Rangahau Hauora a Eru Pōmare researchers' Kaupapa Māori methodology for studying the effects of the closure of the Works was the researchers' focus on axiology. This was expressed in an early paper titled "Kaupapa Māori Meets Retrospective Cohort" where the researchers describe their use of a standard research tool (epidemiology) within a Māori research methodology. The retrospective cohort examined whether the risk of death or hospital admission was higher among ex-Whakatu workers, compared with those working at the Tomoana Freezing Works from 1986 to 1994. The researchers argue that the study was only possible because they and the research were centered within Te Ao Māori (the Māori world).

Four values—*whānau* (family), consultation, *whakapapa* (kinship), and reciprocity—underpinned the research. The concept of whānau provided a way to organize the research group (with many members being related or like family), to conduct ethical research, and to engage with and report back to the community. "Whānau is a way of distributing and sharing tasks; of incorporating people with particular expertise, and of keeping Māori values central to the project" (Keefe et al., 1999, p. 14). Consultation processes recognized the authority of the local tribe, Ngāti Kahungunu, and helped ensure that the research had the best chance of contributing to Māori well-being. Communications were done face-to-face, with *kanohi kitea* (as face that is seen) an overarching principle of the researchers. Community consultation and dissemination of research findings were facilitated by whakapapa, that is, the kinship connections many of the researchers have with Ngāti Kahungunu. The trust relationships established and strengthened through the research process also helped facilitate reciprocity, that is, the exchange of time, knowledge, and skills. The researchers' reciprocity obligations extended beyond the life of any one research project and were fulfilled through developing local research projects, providing research training, and helping with resource creation. The researchers' relationships with Ngāti Kahungunu Iwi Incorporated and the Hawke's Bay community are still strong and have facilitated a continuation of the retrospective cohort study, as well as other Māori health projects.

Sources: Cram, Keefe, Ormsby, Ormsby, & Ngāti Kahungunu Iwi Incorporated (1997); Keefe et al. (1999, 2002); Te Rōpū Rangahau Hauora a Eru Pōmare (2000).

Transformative Ontological Assumption

The nature of reality can be characterized as an either/or choice: either there is one reality out there that is waiting for us to discover/measure it (post-positivist), or there are multiple socially constructed realities (constructivist). The transformative ontological assumption occupies a point of tension in terms of the nature of reality; it recognizes that there are different opinions about what is real, but it does not take a definitive stance on whether there is one reality (Mertens, 2014). Rather, it recognizes the multifaceted nature of what we consider to be real and explores the sources of those diverse perceptions in terms of the values and social positions that lead to privileging one version of reality over another. In addition, it interrogates the consequences of accepting one version of reality over another. Therefore, reality is viewed as that which has been "shaped by social, political, cultural, economic, ethnicity, and gender values; crystallized over time" (Guba & Lincoln, 2005, p. 193).

The application of the transformative ontological assumption can be seen in the work of Bledsoe (2010) who conducted a transformative mixed methods study of an obesity reduction program in a community that was largely poor and comprised of mixed racial/ethnic minorities. The original reality that was assumed by the program developers from the dominant cultural group was that the students were overweight because of poor self-esteem. Bledsoe suggested a mixed methods approach to test this version of reality by collecting data in the form of quantitative medical information and GIS mapping of available healthy foods and qualitative interviewing. The young people's version of reality

was that they were comfortable being "big," but they wanted to avoid medical problems associated with obesity such as diabetes and heart disease. On the basis of this information, rather than developing a program to improve self-esteem, the program was designed to include community festivals with demonstrations of ways to access and cook healthy foods and exercise programs that were seen as fun and safe, such as dance contests at which pedometers were worn to count the participants' number of steps. This use of mixed methods revealed two different versions of reality and allowed for capture of the effects of the program in multiple ways. It allowed for the interrogation of a version of reality that would have sustained the oppressive status quo and revealed another that facilitated social change needed for a healthier lifestyle.

From an Indigenous perspective, a relational ontology aligns with the relational axiology previously discussed. Smith (1999), S. Wilson (2008), and Chilisa (2012) describe the importance of relationships that people have with themselves, living and nonliving beings in their environment, the earth, and the cosmos. Multimethod and mixed methods are needed to conduct research in culturally diverse groups in ways that respect the multiple layers of relationships associated with exploring realities, their origins, and the consequences of accepting one version of reality over another. Indigenous peoples also describe the importance of the inner self and its inclusion in what is real.

Although there is no lack of discrimination between the experiences of self when awake and when dreaming, both sets of experiences are equally self-related. Dream experiences function integrally with other recalled memory images as far as these, too, enter the field of self-awareness. (Hallowell, 1975, p. 165)

How would research methodologies change if we assumed that knowledge is our relationships with one another, nature, the spirit world, and the cosmos—if knowledge was in our wakefulness as well as our dreaming? As Meyer (2001) notes we would have to use more than five senses to make sense of the world, becoming other-intellectuals. In such a context the use of mixed methods would probably be mandatory. The plant closure example described in the next box illustrates the use of mixed methods that encompasses multiple realities from an Indigenous perspective.

Plant Closure and Kaupapa Māori Mixed Methods Research: Ontological Assumption

Unemployment in a Western sense has long been theorized/known to cause physical and psychological health problems for the unemployed, their families, and their communities (Bethwaite, Baker, Pearce, & Kawachi, 1990). It is said to lead to depression, apathy, and a loss of self-esteem because it removes important sources of structure, identity, and connectedness from people's lives (Jahoda, 1979). However, social class and identity linkages to employment status may not have the same meaning for Māori. As Durie (1985) explains, "Occupation is of comparatively little consequence within Māori society. A manual labourer performing the most menial task not infrequently turns out to be a gifted orator, or a person with exceptional prestige widely regarded by his tribe as healthy; while the professional who is hesitant within Māoridom may evoke the type of pity normally reserved for those in ill health" (p. 485).

In undertaking research about the health effects of involuntary job loss, the concerns of the researchers were three-fold: ensure that the research was collaborative and nonexploitative, represent the experiences of ex-workers in ways that would speak to others in similar situations, and design the research to facilitate use of findings to influence policy and interventions designed to support workers who lose their jobs. The representation of ex-workers was about building an understanding of how involuntary job loss was impacting on them and their whānau without jumping to conclusions about what these effects might be based on a literature that might not be valid for an Indigenous population. The grant application for the qualitative research talked about participants being "in the driver's seat" so that they could tell the stories they needed to tell.

As the researchers explained, Māori studies of unemployment were needed for at least two key reasons (Cram et al., 1997): to challenge the universality of work-based identity and to demonstrate that (un)employment has unrecognized health costs for Māori. The mixed method approach enabled the researchers to tackle this agenda through a quantitative epidemiological view of increased health risks for the population of workers made redundant, and an on-the-ground, largely qualitative view of the place of employment in, and the impact of involuntary job loss on, people's everyday lives.

Transformative Epistemological Assumption

This assumption is related to the nature of knowledge, truth, and the relationship between the researcher (the "knower") and that which would be known (the community, the participants). In transformative terms, knowledge is viewed as being constructed within contexts of power and privilege (Mertens & Wilson, 2012). Scheurich and Young (1997) have argued that "White racism or White supremacy became interlaced or interwoven into the founding fabric of modernist western civilization" (p. 7) through "racially biased ways of knowing" (p. 4). The resulting exclusion of other epistemologies has impacted severely on nonmembers of the dominant culture around the globe (Bishop & Glynn, 1999; Smith, 1999).

What is needed now is to move beyond divisive, dismissive and neocolonial rhetoric which offers no viable solutions to modern ecological and social issues affecting Indigenous communities. What is needed instead is a collaborative environment which allows for traditional knowledge to be articulated, and heard, within its own cosmological worldview. (Walsh, 2011, p. 9)

Kaupapa Māori (by Māori, for Māori) research adds that participants' "voices" must be complemented by a structural analysis of the political, economic, cultural, and other strategies that work to maintain the status quo of Indigenous marginalization and oppression (Pihama, 2010). Opportunities to engage at a structural level are important as the structures of a society cause, minimize, or maintain disparities between groups. This aligns well with the description by Mertens and Wilson (2012) of the transformative paradigm focusing "primarily on the viewpoints of marginalized groups and interrogating systemic power structures through mixed methods to further social justice and human rights" (p. 160).

Scholars whose work is commensurate with the transformative paradigm write about epistemologies such as Chicana feminist epistemology (Delgado Bernal, 1998), African epistemologies (Bewaji, 1995), and endarkened feminist epistemology (Dillard, 2000). These researchers take on roles as activists who are cognizant of their own values and those of the community and who are committed to social justice and human rights. Use of mixed methods is recommended because of the need to be responsive to the range of diversity within the communities and the information needs of those with power to create change. For example, Dillard (2008) advances three tenets of an African-based cosmology—spirituality, community, and praxis—that constitute both a healing methodology and a bridge to new, celebratory knowledge. The principles of the healing methodology are love, allowing researchers to look and listen deeply; compassion, compelling researchers to engage in activist research to facilitate transformation; and reciprocity, encouraging researchers to form reciprocal relationships with research participants and communities.

This relational aspect of epistemology underscores the importance of our ethical responsibilities and how these need to be reflected in all of our research work. It influences how researchers build relationships with the communities in which they work. Access to both quantitative and qualitative data provides researchers with an opportunity to understand the complexity of how to build relationships and how to understand the relationships that are present in communities.

Chilisa's (2012) description of Indigenous knowledge provides useful insights into Indigenous epistemology and implications for research methodologies:

> Indigenous knowledge is embodied in languages, legends, folktales, stories, and cultural experiences of the formerly colonized and historically oppressed; it is symbolized in cultural artifacts such as sculpture, weaving, and painting, and embodied in music, dance, rituals, and ceremonies such as weddings and worshipping. It is the source of literature to draw from to challenge stereotypes of postcolonial societies. Instead of relying on written literature, which is often written from the Euro-American perspective, the above sources assist in giving voice to postcolonial indigenous communities. (p. 100)

The acceptance of knowledge from multiple sources such as those mentioned by Chilisa (2012) extend the possibilities for mixing methods beyond what is traditionally thought of as quantitative and qualitative methods. Motheo Koitsiwe (2013) used multiple methods to understand Indigenous knowledge systems in South Africa. Much of the Indigenous knowledge is held by the elders and has been marginalized, especially during periods of colonization and apartheid. Koitsiwe used Indigenous language and employed multiple methods that incorporated the importance of Indigenous religion in the research, made use of existing tribal councils, and preserved Indigenous knowledge. Researchers visited heritage sites and traditional healers' surgeries to understand the complexity of Indigenous knowledge and to respect its sacredness.

Given this description of Indigenous knowledge, multimethod and mixed methods of research appear to be a logical choice to incorporate these diverse ways of knowing. For example, a researcher would need to use methods that could capture the stories, poems, folklore, dances, and so on that are the embodiment of Indigenous knowledge. This calls on researchers to be open to creative ways to collect and portray data in order to accurately capture the experiences of members of Indigenous communities. Similarly, with transformative studies that are conducted with other oppressed communities, researchers need to be able to respond to different types of knowledge and the modes of expressing that knowledge. This is illustrated in the next plant closure example.

Transformative Methodological Assumption

The transformative methodological assumption derives from the three previously described assumptions in that the approach to systematic inquiry is one that aligns with the ethical imperative to support human rights and social justice, the consciousness of the sources of different versions of reality and the consequences associated with accepting different versions of what is real, and the need to establish trusting relationships that are cognizant of cultural and power-related issues (LaFrance & Crazy Bull, 2009; Mertens, 2014; Mertens & Wilson, 2012). The transformative methodological assumption does not mandate the use of mixed methods; however, multimethod and mixed methods of research appear to be well suited to conducting an inquiry process that has the potential to lead to the necessary understandings and the use of the research as a mechanism for social change, as is exemplified in this passage:

> The transformative paradigm leads us to (1) reconsider data-collection decisions so we are more inclined to use mixed methods; (2) become consciously aware of the benefits of involving community members in the data collection decisions and the appropriateness of methods in relation to the cultural issues involved; (3) build trust to obtain valid data; (4) make the modifications that may be necessary to collect valid data from various groups; and (5) tie the data collected to social action. (Mertens, 2009, p. 60)

The transformative methodological assumption supports the use of a mixed methods cyclical design in which different types of data are collected in different phases of a research study (Mertens, 2010). Results that emerge in early phases are used to inform subsequent data collection decisions for later phases of the study. Typically, researchers associated with the transformative paradigm begin their studies with qualitative data collection in the form of document review to ascertain the historical context and interactions with relevant community members to gain understandings of the range of perspectives about the phenomena under study. This is an opportunity to build relationships and to get a better idea of culturally responsive (Hood, Hopson, & Frierson, 2015) methodological options. This qualitative phase is about letting research participants be in the "driver's seat" so they can take the researchers on the guided tour that they think the researchers need in order to know "how it really is." This beginning phase of research might be followed with either a quantitative or mixed methods phase in which incidence data, disaggregated by relevant characteristics, as well as data from surveys and/or interviews could be collected. It is possible to make use of a randomized control trial in a transformative mixed methods study, if the ethical warrants associated with its axiological assumption can be satisfied.

Sweetman, Badiee, and Creswell's (2010) review of exemplary transformative mixed methods studies illustrates the breadth of applicability of transformative mixed methods. They identified 34 transformative mixed methods that addressed such themes as inequities associated with gender, socioeconomic status, immigration, parenting, disabilities, families facing eviction, and drug use. The qualitative methods included interviews, focus groups, and observation. Quantitative data collection included surveys and physical measures (e.g., body mass index). The most common mixed methods designs were sequential in which the first phase of data collection (quantitative or qualitative) influenced the second phase of data collection. What characterized these studies as transformative was summarized by Sweetman et al. as follows: "The majority of the authors referenced a problem in a community of concern, discussed how results would elucidate power dynamics, and discussed how results would facilitate social change" (p. 446).

Indigenous methodologies provide an extension of the concept of relatedness as a core value in life, in research, and in social transformation. Evans, Hole, Berg, Hutchinson, and Sookraj (2009) summarized Indigenous methodologies as research "by and for indigenous peoples, using techniques and methods drawn from the traditions of those peoples. . . . [Indigenous methodology] situates and is reflected on by research/researchers at the location most relevant to that being gazed on, the indigenous experience (p. 894)." Māori scholars have written extensively about Kaupapa Māori research methodology, which means that research is done in the Māori way, in keeping with Māori traditions and ways of thinking and valuing (Bishop, 1996; Cram, 2006; Smith, 1999, 2012).

Methodologies need to be employed that recognize the need for various culturally appropriate strategies for engaging with community members. Storytelling is generally accepted as an appropriate strategy for sharing experiences in Indigenous communities. Storytelling can be a form of data collection that allows for a counter-narrative to emerge that challenges the dominant version of history and current circumstances. Storytelling can reflect the values of the community, including values related to spirituality that might be difficult to convey through other data collection strategies. Other strategies might involve "sharing food, exchanging gifts, and communicating with the nonliving in prayer, in song, in dance or in speech" (Chilisa, 2012, p. 141). Swadener and Mutua (2008) set the tone for "performative" research approaches: the visual and plastic arts, song, oral storytelling, dance, poetry, rituals, "zines," popular media, and the Internet.

The main question always and forever for research praxis remains, "Who benefits?" Decolonizing methodologies constitute activist agendas of social justice, sovereignty, self-determination, and emancipation, realized in collaborative alliance. Again, the plant closure example illustrates the use of mixed methods to this end.

Plant Closure and Kaupapa Māori Mixed-Methods Research: Methodological Assumption

Researchers at Te Rōpū Rangahau Hauora a Eru Pōmare wanted to influence policy and interventions to buffer the negative impacts of involuntary job loss for workers who might lose their jobs by future factory closures. The researchers chose research methods to do that in powerful ways through comparing populations and collecting personal and whānau (family) stories.

A retrospective cohort study offered the opportunity to quantitatively examine the health effects of unemployment (i.e., hospital admissions, cancer registrations, and mortality) when job loss was not about the individual characteristics of workers (e.g., lifestyle, health status). The study followed these workers for eight years, from 1986 to 1994. The findings from the post-closure study found that, compared to the Tomoana worker cohort who retained their jobs, those workers who lost their jobs when Whakatu closed were at more than double the risk of serious self-harm leading to hospitalization or death. They were, however, at no more risk of admission to the hospital with a mental health diagnosis (Keefe et al., 2002). These findings point to the heightened mental distress brought about by involuntary job loss.

While this study fulfilled the majority of characteristics of an ideal factory closure study, it lacked workers' perspectives on the impact of the Works' closure (Morris & Cook, 1991); for example, workers' self-reported health in the years following the closure and what helped and hindered their and their families' wellness. The qualitative component of the study combined personal and focus group interviews with the use of a Memorywork method (Keefe-Ormsby, 2008). Memorywork, developed by Frigga Haug (1987), asserts that the events people remember and how they remember them says a lot about who they currently are. Within a group session, participants' memories are produced in response to a cue and discussed, interpreted, and theorized. Over the course of three nights, eight Māori men met with the researchers and verbally recounted stories related to working at Whakatu, the closure of the Works, and life after Whakatu. Following the telling of the stories, the men identified key themes and then discussed each theme. Separate focus groups were held with women and with young people who had had some connection with Whakatu. Finally, 14 key informants, selected for their overview of events at the Whakatu Works, were interviewed.

Participants described the importance of Whakatu for workers. It was a "university" where employees learned life skills, including Māori culture, as well as work skills. Personal and social networks were forged, with the union's stronghold overriding competing gang memberships among workers, and ensured that workers were well paid. Within this context, the closure of Whakatu came with little warning, and workers were left shocked and disbelieving. The financial difficulties workers faced after the closure were relieved by unemployment payments negotiated by the union. The loss of camaraderie and the Works being a "home away from home" was also eased somewhat by post-closure initiatives to support workers (e.g., buying and distributing bulk vegetables). However, many people left the community, and the break-up of marriages was common. Ten years after the closure, people talked about opportunities that had opened up for them through reemployment, retraining, and education, including Māori language education. Over the 10 years since its closure, people were able to reestablish themselves and move ahead with their lives. This may well be pivotal to why the cohort study did not find more wide-ranging health impacts of the closure.

The qualitative component of the study also highlighted the importance of other opportunities for ex-workers to experience camaraderie, access financial supports, and find out about reemployment, retraining, and education opportunities. The Tomoana Resource Centre, opened five days after the closure of the Tomoana Freezing Works, was about "respecting their contribution to community, supporting them to maintain control over their lives, and valuing their humanity" (Te Rōpū Rangahau Hauora a Eru Pōmare, 2000, p. 55). In this way the center offered emotional and practical support to help ex-workers move forward with their lives. Whereas this support had been rather ad hoc when Whakatu closed, when Tomoana closed, the community had more knowledge about what was needed and was able to successfully lobby for more formal support mechanisms.

Te Rōpū Rangahau Hauora a Eru Pōmare set out to conduct a multimethod study of the impact of the closure of the Whakatu Freezing Works, with this extending to Tomoana Freezing Works when it closed. Their research highlighted the seriousness of involuntary job loss for the health and well-being of ex-workers, their families, and their community.

Examples of Transformative and Indigenous Multimethod and Mixed Methods Research Studies

During the 1992 Royal Commission on Aboriginal Peoples in Canada, an Aboriginal elder quietly stated "If we have been researched to death, maybe it's time we started researching ourselves back to life" (Castellano, 2004, p. 98). The poignant element of this statement is that being "researched to death" is not necessarily a metaphor; on average Indigenous peoples die at a much younger age than the non-Indigenous peoples who reside within their lands (UN Permanent Forum on Indigenous Issues, 2009). As a metaphor the statement is also about the need for research to give life to the traditions, values, cultures, realities, and diversity of Indigenous peoples so that they might be seen as fully human (Smith, 2012). In this section we describe two transformative mixed methods studies in Indigenous communities that are helping, as noted earlier, to research Indigenous peoples back to life. The first is mixed method ecological research with the Nauiyu Nambiyu Aboriginal community in the Northern Territory of Australia. The second is a mixed method evaluation of a program for Native youth at the University of Washington.

Indigenous Ecological Knowledge

In the Northern Territory of Australia, mixed method research by Woodward, Jackson, Finn, and

McTaggart[3,4] (2012) examined Indigenous ecological knowledge about the Daly River, that is "a cumulative body of knowledge and beliefs handed down through generations by cultural transmission about the relationship of living beings (including humans) with one another and with their environment" (Berkes, 1993, p. 3). The axiological assumptions of the project included acknowledgement of and respect for the intellectual property rights of Indigenous knowledge authorities (Woodward, 2010). An important part of the collaboration was an acknowledgement that the collaborators, researchers from the Commonwealth Scientific and Industrial Research Organisation and members of the Aboriginal community had different epistemological and ontological foundations, and that a respectful and inclusive space had to be created for dialogue about the representation of Indigenous knowledge (Woodward, 2010).

The research compared quantitative harvesting and fishing resource-use data collected in a household survey with qualitative phenological (i.e., periodic plant and animal life cycle events) knowledge. The qualitative component of the project focused on the creation of a seasonal calendar of aquatic resource use, developed by the researchers joining community members in hunting, gathering, and fishing expeditions during a full cycle of the seasons. In the quantitative component, 24 households (one-fifth of the Indigenous population) were surveyed twice every three months over two years.

The researchers found that the qualitative data complemented and confirmed the household quantitative data. The quantitative findings provided details about harvesting rates and locations; the qualitative data showcase the ecological knowledge behind this harvesting and how this informed people's subsistence strategies and decision-making. The researchers also recorded oral histories that showed the changing patterns of resource use over an extended time period, as well as changing techniques.

The collaboration with the community over the three years of this study led to the community suggesting other research techniques, including Photovoice. Photovoice is a participatory photographic method whereby people create and then discuss photographs to identify and represent their community in ways that privilege their understandings, issues and aspirations (Wang, Cash, & Powers, 2000). In Woodward et al.'s (2012) research, several communities engaged in a Photovoice project under the guidance of Indigenous experts. A number of visual outputs were produced, including seasonal calendars. The calendars captured more information about species and harvesting than found in the household surveys. "Significantly, the Ngan'gi Seasons calendar reveals that Indigenous people take their cues from some ecological observations that fall outside the realm of orthodox scientific knowledge" (Woodward et al., 2012, p. 62). The research was therefore able to articulate an Indigenous epistemology and ontology, creating a foundation for decolonization (Sium et al., 2012).

Evaluation of the Native Youth Enrichment Program

Joan LaFrance (2011) of Mekinak Consulting in Seattle, Washington, conducted a mixed method external evaluation of the Native Youth Enrichment Program. The program, directed by Polly Olsen at the University of Washington's Indigenous Wellness Research Institute, was designed to redress the underrepresentation of Native American students in science, technology, engineering, and mathematics (STEM). The program consisted of summer and semester programs delivered in 2010–2011 and designed to expose senior high school students to aspects of science and technology and encourage them into tertiary STEM education.

The Indigenous Evaluation Framework (LaFrance & Nichols, 2009) describes the agenda of education for American Indian and Alaskan Natives as the maintenance, restoration, and preservation of Indigenous values, wisdom, knowledge, and pedagogies. Within this context, Indigenous evaluation should lead to transformations that include program improvements, the development of a knowledge base of successful practices and strategies, and education programs that result in increased student participation and success along with tribal community prosperity.

From an epistemological perspective, LaFrance and Nicols (2009) write that understanding Indigenous "ways of explaining what is known" is the foundation step in Indigenous evaluation (p. 20). These ways are about being connected to and participating in nature and everyday communal life. The program's story is understood through the use of careful observation, measurement, and listening. LaFrance and Nichols write that what is now known as "mixed methods" has always been a part of traditional Indigenous knowledge creation.

LaFrance (2012) used three main methods for the evaluation of the Native Youth Enrichment Program, namely, quantitative pre-/postprogram student surveys; qualitative review of students' digital stories, produced as part of the program; and qualitative interviews with students, parents, and program staff. Parents also provided information about parental education, students' grade point average, and family income. Notes from a staff retreat held immediately after the summer program were also examined. Finally, at the end of the digital story workshops, students shared their stories at a community event and talked about their experiences.

The evaluator recommended caution in interpreting the findings from the quantitative surveys of students in the academic year workshops, as participant numbers were low (i.e., less than 30). Students' identity as American Indians was more positive following the workshops, and they were more excited about their future. The digital stories developed by students related to their identity and were often very personal. As the evaluator noted, "Themes that emerge across the stories include: having pride in one's ethnicity or ethnicities, having pride in family and heritage, making difficult choices to seek opportunities for a good education, facing personal challenges and learning important lessons" (LaFrance, 2011, p. 11). Telephone interviews with students' parents found that they were mostly satisfied because their children enjoyed and benefited from the program.

The evaluator argued that taken together these findings indicated that the summer program might have disrupted students' existing career choices, causing them to reconsider their plans. She concluded that "Overall, [the program] was successful in serving youth and their families and demonstrating the potential for more programs for American Indian youth who have the ability to become leaders and contributors to a STEM workforce" (LaFrance, 2011, p. 32).

These two examples illustrate how researchers can apply the transformative and Indigenous frameworks in the conduct of mixed methods studies. In the following section, we provide a critical analysis of the strengths and challenges associated with these approaches.

Critical Analysis of the Transformative and Indigenous Research Frameworks

The transformative paradigm is most closely linked with research undertaken with communities and groups that are marginalized and vulnerable, that experience discrimination and oppression, and that are just not quite the right "fit" within our societies. Indigenous peoples may be all these things, and so a natural affinity was struck between transformative and Indigenous research in this chapter. This affinity and the longevity of the dialogue between transformative and Indigenous research will be tested when social justice movements exclude decolonizing transformation from their research agendas. This exclusion of decolonization was the case when some of those involved in the recent Occupy movement in the United States were reluctant to accept they were occupying Indigenous land and therefore failed to express genuine solidarity with Indigenous peoples (Barker, 2011; Walla, 2011). Within mixed method research this exclusion can involve a failure to collect enough (or even any) quantitative data from Indigenous participants so that an analysis of findings from the Indigenous sample is not possible; there is a failure to separate quantitative data by race or ethnicity or, when data is disaggregated, a failure to explore structural explanations for Indigenous disparities (Reid & Robson, 2007). The qualitative component of a mixed method study can maintain or even strengthen Indigenous marginalization and stigma through the questions that are asked, the way dialogue is analyzed, and the representation of Indigenous voices within research reporting (Cram, 2006).

Sometimes, however, the lack of respect for Indigenous peoples can be both subtle and arrogant. Chary, Greiner, Bowers, and Rohloff (2012), for example, combined structured participant interviews with clinic data to explore type 2 diabetes among Guatemala's Indigenous population. Twenty-three people attending a rural clinic with type 2 diabetes were interviewed about their knowledge, healthcare access, lifestyle, and social supports. Researchers collected data from 80 adult patients on modifiable risk factors and disease characteristics. Educational levels among participants were low, and they preferred to talk in the Mayan language. The researchers saw both these factors as important considerations for any health education programs. However, the researchers note that a limitation of their research was that the interviewers were non-Mayan speaking North Americans not known to participants. This lack of a respectful relationship context is at odds with what we have presented in this chapter.

Table 6.1 Transformative Assumptions Applied

Transformative Assumption	Research Application
Axiology	Focused on resilience in the community; engaged with members of the community to insure that the researchers understood cultural complexities and how to interact in respectful ways; focused on solutions
Ontology	Did not assume that they knew what the problems were; collected qualitative data from interviews with diverse constituencies; collected quantitative data and disaggregated it by salient characteristics to determine prevalence for different subgroups and identify resilience (protective) factors
Epistemology	Established a steering committee representative of the diversity in the community; recruited and trained Indigenous researchers; included multiple formats and opportunities for communication with participants; community owned the data
Methodology	Used a community-based cyclical design that included a baseline survey of youth's knowledge, behaviors, and attitudes; analyzed preliminary data; consulted with elders and other community members to determine how to use the data to develop a culturally appropriate intervention; pilot tested it; collected quantitative and qualitative data on process and impact

Source: Andersson et al., 2008.

Within a research context, MMR is well placed to explore the tensions and promote the dialogue needed between transformative and Indigenous aspirations. Researchers are also grappling with common transformative and Indigenous research issues under the transformative umbrella. The transformative paradigm expands easily to embrace the importance of relationships, whereby research occurs within the context of a longer term, relational context that binds people and calls on them to be responsible, respectful, and reciprocal. Within this web of relationships it has been argued here that MMR is needed to explain, examine, and resolve the complex and wicked problems that face marginalized groups. However, the research capacity of many marginalized groups is still in its infancy, so it may be unlikely that insiders alone (i.e., people from those same groups) can carry out all the MMR that is needed. An issue then becomes which outsiders to include to gain both methodological expertise and axiological alignment. Cram and Phillips (2012) propose a transdisciplinary research readiness scale as a way for researchers to assess their own level of comfort and readiness to collaborate across disciplinary and cultural boundaries (e.g., "The time taken to meet and discuss research with colleagues from other disciplines and cultures is well worth it"). An impetus for this scale is the need to move beyond old-fashioned models of outsiders doing research on marginalized communities to more contemporary models of research teams that include insider and outsider researchers who are able to find common ground and understandings.

For example, Andersson and colleagues (2008) undertook a mixed methods study of resilience in the Canadian Aboriginal communities using the transformative indigenous lens. The researchers noted that the rate of infection for sexually transmitted diseases and HIV were significantly higher in the Aboriginal communities. They designed a study that exemplifies the transformative approach (as displayed in Table 6.1) that involved significant engagement with and capacity building for members of the community. Their goal was to contribute to the development of an intervention to prevent infections of this nature that the community would welcome and that would be effective because the community owned it. To this end, they involved the community in the development of quantitative instruments to collect data about risk and resilience factors; interviewed elders, youth in urban and rural areas, and service providers; mapped local services and community contexts; and reviewed the results with the elders and through focus groups and talking circles.

Conclusion

The principles found in the United Nations declarations and conventions may be idealistic and aspirational, but they offer researchers seeking a transformed world some welcome guidance about what needs to be challenged and undone (e.g., discrimination) and what needs to be asserted and upheld (e.g., Indigenous self-determination). In this chapter, these first principles provided a starting point for a dialogue between transformative and Indigenous research and the testing of whether there was room under the transformative umbrella for an Indigenous research agenda of decolonization and sovereignty. The dialogue that ensued took place at a paradigmatic level about the what, why, and how of knowledge and knowing about our world, the advantages of MMR, and how such research might stimulate transformative change.

The axiological assumption is privileged within the transformative paradigm, so there can be no misunderstanding that the goal of transformative research is social justice and the elimination of inequities. The axiological assumption is of a relationship ethic that lays a firm foundation for culturally respectful research engagement. Within this context, MMR enables a full picture to be built of people's lives, knowledge, needs, and aspirations. In this way a people's understanding of their local ecology can be well represented in research findings (Woodward et al., 2012), and the impacts of involuntary job loss on workers and their communities can be more fully documented (Keefe-Ormsby, 2008). Reciprocity operates well within MMR, as researchers' responsiveness to participant requests to use a research method can be embraced as adding value to the knowledge being assembled. The third *R* of Weber-Pillwax's (2001) healthy relationships entreats researchers to act responsibly in their use of all methods, so that no method can be seen as more objective or subjective, as all are implemented within a relationship ethic.

The ontological assumption of transformative research is about people's reality being shaped by values. Transformative MMR begins with participants' values and works within their reality. In this way a transformation in understandings can happen early in research, such as turning a self-esteem explanation for teenagers being overweight on its head and aligning an intervention more with their desire to avoid health complications (Bledsoe, 2010). The importance of relationships and communality was again stressed by Indigenous ontology, with MMR fit for purpose for exploring the multiple layers of people's relationships with one another, their world, and the cosmos.

The transformative epistemological assumption acknowledges relationships of power and privilege, looking inward to how research participants are experiencing their world and outward to how those experiences are framed/constrained by the larger society within which they live out their day-to-day lives. In MMR, population data can document disparities between groups of people as a way to highlight inequalities, while qualitative methods can examine the discourses of power and resistance among those at both ends of the socioeconomic spectrum. Many other mixes of methods are also possible. Indigenous peoples and others incorporate spiritual and cosmological elements into the epistemological assumptions of transformative research and push the discussion of mixing methods beyond a quantitative/qualitative dyad (Chilisa, 2012).

The transformative methodological assumption establishes principles to guide the selection and mixing of research methods and tools. We acknowledge that MMMR is not compulsory within a transformative paradigm. Our advocacy for it here reiterates our earlier statement that MMR allows for exchanges between the findings gathered through different methods. These methods will often approach a research question from different angles, and their integration will allow for both consistencies and contradictions to exist within the knowledge accumulated. This is important, as no marginalized, colonized, or vulnerable group is homogenous. We therefore need research that acknowledges not only the complexity of the issues they face but also the complexity of characteristics, tensions, attitudes, skills, and talents within their own midst.

Finally, the inclusion of Indigenous research within the transformative paradigm has reinforced the importance of relationships. These relationships extend beyond those between people to the relationships people have with their environment and with the cosmos. The deployment and artful mixing of research methods will enable us as researchers to walk alongside people and research with them, that is, look at their world through their eyes and with their values. In a relationship context that is about respect, responsibility, and reciprocity, we can also stretch our own capabilities as researchers to embrace traditional (e.g., talk-story) as well as contemporary (e.g., hip-hop) research methods. In this way the future of transformative MMR is like the growth of a pantry containing more and more ingredients/methods, more people in the kitchen sharing cooking/mixing techniques, and laughter and dialogue around the dinner table as results are consumed and plans made for future sessions. The role of those committed to social justice, the elimination of inequalities, and decolonization is to help ensure that these gatherings happen

Ko te kai a te rangatira he kōrero	Discussion is the food of leaders
Ko te tohu o te rangatira he manaaki	Hospitality is the mark of leaders
Ko te mahi a te rangatira hei whakatira te iwi	The work of leaders is bringing people together

Discussion Questions

1. What is your understanding of the transformative paradigm and how it supports the use of mixed methods?

2. What is your reaction to the integration of the transformative paradigm and Indigenous approaches to research?

3. What types of mixed methods designs would you propose for research that is designed to address issues of social transformation?

4. What strategies would you use to engage with communities to increase the cultural responsiveness of data collection methods?

Suggested Websites

karda.curtin.edu.au/

The Centre for Aboriginal Studies is located in Australia and focuses on conducting and using research to enhance positive social change for Aboriginals and Torres Strait Islanders.

http://www.maramatanga.co.nz

The Māori center of research excellence is located at the University of Auckland, New Zealand, and partners with a range of participating research entities throughout the country. Their mission is to conduct transformative Māori research.

http://www.nativecairns.org/CAIRNS/CAIRNS.html

The Center for American Indian Research and Native Studies is an Indian-controlled research center that focuses on education and Indian culture in South Dakota.

http://www.ub.edu/web/ub/en/recerca_innovacio/recerca_a_la_UB/instituts/institutspropis/crea.html

The Centre of Research in Theories and Practices that Overcome Inequalities is affiliated with the University of Barcelona; it conducts community-based research designed to provide solutions to "wicked" social problems.

Notes

1. This whakatauāki or traditional saying was given to the research by kaumātua (elder) Tama Tomoana and translates as "Industry begets prosperity (security); idleness begets poverty (insecurity)" (Parker, 1966, p. 10).

2. Vera was still leading this research up until her untimely death in August 2005.

3. Patricia Marrfurra McTaggart is a member of Nauiyu Inc.

4. Our methodologies are the logic that underpin our methods choices; methods are the research techniques and tools that we use.

References

Andersson, N., Shea, B., Archibald, C., Wong, T., Barlow, K., & Sioui, G. (2008). Building on the resilience of aboriginal people in risk reduction initiatives targeting sexually transmitted infections and blood-borne viruses: The Aboriginal community resilience to AIDS. *Pimatisiwin, 6*(2), 89–110.

Barker, J. (2011, October 30). What does "Decolonize Oakland" mean? What can "Decolonize Oakland" mean? [Web log post]. Retrieved from http://foroccupierstodecolonize.blogspot.co.nz/2011/12/what-does-decolonize-oakland-mean-what.html

Berkes, F. (1993). Traditional ecological knowledge in perspective. In J. T. Inglis (Ed.), *Traditional ecological knowledge: Concepts and cases* (pp. 1–9). Ottawa, ON: International Program on Traditional Ecological Knowledge and International Development Research Centre.

Bethwaite, P., Baker, M., Pearce, N., & Kawachi, I. (1990). Unemployment and the public health. *New Zealand Medical Journal, 103*, 48–49.

Bewaji, J. A. I. (1995). Critical comments on Pearce, African philosophy and the sociological thesis. *Philosophy of the Social Sciences, 25*(1), 99–120.

Bishop, R. (1996). *Collaborative research stories: Whakawhanaungatanga.* Palmerston North, New Zealand: Dunmore Press.

Bishop, R., & Glynn, T. (1999). *Culture counts: Changing power relations in education.* Palmerston North, New Zealand: Dunmore Press.

Bledsoe, K. (2010, November). *A transformative mixed methods evaluation of an obesity reduction program.* Paper presented at the annual meeting of the American Evaluation Association, Anaheim, CA.

Broom, D. H., D'Souza, R. M., Strazdins, L., Butterworth, P., Parslow, R., & Rodgers, B. (2006). The lesser evil: Bad jobs or unemployment? A survey of mid-aged Australians. *Social Sciences & Medicine, 63*, 575–586.

Brown, V. A., Deane, P. M., Harris, J. A., & Russell, J. Y. (2010). Towards a just and sustainable futre. In V. A. Brown, J. A. Harris, & J. Y. Russell (Eds.), *Tackling wicked problems: Through transdisciplinary imagination* (pp. 3–16). New York, NY: Earthscan.

Castellano, M. B. (2004). Ethics of Aboriginal research. *Journal of Aboriginal Health, 1*(1), 98–114.

Chary, A., Greiner, M., Bowers, C., & Rohloff, P. (2012). Determining adult type 2 diabetes-related health care needs in an indigenous population from rural Guatemala: A mixed-methods preliminary study. *BMC Health Services Research, 12*, 476.

Chilisa, B. (2012). *Indigenous research methodologies.* Los Angeles, CA: Sage.

Cram, F. (2006). Talking ourselves up. *Alternative: An International Journal of Indigenous Scholarship* (Suppl 2), 28–45.

Cram, F., Chilisa, B., & Mertens, D. (2013). The journey begins. In D. Mertens, F. Cram & B. Chilisa (Eds.), *Indigenous pathways into social research: Voices of a new generation* (pp. 11–40). Walnut Creek, CA: Left Coast Press.

Cram, F., Keefe, V., Ormsby, C., Ormsby, W., & Ngāti Kahungunu Iwi Incorporated. (1997). Memorywork and Māori health research: Discussion of a qualitative method. *He Pukenga Kōrero, 3*(1), 37–45.

Cram, F., & Phillips, H. (2012). Reclaiming a culturally safe place for Māori researchers within multi-cultural, transdisciplinary research groups. *International Journal of Critical Indigenous Studies, 5*(2), 36–49.

Delgado Bernal, D. (1998). Using a Chicana feminist epistemology in educational research. *Harvard Educational Review, 68,* 555–582.

Dillard, C. (2000). The substance of things hoped for, the evidence of things not seen: Examining an endarkened feminist epistemology in educational research and leadership. *Qualitative Studies in Education, 13*(6) 661–681.

Dillard, C. B. (2008). When the ground is black, the ground is fertile: Exploring endarkened feminist epistemology and healing methodologies in the spirit. In N. K. Denzin, Y. S. Lincoln, & L. T. Smith (Eds.), *Handbook of critical and Indigenous methodologies* (pp. 277–292). Thousand Oaks, CA: Sage.

Durie, M. H. (1985). A Māori perspective of health. *Social Science Medicine, 20,* 483–486.

Evans, M., Hole, R., Berg, L. D., Hutchinson, P., & Sookraj, D. (2009). Common insights, differing methodologies: Toward a fusion of Indigenous Methodologies, Participatory Action Research, and White Studies in an urban Aboriginal research agenda. *Qualitative Inquiry, 15*(5), 893–910.

Guba, E. G., & Lincoln, Y. S. (1989). *Fourth generation evaluation.* Newbury Park, CA: Sage.

Guba, E. G., & Lincoln, Y. S. (2005). Paradigmatic, controversies, contradictions, and emerging confluences. In N. Denzin & Y. Lincoln (Eds.), *The SAGE handbook of qualitative research* (pp. 191–216). Thousand Oaks, CA: Sage.

Hallowell, A. I. (1975). Ojibway ontology, behavior, and world view. In D. Tedlock & B. Tedlock (Eds.), *Teachings from the American earth: Indian religion and philosophy* (pp. 141–178). New York, NY: Liveright.

Harris, R., Holmes, H., & Mertens, D. M. (2009). Research ethics in the sign language communities. *Sign Language Studies, 9*(2), 104–131.

Haug, F. (1987). *Female sexualisation: A collective work of memory* (E. Carter, Trans.). London, England: Versa.

Hood, S., Hopson, R., & Frierson, H. (Eds.) (2015). *Continuing the journey to reposition culture and cultural context in evaluation theory and practice.* For the Evaluation and Society Book Series. Charlotte, NC: Information Age.

Howitt, R., & Suchet-Pearson, S. (2003, October). *Changing country, telling stories: Research ethics, methods and empowerment—working with Aboriginal women.* Paper presented at the Fluid Bonds: Gender in Water Resource Management Conference, Canberra, Australia.

Jahoda, M. (1979). The impact of unemployment in the 1930s and 1970s. *Bulletin of the British Psychological Society, 32,* 309–314.

Keefe, V., Ormsby, C., Robson, B., Reid, P., Cram, F., & Purdie, G. (1999). Kaupapa Māori meets retrospective cohort. *He Pukenga Kōrero, 5*(1), 12–17.

Keefe, V., Reid, P., Ormsby, C., Robson, B., Purdie, G., Baxter, J., & NKI Inc. (2002). Serious health events following involuntary job loss in New Zealand meat processing workers. *International Journal of Epidemiology, 31,* 1155–1161.

Keefe-Ormsby, V. (2008). *Tihei Mauri Ora: The human stories of Whakatu. A qualitative study of involuntary job loss following the closure of the Whakatu Freezing Works.* Wellington, New Zealand: Te Rōpū Rangahau Hauora a Eru Pōmare.

Koitsiwe, M. (2013). Prospects and challenges of becoming an Indigenous researcher. In D. M. Mertens, F. Cram, & B. Chilisa (Eds.), *Indigenous pathways to social research* (pp. 261–276). Walnut Creek, CA: Left Coast Press.

Kuhn, Thomas, S. (1970). *The structure of scientific revolutions* (2nd ed.) Chicago, IL: University of Chicago Press. (Originally published 1962)

LaFrance, J. (2011). *Native Youth Enrichment Program 2010–2011 academic year and summer programs: Evaluation report.* Seattle: Mekinak Consulting.

La France, J., & Crazy Bull, C. (2009). Researching ourselves back to life: Taking control of the research agenda in Indian Country. In D. Mertens & P. Ginsberg (Eds.), *The handbook of social research ethics* (pp. 135–149). Thousand Oaks, CA: Sage.

LaFrance, J., & Nichols, R. (2009). *Indigenous evaluation framework: Telling our story in our place and time.* Alexandria, VA: American Indian Higher Education Consortium.

Lake, A. (2013, February 19). Speech by Anthony Lake, UNICEF Executive Director, to the Global Consultation on Addressing Inequalities in the Post-2015 Development Agenda. Copenhagen. Retrieved from http://www.unicef.org/media/media_67945.html.

Lather, P. (1992). Critical frames in educational research: Feminist and post-structural perspectives. *Theory and Practice, 31*(2), 1–13.

Mertens, D. M. (1998). *Research and evaluation in education and psychology* (1st ed.). Thousand Oaks, CA: Sage.

Mertens, D. M. (1999). Inclusive evaluation: Implications of transformative theory for evaluation. *American Journal of Evaluation, 20*(1), 1–14.

Mertens, D. M. (2009). *Transformative research and evaluation.* New York, NY: Guilford Press.

Mertens, D. M. (2010). *Research and evaluation in education and psychology: Integrating diversity with quantitative, qualitative, and mixed methods* (3rd ed.). Thousand Oaks, CA: Sage.

Mertens, D. M. (2014). *Research and evaluation in education and psychology* (4th ed.). Thousand Oaks, CA: Sage.

Mertens, D. M., & Wilson, A. T. (2012). Program evaluation theory and practice: A comprehensive guide. New York, NY: Guilford Press.

Meyer, M. A. (2001). A cultural understandings of empiricism: A Native Hawaiian critique. *Canadian Journal of Native Education, 25*(2), 188–198.

Morris, J. K., & Cook, D. G. (1991). A critical review of the effect of factory closures on health. *British Journal of Industrial Medicineq, 48,* 1–8.

National Health Committee. (2003). *To have an "ordinary" life, Kia whai oranga "noa."* Wellington, New Zealand: National Health Committee.

Nightingale, A. (2003). A feminist in the forest: Situated knowledges and mixing methods in natural resource management. *ACME: An International E-Journal for Critical Geographies, 2*(1), 77–90.

Parker, B. (1966). Nga Whakatauki—Maori proverbs and sayings. *Te Ao Hou, 54,* 10–11.

Pihama, L. (2010). Kaupapa Māori theory: Transforming theory in Aotearoa. *He Pukenga Korero*, *9*(2), 5–14.

Reid, P., & Robson, B. (2007). Understanding health inequalities. In B. Robson & R. Harris (Eds.), *Hauora: Māori standards of health: Vol. 4* (pp. 3–10). Wellington, New Zealand: Te Rōpū Ranaghau Hauora a Eru Pōmare.

Scheurich, I., & Young, M. (1997). Coloring epistemologies: Are our research epistemologies racially biased? *Educational Researcher*, *26*(4), 4–16.

Sefa Dei, G. J. (2006). Introduction: Mapping the terrain—Towards a new politics of resistance. In G. J. Sefa Dei & A. Kempf (Eds.), *Anti-colonialism and education: The politics of resistance* (pp. 1–24). Rotterdam, The Netherlands: Sense Publications.

Sium, A., Desai, C., & Ritskes, E. (2012). Towards the "tangible unknown": Decolonization and the Indigenous future. *Decolonization: Indigeneity, Education & Society*, *1*(1), 1–13.

Smith, L. (1999). *Decolonising methodologies: Research and indigenous peoples*. New York, NY: Zed Books.

Smith, L. T. (2012). *Decolonizing methodologies—Research and indigenous peoples* (2nd ed.). New York, NY: Zed Books.

Swadener, B. B., & Mutua, K. (2008). Decolonizing performances. In N. K. Denzin, Y. S. Lincoln, & L. T. Smith (Eds.), *Handbook of critical and Indigenous methodologies* (pp. 31–43). Thousand Oaks, CA: Sage.

Sweetman, D., Badiee, M., & Creswell, J. W. (2010). Use of the transformative framework in mixed methods studies. *Qualitative Inquiry*, *16*(6), 441–454.

Sullivan, M. J. (2009). Philosophy, ethics, and the disability community. In D. Mertens & P. Ginsberg (Eds.), *The handbook of social research ethics* (pp. 69–84). Thousand Oaks, CA: Sage.

Te Rōpū Rangahau Hauora a Eru Pōmare. (2000). Mauri Tu: The Tomoana Resource Centre—An intervention following job loss. *Social Policy Journal of New Zealand*, *15*, 55–68.

Tuck, E., & Yang, K. W. (2012). Decolonization is not a metaphor. *Decolonization: Indigeneity, Education & Society*, *1*(1), 1–40.

United Nations. (2007). *United Nations Declaration on the Rights of Indigenous Peoples*. Geneva, Switzerland: Author.

United Nations. (2010). *United Nations Convention on the Rights of Peoples with Disabilities*. Geneva, Switzerland: Author.

Walla, H. (2011, October 16). Moving beyond a politics of solidarity towards a practice of decolonization [Web log post]. Retrieved from http://infrontandcenter.wordpress.com/tag/indigenous-sovereignty/

Walsh, D. (2011). Moving beyond Widdowson and Howard: Traditional knowledge as an approach to knowledge. *International Journal of Critical Indigenous Studies*, *4*(1), 2–11.

Wang, C. C., Cash, J. L., & Powers, L. S. (2000). Who knows the streets as well as the homeless? Promoting personal and action through Photovoice. *Health Promotion Practice*, *1*(1), 81–89.

Weber-Pillwax, C. (2001). Orality in Northern Cree Indigenous worlds. *Canadian Journal of Native Education*, *25*(2), 149–165.

Wilson, S. (2008). *Research is ceremony: Indigenous research methods*. Black Point, Nova Scotia: Fernwood.

Woodward, E., Jackson, S., Finn, M., & McTaggart, P. M. (2012). Utilising Indigenous seasonal knowledge to understand aquatic resource use and inform water resource management in northern Australia. *Ecological Management & Restoration*, *13*(1), 58–64.

Woodward, E. L. (2010). Creating the Ngan'gi seasons calendar: Reflections on engaging Indigenous knowledge authorities in research. *Learning Communities: International Journal of Learning in Social Contexts Australia*, *2*, 125–137.

Wronka, J. (2008). *Human rights and social justice: Social action and service for helping and health professions*. Thousand Oaks, CA: Sage. Retrieved from www.humanrightsculture.org.

Understanding and Emphasizing Difference and Intersectionality in Multimethod and Mixed Methods Research

Olena Hankivsky *and* Daniel Grace

Abstract

This chapter provides an overview of the complexity of intersectionality, including its research typologies, guiding research questions, and principles. We review the current state of intersectionality research by analyzing qualitative and quantitative intersectionality-informed research, focusing specifically on data collection, measurement, analysis, and interpretation. We provide in-depth case studies in the areas of education and HIV research that integrate intersectionality into mixed methods research projects. We end with a discussion of issues that arise in intersectionality mixed methods research and directions for the future.

Key Words: intersectionality, complexity, mixed methods, HIV, education

Introduction

The intellectual roots of intersectionality date back more than half a century and are found in US Black feminism, Latina and Asian American feminism, Indigenous feminism, and third-world feminism (Collins, 1990; Combahee River Collective, 1977; hooks, 1984). The term *intersectionality* was coined by critical race legal scholar Kimberlé Crenshaw in 1989. The general thrust of the "intersectional turn" stems from the discontent by scholars and activities in relation to single-axis and unitary frameworks that prioritize gender in feminist studies or race/ethnicity in antiracist studies as primary analytical categories (Nash, 2008). The concern about what researchers may be missing when they prioritize certain categories over others, or fail to acknowledge the interacting factors that contribute to experiences of inequality and the dynamics of subjection, has led to a recognition of intersectionality as a significant research paradigm and theoretical resource.

Intersectionality has been referred to as transformative research, a groundbreaking theory (McCall, 2005), an innovative method (Hankivsky, 2010, 2011), an analytical lens (Wilson, 2013), a policy paradigm, (Dhamoon, 2011), and an innovative framework (Hankivsky, 2011, 2012). For the purposes of this chapter, we refer to intersectionality as a framework, which we conceptualize as a flexible, adaptable, and critical research strategy for moving beyond single or typically favored categories of analysis (e.g., sex, gender, race, and class) to consider simultaneous interactions between different aspects of social identity (e.g., race/ethnicity, Indigeneity, gender, class, sexuality, geography, age, ability, immigration status, and religion) and systems and processes of oppression and domination (e.g., racism, classism, sexism, ableism, and heterosexism; Hankivsky & Cormier, 2009).

Intersectionality frameworks distinguish themselves by their attention to the myriad of interacting factors, including processes of oppression (e.g., racism, classism, sexism, ableism, ageism, and heterosexism) that influence people's everyday lives and identities. Intersectional analysis is not, however, achieved by adding together several inequities or systems of oppression, as evidenced by additive and multiple approaches in research. Additive and multiple approaches assume the coherence and separation of different social locations. Moreover, these approaches often lead to the ranking of identities in shaping inequalities and processes of discrimination (Collins, 1990; Cuadraz & Uttal, 1999; Weber & Parra-Medina, 2003). Conversely, intersectionality foregrounds power and investigates its role in interactive relationships across social locations and mutually constituting processes that create and perpetuate both discrimination and privilege (Dhamoon & Hankivsky, 2011).

Many intersectionality scholars emphasize the need to explore how multiple and interacting social locations position individuals and groups in asymmetrical relation to one another, affecting their perceptions, experiences, and outcomes (Grace 2013a; Hankivsky et al., 2012). Rather than *additive*, these are often operationalized as *multiplicative* approaches in intersectionality research. Explicit attention to interactions ensures an understanding of how constructs such as race, gender, and class are the result of social processes rather than primarily characteristics of individuals. Weber and Parra-Medina (2003) have emphasized the need to distinguish between (a) looking "downstream" for causes that might be associated with social category membership (e.g., individual behaviors) and (b) looking "upstream" at "the group processes that define systems of social inequality" (p. 190), such as laws, institutional practices, and public policies, which are mechanisms that create political, material, and social inequities.

Additionally, rather than predetermining the significance of, and relationships between, any one set of structures and/or social locations, intersectionality expects these to be determined and made politically relevant through inductive research processes (Hankivsky et al., 2012). For example, researchers would typically not start with an a priori assumption that socioeconomic status, gender, or race are the most salient categories of analysis but rather would make these determinations during the course of undertaking the research. Intersectionality researchers also understand that the whole of any complex problem or phenomenon cannot be addressed in one study (Rogers & Kelly, 2011). Although often focused on the social inclusion of previously ignored and excluded populations, the insights gleaned through intersectionality frameworks make this research tradition applicable to the analysis of any group of people, advantaged as well as disadvantaged. Intersectionality advances understandings of how social organization shapes all human lives (Weldon, 2008; Yuval-Davis, 2006).

Because intersectionality emphasizes that privilege and penalty can be simultaneously experienced (Collins, 1990), this approach also challenges common practices of constructing certain groups in opposition of one another (e.g., man vs. women, immigrant vs. nonimmigrant, Aboriginal vs. non-Aboriginal; Hankivsky, 2012). For example, intersectionality brings to the fore that differences among women and among men are often as significant, if not more so, than those between women and men (Crashaw & Smith, 2009; Varcoe, Hankivsky & Morrow, 2007). Furthermore, intersectionality research has highlighted the contexts in which some groups of women exercise power over some groups of men (Pease, 2006), illustrating the complexity of power dynamics and the multiple, shifting social locations individuals occupy across time and space.

Despite being recognized for having enormous potential to transform how researchers think about and respond to human differences, the promise of intersectionality has not been fully realized, and examples of transformative applications remain sparse. Since the late 1990s, the challenges of operationalizing intersectionality have been at the forefront of intersectional scholarship. For example, Cuádraz and Uttal (1999) have argued that "translating the theoretical call for studying the interlocking systems of oppression and intersectionality. . . into methodological practices is not easy" (p. 158). Until very recently, strong claims were made that effective methodologies do not exist or are extremely limited and that scholars have little practical guidance on how to undertake intersectionality-informed research (Hancock, 2007; Nash, 2008; Phoenix & Pattynama, 2006). According to Bowleg (2008), "researchers interested in conducting intersectionality research often have to self teach and learn through trial and error" (p. 313).

Nevertheless, the situation is rapidly changing. As detailed in the following sections, intersectionality scholars are focusing on advancing conceptual clarity and precision. Normative and operational guidance for intersectionality applications in both research and policy is emerging (e.g., Bowleg, 2008; Choo & Ferree, 2010; Cole, 2009; Grace, 2013a; Hancock, 2007, 2011, 2012, 2013; Hankivsky & Cormier, 2009; Hankivsky et al., 2010; McCall, 2005).

Because the relationship between intersectionality and mixed methods is in nascent stages of development, the aim of this chapter is to investigate how researchers have attempted to bring intersectionality into their mixed methods research (MMR) projects. We begin, however, by reviewing the current landscape of intersectionality research literature. We start with a brief overview of intersectionality, including its research typologies, guiding research questions, and principles. This is an essential step because many scholars continue to press for such conceptual clarity due to the ongoing challenges they face when applying intersectionality in their fields of research. We then move on to analyze the insights gleaned from qualitative and quantitative intersectionality-informed research to date, focusing specifically on data collection, measurement, analysis, and interpretation. In this section we also highlight some of the tradeoffs involved from the perspective of intersectionality when collecting and interpreting quantitative and qualitative data.

We then move on examine two specific areas that are making important advancements in this regard: HIV and education. Even though these fields of scholarship represent preliminary efforts, scholars engaging with mixed methods are motivated to challenge essentialist categories of experiences in their research. As we illustrate, their scholarship helps to further reveal the significance of meaningfully accounting for diversity in research that is often obfuscated by the use of isolated analytical categories (e.g., gender, race, socioeconomic status). Moreover, the emerging mixed methods work demonstrates the importance of uncovering the foundations and functions of power in the creation and perpetuation of both power and privilege as precursors to achieving social justice and institutional transformation (Hankivsky, 2011; Hankivsky & Cormier, 2009; Thornton Dill & Kohlman, 2012). While it is useful to review this emerging literature, we do not, however, create a prescription for any one interpretation of mixed or multimethods. Instead, we focus on identifying emergent trends in mixed methods intersectional research and explicate these in relation to the central tenants of intersectionality that have been established in the literature (Hankivsky et al., 2012). In the process, we seek to provide some direction and insights for

the advancement of mixed methods work. We conclude that while it is useful to review the research that has been conducted to date, intersectionality in the context of mixed methods remains underinvestigated, and thus its full transformative potential is largely unrealized.

Conceptual and Research Typologies of Intersectionality

Among the first attempts to formulate questions that could guide researchers interested in pursuing an intersectionality-informed analysis was made by Weber and Parra-Medina (2003). First, Weber and Parra-Medina question the meaning of social categories and structures of inequality: "What is the meaning of race, ethnicity, class, sexuality and other systems of inequality across the ideological, political, and economic domains of society in institutional structures and individual lives?" (p. 184). Second, they ask researchers to consider the relational nature of systems: "How are these co-constructed systems of inequality simultaneously produced, reinforced, resisted, and transformed—over time, in different social locations, and in different institutional domains (for example, health, education, economy, religion, polity, and family)?" (p. 184). Finally, the focus on social justice for intersectionality is emphasized (e.g., how can our understandings of the intersecting dynamics of these systems guide us in the pursuit of social justice?; Weber & Parra-Medina, 2003, p. 184; see also Hankivsky et al., 2012, p. 38).

In her attempt to differentiate intersectionality from what she refers to as "unitary" or "additive/multiple" approaches, Hancock first developed a conceptual table in 2007, which she has recently revised (Hancock, 2013) that makes explicit the distinction between the three methods of conceptualizing categories of difference like race, gender, class, and sexuality. According to Hancock (2013), "each conceptualization strategy. . . has important ramifications for research design and methodology that have not yet been systematically interrogated in the intersectionality literature" (p. 109). This table provides a succinct overview of unitary, multiple, and intersectional approaches by reviewing key differences regarding how each tradition conceptualizes and empirically examines difference. For example, while a unitary approach has one relevant category of analysis, multiple and intersectional approaches have more than one. The table also notes that while relationships between categories are not posited in a unitary approach, in multiple approaches they are both predetermined and conceptually distinguishable, while in an intersectionality approach relationships are open to reveal themselves through the process of research and discovery.

McCall (2005) and Choo and Ferree (2010) have also developed classification systems of intersectionality research practices. McCall's typology differentiates between anticategorical, intracategorial, and intercategorical analyses. Anticategorical analysis questions the process of categorization itself and leads researchers to focus on research participants' points of intersection as gleaned through personal narratives, case studies, and in-depth interviews (Rogers & Kelly, 2011, p. 402). Intracategorical analysis seeks to highlight diversity within groups by taking marginalized intersectional identities as an analytic starting point in order to reveal the complexity of lived experience within such groups (McCall, 2005, p. 1774). Using this approach, researchers choose a particular social group and focus on understanding the complexity of lived experiences within this group (e.g., immigrant women, Aboriginal women, women of color). Finally, intercategorical analysis focuses on the nature of relations of inequality among already constituted groups. This approach entails using preexisting categories of difference to explore inequalities within and across social groups (e.g., comparing Black women with poor White men). Grace (2010) calls this a "provisional categorical" strategy and argues it may be most amenable to research involving quantitative measures, as the (provisional) use of socially constructed categories of difference is a requirement of most survey methods (p. 3). Further, McCall favors this conceptualization since it exposes the relationships between inequality and the social categories themselves in order to display the linkages between social categories and disadvantages/inequalities.

Choo and Ferree (2010) distinguish between group-centered, process-centered, and system-centered intersectionality research practices. They explain that group-centered practices seek to take into account multiply marginalized groups and explore intersectional dynamics in data analysis. However, Choo and Ferree argue that group-centered approaches contribute to "overemphasizing the differences of the group under study from an assumed middle-class readership and obscuring the norm-constructing operations of power" (p. 137). In comparison, process-centered practices are intended to bring attention to how

structural processes organize power and how identities and social locations are constructed and/or co-constructed with macro and meso categories and relations (Choo & Ferree, 2010, p. 134). However, Choo and Ferree observe that process-centered approaches fall short of such intentions because they start their analysis with assumptions around primary forms of oppression. The approach favored is what they refer to as a system-centered intersectional analysis, which "moves away from associating specific inequalities with unique institutions, instead looking for processes that are fully interactive, historically co-determining, and complex" (p. 129).

In addition to typology advancement, others have moved to provide more concrete guidance on how to proceed with applying intersectionality into the research process. Scholars have also provided concrete, step-by-step advice for how to make qualitative research congruent with intersectional thinking at various stages in the research process. For example, Hankivsky and Cormier (2009, p. 22) provide key questions that are intended to capture the essence of intersectionality when defining one's research question. The questions they provide are intended to encourage researchers to think through how they frame, understand, and engage their research participants and ensure that researchers consider the necessity and social justice aims of the research. These questions ask researchers to consider why their research is essential and how matters of social justice will be meaningfully addressed. Drawing on the work of Cole (2008), Hankivsky and Cormier ask

> With regards to the relationship between the researcher and the researched: How can coalitions among members of social groups with unequal political and economic power avoid reproducing existing inequality in their practice? What procedures will safeguard the voices and interests of the less powerful? How will agendas be set?" (p. 22)

Additional questions focus on the need for researchers to not simply reproduce what they "want to see" in their studies and asks about processes of collaboration in the research process, including the representation of key stakeholders (Hankivsky & Cormier, 2009, p. 22).

In addition, Hankivsky (2012, pp. 1715–1716) has developed a broader set of questions intended to guide researchers throughout the entire research process, understanding that each line of inquiry will have different relevance to qualitative, quantitative, and MMR designs. They are intended to prompt researchers to provide an explicit rationale about whom they are studying, how they frame individuals and groups under investigation, and whom the research will benefit. Importantly, they are designed to provide a robust method for understanding the significance and effects of intersections—the intersections of social locations, institutions, and structures that reveal how power creates and perpetuates differences that result in oppression and privilege.

But even beyond the kind of questions that are asked, or even which methods are employed, intersectionality scholars have recognized the importance of having research underpinned by key principles that advance the central tenants of intersectionality. For example, Hankivsky et al. (2012) have put forward the following principles: intersecting categories, multilevel analysis, power, reflexivity, time and space, and diverse knowledge. These principles, taken together, are intended to provide a kind of "terms of reference" for an intersectionality-informed approach that should inform at all stages of research and/or policy analysis.

Beginning in 2007, Hancock, an internationally recognized intersectionality scholar, claimed that rather than being solely a content specialization, intersectionality is both a normative and research paradigm. She based this argument on her interpretation of paradigms as representing worldviews that precede any questions of empirical investigation (Hancock, 2007, p. 64; see also Hesse-Biber, Leavy, & Yaiser, 2004). Most recently, Hancock has proposed the concept of "paradigm intersectionality." According to Hancock, paradigm intersectionality provides a comprehensive empirical operationalization of intersectionality. As Figure 7.1 outlines, it allows researchers to simultaneously incorporate five relevant dimensions of intersectional complexity, including complexity within categories (diversity within) and between categories (categorical multiplicity, categorical intersection); complexity in a given historical moment as well as over time (time dynamics); and complexity in terms of how categories like race, gender, class, and sexual orientation are shaped by dynamic processes engaged in by individuals, groups, and institutions (individual–institutional interactions) (Hancock, 2013).

Nevertheless, Hancock acknowledges that translating intersectionality to research and policy is an ongoing challenge, and this is certainly evidenced by the overview and analysis of qualitative, quantitative, and MMR that follows.

Intersectionality and Qualitative Research

It is generally thought that because qualitative methodology prioritizes capturing the multidimensional lived experiences of people in the full context of their social lives, it is especially well suited for carrying out intersectionality-informed research. Qualitative researchers have identified methods they see as compatible with the demands of intersectionality. For example, ethnographic methods, including case studies and personal narratives, are

> notably useful in terms of providing detailed accounts that illustrate complex social relationships and dynamics in some depth and contribute to an understanding not only of relationships between concepts, but the processes and the meanings that those processes and relationships hold. (Schulz & Mullings, 2006, p. 7)

Narváez, Meyer, Kertzner, Ouellette, and Gordon (2009) explain that participant observation, personal narrative, and classic or critical ethnography help researchers understand both individual and collective identity processes required for an intersectional analysis. Community-based or participatory action research is favored by intersectionality researchers because "it is informed by the experiences of the people and communities who are being considered, and is conducted in the environments in which interventions will be implemented, assuring 'real world' application of the research findings" (Rogers & Kelly, 2011, pp. 402–404). Based on emerging research in the field, it is possible to pinpoint important considerations and insights relating to data collection and measurement, analysis, and interpretation within intersectionality-informed qualitative research projects.

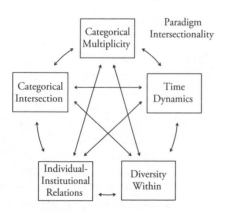

Fig. 7.1 Paradigm intersectionality.

Qualitative Data Collection and Measurement

Warner (2008) suggests that when decisions about which intersections to research (i.e., as a unit of study) are not carefully considered or explicitly documented, there is a potential to exclude intersecting subordinate identities. For example, this may include ignoring identities that go beyond race and class (e.g., gender identity, religious beliefs, age, ableness, and immigration status). Consequently, identities that are involved in particular research can be perceived as prototypical for that social category. This invisibility leads to consequences such as misrepresentation and marginalization of a wide segment of the population. However, it is also important to highlight that in inductive qualitative research, it is often *the research itself* (e.g., revealed through the participants of the research) that make visible which interactions are most significant.

Another important consideration at this stage of the research process is the sampling method. Sample size and composition depends on the analysis to be performed. Qualitative research is concerned with "saturation"—a deep understanding of the phenomenon to be studied. The sample should be representative of the community or population of interest, and it should be sufficiently heterogeneous to allow for inductive explorations of how multiple categories intersect to form a diversity of social locations.

Bowleg (2008) argues that the wording of questions shapes how participants respond, and thus researchers should avoid interview questions that focus on or separate out identities. Instead she contends that researchers should pose general and broad queries that are able to capture the complexity of participant experiences. Bowleg provides the following examples to delineate between additive and intersectional questions that go beyond separating identities to understanding the way they are inextricably linked:

Additive Question:
• What would you say about your life as a Black person? woman? lesbian?

Intersectional Question:
• What are some of the day-to-day challenges that you face in terms of your race, gender and/or sexual orientation? (p. 315)

The distinction Bowleg offers between these questions is consistent with the review of Hancock (2007, 2012; see Table 7.1) provided earlier. With her intersectional question, Bowleg is considering how research participants experience dynamic interactions related to their different social locations and identities. For Bowleg, it is essential that questions about intersectionality focus on constructs such as stress, prejudice, and discrimination rather than relying on demographic information alone. Bowleg provides a compelling example about the efficacy of such question construction by explaining how Nancy, a 44-year-old lesbian with a physical disability, replied to the second question. She explained: "Getting listened to. I think that a lot of time people discredit me because I am a Black lesbian, who walks with a cane most of the time"

Table 7.1 Three Empirical Approaches to Conceptualizing Categories of Difference

	Unitary Approach	Multiple Approach	Intersectional Approach
Number of relevant categories/processes	One	More than one	More than one
Posited relationship between categories/processes	None	Predetermined and conceptually distinguishable relationships	Relationships are open, empirical questions to be determined
Conceptualization of each category	Static at individual or institutional level	Static at individual or institutional level	Dynamic interaction between individual and institutional factors
Case makeup of category/class	Uniform	Uniform	Diverse; members often differ in politically significant ways
Approach to intersectionality	Lip service or dismissal	Intersectionality as testable explanation	Intersectionality as paradigm/research design

(Bowleg, 2008, p. 315). According to Bowleg, this narrative clearly demonstrated the intersection of sex, sexual orientation, and disability in Nancy's life experiences. At the same time, Bowleg also cautions that respondents' interpretation of the question can in fact result in additive responses where different identities are in fact ranked and seen as separate from others.

Qualitative Data Analysis and Interpretation

To be consistent with intersectionality guiding principles, it is critical that analyses capture multiplicative experiences. A number of researchers have proposed multistage analyses to achieve such a goal. For example, according to Bowleg (2008), analyzing a text or narrative using an intersectionality lens requires specific coding processes. According to Bowleg's approach, which she argues is in accordance with grounded theory, coding involves three steps—open, axial, and selective—which allow movement from an additive to interactive analysis. Using her example of black lesbian women, Bowleg explains that data would be analyzed first using *open coding*, which involves coding a passage using multiple and overlapping codes (e.g., there would be a code for heterosexism, another for violence, sexism, and intersectionality). This would be followed by *axial coding* that focuses on how to separate each code and further refine it into more distinct codes (e.g., intersections of racism and sexism). Axial coding is associated with the data-driven inductive approach. Finally, *selective coding* would be utilized to further refine the codes to reflect a specific dimension of an intersectional experience to highlight, for example, how Black lesbians' experiences

of violence reflect intersections of racism, sexism, and heterosexism (Bowleg 2008; see also Narváez et al. 2009, p. 72).

Sirma Bilge (2009) has developed a two-step hybrid approach combining inductive thematic analysis and a deductive template approach (Table 7.2). The first level of analysis—*the data-driven inductive approach*—focuses on open and axial coding identifying emergent themes and patterns and their connections that emerge from qualitative interview data. During this stage of analysis the interviewer works to avoid treating individual interviews as representative accounts of social categories such as gender, race, class, and sexual orientation. In the second stage of analysis—*the theory-oriented deductive approach*—the data analyzed in the inductive approach is reinterpreted through a deductive analytical template. At this stage intersectionality is applied in the analysis of the data collected and individual participant accounts are related to broader social relations structured by social categories.

This type of approach can be seen as consistent with McCall's (2005) intercategorical approach outlined earlier. According to Bilge (2009), her approach is effective for helping to unpack the often hidden processes that shape diverse (and often stigmatized and pathologized) experiences of masculinities that are not recognized when researchers focus only on gender and the experiences associated with dominant groups.

Despite the promising developments made in the qualitative field in relation to intersectionality, one of the persistent critiques of this tradition—whether informed by intersectionality or not—is that the evidence collected is not, as Hancock has

Table 7.2 Intersectionality and Mixed Methods Research: Key Shared Assumptions

	Theory of Intersectionality	Mixed-Methods Research
Holistic inquiry	Reject dichotomous, binary thinking	Reject choice between constructivism and positivism
Centering contradictions and tensions	Focus on converging identities and discriminations Focus on intersection of oppressions	Focus on approaching knowledge production in ways that accounts for diverse, converging perspectives and multiple ways of knowing
Interplay between agency and structure	Allows for a critical conceptualization of power and identity Allows for contextual analysis (e.g., analyzing role of institutional structures)	Allows for a collection of data (e.g., quantitative and qualitative) that accounts for power, history, and context

Source. Adapted from Perry (2009, p. 237).

argued elsewhere (2013), particularly amenable to generalizable policy solutions beyond those on extremely localized levels. Generalizability and transferability of qualitative research (i.e., the extent to which findings from a study are applicable to wider populations and/or different contexts) have been widely discussed, largely because qualitative work typically focuses on purposeful samples aimed at generating "thick descriptions" of a particular phenomenon. Because qualitative research often does not seek "generalizable" accounts, quantitative research—in which large random samples are collected and analyzed—is considered to be far more robust and reliable in terms of drawing inferences that can be expanded to a broader population base (Hancock, 2013; Hankivsky, 2011). Not surprisingly, intersectionality scholars have started to explore the potential of quantitative methods as an empirical strategy for advancing intersectionality.

Intersectionality and Quantitative Research

The potential of intersectionality in quantitative research and statistical data analysis is only starting to be realized. However, the inherent challenges confronted in applying intersectionality within quantitative research have also been recognized (Barker, 2005; Phoenix & Pattynama, 2006; Shields, 2008; Weldon, 2005). And as Dubrow (2008) has so aptly concluded, the few guides that exist speak in very broad terms and do not provide empirical illustrations that support the theoretical framework of intersectionality.

A major challenge of incorporating intersectionality into quantitative research is that study designs are often not developed with intersectionality in mind, and thus sample sizes often lack the diversity of demographics to construct meaningful intersections for the purposes of analysis, including for example, sexual orientation, gender identity, immigration status, and religion (Bowleg, 2008, pp. 314–317; Dubrow, 2008; Hancock, 2007, p. 66; McCall, 2005, p. 1787). A related problem is finding a data set with large enough sample sizes to be able to analyze the complexities of subgroup experiences, which are often a smaller subset of the general population. Moreover, as Dubrow has noted, another challenge is how to select among demographic categories. While most research has primarily tested the intersections of gender/sex, race/ethnicity, and socioeconomic status/class, quantitative analyses should not be limited to a few categories but should rather make use of a wide array of demographic variables that are theorized to encompass diverse axes of an individual's identity and social location.

Scholars have also posited that the quantification of intersectional experience is incompatible with the focus of this paradigm on resisting notions of an unchanging fixed reality (Bowleg, 2008) and risks oversimplifying the complex, relational social factors that intersectionality theory seeks to capture (Shields, 2008). Within conventional statistical analyses, as Shields argues, "it is neither an automatic nor easy step to go from *acknowledging* linkages among social identities to *explaining* those linkages or the processes through which intersecting identities define and shape one another" (p. 304).

Further, debates surrounding the "right" intersections or data categories to study and the most appropriate line of inquiry have highlighted the complexity inherent in the design and application of intersectionality research (Bowleg, 2008; Shields, 2008; Warner, 2008). A major difficulty lies in the increased complexity encountered when expanding the research scope to include multiple dimensions of social identity (McCall, 2005), especially when researchers are confronted the need to examine interactions between more than two variables simultaneously.

Quantitative Data Collection and Measurement

From an intersectionality perspective, an additive approach (e.g., *women + ethnic minority + low socioeconomic status*) is inadequate for understanding the synergistic effects of social locations (Dubrow, 2008). Treating variables independently suggests that these social categories are static and primarily properties of individuals rather than reflections of macro-level social practices linked to inequality (Weber & Parra-Medina, 2003). Bowleg (2008) acknowledges this problem but nevertheless argues that some quantitative lines of inquiry may not be able to avoid an additive approach. In reflecting on her own research, Bowleg suggests that the best possible solution in trying to determine the relationship between stress and discrimination would be to pose a question that would allow respondents to pick more than one social location. She provides the following example:

> In the past year, would you say that you have experienced stress as a result of discrimination due to your race, sex, and or/sexual orientation? If so,

please indicate by *checking all that apply* below, the response that best describes the basis for the discrimination you experienced.

Was it primarily because of your:

☐ race ☐ sex ☐ sexual orientation (Bowleg, 2008, p. 316)

While this does not move beyond an additive approach per se, it does avoid giving primacy to any one explanatory factor a priori.

The second approach to applying intersectionality theory in quantitative analysis is multiplicative. In this approach, interaction terms of demographic categories are used to account for the conditional effects of the intersecting categories on the social outcome (Dubrow, 2008). The main question is: To what extent do intersections of disadvantage within gender, ethnicity, and class groups influence participation? The main hypothesis is that intersectional identities influence political participation so that it is lower for those with cumulative disadvantage. And, to ensure movement beyond a traditional additive approach to cumulative disadvantage, Dubrow includes the following interactions in his study: gender–ethnicity, gender–class, ethnicity–class, and gender–ethnicity–class. Similarly, according to Hancock (2013), the most commonly used methodological strategy by researchers who embrace intersectionality involves the inclusion of additional variables and relevant interaction terms as illustrated in Dubrow's work on political participation.

Quantitative Data Analysis and Interpretation

The inclusion of multiple categories and/or statistical interactions between social identities such as race, sex, or sexual orientation is not sufficient for the kind of interactive model envisioned by most intersectionality scholars. First and foremost, such quantitative approaches do not problematize the static and unchanging nature often assumed in the use of such categorical data. Second, it assumes a type of unitary and separable nature of these social locations.

As a result, quantitative research that claims to be informed by intersectionality often involves examinations of two-way statistical interactions between axes of inequality in regression modeling (Read & Gorman, 2006; Nomaguchi, 2007; Veenstra, 2011, 2013). Other studies have attempted to capture social positions arising from intersections among three axes of inequality (Jackson & Williams, 2006; Roxburgh, 2009; Sanchez-Vaznaugh, Kawachi, Subramanian, Sanchez, & Acevedo-Garcia, 2009;

Zambrana & Dill 2006). In a recent collection of articles on intersectionality research on gender, lesbian/gay/bisexual/transexual, and racial/ethnic identities, Parent, DeBlaere, and Moradi (2013) explain that few studies examined three-way interactions. Echoing the work of Babbitt (2011), they postulate that "boundaries or limitations in theoretical underpinnings for three-way statistical interactions or challenges in achieving the sample size and statistical power needed to test such interactions may be among the barriers to fully exploring data in this way" (p. 642).

Scholars have made additional suggestions on how to advance quantitative techniques. For example, Wilkinson (2003) has argued that to explore statistical intersections, individual identity markers that are highly correlated should be combined into a single variable (e.g., immigrant status and visible minority) and then compared to nonvisible minorities looking at outcomes of interest. Dubrow (2008) has suggested that interaction terms are the best method to measure intersections in quantitative research and advises the use of dichotomous variables as the optimal approach. For Dubrow, using dichotomous variables allows differentiating and grouping disadvantaged groups from the nondisadvantaged members of the population into meaningful categories.

Cole (2009) has also argued that there are ways to interpret statistical interactions between variables based on category membership that are not antithetical to intersectionality. She cites the work of Shih, Pittinsky, and Ambady (1999), who report on two studies that demonstrated how different identities (e.g., gender identities and racial identities) can coexist in an individual and manifest differently depending on different contexts. Through processes of priming manipulation and cross-cultural examinations, Cole concludes that intersectionality depends less on what method is used than on how social categories are conceptualized. In the two studies, the "ethnicity effect" did not consistently replicate in relation to math performance among Asian American women in different geographic contexts, highlighting the importance of other interactive factors such as gender and geographic location. The outcomes of the research are important because they also challenge dominant stereotypes regarding the academic performance of Asian Americans.

Arguably, the best intersectionality practices within the quantitative tradition pursue a multi-stage analysis and interpret quantitative research findings within the social, cultural, political, and historical contexts of structural inequity for groups positioned in social hierarchies of unequal power (Bowleg, 2008; Cole, 2009). Categories such as race, gender, and class do not simply describe groups that may be different or similar; they encapsulate historical and continuing relations of political, material, and social inequity and stigma that create barriers to accessing political, economic, and social power, resources, and privileges. Despite the progress that has been made, there are a number of salient characteristics of quantitative strategies that create shortcomings from the perspective of intersectionality scholars. These include (a) predetermination of categorical relationships, (b) static conceptions of each category, and (c) uniformity of cases within each category (Hancock, 2013). According to Hancock, "all three assumptions are hallmarks of good positivist net effects scholarship, but they are not necessarily in line with normative intersectionality theory, which posits non-disaggregability and intersections as a priori assumptions within the theory" (p. 121). With this review of quantitative and qualitative intersectionality research provided, we now turn to discuss how this critical framework informs MMR.

Intersectionality and Mixed Methods Research

A number of intersectionality scholars have highlighted the benefits of engaging with MMR across diverse disciplinary fields (Hankivsky, 2012; Thornton Dill & Kohlman, 2012). Researchers argue this would involve marrying the strengths of quantitative and qualitative methods in order to fully explore individuals' lives across various levels in society, including macro (e.g., global and national-level institutions and policies), meso or intermediate (e.g., regional-level institutions and policies), and micro levels (e.g., community level, grassroots institutions and policies, as well as the individual or "self") (Bowleg, 2012; Dubrow, 2013; Hancock, 2007, 2013; Hankivsky & Cormier, 2009; Hankivsky et al., 2012; Perry 2009; Thornton Dill & Kohlman, 2012; Ungar & Liebenberg, 2011; Weber & Castellow, 2012; Weber & Fore, 2007). Dubrow asserts that both qualitative and quantitative methods are required to "produce a full and complete portrait of intersectionality, and to test its main assumptions" (p. 164). For example, he notes that while qualitative methods can provide valuable insights into social stratification processes, quantitative data is needed to help produce results that are generalizable to larger population groups.

Some scholars have gone so far as to assert a close compatibility of MMR and intersectionality. For example, Perry (2009) argues that mixed methods and intersectionality share a similar epistemological stance that is grounded in shared commitments to holistic and/or integrated inquiry, assessing the interplay between human agency and systemic structures, and centering tensions and contradictions of lived experiences in assessment of social and behavioral realities. In short, according to Perry, intersectionality and MMR have important conceptual and epistemological overlaps. Perry notes how intersectionality focuses on *converging identities* and discriminations, and mixed methods researchers approach knowledge production in ways that accounts for diverse, *converging perspectives* and multiple ways of knowing.

At the same time that there may be shared grounds for inquiry, methodological tensions also must be acknowledged. For example, Kelly (2009) has noted the challenges of bringing together two preferred but often antagonistic research methods when conducting intersectionality research (which frequently involves qualitative methods) and biomedical research (which involves methods such as the "gold standard" of randomized control trials). Kelly writes that there are inherent tensions between intersectionality and biomedicine in terms of underlying assumptions and preferred methods. Both research fields have been discounted by proponents of the other using arguments of scientific fallibility. Feminist intersectionality scholars critique the positivism, dualism, and reductive analysis of the research methods used in biomedicine and its failure to recognize the power relations and multiple oppressions that situate health. Reflecting on positivism more broadly, Hesse-Biber, Leavy, and Yaiser (2004) note how feminists have illuminated the ways in which "epistemological assumptions upon which positivism is based have been shaped by the larger culture and perpetuate the hierarchies that characterize social life: patriarchy, elitism, heterosexism and racialized modes of social power" (p. 11). Biomedical scientists object to the politicized nature of feminist intersectionality and fault it for failing to control for the confounding influences of differences among research subjects, rendering research findings unreliable and invalid (Kelly, 2009, p. 54). However, Kelly argues that both biomedical and intersectional research are essential to advancing the field of health disparities.

Given the growing interest in how to employ intersectionality in MMR, it is instructive to examine and critically evaluate scholarship emerging in two fields of research where intersectionality is being applied in mixed methods studies: HIV research and education research. Through the process of literature review, these diverse fields emerged as two key areas of growth in the literature.

Mixed Methods HIV Research

The field of HIV research offers a number of important examples of MMR that are informed by intersectionality. A review of literature in this field illuminates how mixed method study designs can successfully account for intersectionality throughout the research process while accounting for differences that matter and complex matters of power and inequity.

Using a community-based research design informed by intersectionality, Logie, James, Tharao, and Loutfy (2012, 2013) sought to uncover the needs and research priorities of diverse women living with HIV in Ontario, Canada. Their multimethod design and analysis involved working closely with peer research assistants over two primary phases of data collection: qualitative inquiry into the needs of women living with HIV (through the use of focus groups) followed by a focused quantitative investigation of African Black and Caribbean women living with HIV to assess relationships between intersecting forms of stigma, discrimination, and health outcomes (through the use of cross-sectional surveys). According to the researchers, the project aimed to "implement anti-oppressive, gender and culture-sensitive multimethod research that is methodologically rigorous, empowering, relevant, and meaningful for PRAs [peer research assistants], participants, service providers, and larger communities of PLHIV [people living with HIV]" (Logie et al., 2012, p. 11). The methodological reflections offered by Logie et al. raise important questions for intersectional researchers conducting community-based research. For example, they define a peer research assistant as "a person who shares in common at least one lived experience with focus group participants, such as female gender, race/ethnicity, or HIV-positive serostatus" (Logie et al., 2012, p. 11). The allied commitments of community-based research and intersectional research traditions raise important considerations, including but not limited to the power dynamics involved in the production of knowledge and how research can be used to advance matters of social justice.

Recent intersectionality-informed policy analysis in the field of HIV has also demonstrated the value of drawing on quantitative and qualitative data sources. This is different, albeit related to, conducting a single mixed methods study involving primary quantitative and qualitative data. For example, Grace (2013) utilizes multiple data sources when conducting Intersectionality-Based Policy Analysis (IBPA; Hankivsky et al., 2012). IBPA is an analysis method for understanding the equity-relevant implications of policy. The IBPA framework was developed and refined through an iterative, participatory process (Hankivsky et al., 2012). Grace's IBPA examines the issue of advances in HIV testing technologies and the criminalization of HIV nondisclosure in Canada. While an IBPA need not involve mixed methods per se, Grace demonstrates the importance of drawing on epidemiological and statistical data (e.g., trends of both HIV infections and the increasing application of the criminal law among diverse population groups), qualitative data (e.g., interviews with HIV positive and negative gay and bisexual men in Canada), and other forms of related evidence (e.g., ongoing work by community organizations and civil society to address the structural drivers of the epidemic). Such mixed methods policy analysis makes visible the need to reconceive the "problem" of HIV prevention through an intersectional analysis of the "constructions of policy problems and the empirical actualities of inequity" (Grace, 2013a, p. 178; see also Grace, 2013b). Mixed methods intersectionality research in the field of HIV has worked to focus attention on diverse population groups who may be rendered invisible in other MMR strategies.

Mixed Methods Research on Education and Racialized Students

A growing body of mixed methods intersectional research in the field of education and racialization has focused on themes of identity and belonging for young and emerging adults. A recent collection in the field of higher education research argues that the use of MMR and intersectional frameworks may help to advance this area of scholarship beyond the all-to-frequent overreliance of researchers on static, one-dimensional analyses of both individuals and groups (Griffin & Museus, 2011). This growing scholarship in the area of higher education has focused largely, albeit not exclusively, on how race and ethnicity intersect with other identities and social locations (see Harper, 2011; Maramba &

Museus, 2011). Museus and Griffin (2011) argue that intersectional analysis may advance this field in at least four respects:

(1) *By more accurately accounting for diversity within institutions of higher education* (for example, experience of mixed raced individuals who identify with multiple ethnic backgrounds; how sexual orientation and racial background may inform experiences of female faculty);

(2) *By elucidating voices and lived actualities at the margins* (for example, by considering the convergence of racialized and gendered stereotypes of persons who are at the margins of multiple groups such as Asian American female faculty);

(3) *By illuminating how inequality may result from converging identities and highlight failure among much previous research* (for example, only recently have researchers begun to attend to the intersections of gender and race and "the failure of higher education researchers to make the intersections of social identities and groups more central in research and discourse limits the existing level of understanding of and progress in addressing equity issues in higher education");

(4) *By avoiding the perpetuation of inequality including the recognition of in-group heterogeneity* (for example, recognizing possible differences in college entrance and graduation rates according to multiple ethnic subgrouping of Asian Americans and not ignoring this group due to previous data which demonstrates historically high levels of access and success). (pp. 9–11)

In summary, Museus and Griffin's review helps to make explicit the ways in which intersectionality research can advance scholarship in this field by focusing on complexity and difference within higher educational institutions, making visible the experiences of persons at the margins and avoiding reproducing research processes that further render some groups of persons invisible.

Harper (2011) raises important methodological questions concerning how institutional researchers may robustly capture, measure, and analyze students' intersecting experiences of their identities. For example, the fluid nature of student identities over their educational trajectory (e.g., shifting identities during college years) means that quantitative data collected at the point of admission may not accurately reflect changes in identity for the student at a later point in time. Harper echoes concerns that purely quantitative approaches to intersectionality may "perpetuate categorization and oversimplification" (p. 107; see

also Shields, 2008). As such, she conducted mixed methods longitudinal research to examine racial identification patterns over time and context for college students of mixed race. While race was a focus of Harper's investigation a priori, other dimensions to student identity revealed themselves during the process of investigation.

Harper's (2011) mixed methods analysis sought to illuminate the "intersectionality of identity and how quantitative and qualitative research can be used to understand the complex issues related to quantitative inquiries about students' identities, and used to uncover nuance and complexity within seemingly one-dimensional, static categories" (p. 111). Analysis of quantitative survey data revealed that students are more likely to identify as more than one race (e.g., mixed race) during their senior year of college as opposed to at the point of admission, which "raises questions of whether other identity dimensions such as class, gender, or religion, are similarly dynamic but are treated as static" (Harper, 2011, p. 105). Quantitative analysis revealed the importance of individual and institutional variables on changing/maintaining one's racial identity, yet a number of results in this analysis appeared counterintuitive or presented unclear designation patterns and highlighted the need for qualitative research to uncover issues of meaning and context. Qualitative interviews were designed to provide a nuanced "descriptive portrait" and elicit data relevant to the ethnic and racial identification decisions of mixed race students across diverse campus contexts in which they may be asked about matters of ethnicity, race, and identity (Harper, 2011, p. 108). While Harper used her quantitative research to inform subsequent qualitative analysis, other work in this field has relied on a triangulation mixed methods design allowing for the concurrent collection of quantitative and qualitative data (Maramba & Museus, 2011).

In another example of MMR using intersectionality in the field of higher education, Maramba and Museus (2011) discuss the "utility" of their seven-phase research strategy that "generated a more holistic and accurate picture of the relationship among gender, campus climate, and sense of belonging than would have emerged from using mono-methods techniques' (p. 99). Maramba and Museus enumerate three central lessons learned from their MMR.

(1) *Do not rely on aggregated data* (for example, aggregated data may be misleading and

researchers must consider how to disaggregate data to understand individuals, groups, and organizational processes more accurately).

(2) *Use qualitative research to conceptualize quantitative research* (for example, "how researchers can use the nuances found via qualitative methods to rethink making decisions on disaggregating data, designing quantitative analysis, and redesigning those examinations").

(3) *Keep in mind the multiple purposes of mixed methods approaches* (for example, researchers must maintain flexibility regarding the combinations and sequences of mixed methods use across the process of research and analysis. (p. 99)

We argue that these are important lessons when considering the potential "value added" of using intersectionality when conducting MMR. To further exemplify the second enumerated objective, Maramba and Museus explain that while they designed a concurrent, triangulated study, a post hoc analysis was performed. They explain:

> initial quantitative findings revealed no relationship between gender and perceived hostility of the racial climate or sense of belonging. The qualitative findings, however, indicated there were nuanced differences that helped us rethink how we analyzed the quantitative data, and this led to a post hoc quantitative analysis that accounted for class level and revealed a more complex picture, including a relationship between gender and sense of belonging among an upper-class subsample. (pp. 98–99)

While Maramba and Museus note that these lessons learned may have implications for institutional researchers conducting investigations related to campus climates and one's sense of belonging, we argue these methodological insights may be relevant to other research contexts and mixed method study designs (e.g., as researchers consider the use of *aggregated data* in this MMR design).

While not dealing with campus experiences of identity and belonging, the conceptually allied work of Khanlou and Gonsalves (2011) examined the immigrant and second-generation youth experiences of psychosocial integration into Canada. Khanlou and Gonsalves draw on two mixed methods studies informed by intersectionality in efforts to break down disciplinary silos and examine positions of power, oppression, and relative privilege:

> Disciplinary approaches to understanding identity tend to remain in their silos. Intersectionality provides a space for interdisciplinarity and cross-fertilization of ideas. It recognizes the connection between the psychological and social aspects of identity, where institutional practices (including hiring policies and how they may affect the second generation), and global structures (in particular, large financial institutions that regulate banking and governmental policies that control the flow of migration), inscribe individual and collective identities. And these collective identities in turn influence broader global processes. (p. 177)

The first study they draw on, *Immigrant Youth and Cultural Identity in a Global Context* (Khanlou, Siemiatycki, & Anisef, 2003–2006), applied a comparative longitudinal design to examine self-esteem, cultural identity, and the migration experiences of youth (for further details see Khanlou, 2008; Khanlou, Koh, & Mill, 2008). A second study, *Mental Health Services for Newcomer Youth: Exploring Needs and Enhancing Access* (Khanlou, Shakya, & Muntaner, 2007–2009) used a participatory research approach to mixed methods data collection of the experiences of newcomer male and female youth who had arrived in Canada within the past five years from Afghan, Colombian, Sudanese, and Tamil communities (Khanlou & Gonsalves, 2011, p. 169). While both of these studies are important, limited details are provided in existing published literature to provide a rich account of how intersectionality informed the research questions and overall study design. As we later note, such rich accounts would be a welcome contribution to the mixed methods literature and help to advance the field of intersectionality research.

Finally, in a last example, Graham (2009) conducted mixed methods intersectionality research to understand the experiences of Black female college students. Her sample consisted of 85 Black American women attending either (a) a predominantly White university in the Midwest or (b) a historically Black university in the South. Two overarching research questions guided the study:

1. Qualitative—How is gender constructed among Black women in relation to sexism?
2. Quantitative—What is the relationship between the construction of gender and psychological outcomes among Black women? (p. 26)

Graham's study offers readers a collection of qualitative questions and diverse quantitative measures and standardized scales. However, linking to our earlier review of quantitative research traditions, a review of the scales used reveals some of the limits of using single-axis validated quantitative measures (e.g., race or sex) in a mixed methods study (Graham, 2009, pp. 113–118; e.g., see the Ambivalent Sexism Inventory and the Perceived Gender Discrimination Scale). In the interdisciplinary field of education and racialization, the mixed methods intersectionality research that has been produced to date demonstrates the theoretical and methodological resource of intersectionality throughout the iterative process of study design, data collection, and analysis.

Conclusion

The review of the mixed methods and broader literature to date leads us to make a number of important observations. First, intersectionality does not prescribe or insist on any particular research method or design, nor does it assert any unified way to conduct research (Hankivsky, 2012). As the diversity of quantitative, qualitative, and mixed methods intersectionality literature surveyed can attest to, this is supported across various methods used. In short, the flexibility of intersectionality is an important strength on which we should build.

Second, the benefits of intersectionality for any type of research strategy, including that of mixed methods, are contingent on incorporating and integrating principles of intersectionality theory (Hankivsky et al., 2012). Arguably, at the end of the day "what is needed is an intersectionality-informed stance" (Bowleg, 2012, p. 1270). The ways in which scholars engender their studies with principles of intersectionality across the research lifecycle are diverse and include in some instances an explicit foregrounding of intersectional principles (Grace, 2013a; Hancock, 2011, 2013; Hankivsky et al., 2012). For example, both Hancock (2011, 2013) and Hankivsky et al. (2012) argue that principles such as accounting for temporal, categorical, and multilevel relations are required in the process of intersectional research and analysis.

Third, attention to intersectionality tenets can have transformative effects on the kinds of phenomenon that are examined, the conceptualizations of the populations investigated, the approaches to data collection and measurement, and the way data is ultimately measured and analyzed. This transformation begins with self-reflection on the part of the researcher, which can lead scholars to reassess and critique their methods anew (Kallenberg, Müller, & Meyer, 2013). As Perry (2009) puts it: "Like all

MMR, the effectiveness of one's analysis is highly contingent upon the meticulous and nuanced ideas that inform the research design" (p. 241).

Emerging research signals that intersectionality-inspired ideas cause researchers to pay attention to the needs of understudied populations. According to Warner (2008), researchers using this perspective not only reflect on what they are currently examining but also critically evaluate "who is granted attention, who is not, and the consequences of these actions for the study of social issues" (p. 462). For instance, Dworkin (2005) argues that "who is epidemiologically fathomable in the HIV/AIDS epidemic?" (p. 615) is a central question for researchers to take-up when examining the nature of epidemiological classifications.

Related to this is a conceptual shift that occurs in how researchers understand social categories, as well as their relationships and interactions. Warner and Shields (2013) argue that "intersectionality is not determined by *who* you study but, *how* you study" (p. 809). However, we assert that intersectionality is determined by both these considerations. The examples featured in this chapter demonstrate the importance of examining understudied, marginalized, and traditionally invisible populations. They also illustrate the serious shortcomings of pursuing unitary and one-dimensional examinations of human needs and experiences. Further, the studies show the importance of foregrounding the voices of affected populations, highlighting in-group differences, interrogating intersectional phenomena (e.g., stigma, discrimination, and health outcomes), and illustrating how power and privilege can be simultaneously experienced, shifting over time and place. Additionally, this literature underscores the importance of multistaged investigations that allow for the refinement of categories on which to focus (Logie et al., 2012). Such multistage investigations may be optimally positioned to reveal persons who remain socially invisible—what Purdie-Vaughn and Eibach (2008) call "marginal members of marginal groups" (p. 381).

Further, intersectionality leads researchers to rethink how quantitative and qualitative data is analyzed (Perry, 2009), taking into account the causal complexity of social problems, which explicitly lead to an understanding of within-group variations (Hancock, 2013). In addition, the analysis of all data, from an intersectionality perspective, requires proper contextualization. As Bowleg (2008) notes, "intersectionality researchers, regardless of whether they are using qualitative or quantitative methods, bear the responsibility for interpreting their data within the context of sociohistorical and structural inequality" (p. 321).

An aspect that has not been addressed head-on within mixed methods work is the challenge of different disciplinary research conventions, which Cho, Crenshaw, and McCall (2013) assert may in fact lead practitioners to misrecognize or misinterpret intersectional methodologies. This is clearly a challenge given that intersectionality has been deployed across a diversity of disciplines, all which potentially may have different conceptions of what an intersectionality-informed mixed methods analysis entails. Not surprisingly, Cho et al. urge for "collaborative sensibility"—that is, working toward a methodological literacy across disciplines and contexts—as key to facilitating the growth of intersectionality in various sectors and disciplinary fields.

Another neglected issue in the literature is the power of various types of research methods. It is essential for researchers interested in using multiple methods to be cognizant of the relative power attached to the use of qualitative and quantitative data (Weber & Castellow, 2012). Weber and Castellow, drawing on the work of Fonow and Cook (2005), caution that intersectionality-informed researchers who choose to employ multiple methods, as well as mixed methods, must examine power inequities in the structure of dominant institutions and, in particular, whether qualitative research should always serve as the "'maidservant' to the more powerful quantitative master" (Weber & Castellow, 2012, p. 443). In a similar vein, Bowleg (2012) has also asserted that intersectionality scholars who want to meaningfully engage with mixed methods must actively challenge what counts as sources of data and information (e.g., historic materials, tacit knowledge) beyond empirically collected data. Another issue that has not been fully resolved is the role of the researcher in responding to conflicting results between different methods and how one can resolve such tensions in a mixed methods design, especially when one is attempting to be consistent with an intersectionality paradigm.

Reflecting on the growing body of intersectional scholarship in diverse disciplinary fields over the past 20 years, Kimberlé Crenshaw (2011) recently argued that "to assess what intersectionality can produce is to canvas what scholars, activists and policy makers have done under its rubric" (p. 222). Similarly, Cho et al. (2013) assert that "we think answers to questions about what intersectionality

analysis is have been amply demonstrated by what people are deploying it to do" (p. 789). Canvassing is part of the work we have undertaken in this chapter. While Crenshaw's and Cho et al.'s points are well taken, we argue that the possibilities of intersectional research are only beginning to be realized. Scholars continue to press forward with advancing conceptual understandings of intersectionality, providing practical advice for intersectionality applications and producing concrete research and policy examples.

Researchers exploring the links between the theory of intersectionality and its applications to mixed methods are in many ways entering unchartered territory. In general, there is a paucity of examples that can be drawn on. Moreover, with few exceptions, there is little discussion of the advancements in MMR that have been realized through applications of intersectionality. Researchers are not always explicit about how the theory of intersectionality informs their research design, starting with the formulation of their research question. From all the mixed methods studies we have reviewed in this chapter, researchers do not always make their assumptions clear; they do not consistently detail how intersectionality changes their approach to research, including their research design, data collection, analysis, and/or conclusions. They often fail to articulate how intersectionality differs from or expands on other theoretical frameworks that address inequity. These shortcomings are consistent with Choo and Ferree's (2010) observations elsewhere that scholars undertheorize what intersectionality means in their research and that this undermines the power of their analysis (p. 145). We call on current and future researchers of intersectionality to more robustly account for how their work is informed by intersectionality throughout the research lifecycle.

At the same time, undertaking intersectionality-informed MMR is challenging and complicated. It requires not only expertise in both intersectionality and mixed methods but also in-depth knowledge of the ongoing theoretical and practical insights emerging from intersectionality research literature. Fortunately, there are growing resources, insights, and cautionary notes from intersectionality researchers that can guide these efforts. Most important, however, there is a growing recognition that engaging in such efforts is worthwhile. Intersectionality does offer a unique and transformative framework for rethinking how to address issues of social difference, inequity, and power in the ongoing pursuit of social justice. In the area of mixed methods, we believe that intersectionality can produce much more than the current landscape suggests. The challenge is to continue empirical applications and to realize its full potential for transforming MMR and, in the process, advancing issues of social justice (Canales, 2013; Mertens, 2013).

Discussion Questions

1. How would you apply an intersectionality approach to your area of research and analysis? How might this be different from an additive or multiple approach?

2. What makes intersectionality a valuable framework for thinking about different population groups in MMR?

3. What lessons can be learned from current applications of intersectionality in qualitative and quantitative research that may be used in MMR?

Suggested Websites

www.sfu.ca/iirp/

The Institute for Intersectionality, Research and Policy (IIRP) anchors a vibrant interdisciplinary community of nationally and internationally recognized researchers, scholars, activists, and practitioners who are on the cutting edge of advancing the theory and practical applications of intersectionality in research, policy, and praxis. The IIRP website offers information about key resources and events related to intersectionality.

www.intersectionality-center.org/

Founded by Kimberlé Crenshaw, the Centre for Intersectionality & Social Policy Studies aims to foster the development of interdisciplinary research networks and facilitate dialogue between intersectionality scholars. The website features audiovisual resources as well as information about current intersectionality research and events.

www.cbrc.net/

The Community-Based Research Centre (CBRC) is a nonprofit charitable organization that is dedicated to using community participatory research to develop knowledge about gay men's health and to help guide community practice and theorizing on diverse health and social issues. The CBRC website has diverse resources related to intersectionality, including videos from conference presentations, workshop reports, research papers, and blog posts.

References

Babbitt, L. G. (2011). An intersectional approach to Black/White interracial interactions: The roles of gender and sexual orientation. *Sex Roles, 68*(11–12), 791–802.

Barker, D. (2005). Beyond women and economics: Rereading "women's work." *Signs, 30*(4), 2189–2209.

Bowleg, L. (2008). When Black + Lesbian + Woman ≠ Black Lesbian Woman: The methodological challenges of qualitative and quantitative intersectionality research. *Sex Roles, 59*(5-6), 312–325.

Bowleg, L. (2012). The problem with the phrase women and minorities: Intersectionality—An important theoretical framework for public health. *American Journal of Public Health, 102*(7), 1267–1273.

Canales, G. (2013). Transformative, mixed methods checklist for psychological research with Mexican-Americans. *Journal of Mixed Methods Research, 7*(1), 6–21.

Cho, S., Crenshaw, K. W., & McCall, L. (2013). Toward a field of intersectionality studies: Theory, applications, and praxis. *Signs, 38*(4), 785–810.

Choo, H. Y., & Ferree, M. M. (2010). Practicing intersectionality in sociological research: A critical analysis of inclusions, interactions, and institutions in the study of inequalities. *Sociological Theory, 28*(2), 129–149.

Cole, E. R. (2008). Coalitions as a model for intersectionality: From practice to theory. *Sex Roles, 59*(5–6), 443–453.

Cole, E. R. (2009). Intersectionality and research in psychology. *American Psychologist, 64*(3), 170–180.

Collins, P. H. (1990). *Black feminist thought: Knowledge, consciousness, and the politics of empowerment.* New York, NY: Routledge.

Combahee River Collective. (1995). Combahee River Collective statement. In B. Guy-Sheftall (Ed.), *Words of fire: An anthology of African American feminist thought* (pp. 232–240). New York, NY: New Press. (Originally published 1977).

Crawshaw, P., & Smith, J. (2009). Men's health: Practice, policy, research and theory. *Critical Public Health, 19*(3), 261–267.

Crenshaw, K. (2011). Postscript. In H. Lutz, M. T. H. Vivar, & L. Supik (Eds.), *Framing intersectionality: Debates on a multi-faceted concept in gender studies* (pp. 221–233). London, England: Ashgate.

Cuadraz, G. H., & Uttal, L. (1999). Intersectionality and in-depth interviews: Methodological strategies for analyzing race, class, and gender. *Race, Gender and Class, 6*(3), 156–186.

Dhamoon, R. (2011). Considerations on Mainstreaming Intersectionality. *Political Research Quarterly, 64*(1), 230–243.

Dhamoon, R. K., & Hankivsky, O. (2011). Why the theory and practice of intersectionality matter to health research and policy. In O. Hankivsky (Ed.), *Health inequities in Canada: Intersectional frameworks and practices* (pp. 16–50). Vancouver: University of British Columbia Press.

Dubrow, J. K. (2008). How can we account for intersectionality in quantitative analysis of survey data? Empirical illustration for Central and Eastern Europe. *ASK Research & Methods, 7*, 85–100.9

Dubrow, J. K. (2013). Why should we account for intersectionality in quantitative analysis of survey data? In V. Kallenberg & J. Meyer (Eds.), *Intersectionality und Kritik* (pp. 161–177). Wiesbaden, Germany: Springer Fachmedien.

Dworkin, S. (2005). Who is epidemiologically fathomable in the HIV/AIDS epidemic? Gender, sexuality, and intersectionality in public health. *Culture, Health & Sexuality, 7*(6), 615–623.

Grace, D. (2010). When oppressions and privileges collide: A review of research in health, gender and intersectionality in late (post) modernity. *Canadian Journal of Humanities and Social Sciences, 1*(1), 19–23.

Grace, D. (2013a). Intersectional analysis at the medico-legal borderland: HIV testing innovations and the criminalization of HIV non-disclosure. In A. R. Wilson (Ed.), *Situating intersectionality: Politics, policy, and power* (pp. 157–187). New York, NY: Palgrave Macmillan.

Grace, D. (2013b). Legislative epidemics: The role of model law in the transnational trend to criminalize HIV transmission. *Medical Humanities, 39*(2), 77–84.

Graham, E. T. (2009). *"She's Black more than she's a woman": A mixed method analysis of the construction of gender and psychological outcomes among Black female college students* (Doctoral dissertation), University of Michigan, Ann Arbor.

Griffin, K. A., & Museus, S. D. (Eds.). (2011). *Using mixed-methods approaches to study intersectionality in higher education: New directions for institutional research.* San Francisco, CA: Jossey-Bass.

Hancock, A. M. (2007). When multiplication doesn't equal quick addition: Examining intersectionality as a research paradigm. *Perspectives on Politics, 5*(1), 63–79.

Hancock, A. M. (2011). *Solidarity politics for millennials: A guide to ending the oppression Olympics.* New York, NY: Palgrave MacMillan.

Hancock, A. M. (2013). Empirical intersectionality: A tale of two approaches, *UC Irvine Law Review, 3,* 259–296.

Hankivsky, O. (Ed.). (2011). *Health inequities in Canada: Intersectional frameworks and practices.* Vancouver: University of British Columbia Press.

Hankivsky, O. (Ed.). (2012). *An intersectionality-based policy analysis framework.* Vancouver: Institute for Intersectionality Research and Policy, Simon Fraser University.

Hankivsky, O., & Cormier, R. (2009). *Intersectionality and women's health research: A primer.* Vancouver, BC: Women's Health Research Network.

Hankivsky, O., Grace, D., Hunting, G., Ferlatte, O., Clark, N., Fridkin, A., . . . Lavoilette, T. (2012). Intersectionality-based policy analysis. In O. Hankivsky (Ed.), *An intersectionality-based policy analysis framework* (pp. 33–45). Vancouver: Institute for Intersectionality Research and Policy, Simon Fraser University.

Hankivsky, O., Reid, C., Cormier, R., Varcoe, C., Clark, N., Benoit, C. & Brotman, S. (2010). Exploring the promises of intersectionality for advancing women's health research. *International Journal for Equity in Health, 9*(5), 1–15.

Harper, C. E. (2011). Identity, intersectionality, and mixed-methods approaches. In K. A. Griffin & S. D. Museus (Eds.), *Using mixed-methods approaches to study intersectionality in higher education: New directions for institutional research* (pp. 103–115). San Francisco, CA: Jossey-Bass.

Hesse-Biber, S. N., Leavy, P. & Yaiser, M. L. (2004). Feminist approaches to research as a process: Reconceptualizing epistemology, methodology, and method. In S. N. Hesse-Biber & M. L. Yaiser (Eds.), *Feminist perspectives on social research* (pp. 3–26). New York, NY: Oxford University Press.

Hooks, B. (1984). *Feminist theory: From margin to center.* Boston, MA: South End Press.

Jackson, P. B., & Williams, D. R.(2006). The intersection of race, gender, and SES: Health paradoxes. In A. Schulz & L. Mullings (Eds.), *Gender, race, class, and health: Intersectional approaches* (pp. 131–162). San Francisco, CA: Jossey-Bass.

Jackson, R., & Reimer, G. (2008). *Canadian Aboriginal people living with HIV/AIDS: Care, treatment, and support issues.* Ottawa: Canadian Aboriginal AIDS Network.

Kallenberg, V., Müller, J. M., & Meyer, J. (2013). Introduction: Intersectionality as a critical perspective for the humanities. In V. Kallenberg & J. Meyer, *Intersectionality und Kritik* (pp. 15–35). Wiesbaden, Germany: Springer Fachmedien.

Kelly, U. A. (2009). Integrating intersectionality and biomedicine in health disparities research. *Advances in Nursing Science, 32*(2), E42–E56.

Khanlou, N. (2008). Young and new to Canada: Promoting the mental wellbeing of immigrant and refugee female youth. *International Journal of Mental Health and Addiction, 6*(4), 514–516.

Khanlou, N., & Gonsalves, T. (2011). An intersectional understanding of youth cultural identities and psychosocial integration: Why it matters to mental health promotion in immigrant-receiving pluralistic societies. In O. Hankivsky (Ed.), *Health inequities in Canada: Intersectional frameworks and practices* (pp. 166–179). Vancouver: University of British Columbia Press.

Khanlou, N., Koh, J. G., & Mill, C. (2008). Cultural identity and experiences of prejudice and discrimination of Afghan and Iranian immigrant youth. *International Journal of Mental Health and Addiction, 6*(4), 494–513.

Khanlou, N., Shakya, Y., & Muntaner, C. (2007–2009). "Mental health services for newcomer youth: Exploring needs and enhancing access." Funded by Provincial Centre of Excellence for Child and Youth Mental Health at CHEO.

Khanlou, N., Siemiatycki, M., & Anisef, P. (2003). "Immigrant Youth and Cultural Identity in a Global Context." Funded by the Social Sciences and Humanities Research Council of Canada (2003–2006).

Logie, C., James, L., Tharao, W., & Loutfy, M. R. (2012). Opportunities, ethical challenges, and lessons learned from working with peer research assistants in a multi-method HIV community-based research study in Ontario, Canada. *Journal of Empirical Research on Human Research Ethics, 7*(4), 10–19.

Logie, C., James, L., Tharao, W., & Loutfy, M. R. (2013). Associations between HIV-related stigma, racial discrimination, gender discrimination, and depression among HIV-positive African, Caribbean and Black women in Ontario, Canada. *AIDS Patient Care and STDs, 27*(2), 114–122.

Maramba, D. C., & Museus, S. D. (2011). The utility of mixed methods and intersectionality approaches in conducting research on Filipino American students' experiences with campus climate and on sense of belonging. In K. A. Griffin & S. D. Museus (Eds.), *Using mixed-methods approaches to study intersectionality in higher education: New directions for institutional research* (pp. 93–101). San Francisco, CA: Jossey-Bass.

McCall, L. (2005). The complexity of intersectionality. *Signs, 30*(3), 1771–1800.

Mertens, D. M. (2013). Emerging advances in mixed methods: Addressing social justice. *Journal of Mixed Methods Research, 7*(3), 215–218.

Museus, S. D., & Griffin, K. A. (Eds.). (2011). Mapping the margins in higher education: On the promise of intersectionality frameworks in research and discourse. In

K. A. Griffin & S. D. Museus (Eds.), *Using mixed-methods approaches to study intersectionality in higher education: New directions for institutional research* (pp. 5–13). San Francisco, CA: Jossey-Bass.

Narváez, R. F., Meyer, I. H., Kertzner, R. M., Ouellette, S. C., & Gordon, A. R. (2009), A qualitative approach to the intersection of sexual, ethnic, and gender identities. *Identity: An International Journal of Theory and Research, 9*(1), 63–86.

Nash, J. C. (2008). Re-thinking intersectionality, *Feminist Review, 89*(1), 1–15.

Nomaguchi, K. M. (2007). Are there race and gender differences in the effect of marital dissolution on depression? In B. Landry (Ed.), *Race, gender and class: Theory and methods of analysis* (pp. 394–410). Upper Saddle River, NJ: Pearson Education.

Parent, M. C., DeBlaere, C., & Moradi, B. (2013). Approaches to research on intersectionality: Perspectives on gender, LGBT, and racial ethnic identities. *Sex Roles, 68*(11-12), 639–645.

Pease, B. (2006). Governing men and boys in public policy in Australia. In G. Marston & C. McDonald (Eds.), *Analysing social policy: A governmental approach* (pp. 127–143). Cheltenham, UK: Edward Elgar.

Perry, G. K. (2009). Exploring occupational stereotyping in the new economy: The intersectional tradition meets mixed methods research. In M. T. Berger & K. Guidroz (Eds.), *The intersectional approach: Transforming the academy through race, class and gender* (pp. 229–245). Chapel Hill: University of North Carolina Press.

Phoenix, A., & Pattynama, P. (2006). Intersectionality. *European Journal of Women's Studies, 13*(3), 187–192.

Purdie-Vaughn, V., & Eibach, R. (2008). Intersectional invisibility: The distinctive advantages and disadvantages of multiple subordinate-group identities. *Sex Roles, 59*(5-6), 377–391.

Read, J. N. G., & Gorman, B. (2006). Gender inequalities in U.S. adult health: The interplay of race and ethnicity. *Social Science & Medicine, 62*(5), 1045–1065.

Rogers, J., & Kelly, U. A. (2011). Feminist intersectionality: Bringing social justice to health disparities research. *Nursing Ethics, 18*(3), 397–407.

Roxburgh, S. (2009). Untangling inequalities: Gender, race, and socioeconomic differences in depression. *Sociological Forum, 24*(2), 357–381.

Sanchez-Vaznaugh, E. V., Kawachi, I., Subramanian, S. V., Sanchez, B., & Acevedo-Garcia, D. (2009). Do socioeconomic gradients in body mass index vary by race/ethnicity, gender, and birthplace? *American Journal of Epidemiology, 169*, 1102–1112.

Schulz, A. J., & Mullings, L. (2006). *Gender, race, class, and health: Intersectional approaches*. San Francisco, CA: Jossey-Bass.

Shields, S. A. (2008). Gender: An intersectionality perspective. *Sex Roles, 59*(5-6), 301–311.

Shih, M., Pittinsky, T. L., & Ambady, N. (1999). Stereotype susceptibility: Identity salience and shifts in quantitative performance. *Psychological Science, 10*(1), 80–83.

Thornton Dill, B., & Kohlman, M. H. (2012). Intersectionality: A transformative paradigm in feminist theory and social justice. In S. Hesse-Biber (Ed.), *The handbook of feminist research: Theory and praxis* (pp. 154–174). Los Angeles, CA: Sage.

Ungar, M., & Liebenberg, L. (2011). Assessing resilience across cultures using mixed methods: Construction of the child and youth resilience measure. *Journal of Mixed Methods Research, 5*(2), 126–149.

Varcoe, C., Hankivsky, O., & Morrow, M. (2007). Introduction: Beyond gender matters. In M. Morrow, O. Hankivsky, & C. Varcoe (Eds.), *Women's health in Canada: Critical perspectives on theory and policy* (pp. 3–30). Toronto: University of Toronto Press.

Veenstra, G. (2011). Race, gender, class, and sexual orientation: Intersecting axes of inequality and self-rated health in Canada. *International Journal for Equity in Health, 10*(3), 1–11.

Veenstra, G. (2013). The gendered nature of discriminatory experiences by race, class and sexuality: A comparison of intersectionality theory and the subordinate male target hypothesis. *Sex Roles, 68*(11-12), 646–659.

Warner, L .R. (2008). A best practices guide to intersectional approaches in psychological research. *Sex Roles, 59*, 454–463.

Warner, L. R., & Shields, S. A. (2013). The intersections of sexuality, gender and race: Identity research at the crossroads. *Sex Roles, 68*(11-12), 803–810.

Weber, L., & Castellow, J. (2012). Feminist research and activism to promote health equity. In S. Hesse-Biber (Ed.), *Handbook of feminist research: Theory and praxis* (2nd ed., pp. 434–454). Thousand Oaks, CA: Sage.

Weber, L., & Fore, E. (2007). Race, ethnicity, and health: An intersectional approach. In J. Feagin & H. Vera (Eds.), *Handbook of the sociology of racial and ethnic relations* (pp. 191–218). New York, NY: Springer.

Weber, L., & Parra-Medina, D. (2003). Intersectionality and women's health: Charting a path to eliminating health disparities. In V. Demos & M. T. Segal (Eds.), *Advances in gender research: Gendered perspectives on health and medicine* (pp. 183–226). Boston, MA: Elsevier.

Weldon, S. L. (2005). *Rethinking intersectionality: Some conceptual problems and solutions for the comparative study of welfare states*. Paper presented at the annual meeting of the American Political Science Association, Washington, DC.

Weldon, S. L. (2008). Intersectionality. In G. Goertz & A. Mazur (Eds.), *Politics, gender and concepts: Theory and methodology* (pp. 193–218). New York, NY: Cambridge University Press.

Wilkinson, L. (2003). Advancing a perspective on the intersections of diversity: Challenges for research and social policy. *Canadian Ethnic Studies, 35*(3), 26–39.

Wilson, A. R. (2013). *Situating intersectionality: Politics, policy, and power*. New York, NY: Palgrave Macmillan.

Yuval-Davis, N. (2006). Intersectionality and feminist politics. *European Journal of Women's Studies, 13*(3), 193–209.

Zambrana, R. E., & Dill, B. T. (2006). Disparities in Latina health: An intersectional analysis. In A. J, Schulz & L. Mullings (Eds.), *Gender, race, class, and health: Intersectional approaches* (pp. 192–227). San Francisco, CA: Jossey-Bass.

Interdisciplinary and Transdisciplinary Multimethod and Mixed Methods Research

Rick Szostak

Abstract

This chapter explores the connections between the complementary but distinct literatures on interdisciplinarity or transdisciplinarity and on multimethod and mixed methods research (MMMR). These literatures reflect similar motivations and challenges. After defining interdisciplinarity and transdisciplinarity, the chapter explores the insights that MMMR researchers might draw from the literatures on interdisciplinarity and transdisciplinarity. Several techniques and strategies developed in those literatures, as well as their shared emphasis on disciplinary perspective, could usefully inform MMMR. The literatures on interdisciplinarity and transdisciplinarity also explore epistemological issues and identify attitudes conducive to interdisciplinary research; these too are shown to be applicable to MMMR. Comparisons with the literature on epistemological approaches to MMMR are drawn. The chapter encourages a closer collaboration between scholars of interdisciplinarity or transdisciplinarity and scholars of multimethod and mixed methods research.

Key Words: interdisciplinarity, transdisciplinarity, disciplinary perspective, epistemological approaches, attitudes, disciplinary, mixed methods

The main purposes of this chapter are to (a) distill insights for the performance of multimethod and mixed methods research (MMMR) from the growing literature on interdisciplinary and transdisciplinary practice and (b) encourage a collaborative relationship between our communities where we learn from each other. As we shall see, the two literatures have similar philosophical outlooks. MMMR and interdisciplinarity research face a similar challenge in convincing scholarly communities to accept novel approaches. Yet there are also differences in how the two literatures address methods and how they see methods fitting within broader perspectives or paradigms.

Interdisciplinarity has long been critiqued on the grounds that scholars can truly master only one discipline. MMMR research is likewise criticized in terms of the difficulty of mastering more than one method. Both literatures recognize the advantages of expertise but argue that there are huge advantages associated with integration and that scholars can develop the necessary expertise for drawing on multiple methods and/or disciplines in order to investigate a particular problem.

In the first section of this chapter I define *interdisciplinarity* and *transdisciplinarity*, distinguishing each from *multidisciplinarity*. The second section examines the literature on how best to perform interdisciplinary research, drawing lessons for MMMR. The third section extends this analysis to transdisciplinary research. While the second and third sections focus on practical advice, the fourth section turns to attitudes: What attitudes are conducive to inter/transdisciplinarity, and do these apply also to MMMR? A brief concluding section follows.

Definitions

Interdisciplinarity and *transdisciplinarity* are contested terms in the academy. As granting councils and university presidents increasingly laud the merits of interdisciplinary research and teaching, many scholars have naturally claimed that they are interdisciplinary in orientation. Scholars of interdisciplinarity and transdisciplinarity worry that these terms thus take on too diffuse a meaning. If any scholar who cites a paper from another discipline claims to be an inter- or transdisciplinarian, then these terms mean very little. Moreover, concerns long voiced by disciplinary specialists that interdisciplinary research is inevitably superficial will be reinforced if scholars claim to be interdisciplinary or transdisciplinary without really engaging with the thinking of multiple disciplines.

This chapter applies very specific meanings to the terms *interdisciplinary* and *transdisciplinary*; these meanings reflect a considerable degree of consensus among scholars who actually study interdisciplinary and transdisciplinary practices.

Defining Interdisciplinarity

An emerging consensus around a definition of *interdisciplinarity* has several key components:

• Interdisciplinarians focus on particular problems or questions that are too complex to be answered satisfactorily by any one discipline.

• Interdisciplinarians draw on the insights of (topically) specialized research. Specialized research is performed by communities of scholars who share a set of guiding questions, concepts, theories, and methods.

• Interdisciplinarians evaluate the results of specialized research.

• Interdisciplinarians utilize multiple theories and methods. They are conscious that all theories, methods, and disciplines are useful for some purposes but also have weaknesses.

• Interdisciplinarians appreciate that each discipline is characterized by an (evolving) "disciplinary perspective" or way of looking at the world. We should nevertheless be careful of stereotypes, for members of that discipline will deviate from disciplinary perspective to varying degrees.

• Interdisciplinarians integrate the best elements of disciplinary insights in order to generate a more comprehensive (and often more nuanced) appreciation of the issue at hand. (This may come in the form of a new understanding, new product, or new meaning.) As we shall see later interdisciplinarians often stress "integration" as the defining element of interdisciplinarity.

The following definition provided by Klein and Newell (1998, pp. 393–394) is widely cited and reflects the previous bullet points:

> A process of answering a question, solving a problem, or addressing a topic that is too broad or complex to be dealt with adequately by a single discipline or profession. IDS draws on disciplinary perspectives and integrates their insights through construction of a more comprehensive perspective.

The definition from the National Academy of Science, National Academy of Engineering, and Institute of Medicine (2004, p. 26) is broadly similar:

> Interdisciplinary research (IDR) is a mode of research by teams or individuals that integrates information, data, techniques, tools, perspectives, concepts, and/or theories from two or more disciplines or bodies of specialized knowledge to advance fundamental understanding or to solve problems whose solutions are beyond the scope of a single discipline or area of research practice.

This definition—and this chapter—refer to what is often termed *instrumental* or problem-oriented interdisciplinarity. There is also *conceptual* interdisciplinarity, which critiques the contemporary role and structure of disciplines. One need not be familiar with these conceptual critiques to pursue instrumental interdisciplinarity (see Salter & Hearn, 1997, on conceptual interdisciplinarity).

Defining Transdisciplinarity

The word *transdisciplinarity* was once associated with the pursuit of a unified theory of everything. Today, transdisciplinarity (especially as practiced by those associated with td-net, a network of scholars funded by the Swiss Academy of Sciences) has come to mean something very close to the definition of interdisciplinarity provided earlier, *plus* an emphasis on integrating insights generated outside the academy as well as within it.[1] Interdisciplinarians are generally open to this—and indeed have often noted that integrating across any sort of social or cultural division requires similar strategies to integrating across disciplines—but have stressed interaction beyond the academy to a much lesser degree. Transdisciplinarians are generally interested in generating knowledge that has both academic and practical implications. Again, interdisciplinarians often do the same but do not insist on this to the same degree.

To avoid the infelicitous phrase "interdisciplinary and transdisciplinary" in what follows, we generally speak only of interdisciplinarity but refer to transdisciplinarity when perspectives from beyond the academy are important.

Defining Multidisciplinarity

Multidisciplinarity involves the juxtaposition of insights from different disciplines. It thus eschews the integration that is so critical for interdisciplinarity and transdisciplinarity. Multidisciplinarians are also less likely to evaluate the insights on which they draw. Multidisciplinarity can still be useful in some situations, notably where the insights of different disciplines are not in conflict and can be simply added together. For most complex problems in natural or human science, though, evaluation and integration are critical.

Interdisciplinary Process

Much of the literature on interdisciplinary research has sought to identify best practices.[2] This in turn has required the identification of a set of iterative steps (reviewed later) for the performance of interdisciplinary research—and then strategies for each of these. The best exemplar of this research process is Repko (2012b). Since his book is intended in large part as an undergraduate textbook, it devotes little space to both team-building and the actual performance of MMMR. It does nevertheless provide a number of strategies that are useful to MMMR, and the broader literature speaks even more directly to the performance of MMMR. It is not possible in this section to capture every useful piece of advice in that growing literature, but we can provide a sense of the types of advice given and some key references.

It is critically important at this point in the development of the field to identify such a set of interdisciplinary best practices. At present it is all too easy for any scholar to claim that he or she is interdisciplinary. Whereas the main intellectual challenge to quality interdisciplinary research a couple of decades ago came from disciplinarians claiming that interdisciplinarity was inherently superficial (because of the years it takes to master even one discipline), the challenge today comes from disciplinarians who claim that anyone can be (or indeed is) interdisciplinary. Though it is common in the history of ideas for an idea to progress from being thought wrong to being thought obvious within a generation, such "progress" always carries the danger that the essence of the idea is forgotten along the way. Arguably, those who disdained interdisciplinarity decades ago had a better sense of what interdisciplinarians were trying to achieve than those who casually claim to be interdisciplinary today. Quality interdisciplinary work requires a serious engagement with each discipline on which one draws: this is far from impossible but also far from being easy.

Most scholars of interdisciplinarity are keenly aware of how constraining disciplinary methodologies are: by emphasizing certain theories, methods, and variables, these methodologies strongly discourage the exploration of others. Some interdisciplinary scholars worry that any recognition of interdisciplinary best practices may constrain interdisciplinary research. It is thus critical that such best practices be suggestive rather than prescriptive. And such best practices should always allow and indeed encourage exploration of all relevant methods, theories, and variables.

It is hardly surprising that there has been a similar discussion within MMMR about whether it is advisable to recognize core principles of MMMR. In MMMR there is also considerable consensus that a set of inclusive principles is advisable (Johnson 2011).

Most MMMR scholars believe that the particular research problem should determine the choice of research methods (Johnson, Onwuegbuzie, & Turner, 2007). Advocates of identifying interdisciplinary best practices accept this principle but argue that best practices can be identified that are useful across quite different research questions. This is the explicit position of Bergmann et al. (2012, preface) who note that while they describe particular strategies in the context of research case studies in which these proved successful, they expect each strategy to have wide applicability.

Team-Building

One way to handle the expertise challenge of MMMR is to engage in team research. This is a common approach in interdisciplinary research as well, though the individual interdisciplinary researcher is also often observed. Transdisciplinarity necessitates some sort of team approach. A great deal of current research has drawn lessons from both successful and unsuccessful team efforts. Much of this research focuses on the social aspects of team-building. It identifies helpful personality characteristics for team members such as openness, curiosity, and ability to cope with complexity, as well as less obvious characteristics such as perseverance and time management. Desirable personality characteristics for team leaders include the ability to empower, foster inclusiveness, and effectively provide feedback to team members (though there are different successful leadership styles). Advice regarding helpful team dynamics also abounds: for example, homogeneity makes cooperation easier but limits novelty; teams can emphasize either individual or group rewards.

Increasingly, this literature also addresses the cognitive challenges of teamwork. Because the value of teams comes from the different expertise of team members, identifying differing epistemological and methodological assumptions at the outset is critical. We must develop "shared conceptual frameworks that integrate and transcend the multiple disciplinary perspectives represented among team members" (Stokols, Misra, Moser, Hall, & Taylor, 2008, p. S97). That is, the process of integration needs to start early; the team cannot wait until each member has produced results before successfully integrating these. In addition to working toward epistemological understanding, team members should also appreciate the strengths and weaknesses of each other's favored theories and methods and develop shared understandings of key concepts. Finally, they need to appreciate different publication expectations in different disciplines and agree on what they hope to produce, for which audiences, when, who will do the writing, and how resources will be allocated.

Formulating Research Questions

This seemingly banal early step carries manifest dangers for the unwary. As hinted at earlier, team research can be destroyed if team members do not agree on guiding questions at the outset or—worse yet—think they agree but actually interpret questions quite differently. Even the individual researcher needs to beware of hidden assumptions within research questions. The researcher(s) must consciously ask if the way a question is stated presumes a certain answer or biases the research toward a certain discipline or method.

It can also be critical to address at the outset key subsidiary questions. For example, economists had for decades assumed that the question "What are the causes of economic growth?" was an exclusively economic question to be answered by statistically estimating the relative importance of such variables as investment, labor-force growth, and productivity advance. But if one then asks a question such as "Why do some countries invest more than others?"

then insights from many other disciplines become important (see Szostak, 2009).

Along with clarity and even-handedness, good questions should be precise, jargon-free if possible (if not, jargon should be carefully defined), important, and manageable.

Enhancing Interdisciplinary Communication

Whether communicating within a research team or trying to communicate with a wider audience (in both directions), interdisciplinary communication suffers from two main problems. First, disciplines define key concepts differently, as do social groups, an important fact to keep in mind if stakeholders beyond the academy are involved in a particular research project. Economists define *investment* to mean only expenditures that enhance a firm's ability to produce goods or services. An accountant may employ the term to mean any expenditure (such as buying a bond) intended to earn a financial return. A conversation about the economic impact of investment will quickly derail if a shared definition is assumed. Second, and less obviously, different disciplines are characterized by different perspectives. This results in misunderstanding when the implicit assumptions of a scholar from one discipline are not shared by a scholar from another. (The particular challenges associated with communicating final research results are addressed later.)

Two techniques exist for tackling the first challenge. The most common is for scholars from two disciplines to develop some sort of "pidgin" or "Creole" language that allows them to understand each other (Galison, 1997; Gorman, 2010). Physicists and engineers working together on radar, for example, developed the concept of "equivalent circuits," which was defined in a complementary but different fashion by the two groups to accord with field theory by physicists and radio technology by engineers. Note that these scholars did not need to develop shared understandings of all concepts in physics or engineering,—just those relevant to their collective enterprise. Nor did they need to have precisely the same understanding of relevant concepts as long as these were consistent and guided them well in their interactions. Kessel, Rosenfield, and Anderson (2008) report that in the cases they studied, health science research scholars did become conversant over time. But they note that this process requires both commitment and time, and this challenge expands geometrically as the number of disciplines involved in a research project expands.

A second technique seeks a more general approach to translation. The complex concepts that generate different understandings across disciplinary and social boundaries can be broken into more basic concepts for which shared understandings are possible. Let us imagine that a research group is studying some aspects of "globalization." In breaking this complex concept into basic concepts, it would become clear that globalization involves how economic and political integration, and the spread of cultural elements through mass media, affect political sovereignty, local economies, and local cultures. It would clearly be useful for the researchers in the group to appreciate which of the causal forces and which of the effects is stressed by each researcher (prototype theory would guide us to appreciate that some see globalization as primarily economic while others see it as primarily cultural). While *globalization* lends itself to considerable ambiguity, we could anticipate a much greater degree of shared understanding of elements of globalization such as "increase trade flows as a share of GDP," "increased flows of foreign investment" (though, as discussed earlier, we need then to clearly define *investment*), "increased international access to songs via the Internet," and so on (Szostak, 2013).

It should be noted that ambiguity is not entirely bad. In scholarship (and even moreso in poetry), a bit of ambiguity can stimulate curiosity. Thus it is not such a bad outcome that the aforementioned strategies reduce (substantially) rather than eliminate ambiguity altogether. Yet trying to achieve some degree of conceptual clarity is good scholarly practice: ambiguity at its worst facilitates research that is neither replicable nor convincing.

It is likewise a useful exercise for scholars to become self-aware of their disciplinary perspective. The best strategy for making researchers aware of the hidden assumptions that guide their work is to have them answer questions of an epistemological and methodological nature and then engage in a conversation with those who answer differently (Eigenbrode et al., 2007, O'Rourke et al., 2014). O'Rourke and his colleagues have found that this process does facilitate communication within research teams. Notably, when participants are given the questionnaire a second time, after conversing with peers about their different answers, they often moderate their responses. That is, differences in epistemological and methodological

outlook can be alleviated through a process that first identifies differences and then discusses these. While this research has so far been carried on only within formal research teams, it may well be transferable to any group of scholars with an interest in interdisciplinarity.[3]

Identifying Disciplinary Insights

Any exercise in MMMR requires decisions about what concepts and variables are to be examined and what theories are to be developed and tested. These decisions are often made early in a research project, though they are often revised later. As noted earlier the interdisciplinary research process is itself iterative: it is expected that early steps are revisited as research proceeds.

How can researchers be confident that they are aware of and have considered all relevant variables? One real danger is that researchers are captured by previous research and do not look beyond the variables that others have studied. And of course this danger is magnified if they consult the literature in only one discipline, which will tend to ignore variables studied by other disciplines.

Repko (2012b) outlines two complementary strategies for this exploratory phase of research. One involves first identifying relevant disciplines and then searching within each disciplinary literature for relevant studies and relevant variables. The advantage here is that different disciplines may employ quite different terminology, and thus a general search for relevant works and variables may miss much that is important. One disadvantage is that it may not be obvious at first what the relevant disciplines (and interdisciplinary fields) are—though familiarity with the disciplinary perspectives of different disciplines can be very helpful here. A second challenge is that this strategy does not encourage the exploration of variables that may have been ignored by all previous research.

The second strategy thus suggests instead consulting a list of the key variables—say, cultural attitudes, or membership in social groups, or types of economic output—studied by scholars and asking which might be relevant. Such a list was compiled by Szostak (2004) for human science, with suggestions on how this could be extended to natural science. The advantage here is that one may identify variables that have been ignored by previous research on the topic. A disadvantage is that one may have to master relevant terminologies to identify research involving these variables across disciplines.

The same two approaches—with the same advantages and disadvantages—can be taken with respect to theories. Note that terminological confusion rages here: the same theory often goes under different names in different disciplines, while the same name is applied to quite different theories. Szostak (2004) developed a five-dimensional typology of theory types: (a) who is the agent in the theory? (b) what does the agent do? (c) why does the agent do this? (d) how does the resulting process of change (or not) unfold through time? and (e) how generalizable is the theory? There are a handful of main possibilities along each dimension. This typology can aid the researcher in identifying relevant types of theory for any research question. But it will still be challenging to identify particular instances of these theory types in the literature.

Evaluating Disciplinary Insights

Scholarship is a conversation, and MMMR research will often begin from an appreciation of the limitations or biases in previous research and the possibilities of future research. Certain limitations may be best identified by scholars with expertise in the methods (and theories) employed in previous research: these are best placed to identify misapplications of a method (or theory). But such experts are unlikely to see the limitations of the method itself. The literature on interdisciplinarity stresses that interdisciplinarians can bring many useful strategies to the evaluation of previous research and that these strategies complement the evaluation that might be undertaken within the discipline.

Most obviously, the interdisciplinarian can compare and contrast insights generated by different disciplines. The interdisciplinarian can then ask why these insights are in conflict. (Note that doing so is critical for the later step of integration.) The interdisciplinarian can also ask to what extent the discipline's insights reflect its disciplinary perspective. The disciplinarian that is not self-conscious of disciplinary perspective cannot ask such a question.

While the disciplinarian may have more detailed knowledge of a particular theory or method, the interdisciplinarian can bring an understanding of the relative strengths and weaknesses of different theories and methods (see later discussion). This may allow identification of problems missed by the disciplinarian (because each discipline tends to downplay the limitations of favored theories and methods). It also facilitates the identification of alternative theories and methods that might generate different conclusions

Finally, the interdisciplinarian, by mapping a complex system of interactions among variables, can place any disciplinary insight in context. All too often, disciplinary researchers will examine a particular relationship (how B influences C) in detail but then (often implicitly) assume that other relationships (A influencing B or C influencing D) operate in a particular way and then reach a conclusion about a much more complex chain of relationships (how A influences D through B and C) than they have actually studied. The interdisciplinarian may be able to draw on other disciplines that actually study these other relationships. More generally, the interdisciplinarian can ask whether the disciplinary analysis has ignored critical variables studied by other disciplines (or perhaps ignored by all) and analyze how the discipline's conclusions would change if these were included.

Mapping a Complex Problem or Question

It is generally useful to visually map different insights into a complex problem. Figure 8.1 provides a rather complex map of the causes of economic growth, which attempts to distinguish the proximate causes of growth from important but indirect influences. Researchers will often have recourse to simpler maps with just a handful of interacting variables. Visually mapping the relationships among phenomena serves several purposes (see Keestra, 2012):

• The map helps to identify relevant variables (see previous discussion).
• The map clarifies which relationships among variables may be most important.
• The map allows researchers to identify positive or negative "feedback loops" that may encourage the system of relationships either toward stability or change. (Note that disciplinary researchers may not fully appreciate feedback loops that involve phenomena studied by other disciplines.)
• The researcher can then usefully ask which relationships have been studied by which disciplines.
• The researcher can usefully identify relationships that have been understudied or ignored, or analyzed using a limited set of theories or methods or data.
• Disciplines will often seem to be disagreeing because they are actually focusing on different relationships within a larger system. The mapping exercise can usefully identify such situations.

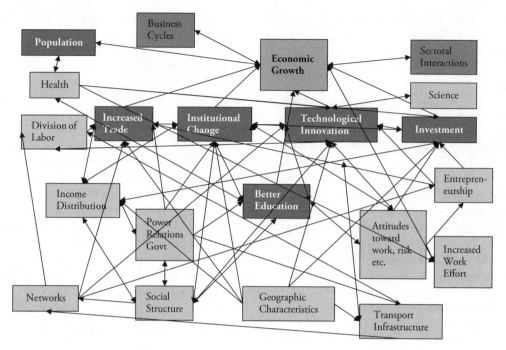

Fig. 8.1 The causes of economic growth.
Source: Repko, 2014, p. 174

• If the goal of the research is to suggest ways that the results emanating from the system might be changed, then the mapping exercise may serve to identify the best place(s) in the system to intervene to effect change. Achieving desired change in complex systems may require multiple interventions that work together toward desired changes but counteract negative side effects.

• One key challenge of interdisciplinary analysis is to study the parts of the system while appreciating the whole (and that the whole may be more than and different from the sum of the parts). A map can be very useful in this respect.

• In team research, a map may allow team members to better appreciate how their respective interests, expertise, and hypotheses fit together (Bergmann et al., 2012).

It is of particular importance for MMMR that different relationships within the system are best studied with different (theories and) methods. Mapping the system allows the researcher to reflect on how best to study each relationship.[4] One possibility among many is that analyses of different causal linkages can feed into some attempt to model mathematically the entire set of relationships.

Henry and Bracy (2012) explore the complex issue of teen violence. Though they do not draw visual maps themselves, they identify several situations that the interdisciplinary researcher is likely to encounter when mapping a complex problem (see also Repko, 2012b, ch. 13). In one common situation, different authors speak of different stages in a causal process. One speaks of how A influences B and another of how B influences C. Mapping the entire causal process may be all that is necessary to integrate these understandings. The greatest challenge may involve clearly identifying what each author is actually talking about.

Alternatively, different authors may stress different causes of a particular result. If these are complementary, then again mapping may be all that is necessary for integration. If they conflict, then a more complicated type of integration is called for and should be reflected in the final map. It may be that the causal variables stressed by different authors interact. Mapping these interactions can aid in assessing whether different understandings are complementary.

It may at times be necessary to map phenomena at different levels: individuals versus groups; atoms versus molecules; watch springs versus watches. While these different levels need to be appreciated, they need not unduly complicate the mapping process (see Keestra, 2012). Special problems arise if there are emergent properties such that activities at one level are more than the sum of activities at lower levels.

Finally, Henry and Bracy (2012) note that different causal relationships may unfold in different places or at different times. It may thus be important to keep track of spatial or temporal locations.

Integration

As noted previously, integration is a defining feature of interdisciplinary research. How can the insights of different disciplines be synthesized into a more holistic understanding? The mapping exercise may show that disciplinary insights are really complementary though they address different relationships. Sometimes the only real conflict between disciplinary insights is that each discipline tends to assume that the things they study are of paramount importance. But often, especially in human science, we must integrate across conflicting understandings of the same relationships.

Integration in the face of conflict requires the creation of some sort of "common ground": some shared concept or theory or other element that allows the conflict to be alleviated. Special note should be made of the word *creation* in this sentence. While there are techniques for creating common ground, it is nevertheless a creative act in which the interdisciplinarian should let intuition work in concert with reason (Welch, 2007).

Scholars of interdisciplinarity have identified four key techniques for creating common ground (Repko, 2012b). The first, *redefinition*, involves altering the way a concept is employed by different authors in order to achieve a common meaning. This technique is powerful when authors appear to be disagreeing because they are using the same concept in different ways. When an interdisciplinary researcher redefines a concept and then restates the authors' insights in terms of the redefined concept, the apparent conflict vanishes. In other cases, redefinition resolves only some of the conflict between insights but by clarifying the nature of this conflict sets the stage for the use of other techniques. Tayler (2012) redefines the meaning of *democratic* in creating common ground in her analysis of marriage laws in Israel. Van der Lecq (2012) redefines both *evolution* and *communication* in creating common ground regarding the first use of language by humans. Bergmann et al. (2012), providing examples from a variety of cases, stress that redefinition may sometimes result in one new term but other times in multiple new terms in order to capture different meanings; they also appreciate the value of breaking complex concepts into their constituent parts (see previous discussion).

A second technique, *extension,* involves extending a theory, or the assumptions underlying a theory, so that it includes elements identified by other authors. This technique works best when different insights are not necessarily in conflict. Different authors emphasize different causal factors, but there is no reason why these cannot work in concert. If one is extending a theory, it is generally best to extend the theory that is already the most comprehensive. If no theory is very comprehensive, then the interdisciplinary researcher can usefully explore whether there is some common set of assumptions that might allow theories to be combined. The extended theory or assumption is the common ground. Repko (2012a), for example, extends identity theory in order to incorporate other key elements of theories of suicide terrorism.

The third technique, *organization,* involves using a map to show how different insights are related. If one author stresses cultural influences on a particular behavior and another stresses personal influences, organization might involve showing how culture influences personal decisions that affect behavior. The map becomes the common ground (see Keestra, 2012). Note that it will often prove useful to group the phenomena emphasized by different authors into broader categories (such as cultural attitudes).

Finally, *transformation* is a technique for addressing opposites by placing these on a continuum. If one author assumes that agents behave rationally in a particular situation but another author assumes irrationality, the interdisciplinarian can appreciate that there is a continuum between perfect rationality and perfect irrationality, identify where on that continuum agents are likely to lie in a particular situation, and then draw on each of the opposing insights appropriately. The continuum is the common ground.

These four different techniques respectively represent different means of integration: (a) Sometimes, integration is primarily semantic: the meanings of concepts are adjusted to carry a similar meaning across communities; (b) sometimes integration occurs by adjusting theories so that these are more inclusive; (c) sometimes integration involves placing competing theories within an overarching framework; and (d) sometimes integration involves seeing conflicts as differences of degree. As should be clear by now, these different integrative strategies can be seen as complementary.[5]

Researchers in MMMR may be particularly interested in cases in which disagreements stem from differences in methods or data sets employed. In such cases MMMR itself can serve as common ground: just as conflicting assumptions can be placed on a continuum, it is possible to appreciate that different methods have compensating strengths that the appropriate use of MMMR will capture. But it would be a mistake for researchers in MMMR to focus exclusively on methods when evaluating the existing literature: researchers choose methods that are good at investigating the theories they like as applied to their favored variables (see Szostak, 2004). It is thus critically important to also appreciate the theories, concepts, and philosophical assumptions at work in previous research.

Integration has been employed in this section to refer to integration of scholarly insights regarding a particular question, problem, or theme. There are two critical defining elements of integration (or synthesis): (a) creation of some common ground (for the previous techniques, this would be, respectively, the redefined concept, the extended theory, the map, and the continuum) that facilitates cross-disciplinary understanding and (b) production as a result of a more comprehensive understanding of the issue being examined. The literature on transdisciplinarity often employs the word *integration* to refer also to the integration of research teams: the achievement of common purpose and understanding among collaborators (which, as we have seen, has both social and intellectual aspects; Bergmann et al., 2012). We used the phrase *team-building* so as to maintain a more precise meaning of *integration*.

Communicating and Disseminating Research Results

Researchers will generally wish to reach multiple audiences. They will then need to use language appropriate to each audience. They must also relate their research outcomes to the concerns of each audience, and they must be both clear and memorable. Being memorable generally requires recourse to metaphor, model, or narrative. Elucidation of a new policy, product, and/or research question is also useful. Providing real-world examples of at least the problem and ideally the solution can be very powerful. Scholars should emphasize the surprising elements of their research.

Disciplinary scholars may be able to meet these criteria intuitively when addressing their own disciplinary colleagues. They have spent years of their life mastering disciplinary terminology and

literature and may find it straightforward to situate their work within the broader literature of their own discipline (though young scholars may struggle to communicate why others should care about their work). Interdisciplinary scholars need to be far more purposeful here. They must recognize the sort of communication problems discussed previously and ensure they write in a way that will be comprehensible to their multiple audiences. One cannot hope to be heard by, say, political scientists, if one has not read some political science in order to know what they are talking about. There must be a hook: for example, "your literature talks about X and my research sheds new light by approaching X from a different angle." Only then might the disciplinary reader be tempted to engage with whatever novel theories or methods or variables that one engages.

Many researchers also hope and some attempt to communicate important theories and findings to policymakers. Indeed, since both interdisciplinarians and transdisciplinarians generally address complex real-world problems, influencing policy is an important goal. This sort of cross-communication presents its own challenges. Communications need to be clear, tightly focused, and jargon-free. But there is a far more important lesson in the literature: it is naïve to hope that policymakers can be influenced by simply communicating one's research results. They are much more likely to be persuaded if they have been involved in a conversation along the way, and especially if they have had input into research design.

This observation holds for all types of research but is especially critical for interdisciplinary research. If interdisciplinarians will investigate complicated systems of relations among diverse sets of phenomena, then there is likely to be a great deal of uncertainty surrounding any policy recommendations that might result from interdisciplinary research (indeed, Bammer and Smithson[2008] identify uncertainty as one of the hallmarks of interdisciplinary research). These recommendations must thus be explained carefully to policymakers and the public and carefully tested in practice. Academics, policymakers, and the public should work together in testing policy recommendations (see Henry & Bracy, 2012, for a discussion of how testing might proceed).[6]

While two-way communication with policymakers is valuable, scholarly researchers must be careful not to be "captured" by political interests and thus produce research designed to justify desired policies (see Connor, 2012). In particular, interdisciplinary researchers should be aware that even good policies may have undesirable side effects and should be ready to evaluate these and investigate possibilities for alleviating them.

Multimethod and Mixed Methods Research and the Interdisciplinary Research Process

Since MMMR is a methodology rather than just a combination of methods (at least for most MMMR researchers; Johnson et al., 2007), MMMR practitioners should find much of interest in the entire interdisciplinary research process. But different types of MMMR research (Johnson et al., 2007) may especially benefit from particular strategies. As noted earlier, mapping may be particularly important to those who apply different methods to different elements of a complex research problem. Those who see MMMR as a methodology for triangulating will find the strategies for achieving integration particularly useful in understanding the sources of different empirical results. Those who pursue MMMR because they find that different methods elucidate different aspects of a particular causal relationship (as when interviews are performed with members of groups identified through statistical analysis) will want to be particularly careful in defining their research question. And of course team researchers pursuing any of these strategies will want to appreciate that mixing of their individual methodological predispositions is necessary from the start. Though it has not been our focus here, it is likewise the case that interdisciplinary researchers have much to learn from the MMMR literature about how best to mix different methods. Since both literatures emphasize integration, we can hope for increased efforts to integrate the insights of the two literatures.

Transdisciplinary Research

Transdisciplinary research embraces all of the interdisciplinary research process but adds nonacademic participation. This has important implications throughout the research process.

Nonacademic participants should be involved in the design of the research questions. Often they will prefer a more practical and context-specific question than academic participants. The research team needs to reflect from the outset on how they can produce results that may provide both practical advice as well as scholarly insights with some capability of generalization. This balance between the practical and the theoretical/scholarly must be maintained throughout the research process.

We stressed earlier the importance of drawing on insights from all relevant disciplines. Interdisciplinary scholars have long appreciated that it is often important to draw on insights from beyond the academy as well. This becomes crucial in transdisciplinary research. The views of nonacademic stakeholders need to be heard and integrated with scholarly analyses of the problem at hand.

Certain participatory methods are especially valuable when stakeholders are involved in the research team (Bergmann et al., 2012). Stakeholders can participate in focus groups where issues are discussed, deliberative discussions where policy proposals are debated (and even voted on), and scenario planning exercises in which desirable futures are identified and strategies for achieving these discussed.

Notably, all of these methods allow for a two-way conversation. Obviously, each allows for the ideas of nonacademic stakeholders to be clarified and communicated to academic researchers. Yet these methods also allow academic analyses to be communicated to stakeholders and discussed with and by them.

Johnson et al. (2007) note that some in the MMMR community see MMMR as an inherently emancipatory project. Transdisciplinarians (and interdisciplinarians) also often stress the critical importance of ensuring that the voices of small and or powerless groups are heard and their insights integrated. And they believe that these views need to be heard both within the academy and in concrete policy proposals.

Interdisciplinary Attitudes With Respect to Methods

This section opens with a discussion of interdisciplinary attitudes with respect to methods. Two key points are stressed: (a) there are key differences among both qualitative and quantitative methods and (b) disciplinary preferences regarding methods are closely aligned with preferences regarding theories and subject matter. Several other attitudes of interest are addressed more briefly.

The Strengths and Weaknesses of Different Methods

Interdisciplinarians believe that every discipline has both strengths and weaknesses. Each has much to contribute to human understanding but also inherent weaknesses that cause them to miss much that is important. The same logic must apply at the level of methods. Each scholarly method has useful insights to provide but also limitations.

This attitude accords well with the approach of MMMR. But there is a critical difference. When Johnson et al. (2007) surveyed leaders in the MMMR field on the meaning of MMMR, the vast majority stressed that MMMR is about mixing quantitative and qualitative approaches. Only one respondent emphasized that MMMR could be applied within the set of qualitative or quantitative methods.[7] Scholars of interdisciplinarity appear to be much more cognizant of the huge differences between methods within each of these two categories (i.e., qualitative and quantitative methods). Disciplines tend to be associated more strongly with particular methods than with these two categories: economists like statistical analysis but have been as suspicious of experiments as of interviews, and literary scholars have stressed close reading of texts but have arguably been at least as open to statistical analyses of those texts as to interviews with authors (and would certainly disdain observation of authors).

MMMR researchers often refer to the existence of quantitative and qualitative paradigms. Indeed, the *methods* in *mixed methods* really means—at least for most practitioners—a much broader *mixed methodologies*. Scholars of interdisciplinarity stress instead the existence of multiple *disciplinary perspectives*. Both literatures appreciate that these paradigms or perspectives contain a set of mutually reinforcing elements that strongly influence the sort of research performed. These disciplinary perspectives contain the sort of epistemological and metaphysical attitudes that MMMR researchers address when they worry about competing paradigms. But the disciplinary perspective also embraces theory to a much greater extent than is stressed in the MMMR literature. In addition, scholars of disciplinary perspective stress the importance of a discipline's subject matter: though scholars of MMMR are well aware that some phenomena are hard to quantify, this also receives less attention.

Economics (in the Western world) embraces rational choice theory, which emphasizes individual-level rational decisions. This theory lends itself to statistical analysis: if one assumes individual rationality, one can predict human behavior from data regarding the choices individuals face. Economists have thus studied a fairly small set of quantifiable variables. It has turned out that experiments often uncover irrational decision-making; most economists have opined that laboratory experiments do not capture how people behave in the real world. It is no surprise that the emerging subfield of behavioral economics simultaneously relaxes the rationality assumption, likes experiments, and is willing to discuss hard-to-quantify variables such as cultural attitudes. Method, theory, and subject matter (and philosophical attitudes) go together.

As was discussed briefly earlier, Szostak (2004) developed a five-dimensional typology of theory types. We can ask of any method how well it allows us to investigate different theory types along each of these dimensions. For each dimension, a subsidiary question arises, leaving us with a set of 10 questions[8]:

1. What sort of agent can the method investigate well? (Agents can have intentionality [or not] and be individuals, groups, or relationships.)
2. How many agents can be investigated?
3. Does the method investigate actions and/or attitudes well?
4. Can the four key elements of a causal argument (correlation between cause and effect, temporality [cause occurs before effect], lack of alternative explanations, and elucidation of intermediate variables/processes) be investigated?[9]
5. What types of decision-making (rational, rule based, value based, intuitive, peer/tradition based) can the method investigate well? (This is for intentional agents; for nonintentional we can instead ask if the method allows us to perceive the internal nature of an agent that generates certain effects.)
6. Does the method allow for induction?
7. Is the method best suited to highly generalizable theory or to the investigation of particular cases?
8. Does the method allow us to follow processes through space?
9. What sorts of causal process (equilibrium, stochastic, cyclical, or unidirectional) can the method investigate well?
10. Does the method allow us to follow processes through time?

Since every second question on this list duplicates a question asked of theories, Szostak (2004) was able to establish empirically that disciplines do indeed choose mutually reinforcing sets of theory and method. It is no coincidence that the mathematical models and statistical analysis favored by economists are good at investigating many intentional rational individuals in a highly generalizable manner in accord with the rational choice theory favored in the discipline. Table 8.1 reports how 10 key methods fare when asked these 10 key questions. The lesson is that there are substantial differences among different qualitative methods and among different quantitative methods, as well as across the two groups. These differences are in turn associated with differences in theories and subject matter (and likely philosophical attitudes). A discipline employing statistical analysis will focus on easily quantifiable variables, while a discipline stressing interviews will not.

Table 8.1 Typology of Strengths and Limitations of Methods

Criteria	Classification	Experiment	Interview	Intuition/ Experience	Mathematical Modeling
Type of agent	All	All; but group only in natural experiment	Intentional individuals; relationships indirect	Intentional individuals; others indirect	All
Number investigated	All	Few	Few	One	All
Type of causation	Action (evolutionary)	Passive, action	Attitude; acts indirectly	Attitude	All
Criteria for identifying a causal relationship	Aids each but limited	Potentially all four	Might provide insight on each	Some insight on correlation, temporality	All; limited with respect to intermediate, alternatives
Decision-making process	Indirect insight	No	Some insight; biased	Yes; may mislead	Some insight
Induction?	Little	Some	If open	Yes; bias	Little
Generalizability	Both	Both	Idiographic	Idiographic	Both
Spatiality	Some	Constrained	From memory	From memory	Difficult to model
Time path	No insight	Little insight	Little insight	Little insight	Emphasize equilibrium
Temporality	Some	Constrained	From memory	From memory	Simplifies
Criteria	**Participant Observation**	**Physical Traces**	**Statistical Analysis**	**Survey**	**Textual Analysis**
Type of agent	Intentional individual; relationships groups?	All; groups and relationship indirect	All; groups and relationship indirect	Intentional individuals; groups indirect	Intentional individuals; others indirect
Number	Few; one group	Few	Many/all	Many	One/few
Type of causation	Action (attitude)	Passive, action	Action, attitude	Attitude; acts indirectly	Attitude, action

(continued)

Table 8.1 Continued

Criteria	Participant Observation	Physical Traces	Statistical Analysis	Survey	Textual Analysis
Criteria for identifying a causal relationship	All but rarely done	Some insight to all four	Correlation and temporality well; others maybe	Some insight on correlation	Some insight on all
Decision-making process	All	No	No	Little	Some insight; biased
Induction?	Much	Much	Some	Very little	Much
Generalizability	Idiographic; nomothetic from many studies	Idiographic; nomothetic from many studies	Both	Both	Idiographic; nomothetic. from many studies
Spatiality	Very good; some limits	Possibly infer	Limited	Rarely	Possible
Time path	Some insight	Some insight	Emphasize equilibrium	Little insight	Some insight
Temporality	Very good up to months	Possibly infer	Static, often frequent	Longitudinal somewhat	Possible

Source: Szostak (2004, pp. 138–139).

Note: The "criteria" reflect the 10 questions listed in the text.

Both/And Thinking

Much scholarship is characterized by either/or thinking. One theory is stressed as being superior to another. One method is urged over another, or one tool or technique within a broader method is celebrated over others. Even philosophers, though aware that there is no perfect argument, tend to devote most of their time to emphasizing one theory over another.

It thus deserves emphasis that interdisciplinary analysis—and likely MMMR as well—requires both/and thinking. Interdisciplinarians expect that there will be some kernel of truth in opposing points of view. They thus seek to integrate the best in each rather than choose one over another. The result will often be "messy," a combination of different theories applied to different facets of a problem. Interdisciplinary researchers must consciously transcend either/or thinking in order to integrate insights.

MMMR also requires an appreciation of the advantages both of different methods and the perspectives in which these nest. Research reports are inherently messy relative to the typical write-up of the results of one application of one method.

Synergy

Though some interdisciplinarians might seek to destroy disciplines, and most might like to alter the disciplinary structure of universities, there is nevertheless a general appreciation of synergy between specialized research and integrative research. Interdisciplinary scholars build on and integrate the insights generated by specialized researchers. They in turn feed back these nuanced understandings to specialized researchers, with advice on how these might broaden the scope of their investigations. MMMR scholars may recognize a similar synergy between their efforts and those of more specialized researchers.

An Overarching Philosophy?

Johnson et al. (2007) wonder if pragmatism can and should serve as the guiding philosophy of MMMR. They worry that any guiding philosophy must be flexible enough that all MMMR scholars feel comfortable with it. They note that quantitative researchers are often guided by a postpositivist philosophy and qualitative researchers are often guided by a poststructuralist philosophy. An MMMR philosophy would likely lie somewhere in between these.

Szostak (2007) investigated how *interdisciplinarity*, as understood in this chapter, relied on a set of (generally implicit) philosophical attitudes that generally lay between what were termed *modernist* and *postmodernist* approaches.[10] Indeed, these "interdisciplinary" attitudes could generally be seen as Aristotelian "Golden Means." Notably many of these might be embraced by affirmative postmodernists—who accept various postmodern concerns but still believe it is possible to enhance human understanding (Rosenau, 1992)—as well as many who might be thought to be modernist in outlook. Moreover, several of these interdisciplinarity attitudes are shown to be complementary to (parts of) diverse intellectual traditions, including complexity, critical theory, critical thinking, discourse analysis, feminism, pragmatism, rhetoric, and social constructionism.[11] Several attitudes that can be identified as interdisciplinary might also well serve the MMMR community:

- Proof and disproof are impossible, but we can increase our confidence in any statement by compiling arguments and evidence in favor.
- It is possible to integrate across perspectives associated with disciplines or social divisions.
- Scholars should reflect on their own biases and those of scholarly communities.
- There is an external reality, though humans are limited in their abilities to accurately and precisely perceive this.
- There are empirical regularities in the world, but these must often be contextualized since all variables are causally related to variables outside of any research study.
- Language is ambiguous, but ambiguity can be lessened (by both classification and interdisciplinary practices).
- Different communities are characterized by overarching perspectives that influence what is said and thought. While barriers to communication exist, these are surmountable to a considerable extent.

These attitudes are complementary. Improved understanding and integration are possible because we can imperfectly perceive, identify contextual regularities, and converse. Special note might be made here of reflection. While interdisciplinarians back away from extreme arguments that scholarly biases and errors are so profound as to prohibit enhanced understanding, they are guided by an appreciation that specialized scholarly research is necessarily biased. Only by constantly reflecting on such biases—and Repko (2012b) urges reflection throughout the interdisciplinary research process—can we hope to transcend these.

Concluding Remarks

The MMMR and inter/transdisciplinarity literatures inevitably overlap. They share similar motivations and face similar challenges. But they are different enough that practitioners of each have much to learn from the other. Interdisciplinarians could be more cognizant of the challenges of integrating different methods within a single discipline. They could better appreciate that an important quantitative/qualitative distinction spans disciplinary boundaries. They could recognize the important distinction between mixing methods in parallel and mixing methods sequentially. And of course they could better appreciate the many practical lessons that can be gleaned from MMMR on how best to mix methods.

In turn, MMMR practitioners can benefit from an enhanced appreciation of disciplinary perspective in general and its key elements: methods are chosen in concert with theories and subject matter. They can better appreciate the important distinctions among particular quantitative or qualitative methods. And they can draw diverse lessons from the interdisciplinary research process

It is in the nature of interdisciplinary scholarship to seek common ground across scholarly communities. In this case, the task is fairly easy. The two literatures do not conflict but rather have different emphases. While they use different terminology, the philosophical underpinnings of each appear to be broadly similar. Also, the research processes that they advocate are complementary. One can simultaneously appreciate the qualitative/quantitative distinction and the importance of disciplinary perspective. One can appreciate the differences both between and within quantitative and qualitative methods. One can integrate methods as well as the insights generally embedded in theories.

Acknowledgments

The author thanks Burke Johnson and Allen Repko for very helpful comments on an earlier draft of this chapter.

Discussion Questions

1. What does the MMMR community gain by exploring in greater detail the differences

between methods within both the qualitative and quantitative paradigms?

2. How useful for MMMR is the concept of *disciplinary perspective* and the analysis of its key components (including theories, methods, subject matter, and concepts)?

3. How in practice can we best encourage more communication between the MMMR and interdisciplinary research communities?

4. Does MMMR reflect both/and thinking?

5. Are the philosophical principles guiding the two communities the same?

Suggested Website

http://www.oakland.edu/ais

The website of the Association for Interdisciplinary Studies provides a host of resources, including links to the websites of kindred organizations. The "About Interdisciplinarity" section provides an overview of the literature on definitions, history, and best practices.

Notes

1. Transdisciplinarians often also stress a case study approach.

2. Not without controversy. Szostak (2012) reviews some of the arguments against identifying best practices and finds them wanting. The interdisciplinary research process "provides structure without interfering with freedom, it facilitates normal research by interdisciplinarians, it encourages use of the widest range of theories and methods and phenomena, it encourages standards grounded in this sort of flexible structure, and it strengthens the case for a role for interdisciplinary within the academy that is clearly symbiotic with specialized research" (p. 18).

3. A strategy of surveying the philosophical attitudes of scholars has also been pursued by MMR researchers. See Sheehan and Johnson (2012).

4. Two of the strategies for "theoretical framing" identified in Bergmann et al. (2012) involve mapping. The same is true of two of their three strategies for integrating methods. They later stress the critical importance of some sort of model to transdisciplinary research.

5. This understanding is echoed in the literature on transdisciplinarity. The focus on integration varies by project: Sometimes developing shared understandings of concepts is critical; in other cases theories must be integrated, in other cases models, and in still other cases policy developments (Pohl & Hadorn, 2008, p. 416).

6. Bergmann and Jahn (2008, p. 96) argue that policy recommendations and academic insights require different types of integration. Scholarly audiences may be most interested in integration at the level of theories and methods. Policymakers will seek integration of diverse policy proposals. Ideally, of course, the first sort of integration should support the second. Bergmann and Jahn feel that very few interdisciplinary research projects succeed on both counts.

7. Johnson (2011) reports that it is useful to mix methods that have little in common. Most respondents in Johnson et al. (2007) appreciate that methodology is chosen in accord with the demands of the particular research question.

8. The original five questions can be stated in a who, why, what, where, and when format, in which case the connection with the subsidiary question to follow becomes more obvious.

9. The first three of these were stressed by Aristotle. The fourth was added and emphasized by Singleton and Strait (1999).

10. Newell (1998) noted that, until the assumptions underlying interdisciplinarity are clearly articulated, it is all too easy for critics "to ascribe to all interdisciplinarians the assumptions and worldview of a minority of the profession" (p. 561). He continues: "It becomes important then to disentangle the characteristics of interdisciplinarity from the characteristics of valuable complementary perspectives such as feminism, postmodernism, anti-logical positivism, and left-wing politics" (p. 561). Welch (2011) provides a (complementary) overview of epistemological issues in interdisciplinarity.

11. Johnson (2011, p. 36) is sure that MMR scholars agree on the need to respect and dialogue with different people and perspectives.

References

Bammer, G., & Smithson, M., eds. (2008). *Uncertainty and risk: Multidisciplinary perspectives*. London, England: Earthscan.

Bergmann, M., & Jahn, T. (2008). CITY:Mobil: A model for integration in sustainability research. In G. H. Hadorn, H. Hoffmann-Riem, S. Biber-Klemm, W. Grossenbacher-Mansuy, D. Joye, C. Pohl,. . . E. Zemp (Eds.), *Handbook of transdisciplinary research* (pp. 89–102). Dordrecht, The Netherlands: Springer.

Bergmann, M., Jahn, T., Knobloch, T., Krohn, W., Pohl, C., & Schramm, E. (2012). *Methods for transdisciplinary research: A primer for practice*. Berlin, Germany: Campus.

Connor, M. A. (2012). The metropolitan problem in interdisciplinary perspective. In A. F. Repko, W. H. Newell, & R. Szostak (Eds.), *Case studies in interdisciplinary research* (pp. 53–90). Thousand Oaks, CA: Sage.

Eigenbrode, S. D., O'Rourke, M., Wulfhorst, J. D., Althoff, D. M., Goldberg, C. S., Merrill, K., . . . Bosque-Pérez, N. 2007. Employing philosophical dialogue in collaborative science. *Bioscience*, *57*(1), 55–64.

Galison, P. (1997). *Image & logic: A material culture of microphysics*. Chicago, IL: University of Chicago Press.

Gorman, M. E. (Ed.). (2010). *Trading zones and interactional expertise: Creating new kinds of collaboration*. Cambridge, MA: MIT Press.

Henry, S., & Bracy, N. L. (2012). Integrative theory in criminology applied to the complex social problem of school violence. In A. F. Repko, W. H. Newell, & R. Szostak (Eds.), *Case studies in interdisciplinary research* (pp. 259–282). Thousand Oaks, CA: Sage.

Johnson, R. B. (2011). Do we need paradigms? A mixed methods perspective, *Mid-Western Educational Researcher*, *24*(2), 31–40.

Johnson, R. B., Onwuegbuzie, A. J., & Turner, L. A. (2007). Toward a definition of mixed methods research. *Journal of Mixed Methods Research*, *1*(2), 112–133.

Keestra, M. (2012). Understanding human action: Integrating meanings, mechanisms, causes, and contexts. In A. F. Repko, W. H. Newell, & R. Szostak (Eds.), *Case studies in interdisciplinary research* (pp. 225–258). Thousand Oaks, CA: Sage.

Kessel, F. S., Rosenfield, P. L., & Anderson, N. B. (Eds.). (2008). *Interdisciplinary research: Case studies from health and social science* (2nd ed.). New York, NY: Oxford University Press.

Klein, J. T., & Newell, W. H. 1998. Advancing interdisciplinary studies. In W. Newell (Ed.), *Interdisciplinarity: Essays from the literature* (pp. 3–22). New York, NY: College Board.

National Academy of Science, National Academy of Engineering, & Institute of Medicine. (2004). *Facilitating interdisciplinary research*. Washington, DC: National Academies Press.

O'Rourke, M., Crowley, S., Eigenbrode, S. D., & Wulfhorst, J. D. (Eds.). (2014). *Enhancing communication and collaboration in interdisciplinary research*. Thousand Oaks, CA: Sage.

Pohl, C., & Hadorn, G. H. (2008). Core terms in transdisciplinary research. In G. H. Hadorn, H. Hoffmann-Riem, S. Biber-Klemm, W. Grossenbacher-Mansuy, D. Joye, C. Pohl, . . . E. Zemp (Eds.), *Handbook of transdisciplinary research* (pp. 427–432). Dordrecht, The Netherlands: Springer.

Repko, A. F. (2012a). Integrating theory-based insights on the causes of suicide terrorism. In A. F. Repko, W. H. Newell, & R. Szostak (Eds.), *Case studies in interdisciplinary research* (pp. 125–158). Thousand Oaks, CA: Sage.

Repko, A. (2012b). *Interdisciplinary research: Process and theory* (2nd. ed.). Thousand Oaks, CA: Sage.

Repko, A., with Szostak. R., & Buchberger, M. (2014). *Introduction to interdisciplinary studies*. Thousand Oaks, CA: Sage.

Rosenau, P. M. (1992). *Post-modernism and the social sciences*. Princeton, NJ: Princeton University Press.

Salter, L., & Hearn, A., eds. (1997). *Outside the lines: Issues in interdisciplinary research*. Montreal, QC: McGill-Queen's University Press.

Sheehan, M., & Johnson, R. B. (2012). Philosophical and methodological beliefs of instructional design faculty and professionals. *Educational Technology Research and Development, 60*(1), 131–153.

Singleton, R. A., & Strait, B. C. (1999). *Approaches to social research* (3rd ed.). New York, NY: Oxford University Press.

Stokols, D., Misra, S., Moser, R. P., Hall, K. L., & Taylor, B. K. (2008). The ecology of team science: Understanding contextual influences on transdisciplinary collaboration. *American Journal of Preventive Medicine, 35*(2 Suppl), 96–115.

Szostak, R. (2004). *Classifying science: Phenomena, data, theory, method, practice*. Dordrecht, The Netherlands: Springer.

Szostak, R. (2007). Modernism, postmodernism, and interdisciplinarity. *Issues in Integrative Studies, 26*, 32–83.

Szostak, R. (2009). *The causes of economic growth: Interdisciplinary perspectives*. Berlin, Germany: Springer.

Szostak, R. (2012). The interdisciplinary research process. In A. F. Repko, W. H. Newell, & R. Szostak (Eds.), *Case studies in interdisciplinary research* (pp. 3–20). Thousand Oaks, CA: Sage.

Szostak, R. (2013). Communicating complex concepts. In M. O'Rourke, S. Crowley, S. D. Eigenbrode, & J. D. Wulfhorst (Eds.), *Enhancing communication and collaboration in interdisciplinary research* (pp. 34–55). Thousand Oaks, CA: Sage.

Tayler, M. R. (2012). Jewish marriage as an expression of Israel's conflicted identity. In A. F. Repko, W. H. Newell, & R. Szostak (Eds.), *Case studies in interdisciplinary research* (pp. 23–52). Thousand Oaks, CA: Sage.

van der Lecq, R. (2012). Why we talk: An interdisciplinary approach to the evolutionary origin of language. In A. F. Repko, W. H. Newell, & R. Szostak (Eds.), *Case studies in interdisciplinary research* (pp. 191–224). Thousand Oaks, CA: Sage.

Welch, J. IV. (2007). The role of intuition in interdisciplinary insight. *Issues in Integrative Studies, 25*, 131–155.

Welch, J. IV. (2011). The emergence of interdisciplinarity from epistemological thought. *Issues in Integrative Studies, 29*, 1–39.

Putting Ethics on the Mixed Methods Map

Judith Preissle, Rebecca M. Glover-Kudon, Elizabeth A. Rohan,
Jennifer E. Boehm, *and* Amy DeGroff[1]

Abstract

The literature on ethics in social science research and evaluation practice indicates how mixed and multimethods increase complexity for ethical and moral decision-making. Paradoxically, mixed methods research (MMR) also offers a larger set of more flexible tools for tackling ethical quandaries in complex, real-world contexts than single-method approaches. This chapter draws both on the literature and on evaluation research in two public health projects to examine ethical challenges across the phases of MMR, from designing a study to reporting findings. Among the various ethical approaches advocated are reflexivity and transparency. Research ethics involves both compliance and integrity but is broader than either of these common standards, and it requires ongoing thought and judgment specific to each research project.

Key Words: ethics, mixed methods research, MMR, integrity, compliance, reflexivity, transparency

We cannot be taught wisdom, we have to dis-cover it for ourselves by a journey which no one can undertake for us, an effort which no one can spare us.

—*Marcel Proust (quoted in de Botton, 1997, p. 67)*

We have arrived at the third methodological movement in social science and behavioral research (Tashakkori & Teddlie, 2003; Teddlie & Tashakkori, 2003). Forty years in the making, we have survived the reign of positivism, the constructivist revolution, and paradigm wars to reach this place of greater method-ological heterogeneity. With proposed roots in philo-sophical pragmatism (e.g., Greene, 2007; Johnson & Onwuegbuzie, 2004; Maxcy, 2003), multimethod and mixed methods research (MMMR) allows us the flexibility to prioritize *what is to be learned* over *how to learn it*. No longer confined by the boundaries of a single method or epistemology, we marvel at the options in combining various approaches to suit the research problem and context.

We recognize that the new frontier, while excit-ing and full of opportunity, is also rife with chal-lenges. As Creswell (2010) mapped it, the MMMR landscape is still developing, and what is viewed as legitimate evidence remains politicized. Over the past decade, early settlers have struggled with common language, rules, and cultural practices for conducting MMMR and with how best to teach MMMR to new explorers. Given the unfa-miliar territory, Denzin (2010) called for a map to guide the MMMR enterprise. As evidenced by the expanding horizon of MMMR literature, such as this handbook, many researchers are staking their claims. As more topographical features are added to the map, we notice that ethics in MMMR remains uncharted. In writing this chapter, we contend that MMMR requires a moral compass, as all research endeavors do. Our charge is to explore the specific and possibly unique ethical dilemmas encountered when conducting MMMR. In other words, we aim to draw ethics on the mixed methods map.

In getting our bearings, we concede that "true north" does not yet exist, if it ever will or should. However, the MMMR journey can still be a morally guided one, and we are pleased to serve as early cartographers.

Our multidisciplinary team has worked together for seven years. Our packs are filled with nine advanced degrees and 123 years of combined experience in our respective fields: education, public health, social work, anthropology, sociology, public policy, program evaluation, and research methodologies. We have experience as researchers, practitioners, and administrators in academia, nonprofit organizations, practice and clinical settings, public schools, and government. For all of us, public stewardship and ethical practice is a shared value and professional obligation. The lead author, in particular, is an expert in research ethics, having published widely on the topic and having served for over 20 years on her university's institutional review board (IRB). The five of us first collaborated as a team on an evaluation of a federally funded demonstration program (the Colorectal Cancer Screening Demonstration Program [CRCSDP]) examining the feasibility of providing colorectal cancer screening to low-income, underinsured populations (Boehm, Rohan, Preissle, DeGroff, & Glover-Kudon, 2013; Glover-Kudon, DeGroff, Rohan, Preissle, & Boehm, 2013; Rohan, Boehm, DeGroff, Glover-Kudon, & Preissle, 2013). We developed the longitudinal, multiple-case study portion of a larger multimethods project, with the qualitative case running simultaneously with quantitative clinical and cost studies. Together, we possess methodological experience in qualitative and quantitative inquiry as well as MMMR. These years of research practice have earned us an eclectic positioning toward all approaches to investigation. However, we caution readers that expertise takes us only so far. As Proust reminds us, knowledge must be put to work in experience to produce wisdom, and all five of us are still journeying on that path. We meet ethical challenges regularly in our work and continue to build our knowledge.

Reading a map, of course, is different from taking the journey itself. Readers must experience the ethical issues involved in mixed methods research (MMR) for themselves to truly appreciate them. As we blaze the trail, we encourage others to forge their own paths, explore the terrain from their own perspectives, and contribute to our ongoing and shared enterprise.

Ethics in the Practice of Human Research

Ethics and morality focus attention on research decisions about good and bad, virtue and evil. Philosophers use the terms *ethics* and *morals* interchangeably, but sometimes morality is limited to conventional expectations for what is good and bad whereas ethics is the broader attention to standards and principles for making good decisions and reflecting on what standards are applicable to given situations (Hinman, 2003). We address both professional ethical research conventions and the harder decision-making beyond rule-following. In the past 50 years, goodness in research has come to be discussed using two additional terms: *compliance* and *integrity*.

Compliance is the term used in the United States and elsewhere for conforming to federal guidelines for the treatment of human and animal subjects of research. Compliance requires that research projects be subject to peer review and that human participation in research reflect the ethical principles of respect for persons, beneficence, and justice (Bankert & Amdur, 2006; Mazur, 2007). Scholars assume that these values are practiced by informed consent, balancing risk with benefit, and selecting participants fairly so that risks and benefits are distributed equitably among people. Risk includes invasion of privacy as well as other kinds of harms—such as physical, mental, emotional, social, and economic. Human participation and consent requires consideration of people's abilities for decision-making. Minors, those incarcerated, or people incapacitated by disease or other conditions may be regarded as vulnerable populations needing special care when involved in research. The focus of compliance, then, is the ethical treatment of participants in qualitative, quantitative, and mixed methods research.

However, research ethics involves more than how scholars treat those they study. *Research integrity*, a more global term, has come to refer to the quality or the goodness of the research: whether the topic or question pursued has some scholarly or professional significance; whether research practices are defensible by some criteria; whether researchers are honest about their standpoints, interests, and procedures; and whether such violations as falsification, fabrication, or plagiarism are involved (Macfarlane, 2009). A study's integrity, then, is to some extent reliant on its compliance. Research may generate useful knowledge but still be morally and ethically suspect (e.g., Reverby, 2009).

Supplementing compliance and elaborating on practices ensuring integrity are the ethical guidelines and standards adopted by professional and scholarly organizations. Summarizing these is beyond the scope of this chapter, but we offer the resources in Appendix A to indicate the endeavors of social, behavioral, health, evaluation, and medical scientists to articulate ethical practice in these various fields. We also note that compliance and adherence to professional expectations do not prevent ethical dilemmas or guarantee research of high integrity. In the past decade a growing literature documents ways that compliance and oversight may impede study of important topics and hamper complex investigations (e.g., Gabb, 2010; Green, Lowery, Kowalski, & Wyszewianski, 2006; Schrag, 2010), and we view continuing discussion of these frameworks and regulations as crucial to scholarly advance.

All of these standards and guidelines draw to a large extent on the same ethical principles (Freeman & Preissle, 2010)—sometimes called moral theories—that guide behavior and conduct in daily lives around the modern world: fairness, duty, consequences, reasonableness, virtuousness, sociability, and caring. The first four compose the foundations for the aforementioned principles guiding compliance. Researchers have a duty to respect participants, to treat them fairly, and to assure that the consequences of the research are balanced. In practice, the other three principles also come into play. For example, we are to deceive—to be untruthful—only with peer review and according to strict guidelines. Sociability and caring come into play as we work through the details of consenting and judging vulnerabilities.

What makes the ethical conduct of research especially challenging, however, is not necessarily compliance or conformity to a particular professional practice. What troubles and puzzles researchers are, first, the trade-offs and balances of guiding principles and practices and, second, the unexpected developments that occur in conducting research or other human activity. For any set of decisions we make, multiple goods or priorities compete. While most people recognize those goods and priorities, balancing them complicates ethical decisions (Kidder, 1995). For instance, acquiring and documenting consent may itself pose risks for privacy. Distributing the burdens of research fairly may place the most vulnerable at greater risk than the least vulnerable. Even when we balance these choices in advance and with peer review, we are often faced with myriad choices once the study is underway (e.g., Patton, 1990). We may find out that our instruments were improperly or ineffectually administered, that our participants were subtly coerced into consenting by their superior, or that an anonymous questionnaire that seemed mild to us is distressing to our participants. In addition to what happens beyond our control are the ordinary, everyday mistakes we make because we ourselves are fallible beings: we forget to do things, we become distracted by one procedure so we neglect another, we respond habitually rather than reflectively, we resist the inconvenience that compliance demands, and we unintentionally breach a professional expectation because we are trying to balance too many different demands. And then, as if doing an experiment or running a survey or conducting observations and interviews were not complicated enough, we decide to use mixed and multimethods. The conventional wisdom of many qualitative and quantitative scholars in the 1980s and 1990s that kept research traditions separate is hardly surprising. One approach was complicated enough! However, in this chapter we argue that the mixes of approaches themselves may permit us to do more ethical research with greater integrity while conceding that the evidence for this claim has yet to be produced. Although the literature on ethics in qualitative and quantitative traditions is substantial (e.g., Mertens & Ginsberg, 2009; Preissle & Han, 2012; Trimble & Fisher, 2006), scholars in multimethod and mixed methods traditions have only recently begun to address their ethical puzzles.[2]

To plot our course, we consider the ethical and moral dimensions of five decisions that any mixed methods researcher studying human beings addresses: what mixed methods design to adapt for what purposes, how to select or sample human participants, what data collection and analysis methods to use, how to formulate and develop relationships with participants and other stakeholders in the research, and what formats to use for representing the research and its findings. For each decision area, we draw on examples from our own research experiences, independently and as a team, and on the limited extant literature on ethics in MMMR.

Although we discuss these decisions in linear order, our experiences in quantitative, qualitative, and mixed methods research are that the decisions are recursive—each affects the others. Limitations of space and the linearity of printed text do not do justice to constructs such as reflexivity that should permeate all research decisions and practices (Hesse-Biber & Piatelli, 2012). We focus on reflexivity in the section on researcher relationships but emphasize its significance from the start to the finish of research projects. We also highlight how mixing methods may produce ethical complexity and argue that mixed methods research offers a larger set of more flexible tools for tackling ethical quandaries in their various contexts. We conclude the chapter with considerations for addressing ethics in MMMR, grounded in our discussions of decision-making.

Ethics of Research Purpose and Design

Researchers must make as many as 13 major decisions when planning and conducting MMMR (Collins, Onwuegbuzie, & Sutton, 2006; Johnson & Onwuegbuzie, 2004; Creswell, Klassen, Plano Clark, & Smith, 2011). In addition to decisions made in single-method studies (e.g., data collection, analysis, interpretation), MMMR further involves specifying the rationale and purpose of mixing data, developing a mixed methods design, establishing data prioritization and implementation sequencing, and delineating how and when data integration will occur throughout the research process (Creswell & Plano Clark, 2007).

A primary ethical concern for design in MMMR is research integrity (Johnson & Onwuegbuzie, 2004). Mixed methods researchers must demonstrate how their designs add value (e.g., improved reliability) over inquiry using a single method (Salehi & Golafshani, 2010), especially when resources are limited. Other fundamental issues are ensuring that the research questions call for a MMMR design and then matching a specific design to articulated purposes for data mixing. Such purposes may include triangulation, exploration, explanation, development, expansion, initiation, and social transformation (Bryman, 2006; Greene, 2007; Mertens, 2012; Newman, Ridenour, Newman, & DeMarco, 2003).

As a particular weakness, critics of MMMR cite failures to integrate findings from different data streams in forming meta-inferences (Bryman, 2007; Maudsley, 2011). However, given the complexities of practicing MMMR, lack of transparency about the research process may be the real issue, aggravated by confusing and conflicting nomenclature (Johnson, Onwuegbuzie, & Turner, 2007) and lack of consensus around design descriptions (Creswell & Plano Clark, 2007; Hanson, Creswell, Clark, Petska, & Creswell,

2005; Onwuegbuzie & Johnson, 2006; Teddlie & Tashakkori, 2006). Fortunately, scholars continue to refine conceptualizations to advance the field of MMMR (Guest, 2012; Hesse-Biber, 2010; Morse, 2010). Standards for assessing the quality of MMMR, thus supporting research integrity, while not uniformly accepted, are increasingly found in the literature (Bryman, Becker, & Sempik, 2008; Creswell et al., 2011; Sale & Brazil, 2004). To improve transparency, for example, researchers suggest ways to enhance discussion and depiction of the research process, including how, when, and for what purpose data mixing and integration occur under various designs (Ivankova, Creswell, & Stick, 2006; Morse, 2003). These descriptions of various mixed methods approaches have typically been conceptualized as design typologies. Scholars offer numerous MMMR typologies for consideration (e.g., Creswell, Plano Clark, Gutmann, & Hanson, 2003; Greene, 2007; Morse, 2003, 2010; Teddlie & Tashakkori, 2006; Terrell, 2011), while reminding us that no schematic is exhaustive or mirrors exactly the complexities of real-world practice (Maxwell & Loomis, 2003; Tashakkori & Teddlie, 2003). Offering a critique of such formulations, Guest (2012) rejects choosing one overall design typology in favor of richer description about the actual research process. Regardless of using common or alternative typologies, we do agree that clarity in planning for, conducting, and reporting common design elements is crucial for supporting integrity in MMMR. Absent that, we are hindered in our ability to assess inference quality, one ultimate product of our research efforts.

Making Design-Related Choices

Mixed methods scholars generally recommend choosing one distinct mixed methods design as a solid framework to guide the research (Creswell & Plano Clark, 2007). For evaluation studies, an additional ethical concern is whether the design will produce the strongest possible evidence to assess the effectiveness of social programs. At stake is stewardship of limited resources and protection of the public's welfare through high-quality, rigorous evaluation (Morris, 2011; Thomas, 2010). The issue of rigor, however, produces much debate. When is a design sufficiently rigorous, and who gets to decide?

As is the case for research generally, systematic inquiry is a guiding principle for evaluators (American Evaluation Association, 2004; Morris, 2011), and accuracy is a related standard in evaluation conduct (Joint Committee, 1994). Achieving a high degree of rigor and accuracy in all designs involves trade-offs with other standards—utility, feasibility, and propriety. For example, meticulously derived findings not used or acted on by stakeholders have minimal value (Patton, 1997; Weiss, 1977). Implementing complicated study designs may not be financially feasible for many organizations or timely for decision-making purposes. Empowerment designs (Fetterman & Wandersman, 2005) involving self-evaluation have been endorsed for democratizing participation and enhancing accountability, although lack of objectivity and perceived credibility are deemed weaknesses of these approaches (Cousins, 2005; Morris, 2011).

Mixed methods studies in particular provoke varied opinions about rigor and the ability to make strong inferences with valid and reliable data. Different disciplines have various levels of acceptance of mixed methods (Plano Clark, 2005). Methodological purists have historically advocated incompatibility in combining quantitative and qualitative methods and data and the epistemologies associated with them (Denzin, 2010; Johnson & Onwuegbuzie, 2004). Mixed methods researchers working with the philosophical tenets of pragmatism (Greene, 2007; Maxcy, 2003) assert that multiple forms of evidence allow stronger inferences to be made through convergence and corroboration (Johnson & Onwuegbuzie, 2004). Onwuegbuzie and Johnson (2006) acknowledge the potential for additive or multiplicative threats to validity when integrating data types and their inherent limitations yet offer nine distinct forms of validity in MMMR, termed *legitimization*, using their bilingual nomenclature. They argue that legitimization in its various forms "represents a process that is analytical, social, aesthetic, emic, etic, political, and ethical, and which must involve the community of quantitative and qualitative scholars alike who are committed to addressing the multiple problems that can occur in mixed research" (p. 60).

In certain situations MMMR may be regarded, in itself, as a more ethical design choice. For example, scholars laud the importance of having fluid designs in real-world settings (Patton, 2002) particularly when sensitive topics (e.g., domestic violence) are explored requiring action out of ethical or legal responsibility (Luxardo, Colombo, & Iglesias, 2011). Mertens (2012) observes that studies aimed at social justice under a transformative paradigm are more likely to have multimethod and mixed methods designs with a qualitative component, allowing the research to be formulated and carried out in culturally appropriate ways. Chen (2010) introduces a new model of validity in real-world evaluation contexts called integrative validity that *requires* mixed methods research involving quantitative and qualitative approaches. Chen's model defines credible evidence about social betterment programs as stemming from internal validity (effectiveness), external validity (generalizability), and *viable validity*, which takes real-world implementation experiences into account. Viability, for example, includes exploring contextual contingencies and community acceptance, as well as assessing and mitigating an intervention's unintended consequences. Integrative validity, therefore, bridges the academic–practice divide by valuing both traditional scientific criteria and practice-based realities. In sum, when deciding to undertake a mixed methods study, researchers must consider myriad contextual factors. Next, we turn to how to anticipate ethical challenges that may stem from design-related choices.

Anticipating Ethical Challenges

How investigations are formulated may create, evade, or prevent ethical dilemmas. One murky area, for example, is whether work labeled *evaluation* is exempt from IRB review on the basis that it is not research. This issue occurred in our own work together on the aforementioned CRCSDP project. One of the institutions we worked for viewed the project as a research study that required IRB clearance; the other exempted it as evaluation, not research, and thus not requiring IRB clearance. Because the means devised to protect participants for the evaluation met what are sometimes the more stringent IRB requirements, we were able to work as a team with no conflicting ethical pressures.

How may mixed methods designs both address and raise ethical challenges? Hesse-Biber (2010) discusses various purposes in mixing quantitative and qualitative data within an overall qualitative methodology. Of nine rationales for mixing data, at least three speak to issues of ethics, depending on study context: using quantitative methods to locate and then qualitatively give voice to a hard-to-reach population; identifying and examining unexpected outlying cases through quantitative and qualitative inquiry, respectively; and using qualitative inquiry to investigate contradictions found in quantitative data, which may include unintended consequences or outcomes.

With sequential designs, where the two strands of the study occur consecutively with one usually informing the other, anticipating ethical challenges is difficult because aspects of the designs are emergent. This means that IRBs also have a harder time assessing the protections in place for participants (Creswell & Plano Clark, 2007). The phased, potentially longer duration of such studies requires researchers and participants to make additional commitments to each other. Passage of time may also introduce new contextual complexities and inconsistencies in the data that demand examination. In sequential mixed methods designs research integrity may be supported, for example (see Glover-Kudon, 2008), when unexpected quantitative results are empirically explained by qualitative follow-up. However, for concurrent triangulation mixed methods designs, reconciling potentially discrepant results can be problematic. What should researchers do when mixed data are contradictory (Bryman, 2006; Salehi & Golafshani, 2010; Zhou & Creswell, 2012)? Research integrity demands that investigators disclose the criteria used to resolve any such discrepancies.

We contend that ethics should be a central and routine part of multimethod and mixed methods researchers' "armchair walkthrough" process of developing study proposals; researchers should envision details of study implementation (e.g., developing IRB packages, hiring staff, arranging funding, specifying timelines), all of which, later, should be reflexively compared to actual experience captured by an audit trail (Morse, 2010). In subsequent sections of this chapter we indicate how that might be done. We stress here that, in MMMR, whom we study, generally or specifically, may be decided prior to or simultaneously with deciding what about them to study and how. In the aforementioned CRCSDP research we knew generally whom we wanted to study as we were figuring out how best to study them about what features of colorectal cancer screening. Having considered some of the ethical issues involved in what we study and how, we move next to who are studied and how they are selected.

Ethics of Mixed Methods Sampling and Selection

The two well-documented sampling and selection methods in research and evaluation, probability sampling and purposive selection, are also the foundation for sampling in MMMR, which incorporates techniques from both (Creswell & Plano,

2007; Kemper, Stringfield, & Teddlie, 2003). Both strengthen research integrity, probability sampling by accurately representing the population under study (Teddlie & Yu, 2007), and purposive selection by allowing researchers to gather rich data from knowledgeable or informative participants for deeper understanding of a phenomenon (Hill, Pace, & Robbins, 2010; Patton, 2002). Both approaches lead to ethical challenges as stand-alone methods, and these may or may not be addressed when using more than one sampling method in a mixed methods study. Two overall concerns are the possibility of compromising methodological rigor and consideration for the involvement of participants of MMR. These factors relate to the integrity of research methods and the protection of human subjects participating in research.

Research Integrity in Sampling and Selection

Dattalo (2010) identifies multiple ethical pitfalls in probability sampling. Designing a sampling scheme to achieve representation can be costly and complicated in real-world settings, such as evaluating interventions in public health, so decisions are made that compromise rigor and integrity (Brady & O'Regan, 2009). Telephone surveys are notoriously limited to those who have telephones and will answer them (Dillman, Smyth, & Christian, 2009). Sometimes probability sampling might be theoretically possible but not feasible because of constraints such as time and cost. In a study of breast cancer risk perception among adopted women in the United States, Glover-Kudon (2008) used snowball sampling methods, as opposed to probability, for the quantitative strand of her MMR because of legal and political constraints around creating a sampling frame.

Assuring representation is also an ethical challenge when using purposive sampling. The researcher chooses participants on the basis of which points of view best serve the study, inevitably disregarding other potential contributions. During the longitudinal case study of the CRCSDP, our sampling strategy evolved over time. For the first wave of data collection, we decided to cast a wide net, interviewing program staff, contracted-site staff, and stakeholders. As the case study progressed, smaller numbers of participants were selected for later interviews. The trade-off was focusing on the most program-knowledgeable participants, foregoing the views of those further removed from daily operations (see Curtis, Gesler,

Smith, & Washburn, 2000, for other ethical challenges in purposive sampling).

An overarching moral challenge in research sampling is the inclination of different traditions to privilege one sampling method over the other. Methodological privileging may unnecessarily limit the possibilities of inquiry. In some cases, privileging is so overwhelming that Bryman (2006) questions whether a study can even be considered mixed or multimethod, such as when a quantitative data collection tool includes several open-ended questions or when some quantitative data are collected during a semistructured interview. Hesse-Biber (2010) provides compelling arguments that MMR has so far favored quantitative methods as the predominant methodology, with qualitative methods playing a subordinate role.

When describing mixed methods sampling techniques, Teddlie and Yu (2007) describe the trade-off researchers must make when implementing both probability and purposive sampling techniques within a mixed methods study. The trade-off is the compromise between meeting the standards of sampling to achieve representativeness while also sampling participants to achieve saturation for a rigorous qualitative component. If the ultimate strength of MMR is the ability to compensate for the weaknesses of individual methods by creating a balance, then compromises should provide some kind of specified balance in sampling. However, in real-settings, researchers must make decisions based on limited resources, time, and other pressing concerns that result in sampling imbalances.

Sampling trade-offs can pose ethical challenges when they compromise the integrity of a study. Placing too strong an emphasis on one technique over the other may threaten the key strength of balancing methods. Researchers must consider the ethical implications of reporting results based on incongruent sampling. Are the claims made while reporting based on balanced and reasonable sample sizes? Was it possible to answer the research questions and support or reject hypotheses with the sample size selected? Researchers should strive to develop evenly scaled sampling strategies that provide external validity while also addressing key research questions and remaining accountable for requirements of each sampling method.

Protecting Participants and Compliance in Sampling and Selection

The selection and involvement of participants is the second, and arguably most important,

ethical consideration for mixed methods sampling. Although all investigatory methods require researchers to weigh risks and benefits for their participants, MMR may have an amplified effect on risks. Aside from the criteria of informed consent, other considerations include burden of participation, over- or undersampling, attrition, disclosure, and justice. We elaborate on these next.

Depending on study design, participants may be sampled multiple times over the course of months or even years to participate in a mixed methods study. Sequential designs may be time-consuming and burdening to participants because of the lengthy nature of their involvement (Creswell & Plano Clark, 2007; Teddlie & Yu, 2007). Likewise, concurrent designs may burden participants because of the intensity of their involvement over a shorter time span. During the CRCSDP study discussed previously, one participant noted feeling overwhelmed by data collection between the two quantitative components of the study, as well as the qualitative component. Being both concurrent and longitudinal, this participant felt the burden of intensity and duration. However, he also described the qualitative interviews as "therapy" for his overall experience participating in the project and evaluation. This was an unplanned and unexpected, yet positive, outcome. Researchers should consider not only the burden to participants of being sampled for each strand of a mixed methods study is worth what the participant risks and receives but also if the value of the research results justifies the burden of selected participants.

Another concern for mixed methods sampling is participant attrition over the course of the study. Mixed methods sampling strategies may select a subgroup of participants to contribute to both qualitative and quantitative data collection over time, but when participants leave the study early, sampling plans may be compromised. Participants discontinue participation for reasons, such as staff turnover, disinterest, or even death. Krishnasamy (2000) describes the high rate of death-related attrition while attempting to sample lung cancer patients, which eventually resulted in the need to include retrospective data. Another example of attrition is staff turnover among sites evaluated from the CRCSDP. Because of the purposive sampling involved in the qualitative case study component, we continued to interview individuals who filled key roles in the program while they were on staff, despite personnel changes over time. Interviewing people serving in the same roles across cases, such as program directors, provided continuity, while personnel changes between cycles allowed alternative points of view into the study.

A broader ethical consideration for sampling human subjects for the purposes of research, including mixed methods studies, relates to the justice principle discussed previously. When sampling strategies become complicated across strands, what ethical compromises may be necessary? By this we refer to the choices researchers must make on who to include and who to leave out, among other potential quandaries. Harris et al. (2008) raise the ethical issue of researchers automatically excluding terminally ill cancer patients because they consider them too vulnerable rather than offering them a choice to participate. The question then becomes: How may mixed methods designs ameliorate complications? Adding a qualitative component to a quantitative sampling approach may offer the opportunity to give voice to those whose data are discarded because of being outliers. For example, follow-up qualitative study components may be added to explore the perspectives of these outliers to gain a broader view of phenomena.

Unfortunately, some studies in the past have selected sites for sampling because of the accessibility of participants, sometimes in exploitative ways and often in low-resource communities, requiring participants to take on undue risk so that others eventually benefit from the research results (Presidential Commission for the Study of Bioethical Issues, 2011). Considerations for who risks and who benefits must continue to be critical in sampling designs as strategies become more complicated across MMR.

A final consideration for selecting participants for MMR is participants' understanding about how their contributions will be used. If participants are providing valuable data across the span of a study, does informed consent include full disclosure about the time required of them and how their contributions may be represented or omitted? How much candid information will be revealed to participants across phases of a MMMR study? Researchers make decisions about how to use collected data, identify results, and report those findings. Informed consent should mean that participants understand how their role fits within a mixed methods study. Our position is that mixed methods studies, like most qualitative research, require some face-to-face relationships between researchers and participants. These relationships as well as those among research team members and stakeholders pose particular ethical challenges, which we explore in the next section.

The Ethics of Research Relationships

Research and scholarship are community activities. We study with other people, about other people, for other people—for others in our research areas and for others globally who use and apply knowledge. All human relationships involve ethical decision-making. A MMR study may, for example, include a double-blind study in which the investigators have no contact with participants; regardless, those researchers are still responsible for the protection of those participants and accountable to their professional communities for their relationships among themselves and with their stakeholders. In this section we consider the ethical challenges of all these relationships.

Relationships Between Researchers and Participants

The participant–researcher relationship in MMMR varies considerably because the overall mixed methods design influences the level of interaction researchers and participants have with one another. Nonetheless, we can address the relationship generally, and we take the position that reflexivity is important in all aspects of MMR (Walker, Read, & Priest, 2013). Reflexivity involves locating the researchers in the work—including how researchers' perspectives, experiences, and values influence the entire research process (Charmaz, 2006; Dowling, 2006; Mauthner & Doucet, 2003; Mruck & Mey, 2007; Padgett, 2004; Riessman, 1994; Stake, 2006). Without imposing any particular theoretical or methodological framework on others, we draw from current philosophy of science to claim that any scientific practice is a human practice and thus is vulnerable to human failings, errors, and mistakes (Godfrey-Smith, 2003; Rosenberg, 2012). Part of our responsibility as scholars, then, is to account for ourselves.

In this way, reflexivity can be seen as an ethical practice in and of itself, because it specifies researchers' relationships with participants, and, as a corollary, to the data and the research. Two examples of MMR (Rohan, 2009; Walker et al., 2013) describe what it was like to include former work colleagues in the data collection process, underscoring the importance of maintaining professional boundaries and integrity in the research. In both cases, researchers reported experiences and interpersonal encounters that both helped and hindered the research process.

Another ethical consideration on relationships between researchers and participants in MMR stems from the notion that interaction between researchers and participants is vital to unearthing "subjugated knowledge" (Hesse-Biber, 2010), the lived experiences of research participants and the meanings they ascribe to those experiences. Researchers typically have more power and resources than those they study, and part of that power can be imposing meanings through standardized instrumentation. Mixed methods designs with qualitative components can provide balance (e.g., Chiu, Mitchell, & Fitch, 2013). As such, MMR can be instrumental in promoting social justice and social change (e.g., Botha, 2011). Although advocacy perspectives are valued in some areas of qualitative research (Mertens, 2012; Padgett, 2009), these positions are less common in quantitative research. Marrying differing perspectives from the divergent epistemologies that underlie qualitative (e.g., constructivism, feminism) and quantitative (e.g., postpositivism) approaches does not have to mean one side dominates; rather, it can be a constructive enterprise that clarifies the overall purpose of the research and buoys the utility of mixed methodology.

Finally, the content of the research may influence both the researchers and the participants. Harris et al. (2008) conducted a systematic review of MMR in terminal cancer and cautioned that investigators may emotionally jeopardize themselves by studying people who are dying. The same is true of researchers who study other vulnerable groups, such as those who are marginalized or victims of abuse (Addington-Hall, 2002). Researchers may, on the other hand, be transformed by the research, witnessing how people manage and derive meaning from painful circumstances. Concomitantly, research participants may react, both positively and negatively, to the content of the research. We noted previously that one of the participants in our CRCSDP study experienced the qualitative interviews as therapeutic; however, in their review Harris et al. (2008) found that participants varied in their responses to such data gathering. An important resource for both researcher and participants can be the presence of multiple researchers, as we discuss next.

Relationships Among Team Members

Mixed methods research is time-consuming and requires expertise in mixed methods design as well as quantitative and qualitative methods. Mixed methods research is certainly conducted by solitary researchers—some of us are testament to that. However, MMMR is especially well suited to a team of researchers, perhaps from multiple disciplines. When undertaken alone, researchers should begin by questioning the extent to which they require additional training—a common challenge for doctoral students—or might benefit from partnering with others who have different skills and preparation (Hesse-Biber, 2010).

When MMR is undertaken with an interdisciplinary team, ethical considerations arise from disciplinary borders that need to be bridged (Hemmings, Beckett, Kennerly, & Yap, 2013). For example, different team members may have various levels of expertise with the topic being studied. What if different levels of knowledge lead researchers to have assumptions about what the data may reveal? Additionally, team members' disciplinary (and methodological) perspectives may lead them to interpret the data differently. How does the team reconcile different interpretations of the data? While formal and informal power dynamics certainly play a role in the resolution of both of these issues, Hemmings et al. assert that disciplinary "border crossings," including team members' teaching each other about both the content of the research endeavor and their disciplinary perspectives and language, are necessarily the solution. They stress that such crossings "depend on intragroup socialization into different disciplines and the formation of a group social identity" (p. 270). They contend that, although these processes can be time-consuming and challenging at times, they are essential to the integrity of interdisciplinary MMR. For example, in our previously cited CRCSDP work (Boehm et al., 2013; Glover-Kudon et al., 2013; Rohan et al., 2013), team members had backgrounds in public health, education, anthropology, sociology, public policy, and oncology social work. Although the multidisciplinary team composition was a rich resource for our case study, it necessitated lengthy but valuable discussions whereby each team member taught the others her perspectives. Ultimately, we approached the analysis in a transdisciplinary manner (Gelhert et al., 2010; Hemmings et al., 2013; Rosenfield, 1992); that is, our teamwork transcended disciplinary boundaries in an effort to appreciate complexity and create new conceptual frameworks from which to understand the issues we were studying.

Relationships in MMR pose multiple ethical challenges, the resolution of which should be identified somewhere in the reporting of the work. In using reflexive techniques, derived from qualitative methods, for all components of mixed methods studies, MMR can normalize the use of such practices in straight quantitative methods, thereby fostering more candor in such endeavors. This candor in reporting, labeled *transparency* in qualitative design and in discussions about integrity, is also invaluable for reporting methods of data collection and analysis, the topic we consider next.

Ethics of Data Collection and Analysis

As in single-method studies, ethical issues may emerge during data collection and analysis in MMR. Use of mixed methods mandates that researchers be prepared to identify and negotiate ethical issues relevant to each methodological approach as well as those that emerge because of the mixing itself. With both quantitative and qualitative methods, the type of instrumentation (e.g., telephone or online survey, personal interview), the data collected (e.g., personally identifiable, sensitivity of data), and the sources of data (e.g., vulnerable populations) significantly influence the ethical issues for a given study. Electronic forms of data collection introduced over the past two decades are noteworthy and have led to new and complex ethical issues, including determining whether such data are public or private, carrying out informed consent, and making the presence of the researcher known during online data collection (Griffiths, 2010; Hesse-Biber & Griffin, 2013). In this section, we address ethical issues related to data collection first, followed by those relevant to data analysis.

Ethical Issues in Data Collection

To illustrate ethical issues in mixed methods data collection, we draw from the project that followed the CRCSDP evaluation research cited in previous sections of the chapter. A team at the Centers for Disease Control and Prevention (CDC) is currently evaluating a strategy called patient navigation (PN) intended to increase adherence to colorectal cancer screening (Paskett, Harrop, & Wells, 2011), examining a model of PN used by a grantee of the CDC's Colorectal Cancer Control Program. To determine program impact, the team is using a mixed methods approach that includes a matched comparison group design (quantitative), an in-depth case study (quantitative and qualitative), and a cost study (quantitative). Primary data collection includes observations of patient navigators and interviews with key stakeholders.

Secondary data include medical chart abstraction, information on program delivery (e.g., participant demographics, navigation activities, time spent delivering navigation), document review (e.g., program reports), and cost data (e.g. cost of colonoscopy, staff salaries). Using a mixed methods approach, we are able to assess effectiveness on key outcomes (matched comparison group design), better understand program implementation and the potential for transferring the model to other contexts (case study), and determine feasibility of using the model given limited resources (cost study).

But what ethical issues for data collection are we facing in choosing this design? First is an ethical obligation to ensure the technical capacity to carry out each component of the study (Brazeley, 2010). As noted previously, MMMR may demand both quantitative and qualitative methods expertise. In this case, we convened a team with quantitative, qualitative, and mixed methods research experience.

Second is the obligation for anticipating ethical concerns in planning for data collection. Table 9.1 summarizes the ethical concerns we are addressing in the PN study, involving six different data collection methods or data sources. For instance, we will abstract patient medical records to gather information needed to assess screening adherence, confronting several ethical issues of privacy, confidentiality, and informed consent. These include compliance with the Health Insurance Portability and Accountability Act or HIPAA, a law protecting the privacy of patients' health information. Adhering to professional standards and ensuring research integrity, we applied strict data abstraction practices, including specifying an abstraction protocol and incorporating quality checks at various points. To protect the identity of the facility, as requested by its leadership, we refer to the site as simply "Clinic A" in all conversation and study documentation.

We will also use existing program delivery data recorded by the navigators into a data system designed for their program. Analysis of these data will help us to describe patient clinical outcomes and program implementation, including the demographics of patients navigated, navigation services provided (e.g., assistance with transportation, patient education), and the time navigators spent with patients. An ethical issue emerged at this point because the program staff members do not secure informed consent from patients receiving navigation because they are implementing a

Table 9.1 Ethical Issues in Data Collection for a Mixed Methods Evaluation of a Patient Navigation Program for Colorectal Cancer Screening

Data Collection Method or Data Source	Ethical Concerns
Primary data collection	
Stakeholder interviews	Informed consent of participants Privacy protections and confidentiality (e.g., use of pseudonyms) Data protections Burden on participants Member checking of transcripts and/or descriptive findings
Participant observations	Informed consent of participants Privacy protections and confidentiality Data protections Burden on participants
Secondary data	
Abstraction of patient medical records	Absence of patients' informed consent Compliance with the Health Insurance Portability and Accountability Act Deidentified analytic data set to ensure privacy protections and confidentiality Data sharing agreements Data handling and related protections
Document review	Privacy protections and confidentiality (e.g., redacting personal identifiers) Data protections
Program delivery data	Absence of patients' informed consent Deidentified analytic data set to ensure privacy protections and confidentiality Data sharing agreements Data handling and related protections
Cost data	Data protections

program, not doing research. Our team is using the data collected by the navigators as secondary data. To ensure the confidentiality of clients, the PN program staff participants are providing us with a deidentified data set in which each patient is assigned a unique patient identifier and all personal identifiers are removed. Others have described this issue in more depth (Leahey, 2007). Next, some information about the navigation services provided is entered as text data in a "navigator notes" section of the data system. This poses a new problem: individually identifying information in the notes sections must be redacted by program staff before the data set can be shared with us. Finally, we will establish a data sharing agreement between the research team and program staff explicating details about the data variables, analyses, and efforts to keep the data secure. Use of a data sharing agreement is intended to strengthen ethical practices.

Some ethical concerns unique to mixed methods also demand attention during data collection. These include the potential for greater burden on participants if they are involved in multiple forms of data collection, discussed previously in the sampling section, and the likelihood that researchers make unexpected discoveries during data collection that introduce ethical dilemmas. Patton (1990) describes numerous such examples in qualitative fieldwork (e.g., teachers cheating on test scores, fraudulent payments, child abuse, sexual impropriety), and these situations are even more likely in mixed methods using multiple data. For instance, in the case study of the CRCSDP, an interviewee revealed that she was enrolling patients in their program who did not meet the study criteria. As evaluators, we had ensured confidentiality in the interview, but we also felt an ethical obligation to tell our colleagues at CDC who led the project to clarify the policy for all the sites. We did so in a manner to preserve the confidentiality of the source.

Ethical Issues in Data Analysis

In mixed methods studies, researchers confront unique ethical challenges during data analysis. We are highlighting several here: ethical issues in data integration, in method preferencing, in triangulation and contradictory results, and in inferences (team power).

When and how data are integrated in MMR vary. Brazeley (2010) defines integration as combining data elements and analysis strategies "throughout a study in such a way as to become interdependent in reaching a common theoretical or research goal, thereby producing findings that are greater than the sum of the parts" (p. 432), observing that conceptual and theoretical frames for integration are currently limited. Approaches to integration are directed by the research purpose and design (Greene, 2007). However, do researchers have an ethical obligation to maximize the opportunity provided by integration? Some leaders in the field have suggested that integration is usually inadequate or underdeveloped (Bryman, 2006; Greene, 2007; Plano Clark, 2010). In the PN study described previously, data will be integrated across diverse methods to assess program impact. We are applying a framework of impact considering not just effectiveness but constructs better reflecting impact in real-world circumstances: affordability, viability, feasibility, and transferability (Chen, 2010). Our goal is to fully mix and integrate data to assess impact based on our comprehensive framework.

As data are integrated during analysis, some specific ethical problems can arise. First is an increased chance of participants being identified as data collected via different methods are combined, linking participant information and posing increased threats to privacy (Leahey, 2007). Concerns for data quality and integrity can also increase during analysis when data are mixed or transformed (Greene, 2007). In the PN study, we are struggling to define protocols to ensure accurate transformation of qualitative data from the navigator "notes" to quantitative variables needed for regression analysis.

Another area for ethical concern in data collection and analysis, discussed in preceding sections, is knowingly privileging one method over another, typically quantitative methods over qualitative methods (Hesse-Biber, 2010). Bryman (2006), for example, suggests that MMR often has a positivist orientation, with the quantitative component more often dominating. Hesse-Biber argues for greater parity of methods, "dialoguing" with qualitative and quantitative findings, recognizing that researchers must be "comfortable residing on multiple levels and in multiple realities that inform one another" (p. 458). As we have already emphasized, power relationships among team members likely influence data preferencing. In the PN study, we promote principles of respect and mutual learning among team members through collaborative planning and training. For example, members of the team leading the quantitative analysis recently participated in a training for qualitative team members to use a structured observation guide. The experience gave quantitative team members a new-found respect for the level of methodological rigor incorporated by the qualitative team.

Next, ethical issues can develop around one of the traditional purposes of mixed methods, triangulation. Triangulation is meant to improve the validity of a study by offsetting the biases of an individual method by using multimethods in a given study (Greene, 2007). Through triangulation, results may, however, not converge but be partially consistent or even contradictory (Mathison, 1988), and researchers must also take into account any possible collusion among sources. We became suspicious of impression management, for example, when all the staff members at one of our five CRCSDP sites relayed the same positive message. As we have emphasized previously, in these cases, researchers have an ethical responsibility to explore unexpected agreements as well as contradictions and, potentially, to represent the varied perceptions of the phenomenon under study without unduly preferencing one particular view. These and other issues we have discussed may be addressed directly in how mixed methods researchers report their studies.

The Ethics of Representation and Reporting

Representation and reporting are how research is presented and published. Academic fields and subject areas have developed conventions or customary formats for how this is done. In the social and professional sciences, research may be reported at professional conferences, in journals and periodicals, in dissertations and theses, in books, and, since the 1990s, online in a variety of formats. Arguably the most common format for publishing research studies has been the journal article, and most professional organizations specify a preferred organization and style for it (e.g., American Psychological Association, 2010; University of Chicago Press, 2003). Representation in qualitative traditions has taken these and diverse other forms. In anthropology, for example, reporting research results in ethnographic film has a long history (Heider, 1976; Hockings, 1975). Over the past 20 years, qualitative scholars across fields and subject areas have been exploring forms of representation other than text presentations and the conventional journal article, borrowing from the humanities, the arts, and emerging media formats like online venues (e.g., Blumenfeld-Jones, 1995; Faulkner, 2009; Gergen & Gergen, 2012; Hesse-Biber & Leavy, 2008; Saldaña, 2011; Tierney & Lincoln, 1997). These include research rendered as performance pieces such as plays and dance, as fiction and poetry, as video and film, and in multimedia formats permitted by digital technologies.

The forms of representation that mixed methods will come to take are continuing to emerge. However, thus far, venues like the *Journal of Mixed Methods Research* appear to be depending on the conventional, American Psychological Association style of report and discussion. We also found this pattern used consistently in our search for citations on ethics and MMR (see endnote 1), but that is partly because the search focused on professional research journals. Padgett (2009) notes the limitations of the format for MMR for full disclosure of research design and methods and for presentation of discrepant results. Finally, we ourselves have thus far presented our own reports from CDC's CRCSDP research in this format. Consequently our discussion here centers on ethical and moral choices when using this convention.

Ethical issues around research reports once focused on how accurate and truthful scholars are in their findings, claims, and interpretations. Research integrity continues to emphasize the obligation to produce honest reports, and periodically the media cover stories about researchers caught inventing and otherwise misrepresenting their material or even their relationships to the work (for a recent incident on falsifying results, see Sutherly, 2012; for an example of researcher bias, see Harris, 2008; for a meta-analysis of surveys on researcher misconduct, see Fanelli, 2009). We speculate that this may be more of a temptation when data are collected anonymously, and no one comes forward to dispute responses on surveys and written tests. However, the checks and balances inherent to many quantitative designs as well as comparison to prior research may signal when data and patterns are questionable.

The labor involved in falsifying qualitative data may discourage similar invention, but it is certainly possible, and the more common issue may be misrepresentation through omission. No one can report everything that occurs during data collection, and selection of what to include involves ethical as well as analytic choices. Scholars need not have economic interests in their results to have biases, and current practice for all researchers is to disclose these as limitations. Furthermore, human interactions are inherently multilayered: meanings nest within other meanings. People honestly disagree about what they observe and what those observations mean. Here the availability of information from multiple sources is a crucial check

on research integrity. Nevertheless, misrepresentation occurs. Ethical controversies in ethnographic film making, for example, surfaced early around whether the events recorded were naturally occurring or scripted (Asch, 1992), and digital film editing adds yet more possibilities for alternative views of human activity if not outright misrepresentation.

For qualitative researchers the ethics of representation is intricately involved with their relationships with participants. The issue is the consequences or effects of research reports on and for the research participants. Through the first half of the 20th century, scholars assumed that their reports were read only by other researchers and that the images portrayed were rarely accessible to the public, much less to the research participants themselves. By midcentury, however, increasing global literacy and wider use of research for policymaking meant that most reports could be read or viewed by almost anyone. People who have consented to being studied may find out they are being portrayed in unexpected and sometimes unwelcome ways. This is captured well in the title of the anthology *When They Read What We Write* (Brettell, 1993). By the 21st century, the instant access provided by digital information systems has democratized knowledge such that all researchers may have an ethical responsibility to assure their findings are available to everyone in accessible formats.

What research reports reveal about people and how the reports characterize individuals and groups have provoked considerable ethical debate (Glazer, 1972). These issues have not been prevented by ethics reviews, as the disclosures about research with the Havasupai have indicated. This small Indigenous population in North America was misled about how their blood samples would be used; rather than addressing the medical condition to which the group had consented, results were used to examine and report Indigenous migration patterns contradicting Havasupai origin beliefs (Harmon, 2010).

In response to such disclosures, scholars such as anthropologists in some periods have been enjoined by ethical codes to place the well-being of the people they study above all other considerations. Some researchers may have felt impelled to present findings that showed participants in the best possible light or that otherwise distorted representations. Subsequent discussions in fields like anthropology have acknowledged the competing priorities that pressure researchers (Fluehr-Lobban, 2002): the integrity of the research, and the other stakeholder interests. Even for scholars whose primary obligations are to priorities other than participants, however, the responsibility to represent participants in respectful and fair ways is acknowledged, and expectations for appropriate representation and reporting to support accountability and transparency may be stronger than ever before. The ethics review issues for these situations would be avoiding reporting and representation practices that place participants at unnecessary risk without consent and peer deliberation and reconsenting participants when research purposes change.

How do these issues play out in MMMR? Mixed methods reports often draw from complex findings; because only some of this can be represented in a particular publication, it becomes crucial to develop presentations and publications that indicate the other parts of the story of the research and the participants. In combining designs across traditions like quantitative and qualitative, researchers should consider at the outset what their expectations are for participant involvement in reports. Although some qualitative practice includes member checking and much evaluation research practice involves stakeholder input, clearing manuscripts with participants in quantitative research is rare. We believe that MMMR may be an opportunity to include participant input more widely. This need not mean rewriting reports to suit those studied; the input and even disagreements can become part of the research record, where participants are provided opportunities to offer their own accounts to balance those of the researchers.

The representation issue we faced in the CRCSDP research occurred during the period when our participants were reviewing our initial three research reports. The cost and clinical reports indicated success in outcomes at each site, and two of the qualitative reports candidly discussed issues common to all five sites. We were therefore taken aback when participants at one site took exception to how we interpreted program development, the topic of the third manuscript. Some of the more quantitatively oriented researchers on the CDC team themselves were uneasy about the metaphoric language used in the original report draft. What followed was a rewording of material to remove implications we had not intended and to connect material in the data to interpretations using more concrete language. Our discussion of the uncertainties of the beginnings of the program development across the five sites was balanced by the two other qualitative reports that indicated the competence

and creative problem solving of site staff and by noting that such uncertainties are endemic to any new programming.

In advocating for taking participant and public perceptions into account in our reporting and representation, we are recognizing researchers' accountabilities to those they study and to the public for whom knowledge is created. Sometimes this means delivering unwelcome messages, but other times it means taking the care to avoid misinterpretations.

Conclusion: Ways Forward

In this chapter, we have aimed to elevate the issue of ethics on the topographic map of MMMR. In surveying the area, our path has covered five coordinates that all researchers in the social sciences must trek: study design, sampling, participant and stakeholder relationships, data collection and analysis, and representation. We have sought to put into the relief the contours of complex moral issues and unique ethical dilemmas inherent in MMMR. We conclude with some recommendations for ensuring ethical mixed methods practice.

Multimethod and Mixed Methods Research—Increased Ethical Challenges and Solutions

Researchers and evaluators should carefully examine the ethical issues for each method used as well as those relevant when mixing these methods before beginning data collection. Anticipating these issues is critical to planning how to manage them. Next, researchers should address ethical issues quickly and promptly as they arise. If needed, professional advice should be sought from an IRB or others to effectively resolve unexpected challenges. Finally, documenting all ethical concerns and their resolution encountered throughout the data collection and analysis process is imperative. As Guest (2012) notes, "a study gains legitimacy from the strength of the research design, the use of a cogent argument, and the transparency of the research process" (p. 144).

More so than using single-method designs, MMR yields the potential for complex or even amplified ethical problems. We have offered examples throughout the chapter as they relate to aspects of the research process. Despite this challenge, however, we argue that MMR designs may provide a greater flexibility and a range of tools for ameliorating ethical dilemmas as they arise. For example, a second method may be added to compensate for a sampling choice that entails ethical repercussions. Likewise, to address the exclusion of outliers in a quantitative component, a qualitative component may be added so that the voices of all participants are included.

Embracing Transparency in Multimethod and Mixed Methods Research

Transparency through the use of reflexive practices should be part of any mixed methods study. Consumers of research are the ultimate arbiters of our work. Consequently, researchers are obliged to demonstrate the goodness of their work. Was IRB obtained? Were appropriate methods applied with adequate rigor? When and how were methods mixed? How were unexpected ethical dilemmas addressed? Research teams should continuously reflect on these decisions and practices. An audit trail, a traditional tool of qualitative research, is essential for documenting decisions throughout the research process.

We further propose that multimethod and mixed methods researchers study the diversity of formats used by qualitative scholars and evaluation practitioners for opportunities not only to make findings more accessible but also to highlight the complexity of discrepant data (Torres, Preskill, & Piontek, 1996). We recommend considering the widest possible audiences and stakeholders for research as well as the formats for presenting research that would be most convincing to different people (Coyle & Williams, 2000). What might be compelling for, say, a hearing-impaired community might be less effective for others. Our intent here is to provoke thinking about venues beyond scholarly colleagues. The public has access to the knowledge we are generating. How can multimethod and mixed methods researchers facilitate that access?

While the practice of MMMR has grown tremendously over the past decades, dialogue about related ethical issues has been neglected. However, the community of mixed method researchers and the institutions that support them are poised to move this issue forward. As we outlined here, there are a multitude of ethical issues inherent in MMMR—some unique to each method and others a product of MMMR practice itself. Transparency is central to advancing ethical practice—illuminating the choices made and our related value stances. Transparency may be promoted, even required, by IRBs, professional organizations, journal editors and peer reviewers,

and researchers themselves (for a recent anthology focusing on reflexivity in ethical issues in qualitative, quantitative, mixed methods, and online research, see Rhodes & Weiss, 2013).

Need for Experienced Multimethod and Mixed Methods Research Peer Reviewers

This chapter advances a topic currently underrepresented in the MMMR literature—the discussion of ethics in MMMR practice. Although the conversation is nascent, the community of multimethod and mixed methods researchers is positioned to further this dialogue. In particular, editors of journals might consider including peer reviewers with MMMR expertise when appropriate (Padgett, 2009) to ensure that manuscripts meet the necessary criteria for inclusion, including addressing ethical practice. Those with MMR experience might be called on as reviewers, and attempts might be made to balance the possibility of methodological preferencing throughout the peer review process. Further, editors and organizers of professional conferences may consider expanding invited manuscripts and abstracts to include those examining ethical issues in MMMR. As example, the *American Journal of Evaluation* has included an ethics section in its journal since 1998. *AJE* began an Ethical Challenges section in 1998, but it does not appear in each numbered volume (although does appear every year). In 2014, the section name changed to Professional Values & Ethics.

Ethics in Practice—Standards and Judgment in Multimethod and Mixed Methods Research

Conducting ethical research mandates assiduous attention to standards and judgment. While researchers have an obligation to ensure the necessary competencies needed to conduct varied methods applied in MMMR, they might also be well versed in issues of compliance and integrity, central components of ethical conduct. Moving beyond the standard rules of behavior, researchers might apply ethical principles in considering study purpose, design, implementation, and reporting. Additionally, researchers may attend to both the expected and unexpected ethical dilemmas that emerge in the conduct of MMMR. To advance the field, developing standards for assessing the quality of MMMR as it relates to ethical practice for the varied fields of social and behavioral inquiry may be considered. Such standards as well as additional and candid dialogue about ethical issues and challenges will advance and improve MMMR by providing more detailed maps for both the novice and the experienced as they navigate the new terrain uncovered by any fresh research study.

Discussion Questions

1. What ethical issues have you encountered in your own research? How are these issues represented in the literature? How might you report your experiences to add to the literature on ethics in MMMR?

2. How have mixed methods approaches helped you to address ethical issues in your research? How have they complicated the ethical issues in your research?

3. Planning for a MMR project, what ethical issues and challenges do you anticipate? How might you address these in your research protocol and human subjects application?

4. How could mixed and multiple research approaches be more ethical than either qualitative or quantitative designs alone?

Suggested Websites

http://www.ethics.org/

The Ethics Resource Center is a nonprofit, nonpartisan group for organizational ethics established in 1922. The website provides resources for professional and research endeavors.

http://ethicscenter.csl.illinois.edu/

The National Center for Professional and Research Ethics is a central clearinghouse for professional and research ethics. The website offers information on best practices in ethics and moral decision-making.

http://www.hhs.gov/ohrp/

The website of the US Department of Health and Human Services, Office for Human Research Protections is an example of a US government resource for the protection of human subjects and participants in research. This office oversees the well-being of subjects involved in research sponsored by the US Department of Health and Human Services and provides resources, including guidance and educational materials, on ethical issues in social-behavioral and biomedical research. Researchers based in other countries may locate similar frameworks sponsored by other national governments.

http://poynter.indiana.edu/

The website for the Poynter Center for the Study of Ethics and American Institutions examines the range of moral and ethical decision-making in the United States and offers special preparation in "bioethics; professional ethics; religion, culture, and society; political ethics; research ethics; and teaching ethics in the sciences and humanities." It provides resources for researchers and scholars that view ethics and morality broadly and inclusively.

For examples of the variety of ethical codes endorsed by professional organizations, see the websites listed in Appendix A.

Notes

1. The findings and conclusions in this chapter are those of the authors and do not necessarily represent the official position of the Centers for Disease Control and Prevention.

2. We searched the electronically indexed literature published in English from 1985 to present. Using derivative search term combinations of "multi*- or mixed-method* and ethic*" in either the title or abstract, a search of PubMed, Sociological Abstracts, Social Services Abstracts, and CINAHL yielded 255 articles after removal of duplicates. After further examination of the titles and abstracts, we discovered only 36 articles to be relevant to our general topic of ethics in MMR. Of the remaining 219 articles, most reported results from mixed-methods studies in specific content areas. We have cited 16 of 36 references we generated from the original literature search. The 36 references fell into these general categories: 6 articles describing MMMR on practice-based ethics and/or professional conduct (e.g., in social work, in business); 12 articles described application of MMR in studying complex social phenomena or sensitive topics, or in advancing a particular field; 18 articles centered on some aspect of ethical research conduct or the research process when MMR is involved (e.g., dealing with IRBs, ethics panels, respecting participants).

References

Addington-Hall, J. (2002). Research sensitivities to palliative care patients. *European Journal of Cancer Care, 11*(3), 220–224.

American Evaluation Association. (2004). Guiding principles for evaluators (Rev. ed.). Retrieved from http://www.eval.org/p/cm/ld/fid=51

American Psychological Association. (2010). *Publication manual of the American Psychological Association* (6th ed.). Washington, DC: Author.

Asch, T. (1992). The ethics of ethnographic film-making. In P. I. Crawford & D. Turton (Eds.), *Film as ethnography* (pp. 196–204). Manchester, UK: Manchester University Press.

Bankert, E. A., & Amdur, R. J. (2006). *Institutional review board: Management and function*. Sudbury, MA: Jones and Bartlett.

Blumenfeld-Jones, D. S. (1995). Dance as a mode of research representation. *Qualitative Inquiry, 1*(4), 391–401.

Boehm, J. E., Rohan, E. A., Preissle, J., DeGroff, A., & Glover-Kudon, R. (2013). Recruiting patients into the CDC's Colorectal Cancer Screening Demonstration Program. *Cancer, 119*, 2914–2925.

Botha, L. (2011). Mixing methods as a process towards indigenous methodologies. *International Journal of Social Research Methodology, 14*(4), 313–325.

Brady, B., & O'Regan, C. (2009). Meeting the challenge of doing an RCT evaluation of youth mentoring in Ireland: A journey in mixed methods. *Journal of Mixed Methods Research, 3*(3), 265–280.

Brazeley, P. (2010). Computer-assisted integration of mixed-methods data sources and analyses. In A. Tashakkori & C. Teddlie (Eds.), *Mixed methods in social and behavioral research* (2nd ed., pp. 431–468). Thousand Oaks, CA: Sage.

Brettell, C. B. (1993). *When they read what we write: The politics of ethnography*. Westport, CN: Bergin & Garvey.

Bryman, A. (2006). Integrating quantitative and qualitative research: How is it done? *Qualitative Research, 6*(1), 97–113.

Bryman, A. (2007). Barriers to integrating quantitative and qualitative research. *Journal of Mixed Methods Research, 1*(1), 8–22.

Bryman, A., Becker, S., & Sempik, J. (2008). Quality criteria for quantitative, qualitative and mixed methods research: A view from social policy. *International Journal of Social Research Methodology, 11*(4), 261–276.

Charmaz, K. (2006). *Constructing grounded theory: A practical guide through qualitative analysis.* London, England: Sage.

Chen, H. T. (2010). The bottom-up approach to integrative validity: A new perspective for program evaluation. *Evaluation and Program Planning, 33*(3), 205–214.

Chiu, C. G., Mitchell, T. L., & Fitch, M. I. (2013). From patient to participant: Enhancing the validity and ethics of cancer research through participatory research. *Journal of Cancer Education, 28*(2), 237–246.

Collins, K. M., Onwuegbuzie, A. J., & Sutton, I. L. (2006). A model incorporating the rationale and purpose for conducting mixed-methods research in special education and beyond. *Learning Disabilities: A Contemporary Journal, 4*(1), 67–100.

Cousins, B. (2005). Will the real empowerment evaluation please stand up? A critical friend perspective. In D. M. Fetterman & A. Wandersman (Eds.), *Empowerment evaluation principles in practice* (pp. 183–208). New York, NY: Guilford Press.

Coyle, J., & Williams, B. (2000). An exploration of the epistemological intricacies of using qualitative data to develop a quantitative measure of user views of health care. *Journal of Advanced Nursing, 31*(5), 1235–1243.

Creswell, J. W. (2010). Mapping the developing landscape of mixed methods research. In A. Tashakkori & C. Teddlie (Eds.), *Mixed methods in social and behavioral research* (2nd ed., pp. 45–68). Thousand Oaks, CA: Sage.

Creswell, J. W., Klassen, A. C., Plano Clark, V. L., & Smith, K. C. (2011). *Best practices for mixed methods research in the health sciences.* Bethesda, MD: National Institutes of Health. Retrieved from http://obssr.od.nih.gov/mixed_methods_research

Creswell, J. W., & Plano Clark, V. L. (2007). *Designing and conducting mixed methods research.* Thousand Oaks, CA: Sage.

Creswell, J. W., Plano Clark, V. L., Gutmann, M., & Hanson, W. (2003). Advances in mixed method design. In A. Tashakkori & C. Teddlie (Eds.), *Handbook of mixed methods in social & behavioral research* (pp. 209–240). Thousand Oaks, CA: Sage.

Curtis, S., Gesler, W., Smith, G., & Washburn, S. (2000). Approaches to sampling and case selection in qualitative research: Examples in the geography of health. *Social Science & Medicine, 50*(7–8), 1001–1014.

Dattalo, P. (2010). Ethical dilemmas in sampling. *Journal of Social Work Values and Ethics, 7*(1). Retrieved from http://www.socialworker.com/jswve/spring2010/2dattalo.pdf

de Botton, A. (1997). *How Proust can change your life.* New York, NY: Pantheon Books.

Denzin, N. K. (2010). Moments, mixed methods, and paradigm dialogs. *Qualitative Inquiry, 16*(6), 419–427.

Dillman, D. A., Smyth, J. D., & Christian, L. M. (2009). *Internet, mail, and mixed-mode surveys: The tailored design method* (3rd ed.). Hoboken, NJ: Wiley.

Dowling, M. (2006). Approaches to reflexivity in qualitative research *Nursing Researcher, 13*(3), 7–21.

Fanelli, D. (2009). How many scientists fabricate and falsify research? A systematic review and meta-analysis of survey data. *PLoS One, 4*(5), e5738. Retrieved from http://www.plosone.org/article/info%3Adoi%2F10.1371%2Fjournal.pone.0005738

Faulkner, S. L. (2009). *Poetry as method: Reporting research through verse.* Walnut Creek, CA: Left Coast Press.

Fetterman, D. M., & Wandersman, A. (2005). *Empowerment evaluation: Principles in practice.* New York, NY: Guilford Press.

Fluehr-Lobban, C. (Ed.). (2002). *Ethics and the profession of anthropology: Dialogue for ethically conscious practice.* Walnut Creek, CA: AltaMira Press.

Freeman, M., & Preissle, J. (2010). Pedagogical ethical dilemmas in a responsive evaluation of a leadership program for youth. *International Journal of Qualitative Studies in Education, 23*(4), 463–478.

Gabb, J. (2010). Home truths: Ethical issues in family research. *Qualitative Research, 10*(4), 461–478.

Gelhert, S., Murray, A., Sohmer, D., McClintock, M., Conzen, S., & Olopade, O. (2010). The importance of transdisciplinary collaborations for understanding and resolving health disparities. *Social Work in Public Health, 25*(3), 408–422.

Gergen, M. M., & Gergen, K. J. (2012). *Playing with purpose: Adventures in performative social science.* Walnut Creek, CA: Left Coast Press.

Glazer, M. (1972). *The research adventure: Promise and problems of field work.* New York, NY: Random House.

Glover-Kudon, R. (2008). *When family history is a mystery—How adult adoptees cope with ambiguous risk for breast cancer: A mixed-methods study* (Doctoral dissertation). University of Georgia, Athens.

Glover-Kudon, R., DeGroff, A., Rohan, E. A., Preissle, J., & Boehm, J. E. (2013). Developmental milestones across the programmatic life cycle. *Cancer, 119,* 2926–2939.

Godfrey-Smith, P. (2003). *Theory and reality: An introduction to the philosophy of science.* Chicago, IL: University of Chicago Press.

Green, L. A., Lowery, J. C., Kowalski, C. P., & Wyszewianski, L. (2006). Impact of institutional review board practice variation on observational health services research. *Health Services Research, 41*(1), 214–230.

Greene, J. C. (2007). *Mixed methods in social inquiry.* San Francisco, CA: Jossey-Bass.

Griffiths, M. D. (2010). The use of online methodologies in data collection for gambling and gaming addictions. *International Journal of Mental Health and Addiction, 8*(1), 8–20.

Guest, G. (2012). Describing mixed methods research: An alternative to typologies. *Journal of Mixed Methods Research, 7*(2), 141–151.

Hanson, W. E., Creswell, J. W., Clark, V. L. P., Petska, K. S., & Creswell, J. D. (2005). Mixed methods research designs in counseling psychology. *Journal of Counseling Psychology, 52*(2), 224–235.

Harmon, A. (2010, April 21)Indian tribe wins fight to limit research of its DNA. *The New York Times.* Retrieved from http://www.nytimes.com/2010/04/22/us/22dna.html?pagewanted=all&_r=0

Harris, F. M., Kendall, M., Bentley, A., Maguire, R., Worth, A., Murray, S., . . . Sheikh, A. (2008). Researching experiences of terminal cancer: A systematic review of methodological issues and approaches. *European Journal of Cancer Care, 17*(4), 377–386.

Harris, G. (2008, March 28). Cigarette company paid for lung cancer study. *The New York Times.*

Heider, K. G. (1976). *Ethnographic film.* Austin: University of Texas Press.

Hemmings, A., Beckett, G., Kennerly, S., & Yap, T. (2013). Building a community of research practice: Intragroup team social dynamics in interdisciplinary mixed methods. *Journal of Mixed Methods Research, 7*(3), 261–273.

Hesse-Biber, S. N. (2010). Qualitative approaches to mixed methods practice. *Qualitative Inquiry, 16*(6), 455–468.

Hesse-Biber, S. N., & Griffin, A. J. (2013). Internet-mediated technologies and mixed methods research: Problems and prospects. *Journal of Mixed Methods Research, 7*(1), 43–61.

Hesse-Biber, S. N., & Leavy, P. (Eds.). (2008). *Handbook of emergent methods.* New York, NY: Guilford Press.

Hesse-Biber, S. N., & Piatelli, D. (2012). The feminist practice of holistic reflexivity. In S. N. Hesse-Biber (Ed.), *Handbook of feminist research: Theory and practice* (2nd ed., pp. 557–582). Los Angeles, CA: Sage.

Hill, J. S., Pace, T. M., & Robbins, R. R. (2010). Decolonizing personality assessment and honoring indigenous voices: a critical examination of the MMPI-2. *Cultural Diversity & Ethnic Minority Psychology, 16*(1), 16–25.

Hinman, L. M. (2003). *Ethics: A pluralistic approach to moral theory* (3rd ed.). Belmont, CA: Thomson/Wadsworth.

Hockings, P. (Ed.). (1975). *Principles of visual anthropology.* The Hague, The Netherlands: Mouton.

Ivankova, N. V., Creswell, J. W., & Stick, S. L. (2006). Using mixed-methods sequential explanatory design: From theory to practice. *Field Methods, 18*(1), 3–20.

Johnson, R. B., & Onwuegbuzie, A. J. (2004). Mixed methods research: A research paradigm whose time has come. *Educational Researcher, 33*(7), 14–26.

Johnson, R. B., Onwuegbuzie, A. J., & Turner, L. A. (2007). Toward a definition of mixed methods research. *Journal of Mixed Methods Research, 1*(2), 112–133.

Joint Committee on Standards for Educational Evaluation. (1994). *The program evaluation standards: How to assess evaluations of educational programs* (2nd ed.). Thousand Oaks, CA: Sage.

Kemper, E. A., Stringfield, S., & Teddlie, C. (2003). Mixed methods sampling strategies in social science research. In A. Tashakkori & C. Teddlie (Eds.), *Handbook of mixed methods in social & behavioral research* (pp. 273–296). Thousand Oaks, CA: Sage.

Kidder, R. M. (1995). *How good people make tough choices: Resolving the dilemmas of ethical living.* New York, NY: Simon and Schuster.

Krishnasamy, M. (2000). Perceptions of health care need in lung cancer. Can prospective surveys provide nationally representative data? *Palliative Medicine, 14*(5), 410–418.

Leahey, E. (2007). Convergence and confidentiality? Limits to the implementation of mixed methodology. *Social Science Research, 36*(1), 149–158.

Luxardo, N., Colombo, G., & Iglesias, G. (2011). Methodological and ethical dilemmas encountered during field research of family violence experienced by adolescent women in Buenos Aires. *Qualitative Report, 16*(4), 984–1000.

Macfarlane, B. (2009). *Researching with integrity: The ethics of academic enquiry.* New York, NY: Routledge.

Mathison, S. (1988). Why triangulate? *Educational Researcher, 17*(2), 13–17.

Maudsley, G. (2011). Mixing it but not mixed-up: Mixed methods research in medical education (a critical narrative review). *Medical Teacher, 33*(2), e92–e104.

Mauthner, N. S., & Doucet, A. (2003). Reflexive accounts and accounts of reflexivity in qualitative data analysis. *Sociology: The Journal of the British Sociological Association, 37*(3), 413–431.

Maxcy, S. J. (2003). Pragmatic threads in mixed methods research in the social sciences: The search for multiple modes of inquiry and the end of the philosophy of formalism. In A. Tashakkori & C. Teddlie (Eds.), *Handbook of mixed methods in social & behavioral research* (pp. 51–89). Thousand Oaks, CA: Sage.

Maxwell, J. A., & Loomis, D. M. (2003). Mixed methods design: An alternative approach. In A. Tashakkori & C. Teddlie (Eds.), *Handbook of mixed methods in social & behavioral research* (pp. 241–271). Thousand Oaks, CA: Sage.

Mazur, D. J. (2007). *Evaluating the science and ethics of research on humans: A guide for IRB members.* Baltimore, MD: Johns Hopkins University Press.

Mertens, D. M. (2012). Transformative mixed methods: Addressing inequities. *American Behavioral Scientist, 56*(6), 802–813.

Mertens, D. M., & Ginsberg, P. E. (2009). *The handbook of social research ethics.* Los Angeles, CA: Sage.

Morris, M. (2011). The good, the bad, and the evaluator: 25 years of AJE ethics. *American Journal of Evaluation, 32*(1), 134–151.

Morse, J. M. (2003). Principles of mixed- and multi-method research design. In A. Tashakkori & C. Teddlie (Eds.), *Handbook of mixed methods in social & behavioral research* (pp. 189–208). Thousand Oaks, CA: Sage.

Morse, J. M. (2010). Simultaneous and sequential qualitative mixed method designs. *Qualitative Inquiry, 16*(6), 483–491.

Mruck, K., & Mey, G. (2007). Grounded theory and reflexivity. In A. Bryant & K. Charmaz (Eds.), *The SAGE handbook of grounded theory* (pp. 515–538). London, England: Sage.

Newman, I., Ridenour, C. S., Newman, C., & DeMarco, G. M. P. (2003). A typology of research purposes and its relationship to mixed methods. In A. Tashakkori & C. Teddlie (Eds.), *Handbook of mixed methods in social & behavioral research* (pp. 167–188). Thousand Oaks, CA: Sage.

Onwuegbuzie, A. J., & Johnson, R. B. (2006). The validity issue in mixed research. *Research in the Schools, 13*(1), 48–63.

Padgett, D. K. (2009). Qualitative and mixed methods in social work knowledge development. *Social Work, 54*(2), 101–105.

Padgett, D. K. (Ed.). (2004). *The qualitative research experience.* Belmont, CA: Wadsworth/Thomson Learning.

Paskett, E. D., Harrop, J. P., & Wells, K. J. (2011). Patient navigation: An update on the state of the science. *CA: A Cancer Journal for Clinicians, 61*(4), 237–249.

Patton, M. Q. (1990). Ethical dimensions of qualitative inquiry: Cultural and research contexts. In M. J. McGee-Brown (Ed.), *Processes, applications, and ethics in qualitative research: Proceedings from the third annual conference of the Qualitative Interest Group* (pp. 7–38). Athens: College of Education, University of Georgia.

Patton, M. Q. (1997). *Utilization-focused evaluation: The new century text* (3rd ed.). Thousand Oaks, CA: Sage.

Patton, M. Q. (2002). Two decades of developments in qualitative inquiry: A personal, experiential perspective. *Qualitative Social Work, 1*(3), 261–283.

Plano Clark, V. L. (2005). Cross-disciplinary analysis of the use of mixed methods in physics education research, counseling psychology, and primary care (Doctoral dissertation, University of Nebraska–Lincoln). *Dissertation Abstracts International, 66*, 02A.

Plano Clark, V. L. (2010). The adoption and practice of mixed methods: U.S. trends in federally funded health-related research. *Qualitative Inquiry, 16*(6), 428–440.

Preissle, J., & Han, Y. (2012). Feminist research ethics. In S. N. Hesse-Biber (Ed.), *Handbook of feminist research: Theory and practice* (2nd ed., pp. 583–605). Los Angeles, CA: Sage.

Presidential Commission for the Study of Bioethical Issues. (2011). *Moral science: Protecting participants in human subjects research.* Retrieved from http://bioethics.gov/sites/default/files/Moral%20Science%20June%202012.pdf.

Reverby, S. M. (2009). *Examining Tuskegee: The infamous syphilis study and its legacy.* Chapel Hill: University of North Carolina Press.

Rhodes, C. S., & Weiss, K. J. (2013). *Ethical issues in literacy research.* New York, NY: Routledge.

Riessman, C. K. (1994). *Qualitative studies in social work research.* Thousand Oaks, CA: Sage.

Rohan, E. A. (2009). *Laboring at the edge: Effects of repeated exposure to death and dying on oncology doctors, nurses, and social workers.* Saarbrücken, Germany: VDM Publishing.

Rohan, E. A., Boehm, J. E., DeGroff, A., Glover-Kudon, R., & Preissle, J. (2013). Implementing the CDC's Colorectal Cancer Screening Demonstration Program: Wisdom from the field. *Cancer, 119*, 2870–2883.

Rosenberg, A. (2012). *Philosophy of science* (4th ed.). Boulder, CO: Westview Press.

Rosenfield, P. L. (1992). The potential of transdisciplinary research for sustaining and extending linkages between the health and social sciences. *Social Science & Medicine, 35*(11), 1343–1357.

Saldaña, J. (2011). *Ethnotheatre: Research from page to stage.* Walnut Creek, CA: Left Coast Press.

Sale, J. E. M., & Brazil, K. (2004). A strategy to identify critical appraisal criteria for primary mixed-method studies. *Quality & Quantity, 38*, 351–365.

Salehi, K., & Golafshani, N. (2010). Using mixed methods in research studies: An opportunity with its challenges. *International Journal of Multiple Research Approaches, 4*(3), 186–191.

Schrag, Z. M. (2010). *Ethical imperialism: Institutional review boards and the social sciences, 1965–2009.* Baltimore, MD: Johns Hopkins University Press.

Stake, R. E. (2006). *Mutliple case study analysis.* New York, NY: Guilford Press.

Sutherly, B. (2012, December 12). OSU prof falsified research results, probes find. *The Columbus Dispatch.* Retrieved from http://www.dispatch.com/content/stories/local/2012/12/22/osu-prof-falsified-research-results-probes- find.html

Tashakkori, A., & Teddlie, C. (2003). Preface. In A. Tashakkori & C. Teddlie (Eds.), *Handbook of mixed methods in social & behavioral research* (pp. ix–xv). Thousand Oaks, CA: Sage.

Teddlie, C., & Tashakkori, A. (2003). Major issues and controversies in the use of mixed methods in the social and behavioral sciences. In A. Tashakkori & C. Teddlie (Eds.), *Handbook of mixed methods in social & behavioral research* (pp. 3–50). Thousand Oaks, CA: Sage.

Teddlie, C., & Tashakkori, A. (2006). A general typology of research designs featuring mixed methods. *Research in the Schools, 13*(1), 12–28.

Teddlie, C., & Yu, F. (2007). Mixed methods sampling: A typology with examples. *Journal of Mixed Methods Research, 1*(1), 77–100.

Terrell, S. R. (2011). Mixed-methods research methodologies. *Qualitative Report, 17*(1), 254–280.

Thomas, V. (2010). Evaluation systems, ethics, and development evaluation. *American Journal of Evaluation, 31*(4), 540–548.

Tierney, W. G., & Lincoln, Y. S. (Eds.). (1997). *Representation and the text: Re-framing the narrative voice.* Albany: State University of New York Press.

Torres, R. T., Preskill, H. S., & Piontek, M. E. (1996). *Evaluation strategies for communicating and reporting: Enhancing learning in organizations.* Thousand Oaks, CA: Sage.

Trimble, J. E., & Fisher, C. B. (2006). *The handbook of ethical research with ethnocultural populations and communities.* Thousand Oaks, CA: Sage.

University of Chicago Press. (2003). *The Chicago manual of style* (15th ed.). Chicago, IL: Author.

Walker, S., Read, S., & Priest, H. (2013). Use of reflexivity in a mixed-methods study. *Nurse Researcher, 20*(3), 38–43.

Weiss, C. (1977). Introduction. In C. H. Weiss (Ed.), *Using social research in public policy making* (pp. 1–22). Lexington, MA: D. C. Heath.

Zhou, Y., & Creswell, J. W. (2012). The use of mixed methods by Chinese scholars in East China: A case study. *Multiple Research Approaches, 6*(1), 73–73.

Appendix A

Ethical Guidelines and Standards Adopted by Professional and Scholarly Organizations and Agencies

Source	URL[a]
American Anthropological Association, 1998, 2009, 2012. *Statement on Ethics—Principles of Professional Responsibility.*	www.aaanet.org/profdev/ethics/
American Educational Research Association, 2011. *Code of Ethics.*	www.aera.net/AboutAERA/AERARulesPolicies/ CodeofEthics/tabid/10200/Default.aspx
American Evaluation Association, rev. 2004. *Guiding Principles for Evaluators.*	http://www.eval.org/p/cm/ld/fid=51
American Psychological Association, 2010. *Ethical Principles of Psychologists and Code of Conduct.*	www.apa.org/ethics/code/index.aspx
American Sociological Association, 1999. *Code of Ethics.*	www.asanet.org/about/ethics.cfm
Association of Schools of Public Health. 2003. *Ethics and Public Health: Model Curriculum*	http://www.aspph.org/wp-content/uploads/2014/02/ EthicsCurriculum.pdf
Centers for Disease Control and Prevention, 2011. *Public Health Ethics.*	www.cdc.gov/od/science/integrity/phethics/index.htm
Joint Committee on Standards for Educational Evaluation, 2011. *The Program Evaluation Standards,* 3rd ed.	http://www.jcsee.org/program-evaluation-standards/ program-evaluation-standards-statements
National Association of Social Workers, 1996, 2008. *Code of Ethics.*	www.socialworkers.org/pubs/code/default.asp
National Commission for the Protection of Human Subjects of Biomedical and Behavioral Research, 1979. *The Belmont Report: Ethical Principles and Guidelines for the Protection of Human Subjects of Research.*	www.hhs.gov/ohrp/humansubjects/guidance/belmont. html
Oral History Association, 2009. *Principles for Oral History and Best Practices for Oral History.*	www.oralhistory.org/do-oral-history/ principles-and-practices/
Public Health Leadership Society, 2002. *Principles of the Ethical Practice of Public Health,* version 2.2.	http://phls.org/CMSuploads/Principles-of-the-Ethical- Practice-of-PH-Version-2.2-68496.pdf
Society for Applied Anthropology. *Statements of Ethics and Professional Responsibilities.*	http://www.sfaa.net/about/ethics/
United Nations, 1948. *Universal Declaration of Human Rights.*	www.un.org/Overview/rights.html
World Medical Association, 1964–2008. *The Declaration of Helsinki.*	www.wma.net/en/30publications/10policies/b3/index. html

[a] In addition to research-related ethics, many of these sites include ethics of professional practice.

Conducting Exploratory, Confirmatory, and Interactive Multimethod and Mixed Methods Research

Conducting Mixed Methods Literature Reviews: Synthesizing the Evidence Needed to Develop and Implement Complex Social and Health Interventions

Jennifer Leeman, Corrine I. Voils, *and* Margarete Sandelowski

Abstract

Systematic literature reviews serve the purpose of integrating findings from reports of multiple research studies and thereby build the evidence base for both research and practice. Mixed methods literature reviews (MMLRs) are distinct in that they summarize and integrate findings from qualitative, quantitative, and mixed methods studies via qualitative and/or quantitative methods. Although MMLRs encompass a range of approaches, the focus of this chapter is on their potential to contribute to the evidence base for complex social and health interventions. The chapter includes examples illustrating how MMLRs have been applied to synthesize evidence for complex interventions and concludes with a discussion of the challenges involved and suggestions for surmounting them.

Key Words: mixed methods, literature reviews, complex interventions, systematic literature review, evidence base

Introduction

Systematic literature reviews serve the purpose of integrating findings from reports of multiple research studies and, thereby, build the evidence base for both research and practice. Like mono-method research reviews, mixed methods literature reviews (MMLRs) are systematic in that they follow specified research protocols for retrieving literature and extracting and synthesizing data from that literature. MMLRs are distinct in that they summarize and integrate findings from qualitative, quantitative, and mixed methods studies via qualitative and/or quantitative methods. In MMLRs "what is 'mixed' are both the object of synthesis (i.e., the findings appearing in written reports of primary qualitative, quantitative, and mixed methods studies) and the mode of synthesis (i.e., the qualitative and quantitative

approaches to the integration of those findings)" (Sandelowski, Voils, Leeman, & Crandell, 2012, p. 317). Although MMLRs encompass a range of approaches (e.g., Harden & Thomas, 2010; Pope, Mays, & Popay, 2007), in this chapter, we focus on MMLRs used for the purpose of building the evidence base for practice. We focus, in particular, on the use of MMLR as an approach to developing and implementing complex social and health interventions, in other words, interventions that aim to improve the well-being of individuals and populations either directly (e.g., behavioral and education interventions) or indirectly via changes to policies, systems, and environments.

Although MMLRs constitute a relatively small percentage of published reviews of the literature, their numbers are increasing rapidly. Much of this growth is being driven by calls for greater use of research findings in practice coupled with the recognition that this will require greater understanding of the contexts and perspectives of the potential users of those findings (Chalmers & Glasziou, 2009; Glasgow et al., 2012; Tunis, Stryer, & Clancy, 2003). Because MMLRs include methodologically diverse findings and multiple methods, they are well suited to the goal of capturing and analyzing the breadth of evidence needed to incorporate users' contexts and perspectives into the understanding and use of interventions. The inclusion of diverse findings and use of multiple methods also present distinct challenges to those conducting MMLRs. Accordingly, in this chapter, we present an overview of MMLRs' potential to contribute to the science and practice of complex interventions followed by illustrations of how MMLRs may be applied to build the evidence base. The chapter concludes with a summary of challenges involved in conducting MMLRs of complex interventions and suggestions for surmounting them.

Mixed Methods Literature Reviews' Potential to Contribute to the Science and Practice of Complex Interventions

Interventions include programs, processes, policies, or guidelines that are intended to improve the well-being of individuals and populations. Historically, generating the evidence base for these interventions has been focused on assessing their effectiveness at achieving targeted outcomes via single-method "effectiveness reviews" of single-method findings. The Cochrane Collaboration, National Institute for Health and Clinical Excellence, and Campbell Collaboration are among the major producers of effectiveness reviews.

Effectiveness reviews involve the use of quantitative methods (e.g., meta-analysis) to summarize and synthesize quantitative findings of an intervention's effects on outcomes (Pope et al., 2007). For example, Ellis et al. (2004) systematically reviewed diabetes education interventions and applied meta-analysis to synthesize findings on the 28 identified interventions' effectiveness at improving glycemic control. They identified diabetes education interventions as effective based on the finding that glycemic levels for participants in the intervention groups were .32% lower than for those in the control groups. In many cases, the studies testing an intervention are too few or too dissimilar to synthesize via meta-analyses. In such cases, vote counting can be used to quantify the number of

studies in support versus not in support of an intervention's effectiveness, frequently with additional weight given to studies deemed to have greater methodological rigor (Cooper, 2010). Vote counting is illustrated in Goode, Reeves, and Eakin's (2012) systematic review of telephone-delivered interventions to increase physical activity and/or improve dietary behavior, in which they counted the number of cases in which the intervention groups' outcomes were significantly better than the comparison groups' ($n = 20$) versus the number in which they were not ($n = 7$).

Although effectiveness reviews have made invaluable contributions to the evidence base for intervention effectiveness, they have been criticized for failing to provide the full range of evidence necessary to generalize findings to new contexts and implement them in real-world settings. As is described in greater detail later, effectiveness reviews have been critiqued for decontextualizing findings, excluding available evidence, and taking a largely atheoretical approach to the assessment of interventions and their effects. Thus they provide information on the net effectiveness of an intervention but fail to detail contextual factors or to build theory that might explain variations in effectiveness across different settings, populations, providers, and approaches to intervening.

The limitations of effectiveness reviews are especially evident for complex social and health interventions. Interventions are complex to the extent that they include multiple components, function at multiple levels, target multiple outcomes, and/or are designed to be tailored and individualized to recipients' needs and preferences (Craig et al., 2008). Complex interventions may include intervention programs, such as a multicomponent diabetes self-management intervention tailored to recipients' self-management priorities. They may also include professional, organizational, and public policies such as a public policy requiring that elementary schools implement specific nutrition standards or guidelines specifying the optimal approach to depression screening. To further complicate the issue, complexity encompasses not only the intervention but also the systems within which interventions function (Sterman, 2006). With few exceptions, social and health interventions function within complex systems comprised of numerous heterogeneous components and actors interrelating across multiple levels, such as cafeteria staff working in local schools that operate as part of school districts and food distribution systems or patient-care teams functioning within a medical center that is part of a larger healthcare system (Hammond, 2009; Sterman, 2006).

Effectiveness reviews assess the evidence on "what works" by documenting the regularity of the relationship between an intervention and its outcomes (Howe, 2012). In assessing effectiveness, reviewers apply a largely reductionist analytic approach that views interventions as something that can be extracted and understood independent from the broader contexts in which they function. This reductionist approach is consistent with the conventional approach to knowledge translation whereby interventions are viewed as something that can be identified, "commodified," and then "rolled out across organizations" (Greig, Entwistle, & Beech, 2012, p. 305).

Complex interventions challenge a reductionist approach on multiple fronts. Because they involve multiple, flexible, and often interacting activities, complex interventions are difficult to standardize (Ogilvie, Egan, Hamilton, & Petticrew, 2011), and reviewers are challenged to identify the configuration of activities that constituted "the intervention" and achieved the intended outcomes. Furthermore, intervention activities often affect intended outcomes through their effects on a chain of intermediate outcomes (i.e., mediators) that are essential to understanding why an intervention works (Sidani & Braden, 1998).

The effects of intervention activities on intermediate and longer term outcomes are largely a function of how activities interact with contexts. The extent of this interaction is so integral to complex interventions as to trouble the legitimacy of trying to understand interventions separate from the contexts in which they occur (Greig et al., 2012). Reviewers have attempted to capture the interaction between contextual factors and interventions by assessing the moderating effects of factors such as intervention setting or characteristics of interveners or participants (e.g., race/ethnicity, literacy level). These reviewers often report that data are insufficient to assess variations in outcomes relative to different contextual factors (e.g., Rueda et al., 2006). Even when data are sufficient, this approach does not capture the interaction of interventions with the dynamics of complex systems (Hawe, Shiell, & Riley, 2009). Therefore, the evidence base to guide interventions cannot be garnered solely, or even principally, via systematic reviews that take a reductionist approach. Developing the evidence base for intervening requires evidence on how intervention activities, contextual factors, and intermediate and longer term outcomes interact as part of complex systems. In other words, it requires evidence in the form of theories explaining "what works for whom in what circumstances and in what respects" (Pawson, 2006, p. 74).

Traditional effectiveness reviews offer conclusions about whether complex interventions have worked, but they do so by "establishing black box associations" between interventions and outcomes (Howe, 2011, p. 169). These reviews provide little guidance on how and why the interventions worked or how they functioned differently across contexts (Pawson, 2006). For example, an effectiveness review may quantify the extent to which a problem-centered math intervention led to improvements in sixth graders' ability to correctly answer word problems. The review typically does not, however, identify which intervention activities (or combination of activities) were effective (i.e., the intervention's "active ingredients"; Miller, Druss, & Rohrbaugh, 2003). In other words, did students improve because the intervention included small work groups, didactic content, tailored practice problems, and/or peer coaching? The findings also will not address the mechanisms through which the intervention affected students' performance (i.e., intermediate outcomes or mediators). Did students improve because they became more confident, developed new strategies, gained new knowledge, and/or became more motivated? The reviews also provide little evidence on how the effects of active ingredients on mediators and outcomes may have varied across differences in contextual factors (i.e., moderated mediation) such as subgroup and/or community cultures, teachers' training and experience, students' prior educational experiences, students' math aptitudes, or class size. Review findings also do not provide guidance on how to navigate multiple levels and negotiate with diverse actors within the school system to promote widespread intervention adoption and implementation.

To build the evidence base for complex interventions, "the evidence for their effectiveness must be sufficiently comprehensive to encompass that complexity" (Rychetnik, Frommer, Hawe, & Shiell, 2002, p. 119). As detailed in the following section, MMLRs are well positioned to encompass complexity (i.e., multiple components, levels, or outcomes) by virtue of the fact that they capture more of the available data, apply and often integrate both inductive and deductive approaches, and prioritize the development of theories.

Mixed Methods Literature Reviews Include More of the Available Data

By design, effectiveness reviews include only a subset of the literature reporting the development and testing of an intervention, and they thereby exclude much of the available evidence. The exclusion of evidence is largely the result of the priority placed in effectiveness reviews on internal validity and resulting restrictions on the types of studies and publications included (Glasgow et al., 2012). A Cochrane review, for example, "would typically seek all rigorous studies (e.g. randomized trials)" testing the effectiveness of an intervention (Higgins & Green, 2011, 5.1.2). Restrictive inclusion criteria may be appropriate for making claims about an intervention's effect on outcomes, but these criteria limit the inclusion of evidence on how interventions work and how they vary across contexts (Lewin et al., 2012). They may exclude data on participants' and providers' perceptions of the intervention or on contextual factors that impeded or facilitated intervention implementation, delivery, and receipt. MMLRs, however, have the potential to include a broader range of studies that provide additional evidence, including studies that are preliminary to controlled trials (e.g., pilot studies with quasi-experimental designs) or that, by design, prioritize a deep understanding of the interplay of contexts and effects, such as case studies or ethnographies. They also have the potential to capture more data from publications included in the review, such as data on intervention feasibility or acceptability or users' experiences with an intervention. Broader inclusion criteria are particularly important in areas where most of the available evidence is from observational or quasi-experimental designs, such as public policy and health systems research (Baxter, Killoran, Kelly, & Goyder, 2010; Kelly et al., 2010; Lewin et al., 2012; Rockers et al., 2012).

Mixed Methods Literature Reviews Apply and Often Integrate Inductive and Deductive Approaches

When developing research questions, reviewers determine the extent to which their review will be guided by questions and constructs that emerge during the course of the literature review (inductive) as opposed to those that are predefined (deductive). Conventional effectiveness reviews take a predominantly confirmatory or deductive approach. In fact, guidelines for conducting and critiquing these reviews specify that review questions, variables, and constructs be identified a priori (The Cochrane Collaboration, 2011; Shea et al., 2007). MMLRs, on the other hand, often apply an inductive approach, with reviewers identifying one or more broad research questions and then iteratively identifying and conceptualizing phenomena and their interrelationships as they emerge during the review (Dixon-Woods, Agarwal, Jones, Young, & Sutton, 2005). The evidence base for many complex interventions is in the early stages of development, and, therefore, an inductive approach is critical to discovering unknown and therefore unanticipated phenomena and relationships. For example, Jagosh et al. (2012) conducted a MMLR of the benefits of participatory research, or research that involves an ongoing partnership between the researchers and the people affected by the problems being studied. Although previous reviewers had assessed the value of participatory research, their review methodologies "failed to embrace the complexity of programs or address mechanisms of change" (p. 313). In light of the limited knowledge of how participatory research works, Jagosh et al. took an inductive approach to their review. Rather than identifying variables and constructs a priori, they extracted data on any findings describing how any participatory research process led to an outcome, organized data into themes, and created visual maps of each partnership to depict the evolving relationships among contexts, mechanisms, and outcomes. They then sought patterns of relationships across the projects' maps with the goal of developing theory to describe the outcomes of participatory research and explain how they occur and why they vary across projects.

Similar to primary mixed methods studies, MMLRs often incorporate inductive and deductive approaches over a series of stages by connecting the findings from an initial inductive analysis of data with findings from subsequent deductive analyses to confirm identifed relationships. Findings from one analysis can be placed beside, "sprinkled" onto, or "mixed" into the findings from a review of the other type of evidence, as when quotations are inserted into findings from a quantitative synthesis (Bazeley & Kemp, 2012, pp. 59–60). An analysis of one type of data (e.g., quantitative) may be used to confirm, explain, or explore findings from analysis of another type of data (e.g., qualitative; Creswell, Klassen, Plano Clark, & Clegg Smith, 2011). For example, Thomas et al. (2003) conducted a meta-analysis to assess the effects that healthy eating interventions had on children's fruit and vegetable consumption. They also synthesized qualitative and quantitative findings on children's views of healthy eating and then integrated findings from both analyses to explore whether interventions were more effective when they were consistent with children's views. The ability to transition between types of evidence and synthesis methods allows MMLRs the flexibility to draw on the strengths of both qualitative and quantitative data and both inductive and deductive approaches.

Mixed Methods Literature Reviews Prioritize Theory Development

Greater use of theory has been recommended as a central approach to addressing the challenges introduced by the complexity of interventions and the systems in which they function (Craig et al., 2008; Kelly et al., 2010; Ogilvie et al., 2011). MMLRs may be used to focus on refining or creating theories or conceptual frameworks. The inductive approach afforded by MMLRs offers the advantage of allowing for the discovery of new phenomena and relationships and thereby the development and refinement of theory. Reviewers contribute to theory development and testing via the configuration or aggregation of data, the two defining logics of MMLRs (Sandelowski et al., 2012). Synthesis by configuration involves arranging thematically different phenomena into "a coherent theoretical rendering of them" (Sandelowski et al., 2012, p. 325). Reviewers applying logic of configuration explore interrelationships among phenomena with the goal of developing theory to explain why, how, and when they are related. Quantitative approaches to configuring mixed data include structural equation modeling and mediation meta-analyses. Qualitative approaches include meta-ethnography, framework-based synthesis, realist synthesis, meta-synthesis, and grounded theory (Dixon-Woods, 2011; Harden & Thomas, 2010; Pawson, 2006; Sandelowski & Barroso, 2007). The Jagosh et al. (2012) review described earlier is an example of a review that applied logic of configuration to develop beginning theory to explain how participatory-research interventions work and why they vary across contexts.

Synthesis by aggregation, on the other hand, involves pooling or merging findings considered to address similar phenomena and relationships in order to quantify the extent and nature of those relationships (Sandelowski et al., 2012). Aggregation methods may be used to test and refine theory by, for example, assessing the weight of evidence in support of relationships posited by existing or reviewer-developed theories and then modifying theory accordingly. Although inherently quantitative, the logic of aggregation may be applied to merge quantitative and qualitative data. Review methodologies that fall within this logic include meta-analysis, meta-summary, and vote counting (Sandelowski et al., 2012). Meta-analysis is a method in which effect sizes (i.e., a statistic representing the difference between the intervention and control group or between two interventions) are pooled across studies. Bayesian meta-analysis is a specific type of meta-analysis in which the findings from prior studies are updated with new evidence as it is obtained. Meta-summary is a quantitatively oriented approach to synthesizing qualitative data whereby the prevalence of findings across reports indicates the extent of replication (Sandelowski & Barroso, 2007). Vote counting is a method in which the proportion of studies reporting a statistically significant finding or reporting a finding of a minimum effect size is calculated.

How Mixed Methods Literature Reviews May be Applied to Build the Evidence Base for Complex Interventions

In the following section, we review a range of questions that MMLRs may address and illustrate how MMLRs may be applied to build the evidence base for complex interventions (see Table 10.1 for an overview). This section is organized around the conceptualization of complex interventions as the interaction of intervention and implementation activities, contextual factors, and intermediate and longer term outcomes within complex systems.

Mixed Methods Literature Reviews Contribute to Understanding Intervention and Implementation Activities

In the implementation science literature, a distinction typically is made between intervention and implementation activities, with intervention activities targeting change in the intervention's intended outcomes and implementation targeting the adoption or integration of interventions within organizations or systems (*Dissemination and Implementation Research in Health*, 2010). We maintain this distinction, recognizing that the line between intervention and implementation activities often is blurred for complex interventions, particularly those that target change at the level of policies, systems, and environments rather than at the level of individuals or populations. For example, creating a system to remind physicians to screen for colorectal cancer may be conceived

Table 10.1 MMLR's Contribution to the Science and Practice of Complex Interventions

Contribution to Understanding	Review Questions
Intervention and implementation activities	What are the active ingredients of an intervention or implementation activity?
	What have others learned about how to deliver and implement the intervention in practice?
Intermediate outcomes	What are the mediators through which intervention activities affect outcomes?
	What are the mediators through which implementation activities affect adoption and implementation?
	How might an intervention activity contribute to or support other intervention activities' effects on outcomes?
	What are possible proximal measures of success on the pathway to longer term outcomes?
Perspectives of intervention decision-makers, providers, and recipients	What problems do intervention decision-makers, providers, and recipients view as high priority?
	What approaches to intervening do intervention decision-makers and potential users view as acceptable?
	How do intervention providers and recipients experience an intervention?
How intervention and implementation activities interact with contexts to affect outcomes	For whom and under what circumstances does an intervention work?
	What contextual factors influence providers, settings, and systems adopt an intervention, implement it with fidelity, and maintain it over time?
	When will intervention, implementation, and/or context need to be adapted to enhance fit?
Identification of promising interventions	What practice-developed interventions have demonstrated potential for broad reach and implementation in practice?

as an intervention activity to improve rates of colorectal screening in the clinic's population or as an implementation activity to increase physicians' use of an intervention (colorectal screening guidelines) within a clinic system. Taxonomies have been created for use in systematically reviewing organization-level implementation activities, which include, among others, use of reminder systems and change agents, audit and feedback, technical assistance, coaching, and a range of quality improvement methods (Effective Practice and Organisation of Care, 2002; Fixsen, Naoom, Blase, Friedman, & Wallace, 2005; Shojania et al., 2004). Michie et al. (2011) created a taxonomy of policy-level activities such as legislating, regulating, and environmental/social planning that may be applied to either intervention or implementation activities.

MMLRs may contribute to describing intervention components and identifying those intervention components (i.e., active ingredients) required to achieve intermediate or longer term outcomes.

Abraham and Michie (2008) created a taxonomy of intervention components for use in systematic reviews of behavioral change interventions, which includes components such as providing information, encouraging, setting goals, and providing feedback. Identifying an intervention's active ingredients will aid in determining those components that must be retained versus those that might be adapted when an intervention is transferred to new contexts (Baker et al., 2008; McKleroy et al., 2006). What is referred to here as active ingredients may also be referred to as *core elements* (Galbraith et al., 2011) or as *causal mechanisms* (Pawson, 2006). Care should be taken with the term *causal mechanism* because its use often conflates components of the intervention (i.e., active ingredients) with intermediate outcomes that mediate the intervention's effects on longer term outcomes.

To illustrate the use of MMLR for identifying active ingredients, O'Campo, Kirst, Tsamis, Chambers, and Ahmad (2011) conducted a MMLR of intimate partner violence screening programs in healthcare settings with the goal of identifying the active ingredients responsible for screening programs' success in increasing provider self-efficacy and rates of universal screening (program outcomes). They identified four active ingredients (institutional support, staff training, screening protocols, and access to on- and off-site support services) and created a conceptual model to configure the relationship of these ingredients to program outcomes.

MMLRs may also be used to describe components of implementation activities. For example, Rycroft-Malone et al. (2012) conducted a MMLR to configure a beginning theory of active ingredients of "change agents" as an approach to implementing change. The term *change agents* encompassed the roles of, among others, opinion leaders, facilitators, and knowledge brokers, and was used to refer to individuals who were successful in promoting the adoption and implementation of change (e.g., interventions). Rycroft-Malone et al. found, for example, that serving as a role model for a desired change in practice may be one of the active ingredients by which change agents promote implementation of change.

In addition to identifying the core components of intervention and implementation activities, MMLRs may contribute to providing practical guidance on how to deliver and implement specific interventions. Rogers (2003) described this as "how to" guidance, which may include training and oversight of those implementing and delivering the intervention, deviations between the intervention as planned and delivered, resources required, barriers encountered, how barriers were overcome, and other lessons learned from prior implementations of the intervention (Baker et al., 2008; Leeman, Sommers, Leung, & Ammerman, 2011). Efforts to use MMLRs to identify implementation guidance have been limited by the lack of implementation data provided in published reports (Arai et al., 2005; Egan et al., 2009; Roen et al., 2006).

Mixed Methods Literature Reviews Contribute to Understanding Intermediate Outcomes

MMLRs also may be used to identify the intermediate outcomes through which intervention activities both cause and contribute to intended outcomes, a central component of an intervention's theory of change (McKleroy et al., 2006; Michie, van Stralen, & West, 2011). Michie et al. (2005) developed a widely used taxonomy of the intermediate outcomes (i.e., mediators) through which interventions cause behaviors to change, such as knowledge, skills, and motivation. To illustrate how MMLRs may be applied to better understand mediators, Leeman, Chang, Voils, Crandell, & Sandelowski (2011) conducted an initial inductive review of qualitative and quantitative observational studies to identify potential mediators of individuals' adherence to antiretroviral regimens. They then used the identified list of eight mediators (e.g., social support) to guide a deductive mediation meta-analysis of both quantitative observational and intervention studies to assess the strength of evidence in support of their potential role as mediators of intervention effects on individuals' adherence.

Not all intermediate outcomes function as mediators in that they may not be directly linked into a causal chain between interventions and the intended outcomes. Many intermediate outcomes may best be conceived as one of multiple strands that contribute to or support intended outcomes without directly or indirectly "causing them." For example, as Figure 10.1 illustrates, although intervening to create more sidewalks may not directly cause improvements in physical activity and health

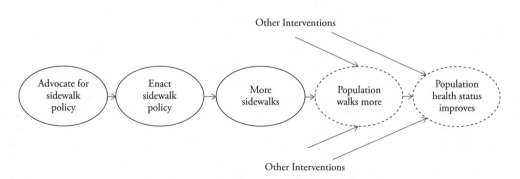

Fig. 10.1 Intermediate outcomes in a sidewalk intervention's effects on health status

status among the population, it may contribute to and support those changes. Multiple other interventions will need to occur to achieve changes in population physical activity and health status. Lavis et al. (2012) developed a taxonomy of organizational and public policy changes generally supportive of longer term outcomes that include changes to governance (e.g., what entities set policies and how they are enforced), finances (e.g., how providers are remunerated, the fees consumers pay), and delivery arrangements (e.g., who delivers services, where and with what level of support). Supportive intermediate outcomes also include changes in environments and sociocultural mechanisms (Baxter et al., 2010). Developing the evidence base for the value of supportive interventions is difficult because most research tends to "deal with end points and outcomes rather than the many and interrelated social and behavioural, structural and cultural intermediate points along the causal chain" (Kelly et al., 2010, p. 1060). MMLRs address this challenge by enabling the development of theories of change and synthesis of evidence in support of the intermediate, interrelated outcomes along the causal chain (Baxter et al., 2010; Kelly et al., 2010). Identifying intermediate outcomes will also be helpful in identifying proxy measures of success for interventions (Lewin et al., 2012). Using the example of sidewalks, successful enactment of policy and construction of more sidewalks are both measures of success on the road to increasing population-level physical activity.

Mixed Methods Literature Reviews Incorporate the Perspectives of Intervention Decision Makers, Providers, and Recipients

The engagement of numerous actors is critical to the implementation and effectiveness of intervention activities. These actors include the formal and informal leaders who decide which interventions to promote and support; staff, community members, and teams who provide intervention services; and the individuals, social groups, and populations who participate in or are reached by the intervention. Understanding the perspectives of these actors is essential to developing interventions that address problems recognized as high priority and use approaches considered acceptable (Chalmers & Glasziou, 2009; Glasgow et al., 2012; Tunis et al., 2003).

MMLRs may be used to incorporate qualitative research findings documenting actors' perspectives with a range of other findings to derive a more complete understanding of problems that may be amendable to intervention. For example, Alderson, Foy, Glidewell, McLintock, and House (2012) conducted a sequential, mixed methods synthesis of patients' beliefs about depression for the purpose of building the evidence base to better engage patients in depression screening. Using Leventhal's Illness Representations as a guiding framework, these reviewers conducted a content analysis of interview data, during which they revised the framework to more fully capture findings. They then mapped quantitative findings onto the themes and summarized and explained findings specific to each identified theme.

MMLRs may be used to assess participants' perspectives on the acceptability of different intervention options. Proctor and Brownson (2012) defined "acceptability" as the perception among potential users that an intervention is "agreeable, palatable, or satisfactory" (p. 265). An intervention's acceptability will likely play a critical role in determining whether it is used in practice, which is critical to determining its potential effectiveness in improving health (Bowen et al., 2009). To illustrate MMLRs' use in advancing understanding of acceptability, Harden, Brunton, Fletcher, and Oakley (2009) reviewed reports of controlled trials of teenage pregnancy prevention interventions and then reviewed findings from research examining teenagers' perceptions of the need and appropriateness of different approaches to intervening. They aligned the findings from the two reviews to assess the extent to which existing interventions addressed the needs and concerns of teenagers.

MMLRs may be applied to better understand individuals' experience of receiving an intervention. To illustrate, Voils, Sandelowski, Barroso, and Hasselblad (2008) aggregated qualitative and quantitative findings on factors influencing HIV-positive women's adherence to their antiretroviral therapies. They initially aggregated the qualitative data inductively to identify factors and their frequencies across studies. They then integrated the quantitative and qualitative data to ascertain their relationships, that is, whether findings confirmed, refuted, or extended each other. For example, from the review of qualitative findings, they found that women reported greater success with incorporating regimens into their routine schedules when the regimens were less complex, and this was confirmed by the finding from quantitative studies that having a regimen with less (as compared to more) complex dosing was associated with greater adherence.

Mixed Methods Literature Reviews Contribute to Understanding How Interventions Interact with Contexts to Affect Outcomes

Understanding how interventions interact with contexts to affect outcomes is essential to assessing an intervention's generalizability. Understanding the interaction of interventions and contexts also is needed to determine when intervention, implementation, and/or context may need to be modified or adapted to enhance intervention/context fit and thereby achieve intended outcomes (Glasgow, 2008). The effects of interventions vary across contexts because contextual factors modify (i.e., moderate) interactions among activities, mediators, and outcomes (Ramsay, Thomas, Croal, Grimshaw, & Eccles, 2010). Contextual factors at the level of intervention recipients may include, for example, race, ethnicity, socioeconomic status, literacy levels, or readiness to change. Contextual factors also include the characteristics of the complex systems in which interventions occur, for example, multiple interacting social networks, organizational infrastructures, socioeconomic pressures, and incentives (Damschroder et al., 2009). MMLRs can be used to synthesize evidence on how contextual factors interact with intervention and implementation activities, and intermediate and longer term outcomes. This evidence may be synthesized via aggregation or configuration to develop theory to explain how activities interact with contexts to affect intermediate and long-term outcomes.

Wong, Greenhalgh, and Pawson (2010), for example, applied a configuration logic to develop theory to explain what types of Internet-medical education worked for whom under what circumstances. They then used vote counting to quantify the number of studies that either supported or refuted specific theoretical constructs. They determined that physician and medical student response to Internet courses was contingent on the fit between their needs and priorities and the technical attributes of the course.

Contandriopoulos, Lemire, Denis, and Tremblay (2010) conducted a MMLR to configure interrelationships among actors, contexts, and knowledge in interventions aimed at influencing behaviors or opinions through the communication of information at the organizational or policymaking level. They identified three central dimensions of context: the extent of polarization in actors' perceptions of the problem and its potential solutions, the way intervention activity costs were distributed within the system, and characteristics of the social networks through which information was communicated. Based on review findings, they posited that the most effective approach to promoting knowledge use (i.e., implementation) would be contingent on the interaction between the extent of polarization and distribution of costs.

For an intervention to have an impact on a population's health, it must not only be effective but also have broad reach, particularly to the populations at greatest risk and the providers and settings that serve those at-risk populations. To have maximal impact, interventions also need to be implemented with fidelity to their active ingredients and maintained over time (Glasgow, Lichtenstein, & Marcus, 2003; Rychetnik et al., 2002). Therefore, to ensure population impact, evidence is needed on the contextual factors that influence whether providers, settings, and systems adopt an intervention, implement it with fidelity, and maintain it over time.

Leeman et al. (2010) conducted a MMLR to identify barriers and facilitators encountered in implementing antiretroviral therapy interventions. They configured implementation to include providers delivering the intervention and participants enrolling in, attending, and continuing the intervention over time. They then explored the effects that contextual factors had on each link in the implementation chain, with contextual factors including characteristics of the intervention, intervention participants and providers, and settings. Based on review findings, the researchers developed a beginning theory that posited that individuals with HIV would be more likely to enroll in interventions that protected their confidentiality and to attend when interventions were scheduled to meet their needs and when they facilitated a strong relationship with the intervener. Dropout rates were likely to be lower for individuals who had less (as opposed to more) prior experience with antiretroviral therapy and were likely to be higher when interventions were integrated into existing delivery systems than when offered as stand-alone interventions (Figure 10.2).

Mixed Methods Literature Reviews Contribute to the Identification of Promising Interventions

Numerous scholars have called for a shift from the prevailing approach of testing the internal

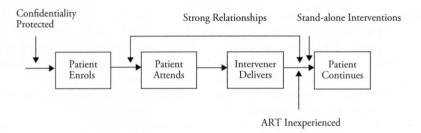

Fig. 10.2 Contextual factors influencing each step in an implementation chain

Source: Reprinted from Leeman, Jennifer, Yun Kyung Chang, Eun Jeong Lee, Corrine Voils, Jamie Crandell, and Margarete Sandelowski. (2010). Implementation of antiretroviral therapy adherence interventions: a realist synthesis of evidence. *Journal of Advanced Nursing 66*(9), 1915–1930.

validity of researcher-developed interventions and then attempting to translate them into real-world practice settings (e.g., Kessler & Glasgow, 2011). This approach has been critiqued not only for its limited attention to external validity but also its inattention to viability validity (Chen, 2010). In designing interventions, researchers have often not attended to whether ordinary people, particularly those in greatest need of an intervention, will participate in or be reached by the intervention or whether busy clinicians, educators, and other practitioners will be able to implement it in their practice settings (Klesges, Estabrooks, Dzewaltowski, Bull, & Glasgow, 2005). To identify more viable interventions, some scholars are advocating looking to identify and carry out interventions that have achieved high levels of reach, adoption, and implementation (i.e., have high viability validity) and then formally testing those interventions in studies (Chen, 2010; Leviton, Khan, Rog, Dawkins, & Cotton, 2010). MMLRs may be used to identify promising interventions. For example, Brennan, Castro, Brownson, Claus, and Orleans (2011) reported on methods they were using in a systematic review of both research-tested and practice-based interventions for the purpose of identifying promising policy and environmental change interventions to prevent obesity in children.

Challenges in Conducting Mixed Methods Literature Reviews to Develop the Evidence Base for Complex Interventions

Like other systematic reviews, MMLRs entail the formulation of purpose and research questions, search for and retrieval of relevant literature, extraction and evaluation of data from retrieved literature, and analysis and integration of extracted data (Cooper, 2010). These activities are not sequential but rather cyclical in that one

activity (e.g., searching for literature) often leads to revisions in a prior activity (formulation of purpose).

Multiple resources are available that provide guidance on how to conduct mono- and mixed methods systematic reviews of quantitative and/ or qualitative research findings (e.g., Cooper 2010; Pope, Mays, & Popay, 2007; Sandelowski & Barroso, 2007; Sandelowski et al., 2012). In previous publications, we have addressed the challenges of conducting MMLRs such as managing data derived from different sampling (i.e., purposeful vs. probability) and data collection imperatives (open vs. closed ended), aggregating data at the study vs. subject level, and data that were adjusted versus unadjusted (Crandell, Voils, & Sandelowski, 2012; Sandelowski, Voils, Crandell, & Leeman, 2013; Voils, Crandell, Chang, Leeman, & Sandelowski, 2011).

Accordingly, we highlight here only those issues distinctive to conducting MMLRs for the purpose of building the evidence base for complex interventions. Specifically, we address issues related to the extraction of findings from primary research reports and to aspects of MMLRs that have been the subject of critique, namely limitations in the way reviewers address the quality of included studies, describe their methods, and link review findings to their sources (Table 10.2).

Extracting Findings from Primary Research Reports

When conducting systematic reviews, reviewers typically separate contextual data from data on the intervention's effects. In the predominant approach to data extraction, reviewers create, pilot, and then use an extraction form to standardize the collection of data on study sample, context, methods, and findings. In the typical extraction form, findings are separated from the information in

Table 10.2 Overcoming Challenges in Conducting MMLR to Inform Complex Interventions

Challenge	Strategies for Overcoming Challenge
Decontextualizing findings during extraction	Configure findings within each study and then look for patterns across configurations
	Extract findings in the form of statements that anchor findings to relevant contextual information
Accounting for the methodological quality of studies reviewed	Resist excluding publications based on a priori quality criteria
	Select and justify quality criteria in relation to study's purpose
	During analysis, address design and execution as potential moderators of review findings
	Give differential weight to findings from studies depending on design and execution
Explicating review methods clearly and completely within page limits	Adapt the PRISMA approach to diagram literature search and retrieval
	Use diagrams to summarize data extraction and analysis
	Submit additional detail on methods as online supplements
Linking review findings to their sources	Link review findings to their sources in tables, text, graphics, and online supplements

other sections of the form that make those findings meaningful. Indeed, Pawson (2006) argued that the best way to avoid separating findings from context was to reject the data extraction process altogether. In his realist synthesis approach to MMLR, Pawson argued that rather than extracting data and then reintegrating it, reviewers should configure the findings from each study and then look for demi-regularities across the configurations created for included studies (e.g., Jagosh et al., 2012). Concerns have been raised, however, that this approach may be very time-consuming and the findings may not justify the resources required to generate them (Sheldon, 2005).

Sandelowski et al. (2012) developed an approach to the extraction of primary study findings intended to preserve key aspects of the context of those findings in a comparable form regardless of whether they were produced in qualitative or quantitative studies. Findings from qualitative and quantitative studies are transformed into complete and portable statements that anchor those findings to features likely to be most relevant to understanding the context of their production. These include aspects of the sample, the source of the finding (e.g., mother-reported child depression vs. child-reported child depression), time, comparative reference point (e.g., mothers vs. fathers), magnitude and significance, and study-specific conceptualization of phenomena (e.g., family functioning defined as balance

between cohesion and conflict). An example of such a statement of findings from a quantitative study is: In families with infants with a congenital heart defect, more mother-reported family cohesion immediately after diagnosis was significantly associated with more father-reported family cohesion one year after diagnosis; neither mother- nor father-reported family cohesion was related to marital satisfaction at any time. All statements addressing family cohesion—whether derived from qualitative or quantitative studies—might then be grouped together to ascertain their topical (e.g., about families with infants as opposed to older children, about congenital heart defect as opposed to other condition) and thematic (whether they confirm, refute, or otherwise modify each other) relationships to each other in preparation for synthesizing them on the basis of common relationships.

Applying Quality Criteria

Methodological problems within the primary studies included in a systematic review are a central threat to the validity of findings for all types of systematic literature reviews. Mono-method reviewers often minimize this potential for bias by excluding studies that fall below predetermined criteria for methodological quality. Yet this a priori, gate-keeping approach to research synthesis has recurrently been shown to be idiosyncratic, unreliable, and a major reason why reviews often cover only a fraction of the potentially relevant research literature available in a target domain (Cooper, 2010; Ogilvie, Egan, Hamilton, & Petticrew, 2005; Pawson, 2008; Sandelowski & Barroso, 2007). Because the goal is to maximize the amount of data available, MMLR reviewers typically choose not to exclude studies a priori for quality reasons. With the goal of maximizing the available data, reviewers may include findings from pilot studies conducted preliminary to more rigorous tests of an intervention. By design, these studies may provide valuable information on intervention acceptability, feasibility, and approaches to increasing the fit between the intervention and variations in context (Bowen et al., 2009). Reviewers may also include studies that employed quasi-experimental or case study designs to assess and explore relationships between interventions and outcomes and the range of contextual factors that may influence those relationships. Although the breadth of findings will contribute to the richness of the MMLR, the design and execution of included studies may fall short of meeting established criteria for methodological rigor in the varieties of qualitative and quantitative methods used. In their review of systematic literature reviews, Bouchard, Dubuisson, Simard, and Dorval (2011) found that authors of MMLRs were significantly less likely to account appropriately for the quality of included studies than were authors of mono-method quantitative reviews.

Yet there is no consensus on the best approach to judging the methodological quality of studies included in MMLRs (Dixon-Woods et al., 2005). Efforts to establish quality criteria are challenged by the absence of widely agreed-on and reliable standards for evaluating qualitative studies (Sandelowski, 2012). They are further challenged by the fact that MMLRs will require different criteria for different types of included studies and because the importance of different aspects of study design and execution varies depending on the purpose of the review (Lewin et al., 2012; Pope et al., 2007). The problem of study quality becomes even greater when MMLRs include literature other than empirical research reports, such as theoretical papers and grey literature (e. g., unpublished or conference reports). Establishing a standardized approach to evaluating quality may not even be appropriate for MMLR, given the variety and breadth of study aims and methods at the level of both the MMLR and the included studies.

Reviewers have multiple options for addressing the quality of the studies included in a MMLR. First and foremost they need to consider the purpose of their reviews and the types of studies to be included and then select quality criteria that are most relevant to assessing validity within the distinct context of their MMLR. Different criteria will apply if the purpose of the review is to determine the weight of evidence in support of the relationship between two phenomena (e.g., gender and adherence) than if the purpose is to explore contextual factors that may explain differences in implementation. Next, reviewers need to identify criteria appropriate to their review and then justify the selected criteria in their reports of MMLR findings. A vast literature details characteristics of study design and execution that are most relevant to assessing the validity of study findings (e.g., Boeije, van Wesel, & Alisic, 2011; Higgins & Green, 2011; Pluye, Gagnon, Griffiths, & Johnson-Lafleur, 2009; Wong, Greenhalgh, Westhorp, Buckingham, & Pawson, 2013).

As with other types of systematic reviews, researchers conducting MMLRs may document concerns related to the quality of the primary literature included and then address those concerns during analysis (Pawson, 2006) by addressing quality appraisal as a moderator of review findings or by giving greater weight to findings from studies that are methodologically stronger (Pope et al., 2007). Reviewers also may include critical exploration of threats to validity as an integral part of the synthesis process. Dixon-Woods et al. (2006) incorporated a critical review of methods into an inductive synthesis of literature on vulnerable group's access to healthcare and identified a concern with the predominant approach used to conceptualize and measure access. They then developed an alternative conceptualization of access they used to guide the subsequent phase of the review.

Explicating Mixed Methods Literature Reviews Methods

Of necessity, MMLRs of complex interventions often are methodologically and conceptually complicated. Reviewers retrieve a broad variety of literatures, use multiple synthesis methods, and employ an iterative approach to both retrieval and synthesis. The complexity of review methods challenges reviewers to explicate methods clearly and completely within the page limits allowed by most journals. Reviewers conducting effectiveness and other types of mono-method reviews often have the advantage of predetermined protocols that prescribe the overall design and methods for the review. The Cochrane Collaboration (Higgins & Green, 2011), for example, provides reviewers with 22 chapters of guidance on how to structure their effectiveness reviews. In contrast, MMLR is a fairly new field with a growing menu of diverse and evolving designs and methods. MMLR by its very nature offers reviewers the opportunity and the challenge to select, revise, and shape their methods as the review progresses. This provides reviewers with the opportunity to select and develop approaches to fit the available literature, the data within that literature, and their evolving research purposes and questions. Although this flexibility enhances reviewers' capacity to capture the evidence base for complex interventions, it may challenge their efforts explicitly to communicate the details of their methods.

The comprehensive and iterative nature of MMLRs mandates that reviewers take care to document and justify their methodological decisions in ways that are explicit but that accommodate journal word limits. Reviewers may make their methods more explicit by following Preferred Reporting Items for Systematic Reviews and Meta-Analyses (PRISMA) guidelines for documenting publication yields and exclusion decisions at each phase of the search and retrieval process (Liberati et al., 2009; e.g., Alderson et al., 2012). Wong et al. (2013) proposed an approach similar to the PRISMA guidelines that reviewers conducting realist MMLRs may use to depict their iterative literature retrieval process within a single flow diagram (see Figure 10.3). Transparency also is enhanced by describing who extracted what data and from which parts of the reports, if and how data were transformed during the extraction process, and how discrepancies between extractors were reconciled.

Reviewers may also take advantage of opportunities to submit additional details of their methods in online journal supplements where available. Additional materials may include search criteria and strategy, extraction tools, and coding schemas. For example, Rycroft-Malone et al. (2012) provided a graphic summarizing the search and retrieval process and also included multiple tables within the text and as online supplements to describe the data extraction form, search terms and strategy, and stages of the synthesis process. Reviewers also may use graphics more thoroughly to describe methods; graphical approaches to methods presentations are especially useful in mixed methods reports of any kind (Onwuegbuzie & Dickinson, 2008).

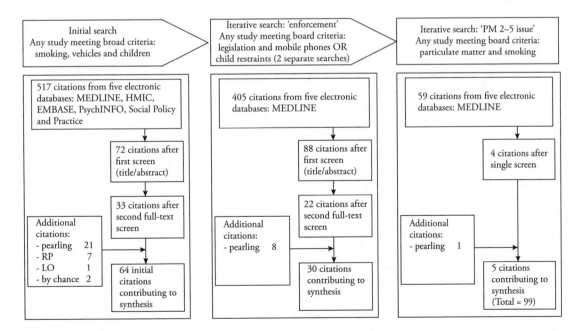

Fig. 10.3 Adapting the PRISMA approach to document an iterative MMLR search

Source: Reprinted with permission from Wong, Geoff, Trish Greenhalgh, Gill Westhorp, Jeanette Buckingham, and Ray Pawson. (2013). RAMESES publication standards: Realist syntheses. *Journal of Advanced Nursing*. doi:10.1111/jan.12095

Linking Included Studies, Extracted Data, and Review Findings

In reporting their MMLRs, reviewers often fail to link their integrated findings to the primary sources of those findings. Linking findings to sources is particularly difficult in largely inductive studies where the findings emerge and evolve over the course of the review. To counter this critique, reviewers might link review findings to their sources in tables, text, graphics, and online supplements. For example, Hage, Roo, van Offenbeek, and Boonstra (2013) used tables to link the themes identified in an inductive review to the source documents that included each theme. Wong et al. (2010) provided supplementary documents providing examples of extracted text in support of their study findings.

Conclusions

Tackling society's most challenging social and health problems requires the development, evaluation, and implementation of complex interventions. The explicit reporting of methods and findings is essential to ensuring that MMLRs fully contribute to improvements in complex interventions. Yet reporting is often difficult due to the diversity of the included literature and review methods. To increase the clarity of reporting, reviewers are advised to use the PRISMA guidance to detail their literature search and retrieval methods. They also might employ tables, diagrams, and online supplements to facilitate reporting of their methods and the linkage of findings to their resources.

Those conducting MMLR often also have difficulty addressing differences in the quality of the studies included in their reviews. A seemingly endless array of evermore cumbersome checklists and standards (e.g., Pluye et al., 2009) have been, and continue to be, advanced whereby the quality of studies is judged with a view to excluding, or severely limiting the contribution of, studies found to be deficient for research synthesis projects. Yet the value of a study cannot be determined a priori without reference to specific purposes. Moreover, methodological deficiencies do not necessarily invalidate findings or make them unusable (Pawson, 2006, 2008; Sandelowski & Barroso, 2007). Therefore, additional research is needed to develop methods to identify and assess the aspects of study quality that are relevant to the varying aims of different syntheses projects and to then incorporate these aspects of quality assessment into the analysis of synthesis findings.

Because MMLRs include methodologically diverse findings and multiple methods, they are well suited to the task of capturing and analyzing the breadth and depth of evidence needed to understand the activities involved in intervening and implementing complex interventions. The incorporation of both inductive and deductive approaches makes MMLRs particularly well suited to the development of theory and the exploration of interactions among intervention activities, contextual factors, and outcomes. Thus MMLRs can be used to identify gaps in knowledge regarding the generalizability of complex interventions for various settings and populations. These gaps, in turn, can lead to informed decisions about whether to obtain additional effectiveness data prior to implementation in various settings. This information ultimately can facilitate the translation of effective interventions to improve population health and well-being.

Discussion Questions

1. In what ways do MMLRs diverge from mono-method reviews?

2. Compare the use of systematic reviews designed to synthesize evidence of effectiveness to those designed to synthesize evidence of their utility in real-world contexts.

3. What are the distinctive contributions of MMLRs to the science and practice of implementation?

4. What are the distinctive challenges for conducting MMLRs for the purpose of building the evidence base for complex interventions?

Suggested Websites

www.cochrane.org

The Cochrane Collaboration promotes systematic literature reviews with a primary focus on building the evidence base for the effectiveness of healthcare interventions. The site includes access to over 5,000 systematic reviews and to resources detailing Cochrane review methods and quality criteria.

www.joannabriggs.edu.au

The Joanna Briggs Institute promotes systematic literature reviews with a primary focus on building the evidence base for healthcare. The site includes access to systematic reviews and also to resources detailing methods for appraising and synthesizing the findings from qualitative research studies.

www.campbellcollaboration.org

The Campbell Collaboration is a sibling organization to the Cochrane Collaboration. The Campbell Collaboration promotes systematic literature reviews in areas such as education, criminal justice, and social policy, among others.

References

Abraham, C., & Michie, S. (2008). A taxonomy of behavior change techniques used in interventions. *Health Psychology, 27*, 379–387.

Alderson, S. L., Foy, R., Glidewell, L., McLintock, K., & House, A. (2012). How patients understand depression associated with chronic physical disease: A systematic review. *BMC Family Practice, 13*, 41. Retrieved from http://www.biomedcentral.com/1471-2296/13/41

Arai, L., Roen, K., Roberts, H., & Popay, J. (2005). It might work in Oklahoma but will it work in Oakhampton? Context and implementation in the effectiveness literature on domestic smoke detectors. *Injury Prevention, 11*, 148–151.

Baker, E. A., Brennan Ramirez, L. K., Claus, J. M., & Land, G. (2008). Translating and disseminating research- and practice-based criteria to support evidence-based intervention planning. *Journal of Public Health Management and Practice, 14*, 124–130.

Baxter, S., Killoran, A., Kelly, M. P., & Goyder, E. (2010). Synthesizing diverse evidence: The use of primary qualitative data analysis methods and logic models in public health reviews. *Public Health, 124*, 99–106.

Bazeley, P., & Kemp, L. (2012). Mosaics, triangles, and DNA: Metaphors for integrated analysis in mixed methods research. *Journal of Mixed Methods Research, 6*, 55–72.

Boeije, H. R., van Wesel, F., & Alisic, E. (2011). Making a difference: Towards a method for weighing the evidence in a qualitative synthesis. *Journal of Evaluation in Clinical Practice, 17*, 657–663.

Bouchard, K., Dubuisson, W., Simard, J., & Dorval, M. (2011). Systematic mixed-methods reviews are not ready to be assessed with the available rools. *Journal of Clinical Epidemiology, 64*, 926–928.

Bowen, D. J., Kreuter, M., Spring, B., Cofta-Woerpel, L., Linnan, L., Weiner, D., . . . Fernandez, M. (2009). How we design feasibility studies. *American Journal of Preventive Medicine, 36*, 452–457.

Brennan, L., Castro, S., Brownson, R. C., Claus, J., & Orleans, C. T. (2011). Accelerating evidence reviews and broadening evidence standards to identify effective, promising, and emerging policy and environmental strategies for childhood obesity prevention. *Annual Review of Public Health, 32*, 199–223.

Chalmers, I., & Glasziou, P. (2009). Avoidable waste in the production and reporting of research evidence. *Lancet, 374*(9683), 86–89.

Chen, H. T. (2010). The bottom-up approach to integrative validity: A new perspective for program evaluation. *Evaluation and Program Planning, 33*, 205–214.

Contandriopoulos, D., Lemire, M., Denis, J. L., & Tremblay, E. (2010). Knowledge exchange processes in organizations and policy arenas: A narrative systematic review of the literature. *Milbank Quarterly, 88*, 444–483.

Cooper, H. (2010). *Research synthesis and meta-analysis: A step-by-step approach* (4th ed.). Los Angeles, CA: Sage.

Craig, P., Dieppe, P., Macintyre, S., Michie, S., Nazareth, I., & Petticrew, M. (2008). Developing and evaluating complex interventions: The new medical research council guidance. *BMJ, 337*, a1655. Retrieved from http://www.bmj.com/content/337/bmj.a1655

Crandell, J. L., Voils, C. I., & Sandelowski, M. (2012). Bayesian approaches to the synthesis of qualitative and quantitative research findings. In K. Hannes & C. Lockwood (Eds.), *Synthesizing qualitative research: Choosing the right approach* (pp. 137–159). Oxford, UK: Wiley-Blackwell.

Creswell, J. W., Klassen, A. C., Plano Clark, V. L., & Clegg Smith, K. (2011). *Best practices for mixed methods research in the health sciences*. Bethesda, MD: National Institutes of Health Office of Behavioral and Social Sciences Research.

Damschroder, L. J., Aron, D. C., Keith, R. E., Kirsh, S. R., Alexander, J. A., & Lowery, J. C. (2009). Fostering implementation of health services research findings into practice: A consolidated framework for advancing implementation science. *Implementation Science, 4*, 50. Retrieved from http://www.implementationscience.com/content/4/1/50

Dissemination and Implementation Research in Health (R01). (2010). Washington, DC: National Institutes of Health, Department of Health and Human Services. Retrieved from http://grants.nih.gov/grants/guide/pa-files/PAR-10-038.html

Dixon-Woods, M. (2011). Using framework-based synthesis for conducting reviews of qualitative studies. *BMC Medicine, 9*, 39. Retrieved from http://www.biomedcentral.com/1741-7015/9/39

Dixon-Woods, M., Agarwal, S., Jones, D., Young, B., & Sutton, A. (2005). Synthesizing qualitative and quantitative evidence: A review of possible methods. *Journal of Health Services Research & Policy, 10*, 45–53.

Dixon-Woods, M., Cavers, D., Agarwal, S., Annandale, E., Arthur, A., Harvey, J., . . Sutton, A. J. (2006). Conducting a critical interpretive synthesis of the literature on access to healthcare by vulnerable groups. *BMC Medical Research Methodology, 6*, 35. Retrieved from http://www.biomedcentral.com/1471-2288/6/35

Effective Practice and Organisation of Care. (2002). EPOC taxonomy of professional and and organisational interventions. Ottawa:. Cochrane Effective Practice and Organisation of Care Group. Retrieved from http://epoc.cochrane.org/epoc-author-resources

Egan, M., Bambra, C., Petticrew, M., & Whitehead, M. (2009). Reviewing evidence on complex social interventions: Appraising implementation in systematic reviews of the health effects of organisational-level workplace interventions. *Journal of Epidemiology and Community Health, 63*, 4–11.

Ellis, S. E., Speroff, T., Dittus, R. S., Brown, A., Pichert, J. W., & Elasy, T. A. (2004). Diabetes patient education: A meta-analysis and meta-regression. *Patient Education and Counseling, 52*, 97–105.

Fixsen, D. L., Naoom, S. F., I, K. A., Friedman, R. M., & Wallace, F. (2005). *Implementation research: A synthesis of the literature*. Tampa, FL: National Implementation Research Network. Retrieved from http://ctndisseminationlibrary.org/PDF/nirnmonograph.pdf.

Galbraith, J. S., Herbst, J. H., Whittier, D. K., Jones, P. L., Smith, B. D., Uhl, G., & Fisher, H. H. (2011). Taxonomy for strengthening the identification of core elements for evidence-based behavioral interventions for HIV/AIDS prevention. *Health Education Research, 26*, 872–885.

Glasgow, R. E. (2008). What types of evidence are most needed to advance behavioral medicine? *Annals of Behavioral Medicine, 35*, 19–25.

Glasgow, R. E., Green, L. W., Taylor, M. V., & Stange, K. C. (2012). An evidence integration triangle for aligning science with policy and practice. *American Journal of Preventive Medicine, 42*, 646–654.

Glasgow, R. E., Lichtenstein, E., & Marcus, A. C. (2003). Why don't we see more translation of health promotion research to practice? Rethinking the efficacy-to-effectiveness transition. *American Journal of Public Health, 93,* 1261–1267.

Goode, A. D., Reeves, M. M., & Eakin, E. G. (2012). Telephone-delivered interventions for physical activity and dietary behavior change: An updated systematic review. *American Journal of Preventive Medicine, 42,* 81–88.

Greig, G., Entwistle, V. A., & Beech, N. (2012). Addressing complex healthcare problems in diverse settings: Insights from activity theory. *Social Science & Medicine, 74,* 306–312.

Hage E., Roo, J. P., van Offenbeek, M. A. G., & Boonstra, A. (2013). Implementation factors and their effect on e-health service adoption in rural communities: A systematic literature review. *BMC Health Services Research, 13,* 19.

Hammond, R. A. (2009). Complex systems modeling for obesity research. *Preventing Chronic Disease, 6*(3), A97. Retrieved from http://www.ncbi.nlm.nih.gov/pmc/articles/PMC2722404/

Harden, A., Brunton, G., Fletcher, A., & Oakley, A. (2009). Teenage pregnancy and social disadvantage: Systematic review integrating controlled trials and qualitative studies. *BMJ, 339,* b4254. Retrieved from http://www.bmj.com/content/339/bmj.b4254

Harden, A., & Thomas, J. (2010). Mixed methods and systematic reviews: Examples and emerging issues. In A. Tashakkori & C. Teddlie (Eds.), *The SAGE handbook of mixed methods in social & behavioral research* (pp. 749–774). Los Angeles, CA: Sage.

Hawe, P., Shiell, A., & Riley, T. (2009). Theorising interventions as events in systems. *American Journal of Community Psychology, 43,* 267–276.

Higgins, J. P. T., & Green, S. (2011, March). *Cochrane handbook for systematic reviews of interventions.* Cochrane Collaboration Version 5.1.0. Retrieved from http://handbook.cochrane.org/

Howe, K. R. (2011). Mixed methods, mixed causes? *Qualitative Inquiry, 17,* 166–171.

Howe, K. R. (2012). Mixed methods, triangulation, and causal explanation. *Journal of Mixed Methods Research, 6,* 89–96.

Jagosh, J., Macaulay, A. C., Pluye, P., Salsberg, J., Bush, P. L., Henderson, J., . . . Greenhalgh, T. (2012). Uncovering the benefits of participatory research: Implications of a realist review for health research and practice. *Milbank Quarterly, 90,* 311–346.

Kelly, M., Morgan, A., Ellis, S., Younger, T., Huntley, J., & Swann, C. (2010). Evidence based public health: A review of the experience of the National Institute of Health and Clinical Excellence (NICE) of developing public health guidance in England. *Social Science & Medicine, 71,* 1056–1062.

Kessler, R., & Glasgow, R. E. (2011). A proposal to speed translation of healthcare research into practice: Dramatic change is needed. *American Journal of Preventive Medicine, 40,* 637–644.

Klesges, L. M., Estabrooks, P. A., Dzewaltowski, D. A., Bull, S., & Glasgow, R. E. (2005). Beginning with the application in mind: Designing and planning health behavior

change interventions to enhance dissemination. *Annals of Behavioral Medicine, 29,* 66–75.

Lavis, J. N., Rottingen, J. A., Bosch-Capblanch, X., Atun, R., El-Jardali, F., Gilson, L., . . . Haines, A. (2012). Guidance for evidence-informed policies about health systems: Linking guidance development to policy development. *PLoS Medicine, 9*(3), e1001186. Retrieved from http://www.plosmedicine.org/article/info%3Adoi%2F10.1371%2Fjournal.pmed.1001186

Leeman, J., Chang, Y. K., Lee, E. J., Voils, C. I., Crandell, J., & Sandelowski, M. (2010). Implementation of antiretroviral therapy adherence interventions: A realist synthesis of evidence. *Journal of Advanced Nursing, 66,* 1915–1930.

Leeman, J., Chang, Y. K., Voils, C. I., Crandell, J., & Sandelowski, M. (2011). A mixed-methods approach to synthesizing evidence on mediators of intervention effects. *Western Journal of Nursing Research, 33,* 870–900.

Leeman, J., Sommers, J., Leung, M. M., & Ammerman, A. (2011). Disseminating evidence from research and practice: A model for selecting evidence to guide obesity prevention. *Journal of Public Health Management and Practice, 17,* 133–140.

Leviton, L. C., Khan, L. K., Rog, D., Dawkins, N., & Cotton, D. (2010). Evaluability assessment to improve public health policies, programs, and practices. *Annual Review of Public Health, 31,* 213–233.

Lewin, S., Bosch-Capblanch, X., Oliver, S., Akl, E. A., Vist, G. E., Lavis, J. N., . . . Haines, A. (2012). Guidance for evidence-informed policies about health systems: Assessing how much confidence to place in the research evidence. *PLoS Medicine, 9*(3), e1001187. Retrieved from http://www.plosmedicine.org/article/info%3Adoi%2F10.1371%2Fjournal.pmed.1001185

Liberati, A., Altman, D. G., Tetzlaff, J., Mulrow, C., Gotzsche, P. C., Ioannidis, J. P., . . . Moher, D. (2009). The PRISMA statement for reporting systematic reviews and meta-analyses of studies that evaluate healthcare interventions: Explanation and elaboration. *BMJ, 339.* Retrieved from http://www.bmj.com/content/339/bmj.b2700

McKleroy, V. S., Galbraith, J. S., Cummings, B., Jones, P., Harshbarger, C., Collins, C., . . . Carey, J.W. (2006). Adapting evidence-based behavioral interventions to new settings and target populations. *AIDS Education and Prevention, 18*(4 Suppl. A), 59–73.

Michie, S., Johnston, M., Abraham, C., Lawton, R., Parker, D., & Walker, A. (2005). Making psychological theory useful for implementing evidence based practice: A consensus approach. *Quality and Safety in Health Care, 14,* 26–33.

Michie, S., van Stralen, M. M., & West, R. (2011). The behaviour change wheel: A new method for characterising and designing behaviour change interventions. *Implementation Science, 6,* 42. Retrieved from http://www.ncbi.nlm.nih.gov/pubmed/21513547

Miller, C. L., Druss, B. G., & Rohrbaugh, R. M. (2003). Using qualitative methods to distill the active ingredients of a multifaceted intervention. *Psychiatric Services, 54,* 568–571.

O'Campo, P., Kirst, M., Tsamis, C., Chambers, C., & Ahmad, F. (2011). Implementing successful intimate partner violence screening programs in health care settings: Evidence generated from a realist-informed systematic review. *Social Science & Medicine, 72,* 855–866.

Ogilvie, D., Cummins, S., Petticrew, M., White, M., Jones, A., & Wheeler, K. (2011). Assessing the evaluability of complex public health interventions: Five questions for researchers, funders, and policymakers. *Milbank Quarterly, 89*, 206–225.

Ogilvie, D., Egan, M., Hamilton, V., & Petticrew, M. (2005). Systematic reviews of health effects of social interventions: 2. Best available evidence: How low should you go? *Journal of Epidemiology and Community Health, 59*, 886–892.

Onwuegbuzie, A. J., & Dickinson, W. B. (2008). Mixed methods analysis and information visualization: Graphical display for effective communication of research results. *The Qualitative Report, 13*, 204–225.

Pawson, R. (2006). *Evidence-based policy: A realist perspective.* London, England: Sage.

Pawson, R. (2008). Method mix, technical hex, and theory fix. In M. M. Bergman (Ed.), *Advances in mixed methods research: Theories and applications* (pp. 120–137). London, England: Sage.

Pluye, P., Gagnon, M. P., Griffiths, F., & Johnson-Lafleur, J. (2009). A scoring system for appraising mixed methods research, and concomitantly appraising qualitative, quantitative and mixed methods primary studies in mixed studies reviews. *International Journal of Nursing Studies, 46*, 529–546.

Pope, C., Mays, N., & Popay, J. (2007). *Synthesizing qualitative and quantitative health evidence: A guide to methods.* Berkshire, UK: Open University Press.

Proctor, E. K., & Brownson, R. C. (2012). Measurement issues in dissemination and implementation research. In R. C. Brownson, G. A. Colditz, & E. K. Proctor (Eds.), *Dissemination and implementation research in health* (pp. 261–281). New York, NY: Oxford University Press.

Ramsay, C. R., Thomas, R. E., Croal, B. L., Grimshaw, J. M., & Eccles, M. P. (2010). Using the theory of planned behaviour as a process evaluation tool in randomised trials of knowledge translation strategies: A case study from UK primary care. *Implementation Science, 5*, 71. Retrieved from http://www.implementationscience.com/content/5/1/71

Rockers, P. C., Feigl, A. B., Rottingen, J.A., Fretheim, A., de Ferranti, D., Lavis, J., & Barnighausen, T. (2012). Study-design selection criteria in systematic reviews of effectiveness of health systems interventions and reforms: A meta-review. *Health Policy, 104*, 206–214.

Roen, K., Arai, L., Roberts, H., & Popay, J. (2006). Extending systematic reviews to include evidence on implementation: Methodological work on a review of community-based initiatives to prevent injuries. *Social Science & Medicine, 63*, 1060–1071.

Rogers, E. M. (2003). *Diffusion of innovations* (5th ed.). New York, NY: Free Press.

Rueda, S., Park-Wyllie, L. Y., Bayoumi, A. M., Tynan, A. M., Antoniou, T. A., Rourke, S. B., & Glazier, R. H. (2006). Patient support and education for promoting adherence to highly active antiretroviral therapy for HIV/AIDS. *Cochrane Database of Systematic Reviews, 3*, Art. No. CD001442. Retrieved from http://onlinelibrary.wiley.com.libproxy.lib.unc.edu/doi/10.1002/14651858.CD001442.pub2/pdf

Rychetnik, L., Frommer, M., Hawe, P., & Shiell, A. (2002). Criteria for evaluating evidence on public health interventions. *Journal of Epidemiology & Community Health, 56*, 119–127.

Rycroft-Malone, J., McCormack, B., Hutchinson, A. M, Decorby, K., Bucknall, T. K., Kent, B., . . . Wilson, V. (2012). Realist synthesis: Illustrating the method for implementation research. *Implementation Science, 7*, 33. Retrieved from http://www.implementationscience.com/content/7/1/33

Sandelowski, M. (2012). Metasynthesis of qualitative research. In H. Cooper (Ed.), *APA handbook of research methods in psychology: Vol.2. Research designs: Quantitative, qualitative, neuropsychological, and biological* (pp. 19–36). Washington, DC: American Psychological Association.

Sandelowski, M., & Barroso, J. (2007). *Handbook for synthesizing qualitative research.* New York, NY: Springer.

Sandelowski, M., Leeman, J., Knafl, K., & Crandell, J. L. (2013). Text-in-context: A method for extracting findings in mixed-methods mixed research synthesis studies. *Journal of Advanced Nursing, 69*, 1428–1437.

Sandelowski, M., Voils, C. I., Crandell, J., & Leeman, J. (2013). Synthesizing qualitative and quantitative research findings. In C. T. Beck (Ed.), *Routledge international handbook of qualitative nursing research* (pp. 347–356). New York, NY: Routledge.

Sandelowski, M., Voils, C. I., Leeman, J., & Crandell, J. L. (2012). Mapping the mixed research synthesis terrain. *Journal of Mixed Methods Research, 6*, 317–331.

Shea, B. J., Grimshaw, J. M., Wells, G. A., Boers, M., Andersson, N., Hamel, C., . . . Bouter. L. M. (2007). Development of AMSTAR: A measurement tool to assess the methodological quality of systematic reviews. *BMC Medical Research Methodology, 7*, 10. Retrieved from http://www.biomedcentral.com/1471-2288/7/10

Sheldon, T. (2005). Making evidence synthesis more useful for management and policy-making [Editorial]. *Journal of Health Services Research & Policy, 10*(Suppl. 1), 1–5.

Shojania, K. G., Ranji, S. R., Shaw, L. K., Charo, L. N., Lai, J. C., Rushakoff, R. J., . . . Owens, D. K. (2004). *Closing the quality gap: A critical analysis of quality improvement strategies: Vol. 2: Diabetes care.* Technical review 9. Rockville, MD: Agency for Healthcare Research and Quality. Retrieved from http://www.ahrq.gov/downloads/pub/evidence/pdf/qualgap2/qualgap2.pdf

Sidani, S., & Braden, C. J. (1998). *Evaluating nursing interventions: A theory-driven approach.* Thoursand Oaks, CA: Sage.

Sterman, J. D. (2006). Learning from evidence in a complex world. *American Journal of Public Health, 96*, 505–514.

Thomas, J., Sutcliffe, K., Harden, A., Oakley, A., Oliver, S., Rees, R., . . . Kavanagh, J. (2003). *Children and healthy eating: A systematic review of barriers and facilitators.* London: EPPI Centre, Social Science Research Unit, Institute of Education, University of London. Retrieved from http://eppi.ioe.ac.uk/EPPIWebContent/hp/reports/healthy_eating02/Final_report_web.pdf

Tunis, S. R., Stryer, D. B., & Clancy, C. M. (2003). Practical clinical trials: Increasing the value of clinical research for decision making in clinical and health policy. *JAMA: Journal of the American Medical Association, 290*, 1624–1632.

Voils, C. I., Crandell, J. L., Chang, Y., Leeman, J., & Sandelowski, M. (2011). Combining adjusted and unadjusted findings in mixed research synthesis studies. *Journal of Evaluation in Clinical Practice*, *17*, 429–434.

Voils, C. I., Sandelowski, M., Barroso, J., & Hasselblad, V. (2008). Making sense of qualitative and quantitative findings in mixed research synthesis studies. *Field Methods*, *20*, 3–25.

Wong, G., Greenhalgh, T., & Pawson, R. (2010). Internet-based medical education: a realist review of what works, for whom and in what circumstances. *BMC Medical Education*, *10*, 12.

Wong, G., Greenhalgh, T., Westhorp, G., Buckingham, J., & Pawson, R. (2013). RAMESES publication standards: Meta-narrative reviews. *BMC Medicine*, *11*, 20. Retrieved from http://www.biomedcentral.com/1741-7015/11/20/

Designing Multimethod Research

Albert Hunter *and* John Brewer

Abstract

The chapter begins with the "spirit of multimethod research," which refers to an openness to serendipity and humble recognition that all methods have strengths and weaknesses and that by combining different methods one has compensating strengths leading to more credible results in the face of a series of skeptics' questions. "Multimethods" involves combining any different methods while" mixed methods" more specifically focuses on combining qualitative and quantitative methods. Typologies of multimethod research from the literature based on characteristics and sequencing of methods themselves are briefly explored. The focus of the chapter is on the design of multimethod research in different subfields elucidating early historical exemplars and current developments. The selective and nonexhaustive subfields include words and deeds, rational actor, contextual effects, biomedical-social, evaluation, historical/comparative, and disaster research. Much of the chapter uses a positivist framework but concludes with a discussion of how multimethods are relevant for postpositive rhetorical and narrative frames.

Key Words: multimethod research, compensating strengths and weaknesses, skeptics' questions, exemplars, post-positivist, rhetorical, narrative frames, design, multimethod, mixed method, historical exemplars

Preamble: The Spirit of Multimethod Research

In addressing the question of research design we do not provide a "cookbook" or textbook normative approach to design where all is codified in a sequence of steps such that by doing A then B and combining with C one will produce D, an optimal outcome of research findings. We would rather stress the "art" of multimethod research—recognizing that good science exists to the degree it addresses a limited but profound set of questions. We have referred to these as the skeptics' questions: an overarching concern with content, not a fetishsized concern with form—what some have labelled *scientism*.

We must not have an overreified notion of what science is but rather a more realistic empirical understanding of how science is actually done.

As repeated studies in the sociology of science, or science studies suggest, it is better to pay attention to what practitioners say they really did, not what the methods textbooks say one should do (Denzin, 1970). As Paul Lazarsfeld (1945), an early practitioner of multimethod as well as survey research, stressed, "A good methodological investigation is not concerned with what a science should be: it tries to clarify what a science is and how it obtains its results" (p. vii; see also Jahoda, Lazarsfeld, & Zeisel, 1933/1971).

If one is to learn by studying then perhaps it is best to study exemplars, reports on research itself, not rules. This same spirit we suggest may carry over into the teaching and mentoring of science education. In the hard sciences (physics, chemistry, biology, zoology) one does not have courses in methods per se; rather one acquires methods through the older apprentice model of working in labs, and as a research assistant one learns methods by doing research, not reading about how one should do research. This is a distinction we will see shortly is akin to distinguishing between "saying versus doing" or "words versus deeds." Methods are what one does—not to say there are no limits and boundaries, but these are few and easily communicated as ideals—reliability and reproducibility, openness, no fabrication or fraud, and so on. Beyond that, researchers should show their data, explain how they obtained their data, how they analyzed their data, and consider alternative interpretations, summarizations, and generalizations as well as limitations and threats to validity. The objective is to build an argument that is *consistent* (logical), *corresponding* (to the data), and *convincing* (believable).

The Skeptics' Questions

Research methods, in short, must address a few very basic questions true of all scientific investigations, and these normative ideals ask that research be systematic, open, reproducible, reliable, valid, and believable after scrutiny with a healthy skepticism.

Elsewhere we have enumerated some of these basic skeptics' questions as follows:

(1) *Absolute theoretical adequacy*—to what degree does a theory explain the full set of empirical findings?

(2) *Relative theoretical adequacy*—how well does a theory explain data compared to other possible theories?

(3) Questions of *methodological bias*—how might the data to be explained be influenced by the particular method(s) used to obtain the data?

(4) Questions of *measurement* and conceptualization—how well have the concepts of a theory been measured?

(5) Questions of *causal inference*—how well have research methods addressed the cause-and-effect relationships of a theory's hypotheses

(6) Questions of *generalizability*—how generalizable are the findings of research given the methods used?

(7) Questions of *realism* versus simplification—how much realism versus simplification do the research's methods provide? (Brewer & Hunter, 1989, 2006)

All research, whatever the method, should address these questions, and different methods may address one or another of the questions better than others. The multimethods we suggest may be particularly helpful in addressing more of them, thereby reducing the skepticism about the research results or, conversely, increasing their credibility.

The overarching purpose of our conceiving and writing *Multimethod Research* (Brewer & Hunter, 1989) over some three decades ago was to overcome the continuing and at times acrimonious debates between practitioners of different techniques of research, especially but not exclusively between quantitative and qualitative approaches in the social sciences. It was a disciplinary concern as much as a narrow methodological one—with an overall objective of reasserting the centrality of the old Baconian generic goal of an eclectic but rigorous method of science itself.

The earlier debates were useful for self-reflection and continuing refinement of different techniques highlighting the limitations noted by critics as well as the strengths asserted by proponents often in hyperbolic rhetoric on both sides. Our goal was to discipline but not stifle the debates and to bring about a tolerance and mutual understanding of a unified endeavor—advancing the singular overarching method of science itself.

What Do We Mean By "Design"?

Design means (for us) a number of different things. Design may, on the one hand, be the outcome of prescriptive planning as in research proposals where specification and selection of such elements as units of investigation, universes, sampling frames, sampling techniques, measurement, data transformation, and modes of analysis are thoughtfully defined in detail. On the other hand design may be discerned in post hoc pattern recognition of what has been an unfolding, evolutionary, pragmatic adaptation in the research process. In short, design can consciously occur before starting the research, or the process can occur as the research unfolds in an organic, opportunistic, and serendipitous fashion. We try to encompass both of these meanings—the enacted and the emergent—in our discussion of design. We suggest that most research progresses as a combination of some preplanning coupled with judicious emergent decision-making as the research is carried out. We would encourage a spirit of a competently trained pragmatic openness to serendipity; in short, the idea of "design" in designing multimethod research is more of a Darwinian notion of evolution and adaptation rather than an overreliance on an authoritative "Intelligent Designer."

The evolution of multimethod designs, as with all methods, can occur at two levels—at the micro level with the opportunistic unfolding and combining of specific techniques of data collection and analysis present in a single research project, and at the macro level of a discipline as a whole as Mario Small (2011) demonstrated in his comprehensive review of multimethod research in sociology as he traced the unfolding natural history of specific combinations of different types of methods over recent decades. The multimethod spirit is one that is open to new, innovative, and at times unanticipated techniques.

Prepared Contingency

One way individuals learn different methods is through the study of prior exemplars and also through an apprenticeship in mentoring relationships during the actual conduct of research itself. An exposure to, understanding of, and capacity to use different methods is an ongoing learning experience throughout one's career, a learning process greatly aided by an openness to a multimethod perspective. Some individuals may develop varying degrees of mastery of a variety of techniques, say for data collection or data analysis, while others may become highly specialized in this or that singular technique. The former person may craft a multimethod piece of research on his or her own, while the latter may still participate in multimethod research through a division of labor within a collective research project. Such was the case for example with the Reactions to Crime Project carried out by Northwestern University's Center for Urban Affairs and Policy Research in the 1970s and 1980s (Hunter & Maxfield, 1980). But, to work, the collective multimethod research project must have a collective spirit that recognizes the strengths and limitations of the different methods, a spirit that does not just tolerate but emphasizes and appreciates the need for rigor and quality in the application of different methods in the overall scientific enterprise. In sum, multimethod research does not disparage monomethod research and in fact encourages more reflexive and refined sophistication in the mastering of each method with the goal of enacting the highest quality competent research. At the same time, the multimethod spirit encourages a "design for serendipity" recognizing that opportunistic and creative insights come to the well-prepared and reflective mind.

Methods Are What Researchers Do

Case studies in the ethnography of science have shown repeatedly that actual research is different than any ideal, and, we suggest, this is true of multimethod research as well. The oft told story of W. I. Thomas (1923) discovering a packet of letters thrown out in an alley and seeing them as a potential data source for studying Polish peasants who had immigrated to America is perhaps apocryphal but underscores the need for openness to diverse data and methods. We are not interested in prescription or preaching with respect to multimethod research. It is an approach we highly recommend when and where appropriate. Monomethod research is at times under certain conditions and contexts the way to go. We definitely prefer well-executed monomethod research to less competent multimethod research. The use of multimethods alone does not exonerate nor should it be a cloak for incompetence.

Multimethod Research Design

Multimethod research may be broadly defined as the practice of employing two or more different methods or styles of research within the same study or research program rather than confining the research to the use of a single method (Brewer & Hunter, 1989, 2006). Unlike mixed method research, it is not restricted to combining qualitative and quantitative methods but rather is open to the full variety of possible methodological combinations.

As there are numerous methods available to social researchers, and a variety of ways in which these methods can be combined, the topic of multimethod research design involves foremost asking (a) which methods are combined with which other methods and (b) how are the different methods deployed and implemented in relation to one another in the research process.

Typologies of Mixing

Prior commentators on multimethod research have produced a number of typologies reflecting the "what" and "how" of combining or mixing different distinct methods. We will briefly explore a few of these as developed by others. We note that most commonly in the literature "mixed methods" is used to refer to mixing quantitative and a qualitative method, while "multimethod" more broadly refers to mixing of two or more methods—regardless of whether they are qualitative or quantitative. In short, mixed method is a subset of multimethod.

One of the more formal and systematic typologies is that by Janice Morse (2003) who began with the basic qualitative quantitative distinction that she equated with a deductive and inductive drive, respectively. She then paired each with either a second quantitative or qualitative method and then subdivided each of those four cases in turn into a simultaneous or sequential timing of the deployment of the methods. The result was an eight-fold typology that she then analyzed in more depth as to their contribution to theory.

Johnson and Turner (2003) derived a typology based on the principal method of data collection by first distinguishing among the methods of questionnaires, interviews, focus groups, tests, observation, and secondary data. They then considered that each of these methods may in and of itself use mixed data collection strategies that could include two quantitative, two qualitative, or one qualitative and one quantitative. The first two "mixes" would be multimethod, while the third would be defined as an example of "mixed methods." Finally, they suggested the six different methods themselves may be combined to create a "continuum" of a variety of methods and varied qualitative/quantitative combinations.

We will look at two other typologies that are more inductive in their derivation by Jerry Jacobs (2005) and Mario Small (2011), respectively. Let us begin by examining research published recently by Jerry Jacobs in the *American Sociological Review*, the official journal of the American Sociological Association. This seems a promising way to lay out the basic dimensions of multimethod and mixed methods research design as now practiced in the discipline with which we are most familiar. Jacobs has helpfully published a brief survey of the papers published between 2003 and 2005, a period when he was editor of the *American Sociological Review*. He reported that a quarter of the papers he accepted for publication (17 out of 65) involved multiple method research, by which he means studies that "draw on data from more than one source and present more than one type of analysis" (Jacobs, 2005).

Jacobs (2005) found several different combinations of methods in this group of studies. He noted that these multiple method studies "often but not always combined quantitative and qualitative data." First, statistical surveys were combined with qualitative interviews. The interviews might either precede the survey to refine its questions or be conducted later to increase understanding and deepen interpretation of the survey data. Second, there were multiple quantitative approaches: for example, a field experiment followed later by a survey of the same subjects to test and compare with

the experimental results; analysis of survey data from 30 countries to bolster a hypothesis derived from aggregate data from those countries. Finally, historical analyses employed qualitative and quantitative analyses of historical documents and archival data, and quantitative analysis of survey data were available as well as qualitative interview data from still-living participants. These different sorts of data were sometimes used concurrently to provide a more complete picture and sometimes in sequence to form and test hypotheses.

To put Jacobs's (2005) report in perspective we have examined two other samples of the *American Sociological Review*, one roughly 20 years earlier (1984 and 1985) and the second from 2011 to the present. A striking contrast in these different time periods is that while Jacobs identified 17 multiple method studies in the 2003–2005 period, there were 10 such studies during 1984 and 1985, and 32 during 2011 and 2012. Clearly there is a linear trend of increasing publication of multimethod studies within sociology.

Mario Small (2011) in an *Annual Review of Sociology* article similarly developed an inductive typology based on an extensive review of the sociological literature. He too first noted the burgeoning number of studies that have come to use multiple methods in recent decades. He also noted that the usual combined qualitative/quantitative meaning of the category is unnecessarily restrictive as different qualitative methods and different quantitative methods may also be combined, and that furthermore the distinction of what constitutes quantitative and qualitative is itself a "fuzzy" distinction.

He began his typology by distinguishing between data collection and data analysis, recognizing, for example, that one could have a qualitative analysis of quantitative data and conversely a quantitative analysis of qualitative data. He then proceeded to elucidate examples of these varying types. He also considered the epistemology of multimethod research, which he noted is heavily rooted in pragmatism, and the primary motivations of researchers, which are either confirmation or complementarity. He further explored questions of sequencing and nesting in data collection and cross-over and integration in data analysis. Finally he noted the enduring questions of commensurability and specialization among methods. As he concluded:

the challenges of mixed methods research reflect those of sociology writ large, a discipline whose core methodological pluralism has produced, over its history, periods of conflict and cooperation, but few of lasting resolution. . . . Mixed method projects provide both the challenge and the opportunity for researchers to resolve some of the ambiguities that result from pluralism. (Small, 2011, p. 79)

An Inductive Typology of Fruitful Substantive Arenas for Multimethod Social Science Research

The previous discussion of multimethod research highlights typologies of different combinations of methods that are derived from characteristics of the methods themselves—such as the basic quantitative qualitative distinction, or relative significance as to which method has primacy in the research versus which plays a supportive role, or the mere sequencing and timing as to which comes first and which follows. These typologies are valuable for giving some coherence and organization to the rapidly expanding accumulation of multimethod studies. One must be careful, however, to not over-reify these typologies and potentially advance them as normatively prescriptive strategies for conducting multimethod research. All research, multimethod included, is, we contend, a combination of science and art, design and serendipity, thoughtful planning and pragmatic opportunism.

We use here a more inductive approach following the lead of Jacobs (2005) and Small (2011) and develop a typology of multimethod research that begins not from first principles about methods but from different generalized types of substantive questions that have already been explored in the literature using multimethod research. The types of substantive questions are varied, and some that we identify, like that exploring the differences between words and deeds, have a long history in the literature, while others, such as combing biomedical markers and interview data, are relatively recent in origin. We present this typology as neither exhaustive nor necessarily mutually exclusive and do so in the hopes of presenting categories that will be useful in organizing and bringing some order to the field. But, in contrast to most multimethod typologies, we offer these less as prescriptive normative guides and more as sensitizing exemplars. As one prepares to conduct a piece of research and thinks about how to possibly incorporate a multimethod style, one can ask substantively, not just methodologically: What kind of research question is this? In such a case, one is being more true to the old adage that research questions should be driven by theoretical substance not methodological proclivities. Substance should dictate methods, not the reverse. This is an admonition shared widely across science in general, not just the social sciences.

For example, a recent article in *Science* (Joppa et al., 2013) reporting a survey study of 400 biologists using canned modeling programs in the substantive area of "species distribution modeling" quotes one scientist: "The research question and the data should be king, with an approach being selected on the basis that it is appropriate to both the research question and the data rather than the research question and the data being selected to fit the approach which a person knows how to use." While another biologist echoed a multimethod thesis: "We don't need fancier software, we need people who understand ecology and the importance of multiple types of data. . . The key is the ability to think in ecological terms"(p. 815).

Substantive Arenas

The following are a few of these types of substantive arenas often using multimethod research that we have begun to explore and that we briefly elaborate in the following discussion:

(1) Words and Deeds
(2) Rational Action
(3) Contextual Effects
(4) Biomedical Social Research
(5) Evaluation Research
(6) Historical/Comparative
(7) Disaster Research

Words and Deeds

Words are what people say and are windows into what they think, while deeds are what people do—their behavior. We are most interested in the latter, because that is what has direct consequences for us and that is what we are most interested in anticipating so we may adapt our own behavior accordingly.

We acknowledge that words may be thought of as a form of behavior, so in this light we are comparing two different forms of behavior with one another. The words, which give the participants' "meanings," are closer to thoughts and ideas, or, using a more social psychological vocabulary, they are "attitudes" and "opinions" (things in people's heads) and so "words and deeds" are linked to the "attitude behavior" distinction. Attitudes are seen as "predispositions" that may or may not match "dispositions" or behavior itself.

In comparing words and deeds, the approach is most often to compare prior words to subsequent deeds and to ascertain the degree of agreement or divergence between the two. The classic case of "cognitive dissonance" is but one type of divergence between word and deed.

Words as data can be gathered in a variety ways that often require direct interaction: they are "voiced" and may take the form of responses to questions on a survey instrument, recorded phone conversations, or written documents.

By contrast, deeds as data ideally require direct observation of behavior and so often require different methods than those used to gather "words." Hence the multimethod approach is routinely found in such studies where two different data sets are compared.

Richard Lapiere's (1934) work is generally cited as being among the earliest multimethod studies of the relationship between words and deeds or, in his words, attitudes and actions. In 1930 Lapiere conducted a field experiment consisting of 251 visits across the United States to assess the responses of hotel and restaurant proprietors to a young Chinese couple's requests for service. Only once was the couple turned away. He followed up this action research component six months later with an attitude component, a mail survey asking the proprietors whether or not they would "accept members of the Chinese race" at their establishments. Contrary to their prior actions, very few of the proprietors expressed an accepting attitude (Lapiere, 1934).

Lapiere's work has proven to be exemplary in several ways. First, it demonstrated that individuals' actions and attitudes could not necessarily be inferred directly from one another. Second, it demonstrated a methodology for measuring attitudes and actions separately and then empirically determining their interrelationships. Finally, the study has inspired and informed later research, particularly in the study of discrimination but also in the wider theoretical area of attitude–behavior relations (e.g., Ajzen & Fishbein, 1977; Ajzen, 2005). Pager and Quillian (2005) provided an overview of this more recent and more broadly theoretical work in the introduction to their own research, which is evocatively titled "Walking the Walk? What Employers Say Versus What They Do." It is a sophisticated contemporary analogue of Lapiere's study. They investigated employment discrimination based on the applicants' race and criminal record.

The study was conducted in two stages. In the first "employers' responses to job applicants were measured in real employment settings using an experimental audit methodology. . . . The preferences of employers were measured based on the number of call-backs to each of the applicants" (Pager & Quillian, 2005, p. 362). "The findings of the audit showed large and significant effects of both race and criminal record on employment opportunities" (p. 362). The second stage of the study was a telephone survey carried out several months later in which employers were asked to express their hiring preferences for hiring offenders. They found that employers who in the survey expressed "a greater likelihood of hiring ex-offenders were no more likely to do so in practice, and that large differences in racial hiring preferences were found in the experiment, but not in the survey" (p. 362).

Pager and Quillian (2005) concluded that "these comparisons suggest that employer surveys—even those using an experimental design to control for social desirability bias—may be insufficient for drawing conclusions about the actual level of hiring against stigmatized groups" (p. 355).

Rational Action

A central, and some say defining, assumption in classical economic theory is that individuals act rationally in pursing their own self-interest. From an economic perspective, words may be seen as a verbal expression of preferences, as illustrated in surveys of marketing research such as when people are asked which brand of detergent they prefer. The ultimate behavior or "deed" one is interested in, however, is: "Which detergent do they buy?" "What do they spend their money on?" According to Paul Samuelson (1948), who developed the theory of revealed preferences, preferences are revealed in the behavior of how money is spent. Economists often eschew any other indicator of preferences other than that. In short, revealed preference is

> an economic theory of consumption behavior which asserts that the best way to measure consumer preferences is to observe their purchasing behavior. Revealed preference theory works on the assumption that consumers have considered a set of alternatives before making a purchasing decision. Thus, given that a consumer chooses one option out of the set, this option must be the preferred option. (Investopedia, 2014)

One of the critics of the revealed preference theory states that "Instead of replacing 'metaphysical' terms such as 'desire' and 'purpose'" they "used it to legitimize them by giving them operational definitions" (Wade, 2004, p. 958). Thus in psychology, as in economics, the initial, quite radical operationalist ideas eventually came to serve as little more than a "reassurance fetish" for mainstream methodological practice.

A common critique of this rational economic approach is that it is often based on sophisticated modeling relying on monomethod data points of either an experimental type, as in "prisoners' dilemma" research, or monetized aggregated market data. In a circular self-referential manner, monetary expenditure is the "revealed preference" of economic researchers about how best to measure rationality itself. When the same propositions are explored with multimethods, different types of data, and other measures, researchers are often able to more realistically address the simplifying assumptions of such models and provide more robust analyses. For example, the seminal work of Amos Tversky and Daniel Kahneman (1974, 2011) speaks to a variety of different methods that suggest that economic decision-making may be other than rational. Their research begins from a psychological experimental approach but is elaborated to include in-depth interviews, aggregate market data, and historical examples. Their results suggest that individuals operate in their decision-making by the use of heuristics or rules of thumb that are often less than optimally rational in economic terms or payoffs.

Mark Granovetter's (1985) work on the socially embedded nature of economic transactions again relied on different data and methods that led to a reconsideration of the "rational individual" assumptions of traditional economics. The study of social networks required the addition of different methods and types of data beyond that provided by either aggregated economic or individualistic experimental methods. Studying the impact of people's embeddedness in social contexts and social networks has become both a conceptual and a methodological addition to prior research on individualized and aggregated data methods and has been used to study everything from obesity to getting a job or a loan from a bank (Granovetter, 1985; Uzzi, 1999; Cohen-Cole & Fletcher, 2008).

Contextual Effects

All social behavior occurs in a specific context or situation, and observed patterns of behavior may be generalized from one context to another, leading to more generalized understanding, or may be seen to be limited to specific contexts. The idea of seeing individuals' behaviors as related to their context is exemplified by W. I. Thomas's (1923) older notion of "the definition of the situation" and in more current discussions of structural effects and in empirical analyses employing hierarchical linear modeling. In short, individuals' behaviors may not be simply a product of their individual attributes and attitudes but may be "influenced" by the fact that they are embedded in socially specific time and space contexts such as networks of friends and kin, institutions of school, church, and work, or small and large communities from neighborhoods to nations. A current example of such a research area is the discussion of "neighborhood effects" on such specific outcomes as academic achievement, mental and physical health, delinquency, and employment (Sampson, Morenoff, & Gannon-Rowley, 2002).

The study of such contextual effects often requires an explicit multimethod perspective in that one is simultaneously gathering data on two different types of units—individuals and the collective context in which they are embedded. Researchers attempt to assess the degree to which individual attributes versus collective characteristics (such as "race" or "class," for example) have similar or different effects on people's behavior. A typical structural effects question would ask: "Do poor people in rich neighborhoods behave differently than poor people in poor neighborhoods?"

Some subsets or types of contexts whose effects have been explored include the following:

1. Geo-political units that may vary in scale from neighborhood to cities and metro areas to states/provinces and nations. (See the voluminous research on neighborhood effects summarized in Sampson et al., 2002).

2. Organizational/institutional contexts such as schools, firms, agencies (Scott & Meyer, 1994).

3. Small group/social network/social tie contexts such as friendship, coworkers, family, and kin.

This is what theorist Georg Simmel (1971) referred to as "social circles" and what Gary Fine (2012) documented in his numerous ethnographic studies of what he calls "tiny publics," ranging from boys' Little League teams to mushroom hunters to restaurant kitchens.

The idea of contextual effects is that one is collecting data at different scales, levels, or units of analysis and these different types of data require different methods of data collection. For example, at the collective level, there is census or economic data on geopolitical units or archival data on organizations. These collective levels of data are then coupled with individual-level data obtained through surveys, interviews, observation, or records.

Examples of structural effects are seen in the early work of reference group researchers such as Robert Merton, Samuel Stouffer, and Herbert Hyman among others (Merton & Lazersfeld, 1950). The classic case is from Stouffer et al.'s (1949), *The American Soldier*, where they discovered that satisfaction with the promotion system in different branches of the military depended on the varying rates of promotion between the branches (Air Force vs, Marines). The counterintuitive outcome was that higher rates of promotion produced less satisfaction with the system (Air Force) with lower rates producing greater satisfaction (Marines). James A. Davis, Spaeth, and Huson (1961) later elaborated these into systematic comparisons of individual- and collective-level variables producing a "typology of effects:" (a) Additive effects in which both individual-level and collective-level variables operate to combine their effects; (b) interaction effects in which the effect of either the individual-level or the collective-level variable is different depending on the value of the other; and (c) spurious effects in which the effect of either the individual-level or the collective-level variable disappears once one has "controlled" for the other level. More recent techniques of hierarchical linear modeling and their variants similarly attempt to disentangle these multimethod data to uncover contextual effects (Raudenbush & Bryk, 2001).

Biomedical Social Research

There is an increasing interdisciplinary perspective on healthcare-related issues that has led to an explosion of multimethod research using combined methods of collecting biomedical data, social, and psychological data of individuals. From blood samples to mouth swabs to more detailed use of medical charts and the numerous "test results" they may contain, such data can be coupled to interview, survey, or field observational data on individuals. Such research is often motivated to finding causes or the etiology of disease or "cures" that may mitigate the consequences. Beyond causal analyses and questions of social causes of "illness," or the reverse causation of medical conditions affecting social and psychological outcomes, lies the measurement

and conceptual question of validity of medical conditions and symptoms. Such assessments may use multimethods research to actually identify and diagnose or define a syndrome or medical condition, for example posttraumatic stress disorder.

Such research has become especially significant with increasing use of genetic markers and some researchers attempts, perhaps too often naively, to link specific genes to specific behaviors—thereby short-circuiting what are likely much more complex processes at work. One is reminded of the early attempts of Cesare Lombroso to see a causal link between skull sizes and shapes and William Sheldon's "biological body types" of ectomorphs, mesomorphs, and endomorphs and predilections to engage in criminal/delinquent behavior.

The multimethod perspective of this research extends beyond different types of data and data collection to include various analytic frameworks and strategies. Often relying on very large data sets of tens of thousands of cases, the analytic strategies point to "statistically significant" correlations between genetic markers and health or behavioral outcomes, even when the amount of variance explained is miniscule by comparison to the vast amount of unexplained variance still left to be explained by nongenetic factors. Such results are too readily overly interpreted from a "genetic determinist" argument by some, even when the authors of the research caution against such interpretations.

What a multimethod perspective brings to such questions is a need for other types of data and analyses that would fill in the black box of mechanisms and multifaceted chains of contingent causation that might link the genetic marker to some specific outcome. The perennial question of correlation and causation becomes entangled in the nature versus nurture debate. Jeremy Freese has perhaps been one of the leading sociological spokespersons calling for more cautionary conclusions based on multimethod strategies, especially when they are advanced in consideration of policy recommendations and programs. A recent research article in *Science* reporting a link between specific genetic markers and "educational outcomes" cautioned "the main lesson of the research, experts say, should be that attributing cultural and socioeconomic traits to genes is a dicey enterprise. " 'If there is a policy implication, it's that there's even more reason to be skeptical of genetic determinism', says Jeremy Freese of Northwestern University in Evanston Illinois" (Saey, 2013).

How does multimethod research help address genetic/social issues? Research aimed at relating genetics and social behavior is, of course, inherently multimethod in the broadest sense of the term because it employs methods derived from biology to study the genetic components and social science methods for the social components. Moreover, there are multiple biological research techniques and designs (e.g., blood vs. saliva DNA tests; twin, sibling, adoption, and molecular genetic studies). However, as sociological research interest has grown in the past two decades, the area has also become more multimethod in the general sense of employing varieties of social science methods in conjunction with one another and also as well with varieties of genetic data.

Survey research is the primary data collecting method currently employed in many social genetic studies. It allows for large sample studies that may be put to wide use. For example, the National Longitudinal Study of Adolescent Health was started through the University of North Carolina–Chapel Hill by Bearman, Udry, and Harris

> to capture as much information as possible about the social circumstance, friendship networks and family conditions of 21,000 teenagers in 132 schools, from grades 7 through 12. The survey included a disproportionate number of twins, fraternal and identical, full and half siblings, and adopted children. . . Follow-up interviews were conducted a year later. Then, for the third wave. . . (in 2002), 2500 siblings were asked for DNA samples (via cheek swabs). (Shea, 2009, p. B6)

A fourth wave collected DNA with saliva samples for all respondents.

Data from surveys such as this have been employed to investigate the possible main and interaction effects of genetic characteristics on social behavior and are often supplemented by additional methods to improve upon the surveys. Guo, Elder, Cai, and Hamilton (2009), for example, tested the hypothesis that "the genetic contribution to adolescent drinking depends on the drinking behavior of their friends" (p. 355) with data from a sample of clusters of siblings and their friends from the larger National Longitudinal Study of Adolescent Health. They reinterviewed respondents at home, beyond the survey, to construct the clusters of friends. A special problem in determining friends' drinking behavior is that there may be a projection effect when respondents themselves are asked to report their friends' behavior. To avoid this possible bias, the researchers identified and then directly interviewed the respondents' friends.

In another study, Guo et al. (2009) addressed the issue of selection bias in studying the influence of friends on behavior in their study of peer impacts on attitudes and drinking behavior. The study was a survey of a sample of roommates in a large university. The issue was that adolescents in particular tend to choose as friends people similar to themselves (Guo et al., 2009). To address this issue, the researchers introduced an experimental component to their study by separately studying students who had been randomly assigned to roommates by the university housing office, a procedure that in their words "avoids the confounding effects of residential choice" (p. 4). The authors report that "This is the first time that gene-environmental interactions have been investigated using randomly assigned environmental influences" (p. 6). They conclude that the "genetic contribution" to adolescent drinking depends on the drinking behavior of their friends. That is, friend behavior moderates the genetic contribution to alcohol use.

Evaluation Research

Multimethod research has found a ready application in the burgeoning area of evaluation research. Evaluation research emerged explicitly from a policy-oriented set of questions about the effectiveness of programs designed to deal with specific social problems (Rossi, Lipsey, & Freeman, 2004). The call for evaluation of such programs has been heightened under the current antitax political context of doing away with programs that cannot demonstrate their *effectiveness* and more stringently their *efficiency* in a cost/benefit calculus. Evaluation research is therefore explicitly geared to providing data and analysis that can inform decision-making about supporting or negating specific programs. As a rubric in rational decision-making quantification is seen to be particularly valued as able to provide objective, universalistic, summary, comparative criteria by which to judge such programs. Coupled with the "natural" quantification provided by a "money" calculus, costs and benefits can be rendered commensurable and evaluated accordingly (Espeland & Stevens, 1998).

An additional more refined consideration beyond assessing efficacy and efficiency is that of equity. Here the question becomes: "Who bears the cost, and who reaps the benefit?" The answer to this question may require different kinds of data and still different methods of research to distinguish how the costs and benefits are differentially distributed.

This logic of evaluation research has had a number of consequences. One is to focus on outcomes, more explicitly outcomes that are quantifiable, and even more explicitly quantifiable outcomes that can be given a dollar value. Second, the most valued research design is the true experiment with pre- and posttest measurement of outcomes (or "dependent" variables) coupled with random assignment to control and experimental groups that "do" or "do not" get the treatment of the program (the independent variable). These "ideal" research designs are often difficult to implement for any number of cost, time, practical, and ethical reasons, and this has led to a variety of quasi-experimental designs that relax one or another of the criteria (Campbell & Stanley, 1963, Cook & Campbell, 1979; Cook, 2002; Shadish, Cook, & Campbell, 2002). The actual implementation and process of carrying out the program are often left relatively unexplored in such designs. This is the point at which more qualitative and ethnographic methods are brought to bear in a fuller understanding of the evaluation of programs (Cook, Shadish, & Wong, 2008). Such qualitative research (e.g., in-depth interviews and field observation) may provide an understanding of the "causal process," the detailed concatenated sequential "mechanisms" by which certain outcomes were obtained. Furthermore, such qualitative research may heighten the possibility of serendipitous discovery of unanticipated outcomes not previously considered, especially given a specific focus on monetized quantitative measurable outcomes.

As a result of the these considerations, evaluation research has increasingly come to incorporate a multimethod perspective—combining a variety of methods that more robustly evaluate programs in terms of process and outcomes and varieties of methods both within and between qualitative and quantitative methods. The "approximations" to what some see as the ideal of randomized experimental designs in "quasi-experiments come with appropriate caveats as to their limitations (Cook & Campbell, 1979), and as Cook et al. (2008) later note, the use of different methods in combination have utility for answering a variety of different questions in evaluation research.

A number of major experimental social policy programs have been evaluated using multimethod research. For example researchers at the Seattle Income Maintenance Experiment and the Denver Income Maintenance Experiment randomly assigned poor people to various regimes and levels of welfare expenditure and assessed through multiple methods, such as surveys, interviews, diaries, and various specific outcomes in the life and welfare of recipients (US Department of Health and Human Services, 1983). More recently, Move to Opportunity Programs have been evaluated with a variety of methods to assess the effects of moving poor families out of concentrated inner-city public housing to better neighborhoods and assessing various outcomes such as health, employment and educational performance of children (Briggs, Popkin, & Goering, 2010).

Greene, Caracelli, and Graham (1989) developed a systematic rationale and prescription for the use of multimethods in evaluation research for five distinct purposes: (a) triangulation for convergence and corroboration, (b) complementarity for elaboration and enhancement, (c) development for helping to inform one method by another, (d) initiation for discovering paradox and contradiction, and (e) expansion for extending breadth and range. These were assessed empirically by looking at 53 evaluation studies and resulted in recommendations for ideal mixing of particular combinations of qualitative and quantitative methods. The combinations took into account their similarity and difference in phenomena studied, paradigm used, primacy of one over the other, integration or independence, and timing. One of the key distinctions noted was between product (outcome)-oriented evaluation and process-oriented evaluation and the finding that those that evaluated both product and process constituted the majority of mixed method studies.

Comparative Historical Causation, Trends, and Character Types

Our initial formulation of the multimethod perspective in multimethod research (Brewer & Hunter, 1989) clearly called for a broad conception of multimethods beyond the narrow question of measurement as in Campbell and Fiske's (1959) landmark article on triangulation. Multimethods we suggested should apply to all stages of the research to include for, example, multiple theoretical perspectives, and also different analytical strategies.

HISTORICAL CAUSATION

The question of varying analytical strategies has emerged in a number of arenas of social science but perhaps no more clearly than in the field of comparative/historical analysis. This becomes especially apparent in addressing the question of causation and its complexities (Abbott, 1990). Should one pursue a variable-based statistical linear approach of a large numbers of cases isolating the impact of causal variables on selected outcomes, or should one pursue a small-N comparative analysis based on detailed exposition of selected cases using a logic of similarity/difference and presence/absence and being sensitive to sequence and timing in trying to isolate necessary and sufficient causes (Skocpol & Somers, 1980; Skocpol, 1984)? This is where Andrew Abbott's (1997) reflections on the early Chicago School stressing "contingency and context" suggest the need for multimethod strategies. Abbott distinguished, for example, between those comparative historians who rely on variable analyses of large-N studies of nation/states statistically parsing out the effects of independent variables on selected dependent variables of interest versus those who rely on a small-N more comparative case-based analysis of specific events that have unfolded at varying points in time.

Among comparative historical analysts, Charles Ragin (1987) has developed a synthetic approach that reflects a multimethod merger of qualitative and quantitative methods. He uses the logic of Boolean algebra and "fuzzy sets" that produces a rigorous quantifiable assessment of varying combinations of qualitative characteristics that permit one to assess the contribution of necessary and sufficient causes for given outcomes. In short, he marries the rich detailed knowledge of qualitative data and small-N comparative logic with larger N data sets and develops quantitative statistical assessments of the likelihood of different combinations of contexts and conditions producing specified outcomes. Walton and Ragin (1990) have applied this technique to a study of which combinations of factors contributed to countries experiencing middle-class riots in response to International Monetary Fund policies. James Mahoney and Dietrich Rueschemeyer (2003) posed similar concerns in their landmark compilation *Comparative Historical Analysis in the Social Sciences*. Focused especially on questions of causation such as necessary and sufficient causes and temporal order, sequence, and duration in societal level events—such as revolutions and depressions—they were concerned with the different logics and modes of analysis in this emergent field. Specifically addressing the concerns that a multimethod strategy is designed to address, they noted

First of all, across the relevant disciplines, methodological disagreements of varying intensities have emerged between qualitative and quantitative approaches. In comparative social science this is represented by disputes between comparative historical researchers and cross-national statistical researchers who work with large numbers of cases. (p. 16)

However, they note that the advocates of large-N and small-N methods are more recently "acknowledging that there is a place for both in the cycle of research" (p. 17). For example, methodologists report on iterative research programs in which comparative historical research supplements the initial findings of statistical studies and vice versa. They quote King, Kehone, and Verba's book *Designing Social Inquiry* (1994) to the effect that "the differences between the quantitative and qualitative traditions are only stylistic and are methodologically and substantively unimportant. All good research can be understood—and is indeed best understood—to derive from the same underlying logic of inference" (p. 4). Mahoney and Rueschemeyer (2003) conclude with an invocation to the spirit of multimethod research "comparative historical researchers do their best research when they remain open to the use of diverse methodologies and analytic tools" (p. 24).

TRENDS

Debates over causal analysis in comparative and historical social science are often predicated on documenting broad historical trends of social change such as urbanization, industrialization, bureaucratization, and secularization, all of which are often captured in theories of modernity (Moore, 1958, 1966). Such studies—both historical analyses of changes over time and comparative analyses of different societies considered to be at different stages in an historical linear development from primitive to modern—often rely on a variety of data and different methods to demonstrate these broad trends of social change. We are not debating here the "Western bias" of theories of modernity or their assumptions of linear societal development (see Wallerstein, 1974, 2004 on world systems theory and others for such questions and critiques), nor are we entering the debate as to whether or not such trends can be variously couched as upward positive "progress" versus downward declining trajectories, or combinations in various cyclical rise and fall theories. Rather we are highlighting here the degree to which such studies often rely on a multimethod accumulation of diverse sets of data as the basis of their assertions. We will briefly look at two such empirically based landmark exemplars, David McClelland's (1961) research reported in *The Achieving Society* and Robert Putnam's (2001) more recent research on the decline of civil society reported in *Bowling Alone*.

As a social psychologist, McClelland (1961) became fascinated with the psychological trait that he identified as "the need for achievement" or *nAch* as it became known, which is an internalized motive of people to continue to strive for ever greater accomplishments. Drawing on the work of the sociologist Max Weber (1905) and his landmark study of the rise of modern capitalism documented in *The Protestant Ethic and the Spirit of Capitalism*, McClelland saw this need for achievement as a cultural variable that socialized individuals from different cultures into varying needs for achievement. In his experimental research, he documented the ways in which this need for achievement could be manipulated and heightened or depressed under varying conditions. But he extended his line of research far beyond the laboratory to include other data and other methods, such as analyses of artifacts of different cultures over time and content analysis of myths and stories from different cultures as to their emphasis on "achievement." He correlated these with data from still other methods such as governmental statistics and showed, for example, a correlation between socialization into need for achievement as indicated by children's stories and GDP as an outcome variable reinforcing one of Weber's central tenants of the *Spirit of Capitalism*.

Robert Putnam (2001) begins his analysis of the decline of civil society in America by focusing on the questions of "trust" and "trustworthy," which are seen to rest ultimately on the idea of keeping one's word—meaning one's subsequent behavior is in line with one's prior verbal commitment. Trust is not just an attribute of individual dyadic relationships but may be generalized not only to people in general, including even strangers, but to institutions as well, as in people's trust in government. The idea of civil society, that is, voluntary social relationships among individuals who have minimal social ties and may even be strangers to one another, is predicated on this element of a presumption of trust. To explore this realm of informal voluntary social ties, that is, civil society, which is distinct from primary ties of friends and kin and more formal ties governed by laws and the institutions of

social control of the state (Shils, 1957), requires a variety of different methods and data sources. This is clearly demonstrated by Putnam in his contemporary classic, *Bowling Alone: The Collapse and Revival of American Community*. In this summary volume, he argues there has been a decline and transformation of the civil sphere in American life. In building his argument he presents a variety of data derived from different methods, including survey research on participation in voluntary associations, attitudes toward government, and generalized trust of others, as well as historical and archival data such as organizational memberships, voting records, and content analyses of media. As he states in his methodological appendix in *Bowling Alone*, "My primary strategy, as explained in Chapter 1, has been to triangulate among as many independent sources of evidence as possible, following the model of researchers into global warming" (p. 315). Overall he finds there is a decline in people's expressed trust of major traditional institutions in society – from government, to religion to business—which is seen to be the result of broken promises in the conduct of these institutions due to incompetence and corruption that undermines their legitimacy. It is the sheer volume and variety of data derived from different methods that makes his argument and analysis so persuasive. This is in part because he is able to provide a litany of data that support his argument and also because of the variety and types of data through which he is able to demonstrate a subtle and nuanced analysis that shows exceptions, qualifications, and limitations that increase the credibility of his overall argument. In short, he comes across as an objective researcher rather than a true believer polemicist.

CHARACTER TYPES

C. Wright Mills (1959) in *The Sociological Imagination* roots the understanding of social life in the intersection of biography and history. Combining these two elements has been a continuing concern in social science research and has often involved different data and methods—a multimethod perspective—to capture and tease out this critical intersection. We have already briefly looked at macro-level multimethod approaches to history in considering causation and trends. Cultural shifts over time have social consequences and vice versa, not the least in producing different emerging types of characters as a consequence.

With respect to biography, there is an old tradition within sociology of producing life histories or characterizations of a type of person: a composite summarization of data obtained from numerous discrete individuals. These include *The Unadjusted Girl* (Thomas, 1923), *The Jack-roller* (Shaw, 1930/2013), *The Professional Thief* (Sutherland, 1937), *The Hobo* (Anderson, 1923), and others. James Bennett (1981) wrote of this approach as a typification or characterization of what theorists like Robert Merton (1968) would call statuses and roles, that is, structural positions that are distinct from the more individualistic psychology of personality. The composite character was a fictionalized distillation and amalgamation, with data selectively organized and summarized, but it was all true in the sense that all of the facts were verified and valid or, as one commentator put it, "nothing in here was made-up" (Howard Becker in personal communication at Rhetoric of Research Conference Northwestern University, May 1980). This is one type of biography that may result from an analysis of numerous discrete individual biographies. By contrast, the focus on discrete individual biographies—the archetypal literary biography such as James Boswell's *The Life of Samuel Johnson* (1998) or William Manchester's (1978) *American Caesar: Douglas MacArthur, 1880–1964*—are in effect case studies of a single individual while the composite biography constitutes the case itself (see Ragin and Becker's *What Is a Case?* [1992]). Here, different methods and different types of data would be employed to produce the distinction between an individual personality and a social type or character.

The former would more likely involve archives and perhaps interviews of those who knew the focal person, while the latter would more likely draw on interviews and observations of numerous individuals representative of that type. An example of the latter is Martin Jankowski's (1991) development of the summary gang character defined by defiant individualism (as opposed to a specific individual's personality). He synthesized and distilled the characteristics of a typical gang member based on his decade-long participant observation of 29 gangs in three cities. A focus on character requires a multimethod strategy that incorporates cultural (e.g., ideas, beliefs) and structural (e.g., network) data about the milieu within which character types are formed. Context produces similarity that is distilled in similar character traits. Fitting individuals into history is a multimethod strategy of placing different types of characters into different historical trends and causal processes. The life histories are typified characters who are the outcomes of these processes.

Disaster Research

Disaster research is one of the earliest sociological research areas to develop an explicitly multimethod approach. The impetus was the immediacy and transience of the events being studied.

On December 5, 1917, a munitions ship exploded in Halifax Harbor, inflicting severe damage on the city and injury to its inhabitants. Close to 2,000 people were killed and 9,000 more injured (in all about 22% of the city's population). Samuel Henry Prince, who was then serving as an episcopal priest in Halifax, was both a participant and an observer of this explosion and its results. He later recorded his observations in his Columbia University doctoral dissertation, in what is generally regarded as the first sociological study of disaster (Prince, 1920). Prince introduced his study with a methodological note that has resounded in the design of disaster research ever since:

> The whole field. . . is a virgin subject in sociology. Knowledge will grow scientific only after the most faithful examination of many catastrophes. But it must be realized that the data of greatest value is left sometimes unrecorded and fades rapidly from the special memory. Investigation is needed immediately after the event. (p. 22)

In short, disaster studies to capture these fleeting memories and events must be based on quick response and firsthand research.

Following the disastrous experiences of World War II and the onset of the Cold War (Form & Nosow, 1958), a number of quick-response disaster research programs were established at the National Opinion Research Center and elsewhere (see Barton, 1969). In 1963 the Disaster Research Center was established to more regularly monitor disasters with field and survey research. It has conducted over 600 such studies since its inception. Thus, in contrast to the 1917 Halifax explosion, the September 11, 2001, attack on New York City's World Trade Center, while equally unexpected, had trained and experienced observers from the Disaster Research Center ready to respond almost immediately.

However, the routinization of disaster research readiness does not routinize the disastrous events themselves or the research into them. For example, one of the lead Disaster Research Center 9/11 researchers writes in her dissertation:

> Direct observation of ongoing emergency activities was particularly valuable in this case precisely

because the event itself seriously hampered record-keeping and clouded the memory of some emergency responders. With key decision makers often unable to recollect what was happening literally from one moment to the next, the ability to actually be present as decisions were made was critical for later efforts to reconstruct events. . . also facilitated rapport in later face-to-face interviews and added validity to information obtained in those conversations. To contend with the. . . research challenges. . . I draw upon the variety of data sources and employ multiple qualitative strategies—among them direct exploratory observation, primary data collection and analysis, as well as in-depth face-to-face and telephone interviews—to triangulate emergency response information. (Kendra & Wachtendorf, 2003, pp. 41–42)

More generally, Stallings (1997) has suggested that

The "challenge" of disaster research. . . is the lack of time between the occurrence of a disaster and the fielding of research: lack of time to develop theory and hypotheses; lack of time to develop research instruments; lack of time to decide which events are worthy of study. (p. 9)

This highly specialized area of research highlights another key factor that a multimethod perspective has proven be helpful in addressing the time element and a need for pragmatic quick response to an often unanticipated research situation and the need to address the multiple audiences and consumers of research.

One example of this pragmatic adaptation in a manmade disaster was the "experimental/survey" research of Bobo, Zubrinsky, Johnson, and Oliver (1994) in Los Angeles during the time of the Rodney King riot following the "not guilty" verdict of police officers captured on tape beating Mr. King. A survey had been launched days prior to the riot, which, among other things, had a series of items focused on race relations. After the riots the survey continued, and the researchers had a "natural experiment" or quasi-experimental design of before and after measures with the riot as the experimental variable. This piece of research beautifully represents two key aspects of the spirit of multimethod research—a pragmatic adaptive response to the serendipity of the research situation and a melded multimethod design combining survey and experimental logics.

The fact that "disaster research" often has multiple purposes for different audiences is another factor that makes multimethod research particularly attractive as a purposeful design. This was clearly the case, for example, in Kai Erikson's (1976) research following the Buffalo Creek disaster in West Virginia reported in *Everything in Its Path: Destruction of Community in the Buffalo Creek Flood.* Erikson was initially approached by a law firm involved in the litigation of the case on behalf of residents whose homes and hamlets had been wiped out by the floodwaters released by a failed earthen dam built by a mining company. Erikson's multimethod research relied predominantly on in-depth interviews with displaced residents and, perhaps most poignantly and empathetically, firsthand field observations of the everyday disrupted lives of residents of the hills and hollows of the area. Documenting the effects of the disaster for the legal audience may have been the initial impetus of the research, but other audiences included welfare services and various governmental agencies. Drawing on officially compiled statistics and archives, including the history of actions by the mining company, permitted Erikson's multimethod research to both draw from and be of use to multiple sources and audiences. The simple profound conclusion for the sociology of disasters was to qualify the commonly stated proposition that disasters create a heightened sense of community in response to the shared fate. Erikson's research concluded that if the disaster was sufficiently severe, as in the case of Buffalo Creek, it could in fact destroy community.

Another example of disaster research employing multimethods is Eric Klinenberg's (2003) study of the Chicago summer heat wave of 1995, which resulted in the death of hundreds of Chicagoans, especially the elderly in certain poor minority neighborhoods. Again, relying on official statistics, in-depth interviews, and field observations Klinenberg concluded that the deaths were differentially distributed by neighborhood and that a critical factor was the variable density of networks of elderly found in two adjacent neighborhoods—dense in a Latino community that had relatively fewer deaths and relatively sparse in an adjacent Black community that had greater deaths. The relative isolation or connectedness affected whether or not others were there to check on how the elderly were faring in the heat and to offer assistance if needed. In a broadened autopsy of the disaster, Klinenberg's research also explored the response and programs in place of various city agencies and departments, from police and fire to health and welfare, and concluded that they too bore some culpability.

One policy implication of the research has now been instituted by the mayor's office: repeated public service announcements during subsequent heat waves for residents of the city to contact and check on the welfare of elderly kin and neighbors and for city employees such as police and fire and welfare workers to do the same. Klinenberg's (2003) research has also been important for thinking about the quality of multimethod research and raising the question: Does the use of multimethods ipso facto produce better research results? Critiques of Klinenberg's research by Duneier (2004, 2006) and others generated some controversy and debate as to the adequacy and "thinness" of the field research he conducted. The implication is that time and effort spent on collecting other types of data might have been better spent in a greater immersion in the field providing more "thick description" rather than the more superficial observations reported. The lesson is, in short, that multimethods may be valuable but that simply having more methods and different data does not ensure greater validity if the methods themselves are inadequately employed.

Disaster research often attempts to distinguish between what is natural, as in a natural disaster, and what is the result of human agency and in the latter case to parse out "blame" and accountability This research gets readily translated into legal conceptual frameworks of culpability. Recent legal cases, for example, have held meteorologists "guilty" for having failed to predict and warn residents of impending storms or geologists for failure to warn of earthquakes (Erikson, 1994; Freudenburg, Gramling, Laska, & Erikson, 2009).

The art of translating scientific and social science research results to multiple audiences was exemplified in the case of research on Love Canal, the toxic chemical site in Upstate New York where different publics, which included fellow scientists, evacuated former residents eager to learn if they could safely return to their homes and public officials and governmental decision-makers all eager for a simplified "yes or no" recommendation. Different data obtained through different methods, and perhaps equally significant, from different disciplines proved useful in communicating an understanding of the facts of the case and their implications for what people might decide to do (Hunter, 1986).

Rhetoric, Narrative, and Postpositive Postmodern Multimethods: Turn, Turn, Turn

Science is a social process, and social science is social in both form and substance. The idea that methods of systematic research are employed to discover truth may be a central and noble teleological goal, but it is an oversimplified, reified, and idealized conception of what we actually do. We are not mere scientific automatons programmed to follow fixed procedures for probing reality, like the Mars rovers (Spirit, Opportunity, and Curiosity), but rather we are active social agents who talk to one another, read one another's work, and debate and argue about the direction, meaning, and credibility of one another's research and our assertions about the "truth" of what we have observed. This social constructionist perspective on science has a number of implications often defined as postmodern or postpositivist critique. Two of the more significant ones are the role of "the new rhetoric" and the "narrative" emphasis that sees science as a collection of stories. We briefly explore elements of rhetoric and narrative in turn.

The Rhetorical Turn

The social and rhetorical aspect of science is evidenced in a multimethod perspective with respect to the following:

1. The social goal of science is to convince others of the tentative truth of one's assertions about questions posed. The tentativeness arises for a number of reasons, such as method limitations and historical and spatial limitations. These result in varying degrees of generalizability—from modest, limited claims of local truths to broader claims and heroic ones of universal truths. The convincing part entails the art of persuasion and being attentive to one's audiences and the criteria by which they will judge the validity of one's assertions.

2. Multimethods permit a variety of different questions to be posed about a given phenomenon of interest. For example, is the question/assertion one of descriptive fact or causal explanation (correlation vs. causation), one dealing with macro structural/cultural phenomena or the micro level of agency and intent, one focused

on process and outcome, or one concerned with understanding alone or prescriptive policy implications?

3. Diverse others may have a variety of criteria by which they evaluate and are convinced of the truth value of one's assertions. Multimethods allow one to address these different criteria. Different methods are varyingly adept at addressing each of the skeptic's questions, and beyond these there may be other criteria in addition—some more general and some more specific that go to ontological assumptions: for example debates over the best mode of analysis in studying social change from "interrupted time series with switching replications" (Cook & Campbell, 1979) to event history analysis (Allison, 1984) to patterned sequences of nomothetic narrative (Abbott 1995).

4. Multimethods address diverse criteria and answer a variety of skeptic's questions, thereby becoming more convincing to more people and more types of people, as different types of texts and rhetorics are employed. These *others* may range from fellow academics concerned with the skeptics' questions to policy planners concerned with cost/benefit analyses of effectiveness and efficiency to the broader public concerned with issues of equity and ethics. The variety of rhetorical arguments contained in a multimethod perspective may range from quantitative survey results to numbers to a sample of personal accounts to historical archives.

The rediscovery of rhetoric as a central component of scientific argument and social research is based on this social aspect of science. From these rhetorical perspective methods and the varying rules, procedures, techniques, and norms of science we derive tools for building an argument about the link between observations and data about the world and one's ideas or theories. Scientific method narrowly construed is concerned about "persuading skeptics" by satisfying them that one has followed these rules in the research. According to The *British Strong Programme* (Bloor, 1976/1991; Mulkay 1979). science is, from this perspective, subsumed under rhetoric as a method or "tool" of argumentation and persuasion. The "strong" assertion is that it is all rhetoric through and through. Hunter (1990) in *The Rhetoric of Social Research* sees social science research as a set of rhetorical relationships among the researcher, the subjects, and the audience tied together by texts or research reports.

Not only are there "conventions" of science that must be followed to be convincing, but the reports of research, from published articles to PowerPoint presentations, must be similarly stylized to persuade specific audiences. The multimethod approach, which is a "synthesis of styles" of research (Brewer and Hunter, 1989), lends itself to being more persuasive (believable) not merely due to a greater number of methods but to their addressing different criteria of credibility. As poet John Donne noted about An Obscure Writer

> Philo, with twelve years study hath been grieved
> This is to be understood as when will he be believed.
> *(Donne, 1986, p. 210)*

Margarete Sandelowski (2003) in *Tables or Tableaux? The Challenges of Writing and Reading Mixed Methods Studies* distinguished between method and methodology and also paradigms and techniques and added, "A major—and arguably the most important—criterion in evaluating the merits of a study lies in the ability of writers to persuade readers of its merits in their research reports (p. 321). Invoking Fish (1980), she directly addressed the rhetoric of multimethods by noting that qualitative and quantitative belong to different interpretive communities. She considered this an "aesthetic criteria, including the sense of rightness and comfort readers experience that is crucial to the judgment they make about the validity of a study." She therefore explores the need for" mixed media for mixed methods for mixed audiences" (p. 335).

The issue of different genres of research reports are seen in two chapters from Hunter's edited volume (1990)—Joseph Gusfield's (1990) comparison of Liebow's (1967) *Tally's Corner* based on qualitative research versus Blau and Duncan's (1978) quantitative analysis of the *American Occupational Structure*—and in Marjorie DeVault's (1990) comparison of Kanter's (1993) *Men and Women of the Corporation* versus Krieger's (1983) *The Mirror Dance*, both dealing with women's roles and identities bur the former with a traditional organizational analysis and the latter with a more feminist perspective. To paraphrase DeVault: same subject, different methods. Quoting Wolfer (1991), Sandelowski (2003) noted that "different aspects of reality lend themselves to different methods of inquiry" (p. 327), and, she added, "there is no uniform paradigm-method link, there is a method reality link" (p. 327).

Sandelowski (2003) further suggests the mixing may have one of two purposes "to achieve a fuller understanding of a target phenomenon and to verify one set of findings against the other or a comprehensive kaleidoscopic sense of understanding versus truth or validity 'representation'." She posed a great question: What is mixed? And what kind of mixing occurs? Through focusing on the qualitative quantitative distinction she recognizes the ambiguity in distinguishing between them and the difficulty of crafting research reports incorporating both in a convincing manner.

Johnson and Turner's (2003) chapter in the *Handbook of Mixed Methods* uses the key idea of "trustworthy," which they equate with validity and which in the title of Hunter's book would be "believable." They say, "Valid research is plausible, credible, trustworthy, and, therefore, defensible. . . . We treat the terms *valid* and *trustworthy* as synonyms" (p. 300; italics in original). This may be directly linked to multimethods in that we are prone to trust the many over the few, if confirmatory, and to have if not "mistrust" then at least doubt over the disconfirming or specification of differences due to method itself (Lever, 1978).

Narrative

The rhetorical turn is closely allied with another postmodern humanistic approach to social science research and that is the idea that what we do is basically tell a story—create a narrative. The iconic corollary to multimethod research from the narrative perspective is like the "Rashomon effect," the stories of a single event or phenomenon told from the perspectives of different witnesses and participants. This, of course, raises the larger phenomenological question—is it many versions of one event or many different events? We operate from the assumption that the real world does exist (physicalism) and yet recognize that our knowledge of that real world is a varied and imperfect product of the observations we make of it (relativism).

As Andrew Abbott (1992) has observed in his landmark paper "From Causes to Events: Notes on Narrative Positivism":

In the last decade, a number of writers have proposed narrative as the foundation for sociological methodology. By this they do not mean narrative in terms of words as opposed to numbers and complexity as opposed to formalization. Rather, they mean narrative in the more generic sense of process, or story. . . . In the context of

contemporary empirical practice, such a conception is revolutionary. Our normal methods parse social reality into fixed entities with variable qualities. They attribute causality to the variables – hypostatized social characteristics—rather than to agents; variables do things, not social actors. Stories disappear. (p. 428)

The key trope (Booth, 1961/1983) that governs narratives of science, including social science, is that of a "quest." It is a quest that begins with a question leading to a search using research to explore the unknown. It is a purposeful journey to find a treasured goal, to go out into that real world and make the unknown known—in a word to acquire knowledge. One hopes that the knowledge one acquires has some validity that it is "true" and that what one believes to be true about the phenomena bears some close approximation to reality. From a pragmatic perspective—it is valid if the knowledge works, if it allows one to accomplish what one wishes to get done; if it doesn't work it is useless (Dewey, 1938).

Some might think the narrative is merely the story about how one does science—that it is not the doing of science itself. We suggest that the narrative is in fact a critical part of the doing of science itself, and the stories we tell about what we do serve to reflexively construct and reconstruct the actual quest itself.

As noted by Scott Baker (1990):

In studying the discourse of scientific communities, in fact, we find these communities employing multiple rhetorics as often as they use strict singular logics. . . . We note moreover, that scientists do not exclusively depend upon, or even follow, the strict guidelines of their field's logic or method. They convince each other and the lay public that their theories are reliable by means of persuasion not provided for or sanctioned by the accepted methodology. . . these communication strategies are outside the formal rules of method, [yet] they do persuade. (pp. 233–234)

But the postmodernist idea of narrative is more than just telling a story about how science is conducted; narrative is seen to be an ontological aspect of how we as "sensate human beings" "make sense" of the real world. Abbott (1997) claims we do so by taking into consideration "context and contingency," and Ragin (1987) suggests we tell narratives of constellations of characteristics defining our objects of study (our cases) as they alter through time. To highlight a quote presented previously that focused on the mechanism or the black box of explanation (Guo & Adkins, 2008):

> It should be pointed out that significant statistical findings alone are rarely, if ever, considered proof of a link between a genetic variant and a human complex phenotype. This contrasts with the usual practice in social sciences. Repeated significant results in social sciences showing a connection between, for example, parental education and children's education attainment are often considered sufficient evidence for such a connection. The credibility of the evidence is not only from the replicated statistical results but also from real-life observation. Drawing from personal experiences, most people would probably agree that a higher level of parental education would lead to a higher level of education in children on average. Such confirmation from life experiences is not available for interpreting genetic findings. Genotypes are not visible in everyday life. *To develop a credible story* that supports statistical findings, other evidence is needed, such as those from animal studies and biochemical studies. (p. 224; italics added)

The Narrative Moral of Multimethod Research Design

We return to the opening of our discussion about multimethod research design, just as Ulysses eventually returned to Greece after a meandering Odyssey, and that is to stress the spirit of multimethod research with which we began. True believers of one or another method, positing different ontological assumptions, will continue to debate the appropriateness of different methods, as they should in the full spirit of free inquiry. But in the further spirit of multimethod research such assumptions should be open to challenge, and a tolerance for entertaining alternative assumptions should be considered. The spirit of humility, not hubris, and the recognition of limitations in methods are more likely to advance the cause of science than any authoritative dictates of idealized methods. Context and contingency apply to research itself, and understanding the broader social context and the pragmatic contingent decisions made in the conduct of research must be taken into accounts. What we claim to know is dependent on how we came to know it. And the multimethod perspective still holds out the promise of closer approximations to truth about reality or, at a minimum, more moderated contingent claims to truth that reflect the reality of science itself.

We previously stated our criteria of good scientific research that it be

- Consistent—logically consistent, not random or contradictory
- Corresponding—data and ideas linked in measurement
- Convincing—rhetorically persuasive
- To this we add another—that it be "competent"

Multimethod research is not a magic bullet to truth but a style that still demands rigor and reflection in addressing the skeptic's central question: "How do you know?"

Discussion Questions

1. Can one consider mixed methods research a subset of multimethod research?
2. What parts of reality and the world does multimethod research focus on?
3. In what ways is multimethod research frequently superior to single or monomethod research?
4. Is multimethod research multidisciplinary?
5. What are some classic multimethod studies provided in this chapter, and what makes them important?

Suggested Websites

http://www.sociology.northwestern.edu/people/faculty/albert-hunter.html
Information about the authors of this chapter.

References

Abbott, A. (1990). Conceptions of time and events in social science methods: Causal and narrative approaches. *Historical Methods: A Journal of Quantitative and Interdisciplinary History, 23*(4), 140–150.

Abbott, A. (1992). From causes to events notes on narrative positivism. *Sociological Methods & Research, 20,* 428–455.

Abbott, A. (1995). Sequence analysis: New methods for old ideas. *Annual Review of Sociology, 21,* 93–113.

Abbott, A. (1997). Of time and space: The contemporary relevance of the Chicago School. *Social Forces, 75,* 1149–1182.

Ajzen, I., & Fishbein, M. (1977). Attitude-behavior relations: A theoretical analysis and review of empirical research. *Psychological Bulletin, 84*(5). doi: 10.1037/0033-2909.84.888

Allison, P. D. (1984). *Event history analysis: Regression for longitudinal event data.* Newbury Park, CA: Sage.

Anderson, N. (1923). *The hobo: The sociology of homeless men.* Chicago, IL: University of Chicago Press.

Baker, S. (1990). Reflection, doubt, and the place of rhetoric in postmodern social theory. *Sociological Theory, 8,* 212–245.

Barton, A. H. (1969). *Communities in disaster: A sociological analysis of collective stress situations.* Garden City, NJ: Doubleday.

Bennett, J. (1981). *Oral history and delinquency: The rhetoric of criminology.* Chicago, IL: University of Chicago Press.

Blau, P. M., & Duncan, O. D. (1967). *American occupational structure.* New York, NY: Free Press.

Bloor, D. (1991). *Knowledge and social imagery.* Chicago, IL: University of Chicago Press.

Bobo, L., Zubrinsky, C. L., Johnson, J. H. Jr., & Oliver, M. L. (1994). Public opinion before and after a spring of discontent. In M. Baladassare (Ed.), *The Los Angeles riots: Lessons for the urban future* (pp. 103–133). Boulder, CO: Westview.

Booth, W. C. (1983). *The rhetoric of fiction.* Chicago: University of Chicago Press.

Boswell, J. (1998). *Life of Johnson.* Edited by R. W. Chapman. Oxford, UK: Oxford University Press.

Brewer, J., & Hunter, A. (1989). *Multimethod research: A synthesis of styles.* Newbury Park, CA: Sage.

Brewer, J., & Hunter, A. (2006). *Foundations of multimethod research: Synthesizing styles.* Thousand Oaks, CA: Sage.

Briggs, X. S., Popkin S. J., & Goering J. M. (2010). *Moving to opportunity: The story of an American experiment to fight ghetto poverty.* New York, NY: Oxford University Press.

Campbell, D. T., & Fiske, D. W. (1959). Convergent and discriminant validation by the multitrait-multimethod matrix. *Psychological Bulletin, 56,* 81.

Campbell, D. T., & Stanley, J. C. (1963). *Experimental and quasi-experimental designs for research.* Chicago, IL: Rand McNally.

Cohen-Cole, E., & Fletcher, J. M. (2008). Is obesity contagious? Social networks vs. environmental factors in the obesity epidemic. *Journal of Health Economics, 27,* 1382–1387. doi: 10.1016/j.healeco.2008.04.005

Cook, T. D. (2002). Randomized experiments in educational policy research: A critical examination of the reasons the educational evaluation community has offered for not doing them. *Educational Evaluation and Policy Analysis, 24*(3), 175–199.

Cook, T. D., & Campbell, D. T. (1979). *Quasi-experimentation: Design and analysis issues for field settings.* Boston, MA: Houghton Mifflin.

Cook, T. D., Shadish, W. R., & Wong, V. C. (2008). Three conditions under which experiments and observational studies produce comparable causal estimates: New findings from within-study comparisons. *Journal of Policy Analysis and Management, 27,* 724–750. doi: 10.1002/pam.20375

Davis, J. A., Spaeth, J. L., & Huson, C. (1961). A technique for analyzing the effects of group composition. *American Sociological Review, 26,* 215–225.

Denzin, N. K. (1970). *The research act in sociology: A theoretical introduction to sociological methods.* Piscataway, NJ: Aldine.

DeVault, M. L. (1990). Women write sociology: Rhetorical strategies. In A. Hunter (Ed.), *The rhetoric of social research: Understood and believed,* (pp. 97–110.). New Brunswick, NJ: Rutgers University Press.

Dewey, J. (1938). *Logic: The theory of inquiry.* New York, NY: Holt, Rinehart and Winston.

Donne, J. (1896). Epigrams. In E. K. Chambers (Ed.) *Poems of John Donne* (Vol II, p. 210). London: Lawrence & Bullen.

Duneier, M. (2004). Scrutinizing the heat: On ethnic myths and the importance of shoe leather. *Contemporary Sociology, 2,* 139–150.

Duneier, M. (2006). Ethnography, the ecological fallacy, and the 1995 Chicago heat wave. *American Sociological Review, 71,* 679–688.

Erikson, K. T. (1976). *Everything in its path: Destruction of community in the Buffalo Creek flood.* New York, NY: Simon and Schuster.

Erikson, K. (1994). *A new species of trouble: The human experience of modern disasters.* New York, NY: W. W. Norton.

Espeland, W. N., & Stevens, M. L. (1998). Commensuration as a social process. *Annual Review of Sociology, 24,* 313–343.

Fine, G.A. (2012). *Tiny publics: A theory of group action and culture.* Ithaca, NY: CUP Services.

Form, W. H., & Nosow, S. (1958). *Community in disaster.* New York, NY: Harper.

Freudenburg, W. R., Gramling, R., Laska, S. & Erikson, K. (2009). *Catastrophe in the making: The engineering of Katrina and the disasters of tomorrow.* Washington, DC: Island Press.

Granovetter, M. (1985). Economic action and social structure: The problem of embeddedness. *American Journal of Sociology, 91,* 481–510.

Greene, J. C., Caracelli, V. J., & Graham, W. F. (1989). Toward a conceptual framework for mixed-method evaluation designs. *Educational Evaluation and Policy Analysis, 11,* 255–274.

Guo, G., & Adkins, D. E. (2008). How is a statistical link established between a human outcome and a genetic variant? *Sociological Methods Research, 37,* 201–226.

Guo, G., Elder, G. H., Cai, T., & Hamilton, N. (2009). Gene–environment interactions: Peers' alcohol use moderates genetic contribution to adolescent drinking behavior. *Social Science Research, 38,* 213–224.

Guo, G., Hardie, J. H., Owen, C., Daw, J.K., Fu, Y., Lee, H . . . Duncan, G. (2009). DNA collection in a randomized social science study of college peer effects. *Sociological Methodology, 39,* 1–29.

Gusfield, J. R. (1990). Two genres of sociology: A literary analysis of the American occupational structure and tally's corner. In A. Hunter (Ed.), *The rhetoric of social research: Understood and believed,* (pp. 62–96.). New Brunswick, NJ: Rutgers University Press.

Hunter, A. (1986). *Love Canal emergency declaration area: Proposed habitability criteria study: Vol. 1. Technical Review Committee.* New York, NY: US Environmental Protection Agency, US Department of Health and Human Services/Centers for Disease Control, New York State Department of Health, New York State Department of Environmental Conservation.

Hunter, A. (Ed.). (1990). *The rhetoric of social research: Understood and believed.* New Brunswick, NJ: Rutgers University Press.

Hunter, A., & Maxfield, M. G. (1980). *Reactions to Crime Project: Vol. 1. Methodological overview of the Reactions to Crime Project.* Evanston, IL: Northwestern University, Center for Urban Affairs.

Investopedia. (2014). Revealed preference. Retrieved from http://www.investopedia.com/terms/r/revealed-preference.asp

Jacobs, J. A. (2005). Multiple methods in ASR. *Footnotes: Newsletter of the American Sociological Review, 33*(9). Retrieved from http://www.asanet.orgwww.asanet.org/footnotes/dec05/indextwo.html.

Jahoda, M, Lazarsfeld, P. F., & Zeisel, H, (1971). *Marienthal: The sociography of an unemployed community.* New Brunswick, NJ: Transaction. (Originally published in 1933)

Jankowski, M. S. (1991). *Islands in the street: Gangs and American urban society.* Berkeley: University of California.

Joppa, L. N., McInerny, G., Harper, R., Salido, L., Takeda, K., O'Hara, K., . . . Emmott, S. (2013). Troubling trends in scientific software use. *Science, 340*, 814–815.

Johnson, B., & Turner, L. A. (2003). Data collection strategies in mixed methods research. In A. Tashakkori & C. Teddlie (Eds.), *Handbook of mixed methods in social & behavioral research*, (pp. 297–319). Thousand Oaks, CA: Sage.

Kahneman, D. (2011). *Thinking, fast and slow.* New York, NY: Farrar, Strauss & Giroux.

Kanter, R. M. (1993). *Men and women of the corporation.* New York, NY: Basic Books.

Kendra, J. M., & Wachtendorf, T. (2003). Elements of resilience after the World Trade Center disaster: Reconstituting New York City's Emergency Operations Centre. *Disasters, 27*(1), 37–53. doi:10.1111/1467-7717.00218

King, G., Keohane, R. O., & Verba, S. (1994). *Designing social inquiry: Scientific inference in qualitative research.* Princeton, NJ: Princeton University Press.

Klinenberg, E. (2003). *Heat wave: A social autopsy of disaster in Chicago.* Chicago, IL: University of Chicago Press.

Krieger, S. (1983). *The mirror dance: Identity in a women's community.* Philadelphia, PA: Temple University Press.

LaPiere, R. T. (1934). Attitudes vs. actions. *Social Forces, 13*, 230–237.

Lazarsfeld, P. F. (1945) Foreward to Ernest Greenwood, *Experimental Sociology.* New York, NY: King's Crown Press.

Lever, J. (1978). Sex differences in the complexity of children's play and games. *American Sociological Review, 43*, 471–483.

Liebow, E. (1967). *Tally's corner: A study of Negro streetcorner men.* New York, NY: Rowman & Littlefield.

Mahoney, J., & Rueschemeyer, D. (Eds.). (2003). *Comparative historical analysis in the social sciences.* Cambridge, UK: Cambridge University Press.

Manchester, W. (1978). *American Caesar: Douglas McArthur.* New York, NY: Dell.

McClelland, D. C. (1961). *Achieving society.* Princeton, NJ: Van Nostrand.

Merton, R. K. (Ed.). (1968). *Social theory and social structure.* New York, NY: Free Press.

Merton, R. K., & Lazersfeld, P. F. (Eds.). (1950). *Continuities in social research: Studies in the scope and method of "The American Soldier."* New York, NY: Free Press.

Mills, C. W. (1959). *The sociological imagination.* New York, NY: Oxford University Press.

Moore, B. (1958). *Political power and social theory: Six studies.* Cambridge, MA: Harvard University Press.

Moore, B. (1966). *Social origins of dictatorship and democracy: Lord and peasant in the making of the modern world.* Boston, MA: Beacon Press.

Morse, J. M. (2003). Principles of mixed methods and multimethod research design. In A. Tashakkori & C. Teddlie (Eds.), *Handbook of mixed methods in social & behavioral research* (pp. 189–208). Thousand Oaks, CA: Sage.

Mulkay, M. J. (1979). *Science and the sociology of knowledge.* London: Allen & Unwin.

Office of Income Security Policy, Office of the Assistant Secretary for Planning and Evaluation, US Department of Health and Human Services. (1983). *Overview of the Seattle–Denver income maintenance experiment final report.* Washington, DC: Author.

Pager, D., & Quillian, L. (2005). Walking the talk? What employers say versus what they do. *American Sociological Review, 70*, 355–380. doi: 10.1177/000312240507000301

Prince, S. H. (1920). *Catastrophe and social change, based upon a sociological study of the Halifax disaster.* Studies in History, Economics, and Public Law 212. New York, NY: Columbia University Press.

Putnam, R. D. (2001). *Bowling alone: The collapse and revival of American community.* New York, NY: Simon and Schuster.

Ragin, C. C. (1987). *The comparative method: Moving beyond qualitative and quantitative strategies.* Berkeley: University of California Press.

Ragin, C. C., & Becker, H. S. (Eds.). (1992). *What is a case? Exploring the foundations of social inquiry.* Cambridge, UK: Cambridge University Press.

Raudenbush, S. W., & Bryk, A. S. (2001). *Hierarchical linear models: Applications and data analysis methods.* Advanced Quantitative Techniques in the Social Sciences 1. Thousand Oaks, CA: Sage.

Rossi, P. H., Lipsey, M. W., & Freeman, H. E. (2004). *Evaluation: A systematic approach.* Thousand Oaks, CA: Sage.

Saey, T. H. (2013, June 29). Gene weakly linked to education level. *Science News.* Retrieved from https://www.sciencenews.org/article/genes-weakly-linked-to-education-level

Sampson, R. J., Morenoff, J. D., & Gannon-Rowley, T. (2002). Assessing "neighborhood effects": Social processes and new directions in research. *Annual Review of Sociology, 28*, 443–478.

Samuelson, P. (1948). *Economics.* New York, NY: McGraw-Hill.

Sandelowski, M. (2003). Tables or tableaux? The challenges of writing and reading mixed methods studies. In A. Tashakkori & C. Teddlie (Eds.), *Handbook of mixed methods in social & behavioral research*, (pp. 321–350). Thousand Oaks, CA: Sage.

Scott, W. R., & Meyer, J. W. (Eds.). (1994). *Institutional environments and organizations: Structural complexity and individualism.* Thousand Oaks, CA: Sage.

Shadish, W. R., Cook, T. D., & Campbell, D. T. (2002). *Experimental and quasi-experimental designs for generalized causal inference.* Boston, MA: Houghton Mifflin.

Shaw, C. R. (2013). *The jack-roller.* Eastford, CT: Martino. (Originally published in 1930)

Shea, C. (2009). The nature–nurture debate, redux: Genetic research finally makes its way into the thinking of sociologists. *The Chronicle of Higher Education, 54*(31), B6.

Shils, E. (1957). Primordial, personal, sacred and civil ties: Some particular observations on the relationships of sociological research and theory. *The British Journal of Sociology, 8*(2), 130–145.

Simmel, G. (1971). *On individuality and social forms.* Chicago, IL: University of Chicago Press.

Skocpol, T (Ed.). (1984).*Vision and method in historical sociology.* New York, NY: Cambridge University Press.

Skocpol, T., & Somers, M. (1980). The uses of comparative history in macrosocial inquiry. *Comparative Studies in Society and History, 22*(2), 174–197.

Small, M. L. (2011). How to conduct a mixed methods study: Recent trends in a rapidly growing literature. *Annual Review of Sociology, 37*, 57–86. doi: 10.1146/annurev.soc.012809.102657

Stallings, R. A. (1997). *Sociological theories and disaster studies.* Newark, DE: Disaster Research Center.

Stouffer, S. A., Lumsdaine, A. A., Lumsdaine, M. H., Williams R. M. Jr., Smith, M. B., Janis, I. L., . . . & Cottrell L. S. Jr.

(1949). *Studies in social psychology in World War II: Vol. 2. The American soldier: Combat and its aftermath*. Oxford, UK: Princeton University Press.

Sutherland, E. H. (Ed.) (1937). *The professional thief*. Chicago, IL: University of Chicago Press

Thomas, W. I. (1923). *The unadjusted girl*. Oxford, UK: Little, Brown and Co.

Tversky, A., & Kahneman, D. (1974). Judgment under uncertainty: Heuristics and biases. *Science, 185*, 1124–1131.

Uzzi, B. (1999). Embeddedness in the making of financial capital: How social relations and networks benefit firms seeking financing. *American Sociological Review, 64*, 481–505.

Wade, H. D. (2004). On operationalisms and economics. *Journal of Economic Issues, 38*(4), 953–968.

Wallerstein, I. M. (1974). *The modern world-system: Vol. 1. Capitalist agriculture and the origins of the European world-economy in the sixteenth century*. New York, NY: Academic Press.

Wallerstein, I. M. (2004). *World-systems analysis: An introduction*. Durham, NC: Duke University Press.

Walton, J., & Ragin, C. (1990). Global and national sources of political protest: Third world responses to the debt crisis. *American Sociological Review, 55*, 876–890.

Weber, M. (1905). *The protestant ethic and the spirit of capitalism*. New York, NY: Routledge. 2001.

Issues in Qualitatively-Driven Mixed-Method Designs: Walking Through a Mixed-Method Project

Janice M. Morse

Abstract

The objectives of this chapter are to illustrate issues in qualitatively-driven mixed-method designs by walking the reader through a project from idea to proposal completion. In this chapter I illustrate the process of conducting a mixed-method project using a hypothetical project. Strategies for maintaining rigor in mixed-method designs are addressed, using diagramming as a tool, the theoretical drive, the mechanisms of pacing, and the strategies for maintaining rigor. In addition, the chapter explores design issues and pitfalls that may occur when using qualitative methods with mixed-method design.

Key Words: qualitatively-driven, mixed-method, research, design, diagramming, rigor

Introduction

I recently read an article evaluating the delivery of care in an emergency department in a third-world country. The authors used focus groups—lots of them. Data were rich and descriptive. There were descriptions of injuries and the inability of the department to manage the injured. Relatives filled the department, impeding access to patients for critical treatments and even assisting with care. In fact, relatives were providing care that would elsewhere be considered the purview of nursing. The authors' made an important case for *change,* and the reader could recognize that the care provided was far less than optimal and appropriate.

But the article lacked real substance. There were numbers—I read in excruciating detail exactly who was interviewed by gender, age, ethnicity, profession, and many other less important details, which were included in a two-page table. I was given geographic details, population density, and details about the hospital census. But most of all what was lacking from this focus group study were all the statistics that I would need, as a health planner, to

do anything about the presenting problem and to implement change. In other words, the study presented a case that was interesting to read and that pulled at my heart—let's call this representative of *subjective need*—but when the author's intention was to provide the basis for developing the necessary change, the article lost significance. The wrong method had been used to convey a useful message for health research.

A decade ago this study might have been conducted as an ethnography, including numbers as well as firsthand descriptions of incidents, various measures of time, preventable deaths, along with detailed case studies as examples and perhaps even suggesting solutions: time consuming to do but with impact and usefulness. Then, in later years, the study might have been conducted as a qualitative and quantitative evaluation project. Perhaps we still have that choice. But when focus groups and interviews are used alone, the investigator is relying solely on participant-reported data—on what people have seen and experienced, have remembered, thought, and now think—rather than investigator-obtained, firsthand participant observation. Worse, when using focus groups alone as a method, one cannot *count* these opinions. As all participants in the group are not asked the same questions, we have, at the end of the study, general agreement or disagreement with the questions, or differing opinions within the group, and from these we construct themes. I am not criticizing focus groups as a method but only noting that in some situations, it is inappropriately used as a replacement for a survey and other types of "hard" data and, with the use of themes, cannot provide *numbers*. Findings that lack such quantitative facts result in a much weaker study. Similarly, with studies that use unstructured interviews, when the interviewer is learning as the study progresses, the questions change accordingly, and counting is not a strategy that may be used.

This means that researchers are forced to present their case without the necessary data—that is, statistics for the reader to assess the situation: how many cases were observed, the treatment patterns, and detail about the outcomes. There is no supporting hospital chart data and statistics and not even a survey. Researchers do not have the numbers necessary for making their case. These researchers are forced to present their case using *reported subjective data*, rather than a report that includes their own observations.

With our abhorrence for statistics, we are losing ground. Qualitative researchers are replacing meticulous detail that provided a foundation to understanding and change by focusing on finding out what others think—using second-hand reports, which lends a type of distortion to our research. The distortion may not actually be a bias, but it is a distortion that comes about because the data "floats over" the real issues and concrete facts. In our rush to do research, we are forgetting why we are doing it, what we need to know, and why.

Unstructured interviews and focus group research do provide an important type of data. For instance, used early in the study, they can inform the researcher regarding where to look as the study proceeds or help them scope the area for a position to start their investigation. Interviews provide subjective data that provides rich description, adding context and meaning and even information that is outside the study boundaries: "and then, he was never the same; two years later he died," and so forth.

But a new way to balance our research has recently become available to us: that of mixed-method research. We now have the option, depending on our study aims, to approach our research problems using both subjective and objective data. We can keep our focus groups *and* collect the necessary hard data. We can use both qualitative and quantitative data, and even add more components exposing additional qualitative or quantitative strategies until the problem is appropriately understood and documented. We can approach the study qualitatively and then add the necessary "hard data" once we know what we are looking for and what needs to be justified. Qualitatively-driven (QUAL-*quan*) mixed-method designs provide us with a way to add hard data that reinforce our interviews and observations; alternatively, for quantitatively driven QUAN-*qual* designs, qualitative data provides us with description that illustrates and makes sense of our hard data.

But these choices do not mean that we approach the setting blindly, without design. Rather, mixed-method designs provide the limited freedom needed to be reflexive and responsive to interim results and enough design so as to maintain control. It does not mean that the study will be easyf or without validity traps. We must attend to design and be always aware of whether we are doing qualitative or quantitative analysis. Without design, mixed-method research may rapidly become jumble of data, of missed and unanswered questions, violated assumptions and forgotten goals. But with attention to design, the researcher can maintain control, avoid making errors that violate rigor, and move through the project smoothly and sanely.

In this chapter, I show the significance of such necessary planning and how to prepare a schematic representation or diagram of a project before its start. Then, if one works reflexively and wishes to make changes during the project, this diagram may be used as an audit trial (Morse & Niehaus, 2009) to keep the project in control and to maintain rigor. Here I use a qualitatively-driven project examining the role of stigma in the diagnosis and treatment of lung cancer. I will work through a project, so readers can see that the process is not a blind, fumbling in the dark, hit-or-miss endeavor. On the other hand, while it appears to have a definite process, the order of the research process also allows for reflexivity, additions, and changes of direction.

Qualitatively-Driven Mixed-Method Design

Mixed-method design consists of a complete, cohesive core component (or project), with an additional supplementary component[1] or strategy

(Morse 1991, 2003). We must think of mixed-method design as one-and-a-half studies; the supplemental component uses strategies that add data, which cannot be accessed by the core component, but is not a complete project in itself.[2] Thus mixed-method designs increase the scope, and possibly the dimensions, of the project. They provide an answer to an additional subquestion, often a question that is significant to the project as a whole but that cannot be answered by the core project alone. By answering a secondary, accompanying question (or questions), the supplemental component makes the project better and broader, adds depth, and saves the researcher the trouble of conducting a second study to answer the supplemental question. The great benefit of mixed-method design is that, if done well, it enables a means for inquiry to move forward more quickly, efficiently, and as effectively as possible.

Because these different data are an incompatible analytic fit, the supplementary component cannot be incorporated into the core component until the results are separately analyzed. Examples of "incompatible analytic fit" include designs in which the results of two different qualitative analytic techniques (QUAL-*qual*) are deliberately brought together and integrated as a narrative report. For example, there may be

1. different types of data, requiring a different mode of analysis, most commonly numerical data and textual data. But there may be observational data, photographs, documents, maps, or anything that requires different handling or mode of analysis.

2. different levels of analysis—for instance, group data and micro-analytic data.

3. different groups that cannot be combined but are discussed separately to meet the needs of a research question: male and female, individual data and family data, data from a different ethnic groups, or data from two time periods.

The defining characteristic of mixed-method design is that the findings of the two different types of data are bought together in the results narrative to build expanded results. Another important characteristic of mixed-method designs is its *internal design*—an organized process and procedure that prevents threats to rigor when two different types of data (in this example, qualitative and quantitative data) are being used. These organizations of internal design processes and procedures are dissimilar from those used in

ethnography: ethnography involves more "thinking on your feet" and grants the researcher total flexibility during data collection and analyses and with outcomes that often cannot be foreseen at the outset. On the other hand, the internal design of mixed-method designs allows for much more predictability, organization, and control. The major design is determined with the writing of the proposal, apart from relatively minor additional supplemental components that are added as a results if *dynamic reflexivity* and questions that arise from the ongoing analysis of the QUAL component. The additional supplementary components may be added at the completion of the project (sequential) or partway through the conduct of the core QUAL component.[3]

Does Stigma Interfere With Diagnosis and Treatment of Lung Cancer?

To illustrate the design and construction of mixed-method, let's consider the development of a qualitatively-driven study by setting up a fake project. It is "fake" because smoking, stigma, and lung cancer are not my areas of expertise, and I do not want anyone to use this project based on my meager and superficial knowledge of the topic; please excuse any substantive errors. The purpose of my diving into this area is simply to show how to think through a project when designing a mixed-method study.

Qualitatively-driven designs are those designs in which the core component is qualitative, the overall thrust is inductive, and the aim is usually that of discovery. In qualitatively-driven designs, the core component of the study is qualitative (QUAL), and the minor supplemental component(s) may be quantitative (*quan*), qualitative (*qual*) or even both. Note that the core component is represented by uppercase letters, and the supplemental component is represented by lowercase italics.

Identifying the Aim

Research always begins with a hunch, and this hunch becomes (or is modified postliterature review) to form the *aim*. Supposing we have a hunch that people who smoke and have been diagnosed with lung cancer feel responsible for causing their own disease, yet they are unable to stop smoking. As a result, they hide their smoking behaviors, do not accurately report these to physicians when asked, and cognitively diminish or deny that the relationship in the risks between smoking and lung cancer is applicable in their case. If they do recognize this relationship, they feel ashamed and self-stigmatized but cannot stop smoking. They are also stigmatized by the health providers, who feel frustrated that the people they are trying to help are not helping themselves.

So our first articulation of the aim is to explore the doctor–patient relationship with people who smoke and are undergoing treatment for lung cancer. This aim is not carved in stone but only serves to guide our review of the literature. As we analyze that literature, and as our thinking on this topic matures, we can modify the aim.

The Literature

Next we retrieve the literature—a huge pile of research. In looking to see what is known, we examine both qualitative and quantitative inquiries, conducting a content analysis of these articles. Briefly, we learn that the relationship between and lung cancer is well established, yet 50% of lung cancer patients are smokers at the time of diagnosis, and, of these, 83% continue to smoke during treatment (Cataldo, Dubey, & Prochaska, 2010). Those who continue to smoke double their risk of dying (Parsons, Daley, Begh, & Aveyard, 2010).

It is evident that the focus of the social science research has been on smoking cessation, but quitting smoking causing stress and emotional distress. For the highly dependent smoker, smoking-cessation programs combining intensive behavioral and pharmaceutical interventions may be helpful, but according to Parsons et al. (p. 289), by 2010 only three inconclusive studies had been conducted with lung cancer patients.

A cluster of studies about the stigmatization of smoking exist. As public health policies increased to limit smoking ("denormalization"; Bell, Salmon, Bowers, Bell, & McCullough, 2010) increased, negative responses of others toward the smokers led to the "internalization of stigma and self-blame" in the smokers (Else-Quest, LoConte, Schiller, & Hyde, 2009). Clearly, smoking during lung cancer treatments becomes a stigmatized state, both within oneself and derived from the attitudes of others toward the smoker (Lebel & Devins, 2008; Stuber, Galea, & Link, 2008). Within patients, qualitative researchers have documented feelings of stigma, shame, and blame in persons who continue to smoke with lung cancer (Chapple, Ziebland, & McPherson, 2004). This stigma may be so strong as to result in delay of seeking diagnosis and treatment (Tod, Craven, & Allmark, 2008).

At this point, the perspective in the literature is clear. With few exceptions, these studies focus on the patient (although Bottorff, Robinson, Sullivan, & Smith, 2009, did include family relations); few have explored the impact of stigma on treatment and its influence on the therapeutic relationship during treatments. Inequities in stigma related to asbestos-related lung cancer have been reported between physician specialties (Verge et al., 2008). But the effects of the health provider stigma, how the patient perceives this, and how it interferes with the treatment protocol have not been studied, at least for the purposes of this illustration.

Theoretical Perspective

Qualitative research questions are not neutral, but they invariably have an underlying and/ or embedded value, providing the researcher with a theoretical lens through which data are viewed and the analysis interpreted. In this way, the theoretical perspective is a type of bias because the reason one is conducting the study underlies the questions. These questions direct how and where the researcher focuses the data and, in turn, directs which data are considered more important than other data. Most important, the theoretical perspective is the organizing frame for reporting the data and determining its ramifications. This perspective must be considered a conscious bias and deliberate bias; if unrecognized, a theoretical perspective is harmful, for as Popper (1963) noted, it is invalid to subconsciously *prove* a point using inductive methods. Therefore some researchers, particularly phenomenologists, deliberately *bracket* these assumptions (van Manen, 1990, 2014) and enter the field as blank slate, trusting their analysis to inductive processes.

In our case, our theoretical perspective is in relation to stigma: we assume that the physicians have been taught that smoking causes lung cancer, yet some patients who smoke and who have lung cancer will not stop smoking, despite the fact that research shows that continuing smoking decreases their prognosis (Parsons et al., 2010). This makes for an extremely frustrating experience for physicians—I have even discovered a patient sneaking a cigarette in the hospital, within the proximity of oxygen.

Refining the Questions

Having made a theoretical argument justifying the exploration of stigma and its impact on care, this position must be argued logically in the literature review and must be reflected in the aim and in the research question(s). Our arguments force us to use a comparative design, comparing those with and without the undesirable behavior (smoking) in the core component, and to analyze our data accordingly. We must be able to show differences between groups.

Thus, having made this decision, we must now revisit our aim and our questions. The first aim was

> To explore the doctor–patient relationship in smokers undergoing treatment for lung cancer.

A refocused aim clarifies the purpose of the study:

> To explore stigma in the doctor–patient relationship with patients who are smokers undergoing treatment for lung cancer.

Thus our research question for the QUAL component will be

> What is the experience of stigma in the doctor–patient relationship when patients who smoke are undergoing treatment for lung cancer?

The Armchair Walkthrough

In research, thinking always precedes the doing. Whenever planning a study, one must first identify the overall purpose (the aim) and, at the same time, decide what one expects or needs to know at the end of the study. Research is always guided; the beginning and ends must match. That is, one must deliberately set up the study to answer the research question, so that it is supported (explained) or not supported with an alterative explanation presented in the results. This procedure does not invalidate the study by making a qualitative study deductive or biased; it simply gives it a goal and endpoint. Of course, in qualitative inquiry, while we recognize that the study question may be modified or changed once the study begins, so may the endpoint be altered, discarded, or downsized and made more achievable. However, this is done with deliberation and care, not spontaneously in a fit of despair. For instance:

> Our purpose in this study may be to explore the doctor–patient relationship where doctors are caring for patients who smoke and are undergoing treatment for lung cancer. We came to this topic by examining the literature within our area of interest. The goal is to study the ways in which stigma is manifest as the patients' feeling of shame and self-stigma and how the physicians'

own stigmatizing behaviors are evident in their behavior interfering with the provision of care for lung cancer patients. By the end of the study, we hope to show that all patients are treated equally, while considering the patients' feelings of self-stigma or the physician stigmatizing the patient. Note that this is a kind of a null hypothesis that if disproved will demonstrate clearly the nature of the effects of stigma on the relationship of doctor and lung cancer patients who smoke.

At this stage, the researchers must decide on the theoretical rationale of their study. Our interest is in stigma and its impact on care. This perspective has ramifications for the entire design: how the interview questions are asked, the sampling, the analysis, and how the results are presented. The theoretical rationale is not something that is simply written in at the front of the article—qualitative inquiry theory runs right through the project. It has implications for how data are collected and analyzed and the way the results are presented. This is an aspect that distinguishes a qualitatively-driven mixed-method design from a quantitatively driven design. In quantitative designs, the investigator keep theory out of the method component, for this is actually a part of what is being tested.

Already we know that our design will be comparative, for, by the end of the study, we must be able to demonstrate differences between the stigmatization of smokers (both from the self and from the physicians) from nonsmokers. Therefore, we will compare a group of nonsmokers (preferably those who have never smoked) who have lung cancer and are undergoing the same treatment as smokers with lung cancer.

Once we have identified the aim, the main question, and where we plan to finish the study, the next task is much less frightening, which is to develop the questions and identifying methods that will give the necessary data. The researcher's questions are developed directly from the aim. Our main research question, "What is the experience of stigma in the doctor–patient relationship when patients who smoke are undergoing treatment for lung cancer?" has the following question for the core component: "Will the physicians' stigmatizing of smokers with lung cancer impact the care of patients who smoke and who have lung cancer?" This question will be addressed in the core component.

THE CORE COMPONENT

The core component is a cohesive component (or project) that is a complete project. It is publishable alone as a single qualitative study (or quantitative, if that is the case; Morse 1991, 2003). Thus for the QUAL component, we could adequately address the first question regarding the experience of stigma in the doctor–patient relationship by using unstructured interviews with physicians, as well as nonsmoking and smoking patients with lung cancer. The method we choose to elicit rich description and interpretation is interpretative description (Thorne, 2008). We will conduct unstructured recorded exploring for differences in their care of patients with lung cancer, those who smoke and those who do not smoke. Because suggesting that the care provider may stigmatize a particular patient group (which is not a desirable aspect of care to explore), the necessary information may not be obtained from the interviews with the physicians, who may consciously or unconsciously conceal or cover their actual beliefs and practices. Therefore we will also observe physician–patient interactions and interview patient smokers and nonsmokers who are undergoing lung cancer treatment. Do we have to observe the same patients that we interview? No—in fact it will be better if we do not, for if there is a change in the physicians' behavior because of the study, then this will be a confounding factor in the design.

These interviews, conducted in the three groups of participants, will each be analyzed separately (i.e., physicians, the patients who smoke, and the nonsmoking patients). Once the three groups have been analyzed, we will compare each of the results of the physician interaction with the patients who smoke to with the patients who do not smoke. This will provide us with a solid database of the *perceived* presence or absence of caregiver stigma.

But we still have one threat to validity. If we apply institutional review board (IRB) ethical approval, the physicians and the patients may be able to surmise that we are looking for discriminations in care. Will this bias the study? Certainly there will be bias (Morse, 2006, 2008). Therefore, we must create a more neutral title, develop a new explanation for the consent form, argue for the use of neutrality with the IRB, and develop a debriefing program for all participants (physicians and patients) after the study.

The core component, QUAL, serves as the theoretical drive for the project. The entire study (both the core and the supplementary component) will be

considered inductive (Morse, Niehaus, Wolfe, & Wilkins, 2006). This encompasses even the supplementary *quan* component, because it adds detail to the QUAL component. Most important, the inductive theoretical drive is primary in the integration of the results in the results narrative.

THE SUPPLEMENTARY *quan* COMPONENT

At this point we have designed the study without quantitative data. As a part of the armchair walkthrough,[4] we now determine what can be "added" to build the necessary quantitative data by adding "supplemental components." In a mixed-method design, it is the supplemental project that adds the comprehensiveness or information that cannot be obtained from the core component. Thus the supplemental component further expands and enriches the scope of the study. This expansion is not possible when using a single method or the core component alone, but it is our role to make certain that the core and the supplemental projects are complementary and will fit together in the analysis.

The supplementary project answers a research subquestion, but this question is usually quite narrow in scope and more limited than questions used for the core component. This supplementary component cannot stand alone—it is not saturated, it lacks major significance, and, importantly, it is not interpretable without reference to the core component. It does not pass the acid test, which means that it is not publishable alone. If the supplementary component is quantitative (*quan*), it may consist of scores—even single measures—that will illuminate some aspect of the core QUAL component.

The tricky question is how complete should the supplemental project be? The answer depends on the research goals (and supplemental question[s]) and how the component will be used in support of the core. Note that the subquestions developed for the supplementary component are narrow and specific. If one has a *qual* supplementary component, it may be used simultaneously to develop case studies, exemplars, and examples in order to answer questions that are beyond the reach of the core method or for sequentially clarifying questions that have arisen from the core. Remember, these questions are usually narrow and specific; if not, researchers may find themselves conducting an entire separate study (and a multimethod design). The important point is that the interviews, focus groups, observations, and so on are conducted only until the researcher is *certain* about the answer needed for the supplementary question (Morse & Maddox, 2014). Saturation

(Morse, 2004) is not the goal, for if saturation were reached, the supplemental project would then have developed into a complete project and the design transformed to a multiple methods project. Rather, again, the criterion of *certainty* is used when the answer is adequate for the study purposes, makes sense, fits with other emerging ideas, and has been confirmed in secondary interviews or in the pertinent literature (Morse & Maddox, 2014).

DETERMINING THE SUPPLEMENTAL QUESTIONS

Recognizing that the QUAL core will provide us with the subjective descriptions, our next task is to add indicators that the care of the two groups of patients (those who smoke and those who do not) are being treated the same or differently. What quantitative measures will reveal differences in treatment?

We wonder if there would be a difference in the duration of the physician–patient contact time. Our theoretical rationale for expecting differences is that physicians may take more time interacting with patients with whom they feel are more worthwhile.

RQ S1: *What is the duration of the physician–patient visit, from the time the physician enters the room until he or she leaves?*

We will obtain these data from our observations in the clinic, sorted by physician and by patient status as a smoker or nonsmoker.

We examine the literature and notice that Veger et al. (2008) found that physicians were less likely to recommend filing lung cancer claims for patients who were smokers. We decide to add this as a *quan* indicator in our design.

RQ S2: *Are there differences in the filing claims for asbestos-related lung cancer between smoker and nonsmokers?*

We will use recorded data for all physicians in the study from the previous two years, for all newly diagnosed lung cancer patients, by physician and sorting the data by smoking and nonsmoking. There may be other quantitative measures to add, and there are no restrictions on these components, provided one has a theoretical rationale for adding each one.

Finally, we will create a form to record patients' demographic data, including smoking history. In some studies there may be comparisons by variables, such as gender or other demographic factors, but in this study we will use these data only for describing the participants.

CONTEXT

Next we select the context for the study: one site, or two, or three? The context is often closely considered in relation to sample size. How many physicians are seeing clinic patients at each site? We know we must collect data until data are saturated, and, as each physician will have a caseload, we decide we must observe at least five physicians as they provide care to a number of lung cancer patients, and it will be necessary to enter three sites simultaneously. The other disadvantage of using one site is that we will be interviewing and observing only one group of staff. Are the behaviors we are interested in (those in providing care without stigma for smoking patients) "contagious"? That is, is stigmatized care tolerated or modeled in a single setting? However, realizing we may be compromising loss of validity for feasibility; we decide to select three sites, and we will analyze data separately. Data collection with the core data will continue until we are convinced that there are real differences in stigmatizing behaviors.

SAMPLE

We decided to sort the data into three groups: physicians and two groups of patients. We decided not to sort data further by gender or ethnicity, as each of these groups would have to be saturated, and by then our sample would be too large to be feasible. Our study design, thus far, is:

QUAL: Interviews with physicians, patients who smoke, patients who do not smoke, and observations of the physician-patient interaction. *quan 1*: the time of physician-patient consultations and *quan 2* a comparison of the number of claims filed for smokers and nonsmokers.

A core data set (QUAL) is the interviews and observations, and two supplemental data sets that will be conducted simultaneously during the same time period as the interviews are being conducted and analyzed. The *design* notation for this project will be QUAL + *quan* + *quan* design. With three groups of participants, we ask: How many participants? How many observations?

Adequacy of the interview data occurs in two stages. The first is a discovery stage, in which stories of giving or receiving care will be obtained, and the researcher is busy finding out what is going on. Later, once the researcher has developed a theoretical scheme, sampling becomes more directed and is aimed at confirming hunches and verifying thin data. For the purposes of our proposal, we overestimate the number of participants (especially if applying for funding) because one never knows at the proposal stage exactly how many participants will be needed. So we estimate 15 physicians and 30 patient participants in each group and hope that saturation occurs earlier rather than later in the data collection and analysis. This will give us 75 interviews. Observations are estimated in number of hours during clinic days. If the clinic schedules 20 patients per physician per 4-hour clinic, we estimate 100 hours of observations, which will give us observations on 500 patients.

Diagramming the Study

Once we have identified most of the crucial design features, the next step is to prepare a diagram of the study (see Creswell & Plano Clark, 2007; Hesse-Biber, 2010, p. 110, Morse, 2003; Morse & Maddox, 2014) to visualize and communicate the study design. A diagram allows one to quickly view all to the components of the study, their relationship to all components, and how they will be paced—that is, how they relate to one another and the order in which they will be conducted.

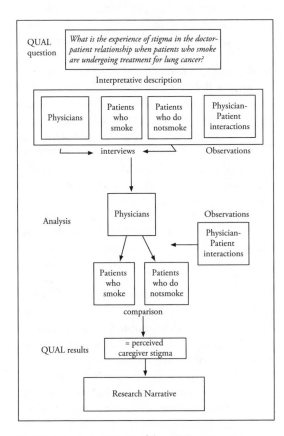

Fig. 12.1 Analytic strategies of the QUAL component.

DIAGRAMMING THE QUAL CORE

Whether an inductive or deductive theoretical drive and core component, these flow charts are read from the top down. The QUAL component is outlined on Figure 12.1. Note that this diagram is the normal research process for any qualitative study. So far, there is nothing complex or new here.

For our study we have shown the three groups to be interviewed and that each group of interviews will be analyzed separately. These observations are initially kept separate, but as we write our findings from the interviews and compare and contrast what we have seen in each group, we will add our findings from the interview studies to support or contradict the interviews. This will be the first part of the analysis. Note how diagramming makes these procedures less muddled and the researchers less confused.

THE SUPPLEMENTAL COMPONENTS

At first glance the supplemental data appears complex. For RQ S1 and to calculate the average consultation time by the patients smoking status, we need to obtain the amount of time (in minutes) from when the physician enters the patient's room until he or she leaves the room. We will combine this time for all physicians by patient smoking status and that will give us two values: the average length of time spent consulting with smoking and with nonsmoking patients with lung cancer. It will not give us time consulting with other physicians or reviewing the chart.

The filing of asbestos-related claims comparing patients smoking status is also difficult, because the filing is a relatively rare event. To answer RQ S2 and determine differences in filing status, we need to find a governmental database that can provide these data nationally and state by state. We request data on the number of cases of lung cancer reported for two years by smoking status and the number of asbestos claims filed for a period of two years by patients' smoking status. These epidemiological data will show the differences between lung cancer patients by smoking status, and the difference in numbers of lung cancer asbestos claims filed by smoking status should provide us with any discrepancies filed by smoking status, as was show in France (Verger et al. 2008). Thus the supplemental components may be observed as shown in Figure 12.2.

POINT OF INTERFACE

Once each data set is analyzed, all data sets are moved to the point of interface and into the results narrative so that all components may contribute to

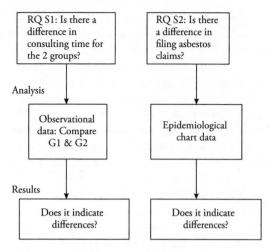

Fig. 12.2 Supplemental *quan* design (*quan* + *quan*).

the analysis. The point of interface is the position in the design where the different type of data from the core and supplemental components are brought together (Morse & Neihaus, 2009). In this case, data are bought together with the analysis of each component completed: the QUAL interview data will be analyzed as narrative data according to the methods of interpretive description (Thorne, 2008). Then we need to analyze data separately by physicians, by smokers and by nonsmokers, and the observational data. We have two scores for physician average times in rooms of lung cancer smoker and nonsmoker patients; we have epidemiological data on the number of physicians filing for asbestos-related claims. At the point of interface, these individual sets of results are now integrated as we write the result in section called the results narrative (see Figure 12.2).

THE RESEARCH NARRATIVE

Now the QUAL results from the interpretive description will tell the story from the synthesized interview data, based on the presence or absence of caregiver stigma. These results will be conceptually rich and dense. By reading these results we will have an understanding of the experiences of physicians providing care and the two groups of lung cancer patients receiving care. If there are no differences, we will be able to show that; if there are, we will be able to describe them.

The QUAL results are written to provide the theoretical base (or the foundational story). The supplemental results from the two *quans* provide supplemental detail of the main story, exemplifying and supporting or expanding the descriptions. We write, integrating the observational data, and as pertinent, the *quan* analysis from RQ 1 and RQ 2, on physician

time and reporting, is integrated into the QUAL narrative wherever appropriate to show that stigma does or does not occur in the care of these patients.

It is important that this integration of findings occurs in the results narrative. Some researchers place this in the discussion, but this integration is the purpose and the strength of the mixed-method design. It is a separate operation, and it must be allotted the necessary space in the article and the highlighting that a separate section provides.

The discussion will be written in the usual form, providing clear information about the unique contribution of this study, how the results fit into others' research, limitations, and implications. The discussion about any new concepts or about the theory and its application is particularly important, as is the discussion about the relationship between the QUAL and the *quan* data. The researcher then makes recommendations for implementation of any findings. Also consider: Is the research more generalizable than a single, stand-alone qualitative study? Is the resulting theory more "solid" than a qualitative study on its own? These are important considerations when a mixed-method study is used. Thus the completed study will be diagrammed as shown in Figure 12.3, but before applying for a grant and doing the study, let's discuss more about the process of doing mixed-method research.

Reflexivity and the Use of the Proposal Diagram While Conducting the Research

While the investigator may have research design plans at the beginning of the study, insights that occur during the course of the project often waylay, divert, or alter the course of the inquiry. Once beneath the superficial layer of a problem and doing the analysis of the QUAL interviews, researchers find that projects that appeared straightforward at the time of the literature review and proposal writing suddenly become complex and confusing—yet intriguing—and researchers are often compelled to add components to the design. This is what reflexivity is all about: letting the problem lead the design.

As stated earlier, when conducting a qualitatively-driven mixed-method study, the proposal appears rigid and fixed. But to a seasoned qualitative researcher, this is not so. The inductive nature of doing a qualitative study makes the conduct of research rather like a life-size puzzle. With QUAL mixed-method, designs are particularly adaptable. If the early interviews indicated interesting and relevant findings, then the researcher "follows his (or her) nose" within the QUAL component.

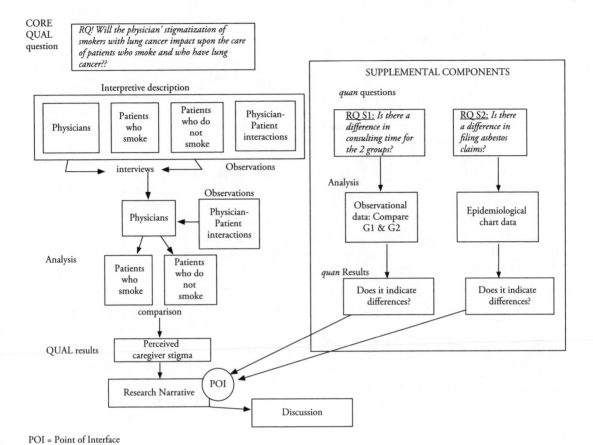

CORE QUAL question

RQ! Will the physician' stigmatization of smokers with lung cancer impact upon the care of patients who smoke and who have lung cancer??

SUPPLEMENTAL COMPONENTS

Interpretive description

Physicians | Patients who smoke | Patients who do not smoke | Physician-Patient interactions

interviews → Observations

Observations

Physicians ← Physician-Patient interactions

Analysis

Patients who smoke | Patients who do not smoke

comparison

QUAL results

Perceived caregiver stigma

Research Narrative → POI

Discussion

quan questions

RQ S1: *Is there a difference in consulting time for the 2 groups?*

RQ S2: *Is there a difference in filing asbestos claims?*

Analysis

Observational data: Compare G1 & G2 | Epidemiological chart data

quan Results

Does it indicate differences? | Does it indicate differences?

POI = Point of Interface

Fig. 12.3 Proposed complete mixed method project design.

But more important, if the researcher identifies an interesting part of the data for which a supplemental measure would assist with clarifying, the researcher can add a supplemental component, a *quan* or *qual* at that time—of course, subject to the appropriate permissions and IRB approvals. Thus a QUAL-*quan* mixed-method design has all of the advantages of reflexivity associated with qualitative research *and* the freedom to add confirming quantitative measures. This characteristic makes mixed-method designs powerful.

With the QUAN component in our lung cancer project, as the study progresses and as the early findings are verified, we develop understanding and a new question arises. Practicing reflexivity, if the findings indicate that we should look in another direction, we have the freedom to do so, and we may add another supplemental component.

When adding a supplemental component midway through, a new subquestion must be identified, and we again walk through the new design. We consider what data might be required to answer the new question, what sample is necessary and

acceptable (and what size may be needed), how these data will be analyzed, the point of interface, and how these results will fit into the results analysis. These design issues must always be decided before applying to the IRB for permission to expand the study.

Diagramming Mixed-Method Designs

Adding components to a mixed-method design in progress may make the mixed-method project go out of control very quickly. There are two golden rules:

1. *Add a component only if certain that the results will facilitate the inquiry.* The additional component has to be worth all of the work that it entails, and often the supplemental components may rapidly resemble a new study. On the other hand, a supplemental sequential component (one added at the end of a core component) may circumvent the necessity to conduct a new and separate study. It may provide the remaining answer to a question needed to move onto the next full study.

2. Use the flow chart diagram as an audit trial, even as a wall chart if necessary. On it, write all research questions, samples, and all details. Keep it up-to-date.

The Role of qual *in a QUAN Project*

Suppose we had set up the previously described lung cancer/stigma project as a quantitative study, QUAN, with a supplementary *qual* component. How would that have changed the role of the *qual*?

QUAN mixed-methods designs have a deductive theoretical drive. They are designed to test or to measure. The role of the *qual* supplementary component is for illustration, to elicit information that is not otherwise obtainable using a quantitative method, and to investigate phenomena that cannot be otherwise measured.

ILLUSTRATION

Researchers often wish to complement the quantitative analysis by providing exemplars to illustrate the main findings, for instance, to add explanation or to illustrate by adding the participant's voice. This is the most common use of qualitative data in quantitative research. Unfortunately, data obtained is often thin, with the sample size too small, and a superficial "cherry-picking" analysis. Reasons for adding a *qual* component include

1. To investigate the immeasurable. When using quantitative scales or tools, often some aspect of the phenomena cannot be measured. For example, because one cannot identify all of the answers as preselected clusters, a questionnaire, or even a forced-choice survey may have some areas that cannot be included in the QUAN portion, and several open-ended semi-structured questions may be used to obtain data that would otherwise leave a gap. Therefore, the *qual* component consists of semistructured questions designed to elicit this missing information.

In this case, a QUAN questionnaire is being administered to a large sample along with the several *qual* unstructured supplemental questions (see endnote 1). The responses to these unstructured questions are cumbersome for qualitative analysis, even content analysis, due to the large sample size used in the core component. It is therefore recommended that these open-ended questions be transposed to numerical data and used as an analytic point of interface, creating a new variable in the quantitative data set and transferring the coded responses into the data set for quantitative analysis (Morse & Neihaus, 2009).

2. To elicit unobtainable information. This happens frequently in a particular area or part of the questionnaire that is not amenable to quantitative analysis, as this area is too broad or complex to be covered by several semistructured questions, as suggested earlier. For instance, if the researcher does not know and cannot develop choices in the structured questionnaire, he or she is forced to use an open-ended questionnaire. When conducting *qual*, researchers usually use unstructured interviews that, while open ended, are quite targeted (or narrow), focusing on the particular information that is needed in the study. Others may use focus groups to elicit opinions. Alternatively with a sequential design, the researcher needs an explanation for some unexpected findings from the QUAN components.

QUAN-qual EXAMPLE

Already we have problem, because we cannot locate a measure of caregiver stigma toward patients with lung cancer who smoke. (Remember, we do qualitative studies because we cannot find a measure for what we want to investigate.) So we will refocus our study, with the aim focused on *patients* with lung cancer, rather than on the differential care of caregivers. Thus the revised QUAN-qual aim is: *To explore the perceptions of self-stigma in patients who are presently smoking, former smokers, and nonsmokers, who are undergoing treatment for lung cancer and impact of their smoking behaviors on received care.* First, the QUAN core research question will have to be revised as a quantitative question:

R Q1: *Are there are differences in perceived stigma in patients undergoing treatment for lung cancer who continue to smoke compared with patients who have stopped smoking and those who have never smoked?*

There will be two *qual* subquestions, with the physicians' "management of care" and the patients perceptions of care received.

RQ S1: *What are the expressed attitudes of physicians toward "managing" the care for patients who smoke, former smokers, and nonsmokers, while being treated for lung cancer?*

RQ S2: *What are the perceptions of the quality of care received by patients with lung cancer who are smokers, former smokers, and those who have never smoked?*

As we reconceptualize this study we realize that we must first increase its scope in order to have an adequate sample for the QUAN core component. We therefore decide to use a sample of patients drawn from the support website for patients "Living with Lung Cancer."

(a) For the QUAN component, we will need a measure of stigma from an adequate sample of patients presently undergoing therapy for lung cancer who continue to smoke and also from patients who are former smokers and nonsmokers. We identify the Cataldo Lung Cancer Stigma Scale (Cataldo, Slaughter, Jahan, Pongquan, & Hwang, 2011).

(b) For the *qual* supplemental component, we know the QUAN sample is too large for the *qual* data but realize we must use the same *population* as approached for the QUAN component. We decide to use focus groups to obtain data about the perceived care provided (RQ S1) and the patients' perceptions of care received (RQ S2). Therefore we decide that the *qual* supplemental component to elicit physicians' perceptions of care may be obtained from physicians attending the annual convention of pulmonary oncologists. We decide to conduct two focus groups each attended by 8 to 10 physicians.

Thus, the focus group samples of patients (RQ S2) may be solicited from patients attending the annual meeting for the support of oncology patients and their families. We recruit patients from the conference attendees who are undergoing treatment for lung cancer and who have smoked or are presently smoking. We prepare guiding questions to ask about their experiences as patients who continue to smoke or who have recently smoked and who are undergoing treatment. Because we do not saturate these data but rather collect data until we are certain of the results, we initially plan to conduct four focus groups (two with presently smokers and two with former smokers). We will use these data to develop themes that will illustrate the core QUAN findings.

How will we compile and write the results of the study? First, all data sets are analyzed separately. Because the study is quantitatively driven, the quantitative results provide the *base* of the description. Scores may be presented in the results narrative by comparing the scores of the present smokers with the scores of the former smokers, or by high and lower scores on the Stigma and Shame subscale. The *qual* focus group findings are used

to add description, quotations, and even exemplars that may have been offered in the focus groups. The two data sets should be compatible—that is, there should not be large discrepancies between the two sets of data. In the discussion section, these results are linked to the literature.

Deviations in Design and Other Pitfalls

In this section, I address some common and less obvious difficulties and confusions that occur in mixed-method designs.

What Is the Best Way to Make Mixed-Method Design Clear to the Reader?

Mixed-method design is confusing. First, without diagramming, there is a lack of clarity, which may even result in the misidentification of the theoretical drive of the project. Major problems include confusing the study context with the theoretical drive and the methodological components. Identifying the study components by diagramming assists the researcher in avoiding confusion about the design. For instance, in medical sciences, several investigators have conducted studies exploring randomized control trials (RCTs) using embedded designs. The RCT is, of course, then considered the quantitative core, QUAN, designed to determine the effectiveness of a certain drug. The purpose of the additional supplemental *quan* components is, for instance, to qualitatively explore the experience of participating in the trial.

The qualitative components are erroneously described as a *supplemental* (embedded) design, so the entire project is called quantitatively driven, with the RCT as the dominant component (QUAN + *qual* + *qual*) and may be diagrammed illustrating the RCT as the dominant component.

However, this design has two problems:

1. In the clinical setting, the RCT design determines when data are collected for both the QUAN and the *qual* components—which is when the participants attend for data collection for the RCT. However, often investigators fail to recognize that the RCT is actually the *context* of the study, that the RCT does not *drive* the qualitative components, and that the RCT's regulation of the sampling is only circumstantial and contextual.Actually, all clinical qualitative inquiry is "constrained" by the routines of examinations, treatments, diagnostic tests, patients' condition, care practices, meal times, and even visitors. In this case, sampling was dictated by the RCT treatment schedules.

2. In these studies, the placebos in the QUAN component means there is no interaction or *dynamic reflectivity* between QUAN and the *qual* components, so there is no characteristic of a mixed-method (or "embedded") study; there are no points of interface between the QUAN and the *qual* components and no complementary integration of these components in the research narrative, thus an essential characteristic of a mixed-method study is missing.

The study is actually a qualitative mixed-method study (QUAL + *qual*) exploring the experience of participating in a quantitative RCT, not a QUAN + *qual* design.

Remember: if a study is to fit the criteria of a mixed-method, it must meet the following criteria: At the end of the data analysis of the qualitative subcomponents, the results must be brought to the point of interface and merged with the QUAN results. It is not enough to simply make recommendations from the *qual* supplementary component about the QUAN component. In mixed-method design these components must be integrated.

Must Mixed-Method Projects Have an Internal Design?

Some researchers may or may not have a developed design when conducting mixed-method research, but my students complain that they cannot determine from the written descriptions of the design, particularly when there is no diagram, what design has actually been used. Subsequently, attempting to diagram these studies, we have identified several problems.

THE JELLYFISH DESIGN

These studies look beautiful, but there is no real form. The results are reported without any link to the methods. The reader cannot discern how and from where each finding was developed. An audit trial would not be helpful because the researcher has not linked the result with the method, and because several strategies different analyses were used, the reader is forced to take the results at face value.

MISH-MASH DESIGN

Can a mixed-method design exist without a core project? Can all of the components be incomplete, simply as a collection of supplemental components? Perhaps. Let us consider the case of evaluation research. Here the evaluator must use sets of data provided or requested, depending on what one is evaluating. But for each of these pieces of data or data sets, the evaluator has an external criterion, perhaps of adequacy or excellence. Or he or she may have an overall statement of objectives or even a mission statement. In these cases the external criterion plays an important role and the "supplemental" data sets are evaluated against these criteria.

But in a research mixed-method project, a core is essential for validity of the project. As I have defined "supplemental project" here, as a strategy and using criteria of *certainty* rather than saturation for completion, then even a collection of supplemental projects are nothing more than glimpses or suggestions, without the contextualization of the core project.

Consequences of mish-mashing are important. There is the "This is what I found design" in which the components are not integrated, and the findings are written as simply a collection of findings, and not integrated with one another. There is no attempt at theory building, and often the findings are not linked with the literature.

Do the Result Narratives in Mixed-Method Qualitative Research Need to Have a Core Method as the Theoretical Backbone?

The core project provides the supplemental component with the necessary methodological context to be a complete project. It is within the core component that the supplemental findings "make sense." The point of interface, for most of these designs, is in the results narrative rather than integration in the analysis.

The core project—the complete method—is first analyzed as a single component. Similarly the *qual* or *quan* supplemental component are analyzed apart from the core component. Then the two (or more) sets of results are merged, that is, brought together, in a separate section of the article in the results narrative. The core component becomes the foundation for the writing of the results. The core results "tell the story" in a cohesive manner answering the research question for that component, with the supplemental component (*qual* or *quan*) adding essential detail. It is not possible to write the results by inverting this relationship and trying to make the supplemental component serve as the theoretical base. One frequent mistake is when researchers neglect to write the supplemental *quan* results as a cohesive narrative (or even the findings of a QUAN project) but rather to present results and an unconnected collection of facts.

Can We Have Equally Weighted Components?

Using the definitions in this chapter and elsewhere (Morse, 1991), two core (complete) components would be classified as a multiple methods study, not a mixed-method study.

Consider: if it is a mixed-methods study, must the supplementary component always contribute to the core component? Or can the core and the supplemental components both be somehow integrated and given equal weight in the results narrative? This question is easily answered with mixed-method designs, for one of the two components is a complete project and directly supports the study aim. The core component must, therefore, always provide the theoretical base. The supplemental component is used to enhance the description of the core component. The components cannot be equally weighted.

This question of equal weight is more difficult with multiple method design, in which both components are complete. The answer lies in the aim, and the primary overall research question dictates which project forms the theoretical base in the results narrative, which is usually a separate article.

Even with multiple method designs, the overall aim determines the theoretical thrust of the research program as inductive or deductive. Even quantitative projects under the rubric of a QUAL aim fit into the criteria for an inductive QUAL theoretical thrust, with the overall writing of the results as explanation.

Perhaps one exception is when, for instance, the investigator is comparing males and females in a multiple methods design, with one project conducted on each gender. Such a study may be considered multiple methods, equally weighted—or it may not be considered a multiple methods project at all but simply a comparative study.

Can a Project Begin with a Supplementary Project?

Sometimes we see a design that is written as *qual* → QUAN, with the first study presented as a minor component, in terms of the amount of work involved. Examples are

(a) A "few" focus groups that precede a community survey. The focus groups are used to determine the sampling frames, and the appropriateness of and instruments, and to pilot the instrument.

(b) Focus groups that are used to analyze and to create an instrument. The focus groups

determine the theoretical structure of the instrument, hypothesized factors, the items, and even the wording of the items.

In both of these cases, the rigor of the entire project rests on the "few focus groups." Those data are providing the overall theoretical foundation for the study. Granted the *product* of the study will be emerging from the *quantitative* component, but the quality of the instrument relies on the first component. The theoretical drive designation does not arise (or is awarded) from the component that is the most work or actually creates the instrument but on the theory on which is created. If the qualitative component is theoretically significant and required to develop the quantitative component, such designs must be treated as QUAL → *quan*. Therefore, *qual* → QUAN designs are mislabeled, and the contribution of the qualitative component to the research undervalued.

What Is the Consequence of Compartmentalizing Components?

Often the two components of the mixed-methods design are not integrated following their analysis in the narrative results section but remain separate throughout the entire project: These are discussed in separate sections in the methods and results and are not integrated by the researcher even in the discussion. As such they do not meet the criteria for a mixed-method project.

Worse, some authors confuse the terms *mixed-method* and *multiple methods* and publish their works in pieces, in different journals, sometimes not even referencing the other journals but teasing the reader with, "This is a part of the mixed-methods study. . . ." They may not even provide references for the readers to track the other parts of the study.

Can QUAL—qual *Share the Same Data?*

Only under special circumstances can QUAL-*qual* share the same data. In this case the method for each is distinctive and very different. For example, the core may be grounded theory, with some of the data consisting of videotaped data, and the *qual* may be conversational analysis, developed from the dialogue from the same videotapes. Usually, however, mixed-method studies do not use the same data.

On the other hand, the same subjects may be used. In QUAL-*quan* this introduces problems of sample size for the *quan* component, and if the *quan* consists of measures, external comparisons for interpreting the meaning of those measures should be used (Morse, 1991; Morse & Niehaus, 2009, ch. 6). If the study is QUAN-*qual,* the quantitative core sample is too large for qualitative use, and the trick becomes how to select participants for the qualitative component. Some researchers select participants by scores on the quantitative components; others select them by asking the research assistants to select participants according to characteristics usually used in qualitative inquiry, such as the characteristics of a good informant (Spradley, 1979); others draw a new sample from the same subpopulation as used in the QUAN.

Destroying Cohesiveness: Can a Mixed-Method Design Be Published in Components?

With the pressure to publish as many articles as possible to achieve tenure, mixed-method design appears to be something that lends itself naturally for "splitting" the qualitative and the quantitative component into two different publications. Actually this should not be possible with mixed-method designs as they have been defined here—the supplemental component should not be meaningful without the core project. The supplemental, if *qual,* will be considered "thin," "not saturated," and often the reviewers will not be able to see the worth of the study. If *quan,* the study measures may be used for an inadequate *n* in the QUAL sample.[5]

In short, by removing the supplemental component from the core, the researcher destroys the mixed-method aims, and the publication resulting from the core component is more limited (and less interesting) than it would be if it were published as an integrated mixed-method study.

Multiple methods studies are different. Here (as with a research program) each study may be published, and then finally a publication appears integrating all of the studies. In this case, it is important that readers can locate all of the studies. Some research teams give themselves an acronym and use this in the authorship line so that search engines can find all of the threads.

Conclusion

Qualitatively-driven mixed-method designs provide an innovative way for the researcher to make a qualitative case, describing the issue with powerful subjective logic, and at the same time include strong quantitative measures. This dual perspective gives the researcher the tools to provide the theoretical and practical information and the data that will result in change, may be used as a baseline, and may even provide the guidelines for what that change may be. It builds the case and is pragmatic, directive, and powerful.

But mixed-method designs are not without pitfalls. An example of how to do such research was created here to clarify the process for planning a mixed-method study and to clarify the ways to enhance the process.

The importance of diagramming cannot be stressed enough: diagramming keeps the project in control, illustrates the tracing of the theoretical perspective, and describes how the questions were answered throughout. It enables the viewing of all of the project components and clarifies how results of each component are integrated in the results narrative.

Frequent problems and pitfalls that occur when diagramming is *not* used are

- failure to identify the context or the theoretical drive.
- lack of internal design in the project.
- failure to identify the core component.
- neglecting to use dynamic reflexivity.
- initiating the project with the supplemental components; equally weighting the core and the supplemental component.
- writing the project without integration of the results of each component.

Each of these problems is a threat to validity of a mixed-method design. But recall, mixed-methods are defined differently in this chapter than they are in others. If the term *mixed-methods* is being used, not as "one and a half projects" but as two complete methods, (what I refer to as a multiple method design), then some of these problems may not apply. On the other hand, are they really a mixed-method?

Used correctly and wisely, mixed-method design is a powerful design. It has the strengths of qualitative inquiry, that is, the validity of induction, combined with processes of dynamic reflexivity that enable midcourse corrections as new and unexpected findings are revealed. It has the advantages of logic and measurement of quantitative inquiry in answering *how* as well as *how many.* Finally, it moves major ideas and research programs forward, on course, with efficiency.

Future Directions

What difference will mixed-method designs make to health research? The work of the Patient

Centered Outcomes Research Institute (http://www.pcori.org/) is placing calls not only for patient-centered research but for research that incorporates "the patient's voice." Mixed-method design is optimally suited for such an approach, and the Institute is sponsoring grant competitions to facilitate the development of mixed-method designs.

The fact that using mixed-method can expedite a research program is incredibly important at this time of shrinking grant support for research. Diagramming assists reviewers in gaining a quick overview of the project, understanding how the components are interfacing, and determining what the researcher will know and how significant the results will be at the end of the study.

Such a diagram clarifies the text; it does not replace it. The flow chart may contain as many cells are necessary. For instance, if the diagram is to show the overall components of the research and how the different components will be linked, it will be broadly schematic. If, on the other hand the researcher wishes to illustrate sampling decisions, or the intricacies of methods, the diagram will be much more detailed and may even focus on a part of the research process rather than the entire study. Descriptive text may be included in the cells or written beside the diagram. Again, such text clarifies the main text, but the full explanation remains in the body of the text.

I am concerned that the majority of the mixed-method research appears to be quantitatively driven, with a minor qualitative component used to illustrate, rather than allowing the qualitative component to delve into unknown areas with the patient experience. Torrance (2103) has called this "uneasy truce" between qualitative and quantitative researchers that has occurred in the context of mixed-methods. As team research comes to the fore and research grants become larger and more focused, there is a risk that qualitatively-driven mixed-method research will be smothered by quantitatively driven designs (Torrance, 2013). While quantitative researchers reach out to include quantitative researchers in their projects, and as granting bodies insist on the inclusion of the patients' voice (see Patient-Centered Outcomes Research Institute, http://www.pcori.org/about-us/landing/), how this qualitative research is used and contributes to the overall project is a political quagmire. Projects are designed with qualitative researchers serving as principal investigators less often, with the quantitative researchers responsible for minor components within the overall project, perhaps because these projects are still are less likely to be supported by funding agencies. The politics and changing roles between qualitative and quantitative research are still being constantly negotiated despite the rise of mixed-methods and team research.

Overall, mixed-methods continues to be a confusing field with a jumble of overlapping terms. In the future, as quantitative researchers gain facility in qualitative inquiry and appreciative of the strength and contribution of qualitatively-driven mixed-method research. This imbalance will correct itself; meanwhile the linking of qualitative components to quantitative research will remain the major source of funding for qualitative inquiry at the federal level.

Key Points

Researchers must be clear about terminology and design, especially with regard to the following:

• The use of the term *mixed-method*. Use "mixed-method" to apply to designs in which one project is complete and the supplemental component is incomplete, often another strategy used for additional data collection and analysis, and these two components are combined in the results narrative. I use *mixed-method* as the singular form and *mixed-methods* to refer to the entire class of mixed-methods.

• Difficulty of mixed-method design. Mixed-method design is the most of the difficult to conduct. For instance, in QUAN-*qual* design it is difficult to work with a qualitative strategy (rather than a complete method) and to know when to stop data collection. I introduce the term *certainty* rather than *saturation* as criterion for ceasing supplemental data collection.

• The importance of diagramming. Diagramming clarifies the design and illustrates sampling, pacing, points of interface, and the results narrative.

Discussion Questions

1. In an emerging field, it is important that terms and definitions be standardized? Develop a list of pros and cons for standardization.

2. Select two or three published mixed-method studies that have not been diagrammed by the author and diagram them. Compare the details of your design with those of the authors.

3. Select a published study in which the authors have described the supplemental project preceding the core project (i.e., as *qual* → QUAN or *quan* → QUAL). Identify the contribution of the first supplemental component to the project as a whole. Do you agree that the theoretical contribution of the first project is the supplemental or the core component?

Notes

1. Researchers have various definitions for mixed-methods (Leech, 2010): some consider it to be a qualitative and quantitative project, while some refer to my definition as *embedded design* (Greene, Caracelli, & Graham, 1989) or *nested* (Creswell, Klassen, Plano Clark, & Smith, 2011) Here, *mixed-method* design refers to a single project; *multiple methods* to two or more complete projects meeting the same aim; and *mixed-methods* to the entire class of research. I refer to the component in the embedded design as the *supplemental component*.

2. On the other hand, *multiple methods* consist of two or more or complete projects addressing the same topic, and the results of these are combined in a third publication.

3. This design is not a case approach; data are synthesized within groups.

4. The armchair walkthrough is a cognitive process, in which the researcher mentally goes through the project, using if-then statements, so that all the phases of the research may be planned (Morse, 1994).

5. If this occurs, the score from each participant must be compared with population normative scores and not presented as descriptive statistics with the small sample.

References

Bell, K., Salmon, A., Bowers, M., Bell, J., & McCullough, L. (2010). Smoking, stigma and tobacco "denormalization": Further reflections on the use of stigma as a public health tool. A commentary on *Social Science & Medicine. Stigma, Prejudice, Discrimination and Health Special Issue 67*(3). *Social Science & Medicine, 70*(6), 795–799.

Bottorff, J. L., Robinson, C. A., Sullivan, K. M., & Smith, M. L. (2009). Continued family smoking after lung cancer diagnosis: The patient's perspective. *Oncology Nursing Forum, 36*(3), E126–E132. doi 10.1188/09.ONF.E126-E132

Cataldo, J. K., Dubey, S., & Prochaska, J. J. (2010). Smoking cessation: an integral part of lung cancer treatment. *Oncology, 78*(5–6), 289–301. doi: 10.1159/000319937

Cataldo, J. K., Slaughter, R., Jahan, T. M., Pongquan, V. L., & Hwang, W. J. (2011, January). Measuring stigma in people with lung cancer: Psychometric testing of the Cataldo lung cancer stigma scale. In *Oncology Nursing Forum, 38*,(1), pp. E46–E54. doi: 10.1188/11.ONF.E46-E54

Chapple, A., Ziebland, S., & McPherson, A. (2004). Stigma, shame, and blame experienced by patients with lung cancer: qualitative study. *BMJ, 328*(7454), 1470. doi:10.1136/bmj.38111.639734.7C

Creswell, J. W., Klassen, A. C., Plano Clark, V. L., & Smith, K. C. (2011). *Best practices for mixed methods research in the health sciences.* Bethesda, MD: National Institutes of Health.

Creswell, J. W., & Plano Clark, V. L. (2007). *Designing and conducting mixed methods research.* Thousand Oaks, CA: Sage.

Else-Quest, N. M., LoConte, N. K., Schiller, J. H., & Hyde, J. S. (2009). Perceived stigma, self-blame, and adjustment among lung, breast and prostate cancer patients. *Psychology and Health, 24*(8), 949–964.

Greene, J. C., Caracelli, V. J., & Graham, W. F. (1989). Toward a conceptual framework for mixed method evaluation designs. *Educational Evaluation and policy Analysis, 11*(3), 255–274.

Hesse-Biber, S. N. (2010). *Mixed methods research: Merging theory with practice.* NY: Gilford Press.

Lebel, S., & Devins, G. M. (2008). Stigma in cancer patients whose behavior may have contributed to their disease. *Future Oncology, 4*(5), 717–733.

Leech, N. (2010). Interviews with the early developers of mixed methods research. In A. Tashakkori & C. Teddlie (Eds.), *Mixed methodology: Combining qualitative and quantitative approaches.* (pp. 253–274). Thousand Oaks, CA: Sage.

Morse, J. M. (1991). Approaches to qualitative-quantitative methodological triangulation. *Nursing Research, 40*(2), 120–123.

Morse, J. M. (1994). Designing qualitative research. In Y. Lincoln & N. Denzin (Eds.), *Handbook of qualitative inquiry* (pp. 220–235). Menlo Park, CA: Sage.

Morse, J. M. (2003). Principles of mixed and multi-method research design. In A. Tashakkori & C. Teddlie (Eds.), *Handbook of mixed methods in social and behavioral research.* Thousand Oaks, CA: Sage.

Morse, J. M. (2004). Theoretical saturation. In M. Lewis-Beck, A. Bryman, & T. Futing Liao (Eds.), *Encyclopedia of social science research methods* (Vol. 3, pp. 1122–1123). Thousand Oaks, CA: Sage.

Morse, J. M. (2006). Biased reflections: Principles of sampling and analysis in qualitative enquiry. In Jennie Popay (Ed.), *Moving beyond effectiveness in evidence synthesis: Methodological issues in the synthesis of diverse sources of evidence* (pp. 53–60). London, England: HAD.

Morse, J. M. (2008). Does informed consent interfere with induction? *Qualitative Health Research, 18*(4), 439–440. doi:10.1177/1049732307313614.

Morse, J. M., & Maddox, L. (2014). Analytic strategies with qualitative components in mixed method research. In U. Flick (Ed.), *The SAGE handbook of qualitative data analysis.*(pp. 524–539). London, England: Sage.

Morse, J. M., & Niehaus, L. (2009). *Mixed method design: Principles and procedures.* Walnut Creek, CA: Left Coast Press.

Morse, J. M., Niehaus, L., Wolfe, R., & Wilkins, S. (2006). The role of theoretical drive in maintaining validity in mixed method research. *Qualitative Research in Psychology, 3*(4), 279–291.

Parsons, A., Daley, A., Begh, R., & Aveyard, P. (2010). Influence of smoking cessation after diagnosis of early stage lung cancer on prognosis: Systematic review of observational studies with meta-analysis. *BMJ, 340*, b5569.

Popper, K. (1963). *Conjectures and refutations: The growth of scientific knowledge.* New York, NY: Routledge.

Spradley, J. P. (1979). *The ethnographic interview.* New York, NY: Holt, Rienhart & Winston.

Thorne, S. (2008). *Interpretive description.* Walnut Creek, CA: Left Coast Press.

Stuber, J., Galea, S., & Link, B. G. (2008). Smoking and the emergence of a stigmatized social status. *Social Science & Medicine, 67*(3), 420–430.

Tod, A. M., Craven, J., & Allmark, P. (2008). Diagnostic delay in lung cancer: a qualitative study. *Journal of Advanced Nursing, 61*(3), 336–343.

Torrance, H. (2013). The practice of educational and social research: Running a small research institute. *International Review of Qualitative Research, 6*(3), 323–336.

Van Manen, M. (1990) *Researching lived experience.* London, England: Althouse Press.

Van Manen, M. (2014) *Phenomenology of practice.* Walnut Creek, CA: Left Coast Press.

Verger, P., Arnaud, S., Ferrer, S., Iarmarcovai, G., Saliba, M. L., Viau, A., & Souville, M. (2008). Inequities in reporting asbestos-related lung cancer: Influence of smoking stigma and physician's specialty, workload and role perception. *Occupational and Environmental Medicine, 65*(6), 392–397. doi:10.1136/oem.2007.035808

Designing Integration in Multimethod and Mixed Methods Research

Joseph Maxwell, Margaret Chmiel, *and* Sylvia E. Rogers

Abstract

The integration of data and results derived from different methods is intrinsic to multimethod and mixed methods research but has been, for many researchers, a difficult goal to achieve. This chapter examines a broad range of studies, from the natural as well as social sciences, to develop insights into, and strategies for, achieving this integration. The type of design, and the paradigm views of the researchers, are less important for integration than the ability to view the results using different mental models or "lenses." Direct engagement of the researcher(s) with both types of data, and ongoing interaction between quantitative and qualitative researchers, facilitates integration, as does systematically developing and testing conclusions using both types of data.

Key Words: integration, mixed methods, multimethod, design, qualitative, quantitative

Approaches to Integrating Qualitative and Quantitative Methods and Results

This chapter is based on a different conception of "design" than that of most of the preceding chapters. These chapters assume that "research design" refers to a *type* of design (an exception is Chapter 3, by Pearce). This is a widely held view of design—that design primarily involves selecting a particular design from an existing set and then using that design as a model to plan the study (e.g., Creswell & Plano Clark, 2011; Morgan, 2013; Morse & Niehaus, 2009; Teddlie & Tashakkori, 2009). However, this is not the only possible way of thinking about design. We discuss "integration" from an alternative understanding of, and approach to, design (Maxwell, 2012a; Maxwell & Loomis, 2003). This understanding is of design as the actual relationships among all of the components of a study, not just a categorization of the study as a particular type of design.

Maxwell (2012a) identified five components of a study's design: (a) goals (what the study is intended to contribute or accomplish); (b) conceptual framework (the researchers' theory and assumptions about the phenomena studied and how best to study this); (c) research questions; (d) methods (including the relationships that the researchers establish with participants, as well as sampling/selection, data collection, and analysis); and (e) validity (the potential threats to the study's conclusions that the researchers identified and the strategies they employed to address these). These five components, as well as external influences such as researchers' skills, situational constraints, ethical standards, funding and funders' agendas, and prior research, all interact to influence the design and how it may change during the research. In adopting this approach, we view designing a study as thinking through each of these components of the research and how they will relate to the other components and the larger environment, as well as paying attention to how these relationships play out as the study develops.

These two views of design were labeled "typological" and "interactive" (or "systemic"), respectively, by Maxwell and Loomis (2003); Creswell and Plano-Clark (2011) referred to these as "typology-based" and "dynamic" approaches. Although most published textbooks and handbook chapters on designing a mixed methods study have used a typological approach, some disadvantages of this approach have been described by Bryman (2006; 2007), Guest (2013), Hesse-Biber (2010), Maxwell and Loomis, and Morse (2006). Hall and Howard (2008) have proposed combining the two strategies in what they call a "synergistic approach."

We believe that, for the purposes of understanding and achieving the integration of qualitative and quantitative approaches, methods, and data, a systemic or interactive concept of design is better able to represent the actual process of planning and conducting a mixed methods study. Typological approaches, because they focus on the initial decision about the sequence and priority of the qualitative and quantitative components of the study, fail to capture other aspects of the research or the modifications to these that frequently occur in the course of doing the research. A systemic approach addresses not only the prior intentions of the researchers, but also what Kaplan (1964) called the "logic-in-use" of the study itself—the actual relationships among the components as the study develops, which may differ substantially from the original plans. These relationships (and the resulting integration) are often far more complex than typologies can adequately represent.

A similar critique of design typologies has been made by Shadish, Cook, and Campbell (2002) in what is widely regarded as the preeminent work on experimental and quasi-experimental research design. They emphasized focusing on design *elements,* rather than a finite series of designs; this allows the creation of new designs and the use of specific elements of experimental design in nonexperimental research. They stated that "we hope to help readers acquire a set of tools that is flexible enough so that some of them will be relevant. . . in almost any research context" (p. xviii).

While we believe that the *dimensions* on which mixed methods studies vary, and on which typologies are based, are useful conceptual tools, we do not think that they are the most useful approach to *planning* a study. We see typologies of mixed methods designs as potentially most useful as tools for making better sense of a study *during and after* the research, as part of an overall toolkit of concepts and strategies (Maxwell, 2011b), rather than as the initial decision or starting point for designing a study.

This chapter is not simply a compilation of generally accepted ideas about, and strategies for, integration; in some places, we challenge current orthodoxy and advance "outside-the-box" ways of thinking about mixed methods research. Our purpose is to provide useful conceptual and methodological tools for researchers who want to genuinely integrate qualitative and quantitative approaches.

We begin by addressing three questions that we feel are central to the issue of how to design mixed methods studies in which the qualitative and quantitative components are genuinely integrated:

1. What is a mixed methods study?
2. What are qualitative and quantitative methods and approaches?
3. What does it mean to "integrate" methods?

What Is a "Mixed Methods" Study?

The precise definition of "mixed methods research" is problematic (Small, 2011; Tashakkori & Creswell, 2007). Symonds and Gorard (2008) challenged the validity of the concept of "mixed methods," and Giddings (2006) argued that mixed methods research is simply "positivism dressed in drag" (p. 195). However, there is a growing belief within the mixed methods community that mixed methods research involves not just the joint use of qualitative and quantitative methods or data but the integration of these (e.g., Bryman, 2007; Greene, 2007; Hesse-Biber, 2010; Morgan, 2013; Yin, 2006). Tashakkori and Creswell, in the inaugural issue of the *Journal of Mixed Methods Research,* defined mixed methods research as "research in which the investigator collects and analyzes data, integrates the findings, and draws inferences using both qualitative and quantitative approaches or methods" (p. 4), and Teddlie and Tashakkori (2006) labeled studies that lack integration "quasi-mixed studies." Slonim-Nevo and Nevo (2009) stated, as a self-evident truth, that "mixed methods researchers have to integrate the inferences generated by the qualitative and the quantitative phases of the study" (p. 110), and Bryman argued that

> mixed methods research is not necessarily just an exercise in testing findings against each other. Instead, it is about forging an overall or negotiated account of the findings that brings together both components of the conversation or debate. The challenge is to find ways of fashioning such accounts when we do not have established templates or even rules of thumb for doing so. It is being suggested

here that more attention needs to be given to the integration of findings and to the representation of those findings in publications. (p. 21)

It is clear that integration is felt by many mixed methods scholars to be intrinsic to mixed methods research, not something that is limited to a particular type of mixed methods design. While mixed methods studies vary in what is integrated and in the nature and extent of the integration, we believe that virtually all studies that would be considered mixed methods (ones that involve both qualitative and quantitative methods or approaches) exhibit some sort of integration in the actual conduct of the study, even if this is not obvious in the published reports.

We also believe that, if these definitions are taken seriously, the actual practice of mixed method research is far broader than what is typically discussed in the mixed methods literature. The origin of mixed methods is usually identified with the work of Campbell and Fiske (1959) on triangulation, with a full flowering of actual mixed method studies in the 1980s. A typical statement is that by Creswell and Plano Clark (2011): "The formative period of mixed methods began in the 1950s and continued up until the 1980s. This period saw the initial interest in using more than one method in a study" (p. 25).

Such statements ignore the widespread combined use and integration of qualitative and quantitative approaches, methods, and data for over a century before this. Small (2011) noted that "one can find mixed methods studies throughout the history of the social sciences" (p. 60); some of these earlier studies have been discussed by Alastalo (2008), Johnson and Gray (2010), Maxwell and Loomis (2003), and Platt (1996). Johnson and Gray quote a 1934 research methods textbook stating that "the really creative part of a social inquiry is deciding how different approaches should be combined to yield the most fruitful results" (Fry, 1934, p. 136).

In this chapter we attempt to include a broader range of studies than is usual in discussions of mixed methods research, believing that this wider and more diverse sample contains some useful insights and lessons for integrating qualitative and quantitative approaches, methods, and results. Such strategies developed first in the natural sciences, and are most apparent in disciplines that often involve field research, such as geology and biology. They were a somewhat later development in the social sciences, but clear examples emerged in the 1920s and 1930s; some of these are described later in this chapter.

In addition, published accounts of a study's design and methods—what Kaplan (1964) called the "reconstructed logic" of a study—often are potentially misleading with respect to the actual integration that occurred during the research. It is often the case for research publications, as Kuhn (1977) argued for history, that "the finished product of research disguises the nature of the work that produced it" (p. x). Platt (1996), in her history of sociological research methods, likewise noted that "what is written up may not correspond closely to practice" (p. 65).

Similarly, Bryman (2006) found that, in his sample of multimethod studies, "practice does not always tally with the reasons given for using the approach, if indeed reasons are given at all" (p. 109) and that "what these findings suggest is that there is quite often a mismatch between the rationale for the combined use of quantitative and qualitative research and how it is used in practice" (p. 110). This is similar to Kaplan's (1964) distinction between the "reconstructed logic" and the "logic-in-use" of a study but focuses on the difference between the *intended* logic and the logic-in-use. It is important to recognize, however, that neither of these is directly given; both must be inferred from what the researcher *wrote* about the research, and, as noted previously, the actual practice may be distorted or missing in the published work.

This discrepancy between the presentation of results in publications and the actual process of developing these results casts doubt on conclusions about the integration of qualitative and quantitative approaches and data that are based solely on the organization of the published results, and problematizes the finding by Greene, Caracelli, and Graham (1989) and Niglas (2004) that data integration was rare in the studies they reviewed. The actual process of integrating data may not be reported in journal publications because of space limitations, and such presentations may give a distorted impression of this process. For these reasons, we have tried to find examples in which the methods were described in detail, rather than simply categorized; this partly accounts for the preponderance of book-length publications in our examples, as opposed to journal articles. We believe that a case-based approach, examining particular studies to understand what integration was achieved and how, will be more useful to researchers than presenting a classification of studies based on the types of integration that are present.

What Are Qualitative and Quantitative Methods/Approaches?

As with the definition of mixed methods research, defining the distinction between qualitative and quantitative approaches and methods has been controversial within (and outside) the mixed methods community, and varied definitions of the two approaches were in use long before the explicit emergence of "mixed methods" as an approach. The simplest, and one of the oldest, ways of making the distinction is that qualitative research uses words and quantitative uses numbers. This is consistent with the usual definition of "qualitative" in the physical sciences—that it refers to categorical or nominal-level (or sometimes ordinal-level) measurement, rather than numerical interval- or ratio-level measurement (e.g., qualitative analysis in chemistry only detects the presence of particular elements, while quantitative analysis determines the amount of the element present).

This definition has also been used in the social sciences (e.g., King, Keohane, & Verba, 1994, p. 6). However, it fails to capture what is most distinctive and important about qualitative research. In addition, it is not particularly useful in understanding how qualitative and quantitative approaches are, or can be, integrated. Qualitative researchers often use numbers in the form of simple counts of things, in order to make statements of "many," "frequent," and "unusual" more precise (Becker, 1970), but this does not make the research a mixed methods study (Maxwell, 2010), any more than verbal labels for categories make a study qualitative.

Hammersley (1992) argued that the qualitative/quantitative distinction is not a unitary one, and identified seven dimensions of this distinction, which he held were logically independent of one another. For the purposes of this chapter, four of these dimensions seem important: qualitative and quantitative data, natural and artificial settings, meanings and behavior, and inductive and deductive approaches. However, although these are important aspects of the qualitative/quantitative distinction, none of these dimensions is absolute; each represents a continuum or a multidimensional space. Thus, as sociologist Peter Blau (1963) commented in his classic work *The Dynamics of Bureaucracy*, "the idea that research methods can neatly be classified into hypothesis-testing and insight-supplying ones is grossly misleading, since these are polar types that appear in actual investigations in various admixtures" (p. 272). Small (2011) argued more broadly that "when used as

all-encompassing markers, qualitative and quantitative refer to categories that are neither clearly bound nor mutually exclusive" (p. 59).

A dimensional approach to mixed methods research also is seen in Johnson and Christensen (2014), in what Johnson calls the multiple-dimension process approach to mixed design. Johnson provides a large set of dimensions built on the work of Greene (2007) and Teddlie and Tashakkori (2009) and the process logic (or interactive model) of Maxwell (2012a) and Maxwell and Loomis (2003). The basic concept is to center one's study on the research questions and to construct a flexible processual design (that operates dynamically during a study). A few of the dimensions include the nature of the phenomena studied, use of substantive theory, purposes of mixing, interaction of sampling methods, number of methodological approaches, nature of the implementation setting, degree to which methods are similar or different, use of a combination of multiple traditional designs, ideological drive, "validity" criteria and strategies, and how and where integration occurs. Additional dimensions are seen in the dualisms debated by researchers, producing a specific signature (or relatively unique) design for each research study. This approach is not focused on a qualitative versus quantitative distinction, and views all current design typologies as strongly limited in their usefulness.

Similar critiques of the qualitative/quantitative distinction have been made by Sandelowski, Voils, and Knafl (2009) and by many of the contributors to a volume edited by Bergman (2008a). Bergman (2008b) argued that both qualitative and quantitative research consist of a collection of disparate concepts and strategies that have only a tenuous relationship to one another, and that "the conventional divide between [qualitative and quantitative] methods is based on highly questionable premises" (p. 19). He also claimed that the separation of qualitative and quantitative methods is to a considerable degree related to "delineating and preserving identities and ideologies rather than to describe possibilities and limits of a rather heterogeneous group of data collection and analysis techniques" (p. 29).

However, another way of making the distinction seems to us to embody important aspects of the "mental models" of quantitative and qualitative researchers, respectively. This is Mohr's (1982) distinction between variance theory and process theory; similar distinctions are those between variable analysis and the process of interpretation (Blumer, 1956), variable-oriented and case-oriented approaches (Ragin, 1987), and factor theories and explanatory theories (Yin, 1993).

Variance theory deals with variables and the correlations among them; it is based on an analysis of the contribution of differences in values of particular variables to differences in other variables. Variance theory tends to be associated with research that employs experimental or correlational designs, quantitative measurement, and statistical analysis. As Mohr (1982) noted, "the variance-theory model of explanation in social science has a close affinity to statistics. The archetypal rendering of this idea of causality is the linear or nonlinear regression model" (p. 42). The model of causality involved is usually what is called the "regularity" or "successionist" theory of causality, which sees causality as simply the regular association of events or variables and rejects the idea that there is anything "behind" this association.

Process theory, in contrast, deals with *events* and the processes that connect them; it is based on an analysis of the *processes* by which some events influence others. It is fundamentally different from variance theory as a way of thinking about scientific explanation. Maxwell and Loomis (2003) applied this distinction to mixed methods research, but it has rarely been used in the mixed methods literature. The causal model informing this approach has been termed a "process" or "realist" theory, which sees causality as the actual mechanisms or processes by which one event or phenomenon influences another (for a detailed discussion of these two views of causation, see Maxwell, 2011a).

In addition, the researcher's own presentation of what constitutes qualitative and quantitative methods in a particular study is not always trustworthy. Bryman (2006) discovered cases in which the researcher claimed to have used a qualitative approach or to be using qualitative data, but in fact the "qualitative data" were based on a quantitative analysis of unstructured data—for example, of responses to open questions. Articles in which this occurred and where such data were the only source of the qualitative component were not included in his sample, because it is very debatable whether they can be regarded as indicative of a qualitative approach. This kind of quantification of qualitative data is more properly regarded as indicative of a quantitative research approach (p. 100).

In this chapter, we view mixed method research as involving the use of both qualitative and quantitative mental models (not just qualitative and quantitative methods or data) in a single study (Greene, 2007). These mental models do not necessarily constitute "paradigms" in a strict sense (Maxwell, 2011b), nor are they intrinsically "incommensurable." They simply represent different ways of approaching or conceptualizing the phenomena studied.

What Does it Mean to "Integrate" Methods?

How to integrate qualitative and quantitative methods and data has also been problematic in mixed methods research. Bryman (2007) stated that

> how to present mixed methods findings in such a way that the quantitative and the qualitative findings are genuinely integrated, rather than standing as separate spheres or barely referring to each other, has not been touched upon to any significant extent in the burgeoning literature in this field. In genuinely integrated studies, the quantitative and the qualitative findings will be mutually informative. They will talk to each other, much like a conversation or debate, and the idea is then to construct a negotiated account of what they mean together. (pp. 20–21)

Greene (2007) similarly argued that "the interaction challenge in integrated designs is under-theorized and understudied. . . [but] constitutes the very heart of integrative mixed methods inquiry" (p. 125).

Consistent with the dominant approach to mixed methods design described previously, most discussions of integrating qualitative and quantitative methods have been typological and closely parallel the design typologies, based on the purposes, sequence, degree of separation, and relative dominance of the qualitative and quantitative "strands" of the research. Bryman (2006) stated that, in this approach,

> most of the typologies have been constructed in largely theoretical terms and have not been apparently influenced in a systematic way by examples of multi-strategy research. To a large extent, they are exercises in logically possible types of integration, rather than being built up out of examples. (p. 98)

For example, Greene (2007) distinguished component and integrated designs, the former integrated only in the interpretation and conclusion phases of a study. This distinction has been widely adopted in textbook accounts of mixed methods design. However, it neglects the fact that "interpretation and conclusions" can occur throughout a study; they are not a discrete "stage" in many studies. An example is a study of the relationship between expressed emotion and sales in convenience stores (Sutton & Rafaeli, 1988, 1992). The quantitative and qualitative data were sequentially collected, and were, as Greene defined "component" studies, "separate and discretely identifiable throughout the study" (p. 122). However, the qualitative component was designed to address the unexpected results of the initial quantitative analysis, and the qualitative findings completely reshaped the final quantitative analysis; this would seem to fit Bryman's (2007) criterion that the qualitative and quantitative components of a mixed methods study be "mutually illuminating" (p. 8). (For a more detailed discussion of this study, see Maxwell & Loomis, 2003, pp. 257–259; similar examples can be found in Weisner, 2005.)

Bryman's statement would seem to require the influence of the *results* of each approach on the other, not just the joint use of two approaches. A questionnaire that contains both forced-choice and open-ended questions is not "integration" if the two are analyzed and reported separately, with no merging of results or influence of the results of one on the other. However, we disagree with Bryman's (2007) claim that if the qualitative results simply influence the quantitative design, research questions, or methods (or vice versa), so that, for example, the qualitative element is "solely a springboard for hypotheses to be tested using a quantitative approach" (p. 8), this is not integration; we see this as one type of integration.

Irwin (2008), in an important contribution to the discussion of integration, focused specifically on the integration of qualitative and quantitative data, not on methods in general. Her approach to this involved seeing data primarily as *evidence* for or against a particular conclusion or theory about the issue being investigated. She emphasized that all data (and methods) carry with them specific conceptions of the phenomena being studied, particular "lenses" for viewing these phenomena, and that we need to critically examine the concepts and categories that we use to organize our data (and thinking); "developing adequate conceptualizations of the phenomena and processes under investigation must remain at the heart of social analysis" (p. 416).

Irwin's (2008) analysis of causality, and her critique of variable-centered quantitative modeling strategies for identifying causal relationships, draw on a process approach that is similar to that presented by Freedman (2010) and Maxwell (2004a, 2004b, 2011a, 2012b). She sees quantitative data as mainly addressing the macro level of general patterns and social structure, and qualitative data as mainly addressing the micro level of individual action and meaning. However, it is not clear to us that the macro/micro distinction is coterminous with the social-structural/individually meaningful distinction; we see meaning and social relationships as both involved in micro *and* macro phenomena. For example, cultural patterns are symbolic/meaningful but macro, while individual relationships are social but micro (see Maxwell, 2011a, ch. 2, for a more detailed discussion of this issue). We believe that both qualitative and quantitative approaches and data are relevant to causal inference, and can be productively integrated.

Based on interviews with researchers who have combined qualitative and quantitative methods, Bryman (2007) identified a number of barriers to the integration of qualitative and quantitative findings. Some of his findings, such as that the researchers he interviewed had trouble coming up with exemplary mixed method studies, are important for understanding the integration of qualitative and quantitative approaches. He also emphasized a point that we think is insufficiently appreciated—that mixed method research has to be *written up* (p. 20), and that the ways we write about research have a major influence on both how we integrate findings and how we understand the integration of approaches in these studies.

In the remainder of this chapter, we discuss a range of published studies that, in our view, provide valuable insights into the strategies, outcomes, and difficulties of integrating qualitative and quantitative methods, data, and mental models. We begin by discussing examples of integration in the natural sciences, the first to clearly use mixed methods, and then take up integration in the social sciences.

Examples of Integrated Mixed Method Studies in Various Fields
Natural Sciences: Geology

Geology presents one of the earliest and clearest cases in the natural sciences of the integration of qualitative and quantitative approaches, methods, and data. In Charles Lyell's *Principles of Geology* (1830–1833), his arguments were supported primarily by the qualitative description of rock formations, including drawings and maps, but also contained numerous measurements of elevation and distance. The most detailed example of integration is in Lyell's presentation of his classification of different strata by the proportion of fossil shells of current versus extinct species, in Appendix I of Volume 3, based on a detailed table of the more than 7,000 fossil genera. Lyell combined the quantitative analysis of shell proportions with his qualitative descriptions of superposition, folding, and unconformities to generate a detailed chart of the chronological ordering of the strata, and used the fossil shell proportions to test some of his previous conclusions that were based on the stratigraphy alone (an example of triangulation).

A major reason that geology exhibits such an early integration of qualitative and quantitative methods and data is that it is essentially a historical science; its main task is reconstructing the sequence of events and processes that led to the currently observable features of the earth (McPhee, 1998). Compton (1985), in a widely used manual of geological fieldwork (a more recent but very similar manual is Coe, 2010), argued that "every geological event is unique and each rock and structure thus has intrinsic uniqueness, a dependency differing radically from those of broadly abstract science" (p. 1). This uniqueness, and geology's concern with process and context, thus gives great importance to qualitative description and inference.

However, the fixed, physical nature of the phenomena that geology studies also makes quantitative measurement and analysis very feasible, and provides a greater degree of precision for the description of some properties of these phenomena. These complementary strengths lead to an intimate integration of qualitative and quantitative methods and data in geological fieldwork. Compton's (1985) manual contains detailed instructions for both observational methods (e.g., using a hand lens, drawing formations) and the use of different instruments to provide quantitative measurement (e.g., compass, clinometer, alidade and plane table, and measuring tape). Compton's example of geologic field notes (pp. 28–29) is primarily a verbal description of the area and the outcrops visited, interspersed with measurements (e.g., strike and dip, thickness of beds, size of fossil shells, percentages of different minerals, etc.), drawings of formations, and tentative interpretations.

We argue that geologic fieldwork thus represents a clear example of mixed methods research, integrating qualitative observations and the recording of these with quantitative measurement. Some qualitative researchers might object that the sorts of qualitative methods and data that we have described for geology are not actually "qualitative" in the sense typically involved in the social sciences, since they are not "interpretive" in the sense of investigating participants' meanings and perspectives. The latter is certainly one of the meanings that "qualitative" has had, and one that played a prominent role in the paradigm wars. However, it is not the only meaning the term possesses, as discussed previously. Geological fieldwork is indisputably qualitative in several other senses. First, it is inherently particularistic rather than generalizing, focusing on the description and interpretation of specific, local phenomena, rather than aiming at generalizations. Second, it is naturalistic, studying existing settings rather than manipulating or intervening in order to determine the effect of particular variables. Third, much of the data is in the form of words and drawings, rather than numbers. Fourth, it is inductive, rather than simply testing prior hypotheses. Compton (1985) stated that "mapping is likely to be exploratory and deliberate until the principal rocks have become familiar. . . .Recesses may be needed to do laboratory work on critical fossils or rocks" (p. 7).

Finally, geologic fieldwork is directed at a descriptive understanding of the processes that created these local phenomena, what Miles and Huberman (1984) called "local causality," rather than the establishment of a correlation or experimental relationship between variables. The measurements of particular features of these phenomena are directed toward a more precise description and explanation of the phenomena rather than toward a general, variable-based theory. McPhee (1998), in his acclaimed account of the development of the theory of plate tectonics, stated that a geologic map "should serve as an epitome of what is known and not known about a region. . . geology is a descriptive, interpretive science" (pp. 378–379).

This integration of qualitative and quantitative methods and data is present in several forms. First, as described earlier, the initial collection of geological field data involves a fine-grained integration of qualitative (observation, sketching, verbal notes) and quantitative (location and distance, strike and dip, measurement of beds) methods and data; this integration is omnipresent in geological fieldwork and is simply not seen as problematic in any way. Both qualitative and quantitative data are used to provide a more detailed and complete description of an outcrop or formation than could be obtained by either method alone.

This integration is not just a result of the concurrent use of the two types of methods but of the fact that they are done by the same person at the same time, alternating in rapid succession between observation, measurement, and the recording of both. (This depth of integration during data collection is facilitated by two features of geologic fieldwork: the fixed, physical nature of the phenomena studied, and the discrete nature of the quantitative measurements involved; the measurements are directly related to the description of specific, local features rather than being collected for later statistical analysis in the aggregate.)

These features are not as uniformly present in the social sciences. However, such integration often occurs when, for example, an observer of some setting is both recording particular events on a quantitative form and also taking descriptive notes on the activity, or when someone is engaged in educational or psychological testing of a child and at the same time recording descriptive observations, if these two types of data both inform the conclusions drawn. To our knowledge, this has not been discussed as a form of integration in the mixed methods literature.

Second, qualitative and quantitative data are closely integrated in the preparation of the basic findings of a geologic study—the interpretation of the processes that created the observable features of the landscape. Here, both qualitative and quantitative data are used to develop and test the interpretation (theory) of what took place. A credible interpretation has to be consistent with both types of data; this can be seen as a form of triangulation, but this is not simply a matter of testing a conclusion based on one method against the results of a second method. Both sorts of data are integrally involved in the *development* of the conclusions. Such a strategy blurs the distinction between triangulation and what Greene (2007) calls "initiation"—the use of different methods to generate "fresh insights, new perspectives, original understandings" (p. 103).

Natural Sciences: Ethology

Fieldwork in ethology (the study of animal behavior) has some similarities to fieldwork in geology, but there are also some important differences, due to the fact that animals, unlike rocks, move and interact with other animals on an observable timescale. The primary qualitative and quantitative data are often gathered concurrently by a single person or team. However, in many studies much of the quantitative data are created by categorizing, aggregating, and statistically analyzing the qualitative behavioral data. In addition, animals lend themselves to experimental manipulation of stimuli or other environmental factors. All of these features are found in early work in ethology and are prominent in more recent studies as well (e.g., de Waal, 1982, 1989, on bonobos; Goodall, 1986, 1992, on chimpanzees; Heinrich, 1999, on ravens; Mech, 1970, on wolves).

A study that illustrates these features, and the integration that they involve, is a report by Minta, Minta, and Lott (1992) on hunting associations of badgers and coyotes, drawn from a 3-year study of badger ecology using implanted radio transmitters. The researchers observed 214 such associations in hunting ground squirrels; the coyotes' behavior, and that of the badgers when above ground, could be directly observed, while the badgers could be tracked below ground using the radio transmitters. The qualitative data consisted of descriptions of the animals' behaviors and of the surrounding environment; the quantitative data consisted of counting or timing of associations and of specific behaviors, and estimates of spatial distance between the animals, and also of aggregate data (such as success rates for coyotes hunting alone and with badgers), presented as descriptive data and also analyzed using inferential statistics.

The integration of these data is similar to that in geology. Both qualitative and quantitative data are presented in the basic description of the activities studied, although the qualitative data are less detailed than in the book-length reports by Goodall (1992), de Waal (1982), and Heinrich (1999), mentioned earlier. In addition, the two types of data are integrated in presenting and supporting the authors' conclusions:

> We used two types of indices of the association's costs and benefits to each species: first, we compared rates of prey capture and activity budgets of each species hunting alone and hunting in an association. Then we recorded each species' response to the other's presence assuming that behavior that initiates or maintains the association is evidence that the net outcome for the behaving animal is

neutral or positive, while behavior that tends to avoid or terminate the association is evidence that the net outcome is negative. (Minta, Minta, & Lott 1992, p. 815) [The term "then" does not refer to chronological sequence; both types of data were collected concurrently.]

Their conclusion, that the association represents mutualism (joint benefit) rather than parasitism or competition, is supported by both types of data, as well as by the description of features of the habitat that would make individual hunting less productive, for both species, than hunting in association.

Probably because of the space limitations of journal papers, there is relatively little explicit description of the *processes* involved in the association. Such description is more prominent in longer works, such as those cited earlier. A particularly striking example is Goodall's (1986) 600-page *The Chimpanzees of Gombe: Patterns of Behavior*, a summary of 25 years of work with these chimpanzees. The entire book is a fine-grained integration of tables, graphs, and other quantitative data with verbal descriptions of the behavior of particular individuals, often supplemented by photographs, showing the processes of problem solving and social interaction that these individuals engaged in.

There is also relatively little attempt in the paper by Minta et al. (1992) to interpret the animals' behavior in terms of motives, feelings, or perceptions of the world, or attempts to integrate this with behavioral observations or experimental results. Such an approach was more common in early work in ethology, such as that of Portmann (1961) and Tinbergen (1961), who used concepts such as "image" and "mood" to represent the minds of animals, but this sort of description declined with the increasing influence of behaviorist views in ethology (e.g., the dismissal of Goodall's early work by other ethologists, described in Goodall, 1992, p. 14 ff.). This attention to the *minds* of animals has seen a more recent resurgence in biology (e.g., Shettleworth, 2010), and such research typically combines qualitative and quantitative methods and data. For example, biologist Bernd Heinrich's (1999) report on his extensive studies of ravens, *Mind of the Raven*, integrates systematic experimental results and descriptive statistics with detailed observation and interpretation of individual ravens' behaviors and their social interactions.

Social Sciences

Even in the social sciences, the use of, and explicit justification for, integrating qualitative and quantitative methods preceded the definition of this as a "type" of research; this challenges prevalent assumptions about the "origin" of mixed method research in the social sciences (Johnson & Gray, 2010; Johnson, Onweugbuzie, & Turner, 2007; Maxwell & Loomis, 2003). In the remainder of this section, we attempt to identify and synthesize the integration strategies of some of these early studies to see what can be learned from this body of work. While the call for *combining* qualitative and quantitative approaches can be found even earlier, for example, in the work of the psychologists Wilhelm Wundt and Ernest Burgess (Alastalo, 2008) and the anthropologist Bronislaw Malinowski (1922), we focus on studies that explicitly exhibit such integration and that we believe can contribute to our understanding of how to integrate the two approaches.

Three early studies are particularly noteworthy as examples of the integration of qualitative and quantitative approaches in the social sciences: *Middletown: A Study in American Culture*, by Robert Lynd and Helen Merrell Lynd (1929); *Marienthal: The Sociography of an Unemployed Community*, by Marie Jahoda, Paul Lazarsfeld, and Hans Zeisel (1933/1971); and *The Social Life of a Modern Community* (the first volume of the *Yankee City* series), by W. Lloyd Warner and Paul Lunt (1941). In the following description, we focus on the second of these studies, because it exhibits the clearest and most detailed discussion of this integration and of the authors' rationale for this. However, this integration was explicitly present in all three studies.

The research for *Marienthal* was conducted in 1930, and the report was published in 1933 in German (an English translation by the authors was published in 1971). In the first paragraph of the book, the authors described the existing state of research on unemployment:

> There are some statistics available on the extent of unemployment and the amount of relief provided. . . . There is also a literature on social problems: newspapermen and other writers have most effectively portrayed the life of the unemployed, bringing home their condition through example and description. . . . But there is a gap between the bare figures of official statistics and the literary accounts. . . . The purpose of our study

of the Austrian village, Marienthal, is to bridge this gap. (Jahoda et al., 1933/1971, p. 1)

They continued

Our idea was to find procedures which would combine the use of numerical data with immersion (*sich einleben*) into the situation. To this end it was necessary to gain such close contact with the population of Marienthal that we could learn the smallest details of their daily life. At the same time we had to perceive each day so that it was possible to reconstruct it objectively. . . [this apparently refers to quantification of the qualitative data].

As this report proceeds, it will become clear how we have tried to build up a comprehensive picture of life in Marienthal, while at the same time accommodating complex psychological situations within an objective framework that is supported by relevant statistics. . . . The testimony of the unemployed themselves brought us face to face with the living experience of unemployment (Jahoda et al., 1933/1971, pp. 1–2)

Lazarsfeld, in his introduction to the English translation of the report, described in more detail the goals and strategy of the study:

In all this work certain norms for empirical study were maintained as a matter of course. It would have been unacceptable just to report that x percent of the people did or thought this or that about some topic. The task was to combine diverse findings into a small number of "integrating constructs." At the same time it was imperative to explicate as clearly as possible the procedure by which such greater depth was achieved. In a paper written in 1933 summarizing the Austrian experience, the following four rules were singled out and amply exemplified:

1. For any phenomenon one should have objective observation as well as introspective reports.

2. Case studies should be properly combined with statistical information.

3. Contemporary information should be supplemented by information on earlier phases of whatever is being studied.

4. "Natural and experimental data" should be combined. By experimental, I meant mainly questionnaires and solicited reports, while by natural I meant what is now called "unobtrusive measures"—data derived from daily life without interference from the investigator.

More [mere?] description was not enough. In order to get "behind" it, a variety of data had

to be collected on any issue under investigation, just as the true position of a distant object can be found only through triangulation, by looking at it from different sides and directions. (Lazarsfeld, 1971, p. xiv)

It is clear that this was not simply a mixed methods study, but one that was explicitly *designed* as a mixed methods study, with deliberate attention to how the different methods and types of data should be integrated.

In the appendix to *Marienthal, Toward a History of Sociography*, Hans Zeisel (1933/1971) noted the influence of *Middletown* (Lynd & Lynd, 1929) on the research, but more fundamentally that of Max Weber. However, he stated that Weber's insistence that the social surveys of the *Verein fuer Sozialpolitik* address the entire pattern of life of the workers, subjective and cultural as well as objective, tended to be lost in the focus on detailed and precise analysis of the objective data, and

statements on attitudes and sentiments were supported with no more than impressions, at best with a few quotations taken out of context. . . .The totality that Max Weber had seen as an integral part of the research plan was lost in its execution. (Zeisel, 1933/1971, p. 119)

Several lessons for integrating qualitative and quantitative approaches can be drawn from these three studies. First, in all of the studies a major source of integration was the joint collection of both qualitative and quantitative data by the research team and the frequent and detailed sharing of these data and preliminary findings with other members of the team. Second, both methods were used in drawing and testing conclusions from the study. This involved not only the final conclusions of the study but the revision of initial theories and preliminary findings. For example, in the Yankee City study, the interviews challenged the researchers' initial belief that economic status was the primary basis for social class, and revealed the importance of "acting right" and of residential location in the city, conclusions that were supported by both quantitative analyses and by careful follow-up interviews (Warner & Lunt, 1941, pp. 81–91).

Third, the main goal of all three studies was to provide a comprehensive picture of a community, one in which "objective" and "subjective" perspectives and data were integrated in a holistic portrait. Without this goal, and the belief that such an account was possible, it is doubtful that the fine-grained integration of methods would have occurred. Fourth, although the frequent separation of quantitative and qualitative methods was noted and discussed in all three works, there is no indication that this was seen as a "paradigm" difference, or that the researchers felt any sense of "incompatibility," philosophical or methodological, between the two approaches. The idea of incompatibility was a much later development in the history of mixed methods research and drew substantially from Kuhn's (1970) discussion of paradigms and incommensurability. Staw (1992) argued that even in the 1950s, combining methods was more common than later, and Rabinowitz and Weseen (2001) identified the work of Festinger (e.g., Festinger, Riecken, & Schachter, 1956) and Milgram (1974) as representing a period in psychology when qualitative and quantitative methods were more easily combined than later. (For a discussion of the study of disconfirmation and belief by Festinger et al., 1956, which led to Festinger's theory of cognitive dissonance, see Maxwell & Loomis, 2003.)

Finally, we describe a number of more recent studies that we believe provide useful examples of the integration of qualitative and quantitative approaches. Stanley Milgram's (1974) book *Obedience to Authority*, based on research conducted from 1960 to 1963, is one of the most detailed and complex examples of mixed method research that we know of, and one of the most thoroughly integrated uses of mixed methods. This is in part because it is an account not just of a single study, but of an elaborate series of laboratory experiments on how people respond when they are ordered by authorities to inflict apparent pain and possible serious harm on others (see Maxwell & Loomis, 2003, pp. 265–267, for a more general discussion of this study.). Milgram's book is not simply a description of the study and its results; it is primarily a detailed argument for the validity and importance of his findings and conclusions. How he used qualitative and quantitative evidence in this argument is just as important for understanding the integration of qualitative and quantitative approaches as is his collection and analysis of the qualitative and quantitative data.

In conducting an experimental study, Milgram (1974) was primarily concerned with discovering the effect of particular variables on the subjects' obedience to authority; he recorded and statistically analyzed the level of shock that subjects were willing to administer to a supposed "learner," and manipulated different situational factors to

determine their effect on this level. However, he was also concerned with the *process* by which people responded to the researcher's directions: how they made sense of and reacted to these directions, and why they complied with or resisted the orders. In introducing the individual case studies, Milgram states that

> From each person in the experiment we derive one essential fact: whether he has obeyed or disobeyed. But it is foolish to see the subject only in this way. For he brings to the laboratory a full range of emotions, attitudes, and individual styles. . . . We need to focus on the individuals who took part in the study not only because this provides a personal dimension to the experiment but also because the quality of each person's experience gives us clues to the nature of the process of obedience. (p. 44)

The researchers covertly filmed the subjects' behavior during the experiment, interviewed some subjects at length after the experiment was over to determine their reasons for compliance or refusal, and sent a follow-up questionnaire to all participants that allowed expression of their thoughts and feelings.

The integration of qualitative and quantitative approaches and data is not immediately obvious from the organization of the material in Milgram's (1974) book. The results chapters (chapters 3–9) primarily report the experimental findings; the case studies (chapters 5 and 7) are discussed separately from the quantitative and experimental results. The description of the methods (chapter 2) likewise focuses on the experimental design and procedures, as well as addressing ethical issues, and the theoretical discussions (chapters 1, 10, and 11) contain little actual data. A superficial reading could easily classify this as a "component" study, with little real integration.

Part of the reason for the separation of qualitative and quantitative data in the book is that, to some extent, they address different questions. The quantitative data primarily demonstrate *that* particular factors affected the outcomes, while the qualitative data, as suggested in the previous quote from Milgram (1974), provide evidence for *how* they did so—the *process* by which the effect occurred. However, the fact that the quantitative and qualitative data were collected concurrently by the same team suggests that there might be more integration than this. This is borne out by two features of the presentation. First, the discussion of the experimental results is substantially interspersed with descriptions of the subjects' behavior, photographs of the subjects during the experiment, dialogue between the experimenter and the subject, and lengthy quotes from subjects as they responded to the experimental procedures.

Second, there is a substantial integration of qualitative and quantitative data in the final chapters (chapters 13 and 14), which address an alternative possible explanation for the results (aggression) and the argument that the experiment does not reflect real life. In these chapters, Milgram (1974) used both qualitative and quantitative evidence to counter these validity threats. In addition, much of the qualitative material in the early chapters seems intended to support the "realism" of the experimental design, making it implausible that the results were due to some highly artificial aspect of the study. An important contributor to this integration, we believe, is that the *theory* of obedience that informed Milgram's study, and that his results were intended to support, incorporated both variance and process components, as the previous quote from Milgram makes clear.

A study that exhibits a striking contrast to Milgram's, in terms of the nature of the integration involved, is an account of an evaluation of a federal program to provide housing payments to help low-income families find better housing (Trend, 1979). (The following brief account focuses only on integration; this highly regarded paper deserves to be read in its entirety, not least because it was one of the first to explicitly address conflict between the qualitative and quantitative findings.) The study was described as a "naturalistic experiment" to understand how to best manage the program, comparing different administrative agencies' performances. The quantitative and qualitative data collection were completely separate. Quantitative data were collected by the administrative agency and sent to the contracting agency for the study, and participating families were periodically surveyed by the contracting agency; qualitative data were obtained by having "site observers" (mostly anthropologists) in each of the administrative agencies; the observers interviewed staff and observed activities, and sent their field notes and reports to the contracting agency. The two sorts of data were intended to address different questions: the program outcomes would be determined through analysis of the quantitative data, while the observers' case studies would provide a holistic picture of program processes (Trend, 1979).

The integration of the qualitative and quantitative data and "mental models" occurred only because the report by one site observer directly contradicted the conclusions that the contracting agency staff had drawn from the quantitative data. The agency staff's view was that the observer's conclusions were biased, and he was repeatedly told to rewrite his analysis to fit the quantitative conclusions. However, the observer insisted that the quantitative data were misleading and that the agency's conclusions about the outcomes from this site were suspect. Finally, Trend (1979) and the observer made a sustained effort to get at what had really been going on, using both the quantitative and the qualitative data. They eventually came up with a coherent, process explanation for almost all of the data, one that went well beyond either the quantitative or the initial qualitative conclusions and that revealed serious shortcomings in both accounts.

Although the data collection in this study fits a "component" design, in that the quantitative and qualitative data were collected and analyzed separately, and only combined in developing conclusions, it also resembles the most developed subtype of integrated design described by Caracelli and Greene (1997), the transformative design; Greene (2007) later described this as the "dialectic" stance for mixed methods research. In this stance, diversity, and the generative potential of engaging with difference, are of primary importance, providing a better understanding of the phenomena studied through the engagement and integration of different mental models and perspectives. Although the integration took place only at the end of the research process, it was an unusually deep and comprehensive integration. Trend (1979) noted that "major gains from the Site B analysis accrued to the in-house analysis [at the contracting agency]. They began to think of ways that conflicting interpretations could be used for gains in understanding" (p. 82).

The failure to integrate the data at an earlier point in the study was not the result of different databases; both sides had access to all of the data. Instead, it was due to a preference for different *kinds* of data, as a result of different mental models for understanding the phenomena studied; "each side held so tightly to its own views that it was impossible to brush aside the lack of congruence" (Trend, 1979, p. 84). Rather than a single theory that integrated variance and process aspects, as in Milgram's (1974) study, there were two sharply differing conceptual frameworks for making sense of the data. The contracting agency's mental model was largely a variance-theory one; the analysts seemed to have a bias against site-specific process explanations as not being "policy-relevant." The site observer's mental model, in contrast, was a process model of how the administrators' heavy-handed policies led to staff disaffection and poor implementation of the program.

Counterintuitively, Trend (1979) argued that an earlier attempt to integrate the two types of data might well have led to the suppression of the observer's interpretations, since "observationally derived explanations are particularly vulnerable to dismissal without a fair trial. . . .because the data on which they are based are difficult to check for reliability" (p. 84) and that "earlier harmony would have prevented any additional searching, since nothing would have needed explaining" (p. 84). The initial failure of integration was the result of the rigid adherence of the two parties to different mental models, and of the power differential between them. The final integration, in contrast, was a product of Trend's and the site observer's commitment to taking seriously both approaches and to creating a coherent account that incorporated both. If the contracting agency staff had seriously considered a process model at the outset, this could have forestalled some of the conflict by forcing them to think about what processes in this site could possibly have resulted in high housing quality for clients (a quantitative finding that was later found to be flawed).

Trend's (1979) conclusions are supported by a study (Kaplan & Duchon, 1988) of the effect of the implementation of a computer reporting system on technicians' work in the laboratories of a university medical center. The two authors began the study with very different mental models; Duchon and two other members of the team were quantitatively oriented researchers on organizational behavior, while Kaplan, though she had worked extensively with computer information systems, had a PhD in history of science and was familiar with historians' methods of research, which tend to be qualitative. They had each developed different sets of research questions for the study; Kaplan was interested in studying what happened when a computer information system was installed in a new setting, using interviews and observational fieldwork, while Duchon wanted to test existing theory on job characteristics and job satisfaction, using surveys and statistical analysis, and viewed interviews and observations as "background" rather than "data."

An initial questionnaire was administered to all members of the laboratory staff 7 months after the computer system was introduced. It contained items adapted from standard instruments for measuring job characteristics, Likert-scale measures of expectations and changes, and four open-ended questions that addressed changes caused by the computer system and solicited suggestions for improvement. When Kaplan analyzed the responses to the open-ended questions, she found substantial differences among the laboratories in their evaluation of the change (Kaplan & Duchon, 1988). However, the initial statistical analysis of the quantitative data (by researchers who were unaware of the qualitative results) found high reliability for five factors but no significant differences in responses by laboratory, age, or job experience.

Kaplan was surprised by this, because the variables measured by the survey items were very similar to themes derived from the open-ended questions, which differed markedly among the laboratories, and because these differences were supported by her observations in the laboratories and at meetings of the lab directors. She therefore decided to pursue this further, analyzing her interviews with the lab directors. She eventually developed a theory (based on the qualitative data) that technicians differed in their definition of what their "job" was; one group saw their job as producing lab results reports (a service to the rest of the medical center), while the other saw their job as doing the bench work necessary to producing the reports. This led to quite different views of the computer system: the former group liked it because it improved results reporting, while the latter group disliked it because it increased their workload and hassles (Kaplan & Duchon, 1988). These differences would not have been captured by the quantitative job characteristics measures.

Working out these conflicting interpretations was a challenge; "neither author initially realized the extent to which differing values, assumptions, and vocabularies would interfere with the project" (Kaplan & Duchon, 1988, p. 581). Following her development of the new theory, Kaplan combined scores on different variables to create two new, composite variables that measured technologists' orientation to process or product aspects of their jobs. These two variables were significantly negatively correlated, and when Duchon reanalyzed the quantitative data, statistically significant differences between the labs were found.

This study differed from that reported by Trend (1979) in that the researchers holding the different perspectives were in regular face-to-face communication and had collected some of the data jointly, and there was no power differential to overcome. The authors stated that "our tenacity in holding to our initial independent analyses of the different data—though a problem at the time—and the increased respect each of us developed for the other's approach, in fact, were positive aspects of our research" (p. 582). The integration of the quantitative and qualitative data was not planned (the authors were addressing separate research questions) but occurred because of the discrepancy in interpretations and the researchers' persistence in working to resolve these. It was also helpful that Kaplan was aware of previous work on combining qualitative and quantitative methods, including Trend's paper.

Another study addressing the issue of integrating conflicting findings is that of Slonim-Nevo and Nevo (2009), on the academic and social adjustment of immigrant adolescents in Israel. The authors found several discrepancies in their results, both between the qualitative and quantitative results (some students perceived their progress very differently from what their psychometric scores and grades indicated) and between the different types of qualitative data. In the absence of apparent methodological problems, the authors attempted to interpret these inconsistencies as complementary and to integrate the findings, rather than assuming that one or the other was wrong. However, they found this difficult to do when there was a need to make clinical diagnoses or policy recommendations, rather than simply to better understand their clients. They argued that researchers should not assume that inconsistent findings are necessarily contradictory, and that, when clinical or policy decisions must be made, multiple methods be used to address potential bias in a single method. However, when data do conflict, researchers must ensure that they can justify the decision to prefer one type of data.

A recent paper by Boeije, Slagt, and van Wesel (2013) makes an important contribution to understanding integration. Arguing that integration is "the weakest link in most mixed methods designs" (p. 348), the authors presented the results of a review of 13 studies of childhood trauma, examining the research objectives, motivation for combining methods, data collection, analysis, results, and integration. They found that the kind and degree of integration depended substantially on the research objectives and motivation for combining methods. Studies that used qualitative and quantitative methods to measure a particular construct and to understand the meanings the children gave to situations, respectively, or to understand the outcome and mechanism of an intervention, respectively, were less likely to integrate the results than studies in which the goal was to build theory or to develop and validate an instrument.

Studies that achieved substantial integration include those with a confirmatory as well as a complementary goal, as well as studies with sequential as well as concurrent data collection (Boeije et al., 2013). Although all but one of the studies presented the qualitative and quantitative data separately, this did not prevent many of the authors from integrating the two types in their conclusions; separate presentation is not itself evidence of lack of integration, although alternating or linked presentation may facilitate integration. In addition, nested, rather than separate, *samples* appeared to facilitate integration.

Lessons

In this final section, we discuss the lessons that we draw from the previous discussion. The first lesson is the importance of viewing design as a real property of a research study. Confusing this actual design with the reconstructed design described by the authors, or implied by the way the study's results are presented in publications, can be seriously misleading in understanding the integration of qualitative and quantitative approaches and data in a published study or in accomplishing this integration in one's own research. The emphasis or organization of methods and results in a publication may be largely shaped by the journal's guidelines or the intended audience rather than the actual conduct of the research. Bryman (2007) discussed the difficulty in integrating qualitative and quantitative data in *writing up* a study as a significant barrier to integration, but this is not necessarily the most important form of integration or the best evidence of integration.

Second, integration is substantially influenced by the mental models used by the researcher(s). Greene (2007) strongly urged that researchers integrate multiple mental models in their work, seeing this as the most developed and enlightening form of mixed methods research. A researcher's inability to understand or appreciate the perspective of someone with a different approach to research can seriously inhibit the integration of different approaches, and "ontological divides" is one of the barriers to integration that Bryman (2007, pp. 16–17) identifies. While only one of Bryman's 20 interviewees in this study mentioned this issue spontaneously, it seems very likely to us that many of these researchers were simply unaware of how their ontological and epistemological assumptions were shaping their research and possibly constraining their integration of their data.

Third, the actual engagement of the researcher or team with the collection of both qualitative and quantitative data can importantly facilitate the integration of these data. We saw this in the discussion of the example studies presented previously,, and many more examples could have been described were it not for space limitations. In particular, this allows the researcher to more easily see the possible implications of the qualitative data for quantitative theorizing, research questions, data collection and analysis, and validity concerns. Collecting qualitative data on the same sample as, or a subset of, the quantitative sample, also can facilitate integration.

Fourth, a key use of integrating qualitative and quantitative data and thinking is in drawing and testing interpretations and conclusions; this was the major form of integration identified in geology and ethology and was prominent in the social science studies as well. However, this aspect of integration has not often been specifically addressed in the mixed methods literature (an important exception is Irwin, 2008, discussed earlier in the chapter) and is often confused with the *presentation* of results in a report. Greene's (2007) typology of purposes for combining methods is an important conceptual tool, but does not clearly capture the ways qualitative and quantitative data can jointly be used to develop conclusions. Her sharp distinction between triangulation (seeking convergence) and initiation (seeking divergence), as purposes for mixed method research, does not acknowledge that *both* processes are frequently and inextricably involved in drawing conclusions and that data may be integrated inductively without either being an explicit goal. Systematically listing the qualitative and quantitative findings for comparison may be helpful; "the challenge seems to be explicitly define what each of the components adds to the knowledge" (Boeije et al., 2013, p. 364).

These strategies are not simply additive, so that using more of them always creates a better integrated study. As implied by the design model we have used in this chapter, any strategy has consequences for the rest of the design, including the other integration strategies. Attempting to integrate data during data collection *may*, as Trend (1979) argued, inhibit the final integration of findings. However, whether it does so depends on other aspects of the design, as described here.

For all of these reasons, we urge researchers to *write* more about their experiences with integrating approaches and methods, so that we can gain a better sense of how to do this productively. We believe that it is still true, as Hans Zeisel (1933/1971) wrote 80 years ago in his Afterword to *Marienthal*, that "the task of integration lies still ahead" (p. 125).

Discussion Questions

1. How might your mental models influence how you would integrate a mixed methods study? How might your epistemological and ontological assumptions influence your research?

2. How does your definition of mixed methods research fit in with the definitions discussed in this chapter? How is yours similar or different and why?

3. Think about some recent mixed methods research journal articles that you have read. Did the authors integrate their results? If so, what did they integrate and what strategies did they use?

4. Did this chapter change your thinking about "integration" in mixed methods research? How so?

5. How would you like to design integration into one of your future mixed methods studies?

Suggested Websites

http://web.worldbank.org/WBSITE/EXTERNAL/TOPICS/EXTSOCIALDEV/0,,contentMDK:21189299~pagePK:64168445~piPK:64168309~theSitePK:3177395,00.html

The World Bank: Mixed Methods and PSIA: This website looks at mixed methods research in poverty and social impact analysis.

http://www.principalinvestigators.org/interdisciplinary-research-teams-guide/

Interdisciplinary Research in Teams

References

Alastalo, M. (2008). The history of social research methods. In P. Alasuutari, L. Bickman, & J. Brannen (Eds.), *The SAGE handbook of social research methods* (pp. 26–41). Los Angeles, CA: Sage.

Becker, H. S. (1970). Field work evidence. In H. Becker (Ed.), *Sociological work: Method and substance* (pp. 39–62). New Brunswick, NJ: Transaction Books.

Bergman, M. (Ed.). (2008a). *Advances in mixed method research*. London, England: Sage.

Bergman, M. (2008b). The straw men of the qualitative-quantitative divide and their influence on mixed method research. In M. Bergman (Ed.), *Advances in mixed method research*. (pp. 11–21). London, England: Sage.

Blau, P. (1963). *The dynamics of bureaucracy* (rev. ed.). Chicago, IL: University of Chicago Press.

Blumer, H. (1956). Sociological analysis and the "variable." *American Sociological Review, 21*(6), 683–690.

Boeije, H., Slagt, M., & van Wesel, F. (2013). The contribution of mixed methods research to the field of childhood trauma: A narrative review focused on data integration. *Journal of Mixed Methods Research, 7*(4), 347–369.

Bryman, A. (2006). Integrating quantitative and qualitative research: How is it done? *Qualitative Research, 6*(1), 97–113.

Bryman, A. (2007). Barriers to integrating quantitative and qualitative research. *Journal of Mixed Methods Research, 1*(1), 8–22.

Campbell, D. T., & Fiske, D. W. (1959). Convergent and discriminant validation by the multitrait-multimethod matrix. *Psychological Bulletin 56*(2), 81–105.

Caracelli, V. J., & Greene, J. C. (1997). Crafting mixed method evaluation designs. In J. C. Greene & V. J. Caracelli (Eds.), *Advances in mixed-method evaluation: The challenges and benefits of integrating diverse paradigms* (pp. 19–32). New Directions for Evaluation 74. San Francisco, CA: Jossey-Bass.

Coe, A. (Ed.). (2010). *Geological field techniques*. Milton Keynes, UK: Wiley Blackwell.

Compton, R. R. (1985). *Geology in the field*. New York, NY: John Wiley.

Creswell, J. W., & Plano Clark, V. L. (2011). *Designing and conducting mixed methods research*. Thousand Oaks, CA: Sage.

de Waal, F. (1982). *Chimpanzee politics: Power and sex among apes*. New York, NY: Harper & Row.

de Waal, F. (1989). *Peacemaking among primates*. Cambridge, MA: Harvard University Press.

Festinger, L., Riecken, H. W., & Schachter, S. (1956). *When prophecy fails*. Minneapolis: University of Minnesota Press.

Freedman, D. A. (2010). Statistical models and shoe leather. In D. A. Freedman (Ed.), *Statistical models and causal inference: A dialogue with the social sciences* (pp. 45–62). Cambridge, UK: Cambridge University Press. (Reprinted from *Sociological Methodology, 21*, 291–313 [1991])

Fry, C. I. (1934). *The technique of social investigation*. New York, NY: Harper.

Giddings, L. S. (2006). Mixed methods research: Positivism dressed in drag? *Journal of Research in Nursing, 11*(3), 195–203.

Goodall, J. (1986). *The chimpanzees of Gombe: Patterns of behavior*. Cambridge, MA: Harvard University Press.

Goodall, J. (1992). *Through a window: My thirty years with the chimpanzees of Gombe*. Boston, MA: Houghton Mifflin.

Greene, J. (2007). *Mixed methods in social inquiry*. San Francisco, CA: Jossey-Bass.

Greene, J., Caracelli, V., & Graham, W. F. (1989). Toward a conceptual framework for mixed methods evaluation designs. *Educational Evaluation and Policy Analysis, 11*(3), 259–274.

Guest, G. (2013). Describing mixed methods research: An alternative to typologies. *Journal of Mixed Methods Research, 7*(2), 141–151.

Hall, B., & Howard, K. (2008). A synergistic approach: Conducting mixed methods research with typological and systemic design considerations. *Journal of Mixed Methods Research 2*(3), 248–269.

Hammersley, M. (1992). Deconstructing the qualitative-quantitative divide. In M. Hammersley (Ed.), *What's wrong with ethnography? Methodological explorations* (pp. 159–173). London, England: Routledge.

Heinrich, B. (1999). *Mind of the raven*. New York, NY: HarperCollins.

Hesse-Biber, S. N. (2010). *Mixed methods research: Merging theory with practice*. New York, NY: Guilford.

Irwin, S. (2008). Data analysis and interpretation: Emergent issues in linking qualitative and quantitative evidence. In S. N. Hesse-Biber & P. Leavy (Eds.), *Handbook of emergent methods* (pp. 415–435). New York, NY: Guilford Press.

Jahoda, M., Lazarsfeld, P. F., & Zeisel, H. (1933/1971). *Marienthal: The sociography of an unemployed community*. Chicago, IL: Aldine Atherton.

Johnson, R. B., & Christensen, L. B. (2014). *Educational research methods: Quantitative, qualitative, and mixed approaches* (5th ed.). Los Angeles, CA: Sage.

Johnson, R. B., & Gray, R. (2010). A history of philosophical and theoretical issues for mixed methods research. In A. Tashakkori & C. Teddlie (Eds.), *SAGE handbook of mixed methods in social and behavioral research* (2nd ed., pp. 69–94). Thousand Oaks, CA: Sage.

Johnson, R. B., Onwuegbuzie, A. J., &Turner, L. A. (2007). Toward a definition of mixed methods research. *Journal of Mixed Methods Research, 1*(2), 112–133.

Kaplan, A. (1964). *The conduct of inquiry*. San Francisco, CA: Chandler.

Kaplan, B., & Duchon, D. (1988). Combining qualitative and quantitative methods in information systems research: A case study. *MIS Quarterly, 12*, 571–586.

King, G., Keohane, R. O., & Verba, S. (1994). *Designing social inquiry: Scientific inference in qualitative research*. Princeton, NJ: Princeton University Press.

Kuhn, T. (1970). *The structure of scientific revolutions* (2nd ed.). Chicago, IL: University of Chicago Press.

Kuhn, T. (1977). *The essential tension: Selected studies in scientific tradition and change*. Chicago, IL: University of Chicago Press.

Lazarsfeld, P. (1971). Forty years later. In M. Jahoda, P. F. Lazarsfeld, & H. Zeisel (Eds.), *Marienthal: The sociography of an unemployed community* (pp. vii–xvi). Chicago, IL: Aldine Atherton.

Lyell, C. (1830–1833), *Principles of geology: Vol. I–III*. London: John Murray.

Lynd, R. S., & Lynd, H. M. (1929). *Middletown: A study in American culture*. New York, NY: Harcourt, Brace.

Malinowski, B. (1922). *Argonauts of the western Pacific*. New York, NY: E. P. Dutton.

Maxwell, J. A. (2004a). Causal explanation, qualitative research, and scientific inquiry in education. *Educational Researcher, 33*(2), 3–11.

Maxwell, J. A. (2004b). Using qualitative methods for causal explanation. *Field Methods, 16*(3), 243–264.

Maxwell, J. A. (2010). Using numbers in qualitative research. *Qualitative Inquiry, 16*(6), 475–482.

Maxwell, J. A. (2011a). *A realist approach for qualitative research*. Thousand Oaks, CA: Sage.

Maxwell, J. A. (2011b). Paradigms or toolkits? Philosophical and methodological positions as heuristics for mixed methods research. *Midwest Educational Research Journal*, *24*(2), 27–30.

Maxwell, J. A. (2012a). *Qualitative research design: An interactive approach* (3rd ed.). Thousand Oaks, CA: Sage.

Maxwell, J. A. (2012b). The importance of qualitative research for causal explanation in education. *Qualitative Inquiry*, *18*, 655–661.

Maxwell, J. A., & Loomis, D. (2003). Mixed methods design: An alternative approach. In A. Tashakkori & C. Teddlie (Eds.), *Handbook of mixed methods in social and behavioral research* (pp. 241–271). Thousand Oaks, CA: Sage.

McPhee, J. (1998). *Annals of the former world*. New York, NY: Farrar, Straus, & Giroux.

Mech, D. (1970). *The wolf: The ecology and behavior of an endangered species*. Minneapolis: University of Minnesota Press.

Miles, M., & Huberman, A. M. (1984). *Qualitative data analysis: A sourcebook of new methods*. Thousand Oaks, CA: Sage.

Milgram, S. (1974). *Obedience to authority: An experimental view*. New York, NY: Harper & Row.

Minta, S. C., Minta, K. A., & Lott, D. F. (1992). Hunting associations between badgers (*Taxidea taxus*) and coyotes (*Canis latrans*). *Journal of Mammalogy*, *73*(4), 814–820.

Mohr, L. B. (1982). *Explaining organizational behavior*. San Francisco, CA: Jossey-Bass.

Morgan, D. L. (2013). *Integrating qualitative and quantitative methods: A pragmatic approach*. Los Angeles, CA: Sage.

Morse, J. M. (2006). The politics of developing research methods. *Qualitative Health Research 16*(3), 3–4.

Morse, J. M., & Niehaus, L. (2009). *Mixed methods design: Principles and procedures*. Walnut Creek, CA: Left Coast Press.

Niglas, K. (2004). *The combined use of qualitative and quantitative methods in educational research*. Dissertation on Social Sciences 8. Tallinn, Estonia: Tallinn Pedagogical University.

Platt, J. (1996). *A history of social research methods in America, 1920–1960*. Cambridge, UK: Cambridge University Press.

Portmann, A. (1961). *Animals as social beings*. New York, NY: Harper & Row.

Rabinowitz, V. C., & Weseen, S. (2001). Power, politics, and the qualitative/quantitative debates in psychology. In D. Tolman & M. Brydon-Miller (Eds.), *From subjects to subjectivities: A handbook of interpretive and participatory methods* (pp. 12–28). New York, NY: New York University Press.

Ragin, C. C. (1987). *The comparative method: Moving beyond qualitative and quantitative strategies*. Berkeley: University of California Press.

Sandelowski, M., Voils, C. I., & Knafl, G. (2009). On quantitizing. *Journal of Mixed Methods Research*, *3*(3), 208–222.

Shadish, W. R., Cook, T. D., & Campbell, D. T. (2002). *Experimental and quasi-experimental designs for generalized causal inference*. Boston, MA: Houghton Mifflin.

Shettleworth, S. J. (2010). *Cognition, evolution, and behavior* (2nd ed.). New York, NY: Oxford University Press.

Slonim-Nevo, V., & Nevo, I. (2009). Conflicting findings in mixed methods research: An illustration from an Israeli study on immigration. *Journal of Mixed Methods Research*, *3*(2), 109–128.

Small, M. L. (2011). How to conduct a mixed methods study: Recent trends in a rapidly growing literature. *Annual Review of Sociology*, *37*, 57–86.

Staw, B. M. (1992). Do smiles lead to sales? Comments on the Sutton/Rafaeli study. In P. Frost & R. Stablein (Eds.), *Doing exemplary research* (pp. 136–142). Thousand Oaks, CA: Sage.

Sutton, R. I., & Rafaeli, A. (1988). Untangling the relationship between displayed emotions and organizational sales: The case of convenience stores. *Academy of Management Journal*, *31*(3), 461–487.

Sutton, R. I., & Rafaeli, A. (1992). How we untangled the relationship between displayed emotions and organizational sales: A tale of bickering and optimism. In P. Frost & R. Stablein (Eds.), *Doing exemplary research* (pp. 115–128). Thousand Oaks, CA: Sage.

Symonds, J. E., & Gorard, S. (2008, September). *The death of mixed methods: Research labels and their casualties*. Paper presented at the British Educational Research Association annual conference, Edinburgh, Scotland.

Tashakkori, A., & Creswell, J. W. (2007). Editorial: The new era of mixed methods. *Journal of Mixed Methods Research*, *1*(1), 3–7.

Teddlie, C., & Tashakkori, A. (2006). A general typology of research design featuring mixed methods. *Research in the Schools*, *13*(1), 12–28.

Teddlie, C., & Tashakkori, A. (2009). *Foundations of mixed methods research: Integrating quantitative and qualitative approaches in the social and behavioral sciences*. Thousand Oaks, CA: Sage.

Tinbergen, N. (1961). *The herring gull's world*. New York, NY: Basic Books.

Trend, M. (1979). On the reconciliation of qualitative and quantitative analyses: A case study. In T. D. Cook & C. S. Reichardt (Eds.), *Qualitative & quantitative methods in program evaluation* (pp. 68–86). Thousand Oaks, CA: Sage.

Warner, W. L., & Lunt, P. S. (1941). *The social life of a modern community*. Westport, CT: Greenwood Press.

Weisner, T. S. (Ed.). (2005). *Discovering successful pathways in children's development: Mixed methods in the study of childhood and family life*. Chicago, IL: University of Chicago Press.

Yin, R. (1993). *Applications of case study research*. Thousand Oaks, CA: Sage.

Yin, R. (2006). Mixed methods research: Are the methods genuinely integrated or merely parallel? *Research in the Schools*, *13*(1), 41–47.

Zeisel, H. (1971). Afterword: Toward a history of sociography. In M. Jahoda, P. F. Lazarsfeld, & H. Zeisel, *Marienthal: The sociography of an unemployed community* (pp. 99–125). Chicago, IL: Aldine Atherton. (Originally published 1933)

Validity in Multimethod and Mixed Research

Kathleen M. T. Collins

Abstract

The first purpose of this chapter is to discuss validity and the varying ways that researchers interpret it. The second purpose is to present guidelines designed to facilitate researchers' efforts to devise, to apply, and to evaluate quality criteria that meet the standard of rigor in multimethod and mixed research[1] (MMMR). First, a discussion of MMMR methodology is presented, and embedded in this discussion is the importance of integration as a characteristic defining MMMR as high-quality research. Second, examples of researchers' interpretations of validity are presented. Aspects of quality criteria that are related to the three research paradigms dominating contemporary social science research accompany these examples. Third, examples of high-quality research frameworks applicable for MMMR are detailed. This chapter concludes with an outline of a criterion sample of articles to illustrate how researchers are designing, applying, and evaluating quality criteria in practice.

Key Words: integration, high-quality research, validity, quality criteria, frameworks

Methodological eclecticism defines the synergistic process of conducting (MMMR) because as a concept it leads researchers' efforts to respond to the research question by *"selecting and then synergistically integrating the most appropriate techniques from a myriad of QUAL, QUAN, and mixed methods"* (Teddlie & Tashakkori, 2011, p. 286, italics in original). The concept of synergy resonates as descriptive of MMMR because the goal of *mixing* is to expand researchers' interpretations and explanations about the topic of interest and to draw data-based conclusions and inferences that are different than or potentially superior to the outcome derived by implementing a monomethod approach.

However, a critical distinction of MMMR is the degree that researchers present a persuasive argument that *integration* has occurred at one or more stages of the research process (i.e., conceptualization, design, implementation) and at the outcome stage, when researchers form credible conclusions

and defensible inferences. The degree that research consumers perceive this argument as persuasive distinguishes MMMR as high-quality research. Members within and across intellectual or research communities vary in their interpretations of what constitutes MMMR (e.g., Brewer & Hunter, 2006; Hesse-Biber & Johnson, 2013; Morse, 2003; Tashakkori & Teddlie, 2003a). Variations in interpretations continue to evolve, as evidenced in the interviews of a criterion sample of researchers identified as early developers of mixed research (cf. Leech, 2010). One interpretive perspective is the view of Hesse-Biber and Johnson (2013) who present an inclusive interpretation of MMMR. They characterize

> MM [mixed methods] research and inquiry [as an approach] that includes "multiple and mixed" research projects that facilitate and reside at the intersections of multiple methods, purposes, kinds of data, and levels of analysis (e.g., micro, meso,

macro), as well as a range of academic disciplines, paradigms, axiologies, stakeholders, and cultures of research and practice. (p. 103, quotes in original)

Hesse-Biber and Johnson (2013) advocate that researchers "'*expand the conversation*' about what MM [mixed methods] is in order to grow, challenge and dialogue among diverse approaches" (p. 103, italics in original). The goal of this chapter is to contribute to this conversation by discussing validity and the varying ways that it is interpreted by researchers who engage in research within and across the three research paradigms. This conversation is framed to juxtapose these interpretations as they contribute toward defining high-quality research. High-quality research is characterized as research that is justified; the process is transparent; the outcomes are defensible; and the findings are viewed as applicable by research consumers.

The purpose of this chapter is to discuss a key component of conducting MMMR that characterizes MMMR as high-quality research, namely, design, application, and evaluation of quality criteria that meets the standard of rigor. Quality criteria are defined as the techniques embedded throughout the study, which when used holistically justify that the study's outcomes are warranted and the researcher's inferences are defensible. The dimensions defining high-quality research discussed in this chapter are presented in Figure 14.1. to illustrate the relationship between these dimensions in conceptualizing high-quality MMMR.

The conceptual blueprint structuring the chapter's content is organized into sections. The first section begins with a discussion of MMMR methodology as an exemplar of high-quality research and the importance of integration as a defining characteristic of a MMMR methodology. In the second section, interpretations of validity and specific aspects of quality criteria related to the three research paradigms dominating social science research are detailed. Next, I present examples of high-quality research frameworks comprising quality criteria reflective of the three research paradigms and applicable for MMMR studies. Finally, a criterion sample of published articles is outlined to illustrate how researchers are applying quality criteria in practice.

Methodology in Multimethod and Mixed Research

The role of researchers who use MMMR methodology is that of an "everyday problem solver" who, typically, will devise research questions that are "multidimensional" (Tashakkori & Teddlie, 2010, p. 274). To respond to these questions, researchers conceptualize a model. This model exemplifies an interpretive framework designed to lead researchers toward forming a broader understanding of the topic of interest. This framework comprises intersections of researchers' theoretical and epistemological perspectives that support decisions and actions, which, in turn, influence researchers' values and beliefs about what constitutes credible data and what comprises the best approach (i.e., methods) to collect and analyze these data (Christ, 2014; Collins, Onwuegbuzie, & Johnson, 2012; Guba, 1990; Hall & Howard, 2008; Morgan, 2007).

Greene's (2008) conceptualization of a methodology as including four domains is an illustrative example of an interpretive framework that typifies MMMR. The first domain is *philosophical assumptions and stances*. This domain situates and brings to the foreground researcher and research team worldview(s), including axiological and epistemological assumptions about what kinds of questions are to be addressed, what kinds of data should be collected to understand the phenomenon of interest, and what are the best ways to analyze and to interpret the data. A worldview also is shaped by the shared beliefs and values found in one's chosen intellectual and disciplinary community (Morgan, 2007). Greene states broadly that this domain refers to what philosopher Denis Phillips (1996) called the "'mental model', of the inquirer—a construct that is messier and less rarified than philosophical paradigms, but also fuller and enriched by both substance and experience"

Fig. 14.1 Dimensions of high-quality research in MMMR.

(p. 9, quotes in original). The following philosophical and conceptual stances have been identified by Teddlie and Tashakkori (2010) as prevalent: a-paradigmatic stance, substantive theory stance, complementary strengths stance, multiple paradigms stance, dialectic stance, and alternative paradigm stance (previously single paradigm stance)— meaning that it "has been used (explicitly or implicitly) by groups of scholars who are practicing MMR (mixed methods research)" (p. 14).

Domain 2 is labeled and focuses on *inquiry logics*. This domain includes researchers' justifications for decisions relevant to the methods selected and implemented in terms of rationale, purpose, question, design, sampling design (i.e., sampling strategy to collect data and sample size per approach), data analysis techniques, quality criteria, and dissemination strategies. Domain 3 includes *guidelines for practice*. This domain addresses the researchers' actions as they devise procedures to actualize into practice the decisions made in the preceding domains. Domain 4 is *sociopolitical commitments*, and as a domain it focuses on awareness of the interplay of the research process and the degree that the researchers' and the stakeholders' (i.e., individuals and or groups who are impacted by the research) values influence this process.

Although each of Greene's (2008) domains must be considered in order to address fully research questions, it is the interconnections of the four domains that characterize this framework as a methodology. Domain 1 is especially connected to the sociopolitical commitment domain, because researchers' ideological perspectives guide decisions about types and framing of the research questions. According to Greene's and my perspective, researchers should consider carefully the needs of all key stakeholders, especially those stakeholders with little power and voice, who, consequently, experience societal disparities in areas such as income, education, and social mobility. Research becomes a form of advocacy that affects forming of the research questions, designing and implementing the study, and disseminating the findings with these stakeholders' values and needs in mind. Inherent in this process are the ethical dimensions of the research in terms of collection, analysis, and interpretation of credible data; quality criteria detailing the rigor of the process; and the transparency of reporting the process as a means of justifying the conclusions and inferences.

The process of forming research questions can originate and reflect primarily researchers' perspectives or stakeholders' perspectives, or it can be an exchange between researchers and stakeholders leading to a collaboratively developed research question. Governmental funding agencies and professional organizations also can exert pressure to sway a researcher's decision to use a specific type of research to address the research question(s) (Brannen, 2005).

The interrelationship of the four domains is one framework for conducting MMMR. For an example of an alternative perspective of a MMMR methodology, readers are encouraged to see Castro, Kellison, Boyd, and Kopak (2010). Castro et al. propose a methodology that focuses primarily on the design component of the study and emphasizes techniques to guide an integrative analysis of quantitative and qualitative data.

Integration

A critical component of instantiating MMMR methodology into practice and justifying the process and conclusions is the degree that "researchers 'genuinely integrate' [their findings] in such a way that the quantitative and qualitative components are mutually illuminating" (Bryman, 2007, p. 8). Bryman's conceptualization of "genuinely integrate" requires researchers to explain how the linkage occurred (Bryman, 2007, p. 8, quotes in the original). The idea of "mutually illuminating" also is used descriptively in Woolley's (2009) interpretation of integration as "mutually illuminating, thereby producing findings that are greater than the sum of the parts" (p. 7).

Integration also is conceptualized as a multidimensional continuum that can occur at one or more stages of the research process (Creswell & Tashakkori, 2007; Yin, 2006). Viewing integration as a continuum highlights the evolving conceptualizations of MMMR as researchers devise different approaches to address different research questions. Researchers can integrate or combine different philosophical assumptions and different methods of data collection and analyses, leading to meta-inferences. A meta-inference in mixed research is the combination or integration of researchers' inferences made from the qualitative *and* quantitative findings, concepts, or theories (Tashakkori & Teddlie, 1998). In multimethod research, the meta-inference is the integration of inferences obtained from concepts or theories and the combination of findings across methods typically associated with one paradigm. It is the tensions evolving from these forms of integration that shape the research process and the outcomes of the research—all contributing to the integration of knowledge. As noted by Pohl, van Kerkhoff, Hadorn, and Bammer (2008), integration of knowledge is a way of "improve[ing] societal problem-solving" (p. 414). This interpretation resonates with the intent underlying sociopolitical commitments, Domain 4 of Greene's interpretation of a MMMR methodology.

Successful integration requires the researcher to explicate the links between the rationale for conducting the research, the purpose, and the analysis (Bryman, 2006; Maxwell & Loomis, 2003); however, the dependent interrelationships between rationale, purpose, and analysis tend to be underreported in MMMR studies (Bryman, 2006). One possible reason for this underreporting is that researchers might not be aware of the multiple rationales and purposes for conducting MMMR and the relationships between rationale, purpose, and design considerations.

Collins, Onwuegbuzie, and Sutton (2006) conducted an analysis of the various ways researchers were implementing mixed research in practice. The results of their analysis led to a model that details the following four rationales for mixing: *participant enrichment* to optimize the sample, *instrument fidelity* to maximize the data collection instrument, *treatment integrity* to ensure the fidelity of the treatment program, intervention, and *significance enhancement* to enhance interpretations of findings. Embedded under each rationale are examples of purposes for mixing. The selection of the rationale and the choice of purpose are dependent on the research question. Two other dimensions identified in this model also affect the design of an investigation. The first dimension is the researcher's decision to emphasize one set of findings—either the findings obtained in the qualitative phase or the findings obtained in quantitative phase, or to place approximately equal emphasis on both sets of findings when he or she is forming conclusions and integrating inferences. This decision is dependent on the design of the study (concurrent or sequential), the quality of the data collected and analyzed, and the type of generalization intended. The remaining dimension in this model is determining and making explicit to the research consumer the stage at which the mixing occurred (e.g., beginning of the study, during the implementation of the study, conclusion of the study).

Design considerations also impact successful integration. The design decision of implementing either a concurrent design or a sequential design can affect integration and the emphasis placed on the conclusions in forming inferences per stage (Bryman, 2007). For example, say the researcher decides to implement a concurrent design whereby data collected in stage 1 and stage 2 are analyzed independently. The sample participating in each stage is identical (Onwuegbuzie & Collins, 2007). Data collected in stage 1, via an interview, are intended to provide contextual information of high-risk geographic areas, and data collected in stage 2, questionnaire responses, are intended to obtain prevalence and incidence rates of low birth rates in these areas. In this example, integration is plausible because the same individuals participated in each phase, and the integration of the findings would allow the researcher to address the entirety of the research question. Also, by using an identical sample, the researcher addressed one of the threats, sample integration, identified in the validity framework of Onwuegbuzie and Johnson (2006).

In a second example, the researcher decides to implement a sequential design, whereby the data analyzed in stage 1 informs the design of stage 2. In this example scenario, the purpose of the interview data collected in stage 1 is critical to the process of ensuring rigor because the interview data is designed to optimize the selection of a criterion sample. The criterion sample is the data source for stage 2. In this example, in stage 2 the questionnaire data collected were expanded to obtain contextual information by using open-ended questions as part of the questionnaire. Data in stage 2 provided the data for interpreting prevalence and incidence rates of low birth rates and contextual information about high-risk geographic areas—the specific research question addressed in the study. Subsequently, at the outcome stage, the researcher placed the emphasis on the findings obtained in stage 2 because the data collected in this phase addressed the entirety of the research question. In this scenario, integration between the qualitative stage (stage 1) and the quantitative stage (stage 2) is limited due to the role of the interview data in stage 1. Another validity consideration when implementing a sequential design is the ordering of the stages and the degree to which the ordering of the stages impacts integration and, subsequently, impacts the quality of the inferences. This threat to validity, called sequential threat, is one of the nine threats identified in the validity framework of Onwuegbuzie and Johnson (2006).

Data considerations impact successful integration. Successful integration requires the researcher to collect the data necessary to respond adequately to the research question. Data adequacy is the degree to which the researcher has collected adequate data in terms of quantity and quality necessary to justify the type of analysis used, namely, case oriented, variable oriented, and process/experience oriented (Onwuegbuzie, Slate, Leech, & Collins, 2009). Case-oriented analysis (popular in qualitative research) focuses on a selected case (or several cases for comparison) as the object of analysis, and variable-oriented analysis (popular in quantitative research) identifies probabilistic relationships among variables. Onwuegbuzie, Slate, et al. (2009) coined the term *process/experience–oriented analysis* to refer to "analyses [that involve] evaluating processes or experiences pertaining to one or more cases within a specific context over time" (p. 24).

Addressing the standard of data adequacy also allows researchers the option to transform the data using quantitizing and/or qualitizing strategies (Onwuegbuzie & Teddlie, 2003; Tashakkori & Teddlie, 1998) and conducting cross-over tracks analyses (Li, Marquart, & Zercher, 2000) or cross-over mixed analyses (Onwuegbuzie & Combs, 2010). Collecting the adequate amount of data allows the option of implementing mixed advanced statistical techniques, such as Q methodology, Q factor analysis (e.g., Newman & Ramlo, 2010), canonical correlation (e.g., Onwuegbuzie et al., 2007), and correspondence analysis (e.g., Onwuegbuzie, Frels, Leech, & Collins, 2011).

Data integration is "the extent that different data elements and various strategies for analysis of those elements are combined. . . as to become interdependent in reaching a common theoretical or research goal" (Bazeley, 2010, p. 432). Bazeley (2009) observed that data integration of the quantitative- and qualitative-driven stages has been criticized as "epistemologically unacceptable" (p. 203), but the product of integration, the researcher's conclusions, is often considered acceptable and desirable. This conflict might be based on a pragmatist paradigm judgment of the findings and conclusions: Do they make sense? Do they appear to answer the research questions? Do they produce predicted outcomes? Do they apply in particular situations?

Conducting data integration and documenting its application is complicated further by the language of integration, specifically the metaphors used to describe the integration of analyses (Bazeley & Kemp, 2012). Applicability of a particular metaphor is based on the implicit assumption that consumers and researchers interpret *similarly* the metaphor's meaning (Bazeley & Kemp, 2012). For example, the metaphors used to present integration are not mutually exclusive in terms of characteristics. As an example, Bazeley and Kemp note that triangulation is used to describe two different purposes of triangulation: validation (which is achieved when results converge) and complementarity (which is achieved when results together provide a more complete and more complex picture). They note that too often researchers overlook the fact that whether results converge or diverge is an empirical issue. Although triangulation has been used to refer to a type of result, specifically convergence of results, a purpose for implementing a mixed design could be initiation (Greene, Caracelli, & Graham, 1989). Designing a MMMR study for the purpose of initiation occurs when the researcher's intent is to obtain findings that diverge, contradict. This dissonance could lead potentially to findings, conclusions, and inferences not obtainable using methods for the purposes of validation and complementarity (Greene, 2007). Triangulation also has been used to refer to a design issue (specifically, the use of multiple investigators, methods, data sources, and theories/perspectives; Bazeley & Kemp, 2012). Bazeley and Kemp caution that the word *triangulation* be used carefully and its role in integration should be clarified.

Interpretations of Validity in High-Quality Research

A key factor influencing perspectives about validity and rigor is the interpretation of the words (Dellinger & Leech, 2007). In the realist paradigm in quantitative/experimental research, the researcher assumes that the construct of interest exists independently of the person, and support for constructs is seen in the theoretical positioning of the construct in the empirical literature. Generally, in qualitative/interpretive research constructs are more concrete and are situated in particular historical and cultural contexts. Highly abstract and general constructs are viewed with suspicion, and interpretation and construction of a construct continues to change as the inquiry develops. In both research approaches, however, neither participants nor researchers can claim value neutrality because their perspectives are positioned culturally, historically, and theoretically (Freeman, deMarrais, Preissle, Roulston, & St. Pierre, 2007).

However, there are differences *within* qualitative and quantitative research about what constitutes rigor and the best approach to attain it, as well as what language to use to articulate the meaning of these perspectives in practice. Preissle (2011) observed that "most methodologies from a variety of persuasions used the term validity but their discussions of what *constitutes* validity were richly informed by scholars proposing substitute language [of validity]" (p. 693, italics in the original). For example, compare the following quantitative and qualitative terms for rigor: internal validity (Campbell & Stanley, 1963) and trustworthiness (Lincoln & Guba, 1985); external validity (Campbell & Stanley, 1963) and credibility (Eisner, 1991). Adding to the list are the mixed research terms of legitimation (Onwuegbuzie & Johnson, 2006) and inference quality (Tashakkori & Teddlie, 2008). All of these terms are expressive of the process of designing and conducting high-quality research that meets the standards of rigor.

However, the standards of rigor and the quality criteria to design and to implement rigor in practice are interpreted differently by intellectual and research communities and, subsequently, vary across the three major research paradigms. A researcher's choice of standards of rigor is likely to be to be reflective of his or her particular interpretive framework, and it is this framework that shapes the interpretive meaning and choice of language in high-quality research.

The language of research and the degree that language in terms of "theoretical concepts, models and products" and terminology is interpreted similarly by the research team, a team that might include members of different disciplines, is a factor in achieving successful communication, collaboration, and integration (Pohl et al., 2008, p. 415). Subsequently, researchers of different paradigms need to understand the language of other paradigms for the purpose of communication and collaborative work—especially when conducting MMMR. A MMMR design is a more complex design because it is likely to involve two or multiple stages, and in mixed research these stages are representative of qualitative-based design *and* quantitative-based design. High-quality research requires that researchers meet the relevant research quality criteria associated with each paradigm at these various stages. Decisions made during the conduct of a research study are not static; they evolve as the researcher is immersed in the study, and they are made transparent by strategically addressing and documenting the use of appropriate qualitative, quantitative, and mixed quality criteria throughout the study (Collins et al., 2012; Onwuegbuzie & Johnson, 2006).

A critical dimension of high-quality research is to establish quality criteria for assessing the degree that the process *and* the outcome of the research are interpreted as credible, defensible, and rigorous. A key point of this chapter is that it is up to the researcher or research team to construct the appropriate *validity design* for the research study (i.e., select and use the appropriate quality criteria for the particular research questions and for the particular research study). In conducting high-quality MMMR, the complexity of the design likely will lead the researcher to select strategically quality criteria across the three paradigms. In the following sections, interpretations of validity and selective quality criteria implemented in the quantitative, qualitative, and mixed research paradigms are outlined.

Quantitative Paradigm

The postpositivist paradigm, which is popular in quantitative research, is grounded in the tenets defining the natural sciences. The support for constructs of interest in a study is seen in the theoretical positioning of the construct in the empirical literature. Postpositivists emphasize the hypothetic-deductive model of logic when devising an approach to research. Generally, the researcher approaches the research process with the goal of attaining objective data by conducting empirical observations, implementing statistical analysis to identify potential relationships between independent and dependent variables, and verifying theories. The researcher implements standardized methods, such as designing randomized control studies to minimize potential sources of bias, conducting power analyses to obtain an adequate sample, and addressing the assumptions underpinning the statistical analyses.

In quantitative research the traditional focus has been on design-related validity (Campbell & Stanley, 1963; Cook & Campbell, 1979), specifically, the degree that the research design addresses potential threats to causation (i.e., internal validity), and generalizations (i.e., external validity). Cook and Campbell add statistical conclusion validity and construct validity (in a design context) to the traditional concepts of internal and external validity. The former refers to one's ability "to infer that the independent and dependent variables are related [covariation] and the strength of that relationship" (Johnson & Christensen, 2014, p. 668). The latter is "the extent to which a higher order construct is accurately represented in a particular study" (Johnson & Christensen, 2014, p. 653). One of the many threats to construct validity in a research context is treatment diffusion (i.e., cross-over of some members of the control group to the treatment group due to physical proximity and/or communication). Threats to internal validity are the "causal reasoning errors" (Shadish, Cook, & Campbell, 2002, p. 63) that are "possible causes—reasons to think that the relationship between A and B is not causal, that if could have occurred even in the absence of the treatment and… led to the same outcomes that were observed for the treatment" (Shadish et al., 2002, p. 54). (For more information on validity of research results or research validity and the many threats, see Shadish et al., 2002).

In quantitative research another traditional focus has been on measurement validity. Measurement validity (Messick, 1989, 1995) is a unitary concept with construct validity as the unifying concept. Major kinds of evidence used to establish measurement validity include evidence on content (content-related evidence), evidence based on internal structure of the instrument (e.g., dimensionality is examined with factor analysis), and evidence based on relations to other variables (e.g., criterion-related evidence including concurrent and predictive evidence, convergent evidence, discriminant evidence, and known groups evidence; Johnson & Christensen, 2014). In Messick's model of validity (see American Educational Research Association, American Psychological Association, & National Council on Measurement in Education, 1999; Johnson & Christensen, 2014; Messick, 1989, 1995), validity refers to the "appropriateness of the interpretations, inferences, and actions that we make based on test scores" (Johnson & Christensen, 2014, p. 172). Messick's (1995) model of validity in terms of content-related criterion-related and construct-related validity also has been applied to scores obtained from student teaching evaluations in higher education. The meta-validation model developed by Onwuegbuzie, Daniel, and Collins (2009) is an illustrative example of this application.

Qualitative Paradigm

In qualitative research generally, the issue of representation dominates credibility of the data collected and reported. The communication process that shapes the circumstances surrounding the participants' and the researcher's subjectivity are central to the study's design and the textual analysis and interpretation of data. There are several critical dimensions of validity in qualitative research.

FIRST CRITICAL DIMENSION

A critical dimension of validity in qualitative research and high-quality research is to acquire understanding of the phenomenon of interest and to collect data and implement validity or audit checks leading to conjectures that are trustworthy (Lincoln & Guba, 1986; Maxwell, 1992). Lincoln and Guba (1986) detail the following dimensions of trustworthiness: "credibility" (audits: prolonged engagement, member check), "transferability" (audit: account details context) "dependability" (audit: external review to document the collection process), and "confirmability" (audit: external review to document the product of the process, i.e., "data and reconstructions" p. 77).

Maxwell (1992) delineates his analysis of validity in qualitative research into broad categories. As conceptualized by Maxwell, each category places emphasis on the degree that the researcher's account leads to an understanding in terms of credible inferences about the topic under investigation. *Descriptive* validity emphasizes "factual accuracy" of the reporting and or transcription of the account (e.g., interview, observation; Maxwell, 1992, p. 285). Another component of descriptive validity is the recording of participant's tonal quality and nonverbal behavior (Onwuegbuzie, Leech, & Collins, 2008). *Interpretive* validity is the degree to which the researcher's interpretation of the account captures the meaning of the words used and the experiences of the participants. *Theoretical* validity is the fit between the theoretical explanation derived from the study's findings and the analyzed data (Maxwell, 1992).

Examples of validity or audit checks pertaining to descriptive and interpretive validity are member-checking the account, interviewing participants and researchers at multiple points in the course of the study, and using purposive sampling to identify negative cases. Addressing theoretical validity might require researchers to expand their fieldwork, thereby collecting more data and/or employing multiple theories as part of the interpretive framework (Johnson & Christensen, 2014). (For more information on these categories of validity see Maxwell, 1992; Onwuegbuzie et al., 2008).

SECOND CRITICAL DIMENSION

A second critical dimension is to establish criteria for detecting bias. The five levels of authenticity criteria (Guba & Lincoln, 1989; Lincoln & Guba, 1986) are situated in a naturalistic inquiry associated with the tenets defining constructivist and phenomenological research. Omission of these criteria can compromise the quality of data collected, the degree that the analyses are credible and the potential for introducing bias into the study (Lincoln, Lynham, & Guba, 2011).

The first authenticity criterion, *fairness*, is the degree to which collected data represent a balanced perspective that encompasses the participants' constructions and underlying values. The emphasis is to uncover potentially "conflicting constructions and value structures" of the stakeholders by implementing a deliberate process designed to access and analyze these constructions at the stages of data collection, analysis, and interpretation (Lincoln & Guba, 1986, p. 79). Addressing this criterion of fairness, the researcher implements ". . . deliberate attempts to prevent marginalization, to act affirmatively with respect to inclusion. . . and to ensure [that the participants]. . . have their stories treated fairly and with balance" (Lincoln et al., 2011, p. 122).

The second, *ontological* authenticity, and the third, *educative* authenticity, are the extent to which participants' involvement in the research has increased individually their levels of awareness. The elevation of awareness, subsequently, leads to a change in self-constructions (ontological), and these elevated levels of awareness can lead participants to recognize that the constructions of others might reflect values that are potentially unlike the individual participant's own value system (educative); this recognition leads the participants to formulate a better understanding and appreciation of the constructions, perspectives, and opinions of others.

The fourth, *catalytic* authenticity, is the degree to which participants' evolving constructions promote decisions leading to actions. *Tactical* authenticity, the fifth, is the degree to which the researcher has become empowered to act to encourage and to support the transition of participants' decisions into actions by providing resources (e.g., training in community activism and political advocacy). (For more information on authenticity criteria, see Lincoln et al., 2011).

THIRD CRITICAL DIMENSION

A third critical dimension is reflexivity (Alvesson & Sköldberg, 2009). Reflexivity is interpreted as a "process of reflecting critically on the self as researcher, 'the human as instrument'" (Guba & Lincoln, 2005, p. 210, quotes in original). In qualitative research, the subjectivity of the researcher is recognized as integral to the research implementation (Poggenpoel & Myburgh, 2003). However, as noted by Poggenpoel and Myburgh, researchers can introduce bias, leading to unintended consequences in the research process that can compromise the trustworthiness of the data collected and analyzed. One example of potential bias introduced by a researcher is scholastic bias, whereby the researcher attributes erroneously underlying intent in some form to a research participant's behavior (Bourdieu, 1998).

Reflexive strategies (e.g., interviews, journaling, focus groups) prompt researchers' self-reflections and heighten their awareness that their social background (i.e., class, ethnicity, gender, level of education), beliefs, and assumptions concerning social reality interconnect with the context of the research study (Hesse-Biber & Leavy, 2007). These interconnections intervene concomitantly in the creation of knowledge and thereby affect the process of conducting the research (Alvesson & Sköldberg, 2009). Examples of these reflexive strategies often are found in action research and feminist approaches.

Reflexivity also can enhance researchers' explicit and implicit assumptions about their conceptualizations of the validation audit and the rationale for its selection—one example is triangulation. As noted earlier in this chapter, how the researcher conceptualizes triangulation (e.g., use of multiple investigators, methods, data sources, and theories/perspectives) and explicates the purpose of triangulation (validation, complementarity, initiation) for its use in a study impacts the process of integration. Reflexivity strategies can illuminate researchers' conceptualizations of triangulation as a design strategy, thereby prompting them to make their conceptualizations transparent and potentially enhancing the trustworthiness of the data.

Mixed Research Paradigm

As noted earlier, high-quality research requires strong validity designs. The quality of the validity design leads the researcher to formulate credible conclusions and to support the degree that the researcher can integrate these conclusions into meaningful and defensible inferences. In mixed research, this process of integration and the degree that it is successful is referred to as integrative efficacy, whereby the goal of integration leads to the researcher formulating "theoretically consistent meta-inference[s]" based on integration of findings and conclusions obtained from each strand (Teddlie & Tashakkori, 2009, p. 305). In this context, *strand* refers to the three components of the study: conceptualization (forming the purpose, questions, design), experiential (implementing the methods), inferential (formulating conclusions and inferences). Integrative efficacy is unique to mixed research because within a study there is a minimum of two strands: a quantitative strand and a qualitative strand (Tashakkori & Teddlie, 2003b). Achieving integrative efficacy typically requires researchers to use thoughtfully the appropriate validity standards found in the three prominent paradigms and in multiple intellectual research communities (some examples of communities are in parentheses) who are associated, in varying ways, with these three research paradigms: quantitative-based paradigm (e.g., postpositivists), qualitative-based paradigm (e.g., social constructivists, autoethnographers, critical theorists), and the mixed research-based paradigm (e.g., transdisciplinary, interdisciplinary, and mixed researchers). Addressing the appropriate design of these types of quality criteria during the research process for a particular study is called *multiple validities* by Onwuegbuzie and Johnson (2006). Coining the term *legitimation* to describe validity was Onwuegbuzie and Johnson's attempt to present a term that transcended reliance on one word, such as *validity* or *trustworthiness*, terms associated traditionally with quantitative and qualitative research, respectively.

Forms of Quality Criteria

To construct the appropriate validity design, Bryman (2006) identified three forms of quality criteria: separate criteria, convergent criteria, and bespoke criteria. Application of the first form, *separate criteria*, involves the researcher applying to each methodological approach quality criteria that are associated with each paradigm. Subsequently, these criteria are viewed as applicable for assessing the methodological soundness of that particular approach. Specifically, validity criteria (e.g., internal and external validity, reliability, objectivity) would be applied to the quantitative component, and qualitative criteria (e.g., trustworthiness, authenticity, subjectivity) associated with qualitative paradigm would be applied to the qualitative component. Using separate criteria can be used in a concurrent design. In this design, data collection

and analysis activities per approach are independent. The integration of findings per approach occurs at the conclusion stage of the study. Independence of the two approaches throughout the research process allows the researcher to apply separate criteria to each approach. Separate criteria also can be used in a sequential design depending on the relationship between the phases of the study. In a sequential design, the data collected in the first approach are analyzed, and the results are used to inform decisions implemented in the second approach. Ivankova's (2014) study, which is detailed later in this chapter, is an example of the use of separate criteria in a sequential design.

Application of the second form, *convergent criteria*, means the researcher applies the same criteria to each qualitative and quantitative component in a study. Applying convergent criteria makes sense when researchers are working primarily or entirely from a quantitative or qualitative framework. Bryman (2006) offers the following example: qualitative component is implemented to generate hypotheses and/or to generate measurement guidelines for the quantitative component; however, the framework guiding the design is primarily quantitative. Subsequently, in this example, the types of validity addressed are generalization—external validity and construct validity—measurement validity.

Applying convergent criteria also makes sense in a multimethod design that employs a pluralistic approach to data collection and analysis, *if* the methods used reflect a similar epistemological orientation. The study conducted by Frost et al. (2011) is an example of the application of convergent criteria. These researchers analyzed the transcript of a semistructured interview using four different qualitative analyses: grounded theory, interpretive, phenomenological analysis, narrative analysis, and Foucauldian discourse analysis (Frost et al., 2011). These four analyses are associated with the qualitative paradigm and meet the criterion of sharing a similar epistemological orientation.

The third form, *bespoke criteria*, is developed specifically for a MMMR design and involves employing methods that represent more than one epistemological orientation, and/or implementing at least one quantitative component and one qualitative component, and integrating systematically the quantitative and qualitative components throughout the study. However, criteria defining the methodological soundness of bespoke criteria are grounded in selective aspects of quality criteria reflective of the three research paradigms. Bespoke criteria make sense when the researcher is applying a sequential design. Bespoke criteria also are appropriate when data are transformed.

The degree of integration likely will influence researchers' decisions to use one or more of these forms of criteria in a study. A limited degree of integration would support applying separate criteria (Bryman, 2006). Bespoke criteria would be a more suitable choice when there is a high level of systematic integration at one or more of the following components: philosophical stances, techniques for data collection, and methods of analyses occurring within and across the components of a study (Bryman, 2006).

Bryman (2006) recommends a contingency approach that takes into account the circumstances surrounding the individual study. Two key factors can influence the choice of criteria representative of a contingency approach: level of integration and the degree that one set of findings obtained from one approach dominates when the conclusions and inferences are formed (Bryman, 2006).

Selective Examples of Research Quality Frameworks

Several research quality frameworks are available to facilitate the design of quality criteria. These frameworks are designed as guidelines that researchers adapt to *fit* the circumstances of a study. I use the word *fit* because there are circumstances surrounding each study that require researchers to reflect about what constitutes rigor and the best approach to attain it, given the study's characteristics. In the following sections, I outline five quality frameworks. These frameworks were selected because each demonstrates a different approach to validity design and each can be useful for the construction of specific quality criteria for a particular MMMR study attempting to answer a particular set of research questions. Therefore, when viewed holistically, these frameworks can be complementary for appropriate validity design in MMMR.

Framework Example 1

Onwuegbuzie and Johnson (2006) developed a quality framework detailing nine criteria. Applications of these criteria are applicable for designing contingency criteria specifically for a MMMR methodology. To illustrate, I relate their framework to Greene's (2008) four domains of a research methodology.

First, the following are relevant especially for Greene's (2008) philosophical assumptions and stances domain: paradigmatic mixing, inside-outside or emic and etic perspectives, and commensurability approximation legitimation. Second, these criteria are relevant especially for Greene's inquiry logics domain: weakness minimization, sequential, conversion, and sample integration legitimation. Third, the following are important for Greene's guidelines for practice domain in terms of procedural aspects of the inquiry: sequential, conversion, and sample integration. Fourth, Greene's sociopolitical commitment domain is addressed directly in sociopolitical legitimation.

Perhaps, most important, Onwuegbuzie and Johnson (2006) emphasize the use of multiple validities or multiple legitimation, which is the extent to which the relevant quality criteria from quantitative, qualitative, and mixed research are addressed, used, and resolved successfully in a MMMR study. Placement of each criterion under a specific domain, and in some cases more than one domain, is meant to show that these criteria relate to legitimation of the research process and the research findings/outcomes. (For more information on these types of legitimation see Onwuegbuzie & Johnson, 2006).

Framework Example 2

As emphasized throughout this chapter, MMMR necessitates the inclusion of aspects of quality criteria from both the quantitative and qualitative research paradigms. However, although this is a necessary condition, it is not sufficient for studies that involve a high level of systematic integration. Systematic integration is important especially for distinguishing MMMR as high-quality research, and in practice it likely will necessitate an eclectic approach to the construction of validity designs. The framework developed by Dellinger and Leech (2007) exemplifies this approach. The mixed research criteria serving as the base of their framework are design quality and interpretive rigor (Teddlie & Tashakkori, 2009) and legitimation (Onwuegbuzie & Johnson, 2006). They use traditional quality criteria from qualitative research (credibility, authenticity, thoroughness) and quantitative research (design-related and measurement-related criteria).

Measurement-related criteria include the following elements of construct validation: foundational, inferential consistency, utilization/ historical, and consequential. Foundational element is the quality of the researcher's understanding of his or her potential biases, knowledge, and the literature (e.g., theoretical, analytical, evaluative) surrounding the construct of interest. Validation of the researcher's understanding is based on a comprehensive and critical appraisal of the literature. The results of the appraisal, assuming defensible criteria have been implemented, situate purposefully the study's theoretical framework and methodology in scholarly and historical contexts and examines the degree to which the claims are justified and the conclusions are defensible (Boote & Beile, 2005; Dellinger & Leech, 2007).

Inferential consistency, as an element in this model, validates that the researchers' decisions made relative to implementing the methodology make the best use of the data collected in terms of addressing the research question and formulating credible conclusions and defensible inferences. Utilization/historical element is the degree to which "evidence accrues to a study's inferences, measures, or findings because of the use (appropriate or not) in the extant literature or in other applications, such as decision making or policy development" (Dellinger & Leech, 2007, p. 325). Consequential element provides justification of the results in terms of the degree that the findings and inferences are perceived by the research consumer as having consequential effects in real-world applications. These five criteria help us to see, depending on our reflectivity, that the research process, validity audits, and research outcome are interpreted in multiple contexts. Moreover, these interpretations are shaped by the selection of specific literature, merging of evidence, and applicability of the findings as perceived by the research consumer.

Framework Example 3

The framework developed by Teddlie and Tashakkori (2009) highlights the interrelationship between a study's design and the design of the quality criteria. In their framework, they provide two interrelated ideas of inference quality (i.e., selection of a design) and interpretive rigor (i.e., selection of the appropriate analysis techniques). The following are important for design quality: (a) design suitability (Is the mixed research design appropriate for addressing the research question and purpose for mixing?); (b) design fidelity (Do the sampling design, data collection activities, and data analysis techniques reflect standards of "quality and rigor" and lead to the understanding of "meanings, effects,

and relationships?"); (c) within-design consistency (Are the design components connected in a "logical and seamless manner" and "do the strands. . . follow each other (or are they linked?) in a logical and seamless manner?"; and (d) analytic adequacy (Are the analytical techniques applied appropriately and applicable to addressing the research question?) (Teddlie & Tashakkori, 2009, p. 301).

To achieve interpretive rigor, Teddlie and Tashakkori (2009) recommend the following: (a) interpretive consistency (Do the inferences "follow the relevant findings in terms of type, scope, and intensity?"); (b) theoretical consistency (Are the inferences "consistent with theory and state of knowledge in the field?"; (c) interpretive agreement (Do the inferences resonate as credible to other scholars and "match participants' constructions?"); and (d) interpretive distinctiveness (Are the inferences perceived as "distinctively more credible/plausible" compared to other conceivable conclusions?) (Teddlie & Tashakkori, 2009, p. 301). Also helpful for interpretive rigor are (a) making sure meta-inferences are based appropriately on the data from each approach and carefully evaluating any inconsistencies (integrative efficacy) and (b) making sure inferences based on qualitative and quantitative data correspond to the research purpose and question(s) guiding the design of the study (interpretive correspondence). In sum, inference quality and interpretive rigor should help facilitate a transparent process for using quality criteria throughout the research process and place a strong emphasis on integration (Teddlie & Tashakkori, 2009).

Framework Example 4

O'Cathain (2010) developed a framework that details domains of quality criteria applicable at distinct stages of a research study. It is organized according to the following dimensions: stage of the study (planning, undertaking, interpreting, disseminating, and applying) and the following domains of quality obtained from her critique of published frameworks and articles outlining quality criteria across disciplines: planning quality, design quality, data quality, interpretive rigor, inference transferability, reporting of quality, synthesizability (i.e., quality for inclusion in a systematic review), and utility quality. O'Cathain comments that the feasibility of using the entire framework within a single study could be problematic because addressing one criterion might diminish the efficacy of addressing another criterion. However, she also comments that the researcher can prioritize and select judiciously criteria based on his or her philosophical stance concerning what constitutes rigor given the parameters of the study.

Framework Example 5

The next framework's (Collins et al., 2012) construction expands validity design to a holistic and synergistic legitimation process. The word *holistic* refers to combining and incorporating quality criteria from published works into the research study; the word *synergistic* refers to, for example, incorporating quality criteria such as the four core principles of the Hall and Howard (2008) model. In their model, they label the following core principles: concept of synergy, position of equal value, ideology of difference, and the relationship between the researcher and the study design. Collins et al. rely on this meaning of synergy in developing their framework.

According to Hall and Howard (2008), *synergy* in a MMMR design creates a combined effect that leads optimally to a "greater" outcome, which is interpreted as "greater as more than" what would be gained from separate qualitative and quantitative studies (p. 251). Position of *equal value* requires the researcher to be aware of the possible contributions of multiple epistemologies and theories as well as methodologies when mixing approaches (Hall & Howard, 2008). *Ideology of difference* focuses researchers' attention on "using methods that contribute multiple points of view on the topic of interest" (Hall & Howard, 2008, p. 252). Research integrity is gained by maintaining a dynamic balance between the tensions of the "more quantitatively based position of objectivity and the more qualitatively based position of subjectivity" (Hall & Howard, 2008, p. 252). This balancing of tensions is facilitated through researchers' use of interactive subjectivity (cf. Morgan, 2007) to support interpretations and claims. The final principle stresses the importance of relationships representing collaboration and cooperation between research team members who likely will represent diversity in terms of membership in one or more intellectual research communities and have expertise in either quantitative, or qualitative, or both research approaches. The diversity within the team and the degree that this diversity is reflected in the research process creates the synergism.

In its systematic attempt to obtain synergy and integration, the holistic and synergistic legitimation process framework (Collins et al., 2012) adds to the discussion of high-quality research two criteria applicable for mixed research that relies on ideas and approaches from, at a minimum, the three research paradigms. The first criterion is philosophical clarity. Philosophical clarity refers to researchers' awareness regarding their philosophical assumptions and stances and use of these stances in their decisions and actions in a study, including their decisions regarding legitimation criteria. The second criterion stresses the contribution of integrating disciplinary and research community viewpoints and use of quality criteria of multiple established and creative intellectual research communities. For example, this criterion strategically selects from Patton's (2002) quality criteria for the following five intellectual communities of research practice: (a) traditional scientific research; (b) social construction, constructivist, interpretivist research; (c) artistic and evocative research; (e) critical change research; and (e) program evaluation and research. Collins et al. (2012) in their framework added a sixth community of research practice labeled *mixed research and dialectical pluralism*. They included this second criterion because the conduct of high-quality research often necessitates that researchers carefully *integrate* ideas from these different communities and disciplinary perspectives to address empirical research questions.

Applications of Quality Criteria for Multimethod and Mixed Research

To examine how researchers are interpreting validity and designing, applying, and evaluating quality criteria in practice, I present three selective examples. My selection of the three applications was based on specific criteria. In application 1, the authors detail an application of authenticity criteria (defined earlier) to the development of an interview protocol. This application exemplifies the use of quality criteria documenting rigor as interpreted in the context of constructivist and phenomenological research. It is an illustrative example of the use of quality criteria representative of different intellectual research communities in a MMMR design, as recommended by Collins et al. (2012).

Applications 2 and 3 provide empirical examples of a multimethod study and a mixed research study, respectively. In both examples, the authors explained the rationales for their validity designs and detailed the quality criteria implemented. Rationales and explanations of the use of specific quality criteria supported their conclusions and inferences. Moreover, in both studies the authors' process of integration was transparent.

Application Example 1

Collins, Onwuegbuzie, Johnson, and Frels (2013) discuss how to construct an interview protocol designed to debrief the research team during a research study. A primary intent of the interview protocol is to increase researchers' awareness of their decisions, actions, and use of quality criteria during each phase of the research process. Collins et al. defined debriefing as "the reflective and iterative process of acquiring information, insights, and reflections from members of the research team about their decisions and their actions" (p. 271).

Additionally, the debriefing approach can help document the degree that researchers have met in their study the five principles of authenticity bias (defined earlier), the quality criteria of philosophical clarity, and, when applicable, the integration of multiple viewpoints representing different intellectual and research communities of practice. Collins et al. (2013) recommend conducting a minimum of one focus group interview of the team members to address (a) ontological and educative authenticity and (b) use of an appropriate quality criteria design in the research study. To assist researchers, Collins et al., building on the work of Onwuegbuzie et al. (2008) who detailed example questions assessing authenticity bias, included example interview questions relating to Guba and Lincoln's (1989) authenticity bias as it relates to quality criteria (i.e., inclusive of qualitative, quantitative, and mixed quality criteria thoughtfully and appropriately combined for each research study). Embedded in these questions are probes assessing the researcher's awareness of his or her theory in practice and degree of philosophical clarity. They also developed debriefing interview questions to ask at each of the four phases of the research study because debriefing is done during *and* at the end of a study. Its purpose is to make sure the research process is instantiated appropriately given one's research questions, research purpose, and purpose for mixing.

Application Example 2

Frost et al. (2011) conducted a multiple methods study using a pluralistic approach that involved applying the following four qualitative analytical techniques—grounded theory, interpretive phenomenological analysis, narrative analysis, and Foucauldian discourse analysis—to analyze an interview transcript. Four analysts, each using one of the methods, analyzed a single semistructured interview. The four analyses were cross-analyzed by the team. The integration rationale was significance enhancement, and the integration purpose was complementarity (Collins et al., 2006; Greene et al., 1989). Frost et al. noted that the team's interpretation of integration was "the mixing of realist, interpretive, and constructionist paradigms within qualitative approaches [a position supported by] Moran-Ellis et al., 2006" (p. 94). Frost et al. improved integration by placing similar emphasis on the "use and outcomes of each method used and its role in the process" (p. 109), thereby elevating the team's "multilayered understanding of data" (p. 93). The team also conducted debriefing interviews, a technique recommended by Collins et al. (2013). Each analyst was interviewed individually using a semistructured interview format, and each analyst kept a reflective journal describing the process of conducting the analysis. The analysis of these data detailed the analysts' individual experiences, and the cross-case case analyses created an opportunity to consider the "creative tensions arising from combining epistemologies when analyzing the same piece of data" (Frost et. al., 2011, p. 95).

Frost et al. (2011) could have added another dimension of quality criteria: interviews of the participants to member check the interview data. Asking the interviewee to validate the accuracy of the transcribed data (i.e., member check) would help improve interpretive validity (Maxwell, 1992) by revising interpretations based on the participants' perceptions and, depending on the data quality, adding another dimension of quality criteria.

Application Example 3

Ivankova (2014) proposed a multifaceted approach to validate the meta-inferences generated from the implementation of a sequential QUAN → QUAL mixed design. Separate criteria (Bryman 2006) were implemented to assess the reliability and validity of the quantitative data and the trustworthiness of the qualitative data. Ivankova established credibility of the meta-inferences by implementing the following design strategies particular to a sequential design: "applying a systematic process for selecting participants for qualitative follow-up, elaborating on unexpected quantitative results, and observing interaction between qualitative and quantitative study strands" (p. 48).

Ivankova (2014) presents this approach in the context of designing and implementing an empirical study. The study's purpose was to determine and to assess graduate students' perspectives about learning in an online environment. The quantitative component of questionnaire responses preceded the qualitative component of responses to an open-ended telephone interview. Questionnaire findings were used to craft the interview protocol, which consisted of 12 questions accompanied by probes to elicit elaboration on responses to the questions. This protocol was used to interview a subset of the sample. The subset participated in the quantitative component, the first stage of the study. The integration rationale was significance enhancement, and the integration purpose was complementarity (Collins et al., 2006; Greene et al., 1989).

Separate criteria were used to assess the validity (quantitative) and the trustworthiness (qualitative) of the data collected in each component. Validity in the quantitative component was assessed by calculating reliability coefficients of participants' questionnaire responses. Trustworthiness of the qualitative interview data was documented by using multiple data sources, including transcribed interview data, follow-up e-mails, researcher notes, and intercoder agreement percentages. Each respondent was provided a summary of his or her transcribed interview for member checking. Comparisons of the quantitative and qualitative data resulted in Ivankova (2014) conducting additional statistical analyses on the questionnaire data. The additional analysis led her to conduct additional qualitative interviews. The analyses were conducted and interpreted iteratively, and "provided additional validity checks to secure credible meta-inferences" (p. 24).

Conclusion and Future Directions

This chapter began with a discussion of methodology and integration because it is transparency of the methodology and the degree of integration that characterizes MMMR as a model of *rigorous* high-quality research and good research practice. Greene's (2008) methodology and several perspectives about integration were presented to illustrate these interrelated points. The specificity of the language used to describe integration, as exemplified by the discussion about triangulation, was noted as an important part of the conversation about integration. In this chapter, validity was conceptualized as a design that researchers construct to develop and to evaluate quality criteria throughout the stages of the methodology. Construction of strong validity

designs requires researchers to consider thoughtfully the particular criteria that are relevant and important for each study. Developing the validity design, it is likely researchers will incorporate quality criteria that are aligned to standards of rigor exemplified by their chosen communities of practice. Therefore, I presented examples of selective quality criteria representing validity and rigor that are recognized by communities practicing research within the three dominant research paradigms.

Because of the complexity of MMMR, it also is likely that researchers will apply an eclectic approach to the construction of validity designs. To provide guidelines, I presented examples of published frameworks applicable for MMMR. These frameworks were selected because each demonstrates a different approach to validity design relating to MMMR. The reader can dialogue with these multiple ideas in his or her future research.

I concluded the chapter by outlining three published applications of quality criteria. These applications were included because it is critical that researchers and methodologists, in particular, continue to examine how researchers are interpreting validity and designing, applying, and evaluating quality criteria in practice. Doing so will provide empirical examples for design and support the development of methodological guidelines and frameworks that are empirically based as well as methodologically sound.

Members of intellectual communities are aware of the importance of validity and rigor; the point is how the members of the various communities interpret and converse about these two interrelated concepts when conducting collaborative MMMR. Future directions for researchers of MMMR are to create opportunities to dialogue with different paradigms and intellectual research communities and to participate in continued dialogue about transparency of methodology and integration. The goal of these discussions is the construction of strong validity designs for the instantiation of each MMMR study. Therefore, I hope that this chapter's content will lead to further conversations about these topics by researchers and other stakeholders.

Discussion Questions

1. Discuss the concept of integration as it applies to MMMR.

2. Compare and contrast the various interpretations of validity within and across the three research paradigms.

3. Select an empirical mixed research study (i.e., quantitative and qualitative data are collected or transformed) and critique the study in terms of the degree to which the researcher has addressed criteria described in this chapter.

4. Select an empirical multimethod study (i.e., two or more methods of data collection and analysis that represent a pluralist approach) and critique the study in terms of the degree to which the researcher has addressed criteria described in this chapter.

Suggested Websites

http://www.asanet.org

The American Sociological Association promotes the study of human behavior that represents an interrelated focus on societal structures and culture. The research is multidisciplinary, and its aim is to have an impact at national and global levels.

http://www.eval.org

The goal of the American Evaluation Association is to contribute to the advancement of the field of evaluation. This association promotes evaluation practices and methods that lead to the development of theories and knowledge that will serve as resources for evaluators worldwide.

Note

1. The term *mixed research* evolved because mixed methods research as an approach is not just about methods; rather it also is about the researcher's philosophy and values about what constitutes credible data and what are the best methods to collect and analyze these data.

References

Alvesson, M., & Sköldberg, K. (2009). *Reflexive methodology: New vistas for qualitative research* (2nd ed.). London, England: SAGE.

American Educational Research Association, American Psychological Association, & National Council on Measurement in Education. (1999). *Standards for educational and psychological testing.* Washington, DC: American Psychological Association.

Bazeley, P. (2009). Integrating data analyses in mixed methods research. [Editorial]. *Journal of Mixed Methods Research, 3,* 203–207. doi:org/10.1177/1558689809334443

Bazeley, P. (2010). Computer-assisted integration of mixed methods data sources and analyses. In A. Tashakkori & C. Teddlie (Eds.), *SAGE handbook of mixed methods in social & behavioral research* (2nd ed., pp. 431–467). Thousand Oaks, CA: SAGE.

Bazeley, P., & Kemp, L. (2012). Mosaics, triangles, and DNA: Metaphors for integrated analysis in mixed methods research. *Journal of Mixed Methods Research, 6,* 55–72. doi: org/10.1177/1558689811419514

Boote, D. N., & Beile, P. (2005). Scholars before researchers: On the centrality of the dissertation literature review in research preparation. *Educational Researcher, 34*(6), 3–15. doi:10.3102/0013189X034006003

Bourdieu, P. (1998). *Practical reason.* Palo Alto, CA: Stanford University Press.

Brannen, J. (2005). Mixing methods: The entry of qualitative and quantitative approaches in the research process. *International Journal of Social Research Methodology, 8*(3), 173–184. doi:org/10.1080/13645570500154642

Brewer, J., & Hunter, A. (2006). *Foundations of multimethod research: Synthesizing styles* (2nd ed.). Thousand Oaks, CA. SAGE.

Bryman, A. (2006). Paradigm peace and the implications for quality. *International Journal of Social Science Methodology, 9,* 111–126. doi:org/10.1080/13645570600595280

Bryman, A. (2007). Barriers to integrating quantitative and qualitative research. *Journal of Mixed Methods Research, 1,* 8–22. doi:org/10.1177/2345678906290531

Campbell, D. T., & Stanley, J. C. (1963). *Experimental and quasi-experimental designs for research.* Chicago, IL: Rand McNally.

Castro, F. G., Kellison, J. G., Boyd, S. J., & Kopak, A. (2010). A methodology for conducting integrative mixed methods research and data analyses. *Journal of Mixed Methods Research, 4,* 342–360. doi:org/10.1177/1558689810382916

Christ, T. W. (2014). Scientific-based research and randomized controlled trials, the "gold" standard? Alternative paradigms and mixed methodologies. *Qualitative Inquiry, 20,* 72–80. doi:10.1177/1077800413508523

Collins, K. M. T., Onwuegbuzie, A. J., & Johnson, R. B. (2012). Securing a place at the table: Introducing legitimation criteria for the conduct of mixed research. *American Behavioral Scientist, 56,* 849–865. doi:10.1177/0002764211433799

Collins, K. M. T., Onwuegbuzie, A. J., Johnson, R. B., & Frels, R. K. (2013). Practice note: Using debriefing interviews to promote authenticity and transparency in mixed research. *International Journal of Multiple Research Approaches, 7,* 271–283. doi:org/10.5172/mra.2013.7.2.271

Collins, K. M. T., Onwuegbuzie, A. J., & Sutton, I. L. (2006). A model incorporating the rationale and purpose for conducting mixed methods-research in special education and beyond. *Learning Disabilities: A Contemporary Journal, 4*(1), 67–100.

Cook, T. D., & Campbell, D. T. (1979). *Quasi-experimentation: Design and analysis issues for field settings.* Chicago, IL: Rand McNally.

Creswell, J. W., & Tashakkori, A. (2007). Differing perspectives on mixed methods research. [Editorial]. *Journal of Mixed Methods Research, 1,* 303–308. doi: org/10.1177/1558689807306132

Dellinger, A. B., & Leech, N. L. (2007). Toward a unified validation framework in mixed methods research. *Journal of Mixed Methods Research, 1,* 309–332. doi:10.1177/1558689807306147

Eisner, E. W. (1991). *The enlightened eye: Qualitative inquiry and the enhancement of educational practice.* Upper Saddle River, NJ: Prentice Hall.

Freeman, M., deMarrais, K., Preissle, J., Roulston, K., & St. Pierre, E. A. (2007). Standards of evidence in qualitative research: An incitement to discourse. *Educational Researcher, 36*(1), 25–32. doi:org/10.3102/0013189X06298009

Frost, N. A., Nolas, S. M., Brooks-Gordon, B., Esin, C., Holt, A., Mehdizadeh, L., & Shinebourne, P. (2011). Pluralism in qualitative research: The impact of different researchers and qualitative approaches on the analysis of qualitative data. *Qualitative Research, 10*(4), 1–20. doi: org/10.1177/1468794110366802

Greene, J. C. (2007). *Mixed methods in social inquiry*. San Francisco, CA: Jossey-Bass.

Greene, J. C. (2008). Is mixed methods social inquiry a distinctive methodology? *Journal of Mixed Methods Research, 2,* 7–22. doi:org/10.1177/1558689807309969

Greene, J. C., Caracelli, V. J., & Graham, W. F. (1989). Toward a conceptual framework for mixed method evaluation designs. *Educational Evaluation and Policy Analysis, 11,* 255–274. doi:10.3102/01623737011003255

Guba, E. G. (1990). The alternative paradigm dialog. In E. G. Guba (Ed.), *The paradigm dialog* (pp. 17–30). Newbury Park, CA: SAGE.

Guba, E. G., & Lincoln, Y. S. (1989). *Fourth generation evaluation*. Newbury Park, CA: SAGE.

Guba, E. G., & Lincoln, Y. S. (2005). Paradigmatic controversies, contradictions, and emerging confluences. In N. K. Denzin & Y. S. Lincoln (Eds.), *The SAGE handbook of qualitative research* (3rd ed., pp. 191–215). Thousand Oaks, CA: SAGE.

Hall, B., & Howard, K. (2008). A synergistic approach: Conducting mixed methods research with typological and systemic design considerations. *Journal of Mixed Methods Research, 2,* 248–269. doi:10.1177/1558689808314622

Hesse-Biber, S. N., & Johnson, R. B. (2013). Coming at things differently: Future directions of possible engagement with mixed methods research [Editorial]. *Journal of Mixed Methods Research, 7,* 103–109. doi:10.1177/1558689813483987

Hesse-Biber, S. N., & Leavy, P. L. (2007). *Feminist research practice: A primer*. Thousand Oaks, CA: SAGE.

Ivankova, N. V. (2014). Implementing quality criteria in designing and conducting a sequential QUAN → QUAL mixed methods study of student engagement with learning applied research methods online. *Journal of Mixed Methods Research, 8,* 25–51. doi:org/10.1177/1558689813487945

Johnson, R. B., & Christensen, L. (2014). *Educational research: Quantitative, qualitative, and mixed approaches* (4th ed.). Thousand Oaks, CA: SAGE.

Leech, N. L. (2010). Interviews with the early developers of mixed methods research. In A. Tashakkori & C. Teddlie (Eds.), *SAGE handbook of mixed methods in social & behavioral research* (2nd ed., pp. 253–272). Thousand Oaks, CA: SAGE.

Li, S., Marquart, J. M., & Zercher, C. (2000). Conceptual issues and analytical strategies in mixed method studies of preschool inclusion. *Journal of Early Intervention, 23,* 116–132. doi:org/10.1177/105381510002300206

Lincoln, Y. S., & Guba, E. G. (1985). *Naturalistic inquiry*. Newbury Park, CA: SAGE.

Lincoln, Y. S., & Guba, E. G. (1986). But is it rigorous? Trustworthiness and authenticity in naturalistic evaluation. [Special issue: Naturalistic evaluation]. *New Directions for Program Evaluation, 30,* 73–84. doi:org/10.1002/ev.1427

Lincoln, Y. S., Lynham, S. A., & Guba, E. G. (2011). Paradigmatic controversies, contradictions, and emerging confluences, revisited. In N. K. Denzin & Y. S. Lincoln (Eds.), *The SAGE handbook of qualitative research* (4th ed., pp. 97–128). Thousand Oaks, CA: SAGE.

Maxwell, J. A. (1992). Understanding and validity in qualitative research. *Harvard Educational Review, 62,* 279–299.

Maxwell, J. A., & Loomis, D. M. (2003). Mixed methods design: An alternative approach. In A. Tashakkori & C. Teddlie (Eds.), *SAGE handbook of mixed methods in social & behavioral research* (pp. 241–271). Thousand Oaks, CA: SAGE.

Messick, S. (1989). Validity. In R. L. Linn (Ed.), *Educational measurement* (3rd ed., pp. 13–103). New York, NY: Macmillan.

Messick, S. (1995). Validity of psychological assessment: Validation of inferences from persons' responses and performances as scientific inquiry into score meaning. *American Psychologist, 50,* 741–749.

Morgan, D. L. (2007). Paradigms lost and pragmatism regained: Methodological implication of combining qualitative and quantitative methods. *Journal of Mixed Methods Research, 1,* 48–76. doi:org/10.1177/2345678906292462

Morse, J. M. (2003). Principles of mixed methods and multimethod research design. In A. Tashakkori & C. Teddlie (Eds.), *Handbook of mixed methods in social & behavioral research* (pp. 189–208). Thousand Oaks, CA: SAGE.

Newman, I., & Ramlo, S. (2010). Using Q methodology and Q factor analysis in mixed methods research. In A. Tashakkori & C. Teddlie (Eds.), *SAGE handbook of mixed methods in social & behavioral research* (2nd ed., pp. 505–530). Thousand Oaks, CA: SAGE.

O'Cathain, A. (2010). Assessing the quality of mixed methods research: Towards a comprehensive framework. In A. Tashakkori & C. Teddlie (Eds.), *SAGE handbook of mixed methods in social & behavioral research* (2nd ed., pp. 531–555). Thousand Oaks, CA: SAGE.

Onwuegbuzie, A. J., & Collins, K. M. T. (2007). A typology of mixed methods sampling designs in social science research. *The Qualitative Report, 12,* 281–316.

Onwuegbuzie, A. J., & Combs, J. P. (2010). Emergent data analysis techniques in mixed methods research: A synthesis. In A. Tashakkori & C. Teddlie (Eds.), *SAGE handbook of mixed methods in social & behavioral research* (2nd ed., pp. 397–430). Thousand Oaks, CA: SAGE.

Onwuegbuzie, A. J., Daniel, L. G., & Collins, K. M. T. (2009). A meta-validation model for assessing the score-validity of student teacher evaluations. *Quality & Quantity: International Journal of Methodology, 43,* 197–209.

Onwuegbuzie, A. J., Frels, R. K., Leech, N. L., & Collins, K. M. T. (2011). A mixed research study of pedagogical approaches and student learning in doctoral-level mixed research courses. [Special issue]. *International Journal of Multiple Research Approaches, 5*(1), 169–202. doi:org/10.5172/mra.2011.5.2.169

Onwuegbuzie, A. J., & Johnson, R. B. (2006). The validity issue in mixed research. *Research in the Schools, 13*(1), 48–63.

Onwuegbuzie, A. J., Leech, N. L., & Collins, K. M. T. (2008). Interviewing the interpretive researcher: A method for addressing the crises of representation legitimation, and praxis. *International Institute for Qualitative Methodology, 7*(4), 1–17.

Onwuegbuzie, A. J., Slate, J. R., Leech, N. L., & Collins, K. M. T. (2009). Mixed data analysis: Advanced integration techniques. *International Journal of Multiple Research Approaches, 3,* 13–33. doi:org/10.5172/mra.455.3.1.13

Onwuegbuzie, A. J., & Teddlie, C. (2003). A framework for analyzing data in mixed methods research. In A. Tashakkori & C. Teddlie (Eds.), *Handbook of mixed methods in social & behavioral research* (pp. 351–383). Thousand Oaks, CA: SAGE.

Onwuegbuzie, A. J., Witcher, A. E., Collins, K. M. T., Filer, J. D., Wiedmaier, C. D., & Moore, C. W. (2007). Students' perceptions of characteristics of effective college teachers: A validity study of a teaching evaluation form using a mixed-methods analysis. *American Educational Research Journal, 44*, 113–160.

Patton, M. Q. (2002). *Qualitative research and evaluation methods* (3rd ed.). Thousand Oaks, CA: SAGE.

Poggenpoel, M., & Myburgh, S. (2003). The researcher as research instrument in educational research: A possible threat to trustworthiness? *Education, 124*, 418–421.

Pohl, C., van Kerkhoff, L., Hadorn, G. H., & Bammer, G. (2008). Integration. In G. H. Hadorn et al. (Eds.), *Handbook of transdisciplinary research* (pp. 411–424). New York, NY: Springer.

Preissle, J. (2011). Qualitative futures: Where we might go from where we've been. In N. K. Denzin & Y. S. Lincoln (Eds.), *The SAGE handbook of qualitative research* (4th ed., pp. 685–698). Thousand Oaks, CA: SAGE.

Shadish, W. R., Cook, T. D., & Campbell, D. T. (2002). *Experimental and quasi-experimental designs for generalized causal inference*. Boston, MA: Houghton Mifflin.

Tashakkori, A., & Teddlie, C. (1998). *Mixed methodology: Combining qualitative and quantitative approaches*. Thousand Oaks, CA: SAGE.

Tashakkori, A., & Teddlie, C. (Eds.). (2003a). *Handbook of mixed methods in social & behavioral research*. Thousand Oaks, CA: SAGE.

Tashakkori, A., & Teddlie, C. (2003b). The past and future of mixed methods research: From data triangulation to mixed model designs. In A. Tashakkori & C. Teddlie, (Eds.), *Handbook of mixed methods in social & behavioral research* (pp. 671–702). Thousand Oaks, CA: SAGE.

Tashakkori, A., & Teddlie, C. (2008). Quality of inferences in mixed methods research: Calling for an integrative framework (pp. 101–119). In M. Bergman (Ed.), *Advances in mixed-methods research: Theories and applications*. London, England: SAGE.

Tashakkori, A., & Teddlie, C. (2010). Putting the human back in "human research methodology": The researcher in mixed methods research. [Editorial]. *Journal of Mixed Methods Research, 4*, 271–277. doi:org/10.1177/1558689810382532

Teddlie, C., & Tashakkori, A. (2009). *Foundations of mixed methods research: Integrating quantitative and qualitative approaches in the social and behavioral sciences*. Thousand Oaks, CA: SAGE.

Teddlie, C., & Tashakkori, A. (2010). Overview of contemporary issues in mixed methods research. In A. Tashakkori & C. Teddlie (Eds.), *SAGE handbook of mixed methods in social & behavioral research* (2nd ed., pp. 1–41). Thousand Oaks, CA: SAGE.

Teddlie, C., & Tashakkori, A. (2011). Mixed methods research: Contemporary issues in an emerging field. In N. K. Denzin & Y. S. Lincoln (Eds.), *The SAGE handbook of qualitative research* (2nd ed., pp. 285–300). Thousand Oaks, CA: SAGE.

Woolley, C. M. (2009). Meeting the mixed methods challenge of integration in a sociological study of structure and agency. *Journal of Mixed Methods Research, 3*, 7–25. doi: org/10.1177/1558689808325774

Yin, R. K. (2006). Mixed methods research: Are the methods genuinely integrated or merely parallel? *Research in the Schools, 13*(1), 41–47.

Data Analysis I: Overview of Data Analysis Strategies

Julia Brannen *and* Rebecca O'Connell

Abstract

This chapter enables the reader to consider issues that are likely to affect the analysis of mixed method research (MMMR). It identifies the ways in which data from multimethod and mixed methods research can be integrated in principle and gives detailed examples of different strategies in practice. Furthermore, it examines a particular type of MMMR and discusses an exemplar study in which national survey data are analyzed alongside a longitudinal qualitative study whose sample is drawn from the same national survey. By working through three analytic issues, it shows the complexities and challenges involved in integrating qualitative and quantitative data: issues about linking data sets, similarity (or not) of units of analysis, and concepts and meaning. It draws some conclusions and sets out some future directions for MMMR.

Key Words: mixed method research, MMMR, analysis, integrating, survey data, qualitative study, qualitative data

Introduction

This chapter begins with a consideration of the conditions under which integration is possible (or not). A number of factors that need to be considered before a researcher can decide that integration is possible are briefly discussed. This discussion is followed by a consideration of Caracelli and Greene's (1993) analysis strategies. Examples of mixed method studies that involve these strategies are described, including the ways they attempt to integrate different data, in particular data transformation, examine typologies and outlier cases, and merge data sets. It is shown that these strategies are not always standalone but can merge into each other. The chapter concludes with a discussion of an extended example of the ways in which a study we carried out called Families, Food and Work (2009–2014) sought to employ analysis of relevant questions from different large-scale data sets with data from a qualitative study of how working parents and children negotiate food and eating (O'Connell & Brannen, 2015).

Issues to Consider Before Conducting Mixed Method Research and Analysis

The researcher should consider a number of issues that need to be revisited during the analysis of the data before embarking on multimethod and mixed methods research (MMMR).

The first concerns the *ontological and epistemological assumptions* underpinning the choice of methods used to generate the data. Working from the principle that the choice of method is not made in a philosophical void, the data should be thought about in relation to epistemological assumptions underpinning the aspect of the research problem/question being addressed (see, e.g., Barbour, 1999). Thus in terms of best practice, researchers may be well advised to consider what kind of knowledge they seek to generate. Most multimethod and mixed methods researchers, while not necessarily thinking of themselves as pragmatists in a philosophical sense, adopt a pragmatic approach (Bryman, 2008). Pragmatism dominates in MMMR (Omwuegbuzie & Leech,

2005), especially among those from more applied fields of the social sciences (in which MMMR has been most widespread). However, pragmatism in this context connotes its common-sense meaning, sidelining philosophical issues so that MMMR strategies are employed as a matter of pragmatics (Bryman, 2008). Some might argue that if different questions are addressed in a study that require different types of knowledge, then the data cannot be integrated unproblematically in the analysis phase. However, it depends on what one means by "integration," as we later discuss.

The second issue concerns the *level of reality* under study. Some research questions are about understanding social phenomena at the micro level while others are concerned with social phenomena at the macro level. Thus researchers in the former group emphasize the agency of those they study through an emphasis on studying individuals' subjective interpretations and perspectives and have allegiances to interpretivist and postmodernist epistemologies. Those working at the macro level are concerned with identifying larger scale patterns and trends and seek to hypothesize or create structural explanations, which may call on realist epistemologies. However, all researchers aim to focus to some extent on the relation between individuals and society. If one is to transcend conceptually the micro and the macro levels, then methods must be developed to reflect this transcendence (Kelle, 2001). For example, in qualitative research that focuses on individuals' perspectives, it is important to set those perspectives in their social structural and historical contexts. Whether those who apply a paradigm of rationality will apply both qualitative and quantitative methods will depend on the extent to which they seek to produce different levels and types of explanation. This will mean interrogating the linkages between the data analyzes made at these levels.

The third issue relates to the *kinds of human experience and social action* that the study's research questions are designed to address. For example, if one is interested in life experiences over long periods of time, researchers will employ life story or other narrative methods. In this case, they need to take into account the way stories are framed, and in particular how temporal perspectives, the purposes of the narrator, and the way stories are told influence the stories. The data the researchers will collect are therefore narrative data. Hence how these stories fit, for example, with quantitative data collected as part of a MMMR approach will require close interrogation in the analysis of the two data

sets, taking into account both interpretive and realist historical approaches.

The fourth issue to consider is whether the data are *primary or secondary* and, in the latter case, whether they are subjected to secondary analysis. Secondary data are by definition collected by other people, although access to them may not be straightforward. If the data have already been coded and the original data are not available, the types of secondary analysis possible will be limited. Moreover, the preexistence of these data may influence the timetabling of the MMMR project and may also shape the questions that are framed in any subsequent qualitative phase and in the data analysis. Depending on the nature and characteristics of the data, one data set may prove intrinsically more interesting; thus more time and attention may be given to its analysis. A related issue therefore concerns the possibilities for operationalizing the concepts employed in relation to the different parts of the MMMR inquiry. Preexisting data, especially those of a quantitative type, may make it difficult to reconceptualize the problem. At a practical level, the questions asked in a survey may poorly relate to those that fit the MMMR inquiry, as we later illustrate. Since one does not know what one does not know, it may be only at later stages that researchers working across disciplines and methodologies may come to realize which questions cannot be addressed and which data are missing.

The fifth issue relates to the *environments* in which researchers are located. For example, are the research and the researcher operating within the same research setting, for example the same discipline, the same theoretical and methodological tradition, or the same policy social context? MMMR fits with the political currency accorded to "practical inquiry" that speaks to policy and policymakers and that informs practice, as distinct from scientific research (Hammersley, 2000). However, with respect to policy, this has to be set in the context of the continued policy importance afforded to large-scale data but also the increased scale of these data sets and the growth in the availability of official administrative data. In turn, these trends have been matched by the increased capacity of computing power to manage and analyze these data (Brannen & Moss, 2013) and the increased pressure on social scientists to specialize in high-level quantitative data analysis. As more such data accrue, the apparent demand for quantitative analysis increases (Brannen & Moss, 2013). However, MMMR strategies are also often employed alongside such quantitative analysis, especially in policy-driven research. For example, in cross-national research, governmental organizations require comparative data to assess how countries are doing in a number of different fields, a process that has become an integral part of performance monitoring. But, equally, there is a requirement for policy analysis and inquiries into how policies work in particular local conditions. Such micro-level analysis will require methods like documentary analysis, discourse analysis, case study designs, and intensive research approaches. Furthermore, qualitative data are thought useful to "bring alive" research for policy and practitioner audiences (O'Cathain, 2009).

Another aspect of environment relates to the sixth issue concerning the constitution of the research team and the extent to which it is *inter or transdisciplinary*. Research teams can be understood as "communities of practice" (Denscombe, 2008). While paradigms are pervasive ways of dividing social science research, as Morgan (2007) argues, we need to think in terms of shared beliefs within communities of researchers. This requires an ethic of "precarity" to prevail (Ettlinger, 2007, p. 319), through which researchers are open to others' ideas and can relinquish entrenched positions. However, the success of communities of practice will depend on the political context, their composition, and whether they are democratic (Hammersley, 2005). Thus in the analysis of MMMR, it is important to be cognizant of the power relations with such communities of practice since they will influence the researcher's room for maneuvering in determining directions and outputs of the data analysis. At the same time, these political issues affect analysis and dissemination in research teams in which members share disciplinary approaches.

Finally, there are the *methodological preferences, skills, and specialisms* of the researcher, all of which have implications for the quality of the data and the data analysis. MMMR offers the opportunity to learn about a range of methods and thus to be open to new ways of addressing research questions. Broadening one's methodological repertoire mitigates against "trained incapacities" as Reiss (1968) termed the issue—the entrenchment of researchers in particular types of research paradigms, as well as questions, research methods, and types of analysis.

The Context of Inquiry: Research Questions and Research Design

The rationale for MMMR must be clear both in the phase of the project's research design (the context of the inquiry) and in the analysis phase (the context of justification). At the research design phase, researchers wrestle with such fundamental methodological questions as to what kinds of knowledge they seek to generate, such as whether to describe and understand a social phenomenon or seek to explain it. Do we wish to do both, that is, to understand and explain? In the latter case, the research strategy will typically translate itself into employing a mix of qualitative and quantitative methods, which some argue is the defining characteristic of mixed method research (MMR) (Tashakorri & Creswell, 2007).

If a MMR strategy is employed, this generally implies that a number of research questions will address a substantive issue. MMMR is also justified in terms of its capacity to address *different aspects* of a research question. This is turns leads researchers to consider how to frame their research questions and how these determine the methods chosen. Typically research questions are formulated in the research proposal. However, they should also be amenable to adaptation (Harrits, 2011, citing Dewey, 1991); adaptations may be necessary as researchers respond to the actual conditions of the inquiry. According to Law (2004), research is an "assemblage," that is, something not fixed in shape but incorporating tacit knowledge, research skills, resources, and political agenda that are "constructed" as they are woven together (p. 42). Methodology should be rebuilt during the research process in a way that responds to research needs and the conditions encountered—what Seltzer-Kelly, Westwood, and Pena-Guzman (2012) term "a constructivist stance at the methodological level" (p. 270). This can also happen at the phase when data are analyzed.

Developing a coherent methodology with a close link between the research question and the research strategy holds out the best hope for answering a project's objectives and questions (Woolley, 2009, p. 8). Thus Yin (2006) would say that to carry out an MMMR analysis it is essential to have an integrated set of research questions. However, it is not easy to determine what constitutes coherence. For example, the research question concerning the link between the quality of children's diet in the general population and whether mothers are in paid employment may be considered a very different and not necessarily complementary question to the research question about the conditions under which the children of working mothers are fed. Thus we have to consider here how tightly or loosely the research questions interconnect.

The framing of the research question influences the method chosen that, in turn, influences the choice of analytic method. Thus in our study of children's food that examined the link between children's diet and maternal employment, we examined a number of large-scale data sets and carried out statistical analyzes on these, while in studying the conditions under which children in working families get fed, we carried out qualitative case analysis on a subset of households selected from one of the large-scale data sets.

The Context of Justification: The Analysis Phase

In the analysis phase of MMMR, the framing of the research questions becomes critical, affecting when, to what extent, and in what ways data from different methods are integrated. So, for example, we have to consider the temporal ordering of methods. For example, quantitative data on a research topic may be available and the results already analyzed. This analysis may influence the questions to be posed in the qualitative phase of inquiry.

Thus it is also necessary to consider the compatibility between the units of analysis in the quantitative phase and the qualitative phase of the study, for example, between variables studied in a survey and the analytic units studied in a qualitative study. Are we seeking analytic units that are equivalent (but not similar), or are we seeking to analyze a different aspect of a social phenomenon? If the latter, how do the two analyses relate? This may become more critical if the same population is covered in both the qualitative and quantitative phases. What happens when a nested or integrated sampling strategy is employed, as in the case of a large-scale survey analysis and a qualitative analysis based on a subsample of the survey?

A number of frameworks have been suggested for integrating data produced by quantitative and qualitative methods (Brannen, 1992; Caracelli & Greene, 1993; Greene, Caracelli, & Graham, 1989). While these may provide a guide to the variety of ways to integrate data, they should not be used as fixed templates. Indeed, they may provide a basis for reflection after the analysis has been completed.

1. *Corroboration*—in which one set of results based on one method are confirmed by those gained through the application of another method.

2. *Elaboration or expansion*—in which qualitative data analysis may exemplify how patterns based on quantitative data analysis apply in particular cases. Here the use of one type of data analysis adds to the understanding gained by another.

3. *Initiation*—in which the use of a first method sparks new hypotheses or research questions that can be pursued using a different method.

4. *Complementarity*—in which qualitative and quantitative results are regarded as different beasts but are meshed together so that each data analysis enhances the other (Mason, 2006). The data analyses from the two methods are juxtaposed and generate complementary insights that together create a bigger picture.

5. *Contradiction*—in which qualitative data and quantitative findings conflict. Exploring contradictions between different types of data assumed to reflect the same phenomenon may lead to an interrogation of the methods and to discounting one method in favor of another (in terms of assessments of validity or reliability). Alternatively, the researcher may simply juxtapose the contradictions for others to explore in further research. More commonly, one type of data may be presented and assumed to be "better," rather than seeking to explain the contradictions in relation to some ontological reality (Denzin & Lincoln, 2005; Greene et al., 1989).

As Hammersley (2005) points out, all these ways of combining different data analyses to some extent make assumptions that there is some reality out there to be captured, despite the caveats expressed about how each method constructs the data differently. Thus, just as seeking to corroborate data may not lead us down the path of "validation," so too the complementarity rationale for mixing methods may not complete the picture either. There may be no meeting point between epistemological positions. As Hammersley (2008) suggests, there is a need for a dialogue between them in the recognition that absolute certainty is never justified and that "we must treat knowledge claims as equally doubtful or that we should judge them on grounds other than their likely truth" (p. 51).

Multimethod and Mixed Methods Research Analysis Strategies: Examples of Studies

Caracelli and Greene (1993) suggest analysis strategies for integrating qualitative and quantitative data. In practice these strategies are not always standalone but blur into each other. Moreover, as Bryman (2008) has observed, it is relatively rare for mixed method researchers to give full rationales for MMMR designs. They can involve data transformation in which, for example, qualitative data are treated quantitatively. They may involve typology development in which cases are categorized in patterns and outlier cases are scrutinized. They may involve data merging in which both data sets are treated in similar ways, for instance, by creating similar variables or equivalent units of analysis across data sets. In this section, drawing on the categorization of Caracelli and Greene, we give some examples of studies in which qualitative and quantitative data are integrated in these different ways (Table 15.1). These are not intended to be exhaustive, nor are the studies pure examples of these strategies.

Qualitative Data Are Transformed into Quantitative Data or Vice Versa

In survey research, in order to test how respondents understand questions it is commonplace to transform qualitative data into quantitative data. This is termed *cognitive testing*. The aim here is to find a fit between responses given in both the survey and the qualitative testing. For example, most personality scales are based on prior clinical research. An example of data transformation on a larger scale is taken from a program of research on the wider benefits of adult learning (Hammond, 2005). The rationale for the study was that the research area was underresearched and the research questions relatively unformulated (p. 241). Qualitative research was carried out to identify variables to test on an existing national longitudinal data set. The qualitative phase involved biographical interviews

with adult learners. The quantitative data consisted of data from an existing UK cohort study (the 1958 National Child Development Study). A main justification for using these latter data concerned the further exploitation of data that are expensive to collect. The qualitative component was conceived as a "mapping" exercise carried out to inform the research design and the implementation of the quantitative phase, that is, the identification of variables for quantitative analysis (Hammond, 2005, p. 243). This approach has parallels with qualitative pilot work carried out as a prologue to a survey, although the qualitative material was also analyzed in its own right. However, while the qualitative data were used with the aim of finding common measures that fit with the quantitative inquiry, Hammond also insisted that the qualitative data *not* be used to explain quantitatively derived outcomes but to interrogate them further (Hammond, 2005, p. 244). Inevitably, contradictions between the respective findings arose. For example, Hammond reported that the effect of adult learning on life satisfaction (the transformed measure) found in the National Child Development Study cohort analysis was greater for men than for women, while women reported themselves in the biographical interview responses to be positive about the courses they had taken. On this issue, the biographical interviews were regarded as being "more sensitive" than the quantitative measure. Hammond also suggested that the interview data showed that an improved sense of well-being (another transformed measure) experienced by the respondents in the present was not necessarily incompatible with having a negative view of the future. The quantitative data conflated satisfaction with "life so far" and with "life in the future." Contradictions were also explained

Table 15.1 MMMR Analysis Strategies: Examples

Analytical Strategy	Summary	Example(s)	Why/How Useful
Data transformation	Qualitative data are transformed into quantitative data or vice versa	Hammond, 2005	For example to identify variables for quantitative analysis and interrogate quantitative outcomes
Deepening of the analysis via case selection and typologies	Typologies, extreme, or outlier cases are subjected to scrutiny either at a later time point or in another data set	Glueck and Glueck, 1950, 1968	For example to enrich interpretation and further explanation
Data merging	The same set of variables is created across quantitative and qualitative data sets	Blatchford, 2005; Sammons et al., 2005	For example to make consistent comparisons across data sets

in terms of the lack of representativeness of the qualitative study (the samples did not overlap). In addition, it is possible that priority was given by the researcher to the biographical interviews and may have placed more trust in this approach. Another possibly relevant factor was that the researcher had no stake in creating or shaping the quantitative data set. In any event, the biographical interviews were conducted *before* the quantitative analyses and were used to influence the decisions about which analyses to focus on in the quantitative analysis. Hence the qualitative data threw up hypotheses that the quantitative data were used to reject or support. What is interesting about using qualitative data to test on quantitative evidence is the opportunity it offers to pose or initiate new lines of questioning (Greene et al., 1989)—a result not necessarily anticipated at the outset of this research.

Typologies, Deviant, Negative, or Outlier Cases Are Subjected to Further Scrutiny Later or in Another Data Set

A longitudinal or multilayered design provides researchers with opportunities to examine the strength of the conclusions that can be drawn about the cases and the phenomena under study (Nilsen & Brannen, 2010). For an example of this strategy, we turn to the classic study carried by Glueck and Glueck (1950, 1968). The study *Five Hundred Criminal Careers* was based on longitudinal research of delinquents and nondelinquents (1949–1965). The Gluecks studied the two groups at three age points; 14, 25, and 32. The study had a remarkably high (92%) response rate when adjusted for mortality at the third wave. The Gluecks collected very rich data on a variety of dimensions and embedded open-ended questions within a survey framework. Interviews with respondents and their families, as well as key informants (social workers, school teachers, employers, and neighbors), were carried out, together with home observations and the study of official records and criminal histories. Some decades later, Laub and Sampson (1993, 1998) reanalyzed these data longitudinally (the Gluecks' original analyzes were cross-sectional).

Laub and Sampson (1998) note that the Gluecks' material "represents the comparison, reconciliation and integration of these multiple sources of data" (p. 217) although the Gluecks did not treat the qualitative data in their own right. The original study was firmly grounded in a quantitative logic where the purpose was to arrive at *causal explanations* and *the ability to predict criminal behavior.*

However, the Gluecks were carrying out their research in a pre-computer age, a fact that facilitated reanalysis of the material. When Laub and Sampson came to recode the raw data many years later, they rebuilt the Gluecks' original data set and used their coding schemes to validate their original analyzes. Laub and Sampson then constructed the criminal histories of the sample, drawing on and integrating the different kinds of data available. This involved merging data.

Next they purposively selected a subset of cases for intensive qualitative analysis in order to explore consistencies and inconsistencies between the original findings and the original study's predictions for the delinquents' future criminal careers—what happened to them some decades later. They examined "off diagonal" and "negative cases" that did not fit the quantitative results and predictions. In particular, they selected individuals who, on the basis of their earlier careers, were expected to follow a life of crime but did not and those expected to cease criminality but did not.

Citing Jick (1979), Laub and Sampson (1998) suggest how divergence can become an opportunity for enriching explanations (p. 223). By examining deviant cases on the basis of one data analysis and interrogating these in a second data analysis, they demonstrated complex processes of individual pathways into and out of crime, including identified pathways, that take place over long time periods (Laub & Sampson, 1998, p. 222). They argued that "without qualitative data, discussions of continuity often mask complex and rich qualitative processes" (Sampson & Laub, 1997, quoted in Laub & Sampson 1998, p. 229).

In addition they supported a biographical approach that enables the researcher to interpret data in historical context, in this case to understand criminality in relation to the type and level of crime prevalent at the time. Laub and Sampson (1998) selected a further subsample of the original sample of delinquents, having managed to trace them after 50 years (Laub & Sampson, 1993) and asked them to review their past lives. The researchers were particularly interested in identifying turning points to understand what had shaped the often unexpected discontinuities and continuities in the careers of these one-time delinquents.

This is an exemplar study of the analytic strategy of subjecting typologies to deeper scrutiny. It also afforded an opportunity to theorize about the conditions concerning cases that deviated from predicted trajectories.

Data Merging: The Same Set of Variables Is Created Across Quantitative and Qualitative Data Sets

Here assumptions are made that the phenomena under study are similar in both the qualitative and quantitative parts of an inquiry, a strategy exemplified in the following two studies. The treatment of the data in both parts of the study was seamless, so that one type of data is transformed into the other. In a longitudinal study, Blatchford (2005) examined the relationship between classroom size and pupils' educational achievement. Blatchford justifies using a mixed method strategy in terms of the power of mixed methods to reconciling inconsistencies found in previous research. The rationale given for using qualitative methods was the need to assess the relationships between the same variables but in particular case studies. Blatchford notes that "priorities had to be set and some areas of investigation received more attention than others" (p. 204). The dominance of the quantitative analysis occurred despite the collection of "fine grained data on classroom processes" that could have lent themselves to other kinds of analysis, such as understanding how students learn in different classroom environments. The qualitative data were in fact put to limited use and were merged with the quantitative data.

Sammons et al. (2005) similarly employed a longitudinal quantitative design to explore the effects of preschool education on children's attainment and development at entry to school. Using a purposive rationale, they selected a smaller number of early education centers from their original sample on the basis of their contrasting profiles. Sammons et al. coded the qualitative data in such a way that the "reduced data" (p. 219) were used to provide statistical explanations for the outcomes produced in the quantitative longitudinal study. Thus, again, the insights derived from the qualitative data analysis were merged with the quantitative variables, which were correlated with outcome variables on children's attainment. The researchers in question could have drawn on both the qualitative and quantitative data for different insights, as is required in case study research (Yin, 2006) and as suggested in their purposive choice of preschool centers.

Using Quantitative and Qualitative Data: A Longitudinal Study of Working Families and Food

In this final part of the chapter we take an example from our own work in which we faced a number of methodological issues in integrating and meshing different types of data. In this section we discuss some of the challenges involved in the collection and analysis of such data.

The study we carried out is an example of designing quantitative and qualitative constituent parts to address differently framed questions. Its questions were, and remain, currently highly topical in the Western world and concern the influences of health policy on healthy eating, including in childhood, and its implications for obesity.[1] Much of the health evidence is unable to explain why it is that families appear to ignore advice and continue to eat in unhealthy ways. The project arose in the context of some existing research that suggests an association between parental (maternal) employment and children's (poor) diet (Hawkins, Cole, & Law, 2009). We pursued these issues by framing the research phenomenon in different ways and through the analysis of different data sets.

The project was initiated in a policy context in which we tendered successfully for a project that enabled us to exploit a data set commissioned by government to examine the nation's diet. Somewhat of a landmark study in the UK, the project is directly linked to the National Diet and Nutrition Survey (NDNS) funded by the UK's Food Standards Agency and Department of Health, a study largely designed by those from public health and nutritionist perspectives. These data, from the first wave of the new rolling survey, were unavailable to others at that time. We were also facilitated in selecting a subsample of households with children from the NDNS that we subjected to a range of qualitative methods. The research team worked closely with the UK government to gain access to the data collected and managed by an independent research agency in the identification of a subsample to meet the research criteria and in seeking the consent of the survey subsample participants.

Applying anthropological and sociological lenses, the ethnographically trained researchers in the team sought to *explore inductively* parents' experiences of negotiating the demands of "work" and "home" and domestic food provisioning in families. We therefore sought to understand the contextual and embodied meanings of food practices and their situatedness in different social contexts (inside and outside the home). We also assumed that children are agents in their own lives, and therefore we included children in the study and examined the ways in which children reported food practices and attributed meaning to food. The main research questions (RQ) for the study were:

RQ 1. What is the relationship between parental employment and the diets of children (aged 1.5 to 10 years)?

RQ 2. How does food fit into working family life and how do parents experience the demands of "work" and "home" in managing food provisioning?

RQ 3. How do parents and children negotiate food practices?

RQ 4. What foods do children of working parents eat in different contexts—home, childcare, and school—and how do children negotiate food practices?

The study not only employed a MMMR strategy but was also longitudinal, a design that is rarely discussed in the MMMR literature. We conducted a follow-up study (Wave 2) approximately two years later, which repeated some questions and additionally asked about social change, the division of food work, and the social practice of family meals. The first research question was to be addressed through the survey data while RQ 2, 3, and 4 were addressed through the qualitative study. In the qualitative study, a variety of ethnographic methods were to be deployed with both parents and children ages 2 to 10 years. The ethnographic methods included a range of interactive research tools, which were used flexibly with the children since their age span is wide: interviews, drawing methods, and, with some children, photo elicitation interviews in which children photographed foods and meals consumed within and outside the home and discussed these with the researcher at a later visit. Semistructured interviews were carried out with parents who defined themselves as the main food providers and sometimes with an additional parent or care-provider who was involved in food work and also wished to participate.

In the context of existing research that suggests an association between parental (maternal) employment and household income with children's (poor) diet (Hawkins et al., 2009) carried out on a different UK data set and also supported by some US research (e.g. Crepinsek & Burstein, 2004; McIntosh et al., 2008), it was important to investigate whether this association was born out elsewhere. In addition and in parallel, we therefore carried out secondary analysis on the NDNS Year 1 (2008/2009) data and on two other large-scale national surveys, the Health Survey for England

(surveys, 2007, 2008) and the Avon Longitudinal Study of Parents and Children (otherwise known as "Children of the Nineties") (data sweeps 1995/1996, 1996/1997, and 1997/1999) to examine the first research question. This part of the work was not straightforward. First we found that, contrary to a previous NDNS (1997) survey that had classified mothers' working hours as full or part-time, neither mothers' hours of work nor full/part-time status had been collected in the new rolling NDNS survey. Rather, this information was limited in most cases to whether a mother was or was not in paid employment. Thus it was not possible to disentangle the effects of mothers working full-time from those doing part-time hours on children's diets. This was unfortunate since the NDNS provided very detailed data on children's nutrition based on food diaries, unlike the Millennium Cohort Study, which collected only mothers' reports of children's snacking between meals at home (Hawkins et al., 2009). While the Millennium Cohort Study analysis found a relationship between long hours of maternal employment and children's dietary intake, no association between mothers' employment and children's dietary intake was found in the NDNS (O'Connell, Brannen, Mooney, Knight, & Simon, 2011; Simon et al., forthcoming). However, it is possible that a relationship might have been found if we had been able to disaggregate women's employment by hours.

In the following we describe three instances of data analysis in this longitudinal MMMR study in relation to some of the key analytic issues set out in the research questions described previously (see Table 15.2).

1. Studying children's diets in a MMMR design

2. Examining the division of household food work in a MMMR design

3. Making sense of family meals in a MMMR design

Linking Data in a Longitudinal Multimethod and Mixed Methods Research Design: Studying Children's Diets

THE RESEARCH PROBLEM

Together with drawing a sample for qualitative study from the national survey, we aimed to carry out secondary analysis on the NDNS data in order to generate patterns of "what" is eaten by children and parents and to explore associations with a range of independent variables, notably mothers'

Table 15.2 MMMR Analyses in Working Families and Food Study

Research Questions	Data Sets	Presence of Integration of Analyses
(1) What is the link/association between parental employment and children's diet?	NDNS national survey HSE national survey ALSPAC (regional survey) Qualitative subsample of NDNS (2 time points)	Lack of integration, for example - Different measures and concepts across data sets - Diets of children may have changed by time of interview as children got older
(2) How do households organize the division of food work and how is this influenced by parental employment?	NDNS US (National Panel Study) Qualitative subsample of NDNS (2 time points)	Convergent analysis as similar focus on behavior plus Qualitative data provide outlier cases (compared with survey results) to further scrutiny
(3) What is the relationship between family meals and parental employment?	NDNS data taken from diaries (who was present when children eating) US (National Panel Study) (self-report of meal frequency) Qualitative subsample of NDNS (patterns of eating together in working week; 2 time points)	Lack of integration, for example - NDNS measured who was present when child eating and missing data on working hours - US self-report of frequency of "family meal" (assumes one shared meaning) - NDNS qualitative study asked about patterns of eating together in working week

Note: NDNS = National Diet and Nutrition Survey; HSE = Health Survey for England; ALSPAC = Avon Longitudinal Study of Pregnancy and Childhood.

employment. The NDNS diet data were based on four-day unweighed food diaries that recorded detailed information about quantities of foods and drinks consumed, as well as where, when, and with whom foods were eaten (Bates, Lennox, Bates, & Swan, 2011). On behalf of the NDNS survey, the diaries were subjected by researchers at Human Nutrition Research, Cambridge University, to an analysis of nutrient intakes using specialist dietary recording and analysis software (Bates et al., 2011; Data In Nutrients Out [DINO]).

METHODOLOGICAL CHALLENGES

These nutritional data proved challenging for us as social scientists to use, and they involved discussion with nutrition experts from within and outside Human Nutrition Research who created different dietary measures for the use of the team in the secondary analysis, thereby involving some interesting cross-disciplinary discussion. Working with nutritionists, we developed a unique diet quality index that compared intakes for children in different age ranges to national guidelines, giving an overall diet "score"—a composite measure that could be used to sample children from the survey and also as an outcome measure in the regression analysis described earlier, which set out to answer the first research

question on the relationship between maternal employment and children's dietary intakes (Simon, O'Connell, & Stephen, 2012). While the usefulness of the diet data was constrained by the fact that no data had been collected about mothers' working hours (nor indeed maternal education, an important cofounder), an important impact of our study has been to have these added to the annual survey from 2015 to increase the study's usefulness to social science and social policy.

As noted, another aim of using the NDNS was to help us draw a purposive subsample of children ($N = 48$) in which cases of children with healthier and less healthy diets were equally represented (as well as to select the sample on demographic variables). However, we encountered a challenge because of the small number of children in the age range in which we were interested; we thus had to include a wider age range of children (1.5–10 years) than would have been ideal.

We also sought to link the quantitative diary data from NDNS with the ethnographic and interview data from parents and children concerning their reported food practices. However, while the NDNS dietary data and the diary method used are considered the "gold standard" in dietary surveys (Stephen, 2007), they were less useful for us at the level of the qualitative sample, and in practice this proved not to be feasible. First, the scores were based on dietary data collected over a single brief period of time (four days; Bates et al., 2011). Also, the whole survey was conducted over an extended time period (one year), with a mixture of weekdays and weekend days surveyed, which was unproblematic at the aggregate level. However, at the individual level, it was clear that these four days were not generalizable to dietary intakes over a longer time period. One parent in the qualitative study, for example, said the diary had been collected over a weekend break in Scotland where the family had indulged in holiday eating, including plenty of chips. In addition, since the data we had was about nutrient intakes—we did not have the resources (time or expertise) to examine the raw diary data, which could potentially have been provided—we had no idea what children were actually eating. Furthermore, there was a time lag between when the diet data were collected and when we did the fieldwork for the qualitative study (around six months later). We could have waited for all the NDNS data to be cleaned and analyzed, which would have given us additional information about children's food intakes (e.g., their consumption of fruit and vegetables), but this would have caused a far greater time delay in starting the qualitative study. Given the rapidity with which children in the younger age range change their preferences and habits, the diet data would then have been "out of date" by the time we conducted qualitative interviews. Our decision to construct a diet quality index was therefore a pragmatic one, largely determined in practice by the data available to us within a reasonable time from the diary data collection—those provided as feedback to the study participants after the NDNS visits.[2]

As we were also interested in the foods children were eating, we asked parents and children in the qualitative interviews to describe what they ate on the last weekday and on the last weekend day and about typicality, rather than repeating the diet diaries, which would have been highly resource intensive. Mothers were also asked to assess their children's diets. We could not compare mothers' descriptions and assessments of their child's diet with diaries since we did not have access to the latter. However, in comparing these assessments with the child's NDNS diet score there appeared in some cases to be corroboration, while others appeared to bear no relation. Indeed, some of the apparently "worst" cases, according to mothers' assessments,

did not necessarily have scores suggesting poor diets. Although hours of employment were asked in the qualitative study, no patterns were found in these data between hours of employment or other characteristics such as social class.[3] In analyzing other research questions about patterns of family meals and child versus adult control, for example, diet scores did not generally appear to be related to patterns found in the qualitative data. This may have been explained by the small sample or by lack of validity of the diet data at the individual level or by changes in children's diet between the survey and qualitative study. In a follow-up qualitative study we are conducting with families two years later we will be able to compare analyses over two time points using the same questions put to parents and children about children's food and eating.

In terms of linking dietary data in a MMMR design, the NDNS survey data suffered from a number of limitations. Even though we set aside our particular epistemological assumptions, theoretical interests, and research objectives, which were different from those of the survey, these affected the integration of the data. The usefulness of the NDNS data for addressing the research questions at the aggregate and individual level was questionable, notably the lack of data on the working hours of mothers and the difficulties of accessing detailed diary data collected at one time point as an individual measure of nutrition. The NDNS had rather small numbers of the groups in which we were interested, which compounded the selection of the qualitative subsample. There were also issues concerning the employment of different methods at different time points; this was especially challenging methodologically given the focus on younger children's food tastes and diets, which can change dramatically within a short period of time. A further issue concerned conceptualization across different data sets, in particular relating to issues around food practices such as healthy eating. As noted, in the case of the survey data composite, measures of children's nutrient intake at a particular moment in time were created using food diary data, and the measurements were then compared to national guidelines. In contrast, in the qualitative study latitude was given to parents to make their own judgments about their child's diet from their perspectives while we were able to compare what parents reported at two time points and so take a longer term view. Therefore in integrating and interpreting both sets of data, we wrestled with the epistemological and ontological assumptions that underpinned the study's main research questions concerning the meaning and significance of food and our own expectations about the kinds of "essential" sociodemographic data that we would expect any survey to collect.

Nonetheless, we had to overcome these tensions and demonstrate the societal impact of research that focused on an emotive and politically sensitive topic—maternal employment and diets of young children. In practice, the study's outputs remained divided by approach, with papers drawing on mainly qualitative (Brannen, O'Connell, & Mooney, 2013; Knight, O'Connell, & Brannen, 2014; O'Connell & Brannen, 2014) or quantitative (Simon et al., forthcoming) findings or describing methodological approaches (e.g., Brannen & Moss, 2013; O'Connell, 2013; Simon et al., 2012).

Similar Units of Analysis in a Multimethod and Mixed Methods Research Longitudinal Design: Examining the Division of Household Food Work

THE RESEARCH PROBLEM

Mothers' employment is only one small part of the picture of how food and work play out in households in which there are children. UK evidence suggests that men are more likely to cook regularly and share responsibility for feeding the family when women are absent, usually because of paid employment. However, this research was conducted some time ago (e.g., Warde & Hetherington, 1994).

THE ANALYSIS

The more recent evidence that we analyzed is from the NDNS and the 40,000 UK Household Panel study called Understanding Society. The NDNS (Year 1: 2008/2009) survey findings suggest that mothers are the "main food providers" in 93% of families with a child 18 months to 10 years, with no significant differences according to work status or social class. Data from Understanding Society (Wave 2: 2010/2011) provide data on parental hours of work (10,236 couples with a child age zero to 14 years). Our secondary analysis of these data suggests that mothers working part-time are significantly less likely to share cooking with their partners, compared with mothers working full-time (but not those working 48 or more hours per week).[4] Complementing this, the secondary analysis also found that, in general, the longer the hours worked by a father, the less likely he was to share cooking with his spouse or partner.

In the qualitative study we asked questions (mainly to mothers) about who took charge of the food work, including cooking and food shopping. At the follow-up study (Wave 2) we asked about whether this was the same/had changed, whether children were encouraged to do more as they got older, and how the participants felt about how food work was shared. In their responses, the participants, usually mothers, mentioned other aspects of food work such as planning for meals, washing up, and loading the dishwasher. In classifying the cases, we drew on DeVault's (1991) concept of "domestic food provisioning" and did not limit food work to cooking but also included shopping, cleaning up, and less visible aspects such as meal planning and feeling "responsible" for children's diets. (At Wave 2 we asked a question about which parent worried more about the target child's diet, thus eliciting responses about "responsibility.")

THE METHODOLOGICAL CHALLENGES

The treatment of the households as cases was intrinsic to the way we approached the qualitative analysis. We plotted the households according to the level of fathers' involvement in food provisioning on a continuum. This resulted in a more refined analysis compared with the quantitative data analysis (in the UK panel study Understanding Society). It enabled us to identify features of family life, not only mothers' and fathers' working hours—albeit these were mentioned most often—which were important in explaining the domestic division of food work (Metcalfe, Dryden, Johnson, Owen, & Shipton, 2009, pp. 109–111). Moreover, because we investigated the division of food work over time (two years), we were also able to explore continuities and discontinuities at the household level. Parents accounted for changes in the division of food work accordingly: a mother becoming ill, moving house, the birth of an additional child, loss of energy, children being older and easier to cook for, the loss of other help, and health concerns. We found, therefore, that patterns within households do change, with some fathers doing more food work and some doing less in response to circumstances in their lives (within and beyond the household), albeit only a minority do equal amounts or more. The conceptual approach that was adopted included a focus on routine practices and on accounting for practices to help shift the gaze away from a narrow behavioral "working hours perspective" toward understanding how family (food) practices are influenced by the interpenetration of public and private spheres (home and workplace) and how people make sense of (and thus reproduce or redefine) patterns of paid and unpaid work. Food practices, like other family practices, are shaped by gendered cultural expectations about motherhood and fatherhood—what it means to be "a good mother" and "a good father"—as well as by material constraints of working hours.

In addition to providing a more refined analysis than the quantitative data, the qualitative data also provided a way of examining outliers or cases that did not fit the general pattern shown in the survey results (according to Caracelli & Greene's [1993] categories described earlier). Although the general trend was for a man to share cooking more when his spouse worked longer hours and to do less sharing when he worked longer hours, the qualitative data provided examples of where this did not fit (as well as where it did). For example, in one case, a father worked fewer hours than his wife but did almost no food work as he was said by his wife to lack competence, while another father who worked longer hours took most responsibility for food work as this fitted with his and his wife's shift patterns.

In addressing the research question of how parental employment influences the division of food work, the use of both the survey data and the qualitative material together proved relatively successful since the unit of analysis in both referred to behavior. To some extent the MMMR approach provided corroborating evidence while the qualitative material refined and elaborated on the quantitative analysis. Broadly, the results were comparable and complementary, albeit the research questions relating to each method were somewhat different; notably in the qualitative study, there was a concern to understand the respondents' accounts for the division of food work and to examine food work in the context of the families more holistically and the meaning of mothering and fathering more generally. By contrast, in the survey, food work was conceptualized behaviorally and broken down into constituent "tasks" such as cooking (cf. DeVault, 1991).

Concepts and Meaning in a Multimethod and Mixed Methods Research Longitudinal Design: The Study of Family Meals
THE RESEARCH PROBLEM
Studies have identified an association between frequency of "family meals" and children's and adolescents' body mass index, nutritional status, social well-being, and physical and mental health. These studies suggest that children who eat fewer family meals have poorer health, nutrition, and behavioral outcomes than those who eat more meals with their families (e.g., Neumark-Sztainer, Hannon, Story, Croll, & Perry, 2003). Some longitudinal research implies causality rather than mere association and that family meals are "protective" against a range of less optimal nutritional and psychosocial outcomes, especially for girls (e.g., Neumark-Sztainer et al., 2003). There is widespread agreement about the reduced frequency of eating dinner as a family as children age (e.g., Gilman et al., 2000). Some studies also find an association with socioeconomic status and mothers' paid employment (e.g., Neumark-Stzainer et al., 2003). In Wave 1 of the study we wanted to examine via the qualitative data set the relationship between children's participation in family meals and their parents' employment to establish whether maternal employment seemed important in explaining the social dimension of children's eating practices (in this case meals). We asked about eating patterns on the previous work and nonwork day and their typicality. We also asked about the presence of different family members on different days of the week.

THE ANALYSIS
These questions enabled us to develop a typology of eating patterns in the working week: eating together most days, the modified family meal in which children ate with one parent, and a third situation in which eating together never occurred. In addition we asked what participants understood by the term *family meal* and whether family meals were important to them. Most people suggested that family meals were important, but fewer managed to eat them on most working days. We drew on the concept of synchronicity to shed light on how meals and mealtimes were coordinated in family life and the facilitators and constraints on coordination (Brannen et al., 2013). We found that whether families ate together during the week, on the weekend only, or more rarely was not only influenced by parents' work-time schedules but also by children's timetables relating to their age and bodily tempos, their childcare regimes, their extra-curricular activities, and the problem of coordinating different food preferences and tastes. While we did not report it, as the numbers were small, there was very little difference between the average diet score of children in each group (meals, no meals, and modified meals), which, as explained previously, is perhaps to be expected given that the differences within each group meant there were many factors involved.

At Wave 2 we aimed to extend this analysis by examining quantitatively the relationship between children eating family meals and sociodemographic variables (e.g., child age, maternal employment, social class) and nutritional intake at the aggregate level. To do so we aimed to explore a unique aspect of the archived NDNS data set, which has currently only been analyzed in one other study (Mak et al., 2012). These data are "contextual" in relation to the food and nutrition data in that participants were asked as part of the food diaries to record, in relation to each eating occasion, not only what was eaten but also the time of eating, where, with whom, and whether the television was on (Bates et al., 2011).

THE METHODOLOGICAL CHALLENGES

The main advantage of using these data was that, in contrast to dietary surveys that include a measure of "family meal frequency" and take the meaning of *family meal* for granted, these data were not collected by retrospective self-reports. Given the normative status of "the family meal," as set out in the sociological literature (e.g., Jackson, Olive, & Smith, 2009; Murcott, 1997, 2010) and our own qualitative study (Wave 1), we thought that these data were advantageous.[5] In addition, since the NDNS contains information about overall dietary intake, we could link family meal frequency to diet quality using our score. However, there were also disadvantages, namely that the sociodemographic data (especially maternal education and hours of employment) had not been collected. There were also other methodological challenges for the team, specifically in designing an operationalizable definition of a family meal. In short, we had to define "what is a meal?" and "what is a family?" in relation to the data available. This was limited by the following factors, among others. First, in relation to the variable "who eaten with," we found little within-group variation in that most children were not reported as eating alone. While we thought it feasible to create a dichotomous variable—family/not family—decisions about how to do this were tricky given the data had been coded into categories that were not mutually exclusive ("alone," "family," "friend's," "parent(s)/care-provider," "siblings," "parent(s)/care-provider & siblings," "care-provider & other children," "other"). Second, the number of possible eating occasions throughout the day was considerable, involving consideration of which "time slot" to examine for a possible "family meal." We opted to look at the family evening

meal, as this is implied if not explicitly spelled out in popular understanding and in research about family meals, and, furthermore, we had established that 5 PM to 8 PM was the most common time slot for children's eating in the NDNS data. However, we were aware that this might exclude some younger children who might eat earlier.

Other problems not limited to this data set were that we could not know from these data whether those present were actually eating with the child or whether they were eating the same foods (both of which are thought to be potentially important in explaining any association between family meal frequency and children's and adolescents' overall dietary intakes; (e.g., Centre for Research on Families and Relationships, 2012; Skafida, 2013).

In operationalizing family meals in the NDNS data set, we therefore recognized that we had moved away somewhat from the idea of a family meal as held by most people. While we were avoiding the problem of asking participants to define this themselves, we were creating new problems in that any conclusions would not relate to family meals as they are popularly understood but would rather relate to very particular practices—a child eating between 5 PM and 8 PM with an adult member of his or her family present (or not).

Thus in examining the topic of family meals via a MMMR design, we sought through the qualitative data to explore similar issues to those examined in the quantitative data, namely to determine the frequency of parental presence and child presence at family mealtimes. However, we were also able to tease out whether children and parents were both eating and whether they were eating the same foods and the conditions under which they did and did not do so (Brannen et al., 2013). The qualitative study also provided insight into the symbolic and moral aspects surrounding the concept of family meals as well as practices of eating together, while in the analysis of the quantitative data set the onus was on us to define what constituted eating together.

Given the risk inherent in the experimental nature of our analysis of NDNS data and the political appetite for statistical findings, we sought also to analyze participation in family meal frequency and sociodemographic factors in two other UK large-scale surveys that have asked about children and adults eating together: the Millennium Cohort Survey and Understanding Society. Since these were not dietary surveys, we could not examine associations of self-reported family meal frequency with diet outcomes, but we could examine the relationship with factors such as hours of maternal employment. Albeit the data were limited by their reliance on self-report based on the assumption of a shared understanding of the concept of family meal as outlined earlier, in combining results with findings from our complementary analyses of the qualitative data and the NDNS "contextual data" we hope to foreground the importance of methodology and highlight the complexities of measuring children's participation in family meals and any association with sociodemographic factors or health and behavioral outcomes.

In disrupting common sense and taken for granted assumptions about the association between family meals and other factors such as mothers' work and children's overall diets, our findings based on applying a MMMR approach—while unsettling in the sense of raising methodological uncertainties—speak directly to political and policy concerns in that they caution against the idea that family meals are some sort of "magic bullet," although they are a convenient way for politicians to (dis)place responsibility for children's food intake onto parents (O'Connell & Simon, 2013; Owen, 2013).

Conclusion

We hope we have demonstrated some of the benefits as well as the methodological issues in multi-method research. In particular it is important to take into account that quantitative and qualitative methods each suffer from their own biases and limitations. Survey diary data, while advantageous in measuring behaviors (e.g., what children ate), have the disadvantage that they do not address issues of meaning (in the previous example concerning the study of family meals). Qualitative methods, while providing contextual and symbolic meanings (about food and meals, for example), may not provide detailed information about what is eaten and how much.

However, the combination of these methods may not provide a total solution either, as we have demonstrated with particular reference to our own study of food and families. Qualitative and quantitative methods may not together succeed in generating the knowledge that the researcher is seeking. In researching everyday, taken-for-granted practices, both methods can suffer from similar disadvantages. In surveys, practices may not easily be open to accurate recall

or reflection. Likewise, qualitative methods, even when a narrative approach is adopted, may not produce recall but instead provoke normative accounts or justifications. While survey data can provide a "captive" sample for a qualitative study and the opportunity to analyze extensive contextual data about that sample, the two data samples may not be sufficiently comparable. Survey data conducted at one moment in time may not connect with qualitative data when they are collected at another time point (this is critical, for example, in studying children's diets). Thus it may be necessary to build resources into the qualitative phase of the inquiry for reassessing children's diet using a method based on that adopted in the survey. This may prove costly and require bringing in the help of nutritionists.

Many social practices are clothed in moral discourses and are thereby difficult to study by whatever method. Surveys are renowned for generating socially acceptable answers, but in interviews respondents may not want to admit that they do not measure up to normative ideals. In discussing methodological issues in MMMR, it is all too easy to segment qualitative and quantitative approaches artificially (Schwandt, 2005). As already stressed, MMMR can provide an articulation between different theoretical levels as in macro, meso, and micro contexts. However, these theoretical levels typically draw on different logics of interpretation and explanation, making it necessary to show how different logics can be integrated (Kelle, 2001). Moreover, we should not adopt a relativist approach but continue to subject our findings to scrutiny in order to draw fewer false conclusions.

Translating research questions across different methods of data collection may involve moving between different epistemologies and logics of inquiry and is likely to affect the data and create problems of interpretation, as has been discussed in the example of families and food. Quantitative and qualitative analyzes do not necessarily map on to each other readily; they may be based on different forms of explanation. While sometimes they may complement one another, in other instances analyzes are dissonant. However, we should also expect that findings generated by different methods (or conducted at different points in time) do not match up. It is, for example, one thing to respond to an open-ended question in a face-to-face interview context and quite another to tick an item from a limited set of alternatives in a self-completion questionnaire.

Given the complexities of linking quantitative and qualitative data sets, we suggest a narrative approach be adopted in reporting the data analyses. By this we mean that when writing up their results, researchers should give attention to the ways in which the data have been integrated, the issues that arise in interpreting the different data both separately and in combination, and how the use of different methods have benefited or complicated the process. This is particularly important where MMMR is carried out in a policy context so that policymakers and other stakeholder groups may be enlightened about the caveats associated with different types of data and, in particular, the advantages and issues of employing more than one type of research methodology (typically quantitative data are preferred by policymakers; Brannen & Moss, 2013).

In addition, the researcher should be attentive to the ways in which the processes of "translation" involved in interpreting data are likely, often unwittingly, to reflect rather than reveal the contexts in which the research is carried out. Data have to be understood and interpreted in relation to the contexts in which the research is funded (by whom and for whom), the research questions posed, the theoretical frameworks that are fashionable at the time of study, and the methods by which the data are produced (Brannen, 2005a, 2005b).

Just as when we use or reuse archived data, it is important in primary research to take into account the broad historical and social contexts of the data and the research inquiry. All data analyses require contextualization, and whether this is part of a mixed method or multimethod research strategy, it is necessary to have recourse to diverse data sources and data collected in different ways. MMMR is not only a matter of strategy. It is not a tool-kit or a technical fix, nor is it a belt-and-braces approach. MMMR requires as much if not more reflexivity than other types of research. This means that researchers need to examine their own presumptions and preferences about different methods and the results that derive from each method and be open to shifting away from entrenched positions to which they cling—theoretical, epistemological, and methodological. At a practical level, the multimethod researcher should be prepared to learn new skills and engage with new communities of practice.

Future Directions

In the future, social science research is likely to become increasingly expensive. Primary research may also prove more difficult to do for other reasons, for example the restrictions imposed by ethics committees. Many researchers will have recourse to secondary analysis of existing contemporary data or turn to older archived data. MMMR research will therefore increasingly involve the *analysis of different types of data* rather than the application of different methods. For example, in our own work we have become increasingly engaged not only in examining data from different surveys but also in interrogating the assumptions that underlie the variables created in those surveys and reconciling (or not) these variables with new qualitative data we have collected.

Another possible trend that is likely to promote the use of MMMR is the growth in demand for interdisciplinary research that embraces disciplines beyond the social sciences. This trend will require even more emphasis on researchers working outside their traditional comfort zones and intellectual and methodological silos. For example, in our own research on families and children's food practices we have been required to engage with nutritionists.

A third trend concerns the growing external pressure on social scientists to justify the importance of their work to society at large, while from within social sciences there is pressure on them to reassert the role of social science as publically and politically engaged. In the UK, we are increasingly required by funding bodies—research councils and government—and by universities to demonstrate the societal "impact" of our research. Part and parcel of this mission is the need to demonstrate the credibility of our research findings and to educate the wider world about the rigor and robustness of our methods. In order to understand the conditions of society in a globalized world, it will indeed be necessary to deepen, develop, and extend our methodological repertoire. MMMR is likely to continue to develop an increasingly high profile in this endeavor.

Discussion Questions

1. Discuss the benefits and challenges of linking a qualitative sample to a survey.

2. Identify within a MMMR study a research question that can be addressed both by qualitative and quantitative methods and a research question that can be addressed via one method only; discuss some different ways of integrating the data from these methods.

3. Discuss two or three methodological strategies for integrating dissonant research results based on quantitative and qualitative data.

4. Create a research design for a longitudinal research project that employs MMMR as part of that design.

Suggested Websites

http://eprints.ncrm.ac.uk

UK's National Centre of Research Methods website, where its "e-print" series of working and commissioned papers are found.

http://www.qualitative-research.net/fqs

Website of a European online qualitative journal, *FQS*.

Notes

1. The study titled *Food Practices and Employed Families with Younger Children* was funded as part of a special initiative funded by the UK's Economic and Social Research Council and the UK's Food Standards Agency (RES-190–25-0010) and subsequently with the Department of Health (ES/J012556/1). The current research team includes Charlie Owen and Antonia Simon (statisticians and secondary data analysts), the principal investigator Dr. Rebecca O'Connell (anthropologist), and Professor Julia Brannen (sociologist). Katie Hollinghurst and Ann Mooney were formerly part of the team (psychologists).

2. A "Dietary Feedback" report was provided to each individual participant about his or her own intake within 3 months of the diet diary being completed. This provided information about the individual intakes of fat, saturated fat, non-milk extrinsic sugars, dietary fiber (as non-starch polysaccharide), Vitamin C, folate, calcium, iron and energy (Table 15.1) relative to average intakes for each of these items for children in the UK, these being based on the results for children of this age from the NDNS conducted in the 1990s (Gregory & Hinds, 1995; Gregory et al., 2000).

3. However at the aggregate level, secondary analysis of the NDNS for 2008–2010 (National Centre for Social Research, Medical Research Council Resource Centre for Human Nutrition Research, & University College London Medical School, 2012), a combined data set of respondents from Year 1 (2008–2009) and Year 2 (2009–2010) found that social class and household income were related to children's fruit and vegetable consumption and overall diet quality (as measured by our nutritional score; Simon et al., forthcoming).

4. A feasible explanation for this finding is that mothers working these long hours are more likely to use paid or unpaid childcare in addition to sharing with a partner or spouse.

5. They avoid two key problems associated with self-report of family meals in the extant literature in which "family meals" are not usually defined by interviewers but by interviewees themselves (cf. Hammons & Fiese, 2011): that people will answer the same response but mean different things and, additionally, also because of the normativity surrounding family meals, some participants may overreport their participation in them. In short, such data seemed advantageous compared to poorly designed survey questions that are associated with known problems related to reliability, validity, and bias (cf. Hammons & Fiese, 2011).

References

Bates, B., Lennox, A., Bates, C., & Swan, G. (Eds.). (2011). National Diet & Nutrition Survey: Headline results from Years 1 & 2 (combined) of the rolling programme 2008/9–2009/10. Appendix A. Dietary data collection and editing. London, England: Food Standards Agency and Department of Health.

Blatchford, P. (2005). A multi-method approach to the study of school class size differences. *International Journal of Social Research Methodology, 8*(3), 195–205.

Brannen, J. (1992). *Mixing methods: Qualitative and quantitative research*. Aldershot, UK: Ashgate.

Brannen, J. (2005a). *Mixed methods research: A discussion paper*. NCRM Methods Review Papers NCRM/005. Southampton, UK: National Center for Research Methods. Retrieved from http://eprints.ncrm.ac.uk/89/

Brannen, J. (2005b). Mixing methods: The entry of qualitative and quantitative approaches into the research process. *International Journal of Social Research Methodology* [Special Issue], *8*(3), 173–185.

Brannen, J., & Moss, G. (2013). Critical issues in designing mixed methods policy research. *American Behavioral Scientist, 7*, 152–172.

Brannen, J., O'Connell, R., & Mooney, A. (2013). Families, meals and synchronicity: Eating together in British dual earner families. *Community, Work and Family, 16*(4), 417–434. Retrieved from http://www.tandfonline.com/doi/abs/10.1080/13668803.2013.776514 doi:10.1080/13668803.2013.776514

Bryman, A. (2008). Why do researchers integrate/combine/mesh/blend/mix/merge/fuse quantitative and qualitative research? In M. Bergman (Ed.), *Advances in Mixed methods research: Theories and applications* (pp. 87–100). London, England: Sage.

Caracelli, V.J., & Greene, J. (1993). Data analysis strategies for mixed-method evaluation designs. *Educational Evaluation and Policy Analysis, 15*(2), 195–207.

Centre for Research on Families and Relationships. (2012). *Is there something special about family meals? Exploring how family meal habits relate to young children's diets*. Briefing 62. Edinburgh, UK: Author. Retrieved from http://www.era.lib.ed.ac.uk/bitstream/1842/6554/1/briefing%2062.pdf

Crepinsek, M., & Burstein, N. (2004). *Maternal employment and children's nutrition: Vol. 2. Other nutrition-related outcomes*. Washington, DC: Economic Research Service, US Department of Agriculture.

Denscombe, M. (2008). Communities of practice: A research paradigm for the mixed method approach. *Journal of Mixed Methods Research, 2*, 270–284.

Denzin, N., & Lincoln, Y. (Eds.). (2005). *The SAGE handbook of qualitative research*. Thousand Oaks, CA: Sage.

DeVault, D. L. (1991). *Feeding the family: The social organization of caring as gendered work*. Chicago, IL: University of Chicago Press.

Dewey, J. (1991). The pattern of inquiry. In J. Dewey (Ed.), *The later works* (pp. 105–123). Carbondale: Southern University Illinois Press.

Ettlinger, N. (2007). Precarity unbound. *Alternatives, 32*, 319–340.

Gillman, M. W., S. L. Rifas-Shiman, A. Lindsay Frazier, H. R. H. Rockett, C. A. Camargo Jr., A. E. Field, . . . G. A. Colditz. (2000). Family dinner and diet quality among older children and adolescents. *Archives of Family Medicine, 9*, 235–240.

Glueck, S., & Glueck, E. (1950). *Unravelling juvenile delinquency*. New York, NY: Commonwealth Fund.

Glueck, S., & Glueck, E. (1968). *Delinquents and non-delinquents in perspective*. Cambridge, MA: Harvard University Press.

Greene, J., Caracelli, V. J., & Graham, W. F. (1989). Towards a conceptual framework for mixed-method evaluation designs. *Education, Evaluation and Policy Analysis, 11*(3), 255–274.

Gregory J. R., & Hinds K. (1995). *National Diet and Nutrition Survey: Children aged 1 1/2 to 4 1/2 Years*. London, England: Stationery Office.

Gregory, J. R., Lowe S., Bates, C. J., Prentice, A., Jackson, L. V., Smithers, G., . . . Farron, M. (2000). *National Diet and Nutrition Survey: Young people aged 4 to 18 years: Vol. 1. Report of the diet and nutrition survey*. London, England: Stationery Office.

Hammersley, M. (2000). Varieties of social research: A typology. *International Journal of Social Research Methodology, 3*(3), 221–231.

Hammersley, M. (2005). The myth of research-based practice: The critical case of educational inquiry. *International Journal for Multiple Research Approaches, 8*(4), 317–331.

Hammersley, M. (2008). Troubles with triangulation. In M. Bergman (Ed.), *Advances in mixed methods research: Theories and applications* (pp. 22–37). London, England: Sage.

Hammond, C. (2005). The wider benefits of adult learning: An illustration of the advantages of multi-method research. *International Journal of Social Research Methodology, 8*(3), 239–257.

Hammons, A., & Fiese, B. (2011). Is frequency of shared family meals related to the nutritional health of children and adolescents? *Pediatrics, 127*(6), e1565–e1574.

Harrits, G. (2011). More than method? A discussion of paradigm differences within mixed methods research. *Journal of Mixed Methods Research, 5*(2), 150–167.

Hawkins, S., Cole, T., & Law, C. (2009). Examining the relationship between maternal employment and health behaviours in 5-year-old British children. *Journal of Epidemiology and Community Health, 63*(12), 999–1004.

Jackson, P. Olive. S., & Smith, G. (2009). Myths of the family meal: Re-reading Edwardian life histories. In P. Jackson (Ed.), *Changing families, changing food*, (pp. 131–145). Basingstoke, UK: Palgrave Macmillan.

Jick, T. (1979). Mixing qualitative and quantitative methods: Triangulation in action. *Administrative Science Quarterly, 24*, 602–611.

Kelle, U. (2001). Sociological explanations between micro and macro and the integration of qualitative and quantitative methods. *FQS, 2*(1). Retrieved from http://www.qualitative-research.net/fqs-eng.htm

Knight, A., O'Connell, R., & Brannen, J. (2014). The temporality of food practices: Intergenerational relations, childhood memories and mothers' food practices in working families with young children. *Families, Relationships and Societies, 3* (2), 303–318.

Laub, J., & Sampson, R. (1993). Turning points in the life course: Why change matters to the study of crime, *Criminology, 31*, 301–325.

Laub, J., & Sampson, R. (1998). Integrating qualitative and quantitative data. In J. Giele & G. Elder (Eds.), *Methods of life course research: Qualitative and quantitative approaches* (pp. 213–231). London, England: Sage.

Law, J. (2004). *After method: Mess in social science research*. New York, NY: Routledge.

Mak, T., Prynne, C., Cole, D., Fitt, E., Roberts, C., Bates, B., & Stephen, A. (2012). Assessing eating context and fruit and vegetable consumption in children: New methods using food diaries in the UK National Diet and Nutrition Survey Rolling Programme. *International Journal of Behavioral Nutrition and Physical Activity, 9*, 126.

Mason, J. (2006). Mixing methods in a qualitatively driven way," *Qualitative Research, 6*(1), 9–26.

Metcalfe, A., Dryden, C., Johnson, M., Owen, J., & Shipton, G. (2009). Fathers, food and family life. In P. Jackson (Ed.), *Changing families, changing food*. Basingstoke, UK: Palgrave Macmillan.

McIntosh, A., Davis, G., Nayga, R., Anding, J., Torres, C., Kubena, K., . . . You, W. (2008). *Parental time, role strain, and children's fat intake and obesity-related outcomes*. Washington, DC: US Department of Agriculture, Economic Research Service.

Morgan, D. (2007). Paradigms lost and pragmatism regained; Methodological implications of combining qualitative and quantitative methods. *Journal of Mixed Methods Research, 1*(1), 48–76.

Murcott, A. (1997). Family meals—A thing of the past? In P. Caplan (Ed.), *Food, identity and health* (pp. 32–49). London, England: Routledge.

Murcott, A. (2010, March 9). *Family meals: Myth, reality and the reality of myth*. Myths and Realities: A New Series of Public Debates. London, England: British Library.

National Centre for Social Research, Medical Research Council Resource Centre for Human Nutrition Research, & University College London Medical School. (2012). National Diet and Nutrition Survey, 2008–2010 [Computer file]. 3rd ed. Essex, UK: UK Data Archive [distributor]. Retrieved from http://dx.doi.org/10.5255/UKDA-SN-6533-1

Neumark-Sztainer, D., Hannon, P. J., Story, M., Croll, J., & Perry, C., (2003). Family meal patterns: Associations with socio-demographic characteristics and improved dietary intake among adolescents. *Journal of the American Dietetic Association, 103*, 317–322.

Nilsen, A., & Brannen, J. (2010). The use of mixed methods in biographical research. In A. Tashakorri & C. Teddlie (Eds.), *SAGE handbook of mixed methods research in social & behavioral research* (2nd ed., pp. 677–696). London, England: Sage.

O'Cathain, A. (2009). Reporting results. In S. Andrew & E. Halcomb (Eds.), *Mixed methods research for nursing and the health sciences* (pp. 135–158). Oxford, UK: Blackwell.

O'Connell, R. (2013). The use of visual methods with children in a mixed methods study of family food practices. *International Journal of Social Research Methodology, 16*(1), 31–46.

O'Connell, R., & Brannen, J. (2014). Children's food, power and control: Negotiations in families with younger children in England. *Childhood, 21*(1), 87–102.

O'Connell, R., & Brannen, J. (2015). Food, *Families and work*. London, England: Bloomsbury.

O'Connell, R., Brannen, J., Mooney, A., Knight, A., & Simon, A. (2011). Food and families who work: A summary. Available at http://www.esrc.ac.uk/my-esrc/grants/RES-190-25-0010/outputs/Read/e7d99b9f-eafd-4650-9fd2-0efcf72b4555

O'Connell, R., & Simon, A. (2013, April). *A mixed methods approach to meals in working families: Addressing lazy assumptions and methodologies difficulties.* Paper presented at the British Sociological Association Annual Conference: Engaging Sociology. London, England.

Omwuegbuzie, A., & Leech, N. (2005). On becoming a pragmatic researcher: The importance of combining quantitative and qualitative research methodologies. *International Journal of Social Research Methodology, 8*(5), 375–389.

Owen, C. (2013, July). Do the children of employed mothers eat fewer "family meals"? Paper presented at the Understanding Society Conference, University of Essex.

Reiss, A. L. (1968). Stuff and nonsense about social surveys and participant observation. In H. L. Becker, B. Geer, D. Riesman, & R. S. Weiss (Eds.), *Institutions and the person: Papers in memory of Everett C. Hughes* (pp. 351–367). Chicago, IL: Aldine.

Sammons, P., Siraj-Blatchford, I., Sylva, K., Melhuish, E., Taggard, B., & Elliot, K. (2005). Investigating the effects of pre-school provision: Using mixed methods in the EPPE research. *International Journal of Social Research Methodology, 8*(3), 207–224.

Schwandt, T. (2005). A diagnostic reading of scientifically based research for education. *Educational Theory, 55,* 285–305.

Seltzer-Kelly, D., Westwood, D., & Pena-Guzman, M. (2012). A methodological self-study of quantitizing: Negotiated meaning and revealing multiplicity. *Journal of Mixed Methods Research, 6*(4), 258–275.

Simon, A., O'Connell, R., & Stephen, A. M. (2012). Designing a nutritional scoring system for assessing diet quality for children aged 10 years an under in the UK. *Methodological Innovations Online, 7*(2), 27–47.

Simon, A., Owen, C., O'Connell, R., & Stephen, A. (forthcoming). Exploring associations between children's diets and maternal employment through an analysis of the UK National Diet and Nutrition Survey.

Skafida, V. (2013). The family meal panacea: Exploring how different aspects of family meal occurrence, meal habits and meal enjoyment relate to young children's diets. *Sociology of Health and Illness, 25*(6), 906–923. doi:10.1111/1467-9566.12007

Stephen, A. (2007). The case for diet diaries in longitudinal studies. *International Journal of Social Research Methodology, 10*(5), 365–377.

Tashakorri, A., & Creswell, J. (2007). Exploring the nature of research questions in mixed methods research. *Journal of Mixed Methods Research, 1*(3), 207–211.

Woolley, C. (2009). Meeting the methods challenge of integration in a sociological study of structure and agency. *Journal of Mixed Methods Research, 3*(1), 7–26.

Yin, R. (2006). Mixed methods research: Are the methods genuinely integrated or merely parallel? *Research in the Schools, 13*(1), 41–47.

Warde, A., & Hetherington, K. (1994). English households and routine food practices: A research note. *Sociological Review, 42*(4), 758–778.

Advanced Mixed Analysis Approaches

Anthony J. Onwuegbuzie *and* John H. Hitchcock

Abstract

Because of the complexity of mixed analysis, several authors recently have written methodological works that provide either an introductory- or intermediate-level guide to conducting such analyses. Although all of these works have been useful for beginning and emergent mixed researchers, what is lacking are works that describe and illustrate advanced mixed analysis approaches. Thus, in this chapter, we provide a compendium of advanced mixed analysis approaches. In particular, we outline three advanced quantitative-dominant crossover mixed analyses, three advanced qualitative-dominant crossover mixed analyses, and one advanced equal-status crossover mixed analysis. Most of these advanced crossover mixed analyses previously have not been described as a mixed analysis technique in any published work, illustrating the significance and innovation of our chapter.

Key Words: mixed methods analysis, mixed analysis, crossover mixed analysis, quantitative-dominant crossover mixed analysis, qualitative-dominant crossover mixed analysis, equal-status crossover mixed analysis

In all empirical research studies representing the social, behavioral, and health sciences, data analysis is a process that comprises multiple phases. These phases can include examining, cleaning, reducing, exploring, describing, explaining, displaying, transforming, correlating, consolidating, comparing, integrating, importing, and/or modelling data, with the goal of comprehending phenomena and meaning making. As such, data analysis serves as the bridge between the data collected and the interpretations that emanate from these data. In most instances, data analysis optimally leads to some form of generalization that includes (a) *external (statistical) generalizations* (i.e., making generalizations, judgments, predictions, or inferences based on data yielded from a representative statistical [i.e., optimally random and large] sample to the population from which the sample was selected [i.e., universalistic/probabilistic generalizability]); (b) *internal (statistical) generalizations* (i.e., making generalizations, judgments, predictions, or inferences on data obtained from one or more representative or elite study participants [e.g., key informants, subsample members] to the sample from which the participant[s] was selected [i.e., particularistic generalizability]); (c) *analytic generalizations* (i.e., "the investigator is striving to generalize a particular set of [case study] results to some broader theory"; Yin, 2009, p. 43) are "applied to wider theory on the basis of how selected cases 'fit' with general constructs" (Curtis, Gesler, Smith, & Washburn, 2000, p. 1002); (d) *case-to-case transfer* (i.e., making generalizations, judgments, or inferences from one case to another [similar] case; Miles & Huberman, 1994); (e) *naturalistic generalization* (i.e., each reader makes generalizations entirely, or at least in part, from his or her personal or vicarious experiences; Stake & Trumbull, 1982); or (f) *moderatum generalization* (i.e., generalizations that "resemble the modest, pragmatic generalizations drawn from personal experience which, by bringing a semblance of order and consistency to social interaction, make everyday life possible"; Payne & Williams, 2005, p. 296; see also Williams, 2000). (For a discussion of these generalizations, see Onwuegbuzie, Slate, Leech, & Collins, 2009, and Onwuegbuzie & Collins, 2014.)

As outlined by Onwuegbuzie and Collins (2014), these generalizations or inferences involve some form of probabilistic judgment, whether it represents the theoretical method of assigning probabilities (i.e., via p values, confidence intervals), the relative frequency method of assigning probabilities (i.e., via internal replication, e.g., bootstrapping or jackknife techniques, cross-validation), or—as is typically the case when interpreting findings in qualitative research studies/phases of studies or quantitative-based descriptive research studies—the subjective method of assigning probabilities (i.e., subjective probabilities). This probabilistic judgment arises from the notion that generalization

> represent[s] an adequate level of *confidence* that the phenomenon captured by the underlying data is both real—in the subjective, objective, or intersubjective sense—and stable (e.g., reliable, trustworthy), for the study participants from whom the data are collected, and, in the case when external or internal statistical generalizations are made, for people other than these study participants. (Onwuegbuzie & Collins, 2014, p. 655–656)

Given that sufficient trustworthy data have been collected, the ensuing data analysis moderates the level of confidence that the researcher(s) places on the inferences that evolve. As such, data analysis plays a pivotal role in the research process in answering the underlying research question(s). In any given study, depending on the research question(s), the researcher(s) uses either one data analysis type (i.e., *monoanalysis*; Onwuegbuzie, Slate, Leech, & Collins, 2007, p. 6) or multiple data analysis types (i.e., *multianalysis*; Onwuegbuzie et al., 2007, p. 6). Thus, multianalysis subsumes monanalysis as a special case. Moreover, a multianalysis can involve the use of two or more analyses that represent the same tradition (e.g., multiple qualitative data analyses)—typically a hallmark of what some authors refer to as *multiple methods research* or *multimethod research studies* (cf. this volume)—or two or more analyses that represent both qualitative and quantitative traditions—a common feature of what is known as *mixed methods research*

or *mixed research* (cf. Johnson, Onwuegbuzie, & Turner, 2007). Information abounds about how to conduct a monoanalysis—whether it be a quantitative analysis or a qualitative analysis. However, there is much less information about how to conduct a multianalysis. This is the focus of the present chapter. Specifically, in this chapter, we outline ways of conducting the more complex forms of multianalyses.

Data Analysis in Multiple Methods Research

Because at the most basic level, the data analysis stage of qualitative, quantitative, and mixed research studies involves the use of one or more analysis types combined with one or more methods used at other stages of the research process (e.g., methods of data collection, data interpretation, data validation/legitimation, data interpretation, data reporting), it can be argued that *virtually every study represents a multiple methods research study to some degree*. Indeed, we do not know what a single-method research study looks like. Moreover, we believe that multimethod research approaches either within traditions (i.e., qualitative, quantitative, and mixed research) or across traditions (i.e., mixed research) typically represent the most effective research because, extending Greene, Caracelli, and Graham's (1989) framework to the multimethod situation, it allows researchers to seek one or more of the following integration purposes: *triangulation* (i.e., comparing findings stemming from one data analysis type with results stemming from one or more other data analysis types), *complementarity* (i.e., seeking elaboration, illustration, enhancement, and clarification of the findings from one data analysis type with results from one or more other types), *development* (i.e., using the results from one type to help inform results emanating from one or more types), *initiation* (i.e., discovering paradoxes and contradictions that emerge when findings from two or more types are compared that might lead to a re-framing of the research question), and *expansion* (i.e., expanding the breadth and range of a study by using multiple data analysis types for different study phases). As such, we believe that it would be futile for us to attempt to provide a framework (i.e., a basic structure that promotes conscious selection of data types and connecting them optimally to address a given set of research goals) for conducting multimethod analyses because of the almost infinite number of possible ways that data analyses within and across traditions can be combined within a multiple research study. Thus, for the remainder of this chapter, instead, we will focus on the analysis of qualitative and quantitative data within a coherent and integrated framework—known as a *mixed methods analysis* or more simply as *mixed analysis*. Specifically, we provide a partial compendium of advanced mixed analysis approaches rooted in Greene et al.'s (1989) framework described earlier.

Overview of Mixed Analysis

In mixed research, mixed analysis represents a complex process because, as identified by Onwuegbuzie and Combs (2010), it optimally involves making decisions about the following 13 criteria:

1. rationale/purpose for conducting the mixed analysis
2. philosophy underpinning the mixed analysis
3. number of data types that will be analyzed
4. number of data analysis types that will be used
5. time sequence of the mixed analysis
6. level of interaction between quantitative and qualitative analyses
7. priority of analytical components
8. number of analytical phases
9. link to other design components
10. phase of the research process when all analysis decisions are made
11. type of generalization
12. analysis orientation
13. cross-over nature of analysis

As such, Onwuegbuzie and Combs (2010) state that a mixed analysis involves

the use of both quantitative and qualitative analytical techniques within the same framework that is guided either a priori, a posteriori, or iteratively (representing analytical decisions that occur both prior to the study and during the study) by one of the existing mixed research paradigms (e.g., pragmatism, transformative-emancipatory) such that it meets one or more of the following rationales/purposes: triangulation, complementarity, development, initiation, and expansion. Mixed analyses involve the analysis of one or both data types (i.e., quantitative data *or* qualitative data, or quantitative data *and* qualitative data) that occur either concurrently (i.e., in no chronological order) or sequentially in two phases (in which the qualitative analysis phase precedes the quantitative

analysis phase or vice versa and findings from the initial analysis phase inform the subsequent phase) or more than two phases (i.e., iteratively). The analysis strands might not interact until the data interpretation stage yielding a basic parallel mixed analysis, although more complex forms of parallel mixed analysis might be used in which interaction takes place in a limited way before the data interpretation phase. The mixed analysis can be design-based, wherein it is directly linked to the mixed design (e.g., sequential mixed analysis techniques used for sequential mixed designs). Alternatively, the mixed analysis can be phase based, in which the mixed analysis takes place in one or more phases (e.g., data transformation). In mixed analyses, either the qualitative or quantitative analysis strands might be given priority or given approximately equal priority as a result of a priori decisions (i.e., determined at the research conceptualization phase) or decisions that emerge during the course of the study. The mixed analysis could represent case-oriented, variable-oriented, and process/experience-oriented analyses. The mixed analysis is guided by an attempt to analyze data in a way that yields at least one of five types of generalizations (i.e., external statistical generalizations, internal statistical generalizations, analytical generalizations, case-to-case transfer, naturalistic generalization). At its most integrated form, the mixed analysis might involve some form of cross-over analysis, wherein one or more analysis types associated with one tradition (e.g., qualitative analysis) are used to analyze data associated with a different tradition (e.g., quantitative data). (pp. 425–426)

Because of the complexity of mixed analysis, over the past decade, several authors have written methodological works that provide either an introductory-level (e.g., Bazeley, 2003, 2006, 2009c; Combs & Onwuegbuzie, 2010; Onwuegbuzie & Combs, 2011; Onwuegbuzie & Teddlie, 2003) or intermediate-level (e.g., Bazeley, 2009b; Bazeley & Kemp, 2012; Castro, Kellison, Boyd, & Kopak, 2010; DeCuir-Gunby, Marshall, & McCulloch, 2012; Happ, DeVito Dabbs, Tate, Hricik, & Erlen, 2006; Jang, McDougall, Pollon, & Russell, 2008; Li, Marquart, & Zercher, 2000; Onwuegbuzie & Dickinson, 2008; Onwuegbuzie, Leech, & Collins, 2011; Onwuegbuzie et al., 2007, 2009; Sandelowski, Voils, & Knafl, 2009) guide to conducting mixed analyses. Although all of these works likely have been useful for beginning and emergent mixed researchers, what is lacking are works that outline advanced mixed analysis approaches. This, again, is the purpose of the present chapter. Specifically, in this chapter, we provide a partial compendium of advanced mixed analysis approaches. Readers should note that this chapter provides an overview of how approaches can work, but detailed explication is not possible due to page restrictions. It might be necessary to consult the references cited at the end of this chapter to develop the necessary methodological approaches that can be mixed. Note that we refer to this as a partial compendium because we have identified several additional types of advanced mixed analyses (Hitchcock & Onwuegbuzie, 2015) that are not presented in this chapter because of space

limitations. However, the fact that we do not list all of our ideas here should not be construed as a limitation; rather, we hope that readers will see that adopting Greene et al.'s (1989) framework provides the basis for creativity when mixing. That is, the notions of triangulation, integration, complementarity, development, initiation, and expansion can almost always spur thinking about how to engage in advanced mixed analyses, and this chapter should be thought of as a demonstration of this point.

Conceptual Framework

With respect to qualitative data analysis approaches, Leech and Onwuegbuzie (2008) identified 23 qualitative data analysis approaches (see Table 16.1; see also Leech & Onwuegbuzie, 2007).

Table 16.1 Most Common Qualitative Analyses

Type of Analysis	Short Description of Analysis
Constant comparison analysis	Systematically reducing data to codes then developing themes from the codes
Classical content analysis	Counting the number of codes
Word count	Counting the total number of words used or the number of times a particular word is used
Keywords-in-context	Identifying keywords and utilizing the surrounding words to understand the underlying meaning of the keyword
Domain analysis	Utilizing the relationships between symbols and referents to identify domains
Taxonomic analysis	Creating a system of classification that inventories the domains into a flowchart or diagram to help the researcher understand the relationships among the domains
Componential analysis	Using matrices and/or tables to discover the differences among the subcomponents of domains
Conversation analysis	Utilizing the behavior of speakers to describe people's methods for producing orderly social interaction
Discourse analysis	Selecting representative or unique segments of language use, such as several lines of an interview transcript, and then examining the selected lines in detail for rhetorical organization, variability, accountability, and positioning
Secondary data analysis	Analyzing nonnaturalistic data or artifacts that were derived from previous studies
Membership categorization analysis	Utilizing the role that interpretations play in making descriptions and the consequences of selecting a particular category (e.g., baby, sister, brother, mother, father = family)
Semiotics	Using talk and text as systems of signs under the assumption that no meaning can be attached to a single term
Manifest content analysis	Describing observed (i.e., manifest) aspects of communication via objective, systematic, and empirical means

(continued)

Table 16.1 Continued

Type of Analysis	Short Description of Analysis
Latent content analysis	Uncovering underlying meaning of text
Qualitative comparative analysis	Systematically analyzing similarities and differences across cases, typically being used as a theory-building approach, allowing the analyst to make connections among previously built categories, as well as to test and to develop the categories further
Narrative analysis	Considering the potential of stories to give meaning to individual's lives and treating data as stories, enabling researchers to take account of research participants' own evaluations
Text mining	Analyzing naturally occurring text in order to discover and capture semantic information
Micro-interlocutor analysis	Analyzing information stemming from one or more focus groups about which participant(s) responds to each question, the order in which each participant responds, the characteristics of the response, the nonverbal communication used, and the like
Framework analysis	Analyzing inductively to provide systematic and visible stages to the analysis process, allowing for the inclusion of a priori as well as a posteriori concepts, and comprising the following five key stages: (a) familiarizing, (b) identifying a thematic framework, (c) indexing, (d) charting, and (e) mapping and interpreting
Grounded visualization	Examining spatially a combination of referenced data and ethnographic data, in close relationship to each other, and integrating geographic information systems–based cartographic representations with qualitative forms of analysis and evidence, thereby yielding an inductive and critically reflexive scale–sensitive analysis that combines grounded theory and visualization
Interpretative phenomenological analysis	Analyzing in detail how one or more persons, in a given context, make sense of a given phenomenon—often representing experiences of personal significance (e.g., major life event)
Schema analysis	Searching for cultural schemata (i.e., scripts) in texts, which include identifying semantic relationships between elements of component schemas
Ethnographic decision models	Building a model of the decision process for a behavior of interest, resulting in a display of data, via decision trees, decision tables, or sets of rules that take the form of *if-then* statements

Adapted from "Qualitative Data Analysis: A Compendium of Techniques and a Framework for Selection for School Psychology Research and Beyond," by N. L. Leech and A. J. Onwuegbuzie (2008), *School Psychology Quarterly, 23*, p. 601. Copyright 2008 by American Psychological Association.

Most recently, Onwuegbuzie and Denham (2014) identified 34 qualitative data analysis approaches that were identified from an exhaustive search of the literature, which they arranged in chronological order, starting from 323 BC (word count; cf. DeRocher, Miron, Patten, & Pratt, 1973) to the present day (e.g., nonverbal communication analysis; Denham & Onwuegbuzie, 2013). Further, Miles and Huberman (1994) conceptualized 19 within-case analyses and 18 cross-case analyses. Although this list of qualitative analyses is not exhaustive, it does comprise many of the most popularized qualitative data analysis approaches. In any case, this list illustrates that qualitative researchers have numerous analysis approaches from which to choose.

With respect to quantitative data analysis approaches, Onwuegbuzie, Leech, et al. (2011) identified 58 classes of established parametric quantitative analysis approaches and select nonparametric quantitative analysis approaches (cf. Figure 16.1). These 58 classes of quantitative analyses illustrate

Measurement Techniques	
Name of Analytical Technique	Description
Classical Test Theory	Analyzes the relationship among observed scores, true scores, and error in an attempt to predict outcomes of psychological and behavioral measurement
Item Response Theory (Latent Trait Theory, Strong True Score Theory, Modern Mental Test Theory)	Analyzes the probabilistic relationship between the response that a person provides (e.g. examinee) on a quantitative item(s) and item parameters (e.g., item difficulty, item discrimination, guessing parameter) and person parameters/latent traits (e.g., ability, personality trait)
Multilevel Item Response Theory	Estimates latent traits of the respondent at different levels and examines the relationships between predictor variables and latent traits at different levels
Exploratory Factor Analysis	Explores the underlying structure of correlations among observed variables in an attempt to reduce dimensionality of data, wherein a small(er) number of factors significantly account for the correlations among the set of measured variables; utilizes estimates of common variance or reliability on the main diagonal of the correlation matrix that is factor analyzed
Principal Component Analysis	Explores the underlying structure of correlations among observed variables in an attempt to reduce dimensionality of data, wherein a small(er) number of factors significantly account for the correlations among the set of measured variables; utilizes the total variance of each variable to assess the shared variation among the variables. That is, it uses "ones" on the diagonal of the correlation matrix that is factor analyzed. Principal component analysis typically is conducted for variable reduction because it can be used to develop scores that are combinations of observed variables, whereas exploratory factor analysis is more appropriate for exploring latent constructs and allows for error in estimation models
Confirmatory Factor Analysis	Verifies the factor structure of a set of observed variables; it allows testing of the hypothesis that a relationship between observed variables and their underlying latent constructs exists
Multiple Factor Analysis (optimal scaling, dual scaling, homogeneity analysis, scalogram analysis)	Analyzes observations described by two or more sets of variables, and examines the common structures present in some or all of these set
Hierarchical Factor Analysis	Differentiates higher-order factors from a set of correlated lower-order factors
Assessing One Variable/Participant at a Time	
Descriptive Analyses (i.e., measures of central tendency, variation/dispersion, position/relative standing, and distributional shape)	Summarizes and describes a set of data one variable at a time in quantitative terms
Single-Subject Analysis	Analyzes observations from one or more individuals in which each individual serves as her/his own control (i.e., individual participant is the unit of analysis, although a group such as a classroom also can be the analytic unit); note that it is possible to include several variables at once in a design but analyses typically focus on one variable at a time

Fig. 16.1 Established classes of quantitative data analysis techniques and descriptions

Name of Analytical Technique	Description
Assessing Differences through Variance Analysis	
Independent samples *t* test	Examines the difference between the means of two independent groups
Dependent samples *t* test (paired samples *t* test)	Examines the difference between the means of two groups, wherein the scores in one group is paired or dependent on the scores in the other group
Analysis of Variance (ANOVA)	Partitions the observed variance into components based on different sources of variation; one-way ANOVA examines the equality of several independent groups based on one dependent/outcome variable; factorial ANOVA examines the effects of two or more independent/explanatory/predictor variables and their interactions
Analysis of Covariance (ANCOVA)	Examines whether one or more factors (and their interactions) have an effect or are related to the outcome variable after removing the variance associated with which quantitative predictors (covariates)
Multivariate Analysis of Variance (MANOVA)	Examines whether one or more factors have an effect or are related to two or more outcome variables
Multivariate Analysis of Covariance (MANCOVA)	Examines whether one or more factors (and their interactions) have an effect or are related to two or more outcome variables after removing the variance associated with quantitative predictors (covariates)
Hierarchical Linear Modeling (HLM) (multilevel modeling, mixed effects modeling, covariance components modeling, random-coefficient regression modeling)	Analyzes variance in an outcome variable when data are in nested categories (e.g., students in a class, classes within a school, schools in one school district)
Multivariate Hierarchical Linear Modeling	Analyzes variance in multivariate dependent variables when the covariance structure of the independent variables is of interest
Repeated Measures Analysis of Variance (RMANOVA)	Involves an analysis of variance conducted on any design wherein the independent/predictor variable(s) have all been measured on the same participants under multiple conditions
Mixed Analysis of Variance (Mixed ANOVA)	Examines differences between two or more independent groups whereby repeated measures have been taken on all participants such that one factor represents a between-subjects variable and the other factor represents a within-subjects variable. Observations also may be nested by a unit (e.g., person) where units are generally treated as a between-subject variable
Repeated Measures Analysis of Covariance (RMANCOVA)	Examines whether one or more factors (and their interactions) have an effect or are related to the outcome variables (i.e., repeated measures) after removing the variance associated with quantitative predictors (covariates)
Assessing Group Membership/Relationships	
Cluster Analysis	Assigns a set of observations, usually people, into groups or clusters wherein members of the group are maximally similar
Q Methodology	Involves finding relationships between participants across a sample of variables
Profile Analysis	Classifies empirically individual observations based on common characteristics or attributes measured by an observed variable(s)

Figure 16.1 Continued

Name of Analytical Technique	Description
Multivariate Profile Analysis	Classifies empirically individual observations based on common characteristics or attributes (i.e., multiple dependent variables) measured by observed variables (i.e., multiple independent variables)
Chi-Square Analysis	Involves any test statistic that has a chi-square distribution but generally analyzes the independence of two categorical variables via a contingency table
Chi-Square Automatic Interaction Detection (CHAID)	Examines the relationships between a categorical dependent measure (dichotomous, polytomous, ordinal) and a large set of selected predictor variables that may interact themselves; it involves a series of chi-square analyses (i.e., iterative, chi-square tests of independence) being conducted between the dependent and predictor variables
Multivariate Chi-Square Automatic Interaction Detection (CHAID)	Examines the relationships between two or more categorical dependent measure (dichotomous, polytomous, ordinal) and a large set of selected predictor variables that may interact themselves; it involves a series of chi-square analyses (i.e., iterative, chi-square tests of independence) being conducted between the multiple dependent and predictor variables
Descriptive Discriminant Analysis	Explains group separation (i.e., categorical dependent/outcome variable) as a function of one or more continuous or binary independent variables
Predictive Discriminant Analysis	Predicts a group membership (i.e., categorical dependent/outcome variable) by one or more continuous or binary independent variables
Assessing Time and/or Space	
Time Series Analysis	Involves analyzing, using frequency-domain methods or time-domain methods, an ordered sequence of observations over time, taking into account the serial dependence of the observations for the purpose of modeling and forecasting
Survival Analysis	Analyzes time-to-event data (i.e., failure time data)
Geostatistics	Analyzes spatiotemporal (i.e., existing in both space and time) datasets
Panel Data Analysis	Analyzes a particular participant or group of participants within multiple sites, periodically observed over a defined time frame (i.e., longitudinal analysis)
Correspondence Analysis	Converts data organized in a two-way table into graphical displays, with the categories of the two variables serving as points; this graphical display presents the relationship between the two categorical variables
Canonical correspondence analysis (CCA)	Relates specific variables (e.g., types of species) to variables of interest (e.g., types of environments)
Fuzzy correspondence analysis	Similar to Correspondence Analysis, except uses "fuzzy data"—data that are coded with multiple categories instead of the common "0" or "1"
Multiple Correspondence Analysis	Analyzes the pattern of relationships of several categorical dependent variables
Discriminant Correspondence Analysis	Categorizes observations in predefined groups using nominal variables
Proportional Hazard Model	Estimates the effects of different covariates influencing the times-to-failure of a system (i.e., hazard rate)

Figure 16.1 Continued

Name of Analytical Technique	Description
Explaining or Predicting Relationships Between Variables	
Linear Regression	Examines the linear correlations between one (simple regression) or more (multiple regression) binary or continuous explanatory variables and a single continuous dependent variable
Non-Linear Regression	Examines the non-linear correlations between one or more binary or continuous explanatory variables and a single continuous dependent variable
Probit regression	Examines the non-linear correlations between one or more binary or continuous explanatory variables and a binomial response variable
Regression Discontinuity Analysis	Examines causal effects of interventions, wherein assignment to a treatment condition is determined, at least partly, by the value of an observed covariate that lies on either side of a fixed threshold/cut-score
Logistic Regression (logit regression)	Examines the relationship between one (simple logistic regression model) or more (multiple logistic regression model) binary or continuous explanatory variables and a single categorical dependent variable
Multivariate Logistic Regression	Examines the relationship between one or more explanatory variables and two or more categorical dependent variable(s)
Descriptive Discriminant Analysis	Explains group separation (i.e., categorical dependent/outcome variable) as a function of one or more continuous or binary independent variables
Predictive Discriminant Analysis	Predicts a group membership (i.e., categorical dependent/outcome variable) by one or more continuous or binary independent variables
Log-Linear Analysis (multi-way frequency analysis)	Determines which of a set of three or more variables (and/or interactions) best explains the observed frequencies with no variable serving as the dependent/outcome variable
Canonical Correlation Analysis	Examines the multivariate relationships between two or more binary or continuous predictor variables and two or more binary or continuous outcome variables
Path Analysis	Describes and quantifies the relationship of a dependent/outcome variable to a set of other variables, with each variable being hypothesized as having a direct effect or indirect effect (via other variables) on the dependent variable
Structural Equation Modeling (causal modeling, covariance structure analysis)	Involves building and testing statistical models; it encompasses aspects of confirmatory factor analysis, path analysis, and regression analysis
Multilevel Structural Equation Modeling	Used when the units of observation form a hierarchy of nested clusters and some variables of interest are measured by a set of items or fallible instruments
Multilevel latent class modeling	Analyzes data with a multilevel structure such that model parameters are allowed to differ across groups, clusters, or level-2 units; the dependent variable is not directly observed but represents a latent variable with two or more observed indicators
Correlation coefficient	Measures the association between two variables
Multidimensional Scaling	Explores similarities or dissimilarities in data; it displays the structure of a set of objects from data that approximate the distances between pairs of the objects

Figure 16.1 Continued

Name of Analytical Technique	Description
Social Network Analysis	Involves the identification and mapping of relationships and flows among people, groups, institutions, web sites, and other information- and knowledge-producing units of different sizes; it provides both a visual and a mathematical analysis of complex human systems; the unit of analysis is not the individual, but an element consisting of a collection of two or more individuals and the linkages among them
Propensity Score Analysis	Replaces multiple covariates such that just one score is applied as a predictor rather than multiple individual covariates, thereby greatly simplifying the model; balances the treatment and control groups on the covariates when participants are grouped into strata or subclassified based on the propensity score; it adjusts for differences via study design (matching) or during estimation of treatment effect (stratification/regression)

[a]For many of these analyses, nonparametric versions and Bayesian versions exist.
Source: Adapted from "Toward a New Era for Conducting Mixed Analyses: The Role of Quantitative Dominant and Qualitative Dominant Crossover Mixed Analyses," by A. J. Onwuegbuzie, N. L. Leech, and K. M. Y. Collins (2011) in M. Williams & W. P. Vogt (Eds.), *The SAGE handbook of innovation in social research methods*, pp. 354–356. Copyright 2011 by SAGE Publications.

Figure 16.1 (Continued)

that quantitative researchers also have numerous analysis approaches at their disposal.

Crossover Mixed Analyses

In a crossover mixed analysis, one form of data (e.g., qualitative) collected can be analyzed utilizing techniques traditionally associated with the alternative paradigm (e.g., quantitative) (Greene, 2007, 2008; Onwuegbuzie & Teddlie, 2003), thereby yielding a higher level of integration of quantitative and qualitative analyses than would be the case if a mixed researcher combined the results stemming from the qualitative analysis of qualitative data with the findings stemming from the quantitative analysis of quantitative data (Onwuegbuzie & Combs, 2010). Examples of cross-over analyses include (a) conducting an exploratory factor analysis (i.e., quantitative analysis) of themes emerging from a qualitative analysis (e.g., constant comparison analysis) and (b) constructing narrative profiles (i.e., qualitative analysis) from quantitative data. Consistent with this assertion, Teddlie and Tashakkori (2009) declared that "We believe that this is one of the more fruitful areas for the further development of MM [mixed methods] analytical strategies" (p. 281).

Crossover Mixed Analysis Framework

Crossover mixed analyses can be *quantitative dominant, qualitative dominant*, or *equal status*

(Onwuegbuzie & Combs, 2010). Each of these types of crossover mixed analyses is described in the following sections.[1]

QUALITATIVE-DOMINANT CROSSOVER ANALYSES

Qualitative-dominant crossover mixed analyses involve the researcher taking a stance that is constructivist, critical theorist, or participatory—or any other stance associated with the qualitative research tradition—in terms of the research process in general and the analysis process in particular, while simultaneously operating under the belief that the addition of quantitative data and analysis can help them address the research question(s) to a greater extent. The lowest level of analysis integration would involve combining one or more sets of qualitative analyses with descriptive statistics. At a higher level of integration, the qualitative-dominant crossover mixed analysis would involve combining one or more sets of qualitative analyses with exploratory analysis techniques, such as when conducting an exploratory factor analysis of the emergent themes. At the highest level of integration, the qualitative-dominant crossover mixed analysis would involve combining one or more sets of qualitative analyses with inferential statistics. Whatever the level of integration, the qualitative strand would represent the dominant strand, with the quantitative strand being used in an attempt to fulfill one or more of Greene et al.'s (1989) five purposes for mixing.

QUANTITATIVE-DOMINANT CROSSOVER ANALYSES

Quantitative-dominant crossover mixed analyses involve the analyst adopting a postpositivist stance while at the same time operating under the belief that the inclusion of qualitative data and analysis can help address the research question(s) to a greater extent. The lowest level of analysis integration would involve combining one or more sets of inferential analyses with qualitative analyses that generate some type of frequency data (e.g., word count). Contrastingly, the highest level of analysis integration would involve combining one or more sets of the highest levels of inferential analyses (e.g., hierarchical linear modeling) with the more complex types of qualitative analyses such as Interpretative phenomenological analysis (see Table 16.1).

EQUAL-STATUS CROSSOVER ANALYSES

Equal-status crossover mixed analyses involve the analyst adopting a flexible research philosophical stance (e.g., some form of pragmatism [cf. Biesta, 2010], such as pragmatism-of-the-middle philosophy [Johnson & Onwuegbuzie, 2004], pragmatism-of-the-right philosophy [Putnam, 2002; Rescher, 2000], pragmatism-of-the-left philosophy [Maxcy, 2003; Rorty, 1991], dialectical pluralism [Johnson, 2012], or critical dialectical pluralism [Onwuegbuzie & Frels, 2013]), while at the same time believing that the approximately equal use of both qualitative data analysis and quantitative data analysis can help address the research question(s) to an optimal extent. These types of analyses optimally would involve combining the more complex types of qualitative analyses with one or more sets of the more complex inferential analyses.

The utility of establishing the mixed analysis emphasis—as recommended by Onwuegbuzie and Combs (2010)—is that researchers have flexibility as to the extent to which their mixed analyses *cross over*, and this form of analysis could be driven by their actual philosophical (e.g., postpositivist, constructivist, pragmatist-based) assumptions and stances. A lack of philosophical clarity (i.e., "the degree that the researcher is aware of and articulates her/his philosophical proclivities in terms of philosophical assumptions and stances in relation to all components, claims, actions, and uses in a

mixed research study"; Collins, Onwuegbuzie, & Johnson, 2012, p. 855) could lead to the qualitative-dominant, quantitative-dominant, and equal-status analyst adopting nonoptimal and even poor analytical practices such as not paying due attention to the assumptions underlying both the qualitative and quantitative analyses.

Approaches for Advanced Mixed Analyses

In the remainder of this chapter we outline a partial compendium of advanced qualitative-dominant, quantitative-dominant, and equal-status crossover mixed analysis approaches. All the approaches that we highlight are either very recent or brand new. Specifically, we outline the following three advanced qualitative-dominant crossover mixed analyses:

- Correspondence Analysis
- Qualitative Comparative Analysis
- Micro-Interlocutor Analysis (MIA)

Further, we outline the following three advanced quantitative-dominant crossover mixed analyses:

- Hierarchical Linear Modeling (HLM)
- Social Network Analysis (SNA)
- Bayesian Analyses

Finally, we outline the following advanced equal-status crossover mixed analysis:

- Spatial Analyses

Qualitative-Dominant Crossover Mixed Analyses
Correspondence Analysis

Correspondence analysis is a descriptive and exploratory multivariate analysis and graphical technique that involves factoring categorical (i.e., nominal level) variables and mapping them (i.e., graphing them) in a property space that displays their relationships in multiple (i.e., two or more) dimensions (Greenacre, 1984; Michailidis, 2007). Moreover, correspondence analysis is designed to analyze relationships among entries in large frequency cross-tabulation tables such that the relationship among all entries in the table is represented using a low-dimensional Euclidean space in order that the locations of the row and column points are reflective of their associations in the cross-tabulation table. Moreover, correspondence analysis allows an analyst to examine graphically the relationship between categorical variables and subgroups. As such, as recommended by Onwuegbuzie, Dickinson, Leech, and Zoran (2010), correspondence analysis is a useful technique for conducting a cross-case analysis of emergent themes, allowing the analyst of a qualitative research study or phase to examine relationships (a) among emergent themes, (b) among study participants, and/or (c) between the emergent themes and the study participants. Thus, it is surprising that, to date, (a) only one computer-assisted qualitative data analysis software program (i.e., QDA Miner) allows the analyst to conduct a correspondence analysis of the emergent themes, and (b) correspondence analysis of themes have been used by very few researchers even though this form of crossover mixed analysis ensures that the qualitative data analyst does not engage in what Bazeley (2009a) refers to as a *superficial reporting of themes* in which "qualitative researchers rely on the presentation of key themes supported by quotes from participants' text as the primary form of analysis and reporting of their data" (p. 6).

Onwuegbuzie and colleagues (e.g., Byers et al., 2012; Frels, Onwuegbuzie, Leech, & Collins, 2012; Onwuegbuzie, Frels, Leech, & Collins, 2011) have conducted several studies in which they used QDA Miner to conduct a correspondence analysis of emergent themes. For example, as part of their study, Onwuegbuzie, Frels, et al. (2011) compared and contrasted the pedagogical approaches used by eight first-generation instructors of mixed research courses from institutions around the United States. These instructors were interviewed either face to face or remotely (e.g., via Skype). From a constant

comparison analysis, the researchers extracted three meta-themes: (a) *orientation* (containing the two themes: methodologically focused [containing three subthemes] vs. question/topic focused [containing three subthemes]), (b) *level of application* (containing the two themes: conceptually focused [containing three subthemes] vs. applied focused [containing two subthemes]), and (c) *level of structure* (containing the two themes: exploration focused [containing five subthemes] vs. structure focused [containing three subthemes]). Next, the authors conducted three sets of correspondence analysis, with each analysis mapping the eight participants onto the space that displayed the two dimensions associated with each meta-theme and its associated themes and subtheme. From the three sets of correspondence analyses, the researchers were able to identify pedagogical profiles for each of the eight participants. These profiles are presented in Table 16.2. As such, the researchers' use of correspondence analysis involved both quantitizing (i.e., transferring the meta-themes, themes, and subthemes to frequency cross-tabulation tables) and qualitizing (i.e., forming pedagogical profiles from the three sets of correspondence plots).

As another example, Byers et al. (2013) conducted a collective case study to investigate 10 doctoral students' perceptions about the challenges they encountered while in a doctorate program and the coping strategies that they found to be effective in mitigating these challenges. A constant comparison analysis and classical content analysis revealed the following five themes: compartmentalization of

Table 16.2 Partially Ordered Meta-Matrix: Pedagogical Profiles of Each of the Participants as a Function of Level of Orientation, Level of Application, and Level of Structure

Participant	Orientation	Application	Structure	Total in Group
2	Question/Topic	Applied	Structured	
5	Question/Topic	Applied	Structured	
7	Question/Topic	Applied	Structured	3
1	Methodological	Conceptual	Exploratory	
6	Methodological	Conceptual	Exploratory	2
8	Question/Topic	Conceptual	Exploratory	1
3	Methodological	Conceptual	Structured	1
4	Methodological	Applied	Structured	1

Source: Originally published in *International Journal of Multiple Research Approaches* (Onwuegbuzie, Frels, Leech, & Collins, 2011), p. 193, http://www.ijmra.com; reproduced with permission.

life, outside support systems, justification for participation in program, emotional status, and structure of program. These themes then were subjected to a correspondence analysis, which among other findings revealed that these participants' doctoral experiences occurred as a function of whether or not they had one or more dependent children while they pursued their doctoral degrees. Thus, as can be seen, correspondence analysis represents an advanced crossover mixed analysis that helps analysts get much more out of their qualitative data.

Qualitative Comparative Analysis

Qualitative comparative analysis, which was developed by Charles Ragin (1987), is a case-oriented qualitative data analysis technique that involves a systematic analysis of similarities and differences across cases of interest. Qualitative comparative analysis facilitates theory-building by allowing the analyst to examine links among categories or themes that have been previously identified by the analyst or by another researcher, as well as by testing and developing the categories/themes to a greater extent. In fact, qualitative comparative analysis can be used to analyze categories or themes derived from any of the 32 coding schemes identified by Saldaña (2012), from any of the 19 within-case analyses and 18 cross-case analyses identified by Miles and Huberman (1994), or, most recently, from any of the 34 types of qualitative analyses identified by Onwuegbuzie and Denham (2014). Interestingly, because qualitative comparative analysis builds on one or more previous qualitative analysis techniques, by default it represents a multiple method technique. As described by Miethe and Drass (1999), qualitative comparative analysis always begins with the construction of a truth table, whereby all unique configurations of the study participants and situational variables identified from the data are listed, alongside the corresponding a priori or a posteriori categories or themes for each configuration. Via the truth table, the analyst then identifies which configurations are unique to a category of the classification variable and which configurations are represented by multiple categories. Then, by comparing the numbers of configurations in these groups, an estimate is obtained of the extent to which the categories are similar or unique. As surmised by Miethe and Drass (1999), the analyst then "compares the configurations within a group, looking for commonalities that allow configurations to be combined into simpler, yet more abstract, representations"

(p. 8). Specifically, the analyst concludes that a variable is unnecessary and eliminates it from the configurations if its presence or absence within a configuration has no impact on the outcome that is associated with the configuration. The analyst continues to compare these configurations until no further reductions are possible. Any redundancies among the remaining reduced configurations are eliminated, thereby yielding a final conclusion of the unique features of each category of the typology. By comparing each case with all other cases in the set, the analyst uses the binary logic of Boolean algebra to identify commonalities among these configurations and, in turn, simplifies the typology.

Although not yet fully realized among researchers, qualitative comparative analysis has much potential as a mixed analysis technique. Indeed, as stated by Ragin (2008), qualitative comparative analysis "transcends some of the limitations of conventional quantitative and qualitative research (p. 2)—as does mixed research. Commenting on one of his seminal qualitative comparative analysis books, Ragin stated that "This book demonstrates how to join set theory, *qualitative and quantitative analysis*, and fidelity to theoretical discourse in the effort to redesign social inquiry" (p. 4, emphasis added).

As surmised by Ragin (2008), qualitative comparative analysis involves a focus on calibration of measures—which are derived via external standards—unlike most social and behavioral science researchers. And "the key to 'bringing calibration in' is through the use of fuzzy sets" (Ragin, 2008, p. 8). Fuzzy sets, which subsume classical (i.e., binary) sets as special cases, are sets whose elements have degrees of membership (Zadeh, 1965). For example, in the field of US education in general and K–12 school research in particular, socioeconomic status typically is operationalized as a dichotomous variable (i.e., crisp set) based on the free-and-reduced lunch status of each student. Yet this measure is problematic because of its relative crudeness. Rather, researchers would do well to obtain a calibrated measure of socioeconomic status using either what Ragin refers to as the *direct method* or the *indirect method*. The direct method involves the analyst specifying the value of socioeconomic status on an interval scale that denotes one of three qualitative cut-points that structure a fuzzy set: full membership, full nonmembership, and crossover point. These cut-points then are used to transform the original socioeconomic status values to fuzzy membership scores. The indirect method involves analysts using their qualitative assessment of the degree to which study participants with certain interval-based socioeconomic status values are members of the underlying set. The analyst then assigns each participant into one of six categories and then uses an estimation technique to rescale the original socioeconomic status values such that it is consistent with the qualitative assessment. Although it is beyond the scope of this chapter to demonstrate these two methods of calibration, it should be noted that both techniques lead to fine-tuned calibration depicting the degree of membership of participants in sets, with scores ranging from zero to 1. With respect to software, a useful and free program that can be used is called fsQCA 2.0 (http://www.u.arizona.edu/~cragin/fsQCA/software.shtml).

Thus, using quantitative approaches to a maximal extent to transform uncalibrated interval- and ratio-scaled measures into reliable and well-calibrated fuzzy sets, in turn, transforms qualitative comparative analysis—a qualitative analysis approach—to a mixed analysis approach. As stated by Ragin (2008), fuzzy sets, which simultaneously represent both case-oriented and variable-oriented approaches, "offer a middle path between qualitative and quantitative measurement. . . it transcends many of the limitations of both" (p. 71).

Micro-Interlocutor Analysis

MIA is a relatively new technique for analyzing focus group data. Focus groups are, by and large, associated with qualitative research, representing a form of qualitative interviewing (Morgan, 2008). However, as identified by Onwuegbuzie et al. (2010), regardless of the research question(s) being addressed, in addition to qualitative data, focus group interviews always potentially yield quantitative data. These quantitative data include information regarding how many participants responded to each question, the order in which the participants responded, and the length of response (e.g., number of words spoken). In particular, MIA involves researchers identifying the number of focus group members who contributed to the feeling of consensus underlying each theme that is extracted from the focus group data, the number who provided a dissenting view, the number who did not express any view at all, the number who provided substantive statements or examples that support the consensus view, and the number who provided substantive statements or stories that suggest a dissenting view.

MIA also involves comparing subgroups within a focus group (e.g., male vs. female members) with respect to the members' interaction patterns, such as which subgroup member, if any, tended to speak first in response to a question and which subgroup members spoke the most. As stated by Onwuegbuzie et al. (2010), collecting and analyzing data about dissenting focus group members would facilitate researchers in determining the degree that *within-focus group saturation* (i.e., the degree that data from any single focus group reached saturation) and *across-focus group saturation* (i.e., the degree that saturation occurred across all the focus group interviews) occurred. The analysis involved in MIA most likely would involve descriptive analyses (e.g., consensus counts), univariate analyses (e.g., independent samples t test comparing number of words spoken by male and female focus group members), multivariate analyses (e.g., conducting a discriminant analysis to determine which demographic factors predict consensus vs. dissenters across numerous focus groups), analysis of group membership (e.g., using correspondence analysis to analyze relationships between the emergent themes and the focus groups participants within one focus group or across multiple focus groups). Consequently, MIA transforms the analysis of focus group data from a qualitative analysis to a mixed analysis.

Quantitative-Dominant Crossover Mixed Analyses
Hierarchical Linear Modeling

Many forms of inferential analyses must be conducted under the assumption that observations (i.e., data points) are independent of each other. In other words, one datapoint should not influence (or be correlated) with another. This assumption might make sense if studying the results of aspirin on heart health, assuming patients have no consequential interaction with each other. Take two study participants who are in the same study condition: Patient A and patient B. Patient A's heart health status should not influence patient B's status, and this expectation makes sense for other patients in the study. But observations would not be independent if dealing with many educational and social outcomes (e.g., how well student A learned a concept might be very much related to student B's learning if they have the same teacher, and especially if they interacted with each other when learning the curriculum). Violation of the independence assumption is problematic because, when this occurs, researchers can expect an elevation in the Type 1 error rate associated with an analysis. At the same time, observations that are not independent of each other (i.e., they are clustered or nested) open the door to some interesting research questions because this entails the study of groups (see Kenny & Judd, 1986).

Consider education research. Students are grouped by classrooms, which, in turn, are grouped by schools and so on. It is also the case that observations made about students within classrooms will not be independent as they interact and work together. This is true of both learning and behavioral outcomes. Even if a study starts out in a manner that the independence assumption is reasonable (say students are randomly assigned to one treatment condition or to a control, within a single classroom), any observations of them at the end of a study likely will not be independent as natural working groups form. Clustering is easily seen in other fields as well (e.g., in medical research settings, patients often will be grouped by doctors). It is also the case that repeated observations of an individual yields a form of clustering, in that a person's observation at time point 1 will not be independent from time point 2, time point 3, and so on.

For these reasons, HLM and variants of the procedure that deal with nonlinear data have become a commonly used analytic technique. But like many advanced techniques, we see opportunities for mixing such modeling with qualitative inquiry. This is in terms of not only understanding group structures but also when quantitizing qualitative data. Consider an intercepts and slopes as outcomes model (Raudenbush & Bryk, 2002). This model entails the assumption that each group (e.g., a school) in an analysis will have its own intercept (e.g., average achievement score for the school) and slope (e.g., relationship between student socioeconomic status [SES] and achievement). These estimates are described as outcomes because some set of variables (e.g., school-level SES, principal experience) might be used to predict school-level achievement or the strength of the relationship between two variables (i.e., a slope) within a given school. A common teaching example by Raudenbush and Bryk (2002) demonstrates, for example, how the strength of the relationship between student SES and mathematics achievement is weaker in Catholic than in public schools when examining the High School and Beyond dataset. In other words, a student's SES matters more in terms of mathematics achievement in public schools compared to Catholic ones.

Understanding that this is a teaching example, it offers a great opportunity for the mixing of methods. After all, any researcher should ponder why the SES-mathematics achievement relationship is weaker in Catholic schools than in public schools. Is it because Catholic schools use school uniforms and so SES differences are not as apparent, and this somehow yields a better learning environment for children who contend with poverty? Is there some ethos in these schools that minimize the importance of money and this manifests in curricula and social interactions? Is there something about the types of families that decide to have their children attend Catholic schools (as opposed to public ones) that influence such an ethos?

All of these questions can be informed by qualitative methods. Interviews with stakeholders (e.g., students, parents, teachers, and administrators), observations of lessons and other school activities, and document analyses can all be used to explore reasons for the finding. Indeed, the teaching example involves 168 schools, and quantitative work allows for the identification of outliers. Clearly, these outliers inform purposeful selection approaches where the relationship between student SES and achievement is quite strong, typical, or nonexistent for public and Catholic schools (yielding a multicase study with six schools) where in-depth examination of the phenomenon and how it manifests in different settings becomes possible.

Finally, analysts can assign numerical codes to qualitatively derived themes (this may entail using a link function to handle categorical data, such as when using logistical or multinomial regression). One might reasonably wonder about the costs of doing so. After all, this would undermine rich description of context, participant perceptions, and so on. But at the same time, much of the power of qualitative inquiry can be preserved if the themes were derived from emergent work, extracted from naturalistic settings, and so on. This offers a real advantage when one does not wish to limit potential response data to whatever might be thought of in a survey or other instrument. Rather than using verbal summaries of a code, a number can suffice and open the door to quantitative analyses. Further, any time a quantitized theme is of interest, analysts can revisit initial descriptive themes to extract meaning. Suppose, for example, multiple themes pertaining to school safety were found, and the school generally dealt with the tension between individual privacy and group security. Suppose further that some codes were surprising, or at least not initially considered by researchers, which demonstrates an advantage of qualitative design. One might be able to rank order response sets accordingly, and any representative numbering scheme could be subjected to statistical analyses. In sum, the capacity of HLM to describe relationships within and between clusters might be of considerable interest. One might use HLM to understand typical perceptions of school safety within a cluster (e.g., a classroom or school), compare this across groups, and examine relationships between some predictor variables (e.g., gender) and safety within clusters. A key consideration here is that any subsequent observations would be informed, in part, by emergent design work such that constructs that are assessed could be informed by the flexible and emergent nature of qualitative inquiry.

Social Network Analysis

SNA is the systematic analysis of social networks (Carolan, 2013). These social networks often are displayed via a social network diagram, wherein nodes (which represent individuals within the network) are depicted by points and ties (which represent relationships among individuals) are depicted by lines. Because SNA involves a mathematical analysis of human relationships, it is regarded as a quantitative data analysis technique. Yet, as noted by Hollstein (2011), qualitative data collection and analysis can facilitate social network analysis because qualitative data can "explicate the problem of agency, linkages between network structure and network actors, as well as questions relating to the constitution and dynamics of social networks" (p. 404). More specifically, Hollstein identified six areas where qualitative research can enhance SNA: (a) exploration of networks, (b) network practices, (c) network orientation and assessments, (d) how networks matter, (e) understanding network dynamics, and (f) validation of network data and field access. For example, interview data can be collected whereby clarifying questions are asked while the network data are being collected (Hogan, Carrasco, & Wellman, 2007). The responses to these questions then can be analyzed qualitatively (cf. Miles & Huberman, 1994; Onwuegbuzie & Denham, 2014; Saldaña, 2012) to inform the SNA.

Bayesian Analyses

Bayesian methods often are used when researchers are hoping to predict some outcome or event (O'Hagan & Luce, 2003). An aspect of Bayesian work that should interest mixed

researchers is that the approach requires the establishment of a prior probability distribution (or prior), which is often informed, in part, by the subjective judgment of the researcher. This prior is used as a key point for calculating a posterior probability distribution; taken together, the prior and posterior are used to understand the likelihood of a parameter (a population value) given the observed evidence. If a researcher is completely uninformed about the likelihood of an event (e.g., the chances that a professor is female), then he or she might apply a 50/50 estimate as the prior. If, however, some additional context is known (the professor is in engineering and there are not many female engineering professors), then a more informed prior becomes possible (say there is a 20% chance the professor is a female). Without getting into the mechanics of Bayesian prediction, which is a complex task, it is still reasonable to point out that prior data and knowledge of context are important considerations. This should make sense. If there is some empirical or even intuitive justification for believing an event to be rare, why would this not inform prediction models?

O'Hagan and Luce (2003) deal with the notion of subjectivity. In Bayesian prediction, subjectivity entails making a reasoned judgment about prior evidence. When defining evidence, they write

> It is true that one could carry out a Bayesian analysis with a prior distribution based on mere guesswork, prejudice or wishful thinking. Bayes' theorem technically admits all of these unfortunate practices, but Bayesian statistics does not in any sense condone them. Also, recall that in a proper Bayesian analysis, prior information is not only transparent but is also based on both defensible evidence and reasoning which, if followed, will lead any above-mentioned abuses to become transparent, and so to be rejected. (p. 26)

This idea can mix with qualitative inquiry when conceptualizing designs and conducting analyses. The prior distribution estimate can be informed by detailed information that can be gathered by deep understanding of context. Suppose a researcher is conducting a case study of a large high school that recently adopted an innovative sexual harassment awareness program, and this researcher wanted to know the likelihood that students would report having been harassed after the program had been implemented. Suppose further that the school had poor administrative records about sexual harassment because formally reporting and then labeling harassment as being sexual in nature has not been the norm. What should the prior estimate be? How might it differ by student gender, grade, race, and so on? One can consider national estimates, but how would these apply in the context of a school that was applying an innovative program? This is a good point at which the researcher's perspective can be invoked. But now suppose the researcher had been engaged in intensive observation of school events, interviews with multiple stakeholders (e.g., students, parents, administrators, teachers, paraprofessionals), and documenting analyses for months. The researcher may use findings from qualitative inquiry to inform prediction models. In this sense—and as outlined by Newman, Onwuegbuzie, and Hitchcock (2014)—we think that Bayesian work can be mixed with qualitative inquiry.

Equal-Status Crossover Mixed Analyses

In the previous sections, we presented an array of advanced qualitative-dominant and quantitative-dominant mixed analyses. In this section, we present an equal-status crossover mixed analysis approach that represents one of the most beneficial areas for the further development with respect to mixed analysis, namely, the analysis of place and space. Surprisingly, the analysis of place and space is underutilized by many researchers across the social, behavioral, and health science fields. Indeed, as surmised by Fielding and Cisneros-Puebla (2009), "in a recent review, 15 of 19 leading definitions MMR [mixed methods research] specified that what is mixed is quantitative and qualitative data; none specifically referred to spatial data; see Johnson et al., 2007, p. 118" (p. 350). Thus, Fielding and Cisneros-Puebla (2009) and J. G. Frels, R. K. Frels, and Onwuegbuzie (2011) demonstrated the benefits of using geographic information systems (GIS) applications in mixed research. Generally speaking, as described by Frels et al. (2011),

> GIS applications are used to inventory and to manage aspects in the world through numbers and words from databases and help researchers to position data on a map to show patterns and to address questions such as where, why, and how, with locational information in mind. . . . Further, GIS applications integrate hardware, software, and data for capturing, managing, analyzing, and displaying various forms of geographically referenced

information, enabling researchers to understand, to question, to interpret, and to visualize data in many ways that reveal relationships and trends in the form of maps, globes, reports, and charts. (p. 368)

We contend that GIS is an extremely versatile tool for integrating qualitative and quantitative data because it can transform a quantitative analysis to a quantitative-dominant crossover mixed analysis, and, at the same time, it can transform a qualitative analysis to a qualitative-dominant crossover mixed analysis. For example, with respect to quantitative analyses, an exploratory data analysis can be transformed into an exploratory spatial data analysis wherein, in addition to conducting traditional exploratory data analysis, the analyst can explore spatial data (i.e., visualization) that help to contextualize the quantitative data. For example, the GIS software can highlight "trends, and phenomena within their broader contexts in ways that might be missed with coarser resolution and data aggregation" (Knigge & Cope, 2006, p. 2027); also, visualizations and multiple images that represent change over time can provide richness to temporal data, thereby enhancing the understanding of process (Knigge & Cope, 2006). As an example of the use of GIS at an extremely advanced level, Kandalaa, Brodishc, Bucknerc, Fosterd, and Madisee (2011) conducted a Bayesian geo-additive mixed model based on Markov Chain Monte Carlo techniques to map the change in the spatial distribution of HIV/AIDS prevalence at the provincial level during the 6-year period in Zambia that accounted for important risk factors.

With respect to qualitative analyses, qualitative data, such as ethnographic data (e.g., digital photographs, text, sounds), can be linked with maps to provide rich, contextual data for analysis. Further, tools such as real-time 3D modeling "greatly enhance the visual, iterative exploration of data, allow simultaneous attention to both the particular and the general, the concrete and the abstract, at multiple scales, and accommodate multiple interpretations of the world and diverse views of reality" (Knigge & Cope, 2006, p. 2027). Alternatively, qualitative researchers can conduct *information visualization*, which represents the visual display, exploration, and analysis of qualitative data that are nonnumeric and nongeographic. One emerging type of information visualization is *spatialization*. This technique involves the process of converting abstract text-based information (e.g., keywords of published articles, bibliographic entries) into map-based visualizations called *information spaces* (e.g., spatially based regions of information) that visualize data by using cartographic and other geographic techniques (Skupin & Fabrikant, 2003). These are just a few of the many ways that both quantitative analysis and qualitative data analysis can be combined with GIS applications. And with the emergence of new GIS tools, the role that GIS can play in both the quantitative analysis and qualitative analysis can only increase.

Conclusions

Mixed researchers have almost limitless possibilities for combining quantitative and qualitative data analysis approaches, methods, and techniques—or what are aptly named mixed analyses. However, to date, authors have focused on providing either an introductory- or intermediate-level guide to conducting mixed analyses. As such, the present chapter represents a first attempt to provide a partial compendium of very recent or brand-new advanced mixed analysis approaches. In providing this compendium, we used as our conceptual framework the notion of crossover mixed analyses, which can be quantitative dominant, qualitative dominant, or equal status (Onwuegbuzie & Combs, 2010). Specifically, we outlined three advanced qualitative-dominant, three advanced quantitative-dominant, and one advanced equal-status crossover mixed analysis approaches.

A very useful aspect of classifying these advanced mixed analyses as being qualitative dominant, quantitative dominant, or one equal status is that it opens the door not only for mixed researchers to conduct mixed analyses but also for qualitative researchers and quantitative researchers. In particular, when using frameworks like the one offered by Greene et al. (1989) to the multimethod situation, qualitative researchers and quantitative researchers can conduct mixed analyses without contradicting their philosophical belief systems. For example, quantitative researchers operating under a postpositivist worldview who are conducting analyses to address complex research questions can combine any of the advanced quantitative analysis approaches with one or more qualitative analysis approaches, methods, or techniques. Quantitative researchers with the purist postpositivist orientation likely would be most comfortable combining complex quantitative analyses with qualitative analysis approaches, methods, or techniques that involve a strong use of quantitative analyses such as word count. In contrast, quantitative researchers with a more qualitative orientation likely would be comfortable combining complex quantitative analyses with qualitative analysis approaches, methods, or techniques that involve the strong use of both qualitative analyses and quantitative analyses such as classical content analysis and qualitative comparative analysis. Even more contrastingly, quantitative researchers with the most qualitative orientations likely would be comfortable combining complex quantitative analyses with qualitative analysis approaches, methods, or techniques that involve the strong use of qualitative analyses (e.g., constant comparison analysis). Whatever the role that the qualitative analysis plays in the quantitative-dominant crossover mixed analysis process, it is used to fulfill one or more of Greene et al.'s (1989) five purposes for mixing.

At the opposite end of the methodological spectrum, qualitative researchers with a purist qualitative-based philosophical lens (e.g., some form of constructivism, critical theory, participatory) likely would be most comfortable combining complex qualitative analyses with descriptive analyses or with some form of spatial analysis. In contrast, qualitative researchers with a more quantitative orientation likely would be comfortable combining complex qualitative analyses with univariate inferential analyses. Further, qualitative researchers with a more quantitative orientation likely would be comfortable combining complex qualitative analyses with the most complex quantitative analyses. Whatever the role that the quantitative analysis plays in the qualitative-dominant crossover mixed analysis process, it is used to fulfill one or more of Greene et al.'s (1989) five purposes for mixing. Finally, equal-status crossover mixed analyses are more likely to be conducted by a single mixed researcher with competence in both quantitative and qualitative analyses or a team of qualitative, quantitative, and/or mixed researchers.

The advanced mixed analyses that we have outlined in this chapter show the versatility of mixed analyses. Such analyses have the potential to answer increasingly complex research questions and to reach verstehen, and we see additional opportunities for advanced mixing that we will articulate in forthcoming work. As such, we encourage future authors to build on our framework and to continue to advance the field of mixed analyses.

Discussion Questions

1. How does a mixed analysis approach differ from other types of analysis approaches?

2. How does a crossover mixed analysis approach differ from other types of mixed analysis approaches?

3. What is the difference among a quantitative-dominant crossover mixed analysis approach, a qualitative-dominant crossover mixed analysis approach, and an equal-status crossover mixed analysis approach?

4. Apply one of the crossover mixed analysis approaches to a research question of your choice.

Suggested Websites

http://www.mmira.org

The Mixed Methods International Research Association is "an exciting, new professional association created to promote the development of an international and interdisciplinary mixed methods research community," according to its website.

http://www.aera.net/SIG158/MixedMethods ResearchSIG158/tabid/12201/Default.aspx

The purpose of the American Educational Research Association's Mixed Methods Special Interest Group is "To support, encourage, and increase dialogue and idea exchange among educational researchers utilizing mixed methods and those interested in integrating qualitative and quantitative research approaches."

http://www.eval.org

According to the American Evaluation Association, its mission is "to improve evaluation practices and methods, increase evaluation use, promote evaluation as a profession, and support the contribution of evaluation to the generation of theory and knowledge about effective human action."

Note

1. Please note that we are not suggesting that it is inappropriate to combine multiple qualitative data analysis approaches within the same study. The decision to do so would depend, at least in part, on the research question, as well as the researcher's philosophical assumptions and stance.

References

Bazeley, P. (2003). Computerized data analysis for mixed methods research. In A. Tashakkori & C. Teddlie (Eds.), *SAGE handbook of mixed methods in social & behavioral research* (pp. 385–422). Thousand Oaks, CA: SAGE.

Bazeley, P. (2006). The contribution of computer software to integrating qualitative and quantitative data and analyses. *Research in the Schools, 13*(1), 64–74.

Bazeley, P. (2009a). Analysing qualitative data: More than "identifying themes." *Malaysian Journal of Qualitative Research, 2*, 6–22.

Bazeley, P. (2009b). Editorial: Integrating data analyses in mixed methods research. *Journal of Mixed Methods Research, 3*, 203–207. doi:10.1177/1558689809334443

Bazeley, P. (2009c). Mixed methods data analysis. In S. Andrew & E. J. Halcomb (Eds.), *Mixed methods research for nursing and the health sciences* (pp. 84–118). Chichester, England: Wiley-Blackwell.

Bazeley, P., & Kemp, L. (2012). Mosaics, triangles, and DNA: Metaphors for integrated analysis in mixed methods research. *Journal of Mixed Methods Research, 6*, 55–72. doi:10.1177/1558689811419514

Biesta, G. (2010). Pragmatism and the philosophical foundations of mixed methods research. In A. Tashakkori & C. Teddlie (Eds.), *SAGE handbook of mixed methods in social & behavioral research* (2nd ed., pp. 95–117). Thousand Oaks, CA: SAGE.

Byers, V. T., Smith, R. N., Hwang, E., Angrove, K. E., Chandler, J. I., Christian, K. M.,... Denham, M. A. (2013, June). *Survival strategies used by doctoral students: A critical dialectical pluralistic approach*. Paper presented at the Advances in Qualitative Methods Conference, Edmonton, Alberta, Canada.

Carolan, B. V. (2013). *Social network analysis and education: Theory, methods and applications*. Thousand Oaks, CA: SAGE.

Castro, F. G., Kellison, J. G., Boyd, S. J., & Kopak, A. (2010). A methodology for conducting integrative mixed methods research and data analyses. *Journal of Mixed Methods Research, 4*, 342–360. doi:10.1177/1558689810382916

Collins, K. M. T., Onwuegbuzie, A. J., & Johnson, R. B. (2012). Securing a place at the table: Introducing legitimation criteria for the conduct of mixed research. *American Behavioral Scientist, 56*, 849–865. doi:10.1177/0002764211433799

Combs, J. P., & Onwuegbuzie, A. J. (2010). Describing and illustrating data analysis in mixed research. *International Journal of Education, 2*(2), EX, 1–23. Retrieved from http://www.macrothink.org/journal/index.php/ije/article/viewFile/526/392

Curtis, S., Gesler, W., Smith, G., & Washburn, S. (2000). Approaches to sampling and case selection in qualitative research: Examples in the geography of health. *Social Science and Medicine, 50*, 1001–1014. doi:10.1016/S0277-9536(99)00350-0

DeCuir-Gunby, J. T., Marshall, P. L., & McCulloch, A. W. (2012). Using mixed methods to analyze video data: A mathematics teacher professional development example. *Journal of Mixed Methods Research, 6*, 199–216. doi:10.1177/1558689811421174

Denham, M. A., & Onwuegbuzie, A. J. (2013). Beyond words: Using nonverbal communication data in research to enhance thick description and interpretation. *International Journal of Qualitative Methods, 12*(1), 670–696.

DeRocher, J. E., Miron, M. S., Patten, S. M., & Pratt, C. C. (1973). *The counting of words: A review of the history, techniques and theory of word counts with annotated bibliography*. Syracuse, NY: Syracuse University Research Corporation, pp. 302. Retrieved from http://eric.ed.gov/?id=ED098814

Fielding, N., & Cisneros-Puebla, C. A. (2009). CAQDAS-GAS convergence: Toward a new integrated mixed method research practice? *Journal of Mixed Methods Research, 3*, 349–370. doi:10.1177/1558689809344973

Frels, J. G., Frels, R. K., & Onwuegbuzie, A. J. (2011). Geographic information systems: A mixed methods spatial approach in business and management research and beyond. *International Journal of Multiple Research Approaches, 5*, 367–386. doi:10.5172/mra.2011.5.3.367

Frels, R. K., Onwuegbuzie, A. J., Leech, N. L., & Collins, K. M. T. (2012). Challenges to teaching mixed research courses. *The Journal of Effective Teaching, 12*, 23–44.

Greenacre, M. (1984). *Theory and applications of correspondence analysis*. Orlando, FL: Academic Press.

Greene, J. C. (2007). *Mixed methods in social inquiry*. San Francisco, CA: Jossey-Bass.

Greene, J. C. (2008). Is mixed methods social inquiry a distinctive methodology? *Journal of Mixed Methods Research, 2,* 7–22. doi:10.1177/1558689807309969

Greene, J. C., Caracelli, V. J., & Graham, W. F. (1989). Toward a conceptual framework for mixed-method evaluation designs. *Educational Evaluation and Policy Analysis, 11,* 255–274. doi:10.3102/01623737011003255

Happ, M. B., DeVito Dabbs, D. A., Tate, J., Hricik, A., & Erlen, J. (2006). Exemplars of mixed methods data combination and analysis. *Nursing Research, 55*(2 Suppl. 1), S43–S49.

Hitchcock, J. J., & Onwuegbuzie, A. J. (2015). *Toward a framework for conducting advanced mixed analyses.* Unpublished manuscript, Indiana University, Bloomington, Indiana.

Hogan, B., Carrasco, J.-A., & Wellman, B. (2007). Visualizing personal networks: Working with participant-aided sociograms. *Field Methods, 19,* 116–144. doi:10.1177/1525822X06298589

Hollstein, B. (2011). Qualitative approaches. In J. P. Scott & P. J. Carrington (Eds.), *The SAGE handbook of social network analysis* (pp. 404–416). Thousand Oaks, CA: SAGE.

Jang, E. E., McDougall, D. E., Pollon, D., & Russell, M. (2008). Integrative mixed methods data analytic strategies in research on school success in challenging environments. *Journal of Mixed Methods Research, 2,* 221–247. doi:10.1177/1558689808315323

Johnson, R. B. (2012). Dialectical pluralism and mixed research. *American Behavioral Scientist, 56,* 751–754. doi:10.1177/0002764212442494

Johnson, R. B., & Onwuegbuzie, A. J. (2004). Mixed methods research: A research paradigm whose time has come. *Educational Researcher, 33*(7), 14–26. doi:10.3102/0013189X033007014

Johnson, R. B., Onwuegbuzie, A. J., & Turner, L. A. (2007). Toward a definition of mixed methods research. *Journal of Mixed Methods Research, 1,* 112–133. doi:10.1177/1558689806298224

Kandalaa, N.-B., Brodishc, P., Bucknerc, B. Fosterd, S., & Madisee, N. (2011). Millennium development goal 6 and HIV infection in Zambia: What can we learn from successive household surveys? *AIDS, 25,* 95–106. doi:10.1097/QAD.0b013e328340fe0f

Kenny, D. A., & Judd, C. M. (1986). Consequences of violating the independence assumption in analysis of variance. *Psychological Bulletin, 99,* 422–431. doi:10.1037//0033-2909.99.3.422

Knigge, L., & Cope, M. (2006). Grounded visualization: Integrating the analysis of qualitative and quantitative data through grounded theory and visualization. *Environment and Planning A, 38,* 2021–2037. doi:10.1068/a37327

Leech, N. L., & Onwuegbuzie, A. J. (2007). An array of qualitative data analysis tools: A call for qualitative data analysis triangulation. *School Psychology Quarterly, 22,* 557–584. doi:10.1037/1045-3830.22.4.557

Leech, N. L., & Onwuegbuzie, A. J. (2008). Qualitative data analysis: A compendium of techniques and a framework for selection for school psychology research and beyond. *School Psychology Quarterly, 23,* 587–604. doi:10.1037/1045-3830.23.4.587

Li, S., Marquart, J. M., & Zercher, C. (2000). Conceptual issues and analytical strategies in mixed-method studies of preschool inclusion. *Journal of Early Intervention, 23,* 116–132. doi:10.1177/105381510002300206

Maxcy, S. J. (2003). Pragmatic threads in mixed methods research in the social sciences: The search for multiple modes of inquiry and the end of the philosophy of formalism. In A. Tashakkori & C. Teddlie (Eds.), *SAGE handbook of mixed methods in social & behavioral research* (pp. 51–89). Thousand Oaks, CA: SAGE.

Michailidis, G. (2007). Correspondence analysis. In N. J. Salkind (Ed.), *Encyclopedia of measurement and statistics* (pp. 191–194). Thousand Oaks, CA: SAGE.

Miethe, T. D., & Drass, K. A. (1999). Exploring the social context of instrumental and expressive homicides: An application of qualitative comparative analysis. *Journal of Quantitative Criminology, 15,* 1–21.

Miles, M., & Huberman, A. M. (1994). *Qualitative data analysis: An expanded sourcebook* (2nd ed.). Thousand Oaks, CA: SAGE.

Morgan, D. L. (2008). Focus groups. In L. M. Given (Ed.), *The SAGE encyclopedia of qualitative research methods* (Vol. 1, pp. 352–354). Thousand Oaks, CA: SAGE.

Newman, I., Onwuegbuzie, A. J., & Hitchcock, J. H. (2014, June). Bayes methodology: Mixed methods in drag. Paper presented at the first annual meeting of the Mixed Methods International Research Association, Boston, MA.

O'Hagan, A., & Luce, B.R. (2003). *A primer on Bayesian statistics in health economics and outcomes research.* Bethesda, MD: MEDTAP International.

Onwuegbuzie, A. J., & Collins, K. M. T. (2014). Using Bronfenbrenner's ecological systems theory to enhance interpretive consistency in mixed research. *International Journal of Research in Education Methodology, 5,* 651–661.

Onwuegbuzie, A. J., & Combs, J. P. (2010). Emergent data analysis techniques in mixed methods research: A synthesis. In A. Tashakkori & C. Teddlie (Eds.), *SAGE handbook of mixed methods in social & behavioral research* (2nd ed., pp. 397–430). Thousand Oaks, CA: SAGE.

Onwuegbuzie, A. J., & Combs, J. P. (2011). Data analysis in mixed research: A primer. *International Journal of Education, 3*(1), E13. Retrieved from http://www.macrothink.org/journal/index.php/ije/article/view/618/550

Onwuegbuzie, A. J., & Denham, M. (2014). Qualitative data analysis techniques. In R. Warden (Ed.), *Oxford bibliographies online*. Oxford, England: Oxford University Press. Retrieved from http://www.oxfordbibliographies.com/view/document/obo-9780199756810/obo-9780199756810-0078.xml

Onwuegbuzie, A. J., & Dickinson, W. B. (2008). Mixed methods analysis and information visualization: Graphical display for effective communication of research results. *The Qualitative Report, 13,* 204–225. Retrieved from http://www.nova.edu/ssss/QR/QR13-2/Onwuegbuzie.pdf

Onwuegbuzie, A. J., Dickinson, W. B., Leech, N. L., & Zoran, A. G. (2010). Toward more rigor in focus group research in stress and coping and beyond: A new mixed research framework for collecting and analyzing focus group data. In G. S. Gates, W. H. Gmelch, & M. Wolverton (Series Eds.) & K. M. T. Collins, A. J. Onwuegbuzie, & Q. G. Jiao (Eds.), *Toward a broader understanding of stress and coping: Mixed methods approaches* (pp. 243–285). The Research on Stress and Coping in Education Series (Vol. 5). Charlotte, NC: Information Age Publishing.

Onwuegbuzie, A. J., & Frels, R. K. (2013). Introduction: Towards a new research philosophy for addressing social justice issues: Critical dialectical pluralism 1.0. *International Journal of Multiple Research Approaches*, *7*, 9–26.

Onwuegbuzie, A. J., Frels, R. K., Leech, N. L., & Collins, K. M. T. (2011). A mixed research study of pedagogical approaches and student learning in doctoral-level mixed research courses. *International Journal of Multiple Research Approaches*, *5*, 169–199. doi:10.5172/mra.2011.5.2.169

Onwuegbuzie, A. J., Leech, N. L., & Collins, K. M. T. (2011). Toward a new era for conducting mixed analyses: The role of quantitative dominant and qualitative dominant crossover mixed analyses. In M. Williams & W. P. Vogt (Eds.), *The SAGE handbook of innovation in social research methods* (pp. 353–384). Thousand Oaks, CA: SAGE.

Onwuegbuzie, A. J., Slate, J. R., Leech, N. L., & Collins, K. M. T. (2007). Conducting mixed analyses: A general typology. *International Journal of Multiple Research Approaches*, *1*, 4–17. doi:10.5172/mra.455.1.1.4

Onwuegbuzie, A. J., Slate, J. R., Leech, N. L., & Collins, K. M. T. (2009). Mixed data analysis: Advanced integration techniques. *International Journal of Multiple Research Approaches*, *3*, 13–33. doi:10.5172/mra.455.3.1.13

Onwuegbuzie, A. J., & Teddlie, C. (2003). A framework for analyzing data in mixed methods research. In A. Tashakkori & C. Teddlie (Eds.), *SAGE handbook of mixed methods in social & behavioral research* (pp. 351–383). Thousand Oaks, CA: SAGE.

Payne, G., & Williams, M. (2005). Generalization in qualitative research. *Sociology*, *39*, 295–314. doi:10.1177/0038038505050540

Putnam, H. (2002). *The collapse of the fact/value dichotomy and other essays*. Cambridge, MA: Harvard University Press.

Ragin, C. C. (1987). *The comparative method: Moving beyond qualitative and quantitative strategies*. Berkeley, CA: University of California Press.

Ragin, C. C. (2008). *Redesigning social inquiry: Fuzzy sets and beyond*. Chicago, IL: University of Chicago Press.

Raudenbush, S. W., & Bryk, A. S. (2002). *Hierarchical linear models: Applications and data analysis methods* (2nd ed.). Thousand Oaks, CA: SAGE.

Rescher, N. (2000). *Realistic pragmatism: An introduction to pragmatic philosophy*. Albany, NY: State University of New York Press.

Rorty, R. (1991). *Objectivity, relativism, and truth: Philosophical papers (Vol. 1)*. Cambridge, England: Cambridge University Press.

Saldaña, J. (2012). *The coding manual for qualitative researchers* (2nd ed.). Thousand Oaks, CA: SAGE.

Sandelowski, M., Voils, C. I., & Knafl, G. (2009). On quantitizing. *Journal of Mixed Methods Research*, *3*, 208–222. doi:10.1177/1558689809334210

Skupin, A., & Fabrikant S. (2003). Spatialization methods: A cartographic research agenda for non-geographic information visualization. *Cartography and Geographic Information Science*, *30*, 99–119. doi:10.1559/152304003100011081

Stake, R. E., & Trumbull, D. J. (1982). Naturalistic generalizations. *Review Journal of Philosophy and Social Science*, *7*, 3–12.

Teddlie, C., & Tashakkori, A. (2009). *Foundations of mixed methods research: Integrating quantitative and qualitative techniques in the social and behavioral sciences*. Thousand Oaks, CA: SAGE.

Williams, M. (2000). Intepretivism and generalization. *Sociology*, *34*, 209–224. doi:10.1017/S0038038500000146

Yin, R. K. (2009). *Case study research: Design and methods* (4th ed.). Thousand Oaks, CA: SAGE.

Zadeh, L. A. (1965). Fuzzy sets. *Information and Control*, *8*, 338–353.

Writing Up Multimethod and Mixed Methods Research for Diverse Audiences

Pat Bazeley

Abstract

Mixed methods research demands a level of integration of methods and/or analyses that is often difficult to achieve, especially within the writing phase. An integrated report might be threatened by philosophical, interdisciplinary, and methodological tensions, especially in team projects. Journal policies regarding word length or methodological focus often limit integration. Strategies for resolving these tensions and constraints are suggested, along with practical and innovative strategies for presenting results in an article or report. In particular, mixed methods writers are encouraged to integrate the presentation of results from their studies around the substantive issues generated by their purpose-related questions, having chosen points of relevance to the target audience for that publication. This means their focus will be on the message to be conveyed rather than on paradigms or methods as they plan the organization of sections, chapters, or articles.

Key Words: mixed methods, integration of methods, integrated writing, constraints, strategies

Introduction

When Alan Bryman (2007) interviewed 20 social researchers engaged in mixed methods research about practices in relation to the integration of qualitative and quantitative research, many reported "bringing together the analysis and interpretation of the quantitative and the qualitative data and writing a narrative that linked the analyses and interpretations" as a significant cause of concern (p. 10). Yet, as Jennifer Greene (2007) noted, "writing up constitutes the heart of the communication and presentation process" in social inquiry (p. 181). Part of the issue for Bryman's interviewees in the mid-2000s was the lack of exemplars for writing—a problem that has been redressed to some extent since then as both enthusiasm for mixed methods and avenues for publication have grown.

Greene (2007) observed that the "express purpose" for taking a mixed methods approach to social inquiry was because the multidimensionality and complexity of human experience demanded

more than a single viewpoint. Numbers, words, narratives, poetry, images, and performances can all contribute to a representation of human experience that speaks to people's different ways of knowing and understanding such complexity. She therefore (unlike many of her colleagues) recommended that "the mixed methods inquirer is strongly encouraged to adopt a mixed approach to writing up the results and conclusions of his or her work" (p. 185) and that "effective mixed methods writing is also marbled, like good pastrami. . . not layered or offered separately or sequentially; rather, they are mixed together, interwoven, interconnected" (p. 188).

If researchers focus on the substantive issues raised by the questions for their study, having chosen methods appropriate to those questions, then it makes sense for them to focus their writing similarly. Data and analyses should be assembled to tell a story that meets the purpose of the study and answers its questions. Essentially, if using an integrated mixed methods design is predicated on its adding insights and understanding beyond that which is gained from using a single method or even multiple methods, then it simply does not make sense to use paradigms, methodologies, or methods as the primary basis for determining the content or structure of written outputs from the study.

Challenges to Integration and Integrated Reporting

Despite acknowledging the importance of integrating methods in a mixed methods study, a number of mixed methodologists will advise researchers to establish and separately investigate specific qualitative and quantitative questions as part of a mixed methods project (e.g., Creswell & Plano Clark 2011; Dahlberg, Wittink, & Gallo 2010; Morse & Niehaus 2009). Only then, they suggest, are the different strands integrated by contrasting, comparing, building on, or embedding components (Creswell & Tashakkori, 2007; Teddlie & Tashakkori, 2009). Their recommendations for writing up the research typically follow a similar pattern.

I (and others) instead argue that if mixed methods have been employed to meet a particular purpose, the assumption is that each component method is inadequate or incomplete in itself *to satisfy that purpose*. Therefore the data need to be analyzed together (Bazeley, 2010, 2012) and the results need to be written together to achieve that purpose. Furthermore, because a substantial proportion of analysis occurs during the process of writing research (Richardson, 1994), an emphasis on writing the results of different components jointly will help to foster higher quality analyses as well as better integration.

Barriers to integration are only partly to do with factors intrinsic to the use of different methodological strategies. The predispositions and preferences of researchers, disciplines, and funding agencies also play a significant role (Bryman, 2007; O'Cathain, Murphy, & Nicholl, 2007). These barriers become most evident in the structure of the published output from projects. O'Cathain et al. found, for example, that just 21% of the funded mixed methods projects they reviewed realized their potential for integrated reporting.

In this chapter I explore and offer solutions to points of tension and practical difficulties in writing up and publishing a mixed methods study, and I flag issues to consider in framing and setting out a mixed methods paper or report. I then suggest strategies for writing an integrated report or article so that multiple sources of information and analyses are brought together to address the questions asked. I focus on the write-up of a mixed rather than a multiple methods study because the tensions and writing problems that arise in the latter are much less, and, where they do arise, they share similar characteristics. I use the term *mixed methods* in this context as a generic term that includes any research that involves combining more than one type of data, method of data collection, and/or analysis strategy, in such a way that integration of data and/or analyses (at least in the form of providing iterative understanding across methods during the design and analysis process) occurs prior to writing final conclusions about the topic of investigation. Opinions differ as to whether the components that contribute to a mixed methods study are able to stand on their own, being complete within themselves (Creswell & Tashakkori, 2007), or whether defining a study as mixed methods carries an inherent assumption that at least one of the components will be subservient to and incomplete without the other (Morse & Niehaus, 2009). There is, however, general agreement that for it to be defined as "mixed," the combination of methods in a study must contribute insights and understanding beyond those derived from the component parts. In a multiple methods study, each component method is able to stand on its own and is often reported separately, with the interweaving of conclusions derived from both being an added benefit.

Points of Tension and Practical Difficulties in Preparing a Mixed Methods Report

Points of tension and practical difficulties in writing a report from a mixed methods study focus in two broad areas: (a) philosophical, theoretical, methodological, and methods tensions underpinning the mixed research to be reported—each compounded when multi- or interdisciplinary teams are involved, and (b) practical difficulties that arise once the research is done—related to the audience for and acceptance of a mixed methods report or article. Each has the potential to impact on the overarching issue of *integration*—the integration of data, analyses, and reporting, through which different data sources have become mutually informing and are brought together to address the topics and/or questions addressed by the research.

Philosophical (Paradigmatic) Tensions

Debates about tensions created by combining methods presumed to have conflicting paradigmatic (ontological and epistemological) foundations dominated the early mixed methods literature of the 1980s and 1990s. Around the turn of the century, researchers became more interested in what could be achieved by mixing methods. They adopted a broadly pragmatic approach and began to focus more on the practical problems associated with combining methods—just one of Bryman's (2007) 20 interviewees raised conflicting ontology as an issue in integrating data derived from different methods.

Where authors subscribe to the belief that there is an essential link between a particular methodological approach or use of a particular type of data and a particular paradigmatic viewpoint, they report separate analyses for each methodological component of their study. Others attempt to explain their paradigmatic position (and occasionally everyone else's as well!) but, having done so, they then neglect to link that with their description of their approach to data collection or interpretation and, indeed, might go on to describe methods that conflict with their stated approach. An alternative is to say nothing at all. In evaluation and community studies, with a tradition of using mixed or multimethod approaches that preceded these debates (Rallis & Rossman, 2003), philosophical foundations for methods used are often more implicit than explicit (Mertens, 2010).

Writing an integrated report requires resolution of these paradigmatic tensions:

• The different components of a project (data, analyses) might be conducted from a common philosophical position so that integration can occur at any stage in the research process, including in its writing (Lincoln & Denzin, 2011; Yin, this volume). Most often, the philosophical bases chosen under these circumstances will be pragmatism or critical realism. In a pragmatic approach, methods are often combined in a complementary or extension design in which the experience gained through one approach is complemented and enriched by the experience of another (Johnson & Onwuegbuzie, 2004). A critical realist approach, on the other hand, might be employed to provide a contextualized understanding of social processes. In this approach, consideration is given both to regularities that are assessed through empirical observation of patterns of association and to the context-driven mechanisms behind those patterns, with the latter being identified from people's constructions of their experience and observation of the processes involved (Maxwell, 2004, 2012).

• Alternatively, one might take the approach, described by Greene (2007), of deliberately employing a combination of varying paradigms as a way to initiate fresh ideas and knowledge. This dialectical approach, with its goal of initiation, celebrates tensions created through the use of different approaches and methods as a means of prompting further exploration and deeper understanding of the subject matter of the research and related issues. In contrast to the "flatness" of a forced whole, the "gaps and spaces" that can result recognize the incompleteness of any whole and provide a delightful and disturbing alternative to the blandness of certainty (Freshwater, 2007, p. 140).

Where this tension remains unresolved (i.e., for those who see methods as associated with incompatible paradigms), the report will remain separated according to components (as a multimethod study). While the results might be discussed together in a concluding step, doing so is questionable on the same basis that mixing methods was questionable. Why would it be any more legitimate to combine results of paradigmatically incompatible approaches than it was to combine methods associated with them (Moran-Ellis et al., 2006)?

From my experience of working across all publication types (personally and indirectly through others), the extent to which one needs to explain the paradigmatic basis for a work will depend on whether one is reporting to a sponsor (usually minimal or no expectation), writing a substantive article (usually a brief mention only, if at all, depending on the discipline for which one is writing), writing a methodological article (which requires at least a description of and justification for the position taken), or writing a mixed methods dissertation. For a mixed methods dissertation, researchers are expected to provide a cogent argument for their position, possibly (but not necessarily) placed within the historical and or philosophical context of different positions. Attempts to cover paradigmatic perspectives will potentially be complicated as researchers attempt to meet requests of reviewers with differing opinions and positions—a situation best averted by presenting a confidently and clearly articulated approach in the first version.

Interdisciplinary and Methodological Tensions

Many studies are conducted by teams comprised of researchers from different disciplines because of the range of skills required, posing a further risk to integration and coordinated reporting. Interdisciplinary teams face challenges from differences in epistemology, training, knowledge base, goals, and constituent audiences as well as from interpersonal tensions around trust, power, and the lack of a shared language (Bowers et al. 2013; Curry et al. 2012). For example, in Bowers and colleagues' project investigating the efficacy of different models of care in nursing homes, team members used different terms (*patients, residents, elders*) to describe the people they were studying. The term *impact analysis* also meant something quite different to economists and clinicians.

Researchers from different disciplinary backgrounds are trained to use different methodologies and methods. Those from particular disciplines often lack understanding of research processes associated with alternative disciplines, including sampling, analysis strategies, and interpretation. Methodological differences create varying opinions on what counts as evidence and generate the potential for methodological marginalization and disrespect among team members (Bowers et al. 2013; O'Cathain, Murphy, & Nicholl 2008).

Difference between approaches with respect to timelines for progressing the research is a particular aspect of methodology that will affect publication. Whereas the "goal for some is to publish definitive results in research journals, for others, [the] goal is to use preliminary findings to quickly inform policy and practice" (Bowers et al., 2013, p. 2164). For example, Simons (2007) describes how, in the project of which she was a part, not only was the randomized trial the major funded component but, with a formula to work by, results from it were quickly generated, and so it was the first component to be reported. Analysis of the qualitative component of the trial was completed much later and was reported separately. In concluding that it often does make sense to report different elements separately, she nevertheless emphasized the importance of contextualizing and sequencing the different reports to ensure they built on each other.

A meaningful interdisciplinary or multidisciplinary collaboration involves demonstrating respect for all included methods, sharing knowledge, learning from each other, and avoiding simply contributing to particular (compartmentalized) elements of the study based on individual areas of expertise. Leadership, of course, is critical, but collaboration is helped also by recognizing that individual team members represent a larger group of scholars, that they need to be treated on their own terms as well as jointly, and that some conflict is inevitable. Reading and discussing previous papers of other team members can assist in developing appreciation for others, as can being open about the strengths and limitations of different disciplinary approaches (Bowers et al. 2013; Curry et al. 2012).

Different Writing Traditions

The potential for conflict between disciplines represented within a mixed methods team carries through to tensions in publishing beyond timing and separation of component parts, because researchers from different disciplines have different traditions, guidelines, criteria, and assumptions about what is appropriate and engage in quite different styles of reporting (Becher, 1987). This challenge of different communication traditions in different interpretive communities involves aesthetic as well as rhetorical and technical criteria and norms (Sandelowski, 2003). Writing experimental and statistical methods and results tends to follow a standard linear approach, along with use of third-person and passive tense, suggestive of a dispassionate representation of reality. In qualitative work, however, it can be difficult to distinguish the process of writing from the process of analysis; consequently qualitative approaches to writing are less defined and highly variable but commonly include use of first-person and active tense as the author reflects on and interprets his or her data. The result is work positioned somewhere to the left of, or sitting on the fence between, art and science. In either case, doing things differently from the disciplinary norm can engender distrust in what the article is conveying.

One solution is to recognize these differences and employ rhetorical conventions and strategies appropriate to the kind of data and style of analyses that are being written about at the time while keeping the text accessible by avoiding unexplained, specialized jargon. This means there might well be changes of reporting style within an article. When incorporating results from a survey into a comprehensive consultancy report based on mixed data sources (Bazeley et al., 1996), as well as summarizing descriptive and comparative data in tables, I used footnotes to provide the statistical summaries that supported the many relationships being described in the text, resulting in uninterrupted text for the reader while still satisfying the conventions of statistical reporting. A report on well-being for older women (Older Women's Network,

1993) used the outer margins of each page to juxtapose illustrative quotes alongside reports of patterns in responses from interviews with members, statistical data, and insights from the literature. (This strategy also ensures that the report writer cannot so easily rely on a participant quote as the only evidence to support an argument.)

Quality of the Research

Both the depth of separate analyses and the level and timing of integration of data and analyses affect the quality of inferences reported from mixed methods studies. When reviewing mixed methods studies in health, with a focus on approaches to data analysis, Bazeley (2009) found, too often, that authors provided descriptive results for only one or both components (e.g., descriptive statistics, or a few "themes" identified), with integration of results attempted only in the concluding section (if at all). Instances of reports where further questions might have been answered or conclusions might have been different if qualitative and quantitative data had been effectively combined during analysis were identified. For example, long-term survivors of lung cancer studied by Maliski, Sarna, Evangelista, and Padilla (2003) who scored lower in terms of distressed mood spoke more positively as a group about existential issues, health and self-care, physical ability, adjustment, and support than did those who scored higher on distress. The authors described each of these five themes in detail, relating them to distress on a high–low group basis, but they ignored physiological measures, including spirometry (lung capacity) even though these were described in detail in the method. They also did not take into account a clear association of depression scores with racial and educational differences. A case-based comparison on these variables (individually and together) for each of their five themes might have led them to quite different conclusions.

If the underlying design, data gathering, and analysis for a study is lacking in some way, then there will be no basis for quality reporting from that research. Quality in mixed methods research focuses on the basis for meta-inferences from the study as a whole, but it also assumes that component parts meet acceptable standards for the approaches taken. There are, therefore, three sets of quality criteria that might apply to a mixed methods study: those that focus on the adequacy of each of the qualitative and the quantitative components and those that focus on the integration of those components—essentially, did the combination of methods yield more than separate studies would have?

Eight criteria (with subcomponents) for quality specific to mixed methods projects were synthesized by Alicia O'Cathain (2010) from a comprehensive review of previous work in multiple disciplines. The eight criteria cover planning, design, data and analyses, interpretation, inference transferability, reporting, synthesizability, and utility. These provide useful guidance to anyone planning, conducting, assessing, or reporting a mixed methods study.

Who Is the Audience?

Formats for reporting a mixed methods study vary from more formal academic publications and presentations, through reports to funding bodies and other stakeholders, to communication with the general public. Each form has its own requirements for style, content, and timelines for production. While readers of an academic publication expect transparency in the description of both the theoretical framework for and methods used in a study as a basis for interpreting the results obtained by the research, a report to funders and other stakeholders is likely to focus more on the actual results and the implications of those results for their constituent groups than on the theory and methods behind them.

Writing an article for an academic audience: If you're not sure where to publish, get an idea of potentially relevant journals from your reference list. Consider whether your work is of interest to a local or international audience. Visit the website of a journal you might publish in for information for authors. Check out copies of that journal. What kinds of articles do they normally publish? What length is allowed? Do you want to write for a discipline-based audience (with interest in what you have discovered), or does your writing focus on interdisciplinary concerns or the methods you have used? To what extent will you need to justify and explain your use of a mixed methods approach, if at all? Be respectful of the conventions employed by the particular academic community served by the journal you choose.

Writing a report for (nonacademic) stakeholders: Find out what is expected and how your report will be used. Nonacademic stakeholders are less interested in academic justifications for methods of data collection and analysis than they are in whether you have produced information they can use. Beware political interference with the results of your work, and ensure you substantiate your results and conclusions. Policymakers need numbers, but brief vignettes that are complete in themselves can also be a helpful addition. Use tables and models to present and/or summarize data. Busy stakeholders are less likely to read a full report, so it is critical to provide an executive summary at the start of the report (the evaluation section of the US Government Accountability Office limit theirs to a single page). Smith and Robbins (1982, p. 60) recommended starting each section with a summary and putting the key message for each section into the heading for that section. This means it will show up clearly in the table of contents and again in the text where, usually, it will appear in bold and therefore catch the eye of the reader. Thus instead of "Parent Attendance Patterns" a heading might read "Few Parents Attended Parent Advisory Council Meetings."

Writing for more leisured readers and for a community-based audience: Provide additional illustrative detail through vignettes or mini case studies. Present your results as a newspaper commentary, novel, film, or documentary, while still incorporating information derived from both statistical and hermeneutic sources. For example, Al Gore's *An Inconvenient Truth* and Michael Moore's *Bowling for Columbine* drew on mixed data and analyses to reach a larger audience (Creswell & McCoy, 2011).

Writing for reviewers as audience: A mixed methods article for an academic audience needs to be acceptable to and understood by editors and reviewers who are not used to reading across different paradigms or methods and who might favor particular types of research (Brannen, 2005). Authors can experience conflicting reviews with seemingly opposing requests for clarifications of philosophical and methodological approaches. This can delay publication for many months and may result in a less than clear exposition as the author tries to satisfy too many "masters." Joseph Teye (2012), who wrote one of the more fully integrated articles published in the *Journal of Mixed Methods Research* in 2012, observed, "As the idea of using mixed methods strategy in this study was to enhance quality of explanations, it was thought wise to integrate the two components in the entire manuscript, rather than having two separate components" (p. 386), yet he had problems along the way because reviewers wanted him to separate them. Dahlberg et al. (2010) provide useful guidance on understanding the mentality of reviewers (so you can preempt their criticisms). They also suggest working out your response to the reviewers before modifying the paper, to help you clarify what changes you need to make.

Publication (Journal) Limitations

Apart from disciplinary and/or methodological biases, journal policies that severely limit word counts do not allow the space necessary for reporting a study that involves multiple methods, multiple approaches to analysis, and potentially complex results. Nursing and health journals, for example, often have 3,000 or 5,000 word limits on the length of articles. The consequence is that often only parts of a study can be reported in any one article.

A frequent response is to publish the quantitative and qualitative data components of a multimethod or mixed methods study in separate articles, but if a mixed rather than multimethod approach is the best one to take for the research purpose, then this solution defeats the purpose of having used mixed methods. Sometimes separate articles can be published side by side in the same journal issue (which rather begs the question of why a longer article could not have been allowed). O'Cathain (2010) provides an example of the latter but observes with a tone of regret that it meant publication of the more illuminating and generalizable conclusion drawn from integration of the two sets of findings never happened.

Mixed methods researchers have employed a number of strategies to deal with this problem, some of which are more satisfactory than others. Strategies, which need to be selected to suit the particular conditions of the study, include

• Publish a methodological article first to describe the approach and data sources used in the study, then draw on this for reference in later articles. For example, Sharp et al. (2012) published an article that detailed the four-stage, mixed methods sampling strategy they employed for their multisite case study of the implementation of a statewide policy designed to improve student career choices and outcomes. In a government-funded study of early career researchers that I led (Bazeley et al., 1996), a detailed description of design, sampling, and data collection for each of the multiple data gathering strategies used was provided in an appendix to the main report. As this report was freely available, it was then possible to present the methods relevant to each of several later articles in summary form with a cross-reference to the report and its appendix for further details.

• Alternatively, provide an overview paper at the start of the publication program and/or an inference paper drawing on the entire body of work from the study to "wrap up" the program of publication.

• Focus separate papers on specific aspects of the subject matter of the study or issues raised by it, bringing together all relevant sources of data for the aspect or issue being discussed, as described below (framing the paper). Whenever papers are "drawn off" from a larger study, it is important to locate them within the context of the larger study.

• Seek out journals that allow for longer articles. For example, the *Journal of Mixed Methods Research* allows 10,000 words for empirical reports, *Quality & Quantity* allows 5,000 to 10,000 words, and the *International Journal of Social Research Methodology* allows 8,000 words. Examples among journals with a disciplinary focus include *Social Science and Medicine* (8,000 words), *Academy of Management Journal* (40 pages [10,000 to 12,000 words]), and the *American Educational Research Journal* (20 to 50 pages).

Framing Writing

With the pressure on to start a report or academic paper, the task becomes one of deciding how to frame each of those reports or papers and then to work out what is needed from the data to make each necessary point. Unlike conventions for reporting experimental or other hypothesis-driven studies, there is no standard design framework for reporting qualitative or mixed methods research. The approach to reporting a mixed or multimethod study could depend on the specific study design, the timing of the "point of interface" (Morse & Niehaus, 2009—the point at which methods are integrated in a project), the audience (as noted earlier), the nature of the information communicated, and whether the paper has a methodological or substantive purpose. Over and above all of these is the question of the specific purpose or focus for each publication (or other form of output)— the "take-home message" you want the reader to remember.

Focus Writing on the Message Rather Than the Method

Your research program will have been closely aligned to your primary purpose(s) and question(s), adjusted to what you were finding

in relation to those. These questions will have guided your analyses, but now, in writing up your study, you will need to decide on the focus for each subsection of an overall report or of each paper for presentation or publication. To help clarify the focus for any section or item of written output, think about it as determining the take-home message for the reader (or listener). Thus the first and most important question to consider in writing up any study, including one drawing on mixed methods, is: "What is the story I want to tell with this data in this publication—what is the message I want people to take away from reading it?"

A report to a stakeholder, such as a funding body, usually will necessarily cover the full breadth of the substantive subject matter and related issues encompassed within the aims and objectives of the research proposal, and it should be organized accordingly into sections that deal with each aspect of this subject matter or each issue arising from it, building toward the conclusions and recommendations. Similarly, although written in a different style and with different emphases, a dissertation will comprehensively account for the study program that has been completed. Again, each chapter or section of the results will deal with a particular aspect of the subject matter covered by the research to create a series of related chapters that contribute to arguing a thesis. View the different methods you employed in the research simply as the tools that allowed you to carry out your investigation, not as a basis for organizing the results generated through them.

Plans for academic papers from a mixed methods project will depend on the complexity and breadth of the project. The data and argument supporting the overall conclusion from the study might be written in a single article. For a more complex study, an overview paper (or published report) might be followed (or preceded) by other articles, each of which will be crafted around one of several subcomponents, questions, or related issues identified from within the wider study (see Table 17.1). Each of these separate papers might embrace quite a deal of complexity, but each will be structured so that the reader finishes reading it with a clear picture of its particular take-home message, as well as with a sense of where that fits within the objectives of the whole project.

The content within each paper also will be structured to lead to the conclusion by drawing on whatever information is available and useful, regardless

Table 17.1 Academic Papers Published Following Publication of an Initial, Comprehensive Report

Publication	Focus/Primary Question	Types of Data Used
Bazeley, 1998	Who wins prestigious research funding?	Quantified administrative by-product data, supplemented by interviews with panel members, successful researchers, and heads of departments
Grbich, 1998	The effect of departmental socialization on ECR development and productivity	Qualitative (comparative) case studies
Bazeley, 1999	Factors predictive of continuity as an active researcher after PhD	Survey of PhD graduates supplemented by survey of ECRs, interviews with ECRs, and responses to public advertising
Asmar, 1999	Gender and discipline differences in academic ECR experience, post-PhD	Survey of PhD graduates
Marsh and Bazeley, 1999	Level of agreement in assessor scoring for grant applications	Administrative by-product data (assessor scores) contextualized within other project data
Bazeley, 2003	Describe and justify a definition for early career status for use by academic research funding bodies	Document analysis (grants schemes), surveys of ECRs and PhD graduates, interviews (multiple sources), responses to public advertising.

Note: ECR = early career researcher.

of the method used to obtain it, as you build the argument. Not all articles reporting components from a more complex mixed methods study (or chapters within a report of thesis) will necessarily be based on all data sources used, but each will draw on whatever is needed to answer the questions and/or cover the issues raised for that paper.

For example, at the conclusion of our study on the career development and funding needs of early-career researchers leading to a multidisciplinary definition of "early career" for grant distribution purposes, we provided a comprehensive report to the commissioning agency—the Australian Research Council (Bazeley et al., 1996). Members of the research team subsequently published a number of academic papers, as outlined in Table 17.1. Each individual paper focused on or extended analysis of one specific issue covered by or arising from the broader aegis of the report; four of the six integrated data of more than one type and from more than one source, but the focus always remained on the issue being discussed. This is illustrated by the structure (shown in Table 17.2) of the last-listed paper, which was about the background and rationale for defining who an early-career researcher is (Bazeley, 2003). An excerpt from the text of this article can be

found later in this chapter, illustrating writing based on a combination of statistical and textual data sources.

Setting Out the Mixed Methods Paper

Although there is no accepted template to draw on for reporting mixed methods studies, there are certain expected inclusions. Several chapters, papers, and editorials offer detailed guidance on what to cover in each part of a mixed methods proposal or report for a variety of audiences (e.g., Creswell & Plano Clark 2011; Dahlberg et al. 2010). The degree of variability in how a mixed methods study is conducted is surely a factor contributing to the lack of standardization in the structure of written reports, and in this regard, mixed methods is similar to qualitative research. But perhaps this variability provides the opportunity, sought by Wolcott (2002), to make academic writing "less pompous and less dependent on ritual, more searching and discovery oriented," with literature, methods, and theory included on an as needed basis (p. 102). For example, as well as providing introductory context, literature might be included in with other results (Morse, 2007), especially if exploration of these particular items of literature was prompted by something found in the data.

Table 17.2 The Structure of a Substantively Focused Mixed Methods Paper

Abstract
The "problem" of early career researchers
Research design [and data sources]
Milestones in an academic research career
    Completion of high-level research training
    Obtaining an academic appointment providing a
        stable research environment
    Balancing the demands of teaching with the need/
        desire to research
    Maintaining a research profile when promotion
        brings increased non-research responsibilities
    Achievement of established researcher status
Identifying research potential
    Qualification as a criterion
    Age as a criterion
    Length or stability of employment as a criterion
    The research "track record" as a criterion
A definition for early career
Assessing early career status
Conclusion

Source. Bazeley (2003).

Whatever system or convention you use to guide your writing, a clear and progressive structure to the report or article is critical to giving the reader a sense of direction and confidence in following the material presented. One of the "tricks" to working out structure is to ask: What did the reader *already* need to know to understand the events being described or the point being made now; and what does the reader need to know *now* in order to understand what's coming next? Review the table of contents (the document map in the navigation pane is a great interim substitute) to check the sequencing. In general, description will come before comparative and relational analyses, theory before application, and so on. The importance of structure runs right down to the level of the paragraph and sentence: thus the first sentence in a paragraph identifies the (single) point to be made in that paragraph, which is then developed in the rest of the paragraph, and (in general) a sentence starts with the words to which you wish to give most emphasis. Good linking paragraphs or sentences are another essential feature to lead readers smoothly from one section or chapter to the next so that they always have a sense of knowing where they are going.

Having a plan so "the writer can focus on one sentence or one paragraph at a time, shifting back and forth between the details and the whole [means that] the task is reduced to writing paragraphs, each of which has a job, rather than writing an entire paper from beginning to end" (Dahlberg et al., 2010, p. 778). Planning of this nature is helpful when writing has to be built into an otherwise busy schedule, and it is essential when a team is involved in writing. My strategy is to make extensive use of headings and the document map (Windows) or sidebar (Macintosh), so that as I'm preparing to write I can easily locate a heading and drop random ideas and bits of information under it (very messily!). I then gradually reorganize and rationalize these and fill out each section as I become confident I am close to having sufficient material for writing that section. Once I have a sense of the structure of the whole, I will then work through, more or less completing sections from beginning to end. Final steps involve checking the consistency of each section with the goals and framework for the paper, checking the ordering and that each section links smoothly to the next, and then "sitting on it" for a time before a final read-through and edit.

Describing the Design and Methods

The number and arrangement of methods (each selected on the basis of how they will assist you in answering your questions) and the need to show how these various methods will be integrated in a mixed methods study complicates writing the methods section of a report or paper. Some suggestions for structuring the methodology or methods section follow.

• Start with a reminder of the purpose and provide a one- or two-sentence overview of the study design. Avoid simply applying a design label from a textbook as it might not truly represent your methods.

• Follow with your rationale for why it was necessary to use mixed methods to achieve your specific purpose. You do not need to provide a history of the mixed methods movement or of decades of paradigm debates, nor do you need to elaborate on all the alternative approaches you considered—remember you are not writing a methods (or philosophical) textbook.

• Elaborate on the design features, making clear whether this was how the project was designed, or what actually happened. A visual model showing timing, relative importance, and how each element influenced others at each stage of the project is a useful presentation tool (Creswell & Plano Clark, 2011). Diagrams were employed to supplement descriptions of methods by authors of 7 out of 12 research articles in the *Journal of Mixed Methods Research* in each of two sample years reviewed (2010 and 2012).

• While it might be possible to present a design neatly, what happens in fact is likely to be far more messy, and so you will need to show where modifications occurred or add some descriptive-explanatory text accompanying the design visualization to explain complex details and/or to indicate what was changed during implementation.

• Provide the details of sample, data collection, and analysis strategies, as appropriate, for each phase of the research and/or each method employed and the implications of your choices (e.g., in relation to your capacity to generalize from your study).

• Show when and how the methods and/or analyses were integrated and (if mixed rather than multimethod) what kind of additional benefit was expected from that integration.

• Optionally, use a table to summarize the methods, showing their fit with your questions and, as in Table 17.3, perhaps also with your theoretical framework. A table of this type is useful for summarizing and clarifying the contribution of each component to the objectives of the study. It is especially valuable when you are writing an article or presenting a proposal for mixed methods research and you have limited space.

• Indicate both design and in-practice limitations of your study.

• Comment on the ethical implications of your study.

Transparency in Reporting Methods

Maxwell and Loomis (2003) describe a distinction between an author's characterization of his or her methodology (reconstructed logic) and the reader's reconstruction of methods (logic-in-use), claiming that, historically, there has been "widespread but relatively implicit use of methods, approaches, and concepts from both the qualitative and quantitative paradigms" (p. 242). They illustrate their point by citing a number of classic studies, including those by Blumstein and Schwartz (1983) and Festinger, Riecken, and Schachter (1956), each of which claimed to be quantitative in

design (a more "acceptable" approach at the time) yet each relied heavily on extensive contributions from qualitative data in order to interpret and present their findings.

Transparency in describing methods employed in research is a major criterion for quality in reporting (O'Cathain, 2010). It is important for readers to know how results were generated and what problems were experienced, as this can affect their assessment of the trustworthiness of the results. Transparency of methods also affects a reader's capacity to apply what has been learned from the study to other situations. In a mixed methods report, where and how integration between methods occurred needs to be explained (O'Cathain, 2009), particularly since the initial descriptions of methods used for data gathering and analysis are likely to be presented separately for each data type or source.

Strategies for Integrating Writing of Results

While the content of your results will be determined by your purpose and research questions, researchers using mixed methods are often advised that the structure of their write-up will parallel the design of their study (e.g., Creswell & Plano Clark, 2011; Dahlberg et al., 2010). Thus in a concurrent design with a complementary purpose authors might be advised to present the results from each component and then bring them together; they will almost always be advised that results from a sequential design should be presented as a sequential write-up, revealing or expanding results in accord with the sequence of each method used.

Rather, I would argue, the *methods* section is the place to show details of the methods used for each component and how methods are expected to interrelate. In the *results* section for a substantively focused empirical study, as noted earlier, the emphasis and consequently the rationale for organization will be on the substantive questions and issues that were raised as the subject of the investigation, even if the methods were conducted separately or sequentially. For example:

• When preliminary work is designed to generate appropriate design and wording for questions in a survey, there are two possibilities: (a) If that preliminary work is minimal, regard it as a routine element of designing a survey, historically not seen as warranting classification of the study as a whole

Table 17.3 Data Collection and Analysis Procedures for a Proposed Study of Immunization Compliance[a]

Research Questions	Theoretical/Conceptual Basis	Data Sources and Timing	Data Analysis
Disposition, coping style, experiences and beliefs of the parent	Self-efficacy theory, parental efficacy, health locus of control	Interview about background experience of diseases and expectations and priorities for child—prebirth. Survey questions and scaled items—prebirth and 10 weeks postbirth.	Statistical analyses of scales and survey items, content coding of interviews, comparative analyses and interrelationships between variables and between qualitative concepts and quantitative variables

Social integration of the parent
  - information and social influence
  - availability of social support
	Social influence—normalizing
	Social support theory
		Social network analysis (ego nets) and associated immunization-related accounts regarding members of the ego net—10 weeks postbirth	Extent, centrality, density, considered in relation to description given of belief and support from each network member; interrelationship with other data (e.g., with self-efficacy, locus of control, needle phobia, support to attend clinic, compliance)

Assessing probabilities and decision-making under conditions of ambiguity and risk	Decision-making theory	Narrative regarding process of going (or not going) for immunization; mapping of decision-making—10 weeks postbirth.	Narrative analysis regarding story of the day, coding of decision steps and influences, comparative analyses and relationships with other data

[a] Part of the first two of three phases adapted from a proposal for public health research funding.

as mixed (or even multiple) method. (b) "Serious" qualitative work undertaken as a foundation for a quantitative survey will be foundational to describing and explaining what was found through the quantitative survey. The various questions or issues raised in the initial qualitative work and further explored through the survey should be discussed as interrelated aspects contributing to the primary purpose of the whole undertaking.

• If the design is one in which qualitative work is undertaken to complement or expand on questions raised by a previous quantitative tool, then the expanded understanding needs to be reported along with the initially gained information, with the two sets of information being integrated point by point.

• In a confirmatory design it might have been necessary to keep the methods independent during data gathering and analysis, but that does not necessarily mean they should be reported separately. Rather, show how each element of the study was confirmed (or contested) as you go, using phrases such as "both sources of data

showed that. . ." or "this was confirmed by. . . from the [alternate method]." Further joint analyses might be found necessary to resolve discrepancies or explain results.

Having made a case for integration and described some aspects of what that might look like, I now turn to examples of both routine and more creative strategies that have been used to achieve integrated reporting of results. Reports of analyses (including interpretation of the meaning of specific results as they are presented) should always be completed within the results section(s) of a dissertation, article, or report. The discussion section is then reserved for elaborating on the significance of the results as a whole in relation to the original objective and in the light of the literature—it should not include any new results, and it should not be the place where the results are integrated.

Juxtaposition of Statistical and Textual Data

This is perhaps the most common and most important approach to integrated reporting, where data from different sources are reported side by side. Qualitative data might extend understanding of a statistical pattern, a statistical pattern will add breadth to the qualitative data, or the two might come together as "warranted assertions" based on a review of all available evidence (Greene, 2007). Hall, Phillips, Dubois, Follett, and Pancaningtyas (2010) juxtaposed insights from interview, survey, diary, and observational data to produce an excellent example of an integrated evaluation report that was prepared for both government and community audiences. Similarly, the following extract from Bazeley (2003) includes a "marbling" of comparative analyses of text, statistical analyses, illustrative quotations, relational statements, documentary data and explanatory comment. Together these supported the argument for the second milestone to be passed in building a research career (as outlined in Table 17.2)—the need to gain stable, research-oriented employment.

> While the majority of PhD graduates were in full time work or further study within a short time of graduating, many were unable to find employment which allowed further research or which fostered the development of a career in research, frustrating to those who had spent years pursuing that as their goal. Frustration amongst those who were unable to gain academic employment was most evident in the physical sciences and the humanities, disciplines in which the majority of graduates had to seek new employment and in which the shortage of new academic positions was most acute.
>
> *I cannot convey to you how very disheartening this situation is: to be keen to embark upon an academic career but to be, as so many others are, unable to make a small entrance into a teaching position.*
>
> *My ambition was to become an academic, but I have now almost given up hope of attaining that goal. Hardly any positions in my field have been advertised in the last four years.*
>
> Social science and health graduates were least likely to express problems regarding employment. For the social scientists at least, this was related to their generally being in employment already by the time they graduated with PhD.
>
> The perceived lack of a career structure for young researchers can remain an issue even if employment is obtained. Many seeking academic appointments in particular complained of having to "continually move from institution to institution on contracts lasting one year or less" with consequent impact on ability to apply for research grants. While university

> internal granting schemes were generally designed to benefit new or recently qualified staff, some required a minimum guaranteed period of continuing employment as a condition for award. In such cases, those on one year appointments or in the last year of a three year appointment found themselves unable to apply for research support at the time when they most needed it.
>
> Lack of security in university employment posed some, considerable or a major problem to their research for 42.5% of the early career academics surveyed while the majority (64.5%) rated the prospects for someone wishing to pursue a research career in their field to be only fair or not good at all. Those in postdoctoral research positions experienced particularly high levels of job insecurity, stating that this was a major problem causing them difficulties in their research or in the development of their research career (mean 4.7 on a scale of 1–5). Of the six disciplines specifically studied, physicists consistently rated their employment prospects and future research prospects most poorly ($F = 4.63$, $df = 5,267$, $p < .001$ and $F = 3.37$, $df = 5,285$, $p < .01$ respectively), followed by historians, with those in nursing/health being most optimistic. (Bazeley, 2003, pp. 264–266; used with permission from Springer)

As I reflect on this extract 12 years after writing it, I am thinking that I would now attempt to interweave the statistical data even more effectively with the qualitatively derived text. I would also note (in brackets at the end of each quote) the disciplines of the two quoted graduates (humanities and medical sciences, respectively), as relevant demographic information.

Inclusion of numerical data is integral to conveying patterns, to showing you have accounted for all data and observed absences, but "acontextual counting" needs to be accompanied by details of what was said (Sandelowski, 2003). Statements supporting the observation of a broad pattern should precede illustrative quotes so that the quotes can be seen in context. One of the distinct advantages of using qualitative computer software when analyzing data is that matrix displays of patterns in the data provide both numerical results and give access to the text that supports those numbers, thus supporting integrated reporting of both "how many" and "in what way" (Bazeley & Jackson, 2013).

For example, Dockett and Perry (2004) used a table, a graph, and descriptive text when they reported differences in parents', teachers', and children's experience of issues relating to the children's transition from home to school. They were able to show numerically that both teachers and parents rated adjustment as the predominant issue (of eight altogether) in transition to school but that in their responses teachers focused on the organizational aspects of adjustment (being able to follow directions, demonstrate independence), while parents focused on the social aspects of their child fitting in to the group. Numbers and text provided valuable, if different, insights into the issues of transition; both were necessary for a rounded understanding of those issues.

As well as elaborating on patterns, qualitative data might help to explain statistical patterns, with the explanation logically accompanying the statistical report. A paper derived from the aforementioned study exploring who received research council funding and how accessible it was to early career researchers (Bazeley et al., 1996) provides an example:

> Applicants who had recent ARC or NHMRC funding were significantly more likely to gain funding for their current project (at 26.0%) (particularly if it was for a related project) although it was by no means a guarantee of continuing support, while those who had "other external funding" in the absence of ARC or NHMRC funding had a reduced probability of success (at just 3.8%) ($\chi^2 = 24.51$, $df = 7$, $p = .001$). When chairs of the discipline panels were asked about this latter apparent anomaly, they suggested that much of what is funded by other external sources might be regarded as "consultancy" or "development," rather than "research," indicating that it is therefore questionable that it constitutes a legitimate research activity resulting in the advancement of knowledge rather than merely the application of that knowledge. For track-record recognition to be gained (within the ARC network) from research undertaken with non-ARC funding, publications emanating from that research must include a basic research component and be widely disseminated or, preferably, be presented as peer-reviewed scholarly publications that will contribute to the development of the discipline. (Bazeley, 1998, p. 444)

Conveying Results Using Alternative Modes of Representation

Noting that each inquiry tradition has its own mode of persuasive writing and voice, Greene (2007) offers "multiple representational forms. . . as one valuable strategy to both respect and integrate different writing traditions" (p. 179). She reports a study that demonstrated audience preference for mixed forms of presentation (for the same information) over single forms, hence her recommendation for "marbling" different forms within a presentation, as noted earlier. This means, for example, that statistical data might be accompanied by a (co-located) vignette, or an image, or even a poem to provide contextual understanding or to engage the emotions as well as the intellect. Picture the child in poverty, while taking in statistics about prevalence. Support a narrative account with a visual map of interrelated concepts, perhaps with strength of relationships indicated numerically (Bazeley, 2013). Combinations of these different modes of presentation, as with the harmony created by different instruments in an orchestra, will communicate to a wider audience as different elements engage different facets of the reader's or listener's capacity for understanding. Whether the approving audience would necessarily include the "wardens" of a dominant scholarly journal is uncertain; it would be likely to depend on the forms chosen, their relevance, and the skill with which they are interwoven.

Presenting and Reconciling Alternate Versions

The results of a study might be presented in alternative accounts that convey different understandings of the same event or situation. John Jermier (1985, cited in Frost & Stablein, 1992) presented the same characters differently in two short stories to convey contrasting theoretical perspectives on worker alienation derived from field observations in a phosphate factory. He followed the two stories with a reprise and a tabulated review of the contrasting theoretical implications. The telling of a story or description of an event from different perspectives has been referred to as the Rashomon effect (Heider, 1988), a term derived from a film of that name. The film is based on a 12th-century Japanese story in which four witnesses to an event each gave contrasting but entirely believable evidence about it, with no attempt to resolve the differences. Differences in understanding of an event might cause a problem for a jury in a legal case, but value is created for the mixed methods researcher when the dialectic between paradigms or methods initiates further analysis and attempts are made to reconcile them

(Greene, 2007). Even just the actual process of attempting to write a report from a study with divergent results, through consequent immersion in the problems of the data, helps the writer to work through the differences and reach some resolution.

Integrating Using a (Borrowed) Theoretical Framework

In their article exploring the dynamics of health sciences mixed methods research teams, Curry et al. (2012) used representational group theory from organizational psychology to bring together a diverse set of literature and experiences to understand and provide constructive guidance for the tensions, conflicts, trust issues, and leadership issues that arise when dealing with disciplinary differences, methodological differences, and differences in language between team members. Their use of this theory provided a coordinated framework showing how mixed methods teams can move forward by separating the challenges experienced in the team from the level of interpersonal conflict.

After electronically searching seven years of studies (2004–2010) from the medical and health literature, Evans, Coon, and Ume (2011) found just 28 articles in which the authors reported using an a priori theoretical framework to guide their study, with 11 of these in nursing. Seven of the 11 nursing studies effectively threaded the theoretical framework through the design, data collection, analysis, and discussion. Those that did were more likely than the other four to integrate the qualitative with the quantitative components of the study (6/7 compared with 0/4). The authors of this review then demonstrated the usefulness of a "life course perspective," with its attention to "trajectories, transitions, turning points, timing of life events, adaptive strategies, and cultural and contextual differences" (p. 280) as an integrative theoretical framework for their longitudinal, multisite case study of crucial moments in caregiving for Mexican American families. They juxtaposed data from interviews and scores on standardized measures, gathered over a 15-month period, with critical moments along a timeline to create time-ordered summary profiles for each case. Having a theoretical perspective helped them to focus on relevant constructs and interrelationships as they designed and carried out their study. They expect that it will also contribute to the generalizability of their results.

Use of Displays

Using a model to present results from diverse strands of a study forces the researcher to contemplate how the strands come together, enriching both the analysis and the writing. "You know what you display" was Miles and Huberman's (1994, p. 91) famous maxim. With all forms of display, allow the display to do its work of communicating. Rather than repeating the content of that communication in the text, use text accompanying the model to explain or elaborate on the messages contained within components and connections in the display.

Udo Kelle (2006) used quantitative survey analysis, supplemented by understanding of economic circumstances and occupational culture gained through qualitative analysis, to study the "status passage" of school leavers moving into craft, office, and technical-industrial occupations. He found an anomaly in the data for industrial mechanics who, because of economic circumstances at the time, were restricted to less stimulating and less prestigious employment than they expected. Most came to accept good working conditions and good salary as a sufficient compromise, but a minority of mechanics who desired to optimize their career development took steps to further their education. Using the multiple data sources, and with this added insight, Kelle was able to develop and refine a visual model that supplemented his text as he explained the passage from school education through vocational training to employment for German youth in those occupations (Figure 17.1).

A table, like a model, is also helpful in integrating data from multiple sources to present as part of the results, either to unite elements that have been separately analyzed or to provide the basis in the results for an integrated interpretation and discussion. Lee and Greene (2007) used a joint display of quantitative and qualitative responses as one of two integrative strategies for furthering analysis of their data on the predictive value of standardized test scores for proficiency in English and then to demonstrate discrepancies in scoring in their report of the study. The statistical results suggested a lack of overall correlation between test scores and grade point average, but the joint display of test scores matched with extracts from students' reports of their experience of language difficulties, faculty reports of students' difficulties, and assessment of their academic performance revealed the variability and complexity of this relationship in relation

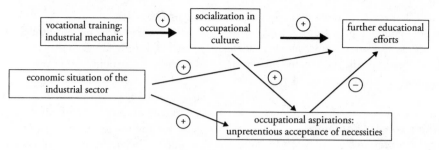

Fig. 17.1 Causal model of the relation between vocational training, macroeconomic influences, and educational efforts of respondents.

Source: Kelle (2006, p. 300, Figure 1). Reprinted with permission from Taylor and Francis.

to both the primary discipline of the student and the kinds of difficulty experienced—aspects that were not taken into account in the overall statistical assessment.

Use of Metaphor

A metaphor uses a concept or process that is readily understood to facilitate comprehension of something more complex. Mixed and multimethod researchers have creatively employed a wide selection of metaphors to describe and convey to the reader what they are doing when they combine data and/or analyses. These range from *sprinkling* one type of data through another, to constructing a *mosaic, bricolage,* or *jigsaw* where different forms of data are placed side by side or are *woven together* to complete a design or picture, through *mixing* or *blending* to *conversation, morphing,* and *fusion* to capture the iterative, sometimes reconstructive and generative nature of combining methods (Bazeley & Kemp, 2012). Lawrenz and Huffman (2002) creatively employed the metaphor of an archipelago, for example, to show how the various elements of their study of the professional development of teachers came together to reveal a "submerged" whole.

Triangulation is perhaps the most used, and misused, metaphor in mixed methods research. How many of those who use this term to explain their design or analysis have really checked the history of the term or thoughtfully considered its meaning as a metaphor? (See, e.g., Bazeley and Kemp's [2012] derivation of different metaphors for triangulating data and the special issue of the *Journal of Mixed Methods Research* on triangulation [2012, 6(2)]. The latter includes Denzin's perspective, past and present, on the term he helped to popularize.) Triangulation has been used in at least two ways in the mixed methods literature: to describe

assessment of the convergence (corroboration, validation) of results obtained by independently using two or more methods and, more commonly, to describe the concurrent use of more than one method in order to gain a fuller understanding of a research problem (complementarity). In neither sense is it a metaphor for mixed research in general. Each of these meanings has different implications for the conduct of research (requiring separation vs. combination) and the way it is reported, so if triangulation is to be used as a metaphor when writing up a mixed or multiple methods study, it needs to be explained.

Narration and/or Progressive Focusing

Present what has been learned as an unfolding narrative, perhaps even a mystery, with a "plot" that builds toward a climax, while drawing in both quantitative and qualitative elements of the data (Leech, 2012). As you progressively focus, you might work from a broad overview of the topic through a more detailed view of its intricacies to eventually arrive at a coherent model, argument, or thesis.

Telling the unfolding story of the research is likely to be more appropriate for a methods-oriented rather than results-oriented paper (because the latter more often requires integration of what has been learned from the different methodological components). For example, Seltzer-Kelly, Westwood, and Peña-Guzman (2012) narrate in a deeply reflexive way the change in focus and shifts in their understanding that occurred through the research process as the three team members, with their different backgrounds, skills, and perspectives, attempted to generate "reliable" coding and then sought to understand and learn from the differences that could not readily be resolved through simple review and discussion.

Conclusion

Despite attempts to classify them, mixed methods studies are infinitely variable in their design. Equally variable are strategies used to integrate the data, methods, analyses, and conclusions in a study that might be defined as having adopted a mixed approach. Explicit and tacit tensions serve to foster division within teams and between methodological components of a study. Paradigms, methodologies, and methods are relevant to choices about the design of research and interpretation of research results, but they are not a deciding factor in how one should structure the report from research. Rather, in writing up a mixed methods study the substantive purpose of the study, reflected in its aims, objectives, and questions, can and should guide planning of the written product(s) from it, and the structure of sections within those products. Keeping this in focus will help to diffuse any tensions and will ensure that the knowledge and understanding that was gained through the research—the message being presented—is clear to the reader. Only when all relevant data are brought together to bear on any issue or question being discussed will the full value of multiple methods or the added benefit from integrating mixed methods become available to readers.

The process of writing is a process of analysis. As you work to structure your writing and to determine what evidence you have to support your claims, you will inevitably be sent back into your data, to think about them further, to "play" a little more, to reflect on what you are finding, until your message is coordinated and clear. This works to the benefit of your research outcomes and your publications from them.

Discussion Questions

1. Review several articles written using mixed methods in your discipline area and ask the following questions:

- What is the primary "take-home message" from each article?
- Is each article reporting an entire study or part of one? If the latter, how is that part contextualized?
- How is each article structured (what is the organizing principle used) to present its message?
- What integrating strategies have been employed to help convey the methods and results from the study (if any)?

2. Compare articles that are more or less successful in conveying their message:

- In what ways do they differ?
- How effectively do they communicate with the reader?

References

Asmar, C. (1999). Is there a gendered agenda in academia? The research experience of female and male PhD graduates in Australian universities. *Higher Education, 38,* 255–273.

Bazeley, P. (1998). Peer review and panel decisions in the assessment of Australian Research Council project grant applications: What counts in a highly competitive context? *Higher Education, 35,* 435–452.

Bazeley, P. (1999). Continuing research by PhD graduates. *Higher Education Quarterly, 53*(4), 333–352.

Bazeley, P. (2003). Defining "early career" in research. *Higher Education, 45*(3), 257–280.

Bazeley, P. (2009). Mixed methods data analysis. In S. Andrew & E. Halcomb (Eds.), *Mixed methods research for nursing and the health sciences* (pp. 84–118). Chichester, UK: Wiley-Blackwell.

Bazeley, P. (2010). Computer assisted integration of mixed methods data sources and analyses. In A. Tashakkori & C. Teddlie (Eds.), *SAGE Handbook of mixed methods research for the social and behavioral sciences* (pp. 431–467). Thousand Oaks, CA: Sage.

Bazeley, P. (2012). Integrative analysis strategies for mixed data sources. *American Behavioral Scientist, 56*(6), 814–828.

Bazeley, P. (2013). *Qualitative data analysis: Practical strategies.* London, England: Sage.

Bazeley, P., & Jackson, K. 2013. *Qualitative data analysis with NVivo.* London, England: Sage.

Bazeley, P., & Kemp, L. (2012). Mosaics, triangles, and DNA: Metaphors for integrated analysis in mixed methods research. *Journal of Mixed Methods Research, 6*(1), 55–72.

Bazeley, P., Kemp, L., Stevens, K., Asmar, C., Grbich, C., Marsh, H., & Bhathal, R. (1996). *Waiting in the wings: A study of early career academic researchers in Australia.* Canberra: Australian Government Publishing Service. Retrieved from www.researchsupport.com.au

Becher, T. (1987). Disciplinary discourse. *Studies in Higher Education, 12,* 261–274.

Blumstein, P., & Schwartz, P. (1983). *American couples.* New York, NY: Simon and Schuster.

Bowers, B., Cohen, L. W., Elliot, A., Grabowski, D. C., Fishman, N. W., Sharkey, S. S., . . . Kemper, P. (2013). Creating and supporting a mixed methods health services research team. *Health Services Research, 48*(6), 2157–2180.

Brannen, J. (2005). *Mixed methods research: A discussion paper.* NCRM Methods Review Papers NCRM/005. Southampton, UK: National Centre for Research Methods. Retrieved from http://eprints.ncrm.ac.uk/89/

Bryman, A. (2007). Barriers to integrating quantitative and qualitative research. *Journal of Mixed Methods Research, 1*(1), 8–22.

Creswell, J. W., & McCoy, B. R. (2011). The use of mixed methods thinking in documentary development. In S. N. Hesse-Biber (Ed.), *The handbook of emergent technologies in social research* (pp. 453–468). New York, NY: Oxford University Press.

Creswell, J. W., & Plano Clark, V. L. (2011). *Designing and conducting mixed methods research* (2nd ed.). Thousand Oaks, CA: Sage.

Creswell, J. W., & Tashakkori, A. (2007). Developing publishable mixed methods manuscripts. *Journal of Mixed Methods Research, 1*(2), 107–111.

Curry, L. A., O'Cathain, A., Plano Clark, V. L., Aroni, R., Fetters, M., & Berg, D. (2012). The role of group dynamics in mixed methods health sciences research teams. *Journal of Mixed Methods Research, 6*(1), 5–20.

Dahlberg, B., Wittink, M. N., & Gallo, J. J. (2010). Funding and publishing integrated studies. In A. Tashakkori & C. Teddlie (Eds.), *SAGE Handbook of mixed methods in social & behavioral research* (pp. 775–802). Thousand Oaks, CA: Sage.

Dockett, S., & Perry, B. (2004). Starting school: Perspectives of Australian children, parents and educators. *Journal of Early Childhood Research, 2*, 171–189.

Evans, B. C., Coon, D. W., & Ume, E. (2011). Use of theoretical frameworks as a pragmatic guide for mixed methods studies: A methodological necessity? *Journal of Mixed Methods Research, 5*(4), 276–292.

Festinger, L., Riecken, H. W., & Schachter, S. (1956). *When prophecy fails.* Minneaplois: University of Minnesota Press.

Freshwater, D. (2007). *Reading mixed methods research: Contexts for criticism. Journal of Mixed Methods Research, 1*(2), 134–146.

Frost, P. J., & Stablein, R. E. (1992). *Doing exemplary research.* Newbury Park, CA: Sage.

Grbich, C. (1998). The academic researcher: Socialisation in settings previously dominated by teaching. *Higher Education, 36*, 67–85.

Greene, J. C. (2007). *Mixed methods in social inquiry.* San Francisco, CA: Jossey-Bass.

Hall, S. J., Phillips, C. B., Dubois, L., Follett, N., & Pancaningtyas, N. (2010). Preventing falls, promoting health, engaging community: Evaluation report of the Greater Southern Area Health Service Physical Activity Leaders Network Tai Chi Program. Canberra, Australia: ANU Medical School. Retrieved from: www.anu.edu.au

Heider, K. G. (1988). The Rashomon effect: When ethnographers disagree. *American Anthropologist, 90*(1), 73–81.

Johnson, R. B., & Onweugbuzie, A. J. (2004). Mixed methods research: A research paradigm whose time has come. *Educational Researcher, 33*(7), 14–26.

Kelle, U. (2006). Combining qualitative and quantitative methods in research practice: Purposes and advantages. *Qualitative Research in Psychology, 3*(4), 293–311.

Lawrenz, F., & Huffman, D. (2002). The archipelago approach to mixed method evaluation. *American Journal of Evaluation, 23*(3), 331–338.

Lee, Y.-J., & Greene, J. (2007). The predictive validity of an ESL placement test: A mixed methods approach. *Journal of Mixed Methods Research, 1*(4), 366–389.

Leech, N. L. (2012). Writing mixed research reports. *American Behavioral Scientist, 56*(6), 866–881.

Lincoln, Y. S., & Denzin, N. K. (2011). Epilogue: Toward a refunctioned ethnography. In N. K. Denzin & Y. S. Lincoln (Eds.), *The SAGE handbook of qualitative research* (pp. 715–718). Thousand Oaks, CA: Sage.

Marsh, H. W., & Bazeley, P. (1999). Multiple evaluations of grant proposals by independent assessors: Confirmatory factor anaysis evaluations of reliability, validity, and structure. *Multivariate Behavioural Research, 34*(1), 1–30.

Maxwell, J. A. (2004). Causal explanation, qualitative research, and scientific inquiry in education. *Educational Researcher, 33*(2), 3–11.

Maxwell, J. A. (2012). *A realist approach for qualitative research.* Thousand Oaks, CA: Sage.

Maxwell, J. A., & Loomis, D. (2003). Mixed method design: An alternative approach. In A. Tashakkori & C. Teddlie (Eds.), *SAGE handbook of mixed methods in social & behavioral research* (pp. 241–271). Thousand Oaks, CA: Sage.

Maliski, S. L., Sarna, L., Evangelista, L., & Padilla, G. (2003). The aftermath of lung cancer: Balancing the good and bad. *Cancer Nursing, 26*(3), 237–244.

Mertens, D. M. (2010). *Research and evaluation in education and psychology* (3rd ed.). Thousand Oaks, CA: Sage.

Miles, M. B., & Huberman, A. M. (1994). *Qualitative data analysis: An expanded sourcebook.* Thousand Oaks, CA: Sage.

Moran-Ellis, J., Alexander, V. D., Cronin, A., Dickinson, M., Fielding, J., Sleney, J., & Thomas, H. (2006). Triangulation and integration: Processes, claims and implications. *Qualitative Research, 6*(1), 45–59.

Morse, J. M. (2007). Quantitative influences on the presentation of qualitative articles. *Qualitative Health Research, 17*(2), 147–148.

Morse, J. M., & Niehaus, L. (2009). *Mixed method design: Principles and procedures.* Walnut Creek, CA: Left Coast Press.

O'Cathain, A. (2009). Reporting mixed methods projects. In S. Andrew & E. Halcomb *Mixed methods research for nursing and the health sciences* (pp. 135–158). Chichester, UK: Wiley-Blackwell.

O'Cathain, A. (2010). Assessing the quality of mixed methods research. In A. Tashakkori & C. Teddlie (Eds.), *SAGE handbook of mixed methods in social & behavioral research* (pp. 531–555). Thousand Oaks, CA: Sage.

O'Cathain, A., Murphy, E., & Nicholl, J. (2007). Integration and publications as indicators of "yield" from mixed methods studies. *Journal of Mixed Methods Research, 1*(2), 147–163.

O'Cathain, A., Murphy, E., & Nicholl, J. (2008). Multidisciplinary, interdisciplinary or dysfunctional? Team working in mixed methods research. *Qualitative Health Research, 18*, 1574–1585.

Older Women's Network. (1993). Well-being for and by older women. Sydney: Author.

Rallis, S. F., & Rossman, G. B. (2003). Mixed methods in evaluation contexts: A pragmatic framework. In A. Tashakkori & C. Teddlie (Eds.), *SAGE handbook of mixed methods in social and behavioral research* (pp. 491–512). Thousand Oaks, CA: Sage.

Richardson, L. (1994). Writing: A method of inquiry. In N. K. Denzin & Y. S. Lincoln (Eds.), *The SAGE handbook of qualitative research* (pp. 516–529). Thousand Oaks, CA: Sage.

Sandelowski, M. (2003). Tables or tableaux? The challenges of writing and reading mixed methods studies. In A. Tashakkori & C. Teddlie (Eds.), *SAGE handbook of mixed methods in social & behavioral research* (pp. 321–350). Thousand Oaks, CA: Sage.

Seltzer-Kelly, D., Westwood, S. J., & Peña-Guzman, D. M. (2012). A methodological self-study of quantitizing: Negotiating meaning and revealing multiplicity. *Journal of Mixed Methods Research, 6*(4), 258–274.

Sharp, J. L., Mobley, C., Hammond, C., Withington, C., Drew, S., Stringfield, S., & Stipanovic, N. (2012). A mixed methods sampling methodology for a multisite case study. *Journal of Mixed Methods Research, 6*(1), 34–54.

Simons, L. (2007). Moving from collision to integration: Reflecting on the experience of mixed methods. *Journal of Research in Nursing, 12*(1), 73–83.

Smith, A. G., & Robbins, A. E. (1982). Structured ethnography: The study of parental involvement. *American Behavioral Scientist, 26*(1), 45–61.

Teddlie, C., & Tashakkori, A. (2009). *Foundations of mixed methods research.* Thousand Oaks, CA: Sage.

Teye, J. K. (2012). Benefits, challenges, and dynamism of positionalities associated with mixed methods research in developing countries: Evidence from Ghana. *Journal of Mixed Methods Research, 6*(4), 379–391.

Wolcott, H. F. (2002). Writing up qualitative research . . . better. *Qualitative Health Research, 12*, 91–103.

Funding for Mixed Methods Research: Sources and Strategies

Jennifer P. Wisdom *and* Michael D. Fetters

Abstract

This chapter describes strategies investigators can use to write compelling mixed methods research (MMR) proposals. The chapter discusses how to identify sources of research funding, including what is typically contained in announcements about funding opportunities and how to determine which funding opportunities are best to pursue. It outlines strategies to prepare a proposal for funding to conduct a mixed methods project, including creating a timeline, assembling a research team, writing the MMR project, preparing the budget and other materials, and obtaining feedback. Last, it describes the review process, because an understanding of how proposals are reviewed can greatly inform proposal writing. The chapter ends with a discussion of additional resources and future directions.

Key Words: research funding, budget, mixed methods research, MMR, writing, review process

Introduction

The need to increase understanding of the human condition and the environment is more important than ever. Public and private organizations around the world are funding research to improve health and education, understand basic science, and develop innovations. Mixed methods research (MMR) offers previously unavailable options for robustly assessing and articulating the research that can inform such decisions. While a recognition of the value of MMR for integrating perspectives on both quantitatively derived findings such as magnitude, associations, causality, and generalizations and qualitatively derived findings about what, how, and the nature of experiences of those involved has been achieved, more of this mixed, complex, integrated research needs to be funded. Indeed, without funding, the complex procedures required in a mixed methods investigation may not even be possible. Consequently, the purpose of this chapter is to describe strategies investigators can use to write compelling mixed

methods proposals based on lessons learned in our previous successful experiences.

There are several elements of securing funding for a mixed methods project. First, the applicant must be pursuing a research question that the funding agency, public or private, considers to merit investigation and is within the funding agency's scope of practice. Second, the question needs to be one that cannot be answered optimally or thoroughly with a quantitative or qualitative approach alone. Third, the proposal and supporting documentation must provide an eloquent and robust explication of both the need for as well as how the mixed methods procedures will provide an answer to the critical questions identified for the study. Fourth, the proposal should provide absolute clarity about what meticulous mixed-methods approaches the investigators will employ, the outcomes that will be achieved, and why the proposed project is the best way to address the research question.

This chapter provides an overview of sources and strategies for obtaining funding for mixed methods projects. First we discuss how to identify sources of research funding, including what is typically contained in announcements about funding opportunities and how to determine which funding opportunities are best to pursue. Next we discuss strategies to prepare a proposal for funding to conduct a mixed methods project, including creating a timeline, assembling a research team, drafting the MMR project, preparing the budget and other materials, and obtaining feedback. We then focus on the review process, as an understanding of how proposals are reviewed can inform proposal writing. The chapter ends with a discussion of additional resources and future directions.

First a few notes about this chapter: We refer to a particular set of mixed methods activities that is being submitted for funding as a "mixed methods project." This includes the possibility that the project is considered research or evaluation and that it may be composed of a single study or a series of studies. Similarly, we refer to the lead applicant for funding and the person who proposes to lead the mixed methods project as the "principal investigator" (PI). We acknowledge that it is possible to have multiple leaders of a study, but we use this term because proposals typically require a single point of contact who is designated the lead, even on studies that are co-led. We refer to others on the study as "investigators" to acknowledge that many mixed methods practitioners may not identify themselves as "researchers" or "evaluators." We also suggest that it is important for investigators who wish to obtain funding for their mixed methods projects to remain open to different conceptions of projects as research, evaluations, studies, or other terms to ensure the broadest possibility of successful funding. Ultimately, the goal is to obtain funding to complete a rigorous mixed methods project that will increase our understanding of an important phenomenon in the world that could not be as robustly understood using a qualitative or quantitative approach alone.

Identifying and Evaluating Sources of Research Funding

Numerous organizations provide funding for mixed methods projects. An assumption of this chapter is that the research team proposing the project will carefully consider the motivation and requirements of the funding organization in order to frame the MMR approach that will be proposed. Most important, the methods proposed will produce answers that address the problem proposed for the mixed methods investigation.

Sources of Funding

Institutions where investigators have affiliations may have funding opportunities. Many universities and other institutions frequently have small grants as seed funding for scholars to start new projects or collect pilot data for a larger project, or as bridge funding when scholars are between other sources of funding. These funds are typically small and require an application for funding. Institutions seek a return on investment, and the applicant often must provide a compelling case of plans for how the funds will be leveraged to acquire further funding.

As mixed methods is an emerging field, an application could qualify under new research efforts, nontraditional collaborations, interdisciplinary activity, or even software for analyses. For institutional applications, the novelty of the mixed methods approach and the specific kinds of pilot data that will be produced and how these will be compelling for future funding should be emphasized. For the mixed methods investigator, such funding affords the opportunity to test qualitative and quantitative data collection procedures, instruments, and analytics. If possible, developing strategies and examples for how integration will be accomplished should be tested and demonstrated through such projects.

Numerous *nonprofit organizations*, including independent philanthropic foundations (e.g., Gates Foundation, MacArthur Foundation), philanthropic foundations associated with corporations (e.g., Gerber Foundation), trade/service organizations (e.g., American Medical Association), and others may provide funding for conducting mixed methods projects. Funding applications to these organizations typically must closely hew to the mission or a specifically stated priority of the organization, which may not be research and which may provide a substantial service component. For example, the Social Sciences Research Council is an independent, nonprofit international organization founded in 1923. The Council's stated mission is to nurture new generations of social scientists, foster innovative research, and mobilize necessary knowledge on important public issues (http://www.ssrc.org/about/). The Social Sciences Research Council provides a succinct, eight-page document on tips for writing an effective research proposal that may have particular relevance for social science applications for funding to foundations (https://s3.amazonaws.com/ssrc-cdn1/crmuploads/new_publication_3/%7B7A9CB4F4-815F-DE11-BD80-001CC477EC70%7D.pdf).

In our experience, foundations often have very specific goals that they are seeking to accomplish and will be less likely to fund investigator ideas unless they are relevant to the foundation's funding priorities. The call for proposals from nonprofits may be more or less clear than calls for federal projects. It may be necessary to clarify with the funding agency both the degree to which a proposed project appeals to the foundation, as well as whether a mixed methods approach will acceptable. It is a good idea to stay in close contact with the project officer. If the foundation likes the work an investigator is doing, the odds are good that the foundation will make further investments through future funding. In a mixed methods application to such organizations, the applicant should make the case for using both qualitative and quantitative data collection strategies from the perspective of how the data will be linked and produce more robust results than by using just one data source.

State, provincial, federal, and multinational sources of funding vary widely by municipality. In the United States, for example, most funding for research and evaluation activities is provided at the federal level, with states and counties providing comparatively less funding. In other countries, regions or provinces may have significant funding opportunities. Many countries and multinational organizations have research organizations with easily searchable websites, such as Canada's National Research Council (http://www.nrc-cnrc.gc.ca/eng/index.html), the Australian Research Council (http://www.arc.gov.au), the European Commission on Research and Innovation (http://ec.europa.eu/research/index.cfm), the Qatar National Research Fund (http://www.qnrf.org/), and South Africa's National Research Foundation (http://www.nrf.ac.za). The US federal government has a free, consolidated search engine for funding opportunities across all US government sources (http://grants.gov).

Note that these sources of funding may provide very different support for applicants: institutional funding may be easier to obtain than external funding but is likely to be in smaller amounts. Institutional and government funding sources likely will provide some feedback about the proposal if it is not funded; nonprofit organizations likely will provide little or no feedback from the review process. In addition, there is a difference in institutional, nonprofit, and government sources' approaches to facilities and administrative costs, which are the indirect costs charged in addition to

the direct costs of conducting the work as a way to recoup the costs of conducting the work that cannot usually be charged to the project (e.g., rent, electricity). Nonprofit sources often pay lower indirect costs or none; and government sources likely will pay the maximum allowable indirect costs.

Locating funding opportunities is frequently a challenge for all investigators but especially for new investigators. Community of Science is a subscription service for educational institutions that allows access to the search engine Pivot. Pivot includes federal and foundation funding opportunities in a database searchable by keyword and by other characteristics (e.g., funding targeted toward students vs. professionals). In the United States, federal funding opportunities are catalogued at http://www.grants.gov. Foundation sources of funding are catalogued at http://www.foundationcenter.org; a subscription is required to access funding. University-affiliated investigators may obtain assistance in locating funding opportunities from their university research office or development office.

Evaluating Funding Opportunities

Although terminology may differ slightly by sponsor, funding opportunity announcements are likely to be characterized as requests for applications (RFAs), program announcements (PAs), or open calls for funding.

RFAs usually indicate there is a certain amount of funding set aside to fund proposals on a specific topic. These are often one-time solicitations that require investigators to respond to specific criteria within a specified amount of time. Since the funding agency has set aside funds, there is a potential advantage of applying for RFAs because the funding agency expects to expend all the funds through the grant cycle. Furthermore, as the funding agency provided a specific conceptual theme for consideration, the applicant must target the specific area of interest. The grant review committee will thus be comparing "apples to apples" by reviewing proposals within a very narrow topic. A potential downside is that the applicant may have only one opportunity for this submission, meaning that there may not be an option to revise and resubmit.

PAs indicate that the sponsor is embarking on a program of research and often includes multiple rounds of deadlines for proposals. The content area described in PAs is often much broader than in a RFA, as it indicates the sponsor would like to set up a series of projects that address the same conceptual theme. As in RFAs, the applicant's proposal in response to a PA will be compared on an apples-to-apples basis with other proposals since the funding organization has chosen a specific program of research. Applying for PAs early may provide a strategic advantage for funding because the first round is when the funding agency will begin establishing its portfolio of projects, and if not funded during the first round, there may be time to revise and resubmit. If applying after the PA has already been open for one or more rounds, the funding agency may become more selective as fills in "vacancies" in its portfolio.

Open calls for funding usually suggest the sponsor is open to solicitations at any time in a broad range of general themes or topics. In this case, it is useful to find out how often the review committee meets. While open calls give the applicant much more freedom in terms of the topic chosen, the downside can be that, when applying, it will not be necessarily clear if the funding agency or reviewers will have an interest in the particular topic submitted. In addition, open calls do not have set amounts for funding in any given cycle, and reviewers will be comparing apples to oranges, since the parameters and type of proposals submitted in any given funding cycle will be much more broad than those submitted to RFAs or PAs.

In addition to funding mechanisms specifically soliciting single research projects, other funding mechanisms can also provide opportunities for mixed methods investigators. For example, the US federal government supports several types of small business innovation research and technology transfer grant mechanisms to facilitate academic–private partnerships in creating and marketing new products or services; these mechanisms can incorporate mixed methods to test a new product or service. Training grants may be available to fund a program of training for an individual (e.g., a predoctoral fellowship) or to fund an institutional research training program (e.g., a program to train physician-scientists in public health) that can include training in mixed methods. Other funding mechanisms can be targeted to fund service projects (e.g., providing free legal services to the economically disadvantaged) or centers (which fund an administrative structure to facilitate multiple, integrated research projects with multiple investigators), many of which can include a MMR or evaluation component.

For all funding proposals, investigators should try to identify the kinds of proposals the sponsor has previously funded and whether the sponsor has funded mixed methods proposals. It is good practice to review funded proposals if available, as this helps inform what particular spin, or argument, will appeal to the sponsor and whether a particular topic is a good fit. Consultation with colleagues who have had previous experience with the funder could also yield useful insights about the funder. Alternatively, the funding agency may be willing to share a funded proposal. The US National Institutes of Health (NIH) website RePORT (Research Portfolio Online Reporting Tools, http://report.nih.gov/) offers information about previously funded projects such as abstracts, award amounts, PI contact information, and study results but not the application itself. The Robert Wood Johnson Foundation also lists all funded awards on its website (http://rwjf.org). Most funders do not make full proposals available online, but intrepid investigators can contact funded PIs and request a copy of their proposal. If the PI refuses, it is still possible to obtain additional information on federally funded proposals under the Freedom of Information Act (http://www.nih.gov/icd/od/foia/), although this can take months or longer.

Once some funding opportunity announcements have been identified, it is important to review them for relevance and applicability to the proposed question(s) the investigator wants to examine using a mixed methods project. A quick review of the purpose/topic of the funding announcement, who is eligible to apply, amount of funding, and due date can often rule out many opportunities as lacking relevance, applicability, scope, or preparation time. After this initial review, a more thorough review of the funding opportunity announcements can narrow down the opportunities to the ones most appropriate for research question(s) of the mixed methods project. Announcements typically contain the following components:

1. *A description of the types of proposals that are sought.*

This description can include a specification about the funder's mission or goals, a brief review of the phenomenon under study, and specific details about what the funder is seeking in proposals to the particular announcement. Some funding opportunity announcements also clarify what kinds of projects are specifically excluded from competition. Questions for investigators to consider include: Are the aims of the mixed methods project consistent with the stated aims of the funder? Would the proposed mixed methods project be consistent with what funders are seeking for the particular announcement? Is the proposed project of similar scope and complexity to what is being sought? If background information on the phenomena is provided, is that information consistent with how the proposed mixed methods project is framed, or could the proposed project be modified to be consistent with that background? Applicants can capitalize on their completed work to apply a new approach to a specific funder's interests. For example, a proposal initially focusing on identifying cultural differences in healthcare quality perceptions for cultural minorities in the United States was reframed by one of us (MF) to examine the primary cultural groups of interest in Qatar and was successfully funded (Hammoud et al., 2012).

The budget limits and expected time period for projects are key components of the scope of work the funder expects to be completed. An award of $5,000 over one year will support a very different project than an award of $200,000 over three years. Some grant opportunities expect "in kind" matching funds from the host institution. When applying for such funding, it is imperative to determine what the host institution is willing to cover in terms of investigator time and other support as specified internally. There may be limits on specific categories of expenditures that funding agencies will allow under their funding mechanism. Thus for in kind host institution support, it may be advantageous to seek matching funds for the category not eligible under the funding mechanism. Finally, investigators should consider the amount of work required for the application in relation to the amount to be awarded in the context of how much project work the award will actually support.

2. A statement of who is eligible to apply.

This typically clarifies which institutions are eligible to apply for the award. For example, the NIH typically indicates that eligible institutions include various types of institutions of higher education; nonprofit institutions; small businesses and other for-profit organizations; city, township, county, tribal, and state governments; school districts; housing authorities; foreign organizations; eligible federal agencies; and faith-based or community-based organizations. If the PI is affiliated with more than one type of eligible organization, he or she should discuss the pros and cons of applying from each organization to decide which would be best. For example, some funding opportunity announcements specifically favor or require community-based organizations as opposed to universities. There may also be a clarification about which individuals are qualified to be a PI on the project. Typically this statement indicates that individuals who have the knowledge, abilities, skills, and experience to be able to successfully complete the project, but there may be other requirements such as nationality or training level. It may be useful to indicate clearly in the proposal and/or the cover letter that the institution and PI are eligible to apply.

3. Specific guidance on the preparation of the application.

The instructions list specific forms to use; all components that should be included; what to include in the budget and how specifically the budget items need to be delineated and described; limitations on the font size, margins, and page limits; and other specifications. Although this guidance typically would not rule out an investigator's choice of funding opportunity, it is useful to review in case there are specific requirements that would need to be considered in deciding whether to move forward with it. For example, a funding opportunity may require or prohibit the inclusion of students in a training capacity, require signoff of the proposal by individuals to whom the investigator would need to arrange access, require the applicant institution to waive its rights to intellectual property created by the project, require or prohibit additional funds provided by the institution to support the project (called cost-matching or cost-sharing), or have budget specifications that are inconsistent with the investigator's current institutional practices. The investigator may wish to consider how logistical issues related to this guidance may impact his or her ability to complete the proposal in a timely manner.

Applicants must follow all directions, as a proposal that is otherwise completely meritorious based on the idea and content could be rejected up front for failure to comply with the application rules. If there are any aspects of the guidance for preparation that are unclear, the applicant should contact the funding agency for clarification. One of the most obvious but critical issues is submission of the funding materials on time. In the age of online submissions, it is not unusual for the funding agency site to have high traffic immediately prior to submission due dates. It is imperative to plan on submission with a time buffer to prevent missing the deadline.

4. *How applications will be evaluated.*

This is a key component of the funding opportunity announcement, as it clarifies to the investigator what the review committee and funders deem most important. In general, it is expected that the proposal is responsive to the specifications in the funding opportunity announcement. In the application, it is wise to state specifically how the proposal is responsive to eliminate any possible confusion. At the US NIH, general review criteria include significance, innovation, investigators, approach, and environment. The US National Science Foundation includes general review criteria of intellectual merit and broader impacts. With private funding agencies, details about the process may be less clear. Under such circumstances, contacting the project officer will be well worth the effort.

5. *Additional details.*

Many funding opportunity announcements indicate a point of contact whom applicants may contact with questions. At smaller organizations, this may be one person for all questions, and at larger organizations, program questions (e.g., about the science, service, or project) and budget questions are directed to different parties. In addition, larger organizations may require submission via the Internet, which may require a registration process. For example, in the United States, the NIH requires most proposals to be submitted via http://www.grants.gov, and the National Science Foundation requires proposals to be submitted via FastLane (https://fastlane.nsf.gov), both of which require separate registrations for the PI and the institution.

Determining a Good Fit Between Mixed Methods Projects and Funding Opportunities

In this section we provide some practical thoughts to keep in mind when choosing whether to pursue a specific funding opportunity.

WALK BEFORE YOU RUN

Investigators should consider how appropriate this opportunity is to their career stage. Although it is good to be ambitious, new investigators rarely are funded to lead center grants and might be more successful by starting with smaller projects and moving up to larger projects. Funding agencies are interested in investing in young investigators who will devote their careers to the funding agencies area of emphasis, and career development awards are particularly appropriate for new investigators. Career awards from both federal and private sources alike want young investigators to learn new skills, and incorporating planning specifically to bolster the applicants' qualitative or quantitative skills or integration for mixed methods may all be attractive options. Demonstrating success with smaller funds is important to funders who want to be assured that their investment is likely to result in a completed, impactful project. Funding organizations often support pilot projects because they want to support not only the specific project but also the applicant's success in a particular content area. Preliminary success by a young investigator will often lead to sustained and increased funding by the applicant on related topics of interest to the funding organization in the future.

SUCCESS BREEDS SUCCESS

Funding agencies will look to see if others have previously invested in a particular investigator. Thus the initial pilot funds are critical. Does the investigator show a history of successfully completed research projects, as demonstrated by timely completion of the grant, presentation of the results at scientific meetings, and production of research papers in respected scientific journals? If so, reviewers and funding organizations consider the initial success a harbinger of potential future success. The funding agency will be more likely to take a risk investing in an applicant and the project if the investigator has achieved success with a previous grant.

RIDE THE HORSE THE DIRECTION IT IS ALREADY RUNNING

It's important to consider the congruence between the applicant's proposed project and what the sponsor wants to fund to ensure it is a good fit. Investigators should consider how this project will fit within their overall career trajectory. For example, investigators in some departments of highly competitive research universities are often encouraged to focus primarily on research activities and are less encouraged to conduct evaluation activities. Other institutions prioritize evaluation activities or may provide equal weight to both. Consider the kind of support available during the proposal preparation period, including collaborators, mentors, and administrators, in light of one's own schedule and availability such as teaching/advising load, other ongoing projects, travel, and personal events. One should think carefully about the commitment to prioritize and finish a quality proposal in the time specified.

"STAND ON THE SHOULDERS OF GIANTS"

Junior investigators should find a senior investigator in the field of study who can be included on the application for funding if possible. For mixed methods proposals in particular that are complex and require teamwork, having a senior investigator who is a recognized "giant in the field" on the proposal, even if only as a consultant or for a minimum amount of time, can add significant credibility to the application. These individuals will not likely have a large amount of time to give to a proposal but can be great resources for addressing problems or issues that arise in the course of a mixed methods project. It is not critical, but such a person may develop as a mentor. If that it is the case, we recommend making specific mention of this on the proposal, particularly in the case of a junior applicant or those with less mixed methods experience.

Strategies for Preparing a Submission for Funding

The most successful and well-funded investigators are those who co-manage the science (or content portion of the project), logistics, and packaging of a proposal. The science or content portion of the project refers to the actual activities proposed in the project, including the study or evaluation itself, all background justification, project design, data collection and analysis, and proposed next steps. Although many investigators focus nearly all of their energy on this portion of the proposal, unless there is substantial assistance in the form of a proposal manager or astute research administrator, most investigators would be well served to also focus on logistics and packaging. Packaging refers to the process of how to "sell" the grant to the reviewers. Investigators who also pay attention to packaging the proposal and use *persuasive* writing to help increase its appeal have an advantage over those who do not.

Step 1: Assemble the Mixed Methods Project Team

First, put together the project team. Consider what expertise will be needed to "sell" the project to the reviewers and what expertise will be needed to do the work. Highlight how the disciplinary diversity of mixed methods teams can strengthen the proposal (Curry et al., 2012). Also be aware that individuals with disciplinary diversity may approach problems differently, so it would be useful to choose individuals who are committed to working through diverse ideas for the project and to working on a mixed methods project.

Team members with different roles have different names, which may vary by funding opportunity, country, and institution. The PI is typically the person responsible for all aspects of the project, including designing the study; conducting or overseeing the conduct of all study activities; ensuring that all activities are conducted in accordance with appropriate ethical standards; compliance with appropriate laws, regulations, and funder guidelines; and managing all financial, logistical, and administrative activities. If there is more than one lead on the study (usually two but no more than three), they can all be designated as co-PIs, although one will need to be designated as the lead for administrative purposes. Other key investigators who contribute substantially to the study are called co-investigators and include experts in content, methods, or study procedures. If co-investigators are not at the submitting institution, there often is a need for a contract (sometimes called a subcontract) to pay that person's salary or expenses. Consultants are typically individuals outside of one's home institution who provide a small amount of expert consultation, such as a few hours a year. Usually these are budgeted as a professional services contract. Graduate research assistants (graduate students who conduct work for the project) or postdoctoral scientists (individuals with a terminal degree who are obtaining advanced training and conducting work for the project) can also play critical roles on the project. Some funding mechanisms specifically prefer proposals that include mentoring of graduate students. Focusing the graduate student's work in mixed methods may be considered an innovative aspect of the grant and may help with the review.

Mixed methods projects almost invariably require working in teams. A mixed methods team should include individuals with content expertise about the topic; members with qualitative, quantitative, and mixed methods expertise; and an openness to integrating qualitative and quantitative findings (Creswell, Klassen, Plano Clark, & Smith, 2011). The leader of a mixed methods team should facilitate integration of each team member's expertise and continuously move the study toward successful completion. As an example of a multi-disciplinary mixed methods team, one of us (JW) participated in a team for a MMR project to understand how individuals with serious mental illness conceptualized recovery from mental illness and how health services could facilitate recovery that was led by a sociologist and included a psychiatrist, clinical psychologist, anthropologist, biostatistician, and advisory panel of patients who all contributed to the study (R01 MH62321, PI: Green; Green et al., 2008, 2013). Reviewers who understand the complexity of mixed methods projects will want to know how the qualitative and quantitative data analysts will work together to integrate the data, which can be described in a clear plan for project management. If there is limited space to describe the team in the scientific narrative, this can be discussed in the budget justification or study personnel as these sections usually do not have word limits.

Although there are growing numbers of investigators with expertise in mixed methods, it is still the case that investigators often are more expert or feel more comfortable in either quantitative or qualitative research techniques. This should be seen as an opportunity rather than a barrier; investigators should use the strengths of other study team members to complement each other. One mechanism for this is the "co-PI approach. Although this particular mechanism is often used to assist multidisciplinary efforts and partnerships, it is also an excellent opportunity for joining methodological forces, such as with a qualitative lead and a quantitative lead. It is important to be explicit about the governance and organizational structure of the partnership, including a communication plan and a formalized conflict resolution plan.

Step 2: Identify All Materials Required and Create a Timeline

Using the steps indicated earlier, review the funding opportunity announcement thoroughly and create a list of all materials that will be required for submission. This will likely include some or all of the following: cover letter, cover page, budget and budget justification, description of staff on the project and their qualifications, description of the environment where the project will be conducted, study narrative, documentation about ethical protection of human subjects, letters of support, appendices or other supporting materials, and institutional signatures. Working backward from the proposal due date, plan when items are due and who will complete them. Include time for mentors and administrators if appropriate to review items and provide feedback or approval. If administrative support is available, meet with them, discuss the timeline, divide duties, and schedule weekly meetings to check in. If administrative support is not available, provide a timeline that will allow the proposal team to complete all necessary activities two to four weeks prior to the deadline to obtain feedback.

New investigators often ask how long they should plan to prepare a proposal. Overall, it depends on a number of factors, including the PI's familiarity with the content area; his or her experience writing proposals in general and in working with his or her current institution; familiarity with the funder and this type of funding opportunity announcement; the research team's size, cohesion, interdisciplinarity, and experience; the availability of assistance to complete proposal; and competing requirements (e.g., teaching obligations). To ensure adequate time for preparation, we recommend that a new investigator spend six to nine months to ensure a high quality proposal. A typical application for an investigator with moderate familiarity with proposals, a relatively cohesive team, and some administrative support should budget about four to five months. Very experienced investigators with strong project and administrative teams can complete competitive proposals in about two to three months. When setting a timeline, adjust for these issues.

Step 3: Inform Relevant Parties About the Proposal and Solicit Assistance

Many funders require proposals to be submitted by the institution on behalf of the PI. Similarly, many institutions require investigators to obtain review and approval from their department chair, dean, or supervisor prior to submission. Identify who in the institution is required to review and approve and how much time they need to review materials. Also identify who in the institution is available to provide feedback and mentoring, and ensure that time for their review is included in the timeline. It is good practice to send an e-mail to all people on the team, including other investigators, administrators, people who need to review the proposal, and mentors that includes an announcement of the intent to submit a proposal in response to the specific funding opportunity announcement (include a link to the announcement) and a few key dates regarding when their assistance will be requested. Emergent, last-minute consultations should be avoided; timely notifications are the best way to start off on the right foot.

Step 4: Draft Project Summary

Most proposals require a summary of the proposed project in addition to the full narrative version. This summary can be called an abstract, concept paper, specific aims section, project summary, or something else, and funders may have specific requirements to include one or more of these as formal sections in the proposal. In general, an *abstract* is structured similarly to abstracts for journal articles and for a proposal describes the background, purpose statement, research questions, research methods, analytic techniques, and expected outcomes. Many funders require an abstract and have specific formatting requirements. A *concept paper* is generally a tool to share with co-investigators or the funding agency to obtain feedback. The US National Institute on Drug Abuse provides an outline for a concept paper that suggests including the grant purpose, problem/background, significance, research question(s), study design, analysis, and team (http://obssr.od.nih.gov/di2007/images/Research%20 Project%20Concept%20Paper.pdf). In the early stages of grant planning, project officers will often be willing to look at a concept paper and give the applicant feedback. Concept papers are generally not submitted with the application and are most often used to obtain feedback. The *specific aims section* required for most US NIH proposals is a one-page summary of the proposal that follows the same general format as an abstract and requires more specificity regarding the purpose statement, study aims, objectives, methods, and significance than an abstract or concept paper. The one-page specific aims section of a proposal should not be confused with the study's specific research questions or goals, which are often referred to as specific aims. The US NIH typically requires both an abstract and a specific aims section in the proposal. *Project summary* is a generic term that can refer to any of these specific structures or any structure that provides an overview of the proposed project. In this section, we use the term *project summary* to refer to any of these formats with the understanding that investigators will use the type of project summary appropriate to their proposal. If a funder requires a specific format to the project summary, it is useful to have the initial draft conform to those requirements.

The project summary is often the most difficult part of the study to create, because it becomes the outline for everything else in the study. A well-developed project summary will serve as an excellent first draft for the proposal. Take the time to get this right, and obtain feedback from mentors and collaborators. In our projects, we often go through multiple iterations of the project summary. Review the funding opportunity announcement guidelines for how the proposal will be evaluated and ensure the project summary addresses each area to the extent possible.

The initial portion of a project summary should provide some information about the nature of the problem that is being addressed and the need for the study. This section should be worded so that it addresses the priorities of the funder or funding opportunity. For example, since the US NIH places great emphasis on significance (e.g., does the project address an important problem?) and innovation (e.g., does the project propose to shift current practice by using novel concepts or approaches?), project summaries to those institutes should start with a statement about the significance of the problem and the proposal's innovative approach to addressing it.

For a mixed methods study, the research methods and analytic techniques portions of a project summary should clearly state that it is a mixed methods study, why mixed methods are most appropriate, specific study aims, the sources of qualitative and quantitative data, and integration techniques. In addition, project summaries should include a statement as to the impact and significance of the proposed study and its anticipated findings.

The project summary should clarify the particular objectives for resolution (also called the specific aims). Often individual aims will have exclusively a qualitative or quantitative focus, and one of the aims, often the final, will have a clear mixed methods aim. In the study of recovery from serious mental illness mentioned earlier (R01 MH62321, PI: Green; Green et al., 2008), three specific study aims were (a) to identify processes, factors, actions, and experiences that facilitate recovery (qualitative); (b) to describe participants' reports of how mental health care providers, and the mental health care system more generally, have facilitated their recovery (qualitative); and (c) to examine patterns in health plan service use (quantitative) to understand how volume and type of service relate to participants' reports of symptom levels, functioning, life difficulties, and life satisfaction (integrating qualitative and quantitative).

The methods section of the project summary should have a succinct discussion of the mixed methods design, including the timing of data collection; the specific methodological procedures for collecting the qualitative and quantitative data; and how the data will be analyzed, including how qualitative and quantitative data will be integrated, such as through comparing or transforming data. The concept paper should end with a clear statement of the expected outcomes of the project, including specific mention of what the qualitative and quantitative data collection of the mixed methods approach will lead to.

Once the draft of the project summary is complete, it provides an opportunity to contact the funder and request feedback on how appropriate this project is for the funding announcement and how to modify the proposal to ensure it is most responsive to what the funder is seeking. By getting all of the study aims, procedures, and outcomes on a single page, all members of a team can literally and figuratively be on the same page.

When the funding agency provides contact information, it is appropriate and often valuable to contact the sponsor to share a project summary (often a concept paper). Through contact with the funder, an applicant comes onto the "radar screen" of the funding agency. In a dialogue with the funder, the applicant can discern how the program of research does or does not fit with the funding agencies priorities. In event of a "poor fit," more often than not the applicant can modify the research objectives in a way that appeals to the funding agency. Early contact with a funding organization helps applicants develop a relationship with the funding organization. The advantage to the applicant is ensuring the ideas and approach proposed will be of interest to the funder. In addition, if the funding organization has spent time communicating with an applicant and the applicant's proposal becomes increasingly responsive through an ongoing dialogue, at some level the funder feels an investment in the applicant has occurred, and the funder wants the applicant's proposal to become successful. In addition, if the funding agency does not support mixed methods proposals, it is better to find out before investing in all the work of writing a full proposal.

An efficient approach to clarifying what should be in the project summary is to create a table or figure of the methods (e.g., Table 18.1) to guide the discussion. Once methods are fully developed in a figure or implementation matrix, the writing of the project summary and then the application involves increasingly detailed description of the procedures portrayed.

In an example of how a project summary can work with a team for a mixed methods study, one of us (MF) was invited to participate in a project involving a mixed methods evaluation of adaptive clinical trials. The purpose of the proposal was to identify effective ways to design and run adaptive clinical trials. Since clinical trials often require years to conduct, adaptive clinical trials may allow for new therapies to be evaluated more quickly and with fewer resources thereby making them available faster to the public. Adaptive clinical trials are unique as they can involve frequent interim analyses, predefined decision rules for adaptations, longitudinal modeling, response–adaptive randomization, dose response modeling, and extensive simulations of trial performance (Berry, 2011; Meurer et al., 2012). Because adaptive trials are still a newly developing approach to the conduct of clinical trials, they have not been completely accepted by the scientific community. In this project, the PIs sought to evaluate how the trial development process would work and to learn lessons for future efforts. An entire aim was devoted to the mixed methods evaluation (Meurer et al., 2012).

To develop the text relevant to the mixed methods evaluation aim, MF convened a conference call with the PIs to understand the procedures that would be involved in the adaptive trial development process. Based on a clear grasp of the proposed process, the investigators hammered out a table with data collection procedures. The features to be included were purpose, approach, data collection, and expected outcome (Table 18.1). The first draft of the table was completed after about a 90-minute conference call. This was then distributed for comment to the PIs and other co-investigators. In a subsequent call one week later, the table was refined, and all agreed on the specific aim and procedures. The overarching goal was to study the collaborative process itself using mixed methods, and the specific aim was finalized as "To identify and qualitatively characterize key steps and barriers related to the acceptance and implementation of adaptive clinical trials." MF then wrote the text for the proposal methodology based on the procedures outlined in the table. Since the proposed procedures were clearly delineated in the table, writing the assigned two pages allocated to this aim occurred efficiently

Table 18.1 Sample Table for Inclusion in Mixed Methods Research Proposal

Purpose	Approach	Data Collection	Expected Outcome
To understand the concerns and strategies of personnel participating in FTF meetings, both prior to initiation of design activities (pre-FTF-1) and after completion of substantial design activities (pre-FTF-4)	• VAS ratings of ACT features • Premeeting MFGIs with 3 expert panels: (1) NETT clinical leadership (2) NETT statistical leadership (3) Statisticians experienced in ACT design	• 7 VAS ratings per person on general ACT features (14 persons for 2 FTF meetings • $N = 6$ MFGIs (3 MFGIs prior to FTF-1 and 3 MFGIs prior to FTF-4)	• Quantitative assessments of 7 general ACT features to be examined pre/post-FTF meetings • Identify variations in views of experts regarding potential value, barriers, risks, and advantages of ACTs • Establish baseline views on ACTs to delineate how those views change after participating in design processes
To understand interactions that occur during FTF meetings with respect to ACT development	• Unstructured observations and audiorecordings during 4 FTF meetings to assess participant nonverbal reactions	• 32 hrs direct observation (8 hours per 4 FTF meetings)	• Process evaluation regarding constructive and unconstructive approaches to resolution of disagreements during the development of ACTs
To determine participants' assessments of each proposed ACT's strengths, weaknesses, and probability of success using both quantitative and qualitative measures	• Administer VAS-based assessments after the discussion of each proposed trial in all 4 FTF meetings • Written, short-answer, qualitative assessments at each FTF meeting by all participants	• 6 VAS ratings per person on each trial (14 persons and 2 trials per meeting for 4 meetings • $N = 72$ (18 per FTF meeting) per 4 trials	• Quantitative assessments of 6 ACT features per trial that will be compared with funding success • Assessment by all participating members regarding the design and meeting processes • Examination of degree that qualitative assessments support or conflict with VAS results
To identify the views of stakeholders external to the project	• Stakeholder Interviews including NIH and FDA personnel, patient advocates, and peer reviewers	• $N = 12$ semistructured telephone interviews of key informants in Year 1 and 2	• Stakeholders' knowledge and views regarding potential value, barriers, risks, and advantages of ACTs
To elicit assessments of participants on the ACT design process	• Summative evaluations, using individual interviews at end of 2 years	• $N = 12$ evaluations conducted in early Year 3	• Global assessments of the clinical trials design development process
To evaluate grant reviewer responses to submissions that include ACTs	• Summary statement ("pink sheets") document analysis of 4 trials submitted for funding	• $N = 4$ documents of around 6 pages each in Year 3	• Grant reviewers' knowledge and views regarding potential value, barriers, risks, and advantages of ACTs

Note. FTF = face to face; VAS = Visual Analog scale; ACT = adaptive clinical trial; MFGI = mini focus group interviews; NETT = neurological emergencies treatment Trials network; NIH = National Institutes of Health; FDA = US Food and Drug Administration.
Source. Adapted with permission from the grant proposal, "Adaptive Designs Accelerating Promising Trials Into Treatment" (ADAPT-IT), Co-PIs of the Adapt IT investigation, William G. Barsan, Donald A. Berry, and Roger J. Lewis, supported jointly by the National Institutes of Health Common Fund and the Food and Drug Administration, with funding administered by the National Institutes of Neurological Disorders and Stroke U01NS073476.

and the initial draft required few changes. Since the grant text was written based on the content of the table, there was complete concordance in the proposed procedures found in the table and the narrative. The project was funded, and reviewers commented positively on the methods. Under the heading of "Approach Strengths" one Reviewer 1 wrote, "The mixed approach will allow a good assessment of the process." Reviewer 3 wrote, "As a part of the second aim, investigators will identify and characterize the key steps and obstacles related to the acceptance and implementation of adaptive clinical trials." These comments speak to having conveyed through the table and narrative a concise explanation of the mixed methods approach.

As illustrated in Table 18.1, full details of the procedures are not needed at the project summary stage. But the specific procedures proposed can include sufficient information to see what will be done, how many subjects will be recruited, and what the expected outcomes of the research will be. During the proposal writing phase, a comment section can be added to the table as a last column to include memos about information to check, threats to validity, and so on. When submitting the proposal, the applicant may choose to leave the table in or take it out depending on the content.

Step 5: Plan and Prepare Budget/Budget Justification and Review Other Logistics

Once the abstract/specific aims and team are complete and have been vetted through several iterations for refinement, investigators should turn attention to the logistics of what will need to be submitted in the proposal other than the narrative. Follow the funding opportunity announcement's instructions to prepare the budget (usually a spreadsheet or chart of charges for personnel, travel, supplies/equipment, payments to participants, software, or other expenses) and budget justification (a narrative document that describes each event in detail and justifies its expense for the project). For example, a budget line item could indicate investigator Juana Ortega, her annual salary, the percentage effort (e.g., 20% of her time), the amount charged to the study (multiplying the annual or academic year salary by the percentage effort), and any fringe costs associated with salary for the institution (many institutions charge a percentage of salary as fringe to cover insurances and other fringe benefits). Note that since budget justifications may not have page limits, it may be possible to elaborate on the methods in this section. A hypothetical narrative budget justification might state

Juana Ortega, PhD, Assistant Professor of Psychology (20%). Dr. Ortega has extensive expertise in qualitative analysis for [the content area of the study]. Under the direction of the PI, Dr. Ortega will train staff and direct qualitative data collection and analysis, including leading the collaborative preparation of the interview guides, training staff on interviewing techniques, reviewing completed interviews with staff for quality control, supervising data entry into qualitative software, training staff on qualitative data analysis, leading the collaborative preparation of the code list, supervising the coding process to ensure adequate reliability, and leading the collaborative interpretation of qualitative findings. She will also participate in qualitative and quantitative data integration and manuscript preparation.

Costs associated with activities in addition to personnel should be similarly justified. Some examples are as follows:

Compensation for interview participants. We will compensate youth and parents for their time for interviews at baseline (Time 1), discharge from treatment (Time 2), and 3 months post-discharge (Time 3). For youth, we will pay $20 for the Time 1 interview and $40 each for Time 2 and Time 3 interviews, for a total of $100/youth (See table 3 below). For parents, we also will pay $20 for Time 1, $40 for Time 2, and $40 for Time 3 interviews ($140 \times \$100 = \$14,000$). A higher payment for the second and third interview will encourage participation in the follow-up interview.

Because this example is somewhat confusing, it would be appropriate to include a table (Table 18.2) that clarifies what is being proposed.

Transcription. Transcription services to transcribe and clean data are required for the interviews conducted with adolescents and their parents. Transcription and cleaning required for 20 one-hour interviews at $60 per interview hour = 20 hrs $\times$ $60/hr = $1,200.

Urinalysis Cups. We also request urinalysis cups from Verian to conduct drug testing for $N = 200$ youth follow-up interviews; OnTrack test cups are $324.50 for a box of 25. We plan to order 9 boxes in Year 3 only plus shipping = $3,000.

Many institutions charge additional costs that need to be included in budgets. For example,

Table 18.2 Sample Table for Participant Compensation

	Number of Time 1 Youth ($N = 140$) and Parent ($N = 140$) Interviews at $20 Each	Number of Time 2 and Time 3 Youth and Parent Interviews at $40 Each	Amount
Y1	40	0	$800
Y2	80	120	$6,400
Y3	80	160	$8,000
Y4	80	160	$8,000
Y5	0	120	$4,800
Total	280	560	$28,000

facilities and administrative costs are charged in addition to the direct costs of conducting the work as a way to recoup the costs that cannot usually be directly charged to a single project (e.g., rent, electricity, chairs). Institutional costs for fringe benefits (e.g., health insurance, disability insurance) are calculated as a percentage of salary. Check with the research office to ensure these are calculated correctly. It is normal to revise the budget multiple times during the process of drafting the proposal. Once the budget is finalized, remember to return to the budget justification to ensure it matches the final budget numbers.

In addition to the budget, this is the time to ensure all letters of support are drafted and sent to individuals for their review and signature; subcontracts are finalized and sent out for signatures; cost sharing is approved (if applicable); and all other sections are reviewed and either drafted, prepared, or put on hold for attention later. This is also a good time to identify any additional details about the application process, such as which review group should be targeted. Priority at this time should go to tasks that require other people's review, signature, or approval because they tend to take the most time.

Step 6: Finalize the Narrative

Once the logistics have been reviewed and given a push toward completion, it is time to focus on the completion of narrative. In all research proposals, applicants are faced with the task of explaining a problem, proposing procedures to address the problem, and writing about relevant methods in a

sufficiently succinct way to convince reviewers that the proposal merits funding. Mixed methods studies are often complex because they use both qualitative and quantitative methods. Moreover, the applicant needs to illustrate how the methods will be integrated. A figure of the overall study can provide the overall procedures and expected outcomes.

Excellent guidelines for conceptualizing a mixed methods study are available, including mixed methods books (e.g., Creswell & Plano Clark, 2007; Teddlie & Tashakkori, 2009), articles, and chapters (e.g., Morse, 2010; Nastasi, Hitchcock, & Brown, 2010). The NIH also offers a resource on best practices for MMR in the health sciences (http://obssr.od.nih.gov/mixed_methods_research/). The NIH guide includes a list of concepts to consider when writing mixed methods applications, which include (a) introducing MMR and study designs, (b) providing detailed description and justification for the rigor of both the quantitative and qualitative data collection and analysis plans, (c) explicitly describing how quantitative and qualitative findings will be integrated, (d) describing potential methodological issues and challenges that may arise during the study and how they will be addressed, and (e) including a timeline for study activities.

With regard to methodological rigor, investigators should remember that reviewers are likely to be quantitative *or* qualitative experts. This emphasizes the need for the proposal to address rigor in a way that satisfies each of those experts as well as meeting the standards for mixed methods studies. In addition, investigators must tailor the discussion about rigor to include the level of detail expected by the sponsor and reviewers and to fit into the page limits; a highly technical discussion about rigor appropriate for a methodological paper will usually be inappropriately long in a research proposal. In general, quantitative portions of mixed methods studies rely on quality criteria such as internal validity, generalizability, and reliability (Campbell 1957; Campbell & Stanley 1963), and qualitative portions of mixed methods studies have roughly comparable quality criteria of credibility, transferability, and dependability (Guba & Lincoln, 1989; Maxwell, 2005; Miles, Huberman, & Saldaña, 2014; Pope & Mays, 2006). Additionally, to illustrate methodological rigor in MMR, proposals should describe how integration will occur in the design, methods, and analytical and interpretation levels (Fetters, Curry, & Creswell 2013). Mixed methods proposals should also address (a) the priority of methods (primarily quantitative, primarily qualitative, or equal priority), (b) the purpose of mixing methods (e.g., triangulation, complementarity, initiation, development, or expansion), (c) the sequence of methods (qualitative first, quantitative first, or simultaneous), (d) the stage of integration of both types of data (e.g., data collection, analysis, interpretation), (e) how qualitative and quantitative components were integrated, (f) the limitations of design, (g) areas of consistency between qualitative and quantitative components, and (h) areas of inconsistency between components (O'Cathain, 2010; O'Cathain, Murphy, & Nicholl, 2007; Wisdom, Cavaleri, Onwuegbuzie, & Green, 2011). Additional information on conceptualizing and writing about rigor in mixed methods studies can be found in Creswell et al. (2011), Creswell and Plano Clark (2007), Teddlie and Tashakkori (2009), and Wisdom et al. (2011).

An example of the process for developing the narrative of a mixed methods proposal, Nease and colleagues (Application 2 R42 CA128117-02, http://fundedresearch.cancer.gov/nciportfolio/search/details?action=abstract&grantNum=2R42CA128117-02&grantID=7908290&grtSCDC=FY%202010&absID=7908290&absSCDC=CURRENT) developed a mixed methods Phase II Small Business Technology Transfer (STTR) proposal titled "Chronic Disease Management System." In the United States, STTR proposals are designed to support research development collaboration between small businesses and research institutions. Investigators first apply for Phase I funding for proof of concept. Highly successful investigators can then apply for the much more competitive and larger in scope and dollars Phase II award. Having successfully completed the Phase I grant, the purpose of this Phase II STTR proposal was to complete the development of an electronic medical record for primary care that would prompt and remind clinicians at the point of care about specific preventive services the patient in the office is eligible to receive. For this mixed methods proposal, the authors developed a figure for inclusion in research application (Figure 18.1). This project received an excellent score and was funded. In the reviewers' comments to the applicant, one reviewer indicated as a strength of the research methods that the "'Agile Development' methodology emphasizes ongoing dialogue between developers and end users [and] iterative development and short, focused stages of development," a concept that is visualized in Figure 18.1. Another reviewer commented

on the design both when addressing the proposed study's impact ("Solid development design based upon solid plan for evaluation and theoretically based principles of dissemination of innovation") and complementing the investigators on their clarity of thinking ("[The figures] were quite helpful and the case illustration was very effective in showing the difference between what you propose and what is available"). Further illustrating the savvy of reviewers, in the "Approach Weaknesses" section, reviewer 3 also noted as a weakness, "Qualitative and mixed methods analysis plans are not detailed. How will trustworthiness be assured? Will qualitative or quantitative data be foremost or are they equal? Will they be collected at the same time or sequentially? Will the mixed methods analysis be throughout or at the end?" These comments highlight further the need for clarity, particularly with regard to the mixed methods analysis.

Reviewers of mixed methods projects will expect robust procedures for the qualitative, quantitative, and mixed methods procedures. There are two facets to making a robust mixed methods proposal. First, the questions, specific aims, design, data collection, and analysis procedures all need to be appropriate to the research question. In our view, a second component of a robust proposal is the need to write with clarity. In our experience on review panels, it is not unusual to have discrepant descriptions of procedures or recruitment targets. Reviewers easily become frustrated when there are conflicting accounts of what the applicant is proposing to do. Consider using the funding criteria (e.g., significance, innovation) as headings and ensure the review criteria are addressed directly. Writing with clarity provides elegance to the proposal that reviewers will appreciate.

Excellent guidelines for conceptualizing a mixed methods study are also available (e.g., Creswell & Plano Clark, 2011; Morse, 2010; Nastasi, Hitchcock & Brown, 2010; Teddlie & Tashakkori, 2009). The NIH also offers a resource on best practices for MMR in the health sciences: (http://obssr.od.nih.gov/mixed_methods_research/).

The ultimate goals of research are to create knowledge and see the translation of that knowledge into improving understanding, practice, or the world. Mixed methods proposals should clarify what the project is seeking to produce, discover, or contribute to and how mixed methods can specifically contribute to the proposed products and outcomes. For example, on a community intervention

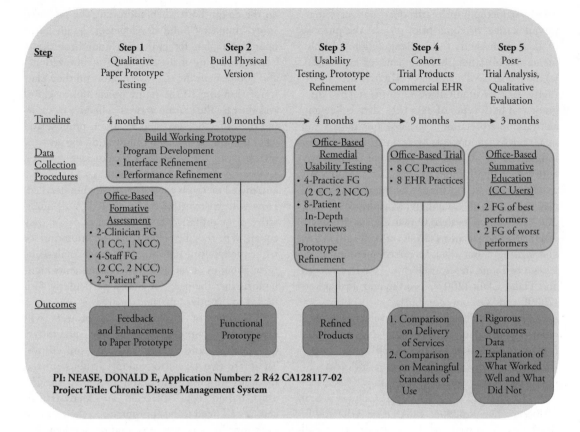

Fig. 18.1 Sample figure for inclusion in mixed methods research proposal.

Used with permission from the grant proposal, "Chronic Disease Management System, PI, Donald E. Nease, that was approved by the National Cancer Institute, Grant 2 R42 CA128117-02.

project, an applicant can explain that qualitative data not only assist the investigator in better understanding the quantitative results but also can be an essential tool for effectively communicating the findings to individuals who may more easily understand or resonate with vignettes versus probability values. Including a section in the proposal that clarifies the proposed products would clarify the study team's thoughtfulness and thoroughness in thinking through the project. For example, in one of our (JW) proposals, we provided the following section describing proposed products:

> The primary manuscripts will evaluate the impact of the intervention on adolescent retention in substance abuse treatment, including a case-mix analysis of adolescent and treatment agency variables. Secondary manuscripts will assess the association between treatment agency management practices and agency characteristics, variables associated with adolescent recovery from substance abuse, and adolescent and parent efforts to maintain

recovery. We will provide summaries of findings to study participants and participating treatment agencies in a "Town Hall" type meeting. We will also disseminate research findings widely to reach both researchers and policy makers nationwide. (R01 DA029745-01A1, p. 88)

Mixed methods can be an effective mechanism to assess the impact of randomized controlled trials (RCTs; Creswell, Fetters, Plano Clark, & Morales, 2009). Due to the rigorous and often constrained nature of RCTs, integration of qualitative approaches can provide rich information about the effects and unexpected outcomes of research that is often produced under heavily formatted designs. Creswell et al. suggest using the strengths of qualitative assessment before, during, and after the experimental intervention. Qualitative data before the trial begins can be instrumental in developing the design and data collection tools and from a pragmatic standpoint, facilitating the recruitment of participants. Qualitative data collection during the trial can help clarify the barriers and facilitators of the intervention and ensure that there is an adequate level of adherence to the implementation of the protocol. Qualitative data after an experiment can help to better elucidate the intervention effects. Grissmer, Subotnik, and Orland (2009) suggest that the examination of quantitative and qualitative data in RCTs can be helpful to explore future directions and hypotheses in subsequent RCT studies. The use of qualitative data and vignettes in the diffusion of RCT results can be especially helpful when communicating outcomes with the community, media, and policymakers.

When an applicant is finishing the narrative, he or she should read back through what has been written and consider how the proposal will look to a reviewer. Consider visual appeal: do not make the proposal a wall of words that will be difficult to read; instead, use headings and tables/figures to break up the text. Include white space. Use persuasive, vivid writing to tell a story and pull the reviewer in. Check that there is no jargon and few if any abbreviations. Applicants should frame and package a proposal differently for reviewers who are all top scientists in the field than for reviewers who are community members. Target the proposal to the funder's criteria and make it easy for the reviewers to write up their review indicating how the proposal excels in each criterion.

Step 7: Obtain Feedback

It is important, especially for new investigators, to obtain feedback on the abstract/specific aims and narrative. Coordinate with co-investigators at the beginning of the proposal process to identify time points at which they will provide feedback. At a minimum, co-investigators should provide feedback on the project summary stage and the draft narrative. Additional mentors who can provide feedback include consultants on the study and other individuals in the institution who are not on the study (such as the director of research or department chair). The institution's research office may be able to provide recommendations for outside readers of the application. Note that individuals who are have conflicts of interest or bias toward the investigator or the project (an investigator who participated in the development of the current proposal or who collaborated on a manuscript or grant with anyone on the project team within, e.g., the past five years) will likely not be allowed to review the application for the scientific review. PIs should ask co-investigators and mentors to focus on specific areas within their expertise. For example, it would make sense to ask the content expert to provide particular attention on the framing of the background and preliminary studies and to assess whether the project is significant and innovative given the state of the field. Ask the methods expert to review the methods carefully for any areas of weakness and ask the department chair or other mentor who may have slightly less familiarity with the particular topic to get a feel for how well the project "sells" and how packaging can be improved to ensure reviewers are delighted.

Step 8: Finalize Proposal and Submit

While the narrative is reviewed by co-investigators and mentors, one should reexamine all logistics. Finalize all budget information, the cover letter, forms, letters of support, description of the environment, human subjects' protection, and any other requirements. Closely review the abstract, specific aims, and narrative to ensure they are all consistent. Ensure the budget and budget justification are consistent and in line with the activities proposed in the narrative. Conduct a final review for packaging to ensure all materials, to the extent possible, are cleanly and crisply presented. Incorporate any last changes to the narrative and prepare for submission.

Institutions have different requirements for submission, ranging from little review and oversight to all-paper routing and approval to all-electronic routing and approval processes. Be aware that all processes can sometimes be delayed. If new to the process, ask a seasoned colleague about how the logistics work locally.

Common Mistakes

Common mistakes with proposals include the following:

• An underdeveloped or incomplete mixed methods plan, especially the integration component, due to a lack of qualitative and quantitative expertise in reviewing the proposal.

• Inadequate justification for: the significance of the proposed project, the expertise of the team members, the budget, the sample selection or sample size, or the use of mixed methods.

• Not following instructions, with mistakes such as going over page limits, using the wrong font size, or failing to include items specifically requested in the funding opportunity announcement.

• Inadequate description or justification for the analytic methods. This includes not sufficiently describing the integration of qualitative and quantitative methods and data and not stating one's expected results.

• The project is more than can feasibly be done on the specified budget, in the specified time frame, or by this investigative team. Reviewers often refer to projects that do not seem feasible as "overly ambitious."

The Review Process

Review committees are designed and members selected to ensure that proposals are selected that meet the sponsor's criteria, whether that is research rigor, geographic distribution, innovativeness of the project, or a combination of these and other criteria. Once proposals are submitted, the sponsor typically reviews proposals for completeness and will identify critical content and methodology from proposals to determine selection of the review committee. Many sponsors want to ensure that a variety of reviewers evaluates each proposal, which can include a content expert, a methodological expert (including a mixed methods, qualitative, and/or quantitative expert), and other types of experts (such as experts on the population under study or other aspect of the studies). For example, reviewers selected to evaluate a proposal on a mixed methods evaluation of adolescent substance abuse treatment intervention would most likely include experts on adolescent substance abuse, dissemination and implementation of treatment interventions, and mixed methods and could also include experts on quantitative methods, qualitative methods, economic analyses, adolescent development, epidemiology, or other topics depending on the nature of the study. Once appropriate reviewers are identified and vetted for potential conflicts of interest, reviewers are assigned proposals and review them prior to the committee meeting. Typically sponsors indicate the format in which they would like the review to be provided. For example, NIH currently has general review criteria and templates for providing written reviews (available at http://grants.nih.gov/grants/peer/reviewer_guidelines.htm).

At the review meeting, typically each proposal is given a short amount of time for the primary reviewer to present comments, other reviewers to provide additional comments, and the entire review committee to ask questions and determine scientific merit of the proposal. In some venues, not all proposals are reviewed. At the US NIH, the review committee members first review proposals individually and assign each proposal a numerical score that reflects its scientific merit. When the committee convenes, the first step is to remove proposals not considered fundable (typically proposals in the lower half of scores), though the committee will sometimes also review a proposal a committee member deems worth reviewing even if it falls below the numerical cutoff line. In considering the scientific merit, reviewers may also consider the experience and expertise of the PI and project team, the feasibility of the project, and the institutional environment or community facilities where the project will be conducted. Some funders have very strict guidelines for numerically ranking proposals' merit; others have a more informal discussion of all proposals. A video describing how the review process works at the NIH is available online at http://www.youtube.com/watch?v=fBDxI6l4dOA.

Participating as a Reviewer

Taking part in a review committee can provide unique insights that are likely to pay strong dividends in writing the next grant. We have both participated in numerous review committees, including both US federal research sponsors (e.g., NIH, Centers for Disease Control and Prevention) and foundation and local sponsors. Benefits to participating in review committees include learning about cutting-edge research and where the field is headed, understanding how ways of framing proposals and elucidating methods are perceived by reviewers, and identifying colleagues who may be good collaborators (as well as provide an opportunity for a quick insight into their character in how they act during the meeting).

Examples of the Review Process

Saint Arnault and Fetters (2011) described how they obtained R01 funding from the NIH to investigate how the symptom and illness experience, cultural interpretations and evaluations, and social structural factors interact to influence help seeking among first-generation Japanese women. The study elucidated clear specific aims to

(a) examine the demographics, symptom experiences, and sociocultural factors that explain help-seeking strategies used by Japanese women recruited from community-based, primary care and mental health treatment sites; (b) describe the ethnographic and psychiatric profiles of an expansion subsample of highly distressed women; and (c) compare ethnographic and psychiatric profiles. (p. 313).

The authors received funding on the first submission (relatively rare) and discussed aspects of the proposal that contributed to its being funded, including the following: (a) stating research questions that required mixed methods to answer, (b) presenting a clear theoretical framework, (c) articulating an innovative research design that highlighted the need for both qualitative and quantitative methods and integrated both types of data in meaningful ways, and (d) using a random sample and large sample size, which increased transferability of the research.

Summary and Future Directions

Evidence from the US and the UK demonstrate an increase in funding mixed methods studies (O'Cathain et al., 2007; Plano Clark, 2010). Writing mixed methods proposals that are compelling, clear, and ultimately funded is a key method to improving the reputation of mixed methods as a rigorous methodology. This chapter identified sources of research funding, strategies to prepare a proposal for funding to conduct a mixed methods project, and the review process in order to assist mixed methods investigators with developing their own proposals.

Mixed methods research has a short but vivid history (Johnson & Gray, 2010) and continues to contribute to the scientific endeavor toward understanding our world. Mixed methods practitioners are uniquely suited to contribute to translating science to the public. The collection of multiple types of data could contribute to increased public awareness of science, particularly for projects with substantial social importance. As mixed methods researchers continue to engage in the public dialogue about science—by writing strong proposals that are funded and conducting strong funded research—they affirm the utility of mixed methods as a rigorous methodology.

Acknowledgments

We extend their appreciation for the sharing of figures and comments of grant reviews to (a) Donald E. Nease, PI of the Chronic Disease Management Systems Grant funded by the National Cancer Institute Grant (2 R42 CA128117-02); (b) the co-PIs of the Adapt IT investigation, William G. Barsan, Donald A. Berry, and Roger J. Lewis, as well as the full research team of the Adaptive Designs Accelerating Promising Trials Into Treatment (ADAPT-IT) that was supported jointly by the NIH Common Fund and the Food and Drug Administration, with funding administered by the National Institutes of Neurological Disorders and Stroke (U01NS073476); and (c) Carla A. Green, PI of the Study of Transitions and Recovery Strategies funded by the National Institute of Mental Health (R01 MH062321).

Discussion Questions

1. How could you identify agencies that fund MMR in your area of study?

2. How would you explain your research purpose in terms appropriate to the funder's needs (lay terms vs. more scientific)?

3. What would be the best way to explain the order of your qualitative and quantitative data collection, and how you will integrate the data?

4. List strategies to organize your work on a proposal to ensure there is time for internal review and to meet deadlines.

Suggested Websites

http://obssr.od.nih.gov/mixed_methods_ research/
National Institutes of Health resource on Best Practices for Mixed Methods Research in the Health Sciences website.

https://s3.amazonaws.com/ssrc-cdn1/crmu ploads/new_publication_3/%7B7A9CB4F4-8 15F-DE11-BD80-001CC477EC70%7D.pdf
Social Sciences Research Council website.

References

Berry, D. A. 2011. Adaptive clinical trials: The promise and the caution. *Journal of Clinical Oncology, 29*(6), 606–609.

Campbell, D. T. (1957). Factors relevant to the validity of experiments in social set- tings. *Psychological Bulletin, 54,* 297–312.

Campbell, D. T., & Stanley, J. C. (1963). *Experimental and quasi-experimental designs for research.* Chicago, IL: Rand McNally.

Creswell, J. W., Fetters, M. D., Plano Clark, V. L., & Morales, A. (2009). Mixed methods intervention trials. In S. Andrew & E. J. Halcomb (Eds.), *Mixed methods research for nursing and the health sciences* (pp. 161–180). West Sussex, UK: Blackwell.

Creswell, J. W., Klassen, A. C., Plano Clark, V. L., & Smith, K. C. (2011). *Best practices for mixed methods research in the health sciences.* Bethesda, MD: National Institutes of Health. Retrieved from http://obssr.od.nih.gov/mixed_methods_research

Creswell, J. W., & Plano Clark, V. L. (2007). *Designing and conducting mixed methods research.* Thousand Oaks, CA: Sage.

Curry, L. A., O'Cathain, A., Plano Clark, V. L., Aroni, R., Fetters, M., & Berg, D. (2012). The role of group dynamics in mixed methods health sciences research teams. *Journal of Mixed Methods Research*, *6*(1), 5–20.

Fetters, M. D., Curry, L. A., & Creswell, J. W. (2013). Achieving integration in mixed methods designs—principles and practices. *Health Services Research*, *48*(6 Pt 2), 2134–2156. Retrieved from http://onlinelibrary.wiley.com/doi/10.1111/1475-6773.12117/abstract;jsessionid=2FC07B370623A4FE8F783D5938346F1C.f02t02

Green, C. A., Polen, M. R., Janoff, S. L., Castleton, D. K., Wisdom, J. P., Vuckovic, N., . . . Oken, S. L. (2008). Understanding how clinician–patient relationships and relational continuity of care affect recovery from serious mental illness: STARS study results. *Psychiatric Rehabilitation Journal*, *32*(1), 9–22.

Green, C. A., Perrin, N. A., Leo, M. C., Janoff, S. L., Yarborough, B. H., & Paulson, R. I. (2013). Recovery from serious mental illness: Trajectories, characteristics, and the role of mental health care. *Psychiatric Services*, *64*(12), 1203–1210.

Grissmer, D. W., Subotnik, R. F., & Orland, M. (2009). *A guide to incorporating multiple methods in randomized controlled trials to assess intervention effects*. Washington, DC: American Psychological Association.

Guba, E. G., & Lincoln, Y. S. (1989). *Fourth generation evaluation*. Newbury Park, CA: Sage.

Hammoud, M. M., Elnashar, M., Abdelrahim, H., Khidir, A., Elliott, H. A. K., Killawi, A., . . . Fetters, M. D. (2012). Challenges and opportunities of US and Arab collaborations in health services research: A case study from Qatar. *Global Journal of Health Science*, *4*(6), 148–159.

Johnson, R. B., & Gray, R. (2010). A history of philosophical and theoretical issues for mixed methods research. *SAGE handbook of mixed methods in social & behavioral research* (2nd ed., pp. 69–94). Los Angeles, CA: Sage.

Maxwell, J. A. (2005). *Qualitative research design: An interactive approach* (2nd ed.). Newbury Park, CA: Sage.

Meurer, W. J., Lewis, R. J., Tagle, D., Fetters, M., Legocki, L., Berry, S., . . . Barsan, W. G. (2012). An overview of the Adaptive Designs Accelerating Promising Trials Into Treatments (ADAPT_IT) project. *Annals of Emergency Medicine*, *60*(4), 451–457.

Miles, M. B., Huberman, A. M., & Saldaña, J. (2014). *Qualitative data analysis: A methods sourcebook* (3rd ed.). Thousand Oaks, CA: Sage.

Morse, J. M. (2010). Procedures and practice of mixed method design: Maintaining control, rigor, and complexity. In A. Tashakorri & C. Teddlie (Eds.), *SAGE handbook of mixed methods in social & behavioral research* (2nd ed., pp. 339–352). Thousand Oaks, CA: Sage.

Nastasi, B. K., Hitchcock, J. H., & Brown, L. M. (2010). An inclusive framework for conceptualizing mixed methods design typologies: Moving toward fully integrated synergistic research models. In A. Tashakorri & C. Teddlie (Eds.), *SAGE handbook of mixed methods in social & behavioral research* (2nd ed., pp. 305–338). Thousand Oaks, CA: Sage.

O'Cathain, A. (2010). Assessing the quality of mixed methods research: Toward a comprehensive framework." In A. Tashakorri & C. Teddlie (Eds.), SAGE handbook of mixed methods in social & behavioral research (2nd ed., pp. 531–557). Thousand Oaks, CA: Sage.

O'Cathain, A., Murphy, E., & Nicholl, J. (2007). Integration and publications as indicators of "yield" from mixed methods studies. *Journal of Mixed Methods Research*, *1*(2), 147–163.

Plano Clark, V. L. (2010). The adoption and practice of mixed methods: U.S. trends in federally funded health-related research. *Qualitative Inquiry*, *16*(6), 428–440.

Pope, C., & Mays, N. (2006). *Qualitative research in health care* (3rd ed.). Malden, MA: Blackwell.

Saint Arnault, D., & Fetters, M. D. (2011). R01 funding for mixed methods research: Lessons learned from the "Mixed-Method Analysis of Japanese Depression" project. *Journal of Mixed Methods Research*, *5*(4), 309–329.

Teddlie, C., & Tashakkori, A. (2009). *Foundations of mixed methods research: Integrating quantitative and qualitative techniques in the social and behavioral sciences* (pp. 40–61). Thousand Oaks, CA: Sage.

Wisdom, J. P., Cavaleri, M. C., Onwuegbuzie, A. T., & Green, C. A. (2011). Methodological reporting in qualitative, quantitative, and mixed methods health services research articles. *Health Services Research*, *47*(2), 721–745.

Mentoring the Next Generation in Mixed Methods Research

Rebecca K. Frels, Isadore Newman, *and* Carole Newman

Abstract

Chapter 19 provides considerations based on the field of mentoring to equip researchers with the tools for understanding and addressing the complexities of multimethod and mixed methods research. A synergistic mentoring framework is distinguished—using a humanistic and developmental supervision process borrowed from the helping professions—for the purposes of conceptualizing skills, goals, and interactive dialogue specific to mixed and multiple research methodology. Finally, the facilitative conditions involved in three potential phases of mentorship are described to help promote professional identity, critical decision-making skills, the art of perspective, and translational research dissemination for current and future multimethod and mixed methods researchers.

Key Words: humanistic mentoring, research mentoring, integrated developmental research model, mixed research

Mentoring the Next Generation in Mixed Methods Research

There is little doubt that mentoring has been foundational in advancing strong researchers and research methodology (Boice, 1992; Johnston & McCormack, 1997; Wanberg, Welsh, & Hezlett, 2003). In the corporate world, Ensher and Murphy (2005) explored the concept of "traditional mentoring" (p. 28) whereby an older, wiser person would offer guidance, emotional support, and serve as an effective role model in the workplace setting. The term *mental models* or *philosophies of mentoring* established that the most powerful mentoring relationships, (i.e., the relationship between a mentor and a protégé) reflect a state of mind for both a mentor and a protégé/mentee (Ensher & Murphy, 2005, p. 102). On the part of the mentor, it upholds reciprocal perspectives, being pragmatic and upfront in approach, recognizing generativity as a concern for the next generation, and being both vulnerable and masterful in growth opportunities. On the part of the mentee, it is demonstrated by

a compelling personal characteristic, performance, or potential and a willingness to learn—deemed as "energy and stamina" (p. 122). Further, in a meta-analysis conducted by Ghosh and Reio (2013), five types of career outcomes were identified as valuable for a mentor: job satisfaction, organizational commitment, lower turnover intentions, higher job performance, and overall perceived career success. Mentoring is valuable to a protégé, or mentee, the mentor, and the overall community/organization as a collective group.

In this chapter, we expand the concept of mentorship to the rapidly growing and complex field of multimethod and mixed methods research. We situate mentoring in research with relational and developmental concepts from the field of counseling to distinguish potential pathways in mixed research—sensitive to stakeholders' values and needs. First, we discuss the importance of mentoring in research overall and in particular for multimethod and mixed methods. Next, we present a graphic to portray the complexities of mixed research decision-making to establish why a mentoring framework is needed. Then we introduce an integrated developmental model of supervision borrowed from the counseling profession (Stoltenberg & McNeill, 2009) that helps to explain how a mentoring relationship might move through phases in time and some of the facilitating components that support what we define as synergistic research mentoring—benefiting both a mentee and a mentor. Throughout the chapter we situate our own mentoring experiences as a mentor and mentee as well as others' short reflections of mentoring. As coauthors of this chapter, it was our hope to reveal creative, imaginative ideas that resulted from interactive, challenging discussions based on evidence-based practices, our differing philosophical stances, emergent new questions, and the synergy that we seek to explicate—a glimpse into the possibilities that result from mentorship.

Background of Mentoring in Research

The term *mentor* has various meanings and values and represents numerous roles. The American Psychological Association's (APA) Presidential Task Force (2006) defined a mentor as a coach who "provides advice to enhance the mentee's professional performance and development" (p. 5) and distinguishes informal mentoring (spontaneously developed) and formal mentoring (within an organizational structure). Research in the area of mentorship suggests that those who are mentored are more committed to their profession than their nonmentored counterparts (Wanberg et al., 2003). Guidelines for choosing a research mentor include considerations of context or research environment, personality of the primary investigator, and specific research program capabilities (National Institutes of Health, n.d.).

Mentoring, per se, can be informally established whereby the mentee or the mentor approaches the other and the dyadic relationship develops on its own, or mentoring can be part of a formal program whereby the mentee and mentor are matched (Buell, 2004). It can be structured, with regular meetings between the mentor and mentee, or it can be unstructured in that the mentee seeks out guidance and coaching from the mentor at various points in time. Further, it is clear that mentees might often have multiple mentors and can benefit from different mentors at different points in their career. Yet, for the most part, each mentoring relationship is unique in terms of its frequency, duration, communication, and collaboration, but "the ultimate goal of the mentor is to establish the

trainee as an independent researcher" (APA, 2006, para. 4). A dyadic exchange, or mentoring, through the lens of humanistic theory (Rogers, 1957), thrives when a safe environment is established. The mentor recognizes the mentee's own abilities in problem solving and self-discovery. Further, mentoring, especially mentoring in research, logically should extend beyond the dyad for influencing the quality of the research process, both methodologically and topic-wise.

Through discussions and feedback based on literature or best practices, whether the dyad meets formally or informally, a mentor in research can influence key characteristics of both the research process and the various relationships that are part of the process, such as the interpersonal relationships with participants, stakeholders, and other researchers in the field. Moreover, research mentoring can impact the intrapersonal relationship whereby the mentee becomes more aware of the personal and professional qualities needed to be a lifelong researcher, including emphasis in the area of ethics in research, which is a focus for institutions of higher education and professional organization (see http://research-ethics.net/topics/mentoring/). In the following section, we review a myriad of principles to frame the need for mentoring in mixed research and to set the stage for exploring researcher characteristics that might result from a synergistic research mentoring process.

A Call for Mentoring in Mixed Research

The mentor's job can be daunting considering the multiple ways a mentee might investigate any one phenomenon, which can include variations of philosophical stances, design elements, methods, analyses, interpretations, and more. Onwuegbuzie and Combs (2011) recognized through a typology of integration that mixing might occur on various layers of the research process—in addition to integration of data. For this reason, mentoring in mixed research becomes even more critical due to the many decisions involved to integrate methodological issues at multiple intersections of inquiry, such as conceptualization, design, implementation, and interpretation. Figure 19.1 illustrates how research traditions (quantitative and qualitative) might be viewed on a schematic, interactive continuum, whereby at any point within one tradition or between the two traditions, variations and combinations exist.

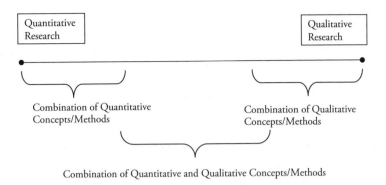

Fig. 19.1 The research continuum and multiple concepts within traditions and between traditions

As seen in Figure 19.1, on each extreme of the continuum, one tradition is represented in isolation or variations of dominance of either or each. Multiple methods might be viewed as closer to one and other and might be considered what Morse (2003) describes as QUAL-qual, or QUANT-quant. In multiple methods, one method might be supplemented by one or more supplementary strategies (quantitative or qualitative) that can be introduced simultaneously or sequentially in design (Morse, 2010). Mixed research, in its most interactive and integrative form, would be nearest to the center of the line, which could be either qualitative dominant research (i.e., the qualitative method is primary and supplemented by quantitative concepts or data) or vice versa. The midpoint of the continuum might be an equal representative of both traditions (Johnson, Onwuegbuzie, & Turner, 2007). Ross and Onwuegbuzie (2010) categorized the complexity within data analysis alone, creating an array of established quantitative techniques into eight levels of complexity. In addition, as posited by Frels and Onwuegbuzie (2013), any one quantitative measure might be used to inform a qualitative inquiry and vice versa, which represents inquiry using both a multimethod and mixed methods approach. For more information pertaining to design typologies and research phases, see Nastasi, Hitchcock, and Brown (2010).

We prelude our discussion of mentoring the next generation by introducing another figure referred to as the interactive continuum, which is defined as a model of mixed research that assumes that most research has aspects that are both qualitative and quantitative and that these aspects are used to inform each other to better answer a research question (Ridenour & Newman, 2008). This continuum is presented in Figure 19.2 and helps to illustrate how someone new to research might benefit from such

a map or guide. It also highlights what Tashakkori and Teddlie (2010) described as "artificial boundaries between qualitative and quantitative approaches" for a platform to recognize the value of various opinions and applications in mixed research (p. xii). As noted by these authors, a scholar is fortunate if learning mixed research methodology is a mentored process. In short, mixed research is inherently complicated. Newman and Benz (1998) and Ridenour and Newman (2008) categorized the many decisions involved in mixed research using this interactive continuum, whereby a researcher reflects, evaluates, and revisits the methodological domains on a continual basis.

The interactive continuum portrays the interdependent decisions that often yield a reevaluation of former decisions. Decision-making in the mixed research process reflects the need for collaborative work, which we define in future sections of this chapter as the cornerstone for research mentoring.

As seen in Figure 19.2, section A begins the process with central decisions regarding an area of interest and theoretical perspective/lens (e.g., topic, questions/speculations); section B involves decisions pertaining to knowledge base/perspective of research (e.g., prior practices/research, philosophical lens/what questions to ask); section C presents the array of qualitative data collection/analysis methods (e.g., case studies, ethnography); and section D lists an array of quantitative considerations (e.g., general hypothesis, research hypothesis, data collection), which is by no means an exhaustive list of decisions that may be made. Depending on the research goal(s) and question(s), inquiry might move from A + B + C; or A + B + D; or A + B + C + D. Regardless as to whether a qualitative, quantitative, or combination route occurs, the *method* stems from the overall *goal* of the research (A) and

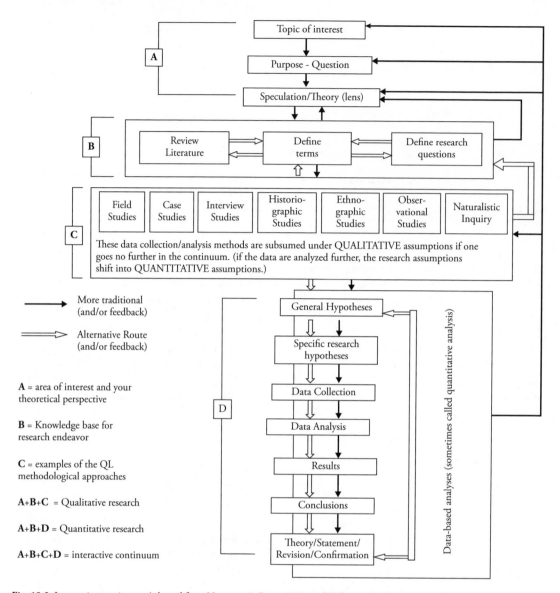

Fig. 19.2 Interactive continuum (adapted from Newman & Benz, 1998, and Ridenour & Newman, 2008)

is influenced by the knowledge base/perspective of research (B). This model brings to the fore that there are numerous decision points in mixed research and that these decisions can be quite difficult to make, especially if a researcher just began his or her career. For example, David, a second-year faculty member in a college of nursing, explains the interactive continuum and how it facilitated his understanding of mixed research:

> When my mentor first showed me this figure, I was amazed at the simplicity of how it integrated the qualitative and quantitative components. That, of course, only lasted for a short time before I digested all of the information provided. Really, looking at the

components allowed me to ask better questions and to gain greater insight. As a professor now who mentors not only my own students but also faculty, I still use this figure when introducing my students and colleagues to mixed methods. I first show them the figure and then have them map out their own research while consulting on it. I answer their questions and provide guidance but the figure is an invaluable teaching tool and it provides a great starting place for discussions.

Based on the multiple combinations of decisions and avenues for research illustrated by David's explanation of the interactive continuum, it is our position that the next generation of scholars are to be *mentored,* and they must be mentored beyond the idea of training or coaching in any one research tradition. To address this need, we present a lens for mentoring in mixed research based on core principals of relationship. Although it is not our intention to present one way for mentoring or to suggest that there might be any one prescription for good research, it is our belief that the following lens can be applied to mixed research mentorship and can expand possibilities, opportunities, and perspectives.

Research Mentoring Using A Humanistic Approach

Considering that relationships grow and thrive as a result of feeling safe and genuine (Rogers, 1957), it is our premise that mentoring in mixed research can focus on the whole person—both mentee and mentor—and recognize what we define as *humanistic mentoring* in a process whereby the mentor and the mentee are very aware and sensitive to each other's personal feelings and cognitive development. This process results in a change in each person's personal, social, emotional, and cognitive development. Furthermore, humanistic mentoring considers the humanness of not only the mentoring dyad but also the human qualities of those who are the participants of our inquiries. This mentoring lens is described by John, in his fifth year as assistant professor and educational researcher working in the field of special populations, and learning needs of children:

Initially, [my mentor] impressed me for that same reasons she impressed others; she was extremely intelligent, yet humble; she was a masterful teacher; she had impeccable integrity and adherence to ethical standards, and she was caring, yet brutally honest, never sugar-coating what she had to say. For these reasons people trusted what she had to say. But there were other aspects of her character that caused me to want her as a mentor. She truly applied the credo of "person-first," not only to individuals with disabilities, but also with everyone. She was more interested in me as a whole person than in any singular aspect of my professional goals, ambitions, or accomplishments. As I worked with her, it became apparent that her caring spirit permeated her research, and she made a point to stress the importance of that to me. Whereas some may see research as a means to an end—getting published—she regularly reminded me that research should have a higher purpose. It should strive to discover that which will improve the lives of

students with disabilities and their families. She regularly encouraged students to take the lead in designing projects that impacted the entire campus as well as the community. To her, the concept of social validity in research was as important as other, more common considerations of validity having to do with research design.

She was also an advocate for faculty/student collaboration in research before it became trendy to do so. Her ideal scenario would be a research team led by college students, with faculty participation, conducting action research based on student-generated ideas, in authentic settings in schools and communities. Considering all I have learned about research—from the technical aspects of designing studies to the care that should be taken in interpreting and reporting results—I believe the lessons learned from my favorite mentor are among the most important. That is, to keep in mind that those who participate in our studies are more than subjects, or merely an "N" value; they are people whose lives can and should be positively affected by our efforts.

Based on practical experiences such as the example of mentorship offered by John, we frame tenets of mentoring using Irby's (2012) description of synergistic mentoring:

A mentor and mentee working together collaboratively to (a) generate a greater good for both, (b) integrate diverse perspectives into the context, and (c) construct together an otherwise unattainable goal attempted independently. (p. 175)

Irby (2012) further explained that synergistic mentoring brings to the fore that mentoring is a verb and is a deliberate action that can bring together diverse perspectives "as a psycho-social endeavor by individuals working together to create a greater good for both mentors and mentees" (p. 175). In addition to creating a greater good for the mentee and mentor, we extend synergistic mentoring to include as a product a greater good for stakeholders and the research community as a whole. Through the lens of what we term as *synergistic research mentoring* (SRM), mentoring becomes a fluid, dynamic process situated in relational factors between a mentee and mentor and the research process. It attends to the unique interaction between the paired relationship that results in a greater good for the mentee, mentor, stakeholders, and research community. It is important to recognize that because mentoring exchange is dynamic, SRM is indeed a process that is influenced by personal factors such as context, personality, learning styles, and other human dimensions. Therefore SRM is not tutoring or coaching, although it may include times of tutoring and coaching. It is much more than that; it emphasizes personal experiences and affirms a better understanding of oneself and others. David also helps to explain this mentor/mentee overlap:

> Last week I was in my office working with a faculty member on conducting Q-methods research and writing-up the results. We were stuck on one aspect, so I called my mentor who provided great advice on which type of rotation we should use and he provided a great rational that I would have never arrived at on my own. About 15 minutes later we were stuck on a technical aspect of the program and I was able to contact another mentor who specialized in the program PQ Methods (a Q-methods program). My mentee was so impressed that I was able to call experts on the topic that she had read in the literature. At that time, I was both mentor and mentee.

Mullen (1999) interpreted the dyadic exchange (mentee and mentor) as an interactive exchange of ideas that are continually being evaluated, adjusted, and reevaluated. Considering that SRM is a process that is fluid and generative, one (of many) potential outputs is what Krathwohl (2002) described as *learning at its highest level,* which is creating, regenerating, planning, or producing something new (Bloom, Engelhart, Furst, Hill, & Krathwohl, 1956). Fink (2003) aligned this high level of learning and generating new ideas with human dimensions that are introspective and psycho-social: (a) discovering how to interact more effectively with oneself and others; (b) caring for developing new interests, feelings, and, values; and (c) learning how to learn. These human dimensions yield important considerations for conceptualizing the SRM relationship. This process of learning requires that researchers tap into their imaginations for new possibilities and options.

When mentoring taps engages a creative spirit, it opens the door for what Moustakas (1990) described as "a unity of intellect, emotion, and spirit" (p. 16). Therefore, SRM establishes and nurtures the very essence of a researcher—which is both intuitive and imaginative. The following account from Rebecca recalls her first memory of being mentored to use intuition in research:

> As a counselor, I always knew that relationships could be messy, but I never realized how research could be so messy. For some reason when taking

my research courses, I believed that if it would be a straightforward process and if I had conceptualized a good design, then I just follow the outline, and the data would reveal the findings—like magic. But I recognized early that everything doesn't always go as planned. I really just wanted my mentor to tell me what to do. Now in retrospect, I realize that my mentor wanted to foster my own knowledge and skills and then just trust.

To set the stage for the process of SRM, we begin with the end in mind. Rather than discuss particular knowledge and skills for the next generation of mixed researchers, we focus on how both a mentor and mentee form a partnership for new learning and for imaginative avenues in inquiry. This relationship occurs beyond the classroom setting and is a unique, personal experience.

Synergistic Research Mentoring for Ways of Being

As outlined by Mullen (1999), mentoring involves a deep examination of ways to establish a safe environment whereby "individuals share processes and purposes, ambiguities and uncertainties, writings and new research" (p. 13). The following sections detail characteristics of what we identify as mixed methods *ways of being* and provide the platform for what we deem as the art of perspective in mixed research.

A Problem-Solving Way of Being

If a partnership for SRM is to be established, it might begin with maintaining a perspective in our very humanness or what Frankl (1988) regarded as being concerned beyond *ontos* (i.e., what kind of things exist) toward *logos*, or an active conviction toward meaning that depends on "a being reaching out beyond himself" (p. 13). This concept relates to understanding the bigger picture of the research—not just the questions but also a focus on the purpose and value of asking those questions. The ability to reach beyond the answer to a question can be facilitated by a synergistic dialogue between the mentor and the mentee. Similar to the idiom of "not seeing the forest for the trees," it is important to establish effective practices that facilitate critical thinking for both a mentee and mentor—especially with respect to mixed research. Therefore, as a way of being, the SRM process includes interactive dialogue that might recognize the human tendency to be "everyday problem solvers [who] use multiple approaches (similar to qualitative and quantitative pathways) concurrently or closely in sequence and examine a variety of sources of evidence in decision making (and in forming impressions)" (Tashakkori & Teddlie, 2010, p. 273). By continuously examining various ways to problem solve and the many facets of any one phenomenon, the SRM process establishes a persona that is genuine and authentic—as well as practical for mixed method researchers in navigating through the complexities of decision-making.

An Expanding Perspective Way of Being

Maxwell (1996) posited an interactive model for research design much "like a philosophy of life; no one is without one, but some people are more aware of theirs, and thus able to make more informed and consistent decisions" (p. 3). If SRM is to be successful, the mentee and mentor dyad should engage one another in a culture of awareness to attend to what is described by Maxwell (1996) as the need for the researcher to have a clear sense of personal motives, desires, and goals in balance with practical and political aspects. Likewise, Ball (2012) established foundational (reflective) practices for expanding perspective: (a) *thoughtful reflection* for "metacognitive awareness concerning the critical role of the need for cooperation among researchers, policy-makers, and practitioners" (p. 288); (b) *introspection*, which involves the researcher looking at personal qualities as a pathway to increased advocacy—specifically revealed through knowledge integration and collaboration to impact practices and policies; (c) *critique of any static levels* of knowledge and practices in which research knowledge is being consumed or not consumed—also referred to in the health science fields as translational research (Nastasi & Hitchcock, 2009; National Institutes of Health, n.d.; Newman, Hitchcock, & Nastasi, 2013); and (d) *personal voice*, which is acquired through inspection of the findings for practical use. Ball (2012) also referred to a zone of generativity, which is the level of potential knowing to "close the knowing-doing gap" (p. 289). Realistically, the higher level thinking attributes as outlined by Bloom et al. (1956) and Ball's foundational practices underscore the importance of interactive dialogue and active imagination to explore avenues for SRM for revealing in practice why at any point in the research process mixing should occur. In fact, it establishes the importance that mixing, at any point in the inquiry, be based on the *purpose for research itself* and how this purpose might be viewed in multiple ways and through multiple approaches

(Newman, Ridenour, Newman, & DeMarco, 2003; Greene, 2007). Therefore, a higher order connection for mentoring research might establish a way of centering that is at the purpose level and not just the question level.

A Purposeful Way of Being

In addition to being aware of expanding perspective, an authentic dialogue in SRM should be not only introspective but also *interspective* to understand translational practices and stakeholder values, beliefs, and needs. As such, SRM should establish as a continuous action/dialogue how in the research process each decision is based on the overall purpose and goal of any specific inquiry. As noted by Greene (2007), purpose yields questions and questions yield design. Further, when creating and generating new ideas in SRM, dialogue might focus on ways to establish rationale for mixing, types of generalizations to be made as a result of inquiry, and levels of mixing (partially mixed vs. fully mixed; concurrent vs. sequential; equal status vs. dominant; Leech & Onwuegbuzie, 2010), to name a few. The pathways to being purposeful in mixed research promotes a persona that is sensitive to continuously linking ideas and decisions directly back to research question(s) and purpose, which is important for credibility and legitimization (Newman & Covrig, 2013). As such, SRM is a fluid weaving of personal foundational practices and perspectives and established research practices. For example, dialogue in mentoring might examine Greene, Caracelli, and Graham's (1989) rationales for mixing, ways to translate stakeholder perspectives, and attending to mono-perspective pitfalls such as Type VI error, which is the act of neglecting to align the typology of purpose, research question(s), and research methods (Newman, Fraas, Newman, & Brown, 2002; Newman, Ridenour, Newman, & DeMarco, 2003).

By discussing and revisiting the purpose for any particular inquiry through SRM, the mentoring exchange might serve as a type of fast-forwarding technique for the mentee to see that the end result is always within sight by helping the mentee to maintain appropriate boundaries in a study, which in turn can minimize feelings of being overwhelmed. For example, if the research goal were to impact institutional change, a decision might be made to obtain a large sample size, which in turn might lead to the decision to integrate quantitative data. If the research goal were to understand better complex phenomena, a decision might be made to collect data within one identified population, using one or more key informants, which in turn leads to the decision to integrate qualitative data. Jennifer, a second-year doctoral student in the field of science education, expressed her interest in refining her skills in mixed methodology as she described her mentoring experiences with respect to interactive dialogue and purposeful research:

> I rely on my mentors for guidance in different aspects of research, including mixed methods. Fortunately, I have multiple mentors who are able to guide me and collaborate with each other. It is like I have a team of research specialists willing and able to help me develop my ideas into sophisticated projects. They not only help shape my thoughts and ideas to refine research questions, but they expand my knowledge and level of comfort in practicing research. For example, some students of research are strictly quan or qual. They shape their questions based on their level of comfort with the technique. My mentors are less concerned with the study's simplicity, and they guide me to develop questions that truly reflect my topics of interest and they provide support and guidance in answering those questions effectively, no matter if the most appropriate technique is mixed, qual, or quan.

In purposeful research, researchers might regard an endeavor more holistically—not only from different research perspectives but also by considering different worldviews and potential scientific and social implications of the research. In sum, there are often critical decision points during the design phase, and these decisions often yield additional questions. Further, by focusing on purposeful research in dialogue and actions, SRM expands awareness to accept contradictory or dissonant findings and to also avoid what Skidmore and Thompson (2012) describe as the human tendency and trappings toward confirmation bias. Building on Jennifer's description of consultation with a "team of research specialists willing and able," the following section expands on the ways of being for approaching SRM already discussed (expanding perspective and purposeful) for personal foundational practices helpful in mixed methods research. Therefore, if research mentoring is going to actually work in creating art of perspective in examining goals and purpose, then it stands to reason that, at the very minimum, mixed researchers might incorporate some type of consultation, which results in a collaborative approach as a way of being.

A Collaborative Way of Being

A collaborative attitude requires first and foremost the idea that alone, one researcher cannot possibly have the knowledge base or perspectives equal to multiple specialists in each area of each tradition. Revisiting Figure 19.2 representing the interactive continuum (Newman & Benz, 1998; Ridenour & Newman, 2008), the potential complexities involved in mixed methods highlights the need for consulting others. Whereby a qualitative researcher might be knowledgeable about phenomenology, case study, ethnography, narrative, and numerous other qualitative research methods, a quantitative researcher might be knowledgeable about descriptive, univariate or multivariate statistical procedures, inferential statistics, or a variety of research designs such as hierarchical linear modeling, structural equation modeling, and a variety of experimental and quasi-experimental designs. As such, a researcher needs to be able to integrate concepts on some level to make meta-inferences. Therefore, to design, conduct, and interpret mixed research, the next generation should recognize the advantages of having a team of researchers, whenever possible, with expertise in the appropriate technique(s) necessary to best align the purpose, research question(s), and methodology. This means that the mixed methods researcher needs to have confidence—in a strength-based approach—to understand different perspectives and how they interact to make the most credible meta-inferences that best represent data.

At this point in time, since there is no established curriculum designed to develop such a researcher, the spirit of collaboration might well be the best way to achieve these results. Specialized mentoring, which is the act of seeking consultation in a specific area, addresses the needed conversations that consider multiple perspectives and potential limitations, multiple collaborations, as well as the need to be introspective and reflective of his or her own practices as a continual, lifelong process. Thus, as we co-created the various ways of being that would weave into a SRM framework, we recognized that inherent in good research is a mindset that takes us back to our natural human instincts—which we distinguish as a *renaissance mindset*. Each way of being presented (expanding perspective, purposeful, collaborative) is interdependent and forges the way for taking risks, or what we define as a renaissance mindset. Finally, all of the attitudes or ways of being help to mold both the mentee and the mentor so that risk-taking and confidence stems from a continual growth model or what we identified as a renaissance in thinking.

A Renaissance Mindset

The debates and dichotomies that are inherent philosophically and methodologically are "not likely to be resolved any time soon, as they are rooted in different, even incommensurable assumptions and stances about reality, knowledge, and especially the purpose and role of social science in society" (Green, 2007, p. 20). It has become increasingly clear that in order to be versatile as a researcher, a researcher cannot exist in only one epistemological space and therefore must adopt "situated views of language" (Onwuegbuzie, 2012, p. 194). This position is one of advocacy in that "good research is good research, whether it stems from the quantitative, qualitative, or mixed research traditions, as long as meaning ensues that represents interpretive consistency" (Onwuegbuzie, 2012, p. 195). As posited by Greene (2007), integrative research reaches beyond the research product or findings for "not only the generative potential of [mixed methods research] but also its potential to respect, appreciate, and accept variation and diversity in the substance of what is being studied" (p. 28).

Recently, Tashakkori, Teddlie, and Sines (2012) conceptualized mixed research as a humanistic methodology and differentiated that varying philosophical frames should not be an obstacle in mixing. Yet it is our interpretation that *multiplicity* implies that a researcher can borrow what is needed to inform a research lens and is respectful of diversity of (a) philosophical assumptions and stances, or the core beliefs within methodology; (b) epistemology, or beliefs about the nature and scope of knowledge; (c) ontology, or issues concerning the nature of knowing such as subjectivity or objectivity; and (d) axiology, or the extent of the role of values. Indeed, multiplicity and dialogue should not require acculturation or assimilation but rather situates dialogue as a mediator for philosophical and methodological positions to address the overall goal(s) or purpose in inquiry. Therefore, variations within the process of inquiry can exist without asking researchers to compromise personal belief systems or worldviews. These variations build dialogue based on respect and usefulness of associated methods (quantitative and/or qualitative) to accomplish the overall goal(s).

As a result, a renaissance mindset is one of revitalization and rebirth of the basic, human tendency to investigate using tools that work. Within this mindset comes a type of give-and-take attitude, much like mediation, with the notion that oftentimes one perspective must yield in order to allow another perspective's voice. A metaphor that closely resembles this concept is that of a musical ensemble, involving more than one instrument with the goal of creating a cohesive, focused, expressive performance. As a group, there is a unified effort for the overall musical message. However, throughout the musical phrases, interpretations of musical notations might vary in personal style during solo opportunities. When one or more instruments move to the background, a soloist is offered personal voice and provides subtle nuances. During the performance, interactions of musical ideas are valued and integration is respectful of unique tones for expressing one needed quality at a specific time. Likewise, a renaissance mindset allows for an "ensemble" approach by negotiating methodological options for rich, variations in meaning toward *versatility* to address stakeholders' missions and visions. Another way of framing this is to remember that good research is good research, and all good research has something in common: it has credibility because the researcher can make logical arguments from many perspectives. It is this openness and willingness to examine a study from as many perspectives as possible, and recognizing the value of doing so through a mentoring relationship, that paves the way for respect to both the qualitative and quantitative understandings of the research. To this end, we have established the aforementioned four ways of being (i.e., problem-solving, expanding perspective, purposeful, collaborative) that we believe are important to address in mentoring the next generation in mixed research, and we imagine that additional attitudes will evolve from these. Because humanistic mentorship also revolves around *identity* development of researchers, it is important for both mentors and mentees to remember that the rapidly changing field of mixed methods requires this type of continual growth model. In essence, ways of being might be perceived as the foundation that allows for the building of value-added research and a renaissance mindset for divergent thinking. To expand on ways that SRM might facilitate identity, per se, we highlight particular points of development that align researcher persona with potential applications specific to mixed methods research.

Mentoring: Valuing the Synergistic Research Process

Mentoring can be highly structured (e.g., meeting formally on a specified day/time) or naturally structured (e.g., consulting when needed). Regardless of structure, what is to be accomplished (the goal of mentoring) at any given time and how it will be accomplished is important to discuss so that both a mentee and mentor are in agreement. A SMR environment depends on the willingness of the mentor and mentee for (a) interaction: each member interacts and appropriately expresses meaningful ideas; (b) appreciative understanding: each member learns to appreciate conflict, utilize empathy, and value diversity; (c) integration: members consider the creative approach of the relationship; and (d) implementation: the mentoring dyad moves toward particular steps for changes (Conner, 1993). Jennifer provides another example and explains how her transformation as a researcher was preceded by mentoring:

> One memorable experience that I felt brought me from mentee to researcher was presenting at my first conference. My mentor guided me through the process and I really believe that without his support and guidance I could have not completed the presentation on my own. As a mentee, there are many moments when I feel uncomfortable with the new knowledge acquired through all the learning experiences, but having a supportive mentor allowed me to reach far beyond what I thought I was capable of at that moment. The trust and confidence I have in my mentor (which is the building block of our relationship) allowed me to push past my own inhibitions and present the results of my study at a national conference. This was the first time I was able to complete a whole cycle of research from the idea development to presenting the findings, and its successful completion added to my development as a researcher.

Working to understand integrative relationships beyond the dyad and within the research process is a justifiable component of SRM. This component is contingent on the interactions that create awareness steps/decisions of inquiry (introspective and collaborative), including awareness of philosophical, methodological, political, and social perspectives. Further, SRM establishes the need for other researchers and collaborative potentials. Last, SRM recognizes the multiple facets of inquiry and all it entails with the vision to co-construct meaningful interpretations with stakeholders for valuable, practical answers. However, it would be naïve to believe that all effective SRM is without difficulty or that negotiating the differences related to power and dynamics is easy. In fact, most often the reason for seeking mentorship by an emergent scholar is to acquire knowledge, confidence, and new opportunities. This undeniable characteristic of mentoring is explained by Randy, a first-year assistant professor in the field of counselor education and supervision:

> Being mentored was not always easy. Having someone you respect tell you that you are wrong and more importantly *why you are wrong* can be hard to hear. It can also be intimidating. Working with someone that always (seemingly) knows more about something than you do can make some people feel *less than*. Most of us have heard the old adage about the only dumb question is the one you don't ask. In some subjects, such as statistics, it can be difficult to even know what questions need to be asked. My mentor was always open to questions. In fact, he encouraged them. I think it takes a special person to be a good mentor. I also believe that one must be open and receptive to mentoring. My mentor and I are on a first name basis now—true colleagues—but he will always be my teacher.

Because most emergent scholars seek mentorship, (APA, 2006), it is important to recognize that the more experienced researcher who typically begins as a mentor has the responsibility to establish an egalitarian relationship and minimize power issues. For this reason, we introduce in the following section a model for SRM that is inclusive of the "learning" facet involved for conducting mixed methods inquiry. According to Munson (1993), for any type of supervision model to be useful, it must have utility, verifiability, comprehensiveness, and simplicity. Therefore, to align with the humanistic aspects of mentoring, we utilized a model of supervision from the counseling field to shed light on ways to mediate power dynamics in a mentoring dyad. This model also integrates important domains of knowledge that we translate for use in mixed research and SRM.

An Integrated Developmental Model for Professional Development

Haynes, Corey, and Moulton (2003) recognized that the term *supervision* in the literal sense would be "to oversee" the development of a new professional, but it also requires a fine balance on the part of the supervisor flexibility in the art and craft of the work while maintaining integrity, ethics, and standards in the field, as well as empowering a new professional. Developed over a period of more than 20 years, Stoltenberg and associates (Stoltenberg, McNeill, & Delworth, 1998; Stoltenberg & McNeill, 2009) established the integrated developmental model of supervision to help contextualize ways to address both the development of professional identity and important knowledge and skills. We borrowed these ideas to explore ways to optimize in which an emergent mixed researcher scholar might utilize awareness, motivation, and autonomy for life-long learning as an outcome of SRM.

In the developmental model, the supervisory relationship focuses on purposeful dialogue with careful considerations of the giving and receiving of feedback (often guided by the supervisor/mentor). The integrated developmental model can help researchers remember that although a final product (research) emerges from mentorship, a parallel process of forming researchers in professional values and ethics also emerges. As explained by one female doctoral student in a reflection of her supervision/mentoring in counseling, development often takes time and is dependent on retrospect. This perspective brings light to the journey toward new possible perspectives for emergent scholars of mixed research:

> The beauty of a graduate program is the ability to take just as much from bad experiences as those that were pleasant; it just might take a few years to recognize the learning that occurred. In my particular case its daily learning from this particular experience I am forever grateful. As a second year master's student I was working with a client that could be framed as my exact opposite. This particular client challenged every aspect of my personal, social, and emotional concepts. Upon supervision my mentor asked the standard questions about my thoughts, and understanding of my client. It was in this supervision session my mentor said something I will never forget: "stop basing a client's norm on what *you* perceive; *you* are not the norm to base your client's goals." My initial response was fear of doing something wrong, followed by failure, then self-disappointment that I let my supervisor down. How could my thoughts, perceived ideas, family history, religious and moral compass *not be* the quote-unquote "normal"? It was with that one statement that I started challenging every personal thought, idea, and emotion to determine if it was my thought and implanted social view. It was this small but powerful statement that helped me recognize that I needed to expand my perceptions.

This reflection brings to the fore the vision we set forth via ways of being and a renaissance mindset previously discussed in this chapter to expand perspective for aligning research goals with *stakeholder values*. This challenging dialogue also highlights how change often occurs over time and often after reflection.

With respect to personal and professional development of professional identity, essential knowledge and skills are categorized in eight critical domains as a roadmap of areas to discuss in supervision (Stoltenberg & McNeill, 2009). Yet these domains are not necessarily explicitly discussed between a mentor and mentee and will vary in intensity, frequency, and duration as needed. By attending to how research mentoring tends to match a more experienced scholar with an emergent mixed research scholar, we highlight supervision considerations using both tenets, or domains for content, and developmental phases, as well as ways to recognize the inherent issues of power between a mentor and mentee. In addition, adapting this integrated developmental model for research mentoring suggests that although covering content relevant to mixing and research practices (e.g., philosophical stance, ethics, cultural differences, social meaning, and perspective) is important; the vehicle for *good research* is nurturing the *good researcher*.

Tenets of Integrated Developmental Supervision

Using the concept of domains/categories of essential content, Stoltenberg and McNeill (2009) explained how supervision/mentorship can be integrative in that it is both training based and relationship based. Dialogue and training should be focused on increasing the values of the previously identified foundational practices of critical thinking processes in everyday problem solving, being purpose driven, collaborative research, and negotiating visions. The relational aspect in SRM examines the same three structures within an emergent research scholar or mentee (motivation, awareness of self and others, autonomy). Stoltenberg and McNeill (2009) also identified eight domains of which we translated to important aspects of mixed research established in the literature. These domains also align with Ridenour and Newman's (2008) schematic representation of the interactive continuum we previously discussed (see Figure 19.2).

For example, by focusing on particular domains/categories to facilitate the knowledge base for a research endeavor (part B of Figure 19.2), the mentoring dyad might determine through feedback a stronger rationale for theoretical perspective (part A of Figure 19.2). In addition, mentoring can reflect the methodological considerations important to legitimation techniques for addressing part C or part D of Figure 19.2, using domains such as those listed in the following as a checklist to (a) facilitate sensitivity in transparency (Newman, Newman, & Newman, 2010) and (b) link typology of purpose (Newman et al 2003; Greene, 2007) to translational research "aimed at enhancing the adoption of best practices in the community" (National Institute of Mental Health, 2007, subsection 1). The following list might serve as a reference for addressing particular domains as part if SRM for mixed research:

- Typology of purpose (research goal)
- Assessment of a problem to explore (research question)
- Intrapersonal assessment of a worldview and belief system (philosophical frame)
- Conceptualization of the research (rationale/ purpose)
- Appropriate design (thoughtful integration)
- Legitimation techniques (integrity and ethics)
- Research planning and collaboration (methodological perspective)
- Translation (interpretation and usefulness for findings)

Both mentors and mentees might recognize how these eight domains can be interactive, interdependent, and recursive. Also, similar to Stoltenberg and McNeill's (2009) supervision model, SRM involves the humanistic approach for mediating comfort levels unique to each domain that might vary due to prior training of the mentee, confidence in the mentee by the mentor, and confidence of the mentee in methodology, just to mention a few. The next sections delineate overlapping phases of development that might be possible in the SRM process. As noted previously, these phases can be overlapping and recursive, and can vary in length for each unique mentoring relationship.

Phases of Development and Synergistic Research Mentoring

In their exploration of perspectives of female school and university co-mentorship, Funk and Kochan (2012) established four phases of mentorship: groundwork, warm-up, working, and long-term status. Similarly, Onwuegbuzie, Frels, Leech, and Collins (2013) distinguished four phases of development with respect to students enrolled in a mixed research course: conceptual/theoretical phase, technical phase, applied phase, and emergent scholar phase. In their evidence-based model of teaching and learning mixed research, Onwuegbuzie et al. (2013) explained how students begin to process the conceptual factors and move

into learning practices such as data collection and analysis. Next, students begin the creative and interactive process of applying their personal approach as a mixed researcher and recognize their emergent identity as a scholar. Although these authors reference a phase development process, they are careful to point out that phases occur oftentimes simultaneously and are interactive. In fact, as explained by one doctoral student in their study, oftentimes movement through the phases are not recognizable:

> The experience I had in mixed methods was one of the most profound learning experiences I have had while pursuing my doctorate. However, I have to say that, during my first few weeks of class, I was in a state of utter confusion. Over the course of almost four months, as I consumed the literature of quantitative, qualitative, and mixed methods inquiry, all of the bits and pieces that I had learned in the three prior semesters came together in one big "aha" moment. Since then, my life as a scholar has begun to take shape. (Onwuegbuzie et al., 2013, p. 152)

Identity development, as a product of engaged reflections, can be a coordinated effort to apply, collaborate, and initiate new ideas if safe and free space is established. In such a safe space, mentees might be more apt to discuss emotions such as feeling discouraged or doubtful, present new ideas, and identify potential collaborators. In supervisee development, Stoltenberg and McNeill (2009) conceptualized three phases that are directly influenced by the working relationship of mentor/mentee, which seeks to build for a mentee greater motivation, awareness of self and others, and autonomy. As such, as a mentoring approach and not solely a supervision approach, SRM is more than an *integrated effort* of researcher identity and mixed research concepts but is rather an *interactive approach* involving methodological perspective(s), the research process, the paired efforts of the mentee and mentor, and the multiple relationships involved. Isadore explained this interactive approach in his account of synergistic mentoring with his son (who happens to be David in our earlier excerpts):

> I now am in the position to have a synergistic mentoring relationship with one of my sons who teaches research methods at a state university. I was initially one of his professors (with the permission of my department head and dean. It's important to note that a faculty member from a different college, who taught a similar course, tested and assigned his grade.) Over the years we have co-authored,

co-consulted, and become colleagues in the field of research. An amusing story was that when my son, David, was presenting at a research conference, my advisor/mentor was his discussant. He was impressed with the quality and sophistication of David's presentation on HLM models, and in conclusion he said he took credit for the quality of the work since, ". . . David learned everything he knows from me and I learned everything I know from him." The collegial relationship I have developed with David, I also have, to varying degrees, with a number of other former students with whom I have worked. These relationships are not only synergetic but also supportive. The point is that a good mentoring relationship, once it is developed, is not unidirectional. Everyone benefits.

The following descriptions of each of the three phases help to identify potential areas for mixed research content. Further, we aligned Stoltenberg and McNeill's (2009) phases of development for a mentee with respect to typical expressions of (a) motivation, (b) awareness of self and others, and (c) autonomy.

Phase 1: Developing Foundations for Identity

Professional identity in mixed research can be nurtured using particular contextual factors or facilitating conditions, much like those described by Rogers (1957) and elaborated by Bennetts (2003) for mentoring as natural or organic process of mutual respect/trust (genuineness), unconditional positive regard (respect), and accurate understanding (empathy). An example of one potential area to discuss in Phase 1 after establishing a tone of respect and empathy (as part of the art of perspective), is to explore ways in which a mixed researcher not only avoids harm but also does good (beneficence) when establishing researcher/participant relationships. This concept was described by Onwuegbuzie and Frels (2013), as having a "communitarian view of power that is represented by reciprocity between the researcher(s) and the participant(s)—a relationship not of domination, but of intimacy and vulnerability" (p. 13). By discussing multiple relationships, SRM can provide a type of openness such as the philosophical frame established by Johnson (2012) as dialectical pluralism, a meta-paradigm for "intellectual process (where one dialogues with ideas, values, concepts, and differences) and a group process (where one, working in a heterogeneous group, strives to produce win-win, or at least complementary, results" (p. 753).

Therefore, through thoughtful and reflective dialogue in the mentoring dyad, more than just research is designed—the researchers (both mentee and mentor) are always being designed and redesigned. That is, both the mentor and mentee can grow by giving and accepting constructive feedback and by actively examining the "how" and "why" involved in mixing.

Phase 1, similar to Onwuegbuzie et al.'s (2013) Phase 1 for teaching and learning mixed research, might also include dialogue relative to mixing and philosophical clarity (Collins, Onwuegbuzie, & Johnson, 2012), especially with respect to all negotiations when working with a team. Also, as noted by Onwuegbuzie et al., the early phase of becoming a mixed researcher is likely to involve confusion pertaining to the dichotomy of traditions portrayed in a respective field and integrating philosophies in a type of "information overload" (p. 147). Although the dialogue in SRM might pertain to knowledge and skills for mixed research it is important for mentors to reflect possible feelings of anxiety, confusion, and challenges, keeping in mind mutual respect, positive regard, and accurate understanding.

Particular to supervision, Stoltenberg and McNeill (2009) recognized that in the first phase of relationship, motivation for a mentee might be high and autonomy might be low. An example of these two structures in SRM would be the way an emergent researcher speaks with enthusiasm about a new study but fails to recognize the myriad of challenges related to the proposed sampling scheme. In addition, in Phase 1, awareness of self and others might include a false or inaccurate sense of relational factors (Stoltenberg & McNeill, 2009) and, in SRM, a low awareness of self and others might be failing to understand how the researcher impacts participants in interview style or the ability to articulate consent. The transition from Phase 1 to Phase 2 might be marked with a more realistic view of research and slightly lower motivation but also with an increased awareness of self and others and greater autonomy. This increased awareness as a developmental "work in progress" is explained by Rebecca in her reflection of SRM toward professional identity:

Thinking back to my experience as a doctoral student, I remember conversations in my dissertation proposal course with respect to deciding a final dissertation topic, and how each of us (my cohort members and I) might explore our prospective topics. We believed a quant study was quick and easy and at the very minimum, we needed to analyze data using ANOVA. Then, my mentor asked me the questions, "What do you want to know" and "Why do you want to know this?" Wow. I needed so much guidance. Concepts such as philosophical stance, a theoretical framework, and how important it was to be transparent as a researcher, were cumbersome and confusing at the time. For some reason, as doctoral students, my peers and I selected topics that were important to us and we selected a method from the course most comfortable for us. Perhaps it was a path of least resistance. Now when I look back on my dissertation research, I recognize that it was through this mentoring experience that I refined my critical thinking skills for the first steps in being a *real researcher*, and not a researcher of convenience.

Phase 2: Developing Collaboration in Research

In movement toward Phase 2, Stoltenberg and McNeill (2009) explained that a supervisee might experience increased motivation, confidence, and awareness of self, particularly with technical aspects relating to knowledge and skills. Yet the second phase of development might bring to the fore a false sense of security in that a mentee might not be aware of what he or she does not know. Therefore, this phase of SRM development might begin to explore some of the collaborative processes in research, requiring justification for decisions. Strategies to structure and increase dialogue might include interview techniques based on Guba and Lincoln's (1989) authenticity criteria. This was conceptualized by Collins, Onwuegbuzie, Johnson, and Frels (2013) as researcher debriefing interviews for exploring questions to conceptualize, design, implement, and utilize research such as: (a) To what extent are you aware of the philosophical assumptions and stances that will drive each component of the mixed research study? (b) To what extent do you think there is consistency between the goal(s), objective(s), rationale(s), purpose(s), and research question(s) and the sampling and research designs toward addressing the research question(s)? (Newman & Covrig, 2013); and (c) To what degree do you think the final research conclusions represent the constructions of all research team members? Frels and Onwuegbuzie (2012a) provided an example of how debriefing prompted a deeper respect for participants of research:

> This might be off subject, but the [question] that I asked [participants] was: "How would others describe you?" Because I'm really trying to look at

the mentors' point of view, this question took so many [participants] by surprise, you know they didn't have any idea! So I asked them to make up a pseudonym. My experience was huge. I never knew how difficult it would be for someone to make up a name for oneself. I learned something from that about the importance of interview questions and things you can learn about participants. . . I was just going to assign names. I'm so glad I asked them. It added another piece of really good descriptive validity because some of them even told me why they picked the name and I think it kind of goes with what I see flowing through their interviews.

In addition to the use of interviewing strategies, SRM in Phase 2 might focus on understanding various positions of subjectivity. For example, phenomenological interview questions based on Nastasi, Bernstein-Moore, and Varjas's (2004) work can facilitate awareness of translational research in that a researcher might better understand and estimate how to interpret empirical probability, which could facilitate understanding a participant's subjective probability. The *subjective probability* is a better estimate of the likelihood that the research would be applied and thus be translational. That is, research is only valuable if and when it is applied. The following prompts might be part of the Phase 2 exchange, and, similar to Onwuegbuzie et al.'s (2013) goals for debriefing, these questions (Newman et al., 2013) are intended to prompt collaborative dialogue and increased methodological perspective. For example: What is the individual's perception of what has been learned? Does the individual think the study was trustworthy (believable, accurate)? How relevant is the research to their interest or need? In their perception, do the findings transfer or generalize to their setting? If implemented, what is their perception of the likely outcomes—both positive and negative?

These collaborative interviewing techniques might also prompt a more systemic view of research or what Nelson, Onwuegbuzie, Wines, and Frels (2013) refer to as family systems thinking within the *research system* to include the researcher, co-researchers, participants, transcribers, research assistants, dissertation/thesis committee members, institutional review boards, peer and professional consultants, funding institutions, and other stakeholders (e.g., from the larger systems such as schools, political entities, or agencies). Regardless of any selected awareness activity in Phase 2, it is important to recognize relationships and potential times of give and take

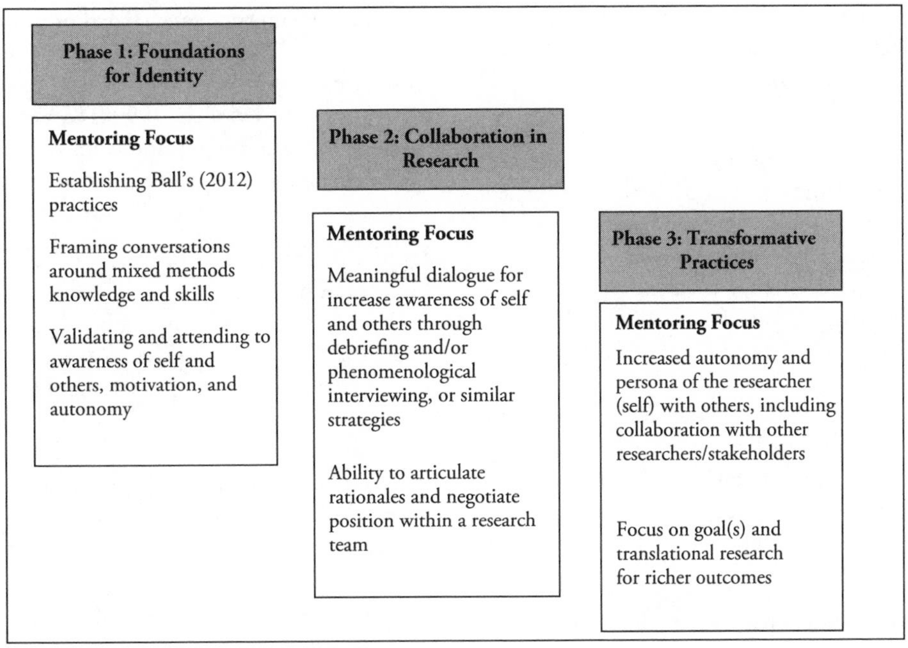

Fig. 19.3 Three overlapping general phases and mentoring focus for professional development in mixed research

in the mixed research process—at the very least—through awareness of the influences for potential research outcomes in a professional field and target community. To this end, particular awareness (of self and others) might include ways in which equal-status mixed research design (i.e., equitable emphasis is given to each method; Johnson, 2012) might be achieved using paradoxes, contradictions, and tensions in decisions and interpretations. Interestingly, when the mentoring dyad moves deeper into discussion of beliefs, ideals, conceptualizations, and considerations in research collaboration, the dyadic exchange in SRM simultaneously negotiates many of the same concepts and becomes more collaborative.

Phase 3: Developing Transformative Practices

Phase 3 is reached when the mentee is highest in the characteristic of autonomy. During this time, a mentee recognizes the importance of being self-supervised, utilizing the strategies outlined in Phase 1 and Phase 2 and also seeking out and sharing new strategies with team members and colleagues. Ultimately, the mentee also becomes a mentor. Isadore recalled becoming aware of his transformation in his account of mentoring:

> During my doctoral studies, my advisor was one of my statistics professors. He was an excellent

teacher who I sought to emulate as a role model. At that point, our relationship was that of professor–student. I'm not sure it met any of the characteristics of a mentoring relationship other than he was my professor who had skills I respected, and he respected my statistical skill. I was also very impressed with how well organized he was for each class and how he valued good research and the people who did it. I learned to see the academic world and the importance of publishing through his eyes. Over the years, after I graduated we became close friends and wrote a number of books and articles together. One of the things he gave me without my realizing it, was that because I, and many others, held him in high academic esteem, he increased my self-efficacy because he made it obvious that he valued me academically. He did this in a number of ways. He invited me to go to conferences where he introduced me to his colleagues as one of his best students. I would tend to share my very nontraditional perceptions about statistical techniques with him and tell him how other traditional statistical thinkers were not positive about how I conceptualized a number of statistical issues. He would tell me I was right and reinforce my "thinking out of the box." This boosted my self-confidence as a researcher. In one of the research books that he wrote in 1996, he autographed it to me writing, ". . . You were my best student, my best colleague and now my best teacher." Obviously, this is an example of a synergistic relationship.

The following figure, Figure 19.3, presents the three potential phases aligned with the possible formative structures associated with development through each phase: (a) Phase 1 foundations for identify, (b) Phase 2 developing collaboration in research, and (c) Phase 3 developing transformative practices. When considering Figure 19.3, note that phases can vary in length and intensity as well as be interrelated, iterative, and overlapping.

In summary, the following key points might serve as an additional guide for SRM and professional identity attributes helpful in mixed research. This list is by no means exhaustive and it is our hope that it serves as a platform for dialogue toward other innovative ideas.

- Introspection of personal qualities for advocacy to impact practices and policies
- Critical thinking of static levels of knowledge
- Personal voice/responsibility for inspecting research findings as translational to practices
- Awareness of dissonance, conflict, and frequent contradictions and the skills to integrate disparate ideas
- Seeking a diverse research team, representative of multiple philosophical stance, methodologies, and perspectives
- Justification for decisions: being well-grounded in mixed research literature (both methodological and philosophical)
- Patience with the process of research and willingness to dialogue about oneself and relationships with others and to be open to learning from that dialogue
- Self-directed, lifelong learning and acceptance that one does not necessarily "know all of the answers" but recognizes many potential answers and the possibility of other sources of data and other perceptions

Although the attributes listed above might appear as a mere list for a mentee only, they are a few of many products or outcomes that are possible for both a mentee and a mentor. In fact, because each dyadic exchange is unique, the aforementioned points are also unique to each mentoring dyad. As noted by Conner (1993), mentoring yields insight and growth for both a mentee and mentor.

Benefits of mentoring, much like those listed above, are maximized if the dyadic exchange is viewed as a form of co-engagement, reeducation, productivity, and innovation (Mullen, 1999). To this end, our final thoughts and implications for SRM relate to both a mentee and a mentor.

Implications for the Present and Next Generation

The crux of mentoring embodies the age-old quote that "the whole is greater than the sum of its parts." Further, by sharing, collaborating, and creating ideas specific to mixed research, SRM can help to articulate philosophical, methodological, and translational practices and the nuances that accompany the often "messy" endeavor of mixed research. When an experienced research scholar takes the lead to establish a safe and empathic environment by *letting go* and being open to discussing his or her own limitations with respect to perspective, knowledge, and skills, the result can be a dynamic, flexible mentoring relationship with limitless imagination. The relational aspects of SRM requires an investment of time and self, but this investment can yield inspiration, a new colleague and friend, greater productivity, renewed trust and motivation—just to mention a few. As noted by Allen, Eby, Poteet, Lentz, and Lima (2004) in their meta-analysis of career mentoring, mentoring relationships associated with career goals (such as research agenda) can be more powerful than without it.

Yet SRM cannot be achieved without being aware of and negotiating various aspects of power differences between an emerging researcher and a more experienced researcher. Illustrating one way to negotiate power in mentoring, Frels and Onwuegbuzie (2012b) applied the conditions established by Axline (1989) relating to work with children for other mentoring relationships: (a) developing warmth and friendliness, (b) acceptance of a person where he or she is, (c) establishing a feeling of permissiveness, (d) recognizing feelings and expressing respect for these feelings, (e) maintaining a deep respect for a person's ability to resolve any problems, (f) not attempting to overly direct, (g) recognizing relationships are a gradual process, and (h) establishing only parameters that are necessary. These qualities might translate into SRM for a generation of empathetic researchers seeking not to alienate but to invest in strong research and strong research relationships. By using established strategies for building rapport and facilitating growth established in supervision literature, the future for mentoring in mixed research might be fueled for representing research that is collaborative, integrative, purposive, warranted, and transparent.

Our vision for this chapter was to promote future efforts of mentorship toward professional researcher identity. In our efforts, we dialogued frequently and at times individually each of us set aside one or more personal perspectives. At various points in our collaboration, if not attending to the very foundational practices distinguished in our framework for SRM, this chapter might have been written from any one dominant perspective. Furthermore at any other point in time, this chapter might have evolved differently and in fact we hope that in 5 years' time, it does! It is our contention that SRM should nurture the idea to *push the envelope* for growth and opportunities for learning. Effective outcomes of SRM

Table 19.1 Facilitating Beliefs and Actions for the Mentor and the Mentee in Synergistic Research Mentoring

Facilitating Mentor Beliefs and Actions	Facilitating Mentee Beliefs and Actions
View self as a motivator and model awareness in self and others	Engage in opportunities for introspection and ways that personal perceptions impact others involved in inquiry
Use a humanistic lens through empathy and validate feelings associated with the research process	Be willing to accept feedback and recognize potential venues for overcoming insecurity with respect to design or analysis skills
Emphasize interactions within (a) methodology, (b) research process, and (c) self	Negotiate times of doubt using literature and other justification for decisions
Share personal experiences, obstacles, times of growth to be more "human" and minimize power issues	Link new learning about self and identity as a researcher to thought process and practical skills
Provide a safe space by encouraging dialogue about doubts or associated fears for conducting mixed research	Engage in self-disclosure about fears for a shared experience and a shared responsibility
Challenge the mentee to examine critically potential decisions for solving practical issues associated with inquiry	Establish rationales based on philosophical lens, methodological perspective, and translational goals
Be grounded in and encourage foundational practices (thoughtful reflection, introspection, critique of static levels, personal voice)	Be faithful to good habits that create a identity and rigorous, transparent research and "trust the process"
Provide discussions involving design and rationale(s) for mixing	Be willing to spend time investigating literature and take the time to contact other researchers that might provide multiple perspectives
Focus dialogue on the overall goal of the inquiry at critical decision points to better bound the study	Recognize that one inquiry cannot address a multitude of problems and notate avenues for possible follow-up studies to stay focused on initial hunches/goals
Encourage the use of new ideas and tools that work for a renaissance mindset	Take the risk to offer suggestions or considerations not imitated by a mentor
Help mentee network and build collaborative relationships with other experienced colleagues and potential stakeholders	Be willing to step out of a comfort zone and ask for help with skills, knowledge, and practices for possible variations of meanings and usefulness of outcomes
Provide opportunities to debrief after critical decisions	Be willing to discuss critical decisions and follow up with any new considerations that emerge through debriefing
Have the ability to let go and recognize that the mentee can work through times of difficulty	Be cognizant of actions and the impact of actions and work with fairness and integrity

involves a look at vulnerability, especially on the part of a mentor for reducing the power differences inherent in mentoring. When a mentor attends to being open and oftentimes vulnerable, the end result can be a sense of normalcy and safety for a mentee and oftentimes, depending on the confidence level of a mentee, vice versa. Brown (2012) illustrated this type of vulnerability as the action of courage. When one person shares particular obstacles and times of growth from personal experiences, he or she models the type of risk-taking behaviors important toward negotiating perspectives. In essence, vulnerability in SRM gives both the mentor and the mentee permission to be human.

Through authentic dialogue, the current and next generation of mixed researchers might recognize and embrace times of disagreement, debate, dissonance, difference, divergence, and dialogue as outlined by Onwuegbuzie (2012) as a reminder that mixing offers choices and that each choice reveals one of many different voices—which oftentimes might not be comfortable. What may follow

SRM is a new/renewed motivation, awareness of intra-actions and interactions, courage, and foundational practices for embracing in essence—a *new culture of researchers.*

In closing, we present a reference guide in the form of two tables outlining qualities/dispositions/ beliefs/actions for SRM that are linked to enriched outcomes from the perspective of a mentee, a mentor, and a mixed researcher persona described in this chapter. First, Table 19.1 summarizes particular beliefs and actions for a mentor and mentee facilitative approaches. Next, Table 19.2 is an overall summation of the moderating qualities for a dyad—which we refer to as facilitating conditions for SRM. By establishing facilitating beliefs and actions and facilitative conditions of SRM, ways of being can lead to interdependent, creative problem-solvers and risk-takers. This new culture of mixed researchers instinctively turns to foundational practices, research collaboration/relationships, rationales/goals, a multimethodological perspective, and translational research as the cornerstone of inquiry.

Table 19.2 Facilitating Conditions for Synergy and Positive Outcomes

Facilitating Condition	Synergy/Outcome in the Dyad
Empathy and trust	Open communication and willingness to take risks
Mutual respect and shared responsibility	Confidence and new ideas
Focus on developing the interdependent, life-long researcher	Detail-oriented implementation of skills using reflexive practices for increased transparency
Co-create goals with agreement on ways to accomplish them	Circular thinking, with the end result in mind
Negotiate a shared vision	Collaborate for translational research for outcomes
Discuss the purpose of research with methodology	Coordinate decisions linked to philosophical considerations
Discussing interactions with others and integrate differing perspectives and interpretations	New possibilities and a broader awareness of various worldviews
Use dialogue, debriefing interviews, journaling, or other reflective tool	Attention to practical, political, and justice issues
Explore multiple avenues and potential benefits/ limitations in various multi- and mixed combinations (rationale for mixing)	Increased motivation, awareness of self and others, and autonomy for mentee Increased understanding and applications for mentor
Dialogue about "good research"	Increased awareness and investment to anticipate limitations and utilize legitimation tools
Discuss interactions of values, perspectives, and avenues of integration for practical answers and added meaning for stakeholders	Avoidance of any one "right" method and addresses methodological considerations and credible meta-inferences Increased confidence in everyday problem solving

Acknowledgments

We would like to thank the contributors of this chapter for sharing their mentoring experiences: Rachael G. Ammons Whitaker, Randy J. Davis, and John D. Mohr of Lamar University, Texas; Jennifer Morales of Florida International University; and David Newman of Florida Atlantic University.

Discussion Questions

1. Examine the interactive continuum and potential pathways for research. In what areas might you need to consult with one or more mentors? How might their perspective and expertise contribute to your growth as a mixed methods researcher?

2. Describe the ways of being for approaching SRM presented in this chapter (Expanding Perspective, Purposeful, Collaborative, Renaissance Mindset). What are areas you deem important in the identity of a mixed methods researcher? How might you approach these topics in a mentoring relationship?

3. Describe the three phases of SRM (foundational phase, collaborative phase, translational phase). What are some challenges that you foresee as a mentee and/or mentor with respect to the complexities of mixed methods in each of the phases? Suggest some methods for dealing with these challenges.

4. Examine Table 19.1. Discuss one or more beliefs and actions that you find to be particularly important/useful as a mentor, such as modeling awareness, sharing personal experiences, or others. What additional beliefs and/or actions would you add to this list, and why are these beliefs/actions important to consider for mixed methods researchers?

Suggested Websites

https://www.training.nih.gov/mentoring_ guidelines

For an understanding other models of mentorship in research, see the *Guide to Mentorship in Research* on the National Institutes of Health website.

http://www.nimh.nih.gov/about/organization/ddtr/index.shtml

http://www.esourceresearch.org/tabid/226/Default.aspx

Both of these websites expand on the goals of translational research in the health and mental health science fields.

http://gsociology.icaap.org/methods/qual.htm

For dialogue pertaining to mixed methods and mentorship opportunities via the Internet, consider becoming a member of the *Methods* forum.

References

Allen, T. D., Eby, L. T., Poteet, M. L., Lentz, E., & Lima, L. (2004). Career benefits associated with mentoring for protégés: A meta-analysis. *Journal of Applied Psychology*, *89*, 127–136. doi:10.1037/0021-9010.89.1.127

American Psychological Association Presidential Task Force. (2006). Introduction to mentoring: A guide for mentors and mentees. Retrieved from http://www.apa.org/education/grad/intro-mentoring.pdf

Axline, V. (1989). *Play therapy*. London, England: Ballantine Books. (Original work published 1947)

Ball, A. F. (2012). To know is not enough: Knowledge, power, and the zone of generativity. *Educational Researcher*, *41*, 283–291.

Bennetts, C. (2003). Mentoring youth: Trend and tradition. *British Journal of Guidance & Counseling*, *31*, 63–76. doi:10.1080/0306988031000086170

Bloom, B. S., Engelhart, M. D., Furst, F. J., Hill, W. H., & Krathwohl, D. R. (1956). *Taxonomy of educational objectives: Cognitive domain*. New York, NY: McKay.

Boice, R. (1992). Lessons learned about mentoring. *New Directions for Teaching and Learning*, *50*, 51–61.

Brown, B. (2012). *The power of vulnerability*. Louisville, CO: Sounds True.

Buell, C. (2004). Models of mentoring in communication. *Communication Education*, *53*, 56–73.

Collins, K. M. T., Onwuegbuzie, A. J., & Johnson, R. B. (2012). Establishing validity standards in mixed methods research. *American Behavioral Scientist*, *56*, 849–865.

Collins, K. M. T., Onwuegbuzie, A. J., Johnson, R. B., & Frels R. K. (2013). Using debriefing interviews to promote authenticity and transparency in mixed research. *International Journal of Multiple Research Approaches*, *7*(2), 271–283.

Conner, D. R. (1993). *Managing at the speed of change*. New York, NY: Villard.

Ensher, E., & Murphy, S. (2005). *Power mentoring: How successful mentors and protégés get the most out of their relationships*. San Francisco, CA: Wiley.

Fink, L. D. (2003). *Creating significant learning experiences: An integrated approach to designing college courses*. San Francisco, CA: Jossey-Bass.

Frankl, V. E. (1988). *The will to meaning: Foundations and applications of logotherapy*. New York, NY: Penguin. (Original work published in 1969)

Frels, R. K., & Onwuegbuzie, A. J. (2012a). Interviewing the interpretive researcher: An impressionist tale. *The Qualitative Report*, *17*, 1–27. Retrieved from http://www.nova.edu/ssss/QR/QR17/frels.pdf

Frels, R. K., & Onwuegbuzie, A. J. (2012b). Principles of play: A dialogical comparison of two case studies in school-based mentoring. *International Journal of Play Therapy*, *21*, 131–148. doi:10.1037/a0028536

Frels, R. K., & Onwuegbuzie, A. J. (2013). Administering quantitative instruments with qualitative interviews: A mixed research approach. *Journal of Counseling & Development*, *91*(2), 84–194. doi:10.1002/j.1556-6676.2013.00085.x

Funk, F. F., & Kochan F. K. (1999). Profiles in mentoring: Perspectives from female school and university voyagers. In C. A. Mullen & D. W. Lick (Eds.), *New directions in mentoring: Creating a culture of synergy* (pp. 87–92). New York, NY: Routledge.

Greene, J. (2007). *Mixed methods in social inquiry*. San Francisco, CA: Wiley.

Greene, J. C., Caracelli, V. J., & Graham, W. F. (1989). Toward a conceptual framework for mixed-method evaluation designs. *Educational Evaluation and Policy Analysis, 11*, 255–274. doi:10.3102/01623737011003255

Ghosh, R., & Reio, T. G. (2013). Career benefits associated with mentoring for mentors: A meta-analysis. *Journal of Vocational Behavior, 83*, 106–116.

Guba, E. G., & Lincoln, Y. S. (1989). *Fourth generation evaluation*. Newbury Park, CA: Sage.

Haynes, R., Corey, G., & Moulton, P. (2003). *Clinical supervision in the helping professions: A practical guide*. Pacific Grove, CA: Thomson Brooks/Cole.

Johnson, R. B. (2012). Dialectical pluralism and mixed research. *American Behavioral Science, 56*, 751–754. doi:10.1177/0002764212442494

Johnson, R. B., Onwuegbuzie, A. J., & Turner, L. A. (2007). Toward a definition of mixed methods research. *Journal of Mixed Methods Research, 1*, 112–133. doi:10.1177/1558689806298224

Johnston, S., & McCormack, C. (1997). Developing research potential through a structured mentoring program: Issues arising. *Higher Education, 33*, 251–264.

Irby, B. (2012). Editor's overview: From mentoring synergy to synergistic mentoring. *Mentoring & Tutoring: Partnership in Learning, 20*, 175–179.

Krathwohl, D. R. (2002). A revision of Bloom's taxonomy: An overview. *Theory into Practice, 41*(4), 221–264. Retrieved from http://www.unco.edu/cetl/sir/stating_outcome/documents/Krathwohl.pdf

Leech, N. L., & Onwuegbuzie, A. J. (2010). Guidelines for conducting and reporting mixed research in the field of counseling and beyond. *Journal of Counseling & Development, 88*, 61–69.

Maxwell, J. A. (1996). *Qualitiative research design: An interactive approach*. Thousand Oaks, CA: Sage.

Morse, J. M. (2003). Principles of mixed methods and multimethod research design. In A. Tashakkori & C. Teddlie (Eds.), *Handbook of mixed methods in social & behavioral research* (pp. 189–208). Thousand Oaks, CA: Sage.

Morse, J. M. (2010). Procedures and practice of mixed methods design: Maintaining control, rigor and complexity. In A. Tashakkori & C Teddlie (Eds.), *SAGE handbook of mixed methods in social and behavioral research* (2nd ed., pp. 339–352). Thousand Oaks, CA: Sage.

Moustakas, C. (1990). *Heuristic research: Design, methodology, and applications*. Newbury Park, CA: Sage.

Mullen, C. A. (1999). Introducing new directions for mentoring. In C. A. Mullen & D. W. Lick (Eds.), *New directions in mentoring: Creating a culture of synergy* (pp. 10–17). New York, NY: Routledge.

Munson, C. E. (1993). *Clinical social work supervision* (2nd ed.). New York, NY: Haworth Press.

Nastasi, B. K., Bernstein Moore, R., & Varjas, K. M. (2004). *School-based mental health services: Creating comprehensive and culturally specific programs*. Washington, DC: American Psychological Association.

Nastasi, B. K., & Hitchcock, J. H. (2009). Challenges of evaluating multi-level interventions. *American Journal of Community Psychology, 43*, 360–376.

Nastasi, B. K., & Hitchcock, J. H., & Brown, L. M. (2010). An inclusive framework for conceptualizing mixed methods design typologies: Moving toward fully integrated synergistic research models. In A. Tashakkori & C. Teddlie (Eds.), *SAGE handbook of mixed methods in social & behavioral research* (pp. 305–338). Thousand Oaks, CA: Sage.

National Institute of Mental Health (2007). Division of Developmental Translational Research (DDTR). Retrieved from http://www.nimh.nih.gov/about/organization/ddtr/index.shtml

National Institutes of Health. (n.d.). Thoughts on choosing a research mentor. Retrieved from https://www.training.nih.gov/mentoring_guidelines

Nelson, J. A., Onwuegbuzie, A. J., Wines, L., & Frels, R. K. (2013). The therapeutic interview process in qualitative research studies. *The Qualitative Report, 18*, 1–17. Retrieved from http://www.nova.edu/ssss/QR/QR18/nelson79.pdf

Newman, I., & Benz, C. (1998). *Qualitative-quantitative research methodology: An interactive continuum*. Carbondale: Southern Illinois University Press.

Newman, I., & Covrig, D. (2013). Building consistency between title, problem statement, purpose, and research questions to improve the quality of research plans and reports. *New Horizons in Adult Education & Human Resource Development, 25*(1), 70–79.

Newman, I., Fraas, J., Newman, C., & Brown, R. (2002). Research practices that produce Type VI errors. *Journal of Research in Education, 12*(1), 138–145.

Newman, I., Hitchcock, J., & Nastasi, B. (2013, April). *Using phenomenological principles to assess stakeholders' perceptions of probability: Applying mixed methods in translational research*. Paper presented at the annual meeting of the American Educational Research Association, San Francisco, CA.

Newman, I., Newman, D., & Newman, C. (2010). Writing research articles using mixed methods: Methodological considerations to help you get published. In T. Rocco & T. Hatcher (Eds.), *The handbook of scholarly writing and publishing* (pp. 191–208). San Francisco, CA: Wiley.

Newman, I., Ridenour, C. S., Newman, C., & DeMarco, G. M. P. (2003). A typology of research purposes and its relationship to mixed methods. In A. Tashakkori & C. Teddlie (Eds.), *Handbook of mixed methods in social & behavioral research* (pp. 167–188). Thousand Oaks, CA: Sage.

Onwuegbuzie, A. J. (2012). Introduction: Putting the MIXED back into quantitative and qualitative research in educational research and beyond: Moving toward the radical middle. *International Journal of Multiple Research Approaches, 6*(3), 192–219.

Onwuegbuzie, A. J., & Combs, J. (2011). Data analysis in mixed research: A primer. *International Journal of Education, 3*, 1–25.

Onwuegbuzie, A. J., & Frels, R. K. (2013). Introduction: Towards a new research philosophy for addressing social justice issues: Critical dialectical pluralism. *International Journal of Multiple Research Approaches [Special Issue on Philosophy, Policy, and Practice], 7*(1), 9–26.

Onwuegbuzie, A. J., Frels, R. K., Leech, N. L., & Collins, K. M. T. (2013). A four-phase model for teaching and learning mixed research. *International Journal of Multiple Research Approaches [Special Issue on Philosophy, Policy, and Practice], 7*(1), 133–156.

Ridenour, C., & Newman, I. (2008). *Mixed methods research: Exploring the interactive continuum*. Carbondale: Southern Illinois University Press

Rogers, C. R. (1957). The necessary and sufficient conditions for therapeutic personality change. *Journal of Consulting Psychology, 21*, 95–103. doi:10.1037/0033-3204.44.3.240

Ross, A., & Onwuegbuzie, A. J. (2010). Mixed methods research design: A comparison of prevalence in *JRME* and *AERJ. International Journal of Multiple Research Approaches, 4*, 233–245.

Skidmore, S. T., & Thompson, B. (2012). Propagation of misinformation about frequencies of RFTs/RCTs in education: A cautionary tale. *Educational Researcher, 41*, 163–170. doi:10.3102/0013189X12441998

Stoltenberg, C. D., & McNeill, B. W. (2009). *IDM supervision: An integrated developmental model for supervising counselors and therapists* (3rd ed.). San Francisco, CA: Jossey-Bass.

Stoltenberg, C. D., McNeill, B., & Delworth, U. (1998). IDM supervision: An integrated developmental model of supervising counselors and therapists. Retrieved from http://www.supervisioncentre.com/docs/kv/IDM_Model.pdf

Tashakkori, A., & Teddlie, C. (2010). Putting the human back in "human research methodology": The researcher in mixed methods research. *Journal of Mixed Methods Research, 4*, 271–277. doi:10.1177/1558689810382532

Tashakkori, A., Teddlie, C., & Sines, M. C. (2012). Utilizing mixed methods in psychological research. In I. Weiner, J. A. Schinka, & W. F. Velicer (Eds.), *Handbook of psychology: Vol. 2. Research methods in psychology* (2nd ed., pp. 429–450). Hoboken, NJ: Wiley.

Wanberg, C. R., Welsh, E. T., & Hezlett, S. A. (2003). Mentoring research: A review and dynamic process model. *Research in Personnel and Human Resources Management, 22*, 38–124.

Contextualizing Multimethod and Mixed Methods Research Within and Across Disciplines and Applied Settings

Multimethod and Mixed Methods Research in the Fields of Education and Anthropology

Jori N. Hall *and* Judith Preissle

Abstract

This chapter considers the differences and similarities of research in education and anthropology and how mixed methods approaches to these fields contribute to the social and professional sciences. The chapter begins with the evolution of research in the fields of education and anthropology and its importance to contemporary mixed and multimethod conceptualizations and research design applications in these fields. In doing so, the chapter identifies key challenges researchers in the fields of education and anthropology face when conducting multimethod and mixed methods research. The chapter offers some important strategies and case studies that discuss the application of mixed and multimethod approaches applied to educational and anthropological research.

Key Words: educational research, anthropological research, multimethod and mixed methods research, social and professional sciences, research

Education and anthropology are two complex research disciplines, each with numerous subfields and a diversity of applications of mixed and multimethod designs. Education is the study of human teaching and learning and the contexts and situations within which these occur, especially in schools. Education has been and continues to be influenced by history, psychology, philosophy, and societal events. Its subfields commonly include social and psychological foundations, curriculum and instruction, and such specialties as educational leadership, higher and adult education, school counseling and student affairs, kinesiology, and education for those with special needs.

Anthropology is the study of the development of human life in its manifest varieties across time and space or history and geography. In the United States anthropology includes cultural anthropology, linguistics, archaeology, and physical or biological anthropology in the so-called four-fields combination (Givens & Skomal, 1993). However, in places like Great Britain cultural anthropology is labeled

social anthropology and is considered distinct from the other three areas (Barnard, 2000). In this chapter our focus is sociocultural anthropology because human communities and their cultures are its focus. Sociocultural anthropology itself is divided into subfields such as applied anthropology, urban anthropology, and the anthropologies of various regions of the world.

Despite the diversity within and across these fields, education and anthropology share common goals: to explain and interpret human behavior and experience and to describe the contexts where these occur. Given these shared goals, we argue, education and anthropology are both social and professional sciences. A social science produces knowledge about societies and the people in them. A professional science likewise uses systematic procedures to produce knowledge on society and its members, but its practitioners and specialists aim to use the knowledge to address needs of individuals and to improve societal conditions. Educational research has been dominated by its professional responsibilities, but scholars of applied anthropology share these concerns for individual and community needs and for improvement of the human condition. The kinds of science (Packer, 2012) practiced in educational research and in anthropology have been hotly debated throughout the development of each field, and these discussions have profoundly affected methodological and research design choices, as we demonstrate in the chapter.

Both educational research and anthropology have been influenced by other scholarly traditions, especially the humanities. Educational research has depended on philosophy and on history in many of its subfields. Sociocultural anthropology has influenced and been influenced by film studies, literature, and such interdisciplinary fields as ethnomusicology. As early as the mid-20th century, however, critics of the academy (e.g., Snow, 1959) warned about increasing specializations and divisions among fields that created chasms of incomprehension between scholars and students, later developing into knowledge silos where experts in one area barely understood constructs and methods common in other areas. This pattern of separation and splintering has been balanced by efforts of other academics to study developments in related fields and to build the plethora of interdisciplinary fields (Finkenthal, 2001; Klein, 1990; Moran, 2002), among them the anthropology of education (deMarrais, Armstrong, & Preissle, 2010), well established by the early 21st century.

Just as important are some key differences between education and anthropology. First, we argue anthropology preceded educational research in its customary use of mixed methods, but both fields share an established tradition of using mixed methods as a set of systematic procedures to investigate different groups of people or individuals with attention to complex cultural, social, and human interactions. Second, we believe that educational research has been far more preoccupied with how something *ought* to be done than with how something *is* done. Anthropologists look at patterns that exist among humans to generate descriptive research. However, educational research is prescriptive; it is preoccupied with how to improve human practices: what is the best way to do something, not just how are people doing something. Anthropologists study teaching practices for comparison across groups; educators study teaching practices to determine what practices work best with which students. Third, we acknowledge that education is a much larger academic field than anthropology in both numbers of faculty members and in numbers of subfields. A rough measure of this is the difference in current size between the American Anthropological Association, founded in 1902, of 12,000 members and the American Educational Research Association, founded in 1916, of 25,000 members. Education serves a larger practitioner body of teachers and administrators than does anthropology, where graduates in applied positions are fewer and work across far more diverse settings than the preschool to secondary schools that employ educators.

Even with these differences, journals such as the *Anthropology and Education Quarterly*, as the name implies, bring together these two fields. The anthropology of education exemplifies the interdisciplinarity that we believe fosters multiple methods investigations and highlights how ethnographic research, which commonly depends on mixed methods, is used to investigate educational issues in the United States and international contexts. Therefore, given the shared foundational aims of educational and anthropological research and the methodological connections between these two social and professional sciences, we discuss mixed methods in the fields of education and anthropology together in this chapter.

Linking these fields in the same chapter permits us to contrast applications of mixed methods in different traditions, traditions in which we each have some expertise. In linking them in the same chapter, we begin with brief overviews of educational and anthropological research. Then we compare and contrast how mixed methods scholarship has manifested itself within these fields. Next we discuss how mixed methods designs are considered within educational and anthropological research, followed by a presentation of selected studies that explore the potential of multimethod and mixed methods research (MMMR) practice. Last we discuss challenges for practicing mixed methods research (MMR) in education and anthropology. We note that our chapter draws from the general literature on research methods in the two fields, as well as on particular MMMR studies within these fields, some of which are explicitly labeled mixed methods and many of which are not so identified.

The Evolution of Research in Education

Educational research currently covers a diversity of subfields, ranging from how contemporary issues such as school choice affect teaching and learning to how emerging frameworks such as complexity theories illuminate ongoing educational problems. Contemporary educational research includes different inquiry types such as basic research, action research, and evaluation research; a variety of methodological designs are used as part of these inquiry types to pursue topics and issues of interest (Johnson & Christensen, 2012). However, the educational research fields and modes of inquiry were not always as diverse as they are today.

In her history and critique of educational research, Lagemann (2000) emphasizes the domination of educational scholarship for most of the 20th century by the theories, concerns, and preferred methods of mainstream psychology. While youths were tested, adults were surveyed to document curriculum, instruction, and administrative approaches in ways that permitted comparisons across classrooms, schools, and districts. Just as behavioral theories of human activity dominated psychological research during the first two-thirds of the 20th century so also were they the foundation for much of educational research.

During the early part of the 20th century, education as a field of study was heavily criticized and not held in high regard by other academic disciplines, including psychology. This lack of respect resulted in educational researchers moving away from these disciplines and scholars to a greater focus on nurturing educational scholarship among themselves. As more of these US educational researchers began to hold appointments at universities, publish in journals, and present at academic conferences, they viewed themselves as education experts (Lagemann, 1997). Their status as specialists facilitated increased credibility and visibility of educational research and professionalization of the field. The early 20th century in the United States also witnessed changes in demographics and in the economy. To address these changes, educational scholars became increasingly concerned with determining the type of curriculum that should be offered. Educational research focused on curriculum studies, using "statistical analysis" or survey research and testing to inform curriculum development and to determine if students were meeting desired educational outcomes (Lagemann, 1997, p. 7).

Interestingly, John Dewey (1859–1962), whose scholarly career spanned the development of educational research as a field of study, advanced a different vision of education and research: pragmatism. Dewey's view of research built on the work of other educators and philosophers such as George Herbert Mead, Charles Sanders Peirce, and William James. Dewey's version of pragmatic educational research, as Campbell (1995) explains, suggests a "turning away from the traditional analyses based in deduction from fixed truths toward self-reflective inquiry based upon broad historical and cross-cultural studies, introduction of research methods and controls, evaluation of results, and so on" (p. 100). In short, for Dewey, educational research should have moved beyond a focus on statistical analysis to a practice of systematic procedures, including careful observation, and an attitude of openness and experimentation.

Parallel to societal events after World War II (i.e., the war on poverty and the civil rights movement), the diversity of educational scholars and scholarship as well as public interest in education increased (Lagemann, 1997, 2000). Public involvement included the support of the federal government and other major funding sources (e.g., philanthropic organizations such as the Ford Foundation). The confluence of these and other complex events in the 1950s and 1960s led to the inclusion of new studies, which overturned some long-standing ideas about schooling practices based on previous quantitatively driven educational research. An example of one such area of new study is the aforementioned educational anthropology. During the portion of the 20th century when survey approaches and experimental designs dominated educational research, roughly the 1920s through the 1960s, various forms of qualitative research in education were carried out along the margins of scholarship by sociologists, anthropologists, and educational researchers. Some of this work, such as Gordon's (1957) examination of a high school, used a collection of mostly, but not exclusively, qualitative methods. Others are what we would label today mixed methods. These include Lortie's (1975) study of US schoolteachers, Hollingshead's (1949) study of the influence of socioeconomic status on teenagers, and Jackson's (1968) synthesis of his reports on classroom life.

Studies such as these fostered and inspired a generation of educational research endeavors more receptive to innovative combinations of different methods and disciplinary orientations (Lagemann, 1997, 2000). By the 1970s, fields such as educational anthropology and the sociology of education were developing institutional support, formal organizations, and journal outlets more amenable to a greater variety of research approaches, as well as to innovative combinations of research designs.

According to Creswell and Garrett (2008), the growth of MMMR in education is also reflected in newly generated conceptualizations and texts, beginning in the 1980s. As evidence, the authors cite the work of US sociology professors John Brewer and Albert Hunter (1989), who authored the book *Multimethod Research: A Synthesis of Styles*, and educator and evaluator, Jennifer Greene, who was the lead author on the paper "Conceptual Framework for Mixed Method Evaluation Designs" with Valerie J. Caracelli and Wendy F. Graham, published in the journal *Educational Evaluation and Policy Analysis* (Greene, Caracelli, & Graham, 1989). The latter piece almost certainly influenced the early adoption of mixed and multiple methods designs in evaluation research, some of which serve educational purposes such as comparing instructional methods and curricular effectiveness.

Creswell and Garrett (2008) cite the increase in published mixed methods books, journals, and conferences, as well as the use of the term *mixed methods* itself when authors describe their studies (see their Table 1 for a listing of educators and their contributions to mixed methods). Further, Creswell and Garrett stress that interest in publishing MMR can be found throughout the world (p. 324). Some examples of published works include research from Japan (Fetters, Yoshioka, Greenberg, Gorenflo, & Yeo, 2007) and the United Kingdom (O'Cathain, Murphy, & Nicholl, 2007).

Another influence on the shift to mixed and multiple methods was the paradigmatic and methodological changes developed from advances in technology, broadly defined. For example, Lagemann (1997) claims

> The school survey movement would not have been possible without tests and statistical devices that allowed researchers to measure the achievement of students and the costs of instruction and, then, through comparative statistical analyses, determine which practices were apparently most effective, least costly, and therefore most efficient. (p. 6)

As further evidence for this, as recently as two decades ago many in the research community were unfamiliar with some of the approaches to sophisticated statistical analysis such as structural equation modeling (Kline, 1998).

Last, we need to acknowledge the paradigm wars of the 1980s that engaged some educational researchers. Quantitative and qualitative "purists" held the "incompatibility thesis" or proposition that scholars cannot mix quantitative and qualitative research because the two approaches were said to be incommensurable. Yet, by the 1990s, many educational researchers discounted the incompatibility thesis and started to promote the thoughtful integration of qualitative and quantitative research (Johnson & Christensen, 2012). This rejection sparked a resurgence of interest in Dewey's philosophy of pragmatism, considered by mixed methods researchers an "alternative paradigm" to the interpretivist and positivistic frameworks (Greene, 2007). Pragmatism rejects the dichotomy of objectivity and subjectivity, depending on the construct of intersubjectivity to acknowledge simultaneous external and internal views on reality and knowledge generation. This alternative paradigm renews the pragmatic stance, which claims "theories or programs or actions that are demonstrated to work for particular groups of people are the ones that we should view as currently being the most valid for those people" (Johnson & Christensen, 2012, p. 32).

As we have briefly recounted, educational research has a history of using multiple paradigms, methodologies, and methods (Tashakkori & Teddlie, 2010, pp. 105–106). Currently, educational researchers use various paradigms or stances such as the dialectical position (Greene & Hall, 2010), dialectical pluralism (Johnson, 2012), realism (Maxwell & Mittapalli, 2010), and the transformative stance (Mertens, 2007) to address the ever-increasing diversity of research questions and concerns (i.e., contextual complexity, causality, and social justice) in education (Rocco, Bliss, Gallagher, & Pérez-Prado, 2003, p. 19). A key contemporary challenge for educational researchers is to appropriately align paradigms with their research questions, purposes, and designs.

To summarize, contemporary educational research has its foundational roots in other disciplines, most notably psychology. The methodological practices of psychologists (survey approaches and experimental designs), diversity of scholars (educators, philosophers, educational anthropologists, etc.), growth in educational subfields, advances in technology, and changes in national demographics represent key contributions to the development of mixed methods in the field of education. Unfortunately, some of these same 20th-century makers and markers of educational research also present challenges to educators conducting mixed methods studies in the 21st century—a topic we return to later when we explore the challenges to MMR in educational and anthropological research.

The Evolution of Research in Anthropology

The driving force in sociocultural anthropology is theory, focusing on human variation in general and cultural variation specifically (Barnard, 2000; Barrett, 1984; Moore, 1997). How can we understand and explain similarities and differences in human experiences, relationships, activities, and organizations? Anthropology developed as a field of study during a period of catastrophic change in human societies. Languages were dying, communities were disappearing, and modernization and globalization were overrunning the diversity of local cultures common around the world prior to the 20th century. Anthropologists were trying to learn about societies before they changed in an effort called salvage anthropology or salvage ethnography (Gruber, 1970). Understanding ourselves meant understanding our variations, and scholars pressed to record the variations while they still existed.

Methods and methodologies in anthropology have served the purpose of describing human communities to develop sociocultural theories to explain and understand the patterns observed (Agar, 1980; Ellen, 1984; Pelto, 1970): methods are the techniques researchers have developed to select, collect, and analyze information, and methodologies have been subsequently formulated to characterize broader philosophies of research such as interpretive ethnography (Geertz, 1973) or cultural materialism (Harris, 1979). Our claim in this chapter is that these methods and methodologies have always been mixed and multiple in anthropology. These mixed or multiple approaches have occurred within the overarching framework of fieldwork or ethnography (Wax, 1971). Fieldwork and ethnography have, from their inception, been composed of varying methods of data selection, collection, and analysis. Anthropologists, beginning in the 19th century, assumed that they had to observe human behavior and interactions in the natural settings where these occurred, hence the centrality of fieldwork and ethnography.

However, from as early as the 19th century, development of the discipline, both the research philosophies and the practices of fieldwork and ethnography, have been hotly debated by anthropologists and other scholars adopting these approaches (Service, 1985). First is the ongoing dialogue about whether anthropology is a science or an art (Carrithers, 1990; Kuznar, 1997; Manners & Kaplan, 1968). Second, assuming that both science and art are somehow involved, what philosophical assumptions ought to and do undergird

anthropological practice of fieldwork and ethnography? What do these assumptions mean for the kinds of knowledge created? A profound challenge to these assumptions arose in the last quarter of the 20th century from poststructural and postmodern critiques: these questioned cultural description based on naïve realism that confused *accounts* of human activity with the *experiences* of human activity of researchers and participants alike (Clifford, 1988; Clifford & Marcus, 1986). In the 1980s and 1990s while scholars in other fields like education discussed the quantitative–qualitative debate or parried shots in the paradigm wars (e.g., Cizek, 1995; Smith & Heshusius, 1986), anthropologists worried about whether culture even exists (Ortner, 1999), not just how to study it, and conversely about how the construct has been so successful that it has been taken up by the business world (Vasavi, 1996). Our point here is that any discussion of mixed and multiple methods in anthropology must take into account these broader currents in the field.

Anthropological fieldwork, generally called ethnography, has from its inception been composed of a wide variety of practices. Central to these practices are observation, participation in people's lifeways, and conversations with those studied. The research approach certainly falls within the overall category of qualitative inquiry. However, collecting, surveying, and a variety of analytic examinations of material thus acquired—qualitative, quantitative, and mixed—have also been integral to what fieldworkers and ethnographers do. Recording in photograph and film and counting linguistic and material items date to 19th-century practices (e.g., Boas, 1940). The extent to which an anthropological study may depend more or less on qualitative or quantitative methods and methodologies revolves around how scholars formulate their topics and the conceptual frameworks used, the subject of the next section.

Approaches to Mixed and Multimethod Research Design in Education and Anthropology

In this section we discuss how mixed and multimethod designs have been applied in education and anthropology. Educational research planning has been dominated by models of effective research process, such as Campbell and Stanley's (1963) recipes for experimental work and more recently Stokes's (1997) hierarchy of design from weak to strong. In contrast, anthropological research planning has been directed more by either theoretical interests of scholars or by interesting developments occurring during field research. The following discussion considers the types of mixed and multimethod designs educators and anthropologists use "on the ground," for what purposes, and under what circumstances. As noted previously, our chapter is based on the general literature on research methods in the two fields, as well as on particular MMMR studies (including evaluations) within these fields, some of which are explicitly labeled mixed methods and many of which are not so identified.

Educational Researchers' Approaches to Research Design

Given that MMR in education has its foundations in evaluation practice, it is not surprising that mixed and multimethod designs typically used by educational researchers rely on quantitative methods to address the "what" questions or issues researchers seek to understand through surveys, questionnaires, or performance tests, whereas interviews, observations, and other forms of qualitative data are used to address the "why" questions involved in the study. Beyond this broad pattern, an abundance of specific mixed and multimethod design frameworks are used by educational researchers (Creswell, 2009; Johnson & Onwuegbuzie, 2004; Tashakkori & Teddlie, 2003, 2010).

To better understand how mixed methods design frameworks (and their purposes) are applied in social science research, a number of prevalence studies have recently been published (e.g., Alise & Teddlie, 2010; Collins, Onwuegbuzie, & Jiao, 2007; Collins, Onwuegbuzie, & Sutton, 2006; Ivankova & Kawamura, 2010; Lopez-Fernandez & Molina-Azorin, 2011; Truscott et al., 2010). These prevalence studies describe the frequency of mixed methods designs across disciplines or within the field of education (Lopez-Fernandez & Molina-Azorin, 2011). Our review of this literature reveals some key findings. First, there were challenges to identify specific mixed methods designs in the field of education because "few researchers disclosed these details of their design" (Truscott et al., 2010, p. 325). Second, when mixed methods designs were identified, the most common designs applied were the quasi-mixed design (i.e., designs that lack integration of quantitative and qualitative findings; Alise & Teddlie, 2010) and the sequential design (Alise & Teddlie, 2010; Collins, et al., 2006; Lopez-Fernandez & Molina-Azorin, 2011).

Last, mixed method approaches were used with a range of purposes (complementarity, development, expansion, and triangulation; Lopez-Fernandez & Molina-Azorin, 2011).

We note that the prevalence rate studies differ in terms of sampling techniques used (types of journals), key terms used (mixed methods, mixed methodology), mixed methods classification of designs, and so on. Yet, when taken together, the prevalence studies do suggest that educational researchers are increasingly using mixed methods designs (Alise & Teddlie, 2010). Indeed, Ivankova and Kawamura (2010) note the growth in MMR

across the countries, [but] the United States ($n = 55$) took the lead in mixed methods methodological discussions, with the United Kingdom ($n = 25$), Canada ($n = 13$), and Australia ($n = 9$) following, and [these] covered a range of social, behavioral, and health disciplines. (p. 584)

We also note that, although this literature indicates an increase in MMR, some subfields (i.e., special education) have witnessed limited growth in the use of mixed methods designs (Collins et al., 2006). Mixed methods designs are also varied across educational subfields such as literacy, mathematics, science, and social studies (Truscott et al., 2010). For instance, Sammons (2010) discusses how mixed method designs such as multilevel and fully integrated mixed methods designs enhance educational effectiveness research in areas such as "school effectiveness, teacher effectiveness and school improvement" through multilayered and interactive investigations (p. 698).

In sum, we do not think the use and variation in mixed methods designs in educational research is surprising, as research ought to be focused on answering research questions using thoughtful and appropriate approaches to mixed methods designs (Johnson & Christensen, 2014). However, we do think the increased attention on MMR design as evidenced by the surge in prevalence studies indicates, to some extent, the priority given to research designs in the field of education. The supremacy of research design in educational research is also demonstrated through federal agencies, funding, and policy that advocate or prescribe mixed methods approaches and reinforce the assumption of a single, correct way to make knowledge (e.g., National Research Council, 2005; What Works Clearinghouse, 2008). We believe this focus on just a few research designs in educational research is unfortunate for the field.

In contrast, anthropologists are not trying to find the correct way to do culture the way some policymakers may hope for a correct way to do school. Therefore, the absence of prevalence studies in anthropology may be due to a more diffuse attention to substance, theory, and emergent design.

Anthropologists' Approach to Research Design

Research in anthropology is far less concerned with particular, structured, or a priori designs than with the substance and theory being pursued in a study. Fieldwork and ethnography are the predominant data collection approaches, but anthropologists incorporate surveys and a variety of standardized and projective instrumentation into their fieldwork. Applied anthropologists occasionally do evaluation research into alternative practices and programs (e.g., Handwerker, 2001), but few anthropologists conduct experiments using randomized clinical trials that are the so-called gold standard for design, according to some educational researchers (Stokes, 1997).

The anthropological assumption is that people ought to be studied in the natural environments where they develop and carry on their daily lives, a focus on naturalistic settings and methods. Sometimes the result of the research is an ethnography, a study of the culture of a group; other times the design is closer to multiple surveys or administered projective and other kinds of tests but typically occurring in the field rather than in a laboratory. The methods of data selection, collection, and analysis are multiple and mixed, but the actual conduct of research is informal in the sense that anthropologists do not customarily use design recipes. They do expect to use observations and interviews, but decisions about data selection and the details of data collection are made in the field, guided in part by what has been learned thus far. (See comparable decision-making patterns advocated for educational research in Johnson & Christensen, 2014, with their multiple-dimension process approach to mixed research design.) This pattern of emergent design is clear in one of the few comments made on research methods by Franz Boas at the turn of the 20th century:

> Boas' instructions had been "to collect certain things and to collect with everything they get information in the native language and to obtain grammatical information that is necessary to explain their texts. Consequently the results of their

journeys are the following: They get specimens; they get explanations of the specimens; they get connected texts that partly refer to the specimens and partly refer simply to abstract things concerning the people; and they get grammatical information." (Hinsley & Holm, 1976, p. 314)

Where materials gathered lent themselves to numerical summary and analysis, Boas used these methods (e.g., Boas, 1940). The emphasis on collecting cultural materials reached its zenith in publications such as *Notes and Queries on Anthropology* (Royal Anthropological Institute of Great Britain and Ireland, 1951), which provided typologies of cultural practices and products to collect, document, and count. This cultural traits approach provides the framework for such texts as Williams's (1967) manual on fieldwork, a midcentury research methods source for anthropologists, and Yale University's Human Relations Area Files' *Outline of Cultural Materials* (1945). Fieldworkers were expected to collect samples of all the material and linguistic objects participants produced—clothes, tools, stories, art—as well as accounts of the objects and of the social organizations using the various objects.

The first half of the 20th century was a period when fieldwork and ethnographic methods were being created by the anthropologists who made decisions on the basis of how best to represent, *scientifically*, the patterns they believed they discerned in people's behaviors. In a 1926 letter to Boas, who was her teacher, Margaret Mead comments on how best to represent her research findings in her study of Samoan girls (1928):

> Ideally, no reader should have to trust my word for anything, except of course in as much as he [sic] trusted my honesty and averagely intelligent observation. . . . Only two possibilities occur to me and both seem inadequate. First I could present my material in semi-statistical fashion. It would be fairly misleading at that because I can't see how any sort of statistical technique would be of value. . . . Then I could use case histories. . . . But how to use it. If I simply write conclusions and use my cases as illustrative material will it be acceptable? Would it be more acceptable if I could devise some method of testing the similarity of attitudes among the [Samoan] girls, in a quantitative way? (Letter quoted in Stocking, 1987, pp. 5–7)

In the end, for this study Mead elected what Boas suggested as a clinical approach to examining cases. About the same time, Bronislaw Malinowsky was wrestling with comparable challenges but advocated a more mixed approach:

> The first cardinal point of method [is that] each phenomenon ought to be studied through the broadest range possible of its concrete manifestations. . . [in what] could be called *the method of statistic documentation by concrete evidence.* . . . Within this frame the *imponderabilia of actual life* and the *type of behavior* have to be filled in. . . [and supplemented with] a collection of ethnographic statements, characteristic narratives, typical utterances, items of folk-lore and magical formulae. . . as documents of native mentality. (Malinowski, 1922/1961, pp. 17, 24; italics in original)

Building field study around observations and interviews, interspersed with relevant life histories, surveys and questionnaires, semantic techniques and projective tests, and a collection of structured behavioral and document content analyses became routine anthropological practice in the second half of the 20th century, as indicated in a variety of research methods texts for sociocultural anthropologists (e.g., Bernard, 1988; Ellen, 1984; Pelto, 1970; Werner & Schoepfle, 1987a, 1987b) and in the primary journal for sociocultural anthropology research methods, *Field Methods* (formerly *CAM: Cultural Anthropology Methods Newsletter*).

Conventions for reporting these research methods and designs were likewise developed by the early fieldworkers. How a study was conducted was sometimes accorded a chapter or an appendix in a book-length presentation of findings, as Malinowski had done in 1922. Design discussions also appeared as separate journal articles such as Mead's 1933 discussion of field methods in her research in Samoa and other locations. They might be the subject of a stand-alone text like Malinowski's (1967/1989) notorious *A Diary in the Strict Sense of the Term*, with its objectionable labels for Indigenous peoples, or Mead's (1977) more decorous *Letters from the Field, 1925–1975*. In addition, in the last decades of the 20th century, commentaries on fieldwork experiences were collected in a diversity of anthologies (e.g., Foster, Scudder, Colson, & Kemper, 1979; Freilich, 1970; Golde, 1986; Messerschmidt, 1981).

Up until the 1980s many anthropologists struggled with combining Malinowski's (1922/1961) "method of statistic evidence" with what he called "documents of native mentality"—what

participants had to say about the evidence. Field reports and ethnographies varied in what they presented as objective material and subjective material. At midcentury, Pike (1954) proposed a new binary, *etic* and *emic*, intended to distinguish between constructs imposed on the field by researchers, similar to phonetic units found across languages, and constructs indigenous to the participants themselves, similar to phonemic units specific to particular languages. From this distinction a new emphasis in anthropology developed called ethnoscience, where ethnographers identified the domains of experience common among people's talk (e.g., Spradley, 1979, 1980) in an effort to connect what was individually held to ideas shared broadly by a community. These approaches led to the formulation of the new subfield of *cognitive anthropology*, focusing on people's cultural knowledge (D'Andrade, 1995) and to a broader discussion led by Clifford Geertz (1973) of the *interpretive* nature of human experience, behavior, and activities. Participants say different things about the evidence researchers collect because human meaning is layered and multiple. Things have multiple, sometimes conflicting meanings, and different people attribute different meanings to what may be shared experiences. Add to this the often-neglected subjectivities of researchers themselves, and the enterprise of studying cultures—scientifically or otherwise—became, and continues to be, hotly debated. As we acknowledged previously, the so-called *crisis of representation* (Marcus & Fischer, 1986) questioned whether cultures and human experiences could even be legitimately represented—whether from a scientific or a humanities perspective.

Meanwhile, despite and alongside of these philosophical worries, anthropologists have gone on studying humans and their cultures, and they have continued to examine human experience using multiple and diverse methods and approaches. However, only in the past couple of decades have anthropologists started to articulate these as mixed or multiple methods. We base this claim on our own examination of the literature.

Using no date limitations, we searched two databases, AnthroSource and Anthropology Plus, for the index terms *mixed* or *multiple methods* or *design*. The AnthroSource search yielded 16 separate items: one from 1990, one from 1997, and the rest after 2000; these articles were from the American Anthropological Association. Anthropology Plus yielded another 10 items; apart from one entry, these were articles from either of two methodological journals, *Qualitative Research* or *Field Methods*. We then combined the index terms with the term *anthropology* to search the Web of Knowledge. These searches yielded larger numbers of items (48) from the 1980s onward in health predominantly but also in fields such as education and physical anthropology. Three out of four items repeated from the anthropology databases in anthropology journals that publish sociocultural anthropology. Many of these entries on MMMR and design referred to anthropology only incidentally.

Most of the explicitly labeled *mixed* or *multiple methods* work is published in psychological and medical anthropology. We suspect that this pattern is connected to the interdisciplinary orientations and teamwork more common to these two specialties. In 2012 Thomas Weisner, a practitioner and advocate of MMR (e.g., Weisner, 2005), called for what he termed *methodological pluralism* in a prominent article in *Anthropology News*, the publication received by all members of the American Anthropological Association. He emphasized the range and diversity of mixed methods in both current anthropological practice and in earlier work, highlighting advantages offered. What we see in anthropology is the practice of mixed and multiple methods designs but little articulation about it.

Based on this review of research designs, we have demonstrated that, while both educational researchers and anthropologists use mixed and multimethod approaches, and even label them as such, the description of the design or reference to the broader mixed methods literature are uneven at best. In the following selected MMMR studies, we illustrate this pattern, highlighting the diverse MMMR studies that do not necessarily cite the mixed or multiple methods literature.

Selected Multimethod and Mixed Methods Research Studies in Education and Anthropology

The mixed methods studies in this section were selected to purposefully showcase studies that are creative, integrative, and reflective. Our review of the mixed methods literature and research indicate studies such as these are not only desired but necessary to encourage and guide the future of thoughtfully innovative mixed and multimethod designs. It is also important to note the mixed methods studies in this section include evaluation research and studies researchers themselves identified as mixed or multimethod research.

Our first two examples are from the field of education. The first is a *mixed methods* evaluation model selected because it incorporates a less known but historical qualitative approach with mixed methods: phenomenography. The second is identified as a *multimethod* approach by the researcher. Both studies address the complexities and subtleties related to how learning is perceived.

Researchers Micari, Light, Calkins, and Streitwieser (2007) explain that phenomenography was developed by Swedish researchers in the 1970s and has been used to "describe variation in the ways people experience learning in various contexts" (p. 459). The authors argue, as we have earlier in this chapter, that the increased call for accountability in education has advanced quantitative evaluations that measure student performance. However, these researchers claim it is just as imperative to understand how students think about learning and how their thinking changes over time when assessing programs.

To illustrate the phenomenographic method, the researchers describe a case when phenomenography was applied to evaluate a program designed to improve teaching and learning strategies at a Midwestern private research university. This case examined faculty approaches to teaching after participating in a faculty development program for one year. This study used a quantitative instrument and a qualitative phenomenographic interview component. First, the researchers conducted 25 faculty phenomenographic interviews and formulated three types of conceptions faculty had of teaching. The first viewed teaching as conveying information without considering students' prior knowledge; the second viewed teaching as helping students gain knowledge by using what they know; and the third conceived of teaching as finding ways to help students independently construct or reconstruct concepts. Next, the researchers asked 31 participants over three years (before and after the program) to complete a standardized Likert-type inventory (developed through previous phenomenographic research), including 16 items to measure variation in the first two conceptualizations of teaching described previously. Evidence from both the inventory and the interviews suggested faculty shifted toward student-centered approaches as the course progressed, and the program played a significant role in developing faculty members' capacities to be student-centered.

The researchers claim that applying the phenomenographic approach gave them access to participants' conceptualizations of teaching and the extent to which these conceptualizations changed over the length of the program. As a result, the researchers "worked to identify areas of the programs (especially workshops and project groups) that can be strengthened to more fully expose participants to the variation between teacher-focused teaching and learner-focused teaching" (Micari et al., 2007, p. 472). In addition, the researchers "created a new survey instrument to follow up participants from the first 5 years of the program to assess their current conceptions of teaching" (p. 472).

Our second educational research example highlights how multiple methods were used in cross-cultural research on students' achievement motivation. The research was implemented by a research team that conducted a series of studies in the United States, Russia, and England to compare students' attributions of academic outcomes, that is, if students believed their academic performance was due to hard work or fixed ability (Elliott, 2004). The multiple methods in this study included student surveys and interviews, teacher interviews and rankings of students, and classroom observations. First, large-scale surveys were completed by over 6,000 9- to 10-year-old and 14- to 15-year-old students. Based on these data, researchers found that the Anglo American students, as compared to their Russian counterparts, were more likely to attribute their achievement to effort and to positive perceptions of themselves as hard workers. To better understand the extent to which these views were held, researchers conducted 144 interviews with 14- to 15-year-old students in a subset of the same US, Russian, and English schools (Elliott, 2004). The majority of the students interviewed reported their ability as determining their academic achievement. However, Russian students reported that both effort and ability determined achievement, depending on the subject matter. Further, when asked what their teachers thought of them, most students' self-perceptions about their ability to work hard aligned with their beliefs about their teachers' perceptions.

Next, to understand what teachers actually believed about students, teacher rankings of students were collected. These rankings revealed Anglo American students overestimated teachers' perceptions about them and Russian youth underestimated teachers' beliefs about them. Then, to understand these different trends across countries, the teachers were interviewed. The interviews revealed the same trends identified in the rankings. Teachers from all three countries claimed to provide praise to students. Interestingly, teacher observations in each country led to nuanced understandings of how praise was actually used in each context. Researchers discovered that Russian teachers provided praise rarely and modestly, as compared to English and US teachers, who used an abundance of elaborate praise. The researchers claimed that, taken together, the multiple methods used in this study helped to clarify differences in perceptions and contributed to understandings of the complex educational contexts and practices that constitute those perceptions. To be sure, they remark,

> By themselves, the surveys informed us of important similarities and differences in reported attitudes, values, and behaviors of our English, U.S., and Russian samples. However, it was only when detailed interviews with children and teachers, and observation of actual practices, were added that we began to recognise more complex and beguiling realities. (Elliott, 2004, p. 145)

The researchers further claim that multiple methods informed by their "study of sociocultural and sociohistorical factors in each context" were critical to understand the "complexities and paradoxes in our informants' responses and appreciate that seeming similarities in informant reports across cultures could mask very different practices" (Hufton, Elliott, & Illushin, 2002, as cited in Elliott, 2004, p. 145). Their multiple methods pointed to, for example, the different cross-cultural uses of praise.

Comparable complexities are reported in uses of mixed and multiple methods in anthropology. We have noted, however, that much mixed and multiple methods work in anthropology is not identified as such. Nevertheless, we have selected for our two examples in this field one labeled *mixed methods* and one using the term *multiple methods*. Both studies are somewhat unusual in anthropology because they examine interventions; however, many anthropology studies labeled *mixed methods* are conducted in interdisciplinary areas like medical anthropology and psychological anthropology where interventions and clinical studies, if not laboratory experiments, are more common.

Thomas Weisner's (2011) summary of research on New Hope (NH), a community-initiated poverty-reduction program operating in the latter part of the 1990s in the Midwestern, urban United

States, is clearly identified as mixed methods. He labels the overall approach as a random-assignment experiment, notes the interdisciplinary nature of its large research team, and frames the study within policy-oriented research in psychological anthropology. More than 1,000 people, predominantly females with children, entered a lottery to be randomly assigned to a control group or to an intervention group. Participants in both groups were eligible for a variety of community services, but the intervention group received additional childcare, healthcare, and occupational services, as well as some direct financial support. The control and intervention groups included 745 individuals who participated in the four-year program and the eight-year research study. All were surveyed, their children were assessed, and documents on their employment and use of social services were collected; baseline data were supplemented with periodic updates. Ethnographic data were collected on a subset of 44 families, half each from the control and treatment groups: interviews and observations occurred during home visits and excursions with the families around the neighborhoods.

The two strongest outcomes were income improvements for participants who had not been employed at all prior to the program and educational improvements for all treatment-group participants' sons but not their daughters. Weisner (2011) explains these quantitative results with the qualitative findings. He notes that the NH program was better suited for the unemployed than for the underemployed, who needed a different set of services than the program provided. He observed that families were able to provide their sons additional resources to protect them from neighborhood dangers to which daughters were less vulnerable (e.g., gang activity), thus addressing the better education results for male children in the families receiving treatment. Weisner comments on the research design:

> The NH study used ethnographic evidence in the context of an experimental, longitudinal design and mixed methods. The cross talk between the evidence from the ethnographic families nested within the larger sample, was important for understanding impacts (experimental-control differences), pathways (how the NH program made a difference overall and for different subgroups, including processes shaping those varied paths), and outcomes (changes over time other than experimental-control group differences). These three kinds of empirical

evidence (impacts, pathways, outcomes) are different and need to be carefully distinguished, and all three are valuable and have been instructive for policy and practice implications. (p. 471)

Wiesner's study is instructive for policymakers because it emphasizes tailoring solutions for unemployment based the context and characteristics of study participants.

Our second example also involves an interdisciplinary team, albeit much smaller than the group of NH researchers, and an intervention but only a few hours rather than a few years. Cox, Kazubowski-Houston, and Nisker (2009) designed a theatrical production as an intervention to provoke public comment on the development of Canadian policy for the controversial practice of preimplantation genetic diagnosis (PGD), genetic testing of embryos created by in vitro fertilization. Sixteen performances of a play about two women considering the practice were held in three Canadian cities in 2005. The audiences for these performances consisted of 741 people whose input on the practice of PGD was sought through a survey of everyone, selected focus-group discussions, and large-group audience discussions. Field notes were recorded of observations of the audience during the performances, and both large-group and focus-group discussions were audio-recorded. Unlike the study reported by Weisner (2011), no input was sought by the researchers from a control group not attending the performance; however, shortly after the PGD performances, a government-sponsored survey on the subject was conducted (but not presented in this report). Cox et al. (2009) found that audience views of PGD varied widely, as might be expected, and were often conflated with other kinds of medical interventions. People expressed concerns about who might have access to PGD and under what circumstances, how the practice ought to be regulated and by whom, what the implications of PGD were for individuals and communities, and how genetic sciences and practices would affect people's lives. Audiences were also asked to assess the use of theatre to present and elicit public commentary on policy issues. They appreciated the theater format as a means of providing information on, and divergent views of, public issues and as an avenue for citizen dialogue with policymakers. They and the researchers, however, noted the limited range of middle- and upper-class people reached by theater attendance. Finally, the researchers noted the differences in people's responses to the survey, the large audience discussion, and the focus-group discussion and stressed the strengths and limitations of each approach, concluding,

> We anticipated that participants would prefer one format and that we would discover patterned interactions characteristic of each. For instance, focus groups would by virtue of their smaller size yield greater participant interaction than large audience discussions. We were not, however, initially as attuned to the pivotal importance of utilizing multiple approaches when a project requires both a method of stimulating ongoing engagement and a method of simultaneously assessing that engagement. (Cox et al., 2009, p. 1478)

Both of these reports by anthropologists (Kazubowski-Houston is the anthropologist on her team) focused on their substantive results and provided only limited information about their research methods and methodologies.

As mentioned earlier, after reviewing the references for the studies highlighted in this section, we find it unfortunate but unsurprising that these articles lack citations to the broader mixed or multiple methods literature, even though these approaches are clearly valued by their authors. For instance, Cox and colleagues (2009) do include citations to the qualitative methods literature, including work on performance studies, but have no references to the survey method they used. Weisner (2011) cites two methods pieces of his own (e.g., Lieber & Weisner, 2010; Lieber, Weisner, & Presley, 2003), but only to account for the software program used in the project. Other facets of a complex design are not referenced at all. This is one of the many challenges of adapting these approaches in this and other fields where research methods and design are discussed less frequently than in education. These challenges are the topic of the following section.

Challenges to Incorporating a Mixed and Multimethod Approach into Educational and Anthropological Research

Challenges to incorporating MMMR into educational and anthropological research are similar to those faced in most fields. In this section, we first discuss some of these general challenges organized by three broad categories: research design issues, practical constraints, and researcher considerations. We then outline what we perceive as major challenges to conducting mixed and multimethod research in the fields of educational and anthropological research, respectively.

General challenges to incorporating mixed and multimethod approaches include the heterogeneity surrounding what constitutes mixed methods (Bazeley, 2004), debates about the mixing of paradigms or the use of alternative paradigms (pragmatism, transformative research, etc.) to support MMR (Greene, 2008; Mertens, 2010; Yin, 2006), the focus on quantitative research or reliance on it to increase the validity of either the results of qualitative research or of MMR (Bazeley, 2004), "pressure for qualitative research from the quantitative community to 'measure up' to quantitative standards without understanding the basic premises of qualitative investigations" (Sale, Lohfeld, & Brazil, 2002, p. 50), and "issues of validity in mixed methods still need[ing] to be addressed" (Dellinger & Leech, 2007, p. 314).

More practical challenges to conducting MMR include the significant time, increased expense, and restrictive timelines encountered when conducting mixed or multimethod research (Bazeley, 2004; Chen, 2006). In addition, other scholars note characteristics of researchers that may present challenges such as the lack of ability and preparation to appropriately conduct a mixed methods study and interpret results (Hesse-Biber & Johnson, 2013).

Challenges From Educational Policy for Multimethod and Mixed Methods Research in Education

A major challenge to incorporating mixed and multimethod designs in the field of education is the influence of national educational policies. Federal governments, resources, and politics have influenced and continue to affect educational policy, which in turn shapes educational research (and evaluation). In the United States and the United Kingdom, educational research has been influenced through respective federal governments by means of grants, policy, mandates, and statutes used to set guidelines for educational reform. An example of polices influencing educational research are the New Public Management (NPM) reforms of the 1980s (Hood, 1995). In general, these reforms refer to a set of policies that focus the efficiency of government services, including public schools, through market-based management approaches. Significant policy convergence around NPM reforms occurred across the United States, Australia, New Zealand, and the United Kingdom, reflecting a high trust in managerialism (i.e., focus on and belief in business practices) and a shift "from process accountability towards a greater element of accountability in terms of results" (Hood, 1995, p. 94). A key justification for these accountability reforms was to make public institutions, such as schools, more accountable to taxpayers, as indicated in the subsequent section.

In the following decades, a component of various educational reform policies (such as the No Child Left Behind legislation in the United States) included accountability practices such as external testing to monitor school and student performance and to serve as evidence measuring school quality. By the 21st century, many of these accountability practices became a common part of the educational policy landscape (Hursh, 2005; O'Day, 2002). Consequently, NPM reforms, including accountability practices, transformed not only the way public school services are delivered but how they are evaluated (Apple, 2004), thus promoting the collection of excessive amounts of quantitative data. This has included greater use of summative evaluations, measurements, assessments, inspections, and so forth, central to the efficient organization and monitoring of schools (Power, 1997; Strathern, 2000).

Recently, the US government's educational policies have shifted roles from highly prescriptive federal accountability policy requirements to providing states and local school districts slightly more flexibility to meet these requirements (Grissom & Herrington, 2012). Despite these shifts in intergovernmental relations in education, educational policies still maintain a managerial orientation that seeks educational accountability through a portfolio of quantitative methods that, for the most part, decontextualize the complexities of the educational enterprise. Therefore, additional use of multiple and mixed inquiry can provide critically needed data to study policy shifts and other changes. In recognition of this need, alternative methodological designs have been offered that attempt to take into account the complexities of educational policy and local educational contexts. One notable example is the extended-term mixed methods evaluation design (Chatterji, 2005). This long-term design approach incorporates formative and summative phases in the mixed methods design to address educational program improvement and delivery.

Understanding this larger sociopolitical context, we argue, is important because the demand for quantitative methodologies, even with shifts toward more state flexibility, have steadily increased as accountability for the use of scarce public resources intensifies. Due to this high demand as well as to advancements in computer technology, both the US and UK governments bring together more quantitative data sets than ever before for educational practice and research purposes. In the United States, the increased demand for quantitative data is reflected in the What Works Clearinghouse, a federal policy tool used to gather and report on the effectiveness of educational programs based on empirical studies that meet strict standards for scientific evidence. For example, in their *Procedures and Standards Handbook 2.1*, the What Works Clearinghouse discusses how studies are reviewed to determine the extent to which they meet evidence standards, with randomized controlled trials viewed as providing the strongest evidence (What Works Clearinghouse, 2008). Given the handbook guidelines, it is no surprise, then, that when mixed or multiple method studies are used in the field of education, often they are conducted with a heavy reliance on quantitative data.

Our thesis is that educational researchers are challenged to use mixed methods designs at the state and federal level. And when they do, qualitative techniques are often used as supplementary or as a triangulation of the initial quantitative results (Tashakkori & Teddlie, 2003). Yet, in addition to the extended-term mixed methods evaluation design discussed previously, other alternative mixed methods designs have been advanced to counter the dominance of quantitatively oriented mixed or multimethod designs. These include qualitatively driven mixed methods designs currently advocated by some multimethod and mixed methods scholars (e.g., Creswell, 2009; Hall & Ryan, 2011; Hesse-Biber, 2010). Such initiatives that champion alternative methodological designs are increasingly important to combat this major challenge of the overreliance on conventional quantitative methods in the field of education. Anthropologists face different challenges, as we discuss subsequently.

Challenges for Multimethod and Mixed Methods Research in Anthropological Research

Anthropology shares with educational research a similar policy climate privileging some design approaches over others at the state and national levels, as discussed previously. National funding agencies and philanthropic organizations provide some support for scholars in anthropology, and this support has also been affected by NPM trends. Lacking the large public sector constituency of teachers and administrators, however, anthropology has been less directly vulnerable to such influences, although anthropology graduates working for social service and evaluation agencies are exposed to similar pressures. Also, as noted previously, except for those working in applied anthropology, anthropological researchers are less pressured for research demonstrating best practices and evidence-based conclusions than educational scholars may be. However, anthropologists in all areas engage in the aforementioned debates about how scientific anthropology is and ought to be, as indicated by the 2010 dispute in the US national organization (Wade, 2010).

The biggest challenges to use of mixed and multiple methodologies in anthropology come from, first, the predilection for qualitative fieldwork; second, an emphasis on design as emergent process rather than dependence on fixed designs; and third, a primary emphasis on substance and theory as more important than design, as discussed in earlier parts of this chapter. Research methods and practice have been assumed to be learnable by fieldworkers on an "as-needed" basis and to be directed by developing field conditions and emergent understandings. Erickson (1986) relates this apocryphal account of planning for fieldwork:

> It is said of Alfred Kroeber that when a doctoral student came for advise [sic] on fieldwork research methods before embarking on a study of a native American society somewhere in California, Kroeber made the following comments:
>
> 1. First, find your Indian (i.e., don't study the wrong group by mistake).
>
> 2. Pads of paper and pencils are very useful.
>
> 3. Be sure to take a frying pan, but don't loan it to anyone; you may not get it back. (p. 140)

We hope that our previous discussion of materials from Margaret Mead and Franz Boas indicate that most anthropologists take their fieldwork practices very seriously indeed, but fieldwork fables such as Erickson's do reveal what he called the romantic vision of anthropological research. This can be compelling, and we believe very misleading, for novice anthropologists as well as for the popular audience for fieldwork accounts. What legitimately challenges the novice is anticipating what quantitative and qualitative approaches are going to be needed once fieldwork commences (for one alternative in multimethod and mixed methods research see Johnson's discussion of interactive mixed inquiry in this volume, ch. 3). An advantage 21st-century anthropologists have over predecessors is readier access to the array of approaches, even after beginning fieldwork far away from their academic homes. Indeed, the variety of approaches available is just one of the many research decisions both educational researchers and anthropologists will have to make when conducting MMMR in the future.

Conclusion

In this chapter we argue for discussing the fields of educational research and anthropology together, as they are both social and professional sciences but provide interesting contrasts. We discuss the history of research within these fields, highlighting how mixed and multiple methods have evolved. With this background in mind, we consider the varying conceptualizations, designs, and challenges to MMMR in each field.

Educational researchers are increasingly using the mixed methods label to identify their designs. However, the use of the label is applied differently, and designs vary across subfields. Educational researchers remain challenged to incorporate alternative paradigms and methods within the larger sociopolitical context of educational accountability. Anthropologists are somewhat less pressured than educational researchers to use particular research designs, but they are also less explicit and direct about describing the designs they do use. Having said that, we commend the field of anthropology for its history of eclectic approaches to research design and suggest that methodological commentaries on anthropological studies be developed to provide models for work in other fields. A synthesis of the many accounts of fieldwork already available for mixed and multiple research practices would be a major contribution to the literature.

Educational researchers can certainly benefit from the responsive and developmental approach to research used by anthropologists. The focus on what is going on in a particular context, rather than how what is going on fits a preconceived model, may direct educational researchers to better understanding of teaching and learning. Anthropologists can learn to be more self-conscious and more articulate about their research decisions and other processes. This reflection and articulation would lead to a better understanding of research results.

We believe the future of MMMR in education and anthropology relies on cutting-edge, empirical studies that include thoughtful reconceptualizations of what can be *mixed* and how the *mixing* can occur. As reflected by our multiple and mixed disciplinary presentation in this chapter, we promote this vision and are convinced that reflective integration will enhance understandings to address needs of individuals and to improve societal conditions.

Discussion Questions

1. How are education and anthropology distinct? What commonalities exist between these two fields?

2. Consider the evolution and contemporary use of MMMR in the fields of education and anthropology. Conduct a web search and locate mixed and multimethod articles in the past several years from your field or discipline. What changes (if any) do you notice in how MMR is used in your field? What are the most common mixed methods designs used in your area?

3. How do the challenges to conducting mixed or multimethod research presented in this chapter help you consider the challenges (if any) faced when conducting MMR in your field? How do these challenges influence how you might carry out a study?

4. What are your views on the information presented in this chapter? What did you find most helpful? What would you like to learn more about?

Suggested Websites

http://www.aaanet.org/

The American Anthropological Association promotes the study of all aspects of human life: archeological, biological, ethnological, and linguistic.

http://anthrosciences.org/xwiki/bin/view/Main/

The Society for Anthropological Sciences advances social science research in anthropology. This research is anchored in theory and appropriate research methodology. The goal of this organization is to describe and explain the difference in human biology, society, and culture across time and space.

http://www.aera.net/

As a national research society, the American Educational Research Association advances educational knowledge and scholarly research to improve education and serve the public good.

References

Agar, M. H. (1980). *The professional stranger: An informal introduction to ethnography.* New York: Academic Press.

Alise, M., & Teddlie, C. (2010). A continuation of the paradigm wars? Prevalence rates of methodological approaches across the social/behavioral sciences. *Journal of Mixed Methods Research, 4,* 103–126.

Apple, M. (2004). Schooling, market, and an audit culture. *Educational Policy, 18*(4), 614–621. doi:10.1177/0895904804266642

Barnard, A. (2000). *History and theory in anthropology.* Cambridge, UK: Cambridge University Press.

Barrett, S. R. (1984). *The rebirth of anthropological theory.* Toronto: University of Toronto Press.

Bazeley, P. (2004). Issues in mixing qualitative and quantitative approaches to research. In R. Buber, J. Gadner, & L. Richards (Eds.), *Applying qualitative methods to marketing management research* (pp. 141–156). London: Palgrave Macmillan.

Bernard, H. R. (1988). *Research methods in cultural anthropology.* Newbury Park, CA: SAGE.

Boas, F. (1940). *Race, language, and culture.* Chicago: University of Chicago Press.

Brewer, J., & Hunter, A. (1989). *Multimethod research: A synthesis of styles.* Newbury Park, CA: SAGE.

Campbell, J. (1995). *Understanding John Dewey: Nature and cooperative intelligence.* Chicago: Open Court.

Campbell, D., & Stanley, J. (1963). *Experimental and quasi-experimental designs for research.* Chicago: Rand McNally.

Carrithers, M. (1990). Is anthropology art or science? *Current Anthropology, 31*(3), 263–282.

Chatterji, M. (2005). Evidence on "what works": An argument for Extended-Term Mixed-Method (ETTM) evaluation designs. *Educational Researcher, 34,* 14–24.

Chen, H. (2006). A theory-driven evaluation perspective on mixed methods research. *Research in the Schools, 13*(1), 75–83.

Cizek, G. J. (1995). Crunchy granola and the hegemony of the narrative. *Educational Researcher, 24*(2), 26–28.

Clifford, J. (1988). *The predicament of culture: Twentieth-century ethnography, literature, and art.* Cambridge, MA: Harvard University Press.

Clifford, J., & Marcus, G. E. (Eds.). (1986). *Writing culture: The poetics and politics of ethnography.* Los Angeles: University of California Press.

Collins, K., Onwuegbuzie, A. J., & Jiao, Q. (2007). A mixed methods investigation of mixed methods sampling designs in social and health science research. *Journal of Mixed Methods Research, 1*(3), 267–294. doi:10.1177/1558689807299526

Collins, K., Onwuegbuzie, A. J., & Sutton, A. (2006). A model incorporating the rationale and purpose for conducting mixed-methods research in special education and beyond. *Learning Disabilities: A Contemporary Journal, 4,* 67–100.

Cox, S. M., Kazubowski-Houston, M., & Nisker, J. (2009). Genetics on stage: Public engagement in health policy development on preimplantation genetic diagnosis. *Social Sciences and Medicine, 68*(8), 1472–1480.

Creswell, J. W. (2009). *Research design: Qualitative, quantitative, and mixed methods approaches* (3rd ed.). Thousand Oaks, CA: SAGE.

Creswell, J. W., & Garrett, A. L. (2008). The "movement" of mixed methods research and the role of educators. *South African Journal of Education, 28,* 321–333.

D'Andrade, R. (1995). *The development of cognitive anthropology.* Cambridge, UK: Cambridge University Press.

Dellinger, A. B., & Leech, N. L. (2007). Toward a unified validation framework in mixed methods research. *Journal of Mixed Methods Research, 1*(4), 309–332. doi:10.1177/1558689807306147

deMarrais, K., Armstrong, J., & Preissle, J. (2010). Anthropology and education. In S. Tozer, B. Gallegos, A. Henry, M. B. Greiner, & P. G. Price (Eds.), *Handbook of research in the social foundations of education* (pp. 76–93). New York: Routledge.

Ellen, R. F. (Ed.). (1984). *Ethnographic research: A guide to general conduct*. London: Academic Press.

Elliott, J. (2004). Multimethod approaches in educational research. *International Journal of Disability, Development and Education*, 51(2), 135–149.

Erickson, F. (1986). Qualitative methods in research on teaching. In M. C. Wittrock (Ed.), *Handbook of research on teaching* (3rd ed., pp. 119–161.). New York: Macmillan.

Fetters, M. D., Yoshioka, T., Greenberg, G. M., Gorenflo, D. W., & Yeo, S. A. (2007). Advance consent in Japanese during prenatal care for epidural anesthesia during childbirth. *Journal of Mixed Methods Research*, 1, 333–365.

Finkenthal, M. (2001). *Interdisciplinarity: Toward the definition of a metadiscipline?* New York: Peter Lang.

Foster, G. M., Scudder, T., Colson, E., & Kemper, R. V. (Eds.). (1979). *Long-term field research in social anthropology*. New York: Academic Press.

Freilich, M. (Ed.). (1970). *Marginal natives: Anthropologists at work*. New York: Harper & Row.

Geertz, C. (1973). *The interpretation of cultures*. New York: Basic Books.

Givens, D. B., & Skomal, S. M. (1993). The four fields: Myth and reality. *Anthropology Newsletter*, 34(5), 1–19.

Golde, P. (Ed.). (1986). *Women in the field: Anthropological experiences*. (2nd ed.). Berkeley: University of California Press.

Gordon, C. W. (1957). *The social system of the high school: A study in the sociology of adolescence*. Glencoe, IL: Free Press.

Greene, J. (2007). *Mixed methods in social inquiry*. San Francisco: Jossey-Bass.

Greene, J. C. (2008). Is mixed methods social inquiry a distinctive methodology? *Journal of Mixed Methods Research*, 2(1), 7–22. doi:10.1177/1558689807309969

Greene, J., Caracelli, V., & Graham, W. (1989). Toward a conceptual framework for mixed-method evaluation design. *Educational Evaluation and Policy Analysis*, 11, 255–274.

Greene, J., & Hall, J. N. (2010). Dialectics and pragmatism: Being of consequence. In A. Tashakkori & C. Teddlie (Eds.), *SAGE handbook of mixed methods in social & behavioral research* (2nd ed., pp. 119–144). Thousand Oaks, CA: SAGE.

Grissom, J., & Herrington, C. (2012). Struggling for coherence and control: The new politics of intergovernmental relations in education. *Educational Policy*, 26(1) 3–14. doi:10.1177/0895904811428976

Gruber, J. W. (1970). Ethnographic salvage and the shaping of anthropology. *American Anthropologist*, 72(6), 1289–1299.

Hall, J. N., & Ryan, K. (2011). Educational accountability: A qualitatively driven mixed methods approach. *Qualitative Inquiry*, 17(1), 105–115.

Handwerker, W. P. (2001). *Quick ethnography*. Walnut Creek, CA: AltaMira Press.

Harris, M. (1979). *Cultural materialism: The struggle for a science of culture*. New York: Random House.

Hesse-Biber, S. (2010). Qualitative approaches to mixed methods practice. *Qualitative Inquiry*, 16, 455–468.

Hesse-Biber, S., & Johnson, R.B. (2013). Coming at things differently: Future directions of possible engagement with mixed methods research. *Journal of Mixed Methods Research*, 7(2), 103–109. doi:10.1177/1558689813483987

Hinsley, C. M., & Holm, B. (1976). A cannibal in the natural museum: The early career of Franz Boas in America. *American Anthropologist*, 78(2), 306–316.

Hollingshead, A. (1949). *Elmtown's youth: The impact of social classes on adolescents*. New York: Wiley.

Hood, C. (1995). The "new public management" in the 1980s: Variations on a theme. *Accounting, Organizations and Society*, 20(2–3), 93–109. Retrieved from http://www.drmanage.com/images/1202965572/Hood_NPM (1995).pdf

Hufton, N., Elliott, J., & Illushin, L. (2002). Achievement motivation: Cross-cultural puzzles and paradoxes. In J. Bempechat & J. Elliott (Eds.), *Learning in culture and context: Approaching the complexities of achievement motivation in student learning* (pp. 65–85). San Francisco: Jossey Bass.

Human Relations Area Files, Inc. (1945). *Outline of cultural materials*. New Haven, CT: Yale University Press.

Hursh, D. (2005). Neo-liberalism, markets and accountability: Transforming education and undermining democracy in the United States and England. *Policy Futures in Education*, 3(1), 1–15. Retrieved from http://spe.library.utoronto.ca/index.php/spe/article/view/6724/3723

Ivankova, N. V., & Kawamura, Y. (2010). Emerging trends in the utilization of integrated designs in the social, behavioral, and health sciences. In A. Tashakkori & C. Teddlie (Eds.), *SAGE handbook of mixed methods in social & behavioral research* (2nd ed., pp. 581–611). Thousand Oaks, CA: SAGE.

Jackson, P. W. (1968). *Life in classrooms*. New York: Holt, Rinehart and Winston.

Johnson, R. B. (2012). Dialectical pluralism and mixed research. *American Behavioral Scientist*, 56, 751–754.

Johnson, R. B., & Christensen, L. B. (2012). *Educational research: Quantitative, qualitative, and mixed approaches* (4th ed.). Thousand Oaks, CA: SAGE.

Johnson, R. B., & Christensen, L. B. (2014). *Educational research methods: Quantitative, qualitative, and mixed approaches* (5th ed.). Los Angeles: SAGE.

Johnson, R. B., & Onwuegbuzie, A. J. (2004). Mixed methods research: A research paradigm whose time has come. *Educational Researcher*, 33(7), 14–26.

Klein, J. T. (1990). *Interdisciplinarity: History, theory, and practice*. Detroit: Wayne State University.

Kline, R. B. (1998). *Principles and practice of structural equation modeling*. New York: Guilford Press.

Kuznar, L. A. (1997). *Reclaiming a scientific anthropology*. Walnut Creek, CA: Altamira Press.

Lagemann, E. C. (1997). Contested terrain: A history of education research in the United States, 1890-1990. *Educational Researcher*, 26(9), 5–17.

Lagemann, E. C. (2000). *An elusive science: The troubling history of education research*. Chicago: University of Chicago Press.

Lieber, E., & T. S. Weisner. (2010). Meeting the practical challenges of mixed methods research. In C. Teddlie & A. Tashakkori (Eds.), *SAGE handbook of mixed methods in social and behavioral research* (2nd ed., pp. 559–579). Thousand Oaks, CA: SAGE.

Lieber, E., Weisner, T. S., & Presley, M. (2003). EthnoNotes: An Internet-based fieldnote management tool. *Field Methods*, 15(4), 405–425.

Lopez-Fernandez, O., & Molina-Azorin, J. F. (2011). The use of mixed methods research in interdisciplinary educational journals. *International Journal of Multiple Research Approaches*, 5(2), 269–283.

Lortie, D. C. (1975). *Schoolteacher: A sociological study*. Chicago: University of Chicago Press.

Malinowski, B. (1961). *Argonauts of the western Pacific: An account of native enterprise and adventure in the archipelagoes of Melanesian New Guinea*. New York: E.P. Dutton. (Original work published 1922)

Malinowski, B. (1989). *A diary in the strict sense of the term*. London: Routledge & Kegan Paul. (Original work published 1967)

Manners, R. A., & Kaplan, D. (1968). Notes on theory and non-thory in anthropology. In R. A. Manners & D. Kaplan (Eds.), *Theory in anthropology: A sourcebook* (pp. 1–12). Chicago: Aldine-Atherton.

Marcus, G. E., & Fischer, M. J. (1986). *Anthropology as cultural critique: An experimental moment in the human sciences*. Chicago: University of Chicago Press.

Maxwell, J. A., & Mittapalli, K. (2010). Realism as a stance for mixed methods research. In A. Tashakkori & C. Teddlie (Eds.), *SAGE handbook of mixed methods in social & behavioral research* (2nd ed., pp. 145–168). Thousand Oaks, CA: SAGE.

Mead, M. (1928). *Coming of age in Samoa: A psychological study of primitive youth for Western civilization*. New York: William Morrow.

Mead, M. (1933). More comprehensive field notes. *American Anthropologist, 35*(1), 1–15.

Mead, M. (1977). *Letters from the field, 1925–1975*. New York: Harper & Row.

Mertens, D. (2007). Transformative paradigm: Mixed methods and social justice. *Journal of Mixed Methods Research, 1*, 212–225.

Mertens, D. (2010). Divergence and mixed methods. *Journal of Mixed Methods Research, 4*(1), 3–5. doi:10.11771558689809358406

Messerschmidt, D. A. (Ed.). (1981). *Anthropologists at home in North America: Methods and issues in the study of one's own society*. Cambridge, UK: Cambridge University Press.

Micari, M., Light, G., Calkins, S., & Streitwieser, B. (2007). Assessment beyond performance: Phenomenography in educational evaluation. *American Journal of Evaluation, 28*(4), 458–476. doi:10.1177/1098214007308024

Moore, J. D. 1997. *Visions of culture: An introduction to anthropological theories and theorists*. Walnut Creek, CA: AltaMira Press.

Moran, J. (2002). *Interdisciplinarity*. London: Routledge.

National Research Council. (2005). *Advancing scientific research in education* (L. Towne, L. L. Wise, & T. M. Winters, Eds.) Washington, DC: National Academies Press.

O'Cathain, A., Murphy, E., & Nicholl, J. (2007) Integration and publications as indicators of "yield" from mixed methods studies. *Journal of Mixed Methods Research, 1*, 147–163.

O'Day, J. A. (2002). Complexity, accountability, and school improvement. *Harvard Educational Review, 72*(3), 293–329.

Ortner, S. B. (1999). *The fate of "culture": Geertz and Beyond*. Berkeley: University of California Press.

Packer, M. (2012). *The science of qualitative research*. Cambridge, UK: Cambridge University Press.

Pelto, P. J. (1970). *Anthropological research: The structure of inquiry*. New York: Harper & Row.

Pike, K. (1954). *Language in relation to a unified theory of the structure of human behavior: Vol. 1*. Glendale, CA: Summer Institute of Linguistics.

Power, M. (1997). *The audit society: Rituals of verification*. Oxford: Oxford University Press.

Rocco, T., Bliss, L., Gallagher, S., & Pérez-Prado, A. (2003). Taking the next step: Mixed methods research in organizational systems. *Information Technology, Learning, and Performance Journal, 21*(1), 19–29.

Royal Anthropological Institute of Great Britain and Ireland. (1951). *Notes and queries on anthropology* (6th ed.). London: Routledge & Kegan Paul.

Sale, J. E. M., Lohfeld, L. H., & Brazil, K. (2002). Revisiting the quantitative-qualitative debate: Implications for mixed-methods research. *Quality and Quantity, 36*, 43–53.

Sammons, P. (2010). The contribution of mixed methods to recent research on educational effectiveness. In A. Tashakkori & C. Teddlie (Eds.), *SAGE handbook of mixed methods in social & behavioral research* (2nd ed., pp. 697–723). Thousand Oaks, CA: SAGE.

Service, E. R. (1985). *A century of controversy: Ethnological issues from 1860 to 1960*. Orlando, FL: Academic Press.

Smith, J., & Heshusius, L. (1986). Closing down the conversation: The end of the quantitative-qualitative debate among educational inquirers. *Educational Researcher, 15*(1), 4–12.

Snow, C. P. (1959). *The two cultures and the scientific revolution*. New York: Cambridge University Press.

Spradley, J. P. (1979). *The ethnographic interview*. New York: Holt, Rinehart and Winston.

Spradley, J. P. (1980). *Participant observation*. New York: Holt, Rinehart and Winston.

Stocking, G. W. (1987). Margaret Mead, Franz Boas, and the Ogburns of science: The statistical and the clinical models in the presentation of Mead's Samoan ethnography. *History of Anthropology Newsletter, 14*(2), 3–10.

Stokes, D. E. (1997). *Pasteur's quadrant: Basic science and technological innovation*. Washington, DC: Brookings Institution Press.

Strathern, M. (Ed.). (2000). *Audit cultures: Anthropological studies in accountability, ethics and the academy*. New York: Routledge.

Tashakkori, A., & Teddlie, C. (2003). Preface. In A. Tashakkori & C. Teddlie (Eds.), *Handbook of mixed methods in social & behavioral research* (pp. ix–xv). Thousand Oaks, CA: SAGE.

Tashakkori, A., & Teddlie, C. (Eds.). (2010). *SAGE handbook of mixed methods in social & behavioral research* (2nd ed.). Thousand Oaks, CA: SAGE.

Truscott, D., Swars, S., Smith, S., Thornton-Reid, F., Zhao, Y., Dooley, C., . . . Matthews, M. (2010). A cross-disciplinary examination of the prevalence of mixed methods in educational research: 1995–2005, *International Journal of Social Research Methodology, 13*, 317–328.

Vasavi, A.R. (1996). Co-opting culture: Managerialism in age of consumer capitalism. *Economic and Political Weekly, 31*(21), M22–M25.

Wade, N. (2010, December 10). Anthropology a science? Statement deepens a rift. *The New York Times*, p. A16. Retrieved from http://www.nytimes.com/2010/12/10/science/10anthropology.html?_r=0

Wax, R. H. (1971). *Doing fieldwork: Warnings and advice*. Chicago: University of Chicago Press.

Weisner, T. S. (Ed.). (2005). *Discovering successful pathways in children's development: Mixed methods in the* study of childhood and family life. Chicago: University of Chicago Press.

Weisner, T. S. (2011). "If you work in this country you should not be poor, and your kids should be doing better": Bringing mixed methods and theory in psychological anthropology to improve research in policy and practice. *Ethos, 39*(4), 455–476.

Weisner, T. S. (2012). Mixed methods should be a valued practice in anthropology. *Anthropology News, 53*(5), 3–4.

Werner, O., & Schoepfle, G. M. (1987a). *Systematic fieldwork: Vol. 1: Foundations of ethnography and interviewing.* Newbury Park, CA: SAGE.

Werner, O., & Schoepfle, G. M. (1987b). *Systematic fieldwork: Vol. 2. Ethnographic analysis and data management.* Newbury Park, CA: SAGE.

What Works Clearinghouse. (2008). Procedures and standards handbook (version 2.0). Washington, DC: US Department of Education. Retrieved from http://ies.ed.gov/ncee/wwc/help/idocviewer/doc.aspx?docid=19&tocid=1

Williams, T. R. (1967). *Field methods in the study of culture.* New York: Holt, Rinehart and Winston.

Yin, R. K. (2006). Mixed methods research: Are the methods genuinely integrated or merely parallel? *Research in the Schools, 13*(1), 41–47.

21 Evolving Mixed and Multimethod Approaches in Psychology

Nollaig A. Frost *and* Rachel L. Shaw

Abstract

This chapter identifies how and why "method" has become so important to the psychology discipline. It considers the social history of the development of qualitative methods in psychology and considers the emergence of mixed methods such as pragmatism and Q methodology. Using discussions and research examples, the chapter considers and illustrates how qualitative methods have been combined with quantitative methods, and with each other, as psychology has demanded more complex and nuanced insights to human behavior. The chapter considers the influence of the underpinnings of the mixing of methods, paradigms, and approaches in psychology and explains how these have been increasingly informed by qualitative approaches to psychological research. The chapter discusses also the emergence of pluralism as a new step in the mixing of methods and paradigms.

Key Words: mixed methods, pluralism, pragmatism, paradigm, Q methodology, qualitative methods, quantitative methods, psychology

Introduction

The discipline of psychology has a long history of experimental approaches to research. From early beginnings that sought to measure and categorize human behavior using scales and surveys, it is now able to measure brain activity and cognition using high-tech electronic equipment. These techniques, which primarily use quantitative methods, have sat alongside qualitative approaches that seek to understand human thinking and actions by observing and talking to research participants, throughout the development of psychology as a discipline. Due to political, pragmatic, and social concerns at the turn of the 19th century, the quest to understand more about human beings became increasingly dominated by the quantitative approach. More recently, there has been a renewed desire to understand the world from the perspective of the research participants, rather than from the perspective of "experts" talking *about* participants, which has led to a proliferation of qualitative methods.

Arguably this development arose out of the "turn to language" taking place in other subject disciplines in the 1970s.

The "Turn to Language" in Psychology

The turn to language sought to challenge the view that language served only to label internal states and external realities and instead regarded language as productive and constructive of realities. This approach became firmly established in psychology in the 1980s with the publication of Potter and Wetherell's (1987) book *Discourse and Social Psychology: Beyond Attitudes and Behaviour*. The book challenged the knowledge and assumptions of cognitivism and experimentalism that dominated psychology at the time by offering a way to go beyond simple research methods to develop an approach that critiqued mainstream psychology. It provided a reconceptualization of language so that it offered a means of constructing social reality and achieving social objectives, rather than being used to simply label preexisting states. This constructionist paradigm was manifest through Potter and Wetherell's introduction of discourse analysis into psychology. The discourse analysis approach makes no assumptions about the social world and, further, seeks to expose the constructedness of existing assumptions (Holt, 2011). Common examples of these "taken-for-granted" assumptions are found in the medical profession where the research focus is often on finding causes of established medical "truths." Using a discourse analysis approach, Ussher (2003) studied women's experiences of premenstrual dysphoric disorder (PMDD) at a time when it was classified by the *Diagnostic and Statistical Manual of Mental Disorders* (fourth edition; American Psychiatric Association, 1994) as a psychiatric disorder. She asked the research question, "What are the effects of the particular hegemonic truth for women experiencing PMDD?" instead of the questions dictated by a realist ontological paradigm that might ask "What causes PMDD?" Ussher's study found that not only had dualistic mind–body Cartesian assumptions that linked causality between biological changes and psychological effects been *talked* into being by professionals but also that they were *practiced* into being by those who experienced them because of the taken-for-granted expectation that menstruation causes psychiatric disorders (Ussher, 2003).

The rapid establishment of discourse analysis within psychology allowed questioning of assumptions through the interrogation of the construction of power relations using language. In turn this led to the development of different approaches to discourse analysis in psychology—Foucauldian analysis, which foregrounds power, and discursive analysis, which foregrounds language. Foucauldian discourse analysis is widely used to interrogate subject positions to understand how humans are afforded or delimited in their particular ways of being by their social locations, for example by renaming women who experience sexual violence as "survivors" instead of as "victims" to minimize the disempowering and disabling effects of "victimhood" that arises from the label (Holt, 2011). Discursive psychology examines the role of language and assumes that accounts vary according to their situational context. It is a particularly useful approach for analyzing social media. A study conducted by Hepburn (2005) examined transcripts of children's calls to a helpline. The use of "active voicing" by the callers with the inclusion of vivid details was identified as a means of persuading the

counsellor of the facticity of her account. Hepburn concluded that institutional requirements of calling helplines demands credibility and motives of children, which can inhibit—or worse, prevent them—from accessing help in this way. With the development of multiple methods within the discourse analysis approach came progress toward combining this approach with other constructionist analytic methods.

Combining Methods Within and Across Paradigms

Combining methods within and across paradigms allows research questions about how human beings talk and practice themselves into particular subject positions *and* what those positions might consist of to be asked. An example is a study by Burck (2004, 2005) in which grounded theory, discourse analysis, and narrative analysis were used as multiple analytical tools to examine the experiences of people who were multilingual and bilingual. The grounded theory method provided initial categories within which the experiences of language were characterized. Discourse analysis of the text allowed scrutiny of the ways the different categories were used by participants to position themselves. Narrative analysis informed the researchers of how the participants presented themselves and made sense of their experiences.

Since the inception of these and other qualitative methods in psychology, there has been a steady increase in studies that combine methods and paradigms in multimethod and mixed methods research. These may be traditional mixed methods approaches, where a realist paradigm (usually associated with quantitative methods) is combined with a constructionist interpretivist paradigm (usually involving qualitative methods) in order to generalize or bring depth to research outcomes, or multimethods approaches, where any number of methods from any paradigm are brought together to answer the research question. One example of where this is key is in the challenges to the status quo of the need for valid evidence on which healthcare practice can be based; to date, this has been almost exclusively reliant on realist paradigm research and pseudo-experimental methods. We will pursue this particular challenging context later on in the chapter.

Pluralistic qualitative approaches, where more than one qualitative method or analysis is combined with others, are emerging in psychology as a way of accessing insight to experience from different in-depth perspectives. The mixing of methods and paradigms may be carried out integratively, whereby each is used to explore one key research question, or in combination, where paradigms, methods, or data are added in as the research evolves and new questions arise. All of these approaches serve to offer access to a more holistic insight to the interpretation of the data. Further, when used together, they can enhance the quality of the research through their individual adherence to theoretical foundations and transparency and, through the emphasis on awareness of reflexive practice by individual researchers working solely with many methods, or with one method as part of a team.

To consider and contextualize the emergence of mixed and multimethods research in psychology, this chapter considers how and why method has become so important to the practice of psychological research. It describes how psychology as a discipline rapidly turned away from what we now call an interpretivist approach to embrace an almost exclusively realist one in the pursuit of the study of human behavior. Having successfully established itself as a science, the psychology discipline has arguably resisted moves toward research that employs methods and paradigms that allow for changing meanings and human dynamics. An overdetermination to retain its scientific status led to excessive focus on method at the risk of losing sight of the research topic, a concept termed *methodolatry* by Curt (1994) and challenged in the past few decades by the emergences and (re)establishment of qualitative paradigms as legitimate means of eliciting, collecting, and analyzing data (Willig & Stainton-Rogers, 2008). The chapter will consider how qualitative paradigms can be combined with quantitative paradigms, when it might be appropriate to do this, how pluralistic qualitative research can add to psychological understanding of experience, and where these developments are taking psychology as a discipline. Throughout the chapter, examples taken from health psychology and other applied contexts will illustrate the points and debates presented.

The Importance of Method in Psychology

The importance of method in psychology can be seen from its very beginnings in mentalism and behaviorism. The recognized founders of psychology as a discipline, Wilhelm Wundt and William James, used subjective and objective means to explore meanings, culture, and identity, employing both participant introspection and measurement of behavior to develop further understanding of the mind (Willig & Stainton-Rogers, 2008). However, when mentalism gave way to behaviorism (Leahy 2000, cited in Willig & Stainton-Rogers, 2008) in the late 1800s, quantitative research came to dominate psychology until 20 to 30 years ago, when qualitative approaches began to (re)emerge. With this came challenges and debates about the reformulation of the discipline of psychology away from being regarded as "the science of behavior" (Willig & Stainton-Rogers, 2008, p. 4), a description that had been established through behaviorism and subsequent experimental approaches, and toward offering insight to individual experience and meaning-making.

The move toward generalization and experimental methods may have lain in the desire to find ways to manage societal concerns such as crime, education, and employment selection. A way to achieve this was through the administration of questionnaires that created and then statistically interrogated large data sets. From this scientific approach, generalizations about people who belonged to groups (often based on socioeconomic definitions) and associated behaviors followed. This dominance of quantitative research approaches held sway until recently in psychology, and increasingly complex statistical analyses have evolved in order to pursue this approach.

However, the establishment and dominance of quantitative methods in psychology was challenged by the psychological research community in response to the social changes and challenges of the 1960s. Psychologists dealing with social phenomena, and those dissatisfied with the positioning of women and other oppressed members of society questioned how psychological knowledge was constructed and its powerful position in shaping experience and sense of self (e.g., Gergen, 1973; Gilligan, 1982). With the recognition that psychology was not simply about describing behavior but also about *shaping* and *informing* behavior came recognition of the need to develop ways to understand how people interact with and understand their environment and those around them. Researchers became interested in pursuing a more naturalistic, contextual, and holistic understanding of human beings, and with this came the employment of ethnographic methods such as observation, documentary analysis, and interviews. With a focus on the ways in which language serves to talk about and represent reality came a discursive approach to psychology that sought out the functions that language serves in constructing the appearance and effects of reality. The development of this approach heralded the turn to language in psychology, outlined earlier, and was followed by a plethora of qualitative methods that enabled researchers to interrogate, deconstruct, and reinterpret the underpinnings of psychological knowledge. The broad range of these methods allows focus on the interpretative, or hermeneutic, understanding of what human actions mean and promotes exploration of unique perspectives of individuals, social institutions, and constructs.

These turns to language and to interpretation in psychological research brought about new ideological standpoints based on the methodologies and methods chosen by different psychologists—those identifying as humanistic psychologists or those working in applied fields such as counseling (Rogers, 1961; Reason & Rowan, 1981). However, the reasons why researchers select quantitative or qualitative methods for psychological research may lie in epistemology and their own assumptions about what knowledge is (paradigms) and how they view the world, the research program, or the theory that they seek to test or explore, rather than in the theory underlying the research study or research question(s). Psychologists using quantitative methods came to regard the interpretivist methodological paradigm used by qualitative researchers as more compatible with the humanities and as a derogation of psychology as a science. Psychologists keen to adopt qualitative methods saw the traditional natural scientific positivist paradigm and its associated quantitative methods as displacing the human individual from the focus of the research. Each methodological standpoint (i.e. quantitative and qualitative) became entrenched in ideological and epistemological positions of the human subject that influenced choice of method depending on whether researchers saw human participants as able to offer insight to their own perspectives or as passive, "mindless subjects" (Willig & Stainton-Rogers, 2008, p. 7) whose behavior could only be understood through observation and objective measurement. The threat of "methodolatry" (Curt, 1994, p.106) crept into research in psychology where method (i.e., what was done with the data and the "truth" of the outcome) became idolized as a way of portraying research as rigorous. The method that qualified was the experimental method and its associated quantitative techniques

for data collection and analysis. This methodolatry in psychological research had the effect not only of positioning research and its outcomes back in the realm of "experts" but also of risking overshadowing the research focus. Arguments about whether the positivist paradigm or the interpretivist paradigm produced valid knowledge deteriorated into the "paradigm wars" (Oakley, 1999), which lasted until a "fragile peace" (Bryman, 2006) was declared several years later.

Since then the growth of qualitative approaches in psychology has been reflected in national psychological societies in the United Kingdom and United States: the British Psychological Society approved the foundation of the Qualitative Methods in Psychology Section in 2005, and in 2012 the Society for Qualitative Inquiry in Psychology became a section of Division 5 of the American Psychological Association. The journal *Qualitative Psychology* was launched by the American Psychological Association as the publication of the Society for Qualitative Inquiry in Psychology, and *Qualitative Research in Psychology*, now published by Taylor & Francis, was created in 2004 by Arnold with an editorial team headed up by UK and US psychologists (other journals dedicated to qualitative research, e.g., the SAGE journals *Qualitative Research* and *Qualitative Inquiry*, have been around a long time). There is also a significant presence in the prestigious medicine journals (e.g., the *British Medical Journal;* Paley & Lilford, 2011) and in health psychology (e.g., *Psychology & Health;* Smith, 2011). *Health Psychology* published a call for papers for a special issue on qualitative health research in 2013. Furthermore, the proliferation of textbooks about qualitative methods in psychology (e.g., Forrester, 2010; Frost, 2011; Smith, 2008; Harper & Thompson, 2011) and conferences, which include qualitative papers that demonstrate how much research activity in psychology uses qualitative methods and/or a multimethod approach. Reaching this level of penetration has meant that qualitative methods have entered the vernacular, leading to many more opportunities for research and development. Skepticism remains, however, with regard to mixing methods. Qualitative research grew out of sometimes vehement arguments against "mainstream" experimental psychology, and many qualitative researchers continue to reject quantitative methods of any kind and continue to position themselves on the margins, which risks prohibiting progress. However, there are many reasons to adopt multimethod approaches and for researchers to combine methods, and it is to this we now turn.

Mixing Paradigms in Psychology

As we have seen, there are a number of challenges to the idea of mixing methods in psychology, springing from its history and the emphasis on method as a definitive factor in the discipline. The first challenge we consider is how one moves from the problem of incorporating new qualitative methods into a predominantly quantitative world to the possibility of selecting more than one type of method, qualitative or quantitative, from a methods toolkit. The second considers the epistemological challenges of mixing methods in psychology; frequently, qualitative researchers argue for a "new paradigm," which emphasizes potentially irreconcilable epistemological differences between qualitative and quantitative research and therefore puts a philosophical halt on the idea of combining methods. The third challenge takes these issues forward within the context of evidence-based healthcare. This provides a good example of how value-laden some methods have become in applied psychology and medical research and the impact of this on the shape of the evidence informing practice. Finally, we think through the implications of mixing methods on the criteria for good-quality research in the context of multimethod approaches.

Getting Over History: Moving Toward a Toolkit Approach

The notion of a methods toolkit has been around a long time (e.g., Bryman, 1988), but because psychology has historically been rather purist about method, it is a concept that has taken a long time to infiltrate psychology research. The hypothetico-deductive logic of inquiry and the experimental method were considered markers of good-quality psychological research since the dominance of behaviorism. This meant other methods were derided as unsystematic and lacking rigor because they did not produce measurements of observable behaviors. Cognitions or talk about behavior and experience were judged as simply anecdotal. However, as discussed earlier, the turn to language saw different (qualitative) methods coming into use. This opened up possibilities for asking different kinds of research questions, rather than being limited to testing hypotheses in experimental settings, and it saw the introduction of methods like collaborative inquiry, interviewing, and discourse analysis being promoted as "new

paradigm" techniques (e.g. Heron, 1981; Potter & Wetherell, 1987; Smith, Harré, & van Langenhove, 1995). This fight for the recognition of qualitative methods in psychology has been rumbling on for at least 50 years, but only now are we safe to argue that qualitative methods have become a solid contender in psychology, as they have elsewhere in the social and medical sciences (Willig & Stainton-Rogers, 2008).

However, since the fight for qualitative approaches in psychology was so passionate and driven by core beliefs about the nature of the human condition, and perspectives from which to study it, it created a marginalized group—an "us and them." It is ironic that social psychology should take up the mantel of creating an ingroup–outgroup battle: critical social psychology constructed itself through a critique of "mainstream" experimental social psychology (e.g., Gough, McFadden, & McDonald, 2013; Stainton-Rogers, 2003). While this helped enormously with the manifesto for qualitative methods in psychology, it also created a divide between those using quantitative or pseudo-experimental methods and those "on the margins" (Willig & Stainton-Rogers, 2008) using qualitative methods.

This quantitative–qualitative divide in psychology is unhelpful (Bryman, 1988) and potentially destructive to qualitative research because it makes assumptions that may not necessarily be true (Paley & Lilford, 2011; Shaw, 2013). In early critical psychology writings and textbooks on qualitative methods in psychology, there was an assumed allegiance to social constructionism, probably because of the dominance of discourse analysis at the time (e.g., Bannister, Burman, Parker, Taylor, & Tindall, 1999; Parker & Shotter, 1990), but as the range of qualitative analysis techniques grew, it became clear that one size did not fit all; those using interpretative phenomenological analysis (IPA), for example, would not stop at language per se as their unit of study but would use language as a route to explore cognition (Smith, 1996). It soon became clear that qualitative research was not a unitary field but an umbrella term for research that uses textual (and other representations) rather than numerical data (Willig & Stainton-Rogers, 2008).

In theory, this acknowledgement of the plurality of methods available within qualitative methodology should lead easily to a toolkit approach where the most appropriate methods are selected for the research question at hand. However, the significance of epistemological allegiance in psychology meant instead that often researchers opted for their preferred method that fit with their worldview and moved forward by always using that method. Consequently, there are now qualitative researchers in psychology known for the method they use rather than their subject of interest. To continue the analogy of a methods toolkit, it is not surprising that some individuals are more skillful with a saw than a hammer, but it is absurd that a saw should always be used regardless of the job, especially when that job is a leaky tap. Nevertheless, we get attached to our methods and all too quickly see questions limited by that method (like the behaviorists did), instead of focusing on techniques that are needed to access and analyze the factors within the research question.

Epistemological Challenges

The fastidious approach to method in psychology has spilled over to create a heightened awareness of "what can be known" (epistemology), as well as what is regarded as knowledge (ontology), and it is these considerations that underlie the choice of methodology in addressing the research questions. To combine epistemologies raises questions of their (in)coherences, and there is often a barrier to doing so. Instead, those who argue against positivism and the experimental method suggest a need for a holistic approach to research to take into account context, subjective experience, and attempts to understand similarity and difference rather than to create predictive universal laws and truths (e.g., Smith et al., 1995), thereby maintaining a mono-paradigmatic dominance. The marriage between epistemology and method has been handed down through textbooks, teaching, and the way researchers have positioned themselves in the papers they have published (see Finlay & Gough, 2003, for examples of different ways of doing this within the context of engaging in reflexivity). What has been forgotten is that one may use qualitative methods (i.e., techniques), without allegiance to any particular epistemological position or theory. The now-landmark paper by Braun and Clarke (2006) about thematic analysis reminded us that this was the case and paved the way for more openness in the choice of method. It also brought back to the fore the logics of inquiry: deduction and induction (Hiles, 2014).

As shown in Hiles' (2014) model (see Figure 21.1), deduction involves using data to test the validity of a theory. The most obvious example of this is the hypothetico-deductive method, which traditionally uses experimental design and quantitative methods to test a hypothesis through deductive reasoning. Induction involves prioritizing the data and working bottom-up to generate theory (e.g., grounded theory). Most qualitative researchers have worked in an inductive way with their data. Nevertheless, Braun and Clarke (2006) remind us that qualitative research can be deductive or indeed involve both deductive and inductive reasoning.

Thinking about the logics of inquiry shifts the debate away from method toward the best-fit approach for the research question. If the question is exploratory, it is likely that an inductive approach will be most appropriate to answer it. This may require an exploratory survey with quantitative analyses, or it may require in-depth interviews with qualitative analysis. Thus we choose the method that is most appropriate, from our toolkit, to perform the tasks we need to answer our research question. This is similar to the school of thought described as pragmatism, discussed later in this chapter. Hiles (2014) has argued recently that the distinction between qualitative and quantitative methods is a red herring and leads to overprescriptive definitions of mixed methods research (MMR) (e.g., research using two types of data, two types of data collection procedures, or data analysis; Tashakkori & Creswell, 2007). Instead, according to Hiles' (1999, 2006) model of disciplined inquiry, we should be focusing on the research question, the strategic decisions made to answer it, the methods of data collection, and analysis, together with a critical evaluation of what is undertaken.

As introduced earlier, historically, qualitative methods have been described as inductive, that is, they are data driven, compared with the theory-driven experimental methods of the

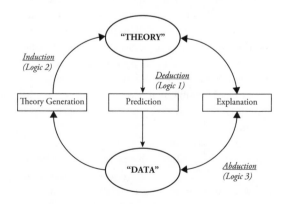

Fig. 21.1 The relation between theory and data and the logics of inquiry.
Adapted from Hiles (2014).

hypothetico-deductive approach. However, it is not necessarily the case that all qualitative methods are inductive or that to be inductive one needs to use qualitative methods. This is a misnomer. Qualitative methods may be used in research, which is deductive, and they may be used in combination with other (quantitative or qualitative) methods, which involve deductive reasoning, as seen in Braun and Clarke's (2006) pluralistic description of thematic analysis. Hiles (2014) reminds us that there is a third, often forgotten logic of inquiry: abductive reasoning. Abduction, following Charles Sanders Pierce (1903), is defined as: "inference to the best explanation" (Harman, 1965; Lipton, 1991). Where deduction is theory driven and induction data driven, abduction is explanation driven (Hiles, 2014). These logics are not exclusive; it is possible to engage in more than one logic within the same study. The possibilities opened up by these logics of inquiry are demonstrated in the example of evidence-based healthcare in the next section.

The logic of inquiry is guided purely by the research question: the type of approach required to answer the research question guides the selection of methods. This means that any method or combination of methods from the toolbox can be used so long as they are appropriate to answer the research question (or series of questions). This more practical approach to method selection has dominated in health research (O'Cathain et al., 2010), probably because of the need to answer a series of questions, which involve the collection of biomedical data, organizational and geographical data, as well as psychosocial and cultural data (Kelly et al., 2009).

A good example of how the practicalities of research need to fit within the requirements or organizations, politics, and assumptions about what constitutes valid knowledge is the field of evidence-based healthcare. Demands of healthcare practice require a practical approach to research, but that is set within the tradition of pseudo-experimental methods and a particular hierarchy of evidence.

Traditional Mixed Methods Research: The Example of Evidence-Based Healthcare

Evidence-based healthcare has been defined by the Cochrane Collaboration (2013) as

> The conscientious use of current best evidence in making decisions about the care of individual patients or the delivery of health services. Current

best evidence is up-to-date information from relevant, valid research about the effects of different forms of health care, the potential for harm from exposure to particular agents, the accuracy of diagnostic tests, and the predictive power of prognostic factors.

This definition sets out some criteria for good-quality evidence: it needs to be the best, up to date, and valid. In medical science, as in psychology, the hypothetico-deductive method dominates. This translates into a hierarchy of evidence (see Figure 21.2), which has historically prioritized experimental and pseudo-experimental research designs because, within the positivist paradigm, these methods were thought to be the only methods to produce valid knowledge. However, applied health research is one field that has embraced mixed and multimethod approaches. The National Institute for Health and Clinical Effectiveness in England and Wales and the Scottish Intercollegiate Guideline Network in Scotland have both recognized the need for diverse evidence when reviewing the literature to write best-practice guidelines. Cochrane systematic reviews focus on reviewing the outcomes of randomized controlled trials, but the National Institute for Health and Clinical Effectiveness (Kelly et al., 2009) and Scottish Intercollegiate Guideline Network (2008) advocate the use of qualitative and other quantitative research designs to answer different questions within the complex challenge of recommending the best care for individual patients and the best-designed health services. The challenge for them is identifying the appropriate methodology

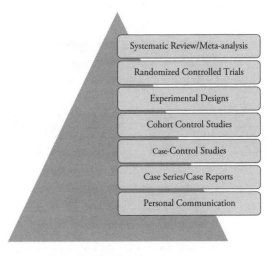

Fig. 21.2 Hierarchy of evidence.
Adapted from Guyatt et al. (1995).

to synthesize the data obtained through different methods in a rigorous and systematic way, though the development of meta-synthesis and mixed studies review techniques open up new possibilities (Pace et al, 2012; Pluye, Gagnon, Griffiths, & Johnson-Lafleur, 2009; Shaw, Larkin & Flowers, 2014). That issue relates to methods for secondary research; here the focus is primary research.

Much applied health research focuses on the design and delivery of health behavior change interventions. Trials of behavioral interventions have been modeled on randomized controlled trials of treatments, but because they involve human behavior within their content, they have been described as complex. The Medical Research Council (2008) has produced a framework for the development and evaluation of complex interventions (see Figure 21.3), which involves a series of steps and incorporates a number of logics of inquiry. An example will help demonstrate this. Adrienne Hudson (a PhD student working with one of the authors) is a qualified nurse and midwife working in a pediatric hospital. She had identified a need for further training for nurses to prepare them for dealing with acute life-threatening events (ALTEs) on the ward. A high level of sickness and staff turnover had begun to raise alarm bells. The objectives of this study were to describe and understand nurses' experiences of dealing with ALTEs on the ward with a view to preparing them for these experiences in the future. Essentially this involved designing a behavioral intervention for nurses in the form of a training package based on a number of studies using multiple methods.

The first step, as guided by the Medical Research Council framework, is to identify the theoretical and substantive evidence in the field. To achieve this, Hudson conducted a systematic review. To establish current practice, an international survey of practice was used (administered by telephone and online; McCabe Hudson, Duncan, Pattison, & Shaw, 2011). Following that, exploratory empirical work was required to examine the experiences of nurses and others attending ALTEs in order to ascertain not only what those events meant to staff but also what proved difficult for nurses to manage. Interviews with nurses and doctors attending ALTEs were conducted, which were then analyzed using IPA (Hudson, Duncan, Pattison, & Shaw, 2012). Using the data from each of these three pieces of work, a training intervention was designed and piloted. As such, this study involved a systematic review, a survey that involved descriptive statistics, interviews that were analyzed qualitatively, and a pilot intervention that involved the use of standardized measures and statistical analysis (Hudson, Mohamed Ali, Duncan, Pattison, & Shaw, 2013). Each of these methods was required in order to fulfill the objectives. Hence, each method was selected because of its appropriateness to answer the research question for each discrete study. When put together, this is an example of a program of work designed within a pragmatic framework. The research was set within the context of evidence-based healthcare, meaning its outcomes could have a real impact on practice and on nurses' clinical competence and confidence. As such, from pragmatism this research used a functional definition of knowledge and in terms of quality appraisal, the studies were evaluated based on whether they addressed the problems in practice adequately and appropriately and led to the development of new ways of working. The multimethod approach employed does not feature the traditional hierarchy of knowledge, so to some it may be considered invalid for use to inform practice. Nevertheless, within the context of an increasing number of studies adopting a pragmatic and mixed methods approach within healthcare, the quality of this program of work is judged based on the rigor of methods used in each component and in terms of whether its outcomes have the potential to impact on practice.

Development of Mixed Methods Research in Psychology

The traditional approach to MMR, in which one quantitative method is employed alongside one qualitative method, was developed primarily

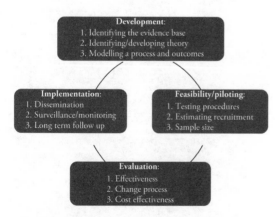

Fig. 21.3 Framework for the design and evaluation of complex interventions.

Adapted from Medical Research Council (2008).

in order to triangulate findings. Despite the view among many qualitative researchers (e.g., Howard, 1983; McLeod, 2005) that qualitative research approaches have much to offer policymakers and practitioners in arenas such as education, healthcare, and clinical practices, the emphasis on subjectivity at the perceived cost of validity means that the findings of qualitative studies are sometimes regarded with skepticism by those seeking "trustworthy evidence" from which to develop policies and good-practice guidelines.

To address this skepticism, advocates for increasing qualitative outcome research in clinical practice (e.g., McLeod, 2005) argue that the use of qualitative inquiry encourages questioning and deconstruction of taken-for-granted concepts such as outcome and change when considering the use and function of therapy (McLeod, 2005). They suggest that instead of seeking evidence based on traditional natural scientific designs and concepts, qualitative research allows for creativity not possible in quantitative work alone (e.g., Mason, 2006). This has led to an increasing use of qualitative approaches alongside traditional quantitative approaches to bring multidimensional research strategies to research questions of lived experience and individual realities (e.g., Bryman, 2007).

Such mixed and multimethod approaches to research have been gaining prominence in psychology research in the UK in recent years as policymakers, practitioners, and academics see the value and complementarities of conjunct numerical and textual analyses (e.g., Bryman, 2007; Kincheloe, 2001, 2005; Mason, 2006; Todd, Nerlich, Mckeown, & Clarke, 2004). The mixed method approach supports methodological pluralism in research into psychological practice and argues that it enables a fuller understanding of humans' needs by applying different core ontological assumptions to the investigation (Howard, 1983). Using mixed method qualitative and quantitative approaches, data can be triangulated and validity of analyses strengthened (Yardley, 2000). However, qualitative data and its analysis are often relegated to a secondary position of contextualizing numerical information or generating hypotheses to be tested numerically.

As we shall see later, one solution to the problem of retaining the value of the qualitative approach without its subjugation to quantitative scientific design is to combine qualitative approaches with each other. By doing this the focus on the differences between paradigms is minimized, and the benefits of each individual approach is highlighted. A multilayered understanding of the data can be obtained from use of different methods, and the research audience can select the approach with the most meaning and value to their area of interest. The combination of qualitative approaches allows investigation of the questions of whether different methods produce different findings and whether different analysts elicit different meanings from data (Frost et al., 2011). Answers to these questions would begin to address concerns about the "quality" of findings reached using qualitative approaches, and they potentially offer new ways of exploring lived experience. The apparent epistemological incompatibility of quantitative and qualitative research approaches has meant that combining the two approaches suffers from, at best, a lack of understanding or expertise in what each approach can offer and, at worst, poor-quality research that is more of an "anything goes" approach than a research process set within a theoretical framework. Within psychology, and elsewhere, efforts have been successfully made to promote the use of mixed methods approaches with arguments to show the appropriateness of topics, and research questions, and with the development of theoretical frameworks. Two of the most widely found in psychology are pragmatism and Q methodology.

Pragmatism

Building on the realization in the late 20th century that "awareness of the world is completely mediated by particular subjective and socio-cultural experiences" (Yardley & Bishop, 2008, p. 354), psychology researchers began to see a new place for qualitative research and its enabling of assumptions and values to be recognized to understand ways in which identity is shaped and activities are decided on and carried out. Extending this traditional approach to MMR, pragmatism is founded on the belief that "all human inquiry involves interpretation and imagination, intentions and values but must also necessarily be grounded in empirical, embodied experience" (Yardley & Bishop, 2008, p. 355). Thus pragmatism allows for both the scientific objective rigor of quantitative approaches and the contextual, interrelational exploration offered by qualitative approaches. Pragmatic researchers aim for a better, richer experience of research that does not seek a truth that is independent of human experience but is founded on the belief that all actions are seen as more or less right.

The pragmatist philosophy developed from the ideas of John Dewey, who proposed that humans know what things are good for and therefore base all judgments on this premise. Common sense is based on, and scientific and moral decisions are made using, these judgments; knowledge gained is therefore linked to intentions and actions. Evaluation of these intensions and actions gives rise to the development of meaning.

Pragmatists do not seek a universal truth in their explorations but instead define "truth" in relation to a particular goal in a particular context, as in the example provided in the previous section. Applying this to the psychological research context, the pragmatist regards all the research actions (observing, interpreting, measuring, and so on) as the right way to set about achieving the goal of understanding more of the topic of inquiry. However, in order to ground the research, all the actions must be evaluated in relation to the external consequences. Thus, for example, the rightness of actions intended to cure cancer must be evaluated by their effects on tumors (Yardley & Bishop, 2008), and knowledge about how young people with chronic illness perceive healthcare must be evaluated by their engagement with healthcare services. Quantitative methods can be used to gain precision measurements in uptake and effect and can be used alongside qualitative methods to gain insight to how and why treatment is taken up or adhered to over the long term.

Perhaps one of the reasons pragmatism has developed a growing following among psychology researchers is its clear openness to qualitative, as well as quantitative approaches and ontologies. Constructivist paradigms maintain that ways in which the world is perceived and shaped by individuals cannot help but be informed by preexisting assumptions and ways of doing. Thus the pragmatic view that the nature of truth and the test of truth are essentially the same, accords closely with the view that the world is seen in the way that people are influenced to see it. The task of the psychology researcher then becomes to identify the best methods of exploring and understanding how humans see the world.

The pragmatic approach offers a framework that incorporates both qualitative and quantitative research approaches under the premise that there is no fundamental contradiction between positivist objective approaches and constructivist interpretivist approaches if all are considered to be appropriate actions in the pursuit of knowledge. The selection

of the correct methods with which to employ the approaches becomes, and in turn is informed by, the research questions, topic under inquiry, and purpose of the research.

However, some critics, and some qualitative researchers, highlight the potential for the methods used to have their integrity compromised by being combined. In practice, it is more commonly the qualitative approach that becomes an adjunct or precursor to the quantitative approach and its outcomes. To reduce the unplanned likelihood of this happening, a clear definition of the proposed use of each approach within the study should be established at the outset—always with the caveat that this may change with the research process. Thus it may be that the qualitative method offers an "external validity" to the study when used to investigate how internally valid claims made from quantitative objective, laboratory-based research correspond to everyday life and contexts. This can be used to explore how particular treatments improve the lives of those with particular illness such as in a study described by Chamberlain, Camic, and Yardley (2004). The authors describe beginning the study with the research question "How does group psychotherapy improve the lives of women with breast cancer?" in order to explore the multifaceted lives of women who have breast cancer and to move away from focusing on medical symptoms toward understanding the effect on everyday life of participating in group psychotherapy. By asking the women about their lives, the researchers gained insight to their a priori knowledge. Using "propositions" developed from theoretical understandings of group psychotherapy participation and experiences of living with breast cancer, the researchers developed a series of hypotheses that could be accepted or rejected according to the data gathered from the women. This helps to define key areas for further attention in the study (Yin, 1994). Using both the research question and the resulting propositions, a unit of analysis is decided upon. In this study this unit was the individual patient/participant so that each member of the group was considered an individual case and all the preceding questions and propositions were considered in each individual case to guide the choice of the most appropriate data collection tools. Those that best provided in-depth information were used, and semistructured interviews were conducted alongside interviews with medical staff, family members, and the group psychotherapist. Coding of the data was carried out using the propositions to guide the development of the analysis so that findings from the first case were compared against a proposition and the proposition revised until it matched the data. It was then compared to all the other cases. The process continued until a final holistic explanation (final proposition) was reached and it could be shown that other explanations were not supported by the data. Three sample propositions reached in this study found that women participating in group psychotherapy gained both from the other participants and from the therapist, that group psychotherapy altered women's perceptions of themselves, and that women engaged in group psychotherapy increased their involvement in activities outside the group. While pragmatism goes a long way to bridging the divide between qualitative and quantitative methods research in psychology by focusing on research outcomes in a holistic way, the next section discusses Q methodology as a way in which the value of each approach is actively retained.

Q Methodology

Q methodology was developed as a way of measuring and manipulating personality traits (Spearman, 1927), but it was later argued (Stephenson, 1982) that because of its focus on the process by which individuals select items, it enabled a systematic exploration of issues toward which different points of view can be expressed. Perhaps not surprisingly then, descriptions and applications of Q methodology can be found both in books about qualitative research in psychology, such as *The SAGE Handbook of Qualitative Research in Psychology* (Willig & Stainton-Rogers, 2008), and in books about MMR in psychology, such as *Mixing Methods in Psychology* (Todd, Nerlich, McKeown, & Clarke, 2004), demonstrating that it is an approach that allies itself both with positivist and interpretivist epistemologies. Q methodology's "foot-in-both-camps" approach led to it being christened a "qualiquantilogical" approach (Stenner & Stainton-Rogers, 2004; Stenner, Watts, & Worrell, 2008).

As a method, Q methodology asks individual participants to sort (Q sort) lists of statements about a topic into groups. The groups generated this way reflect individual personal agreement with them. The Q sorts of a small number of the participants are factor analyzed using a rigorous and systematic approach that identifies small sets of common factors. Correlated clusters of Q-sorted items that have been collated in the same way by different individuals are produced by utilizing an approach

that both seeks a unitary truth about a topic and incorporates insight to individual views and how they are comprised. Coherent and shared views of a topic can be reached through interpretation of the different item configurations that typify each factor. It allows for unexpected or surprising perspectives to emerge because of the self-referential operations of the Q sorters, thus making this way of mixing qualitative and quantitative paradigms of great use to psychology researchers interested in what it feels like to experience a generalizable experience as an individual.

Q methodology is most often applied to health psychology research, where it can separate patients' views from those of professionals to examine misunderstandings and conflict (e.g., Eccleston & Crombez, 1997). It provides a way to explore everyday understandings of issues, such as what it means to be healthy and ill and what factors may be involved in the process of recovery (e.g., Stenner, Dancey, & Watts, 2000). Routes to recovery from substance addiction can be identified (Shinebourne, 2008), as well as shared meanings of emotions such as jealousy, joy, and love (Stenner & Stainton-Rogers, 2004; Stenner, Woodcock, & Ingham, 1992).

One example of the use of Q methodology is its use to explore therapists' understandings and experiences of working with clients with problems of addiction (Shinebourne & Adams, 2007). A set of 60 statements that described personal experiences and reflections on working with clients with problems of addiction was constructed by drawing on published interviews, academic literature, and the media. The statements were presented to 13 participants who were recruited to reflect a range of theoretical orientations, agencies, years of work experience, and supervisory experience as therapists working in this field. The participants were asked to sort the cards on which the statements were printed, initially into three piles according to whether they agreed, disagreed, or were neutral about the statement on each card. They were then asked to continue to sort the cards along a continuum that ranged from −6 (*strongly disagree*) to +6 (*strongly agree*). Beginning with the "agree" pile, participants then selected the two statements they agreed with most, then the three statements they agreed with slightly less, and so on until all the statements in the "agree" pile had been allocated. The process was repeated with the "disagree" pile.

Following the sorting task, participants was asked to comment on the statements they particularly agreed or disagreed with, to comment on those they found difficult to decide on, and to give reasons for this difficulty. In addition they were asked to provide suggestions of other statements to be included in the set. Finally they were asked a few questions about their experience of working with clients with problems of addiction and the theoretical approaches they employ in working with them. A Q statistical package (PCQ; Stricklin & Almeida, 2001) produced a small number of factors that represented shared forms of understanding among participants.

Factors identified included Acceptance; participants who shared this perspective accepted that a client may not aim for acceptance and that a harm-reduction approach may be suitable for working with alcohol/drug users. The Challenge factor was comprised of participants who shared a strong belief that controlled drinking is a myth and therefore that a harm-reduction approach is unsustainable. Addiction is seen by these participants primarily as a substitute for other relational attachments. The third factor identified was Ambivalence, in which participants shared a strong expectation that clients will aim for abstinence and held strong doubts about the possibility of recovering from addiction.

Using Q methodology, this study identified the contrasting views of those working in the field, particularly between the factors of Acceptance and Challenge, in which they differed on abstinence, controlled drinking, and the suitability of the harm-reduction approach. The researchers considered the use of Q methodology in their study and concluded that

> the pilot study has demonstrated that Q methodology can effectively combine statistical techniques and phenomenological research, and can be a useful tool for constructing a unique configuration of each participant's engagement with the topic. . . while at the same time identifying commonalities and diversity in viewpoints that do not conform to a priori conceptualizations. . . [and] that participants were engaging in the sorting task with significant degrees of shared understandings albeit with different loadings (indicating different degrees of agreement with the exemplar account of each factor). (Shinebourne & Adams, 2007, p. 216)

While the use of pragmatism and Q methodology in psychology allows the employment of qualitative and quantitative methods alongside each other in the exploration of human experience and meaning-making, there are emerging approaches that foreground qualitative methods, either in their mixing with quantitative methods or in their combination with other qualitative methods. It is argued that this combining of methods allows for greater representation of the complexity of human experience and thus gives more insight to the ways in which humans make sense of their selves and their relationship to the world. In the next section we briefly discuss each of these mixed methods approaches to show how mixed methods research in psychology is evolving.

Some Future Directions of Mixed and Multimethods Research in Psychology

As we have seen, the development of the mixing of methods in psychology has been both helped and hindered by thinking about how to combine the apparently irreconcilable epistemological differences in paradigms. For some researchers, the paradigm wars that claim the two cannot be combined are maintained; for others, there are ways of working across the differences instead of on either side of them. These researchers suggest that mixing methods in qualitatively driven ways allows for more explanation of the multidimensionality and complexity of lived experiences and social relationships (e.g., Hesse-Biber, 2010; Mason, 2006), albeit in a messier way than is more commonly seen in traditional approaches to research. Others (e.g., Frost et al., 2010; Gabb, 2009) advance the new ways of thinking about mixing methods in order to understand more of relationships, identities, and experiences by mixing methods of one paradigm with each other.

The range of approaches to mixing data methods is now widely accepted (Moran-Ellis et al., 2006). Less explored is the explicit combination of analytical tools that emerge from different paradigms where ontological and epistemological assumptions may vary. As we have seen from the examples throughout this chapter, assumptions about the nature of reality and kind of knowledge being sought by researchers influences the type of research questions asked and informs the interrogation of the data. Thus the mixing of different qualitative methods can seek to access different artifacts such as thoughts, feelings, and actions. By combining different methods, pluralistic qualitative research can enhance the multidimensionality of the investigation. It sees the continuum of dimensions possible in combining qualitative methods, ranging typically from the experiential to the discursive, and from the empiricist to the constructionist, with significant overlapping (Willig, 2008), and it recognizes areas of overlap such as a focus on language (McLeod, 2005). We now consider this in relation to its emergence within the psychology discipline.

Pluralism in Qualitative Research

In its simplest terms, pluralism denotes diversity. This may be a diversity of beliefs, practices, views, or opinions of a phenomenon. When applied to the conducting of qualitative research, pluralism suggests the mixing of paradigms, data, and/or analysis techniques to promote engagement with diversity, to actively seek understanding across lines of difference, and to enter into personal and methodological dialogue to promote and foster understanding of research inquiry and outcomes.

This approach has been used understand more of the experiences of one mother having a second child (Frost, 2006), to investigate anomalous experiences (e.g., Steffen & Coyle, 2010), to enhance research into the development of services for those with mental illness (e.g., Frost & Bowen, 2012; Warner & Spandler, 2012), and to the evaluation of intervention programs (Frost & Nolas, 2013; Nolas, 2009). It recognizes the plurality of paradigms within one approach, in this case the qualitative approach, and it advocates their mixing in order to reduce the likelihood of reductionism of the data or the meanings within it and brings different vantage points to the research. The range of methods available to qualitative researchers allows for combining of visual, verbal, group and individual, and observational data, as well as for other methods and data modalities ranging from participant accounts of events and experiences, to audio representations, official documents, and observations of practice (Dicks, Soyinka, & Coffey, 2006; Bauer & Gaskell, 2000). By considering the content and structure of these data modalities, the language used, and the role the researcher plays in the construction of these research artifacts and their interpretation, data is transformed within a theoretical and intersubjective framework that results in the construction of personal and collective perspectives on lived experience and social worlds.

In a study carried out by the Pluralism in Qualitative Research team (Frost et al., 2010, 2011), an interview transcript of a semistructured interview conducted with Karen, a mother of one child who was six months pregnant with her second child was analyzed by four different researchers, each using one qualitative method. The methods used were narrative analysis, IPA, Foucauldian discourse analysis, and grounded theory. The findings were synthesized by cross-analyzing them with a thematic analysis. Several different interpretations of the same sections of text allowed more in-depth insight to the ways in which this mother made sense of her expectations of and transition to second-time motherhood. For example, all the analysts found that the nature of the bond between Karen and her first child was a visceral one. The four interpretations of the "Visceral Nature of the Mother–Child Bond" described the anxiety provoked by Karen's bond with her child (grounded theory), the descriptions of its intensity using vivid imagery (IPA), the way in which the nature of the bond enabled Karen to construct herself as a mother (Foucauldian discourse analysis), and the contradictions the bond evokes in her as a mother who works (narrative analysis). While each finding taken alone is useful in providing insight into Karen's experience of being a mother, taken together they allow for a more holistic view of the emotional landscape provoked by the strength of the bond, as well as its nature and the purpose it may serve for her (Frost et al., 2010).

Pluralistic use of qualitative methods can be particularly useful for exploring dynamics of relationships, changing or contested meanings, and topics with little or no ontological consensus (Coyle, 2010). However, the enhanced emphasis this approach places on the interpretative lens of individual researchers highlights the importance of the role of the researcher when combining methods across or within paradigms.

The researcher is an important dimension in all research, but qualitative research values and embraces it highly enough to advocate inclusion and awareness of the researcher's assumptions, perspectives, and presuppositions as a quality criteria of the research process. This means that any discussion of the mixing of methods that include the adoption of qualitative approaches or methods must also consider the role and influence of the researcher on the research as it is formulated, as it progresses, and as it reaches and reports its findings. In the next section, we briefly consider some of the issues important to the researcher conducting mixed and multimethod research and to the audience for that research.

The Researcher in Mixed Methods Approaches

Researchers employing different paradigms, different methods, and different epistemologies must consider the worldview they are bringing to the research at any stage during the process and also how they will address the challenges of minimizing the imposition of the assumptions and presuppositions inherent in them or in their choice of method onto the accounts provided by others. This means that they need to find ways to make as explicit as possible the biases they know they are holding and bringing to the research and to be open to the consideration that there will be others of which they are not aware. Researchers in MMR must have the goals being pursued clearly in mind as they select the methods to be brought to the research. The mixed methods researcher must ensure that the methods are utilized as tools in the pursuit of knowledge appropriate to the research question. In mixed methods studies, it is often the case that researchers have a bias, expertise, or skill in one theoretical orientation over another. If they are working alone, they must assess their level of expertise in all the methods to be used and recruit other skills experts if necessary, and they must also reflectively question themselves regarding the purpose of additional methods in enhancing the qualitative understanding of the study. If working within a team, they must find ways to allow for different skills sets, epistemological and ontological values, and beliefs to be brought together in creative dialogue. The responsibility for the richness of the dialogue and the related outcomes of the quality and scope of the explanation lies with each team member's ability to transcend his or her differences and work together as researchers across and within paradigms.

The pluralistic qualitative approach described here acknowledges not only the importance of the role of the researcher in all qualitative research but also that the differences in how this is perceived across different methods can bring different worldviews and dimensions to the research as well. For example, some approaches to narrative analysis incorporate an explicitly critical approach that regards the researcher as a co-constructer of the account (e.g., Emerson & Frosh, 2004; Mishler, 1986), while others look for structure and content of narratives in the data (e.g., Labov, 1972; Gee, 1991).

In recognizing the limitations on expertise of individual researchers, who may be specialists in one qualitative method or another, the pluralistic qualitative approach advocates teamwork and raises awareness of researcher accountability not only for choice of method but also for how individual methods are employed in research. It calls on the distinctions recognized by Mason (2006) and Moran-Ellis et al. (2006) in decisions about whether methods use is developed at the outset of the research (integration) or as the research evolves (meshing).

Team-based research employing pluralistic qualitative methods allows a multilayered understanding of participants' accounts through detailed examination by different researchers of data using different frameworks and paradigms, and by each researcher acknowledging that he or she is bringing different perspectives and worldviews to the understanding of the text. By this process, the Pluralism in Qualitative Research team researchers felt that they came to know Karen better and that they developed an interpersonal relationship with her in the interview and explored her words with different queries in mind.

This emphasis on seeking to make known what is brought by the researcher to the research process is a key quality criterion of research that includes an interpretivist paradigm. Arguably it is a key criterion of all research, because credibility of research is enhanced by the knowledge that assumptions, preconceptions, and biases held by a researcher are known (as far as is possible) and efforts not to impose them onto interpretation of data gathered from participants have been made. The decisions made and choices faced in the research process become more transparent so that trust can be placed in findings that have been reached through the employment of carefully considered methods that best address the research question(s). Through explanation of how methods are employed and the role of the researcher in using them to interpret data, outcomes are substantiated, by reporting them as universal truths, possible meanings, or a synthesis of both. MMR conducted by using different paradigms, with explanation of the role and status of each paradigm, alongside the clear stance adopted by the researcher can lead to credible results that can be both in-depth and generalizable.

Conclusion

We now draw some conclusions about how research in psychology that combines methods of one paradigm or across paradigms offers ways of examining human experience and identity from different methodological (theoretical) perspectives that in turn are linked to methods or methods toolkits.

Initially the psychology discipline was wedded to a positivist paradigm and linked to particular research questions that could be investigated using quantitative methods. In time, and given the dissatisfaction in the reliance on this sole perspective, qualitatively driven approaches and methods were found to provide a set of new questions and perspectives. In this chapter we have demonstrated how multimethod and mixed methods research allows different and complex questions to be asked, and how this research highlights the place of both qualitative and quantitative methods in addressing them. The range of ways in which methods can be mixed, be they with others of the same paradigm or across paradigms, allows the complexity of humanness to be better represented but brings with it a demand for rigor and appropriate evaluation of quality criteria. This may mean moving away from the traditional scientific approach to triangulation to allow for the emergence of gaps, differences, and contradictions in understanding human experiences. The range of ways in which methods can be mixed means researchers must have a range of ways by which to reach outcomes and assess processes. Despite these challenges, there is a hope throughout the research community in psychology that attention to method does not signal a return to a methodolatry, in which the focus of the research, or the people at the center of the research, is obscured by the methods brought to gain understanding of them. It would seem that the emerging approaches of MMR in psychology will enable a greater focus on the researchers and what they bring to the process, as well as on enabling a deeper insight into the experiences of others. However, with these approaches still in their infancy in psychology, debates about the challenges and benefits they bring to the understanding of human behavior and experience continue.

Discussion Questions

1. What types of research questions can be asked using traditional mixed methods approaches that cannot be addressed with use of a single method alone?

2. What are the benefits of using mixed methods in psychology?

3. What are the challenges to employing mixed methods approaches to research in psychology?

4. Can you identify particular fields where the application of MMR would improve our understanding?

Suggested Websites

http://www.casp-uk.net/
Critical Appraisal Skills Programme.

http://cqim.cochrane.org/
The Cochrane Qualitative Methods and Implementation Group advises the Cochrane Collaboration and its networks on policy, practice, and qualitative evidence synthesis. It develops and maintains methodological guidance and provides training. The website provides information and news about training, meetings, and resources for conducting qualitative synthesis.

http://www.bps.org.uk/networks-communities/member-networks/sections/qualitative-methods-psychology-section/qualitative-met
The Qualitative Methods in Psychology Section of the British Psychological Society provides a forum to exchange ideas and promote research into the use of qualitative methods in psychology. The website provides links to news, events, and resources, as well as details about how to join.

http://qualpsy.org/
This newly formed section of Division 5 of the American Psychological Association promotes qualitative research in psychology. The website offers news, links, and resources to encourage and support the development of a forum for enriching and reflecting on forms of qualitative study in psychology.

References

American Psychiatric Association. (1994). *Diagnostic and statistical manual of mental disorders* (4th ed.). Washington, DC: Author.

Bannister, P., Burman, E., Parker, I., Taylor, M., & Tindall, C. (1994). *Qualitative Methods in Psychology: A research guide*. Maidenhead, UK: Open University Press.

Bauer, M. W., & Gaskell, G. (Eds.). (2000). *Qualitative researching with text, image and sound: A practical handbook for social research*. London, England: Sage.

Braun, V., & Clarke, V. (2006). Using thematic analysis in psychology. *Qualitative Research in Psychology, 3*(2), 77–101.

Bryman, A. (1988). *Quantity and quality in social research*. London, England: Routledge.

Bryman, A. (2006). Paradigm peace and the implications for quality. *International Journal of Social Research Methodology, 9*(2), 111–126.

Bryman, A. (2007). Barriers to integrating quantitative and qualitative research. *Journal of Mixed Methods Research, 1*(1), 8–22.

Burck, C. (2004). *Multilingual living: Explorations of language and subjectivity*. New York, NY: Palgrave Macmillan.

Burck, C. (2005). Comparing qualitative research methodologies for systemic research: the use of grounded theory, discourse analysis and narrative analysis. *Journal of Family Therapy, 27*(3), 237–262.

Chamberlain, K., Camic, P., & Yardley, L. (2004). Qualitative analysis of experience: Grounded theory and case studies. In D. F. Marks & L. Yardley (Eds.), *Research methods for clinical and health psychology* (pp. 69–89). Thousand Oaks, CA: Sage.

Cochrane Collaboration. (2013). Evidence-based health care and systematic reviews. Retrieved from http://www.cochrane.org/about-us/evidence-based-health-care

Coyle, A. (2010). Qualitative research and anomalous experience: A call for interpretative pluralism. *Qualitative Research in Psychology, 7*(1), 79–83.

Curt, B. C. (1994). *Textuality and tectonics: Troubling social and psychological science.* Buckingham, UK: Open University Press.

Dicks, B., Soyinka, B., & Coffey, A. (2006). Multimodal ethnography. *Qualitative Research, 6*(1), 77–96.

Eccleston, C., & Crombez, G. (1997). Pain demands attention: A cognitive-affective model of the interruptive function of pain. *Psychological Bulletin, 125*, 355–366.

Emerson, P., & Frosh, S. (2004). *Critical narrative analysis in psychology: A guide to practice.* New York, NY: Palgrave Macmillan.

Finlay, L., & Gough, B. (2003). *Reflexivity: A practical guide for researchers in health and social sciences.* Oxford, UK: Blackwell.

Forrester, M. (Ed.). (2010). *Doing qualitative research in psychology.* London, England: Sage.

Frost, N. A. (2006). Taking the other out of mother: The transition to second-time motherhood, Unpublished thesis, Birkbeck, University of London.

Frost, N. A. (Ed.). (2011) *Qualitative research: Combining core approaches.* London, England: Open University Press.

Frost, N. A., Esin, C., Holt, A., Mehdizadeh, L., Brooks-Gordon, B., & Shinebourne, P. (2011). Pluralism in qualitative research: Consensual findings, individual interpretations. *Qualitative Research in Psychology, 8*(1), 93–113.

Frost, N., & Bowen, C. (2012). Commentary: New pluralistic strategies for research in clinical practice. *Qualitative Research in Psychology, 9*(1), 27–31.

Frost, N., Nolas, S. M., Brooks-Gordon, B., Esin, C., Holt, A., Mehdizadeh, L., & Shinebourne, P. (2010). Pluralism in qualitative research: The impact of different researchers and qualitative approaches on the analysis of qualitative data. *Qualitative Research, 10*(4), 441–460.

Frost, N. A., & Nolas, S.-M. (2013, June). The contribution of pluralistic qualitative approaches to mixed methods evaluations, Special Issue *New Directions in Evaluation*: Addressing the Credibility of Evidence in Mixed Methods Evaluations: Questions, Issues and Strategies.

Gabb, J. (2009). Researching family relationships: A qualitative mixed methods approach. *Methodological Innovation Online, 4*(2), 37–52.

Gee, J. P. (1991). A linguistic approach to narrative. *Journal of Narrative and Life History, 1*(1), 15–39.

Gergen, K. J. (1973). Social Psychology as History. *Journal of Personality and Social Psychology, 26*(2), 309–320.

Gilligan, C. (1982). *In a different voice.* Cambridge, MA: Harvard University Press.

Gough, B., McFadden, M., & McDonald, M. (2013). *Critical social psychology: An introduction* (2nd ed.). New York, NY: Palgrave Macmillan.

Guyatt, G. H., Sackett, D. L., Sinclair, J. C., Hayward, R., Cook, D. J., & Cook. R. J. (1995). Users' guides to the medical literature, IX: A method for grading health care recommendations. *JAMA: Journal of the American Medical Association, 274*, 1800–1804.

Harman, G. H. (1965). The inference to the best explanation, *Philosophical Review, 74*(1), 88–95.

Harper, D., & Thompson, A. (Eds.). (2011). *Qualitative research methods in mental health and psychotherapy: An introduction for students and practitioners.* Chichester, UK: Wiley Blackwell.

Hesse-Biber, S. N. (2010). *Mixed methods research: Merging theory with practice.* New York, NY: Guilford Press.

Hiles, D. R. (1999, June). *Paradigms lost—paradigms regained.* Paper presented at the 18th International Human Science Research Conference, Sheffield, UK.

Hiles, D. R. (2006, August). *The logic of human inquiry: Epistemological and pluralistic issues.* Paper presented at the Sixth European Qualitative Research Conference in Health and Social Care, Bournemouth, UK.

Hiles, D. R. (2014). Qualitative inquiry, mixed methods and the logic of scientific inquiry. *QMiP Bulletin, 17.* Retrieved from http://shop.bps.org.uk/qmip-bulletin-issue-17-spring-2014.html

Holt, A. (2011). Discourse analysis approaches. In N. A. Frost (Ed.), *Qualitative research in psychology: Combining core approaches* (pp. 66–92). Maidenhead, UK: Open University Press.

Howard, G. S. (1983). Research productivity in counselling psychology: An update and generalization study. *Journal of Counselling Psychology, 30*, 600–602.

Hudson, A., Duncan, H., Pattison, H., & Shaw, R. (2012, May). *The experience of nurses and doctors who care for a child who has had an unexpected acute life-threatening event (ALTE) in hospital.* Paper presented at the Seventh International Conference on Rapid Response Systems and Medical Emergency Teams, Sydney, Australia.

Hudson, A., Mohamed Ali, A., Duncan, H., Pattison, M., & Shaw, R. (2013, April). *Bespoke simulation training to improve nurses' self-efficacy and prepare them for caring for children who have an unexpected acute life-threatening event (ALTE) in hospital.* Paper presented at the Fifth International Pediatric Simulation Symposia and Workshops, New York, NY.

Kelly, M., Steward, E., Morgan, A., Killoran, A., Fischer, A., Threfall, A., & Bonnefoy J. (2009). A conceptual framework for public health: NICE's emerging approach. *Public Health, 123*, e14–e20.

Kincheloe, J. L. (2001). Describing the bricolage: Conceptualizing a new rigor in qualitative research. *Qualitative Inquiry, 7*(6), 679–692.

Kincheloe, J. L. (2005). On to the next level: Continuing the conceptualization of the bricolage. *Qualitative Inquiry, 11*(3), 323–350.

Labov, W. (1972). *Language in the inner city: Studies in the Black English vernacular.* Oxford, UK: Blackwell.

Lipton, P. (1991). *Inference to the best explanation.* London, England: Routledge.

Mason, J. (2006). Mixing methods in a qualitatively driven way. *Qualitative Research, 6*(1), 9–25.

McCabe Hudson, A., Duncan, H., Pattison, H., & Shaw, R. (2011, December). *International survey of practice to identify psychological interventions that prepare or support nurses that have cared for a child who has an unexpected acute life threatening event (ALTE) in hospital.* Paper presented at the First PNAE Congress on Paediatric Nursing, Istanbul, Turkey.

McLeod, J. (2005). *Qualitative research in counselling and psychotherapy*. London, England: Sage.

Medical Research Council. (2008). Developing and evaluating complex interventions: new guidance. Retrieved from http://www.mrc.ac.uk/documents/pdf/complex-interventions-guidance/

Mishler, E. G. (1986). *Research interviewing: Context and narrative*. Cambridge, MA: Harvard University Press.

Moran-Ellis, J., Alexander, V. D., Cronin, A., Dickinson, M., Fielding, J., Sleney, J., & Thomas, H. (2006). Triangulation and integration: processes, claims and implications. *Qualitative Research, 6*(1), 45–59.

Nolas, S.-M. (2009). Between the ideal and the real: Using ethnography as a way of extending our language of change. *Qualitative Research in Psychology, 6*(1–2), 105–128.

Oakley, A. (1999). People's way of knowing: Gender and methodology. In S. Hood, B. Mayall, & S. Oliver (Eds.), *Critical issues in social research* (pp. 154–170). Maidenhead, UK: Open University Press.

O'Cathain, A., Murphy, E., & Nicholl, J. (2010). Three techniques for integrating data in mixed methods studies. *British Medical Journal, 341*, c4587.

Pace, R., Pluye, P., Bartlett, G., Macaulay, A.C., Salsberg, J., Jagosh, J., & Seller, R. (2012). Testing the reliability and efficiency of the pilot Mixed Methods Appraisal Tool (MMAT) for systematic mixed studies review. *International Journal of Nursing Studies, 49*, 47–53.

Paley, J., & Lilford, R. (2011). Qualitative methods: An alternative view. *British Medical Journal, 342*, d424.

Parker, I., & Shotter, J. (Eds.). (1990). *Deconstructing social psychology*. London, England: Routledge.

Peirce, C. S. (1903). Pragmatism as the logic of abduction (7th Harvard Lecture). In *The Essential Peirce: Vol. 2*. Bloomington: Indiana University Press.

Pluye, P., Gagnon, M., Griffiths, F., & Johnson-Lafleur, J. (2009). A scoring system for appraising mixed methods research, and concomitantly appraising qualitative, quantitative and mixed methods primary studies in mixed studies review. *International Journal of Nursing Studies, 46*, 529–546.

Potter, J., & Wetherell, M. (1987). *Discourse and social psychology: Beyond attitudes and behaviour*. London, England: Sage.

Reason, J., & Rowan, J. (Eds.). (1981). *Human inquiry: A sourcebook of new paradigm research*. New York, NY: Wiley.

Rogers, C. R. (1961). *On becoming a person: A therapist's view of psychotherapy*. Boston, MA: Mariner Books.

Scottish Intercollegiate Guideline Network. (2008). *SIGN 50: A guideline developer's handbook*. Edinburgh, UK: Health Improvement Scotland.

Shaw, R. L. (2013). Qualitative methods: An alternative view. *British Medical Journal, 342*, d424. Retrieved from http://www.bmj.com/content/342/bmj.d424/rr/63504

Shaw, R. L., Larkin, M., & Flowers, P. (2014). Expanding the evidence within evidence-based healthcare: thinking about the context, acceptability and feasibility of interventions. *Evidence Based Medicine*. Retrieved from: http://ebm.bmj.com/content/early/2014/05/05/eb-2014-101791.extract.

Shinebourne, P., & Adams, M. (2007). Therapists' understandings and experiences of working with clients with problems of addiction: A pilot study using Q methodology. *Counselling and Psychotherapy Research, 7*(4), 211–219.

Shinebourne, P., & Adams, M. (2008). Q-methodology as a phenomenological research method. *Existential Analysis, 18*(1), 103–116.

Smith, J. A. (1996). Beyond the divide between cognition and discourse: Using interpretative phenomenological analysis in health psychology. *Psychology & Health, 11*, 261–271.

Smith, J. A. (2011). Evaluating the contribution of interpretative phenomenological analysis. *Health Psychology Review, 5*, 9–27.

Smith, J. A. (Ed.). (2008). *Qualitative psychology: A practical guide to research methods* (2nd ed.). London, England: Sage.

Smith, J. A., Harré, R., & van Langenhove, L. (1995). *Rethinking methods in psychology*. London, England: Sage.

Spearman, C. (1927). *The abilities of man: Their nature and measurement*. New York, NY: Macmillan.

Stainton-Rogers, W. (2003). *Social psychology: Experimental and critical approaches*. Maidenhead, UK: Open University Press.

Steffen, E., & Coyle, A. (2010). Can "sense of presence" experiences in bereavement be conceptualised as spiritual phenomena? *Mental Health, Religion & Culture, 13*(3), 273–291.

Stenner, P. H. D., Dancey, C. P., & Watts, S. (2000). The understanding of their illness amongst people with irritable bowel syndrome: A Q methodological study. *Social Science & Medicine, 51*(3), 439–452.

Stenner, P., & Stainton-Rogers, R. S. (2004). The example of discriminating between emotions. In Z. Todd, B. Nerlich, S. McKeown, & D. D. Clarke (Eds.), *Mixing methods in psychology: The integration of qualitative and quantitative methods in theory and practice* (pp. 99–118). New York, NY: Psychology Press.

Stenner, P., Watts, S., & Worrell, M. (2008). Q methodology. In C. Willig & W. S. Rogers (Eds.), *The SAGE Handbook of Qualitative Research in Psychology* (pp. 215–239). Thousand Oaks, CA: Sage.

Stenner, K., Woodcock, A. J., & Ingham, R. (1992). Young people talking about HIV and AIDS: Interpretations of personal risk of infection. *Health Education Research, 7*(2), 229–247.

Stephenson, W. (1982). Q-Methodology, interbehavioural psychology, and quantum theory. *Psychological Record, 32*, 235–248.

Stricklin, M., &Almeida, J. (2001). PCQ: Analysis software for Q-technique [Computer software] (Rev.ed.). Portland, OR: PCQ Software.

Tashakkori, A., & Creswell, J.W. (2007). Editorial: The new era of mixed methods. *Journal of Mixed Methods Research, 1*, 3–7.

Todd, Z., Nerlich, B., McKeown, S., & Clarke, D. D. (Eds.). (2004). *Mixing methods in psychology: The integration of qualitative and quantitative methods in theory and practice*. New York, NY: Psychology Press.

Ussher, J. M. (2003). The role of premenstrual dysphoric disorder in the subjectification of women. *Journal of Medical Humanities, 24* (1–2), 131–146.

Warner, S., & Spandler, H. (2012). New strategies for practice-based evidence: A focus on self-harm. *Qualitative Research in Psychology, 9*(1), 13–26.

Willig, C. (2008). *Introducing qualitative research in psychology.* Maidenhead, UK: Open University Press.

Willig, C., & Stainton-Rogers, W. (Eds.). (2008). *The SAGE handbook of qualitative research in psychology.* London, England: Sage.

Yardley, L. (2000). Dilemmas in qualitative health research. *Psychology and Health, 15*(2), 215–228.

Yardley, L., & Bishop, F. (2008). Mixing qualitative and quantitative methods: A Pragmatic approach. In C. Willig & W. Stainton-Rogers (Eds.), *The SAGE handbook of qualitative research in psychology.* London, England: Sage.

Yin, R. K. (1994). *Case study research: Design and methods* (2nd ed.). Thousand Oaks, CA: Sage.

Participatory Mixed Methods Research

Bradley D. Olson *and* Leonard A. Jason

Abstract

This chapter presents *participatory mixed methods research* (PMMR), based on participatory action research, as an alternative to using solely quantitative or qualitative research methods. This approach is illustrated through research with a community-based network of resident-run, substance abuse recovery homes, Oxford House. Participatory input from community members led to a series of mixed methods investigations, the results of which were more informative, revealing, and relevant than they would have been otherwise. The ultimate goal of PMMR is to gain a greater understanding of multiple phenomena of interest (Rappaport, 1987), multiple truths through dialectical pluralism (Johnson, 2012; Johnson & Stefurak, 2013), greater ecological understandings of pressing societal challenges, and ethically putting that knowledge toward action. Future directions are discussed.

Key Words: participatory mixed method research, participatory action research, mixed methods, substance abuse, Oxford House

There are many types and styles of research in the social sciences. On one popular continuum, the work of researchers hovers toward one pole or the other on the quantitative versus qualitative research continuum. Research preferences for either a qualitative or quantitative methodology is often due to one's training, discipline, or worldview, or a combination of these factors. Using multimethod and mixed methods research (MMMR) typically combines aspects of qualitative and quantitative methodologies to gain the benefits of both (Barker & Pistrang, 2012; Campbell, Gregory, Patterson, & Bybee, 2012; Jason & Glenwick, 2012; Johnson & Onwuegbuzie, 2004; Tebes, 2012). We present a model, participatory mixed methods research (PMMR), that goes one step further. PMMR focuses on the merging of diverse epistemologies and considers who participates in collecting, interpreting, and using the newly developed knowledge.

Johnson (2012; see also Johnson & Stefurak, 2013) discusses mixed methods as a form of dialectical pluralism where the dichotomy of qualitative and quantitative methods functions as a practical path toward understanding multiple truths about a particular content area or set of research questions. Dialectical pluralism endorses efforts to discover combined or interactive approaches that can build greater bridges across methods and methodologies, as well as across paradigms and other disciplinary approaches to research. Dialectical situations often require the resolving of paradoxes. Paradoxes, the divergent nature of the social world, are intrinsically helpful in understanding the nature of social scientific research (Rappaport, 1981, 1987).

What follows is a review of methods characterized by quantitative and/or qualitative research, where we highlight differences, similarities, and the complementary features of these approaches in what is known as mixed methods. Next, we present

PMMR, which involves seeking community input throughout a mixed and multimethod research process. Finally we provide examples in our work with a community-based organization, one that was designed and is run by people in substance abuse recovery. The concluding section summarizes the chapter while providing future directions for integrating these diverse methods of conducting community-based research.

Quantitative and Qualitative Methods

The goal of mixed methods is arguably to bring together qualitative and quantitative data into a useful and workable whole. There is rich heterogeneity within each approach, and we contend that there are commonalities across the methods that can bring synergy to the goal of better answering a research question. Yet these commonalities are perhaps too often overlooked.

At the most basic level, quantitative data are seen to be about *numbers*, and qualitative data, in contrast, are about *words*. However, things are not this simple. Quantitative research relies on words in many places, for example, on an attitude questionnaire participants are required to *read* and interpret the questions. Despite the descriptive and inferential statistics in a qualitative research section, every section of a research article (particularly the introduction and discussion but certainly the methods and results too) includes textual descriptions that tend to be dominated by words.

The number–word distinction is no clearer in qualitative research. For example, qualitative researchers may quantify their data by coding interview responses and developing constructs based on recurring themes. Again, at a basic level, social researchers who use qualitative methods know that it is not possible to understand, discuss, and evaluate the world through qualitative means alone.

Quantitative and qualitative approaches often rely on different methods of data collection. For example, more heavily constructed, factor analytic–derived scales are often used in quantitative questionnaires. These traditional quantitative methods differ from the open-ended questions and in-depth interviews in qualitative research.

In MMMR, investigators combine approaches. For example, textual data, obtained using qualitative methods, are sometimes coded on an interval measurement scale (see McAdams, 2009; McAdams & Olson, 2009), so words are translated to numbers by multiple raters (then interrater reliability is examined), and the resulting scores can

then be included in statistical analyses. When the sample size is large enough, the interval-based scores can be used within inferential analyses.

In both quantitative and qualitative research, the idea of "validity" is valued (or at least credibility or justifiability of interpretations is appreciated; Auerbach & Silverstein, 2003). Construct validity, the process within and across scientific research studies, where the meaning of a concept comes into a progressively clearer focus, is particularly important in trying to understand a concept (see our efforts later in this chapter to understand the meaning of *tolerance* [i.e., the opposite of prejudice] and how it grew into *personal growth* through PMMR; Cronbach & Meehl, 1955). One can argue that construct validity is important in both qualitative and quantitative research. In each case, researchers attempt to better understand the meaning behind important constructs they create, they are simply interested in, or that emerge through the research process. Construct validity is about discovering what certain variables mean or finding out if they mean what we once believed them to mean. When construct validity is developed, we are more effective at examining relationships among variables and communicating those relationships across researchers and research projects.

We argue that PMMR may be the best way to, through a research program, piece together the meanings of a construct. Through one's own studies, through the studies of others, through quantitative and qualitative data, and through participatory discussion with community members, we begin to build a "nomological net" (Cronbach & Meehl, 1955)—a metaphorical net whereby constructs and themes are interrelated and where understanding the relationships, the convergences and divergences, we learn more about the phenomenon of interest.

After data has been obtained and it is time for analyses, quantitative data exist as raw scores, whereas qualitative data exist in the form of raw text. Often participants are quoted verbatim as data or as revelatory findings in qualitative research reports. Yet common to both qualitative and quantitative analysis is data reduction—to reduce enough complexity of the information to make it accessible while keeping enough complexity to make it both realistic and meaningful.

Statistical analyses and qualitative coding both work to reduce and organize information. Large amounts of numerical data can easily be analyzed through descriptive statistics, such as measures of central tendency and measures of variability in quantitative research. Likewise, the words from interviews or observations can be coded and quantified through the selection and categorization of chunks of text in qualitative research. All social researchers must deal with complexity, but the goal is to tell a story as accurately and ethically as possible. Parsimony and precision are important elements to telling a theoretically rich story, and this is true in both good statistical analysis reporting and narrative or prose writing.

Throughout the research process, qualitative and quantitative approaches can also have their own rules but also worldviews and styles. Sticking with the theme of dialectical pluralism, some researchers, in terms of style or worldview, see qualitative research as more *flexible*, whereas quantitative research is stereotyped as more *constrained*. There is some truth to these viewpoints, but there are some important exceptions. In his treatise on quantitative methods, Abelson (1995) characterizes a continuum whereby quantitative researchers are either "brash" (flexible or liberal) or "stuffy" (constrained or conservative). Of course many quantitative and quantitative researchers fall somewhere in between, and the two distribution types probably have more overlap than not. Qualitative researchers can be arguably more conservative (careful) in their judgments than many quantitative researchers. Some researchers of both types are brash (and some stuffy), and such styles may vary around interviewing or coding methods or making more cautious or grand claims about findings—often based on the same set of data.

Another popularly believed distinction between quantitative and qualitative research is the position on *generalizability* of findings and claims. Post-positivists strive for generalizability. The goal here is the discovery of universal or relatively universal phenomena, even if the findings of many laboratory studies tend to be most generalizable to university undergraduates. Much qualitative research, in contrast, desires to understand a particular person, set of persons, or local place or program. Even in case studies, though, there is sometimes an aim to find transferability (similar to generalizability) of theoretical concepts (Auerbach & Silverstein, 2003; Denzin & Lincoln, 2000). Quantitative case studies are also common in the history of empirical psychology. In the end, quantitative research tends to be more focused on producing *nomothetic knowledge*, concerns of or findings around the averages across whole populations, and qualitative research

tends to be more focused on producing *idiographic knowledge*, concerns or findings around the unique individual and case. In MMMR, Johnson and Stefurak (2013) support the importance of both levels of knowledge for the enterprise of science. They suggest that science should "learn" from both levels of knowledge and continually integrate them into a dynamic whole.

Many other intersecting dialectics could be considered that are outside the scope of this chapter. For instance, the distinction between *research* and *evaluation*—the idea that "research" is more connected to generalizability and "evaluation" on more local and practical goals. These are the very paradoxes valued by the mixed methods paradigm and the philosophy of dialectical pluralism. Clear answers are difficult to find, and there may be multiple solutions. To value multiple and mixed methods in a participatory framework hints at one solution to become more effective in our search for knowledge within the social sciences. One goal set forth by dialectical pluralism is to dynamically learn from different research worldviews and approaches to obtain fuller and more inclusive outcomes and understandings.

Participatory Mixed Methods Research

We advocate moving a step beyond the mixed methods approach to one of *participatory mixed methods*. The method we are presenting here, PMMR, might be seen as bringing the best of participatory action research (PAR) into the mixed methods community. PAR is in some ways very different from traditional forms of empirical scientific research (Jason, Keys, et al., 2004; Olson & Jason, 2011). PAR is concerned with research–participant interactions, obtaining sound data, and engaging in ethical behavior. The method adds that we must also bring about some *action* through our research to improve our communities and the world. PMMR involves community input at the outset and throughout the research process. Input from community research participants can occur through formal interviewing and informal conversations. Discussions with community members usually involve different levels of partnerships, but always include questions like, "Given your experiential expertise, what is the most important piece for us to study about this topic?" Through PAR and PMMR, the researcher and community members both have power, and they, ideally, operate through dialogue and the mutual sharing of knowledge.

The goal of a collaborative partnership is for all stakeholders of a project to have dialogue in an authentic relationship, with the aim of full and honest sharing of information. Compared to the trained researcher, community partners often know little about experimental or qualitative research designs or about coding and statistical techniques. These more complex research procedures are exactly the places where the expertise of the researchers can be offered to the relationship and initiative. Community members, in contrast, usually have the most to offer in the form of experiential expertise or the "lived experience" around a topic of interest. Participatory communication across stakeholders should be flexible and involve a mutually shared process of education and dialogue (Freire, 1970).

Participatory research is often seen in contrast to more post-positivist, or objectivist, approaches that reflect a value in researchers distancing themselves from the research "subject." While understanding the value of such scientific methods, we argue that such an exclusive focus on objectivity and distance can result in unintentional and unseen negative consequences on the research process, the data, and therefore any hope to have a fully correct interpretation of community-based data. Distancing and hierarchical forms of communication between researcher and research participant can oftentimes lead participants to develop a lack of trust in the research process, which can thereby change their reported beliefs and behavior. Any lack of trust can lead to dishonest surveys or face-to-face interview responses. In PMMR, we recommend dialogue on as equal of a footing as possible among researchers and participants, even if both groups have different assets to offer to the process.

Another way to describe the importance of collaboration, particularly in PMMR, is to say that—to participants or a particular community group—the method sends a better "metacommunication"—that the researcher is coming from a greater place of openness to broader participation in the research process, flexibility in sharing information, and being open to being critiqued by the reality of the community members' lived experiences. Rappaport (2000), who coined the term *metacommunication*, argued that narrative data sent a more respectful, inviting, and collaborative message to participants than quantitative, or objectivist, approaches alone. Quantitative methods, when that is the exclusive approach, can send a message of bureaucratic reductionism—turning humans into numbers. This is not to make a negative judgment of quantitative methods. At times, community members want quantitative data and experimental methods for the very reason that they, or the outside world, views them as more rigorous.

Better metacommunications and dialogue lead to more participant respect for the research process, greater participant investment, increased attention to detail, and a more sustainable research relationship over time. Each of these outcomes has the potential to increase the quality of responses. Rather than researchers simply encouraging socially responsible answers from participants, critical partnerships (i.e., the development of an honest and authentic relationship) can encourage more honest and productive responses and relationships.

PMMR can help prevent irrelevant research. For research to be relevant, it has to be understood and meaningful, and not just to the researchers themselves but also to those the research affects and is about. In the clinical psychological sciences, translational research is often used to make research more "relevant"—to, in essence, "translate" the research into language that can be understood, and used pragmatically, by practitioners. In contrast to translation, PMMR naturally brings alignment across scientific research and community action goals, ensuring, through collaboration, that the alignment occurs from the outset; therefore, making less necessary the later translation to make findings ecologically relevant and actionable.

The PMMR goal of outcomes leading to "action" means real-world impacts. The action-orientation of PAR comes from a sense of urgency, held by all stakeholders, to use data as soon as possible to good effect, e.g., for badly needed policy change. While not all data are actionable, every part of the research process can potentially lead to action in the form of dissemination, program refinement, or advocacy. Of course community participants should play a role in every step, in the research process, and in carrying out subsequent action.

To demonstrate the benefits of using a participatory action approach in MMMR, an extended example helps show how mixed data can be used to better understand the construct of "tolerance," as tolerating other people plays an important role in community-based organizations and society in general.

Oxford House

Oxford House started in 1975 when a group of people in recovery learned that their halfway house was soon to shut down. Because they did not have funds to hire a staff or supervisor, they decided to live together in recovery and allow democratic voting to guide collective decision-making. Over a few years, three rules developed: residents cannot use alcohol or drugs, residents need to pay their fair share of expenses, and residents must do house tasks assigned to them weekly. If residents are willing to abide by these three rules, they can remain in the houses for as long as they want.

As rented, resident-run living settings for people recovering from substance abuse problems Oxford Houses follow a 12-step communal living models, and thus have no professional staff members associated with the homes (Jason, Olson, & Foley, 2008; Olson, Jason, Ferrari, & Hutcheson, 2005). Since the opening of the first Oxford House, there are now over 10,000 people living in 1,600 homes, represented in almost every US state, some solely for men, others for women, and some with children. Residents come from many situations, including many formerly homeless or ex-offender people, and those with lived experience of mental illnesses. Houses have also emerged in Canada, Australia, and Africa.

For more than 20 years, a team of researchers at DePaul University has embraced a participatory action approach with Oxford Houses (Jason et al., 2008). Our research relationship with Oxford House began with a phone call to Paul Molloy, the co-founder and leader of the organization (Jason et al., 1994; Jason et al., 2008). More than a full year of conversations followed, and trust slowly developed between the community organization and the research group. An Oxford House representative was eventually sent to Illinois to set up recovery homes. For the first year, no formal data was collected; instead time was spent attending Oxford House business meetings and building up relationships of mutual trust. Oxford House partners attended research meetings, even tape-recording them so members could research the researchers to have input into the process. The building of a trusting relationship with our community partners helped us determine together what questions should be addressed, what kind of data should be collected, and who should collect that data.

Quantitative Research Using Random Assignment to Groups

During the 1990s, our research group submitted a number of grant proposals to collect longitudinal data from Oxford House members, but National Institutes of Health reviewers kept asking us to conduct a randomized design to determine whether or not the recovery homes could lead to reductions in substance abuse. We kept informing the grant reviewers that a randomized design was not feasible, as each Oxford House voted on whether to allow new members to live in their house. When we finally approached the founder of Oxford House, Paul Molloy, with this predicament, he said that he would work with us toward a randomized study. The willingness of Oxford House leadership was likely a direct result of years of mutual trust building we had been involved in with the organization, as well as conducting a number of collaborative pilot studies. We were later told that another research group had, many years earlier, approached Oxford House with a request for a randomized study. However, because that research group had not built up a trusting relationship, the Oxford House organization refused participation.

The randomized, quantitative, two-year longitudinal study, funded by the National Institute on Alcoholism and Alcohol Abuse, and beginning in 2001, included 150 participants recruited from a variety of inpatient treatment centers throughout Chicago. Participants randomly assigned to the Oxford House condition were separately brought into a variety of houses over time. Each participant was eventually successful in getting voted into a house by other residents. The control condition, or usual aftercare participants, ended up doing what they would have done had the study not existed. Most of the usual care participants moved back into their prior houses (and neighborhoods) while engaging in some form of outpatient care. All participants were interviewed every 6 months for the 24-month period. The tracking rate for participants at the two-year follow-up was over 85%. The participant sample demographics were 62% female, 76% African American, 11% European American, and 8% Latino/a. Participants had previously been incarcerated an average of three times and were in treatment also an average of three times. Random assignment worked well. There were only negligible pretest differences on all relevant variables. In brief, key findings were that those in the Oxford House condition, over a two-year period, had significantly less substance use, higher employment, and lower criminal justice-related outcomes (see Jason et al., 2007).

Tolerance as a Research Topic

In our early studies, we were learning that the underlying mission of the houses involved the residents being able to work in unison with diverse others (Jason et al., 1994). From the mission of the organization, to ensure that the goal of overcoming addiction superseded any distractions, ingroup–outgroup distinctions were prohibited in the houses. Ethnic, socioeconomic status, or any other differences were subservient to the desire to stop using. However, in later studies, we found that some new residents of Oxford House did have concerns about discrimination. For example, in a qualitative data set, one new Latino resident expressed apprehension about "white guys" but also worried about going back anywhere else:

> Not knowing how to deal with people. My only other option was to. . . move in with my parents. That alone in itself is a relapse trigger. They don't use drugs. But the codependency, enabling issues and just being over there in their house. . . creates anxiety for some reason. (Alvarez, Jason, Davis, Ferrari, & Olson, 2004).

Despite worries, this resident reported blending into the house: "The house became my house." And as a female resident described,

> At first, when I moved in, I was afraid to talk much. I kept to myself. I kept really quiet. But in a week or two I started to feel more comfortable. And the other women really tried to get to know me, to draw me out.

She then moved from a sense of marginalization in society to acceptance, a sense of connection, and empowerment:

> I see others in the house with the same addiction problems. Same core issues affect them. Through associating with these gentlemen I'm getting a feeling that I'm a real person. I'm not less than others. I am allowing myself to feel empowered—not marginalized.

As researchers, however, we had not realized the importance of the issue of tolerance in the Oxford House organization. Our early work focused on general characteristics of the houses, reasons for becoming a member, and the active ingredients that might help people stop using drugs. At one annual Oxford House World Convention, after presenting some of our research, an Oxford resident approached the second author and said, "You know I really liked your research. But what you should really be studying is 'tolerance'! That's really what Oxford House is really about." By tolerance,

he meant the ability to overcome prejudice. He continued, "You see that woman over there. She's HIV positive. I would have never talked to her before Oxford House. She is now my girlfriend." In later reflections with the research team we asked ourselves, could tolerance be an essential part of what happens within these houses? Is it important within the recovery process?

We decided to include a tolerance measure in the National Institute on Alcohol Abuse and Alcoholism randomized, longitudinal study that was just beginning. The quantitative measure was the Universality-Diversity Orientation scale (UDO; also known as the Miville-Guzman Universality-Diversity scale; Miville et al., 1999). In this two year study, using hierarchical linear modeling, we found a significant longitudinal trajectory showing that Oxford House residents grew substantially in their tolerance-related attitudes over time, while those in the usual care condition showed no changes in this area whatsoever (see Olson, Jason, Davidson, & Ferrari, 2009, for the published manuscript).

The PMMR approach includes a discovery and testing process. Item interpretation from rating scales (in addition to more casual, participatory discussions with Oxford House residents) helped us understand, to a limited extent, what the quantitative results meant. In trying to understand tolerance, in a construct validity sense, and the commonalities and synergies across mixed methods, we did some informal, interpretive analysis of the universality-diversity items. For each item, we asked ourselves, how does this relate to what occurs in Oxford House?

Looking at the universality-diversity tolerance items, almost in a qualitative sense—to try to understand why the quantitative data showed that Oxford House residents—several themes emerged. For instance, several of the items assessed the desire of respondents to join organizations or attend events where there was a likelihood of encountering people with different views and lifestyles. This made sense for the new life context of Oxford House residents. Compared to a usual aftercare setting, Oxford House living is filled with a wide variety of events around recovery. A resident can attend a Narcotics Anonymous meeting every evening. There are Oxford House business and chapter meetings, Oxford House fundraisers, pool parties, and barbecues (Olson et al., 2005). Each of these events are filled with diverse others—people from all walks of life.

Another specific item on the UDO asked participants about their willingness to learn from people with disabilities—knowledge they could not learn elsewhere. Substance abuse problems have often been considered a disability, making it understandable that participants randomly assigned to Oxford House would increasingly give higher responses on the item. Another universality-diversity item assessed the knowledge respondents tend to gain from the experiences of diverse others. In essence, knowing about others' different experiences helps better understand one's own problems, and this increased over time for our Oxford House participants. This growth experience, as will be better understood with our qualitative data, has a deeper meaning of "recovery" perfectly consistent with the entire 12-step process and how it impacts people's lives.

Although the quantitative results were promising there was much to be learned about tolerance in the houses. Even when taking a qualitative look at individual, standardized survey items, we did not have much more than an outcome that told us more tolerance occurred in Oxford House over time than alternatives. The greatest strength of the quantitative approach was its ability to convince. When the quantitative design is strong (e.g., randomized) and extensive (e.g., longitudinal)— when the results are significant—there is a justified greater sense of collective confidence, a sense that the effect was real. But something more was needed that could only come from a qualitative methodology.

Qualitative approaches have their unique— though not exclusive—strengths. These assets, beyond quantitative methods, include the ability to provide new dimensions of richness, explanation, and extrapolation. The results of the qualitative study explain more than the quantitative research alone. More than anything else, the ultimate conclusions show how the construct of tolerance manifests itself in the daily lives of Oxford House residents. We now examine some of these narratives and group-based methods and then conclude with a broader discussion of the participatory implications of this work and the PMMR approach.

First, the importance of diversity in Oxford House living is clear in the descriptive narratives of participants. One female resident said,

There is a lot of diversity. Lots of different backgrounds. Every individual handles the same situation differently. But there is so much diversity in backgrounds. You kind of get a new light on solutions and coping that you might not have otherwise have thought of.

It is also possible to draw parallels between these qualitatively obtained quotes and the quantitatively structured UDO items. Such comparisons help see the *synergy* across approaches, perhaps the greatest strength of mixed methods.

The quantitative UDO measures the ability of a person to embrace both similarities and differences of others (Miville et al., 1999), as does a quote from an Oxford House resident: "Different opinions, different life styles and experiences. You are always going to find different opinions, people, and cultures. That is life and I think that is how the Houses should be."

UDO items ask participants about their interest in getting to know people of different groups, of ethnicities different from their own. These items also tap into a participant's ability to be at ease with, be comfortable around, or feel close to someone of another ethnicity. Similar content arose spontaneously from our qualitative interviews, even from interview questions that did not explicitly ask about diversity. For instance, one resident referenced race and comfort: "Race isn't an issue. I get along with everyone. Everybody feels like they look out for me and I feel comfortable." A quintessential quote from the qualitative study reflects the importance of tolerance and gets at an even broader form of the growth process: "Alcohol and addicts—we want it our way and right now. We don't care who you are and what. After time, you become open-minded, tolerant, and compassionate in Oxford House."

Social psychological theories of overcoming prejudice and superordinate goals can help explain the tolerance findings. Social psychological research has found that bringing together in-conflict or diverging groups is not enough to bring about tolerance. The secret ingredient is having a superordinate goal—a goal that can only be achieved by all members from both groups working in unison (Allport, 1955; Sherif & Sherif, 1969). Consistent with the superordinate goal, the Oxford House mission statement mentions that to overcome substance abuse, residents must focus on the primary threat—the common enemy—and not let other group differences interfere with their work. Put simply, the superordinate goal of overcoming substance abuse in Oxford House is greater than the tendency to fight over any other form of group divisions. Such a goal can bring diverse individuals together for a sustained period that leads, over time, to a more generalized tendency to be tolerant of others (Olson et al., 2009).

One quote from our qualitative study reveals how staying away from drugs, by "keeping clean," works as a superordinate goal:

> There's really no prejudice in the house. It's not a matter of skin color, it's only a matter of clean, how clean you are, how willing to be a part of this, just your willingness to be clean is all that matters.

The same is reflected in a similar statement: "In this house we don't see each other as different colors, we are a family."

Tolerance may be considered a "social skill" as Oxford House residents progressively realize they gain little by judging others on what are otherwise acceptable and oftentimes interesting forms of difference. Not judging is a skill that involves being comfortable with diverse others. It is a skill that also requires a person to be comfortable in his or her own skin. Consistent with the construct validity process, we began to understand the greater meaning of tolerance and that the growth Oxford House residents are experiencing may be connected to factors that are broader than originally thought—a more general form of *personal growth*. A younger Oxford House resident spoke to an aspect of this broader growth: dealing with others in a more tolerant way, having thicker skin, and being open to more real and effective social connections:

> I am holding resentment. But house members really help me deal with this. I had never dealt with people like that before. Nobody ever yelled, nobody ever talked to me like that. I mean, it's giving me a thicker skin.

The value in diversity, found in living with different people, was also expressed:

> It has to do with the certain people in my house, the balance of people in my house. They are very moody but when it comes down to it, in this house, you know there is a balance. There are people that are quiet, yet they still stand up for themselves. And we have a lot of that going on.

Shared similarity holds diverse people together, as does the superordinate goal:

> To have so many different backgrounds sitting there. . . So much acceptance. . . just immediately sharing a couple little bits about ourselves. We had that common bond, we were all beaten by addiction. We never thought we had a chance to overcome it. And here we all were and just a lot of. . . the dynamics in the house were really good.

Tolerance is a sense of connectedness. It leads to a desire to be with others, bond with others, maintain better relationships, and develop a sense of community (Sarason, 1974). This, sense of community is the broader personal growth beyond tolerance, and may be a key to recovery, to eventually overcoming the need for any or excessive substance consumption.

There are so many societal misunderstandings about addiction, and therefore recovery requires greater understandings and appreciations of other people. This importance of appreciating both what is different among each other and what is similar is also a part of the process of overcoming the trauma from stigma, as noted by one resident:

> People get to the point they don't want to help addicts. We addicts in OH understand each other. We become a family. We know we have a lot of similarities. We come to love each other and to understand each other. With all that help there, all you have to do is to ask.

Tolerance and growth requires empathy and looking at others who are in earlier stages of this social and emotional development. Wisdom involves the empathy and recognition of how far other participants have come in the recovery process:

> I've been through so many meetings with people who have messed up. I have seen them cry, seen them have to walk out the door. I know they had nowhere to go. It's helped me to realize that even though I feel I had hit my bottom, they haven't. And it's sad to see them go. It's sad to learn I could be there too. It's helped me realize that I am an addict and I always will be. And I could trip and fall at any given time just like them. I'm no different than they are. It's a big part of what I've learned.

Multiple forms of diversity and commonality coexist within each house. In the case of women's Oxford houses, commonality is found not only in substance abuse problems but in "sharing" histories of trauma (Olson et al., 2003), as reflected by a young female Oxford House resident:

> We were all chatting about sexual abuse. We talked about different issues and how it affected different women. It was interesting, and so were the diverse backgrounds we all shared: socioeconomically, education-wise, everything. Five out of six of us had all been sexually abused in some way, or went through a rape.

At a women's annual Oxford House conference, a keynote speaker once described how, prior to living in Oxford House, she could never become friends with other women. She described how she had always been competitive with and jealous of other women. This was not because of her personality—abusive men in her life would purposely split up her and other potential friendships. These males kept her physically isolated and dependent. They also made her, she argued, less psychologically accustomed to interacting with other females who were the very "resources" she needed. The path to recovery from substance, physical, and sexual abuse needed an additional step—the development of a greater tolerance for, and an ability to trust, other women and to accept the supports they offered. The following narrative, from a different female resident, illustrates this transition from codependency (i.e., the dependence on the needs of, or control of, another) with men. Her quote shows the necessity of connecting with other women in Oxford House to move toward recovery:

> One of my major things. . . was codependency with men. And living in a house full of women. . . I always have that support; I don't have to run to a man for help or advice. . . .I always have those women really close by that I can always reach out to. That's one aspect I didn't really find until I was about 4 or 5 months clean. I've seen the same sorts of things happen for other women in recovery that have moved in. If you can take the time and be tolerant enough to start bonding with other women in recovery. . . It's so important for women to get to know and like other women. Because the first thing we do is run towards men for everything that we need.

The qualitative study also showed tolerance and growth were about empowerment in the broadest definitions of the term (Rappaport, 1981, 1987). Empowerment, whether psychological or economic, is not simply about gaining power or resources. It involves a liberating sense of growth, individual agency, and a sense of collective efficacy. Empowerment is connected in paradoxical ways with its sibling construct in community psychology, a *sense of community* (Sarason, 1974)—each produces and is produced by the other. It may be this intersection of empowerment and sense of community that brings about a person's "recovery" through a community, improved tolerance toward diverse others, and personal and collective growth. The theoretical connections all require more examination. Of course the best place to turn for such answers is back to community members who are willing to share their lived experiences and perceptions. At this time, as researchers, we can only confirm—from our own experiences—that more on this and other topics can be learned through PMMR than through other, more exclusive and less integrative methods.

Group-Based Participatory Mixed Methods

The prior methods were collected through one-on-one interactions between researcher and participant. PMMR can, however, be expanded to more group-based methods of data collection, perhaps more in the domain of evaluation or needs assessment. Such methods illustrate some of the ways that participatory methods—qualitative and quantitative—can merge in a more unified, integrated process.

The speed at which a quantitative survey instrument can be handed out in a crowded setting—entered and analyzed—is a strength of the quantitative method. While not always true, qualitative methods can often take much longer to collect, transcribe, code, and bring together into meaningful constructs. For this reason we developed a technique called *community narration* that allows commonalities to be found in stories within a community. By the end of a session, the themes are coded by the group and numerically rank-ordered for discussion and evaluation (Olson & Jason, 2011).

This community narration method (Olson & Jason, 2011), used at an Oxford House Convention with roughly 100 residents, led to results comparable to the quantitative and qualitative tolerance findings. The residents came together in small groups of three or four members. In these groups, they were asked to take turns sharing a life episode (story) that best reflected the most important aspect of Oxford House. Once those stories were shared, the small group members were asked to find a commonality, or a theme, across their stories. These common themes were then captured by each group and shared in a one- or two-word concept. These concepts were placed on a large board so the whole room could see. In a dialectical fashion, the whole room was asked to come up with contrast terms to each of the concepts. The bipolar constructs (Kelly, 1955) that resulted were then put on the board. For instance, the group decided that the opposite of *sobriety* was *using* (i.e., *sobriety vs. using*).

Other interesting dichotomies included *empowerment vs. powerlessness, family vs. isolation,* and *diversity vs. uniformity.* Afterward, all the participants voted for the most important dichotomy, numerically rank-ordering which bipolar constructs were most central to the majority of members. Oxford House appears to many as primarily a place to overcome alcohol and drugs. However, consistent with our tolerance and personal growth findings, the most important dichotomy was *growth vs. stagnation.* These bipolar constructs were stimuli for further discussion of the group's mission, its importance, and its community narrative.

Future Directions for Participatory Mixed Methods Research

To summarize and hypothesize future directions of PMMR we (a) discuss the combining of quantitative and qualitative methods and (b) end with the role participatory methods play in maximizing our ability to interpret converging and diverging sets of information from both qualitative and quantitative lenses.

Qualitative and quantitative approaches—at different stages of collection, analysis, and write-up—can be put in different configurations. At different phases of the project, the quantitative and qualitative parts can be ordered and integrated in various ways. Common, required, and often difficult choices will arise with every mixed methods project, rarely with right or wrong decisions or even "best practices." There may be distinct advantages or disadvantages with a particular choice, but what is best may depend on the context and aims of the research project or the community or topic of interest. Greater theory development around how qualitative–quantitative synergies work may provide helpful signposts to more intentionally design a project or set of projects.

Inevitable questions arise in the design phase of a mixed methods study: What proportion of a study or studies will be qualitative, and what quantitative? Will all the data be collected together, from the same participants or at the same time, or separately? And if separately, in what order? Which participants will be chosen for which part of the study? Different choices may be required about whether to discuss the qualitative or quantitative data first, particularly if both types of data have been collected at the same time and from the same participants. What is common to all decisions is the goal to maximize synergy: How do we get the best picture from looking through two different lenses? We might ask: In what contexts to do we follow one path rather than another? What unique value will path A bring about and what value path B? If there is a Study 1 and a Study 2, do we collect the quantitative or qualitative data first? And how do we make these choices based on particular goals? Choices depend on how we think the different types of information will interact, metaphorically "speak to each other", in the most rewarding ways. What we discover through the two lenses will be further triangulated with other information (e.g., the research literature, community input).

We hope to end up with some maximized new understandings around our phenomena of interest. Greater understandings of the unique assets provided by qualitative and quantitative methods help us better understand how different configurations and orderings enhance each other.

If we are designing a sequence of more exploratory studies, we may choose to start with a large sample and the sometimes greater efficiency of quantitative measures or a smaller sample and grounded theory–based coding on qualitative data. Or maybe we would like a qualitative second, follow-up study to provide new dimensions of richness, explanation, and extrapolation beyond a quantitative finding. While the possible combinations and reasons for each may feel infinite, good theories increase the planful nature of helping different sources of information complement each other and bring about new synergies of understanding.

That leaves us with the question about the added value of the participatory aspect of PMMR. Where does the *P* component of PMMR add another layer of value to MMMR? To summarize, community members are often the most knowledgeable sources about a topic of interest. They can often give the best clues about where to look for complements across the two lenses—and help verify the reality of synergies when found. The researcher asks the community participant, "Is the interpretation of this triangulation between qualitative, quantitative and other available information the most sensible one?

If not, what other paths might make more sense?" It is the participatory aspect of this work that allows us, community members and researchers, to sift together through the qualitative–quantitative nomological net. For example,

> Researcher: "Maybe this is not only about being in mere contact with diverse others but what are called superordinate goals, meaning. . ."
> Community member: "Yes, that fits with the traditions of our community, which state. . ."

The more open the dialogue is—the more shared the ownership between community participants and researchers—the better. Shared dialogue and power increases the chance that collective understandings of the phenomena are expanded. PMMR must also be *beyond* dialogue. Like PAR itself, the knowledge must be used toward *action*. Policy decisions, for instance, are often based on the credibility, persuasiveness, and logic of arguments and disseminating that information beyond academic outlets (Olson, Viola, & Fromm Reed, 2011; Jason, 2013). PMMR is therefore in many ways ideal for providing the right combination of hard numbers alongside constituent stories—the combination of which can increase the likelihood that policymakers will act. And to the extent PMMR is used toward action, it is vital to infuse objectivity, rigorous analyses, values, and good ethics into every step of the process.

The ultimate goal of PMMR thus becomes a bit clearer: to gain a greater understanding of multiple phenomena of interest (Rappaport, 1987), multiple truths through dialectical pluralism (Johnson, 2012; Johnson & Stefurak, 2013), and a greater ecological understanding of our most pressing societal challenges and to ethically put that work toward action.

In summary, PMMR can create broader pictures of phenomena, a tighter interconnectedness across methods, and ultimately a greater gestalt of the whole—an understanding of the broader issue that is ultimately above and beyond the sum of its parts. Many of the growing normative rules in participatory mixed methods may involve thinking about how—along every phase of a research project—we can better map the synergies and dialectical choice points according to the pragmatic goals of the research enterprise.

One final future goal for PMMR is to ensure that, through the experiential expertise of community members' lived experience, we, as researchers, along with community members, begin to create ever stronger, more fully integrated synergies between quantitative and qualitative methods. To do this effectively we will need to break down the traditional cultural walls that psychologically separate these methods—that separate different researchers who come from very different forms of training and general research orientations. In other words, we need to build bridges across research participants and researchers, as well as bridges between different types of researchers who often believe they are coming from opposing schools of thought. For the challenge to be overcome, the research community may benefit from lessons provided by Oxford House residents—that we need to better appreciate similarities and differences in others, in their diverse ways of being and we need to value tolerance and a greater sense of universality and integration into our scientific worldviews.

Acknowledgments

We appreciate the support of Paul Molloy, Leon Venable, and the many Oxford House members who have collaborated with our team, as well as Burke Johnson and Deanne Chung for wonderful and extensive editorial advice. We are grateful for financial support provided by the National Institute on Alcohol Abuse and Alcoholism (NIAAA Grant AA12218 and AA16973), the National Institute on Drug Abuse (NIDA Grant DA13231 and DA19935), and the National Center on Minority Health and Health Disparities (Grant MD002748).

Discussion Questions

1. What philosophical connections can you make between the aims of PAR (e.g., participatory approaches or action) and mixed methods research (MMR) (quantitative and qualitative) that can work toward a fuller theory of PMMR model?

2. What are some of the challenges (or paradoxes) likely to be encountered when conducting PMMR?

3. How might PMMR challenges be different at one stage of the research process (e.g., study design and collection) compared to another (e.g., coding and analysis)?

4. Are qualitative research approaches more consistent with the values of "participatory" research? Why or why not? Regardless, can both quantitative and qualitative methods be seen as participatory? Why or why not?

5. Why is it important to include "action" as part of the MMR project?

6. Can the historical differences and conflicts found between qualitative and quantitative research be seen as analogous to other forms of human prejudice (such as ingroup–outgroup divisions)? Can the mixed- and multimethod movement seen as a movement toward greater "openness" and "tolerance"?

Suggested Websites

http://ctb.ku.edu/en/table-of-contents/evaluate/evaluation/intervention-research/main
Community Tool Box.

http://www.scra27.org/
Society for Community Research and Action.

http://www.scra27.org/policy/documents/rapid-response-position-statements/positionstatementrecoveryresidences foraddiction-1Policy statement on Recovery Residences.

References

Abelson, R. P. (1995). *Statistics as principled argument.* Hillsdale, NJ: Lawrence Erlbaum.

Allport, G. (1955). *The nature of prejudice.* Cambridge, MA: Addison-Wesley.

Alvarez, J., Jason, L. A., Davis, M. I., Ferrari, J. R., & Olson, B. D. (2004). Latinos and Latinas in Oxford House: Perceptions of barriers and opportunities. *Journal of Ethnicity in Substance Abuse, 3*, 17–32.

Auerbach, C. F., & Silverstein, L. B. (2003). *Qualitative data: An introduction to coding and analysis.* New York, NY: New York University Press.

Barker, C., & Pistrang, K. A. (2012). Methodological pluralism: Implications for consumers and producers of research. In L. A. Jason & D. S. Glenwick (Eds.), *Methodological approaches to community-based research* (pp. 33–50). Washington, DC: American Psychological Association.

Campbell, R., Gregory, K. A., Patterson, D., & Bybee, D. (2012). Integrating qualitative and quantitative approaches. An example of mixed methods research. In L. A. Jason & D. S. Glenwick (Eds.), *Methodological approaches to community-based research* (pp. 51–68). Washington, DC: American Psychological Association.

Cronbach, L. J. (1957). The two disciplines of scientific psychology. *American Psychologist, 12*, 671–84.

Cronbach, L. J. (1975). Beyond the two disciplines of scientific psychology. *American Psychologist, 30*, 671–84.

Cronbach, L. J., & Meehl, P. E. (1955). Construct validity in psychological tests. *Psychological Bulletin, 52*, 281–302.

Davis, M. I., Jason, L. A., Ferrari, J. R., Olson, B. D., & Alvarez, J. (2005). A collaborative action approach to researching substance abuse recovery. *American Journal of Drug and Alcohol Abuse, 31*, 537–553.

Denzin, N. K., & Lincoln, Y. S. (2000). *The SAGE handbook of qualitative research.* Thousand Oaks, CA: Sage.

Freire, P. (2007). *Pedagogy of the oppressed.* New York, NY: Continuum. (Original work published 1970)

Jason, L. A. (2013). *Principles of social change.* New York, NY: Oxford University Press.

Jason, L. A., & Glenwick, D. S. (Eds.). (2012). *Methodological approaches to community-based research.* Washington, DC: American Psychological Association.

Jason, L. A., Keys, C. B., Suarez-Balcazar, Y., Taylor, R. R., Davis, M., & Durlak, J., Isenberg, D. (Eds.). (2004). *Participatory community research: Theories and methods in action.* Washington, DC: American Psychological Association.

Jason, L. A., Olson, B. D., Ferrari, J. R., Majer, J. M., Alvarez, J., & Stout, J. (2007). An examination of main and interactive effects of substance abuse recovery housing on multiple indicators of adjustment. *Addiction, 102*, 1114–1121.

Jason, L., Olson, B. D., & Foley, K. (2008). *Rescued lives.* New York, NY: Routledge.

Jason, L. A., Pechota, M. E., Bowden, B. S., Lahmar, K., Pokorny, S., Bishop, P., . . . Grams, G. (1994). Oxford House: Community living is community healing. In J. A. Lewis (Ed.), *Addictions: Concepts and strategies for treatment* (pp. 333–338). Gaithersburg, MD: Aspen.

Jason, L. A., Schober, D., & Olson, B. D. (2008). Community involvement among residents of second-order change recovery homes. *The Australian Community Psychologist, 20*, 73–83.

Johnson, R. B. (2012). Dialectical pluralism and mixed research. *American Behavioral Scientist, 56*, 571.

Johnson, R. B., & Onwuegbuzie, A. J. (2004). Mixed methods research: A research paradigm whose time has come. *Educational Researcher, 33*(7), 14–26.

Johnson, R. B., & Stefurak, T. (2013). Considering the evidence-and-credibility discussion in evaluation through the lens of dialectical pluralism. In D. Mertens & S. Hesse-Biber (Eds.), *New Directions for Evaluation* [*Special Issue: Mixed Methods and Credibility of Evidence in Evaluation*], *138*, 103–109.

Kelly, G. A. (1955). *The psychology of personal constructs* (2 vols.). New York, NY: W. W. Norton.

McAdams, D. P. (2009). *The person: An introduction to the science of personality psychology* (5th ed.). New York, NY: Wiley.

McAdams, D. P., & Olson, B. D. (2009). Personality development: Continuity and change over the life course. *Annual Review of Psychology, 61*, 517–542.

Miville, M. L., Gelso, C. J., Pannu, R., Liu, W., Touradji, P., Holloway, P., & Fuertes, J. (1999). Appreciating similarities and valuing differences: The Miville-Guzman Universality-Diversity Scale. *Journal of Counseling Psychology, 46*(3), 291–307.

Olson, B. D., Curtis, C. E., Jason, L. A., Ferrari, J. R., Horin, E. V., Davis, M. I., . . . Alvarez, J. (2003). Physical and sexual trauma, psychiatric symptoms, and sense of community among women in recovery: Toward a new model of shelter aftercare. *Journal of Prevention and Intervention in the Community, 26*, 67–80.

Olson, B. D., & Jason, L. A. (2011). The community narration (CN) approach: Understanding a group's identity and cognitive constructs through personal and community narratives. *Global Journal of Community Psychology Practice, 2*(1), 1–7. Retrieved from http://www.gjcpp.org/

Olson, B. D., Jason, L. A., Davidson, M., & Ferrari, J. R. (2009). Increases in tolerance within naturalistic, intentional communities: A randomized, longitudinal examination. *American Journal of Community Psychology, 44*, 188–195.

Olson, B. D., Jason, L. A., Ferrari, J. R., & Hutcheson, T. D. (2005). Bridging professional and mutual-help: An application of the transtheoretical model to the mutual-help organization. *Applied & Preventive Psychology: Current Scientific Perspectives, 11,* 168–178.

Olson, B., Viola, J., & Fromm Reed, S. (2011). A temporal model of community organizing and direct action. *Peace Review, 23*(1), 52–60.

Rappaport, J. (1981). In praise of paradox: A social policy of empowerment over prevention. *American Journal of Community Psychology, 9,* 1–25.

Rappaport, J. (1987). Terms of empowerment/exemplars of prevention: Toward a theory for community psychology. *American Journal of Community Psychology, 15*(2), 121–148.

Rappaport, J. (2000). Community narratives: Tales of terror and joy. *American Journal of Community Psychology, 28*(1), 1–24.

Sarason, S. B. (1974). *The psychological sense of community: Prospects for a community psychology.* San Francisco, CA: Jossey-Bass.

Sherif, M., & Sherif, C. W. (1969). *Social psychology.* New York, NY: Harper & Row.

Tebes, J. K. (2012). Philosophical foundations of mixed methods research: Implications for research practice. In L. A. Jason & D. S. Glenwick (Eds.), *Methodological approaches to community-based research* (pp. 13–31). Washington, DC: American Psychological Association.

Moving From Randomized Controlled Trials to Mixed Methods Intervention Evaluations

Sarah J. Drabble *and* Alicia O'Cathain

Abstract

This chapter explores why mixed methods intervention evaluations are needed when undertaking randomized controlled trials in order to address a wide range of questions relevant to understanding the effectiveness of an intervention. It describes three frameworks that illustrate different ways in which mixed methods intervention evaluations may be undertaken within the context of a randomized controlled trial: the temporal framework; the process-outcome framework, which includes process evaluations; and the "aspects of a trial" framework. The chapter considers how the language used to describe qualitative research undertaken with trials can represent different underlying assumptions about the relative value of the qualitative research in relation to the trial. The chapter concludes with a discussion of some of the challenges that arise when undertaking mixed method intervention evaluations and the value of including qualitative research in systematic reviews of trials via evidence synthesis.

Key Words: randomized controlled trials, mixed methods intervention evaluations, process evaluation, evidence synthesis, temporal framework, process-outcome framework, aspects of a trial framework

Introduction

Randomized controlled trials (RCTs) are used in social, education, and health research to test whether interventions are effective (Cnaan & Enosh, 2001; Torgerson & Torgerson, 2001), for example, to test the effectiveness of new approaches to delivering foster care, new curriculum in schools, and new ways of delivering self-management advice to people with chronic health conditions. In this chapter we consider the change in use of RCTs to address the single question of "does an intervention work?" to multimethods (Grissmer, Subotnik, & Orland, 2009) or mixed methods (Creswell, Fetters, Plano Clark, & Morales, 2009) intervention evaluations to address a range of questions related to understanding the effectiveness of an intervention. We call these wider designs "mixed methods intervention evaluations" rather than "mixed methods randomized controlled trials" for

reasons we explain later in the chapter. Although multimethod or mixed methods intervention evaluations are undertaken within education and social research—in particular there is a guide to combining multimethods and RCTs produced by the American Psychological Association (Grissmer et al., 2009)—we focus here on health research because RCTs are common within this field and it is our area of expertise.

In the health field a randomized controlled trial is defined as:

> an experiment in which two or more interventions, possibly including a control intervention or no intervention, are compared by being randomly allocated to participants. In most trials one intervention is assigned to each individual but sometimes assignment is to defined groups of individuals (for example, in a household) or

interventions are assigned within individuals. (Cochrane Collaboration, 2013)

The terms *randomized controlled trial* and *randomized clinical trial* are sometimes used interchangeably in the health field because historically they have tested drugs and devices in clinical settings. We prefer the term *randomized controlled trial* (RCT) because this encompasses public health trials that test the effectiveness of interventions that are designed to impact on health behaviors in a range of settings. An example of a public health intervention is peer support delivered in schools to aid smoking cessation among young people (Campbell et al., 2008; Munro & Bloor, 2010).

We have based this chapter on our belief that accepted practice among some communities of researchers has moved from undertaking lone RCTs toward combining qualitative methods and RCTs within mixed methods intervention evaluations. We cannot, however, chart the exact size of this shift and rely on less than ideal methods to suggest its extent. We would ideally compare a random sample of RCTs funded in different decades and measure the proportion using a mixed methods approach within each decade, showing an increase over time. This information is not available, so instead we rely on perceptions that multimethod or mixed methods intervention evaluation is common (Lewin, Glenton, & Oxman, 2009), is increasing (Grissmer et al., 2009), or is a relatively recent phenomenon (Jansen, Foets, & de Bont, 2009). Evidence that mixed methods intervention evaluations are common is available from a range of sources. In a search for pragmatic trials in primary care, Jansen et al. found 33 articles published between 2001 and 2007 reporting the use of qualitative research. Lewin et al. found that between 2001 and 2003, 30% of published trials of changes to organization of health care included qualitative research. In a systematic review of international journal articles reporting qualitative research undertaken with trials in health, we identified 296 articles published between 2008 and September 2010 (O'Cathain, Thomas, Drabble, Rudolph, & Hewison, 2013; O'Cathain et al., 2014).

In this chapter we address why the move from lone RCTs to mixed methods intervention evaluations has occurred and the benefits it can deliver. We also describe three existing frameworks for mixed methods intervention evaluations that can help researchers understand the range of ways in which different methods can be used in conjunction with trials, examine the developing language used to describe this approach, and consider the challenges faced by researchers when making the move to mixed methods intervention evaluations. We provide case studies of published evaluations to illustrate some of these points.

Why Are Mixed Methods Intervention Evaluations Necessary?

In the context of health research, RCTs are used to test whether new drugs, services, or technologies improve health. RCTs are considered the "gold standard" in the hierarchy of providing evidence of effectiveness. However, it appears that within health research, the question "is it effective?" is the gold standard question in an implicit research question hierarchy, with the result that methods that best address other questions may be dismissed as inferior and require defending (Giacomini, 2001). We believe that RCTs are an excellent way of addressing the effectiveness question but that this question needs to be expanded to "effective for whom under what circumstances?" (e.g., Pawson & Tilley, 2004). We identify other important questions relevant to evaluations of interventions that RCTs alone cannot address.

If the Intervention Was Effective in the Trial, Will It Be Effective in the Real World?

Policymakers, clinicians, and patients want to implement evidence from RCTs in the real world. If the intervention was shown to be effective under experimental conditions, those wishing to implement these findings want to know which aspects of the intervention are essential to effectiveness (mechanisms of action) and how relevant the context in which the intervention was tested is to their own circumstances (transferability of evidence). For example, the control arm in a trial may be the care that patients usually receive, but the meaning of *usual care* may be different in different countries and over different time periods, with implications for the comparative effectiveness of the intervention under study. The need to address questions related to *how* and *why* interventions work, that is, to understand mechanisms of action and the transferability of the evidence, has led to inclusion of qualitative methods within these evaluative designs.

Why Was the Intervention Not Effective?

RCTs can be expensive and time consuming to undertake. In theory, RCTs producing null results are as valuable as those with positive results. However, in practice, null RCTs, which identify that an intervention was not effective, can feel like a waste of time and money unless researchers can understand why the intervention was not effective and thus steer other researchers away from evaluating similar types of interventions and toward those that have a better chance of effectiveness. Researchers use qualitative and quantitative methods to facilitate understanding of why interventions do not work. For example, these methods can explore whether interventions have been delivered as planned or met barriers to successful implementation.

What Is the Optimal Intervention to Test?

Undertaking a large and expensive RCT of an intervention that is not well understood may waste resources if the results are that an intervention was not effective because it was not feasible for delivery by health professionals or was not acceptable to patients. Questions about feasibility and acceptability of interventions can be addressed in preparation for an RCT to optimize interventions and their implementation before they undergo expensive evaluation. Qualitative methods such as interviews and focus groups with those delivering the intervention can explore feasibility. For example, the intervention being tested in the RCT may be delivered in busy health service clinics that require health professionals to change their work practices. Interviews and focus groups with those receiving the intervention can explore how the intervention fits into the context of patients' lives and their management of their health condition. Nonparticipant observation or structured observation can be used to consider the fidelity of implementation of the intervention, that is, understand whether the intervention in practice was similar to that planned. All of these methods can help to identify how the intervention can be adapted to operate well in the context in which it will be tested and/or delivered in the real world.

Never Mind the Intervention; Will the Randomized Controlled Trial Work?

It can be challenging to run RCTs. For example, RCTs can struggle to recruit sufficient participants, resulting in low statistical power, or they can lack external validity because they recruit a narrow profile of the population that will actually use the intervention in the real world. Questions around how to improve the conduct of the RCT can be important, and qualitative research has been used for this purpose. For example, interviews with health professionals recruiting patients for RCTs, and interviews with the patients approached for participation, can identify misunderstandings that lead to non-participation in the trial. Observations of recruitment practices can identify poor communication that has led to these misunderstandings.

Have We Really Understood the Complexities of What We Are Researching?

An industry has grown up around RCTs of drugs. Yet much of what is evaluated in health is more complex than a drug and is known as a *complex intervention*. A complex intervention has been defined in different ways. First, it is defined by what it is not: it is not a drug or surgical procedure (Oakley, Strange, Bonell, Allen, & Stephenson, 2006). When defined by what it is, a complex intervention has many components or active ingredients (Campbell et al., 2007; Munro & Bloor, 2010; Oakley et al., 2006), which combine independently and interdependently (Campbell et al., 2007), making the whole more than the sum of its parts (Hawe, Shiell, & Riley, 2004; Oakley et al., 2006). Complex interventions are also defined as organizationally elaborate and socially mediated (Munro & Bloor, 2010). The complexity of the intervention can take different forms, such as the variation in behaviors of the people delivering or receiving the intervention, the different groups or organizations affected by the intervention, and the variation in outcomes (Medical Research Council [MRC], 2008). Examples of complex interventions include the introduction of lifestyle interventions for people with obesity or the reorganization of the way in which a service is delivered.

Complex interventions are particularly challenging and costly to evaluate because of their multifaceted nature and their dependence on the social context. These create methodological challenges for the RCT (Campbell et al., 2007; Oakley et al., 2006) relating to difficulties in standardizing the design and delivery of the intervention and understanding the characteristics of the local context in which the intervention is delivered (MRC, 2008). While an RCT may be the most rigorous way to evaluate the effectiveness of an intervention, there is growing acknowledgement of the contribution of qualitative methods to understand the complexity of interventions (Glenton, Lewin, & Scheel, 2011).

Complexity can be related to more than the intervention: drug trials may be undertaken with complex patient groups (e.g., Romo, Poo, & Ballesta, 2009) or within complex environments (e.g., Shagi et al., 2008), benefiting from qualitative methods to engage with this complexity.

Frameworks for Undertaking Mixed Methods Intervention Evaluations

Three frameworks for multimethod and mixed methods intervention evaluations have been described in the literature: the temporal framework, the process-outcome framework, and the "aspects of a trial" framework. These frameworks can help researchers consider the range of questions relevant to their evaluation and the range and timing of methods within their evaluation. We discuss these frameworks in the following sections.

The Temporal Framework

A common approach to describing the use of qualitative research with RCTs is a temporal framework, which considers how qualitative research can be used before, during, or after a trial (Creswell et al., 2009; Jansen et al., 2009; Lewin et al., 2009; Sandelowski, 1996). It is worth reflecting on what

these authors mean by *trial* before exploring how qualitative research is used before during and after the trial. By *trial* these authors mean what is variously called the "definitive RCT" (MRC, 2000) or "Phase III" trial, which measures the effectiveness of an intervention in large groups of people (US National Library of Medicine, 2008). When testing drugs, other phases occur before and after this Phase III trial. Before the trial, studies are undertaken to test the safety of drugs in a small group of people (Phase I) and to explore effectiveness in a larger group (Phase II); after the Phase III trial, research is undertaken to test the drug's effect in the longer term (Phase IV). A similar phased approach has been described for complex interventions where early phases are carried out before the definitive RCT to prepare for the Phase III definitive trial, and Phase IV occurs after the definitive trial to study longer term implementation of the intervention in the real world (MRC, 2000). This phased approach to trials of complex interventions has been updated to consider development and feasibility phases prior to the trial of effectiveness, which is then followed by implementation studies (Craig et al., 2008). In Table 23.1 we display the different work authors have suggested qualitative research can do before, during, and after the trial, and then we go on to explore these stages in more detail.

Table 23.1 The Use of Qualitative Research With Trials at Different Stages of the Trial

Timing of Qualitative Research	Suggested Uses of Qualitative Research With Trials	References
Before the trial	To "trial" the trial	Sandelowski, 1996
	To develop an instrument when a suitable instrument is not available to measure an outcome in a trial or select appropriate outcome measures	Creswell et al., 2009; Lewin et al., 2009
	To develop recruitment or consent practices, estimate recruitment or retention, and understand the burden placed on trial participants and caregivers	MRC, 2000, 2008; Creswell et al., 2009
	To understand the context in which the trial or intervention occurs to ensure that the intervention will work in a particular context or to identify any issues that may occur	Creswell et al., 2009; Jansen et al., 2009; Lewin et al., 2009
	To support the need for an intervention by identifying the evidence base and identifying or developing theory and hypotheses	MRC, 2000, 2008; Creswell et al., 2009; Jansen et al., 2009; Lewin et al., 2009

(continued)

Table 23.1 Continued

Timing of Qualitative Research	Suggested Uses of Qualitative Research With Trials	References
	To provide baseline information	Creswell et al., 2009
	To obtain information about the feasibility of the intervention	MRC, 2000, 2008; Jansen et al., 2009
	To develop, pilot, and refine the intervention	Jansen et al., 2009; Lewin et al., 2009
During a trial	To validate trial outcomes with participant voices and to identify factors affecting trial outcome measures	Creswell et al., 2009
	To understand how the intervention affects participants (e.g., identifying barriers and facilitators)	Creswell et al., 2009; Jansen et al., 2009; Sandelowski, 1996
	To capture intended and unanticipated experiences of participants during the trial	Creswell et al., 2009; Lewin et al., 2009; Sandelowski, 1996
	To understand processes of change and the context in which the intervention occurs such as its effect on outcomes and alterations to the sociocultural environment.	MRC, 2000, 2008; Creswell et al., 2009; Jansen et al., 2009; Lewin et al., 2009
	To verify fidelity of implementation of the intervention including describing the intervention as delivered, dose delivered, and dose received	Sandelowski, 1996; Creswell et al., 2009; Lewin et al., 2009;
	To identify prospective mediators and moderators of the intervention process	Creswell et al., 2009
	To refine interventions for subsequent trials	Jansen et al., 2009
After a trial	To explore how participants interpret trial results	Sandelowski, 1996; Creswell et al., 2009
	To account for participant feedback in revising a treatment	Creswell et al., 2009
	To understand or explain the trial outcomes (e.g., variation in trial results)	Sandelowski, 1996; Creswell et al., 2009; Lewin et al., 2009
	To establish the long-term effects of the intervention	Creswell et al., 2009
	To understand the trial as an intervention in its own right	Sandelowski, 1996
	To understand in depth how a theoretical model worked	Creswell et al., 2009; Jansen et al., 2009; Lewin et al., 2009
	To verify the fidelity of treatment processes	Creswell et al., 2009
	To consider context when comparing outcomes with baseline data	Creswell et al., 2009
	To generate additional hypotheses	Lewin et al., 2009

BEFORE-TRIAL

According to Creswell et al. (2009), a before-trial design entails the collection and analysis of qualitative data before the trial with the purpose of improving the subsequent trial; Sandelowski (1996) refers to this as "to 'trial' the trial" (p. 361). The qualitative research occurs at the development or feasibility/piloting phases of an evaluation (Craig et al., 2008) and can ensure that the definitive or Phase III trial evaluates the optimum intervention, recruits participants efficiently, and measures the right outcomes in a valid way. The focus of the qualitative research can be on the intervention, the trial conduct, or both. In their study of trials of complex interventions designed to change the organization of care, Lewin et al. (2009) found that half of the studies combining qualitative research and RCTs (14/30) collected qualitative data before the trial. O'Cathain et al. (2013; 2014) found that a quarter of journal articles reporting qualitative research undertaken with RCTs were based on data collection carried out before the definitive trial. The definitive trial can benefit from the before-trial qualitative research findings if the learning is acted upon whereby researchers adapt the intervention, improve recruitment practices, or select outcomes informed by the benefits the patients believe they have gained from the intervention. Although researchers have described the use of qualitative research before the definitive trial, quantitative and qualitative methods can be used at this stage within a mixed methods intervention evaluation. Case study 1 describes how researchers used a mixed methods study prior to a trial to consider adapting an effective intervention for use within a different group before it was then tested in the definitive trial.

Case Study 1: Adherence to Treatment of Cystic Fibrosis in Adolescents

This study (Marciel, Saiman, Quittell, Dawkins, & Quittner, 2010) was conducted in the United States using mixed methods (focus groups, interviews, survey) before an RCT to adapt a peer support group intervention for adolescents, which had previously been tested on preschool and school-age children. The aim of the intervention was to improve adherence to treatment for cystic fibrosis. Focus groups were undertaken with 17 health care professionals and interviews with 18 adolescent patients, 6 adult patients, and 12 parents. The qualitative research

identified that adherence in this age group was particularly difficult due to feelings of invincibility and lack of knowledge about the consequences of nonadherence. It also identified that the mobile phone technology used in the intervention offered other benefits and allowed adolescents to have direct contact with their healthcare team. In the interviews, facilitating adherence was found to be difficult for parents, who identified time constraints, lack of motivation, and forgetting treatments as barriers to adherence. Interviews with adolescents identified the acceptability of the proposed intervention to them. The research facilitated confidence in the proposed intervention prior to testing in an RCT.

DURING-TRIAL

A during-trial design involves the collection of qualitative data during the definitive trial to understand how the intervention is implemented in practice. Lewin et al. (2009) found that 9 of 30 studies collected qualitative data solely during the trial, and 2 studies collected data both before and during the trial. Process-outcome evaluations are a during-trial design, and these are described in detail in the next framework. The purpose of understanding how the intervention was implemented in practice is usually to explain the trial results. Yet, interestingly, authors who use this temporal framework include the use of qualitative research to explain the trial results in the after-design, where qualitative research is used after the trial. There is no doubt that the trial must be complete and the results known before qualitative research can be used to help interpret those results. However, the data collection and analysis of qualitative research can be carried out during the trial. Indeed, explaining the trial results is often the key aim of process evaluations undertaken alongside RCTs.

AFTER-TRIAL

An after-trial design involves collecting qualitative data after the trial has ended to explore the longer term implementation of an intervention (MRC, 2000, 2008). Lewin et al. (2009) found that very few of their studies (4/30) included qualitative research conducted after the trial. Some studies collect qualitative data after a trial that could have been collected during a trial. In Case Study 2, qualitative research was conducted after a trial to help to explain why an intervention was not as effective as expected.

Case Study 2: An Exploration of the Structural and Personal Factors That Might Have Reduced the Acceptability or Feasibility of the Intervention

A cluster RCT (Pope et al., 2010) was carried out in 20 primary-care clinics in the Eastern Cape Province of South Africa. The RCT, which tested an intervention of provider-initiated HIV counseling for newly diagnosed tuberculosis, had a positive result, but the magnitude of the effect was smaller than expected. Once these results were known, a qualitative study of interviews and focus groups was undertaken with the tuberculosis nurses who conducted the education, counseling, and testing sessions to identify barriers to implementation. Three potential barriers to delivery of the intervention were identified: inadequate staffing levels due to the use of nonqualified nurses to provide counseling who then needed to find a qualified nurse to provide HIV testing; a lack of space and privacy in a primary-care environment to conduct counseling sessions; and nurses' beliefs that despite the importance of counseling and testing, the skills required to deliver counseling are innate and therefore cannot be taught, which may have led to inadequate training. In this case, the qualitative research conducted at the end of the RCT enabled the team to understand structural and individual level factors that influenced the success of HIV counseling and testing for newly diagnosed tuberculosis patients. This explained the small effect size in the RCT and highlighted the need for future research to consider innovative and coordinated approaches to service provision in a primary-care environment.

We have used the temporal framework to show how qualitative research can be usefully conducted at different phases of an RCT. In the next section we discuss an alternative framework, the process-outcome evaluation framework, which considers how both quantitative and qualitative research may be used to explore processes within an evaluation where the outcomes are measured using an RCT.

The Process-Outcome Framework

Process evaluations are usually undertaken alongside definitive or Phase III trials and complement the trial's focus on outcomes. They started in health research in the mid- to late 1980s in the context of evaluating applied public health interventions but have a longer history of use within program evaluation (Linnan & Steckler, 2002). Process evaluations were seen as a necessary addition to trials of complex interventions because trials cannot provide insights about the mechanisms behind interventions or how interventions are actually delivered in practice (Glenton et al., 2011; Oakley et al., 2006). Researchers have argued that process evaluations should be an integral part of trials of complex interventions, researching why and how interventions work or do not work (e.g., Linnan & Steckler, 2002; Munro & Bloor, 2010; Oakley et al., 2006; Siu, Shek, & Poon, 2009). Their strength is the ability to distinguish between what is planned in a particular setting and what is actually done in practice, which may depend on factors such as the resources available, the organizational structure in which the intervention is delivered, and the stakeholders involved in delivering the intervention (Aro, Smith, & Decker, 2008). In particular, process evaluations can distinguish between "interventions that are inherently faulty (failure of intervention concept or theory) and those that are badly delivered (implementation failure)" (Oakley et al., 2006, p. 413). This can help to avoid what has been termed "type III errors" (Audrey, Holliday, Parry-Langdon, & Campbell, 2006), that is, where a trial has a null result because the intervention was inadequately implemented rather than a failure in the intervention design itself. It has been argued that process evaluations are particularly useful in cluster or multisite trials to understand the context when the same intervention is delivered at different sites (Oakley et al., 2006) and when an intervention is trying to change the organization of healthcare delivery (Glenton et al., 2011). A process evaluation can help to explain the results of trials with positive results by identifying which aspects of the intervention contributed to its success and trials with null results in terms of why the intervention was not effective (Linnan & Steckler, 2002). Whilst many process evaluations are conducted during the definitive trial, the importance of process evaluations used alongside feasibility and pilot studies prior to the definitive trial has also been highlighted; for example, when used alongside a pilot trial, process evaluations can aid the decision about whether to progress to the definitive trial, and they may inform changes to the intervention to be tested in that definitive trial (Munro & Bloor, 2010).

Linnan and Steckler (2002) present seven key components of a process evaluation that are similar to how qualitative research can be used at the during-trial stage (see Table 23.1), even though process evaluations make use of both qualitative and quantitative methods. Each component is described in the following: context, reach, dose delivered, dose received, fidelity, implementation, and recruitment.

Context includes the broader social, political, and economic setting in which the intervention is delivered (Glenton et al., 2011). For example, a process evaluation undertaken alongside a trial of a treatment for diabetes may use interviews with stakeholders or analysis of policy documents to allow the researcher to consider what is already available for participants in the community, how the intervention fits in with this, and how the intervention is delivered within the existing context of a general practice.

Reach is the proportion of the target population that participates in the intervention. For example, in a trial of medication for blood pressure, it is important to access as many participants who can benefit from the medication as possible, including hard-to-reach subgroups of the population. Interviews with service providers may reveal information about particular groups of patients that have been excluded, even if this was not the intention of the trialist. For example, family practitioners screening patients for inclusion in a trial of medication for reducing high blood pressure may exclude those with diabetes even though they are eligible for the study. This has implications for the generalizability of the RCT results.

Dose delivered is how much of the intervention is intended to be delivered to participants and is often determined by the behavior of the people delivering the intervention; for example, in a trial of cognitive behavioral therapy provided through the Internet, it may be how many sessions were actually delivered to participants. Quantitative methods can be used to record numbers of sessions delivered. Closely related to dose delivered is *dose received*, which in the previous example of cognitive behavior therapy would be the proportion of Internet sessions participants actually accessed and completed.

Fidelity is identified by Linnan and Steckler (2002) as the most difficult component to assess and relates to the quality of the implementation of the intervention, that is, the extent to which the intervention was delivered as planned. Assessment may include quantitative methods such as checklists of how aspects of the intervention were delivered and qualitative methods to make a subjective assessment of whether it was delivered in the "manner and the spirit in which it was intended" (p. 13). This could involve observations of therapy sessions or consultations, or questionnaires for staff delivering the intervention.

Program implementation is a combination of reach, dose, and fidelity and is conceptualized by Linnan and Steckler as a composite score indicating the extent to which the intervention has been implemented and received by the intended population. There is debate about how to calculate implementation and what an acceptable implementation score would be.

Recruitment concerns how trialists attract and approach prospective participants and how they interact with participants once the trial starts. It is important for trialists to recognize sampling bias in the study, identify how this bias might affect the results, and determine how the intervention should be implemented in clinical practice. Researchers should be aware of problems concerning generalizing the findings of the trial to subgroups that were not included in the participant sample or consider whether the trial findings apply to all participants in the trial sample.

While it is possible to see how aspects of process evaluations such as reach, dose delivered and received, and certain features of recruitment or program implementation can be assessed through quantitative methods such as checklists and surveys, others such as context and barriers or facilitators to successful implementation are more readily assessed by qualitative methods such as interviews, focus groups, diaries, and observations. Process evaluations usually include a combination of qualitative and quantitative methods, thereby constituting mixed methods studies (Oakley et al., 2006). Case Study 3 describes how process evaluations for two RCTs for the same intervention addressed different aspects of a process evaluation from the previous list. The process evaluation for the first trial focused on reach, implementation, and participant satisfaction, whereas the one for the second trial focused on dose delivered and received, implementation, and context. This shows how even trials of a similar intervention can utilize different components of process evaluation according to the needs of the evaluation. Indeed, in order to gain the most benefit from process evaluations, Linnan and Steckler (2002) suggest that researchers focus on the most salient processes to reduce the volume of data collected, particularly if cost is an issue. Case Study 3 also highlights the mixed methods approach to these process evaluations, with methods such as questionnaires, interviews, and observations used in both evaluations. Additionally, it is interesting to see process evaluations undertaken at the during-trial phase, where an RCT is used to test the effectiveness of an intervention, and then at the after-trial phase, where an RCT is used to test different strategies for implementing the effective intervention. Finally, it highlights that Linnan and Steckler's components of a process evaluation are not comprehensive and could also include acceptability of an intervention.

Case Study 3: Process Evaluations for the Pool Cool Efficacy and Diffusion Trials

Pool Cool was a skin cancer prevention intervention in the United States initially tested in a RCT in 1999 at 28 swimming pools in Hawaii and Massachusetts (Glanz, Geller, Shigaki, Maddock, & Isnec, 2002; see also Escoffery, Glanz, & Elliott, 2008; Escoffery, Glanz, Hall, & Elliott, 2009). The intervention program was aimed at children aged 5 to 10 years, their parents, lifeguards, and swimming instructors. The intervention included staff training, sun safety lessons, onsite interactive activities, provision of sunscreen, shade and signage, and promotion of safe sun environments in order to improve sun protection. The control groups received an intervention program aimed at bike safety, traffic safety, fire safety, or poisoning and choking prevention. The process evaluation focused on three aspects of the intervention—reach, implementation, and participant satisfaction—assessed using monitoring forms, questionnaires, and post-test observations. The trial showed that the Pool Cool skin cancer prevention program improved sun protection behaviors and environments at swimming pools. The process evaluation showed that the Pool Cool program was successfully implemented at swimming pools and that it was well received by both parents and children.

The Pool Cool trial was followed by a diffusion trial, which ran over four years, evaluating the effects of two strategies for carrying out the Pool Cool program (Escoffery et al., 2008, 2009). The basic strategy was to send a tool kit to sites that included a leaders' guide about how to implement the program, laminated lesson cards and interactive cartoon cards, materials for poolside sun protection activities, a large dispenser of sun cream, and signage targeting poolside tips for sun protection. In the enhanced strategy, pools received the basic strategy materials and additional sun safety items, environmental supports, supplementary guidance, and incentives to promote the Pool Cool program. The process evaluation focused on dose delivered and received, implementation, and context utilizing a mixture of surveys, interviews, observations, and records to assess the maintenance and sustainability of the different implementation strategies employed. In the trial, no difference was found between the effectiveness of the basic and enhanced strategies. The process evaluation identified that the basic strategy, which had higher levels of teaching sun safety lessons and sunscreen use in the first year, was appealing to children and easy to implement whereas the enhanced strategy was not much more intensive in terms of the additional materials offered. The authors suggested that further incentives, training, and monitoring could improve results in the enhanced strategy.

The Aspects of a Trial Framework

We have considered two frameworks for thinking about mixed methods intervention evaluations. A third and final framework is offered by ourselves and detailed in O'Cathain et al. (2013; 2014), where we considered how qualitative research was actually used in practice with RCTs rather than how it *might* be used. That is, this framework was empirically rather than theoretically based. We identified 296 articles published between January 2008 and September 2010 that reported qualitative research undertaken with RCTs and mapped the focus of the qualitative research in relation to the RCT. We found that 28% of these publications had been carried out before the trial. However, it was difficult to distinguish between qualitative research undertaken during or after a trial because data collection might occur during the trial, but analysis and interpretation might occur after the trial results were known. The timing of data collection, analysis, and interpretation of the qualitative research in relation to the RCT was rarely clearly reported in these articles. Thus the temporal framework described earlier was not a helpful way of categorizing these articles in practice, and instead a new framework was developed inductively from reading the 296 publications identified. We found five aspects of a trial that qualitative research could inform (O'Cathain et al., 2013; 2014): the intervention, the trial design and conduct, the outcomes, the process and outcome measures used, and understanding of the health condition at which the intervention was aimed (Table 23.2).

This framework, which is based on articles researchers published from the qualitative research they carried out with RCTs, has some notable differences compared with the two frameworks presented earlier. One of the five aspects of the trial within this framework was the intervention. We identified eight aspects of the intervention addressed in the articles, some of which appeared in the two frameworks presented earlier: intervention development, mechanisms of action, the feasibility and acceptability of an intervention, fidelity,

Table 23.2 Framework of the Focus of Qualitative Research Used With Trials

Category	Subcategory	Description
Intervention content and delivery	Intervention development	Pre-trial development work relating to intervention content and delivery
	Intervention components	Exploring individual components of a complex intervention as delivered in a specific trial
	Models, mechanisms, and underlying theory development	Developing models, mechanisms of action, and underlying theories or concepts relating to an intervention in the context of a specific trial
	Perceived value and benefits of intervention	Exploring accounts of perceived value and benefits of intervention given by recipients and providers of the intervention
	Acceptability of intervention in principle	Exploring stakeholder perceptions of the "in principle" acceptability of an intervention
	Feasibility and acceptability of intervention in practice	Exploring stakeholder perceptions of the feasibility and acceptability of an intervention in practice
	Fidelity, reach, and dose of intervention	Describing the fidelity, reach, and dose of an intervention as delivered in a specific trial
	Implementation of the intervention in the real world	Identifying lessons for "real-world" implementation based on delivery of the intervention in the trial
Trial design, conduct, and processes	Recruitment and retention	Identifying ways of increasing recruitment and retention
	Diversity of participants	Identifying ways of broadening participation in a trial to improve diversity of population
	Trial participation	Improving understanding of how participants join trials and experience of participation
	Acceptability of the trial in principle	Exploring stakeholders' views of acceptability of a trial design
	Acceptability of the trial in practice	Exploring stakeholders' views of acceptability of a trial design in practice
	Ethical conduct	Strengthening the ethical conduct of a trial (e.g., informed consent procedures)

(continued)

Table 23.2 Continued

Category	Subcategory	Description
	Adaptation of trial conduct to local context	Addressing local issues that may impact the feasibility of a trial
	Impact of trial on staff, researchers, or participants	Understanding how the trial affects different stakeholders (e.g., workload)
Outcomes	Breadth of outcomes	Identifies the range of outcomes important to participants in the trial
	Variation in outcomes	Explains differences in outcomes between clusters or participants in a trial
Measures of process and outcome	Accuracy of measures	Assesses validity of process and outcome measures in the trial
	Completion of outcome measures	Explores why participants complete measures or not
	Development of outcome measures	Contributes to development of new process and secondary outcome measures
Target condition	Experience of the disease, behavior, or beliefs	Explores the experience of having or treating a condition that the intervention is aimed at, or a related behavior or belief

Source. Adapted from O'Cathain et al., 2013.

reach and dose, and implementation of the intervention in the real world. However, we also found articles of qualitative research used to describe the intervention in practice, including identifying hidden or unexpected components of the intervention. We also distinguished between qualitative research to identify the acceptability of the intervention in principle for future trials and in practice for current trials because the possibility of fixing problems identified with an intervention is different for each of these. Understanding these aspects of an intervention could help researchers to explain the trial results.

The second aspect of a trial addressed by qualitative research in our framework was design and conduct. Very little of this aspect was addressed by the earlier frameworks presented. There was overlap in terms of understanding ways of improving recruitment and retention within the specific trial or future trials. Indeed, Creswell et al. (2009) give an example of the innovative work by Donovan et al. (2002) who use interviews and observation before the trial to improve recruitment practices iteratively to ensure the successful implementation of the future trial. We found many other uses of qualitative research to explore the acceptability of

the trial in principle and in practice and identify ways of improving the ethical conduct of future trials.

We also found articles focusing on the breadth and variation in outcomes and the development and accuracy of outcome and process measures; these are largely included in the temporal framework. One aspect of the trial that was not identified either by the temporal framework or the process-outcome evaluation framework was the use of qualitative research to explore patient experiences of the disease or behavior at which the RCT intervention was aimed, for example, exploring the lived experience of having a particular illness or condition. Researchers may have set out to explore this, or it may have been a by-product of exploring the intervention itself. We would suggest that it may be problematic to set out with an aim of exploring patient experiences of a health condition using participants in an RCT because trials are rarely representative of the population with that condition. However, it may be an additional bonus for the mixed methods intervention evaluation to understand something more about the health condition, especially if this has implications for the intervention under study.

While presenting these three frameworks we have drawn on language used by scholars discussing this methodology. The temporal framework privileges the RCT by describing other methods undertaken in relation to the RCT. Similarly the aspects of a trial framework considers qualitative research in relation to the trial. The process-outcome evaluation framework offers a more balanced relationship between the mixed methods components and the RCT. The language used to describe the combination of qualitative methods and trials may indicate the value given to different aspects of a mixed methods intervention evaluation, and therefore we discuss it next.

Developing Language for a Developing Methodology

Researchers use a variety of terms to describe the relationship between qualitative research and the trial that is carried out within mixed methods intervention evaluations. Creswell et al. (2009) use the term *embedded* for a qualitative study carried out during a trial. Similar terms used by other researchers include *incorporating, nested, sample from,* and *sub-study*. One could argue that these terms relegate the qualitative research to secondary status, with the trial as the primary method. Indeed Hesse-Biber (2012) identifies how terms such as *embedded* suggest a positivistic lens applied to the qualitative research, where it is given a secondary role as an "add-on" to the more important and valued trial. She argues that this limits the ability of the qualitative research to inform the trial other than in terms of validating or confirming the dominant quantitative results. However, Plano Clark et al. (2013) discuss variations in and disagreements about the definition of the term *embedded* and how it can be used to mean a more integrated approach between methods. They then go on to describe how interpretive qualitative research was embedded in an RCT.

Embedding can occur in other ways. Some researchers describe mixed methods intervention evaluations as trials embedded in qualitative research (Donovan et al., 2002; Hoddinott, Britten, & Pill, 2010), signifying the way in which qualitative research has shaped the trial. Case Study 4 is an example of an innovative study design that does just that by embedding a trial within a broader qualitative study. The case study is interesting because it shows how adopting this different perspective allowed the researchers to step outside the bounds of the single question of effectiveness to consider contextual differences between clusters in a cluster RCT.

Case Study 4: The Breastfeeding in Groups Study

Hoddinott, Britten, and Pill (2010) used the term "prospective mixed method embedded case studies" approach (p. 777) to describe how they assessed the effectiveness of an intervention to improve breastfeeding rates. The breastfeeding in groups trial was a cluster trial of 14 localities in Scotland in which 7 intervention localities were asked to increase group activities related to breastfeeding. The seven control localities did not change their existing group activities. Hoddinott's research team adopted an ethnographic, realist evaluative approach (Pawson & Tilley, 2004) to their trial design and conduct, keeping reflective diaries about meetings, telephone conversations, e-mails, and their thoughts and views about their experiences during the trial. They explored their backgrounds as a general practitioner and a former breastfeeding volunteer and how this interacted with their research roles. They hypothesized that there would be differences between the clusters receiving the intervention related to the local environment in which the intervention was conducted. They carried out focus groups, interviews, and breastfeeding group observations throughout the study. Before conducting analysis of the outcomes of the trial, they used the qualitative research to formulate an explanatory model of factors contributing to the success or failure of the localities in terms of delivering the intervention. The trial itself had a null outcome, with breastfeeding rates declining in three of the seven intervention localities. The model built from the qualitative data helped the researchers to explain differences in outcomes between clusters, identifying problems with the leadership, rooms where the group sessions were held, and a lack of resources in clusters with declining breastfeeding rates.

Another set of terms is also used to describe the relationship between methods in mixed methods intervention evaluations: *alongside, concurrent, in combination with, linked,* and *parallel*. These could suggest a more equal relationship between the RCT and other methods, or alternatively they could suggest separation between the trial and other methods when integration is needed in terms of the qualitative research shaping and impacting the RCT. Concerns about the language used may diminish over time as a variety of relationships between the trial and other methods emerges, and researchers select the language that best describes the relationship between the methods they have used. This may be facilitated by a move to view these types of studies as complex evaluations rather than as trials with extra parts (Song, Sandelowski, & Happ, 2010). We have chosen to use the term *mixed methods intervention evaluation* in this chapter to describe these types of studies, deliberately using the term *evaluation* rather than *RCT* so that no method is privileged. This consideration of the challenge of the language being used to describe studies that combine qualitative research and RCTs highlights that, although there are considerable benefits to this endeavor that we have described earlier in the chapter, there are also challenges involved in moving from RCTs to mixed methods intervention evaluations. We discuss some of these challenges in the next section.

Challenges of Making the Move from Randomized Controlled Trials to Mixed Methods Intervention Evaluations

We now explore some challenges for researchers in moving from an evaluation consisting of a single RCT to a mixed methods intervention evaluation. When more than one method is involved, consideration needs to be given to integration of those methods, since different methods may be associated with different research traditions and paradigms, and to the increase in funding that may be required to deliver them. Additionally, there is a tradition of synthesizing evidence from RCTs, thus if studies are undertaken as mixed methods intervention evaluations, then the challenge of synthesizing this multicomponent evidence arises.

Integration Between Methods

A key value of mixed methods research is that the whole is more than the sum of its parts (Barbour, 1999). For this to happen, one method must influence in some way the objectives, sampling, data collection, analysis, or interpretation of the other method within the study (O'Cathain, Murphy, & Nicholl, 2007). Within mixed methods intervention evaluations, the expectation is that the qualitative research should help to

optimize the intervention to be trialed, improve the efficiency and ethics of the trial conducted, increase the internal validity of the trial by ensuring the right outcomes are measured in the right way, help interpret trial results, or facilitate the transferability of the trial findings to contexts outside the trial (O'Cathain et al., 2013; 2014). Thus the expected integration is one directional, with the qualitative research working to enhance the trial (Popay & Williams, 1998; Song et al., 2010). Examples of this integration are qualitative research showing how differences in staff attitudes and resources between clusters in a cluster RCT could explain differences in the primary outcome of breastfeeding rates between those clusters (see previous Case Study 4; Hoddinott et al., 2010), with qualitative research identifying problems with recruitment practices and the solutions to these problems resulting in increasing recruitment rates so that the trial was viable (Donovan et al., 2002), and qualitative research identifying a problem with an outcome measure in a feasibility study, which resulted in the use of a different outcome measure in the main trial (Farquhar, Ewing, Higginson, & Booth, 2010). However, Lewin et al. (2009) identified that publications from mixed methods intervention evaluations often had no evidence of integration of the findings from the qualitative research and the trial. That is, the promise of qualitative research helping to explain the trial findings was simply not delivered in practice, or at least not in a way that was visible outside the original research team. We drew a similar conclusion from our review of the use of qualitative research with trials (O'Cathain et al., 2013; 2014), as well as identifying examples of visible integration. This lack of visible integration is not surprising given the paucity of visible integration of data or findings within mixed methods studies generally in health research (O'Cathain et al., 2007), but it is disappointing given the potential value of the qualitative research to the endeavor of generating evidence of effectiveness. A challenge to all researchers engaged in mixed methods intervention evaluations is to explicitly report in journal articles the "yield" or insights gained from undertaking qualitative research and RCTs within the same study.

When integration occurs, careful consideration may need to be given to processes of integration. Some researchers have argued that the analysis of process evaluation data needs to be separate from the analysis of the trial outcomes so that researchers can anticipate factors likely to affect outcomes uninfluenced by prior knowledge of the outcome of the trial (Ellard & Parsons, 2010; Munro & Bloor, 2010). This may be difficult where roles within the trial team overlap (Audrey et al., 2006), for example, if the trial manager is also the qualitative researcher. Whether researcher bias is a real issue or not, it is important that data collection processes and integration are addressed up front by the evaluation team, with a clear data collection and analysis plan and reflective and critical engagement about any potential challenges around integration. Otherwise the qualitative research or process evaluation risks being no more than "post-hoc allocation of success or failure," only useful for the development of future interventions (Jansen et al., 2009, p. 224).

Integration may be difficult because some evaluation team members may not feel able to act on findings generated from the qualitative research. The findings may not be available at the time they are needed, the findings may not have credibility among some team members such as the lead researcher, the trialists may be wedded to a particular path for their intervention and trial and be unwilling to deviate from it, or the qualitative research may challenge established ways of thinking and practice. For example, Jansen et al. (2009) raise a concern that researchers do not consider how an intervention can be adapted to fit the context in which it will be delivered but actually focus on adapting the context to fit the intervention. With such a mindset, qualitative research suggesting a need to adapt the intervention to fit the context may be unpalatable to the wider team. To facilitate integration, the whole evaluation team may need to adopt a reflexive approach associated with qualitative research (Hesse-Biber, 2012) and described earlier in Case Study 4. This occurs best at an early stage of study implementation when teams can discuss values and beliefs that shape their actions and reflect on their openness to different possibilities. This is likely to be essential when the qualitative research challenges aspects of the trial in terms of questioning the integrity of the processes utilized during the trial, the ability of the trial to generalize to a population, and the underlying theory on which the intervention is based. Case Study 5 explores this last point, describing how qualitative research can challenge the accepted theoretical basis for an intervention.

Case Study 5: The Use of a Narrative Approach to Understand Smoking Cessation and Challenge Current Thinking

A process evaluation was undertaken alongside a pilot trial of smoking cessation groups in Scotland (Ritchie, Schulz, & Bryce, 2007). The intervention tested in this pilot trial included narrative therapy that encouraged participants to tell stories about their smoking and offered flexibility in group membership, allowing participants to choose whether to attend group sessions or not depending on their needs at a particular time. Ritchie, Schulz, and Bryce (2007) conducted observations of 12 existing smoking cessation groups over a six-week period, debriefing sessions with the group facilitator, and interviews with people who had attended sessions at least three times over six months to assess perceptions and impact of the intervention on smoking behavior. They used narrative analysis to make explicit practitioners' assumptions underlying their work in the cessation groups and participants' views about the groups. The use of narrative therapy was valued and accepted by participants. Facilitators felt that using stories helped the participants to understand information and engage with the group better than simply giving them facts and figures. Many participants perceived that their intention to stop smoking was unstable and that they required long-term support. This long-term support was offered by the intervention in terms of helping with the decision to stop and in continuing not to smoke. Furthermore, participants valued flexibility in making the decision to stop smoking and how and when to attend group sessions. Researchers also found that the inclusion of smokers, those still trying to quit and those who had lapsed, to be beneficial by providing motivation and valuable insights to others at different/earlier stages of the quitting process. The research challenged many previous smoking cessation interventions that were often based on an uncritical adoption of the "one size fits all" "stages of change" model (Prochaska & DiClemente, 1983), which leads to assessment of motivation and readiness to quit as a stable concept.

There may also be tension around expectations for the qualitative research and what can be delivered in practice. Although the qualitative research may enrich understanding of the trial findings, this understanding "will always be nuanced and qualified and rarely determinate" (Munro & Bloor, 2010, p. 710), and the researcher must always remain open to the possibility of other interpretations of the data. Munro and Bloor (2010) discuss a process evaluation carried out alongside a feasibility study for a definitive RCT, highlighting a challenge they faced in practice whereby after completing their data collection for the process evaluation, they were asked to explain unexpected findings from the feasibility study. The feasibility study concerned an intervention to train influential school pupils as "peer supporters" to be able to discuss smoking cigarettes and/or cannabis with their peers in order to educate them about the dangers of smoking. The trial had three arms: two schools had peer supporter training in cigarette smoking, two schools had peer supporter training in cigarette and cannabis smoking, and two schools were controls. One of the outcome measures was the intention to smoke cannabis in three months and at age 16. The researchers found that there was no evidence of an effect of the intervention on intention to smoke cannabis in the intervention schools, but unexpectedly they found an increase in expectations among peer supporters that they would be smoking cannabis by the time they were 16. By the time this unexpected finding emerged, the process evaluation data collection was complete and there was no resource for further data collection. Therefore the researchers had to analyze the data they had already collected in the hopes of finding some reasons for this outcome. Although they suspected that the fatalism of the teenagers in being subjected to drugs through their training as peer supporters underpinned this unexpected outcome, they were unable to provide evidence of this because it had not been explored specifically in their focus groups. Although they did find limited evidence that it was more difficult to talk about smoking cannabis than smoking cigarettes, Munro and Bloor (2010) argued that there is a danger in process evaluations of trying to generalize findings from single cases.

We have presented a number of challenges around integration of the qualitative research and RCT that we consider to be surmountable. We recommend that, in order to gain the benefits of mixed methods intervention evaluations explored earlier, researchers should

• Be explicit in publications about the insights for the trial gained from the qualitative research

so that this learning is visible to other researchers, intervention developers, and research users.

• Plan how and when integration will occur, and who will be involved in it, so that issues such as researcher bias can be explicitly considered and addressed if appropriate.

• Adopt a reflexive approach to the whole evaluation at the beginning, where team members discuss their underlying beliefs and values about the intervention, the methods, and how integration can occur. This can help to prepare team members to be open to any challenging findings from the qualitative research and hopefully help them to take appropriate actions based on those findings.

• Manage expectations of what the qualitative research or process evaluation can deliver within the constraints of the evaluation so that the strengths and limitations are recognized when interpreting the findings.

Paradigmatic Differences

Paradigmatic differences between quantitative and qualitative research tend be ignored in mixed methods intervention evaluations in health (Oakley et al., 2006) but can be a challenge to researchers working on these studies. There can be a tension between the RCT with its assumptions of generalizability, its predetermined protocols, and its determination to control the context in which the research takes place and the more inductive, flexible nature of qualitative research that focuses on context and subjectivity. The ontological position of researchers conducting RCTs is realism: that an objective truth is out there. This ontological position can be shared by the researchers undertaking the qualitative research, and indeed one could argue that qualitative researchers believing in idealism would not be interested in working in the context of an RCT. However, the epistemological positions of trialists and qualitative researchers may be diverse and in tension. Trialists emphasize the objectivity of researchers who must desist from allowing their values to contaminate the research environment (Hesse-Biber, 2012). This can shape the way in which the research is conducted from the formulation of research questions through to how the data is collected and analyzed, who is qualified to do that, and the credibility of the knowledge that is produced (Hesse-Biber, 2012). This may result in the qualitative research being limited in the questions it addresses and having values imposed on it that are more important to quantitative research, for example, large sample sizes. The epistemological stance of the trialists can be dominant because the qualitative research takes an enhancing role within the mixed methods intervention evaluation rather than being viewed as integral to the evaluation (Song et al., 2010). If studies are viewed as evaluations rather than trials with added qualitative components, then teams can pay attention to a variety of epistemological stances and consider the best approach to take within their evaluation.

It is standard practice to publish a protocol for an RCT so that researchers can be held to account, for example in their choice of primary outcome. Oakley et al. (2006) argue that process evaluations should prospectively specify a set of research questions and identify the processes to be studied, the methods to be used, and the procedures for integrating the findings of the process evaluation with the results of the trial. We concord with this view because it encourages planning of the qualitative research and sharing of this plan with the whole team, something that we believe can facilitate integration between relevant components of the study. This approach has been taken up by some research communities where researchers include a process evaluation within published trial protocols (e.g., Murphy et al., 2010) or publish standalone process evaluation protocols (e.g., Ellard, Taylor, Parsons, & Thorogood, 2011; Grant, Dreischulte, Treweek, & Guthrie, 2012).

High-quality RCTs are governed by external trial steering committees, and data monitoring committees, are conducted according to standardized operating procedures, and are reported uniformly in accordance with the Consolidated Standards of Reporting Trials (CONSORT) statement (Schulz, Altman, & Moher, 2010). This raises the question of whether other methods used with trials should be included in these trial practices and procedures. This requires careful thought of the pros and cons

so that qualitative research is not blindly subsumed within all these procedures with an accompanying loss of its key strengths, nor blindly excluded from core aspects of the evaluation. Discussion about the whole study at trial steering committees, rather than only the trial, can ensure more opportunities for integration and that the study is seen as a whole rather than a trial with add-ons. It is also the case that process evaluations can uncover worrying issues about adherence to a planned intervention and the potential for bias within the study, which steering committees may need to be aware of and take action on (Riley, Hawe, & Shiell, 2005). Having a standard operating procedure for the qualitative research undertaken with a trial may ensure that thought is given to any possible damage qualitative research can do to the experiment (Rapport et al., 2013).

For all the potential benefits there might be to including qualitative research in the usual processes and procedures of a trial, we recommend a cautious approach be taken so that a key strength of qualitative research—its flexibility—is not damaged. In particular, a CONSORT statement for reporting qualitative research carried out with trials may be more prohibitive than helpful because of the range of approaches to data collection and analysis, the wide range of possible insights to be gained, and the wide range of ways of reporting these insights. There is also an alternative approach to consider—that the approach to trials is shaped by issues associated with qualitative research. In Case Study 6, Hawe et al. (2004) discuss how using qualitative research in community-based complex interventions may provide an alternative way of conceptualizing the relationship between the variability of the community context and the standardized RCT.

Case Study 6: Community Trial Design

Hawe et al. (2004) argue that RCT design for complex interventions can learn from complexity theory, which allows for real-world contexts by considering the interaction between the context and the intervention. The RCT would measure the effect of an intervention that has integrity, but the integrity is not defined compositionally through standardized processes in the laboratory (form) but rather functionally as being adapted to the local community context (function). For example, in an intervention to educate patients with depression, an intervention that was standardized based on form would distribute the same written patient information to all sites, whereas an intervention based on standardized function would tailor the information at each site based on the local culture, including factors such as the learning styles of the population and their language and literacy needs. Rather than assuming that the "best" evidence comes from a laboratory setting, which becomes gradually compromised in real-world applications, trials should start by conceptualizing communities as complex systems focusing on the standardization of the complex intervention by function rather than form. The study would then be about how the community system recurrently produces the health problem in order to understand how it can be changed in different contexts to achieve the desired outcome.

We have presented a number of challenges related to paradigmatic differences and recommend that researchers:

- Recognize that there are a variety of philosophical and methodological approaches to mixed methods intervention evaluations that they may wish to consider. Undertaking an embedded qualitative study within a trial is not the only option.
- Continue to publish protocols for process evaluations and reflect on the strengths and weaknesses of doing so.
- Proceed with caution in terms of including qualitative research within the formal procedures of trials, thinking about the evaluation as a whole rather than attempting only to squeeze qualitative research into the RCT paradigm.

An Additional Expense?

It costs money to undertake research in preparation for an RCT, process evaluations alongside RCTs, and studies of implementation after RCTs. It has been argued that the additional costs of conducting process evaluations are outweighed by greater explanatory power and an understanding of how well the intervention can be generalized (Oakley et al., 2006). It may also be argued that investment in preparation for a trial is beneficial because optimizing the intervention and having confidence in the feasibility of the full trial can save money by reducing the probability of expensive trials of flawed interventions or failed trials due to inability to recruit.

Even so, mixed methods intervention evaluations occur in the context of limited resources, time, and researchers to collect and analyze data (Linnan & Steckler, 2002). Therefore decisions need to be made about how much qualitative research is necessary for a particular trial, as well as how much can be resourced. Even in the context of ample resources, the volume of data generated by qualitative research can be challenging to analyze, and it may be necessary to focus on salient components in order to gain the most benefit.

There is also the challenge of false economy. Setting up qualitative research that is underresourced by employing unskilled researchers and placing unreasonable limits on time required to complete an in-depth analysis may lead to poor-quality research that lacks credibility.

We believe that qualitative research undertaken with trials is valuable and is worth paying for. We recommend that it is

- Properly resourced for focusing on important aspects of a particular RCT.
- Proves its value by explicitly communicating in publications the impact it has had on the endeavor of evaluating the effectiveness of an intervention.

Moving Beyond Primary Research Toward Evidence Synthesis

Systematic reviews of RCTs are carried out to summarize the evidence of effectiveness of specific interventions. We have shown in this chapter that qualitative research undertaken with trials can help to explain the findings of a specific trial. Qualitative research is also relevant to systematic reviews of trials, potentially adding to their value by helping to explain heterogeneity of trial findings (Noyes, Popay, Pearson, Hannes, & Booth, 2011). An excellent example of this is described in Case Study 7, where an evidence synthesis of qualitative research focusing on different approaches to promoting healthy eating in children helped to explain the different effect sizes found in trials of healthy eating interventions (Thomas et al., 2004).

Case Study 7: Integration of Qualitative Research and Trials in Systematic Reviews of Healthy Eating Promotion Interventions in Children

Thomas and colleagues (2004) conducted a systematic review of trials of interventions to increase healthy eating in children ages 4 to 10 years. First, they conducted a meta-analysis of data from trials showing that interventions increased children's consumption of fruit and vegetables by an average of half a portion per day. However, effect sizes varied between trials; while most trials increased it only by less than one portion, one trial achieved a two portion a day increase. Interested in these differences in effect sizes, Thomas and colleagues next synthesized results from qualitative studies about healthy eating in children, analyzing the authors' findings thematically for barriers and facilitators of healthy eating and ideas for possible interventions from the children's point of view. They found that children see health as the responsibility of their parents and that children prioritize taste over health, so interventions should not actively promote health over taste. They also found that children distinguish between fruit and vegetables rather than perceiving them as both belonging to a healthy food group. Finally, Thomas and colleagues synthesized the results of both reviews in a matrix to explore the relationship between the interventions used in the effectiveness trials and the children's views. They concluded that studies in their sample that had little or no emphasis on health messages were more likely to promote increases in fruit and vegetable consumption. This use of evidence synthesis of both qualitative research and trials can be further mined by synthesizing evidence from mixed methods intervention evaluations so that the qualitative research undertaken with a specific trial is used to understand the context in which those trial results were achieved. Combining learning from each mixed methods intervention evaluation can then lead to an understanding of the important components of interventions and the subpopulations and the health environments in which they may be effective.

Conclusions and Future Directions

In this chapter we have discussed the move from the lone RCT addressing the single question of intervention effectiveness to a mixed methods intervention evaluation addressing a wide range of questions relevant to understanding effectiveness of interventions. We present this as a positive move driven by researchers understanding the complexity of the interventions they evaluate, the trials they conduct, and the environments in which they research. While it can be argued that this move has become part of routine practice in some research communities, we have identified a number of challenges with this approach in health research. These challenges relate to a current and ongoing shift in how researchers evaluate interventions. None of the challenges presented are insurmountable, and indeed reflecting on these challenges is likely to help research communities to understand how to gain the potential benefits of mixed methods intervention evaluations. Our main hope is that, as time goes by, we see a further move from qualitative research taking an enhancement role within trials toward researchers viewing their evaluations as whole studies—mixed methods intervention evaluations—with value placed on all components of these complex evaluations.

Discussion Questions

1. What are the benefits of using mixed methods intervention evaluations rather than standalone RCTs?

2. Why do you think we need to consider the language used to describe the relationship between the qualitative research and the trial?

3. What are some of the challenges in moving from RCTs to mixed method intervention evaluations?

Suggested Websites

http://www.mrc.ac.uk/documents/pdf/complex-interventions-guidance/

The Medical Research Council provides guidance for the development and evaluation of complex interventions, including RCTs and multimethods.

http://www.methodologyhubs.mrc.ac.uk/default.aspx

MRC Hubs for Trials Methodology Research is a focus for the development of trials methodology in the UK.

http://www.bristol.ac.uk/social-community-medicine/centres/conduct2/

ConDuCT-II, the collaboration and innovation in difficult or complex RCTs in invasive procedures, is one of the MRC hubs with a theme of qualitative research with pragmatic RCTs.

http://www.shef.ac.uk/scharr/sections/hsr/mcru/quart/conf

The MRC Hubs for Trials Methodology organization funded a conference on the use of qualitative research with trials, and some of the talks are available here.

http://www.apa.org/ed/schools/cpse/randomized-control-guide.pdf

A guide to multimethod trials in social science and education produced by the American Psychological Association.

References

Aro, A. R., Smith, J., & Dekker, J. (2008). Contextual evidence in clinical medicine and health promotion. *European Journal of Public Health, 18*(6), 548–549. doi:http://dx.doi.org/10.1093/eurpub/ckn082

Audrey, S., Holliday, J., Parry-Langdon, N., & Campbell, R. (2006). Meeting the challenges of implementing process evaluation within randomized controlled trials: The example of ASSIST (A Stop Smoking in Schools Trial). *Health Education Research, 21*(3), 366–377. doi:10.1093/her/cyl029

Barbour, R. S. (1999). The case for combining qualitative and quantitative approaches in health services research. *Journal of Health Services Research & Policy, 4*(1), 39–43.

Campbell, N. C., Murray, E., Darbyshire, J., Emery, J., Farmer, A., Griffiths, F., . . . Kinmonth, A. L. (2007). Designing and evaluating complex interventions to improve health care. *British Medical Journal, 334*, 455–459. doi:10.1136/bmj.39108.379965

Campbell, R., Starkey, F., Holliday, J., Audrey, S., Bloor, M., Parry-Langdon, N., . . . Moore, L. (2008). An informal school-based peer-led intervention for smoking prevention in adolescence (ASSIST): A cluster randomised trial. *Lancet, 371*, 1595–1602. Retrieved from http://dx.doi.org/10.1016/S0140-6736(08)60692-3

Cnaan, R. A., & Enosh, G. (2001). Randomized controlled trials. In B. A. Thyer (Ed.), *The handbook of social work research methods* (pp. 177–192). Thousand Oaks, CA: Sage.

Cochrane Collaboration. (2013). *Glossary.* Retrieved from http://www.cochrane.org/glossary/5#letterr

Craig, P., Dieppe, P., Macintyre, S., Mitchie, S., Nazareth, I., & Petticrew, M. (2008). Developing and evaluating complex interventions: The new Medical Research Council guidance. *British Medical Journal, 337*, 979–983. doi:10.1136/Bmj.A1655

Creswell, J. W., Fetters, M. D., Plano Clark, V. L., & Morales, A. (2009). Mixed methods intervention trials. In S. Andrew & E. J. Halcomb (Eds.), *Mixed methods research for nursing and the health sciences* (pp. 161–180). Oxford, UK: Wiley-Blackwell.

Donovan, J., Mills, N., Smith, M., Brindle, L., Jacoby, A., Peters, T., . . . Hamdy, F. (2002). Quality improvement report—improving design and conduct of randomised trials by embedding them in qualitative research: PROTECT (Prostate Testing for Cancer and Treatment) study. *British Medical Journal, 325*(7367), 766–769. doi: http://dx.doi.org/10.1136/bmj.325.7367.766

Ellard, D., & Parsons, S. (2010). Process evaluation: Understanding how and why interventions work. In M. Thorogood & Y. Coombes (Eds.), *Evaluating health promotion: Practice and methods* (pp. 87–104). New York, NY: Oxford University Press. doi:10.1093/acprof:oso/9780199569298.003.0007

Ellard, D. R., Taylor, S. J. C., Parsons, S., & Thorogood, M. (2011). The OPERA trial: A protocol for the process evaluation of a randomised trial of an exercise intervention for older people in residential and nursing accommodation. *Trials, 12*(1), 28. doi:10.1186/1745-6215-12-28

Escoffery, C., Glanz, K., & Elliott, T. (2008). Process evaluation of the Pool Cool diffusion trial for skin cancer prevention across 2 years. *Health Education Research, 23*(4), 732–743. doi:10.1093/her/cym060

Escoffery, C., Glanz, K., Hall, D., & Thomas, E. (2009). A multi-method process evaluation for a skin cancer prevention diffusion trial. *Evaluation and the Health Professions, 32*(2), 184–203. doi:10.1177/0163278709333154

Farquhar, M., Ewing, G., Higginson, I. J., & Booth, S. (2010). The experience of using the SEIQoL-DW with patients with advanced chronic obstructive pulmonary disease (COPD): Issues of process and outcome. *Quality of Life Research, 19*, 619–629. doi:10.1007/s11136-010-9631-7

Giacomini, M. K. (2001). The rocky road: Qualitative research as evidence [EBM Notebook]. *Evidence Based Medicine, 6*, 4–6. doi:10.1136/ebm.6.1.4

Glanz, K., Geller, A. C., Shigaki, D., Maddock, J. E., & Isnec, M.R. (2002). A randomized trial of skin cancer prevention in aquatics setting: The Pool Cool program. *Health Psychology, 21*(6), 579–587. doi:10.1037//0278-6133.21.6.579

Glenton, C., Lewin, S., & Scheel, I. B. (2011). Still too little qualitative research to shed light on results from reviews of effectiveness trials: A case study of a Cochrane review on the use of lay health workers. *Implementation Science, 6*(1), 53–57. doi:10.1186/1748-5908-6-53

Grant, A., Dreischulte, T., Treweek, S., & Guthrie, B. (2012). Study protocol of a cluster randomized trial to improve the safety of NSAID and antiplatelet prescribing: Data-driven quality improvement in primary care. *Trials, 13*, 154–160. doi:10.1186/1745-6215-13-154

Grissmer, D. W., Subotnik, R. F., & Orland, M. (2009). *A guide to incorporating multiple methods in randomized controlled trials to assess intervention effects.* Washington, DC: American Psychological Association. Retrieved from http://www.apa.org/ed/schools/cpse/activities/mixed-methods.aspx

Hawe, P., Shiell, A., & Riley, T. (2004). Complex interventions: How "out of control" can a randomised controlled trial be? *British Medical Journal, 328*, 1561–1563. doi:10.1136/bmj.328.7455.1561

Hesse-Biber, S. (2012). Weaving a multimethodology and mixed methods praxis into randomised controlled trials to enhance credibility. *Qualitative Inquiry, 18*(10), 876–889. doi:10.1177/1077800412456964

Hoddinott, P., Britten, J., & Pill, R. (2010). Why do interventions work in some places and not others? A breastfeeding support group trial. *Social Science and Medicine, 70*(5), 769–778. doi:10.1016/j.socscimed.2009.10.067

Jansen, Y. J. F. M., Foets, M. M. E., & de Bont, A. A. (2009). The contribution of qualitative research to the development of tailor-made community-based interventions in primary care: A review. *European Journal of Public Health, 20*(2), 220–226. doi:10.1093/eurpub/ckp085

Lewin, S., Glenton, C., & Oxman, A. D. (2009). Use of qualitative methods alongside randomised controlled trials of complex healthcare interventions: Methodological study. *British Medical Journal, 339*, b3496. doi:10.1136/bmj.b3496

Linnan, L., & Steckler, A. (2002). Process evaluations for public health interventions and research. In A. Steckler & L. Linnan (Eds.), *Process evaluations for public health interventions and research* (1–23). San Francisco, CA: Jossey-Bass.

Marciel, K. K., Saiman, L., Quittell, L. M., Dawkins, K., & Quittner, A. L. (2010). Cell phone intervention to improve adherence: Cystic fibrosis care team, patient, and parent perspectives. *Pediatric Pulmonology, 45*(2), 157–164. doi:10.1002/ppul.21164

Medical Research Council. (2000). *A framework for development and evaluation of RCTs for complex interventions to improve health.* London, England: Author. Retrieved from http://www.mrc.ac.uk/documents/pdf/rcts-for-complex-interventions-to-improve-health/

Medical Research Council. (2008). Developing and evaluating complex interventions: New guidance. Prepared on behalf of the MRC by P. Craig, P. Dieppe, S. Macintyre, S. Mitchie, I. Nazareth, & M. Petticrew. London, England: Author. Retrieved from http://www.mrc.ac.uk/documents/pdf/complex-interventions-guidance/

Munro, A., & Bloor, M. (2010). Process evaluation: The new miracle ingredient in public health research? *Qualitative Research, 10*(6), 699–713. doi:10.1177/1468794110380522

Murphy, S., Raisanen, L., Moore, G., Tudor Edwards, R., Linck, P., Williams, N., . . . Moore, L. (2010). A pragmatic randomised controlled trial of the Welsh National Exercise Referral Scheme: Protocol for trial and integrated economic and process evaluation. *BMC Public Health, 10*, 352. doi:10.1186/1471-2458-10-352

Noyes, J., Popay, J., Pearson, A., Hannes, K., & Booth, A. (2011). Qualitative research and Cochrane reviews. In J. P. T. Higgins & S. Green (Eds.), *Cochrane handbook for systematic reviews of interventions* (Version 5.1.0, ch. 20). Hoboken, NJ: Wiley-Blackwell. Retrieved from http://www.cochrane-handbook.org.

Oakley, A., Strange, V., Bonell, C., Allen, E., & Stephenson, J. (2006). Process evaluation in randomised controlled trials of complex interventions. *British Medical Journal, 332*(4), 413–416. doi:10.1136/bmj.332.7538.413

O'Cathain, A., Murphy, E., & Nicholl, J. (2007). Integration and publications as indicators of "yield" from mixed methods studies. *Journal of Mixed Methods Research, 1*(2), 147–163. doi:10.1177/1558689806299094

O'Cathain, A., Thomas, K. J., Drabble, S. J., Rudolph, A., & Hewison, J. (2013). What can qualitative research do for randomised controlled trials? A systematic mapping review. *BMJ Open, 3*(e002889). doi:10.1136/bmjopen-2013-002889

O'Cathain, A., Thomas, K. J., Drabble, S. J., Rudolph, A., Goode, J., & Hewison, J. (2014). Maximising the value of combining qualitative research and randomised controlled trials in health research: The QUAlitative Research in Trials (QUART) study a mixed methods study. *Health Technology Assessment, 18*(38). doi:10.3310/hta18380

Pawson, R., & Tilley, N. (1997). *Realistic evaluation*. London, England: Sage.

Plano Clark, V. L., Schumacher, K., West, C., Edrington, J., Dunn, L. B., Harzstark, A., . . . Miaskowski, C. (2013). Practices for embedding an interpretive qualitative approach within a randomized clinical trial. *Journal of Mixed Methods Research, 7*(3), 219–242. doi:10.1177/1558689812474372

Popay J., & Williams, G. (1998). Qualitative research and evidence-based healthcare. *Journal of the Royal Society of Medicine, 91*(Suppl. 35), 32–37.

Pope, D. S., Atkins, S., DeLuca, A. N., Hausler, H., Hoosain, E., Celentano, D. D. & Chaisson, R. E. (2010). South African TB nurses' experiences of provider-initiated HIV counseling and testing in the Eastern Cape Province: A qualitative study. *AIDS Care, 22*(2), 238–245. doi:10.1080/09540120903040594

Prochaska J. O., & DiClemente, C. C. (1983). Stages and processes of self-change of smoking: Toward an integrative model of change. *Journal of Clinical Psychology, 51*(3), 390–395.

Rapport, F., Storey, M., Porter, A., Snooks, H., Jones, K., Peconi, J., . . . Russell, I. (2013). Qualitative research within trials: Developing a standard operating procedure for a clinical trials unit. *Trials, 14*(1), 54. doi:10.1186/1745-6215-14-54

Riley, T., Hawe, P., & Shiell, A. (2005). Contested ground: How should qualitative evidence inform the conduct of a community intervention trial? *Journal of Health Services Research and Policy, 10*(2), 103–110. doi:10.1258/1355819053559029

Ritchie, D., Schulz, S., & Bryce, A. (2007). One size fits all? A process evaluation—the turn of the "story" in smoking cessation. *Public Health, 121*(5), 341–348. doi:10.1016/j.puhe.2006.12.001

Romo, N., Poo, M., Ballesta, R., & the PEPSA Team. (2009). From illegal poison to legal medicine: A qualitative research in a heroin-prescription trial in Spain. *Drug and Alcohol Review, 28*(2), 186–195. doi:10.1111/j.1465-3362.2008.00015.x

Sandelowski, M. (1996). Using qualitative methods in intervention studies. *Research in Nursing and Health, 19*(4), 359–364. doi:10.1002/(SICI)1098-240X(199608)19:4<359::AID-NUR9>3.0.CO;2-H

Schulz, K. F., Altman, D. G., & Moher, D. (2010). CONSORT 2010 statement: Updated guidelines for reporting parallel group randomised trials. *British Medical Journal, 340*(c332). doi:10.1136/bmj.c332

Siu, A. M. H., Shek, D. T. L., & Poon, P. K. K. (2009). Evidence-based research in community rehabilitation: Design issues and strategies. *Hong Kong Journal of Occupational Therapy, 19*(1), 20–26. doi:http://dx.doi.org/10.1016/S1569-1861(09)70040-3

Shagi, C., Vallely, A., Kasindi, S., Chiduo, B., Desmond, N., Soteli, S., . . . Ross, D. (2008). A model for community representation and participation in HIV prevention trials among women who engage in transactional sex in Africa. *AIDS Care, 20*(9), 1039–1049. doi:10.1080/09540120701842803

Song, M., Sandelowski, M., & Happ, M. B. (2010). Current practices and emerging trends in conducting mixed methods intervention studies in the health sciences. In A. Tashakkori & C. Teddlie (Eds.), *SAGE handbook of mixed methods in social & behavioral research* (2nd ed., pp. 725–747). Thousand Oaks, CA: Sage.

Thomas, J., Harden, A., Oakley, A., Oliver, S., Sutcliffe, K., Rees, R., . . . Kavanagh, J. (2004). Integrating qualitative research with trials in systematic reviews. *British Medical Journal, 328*(1010), 1010–1012. doi: http://dx.doi.org/10.1136/bmj.328.7446.1010.

Torgerson C. J., & Torgerson, D. J. (2001). The need for randomised controlled trials in educational research. *British Journal of Educational Studies, 49*(3), 316–328. doi:10.1111/1467-8527.t01-1-00178

US National Library of Medicine. (2008, April 18). *FAQ. ClinicalTrials.gov—Clinical trial phases*. Retrieved from http://www.nlm.nih.gov/services/ctphases.html

Mixed Methods Evaluation

Donna M. Mertens *and* Michele Tarsilla

Abstract

Understanding mixed methods approaches in evaluation involves understanding the philosophical stances, theoretical perspectives, and practical strategies that have emerged in the evaluation world. Building on such realization, this chapter provides a critical overview of why and how mixed methods have been used in evaluation for decades. After clarifying the definition of mixed and multimethods in evaluation, the chapter identifies five main paradigms underlying the use of mixed methods in contemporary evaluation practice (postpositivist, constructivist, pragmatic, transformative, and dialectical pluralism). Next, real-world evaluations are used to illustrate the assumptions and beliefs of such paradigms across a variety of dimensions (axiology, ontology, epistemology, methodology). The chapter also looks forward to future directions for a more informed use of mixed methods in evaluation.

Key Words: constructivism, dialectical pluralism, evaluation, mixed methods, postpositivism, pragmatismc, transformative

The use of evaluation has dramatically increased over the past two decades across a variety of sectors. In the political arena, policymakers—especially at a time of economic turbulence and fiscal austerity—are constantly pressured by their constituencies to account for the results and economic return of publicly funded programs. Similarly, in the context of social programs, nongovernmental organizations evaluate the effectiveness of their implementation strategies on a routine basis to learn how to serve their beneficiaries better and secure funding for sustaining their programs. Furthermore, project managers in the private sector use evaluation to understand what corrective actions need to be taken to enhance their marketing and sales strategies to boost their clients' satisfaction and increase their profits.

Concurrent with the development and strengthening of the evaluation practice in a number of domains, a plethora of definitions of evaluation have been used to explain what evaluation

is. Despite the undeniable popularity of the term *evaluation* since the late 1960s, common understandings of evaluation's most typical attributes included how evaluative efforts differentiate themselves from apparently similar endeavors, such as research, monitoring, and auditing are missing. In order to fill such a definitional gap and set the stage for informed discussions on mixed methods evaluation (MME), the introductory section of this chapter first clarifies the concept of evaluation by using Fournier's definition:

> Evaluation is an applied inquiry process for collecting and synthetizing evidence that culminates in conclusions about the state of affairs, value, merit, worth, significance, or quality of a program, product, person, policy, proposal or plan. Conclusions made in evaluation encompass both an empirical aspect and a normative aspect (judgment about the value of something). It is the value feature that distinguishes evaluation from other types of

inquiry, such as basic science research, clinical epidemiology, investigative journalism, or public polling. (pp. 139–140)

In line with the classic definitional distinction between research and evaluation, evaluation (and therefore MME) is unique for two main reasons:

1. Evaluation fosters knowledge creation (as research does), but its primary goal (promoting institutional and organizational learning for accountability and programmatic improvement) is broader and somewhat more political than the one pursued by research. As such, evaluation may help identify the positive/negative and intended/unintended effects of implementing an innovative educational policy sponsored by the Department of Education in the United States or it may assist in gauging the extent to which an agricultural value chain program funded by a European foundation in Kenya could be scaled up in two neighboring countries.

2. Evaluation is more intentional about the use of its findings than research is, as it is primarily aimed at influencing program management or decision-making on a variety of issues based on value judgments that are rendered after comparing findings with preestablished benchmarks. As a result, evaluation may, among other sources, inform the future allocation of funding for social programs, the scaling-up of current health or energy policies, and/or the interruption of ineffective projects and programs in a myriad of sectors.

Definitions and Mixed Methods in Evaluation and Research

Now we have defined evaluation's features and main purposes (as distinct from those of research), we next clarify the meaning of MME. However, we first must define mixed methods as generally conceived in relation to the definition of mixed methods research (MMR). A second definition pointing to the distinctive features of MME is then provided.

Defining Mixed Methods Research

The definition of MMR we use is based on criteria that manuscripts submitted to the *Journal of Mixed Methods Research* need to fulfill to be considered for publication. As such, MMR generally includes the following:

1. Data collection and analysis, as well as integration of findings and formulation of

inferences, based on the use of both qualitative and quantitative approaches (i.e., grounded theory or interpretative *and* hypothesis testing or confirmatory) or methods (i.e., structured interviews or surveys coupled with focus group discussions and ethnography);

2. Explicit integration of the quantitative and qualitative aspects of the study in question such as the measurement of quantitative variables associated with specific outcomes of interest (e.g., change in income or employment rate among youth age 18–23 as a result of their participation in a vocational skills training) paired with a more in-depth description of the interactions between the trainers and the training participants coupled with a thorough scan of the environmental factors affecting the implementation of the program;

3. Discussion of how the study in question not only adds to the literature on MMR but also makes a contribution to a substantive area in the scholar's field of inquiry.

Defining Mixed Methods Evaluation

The MMR definition provided in the previous section adequately describes an increasingly popular practice among contemporary researchers. However, as evaluation is characterized by a stronger political connotation than research is (other than accruing knowledge on a given phenomenon, evaluation informs program design and policy-making based on evaluative judgments), a more in-depth discussion is needed before presenting a more exhaustive definition of MME. In particular, some further clarifications on mixed methods is necessary to fully appreciate the distinctive features of MME.

MIXED METHODS ARE MORE THAN DATA COLLECTION METHODS

A definition of MME would not be exhaustive if it were applicable only to data collection methods (e.g., the development of a case study and the administration of a survey for the sake of triangulation). MME are also—more frequently than not—characterized by the combination of both qualitative and quantitative data analysis, as well as hypothesis development processes and conceptual and interpretative frameworks, for either specific (Creswell & Plano Cark, 2007) or multiple (Greene, Caracelli, & Graham, 1989) purposes. More broadly, MMEs are the expression of different philosophical stances (Tashakkori & Teddlie,

1998) and, as such, they honor "emergent and transgressive methodologies, inclusion, and a coloring of epistemologies" (Denzin, 2010, p. 420), such as those of the different evaluation team members and/or the evaluation primary and secondary users (Patton, 2008).

MIXED METHODS EVALUATION: BRIEF HISTORY

Following the publication of the first conceptual framework for MME designs in the late 1980s (Greene, Caracelli, & Graham, 1989) and based on the increased awareness among practitioners of the relevance of mixing methods within the scope of evaluations, a number of important developments occurred in the evaluation world, including the following:

• A groundbreaking *New Directions in Evaluation* issue devoted to mixed methods (Greene & Caracelli, 1997) aimed at summarizing the advances made in the use of mixed methods in evaluation as of the late 1990s.
• The *User-Friendly Handbook for Mixed Method Evaluations*, published by the National Science Foundation (Frechtling & Sharp, 1997).
• The first and second editions of the *Handbook of Mixed Methods in Social and Behavioral Research* (Tashakkori & Teddlie 2003, 2012).
• The launch of a peer-reviewed publication specifically dedicated to mixed methods: the *Journal of Mixed Methods Research* (2007).
• The publication of second *New Directions in Evaluation* volume dedicated to mixed methods in 2013 that focused on the contribution of mixed methods to credibility of evidence (Mertens & Hesse-Biber, 2013).

Concomitantly with the proliferation of these developments, a number of professional groups and communities of practice with a specific focus on mixed methods were established, including the following:

• The Special Interest Group on Mixed Methods created within the American Educational Research Association in 2009.
• The Topical Interest Group on mixed methods established within the American Evaluation Association in 2010.
• The launch of the Mixed Methods International Association in 2013.

Similarly, due to the increased popularity of the topic both within and outside academia, a series of conferences centered on mixed methods were held around the world, such as the following:

• The Mixed Methods International Conference in Cambridge and Leeds (United Kingdom) and Baltimore, Maryland, 2005–2012.
• The Day in Mixed Methods, a full-day learning event organized before the start of the International Qualitative Inquiry Congress Conference in 2012 and 2013 at the University of Illinois, Urbana/Champaign.
• The Mixed Methods International Research Association annual conference in Boston in 2014.

More recently, MME has received special attention within two communities. In the health sciences community, the National Institutes of Health published a guidebook on best practices for mixed methods research (Creswell, Klassen, Plano Clark, & Clegg Smith, 2011) that has influenced the work of many evaluators working in public health both in the United States and overseas. In the international development community, the UK Department for International Development (DFID; Stern et al., 2012) published a working paper on broadening the range of designs and methods for impact evaluations, and Bamberger (2012) wrote a technical note on mixed methods in impact evaluation. More precisely, interest in MME (mainly for the sake of triangulation and a better understanding of implementation processes and root causes of observed phenomena) was recently spurred by two main factors: (a) the identification of the limitations and practical challenges associated with the conduct of randomized controlled trials (RCT) funded generously by a variety of international donors and (b) the realization that the net distinction between qualitative and quantitative is no longer apparent, due to the variety of data collection and analysis tools and techniques available to evaluators today, as confirmed by the authors of the DFID publication mentioned earlier:

> Combining methods has also become easier because the clear distinctions between quantitative (variables) and qualitative methods (cases) have become blurred, with quantitative methods that are non-statistical and new forms of within-case analysis made easier by computer aided tools. (DFID, 2012, p. ii)

RELEVANCE FOR MIXED METHODS EVALUATION IN THEORY AND PRACTICE

The eclectic use of MME is closely linked with the variety of purposes (e.g., exploration, explanation, and triangulation) that the combination of qualitative and quantitative methods generally serves (Greene, Caracelli, & Graham, 1989). As a result, evaluations featuring mixed methods designs attest to the diversity of philosophical frameworks, theoretical lenses, methodological choices, and practices found within the evaluation community. Within the realm of MME, multiple perspectives of what represents evidence and robustness of findings exist, also based on the level of stakeholder participation, as well as the type of disciplinary aspects and the nature of paradigmatic choices. Hence, MME operates at many different levels.

Dialogues around the use of mixed methods are inherently linked with consideration of the credibility of evidence and the criteria used to establish that credibility (Mertens & Hesse-Biber, 2013). Evaluators turn to methodologists from the postpositivist, constructivist, pragmatic, and transformative paradigms for criteria that are associated with credibility and rigor from different philosophical paradigm stances (Mertens & Wilson, 2012). However, far from being solely preoccupied with the robustness of the data on which their findings are based, mixed methods evaluators struggle with how to accurately represent the voices of the less powerful stakeholders from marginalized communities whose views have historically been missing or inaccurately presented in past evaluative endeavors. In response to the question that they often ask themselves about how the inclusion of marginalized communities in evaluation enhances the credibility of their findings, mixed methods evaluators have an embarrassment of riches in terms of the options available to them for justifying their methodological choices. However, such diversity and richness of methodologies poses some challenges to the evaluators wanting to benefit from them, including the need to work within and between standpoints or world perspectives that are in tension with each other.

The Mixed Methods Paradox and the Default Mixed Methods Syndrome

As a result of both the growing body of related specialized literature and the proliferation of professional groups presented in the earlier section, the use of mixed methods is a distinctive feature of many evaluations conducted over the past decade (Mertens & Hesse-Biber, 2013). The effort to combine qualitative and quantitative methods to enhance the validity and credibility of evaluation findings through the use of mixed methods in evaluation represents a commendable endeavor. However, the unsystematic and unquestioned use of mixed methods, referred to here as *default mixed methods*, casts some doubts over the effectiveness of their application. As attested by several evaluations conducted in international development evaluations, for instance, mixed methods are often used during only one of the evaluation stages (data collection) and with the objective of simply meeting the requests made by those who commission the evaluation. Therefore, evaluation teams often use the same dominant approach (in most cases, a quantitative one) that they have been using consistently in their whole career and couple it with some ancillary qualitative data collection methods (e.g., focus group discussions) as if they were "throwing a few M&Ms onto the top of the ice cream to make it look pretty, and it might taste a little bit better" (Kemp, 2001, p. 23). In response to this externally induced demand for the use of mixed methods in evaluation (this is not directly equivalent to a more genuine MME), there is a need for a more shared and solid understanding of mixed methods. Here we provide a rationale for their use.

Why Use Mixed Methods Evaluation?

Traditionally, the most frequent argument provided for justifying the use of MME has been that combining qualitative and quantitative methods helps mitigate the limitations of the "stand-alone" uses of either one. More recently, the use of MME has been associated with broader objectives, including the mix of conceptual frameworks and paradigms. As such, MME are regarded as particularly instrumental for the following:

- "reducing the risk of bias and offset the limitations of a single method and thus increase the robustness of the estimated counterfactual" (Gertler, Martinez, Premand, Rawlings, & Vermeersch, 2011, p. 119)
- "generating a more complete, contextual, contingent and complex understanding of the phenomena of interest than would have a single-method study" (Greene, 2005, p. 410)
- "achieving the best of each method while overcoming their unique deficiencies" (Denzin, 1989, p. 244)

• "celebrating the equality of difference" (McGee, 2003, p. 135)

• throwing "up interesting, often surprising and sometimes counterintuitive relationships and patterns" through inductive qualitative research, as well as ask 'how much?' and establish how confident we can be in these 'working hypotheses' through quantitative research (Garbarino & Holland, 2009, p. 11)

As attested by this broadening of the idea of "methods" and further developing our understandings of why mixed methods are and should be used in evaluation, MME represents an innovation in evaluation. Mixed method evaluation contributes to the definition and pursuit of new approaches characterized by a variety of features, such as expanded epistemological and conceptual frameworks, scope, focus, data analysis approaches, and target audiences (Box 24.1).

The remainder of this chapter explores the diverse philosophical frameworks that provide guidance in the use of mixed methods in evaluation, along with illustrative examples and critical analysis of mixed methods approaches in evaluation.

Box 24.1 Added Value of Mixed Methods Evaluation

Epistemological framework

• MME is geared toward the generation of general findings as well as the promotion of a more solid understanding and explanation of complexity (e.g., of both programs and policies in relation to the multifaceted contexts in which they are implemented) based on the principle that phenomena are often unpredictable and not explained by linear causal mechanisms.

Conceptual framework

• MME enhances triangulation, that is, the use of findings from different data sources in order to address the same evaluation question more effectively: the robustness of evaluation conclusions does not depend exclusively on the degree of convergence of findings but also on the extent to which the evaluator documents the strategies used to mitigate the divergence of findings (including the verification of the divergent finding and the return to the field for further data collection).

• MME informs the use of multiple data collection strategies and instruments that build on one another (e.g., a series of ethnographic case studies on households' dietary patterns, farming practices, and expenditures would allow the identification of the items that could be included in a subsequent survey aimed at measuring changes in nutritional status as a result of a school feeding program).

• MME facilitates different but important understandings of the same evaluand, thus providing a common platform to fully appreciate the contributions of different conceptual frameworks and hypotheses on how changes occur as a result of a given intervention (e.g., as result of the identification, through thematic analysis, of behavioral patterns among program beneficiaries, a new variable could be created and incorporated in a regression analysis, thus increasing the predictive power of the statistical model underlying the program being evaluated.

• MME provides complementarity of qualitative and quantitative findings for a variety of purposes (e.g., some case studies, developed after a training follow-up survey, would allow explaining why female respondents were four times less likely than men to have found a job within nine months from the completion of the training program being evaluated), including "completion, enhancement or detailing a more significant whole" (Bazeley & Kemp, 2012, p. 58).

Scope

• MME combines understanding of the breadth and depth of human experiences.

• MME enhances the accuracy of findings by qualifying them based on spatial and temporal attributes of an intervention as well as characteristics of the population(s) affected by the program being evaluated.

Data analysis

- *MME promotes data transformation*: numerical data are converted to narrative and vice versa for understanding and communication purposes.
- *MME promotes extreme case analysis:* important cases of very high or poor performance are identified and investigated further through a different method;
- *MME promotes theory development and testing:* first, by identifying what should go in a typology rather than just using an a priori theory-driven approach for theory generating purposes, and second, by identifying a theory testing approach, as a sort of mixed methods grounded theory.
- *MME promotes data merging:* qualitative/categorical and quantitative variables are created and merged into the same data set and then used in the statistical analysis of one's explanatory model.

Understanding of the processes/mechanisms leading to the outcomes of interest

- MME helps open the so-called "black box" or "grey box" of a program (Scriven, 1994), by combining the identification of the end results of an intervention with that of the implementation processes and the dynamics (cultural, economic, political, social) influencing the effects of an intervention.

Sampling

MME promotes the use of different samples (both probabilistic and purposely selected) in order to complete one's fuller addressing of the evaluation question.

Target audience

- When MME is conducted in a participatory manner, a plurality of stakeholders' concerns (they capture nuances within the communities/individuals studied) and multiple interests are adequately addressed.
- MME is characterized by a certain flexibility in combining and analyzing both quantitative and qualitative findings in order to improve the effectiveness of findings dissemination and provide a wider understanding and acceptance of the corresponding conclusions and recommendations while also enhancing the accountability of the overall evaluation endeavor

Source: Tarsilla (2013).

Multiple Philosophical and Theoretical Lenses in Evaluation

Alkin (2004) provided a picture of the theoretical roots for evaluation in North America in the first edition of *Evaluation Roots* through the use of a metaphor of a tree to depict three branches of evaluation theories (i.e., Methods, Use, and Values). The Methods branch was populated by those who held that rigor in method achieved by the use of RCTs would produce credible knowledge for evaluators. The Use branch theorists noted that evaluators could rigidly follow postpositivist-based rules, but the results of their studies would not make a difference if no one used them. Hence, their focus was on identifying the intended users and designing studies that would be viewed as credible

by that constituency. The Values branch theorists emphasized the importance of context and multiple stakeholders' constructions of reality as the pathway to creating knowledge that was credible. The first edition of *Evaluation Roots* has been described as providing a good beginning to the process of documenting the evolution of theories in the field of evaluation; however, it has been criticized for not being inclusive of evaluators outside of North America and not having representation of ethnic-minority or Indigenous evaluators' theoretical perspectives (Davidson, 2006; Mertens, 2015).

In the second edition of *Evaluation Roots*, Alkin (2013) used the same three branches to depict theorists in evaluation, and two additional chapters were added to be more inclusive of evaluation theorists around the globe. Stame's (2013) chapter on a European evaluation theory tree mentions the growing need for mixed methods[1] as a tool to settle the tension between an "agricultural-botany" paradigm utilizing the experimental and mental testing traditions in psychology (Parlett & Hamilton, 1977) and the illuminative evaluation paradigm ascribing to anthropology, psychiatry, and participant observation in sociology[2]. Borrowing from Kushner (2000), Stame also reminds the reader that a shift in evaluative thinking is needed from "documenting the program and the lives of the individuals in that context [to] documenting the lives and work of people and to use that as a context within which we read the significance and meaning of programs" (p. 359).

Similarly, Rogers and Davidson's (2013) chapter on New Zealand and Australian evaluation roots mentions the relevance of combining methods in order to both capture the substantive differences of human experiences (often dictated by one's own cultural background as is the case of Aboriginals and Torres Strait Islanders) and making evaluation more culturally responsive (Cram, 2009; Davidson, 2010; Wehipeihana, Davidson, McKegg, & Shanker, 2010).

While the addition of authors from Europe, New Zealand, and Australia certainly widened the scope of the evaluation theorists represented, it did not address the voices of evaluators from marginalized communities and other social justice advocates who are making significant contributions to the field of evaluation. Therefore, Mertens (2012) and Mertens and Wilson (2012) added a fourth branch to the evaluation tree labeled Social Justice. Mertens and Wilson also questioned the metaphor of a tree with separate branches and suggested a metaphor based on ocean currents that have distinct identities while sharing a deep water conveyer belt for sharing ideas. We use this four-branch structure (whether seen as branches of a tree or river or currents in the oceans) to frame our discussion of bases for the use of mixed methods in evaluation. Our main thesis is as follows: Understanding mixed methods approaches in evaluation involves understanding the philosophical stances, theoretical perspectives, and practical strategies that have emerged in the evaluation world associated with advances in mixed methods.

Evaluators lived through what were called the paradigm wars when post-positivists argued with constructivists about which methods would result in the creation of credible evidence (Mertens & Wilson, 2012). The arguments seemed on the surface to be about methods, but they were more fundamentally about the worldviews of the evaluators and their assumptions about axiology (ethics), ontology (reality), epistemology (knowledge), and methodology (systematic inquiry) (Shadish, 1998). Greene (2012) identified one important lesson from the paradigm wars as follows:

> One important lesson from the ensuing "great qualitative-quantitative debate" was the recognition—across *all* methodological divides—that knowledge about human affairs is partially affected by the lenses and stances of the knower, the human inquirer. Accepting the impossibility of positivist raw empiricism and purely objective knowledge about human action meant, in tandem, that social inquirers had to accept the inevitable presence of self as researcher in the knowledge generated by social inquiry. One's philosophical or paradigmatic assumptions about social reality and knowledge—alongside one's favorite theories, the sensibilities of one's mentor, important life experiences, values, and beliefs—all matter to the methodological decisions an inquirer makes and to the interpretive weft and warp of the knowledge attained. (p. 756)

Based on an expanded version of Guba and Lincoln's (1989, 2005) depiction of four paradigms (i.e., postpositivist, constructivist, pragmatism, and critical theory), evaluators are currently operating in a multiparadigmatic world that includes postpositivists, constructivists, pragmatists, and transformativists (Mertens, 2009, 2015; Mertens & Wilson, 2012). Any of these paradigms individually or in combination with each other can be used as a basis for the selection of mixed methods in evaluation. Hence, we use these paradigms and branches as the organizing framework for the next section.

Paradigms and Branches

The four major paradigms align with the four branches in evaluation theory, as depicted in Table 24.1. Postpositivists align with Methods theorists, constructivists with Values theorists, transformativists with Social Justice theorists, and pragmatists with Use theorists. Theorists who choose to work across paradigms are not depicted in this table, however; these theorists are discussed in a later section on dialectical pluralism (DP).

Table 24.1 Philosophical Paradigms and Evaluation Branches

Paradigm	Branch
Postpositivist	Methods
Constructivist	Values
Transformative	Social Justice
Pragmatic	Use

Source: Adapted from Mertens and Wilson, 2012.

Postpositivist Paradigm and the Methods Branch of Evaluation

Table 24.2 depicts the philosophical assumptions associated with the postpositivist paradigm. As the ontological and epistemological assumptions lead to a methodological assumption that prioritizes the use of RCT, one might wonder how mixed methods fit within this branch. Howard White's[3] (2013) recent work tackles this issue and clarifies that the key question asked in impact evaluations (i.e., what difference did the intervention make?) can best be answered with an RCT or quasi-experimental design (if an RCT is not feasible). However, he also admits that impact evaluations can benefit from

Table 24.2 Postpositivist Paradigm Assumptions

Assumption	Beliefs
Axiology	• Respect/privacy (confidentiality) • Beneficence/nonmaleficence (equal opportunity to participate and benefit, especially in the case of RCTs) • Justice (especially in the case of random sampling to avoid bias and targeting of easily accessible subjects/participants)
Ontology	• One reality waiting to be discovered and measured
Epistemology	• Objective; neutral; distant
Methodology	• Quantitative; RCTs or quasi-experimental designs (featuring the use of statistical techniques to make up for the lack of randomization); structured survey research; black box mixed methods

Note. RCT = randomized control trials
Source. Adapted from Mertens and Wilson, 2012.

the addition of qualitative approaches to obtain answers to different types of questions (e.g., What are root causes of the observed changes? What is the quality of implementation? How relevant is the targeting of the intervention being evaluated? What are the barriers to either the adoption of a new behavior or the participation in the program in question?). Otherwise said, evaluations can be strengthened by adding qualitative data collection (Bell, 2006; Briggs, 2006) to an essentially postpositivist study (RCT; Oakley 2005a, 2005b). The postpositivist perspective remains one of the most popular in the research and evaluation community in North America and Europe. However, the fact that qualitative methods are treated as if they were "handmaiden or second best" to quantitative (Hesse-Biber, 2010, p. 457) has not failed to attract criticisms. In particular, often reproached for not having received advanced training in qualitative methodologies (Howe, 2004), postpositivists have been accused of introducing an excessively quantitative lens and jargon in the evaluation community, thus "marginalizing the open-ended, free flowing, emergent nature of qualitative inquiry" and "leaving little space for issues connected to empowerment, social justice, and a politics of hope" (Denzin, 2010, p. 420).

THE POSTPOSITIVIST PARADIGM IN THE REAL WORLD: EXAMPLES

Given the many resources allocated to rigorous impact evaluations across a variety of sectors over the past decade, contemporary evaluation practice abounds with instances ascribed to the postpositivist paradigm, methods-based evaluations. Often suspected to be a sort of "marriage of interest" for either obtaining additional funding or responding to public concerns over the ethical issues associated with randomization (i.e., providing some individuals or communities with some goods and services while denying others access to those very same good and services, for the sake of rigor), the combination of qualitative and quantitative methods has gained increased popularity across a variety of sectors, especially within the international development arena, as illustrated by the following examples.

First, qualitative methods are increasingly used in impact evaluations conducted around the world by the Abdul Latif Jameel Poverty Action Lab affiliated with the Massachusetts Institute of Technology. In the course of over 100 RCT and quasi-experimental impact evaluations conducted over the past decade and based on the realization that findings of purely quantitative evaluations left key policy and programmatic questions unanswered, a certain number of Massachusetts Institute of Technology economists and quantitative evaluators started using (albeit marginally) qualitative methods. Traditionally skeptical about the utility of using nonstatistical methods for research and evaluation purposes, a large number of Jameel Poverty Action Lab impact evaluations in the mid-2000s started using qualitative methods, primarily as a means to identify and explain both the processes and the underlying causes of the impact(s) detected through statistical analysis (e.g., correlational and regression analysis). This is the case of the impact evaluation of the GoBifo[4] community development project funded by the World Bank in Sierra Leone[5] (Casey, Glennerster, & Miguel, 2011). In the course of this evaluation, the organization of focus groups along with the conversion of the corresponding qualitative findings to variables and numbers—which served as the basis for the development of follow-up surveys—proved to be particularly instrumental in explaining social dynamics within the context of the villages targeted by the project.

Second, an illustrative example of this shift in thinking about methods within agencies that favored quantitative methods for decades is the recent hiring of a qualitative evaluator in the Gender Innovation Lab, a new office created within the Poverty Reduction and Economic Management unit of the African Region at the World Bank. Mandated to conduct 12 impact evaluations in the areas of agricultural productivity, entrepreneurship and employment, property rights, assets, and agency in 2012–2015,[6] the newly hired evaluator assists the team in the development of qualitative studies and integration of process- and context-related questions into existing quantitative surveys for the purposes of assessing the impact of development interventions more effectively. Based on the realization that quantitative studies had not highlighted how to provide women with consistent access to economic inputs in the past, the Gender Innovation Lab team acknowledged the critical role that qualitative methods play in the identification of possible solutions.[7]

Third, a variety of predominantly quantitative evaluations recently conducted exemplify some of the key tenets of the postpositivist paradigm. These include, as attested in a recent publication on the use of mixed methods in impact evaluation

(Bamberger, 2012), (a) the impact evaluation of postconflict reconstruction in Liberia, funded by DFID and the International Rescue Committee; (b) the evaluation of a conditional cash transfer program in Kazakhstan, funded by Save the Children; and (c) the impact evaluation of Food and Agriculture Organization of the United Nations emergency and rehabilitation work in rural Democratic Republic of Congo.

Thus the postpositivist paradigm and its associated Methods branch exemplify quantitatively dominant mixed methods designs in which the qualitative component is used to gain insights and understandings related to the phenomenon under study. The Methods branch examples reflect the assumption that a quantitative measure could be used to capture the "reality" of the impact of a program and that evaluators, for the most part, should be objective and neutral in their stance. In the next section, we discuss the assumptions of the constructivist paradigm and how they align with the Values branch of evaluation.

Constructivist Paradigm and Values Branch of Evaluation

As mentioned earlier in the chapter, constructivist evaluators reject the ontological assumption that there is one reality out there waiting to be measured in favor of an ontology that holds that realities are multiple and socially constructed. (See Table 24.3 for a depiction of the philosophical assumptions associated with the constructivist paradigm.) This constructivist assumption leads to an emphasis on the use of qualitative methods because these allow the evaluator to interact with diverse members of the stakeholder community and together create the different versions of social reality needed to fully understand the context and the process of implementing an intervention. Even

Table 24.3 Philosophical Assumptions of the Constructivist Paradigm

Assumption	Beliefs
Axiology	Balanced representation; rapport; multicultural respect
Ontology	Multiple socially constructed realities
Epistemology	Interactive and interpretive
Methodology	Primarily qualitative approaches

Source. Adapted from Mertens and Wilson, 2012.

in the 1980s, constructivists acknowledged that quantitative data could be included as part of a primarily qualitative study (Guba & Lincoln, 1989). Hence, the door has been and continues to be open to consider the character of mixed methods studies within the constructivist paradigm.

Denzin (2012) suggests that mixed methods studies that are rooted in the constructivist paradigm have greater potential to produce findings that can address the social good than can mixed methods approaches more closely aligned with the postpositivist paradigm. Mixed methods that begin in the constructivist paradigm afford the opportunity to assess the interpretive, contextual level of experience where meaning is created and provides a roadmap to address social justice. Constructivists view systematic inquiry as "an interactive process shaped by personal history, biography, gender, social class, race, and ethnicity of the people in the setting (p. 85)." Denzin proposes a moratorium on "mixed methods talk about designs and typologies and get back to the task at hand, which is changing the world" (p. 85). His position is that investigators need to employ constructivist strategies in order to create texts that challenge and stimulate readers to action. Denzin strongly argues for the use of the constructivist paradigm as the framework for social justice oriented research, but there is a large part of the constructivist community that does not embrace this as the primary goal of their work (Merriam, 2009). Many constructivists have long claimed that their work should be descriptive and interpretive rather than activist. The transformative paradigm and Social Justice branch is discussed in the next section; this is a stance that has pursuit of social justice as one of its primary assumptions.

Hesse-Biber (2013) provides additional food for thought as to how a constructivist lens, informed by critical theory, can be used in combination with quantitative approaches, such as RCTs. In contrast to White's (2013) view of the role of qualitative methods in evaluation, Hesse-Biber supports a stronger role for the qualitative aspects of a MME study. She argues that qualitative approaches can be used more extensively to answer such questions as

- How well does the intervention respond to the culture and context of the target population?
- How well do recruitment procedures work?
- To what extent does the target population reflect the range of diversity with regard to the overall goals of the project? Who is left out? Why?

- To what extent is ethics praxis (e.g., cultural responsiveness, attention to power inequities) built into the recruitment and evaluation process?
- How well does the target population understand what they are consenting to?
- To what extent do participants accept the outcome/s of randomization? Are participants willing to be randomized?

She argues that a RCT study would be enhanced by being enveloped within a subjectivist framework. This raises the question: Is it possible that qualitatively framed mixed methods are better suited to the ability of mixed methods researchers to demonstrate a causal relationship between variables? (Mertens & Hesse-Biber, 2012).

THE CONSTRUCTIVIST PARADIGM IN THE REAL WORLD: EXAMPLES

A growing body of impact evaluations funded by DFID and other donors in northern Europe (Swedish International Development Agency and Danish International Development Agency) has given renewed prominence to the constructivist paradigm over the past few years. The idea that qualitative methods help represent the plurality of stakeholders' perspectives on a variety of phenomena of interest was certainly a response to the frustrations and limitations associated with the very finite RCT efforts to measure linear causal links between interventions and effects. Specialized literature seemed to be particularly instrumental in the revitalization of this paradigm and the reaffirmation that qualitative methods ought to be included in the causal analysis toolbox (Brady, 2002; Yin 2003; Pawson, 2007).

Knigge and Cope (2006; cited in Fielding, 2012) illustrate a qualitatively driven approach in their evaluation of community gardens established in a deprived area of Buffalo, New York, to determine their contribution to social capital accumulation. They relied heavily on the use of qualitative methods and modern technologies. Thanks to the use of web-based multimedia environment supported by GIS, the evaluation team first created a map showing community resources and facilities in proximity to the community gardens. Then a visual representation of the community garden blocks was enriched by additional information on ethnicity and land attributes as well as photos of neighborhoods and audio comments by local residents. Based on the specifications provided by the local residents, the evaluation planners agreed to redraw their map to better reflect the reality revealed by the multimedia representation. The methods included the conduct of interviews and observations, including bicycle rides in the target area as a way to gauge participants' opinions about the value of the community gardens project. The evaluation team leader, Knigge, added labor market statistics to the GIS and used the original map's counts of vacant land parcels to show the association of community gardens with adjacent house values. As Fielding (2012) reported in his review of data integration with new technologies:

> Knigge realized that by solely looking at published quantitative data, she "may have missed the existence of community gardens, and a wholly ethnographic study might have missed potential correlations and clusters that were best analyzed through GIS" (Knigge & Cope, 2006, p. 2934, cited in Fielding, 2012, p. 7).

A second illustrative example of the constructivist paradigm in evaluation is the impact evaluation of the India Gram Panchayat Community Development Reform Program (Bamberger, 2012). Following the random assignment of 200 villages (Gram Panchayats) to project and control groups (quantitative conceptual framework), the evaluation relied on exploratory study of land tenure, ownership of public goods, participation, and social networks (qualitative data collection) that informed the content of the baseline survey administered prior to the start of training programs (quantitative data collection). These first few activities were followed by qualitative data collection in five project and five control areas to describe the processes of behavior changes (e.g., new community organization strategies, type and variety of community development projects, extent of women's and scheduled castes' participation). The evaluation, including field visits and community and households interviews, allowed uncovering the processes through which political and social dynamics, corruption, economic change, and network affiliation impacted on the project's effectiveness, measured by the comparison between the effect of the projects before and after two years of implementation.

A third example of constructivism is a MME conducted in a largely rural state in India to examine women's experiences with induced abortion, its determinants, and prevalence. The mixed methods approach included a combination of a quantitative survey that included open-ended questions, case studies, and focus group discussions about attempts and completed abortions, as well as women's motivations and preferences regarding abortion, as influenced by underlying cultural factors. Edmeades et al. (2010) wrote the following:

> The modified narrative approach significantly reduced underreporting of abortions, either through providing women with a safe space in which to discuss abortions or by improving women's recall of past events. As a result, the data on abortions and the circumstances surrounding their use generated by this mixed methods approach are likely to be more representative of the totality of abortion experiences than those based on more conventional data collection approaches. This has the effect of increasing the validity and reliability of the conclusions reached based on the analyses of these data, both of which are of particular importance to policy makers and researchers. (p. 194)

The constructivist paradigm and its embodiment in the Values branch of evaluation is demonstrated in the sample MME studies in that the designs were not only qualitatively dominated but they also focused on constructing understandings of the participants' realities through means that allowed for the complexity of their experiences to surface. Quantitative data also contributed to the quality of the MME, but they were couched within the knowledge gained through the qualitative methods. The next section discusses the pragmatic paradigm and the Use branch of evaluation; here the focus is on identifying the intended users of evaluation findings and designing the evaluation to meet their needs.

Pragmatic Paradigm and Use Branch of Evaluation

The pragmatic paradigm (Morgan, 2007) supports the use of mixed methods based on the assumption that there is not one set of methods that is appropriate; rather, the criteria for choosing methods include what method fits with the evaluation questions. The philosophical assumptions associated with the pragmatic paradigm as it is sometimes depicted in the mixed methods literature appear in Table 24.4.

Biesta (2010), Hall (2009), and Denzin (2012) warn against an overly simplistic application of the pragmatism as a philosophy in evaluation, basically suggesting, "If the method fits the question, then use it." Biesta outlines the basic principles of Deweyan pragmatism as a philosophy that can inform mixed methods evaluators because Dewey

Table 24.4 Philosophical Assumptions of the Pragmatic Paradigm

Assumptions	Beliefs
Axiology	Gain knowledge in pursuit of desired ends and societal improvement as influenced by the evaluator's values and politics and experiences
Ontology	Reality is continually created through experience in interaction and transaction with the "world"
Epistemology	Ideas and knowledge are evaluated according to their consequences; the gold standard evaluators can meet is warranted assertability and provisional truths about situated evaluands
Methodology	Match methods to questions; mixed methods

Source. Adapted from Mertens and Wilson, 2012.

held that no knowledge claim can be documented as providing the "truth." Rather, different knowledge claims result from different ways of engaging with the social world.

Denzin (2012) asks: Have members of the mixed methods community done an injustice to pragmatism as a philosophical frame for mixed methods? Hall (2013) offers a more nuanced version of the pragmatic paradigm based on Dewey's work and opens up possibilities for mixed methods evaluators. She supports the use of Deweyan pragmatism because it emphasizes reflection, ethics, and social justice and using systematic inquiry in the service of addressing societal problems by taking intelligent action. In order to take intelligent action, evaluators need to interact with the communities with which they work and be open to critical reflection about the meanings that are generated in terms of identification of problems and potential solutions. Solutions are not viewed as stagnant entities; rather, the evaluator has a responsibility to continually collect data on the consequences of the solutions and to interact with community members in an ongoing way to insure that adaptations are made to enhance success. Thus collection of evidence needs to be ongoing, responsive, and multifaceted. This provides the rationale for the use of both quantitative and qualitative methods in pragmatically rooted evaluations. Dewey

emphasizes the importance of the consequences of action on the lives of people in a democratic sense (i.e., programs should enhance the lives of all stakeholders, both the privileged and members of marginalized communities).

THE PRAGMATIC PARADIGM IN THE REAL WORLD: EXAMPLES

Robinson et al. (2011) provide an example of a mixed methods study that aligns with the assumptions of the pragmatic paradigm. The study was designed to evaluate the needs and experiences of family members who provided care for their relatives who had dementia. The evaluators justified their choice of mixed methods in this way:

> We judged our objective measures of dementia care recipients and caregivers could be fully meaningful only if considered in the qualitative context of the family carers' lives. This exemplifies why a mixed methods approach is fitting to dementia research: complex research problems warrant a complex research approach. Dementia is a profoundly complicated condition and mixed methods allow for a diverse range of means by which to address the problem. (p. 311)

They specifically mention that they chose the pragmatic paradigm because, according to Morgan (2007), this provides a basis for using quantitative and qualitative methods without needing to give attention to metaphysical concerns such as ontology and epistemology. They also describe the pragmatic paradigm as allowing them to move back and forth between the deductive, quantitative aspects and the inductive, qualitative aspects of their study.

A second example of the pragmatic paradigm is the multilevel multiple methods evaluation of a microloan program managed by a Canadian credit union and primarily targeting unemployed individuals interested in either establishing or expanding their small businesses (Jackson & Tarsilla, 2012, Tarsilla, 2010). Several methods were used to address questions on both the effectiveness of the program (e.g., To what extent did the targeted borrowers strengthen their business as a result of their participation in the program? To what extent did the distributed microloans contribute to the well-being of the borrowers' households?) and implementation processes (e.g., What aspects of the bank–borrower relationship could be strengthened in the near future? What other products would prove to be useful to the borrowers? How could the provincial government assist similar initiatives in the future?). Data collection took place at three different levels: (a) micro level, (the microloan borrowers and their households); (b) meso level (credit union staff); and (c) macro level (provincial and federal government staff). Data collection methods included the following:

- Key-informant interviews with staff from the credit union distributing the microloans and Carleton University faculty members with expertise in community economic development and social return on investment.
- Review of documents on micro-finance and community economic development in Canada and around the world (including audits and annual reports conducted in the past).
- Semistructured questionnaire and focus groups: used to develop a semistructured questionnaire with questions on key outcome indicators (employment, credit status, welfare assistance, etc.).
- Online, semistructured survey consisting of both closed-ended and open-ended questions.
- A second virtual discussion group to validate some of the preliminary findings.
- Case studies: a total of 10 (7 borrowers who had paid back their loan and 3 who had defaulted).
- Expanded value added statement calculations (Mook, Quarter, & Richmond, 2007): to quantify the "hidden" value of nonmonetary contributions from the program (e.g., the provision of free financial literacy sessions and earned articles in the local media).

A third example of this paradigm is the evaluation of children's socialization and movement patterns in the center of an urban center in Denmark. As part of this evaluation, the team combined ethnographic fieldwork with global positioning system technology and used an interactive questionnaire that children completed via mobile phone (Christensen, Mikkelsen, Sick Nielsen, & Harder, 2011). The innovative methodology adopted for this specific evaluative effort highlighted children's subjective experiences with systematic observations, mapping, and survey data. As the evaluation team stated,

> We were brought together by an almost coincidental recognition: two researchers, from transportation and mobility studies, experienced the need for qualitative social science input to understand the subjective and contextual basis for people's

movements, and two anthropologists needed to understand the broader patterning of children's everyday mobility. In this study, therefore, the value of a pragmatic approach that accentuates the flexibility of methods and techniques, and interdisciplinary collaboration, led to the development of an integrated research design unifying our efforts in a holistic approach to understand the everyday mobility patterns of children. (p. 230)

The last example of the pragmatic paradigm is the impact evaluation of integrated community deliberative processes conducted by the National Democratic Institute (in press). The use of survey data collection instruments aimed at gauging changes in local government officials' opinion, knowledge, and attitudes about governance mechanisms was combined with the use of more in-depth interviews with random samples of community members. Qualitative methods were used within the scope of this rigorous impact evaluation in order to assess any unexpected impact and/or identify environmental factors hindering the project effectiveness. The results were quite interesting: while the survey responses suggested that the program was attaining the expected objectives, the qualitative interviews and focus groups highlighted that government officials' corruption and the unjustified land seizure occurring within communities severely hampered the success of the project and significantly questioned the democratic features of the deliberative processes implemented as part of the project.

The preceding examples illustrate the assumptions of the pragmatic paradigm and the Use branch of evaluation in that the primary goal of the studies is to enhance the use of the study findings by the targeted intended users. While some of the studies engaged with participants at the community level, most of the emphasis was on use by those in power. The final paradigm and branch of evaluation, the transformative paradigm and Social Justice branch, focuses on use to enhance the lives of the most marginalized members of society.

Transformative Paradigm and the Social Justice Branch of Evaluation

The transformative paradigm (Mertens, 2009; Mertens & Wilson, 2012) philosophical assumptions emanate from an ethical stance that emphasizes the pursuit of social justice and the furtherance of human rights.[8] The evaluator derives implications for the nature of reality, knowledge, and systematic inquiry that are commensurate with this primary ethical assumption. Hence the nature of reality is looked upon as being multifaceted and reflective of different power positionalities in society. A summary of the transformative philosophical assumptions is presented in Table 24.5.

The transformative axiological assumption prioritizes the values of equal human rights and social justice for all and leads evaluators to ask such questions as: If I start my evaluation with the goal of enhancing human rights and furthering social justice, what does this mean about how I view reality, knowledge, and systematic inquiry? How should this stance influence my philosophical assumptions and my practice as an evaluator? One immediate concern that arises from this primary ethical stance is the need to understand the culture of the community with all its complexity, including issues of power differentials associated with different social, cultural, and economic positionalities. Other issues include the importance of seeing the strengths within the communities and arranging conditions so members of teams are appreciated for the strengths they bring to the study. In addition, evaluators need to design their studies in ways that allow for reciprocity. What do the members of the community get out of the evaluation?

The transformative axiological assumption leads to consideration of the ontological and epistemological assumptions associated with this paradigm. The evaluator needs to engage in data collection in culturally respectful ways that allow for multiple versions of reality to emerge (ontology) and that build relationships of trust (epistemology). Thus mixed methods are not a requirement for doing transformative evaluations; however, they generally provide the opportunity to understand

Table 24.5 Transformative Paradigm Assumptions

Assumptions	Beliefs
Axiology	Cultural respect; promote social justice and human rights; address inequities; reciprocity
Ontology	Multifaceted; consequences of privilege
Epistemology	Interactive; trust; standpoint
Methodology	Transformative, dialogic, emancipatory, mixed methods

Source. Adapted from Mertens and Wilson, 2012.

communities in their full complexity better than monomethods do.

In the transformative paradigm, reality is viewed as being constructed on the basis of different social and cultural positions, such as those related to gender, race, ethnicity, poverty, disability, deafness, religion, age, indigeneity, immigration status, and sexual identity. The evaluator has a responsibility to reveal the different versions of reality, exposing their source and the consequences of privileging one version of reality over another. Different versions of reality emerge from different positions in accord with the earned and unearned privileges associated with occupying different positions within the aforementioned dimensions of diversity. For example, hearing people might have a version of reality that holds that being hearing is better than being deaf. This version of reality contrasts with a deaf version of reality that holds that being deaf means one is a member of a culturally linguistic minority group. If the hearing version of reality is given privilege, this can result in denial of rights for the deaf people in terms of their use of a visual language, such as American Sign Language or British Sign Language. This is exactly what happened in the 1800s at the International Congress on the Education of the Deaf when hearing people decided that an oral approach to communication that requires lip reading and speech was the best method to educate deaf people. The consequence of accepting the hearing version of reality is that, for over a century,[9] deaf people around the world were denied access to a visual language in their education. Is it any wonder that deaf students graduating from high school in the United States read at a sixth-grade level?

Evaluators need to be cognizant of the versions of reality that are associated with unearned privileges within the communities in which they work, and they need to make visible those versions of reality that sustain an oppressive status quo and those that enhance the possibility of furthering human rights. Mixed methods provide a mechanism for revealing different versions of reality, their sources, and the consequences of privileging one version of reality over another. For example, evaluation of court access for deaf and hard-of-hearing people in the United States used qualitative data collection in the form of focus groups with deaf people to reveal the range of different experiences they had with the courts (Mertens, 2009). Their experiences were influenced by the degree of hearing loss (e.g., hard of hearing or deaf), their language use (e.g., American Sign Language, Mexican Sign Language, spoken English), and their ability to benefit from supportive technologies (e.g., hearing aids, cochlear implants, real time captioning). This diversity also needed to be reflected in the training for court personnel and in the quantitative evaluation based on the courts' implementation of plans to enhance accessibility.

Epistemologically, transformative evaluators are aware of the power relations in the communities in which they work, and they are aware of the need to be in a constant state of learning about how to interact in culturally appropriate ways. The nature of knowledge within the transformative paradigm is inclusive of different ways of knowing that are inherent in different stakeholder groups. For example, Indigenous ways of knowing have been explored by Chilisa (2012), Cram (2009), and others in this volume (see Cram and Mertens). This can involve knowledge of a history of oppression, broken treaties, stealing land, and colonialism that might not seem relevant to a non-Indigenous evaluator in the present time. Yet this is knowledge that is carried by members of Indigenous communities that might overshadow the issues that the program developers and evaluators have in mind. Mixed methods in terms of engaging in appropriate cultural rituals or practices may be as important to obtaining good data as is the use of linguistically appropriate data collection instruments.

Methodologically, a cyclical design is recommended for systematic inquiry in order to provide opportunities for understanding the cultural complexity of the community, designing mechanisms for working together, gathering knowledge that already exists, and designing data collection and interventions that are viewed as legitimate and hopeful by members of the community. This can mean beginning with qualitative inquiry in the form of dialogue between and among the stakeholder groups. It can also mean collection of demographic and incidence data that are disaggregated by the relevant dimensions of diversity (e.g., gender, tribal affiliation, age, language). Such qualitative and quantitative data need to be brought to the community to provide guidance on interpretation and to design next steps forward.

THE TRANSFORMATIVE PARADIGM IN THE REAL WORLD: EXAMPLES

Bledsoe (2010) conducted a transformative mixed methods study of an obesity reduction program that was situated in a city in which there was high poverty and many members of ethnic and racial minority groups, as well as immigrants from Africa and Eastern Europe. When Bledsoe joined the development team, they told her that they knew the reason for the obesity in the school: it was poor self-esteem. So they designed a program to raise the students' self-esteem. Bledsoe asked if they had data to support this assumption, but they did not. As a first step, she proceeded to use quantitative and qualitative methods to ascertain the demographic characteristics of the students and their perspectives about obesity. The findings revealed that the students felt good about being big, but they wanted to avoid health problems associated with being obese such as heart problems or diabetes. Thus a different type of program was needed than that which was first planned. Figure 24.1 illustrates the

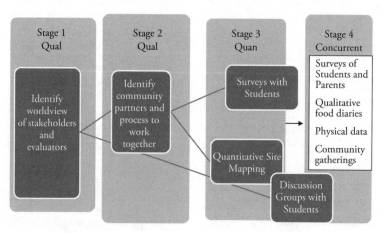

Fig. 24.1 Sample obesity reduction transformative MME.
Adapted from Bledsoe (2010).

full transformative cyclical mixed methods design used. It shows that the evaluators emphasized the importance of understanding the culture of the community and the forces within the community that prevented healthy living choices. The design is cyclical in that information from each stage of the project was used to inform the next stage of the project. For example, once there was an understanding that certain barriers were challenging the students' abilities to lose weight, quantitative site mapping was used to show the lack of access to fresh fruits and vegetables and safe places to exercise. The interventions included things like negotiating with neighborhood food vendors to increase selections of healthy foods, youth wearing pedometers during a dance to count the number of steps taken, and food festivals that demonstrated how to cook traditional foods in a healthier manner.

Another example of transformative MME is the work conducted by Chilisa (2005, 2012) in Botswana. Selected to assess the impact of an intervention designed to reduce the spread of HIV/AIDS in Africa, she started questioning the project design and, through her data collection and analysis, was able to demonstrate the variety of misunderstanding about the culture and language of Botswana. As attested by both the survey and in-depth interviews with youth, Chilisa was able to show that power dynamics between men and women were such that a woman would never have been able to tell a man to use a condom. Likewise, she was able to emphasize that the use of health campaign messages in English was not effective, as those at higher risk of HIV transmission spoke only local languages.

Some additional interesting examples of transformative MME are provided by the growing body of equity-focused evaluations funded by several United Nations agencies over the past few years. In the case of the UNICEF long-term evaluation of the Tostan program (aimed to reduce female circumcision in villages in Senegal), for instance, mixed methods proved to be critical to determine the overall impact of the intervention. In particular, the use of a quantitative district household survey was combined with observations, focus groups and in-depth interviews aimed at assessing the program's implementation process, the dynamics surrounding the villages' commitment to abandon the practice of circumcision, and the perception of the program's impact among the targeted women.

A similar example is the real-time evaluation of the humanitarian response to Pakistan's 2009 displacement crisis (Bamberger & Segone, 2012). Thanks to the use of mixed methods, the findings of this evaluation pointed to the fact that the overall humanitarian response in Pakistan had been planned in consultation only with village elders and male household heads (accounting for the majority of survey respondents and focus group participants) and that no attention had been devoted to the special needs of women and children in the poorest and most vulnerable families. The evaluation of the UNICEF Education Program in Timor-L'Este 2003–2009 is also a good illustration of the transformative use of mixed methods, and it confirmed how the combination of quantitative and qualitative methods, besides serving relevant equity purposes, is key to making up for the limited in-country access to quantitative data. A final transformative example is also the evaluation of the impact of social assistance on reducing child poverty and child social exclusion in Albania. In the course of this evaluation, the mining of national data set allowed the identification of different typologies of vulnerable groups that were then interviewed, thus providing policymakers with actionable recommendations on how to enhance national social safety net mechanisms.

Combining Paradigms: Dialectical Pluralism

A dialectical approach places assumptions, practices, understandings, standpoints, and findings from one or more studies emanating from different paradigmatic positions in conversation with each other (Greene & Hall, 2010; Johnson, 2011). Greene (2012) explains the complex challenges that evaluators encounter in terms of context, values, and the role of inquiry in society. She notes that the different methodological traditions in the evaluation community address these challenges differently, and that, in turn, shapes

> the knowledge generated from a study and the warrants for that knowledge. . . [She] presents a mixed methodological response to these challenges and a primary argument that a mixed methods approach offers dialogic opportunities to generate better understanding of important social phenomena precisely because it legitimizes and respects multiple responses to these critical issues and invites dialogue among them. (p. 755)

DP is a philosophical stance that allows evaluators to engage in MME while experiencing the tensions created when different paradigmatic stances are put in conversation with each other. Johnson and Stefurak (2013) describe DP as encompassing a pluralistic ontology and reliance on a dialectical, dialogical, and hermeneutical process where stakeholders continually interact with differences (e.g., in philosophy, paradigm, culture, methodology, method). Dialectical methods engage parties holding seemingly disparate philosophical and knowledge positions in meaningful dialogue using multiple social psychological, dialogical, and negotiation strategies. They identify the following characteristics of DP: inclusive/heterogeneous team construction, equal power, joint construction of judgment criteria/standards, and commitment to deliberative and transformative democracy. Dialectic pluralism can include observation, experience, experiment, and so on, with the expectation that multiple empirical data will *not* typically converge on a simple conclusion and will often provide divergent results that bring fuller understandings of phenomena. Most human phenomena are complex; hence, there are many perspectives, viewpoints, and smaller truths that can be stated about almost any phenomenon studied.

DIALECTICAL PLURALISM PARADIGM IN THE REAL WORLD: EXAMPLES

An illustrative example of a DP mixed method study is the evaluation of the US Department of Agriculture Personnel Management Demonstration Project (Mark, Fekv, & Button, 1997). The purpose of this evaluation was to test the effectiveness of a new personnel management and human resources strategy aimed at improving the recruitment and selection processes for hiring federal employees (e.g., decentralization and simplification of the administrative tasks and responsibilities associated with the hiring procedures in two of the department's agencies) within the agency. Primarily relying on quantitative data (e.g., review of information about personnel actions and applicants and hired individuals for each vacancy), the evaluation made extensive use of qualitative methods (a theory of change was also developed before the start of the evaluation, based on semistructured interviews and document reviews and a total of 96 follow-up visits at 45 sites). Several features of DP were identified in association with this evaluation. First, the divergence of findings between the survey responses (according to them, managers appreciated the added value of the new hiring system) and in-person interviews (according to them, managers were not satisfied with the new system). Such

plurality of discordant voices among the end users of the new human resources strategy eventually led to the revision of the instrument and the replacement of the term *hiring system* (leading to confusion and misunderstanding) with a more precise label. Second, the interview system in place at the US Department of Agriculture allowed the evaluators to qualify the extent to which the relationship between the applicant and the human resources person influenced the level of employees' satisfaction with the overall hiring experience (qualitative data analysis confirmed the relevance of such relationship whereas the quantitative analysis had erroneously led them to think that this was an "error variance").

A second DP mixed methods example is the evaluation of masculinity ideology conducted among a variety of ethnic groups in South Africa (Luyt, 2011). As part of this evaluation, a quantitative instrument (the MANI-II, a multidimensional measure of masculinity ideology) developed in 2001 was revised based on qualitative findings that recognized basic conceptual differences between cultural groups in understanding masculinity. Based on a thematic analysis of focus group transcripts, the qualitative findings of this evaluation pointed to the lack of equivalence in cross-cultural content across the three versions of the tool (English, Afrikaans, and Xhosa). Simultaneously, a factor analysis of the instrument was conducted to assess the cultural construct validity of the instrument. At the end of this quantitative data collection phase, a large number of responses was analyzed (434 Afrikaans, 890 English, and 273 Xhosa) and the coefficient of congruence (Tucker's phi) was calculated. As the authors put it:

> "small-group descriptive" qualitative data and "large-group normative" quantitative data facilitated thorough exploration into varied participant perspectives within and between cultural groups [. . .] Quantitative data are considered before qualitative data. Yet qualitative data are not considered merely supplementary in that they provide unique as well as supplementary information concerning possible revision. This lends some support for the notion that equal status designs are possible in terms of the sum of their individual contributions. (Edmeades et al., 2010, p. 190)

In summary, DP typically relies on inclusion of methods that are likely to provide different understandings and perspectives of the evaluand. Purposive construction of a participatory multiple-divergent stakeholder team (including those with the least power) is a key strategy to include difference of voices in the evaluation.

Future Issues in Mixed Methods Evaluation and Conclusions

Perhaps because evaluation is inherently situated "out in the world," practitioners embraced the use of mixed methods before philosophical or theoretical frameworks were developed that explicitly addressed the meaning of mixing methods at various levels. Rather than just default mixed methods, evaluators have a rich array of options from the philosophical level to the level of practice to encourage the critical thinking that is necessary in these complex studies. Differences in opinions about the appropriate methodologies and credibility of evidence can be traced back to the philosophical assumptions held by evaluators (or their clients), as has been demonstrated in this chapter. However, in order for that to happen, a serious introspection—a sort of "de-disciplining" process (Richardson, 2006) will first need to take place among those many evaluators who continue to strive for "objectivity" in their profession and, as such, dismiss any remote association between their own design or methodological choices and any specific, value-based understanding of both the evaluand and the reality that surrounds it.

Many questions emerge as we explore the terrain of mixed methods in evaluation from various perspectives. Evaluators with different philosophical frameworks will most likely respond to the challenges in the use of mixed methods differently. For example, evaluators need to address the timing of the mixing methods, the integration of data analysis, and dealing with divergent findings. Also, critical reflection is needed to decide when the use of mixed methods is the better strategy as opposed to the use of multiple methods belonging to only one of the two spheres (quantitative or qualitative).

Given the existing paradox between the infinite opportunities for combining methods and the rather uninventive mix of methods in the current evaluation practice, more MME capacity development programs are needed. Geared toward both those who commission and those who conduct evaluations, such learning events could take the form of either online trainings catering to virtual communities of practice (e.g., American Evaluation Association and EvalPartners webinars, Evaluation Capacity Development Group list-serve, Mymande), research methodologies and evaluation graduate courses (Frels, Onwuegbuzie, Leech, & Collins, 2012) or professional international workshops (International Program in Development Evaluation Training and International Development Evaluation Association workshops).

Building on the radical distinction from MMR and the old paradigm consisting in the often unquestioned combination of data collection methods, practitioners conducting MME will need to broaden the variety of the conceptual frameworks underlying their endeavors, and, by fully embracing the political and systemic functionality of MME, they will need to make epistemological frameworks and their values more explicit in the methodology sections of their evaluation reports.

In conclusion, the popularity of MME increasing and more debates on the why's and how's of MME should take place among evaluation practitioners working in a variety of sectors. Given the dynamic nature of the scholarship, the pervasive involvement of stakeholders, and the rapid developments in mixed methods in recent history in the evaluation field, we expect that evaluators will continue to contribute to the advancement of understandings at multiple levels in the mixed methods community. However, contrary to what happened with mixed methods in research settings, one will need to resist the temptation of developing an excessive number of new MME typologies and theoretical constructs centered around this topic. Evaluators work in a complex reality with a need for responsiveness to political and other contextual variables. Mixed methods in evaluation need to reflect this complexity, the realities the communities in which they work, diversity, and contextual variations in order to provide effective results that can be used to improve decision making and promote the desired social and individual changes.

Suggested Websites

www.eval.org
The American Evaluation Association website contains a list of evaluation organizations across the world and a library of resources for evaluators.

www.interaction.org
Alliance of US-based international nongovernmental organizations who focus on disaster relief and sustainable development programs.

www.ioce.net/
An international partnership of regional and national evaluation organizations that supports capacity development across the globe.

www.mymande.org/

An interactive platform to share knowledge on country-led monitoring and evaluation (M&E) systems and learning resources worldwide

Discussion Questions

1. Which of the paradigms discussed in this chapter resonates with you the most? What reasons can you give for your choice?

2. If applicable, where would your firm and your clients be positioned in relation to the evaluation paradigms, branches, and MM approaches?

3. To what extent do you believe default mixed methods will dominate the discourse within the evaluation community?

4. Is there any trend in MM evaluation that you foresee emerging in the near future and that is not yet adequately captured by any of the paradigms presented in this chapter? Please qualify your response by drawing on your direct evaluation experience and/or your readings.

Notes

1. The use of systematic reviews together with narrative reviews advocated by a number of theorists (Pettigrew & Roberts, 2006) is one of the most illustrative examples of mixed methods in European evaluation theory and practice.

2. One evaluation approach that seems to be well suited to overcome this decade-long tension is realist evaluation. By predicating the possibility to uncover the hidden mechanisms that influence the processes underlying processes (the black box) and assuming the existence of meso-regularities (middle-range theories) in the world's phenomena, the authors that ascribe to such approaches propose an alternative to both the positivist and constructivist movements in evaluation.

3. Howard White was the executive director of the International Initiative on Impact Evaluation (3ie), a special program providing funding and capacity development for the conduct of impact evaluations in conjunction with qualitative studies and systematic reviews of international development policies, projects, and programs. His article titled "Will We Ever Learn?" published by the Center of Global Development in 2007 emphasized the relevance of impact evaluation and stressed the ancillary nature of qualitative methods to address questions on effectiveness and impact of international development interventions.

4. *GoBifo* means "move forward" in the Krio language.

5. The project provided block grants to communities to use toward building local public goods like schools, latrines, and grain-drying floors and/or sponsoring skills training and income-generating activities.

6. Unlike past impact evaluation efforts geared toward the measurement of gender inequalities within the scope of any given development intervention, this new generation of impact evaluation is aimed to identify, develop, and test innovative policy solutions to alleviate underlying gender constraints.

7. In the past, it was through qualitative methods (e.g., case studies and in-depth unstructured interviews) that a series of effective strategies addressing gender issues were identified: (a) the provision of extension for women on the crops that they are currently growing, (b) the delivery of extension closer to women's home (in order to deal with their mobility and time constraints), (c) the combination of extension with subsidies for inputs (given the numerous credit constraints reported during the in-depth interviews), and (d) the training of influential women in how to grow higher value crops that are traditionally male dominated without altering the existing extension programs.

8. Sweetman, Badjee, and Creswell (2010) conducted a literature review on mixed methods studies conducted with a transformative lens. They identified a large number (272) of mixed methods studies, and the most popular form of methods integration was the sequential form, in which one data set extended or added to the other data set.

9. The International Congress on the Education of the Deaf finally apologized for this oppressive policy at their meeting in 2010.

References

Alkin, M. C. (Ed.). (2004). *Evaluation roots: Tracing theorists' views and influences*. Thousand Oaks, CA: Sage.

Alkin, M. C. (Ed.). (2013). *Evaluation roots* (2nd ed.). Thousand Oaks, CA: Sage.

Bamberger, M. (2012). *Introduction to mixed methods in impact evaluation*. Interaction Impact Evaluation Notes No. 3. Retrieved from http://www.interaction.org/document/guidance-note-3-introduction-mixed-methods-impact-evaluation

Bamberger, M., & Segone, M. (2012). *How to design and manage equity-focused evaluations*. New York, NY: UNICEF.

Bazeley, P., & Kemp, L. (2012). Mosaics, triangles, and DNA: Metaphors for integrated analysis in mixed methods research. *Journal of Mixed Methods Research, 6*, 55–72.

Bell, V. (2006). The Cochrane qualitative and implementation methods group. Retrieved from http://cqim.cochrane.org/

Bledsoe, K. (2010, November). *A transformative mixed methods evaluation of an obesity reduction program*. Paper presented at the annual meeting of the American Evaluation Association, Anaheim, CA.

Brady, H. E. (2002, July). *Models of causal inference: Going beyond the Neyman-Rubin-Holland theory*. Paper presented at the annual meeting of the Political Methodology Group, University of Washington, Seattle. Retrieved from http://www.polmeth.wustl.edu/media/Paper/brady02.pdf

Briggs, J. (2006). Cochrane qualitative research methods group. The Cochrane Collaboration. Available from http://www.joannabriggs.org

Casey, K., Glennerster, R., & Miguel, E. (2011). *The GoBifo Project evaluation report: Assessing the impacts of community driven development in Sierra Leone*. New York, NY: World Bank.

Chilisa, B. (2005). Education research within postcolonial Africa: A critique of HIV/AIDS research in Botswana. *International Journal of Qualitative Studies in Education, 18*, 659–684.

Chilisa, B. (2012). *Indigenous research methodologies*. Thousand Oaks, CA: Sage.

Christensen, C., Mikkelsen, M. R., Sick Nielsen, T. A., & Harder, H. (2011). Children, mobility, and space: Using GPS and mobile phone technologies in ethnographic research. *Journal of Mixed Methods Research, 5*, 227–246. doi:10.1177/1558689811406121

Cram, F. (2009). Maintaining Indigenous voices. In D. M. Mertens & P. E. Ginsberg (Eds.), *The handbook of social research ethics* (pp. 308–322). Thousand Oaks, CA: Sage.

Creswell, J. W., Klassen, A. C., Plano Clark, V. L., & Clegg Smith, K. (2011). *Best practices for mixed methods research in the health sciences*. Bethesda, MD: National Institutes of Health. http://obssr.od.nih.gov/mixed_methods_research/pdf/Best_Practices_for_Mixed_Methods_Research.pdf

Creswell, J.W. & Plano Clark, V. L. (2007). Designing and conducting mixed methods research. Thousand Oaks, CA: Sage.

Davidson, E. J. (2006). Book review: *Evaluation roots: Tracing theorists' views and influences. American Journal of Evaluation, 2,* 273–276.

Davidson, E. J. (2010). "Process values" and "deep values" in evaluation. *Journal of Multidisciplinary Evaluation, 6*(13), 206–208.

Denzin, N. K. (1989). *The research act: A theoretical introduction to sociological methods* (3rd ed.). Englewood Cliffs, NJ: Prentice Hall.

Denzin, N. K. (2010). Moments, mixed methods, and paradigm dialogs. *Qualitative Inquiry, 16*(6), 419–427. doi:10.1177/1077800410364608

Denzin, N. (2012). Triangulation 2.0. *Journal of Mixed Methods Research, 6*(2), 80–88.

Edmeades, J., Nyblade, L., Malhotra, A., MacQuarrie, K., Parasuraman, S., & Walia, S. (2010). Methodological innovation in studying abortion in developing countries: A "narrative" quantitative survey in Madhya Pradesh, India. *Journal of Mixed Methods Research, 4*(3), 176–198.

Fournier, D. M. (2010). Evaluation. In S. Mathison (Ed.), *Encyclopedia of evaluation* (pp. 139–140). Thousand Oaks, CA: Sage.

Frechtling, J., & Sharp, L. (Eds.). (1997). *User-friendly handbook for mixed method evaluations*. Arlington, VA: National Science Foundation. Retrieved from http://www.nsf.gov/pubs/1997/nsf97153/

Frels, R. K., Onwuegbuzie, A. J., Leech, N. L., & Collins, K. M. T. (2012). Challenges to teaching mixed research courses. *The Journal of Effective Teaching, 12*(2), 23–44.

Garbarino, S., & Holland, J. (2009). *Quantitative and qualitative methods in impact evaluation and measuring results.* (DFID Issue Paper). London, England: Department for International Development. Retrieved from http://www.gsdrc.org/docs/open/EIRS4.pdf

Gertler, P., Martinez, S., Premand, P., Rawlings, L. B., & Vermeersch C. M. J. (2011). *Impact evaluation in practice.* Washington, DC: World Bank.

Greene, J. C. (2005). Synthesis: A reprise on mixing methods. In T. S. Weisner (Ed.), *Discovering successful pathways in children's development: Mixed methods in the study of childhood and family life* (pp. 405–420). Chicago, IL: University of Chicago Press.

Greene, J. (2012). Engaging critical issues in social inquiry by mixing methods. *American Behavioral Scientist, 56*(6), 755–773.

Greene, J. C., & Caracelli, V. J. (Eds.). (1997). Advances in mixed-methods evaluation: The challenges and benefits of integrating diverse paradigms. *New Directions in Evaluation, 74.* San Francisco, CA: Jossey-Bass.

Greene, J. C., Caracelli, V. J., & Graham, W. F. (1989). Toward a conceptual framework for mixed-method evaluation design. *Education Evaluation and Policy Analysis, 11*(3), 255–274.

Guba, E., & Lincoln, Y. S. (1989). *Fourth generation evaluation.* Newbury Park, CA: Sage.

Hall, J. (2009). Introduction to mixed methods research for nursing and the health sciences. In S. Andrew & E. J. Halcomb (Eds.), *Mixed methods research for nursing and the health sciences* (pp. 3–12). Oxford, UK: Blackwell.

Hesse-Biber, S. (2010). Qualitative approaches to mixed methods practice. *Qualitative Inquiry, 16,* 455–468.

Hesse-Biber, S. (2013). Thinking outside the randomized controlled trials experimental box: Strategies for enhancing credibility and social justice. In *New Directions in Evaluation, 138,* 49–60.

Howe, K. R. (2004). A critique of experimentalism. *Qualitative Inquiry, 10,* 42–61.

Jackson, E. T., & Tarsilla, M. (2013). Mixed methods in social accounting: Evaluating the micro-loan program of Alterna Savings Credit. In L. Mook (Ed.), *Accounting for social value* (pp. 117–138). Toronto: University of Toronto Press.

Johnson, R. B. (2011, May). *Dialectical pluralism: A metaparadigm to help us hear and "combine" our valued differences.* Paper presented at the Seventh International Congress of Qualitative Inquiry, University of Illinois, Urbana-Champaign.

Johnson, R. B., & Stefurak, T. (2013). Dialectical pluralism: A process philosophy for understanding, valuing, and "dynamically combining" our differences. *New Directions in Evaluation, 138,* 37–48.

Kemp, L. (2001, May). *The DNA of integrated methods.* Paper presented at the annual conference of the Australian Association for Social Research, Wollongong, New South Wales, Australia.

Luyt, R. (2011). A framework for mixing methods in quantitative measurement development, validation, and revision: A case study. *Journal of Mixed Methods Research 6*(4), 294–316.

Mark, M., Fekv, I., & Button, S. B. (1997). Integrating qualitative methods in a predominantly quantitative evaluation: A case study and some reflections. *New Directions for Evaluation, 74,* 47–60.

Merriam, S. (2009). *Qualitative research.* San Francisco, CA: Jossey-Bass.

Mertens, D. M. (2009). *Transformative research and evaluation.* New York, NY: Guilford Press.

Mertens, D. M. (2015). *Research and evaluation in education and psychology: Integrating diversity with quantitative, qualitative, and mixed methods* (4th ed.). Thousand Oaks, CA: Sage.

Mertens, D. M., & Hesse-Biber, S. (2013). Mixed methods and credibility of evidence in evaluation. *New Directions in Evaluation, 138,* 5–14.

Mertens, D. M., & Wilson, A. T. (2013). *Program evaluation theory and practice: A comprehensive guide.* New York, NY: Guilford Press.

McGee, R. (2003). Qualitative and quantitative poverty appraisal workshop: Some reflections and responses. In R. Kanbur (Ed.), *Q-squared: Qualitative and quantitative methods of poverty appraisal* (pp. 132–140). Delhi, India: Permanent Black.

Mook, L., Quarter, J., & Richmond, B. J. (2007). *What counts: Social accounting for non-profits and cooperatives* (2nd ed.). London, England: Sigel Press.

Morgan, D. L. (2007). Pardigms lost and pragmatism regained. *Journal of Mixed Methods Research, 1*(1), 48–76.

Oakley, A. (2005a). Paradigm wars: Some thoughts on a personal and public trajectory. In A. Oakley, *The Ann Oakley reader* (pp. 245–250). Cambridge, UK: Polity.

Oakley, A. (2005b). Who's afraid of the randomized controlled trial? Some dilemmas of the scientific method and good research practice. In A. Oakley, *The Ann Oakley reader* (pp. 233–244). Cambridge, UK: Polity.

Parlett, M., & Hamilton, D. (1977). Evaluation as illumination: A new approach to the study of innovatory programs. In D. Hamilton, D. Jenkins, C. King, B. MacDonald, & M. Parlett (Eds.), *Beyond the numbers game: A reader in educational evaluation* (pp. 6–22). London, England: Macmillan.

Patton, M. Q. (2008). *Utilization-focused evaluation* (4th ed.). Thousand Oaks, CA: Sage.

Pawson, R. (2007). *Causality for beginners.* Paper presented at the NCRM Research Methods Festival 2008. University of Leeds. Retrieved from http://eprints.ncrm.ac.uk/245/

Pettigrew, M., & Roberts, H. (2006). *Systematic reviews in the social sciences.* Oxford, UK: Blackwell.

Richardson, V. (2006). Stewards of a field, stewards of an enterprise: The doctorate in education. In C. M. Golde & G. E. Walker (Eds.), *Envisioning the future of doctoral education: Preparing stewards of the discipline.* San Francisco, CA: Jossey-Bass.

Robinson, A. L., Emden, C. G., Croft, T. D., Vosper, G. C., Elder, J. A., Siirling, C. & Vickers, J. C. (2011). Mixed methods data collection in dementia research: A "progressive engagement" approach. *Journal of Mixed Methods Research, 5*(4), 330–344.

Scriven, M. (1994). The fine line between evaluation and explanation. *Evaluation Practice, 15*(1), 75–77.

Shadish, W. (1998). Evaluation theory is who we are. *American Journal of Evaluation, 19,* 1–19.

Stame, N. (2013). A European evaluation theory tree. In M. Alkin (Ed.), *Evaluation roots* (2nd ed.) (pp. 355–370). Thousand Oaks, CA: Sage.

Stern, E., Stame, N., Mayne, J., Forss, K., Davies, R., & Befani, B. (2012). *Broadening the range of designs and methods for impact evaluations* (DFID Working Paper 38). London, England: Department for International Development.

Sweetman, D., Badjee, M., & Creswell, J. W. (2010). Use of the transformative framework in mixed methods studies. *Qualitative Inquiry, 16*(6), 441–454. doi:10.1177/1077800410364610

Tarsilla, M. (2010). *Social impact evaluation of the Alterna Savings Community micro-loan program.* Ottawa, ON: Carleton Centre for Community Innovation, Carleton University.

Teddlie, C., & Tashakkori, A. (2003). Major issues and controversies in the use of mixed methods in the social and behavioral sciences. In A. Tashakkori & C. Teddlie (Eds.), *Handbook of mixed methods in social & behavioral research* (pp. 3–50). Thousand Oaks, CA: Sage.

Wehipeihana, N., Davidson, E. J., McKegg, K., & Shanker, V. (2010). What does it take to do evaluation in communities and cultural contexts other than our own? *Journal of Multidisciplinary Evaluation, 16*(3), 182–192.

White, H. (2013). The use of mixed methods in randomized controlled trials. *New Directions in Evaluation, 138,* 61–74.

Yin, R. K. (2003). *Case study research: design and methods* (3rd ed.). Thousand Oaks, CA: Sage.

Applying Multimethod and Mixed Methods to Prevention Research in Global Health

Stevan Weine

Abstract

Multimethod and mixed methods are well suited to prevention research in global health; however, their application has not yet been adequately discussed or demonstrated. This chapter illustrates key opportunities and challenges through focusing on using multimethod and mixed methods for investigating prevention involving migration. It summarizes one large study focused on labor migrants and HIV/AIDS risk and protection to illustrate how innovative strategies combining different forms of knowledge in multimethod and mixed methods can generate more robust and useful findings. Multimethod and mixed methods in prevention research in global health should strategically utilize multiple study elements (investigators, theories, methods, and data) that are most responsive to the central research problems and questions, through existing and new synergies, so as to most appropriately address the key preventive intervention characteristics and contribute to the overall completeness of the knowledge.

Key Words: multimethods, mixed methods, prevention, migrants, HIV, global health

Multimethod and mixed methods have entered the scientific mainstream in public health research, including prevention science (Zhang & Watanbe-Galloway, 2013) and global health research (Davis & Baulch, 2011). This chapter aims to further advance the applicability of multimethod and mixed methods to prevention research in global health.

Challenges Concerning the Aims of Multimethod and Mixed Methods Research

What is multimethod and mixed methods research (MMMR)? Mixed methods research is "research in which a researcher or team of researchers combines elements of qualitative and quantitative research approaches (e.g., use of qualitative and quantitative viewpoints, data collection, analysis, inference techniques) for the purposes of breadth and depth of understanding and corroboration" (Johnson, Onwuegbuzie, & Turner, 2007, p. 123).

Multimethod research collects several types of qualitative or quantitative data in one study (Creswell & Plano Clark, 2007). This chapter is concerned with both multimethod and mixed methods.

The aspiring multimethod and mixed methods researcher can find a myriad of journals (e.g. the *Journal of Mixed Methods Research*), textbooks (e.g., Creswell & Plano Clark, 2007; Hesse-Biber, 2010; Morse & Niehas, 2009; Padgett, 2012; Tashakkori & Teddlie, 2003), and professional meetings (e.g. International Congress of Qualitative Inquiry and the Mixed Methods International Research Association) to inform designing and conducting MMMR.

In 2011, mixed methods were formalized into "Best Practices for Mixed Methods Research in the Health Sciences" (Best Practices; Creswell, Klassen, Plano Clark, & Clegg Smith, 2011) sponsored by the Office of Behavioral and Social Sciences Research of the US National Institutes of Health. The Best Practices provide an overview of the

"Nature and Design of Mixed Methods Research" and "Teamwork, Infrastructure, Resources, and Training for Mixed Methods Research." This document is currently used to inform developing and reviewing mixed methods grant applicants in the health sciences, which includes research in global health.

Though the existence of these and other finished products could suggest that the majority of key mixed methods questions have been answered and academic debates laid to rest, this is not the case (Creswell, 2011). Within and outside the mixed methods scientific community, substantial disputes persist regarding why, when, how, and to what end mixed methods should be used. There are particular concerns about what should drive mixed methods research projects: qualitative or quantitative methods or a third paradigm? methods or methodology? theory, data, or design?

Commonly mentioned critiques of the Best Practices reflect broader concerns about the efforts to formalize and spread mixed methods research methods and include (a) design type is privileged above theory; (b) qualitative methods are demoted to an inferior position; (c) the discovery phase of research, where problems, questions, and hypotheses are formulated, is given short shrift; (d) designs are insufficiently chosen on the basis of research questions and instead are picked from a finite list of design types; and (e) inadequate consideration is given to incorporating new technologies, such as geosampling (Eng et al., 2007; Keating et al., 2003; Steinberg & Steinberg, 2011), that render multimethod and mixed methods decidedly more complex than simply qualitative plus quantitative methods.

The singular appeal of multimethod and mixed methods are their capacity to embrace diverse forms of knowledge and forge a meaningful synergy between them. The *Oxford English Dictionary* defines synergy as, "The interaction or cooperation of two or more organizations, substances, or other agents to produce a combined effect greater than the sum of their separate effects" ("Synergy," 2013). Generating this "combined effect" depends both on what is being combined and how it is being combined. Some additional key challenges involve: Does genuine combination or interaction really happen? If so, how is it actually achieved and represented?

The Best Practices identifies three means by which the combination of data can occur: (a) *merging* data in the texts or images in the research report; (b) *connecting* data by using knowledge learned from analyzing one dataset to inform data collection in the other set; and (c) *embedding* data, whereby a dataset of secondary priority is embedded within a larger, primary design (Creswell et al., 2011).

One additional approach to the issue of synergy in MMMR has been through the concept of triangulation. In the multimethod and mixed methods fields, triangulation has been defined as a deliberate strategy to strengthen the quality of research in MMMR (Denzin, 1978; Patton, 1990). Four main types of triangulation have been described: investigator triangulation, theory triangulation, method triangulation, and data triangulation (Adami, 2005; Denzin, 1970; Thurmond, 2001). *Investigator triangulation* involves using more than one investigator in the research process (Guion, Diehl, & McDonald, 2011). *Theory triangulation* is using multiple theories to examine a phenomenon, and *method triangulation* involves using more than one data collection method (Denzin, 1970; Mathison, 1988; Shih, 1998; Thurmond, 2001). *Data triangulation* uses a variety of sources of information (Oppermann, 2000). Three types of data sources are person, space, and time (Denzin, 1970; Thurmond, 2011). *Person triangulation* is the collection of data from different groups of people (Knafl & Breitmayer, 1991; Polit & Hungler, 1999). *Space triangulation* is the collection of data from multiple sites (Kimchi, Polivka, & Stevenson, 1991; Rothbauer, 2008). Lastly, *time triangulation* is the collection of data at different points in time (Kimchi et al., 1991; Shih, 1998).

Whether drawing on these multiplicities builds knowledge more through convergence or divergence (McCarthy, Holland, & Gillies, 2003; Sands & Roer-Strier, 2006) remains a matter of debate (Bazeley & Kemp, 2012; Johnson & Christensen, 2004). Multiple papers have been published on triangulation and multimethod designs that explain why triangulation should enhance researchers' understanding of their subjects (Mathison, 1988; Risjord, Dunbar, & Moloney, 2002; Thurmond, 2001). However, Breitmayer, Ayres, and Knafl (1993) explained that researchers who have used the term *triangulation* have failed to provide evidence that actually shows how their methods contributed to confirmation or completeness of the data set. Meanwhile, the term *triangulation* appears to have fallen out of favor in the MMMR community (Bazeley & Kemp, 2012), although the focus on combining multiple study elements remains strong. Alternatively, Johnson and Christensen have described a multiple-dimension process approach in which the researchers start by asking, "what combination of data, methods, and many additional dimensions will provide you with the best chance of obtaining accurate, relatively complete, and useful answers to your research questions" (p. 509).

Bazeley and Kemp (2012) conducted an analysis of how different methodologies and methods might interact in integrated studies. They claim that the approach to integration should always be guided by the goals and purpose of the study. However, creativity is encouraged through exploiting many possible forms of integration. They described both complementary strategies (e.g., combining for completion, combining for enhancement, and combining to detail a more significant whole) and generative strategies (e.g., iterative exchange for initiation and development and transformation for initiation through exploration). The authors concluded, "The product of the integration will be something that would not have been available without that integration" (p. 69).

In summary, the emerging field of multimethod and mixed methods is committed to combining and synergy but still faces fundamental challenges of explaining precisely how researchers should combine different forms of knowledge and toward what ends. When brought into contact with the demands of prevention research in global health, multimethod and mixed methods researchers may find that these challenges can become amplified. But researchers can also find new opportunities for building evidence about how combining different elements in multimethod and mixed methods can generate more robust and useful findings.

Prevention Research in Global Health

Like multimethod and mixed methods, global health is still an emerging field that is endeavoring to clarify its core commitments. These are broader than clinical medicine and distinct from public health in a strictly domestic national context. One recent definition of global health is "Collaborative transnational research and action for promoting for all" (Beaglehole & Bonita, 2010). This definition draws attention to the central roles of collaboration, transnationalism, and transdisciplinarity in global health's quest to connect research and action.

Clearly, prevention should play a core role in global health, given its public health commitment to proactively addressing the health needs of at risk populations. Prevention research has been developed in several areas that are recognized as key global health realms, including the prevention of mental disorders, child maltreatment and youth violence, HIV infection, and violent extremism (Auerbach & Coates, 2000; Bhui, Hicks, Lashley, & Jones, 2012; Guterman, 2004; Patel et al., 2007). Research in these areas has led toward the successful development and evaluation of multiple preventive interventions.

Preventive interventions are typically concerned with promoting those family and ecological factors or processes that lower the risk for health, mental health, and behavioral problems (Albee, 1996; World Health Organization, 2004). Stated otherwise, preventive interventions aim to enhance protective resources at population, community, and family levels so as to stop, lessen, or delay possible negative individual mental health and behavioral outcomes, often using multilevel strategies that address family, social, and structural issues (O'Connell, Boat, & Warner, 2009; Schensul & Tricket, 2009). For example, prevention researchers have studied family and school intervention programs and found that effective preventive interventions build on existing protective resources associated with families and communities (Garmezy, 1971; World Health Organization, 2004). Preventive interventions with families in multiple situations have focused on enhancing the following types of protective processes in families and communities: (a) parental support in families and social support for parents; (b) knowledge, awareness, and skills of parents; (c) communication between youth and parents; (d) links between family members and health or mental healthcare organizations; and (e) links between families and schools or social service providers (Weine, 2009). These protective resources within families, schools, communities, and social environments may be harnessed toward prevention of different problems if they can be identified (Barrio, 2000; Tolan, Hanish, McKay, & Dickey, 2002). They are best approached through a culturally specific lens with cross-culturally sensitive methodology (Matsumoto & van de Vijver, 2011).

A 2009 publication by the Institute of Medicine of the National Academies titled *Preventing Mental, Emotional, and Behavioral Disorders Among Young People* focused new attention on the promise and challenges of further scientific progress regarding prevention interventions (O'Connell et al., 2009). It reviewed a large number of preventive interventions that addressed a myriad of health and mental health problems that have been implemented and evaluated in diverse sociocultural contexts, domestically and internationally. Some of the cited studies and discussions focused on populations such as racial and ethnic minorities, which present challenges for developing preventive interventions. However, few studies focused on prevention in global health settings.

With the growth in global health research, more and more prevention studies in diverse global contexts have begun to appear. One example is the NIMH Collaborative HIV/STD Prevention Trial Group (2007a, 2007b), which investigated a community popular opinion leader intervention in five countries (China, India, Peru, Russia, and Zimbabwe; Rice, Wu, Li, Detels, & Rotheram-Borus, 2012; Sivaram et al., 2004). This study included extensive formative epidemiologic and ethnographic research that was used to refine the intervention and the overall study design and to make particular adaptations in each sociocultural context. However, the study results were disappointing in that the community-level intervention diminished behavioral risk by 33%, which was the same as the comparison condition. This could in part reflect shortcomings in adapting the opinion leader approach to specific sociocultural contexts with diverse populations in low-income countries. In highly different national contexts, opinion leaders may have different roles, communication patterns, gender attitudes, and relations with their cohort, and this would likely impact their capacity to change behavior through spreading HIV prevention messages.

A global health prevention study of this size, scope, and complexity demands that careful attention is paid to how the researchers combine different forms of knowledge and toward what ends. Given that their intervention encompassed both genders and five countries, it is fair to speculate whether the researchers should have depended so highly on Rogers' (1962/1995) diffusion of innovation theory and not done more to integrate gender or cultural theory, or whether they should have collected ethnographic data that examined the intervention processes so that they could have better explained why the intervention did not work as well as anticipated.

It has been said that the global health field was born out of facing the global epidemic of HIV/AIDS (Parker, 2002). If so, then the methodological challenges raised by the community popular opinion leader intervention for men and women in five counties are likely a preview of methodological challenges to come in other realms of prevention research in global health.

The Limits of Best Practices for Approaching Prevention Research in Global Health

What if the existing Best Practices were read from the perspective of an aspiring prevention researcher in global health who was focused on one of the aforementioned areas? That researcher would learn some very helpful general points, but what stands out are the limitations of what could be learned that was specific to prevention research in global health. For example, in my opinion, the Best Practices embrace methodological diversity and the broad range of problems facing public health, including disparities, cultural context, and translation; however, they do not engage with any of the previously discussed areas in adequate depth. The Best Practices embrace the need to address real-life contextual understandings, multi-level perspectives, and cultural influences however limit the focus to quantitative and qualitative data and methods. The Best Practices also call for integrating or combining quantitative and qualitative data but limit the discussion to three approaches (merging data, connecting data, and embedding data). Finally, the Best Practices call for having the nature of the research question drive the formation of a mixed methods research team and the selection of specific designs but limit the focus to four designs types (convergent, sequential, embedded, and multiphase).

Clearly, these Best Practices were not developed with a focus on prevention research in global health or any other specific health sciences topic area. If the Best Practices are to be of use to the aspiring prevention researcher in global health, then they must go further. For starters, the Best Practices would have to embrace several additional claims, including developing a research approach that engages, in sufficient depth, the global contextual challenges of low-resource settings, disparities, sociocultural context, community collaboration, and translation/adaptation. The Best Practices would need to envision multiple mixed methods as more than just combining quantitative and qualitative, taking into account multiple theories, investigators, designs, and data. Additionally, the Best Practices would need to expand the repertoire of approaches for combining or integrating different theories, investigators, designs, and data. Finally, they would have to claim to ground the development of research design in the central research problems and questions.

To inform these additional claims, it could help to draw from some of the particular challenges facing preventive intervention programs in global health and how those have or could be addressed through MMMR. This chapter will do so through focusing on the global health challenges of developing preventive interventions with migrants.

The Challenges of Developing Prevention Interventions With Migrants

One out of every 33 people in the world is a migrant (United Nations, 2009). There are an estimated 214 million international migrants worldwide sending around $414 billion in remittances home annually (United Nations Population Fund, 2013). Migrants also include refugees who have been forced to flee their homes, of which there are 15.4 million worldwide (United Nations High Commissioner for Refugees, 2013). Given the high global rates of migration and forced migration, addressing migrants' health needs is a key challenge for global health. It calls for advances in prevention strategies and the development and evaluation of preventive interventions.

At the University of Illinois at Chicago, since 1995 our multidisciplinary and multinational research team has developed and implemented a half dozen preventive interventions with migrants and refugees, both in the United States and abroad. Based on these experiences, we identified eight key intervention characteristics that could be used to guide their development, implementation, and evaluation (Weine, 2011; see Table 25.1).

These key intervention characteristics and questions can help to inform the development and use of the aforementioned additional claims for the Best Practices. They can assist in identifying the research questions that can drive the design choices, and the types of theories, investigators, designs, and data to be included, and the breadth of underlying global challenges to be considered.

Through conducting prevention research with migrants and refugees, we became aware that to address these eight characteristics in the complex environments where migrants and refugees live requires modifying the process of developmental research from the standard approaches used in clinical trials (e.g., bench research to efficacy research to dissemination; the use of the randomized controlled trial). Specific modifications found

Table 25.1 Key Intervention Characteristics

Feasibility	Is the preventive intervention doable?
Acceptability	Will families and providers accept the preventive intervention?
Prosaicness	Does the preventive intervention use understandable and compelling language?
Culurally tailored	Does the preventive intervention fit the particular characteristics of the situation and group?
Multilevel	Does the preventive intervention address more than one dimension of the problem?
Time-focused	Does the preventive intervention take into account time-dependent processes?
Effectiveness	Will the preventive intervention yield significant positive changes?
Adaptability	Is the preventive intervention flexible?

to be helpful include multimethod and mixed methods, which is the focus of this chapter and book, but also other innovative mental health services research strategies, including a resilience framework (Masten & Powell, 2003; Norris, 2008; Walsh, 2002, 2006), community collaboration (Arcury, 2000; McKay & Paikoff, 2007; Israel, Schulz, Parker, & Becker, 1998), and the comprehensive dynamic trial (Rapkin & Trickett, 2005; Rapkin et al., 2006).

With respect to multimethod and mixed methods, in an earlier publication (Weine, 2011) I identified two general ways (borrowed from Greene, 2007) that MMMR could assist in prevention research in global health. One was the reason of *complementarity*, which is using one method to clarify or illustrate results from another method. Another was the reason of *expansion*, which is providing richness and detail to the study exploring specific features of each method.

Upon further reflection, I concluded that additional consideration should be given to the reason of enhancing the completeness of the knowledge. In the triangulation literature, completeness is described in equally general terms such as *holistic* (Olsen, 2004) and *contextual* (Breitmayer et al., 1993). But why stop there? Based in part on Rubin and Rubin (2011), eight qualities of completeness

Table 25.2 Completeness of Knowledge

Fresh	Exploring new issues or familiar issues in new ways
Real	Including firsthand knowledge of life as people live it
Balanced	Including a range of perspectives
Thorough	Following different lines of inquiry without gaps
Credible	Tightly linking the conclusions to the evidence
Accurate	Explaining the research in a highly clear way
Detailed	Presenting matters step by step or bit by bit
Nuanced	Building layer by layer for richer and deeper results

for multimethod and mixed methods can be articulated (see Table 25.2).

The reason for mentioning these eight qualities of completeness of knowledge is that, like the eight key intervention characteristics and questions, they could also be used to help inform the further development and use of the aforementioned additional claims for the Best Practices as well as other claims. In particular, they could assist in elaborating what completeness could mean with respect to the knowledge built through MMMR in prevention research in global health. This in turn would have implications for design choices and the types of theories, investigators, designs, and data to be included, as well as the breadth of underlying global contextual challenges to be prioritized and addressed.

Research Example of Prevention Research in Global Health Focused on Migration

Earlier I stated that through conducting prevention research in global health, researchers could find opportunities for building evidence about how combining different forms of knowledge in multimethod and mixed methods could generate more robust and useful findings. Collaborative research teams through the International Center on Responses to Catastrophes (Stout, 2009) have been conducting global health research projects using multimethod and mixed methods. Several of the project proposals included methodological

aims that examined whether or not there was added value in gathering several types of data and conducting analysis with different methodologies (Weine, 2008, 2010). The methodological inquiry sought to examine the possible contributions of (a) multiple investigators; (b) multiple theories; (c) multiple methods; and (d) multiple data, specifically persons, spaces, and times. This section summarizes the findings from one large study focused on labor migrants and HIV/AIDS risk and protection regarding the uses of multimethod and mixed methods to address the key preventive intervention characteristics and the completeness of this knowledge. The purpose of the detailed discussion of this one case study is to illustrate how innovative strategies combining different forms of knowledge in multimethod and mixed methods can generate more robust and useful findings, and how research can shine a light on clarifying the additional claims for the Best Practices.

Labor Migrants and HIV Risk

This study addressed the major global health problem of HIV prevention among male labor migrants (Weine & Kashuba, 2012). This five-year, mixed method study focused on married men from Tajikistan working in Moscow and their risks for acquiring HIV through sex with female sex workers and regular partners in Moscow, and the possible transmission of the infection to their wives in Tajikistan. Four hundred surveys were collected with the male migrants, and two ethnographic interviews and two observations each were conducted with a sample of the male migrants ($n = 30$), their wives in Tajikistan ($n = 30$), and their regular partners in Moscow ($n = 30$), as well as ethnographic interviews with sex workers in Moscow ($n = 30$) and providers in Moscow ($n = 16$) and Tajikistan ($n = 16$). (See Figure 25.1 and Table 25.3.)

Methods

The specific aims of this methodological part of the overall study were to address

1. Multiple investigators: How does what was learned through multiple investigators add to or modify what was learned through a single investigator?

2. Multiple theories: How did what was learned through the use of multiple theories add to what was learned through one theory alone?

3. Multiple methods: How did what was learned through minimally structured interviews

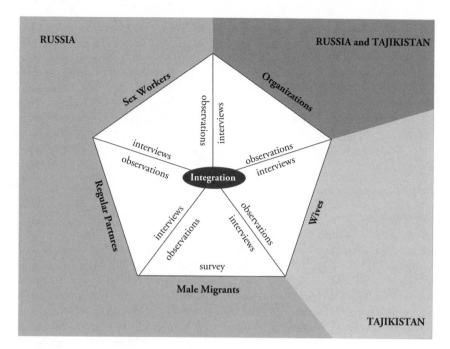

Fig. 25.1 Multiple methods and data

and shadowing observations add to what was learned through surveys alone?

4. Multiple data (persons): How did what was learned from wives, regular partners, and sex workers add to or modify what was learned from the male migrants?

5. Multiple data (spaces): How did what was learned in Moscow, Russia, add to or modify what was learned in Dushanbe, Tajikistan?

6. Multiple data (times): How did what was learned at follow-up time points add to or modify what was learned at the initial time point?

To address these research questions, the researchers used a combination of the following strategies: (a) review of the prior mixed methods research reports and publications generated based upon this data, (b) review of the project's Atlas/ti database with further pattern coding focused on addressing the previous six questions, and (c) discussion and consensus review among members of the research team. As a result of this process, answers emerged in response to each research question. The results section summarizes these answers and provides some illustrative examples.

Results

Overall, the use of multimethod and mixed methods contributed both to addressing key preventive intervention characteristics and to

Table 25.3 Study Domains and Approaches

Domains		Approach
Investigator		Multiple investigators from different disciplines
Theory		Gender schema theory
		Migration theory
		Social cognitive theory
		Human rights theory
		Feminist theory
		Interdependence theory
		Theory of gender and power
Method		Surveys
		Minimally structured interviews
		Shadowing observations
Data	Person	Male migrants
		Wives in Tajikistan
		Regular partners in Moscow
		Sex workers in Moscow
		Providers in Moscow and Tajikistan
	Space	Moscow
		Dushanbe
	Time	Before migrant went home
		After migrant went home

enhancing the completeness of knowledge (Table 25.4). This knowledge was then used to build an overall intervention model that used an opinion leader approach based on *diffusion of innovation* theory (Rogers, 1962/1995). It included three intervention components: *train* for male migrants on the train from Dushanbe to Moscow, *protect* for male migrants living in dormitories in Moscow, and *healthy homes* for male migrants' wives in Tajikistan delivered through primary-care clinics and women's circles.

Multiple Investigators

This study's investigator team came from multiple disciplines, including psychiatry, global health, prevention, epidemiology, ethnography, ethics, public health, and obstetrics/gynecology. Investigators were from both the United States and Tajikistan, including both male and female investigators who came from different backgrounds and work experiences. All team members involved in the project participated in a collaborative study process whereby each member of the team's perspective were shared and contributed to the data collection, analysis, report writing, and intervention development. This was achieved through in-person team meetings, Skype meetings, ongoing e-mail communication, and an overall spirit of collaboration. One example was the Tajik investigators' insider knowledge of diaspora social structures and networks, religious values, and gender and cultural norms, which allowed the team to better access sites and collect and analyze data on the migrants in Moscow. A second example was the US investigators' knowledge of trauma and posttraumatic stress disorder, which helped to reframe the Tajik migrant's experience of being "unprotected" and to examine it in relation to HIV risk, which in turn helped to develop compelling language for how to address the threat of HIV in preventive interventions. A third example involved using the findings to develop feasible and potentially effective preventive interventions for the male migrants and their wives drawing on both the Tajik investigator's familiarity with the local social and organizational contexts and the US investigator's knowledge of HIV preventive intervention and research designs.

Multiple Theories

This study used multiple theories, including gender schema theory (Berm, 1981, 1985),

migration theory (Greenwood, 1985), social cognitive theory (Bandura, 1994), human rights theory (Eisler, 1987), feminist theory (Hesse-Biber, 2007), interdependence theory (Wieselquist & Rusbult, 1999), and the theory of gender and power (Wingood & DiClemente, 2000). Drawing on these multiple theories helped the researchers investigate multidimensional phenomenon involved in HIV risk and protection among male labor migrants and their families. This was achieved through ongoing team dialogue and sharing on theories and models. One example was the use of Connell's (1987) sociostructural theory of gender and power, which helped the researchers focus on women's exposure to gender and power factors that produced gender inequalities that could increase HIV risk for women, such as women's financial dependency and fear of interpersonal violence. Another example was the use of migration theory, which helped to explain the multilevel processes and impact of migration and how these amplified gender inequalities; migration enhanced male migrants' opportunities, which included infidelity and unprotected sex with sex workers, whereas their Tajik wives' opportunities were diminished, including acquiring HIV prevention knowledge and skills (Figure 25.1). It became clear that HIV prevention for both men and women would have to involve addressing gender relations and inequalities.

Multiple Methods

Multiple data collection methods, including surveys, minimally structured interviews, and shadowing observations, were used. Drawing on these three data collection methods especially helped the researchers to better understand the multilevel dimensions of HIV risk and protection and the impact of sociocultural context. The survey results indicated that male labor migrants were at risk for HIV due to risky sexual behaviors, including high rates of sexual relations with sex workers, multiple partnering, unprotected sex with sex workers, and reduced frequency of condom use while drinking alcohol. Multivariate tests indicated the multilevel factors that increased HIV sexual risks including: premigration factors (e.g., used sex workers in Tajikistan); migrant work and lifestyle factors (e.g., greater number of times visited Moscow); migrant sexual and relational factors (e.g., regular partner in Moscow); and migrant health and

Table 25.4 Preventive Intervention Characteristics and Completeness of Knowledge

Domains		Components (Selected)	Preventive Intervention Knowledge (Selected)	Preventive Intervention Characteristics Addressed[a]	Qualities of Completeness of Knowledge Addressed[b]
Investigator		Tajik investigators' insider knowledge	Migrants' diaspora social structures and networks; religious values; gender and cultural norms	F, A,C, M	F, R, B, C, N
		US investigators' knowledge of trauma and PTSD	Migrants' experience of being "unprotected" in relation to HIV risk	F, M	F, R, B, C, N
Theory		Socio-structural theory of gender and power	Gender inequalities related to increased HIV risk for women	F, P, M	B, T, N
		Migration theory	Multilevel processes and impact of migration-amplified gender inequalities	F, P, M	B, T, N
Method		Quantitative	Male migrants at risk for HIV due to risky sexual behaviors	C, E, Ad	C, A, N
		Qualitative	Multilevel protective factors / Challenging commonly held beliefs about HIV prevention among wives / Severity of living environment for migrants in Moscow / Negative impact of migration on wives in Tajikistan / Increased familiarity and trust led to improved sharing and access to more places for observations	A, C, M, E, Ad	C, A, D, N
Data	Person	Examine the key term *trust*	Male migrants' trust in regular partners based on familiarity / Regular partners' trust in male migrants based on perceived commitment to the relationship	P, C, M, E	R, B, T
	Space	Understand characteristics of persons in places	Masculinity in Dushanbe vs. Moscow / Role of religion in Dushanbe vs. Moscow	C, M, E	R, B, T
	Time	Understand dimensions of migration process and family lifecycle	Change in relationships between male migrant and regular partner / Experience of male migrant and wife spending time together in Tajikistan	C, M, T, E	F, D

Note. PTSD = posttraumatic stress disorder;

[a] F = Feasibility; A = Acceptability; P = Prosaicness; C = culturally tailored; M = Multilevel; T = Time focused; E = Effectiveness; Ad = Adaptability.

[b] F = Fresh; R = Real; B = Balanced; T = Thorough; C = Credible; A = Accurate; D = Detailed; N = Nuanced.

mental health factors (e.g., increased frequency of alcohol use). Qualitative findings from the minimally structured interviews and shadowing observations demonstrated how these multilevel premigration and migration factors accounted for HIV risk and protective behaviors in context. One example was understanding possible family-level protective factors, such as visiting relatives, which suggests the potential value of both invoking the migrants' obligation to protect family members and involving these other family members in family-focused HIV prevention. Another example was challenging some important commonly held beliefs about HIV prevention among migrants' wives in Tajikistan. Previous research (Weine, Bahromov, & Mirzoev, 2008) found that wives frequently believed that their husbands were not visiting sex workers in Russia and that if their husbands had a regular partner in Moscow, then they would not visit sex workers. Our study found, however, that having a regular partner in Moscow was associated with having more vaginal sex with women other than the regular partner and with relatively little condom use. Appropriately challenging these beliefs and practices so as to increase protections became a focus of the preventive interventions.

Additionally, through shadowing observations, the researchers were able to witness the harsh living and working environments of the migrants in Moscow, as well as the often negative impact of migration on the wives in Tajikistan. One example was that we observed the migrants' interactions with police, including beatings and arrests. Another example was we saw the wives' conflicts with in-laws leading to their lack of mobility, which wives did not mention in their interviews.

Additionally, through observations, the researchers gained the trust of the participants and were allowed more access to places for observation, where they learned more about where participants go, what activities they do on a daily basis, and who they interact with. One example was that the researchers were able to see the male migrants in the dormitories where they lived together. Another example was being able to attend parties where men drank vodka and met sex workers. These observations then allowed the researchers to ask participants specific questions and probe deeper during the second interview concerning sexual activities and masculine practices.

Multiple Data

PERSONS

This study gathered data form male migrants, their wives in Tajikistan, their regular partners in Moscow, sex workers in Moscow, and organizations in both Tajikistan and Moscow. Drawing on data from these different types of persons helped the researchers to better understand the multiple players and their roles and perspectives regarding HIV risk and protection. One example was examining the key term *trust*, which turned out to mean something very different to male migrants, their wives, regular partners, and sex workers (Golobof, Weine, Bahromov, & Luo, 2011). For the male migrants, trust in their regular partners and sex workers was based on familiarity with the women, whereas from the regular partners' perspective, trust was established once they felt the male migrant was committed to the relationship (Zabrocki et al., 2013). A second example was being able to understand different attitudes and behaviors regarding condom use. The wives had limited HIV knowledge and lacked communication with their husbands about HIV, while the regular partners communicated with the male migrants about HIV risk and protection, and some even taught their male migrant partner how to use condoms.

SPACES

Data was collected in both Moscow (from the male migrant, regular partner, sex workers, and organizations) and in Tajikistan (wives and organizations). Drawing on data from these different spaces helped the researchers to better understand the particular characteristics of HIV risk and protection of persons in social spaces. One way this was approached was through comparative analysis of Dushanbe and Moscow, which revealed some important divergent findings. One finding was that the migrants' sense of being a "real man" changed from Dushanbe (earning money to support and protect the family) to Moscow (working then participating in parties, drinking, and sexual liaisons). Another finding was the changes in the roles of religion from Dushanbe, where it was against their religion to engage in extramarital relations, to Moscow, where the men justified having extramarital relations based on God's forgiveness because they were away from their wives for so long.

TIMES

Data was collected at two different points in time for the male migrant, wives, and regular partners. The initial interview and observation occurred while the male migrant had been in Moscow for a variable period of time. The second interview and observation occurred after the male migrant had been home to Tajikistan in the winter and then returned to Moscow. Drawing on data from these different points in time helped the researchers to better understand important dimensions of the migration process and family lifecycle. One example was being able to understand changes in relationships, as most regular partners and male migrants were no longer in the same relationship at the second point in time. Another example was examining changes in the relationship between husbands and wives such as wives reporting on when their husbands were home.

Conclusions and Implications of the Research Example

Multiple investigators, theories, methods, persons, times, and spaces each strengthened the data collection and analysis and contributed to the overall completeness of the knowledge and to addressing key preventive intervention characteristics. This in turn led to the development of more feasible, acceptable, and potentially effective multilevel preventive interventions. All three of these interventions focused on engaging and educating local opinion leaders (e.g., leaders of groups of migrant men and leaders of women's circles) to disseminate HIV prevention messages using an enhanced opinion leader approach. Each intervention leveraged off of one main set of prevention messages, which were devised from the mixed methods findings, such as "Protect your family and your nation." Results from the pilot studies indicate that all three interventions were effective.

This research example concerning labor migration and HIV illustrates how different strategies combining different forms of knowledge in multimethod and mixed methods can generate more robust and useful findings for prevention. Furthermore, it illustrates how the aforementioned additional claims for the Best Practices can be addressed through research. First, the research approach was able to engage the global challenges of poverty, discrimination, gender disparities, migration context, and translation/adaptation. Second, it was able to incorporate multiple theories, investigators, designs, and data. Third, the research was able to devise a variety of approaches for integrating different theories, investigators, designs, and data, both textually and figuratively. Fourth, the chosen

research design was organized around answering the central research problems and questions and not picked from an a priori list of design types.

Last, it showed how the eight key intervention characteristics and questions and the eight qualities of completeness of knowledge could be used to focus the mixed and multimethod research. These helped to better define the research questions, select the relevant theories, identify requisite investigators from multiple disciplines and backgrounds, devise the appropriate research design, and choose the types of data to be collected.

Research to Practice Models for Overcoming the Challenges of Developing Prevention Intervention Programs

Multimethod and mixed methods can be used in different stages of the longitudinal process of prevention research in global health (Nastasi et al., 2007). In the formative research phase, they could be used to elucidate basic needs, meanings, resources, and strengths that could help in the design of a preventive intervention program (Schensul, Verma, & Nastasi, 2004). In the evaluation phase, they could be used to elucidate both whether or not an intervention worked and how it worked or did not work (Bamberger, Rugh, & Mabry, 2006; Stufflebeam, 2001). They could also be used to focus on community collaborative processes used in designing, refining, implementing, evaluating, or disseminating the preventive intervention (Nastasi et al., 1998).

Responding to the priority of prevention in global health could benefit from multimethod and mixed methods. Prevention in global health entails facing issues of community collaboration, training and education, capacity building, sustainability, multilevel outcome and process evaluation, leadership, organizational buy-in, community perceptions, sociocultural factors and processes, and family factors and processes. One articulation of the complex questions involved in prevention research in global health is: What intervention components implanted at what levels, spaces, and times will potentially best enhance protective processes and mitigate risks so as to achieve targeted outcomes for at-risk persons? The HIV prevention research project in Tajikistan and Russia addressed the questions posed in Table 25.5. The multiplicity and complexity of these questions involved in developing and evaluating a multilevel intervention with migrants called for a multimethod and mixed methods approach.

Table 25.5 HIV Prevention Project Research Questions

Data Sources	Research Questions
Survey and ethnographic research data with male migrants, Tajik wives, Russian regular partners, sex workers, and service providers	**Individual** How do such individual factors as age, education, work, income, health and mental health status, knowledge, attitudes, and behaviors contribute to HIV risk and protective processes? Which of these individual factors are modifiable and how can that be achieved?
	Family How do such family factors as family structure, loss and separation, communication, supports, tensions and conflicts, and solidarity contribute to HIV risk and protective processes? Which of these family factors are modifiable and how can that be achieved?
	Sociocultural How do such sociocultural factors as networks, community, cultural attitudes, gender attitudes, and stigma contribute to HIV risk and protective processes? Which of these sociocultural factors are modifiable and how can that be achieved?
	Structural What do structures such as migration administration, workplace, healthcare institutions, voluntary organizations, and schools contribute to HIV risk and protective processes? Which of these structural factors are modifiable and how can that be achieved?
	Intersections Across Levels Which of the above intersect and how do those intersections further contribute to HIV risk and protective processes? How are these intersections located in spaces, times, and types of events?

However, we should acknowledge that prevention intervention development in global health faces many obstacles. One major challenge concerns how to generate research knowledge that will help to change practices among day-to-day realities in diverse sociocultural contexts. In an attempt to close the gap between prevention science and practice, various research models have been developed. These models' ambitions are to generate knowledge that would more readily translate into practical applications in the field that achieve prevention goals.

However, some of the existing models were considered inadequate, including for example, the Institute of Medicine's five-step model (Wandersman, 2003). It consisted of the following steps: (1) identifying a problem or disorder and its extent; (2) assessing the prevalence of risk and protective factors; (3) designing, conducting, and analyzing a pilot preventive intervention program; (4) designing, conducting, and analyzing a large-scale trial of a preventive intervention program; and (5) facilitating large-scale implementation and evaluation of the preventive intervention

program in the community. However, what this and other similar models tend to lack is sufficient attention as to how to make the leap from research to practice in complex and challenging social settings. In response, new approaches have taken a more deliberate, community-centered focus. These models "begin with the community and ask what it needs in terms of scientific information and capacity building to produce effective interventions" (Wandersman, 2003, p. 230). Two such models are introduced here: community based participatory research (CBPR) and the Interactive Systems Framework for Dissemination and Implementation. Both of these models also create opportunities for using multimethod and mixed methods, as will be discussed.

CBPR has been described as an approach that "equitably involves all partners. . . with a research topic of importance to the community with the aim of combining knowledge and action for social change to improve community health and eliminate health disparities" (Kellog Health Scholars Program, 2013). It not only offers strategies for developing, implementing, and disseminating preventive intervention programs across diverse communities but also for bridging the gap between community and academic partners and advancing social change, such as redressing power imbalances (Wallerstein & Duran, 2010). CBPR assesses the health priorities of communities and then works collaboratively to adapt or design interventions. It attends to and learns from local explanatory models, approaches, and programs. CBPR also builds diverse teams that include community members and ethnic and religious minorities and works within the language of local communities and participants, as well as attends to how changes can be incorporated into community practices and sustained. New modes of community participation, for example, may then become the focus of research to understand how they lead to improvements in the community. To embrace these complexities, researchers need to be able to draw upon multiple investigators, theories, methods, and data.

The Interactive Systems Framework for Dissemination and Implementation was developed in order to better bridge research to practice (Flaspohler, Lesesne, Puddy, Smith, & Wandersman, 2012). It focuses especially on the infrastructure and systems that are needed to undertake implementation and dissemination. This framework consists of three central components: Prevention Delivery System (for implementing prevention), Prevention Support System (for supporting the work), and Prevention Synthesis and Translation System (for distilling the information). Each of these components is briefly described in terms of the types of knowledge they attempt to build through research. This framework and its components pose challenges to prevention research in global health that call for the use of multimethod and mixed methods.

The Prevention Delivery System is focused on understanding practice settings where the preventive intervention program will take place. This entails understanding the individuals, communities, and organizations that will be carrying out the prevention program. For example, this means understanding the individual (e.g., education and experience), organizational (e.g., leadership, commitment, climate), and community (e.g., community readiness and competence) characteristics that could impact implementation.

The Prevention Support System incorporates both innovation-specific support (or capacity building) and general support (or capacity building). This could incorporate understanding the contribution of information about an innovation and/or general knowledge and skill building that is not focused on any particular innovation.

The Prevention Synthesis and Translation System aims to make information about an innovation accessible, user-friendly, and clear to the audience. This also involves understanding how the core elements of a program are identified and then implemented in a new community setting. This depends on understanding the processes of translating or converting scientific knowledge into products that are usable by practitioners.

In summary, both CBPR and the Interactive Systems Framework for Dissemination and Implementation are promising approaches for prevention research in global health that introduce complexities that call for synergy in research approaches for which multimethod and mixed methods could be helpful.

Using Multimethod and Mixed Methods Research in Prevention Research in Global Health

This chapter has focused on the challenges of developing preventive interventions with migrants. It has considered the limitations of the "Best Practices for Mixed Methods Research in the Health Sciences" and proposed additional claims. It described the potential role of eight key preventive intervention characteristics and eight qualities of completeness in informing those claims. It has drawn on one long research example concerning labor migrants and HIV prevention and several other short examples to illustrate how different strategies combining different forms of knowledge in multimethod and mixed methods could generate more robust and useful findings.

The analysis demonstrated that MMMR is far more than a listing of typologies for combining qualitative and quantitative data and analysis. The research example illustrated how combining multiple study elements (investigators, theories, methods, and data) could be used to address the research problems and questions. Additionally, the introduction of several promising research to practice models (CBPR and the Interactive Systems Framework for Dissemination and Implementation) proposed how multimethod and mixed methods could be helpful to address the multidimensional research problems and questions. This leads to the overall conclusion that

> Multimethods and mixed methods in prevention research in global health should strategically utilize multiple study elements (investigators, theories,

methods, and data) that are most responsive to the central research problems and questions, through existing and new synergies, so as to most appropriately address the key preventive intervention characteristics and contribute to the overall completeness of the knowledge.

The following, additional, specific points of guidance are offered:

• Articulate global health prevention research problems and questions that embrace multiplicity and thereby necessitate multimethod and mixed methods. *Multiplicity* refers to research problems and questions that are multilevel, multiperspective, multitemporal, and/or multidimensinsal. Generating these research problems or questions is called for to be responsive to the complexity of global health prevention research, including the aforementioned key preventive intervention characteristics.

• Establish and build capacities for transdisciplinary global health prevention research teams to conduct MMMR. Transdisciplinary means that researchers work jointly using a shared conceptual framework, drawing together disciplinary specific theories, concepts, and approaches to address common problems (Rosenfield, 1992, p. 1351). This requires leadership, resources, and training to build a mixed methods research team (Best Practices).

• Incorporate participatory research approaches into multimethod and mixed methods approaches for global health prevention research. Participatory research, as defined earlier, in terms of CBPR, involves community partners and addresses community concerns in ways that are perceived as helpful and empowering to community members. A participatory research approach, which is more than simply studying community members, yields data with multiplicities that requires multimethod and mixed methods. It means studying not just how an intervention works but also how it is experienced and perceived by community members and how best to enhance the processes that determine its usefulness for communities.

• Invest in the prediscovery phase of multimethod and mixed methods approaches to global health prevention research. *Prediscovery* refers to the period of inquiry, reading, and relationship building that culminates in defining the research problem and questions and choosing the theories, conceptual framework, research design, and data collection approaches. The

newness and complexity of global health contexts in which prevention research will be conducted merits adequate time (often up to several years) before settling on these issues. Sometimes this can be supported by pilot or planning grants, but researchers should be prepared to find ways to conduct it unsupported.

• Incorporate emergent methods and technologies into multimethod and mixed methods approaches to global health prevention research. Emergent methods and technologies include experience sampling (Hektner, 2007; Sullivan, Khondkaryan, Dos Santos, & Peters, 2011), geomapping (Gilliam, Hanchette, Fogarty, & Gibbs, 2008), auto-ethnography (Davis & Ellis, 2008), the biographical-narrative approach (Gubrium & Holstein, 2008), and ethnodrama (Leavy, 2008). Thus MMMR is far more than simply combining quantitative and qualitative methods and calls for innovations.

• Incorporate diverse theories into multimethod mixed methods approaches to global health prevention research. Global health prevention research requires underlying theories that are able to explain the multiple problems or questions at hand, such as theories that focus on behavior change and those that focus on ecological or social context (McAlister, Perry, & Parcel, 2008), violence (Kleinman, Das, & Lock, 1997), cultural transitions (Baumann, 1999), migration (Greenwood, 1985), and gender (Hesse-Biber, 2007).

• Draw on the strengths of qualitative methods in mixed methods approaches to global health prevention research without relegating it to a secondary position. The emphasis on collecting quantitative data and analyzing it with statistical methodologies in prevention science and global health can relegate qualitative methods to a secondary position. The strengths of qualitative methods that can be further drawn on include listening to voices and understanding multiple perspectives, processes of change, social-environmental and sociocultural dimensions, and subgroups.

• Develop integrative results, narratives, and displays for reporting on the results of MMMR in global health prevention research. Combining the MMMR results requires creative approaches to writing and visualizing information. Quantitative research results have generally been displayed using tables, while qualitative data often is not visually displayed, unless through text tables

(Onwuegbuzie & Dickinson, 2008; Tufte, 2001). Nontextal visual representation of data that draws on qualitative and quantitative data, such as graphical displays, can be used to reveal elements that might not have been seen otherwise (Wainer, 1990).

What Can Multimethod and Mixed Methods Researchers Learn From Prevention Research in Global Health?

The aforementioned points of guidance can be generalized beyond prevention research in global health to other areas of MMMR. Stated concisely the overall implication is to *synergistically utilize all available study elements needed to answer the priority research questions.* The specific points of guidance are summarized in Table 25.6. Three additional points of guidance would help to further develop research approaches:

• Conduct studies that demonstrate the contributions of multimethod and mixed methods. As noted earlier, little existing research has provided scientific evidence in support of the roles of multimethod and mixed methods. Systematic literature reviews can show what has been done through prior research. New research is very much needed. One strategy is to incorporate a methods aim into all new multimethod and mixed methods studies.

• Clarify the roles of community collaborative teams in conducting MMMR. There is the potential for confusion between, on the one hand, the diverse community voices collected through qualitative interviews or observations and, on the other hand, the community collaborators who might participate as co-investigators or as members of a community advisory board. These could potentially be redundant, or they could set up conflicts between data sources that could benefit from guidance as to why to collect both and how to manage such potential difficulties.

• Build better bridges between methodologists and researchers. Sometimes it seems like the scholars writing the methodology books and articles have insufficient experience conducting research so as to more fully ground their teachings in current and practical research challenges. This needs correcting, as does the lack of methodology studies by researchers. Methodologists should endeavor to broaden their research experiences, and the persons conducting the studies could build methodological aims into their studies and write about the methodological dimensions of their research.

Discussion Questions

1. This chapter discussed how using multiple investigators, theories, methods, and data can be used to address prevention research in global health. How can integration occur in each of these realms?

2. This chapter introduced community-based participatory research and the interactive systems framework for dissemination and implementation. What mixed methods and methodologies would be useful for studying these areas?

3. What advances in multimethod and mixed methods will come as a result of challenges posed by researching global health?

Suggested Websites
Global Health
http://www.ghrf.org/
The Global Health Research Foundation provides tools of technology and IT expertise to create sustainable development in medically resource poor communities by addressing health issues in the context of the community as a whole.

http://www.globalhealth.gov/
The Office of Global Affairs, part of the US Department of Health and Human Services, promotes the health and well-being of the world's population by advancing global strategies and partnerships and working with US government agencies in the coordination of global health policy.

http://www.globalmentalhealth.org/
The Movement for Global Mental Health is a network of individuals and organizations committed to improving the availability, access, and quality of services for people with

Table 25.6 Points of Guidance

#	Points of Guidance
1	Articulate research problems and questions that embrace multiplicity and thereby necessitate multimethod and mixed methods research.
2	Incorporate diverse theories into multimethod and mixed methods research.
3	Invest in the prediscovery phase of multimethod and mixed methods research.
4	Draw on the strengths of qualitative methods in multimethod and mixed methods research.
5	Incorporate emergent methods and technologies into multimethod and mixed methods research.

mental disorders, with an emphasis on low- and middle-income countries.

Prevention Research

http://www.preventionresearch.org/

The Society for Prevention Research is an organization dedicated to advancing scientific investigation on the etiology and prevention of social, physical, and mental health and academic problems and on the translation of that information to promote health and well-being.

http://www.preventioninstitute.org/

The Prevention Institute is an organization that works to synthesize research and practice, develop prevention tools and frameworks, help design and guide interdisciplinary partnerships, and conduct training and consultation with government, foundations, and community-organizations.

Multimethod and Mixed Methods

http://mmr.sagepub.com/content/6/2.toc

The *Journal of Mixed Methods Research* is an interdisciplinary and international journal that focuses on empirical, methodological, and theoretical articles about mixed methods research in the social, behavioral, health, and human sciences.

Migration

http://www.iom.int/cms/research

The International Organization for Migration (IOM) conducts and supports research designed to guide and inform migration policy and practice. The Migration Research Division monitors IOM migration research activity, gathers lessons learned and develops best practices, and initiates its own research that enables IOM to serve as the primary reference point on migration.

References

Adami, M. F., & Kiger, A. (2005). The use of triangulation for completeness purposes. *Nurse Researcher, 12*(4), 19–29.

Albee, G. W. (1996). Revolutions and counterrevolutions in prevention. *American Psychologist, 51*(11), 1130–1133.

Arcury, T. (2000). Successful process in community-based participatory research. In L.R. O'Fallon, F. Tyson, & A. Dearry (Eds.), *Successful models of community-based participatory research* (pp. 42–48). Washington, DC: National Institute of Environmental Health Sciences.

Auerbach, J. D., & Coates, T. J. (2000). HIV prevention research: accomplishments and challenges for the third decade of AIDS. *American Journal of Public Health, 90*(7), 1029.

Bamberger, M., Rugh, J., & Mabry, L. (2006). *RealWorld evaluation working under budget, time, data, and political constraints.* Thousand Oaks, CA: Sage.

Bandura, A. (1994). Social cognitive theory and exercise of control over HIV infection. In R. DiClemente & J. Peterson (Eds.), *Preventing AIDS: Theories and methods of behavioral interventions* (pp. 25–59). New York, NY: Plenum.

Barrio, C. (2000). The cultural relevance of community support programs. *Psychiatric Services, 51*, 879–884.

Baumann, G. (1999). *The multicultural riddle: Rethinking national, ethnic, and religious identities.* London, England: Routledge.

Bazeley, P., & Kemp, L. (2012). Mosaics, triangles, and DNA metaphors for integrated analysis in mixed methods research. *Journal of Mixed Methods Research, 6*(1), 55–72.

Beaglehole, R., & Bonita, R. (2010). What is global health? *Global Health Action, 3*, 5142.

Berm, S. L. (1981). Gender schema theory: A cognitive account of sex typing. *Psychological Review, 88*, 354–364.

Berm, S. L. (1985). Androgyny and gender schema theory: A conceptual and empirical integration. In T. B. Sondereggar (Ed.), *Psychology and gender* (pp. 179–226). Lincoln: University of Nebraska Press.

Bhui, K. S., Hicks, M. H., Lashley, M., & Jones, E. (2012). A public health approach to understanding and preventing violent radicalization. *BMC Medicine, 10*(1), 16.

Breitmayer, B. J., Ayres, L., & Knafl, K. A. (1993). Triangulation in qualitative research: Evaluation of completeness and confirmation purposes. *Journal of Nursing Scholarship, 25*(3), 237–243.

Connell, R. W. (1987). *Gender and power.* Stanford, CA: Stanford University Press.

Creswell, J. W. (2011). Controversies in mixed methods research. In N. K. Denzin & Y. S. Lincoln (Eds.), *The SAGE handbook of qualitative research* (pp. 269–283). Thousand Oaks, CA: Sage.

Creswell, J. W., Klassen, A. C., Plano Clark, V. L., & Clegg Smith, K. (2011). Best practices for mixed methods research in the health sciences. Bethesda, MD: National Institutes of Health, Office of Behavioral and Social Sciences Research. Retrieved from http://obssr.od.nih.gov/mixed_methods_research/pdf/Best_Practices_for_Mixed_Methods_Research.pdf

Creswell, J. W., & Plano Clark, V. L. (2007). *Designing and conducting mixed methods research.* Thousand Oaks, CA: Sage.

Davis, P., & Baulch, B. (2011). Parallel realities: Exploring poverty dynamics using mixed methods in rural Bangladesh. *The Journal of Development Studies, 47*(1), 118–142.

Davis, C. S., & Ellis, C. (2008). Emergent methods in autoethnographic research: Autoethnographic narrative and the multiethnographic turn. In S. Hesse-Biber & P. Leavy (Eds.) *Handbook of emergent methods* (pp. 283–302). New York, NY: Guilford Press.

Denzin, N. K. (1970). *The research act: A theoretical introduction to sociological methods.* Chicago, IL: Aldine.

Denzin, N. K. (1978). *The research act: A theoretical introduction to sociological methods.* New York, NY: McGraw-Hill.

Eisler, R. (1987). Human rights: Toward an integrated theory for action. *Feminist Issues, 7*(1), 25–46.

Eng, J. L. V., Wolkon, A., Frolov, A. S., Terlouw, D. J., Eliades, M. J., Morgah, K., . . . & Hightower, A. W. (2007). Use of handheld computers with global positioning systems for probability sampling and data entry in household surveys. *American Journal of Tropical Medicine and Hygiene, 77*(2), 393–399.

Flaspohler, P., Lesesne, C. A., Puddy, R. W., Smith, E., & Wandersman, A. (2012). Advances in bridging research and practice: Introduction to the second special issue on the interactive system framework for dissemination and implementation. *American Journal of Community Psychology, 50*(3–4), 271–281.

Garmezy, N. (1971). Vulnerability research and the issue of primary prevention. *American Journal of Orthopsychiatry, 41*, 101–116.

Gilliam, G. A., Hanchette, C. L., Fogarty, K. J., & Gibbs, D. A. (2008). A geospatial analysis of CDC-funded HIV prevention programs for African Americans in the United States: Fiscal year 2000. *Journal of Health Disparities Research and Practice*, 2(2), 39–60.

Golobof, A., Weine, S., Bahromov, M., & Luo, J. (2011). The roles of labor migrants' wives in HIV/AIDS risk and prevention in Tajikistan. *AIDS Care*, 23(1), 91–97.

Greene, J. C. (2007). *Mixed methods in social inquiry*. San Francisco, CA: Jossey-Bass.

Greenwood, M. J. (1985). Human migration: Theory, models, and empirical studies. *Journal of Regional Science*, 25(4), 521–544.

Gubrium, J. F., & Holstein, J. A. (2008). Narrative ethnography. In S. Hesse-Biber & P. Leavy (Eds.), *Handbook of emergent methods* (pp. 241–264). New York, NY: Guilford Press.

Guion, L. A., Diehl, D. C., & McDonald, D. (2011). *Triangulation: Establishing the validity of qualitative studies*. Gainesville: University of Florida Cooperative Extension Service. Retrieved from http://edis.ifas.ufl.edu/pdffiles/FY/FY39400.pdf

Guterman, N. B. (2004). Advancing prevention research on child abuse, youth violence, and domestic violence: Emerging strategies and issues. *Journal of Interpersonal Violence*, 19(3), 299–321.

Hektner, J. (2007). *Experience sampling method: Measuring the quality of everyday life*. Thousand Oaks, CA: Sage.

Hesse-Biber, S. (2010). *Mixed methods research: Merging theory with practice*. New York, NY: Guilford Press.

Hesse-Biber, S. (Ed.). (2007). *Handbook of feminist research: Theory and praxis*. Thousand Oaks, CA: Sage.

Israel, B. A., Schulz, A. J., Parker, E. A., & Becker, A. B. (1998). Review of community-based research: Assessing partnership approaches to improve public health. *Annual Review of Public Health*, 19, 173–202.

Johnson, R. B., & Christensen, L. B. (2004). *Educational research: Quantitative, qualitative, and mixed approaches*. Boston, MA: Allyn & Bacon.

Johnson, R. B., Onwuegbuzie, A. J., & Turner, L. A. (2007). Toward a definition of mixed methods research. *Journal of Mixed Methods Research*, 1(2), 112–133.

Keating, J., Macintyre, K., Mbogo, C., Githeko, A., Regens, J. L., Swalm, C., . . . Beier, J. C. (2003). A geographic sampling strategy for studying relationships between human activity and malaria vectors in urban Africa. *American Journal of Tropical Medicine and Hygiene*, 68(3), 357–365.

Kellog Health Scholars Program. (2013). About us. Retrieved from http://www.kellogghealthscholars.org/about/community.cfm

Kimchi, J., Polivka, B., & Stevenson, J. (1991). Triangulation: Operational definitions. *Nursing Research*, 40, 364–366.

Kleinman, A. M., Das, V., & Lock, M. M. (Eds.). (1997). *Social suffering*. Berkeley: University of California Press.

Knafl, K., & Breitmayer, B. (1991). Triangulation in nursing research: Issues of conceptual clarity and purpose. In: J. Morse (Ed.), *Qualitative nursing research: A contemporary dialogue* (pp. 226–239). Newbury Park, CA: Sage.

Leavy, P. (2008). Performance-based emergent methods. In S. Hesse-Biber & P. Leavy (Eds.), *Handbook of emergent methods* (pp. 343–358). New York, NY: Guilford Press.

Masten, A. S., & Powell, J. L. (2003). A resilience framework for research, policy, and practice. In S. S. Luthar (Ed.), *Resilience and vulnerability: Adaptation in the context of childhood adversities* (pp. 1–25). Cambridge, UK: Cambridge University Press.

Mathison, S. (1988). Why triangulate? *Educational Researcher*, 17(2), 13–17.

Matsumoto, D., & van de Vijver, F. (Eds.). (2011). *Cross-cultural research methods in psychology*. New York, NY: Cambridge University Press.

McAlister, A. L., Perry, C. L., & Parcel, G. S. (2008). How individuals, environments, and health behaviors interact. In K. Glanz, B. K. Rimer, & K. Viswanath (Eds.), *Health behaviors and health education: Theory, reason, and practice* (pp. 169–188). San Francisco, CA: Wiley.

McCarthy, J. R., Holland, J., & Gillies, V. (2003). Multiple perspectives on the "family" lives of young people: Methodological and theoretical issues in case study research. *International Journal of Social Research Methodology*, 6(1), 1–23.

McKay, M., & Paikoff, R. (2007). *Community collaborative partnerships*. New York, NY: Taylor & Francis.

Morse, J. M., & Niehaus, L. (2009). *Mixed method design: Principles and procedures*. Walnut Creek, CA: Left Coast Press.

Nastasi, B. K., Hitchcock, J., Sarkar, S., Burkholder, G., Varjas, K., & Jayasena, A. (2007). Mixed methods in intervention research: Theory to adaptation. *Journal of Mixed Methods Research*, 1(2), 164–182.

Nastasi, B. K., Schensul, J. J., deSilva, M. W. A., Varjas, K., Silva, K. T., Ratnayake, P, & Schensul, S. L. (1998). Community-based sexual risk prevention program for Sri Lankan youth: Influencing sexual-risk decision making. *International Quarterly of Community Health Education*, 18(1), 139–155.

NIMH Collaborative HIV/STD Prevention Trial Group. (2007a). Design and integration of ethnography within an international behavior change HIV/sexually transmitted disease prevention trial. *AIDS*, 21(Suppl. 2), S37–S48.

NIMH Collaborative HIV/STD Prevention Trial Group. (2007b). The community popular opinion leader HIV prevention programme: Conceptual basis and intervention procedures. *AIDS*, 21, S59–S68.

Norris, F. H., Stevens, S. P., Pfefferbaum, B., Wyche, K. F., & Pfefferbaum, R. L. (2008). Community resilience as a metaphor, theory, set of capacities, and strategy for disaster readiness. *American Journal of Community Psychology*, 41, 127–150.

O'Connell, M. E., Boat, T., & Warner, K. E. (Eds.). (2009). *Preventing mental, emotional, and behavioral disorders among young people: Progress and possibilities*. Washington, DC: National Academies Press.

Olsen, W. (2004). Triangulation in social research: Qualitative and quantitative methods can really be mixed. In M. Haralambos & M. Holborn (Eds.), *Developments in sociology*. Ormskirk, UK: Causeway Press.

Onwuegbuzie, A. J., & Dickinson, W. B. (2008). Mixed methods analysis and information visualizations: Graphical display for effective communication of research results. *The Qualitative Report*, 13(2), 204–225.

Oppermann, M. (2000). Triangulation—A methodological discussion. *International Journal of Tourism Research*, 2(2), 141–145.

Padgett, D. K. (2012). *Qualitative and mixed methods in public health*. Thousand Oaks, CA: Sage.

Parker, R. (2002). The global HIV/AIDS pandemic, structural inequalities, and the politics of international health. *American Journal of Public Health, 92*(3), 343–347.

Patel, V., Araya, R., Chatterjee, S., Chisholm, D., Cohen, A., De Silva, M., . . . van Ommeren, M. (2007). Treatment and prevention of mental disorders in low-income and middle-income countries. *The Lancet, 370*(9591), 991–1005.

Patton, M. Q. (1990). *Qualitative evaluation and research methods* (2nd ed.). Newbury Park, CA: Sage.

Polit, D. F., & Hungler, B. P. (1999) *Nursing research: Principles and methods* (6th ed.). Philadelphia, PA: J. B. Lippincott.

Rapkin, B., Massie, M. J., Jansky, E., Lounsbury, D. W., Murphy, P. D., & Powell, S. (2006). Developing a partnership model for cancer screening with community-based organizations: The ACCESS breast cancer education and outreach project. *American Journal of Community Psychology, 38*, 153–164.

Rapkin, B., & Trickett, E. (2005). Comprehensive dynamic trial designs for behavioral prevention research with communities: Overcoming inadequacies of the randomized controlled trial paradigm. In E. J. Trickett & W. Pequegnat (Eds.), *Community interventions and AIDS* (pp. 249–277). Oxford, UK: Oxford University Press.

Rice, R. E., Wu, Z., Li, L., Detels, R., & Rotheram-Borus, M. J. (2012). Reducing STD/HIV stigmatizing attitudes through community popular opinion leaders in Chinese markets. *Human Communication Research, 38*(4), 379–405.

Risjord, M. W., Dunbar, S. B., & Moloney, M. F. (2002). A new foundation for methodological triangulation. *Journal of Nursing Scholarship, 34*(3), 269–275.

Rogers, E. M. (1995). *Diffusion of innovations* (4th ed.). New York, NY: Simon and Schuster. (Original work published in 1962)

Rosenfield, P. (1992). The potential of transdisiplinary research for sustaining and extending linkages between the health and social sciences. *Social Science and Medicine, 35*(11), 1343–1357.

Rothbauer, P. (2008) Triangulation. In L. Given (Ed.), *The SAGE encyclopedia of qualitative research methods* (pp. 892–894). Thousand Oaks, CA: Sage.

Rubin, H. J., & Rubin, I. S. (2011). *Qualitative interviewing: The art of hearing data*. Thousand Oaks, CA: Sage.

Sands, R. G., & Roer-Strier, D. (2006). Using data triangulation of mother and daughter interviews to enhance research about families. *Qualitative Social Work, 5*(2), 237–260.

Schensul, S. L., & Trickett, E. (2009). Introduction to multi-level community based culturally situated interventions. *American Journal of Community Psychology, 43*, 232–240.

Schensul, S. L., Verman, R. K., & Nastasi, B. K. (2004). Responding to men's sexual concerns: Research and intervention in slum communities in Mumbai, India. *International Journal of Men's Health, 3*(3), 197–220.

Shih, F. J. (1998). Triangulation in nursing research: Issues of conceptual clarity and purpose. *Journal of Advanced Nursing, 28*(3), 631–641.

Sivaram, S., Srikrishnan, A. K., Latkin, C. A., Johnson, S. C., Go, V. F., Bentley, M. E., . . . Celentano, D. D. (2004). Development of an opinion leader-led HIV prevention intervention among alcohol users in Chennai, India. *AIDS Education and Prevention, 16*(2), 137–149.

Steinberg, S. J., & Steinberg, S. L. (2011). Geospatial analysis technology and social science research. In S. Hesse-Biber (Ed.) *Handbook of emergent technologies* (pp. 563–591). Oxford, UK: Oxford University Press.

Stout, C. (Ed.) (2009). *The new humanitarians: Inspiration, innovations, and blueprints for visionaries*. Westport, CT: Praeger.

Stufflebeam, D. L. (2001). Evaluation models. *New Directions for Evaluation, 89*, 7–99.

Sullivan, T. P., Khondkaryan, E., Dos Santos, N. P., & Peters, E. N. (2011). Applying experience sampling methods to partner violence research: Safety and feasibility in a 90-day study of community women. *Violence Against Women, 17*(2), 251–266.

Synergy. (2013). In *Oxford Dictionaries Online*. Retrieved from http://oxforddictionaries.com/us/definition/american_english/synergy

Tashakkori, A., & Teddlie, C. (Eds.). (2003). *Handbook of mixed methods in social & behavioral research*. Thousand Oaks, CA: Sage.

Thurmond, V. A. (2001). The point of triangulation. *Journal of Nursing Scholarship, 33*(3), 253–258.

Tolan, P. H., Hanish, L. D., McKay, M. M., & Dickey, M. H. (2002). Evaluating process in child and family interventions: Aggression prevention as an example. *Journal of Family Psychology, 16*, 220–236.

Tufte, E. R. (2001). *The visual display of quantitative information* (2nd ed.). Cheshire, CT: Graphics Press.

United Nations. (2009). *International migrant stock: The 2008 revision*. Geneva, Switzerland: United Nations, Department of Economic and Social Affairs, Population Division. Retrieved from http://esa.un.org/migration/index.asp?panel=1

United Nations High Commissioner for Refugees. (2013). *Facts and figures about refugees*. London, England: Author. Retrieved from http://www.unhcr.org.uk/about-us/key-facts-and-figures.html

United Nations Population Fund. (2013). *Linking population, poverty, and development. Migration: A world on the move*. New York, NY: Author. Retrieved from http://www.unfpa.org/pds/migration.html

Wainer, H. (1990). Graphical visions from William Playfair to John Tukey. *Statistical Science, 5*, 340–346.

Wallerstein, N., & Duran, B. (2010). Community-based participatory research contributions to intervention research: The intersection of science and practice to improve health equity. *American Journal of Public Health, 100*(Suppl. 1), S40–S44.

Walsh, F. (2002). A family resilience framework: Innovative practice applications. *Family Relations, 51*(2), 130–137.

Walsh, F. (2006). *Strengthening family resilience* (2nd ed.). New York, NY: Guilford Press.

Wandersman, A. (2003). Community science: Bridging the gap between science and practice with community-centered models. *American Journal of Community Psychology, 31*, 227–242.

Weine, S. M. (2008). *Migrancy, masculinity, and preventing HIV in Tajik male migrant workers* (1R01HD056954-01A1). Chicago: University of Illinois.

Weine, S. M. (2009). Family roles in refugee youth resettlement from a prevention perspective. *Child and Adolescent Psychiatric Clinics of North America, 17*(3), 515–532.

Weine, S. M. (2010). *Labor migration and multilevel HIV prevention* (K24 HD067095-01). Chicago: University of Illinois.

Weine, S. M. (2011). Developing preventive mental health interventions for refugee families in resettlement. *Family Process, 50*(3), 410–430.

Weine, S., Bahromov, M., & Mirzoev, A. (2008). Unprotected Tajik male migrant workers in Moscow at risk for HIV/AIDS. *Journal of Immigrant and Minority Health, 10*(5), 461–468.

Weine, S. M., & Kashuba, A. B. (2012). Labor migration and HIV risk: A systematic review of the literature. *AIDS and Behavior, 16*(6), 1605–1621.

Wieselquist, J., Rusbult, C. E., Fosterm C. A., & Agnew, C. R. (1999). Commitment, pro-relationship behavior, and trust in close relationships. *Journal of Personality and Social Psychology, 77*(5), 942–966.

Wingood, G. M., & DiClemente, R. J. (2000). Application of the theory of gender and power to examine HIV-related exposures, risk factors, and effective interventions for women. *Health Education & Behavior, 27*(5), 539–565.

World Health Organization. (2004). *Prevention of mental disorders: Effective interventions and policy options: Summary report.* In collaboration with the Universities of Nijmegen and Maastricht, Prevention Research Centre. Geneva, Switzerland: World Health Organization.

Zabrocki, C., Jonbekov, J., Shoakova, F., Bahromov, M., & Weine, S. (2013). Condom use and intimacy among couples of Tajik male migrants and female regular partners in Moscow. *Central Asian Journal of Global Health, 2*(1).

Zhang, W., & Watanabe-Galloway, S. (2013). Using mixed methods effectively in prevention science: Designs, procedures, and examples. *Prevention Science, 15*(5), 654–662. doi:10.1007/s11121-013-0415-5

History and Emergent Practices of Multimethod and Mixed Methods in Business Research

José F. Molina-Azorín *and* Roslyn A. Cameron

Abstract

This chapter presents a history of mixed methods in business research, taking into account the great diversity of this research area. The chapter examines the pioneer studies followed by an analysis of more recent works about mixed methods in the field published after 2004, identifying prevalence studies carried out in several business disciplines over the last decade. Next, this work describes the added value of mixed methods to business research. Furthermore, a range of mixed methods exemplars from within business studies and across several subfields that have employed mixed methods designs is provided. The chapter concludes with our view on the future of mixed methods in the business literature and recommendations for future research and research capacity building within business disciplines.

Key Words: mixed methods, business, management, history, prevalence studies, added value, mixed methods designs

Introduction

Mixed methods research (MMR) is becoming increasingly articulated and recognized as the third major research approach (Johnson, Onwuegbuzie, & Turner, 2007) or the third methodological movement (Tashakkori & Teddlie, 2003), with a burgeoning MMR community. The MMR movement has emerged with a recognized name and distinct identity (Denscombe, 2008). This methodological approach has been championed by methodologists from several fields, including education, evaluation, health sciences, psychology, and sociology. Authors from these fields have published discipline-specific books that include issues on MMR (Andrew & Halcomb, 2009; Greene & Caracelli, 1997; Johnson & Christensen, 2013; Mertens, 2005; Niglas, 2004) and research texts on mixed methods (Axinn & Pearce, 2006; Bergman, 2008; Brannen, 1992; Brewer & Hunter, 2006; Creswell & Plano Clark, 2007,

2011; Greene, 2007; Hesse-Biber, 2010b; Morse & Niehaus, 2009; Plano Clark & Creswell, 2008; Ridenour & Newman, 2008; Tashakkori & Teddlie, 1998, 2003, 2010; Teddlie & Tashakkori, 2009). Moreover, the two founding coeditors of the *Journal of Mixed Methods Research* are researchers in the field of education (John Creswell and Abbas Tashakkori), and the current coeditors (Donna Mertens and Dawn Freshwater) are scholars in the fields of education and health sciences, respectively. In addition, empirical articles that employ a mixed methods approach using this distinct name in the title are also published in these fields, and literature reviews that analyze the application of this methodological approach are carried out.

Although business scholars have combined quantitative and qualitative methods (e.g., marketing research has used focus groups in combination with survey research for many years), in the business field the attention devoted to MMR has been relatively low in comparison to the disciplines from within the social and behavioral sciences identified previously as championing the mixed methods movement. Cameron and Molina-Azorin (2011b), using the framework provided by Creswell and Plano Clark (2007) for judging the current level of acceptance of mixed methods within disciplines (minimal, moderate, or maximum acceptance) concluded that there is a minimal acceptance of mixed methods in the business field. Cameron (2011) called the "first generation" faculty within the business and management fields to begin to take opportunities for instigating change and innovation in relation to the building of mixed MMR capacity. In the editorial of a special issue on MMR in business and management published in the *International Journal of Multiple Research Approaches*, Cameron and Molina-Azorin (2011a) indicated that the business field has not embraced MMR as enthusiastically as other fields. For example, there is no specific book on MMR in business. In addition, although MMR is used in business research (as we examine later), the expression "mixed methods" is not usually used in the title of mixed methods works, and there is no description of specific mixed methods designs in the methods section of these studies. Furthermore, the literature base of MMR is not employed in the published mixed methods studies (Molina-Azorin, 2011).

This chapter presents a history of mixed methods from within business research, taking into account the great diversity of this research area. Regarding this diversity, for example, in the specific field of management, the US-based Academy of Management has 25 management disciplines represented through divisions and interest groups (Table 26.1).

As further evidence to the diversity and breadth of management fields, a quick tally of the conference tracks for major associations can further demonstrate the level of discipline coverage and diversity across management fields. In 2012 the Australian and New Zealand Academy of Management had 19 conference tracks, the European Academy of Management had 27, and the British Academy of Management had 16. Moreover, along with management, other important research areas in the business field are marketing, finance, and accounting. These areas also have several academies and specific research topics. Given this wide ranging discipline coverage and diversity, the task of trying to capture the use of MMR within business research becomes almost overwhelming. Nonetheless, we have taken up the challenge and developed the chapter in a way to ensure we have captured, as best as possible, the history and emergent use of mixed methods from across the business field.

In 2003 two seminal books in MMR were published. The landmark publication edited by Tashakkori and Teddlie (2003), *Handbook of Mixed Methods in Social & Behavioral Research,* played a pivotal role in providing both visibility and credibility to the field of mixed methods (Powell, Mihalas, Onwuegbuzie, Suldo, & Daley, 2008). In the same year, the book by Creswell (2003), *Research Design: Qualitative, Quantitative and Mixed Methods Approaches,* also contributed to the diffusion and growing legitimation of MMR. In addition, we consider another key work to be the article by Johnson and Onwuegbuzie (2004): "Mixed Methods Research: A Research Paradigm Whose Time Has Come" published in the journal *Educational Researcher.* In this article, the authors position MMR as the natural complement to traditional qualitative and quantitative research.

Table 26.1 Divisions and Interest Groups of the Academy of Management (USA)

Business Policy and Strategy	Managerial and Organizational Cognition
Careers	Operations Management
Conflict Management	Organizational and Management Theory
Critical Management Studies	Organizational Development and Change
Entrepreneurship	Organizational Behavior
Gender and Diversity in Organizations	Organizational Communications and Information
Health Care Management	Systems
Human Resources	Organizations and the Natural Environment
International Management	Public and Nonprofit
Management Consulting	Research Methods
Management Education and Development	Social Issues in Management
Management History	Strategizing Activities and Practice
Management Spirituality and Religion	Technology and Innovation Management

Therefore, we consider the years 2003 and 2004 as important dates due to the publication of these key works. We use these dates as a pivotal watershed to perform an analysis of the history of mixed methods in the business field. First, we examine the pioneer studies published before 2004. This is followed by an analysis of more recent works about mixed methods in our field published after 2004, identifying prevalence studies carried out in several business disciplines over the past decade. Next, we examine the added value of mixed methods to business research. We also provide a range of mixed methods exemplars from within business studies and across several subfields that have employed mixed methods designs. Finally, we conclude the chapter with our view on the future of mixed methods in the business literature and recommendations for future research and research capacity building within business disciplines.

Pioneers of Mixed Methods Research in Business

One of the main contributions from the field of business to the mixed methods literature is the work by Jick (1979) titled "Mixing Qualitative and Quantitative Methods: Triangulation in Action." This article was published in the journal *Administrative Science Quarterly,* and it is also included in the book *The Mixed Methods Reader* (Plano Clark & Creswell, 2008). The reader provides a collection of key methodological writings in MMR, and the Jick article is the only work included in the book written by a business scholar. In this article, Jick focuses on the idea of triangulation between methods in order to indicate the main advantages of mixing qualitative and quantitative methods. The convergence or agreement between two methods enhances the belief that the results are valid and not a methodological artefact. Qualitative and quantitative methods should be viewed as complementary rather than as rival camps, underscoring the desirability of mixing methods given the strengths and weaknesses found in single method designs. He also emphasizes the importance of "mixing" the qualitative and quantitative parts. In the article, the author also indicates how the quantitative part can make important contributions to the qualitative part and vice versa.

Although triangulation is related mainly to convergence and corroboration of results, Jick (1979) also emphasizes that sometimes surprises and discrepancies in the multimethod results may lead to unexpected findings. When different methods yield dissimilar results, they demand that the researcher reconcile the differences somehow, and then this divergence can often turn out to be an opportunity for enriching the explanation. In seeking explanations for divergent results, the researcher may uncover unexpected results or unseen contextual factors. Therefore, the process of compiling research material based on multimethods is useful whether there is convergence or not. Furthermore, Jick also indicates the important role of qualitative methods, emphasizing that the firsthand knowledge drawn from qualitative methods can benefit research in business, helping the interpretation phase. As Jick states in the last paragraph of the article, triangulation is not an end in itself. Rather, it can stimulate us to better define and analyze problems in organizational research.

Together with the article by Jick (1979), another relevant pioneer work is the book by Bryman (1988) *Quantity and Quality in Social Research.* After several chapters about the nature of quantitative and qualitative research, Bryman turns to issues related to the combination of quantitative and qualitative research. Specifically, in chapter 5, he focuses on differences, similarities, strengths, and weaknesses of quantitative and qualitative research and examines the broader question of whether quantitative and qualitative research might be combined. In this regard, Bryman points out that there seem to be two distinct versions of the nature of the differences between quantitative and qualitative research that might be referred to as the "epistemological" and "technical" accounts, and these two perspectives may influence the response to the question of combination. Thus the technical version of the differences between quantitative and qualitative research seems to provide few impediments to the possibility of a research strategy that integrates them. However, the epistemological account would seem to pose more problems. If quantitative and qualitative research are taken to represent divergent epistemological packages, they are likely to exhibit incompatible views about the way in which social reality ought to be studied. In any case, Bryman points out that it is very unusual to see this point argued.

In chapter 6 of Bryman's 1988 book, he examines some of the ways in which quantitative and qualitative research may be used in tandem, adopting a technical version of the debate that much more readily accommodates a marriage of the two types of research. The author indicates that the logic of triangulation (mutual confirmation of quantitative and qualitative research) is one of the ways of combining quantitative and qualitative research. Moreover, qualitative research may facilitate quantitative research (qualitative research may act as a source of hypotheses to be tested by quantitative research or may facilitate the construction of scales for quantitative research), and quantitative research may also facilitate qualitative research (quantitative research can prepare the ground for qualitative research through the selection of people to be interviewed or companies to be selected as case studies). Finally, in chapter 7 Bryman asks: Can we genuinely combine the publications deriving from both quantitative and qualitative research and so produce an overall view of a particular substantive area? He points out that quantitative and qualitative research can frequently be found together in particular substantive areas.

These main ideas from Bryman (1988) are included in the first edition of the book by Bryman and Bell (2003), *Business Research Methods*. Specifically, in chapter 21 the authors show that, while there are many differences between quantitative and qualitative methods, there are also many examples of research that transcend this distinction. One way is through research that combines quantitative and qualitative research. Chapter 22 examines this combination. This chapter explores arguments against this combination, the suggestion that there are two versions of the debate about the possibility of mixing quantitative and qualitative research, the different ways in which MMR has been carried out, and the need to recognize that MMR is not inherently superior to research that employs a single research strategy. These ideas have been also used in subsequent editions of this book (see, e.g., the third edition: Bryman & Bell, 2011).

An interesting work about research methods in organization studies is the editorial essay written by the founding editors of the journal *Organization Science*, Daft and Lewin (1990). The title of this editorial is "Can Organization Studies Begin to Break Out of the Normal Science Straitjacket?" The authors indicate that they had heard complaints that manuscripts espousing radical ideas, or topics outside the mainstream, are difficult to publish. Reviewers for established journals seem to value papers whose theses are anchored in established theories or that use "legitimate" methods, thus implicitly creating a publication barrier for research that falls outside mainstream topics or methods. Normal science forces research into conceptual as well as methodological boxes (Kuhn, 1962). Preparadigm thinking produces scholars

without prejudice, who are alert to novel phenomena and are flexible in their approach to discovery. After a paradigm is in place, scholars are trained to elaborate the tradition rather than to challenge it. The boundaries of the paradigm can put the field in an intellectual straitjacket.

In the view of Daft and Lewin (1990), the field of organization studies has prematurely settled into a normal science mindset. These authors point out that if we accept that organizations are variable-rich, multidimensional, and perhaps chaotic, they believe it inappropriate for the field of organizational theory to have settled on a limited set of conceptual and methodological boxes. They emphasize that one challenge for this journal is to encourage diverse perspectives and methods that pursue multiple organizational realities. Related to mixed methods, the authors indicate, for example, that to gain new understanding of an organizational issue, the investigator may need to have direct contact with the organizational phenomena and may need to use qualitative and formal modeling methods to devise new theoretical explanations. Moreover, building theory on the basis of in-depth understanding of a few cases is different from the traditional theory-testing goal of statistical rigor, parsimony, and generalizability. However, this type of research can provide the genesis for new theory that may spawn further research that uses traditional methods. Therefore, the authors implicitly encourage the use of MMR in the field.

Lee (1991) published in *Organization Science* an article titled "Integrating Positivist and Interpretive Approaches to Organizational Research." The intended contribution of this article was to provide a refutation to the widely held notion that the positivist and interpretive approaches are opposed and irreconcilable. The positivist approach makes the claim that its methods (the methods of natural science) are the only truly scientific ones, while the interpretive approach makes the counterclaim that the study of people and their institutions calls for methods that are altogether foreign to those of natural science. Thus the positivist approach and the interpretive approach would appear to be in opposition. The author examines how the two approaches can be integrated so that organizational researchers can simultaneously enjoy the benefits of both, rather than just one or the other. The author develops a framework that integrates the two approaches, examining an example of how the proposed framework applies.

Another important scholar that has advocated multimethodology is John Mingers, who focused his studies in the fields of management science, operational research, and information systems. This author coedited in 1997 the book titled *Multimethodology: Theory and Practice of Combining Management Science Methodologies* (Mingers & Gill, 1997). In this book, Mingers wrote two interesting chapters. In chapter 1, Mingers (1997a) examines multiparadigm multimethodology, that is, the use of more than one methodology from different paradigms. In chapter 15, Mingers (1997b) analyzes critical pluralism, advocating a critical employment of multimethodology. In this regard, the author points out that the process of critical multimethodology is a continual cycle of reflection, judgment, and action, and it brings in and knits together methodologies and techniques as seems appropriate to action. Also in 1997, this author published in the journal *Omega* an article titled "Multimethodology: Towards a Framework For Mixing Methodologies" (Mingers & Brocklesby, 1997). In these works, Mingers examines a number of different possibilities for combining methodologies, emphasizing why such a combination might be desirable for more effective practice, in particular by focusing on how it can deal more effectively with the richness of the real world and better assist through the various intervention stages. Furthermore, Mingers (2003) carried out a review of the use of multimethodology in the information systems literature, and Mingers (2004) examined critical realism as an underpinning philosophy for information systems, indicating relationships of this paradigm with multimethodology.

Business research is dominated by quantitative methods (see Table 26.2). However, qualitative research now also enjoys considerable legitimacy. In any case, Sutton (1997), in an interesting article published in *Organization Science* titled "The Virtues of Closet Qualitative Research," examined an important issue in business research related to mixed methods. Based on his experience as an author, Sutton points out that there are circumstances when qualitative research is best treated as a closet activity. He indicates that there are times when closet qualitative research can be justified, even glorified, because it may lead to better papers. There are other times when qualitative research is a closet activity, because our norms about what is adequate scholarship are too restrictive or because some editors, reviewers, and journals remain unfairly biased against qualitative research. In such cases, authors may decide, or be required, to hide or downplay their qualitative data if they wish to publish the ideas inspired by such evidence.

Sutton (1997) emphasizes that he learned about the virtues of closet qualitative research while trying to write and publish a mix of quantitative, qualitative, and conceptual papers. These experiences led him to publish some papers that were inspired and guided by original qualitative data but in which these data were not mentioned or were deemphasized. Specifically, he found four circumstances when authors, their audiences, or both parties may benefit from treating qualitative research as a closet activity: (a) when weak qualitative data lead to good insights, (b) when describing the qualitative research reduces the quality of the writing, (c) when an outlet does not publish empirical papers, and (d) when writing for an audience that remains biased against qualitative research. The implication of these virtues of closet qualitative research for MMR is that business scholars are using MMR to a greater extent than studies published as mixed methods articles.

Another important work about mixed methods in the field of management is the chapter by Currall and Towler (2003) published in the first edition of the *Handbook of Mixed Methods in Social & Behavioral Research* (Tashakkori & Teddlie, 2003). The title of the chapter is "Research Methods in Management and Organizational Research: Toward Integration of Qualitative and Quantitative Techniques." These authors indicated that most management and organizational researchers have adopted the stance of the natural sciences. This is seen in the attempt to define organizational and management research within a scientific paradigm emphasizing theory testing through quantitative analyses. Therefore, although there is a growing appreciation for qualitative methods, historically quantitative methods have been the techniques of choice by management and business researchers. In addition, the authors emphasized that despite some movement toward greater balance, qualitative and quantitative methods have largely continued to operate on separate tracks. Thus procedures for linking qualitative and quantitative methods within a single study have received little attention in the field. These authors argue in favor of combining qualitative and quantitative methods to examine management and organizational phenomena, showing illustrative studies that integrate qualitative and quantitative methods.

Table 26.2 Prevalence Studies in Business Disciplines

Studies	Prevalence Rates of Empirical Works			Disciplines/No. of Journals	Period	Search Strategy	Total No. of Articles Reviewed
	QUAN	QUAL	MIXED				
Hurmerinta-Peltomaki and Nummela (2006)	68%	15%	17%	International business/4 journals	4 years (2000–2003)	Manual (all articles reviewed)	484 articles (394 empirical)
Hanson and Grimmer (2007)	75%	11%	14%	Marketing/3 journals	10 years (1993–2002)	Manual	1,195 articles (736 empirical)
Molina-Azorin (2008)	78% (80% strategy; 78% operations; 76% entrepreneurship)	10% (5% strategy; 12% operations; 16% entrepreneurship)	12% (15% strategy; 10% operations; 8% entrepreneurship)	Three subfields in management (strategy, operations management, and entrepreneurship/4 journals	5 years (2003–2007)	Manual	916 articles (732 empirical)
Grimmer and Hanson (2009)	65%	21%	14%	Human resource management/1 journal	10 years (1998–2007)	Manual	828 articles (633 empirical)
Molina-Azorin and Cameron (2010)	83% (82% strategy; 87% organizational behavior)	5% (4% strategy; 6% organizational behavior)	12% (14% strategy; 7% organizational behavior)	Two subdisciplines within management (strategy and organizational behavior)/2 journals	7 years (2003–2009)	Manual	871 articles (717 empirical)
Cameron (2010a)	9%	69%	22%	Vocational education and training/1 journal	6 years (2003–2008)	Manual	152 articles (106 empirical)
Cameron (2010b)	51%	43%	6%	Career development/1 journal	6 years (2004–2009)	Manual	99 articles (63 empirical)
Cameron (2011)	46%	40%	14%	Management/Conference papers	1 year (2007)	Manual	281 papers (197 empirical)
Miller and Cameron (2011)	32%	28%	40%	Business administration/ Doctor of business administration research projects	12 years (1996–2007)	Manual	186 research projects

(continued)

Table 26.2 Continued

Studies	Prevalence Rates of Empirical Works			Disciplines/No. of Journals	Period	Search Strategy	Total No. of Articles Reviewed
	QUAN	QUAL	MIXED				
Molina-Azorin (2011)	72% (78% strategy; 67% entrepreneurship)	14% (5% strategy; 23% entrepreneurship)	14% (17% strategy; 10% entrepreneurship)	Two subdisciplines within management (strategy and entrepreneurship)/4 journals	10 years (1997–2006) Strat. 8 years (2000–2007) Entrepreneurship	Manual	1,330 articles (1,072 empirical)
Harrison and Reilly (2011)	–	–	2%	Marketing/9 journals	7 years (2003–2009)	Electronic and manual	2,596 articles
Molina-Azorin (2012)	77%	8%	15%	Strategic management/1 journal	27 years (1980–2006)	Manual	1,431 articles (1,086 empirical)
Molina-Azorin, López-Gamero, Pereira-Moliner, and Pertusa-Ortega (2012)	68%	21%	11%	Entrepreneurship/5 journals	10 years (2000–2009)	Manual	955 articles (742 empirical)
Sankaran et al. (2012)	–	–	1.48%	Project management/3 journals	7 years (2004–2010)	Electronic and manual	1,755 articles (214 identified in search)
Venkatesh, Brown, and Bala (2013)	–	–	3%	Information systems/6 journals	7 years (2001–2007)	Manual	–

Rocco, Bliss, Gallagher, and Pérez-Prado (2003) published an article titled "Taking the Next Step: Mixed Methods Research in Organizational Systems" in the *Information Technology, Learning and Performance Journal*. The authors describe two major positions of mixed method advocates: the dialectical and the pragmatic. In addition, the authors examine the benefits and tenets of MMR, analyze how it is being reported in three studies published in this journal, and offer specific recommendations for clarifying written descriptions of mixed methods used, such as (a) design decisions should be made intentionally through an informed reading of the mixed methods literature, (b) the research should provide the rationalizations or justifications for the use of mixed methods grounded in the mixed methods literature, and (c) regarding data collection and analysis, enough detail should be provided so that readers understand what was done and why it was done. Finally, they indicate positive implications for the organizational systems field for clearly writing about mixed methods in publications.

Hesse-Biber (2010a) has pointed out that the practice of mixing methods was not something readily mentioned in research reports and publications during many years. In fact, most social scientists in the early 1900s up until very recently, even if they used mixed methods, did not explicitly say so. Therefore, much of the early practice has gone under the radar of social research methods history or might have been called something else. In business research, scholars have combined qualitative and quantitative methods before MMR had been "invented" or legitimized as a recognized approach. And literature reviews on the use and application of different methods usually do not take into account mixed methods as a separate category (Scandura & Williams, 2000). This issue has appeared to have changed after 2004, as we discuss in more detail in the next section.

Mixed Methods Research in Business After 2004

Works that examine different aspects of MMR have been published in the business field prior to 2004 (as indicated in the previous section). However, a growing number of studies have been conducted and published after 2004. As a result, there has also been a growing interest in the analysis of the prevalence rates of mixed methods studies in several business subfields over the past decade.

The term *prevalence studies* in relation to MMR was coined by Alise and Teddlie (2010) in their background description to research they conducted and published in the *Journal of Mixed Methods Research* that compared prevalence rate studies across several disciplines. They described mixed methods prevalence studies as a new line of research that has emerged since the mid-2000s, indicating that, in this line of research, investigators determine the percentages of qualitative, quantitative, and MMR studies that occur within journals in the social/behavioral sciences over a specified time period. They go on to explain that they appropriated the term from the field of epidemiology, where prevalence rates are used to describe the number of people within a population that have a particular disease.

Studies related to prevalence rates in the MMR community are used to assist those interested in using mixed methods to estimate the degree of awareness and utility of this methodological approach within a discipline. Table 26.2 provides a summary of 15 prevalence studies conducted across a variety of business disciplines, including career development, entrepreneurship, human resource management, information systems, international business, marketing, operations management, organizational behavior, project management, strategic management, and vocational education and training.

As can be seen from the table, these prevalence studies have emerged in the past few years with the study by Hurmerinta-Peltomaki and Nummela (2006) in international business providing a much-quoted launch pad for the emerging base of prevalence studies across business disciplines and fields.

Of the 15 prevalence rates studies documented in Table 26.2, 13 are articles published in journals. The remaining two studies analyze other forms of research reporting: Cameron (2011) examines conference papers from several management subfields, and Miller and Cameron (2011) analyze research projects as documented in applied doctoral research from across the Asia Pacific region.

From Table 26.2, it can be concluded that quantitative methods are more prevalent and dominate the methodological choice of empirical articles from the chosen disciplines, except for research in vocational education and training (Cameron, 2010a), where qualitative research is more prevalent, and doctor of business administration research projects examined by Miller and Cameron (2011), where a high percentage of the projects are based on a mixed methods approach.

Taking into account only the 13 prevalence studies that examine journal articles, quantitative studies are the most prevalent in the field of organizational behavior (87%) followed by strategic management (several studies reported percentages about 80%) and operations management (78%). Quantitative studies are least prevalent in vocational education and training (9%) and career development (51%). Qualitative are the most prevalent in vocational education and training (69%) and career development (43%) and least prevalent in the fields of strategy (4%–5%) and organizational behavior (6%).

Also seen in Table 26.2, in the 13 prevalence works that included journal articles, mixed methods studies are most prevalent in vocational education and training (22%) followed by international business (17%) and strategic management (several studies, with percentages of 17%, 15%, and 14%). Mixed methods studies are least prevalent in project management (1.48%), marketing (2% in one study, but in other work the percentage is 14%), and information systems (3%). In addition, MMR shows a higher prevalence than qualitative studies in international business, marketing, strategic management, and organizational behavior.

In terms of the period examined by these prevalence studies, the earliest year examined was 1980 (in strategy; Molina-Azorin, 2012) and the latest year studied was 2010 (in Sankaran, Cameron, & Scales, 2012). The longest period analyzed was 27 years (in strategy; Molina-Azorin, 2012) where the sample ranged from 1980 to 2006.

The main search strategy used in these prevalence studies was the manual search; that is, the authors read and reviewed all articles published in the journals in a specific time range. Thirteen studies used this search strategy, and the remaining two works employed a combination of manual and electronic search. Using the manual search strategy, the authors can identify quantitative, qualitative, and mixed methods studies. The use of different search strategies may provide different prevalence rates (Molina-Azorin, 2011). Bryman (2006), using an electronic search, pointed out that this search strategy may provide a biased sample of mixed methods studies in the sense that by no means all authors of articles reporting MMR foreground the fact that the findings reported derive from a combination of quantitative and qualitative research, or do not do so in terms of the keywords that drove the online

search strategy. In the prevalence studies included in Table 26.2, two works used a combination of electronic and manual search, and these two studies had the lowest percentages of mixed methods identified.

Along with prevalence rates, works included in Table 26.2 also examined other interesting issues. Some studies analyzed the characteristics of mixed methods studies (mixed methods purposes and designs). For example, in the field of strategic management, Molina-Azorin (2012) found that development was the main purpose of the mixed methods studies identified. Moreover, the most common type of priority was unequal priority with the quantitative part as the dominant method. Also, the main type of implementation of data collection was sequential, with the first stage the qualitative part. Thus MMR in strategy was described as most commonly being used where the qualitative component is in the service of the main quantitative component. The qualitative part may help develop or extend theory, identify the context-specific dependent and independent variables, improve the measurement instrument of the quantitative phase, and enhance the interpretation of quantitative results. Other issues that are examined in the prevalence studies are the contributions and value added by using a mixed methods approach in these business disciplines. These contributions of MMR to the advancement of business research are examined in the next section.

Together with the studies included in Table 26.2, we have identified other important works published in the past few years in the field of business that discuss aspects of the utility of MMR.

Molina-Azorin (2007) examines the use of MMR in a specific and important strategy theory, namely the resource-based view. The recent advance of this theory has posed new methodological challenges, and the issue need not be reduced to a quantitative versus qualitative methods stance but rather how to combine the strengths of each in a mixed methods approach. Some combinations of quantitative and qualitative methods were found: QUAL → QUAN, QUAN → QUAL, QUAL + QUAN, qual → QUAN, quan → QUAL, QUAL + quan, and QUAN + qual. The author carried out a literature review in relation to the use of mixed methods in the resource-based view and provided an examination of opportunities and challenges associated with the application of mixed methods in order to improve resource-based view research. Some reported opportunities were the contextualization of research, the development of measurement instruments, and the interpretation of findings. Some reported challenges found were the skills and training of strategy scholars to carry out MMR and the explicit clarification of several relevant aspects such as the core reasons for collecting both forms of data and the stage or stages at which integration is carried out.

Bazeley (2008) reviewed 16 research articles in *Administrative Science Quarterly* (June 2005–March 2006) and 19 from the *Academy of Management Journal* (February and April 2006). Of these 35 articles, 21 studies (60%) used a quantitative approach, confirming the continuing predominance of statistical, hypothesis-testing approaches in management studies. Six articles (17%) utilized a pure qualitative approach, employing primarily grounded theory techniques within a case study framework. Eight of the 35 articles (23%) used mixed methods.

A special issue titled "Mixed Methods Research in Business and Management" was published in 2011 in the *International Journal of Multiple Research Approaches*. In the editorial, the guest editors, Cameron and Molina-Azorin (2011), claimed that the business field has not embraced MMR as enthusiastically as other fields, and, based on some indicators, it seems likely that the advantages and potential of this methodological approach may be yet still unknown to many business scholars. Together with encouraging business researchers to consider the possibilities of MMR, the purpose of this special issue was to provide a variety of papers that addressed aspects of the use of mixed methods in business and the value this adds to the research problem under investigation.

The journal *Qualitative Research in Accounting & Management* also published a special issue on "Mixed Methods Research in Accounting" in 2011. The guest editors, Grafton, Lillis, and Mahama (2011) indicated that there is sparse discussion of the application and potential of MMR in the extant accounting literature. They also examined published examples of MMR in this specific field.

Added Value of Mixed Methods in Business Research

Creswell and Plano Clark (2011) point out that, regardless of the design and related procedures, the utility of MMR is tied to whether it is a valuable approach. These authors refer to O'Cathain, Murphy, and Nicholl (2007) who examined the issue of the added value of MMR through the

"yield" of mixed methods projects, taking into account the number of publications and whether the authors actually integrated the data. Moreover, the mixed methods purposes of a study identified by Greene, Caracelli, and Graham (1989; triangulation, development, complementarity, initiation, and expansion) can be considered the added value of mixed methods. Therefore, it seems that there are different perspectives regarding the value added by this methodological approach. In this section we highlight the added value of mixed methods to business research, examining some general advantages of this methodological approach and some specific contributions to business research.

General Added Value of Mixed Methods in Business Research

The central premise of mixed methods studies is that the use of quantitative and qualitative approaches in combination provides a better understanding of the research phenomenon being investigated. As noted previously, Greene et al. (1989) indicated several mixed methods purposes (triangulation, complementarity, development, initiation, and expansion) that can be considered as general advantages, contributions, or added value of mixed methods. These purposes may provide a fuller understanding of the research problem in question.

For example, in the field of strategy, with regard to triangulation, Osborne, Stubbart, and Ramaprasad (2001) indicate that, taken together, the statistical results and the qualitative evaluations are consistent and provide a solid basis of support for the hypothesis of their study. Regarding the purpose of development, Yeoh and Roth (1999) point out that the variables used in the quantitative analysis (the main part of the article) were determined through a previous qualitative phase based on interviews with product and marketing managers as well as with industry experts. In these interviews, informants were requested to identify the types of capabilities that they felt were critical for future success in the pharmaceutical industry. Thus this qualitative phase helped with the quantitative study. With regard to the purpose of complementarity (clarification or interpretation of the results from one method with the findings from the other method), Song (2002) indicates that to enrich the statistical findings, he conducted extensive field interviews, and Kor and Leblebici (2005) conducted phone interviews with a number of senior associates and partners as a reality check for interpretation of their quantitative findings.

Therefore, the purposes of MMR can assist in illuminating, in general terms, the added value mixed methods can have in relation to empirical studies in business research. In addition, another major advantage of MMR is that it enables the researcher to simultaneously generate and verify theory in the same study. For example, Sharma and Vredenburg (1998) carried out an exploratory study in a first phase. This qualitative phase was intended to examine linkages between environmental strategies and the development of capabilities and understand the nature of any emergent capabilities and their competitive outcomes. This first phase ended with two hypotheses. The second phase tested the emergent linkages through a survey study.

Specific Added Value of Mixed Methods in Business Research

Another dimension of the value added by mixed methods is that this methodological approach may contribute to addressing specific issues related to the improvement and development of business research itself. We have identified five main domains where mixed methods can add value: (a) context-specific research, (b) the analysis of outcomes and processes, (c) levels of analysis, (d) relevance of business research to practice, and (e) article impact.

First, MMR can add value in relation to context-specific research. For example, in the field of strategic management, firm strategies, internal resources, and competitive advantages are considered as highly context-specific. As a result, the task of finding a better answer to quantitative research questions could be made easier if, prior to the quantitative inquiry, a qualitative phase were carried out with the aim of acquiring a deeper understanding of the industry context. Examining a single industry arguably reduces the generalizability of the results but can support more accurate measurement of firm-specific resources and their impact on specific firm performance. In fact, the qualitative part may play an important role for determining appropriate independent (strategies, resources, capabilities, competences) and dependent (competitive advantage, performance) variables. In entrepreneurship research, it is also recommended that studies be context specific and that the entrepreneur be placed within a social context. Studies in the entrepreneurship field should pay particular attention to the context of their research and account for its complexity, uniqueness, and richness. In this regard, mixed methods studies may also help in contextualizing entrepreneurship research.

Second, theory building in business research would benefit from a greater integration between process- and outcome-oriented research. Mixed methods studies should be encouraged because they can yield richer insights regarding both process and outcomes. Giving more attention to process research could assist in improving our understanding of content related issues. Thus process studies can clarify which variables are important and why they might influence the outcomes researchers are seeking to explain. For example, in strategy research, whereas the quantitative part of a mixed methods study may focus on the statistical effects of some independent variable (e.g., firm resources and capabilities) on some dependent variable (e.g., competitive advantage or firm performance), the qualitative part may focus on processual characteristics (how these capabilities emerge and develop inside the firm studying the process of evolution).

A third important issue in business research is the level of analysis, and MMR may also add value here. A study with multiple levels of analysis yields a richer understanding than that obtained from the perspective of a single level of analysis. Furthermore, in the field of management, there is a distinction between micro and macro domains. Thus, for example, organizational behavior and human resources management are considered as micro-management research domains (topics studied at individual or group levels and their interactions), whereas strategic management and organization theory are considered as a macro domain within business research (questions studied at the firm or interfirm levels). Research in these subfields of business has been separate. However, the integration of micro and macro aspects is considered a key issue in the development of the field of management (Aguinis, Boyd, Pierce, & Short, 2011). A blending of macro and micro domains bridging different levels of theory and analysis may provide a better understanding of the holistic and interrelated nature of complex organizations. In this regard, for example, quantitative methods can be used to examine higher levels of analysis (firm), and qualitative methods can be employed to analyze lower levels (e.g., individual and team levels). On the other hand, case studies can be done at the firm level, and quantitative survey can be done with individuals. As noted by B. Johnson (personal communication, August 9, 2013), "mixed methods multilevel research" is an approach to be explored more in the future. In sum, mixed methods could be useful for the integration and analysis of several levels of analysis.

Fourth, the application of MMR may facilitate and enhance the interpretation of the results to clarify and emphasize the practical implications of a study. With regard to this practical impact, mixed methods can be used to understand the extent to which a study's results are significant in practice by including practitioners' own discourses. Aguinis et al. (2010), with the goal to bridge the science–practice gap, pointed out that to demonstrate a study's practical significance, there is a need to describe quantitative results in a way that makes sense for practitioners. They suggested that this can be achieved by including practitioners in each research project as part of a qualitative study. Therefore, these authors implicitly defend MMR whereby a quantitative study is completed with a subsequent qualitative part where practitioners become participants. After the application of a quantitative study, a qualitative part is particularly appropriate because the goal is to understand and describe phenomena. Also, qualitative research gives voice to the participants and places importance on their understanding and interpretation of a given research study.

A fifth way to examine the added value of MMR is the analysis of the impact of mixed methods articles in terms of citations. In this regard, Molina-Azorin (2011, 2012) found that mixed methods articles receive more citations than monomethod articles and that the use of a mixed methods design is a predictor of article impact in term of citation counts. Moreover, both the average citations received per year and the cumulating sum of citations were higher for articles reporting studies using mixed methods than for monomethod research designs. Furthermore, in Molina-Azorin (2012), the content analysis of the mixed methods articles showed that there are different types of studies based on several characteristics (purpose, priority, implementation, and design), and all types of mixed methods articles tended to have a higher number of citations than the group of monomethod studies.

Exemplars of Mixed Methods Studies in Business Research

This section of the chapter introduces several exemplars of the use of mixed methods across a variety of business fields and is summarized in Table 26.3. Next, we describe the main characteristics of these mixed methods studies, embellishing the first two works with visual diagrams to depict the mixed methods designs employed.

Table 26.3 Summary of Mixed Methods Studies in the Business Field

Author/Date	Field/Journal	MMR Design
Sharma and Vredenburg (1998)	Strategy *Strategic Management Journal*	QUAL → QUAN
Izushi (2005)	Entrepreneurship *Entrepreneurship and Regional Development*	QUAN→QUAL
Simoes et al. (2005)	Marketing *Journal of the Academy of Marketing Science*	qual → QUAN → (qual+quan)
Challiol and Mignonac (2005)	Organizational behavior *Journal of Organizational Behavior*	QUAN + QUAL
Lee-Kelly (2006)	Project management *International Journal of Project Management*	QUAN → qual
Johnson, Klassen, Leenders, and Awaysheh (2007)	Operations management *Journal of Operations Management*	QUAN → qual
Nielsen, Randall, and Christensen (2010)	Occupational psychology *Human Relations*	QUAN + qual
Bankins (2011)	Human resource management *International Journal of Multiple Research Approaches*	qual → QUAN → qual

Note. MMR = mixed methods research.

Strategy

An exemplar of a QUAL → QUAN design (sequential exploratory, equivalent status) with a mixed methods purpose of development is the article by Sharma and Vredenburg (1998) in the field of strategy. These authors carried out a study conducted in two phases within a single industry context (oil and gas industry). Figure 26.1 shows the visual diagram of this study. The first phase (exploratory) involved comparative case studies through in-depth interviews in seven firms in the Canadian oil and gas industry to ground the resource-based view of the firm within the domain of corporate environmental responsiveness. Interview data were used together with a qualitative content analysis of corporate public documents such as annual reports, environmental reports, company newsletters, and newspapers reports. This exploratory phase was intended to examine linkages between environmental strategies and the development of capabilities and to help understand the nature of any emergent capabilities and their competitive outcomes. This first phase ended with two hypotheses based on previous literature and the qualitative data.

The second phase (confirmatory) involved testing the emergent linkages through a mail survey–based study of the Canadian oil and gas industry. The final written report was structured in two main parts: the exploratory phase included several sections (qualitative data collection, qualitative data analysis, and results with the proposed hypotheses), and then the confirmatory study was carried out (with quantitative data collection, quantitative analysis section, and results). The qualitative phase assisted in understanding the industry and in developing theory, hypotheses, and the measurement instrument. Therefore, this study used a sequential exploratory confirmatory mixed methods design. Regarding the issue of integration, following Creswell and Plano Clark (2007), the mixed methods study by Sharma and Vredenburg (1998) integrated the qualitative and quantitative parts by connecting the results of the qualitative part to the quantitative stage. In other words, the quantitative part, as noted previously, was built on the qualitative part.

Entrepreneurship

As an exemplar of QUAN → QUAL design (sequential explanatory, equivalent status) in the business field of entrepreneurship, Izushi (2005) used quantitative and qualitative methods to study Japan's local technology centres (*kosetsushi* centers) in Nagano and Kyoto. Specifically, the author employed a combination of a mail questionnaire surveys and face-to-face interviews to examine the use of these centers by firms in these areas. The questionnaire was designed to study the use of *kosetsushi* centers by firms and the evaluation of their services and positions within the regional innovation system. Managing directors, technology managers, or individuals in similar senior management positions in 264 companies completed the questionnaire.

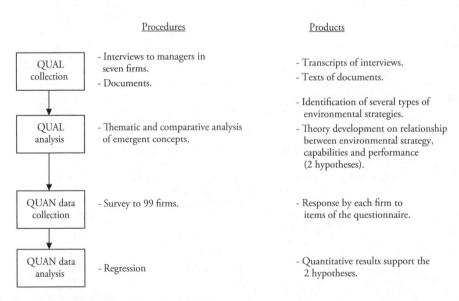

Fig. 26.1 Visual diagram of Sharma and Vredenburg (1998)

To complement the questionnaire survey, a total of 53 individuals were interviewed. They included representatives from the five *kosetsushi* centers and user firms as well as local government and economic development organizations in Nagano and trade associations in Kyoto. Interviews with user firms were aimed at elaborating and clarifying the quantitative results; examining the evolutionary process of usage in greater detail; and asking questions about services used in the first stance and at present, reasons for the shift in services used, and evaluation of *kosetsushi* centers relative to other sources of technical knowledge. Figure 26.2 provides a visual depiction of this work. Integration was carried out by connecting the quantitative and qualitative parts. In this case, the qualitative findings help clarify the quantitative results.

Marketing

In the field of marketing, Simoes, Dibb, and Fisk (2005) carried out a mixed methods study in order to measure the corporate identity management (CIM) construct. A sequential mixed methods design with three phases was implemented. In Phase 1, the authors used qualitative research to gain an in-depth understanding of CIM in the hotel industry. The evidence they collected included published documents, in-depth interviews, and material from tourism and hotel industry events. In-depth interviews with 18 experts helped narrow the search for broad, contextual information to more specific and concrete data. Interviewees included campaign managers from an advertising agency and national

and local tourism boards; directors of national and regional hotel associations; senior managers of international, national, and independent hotel units; and academics. Through this first phase, the authors identified dimensions for the questionnaire, which aided in the design of the corporate identity scale.

Then, in the second phase, the authors developed and tested the survey questionnaire. They used the literature review and the preliminary qualitative phase to generate scale items. After a pilot study, the authors mailed the final questionnaire to 2,150 hotel general managers in England; 533 usable questionnaires were received. The sample included a wide spectrum of hotels with regard to ownership, hotel unit grade, and size. Three main dimensions of the CIM construct were measured: visual identity; communications; and philosophy, mission, and values. In the measurement analysis of this quantitative phase, the authors included exploratory factor analysis and the use of the coefficient alpha. They then conducted confirmatory factor analysis to allow a stricter assessment of construct unidimensionality, using SPSS and LISREL in the analysis.

Finally, in the third phase, the authors further validated the CIM scale through a series of follow-up interviews and a minisurvey of hotel managers. They used this process to support the CIM construct and its main three dimensions. Therefore, in this third phase there was a combination of qualitative (interviews) and quantitative (minisurvey) research.

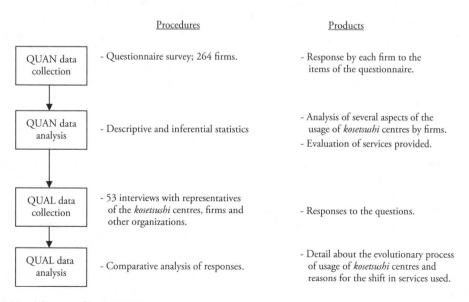

Procedures	Products

QUAN data collection — Questionnaire survey; 264 firms. — Response by each firm to the items of the questionnaire.

QUAN data analysis — Descriptive and inferential statistics — Analysis of several aspects of the usage of *kosetsushi* centres by firms. — Evaluation of services provided.

QUAL data collection — 53 interviews with representatives of the *kosetsushi* centres, firms and other organizations. — Responses to the questions.

QUAL data analysis — Comparative analysis of responses. — Detail about the evolutionary process of usage of *kosetsushi* centres and reasons for the shift in services used.

Fig. 26.2 Visual diagram of Izushi (2005)

Organizational Behavior

In the field of organizational behavior, Challiol and Mignonac (2005) presented the results of two empirical studies related to the geographical mobility of employees. In particular, this paper focused on the relocation decision-making processes of dual-earner couples. The objective was to gain a better understanding of the complex process of the relocation decision-making, and for this reason the authors indicated that two empirical studies, one quantitative and one qualitative, with two independent samples were carried out. The first study was a quantitative survey of 155 management-level employees and focused on variables likely to moderate the influence of the spouse (partner) on the probability of accepting or turning down geographical mobility. The quantitative part examined whether the spouse's attitude toward mobility unconditionally influenced the employee's likelihood of accepting a relocation opportunity or whether it interacted with other factors that the authors identified in their review of the research literature. Willingness to relocate was the dependent variable, and other variables were used as moderators and independent variables such as marital quality, perceived job alternatives for the spouse, spouse's career priority, spouse's willingness to relocate, and employee's relative contribution to household income. Hypotheses were tested using a moderated hierarchical multiple regression procedure.

The second study was qualitative, consisting of 11 in-depth interviews of dual-earner couples within which one of the partners had been required to decide whether or not to accept relocation. It complemented the first study by providing a perspective on the initial results and attempting to identify and isolate the dynamics within the couple when making relocation decisions. The authors indicated that this second study constituted both triangulation across methods (reconciling qualitative and quantitative data) and complementarity by examining overlapping and different facets of a phenomenon. The authors used a snowball sampling technique to identify participants in the qualitative study, and they decided to use two approaches in collecting and analyzing the data: the biographic method and the critical incident technique.

Project Management

Lee-Kelley (2006) combined a survey with a case study in the field of project management. This paper reported a study of the locus of control and attitudes in working with virtual teams. The author refers to this as a two-stage design with two sequential data collection stages. The first stage was quantitative followed by a qualitative stage. The results from both data collection methods were compared to enable the researcher to gain a greater depth of understanding of the issues facing individuals who were initially identified in the quantitative study. Seven hypotheses were derived from the literature, and a quantitative survey was sent to members of the Association of Project Management. The survey was designed to examine the relationships among various constructs: control expectancies, role conflict perception, and job satisfaction. The analysis of the data was undertaken using statistical analysis.

In the second stage, the author conducted 12 semistructured interviews with participants from a service company selected as a case study. The case was an IT company in the UK with approximately 500 project professionals. Interviews were transcribed and coded using QSR NVivo 2.0 software. The qualitative findings coded under the concepts of the constructs measured in the survey were then compared to the survey results for the same constructs as a means to elaborate on the first stage results. After the analysis of the quantitative stage, the qualitative data were analyzed to locate some "typical" expectancy responses by ordering these under either external or internal dimensions according to whether their answers indicated attributions to personal ability and effort or to the project conditions or situation.

Operations Management

In the business field of operations management, Johnson, Klassen, Leenders, and Awaysheh (2007) conducted a study that analyzed the drivers and outcomes of e-business technology use in supply chains. The authors examined how industry context, firm characteristics, and firm-level strategic resources influence the exploitation of e-business technologies and the relationship between e-business technology use and firm performance. Specifically, the authors indicated that a two-phase study employing survey- and case-based empirical methods was undertaken to understand the relationship between the use of purchasing teams, e-business technology adoption, and expected performance outcomes. The methods' purpose was complementarity: survey methods provided a means to examine the generalizability of relationships. Then, by way of follow-up, the qualitative case–based study allowed a greater examination of the mechanisms that underpin the relationships that were statistically supported in the quantitative stage of the study.

In the quantitative stage, a survey instrument was developed to examine the relationships between a firm-level strategic resource, namely purchasing team use and e-business technology use. The target population was large manufacturing and services firms in the United States and Canada. Of the 640 targeted firms, 284 completed questionnaires were returned. In order to identify a taxonomy of e-business technologies and a taxonomy of team use, exploratory factor analysis was used. Then, Tobit regression analysis was carried out to determine the influence of team usage, industry context, and firm characteristics on e-business technology use. Ordinary least squares regression was used to examine the impact of e-business technologies, team use, industry context, and firm characteristics on firm performance. In terms of the qualitative case studies, interviews with managers from four respondent companies were completed to explore the relationship between purchasing teams and e-business technologies. The researcher used theoretical sampling: each site was purposely selected based on the relative use of e-business technologies, purchasing team usage, and performance outcomes to permit comparisons among the sites. A protocol containing some questions was developed, although the interviews were semistructured to allow opportunities for the interviewers to pursue relevant lines of questioning. Multiple sources of evidence were used.

Organizational Psychology

Nielsen, Randall, and Christensen (2010) report on a research project conducted from the field of organizational psychology. The research team was multidisciplinary with the lead author in the field of occupational health psychology, the second author from the occupational psychology/organizational behavior field, and the third a biostatistician. Their study used both qualitative and quantitative data in an 18-month longitudinal quasi-experimental study on the implementation of teamwork. An intervention group (teams with managers who received training) was compared with a comparison group (teams with managers who did not receive training). The data collection involved a combination of both process and effect evaluation using a mixed methods approach.

The rationale was that this approach is a powerful method of strengthening experimental designs through the triangulation of data and different methods. The authors identified the use of mixed methods in quasi-experiential designs as rare but stated that it adds value in terms of providing an important explanatory power when complex and multiple change mechanisms are being studied in complex organizational settings.

The study was undertaken over an 18-month period with the quantitative data collected at Time 1 (pretest) and Time 2 (posttest). This was via questionnaire-based measures conducted preintervention and postintervention. The questionnaire contained questions about the managers' leadership behaviors and team organization and team functioning. Confirmatory factor analysis was used to test the factor structure. Participants of the study were from the elderly care sector in Denmark with the majority of participants being nurses or healthcare assistants who spend the vast majority of their time in the direct care of elderly patients. The manager training intervention was conducted using an action learning theory model with managers having to address real-life issues and problems. The qualitative data collection occurred 15 months after the Time 1 quantitative data collection and involved semistructured interviews with the managers. The authors explained the benefits of using a mixed method approach as achieving three important goals: triangulate data, identify mechanisms behind the changes, and identify the impact of the intervention context. The authors were strong in their conviction that a traditional quasi-experiential design would not have yielded the results that they achieved with the mixed methods approach. "Using a mixed methods approach enabled us to analyze effects at several levels at the same time as investigating hypotheses using several sources of data" (Nielson et al., 2010, p. 1736).

Human Resource Management

The last study discussed in this section of the chapter is another longitudinal and sequentially implemented mixed methods study by Bankins (2011) from the field of human resource management and exemplifies a well thought out and comprehensive account of methodological choices when deciding on the utilization of a mixed methods study. Bankins utilized Teddlie and Tashakkori's (2009) four methodological decision points for formulating the MMR design employed in this study. This resulted in the following longitudinal and sequential-implemented research design (qual → QUAN → qual). The first strand was individual interviews followed by two surveys and individual interviews. The focus was on assessing the change in the psychological contract through the lens of a critical realist philosophy. "The psychological contract has been used extensively as a device to conceptualise, explore and understand the employment relationship" (Bankins, 2011, p. 352). The author's rationale for using a mixed methods design was to draw on the strengths of both modes of inquiry in order to explore the research phenomenon of intra-individual change in the psychological contract. The research questions were aimed at the content of the psychological contract and how it changes over time.

Bankins (2011) used a longitudinal sequential-implemented MMR design and refers to how the adoption of a critical realist philosophy supports the "mixing" of methods. The author documents her research design through a series of methodological decision points devised by Teddlie and Tashakkori (2009) related to (a) the number and type of methodological approaches, (b) the number and type of strands used, (c) the implementation of the research design, and (d) the integration of the research strands. The first strand involved interviews (Study 1) followed by the second (Study 2), which involved four-wave surveys, and the third (Study 3), which were interviews and which gave the study the following design: Qual → QUAN → qual. The participants were 320 organizational newcomers (graduates in graduate development programs) in 2008 from across a range of private-sector organizations in Australia and New Zealand. Study 1 involved 15 interviews with graduates and 8 interviews with managers. Study 2 involved a set of surveys with graduates at four different times over a 16-month period. Study 3 contained 26 interviews with graduates at the end of the 16-month period. The author concludes that the most significant contribution of the study is the innovative longitudinal mixed methods design, in a field of inquiry (psychological contract) that is dominated by cross-sectional quantitative studies.

Vision of the Future of Mixed Methods in Business Research

In this chapter we have attempted to map the history and emergence of mixed methods research in business by signposting the reader to some of the more influential and pioneering pieces of business research that have been published before the pivotal watershed years of 2003–2004. We then directed attention to studies conducted after this period that have mainly examined the prevalence and use of mixed methods across an array of business subfields. Our examination demonstrates the varying uses of mixed methods across subdisciplines but also points to many of the key issues remaining for business researchers when undertaking MMR and attempting to have these published. Our chapter then moved to a detailed discussion of how mixed methods can add value to business research through two main dimensions, general value-added and specific value-added, with the latter including context-specific research, simultaneous outcome and process research, multiple levels of analysis, relevance, and impact. This was followed by exemplars on how MMR has been applied across a variety of business fields to provide concrete evidence of its purposes and application.

So where does this now bring us? What does the future hold for MMR in the business world?

The evidence suggests mixed methods has achieved thus far a relatively minimal acceptance level across business research (Cameron & Molina-Azorin 2011a, 2011b) and yet it has great potential and what Grafton et al. (2011) refer to as "missed opportunities" by business researchers to leverage off this potential through the value-added propositions offered by this methodological approach. The future of mixed methods in business lies with the business faculty, and specifically those tasked with building research capacity, to promote and engage in activities that challenge what Hurmerinta-Peltomaki and Nummela (2006) refer to as the "institutionalised mindsets" found in many business traditions, to begin to acknowledge the contributions mixed methods can make to both theory building and testing and by exploring innovative ways in which to investigate business phenomena in increasingly complex contexts and environments. The business academic community has a crucial role to play in the continued emergence of mixed methods, and we make the following recommendations, based on the call to the "first generation" faculty in business and management research (Cameron, 2011).

First, the use of MMR requires that business scholars develop a broader set of research skills, and the need for such skills has definite implications for how researchers need to be trained. Then, to improve the implementation of mixed methods studies, academic institutions should increase their concern for education about this type of research. We recommend the embedding and teaching of mixed methods within higher research degree programs and the building of MMR capacity through mixed methods doctoral workshops.

This activity should also be targeted at early career and experienced researchers alike and needs to be legitimated through offerings from existing academies and academic professional associations. A prime example is the research methods special interest groups of the existing and well-established academies of management to which there are emerging signs that this is beginning to occur (e.g., the Mixed Methods Research Special Interest Group of the Australian and New Zealand Academy of Management).

Second, we recommend challenging academic promotion and reward structures and traditional career pathways that continue to reinforce the qualitative/quantitative divide. For example, business should make strong links to MMR and involvement in multidisciplinary teams as a distinct career strategy for early career researchers. There is a strong imperative to build research capacity for the future through mentoring and research collaboration, in a time when most academic workforces are aging.

In this regard, academic institutions must take into account that it is not easy to conduct and publish mixed methods studies and, at the same time, to publish a large number of articles. Mixed methods studies require more time, work, effort, and resources than studies that use only a single method. Therefore, carrying out mixed methods studies may lead to the publication of fewer articles than if the strategy is to publish monomethod articles. Thus significant attention must be paid to this issue by academic institutions in evaluation, promotion, and tenure decisions.

Our third recommendation asks that business researchers more frequently extend beyond their own discipline boundaries and traditions and become open to the notion of multi- and interdisciplinary research teams. Innovative forms of research collaboration tend to go hand in hand with this. This is particularly pertinent in a competitive funding environment where funding bodies are looking for the "best value for their research buck."

Last, we recommend that editors, editorial panels, and journal reviewers in the business field develop more inclusive publication policies by explicitly encouraging a range of research approaches that includes monomethods, multimethods, and mixed methods. Business academics in their roles as supervisors, reviewers, assessors, and editors need to be knowledgeable and open to the variety of methodological approaches that are being utilized and freed from the confines of institutionalized practices and socialized traditions. Editors try to increase the impact of their journals, and, as noted earlier in the chapter, the use of a mixed methods approach is related to citation counts. Therefore, journals should encourage the publication of mixed methods articles. Moreover, editors should assign reviewers who have an understanding of mixed methods to review manuscript submissions that use this approach. A barrier to conducting mixed methods studies is the existing constraints to publish these works, such as page limits in journals. We recommend flexibility in manuscript length because by limiting space journals may discourage publication of MMR.

As is the case in the science of change and change management and the study of organizational culture, change comes slowly, with the early adopters or first generation playing a crucial role. We need to enable the new generation. We hope this chapter helps to advance business research through the diffusion of mixed methods literature to this new generation.

Discussion Questions

1. How would you describe the emergence of mixed methods within the field of business research?

2. In what ways does mixed methods add value to business research?

3. What do the mixed methods prevalence studies in Table 26.2 indicate to you?

4. What are some of the challenges facing business scholars who choose to use MMR?

5. What key messages has reading this chapter provided for you?

References

Aguinis, H., Boyd, B. K., Pierce, C. A., & Short, J. C. (2011). Walking new avenues in management research methods and theories: Bridging micro and macro domains. *Journal of Management, 37*, 395–403.

Aguinis, H., Werner, S., Abbott, J., Angert, C., Park, J., & Kohlhausen, D. (2010). Customer-centric science: Reporting significant research results with rigor, relevance, and practical impact in mind. *Organizational Research Methods, 13*, 515–539.

Alise, M., & Teddlie, C. (2010). A continuation of the paradigm wars? Prevalence rates of methodological approaches across the social/behavioral sciences. *Journal of Mixed Methods Research, 4*, 103–126.

Andrew, S., & Halcomb, E. (Eds.). (2009). *Mixed methods research for nursing and the health sciences.* Chichester, UK: Wiley-Blackwell.

Axinn, W. G., & Pearce, L. D. (2006). *Mixed method data collection strategies.* New York, NY: Cambridge University Press.

Bankins, S. (2011). Tracking employees' twists and turns: Describing a mixed methods approach to assessing change in the psychological contract. *International Journal of Multiple Research Approaches, 5*, 351–366.

Bazeley, P. (2008). Mixed methods in management research. In R. Holt & R. Thorpe (Eds.), *Dictionary of qualitative management research* (pp. 133–136). London, England: Sage.

Brannen, J. (Ed.). (1992). *Mixing methods: Qualitative and quantitative research.* Aldershot, UK: Avebury.

Bergman, M. (Ed.). (2008). *Advances in mixed methods research.* London, England: Sage.

Brewer, J., & Hunter, A. (2006). *Foundations of multimethod research.* Thousand Oaks, CA: Sage.

Bryman, A. (1988). *Quantity and quality in social research.* New York, NY: Routledge.

Bryman, A. (2006). Integrating quantitative and qualitative research: How is it done? *Qualitative Research, 6*, 97–113.

Bryman, A., & Bell, E. (2003). *Business research methods.* Oxford, UK: Oxford University Press.

Bryman, A., & Bell, E. (2011). *Business research methods* (3rd ed.). Oxford, UK: Oxford University Press.

Cameron, R. (2010a). Mixed methods in VET research: Usage and quality. *International Journal of Training Research, 8*, 25–39.

Cameron, R. (2010b). Is mixed methods used in Australian career development research? *Australian Journal of Career Development, 19*, 53–67.

Cameron, R. (2011). Mixed methods in business and management: A call to the "first generation." *Journal of Management & Organization, 17*, 245–267.

Cameron, R., & Molina-Azorin, J. F. (2011a). Editorial: Mixed methods research in business and management. *International Journal of Multiple Research Approaches, 5*(3), 286–289.

Cameron, R., & Molina-Azorin, J. F. (2011b). The acceptance of mixed methods in business and management research. *International Journal of Organizational Analysis, 19*, 256–271.

Challiol, H., & Mignonac, K. (2005). Relocation decision-making and couple relationships: A quantitative and qualitative study of dual-earner couples. *Journal of Organizational Behavior, 26*, 247–274.

Creswell, J. (2003). *Research design: Qualitative, quantitative and mixed methods approaches* (2nd ed.). Thousand Oaks, CA: Sage.

Creswell, J. W., & Plano Clark, V. L. (2007). *Designing and conducting mixed methods research.* Thousand Oaks, CA: Sage.

Creswell, J. W., & Plano Clark, V. L. (2011). *Designing and conducting mixed methods research* (2nd ed.). Thousand Oaks, CA: Sage.

Currall, S., & Towler, A. (2003). Research methods in management and organizational research: Toward integration of qualitative and quantitative techniques. In A. Tashakkori & C. Teddlie (Eds.), *Handbook of mixed methods in social & behavioral research* (pp. 513–526). Thousand Oaks, CA: Sage.

Daft, R. L., & Lewin, A. Y. (1990). Can organization studies begin to break out of the normal science straitjacket? An editorial essay. *Organization Science, 1*, 1–9.

Denscombe, M. (2008). Communities of practice. A research paradigm for the mixed methods approach. *Journal of Mixed Methods Research, 2*, 270–283.

Grafton, J., Lillis, A. M., & Mahama, H. (2011). Mixed methods research in accounting. *Qualitative Research in Accounting & Management, 8*, 5–21.

Greene, J. (2007). *Mixed methods in social inquiry.* San Francisco, CA: Jossey-Bass.

Greene, J., & Caracelli, V. (Eds.). (1997). *Advances in mixed-method evaluation: The challenges and benefits of integrating diverse paradigms.* San Francisco, CA: Jossey-Bass.

Greene, J., Caracelli, V., & Graham, W. (1989). Toward a conceptual framework for mixed-method evaluation designs. *Educational Evaluation and Policy Analysis, 11*, 255–274.

Grimmer, M., & Hanson, D. (2009, December). *Qualitative and quantitative research published in the* International Journal of Human Resource Management, 1998–2007. Paper presented at the annual meeting of the Australian and New Zealand Academy of Management, Melbourne.

Hanson, D., & Grimmer, M. (2007). The mix of qualitative and quantitative research in major marketing journals, 1993–2002. *European Journal of Marketing, 41*, 58–70.

Harrison, R. L., & Reilly, T. M. (2011). Mixed methods designs in marketing research. *Qualitative Market Research: An International Journal, 14*(1), 7–26.

Hesse-Biber, S. (2010a). Emerging methodologies and methods practices in the field of mixed methods research. *Qualitative Inquiry, 16*, 415–418.

Hesse-Biber, S. (2010b). *Mixed methods research. Merging theory with practice.* New York, NY: Guilford Press.

Hurmerinta-Peltomaki, L., & Nummela, N. (2006). Mixed methods in international business research: A value-added perspective. *Management International Review, 46*, 439–454.

Izushi, H. (2005). Creation of relational assets through the "Library of Equipment" model: An industrial modernization approach of Japan's local technology centres. *Entrepreneurship and Regional Development, 17*, 183–204.

Jick, T. (1979). Mixing qualitative and quantitative methods: Triangulation in action. *Administrative Science Quarterly, 24*, 602–611.

Johnson, P., Klassen, R., Leenders, M., & Awaysheh, A. (2007). Utilizing e-business technologies in supply chains: The impact of firm characteristics and teams. *Journal of Operations Management, 25*, 1255–1274.

Johnson, R. B., & Christensen, L. B. (2013). *Educational research methods: Quantitative, qualitative, and mixed approaches* (5th ed.). Los Angeles, CA: Sage.

Johnson, R. B., & Onwuegbuzie, A. (2004). Mixed methods research: A research paradigm whose time has come. *Educational Researcher, 33*, 14–26.

Johnson, R. B., Onwuegbuzie, A., & Turner, L. (2007). Toward a definition of mixed methods research. *Journal of Mixed Methods Research, 1*, 112–133.

Kor, Y. Y., & Leblebici, H. (2005). How do interdependencies among human-capital deployment, development, and diversification strategies affect firms' financial performance? *Strategic Management Journal, 26*, 967–985.

Kuhn, T. (1962). *The structure of scientific revolutions.* Chicago, IL: University of Chicago Press.

Lee, A. S. (1991). Integrating positivist and interpretive approaches to organizational research. *Organization Science, 2*, 342–365.

Lee-Kelley, L. (2006). Locus of control and attitudes to working in virtual teams. *International Journal of Project Management, 24*, 234–243.

Mertens, D. (2005). *Research and evaluation in education and psychology: Integrating diversity with quantitative, qualitative and mixed methods* (2nd ed.). Thousand Oaks, CA: Sage.

Miller, P., & Cameron, R. (2011). Mixed method research designs: A case study of their adoption in a doctor of business administration program. *International Journal of Multiple Research Approaches, 5*, 387–402.

Mingers, J. (1997a). Multi-paradigm multimethodology. In J. Mingers & A. Gill (Eds.), *Multimethodology: Theory and practice of combining management science methodologies* (pp. 1–20). Chichester, UK: Wiley.

Mingers, J. (1997b). Towards critical pluralism. In J. Mingers & A. Gill (Eds.), *Multimethodology: Theory and practice of combining management science methodologies* (pp. 407–440). Chichester, UK: Wiley.

Mingers, J. (2003). The paucity of multimethod research: A survey of the IS literature. *Information Systems Journal, 13*, 233–249.

Mingers, J. (2004). Real-izing information systems: Critical realism as an underpinning philosophy for information systems. *Information and Organization, 14*, 87–103.

Mingers, J., & Brocklesby, J. (1997). Multimethodology: Towards a framework for mixing methodologies. *Omega, 25*, 489–509.

Mingers, J., & Gill, A. (Eds.). (1997). *Multimethodology: Theory and practice of combining management science methodologies.* Chichester, UK: Wiley.

Molina-Azorín, J. F. (2007). Mixed methods in strategy research: Applications and implications in the resource-based view. In D. Ketchen & D. Bergh (Eds.), *Research methodology in strategy and management* (Vol. 4, pp. 37–73). Oxford, UK: Elsevier.

Molina-Azorín, J. F. (2008, July). *Mixed methods research in business management: A comparison of the use of mixed methods in three specific areas.* Paper presented at the Fourth Mixed Methods Conference, Cambridge, UK.

Molina-Azorín, J. F. (2011). The use and added value of mixed methods in management research. *Journal of Mixed Methods Research, 5*, 7–24.

Molina-Azorín, J. F. (2012). Mixed methods research in strategic management: Impact and applications. *Organizational Research Methods, 15*, 33–56.

Molina-Azorín, J. F., & Cameron, R. (2010). The application of mixed methods in organisational research: A literature review. *The Electronic Journal of Business Research Methods, 8*, 95–105.

Molina-Azorín, J. F., López-Gamero, M. D., Pereira-Moliner, J., & Pertusa-Ortega, E. (2012). Mixed methods studies in entrepreneurship research: Applications and contributions. *Entrepreneurship & Regional Development, 24*, 425–456.

Morse, J., & Niehaus, L. (2009). *Mixed method design. Principles and procedures.* Walnut Creek, CA: Left Coast Press.

Nielsen, K., Randall, R., & Christensen, K. B. (2010). Does training managers enhance the effects of implementing team-working? A longitudinal, mixed methods field study. *Human Relations, 63*, 1719–1741.

Niglas, K. (2004). *The combined use of qualitative and quantitative methods in educational research.* Tallinn, Estonia: Tallinn Pedagogical University Press.

O'Cathain, A., Murphy, E., & Nicholl, J. (2007). Integration and publications as indicators of "yield" from mixed methods studies. *Journal of Mixed Methods Research, 1*, 147–163.

Osborne, J., Stubbart, C., & Ramaprasad, A. (2001). Strategic groups and competitive enactment: A study of dynamic relationships between mental models and performance. *Strategic Management Journal, 22*, 435–454.

Plano-Clark, V., & Creswell, J. (2008). *The mixed methods reader.* Thousand Oaks, CA: Sage.

Powell, H., Mihalas, S., Onwuegbuzie, A., Suldo, S., & Daley, C. (2008). Mixed methods research in school psychology: A mixed methods investigation of trends in the literature. *Psychology in the Schools, 45*, 291–309.

Ridenour, C. S., & Newman, I. (2008). *Mixed methods research. Exploring the interactive continuum.* Carbondale: Southern Illinois University Press.

Rocco, T. S., Bliss, L. A., Gallagher, S., & Perez-Prado, A. (2003). Taking the next step: Mixed methods research in organizational systems. *Information Technology, Learning and Performance Journal, 21*, 1–29.

Sankaran, S., Cameron, R., & Scales, J. (2012). *The utility of mixed methods in project management research.* 12th EURAM Conference Proceedings, Social Innovation for Competitiveness. Organisational Performance and Human Excellence, Rotterdam, The Netherlands.

Scandura, T. A., & Williams, E. A. (2000). Research methodology in management: Current practices, trends and implications for future research. *Academy of Management Journal, 43*, 1248–1264.

Sharma, S., & Vredenburg, H. (1998). Proactive corporate environmental strategy and the development of competitively valuable organizational capabilities. *Strategic Management Journal, 19*, 729–753.

Simoes, C., Dibb, S., & Fisk, R. (2005). Managing corporate identity: An internal perspective. *Journal of the Academy of Marketing Science, 33*, 153–168.

Song, J. (2002). Firm capabilities and technology ladders: Sequential foreign direct investments of Japanese electronics firms in East Asia. *Strategic Management Journal, 23*, 191–210.

Sutton, R. I. (1997). The virtues of closet qualitative research. *Organization Science, 8*, 97–106.

Tashakkori, A., & Teddlie, C. (1998). *Mixed methodology. Combining qualitative and quantitative approaches.* Thousand Oaks, CA: Sage.

Teddlie, C., & Tashakkori, A. (2009). *Foundations of mixed methods research. Integrating quantitative and qualitative approaches in the social and behavioral sciences.* Thousand Oaks, CA: Sage.

Tashakkori, A., & Teddlie, C. (Eds.). (2003). *Handbook of mixed methods in social & behavioral research.* Thousand Oaks, CA: Sage.

Tashakkori, A., & Teddlie, C. (Eds.) (2010). *SAGE handbook of mixed methods in social & behavioral research* (2nd ed.). Thousand Oaks, CA: Sage.

Venkatesh, V., Brown, S., & Bala, H. (2013). Bridging the qualitative-quantitative divide: Guidelines for conducting mixed methods research in information systems. *MIS Quarterly, 37*, 21–54.

Yeoh, P., & Roth, D. (1999). An empirical analysis of sustained advantage in the U.S. pharmaceutical industry: Impact of firm resources and capabilities. *Strategic Management Journal, 20*, 637–653.

How Does Mixed Methods Research Add Value to Our Understanding of Development?

Nicola A. Jones, Paola Pereznieto, *and* Elizabeth Presler-Marshall

Abstract

Utilizing mixed methods research (MMR) in development evaluations addresses many of the shortcomings of single method approaches, ultimately leading to better informed policy and programming. It allows researchers to harness rigorous quantitative evidence, critical for ascertaining whether and to what extent an intervention has had an effect, as well as to capture the nuance and context-specificity, via qualitative work, which can help explain how and why impacts have or have not been achieved in a given context. Following a discussion of the evolution of MMR in the development arena, this chapter presents case studies that highlight its as-yet unfilled potential to strengthen program design and implementation in ways that respect cultural diversity, engage with high-level outcomes such as "empowerment," and avoid unintended consequences on marginalized groups that jeopardize development goals.

Key Words: mixed methods research, MMR, qualitative, development evaluations, impact evaluation, evidence, policy and programming

The Emergence of "Development" and Development Studies

In order to understand the relative significance of mixed methods research (MMR) within the international development field, it is critical to begin with a brief historical review of the emergence of the development studies discipline. Following the advent of "development" as a political goal in the mid-20th century, development studies began as an interdisciplinary field of inquiry in the 1950s. Buch-Hansen and Lauridsen (2012) argue that the evolution of development studies can be divided into two main periods, respectively characterized by "mainstream, critical and counterpoint approaches" to the study of development. The first period (1950s–1970s) was dominated by the modernization paradigm, whereby development was viewed as an imitative process that would lead to the transformation of traditional societies into modern,

advanced nations. The main driver of change was seen to be state-led economic accumulation and industrialization. This approach was challenged by critical development theories, most notably dependency theories originating in Latin America, which argued that development was really characterized by global processes of unevenness and dependency. Others critiqued the large-scale one-size-fits-all approach of modernization theory and argued for the importance of more diverse, participatory, and equity-oriented development strategies rooted in local culture and thinking.

During the second period (1980s–2000s), there was a shift in focus toward globalization and international governance. Mainstream development economists rejected a separate approach to analyzing developing economies and instead applied a standard neoliberal lens to identifying national development problems, highlighting government failures whereby the state was typically the obstacle to rather than the driver of development (e.g., failed policies, excessive or inappropriate regulations, protectionism, rent seeking, and corruption). Dubbed the Washington Consensus, this neoliberal paradigm was challenged by critical development theorists, who sought to highlight alternative trajectories to development (e.g., East Asian developmentalism), as well as alternative development priorities such as equity, poverty reduction, and sustainable human development, based on Sen's (1999) capability framework. Postdevelopment theorists also critiqued the knowledge–power effects of development discourses, which they argued reproduced misery and oppression. Instead, theorists in this school of thought called for a new approach, one that reflected a variety of "localised and pluralistic histories, cultures, identities and knowledge systems" (Buch-Hansen & Lauridsen, 2012, p. 295) but at the same time did not overly romanticize predevelopment "traditions" (Escobar, 1995, pp. 215–217, quoted in Corbridge, 2007, p. 185).

Development Evaluations "As Usual"

While it is true that development studies are characterized by considerable diversity, development evaluations have been dominated by mainstream paradigms and research questions, with methodological approaches reflecting these underlying foci. The gold standard of development evaluation work is—although this is increasingly called into question, as we discuss later—quantitative impact evaluations that seek, based on counterfactual evidence, to answer the question, "What interventions work across multiple contexts?" In this regard, the development evaluation field has been strongly influenced by the world of medical science, where quantitative experimental methods, especially randomized control trials (RCTs), are predominant and seen as the most rigorous evaluation approach. RCTs depend on counterfactual analysis, randomly selecting control and treatment groups in order to assess the cause and effect of an intervention. This type of approach is championed by institutions such as the Abdul Lateef Jameel Poverty Action Lab, Innovations for Poverty Action, the World Bank's Development Impact Evaluation initiative, the Strategic Impact Evaluation Fund, and the International Initiative for Impact Evaluation—all of which aim to increase the reliability and use of impact evaluation evidence underpinning development interventions.

And indeed, within the context of a broader shift toward evidence-based policy and practice, many policymakers have shown a strong interest in RCTs, as they offer a powerful way of overcoming both selection bias (preselecting groups more likely to exhibit a particular impact) and observer bias (researchers' preconceived beliefs about the likely impact of a particular intervention). As a leading light in this field, Ester Duflo emphasizes that "creating a culture in which rigorous randomized evaluations are promoted, encouraged, and financed has the potential to revolutionize social policy during the 21st century, just as randomized trials revolutionized medicine during the 20th" (*The Lancet*, 2004, p. 731).

Strengths and Shortcomings of Development Evaluations "As Usual"

Not surprisingly, donors and many developing country governments have been very receptive to this type of evaluation evidence, as findings are seen as "scientific" and difficult to dispute on account of their counterfactual analytical approach and because they aim to understand what sorts of interventions work across contexts. Examples that have enjoyed widespread resonance include RCTs demonstrating the role of deworming tablets in increasing school attendance and in turn performance (Miguel & Kremer, 2001) and the RCT evaluation of Mexico's *Progresa-Oportunidades* cash transfer program, which has not only emerged globally as a hallmark for evaluation good practice among poverty reduction interventions but also has contributed to the burgeoning of cash transfer programs globally.[1] Moreover, by focusing on what works where, quantitative impact evaluations speak to "cost-effectiveness" and "value-for-money" agendas, which are on the ascendancy in the international aid world, especially in light of recent global fiscal crises and increasing public pressures to demonstrate how international aid budgets are being spent when domestic hardships abound (Department for International Development, 2011; Dhaliwal, Duflo, Glennerster, Tulloch, & Latif, 2012).

Such considerations are clearly important, not least because development studies from its outset has had as a defining characteristic a commitment to engage with development policy processes (Corbridge, 2007; White, 2009). Sackett (2002), for example, argues that it is irresponsible to intervene in people's lives on the basis of theories unsupported by reliable empirical evidence. That said, what the dominance of quantitative impact RCT evaluation evidence does do is limit the questions the development community, and by extension the broader public, is asking about development interventions and broader development processes and trajectories. Too often there is a focus on the "what" without understanding the "why." So, for example, quantitative impact evaluations can identify whether particular poverty reduction tools such as cash transfers or microcredit alleviate individual vulnerability, but they often fail to shed light on why this is the case. Does a cash transfer program work in reducing poverty because of the economic resources it provides vulnerable households and/or because it helps restore individual dignity and facilitates greater participation in community activities? Does microcredit enhance women's economic empowerment because it helps in overcoming known obstacles to financial institutions or because it also helps shift intra-household dynamics with regard to decision-making about expenditures?

Furthermore, quantitative impact evaluations typically overlook key issues of politics, power, and context, even though there is increasing evidence that these are often at the root of vulnerability and inequality (Chronic Poverty Research Centre, 2009; Hickey, 2010). So, for instance, while quantitative evaluations have found programs that condition beneficiary support on children's nutritional improvements (such as taking supplements, increasing body weight) to be effective, qualitative studies have suggested the impacts are often not translating into embedded behavioral and attitudinal change on the part of caregivers (see Maluccio & Flores, 2005). Parents are reporting changes in supplement use or overfeeding children just before mandatory weigh-ins, reflecting power differentials between themselves and program managers (see Adato, 2008). This suggests that, if unintended and indeed negative effects are to be avoided, understanding why reported behavioral change is happening can be critical. An additional limitation of development evaluations "as usual" is that they tend to focus on discrete interventions (e.g., supply of blackboards in classrooms, deworming tablets, monthly transfers of cash), rather than addressing questions about more complex interventions that seek to catalyze longer term changes regarding sociocultural and political processes, such as questions relating to peace building, governance, and crime reduction (e.g., Jones, Jones, & Walsh, 2008). Cultural norms and attitudes, for instance, may take considerable time

for impact to be realized, and, moreover, are likely to be nonlinear in nature (Bicchieri, 2006). In this vein, recent qualitative work by the World Bank highlights that changing gendered social norms is often a long-term, nonlinear process because of the "sticky" or persistent nature of cultural values and practices. While shifts in norms (e.g., around girls' education or child marriage) may occur in response to short-term incentives (e.g., cash or in-kind support) or sanctions (e.g., fines), once these interventions are discontinued, related practices often resurface (Boudet, Petesch, Turk, & Thumala, 2013).

More recently, in an effort to further strengthen development policy evidence and avoid extrapolating "lessons learned" from cherry-picked cases, a new trend in development evaluation in the form of systematic reviews has emerged. This builds on the principles of impact evaluations but seeks to take the evidence standards further (White & Waddington, 2012). Systematic reviews, again drawing on learning from the biomedical field and in particular the work of the Cochrane Collaboration, differ from regular literature reviews in that they are characterized by a clear protocol for systematically searching defined databases with transparent criteria for the inclusion or exclusion of studies that meet certain methodological standards, as well as the analysis and reporting of study findings (Waddington et al., 2012). Reviews of evaluation evidence in the biomedical field have until very recently been predominantly quantitative. The same can be said for those in development, although considerable debate and interest exist in terms of seeking to broaden the definition of acceptable types of evidence so as to be more inclusive of qualitative methodological approaches (Snilstveit, Oliver, & Vojtkova, 2012; White & Waddington, 2012).

The justification for a systematic approach is that it is inefficient and indeed irresponsible to offer policy advice on a limited number of cases and/or without assessing the quality of evidence on which such advice is based (White & Waddington, 2012). Clearly, there are also powerful arguments, in a field where there is a high moral premium on ensuring research funds are justified on the basis that they have the potential to lead to a greater good in practice, for being well informed about what knowledge already exists rather than blindly reinventing the wheel. Yet, given the resource and time intensiveness of systematic review approaches, as well as the limited evidence evaluation pool on which reviewers can draw in many subject areas in development, the types of evaluation questions that can be illuminated tend to be narrow in scope (Mallett, Hagen-Zanker, Slater, & Duvendack, 2012; Snilstveit, Oliver, & Vojtkova, 2012). Like quantitative impact evaluations that focus on only part of the development landscape, systematic reviews as currently practiced—while potentially useful in some areas of development and to illuminate some questions (primarily on whether an intervention is effective, not how or why)—cannot be seen as a panacea to the evidence demands of development policy more broadly. As Snilstveit et al. (2012) argue, policymakers often want answers as to what works but, where the evidence base on effectiveness is limited, systematic reviews may instead need to refocus on different types of questions:

> They might usefully focus on research that can lead to developing/refining interventions, for instance by synthesising feasibility and acceptability studies. If evidence about effects is heterogeneous, then work needs to focus on identifying the active ingredients or synergistic or antagonistic components of interventions. . . . If interventions do not exist then work reviewing epidemiological studies of risk factors as well as studies of people's views and experiences might be useful in developing a programme theory and designing interventions. (p. 425)

The Emergence of a Mixed Methods Approach to Development in the 2000s

As highlighted from the outset of the chapter, development studies is a diverse enterprise and, since the early stages of the discipline, strong critical voices and approaches have emerged in opposition to the mainstream paradigm. This diversity is also increasingly reflected in the methods employed in the field, especially among scholars interested in issues related to poverty and social exclusion, which are our focus for the remainder of the chapter. As the interest in methodological rigor has grown in mainstream development evaluations, so too have voices interested in methodological pluralism and creativity. Kick-started by the Q2 Poverty Appraisal Conference in 2001,[2] and a subsequent decade of activities led by Ravi Kanbur and Paul Shaffer,[3] the rapid uptake of multimethodological approaches reflects both development studies' cross-disciplinary nature and its growing "openness to the use of all available insights to gain a better understanding of phenomena" (Jones & Sumner, 2009, p. 35). It is of course true that qualitative and

participatory approaches to development evaluations have long existed, but over the past decade they have increasingly been recognized as an important complement to quantitative findings—not only by researchers but also by research consumers in the policy and practice communities.

Defining Mixed Methods Within International Development

Kanbur (2002) and others have argued that using a combination of methods allows us to capture not only macro-level "ifs" and "whats" but also micro-level "whys"—helping us understand the complexities of people's experiences in a way numeric data cannot. Some proponents of MMR approaches have emphasized their ability to "triangulate" or "converge" on truth (e.g., Moser, 2003); others, more in line with the postdevelopment agendas outlined earlier, argue that their real advantage lies elsewhere—in offering "opportunities to meaningfully engage with the differences that matter in today's troubled world, seeking not so much convergence and consensus as opportunities for respectful listening and understanding" (Greene, 2008, p. 20).

Although the "mixed methods paradigm is still in its adolescence" (Leech & Onwuegbuzie, 2009, p. 265), and there are considerable debates about definitions and approaches, the field as a whole has moved toward adopting Becker et al.'s (2006) criteria for judging research quality: seeking not "truth" but "trustworthiness" (p. 37). Within international development, Shaffer, Kanbur, Thu Hang, and Bortei-Doku Aryeetey (2012) observe that mixed methods help researchers distinguish between, and unpack, outcomes versus processes, referring to the fact that, while quantitative data can identify "if," qualitative research is particularly useful for ascertaining "why." In Ecuador, for instance, researchers used quantitative analysis to find that extended households were more likely than nuclear households to be poor. Qualitative analysis found this was because household expansion was a key technique for shielding the old and the young from falling into extreme poverty (Carvalho & White, 1997).

Indeed, it is for its ability to better understand local contextual dynamics that the addition of qualitative research methods to survey findings has gained most recognition among mainstream development analysts. Qualitative research is able to, for example, disentangle cultural norms and practices, including those of a highly sensitive nature, which helps explain noncompliance or unexpected behavioral patterns in response to development interventions that are intended to "help" programme beneficiaries (e.g., Bamberger, Rao, & Woolcock, 2010). Adato's (2008) used mixed methods in Turkey to find out why education stipends for impoverished girls' high school education had limited impacts in some districts. Using ethnographic approaches, the researcher was able to expand on the quantitative survey data that found very limited impacts of education stipends by determining that program design and communication efforts had failed to address parents' concerns about perceived threats to girls'—and in turn family—honor. High school attendance would entail their daughters traveling outside their immediate community, and the risk of loss of honor thus undermined the value of the economic incentive offered. Fairhead, Leach, and Small (2006), in a similar vein, uncovered through in-depth ethnographic work, that resistance to vaccination trial programs in the Gambia stemmed not from the specific program but rather from mixed perceptions about the implementing agency, the Medical Research Council. They found that while the local community perceived the Medical Research Council positively for offering free medication, they also treated the organization with suspicion, as it was seen according to local cultural framings—which, given ritual and occult-related beliefs, view blood as a tradeable commodity—as "stealing blood."

Qualitative research is also increasingly seen as vital in helping unpack the complexity and multidimensionality of many constructs that are pivotal to our understanding of development processes and end goals—such as empowerment, well-being, community cohesion, and leadership. Bamberger et al. (2010) note in this regard that traditional evaluation designs are often reliant on a limited number of unidimensional quantitative indicators to assess project impacts, while qualitative tools such as case studies and in-depth interviews can help in understanding the meaning of statistical indicators.

These strengths notwithstanding, it is also the case that some of the reluctance toward the use of mixed methods approaches that persists within international development evaluations stems from poorly designed and executed qualitative research. Although there is a great deal of high-quality research in the field of international development, there is also a consensus that there exists "a relatively large volume of poor-quality research that fails to adopt a rigorous approach. The boundaries between research and advocacy are often blurred, and such material needs to be treated with caution" (Snilstveit et al., 2012, p. 411). This trend is not helped by a general underfunding of qualitative research, including within mixed methods approaches, whereby the prevailing hierarchy of evidence favors quantitative over qualitative findings (see, e.g., Pereznieto, Jones, Abu-Hammad, & Shaheen, 2014; also see Case Study 2 in this chapter).

There is nonetheless growing sophistication in the field of international development as to how quantitative and qualitative approaches can be combined, depending on the research or evaluation question at hand. Some researchers have focused on the stage at which data are combined; others have seen strategic prioritizing or sequencing as key to design differentiation (Creswell, Plano Clark, Guttmann, & Hanson, 2003; Johnson & Onwuegbuzie, 2004; Bevan, 2005; Teddlie & Tashakkori, 2006). Leech and Onwuegbuzie's (2009) tree-like model first asks about the level of mixing (partial or full?), then about time orientation (concurrent or sequential phases?), and finally about the approach emphasis (do the qualitative and quantitative phases have equal status or is one dominant?) They acknowledge their resulting eight designs are not all-encompassing but note they can represent most mixed methods studies (for a full discussion of design decisions, see also Terrell, 2012).

Bamberger (2012) stretches this model further. His starting point is that evaluations in developing country contexts often face complex resourcing (financial, human, data availability) and political environment constraints and are almost never implemented exactly as envisaged. They therefore demand a higher level of flexibility and creativity than MMR applied in developed country contexts. He argues, for instance, that while strong evaluation designs often require that the same approach be applied across multiple rounds of data collection, mixed methods are better able to address the "monitoring" dimension of monitoring and evaluation work, which scholars and practitioners have somewhat neglected. That is, mixed methods designs can better employ tools that achieve the real-time feedback about service implementation that monitoring allows, enabling projects to learn by doing and to adjust to ground-level realities and rapidly changing circumstances.

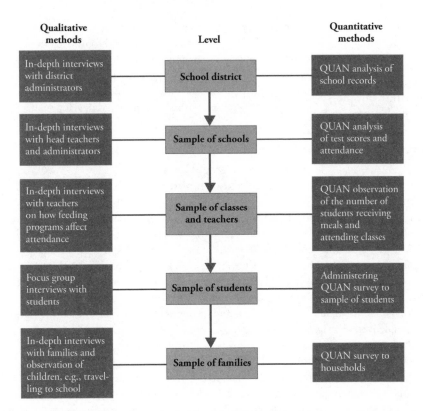

Fig. 27.1 Multilevel mixed methods design: Example of evaluation of effects of school feeding program on school attendance and performance (*Source*: Bamberger, 2012)

Bamberger (2012) also notes that MMR "provides a powerful tool for the evaluation of service delivery that require description and analysis of links between different levels" (p. 13), such as a school feeding program depending on multiple layers of government and cross-sectoral delivery of inputs and staff (see Figure 27.1). In such cases, quantitative and qualitative data can be collected at each level—within a district, a subset of schools, a subset of classes, and, in turn, a subset of teachers, parents, and students. Qualitative techniques including structured observations, key informant interviews, and focus group discussions can also be employed to tease out the interactions between the different levels—for example between district officials and school administrators and teachers.

Finally, some methodologists, including Greene (2008) and Kanbur (2003), go a step further, noting that sociopolitical engagement—"unsettling the settled, challenging the taken-for-granted, offering a discordant voice in an otherwise harmonious choir"—represents "the grand potential of mixed methods social inquiry" (Greene, 2008, p. 20). This type of approach is in keeping with the growing emphasis on the nonlinear and multiplicity of

pathways to development that so-called postdevelopment theories have championed. Corbridge (2007), in his seminal article on "The (Im)possibility of Development Studies," calls attention to the central tension within the development studies discipline: the field emphasizes difference (the "third world" is different, thus demands a separate field of inquiry) but at the same time is committed to similarity (through development policy aimed at molding "them" to become more like "us"; p. 179). He argues nevertheless that, while critics' concerns with development's depoliticizing tendencies on the one hand and their overly close engagement with policymaking on the other have some merit, these do not negate the possibility of carefully nuanced geographical and historical analyses of development processes contributing to meaningful social change.

The good governance agenda, for example, has been described as sickly, vacuous and "apolitical," and it can be all of these things. To the man or woman with no land, however, and no expectation of land reform, it is better than nothing, especially if it increases voice or accountability or the better delivery of an entitlement. . . . Being able to complain effectively is not as glamorous as taking part in a revolution, but in some cases it can count for a great deal. (Corbridge, 2007, p. 203)

It is within this emerging critical approach to development studies more generally that MMR arguably has much to contribute. This is because it has the potential to unpack the complexities and nuances that critical friends of development have long highlighted. In the next section, we present two case studies that highlight this potential within international development.

Case Studies: Applying a Mixed Methods Development Approach

Case Study 1: Combining Survey and Ethnographic Methodologies to Understand Cash Transfer Impacts

As Adato (2008) notes, within development research mixing quantitative and qualitative research methods is often referred to as "Q-squared," suggesting an exponential effect of combining methods. She makes the case that this is indeed true in terms of the explanatory power generated in mixed methods evaluations of large-scale conditional cash transfer (CCT) programs commissioned by governments and donors as part of broader poverty-reduction efforts. While earlier evaluations of the CCT programs in Brazil and Honduras did not include qualitative methods, Adato argues that the fact that governments and development partners increasingly mandate qualitative insights in their evaluation proposals and contractual deliverables signals a growing recognition that the impacts of social policy are mediated by social and institutional processes and relationships. Without understanding these, there is a growing consensus that evaluation evidence is likely to be of limited utility.

What is especially noteworthy about this new trend within the evaluation approach to social assistance programs in developing countries is that evaluations are increasingly becoming a standard feature of cash transfer programs, often built into the initial policy and loan so as to assess the effectiveness of program design and the efficiency of the investment. It is true that the primary interest of governments and lenders such as the World Bank or the Inter-American Development Bank is in quantitative evidence of changes in program targets (e.g., children's enrollment and attendance rates, uptake of health services, improvements in nutritional status, etc.). However, there is also growing interest in understanding implementation issues, how people view the program and respond (or not) to it, and its incentives and ways in which the transparency and accountability of program implementers could be enhanced. It is here that qualitative methods can help shed light in ways that quantitative surveys cannot on shifts in social relationships, including intrahousehold dynamics, gender relations, and community cohesion; institutional and political dynamics; and program beneficiary–service provider interactions.

To illustrate her argument, Adato (2008) draws on the use of quantitative surveys and ethnographic methods by the International Food Policy Research Institute to evaluate cash transfer programs in Nicaragua and Turkey in the mid-2000s. In addition to a large-scale panel household survey with control and intervention groups, involving three rounds of data collection in Nicaragua and two in Turkey, the evaluation drew on an extended case study approach. This involved participant observation to disentangle stated preferences compared with actual behavioral shifts and detailed community and household case studies during residential fieldwork carried out over a four- to five-month period. The evaluation team justified the inclusion of ethnographic (as opposed to shorter and less resource-intensive participatory appraisal techniques) methods by stressing that it allowed for what Burawoy (1998) has described as "multiple dialogues to reach an understanding of empirical phenomenon" (p. 5). The qualitative approach helped in overcoming the problems associated with the brevity that survey methods demand (e.g., in selecting among categorical or continuous variables, respondents are unable to express what they mean by their choice; challenges involved in establishing rapport and trust needed to maximize truthfulness in replies), to capture people's perceptions of the program in their own words and also to uncover less obvious or unintended effects.

So in the case of gender relations, for instance, while there has been some concern in the development literature about women's economic empowerment programs leading to unintended spill-over effects on intrafamilial tensions and power dynamics, in the case of Nicaragua qualitative research, both women and men suggested that both sexes supported women's prominent role in the program (as program beneficiaries), as women were culturally more likely to make spending decisions that would benefit the household and children. Moreover, it was seen as a "women's program," thereby explaining why it did not serve to undermine men's sense of masculinity.

In the Turkish case, a key issue that emerged among program implementers was whether it might incentivize additional pregnancies and larger family size. The survey data and regression analysis found that the CCT program had no statistically significant effect on pregnancy but was unable to explain why. The qualitative findings, however, were able to unpack the underlying sociocultural dynamics at play and offered several compelling explanations as to why the program was unlikely to have an impact on pregnancy decisions. The household and community case studies revealed that not only were there multiple sociocultural pressures on women to get pregnant (e.g., status, social expectations, economics) besides the cash benefit but also that many people also already viewed supporting multiple children when living in poverty as difficult and undesirable—a small cash grant would do little to change this attitude. That said, the fieldwork did uncover the fact that there was a rumor in some locales that the grant was much higher than it really was, which could have acted as a perverse incentive. It thus underscored to program implementers the importance of strengthening information provision and communication channels.

It is, of course, challenging to rigorously attribute evaluation findings to shifts in program design and implementation, as policy changes are often the result of a complex interaction of factors (see, e.g., Jones et al., 2013a). But Adato (2008) notes that the mixed methods findings did contribute to some shifts in CCT rollout in Nicaragua and Turkey, including the programs' continuation into a second phase. She also concludes, however, that, with a relatively greater investment in resources for qualitative evaluation methods, findings could yield greater benefits. More geographical coverage would increase the number of insights and understanding of regional diversity and the relative importance of tailored subnational programming. Additional funding could also facilitate a qualitative panel design that would help in overcoming the limitations of retrospective reflections and more accurately explore changes at baseline and following the cash transfer intervention. And finally, as we argue in the concluding section of this chapter, greater resources could allow for more nuanced explorations of issues relating to policy processes and political economy dynamics, both of which are arguably critical for effective evidence-informed policymaking.

Case Study 2: Triangulating Qualitative and Participatory Methods with a Quasi-Experimental Quantitative Household Survey

To explore the effects of a poverty alleviation program on children and adolescents, particularly when a program has not been designed with a child focus, requires an in-depth understanding of children's and adolescents' experiences of poverty and vulnerability. This is especially relevant in a complex and challenging context such as that of the State of Palestine, where protracted conflict, high levels of insecurity and violence, and extensive internal and external barriers to mobility act as critical constraints to growth and improved welfare for Palestinians.

Pereznieto et al. (2014) conducted a mixed methods evaluation in 2012–2013 of the effects of the Palestinian National Cash Transfer Programme (PNCTP) on children and adolescents and their households. While the donor originally commissioned a quantitative evaluation using a quasi-experimental design, the research team made a case for including a qualitative component, highlighting that a mixed methods analysis not only would be better able to unpack the ways in which the transfer affected (or not) the experiences of children and adolescents living in poverty, but also, through participatory techniques, would reveal what aspects of the program children and adolescents facing specific vulnerabilities valued and what aspects they would like to see improved.

The research team developed a mixed methods approach drawing on a number of qualitative and participatory tools, which included:

1. Small group discussions with up to four adolescents, in separate groups (boys/girls, adolescents with special needs such as disabilities), to solicit perceptions about adolescent-specific vulnerabilities and the extent to which the cash transfer programme and related services were addressing these.

2. Life histories with adolescents whose families received the cash transfer in order to explore the relative significance of the program in their lives as well as intrahousehold effects—both economic and social.

3. Participant observations with a small number of adolescents facing particular vulnerabilities, such as having a disability, living in a camp, or belonging to an ethnic minority group (Bedouin), and their families.

4. In-depth interviews with caregivers whose children were participating in the research to triangulate perspectives about their child's well-being.

5. Focus group discussions with women in the community who received the transfer to discuss their perceptions about the effects of cash transfers on child well-being, especially child psychosocial well-being.

6. Key informant interviews with local and national decision-makers to garner expert views on program history and implementation with regard to addressing child and adolescent experiences of poverty.

Combined, these qualitative tools were used to support findings from the household survey which was conducted to a sample of intervention and comparison households in both Gaza and the West Bank.

Responding to the donor's requirements, the initial focus of the evaluation design was to ensure a large and representative quantitative sample. As such, the resources available for the qualitative component were significantly lower, limiting the scope and scale. Still, due to the layered instrument design outlined earlier—and a relevant purposive sample—important qualitative findings were obtained to help better understand how the cash transfer programme affected different dimensions of child poverty. While the quantitative sample was representative of the PNCTP's target population, the qualitative component zoomed in on particularly vulnerable populations, such as families living in refugee camps, children with disabilities, or households from the Bedouin ethnic minority. The aim of this was to uncover the specific experiences of poverty and social exclusion facing the most vulnerable children and thus nuancing general findings from the quantitative component. For instance, the quantitative survey collected data about household members with a disability and care arrangements for them, but responses came from the caregiver, so it was not possible to explore the implications for adolescents. It was only through the qualitative research that it was possible to understand how the cash transfer had affected the lives of children and adolescents with disabilities in particular. Many adolescents interviewed cited having more access to specialized health care or the ability to buy nappies, which they could not previously afford and which they considered important for their physical and emotional integrity. This said, there was also a widespread view that the program did little to tackle the stigma and social isolation many disabled young people experience.

Further, the qualitative component was sequenced after the quantitative survey, so preliminary quantitative findings could be used to inform the design of the qualitative research methods to better complement data. This was helpful, for example, when it became clear the sample of Bedouin households interviewed in the household survey was very low, given the structure of the ministry's database used for sampling. In the qualitative component, therefore, the research team sought to obtain information from Bedouin households specifically through purposive sampling. Similarly, information from the quantitative survey indicated that violence among children and against children in schools was commonplace, thus attention was given to ensuring relevant questions on violence were asked as part of the qualitative component.

The mixed methods data also helped in identifying policy and programming challenges, which informed a set of recommendations for decision-makers. This was done more effectively through the triangulation of research tools, including program implementation data from the survey as well as a detailed policy mapping based on secondary documentary review and on key informant interviews with relevant policymakers to identify gaps in policy and program design or implementation. Similarly, semistructured discussions with beneficiaries enabled respondents to give more details about problems in service delivery processes than the structured questions of the survey could capture and also to offer their perspectives on possible programming solutions. For example, some explained they had had to use the transfer to pay for medicines that were supposed to be covered by the health insurance to which they were entitled as PNCTP beneficiaries but that tended to be out of stock in government facilities and therefore needed to be purchased in the market.

As a result of this layered analysis, it was possible to generate tailored policy recommendations. For example, while one of the secondary aims of the PNCTP is to enable school attendance for children and adolescents from poor beneficiary households by exempting them from the payment of fees, the quantitative findings found a small difference in school attendance between beneficiary and non-beneficiary adolescent boys (in a context where fewer girls work outside the home). The qualitative component uncovered the fact that, despite fee exemptions, adolescent boys in the poorest families still needed to work to support the family—so the opportunity cost of school was seen as high. The qualitative data also found that pervasive violence by teachers in schools was a common cause of children dropping out of school, sometimes more so than their level of poverty. More important, in the case of Palestine, the qualitative component found that mental health and psycho-emotional challenges significantly compounded the situation of poor households. Thus while the small cash transfer improved household income, enabling the purchase of more and better food and the repayment of debts (the two categories for which the survey data indicated the transfer was most frequently used), lack of economic opportunities, political uncertainty, and the violent environment took a significant toll on caregivers and their children, which the cash transfer alone could do little to relieve. Qualitative respondents spoke about the need for better psychosocial support services to improve families' quality of life.

An additional recommendation, stemming from a deeper understanding of the policy infrastructure, is particularly important to inform the design of child and social protection programming. As a result of the introduction of the PNCTP, which focuses on "family" well-being, some programs that previously catered to important children's needs, particularly in the case of children with disabilities, have been discontinued, so as to focus policy responses at the household level. This has meant that key power dynamics in terms of the intrahousehold allocation of resources have been overlooked, which on occasion has resulted in the marginalization of children with special needs. It also underscores the fact that designers are clearly missing the much greater array of ongoing and periodic expenses disabled children face, which constitute a significant economic burden for these households. The MMR therefore highlighted not only the importance of the PNCTP as an intervention to improve income poverty, but also the need for it to draw on its more comprehensive social protection design to link beneficiaries, based on needs assessments and home visits, with relevant service providers. Only then will it be possible to ensure that children and adolescents who experience poverty across multiple dimensions are cared for more comprehensively.

Incorporating a Mixed Methods Approach into Development Studies: Lessons Learned From the Case Studies
Exploring Unintended Impacts on Specific Social Groups

Mixed methods research can help in uncovering findings that extend beyond direct impacts on the target group in the evaluation but that are relevant for understanding medium- and long-term change processes and well-being trajectories. In the two case studies here, by investing in collecting perception data to go beyond household-level aggregate analysis, it was possible to gain a more nuanced understanding of how the programs were contributing to change processes. In Nicaragua, collecting specific data from men revealed that they did not feel alienated by the cash transfer even though it was seen as a "women-only program." As such, the data identified some program effects on the male role/masculinity that are important to improve program adaptation and redesign by engaging men more effectively. In the case of Palestine, the team used a tool—a quantitative household survey—typically used in the assessment of cash transfer impacts as a practical way of obtaining information on a number of topics (from consumption to schooling) and for different members of the household. However, complementing quantitative data with children's and adolescents' perception data enables a more child-sensitive analysis of intended and unintended effects of the cash transfer on children, which can act positively (e.g., improved self-esteem as adolescent girls are able to purchase some clothes to attend social events) or negatively (some children receiving the transfer feel stigmatized as a result of being identified as "poor").

Engaging with Policy Processes—The Need for Greater Methodological Creativity and Precision

While the core of the development evaluation field remains policy oriented, the extent to which there is a maximum fit between evaluation methods and policy debates remains more tenuous. The real challenge is whether mixed methods evaluation approaches to policy debates "can give policymakers a sense of the effects of policies in the real world beyond government" (Fielding, 2012, p. 127) and lead to the formulation of what is now called "evidence-informed" policy (Pawson, 2001). Unfortunately, it seems donors and policymakers are often receptive to mixed methods approaches if results support existing policy agendas—but less open when their aims are challenged (Barahona & Levy, 2007). The case studies detailed here indicate, however, that there is scope to influence decision-makers through the use of evidence that comes from diverse methodologies, as long as these are robustly designed and justified and the recommendations are anchored in precise findings.

Part of the problem, it would seem, is that there is a striking lacuna in mixed methods evaluations as applied in international development, namely, the limited methodological tools to systematically capture the broader political and policy context in which findings will ultimately be situated, should they successfully avoid a life confined to the library shelf. Our review of development evaluations concerned with poverty and social exclusion suggests only a minority engage in any detail with the policy implications of the research findings, with a good number focusing primarily on areas for further research. While this is not necessarily problematic, especially in fledgling fields of inquiry, we believe there is considerable scope for further innovation in terms of developing stronger policy-relevant and policy-informed research.

As we noted earlier, inspired by the health sciences, development studies has increasingly engaged with debates about evidence-based policy and knowledge translation over the past half decade. As such, there is growing recognition that development research needs to be informed by an understanding of the political economy of a particular context, the types of actors engaged in policy processes, the types of knowledge used to shape policy debates, and the role of knowledge intermediaries—actors who span the boundaries between knowledge and action in ways that enhance the legitimacy and salience of the information they produce (Cash et al., 2003; Jones et al., 2012a). However, translation of this understanding into operationalizable research and evaluation methodologies remains rare, with political and policy context analysis largely relegated as background, if included at all (Taylor & Pereznieto, 2014). In order for knowledge production within development to engage more effectively with the messiness of policy processes, Dodson, Brownson, and Weiss (2012) argue that not only is there a need for closer engagement and collaboration with policy stakeholders throughout the evaluation process but also more disaggregated attention must be paid to policy *processes* and *systems*, which provide the rules and institutional structure through which policy decisions are made and implemented; *policy content*, which is concerned with the specific elements of a policy aimed at affecting change; and *policy outcomes*, which assess the effects of implemented policies. An example of such an approach is outlined in Box 27.1.

Certainly, integrating policy research tools into MMR for international development entails additional complexities. Similar questions about simultaneous or sequenced data collection and data analysis processes as discussed earlier with regard to mixing quantitative and qualitative data need to be considered; capacity to use new tools built and tools piloted; and additional resources sought or trade-offs made. However, embedding research questions and data collection and analysis within the policy systems and processes in which development phenomena unfold has the potential to significantly strengthen the utility of the evaluation findings that emerge. While it could be argued that this is the role of policymakers, in reality policy actors are often compelled to deal with a wide array of issues and frequently do not have the time, skills, or resources to proactively identify then weigh up different options from a complex evaluation. If this legwork were already undertaken, it would likely increase the chances of uptake, as multicountry research funded by the UK Department for International Development and undertaken by SciDevNet and Overseas Development Institute with national and local-level policymakers has shown (Jones et al., 2008). In short, distilling policy implications or recommendations from research findings is an interpretative exercise that could benefit from a more systematic approach and specific tools to aid the process.

Box 27.1 Policy Analysis to Inform Mixed Methods Research in the Context of International Development: An Example of a Multicountry Study on Gender and Social Protection

The Overseas Development Institute undertook a multiyear study funded by the Australian Agency for International Development on gender and social protection in Vietnam and Indonesia, examining to what extent national policies or programs on social protection were taking account of gendered vulnerabilities in their design and implementation. This involved small-scale quantitative surveys to investigate trends in gendered vulnerabilities and coping mechanisms, complemented by more in-depth qualitative research with decision-makers, beneficiaries and nonbeneficiaries, program implementers, and local communities to understand the drivers and maintainers of stasis of gender discriminatory norms and practices.

In order to locate possible entry points to share the evidence gathered, national and local policy analysis was also undertaken to explore the ways gender was integrated into (or excluded from) national policies and with what level of priority. Evaluation tools used included a mix of documentary reviews and interviews, policy mapping, visual tools to explore alignment and influence of key actors, and participatory workshops with local government officials to assess their theoretical and practical knowledge of gender dynamics within the social protection field. Related mapping work also sought to identify gender champions in different spheres of the policy arena who would be interested in utilizing findings to promote better-informed decision-making in this area and who could additionally support capacity-strengthening initiatives aimed at promoting more gender-responsive policy and program implementation.

Sources: Holmes and Jones (2013); Jones et al. (2012b).

Conclusions

The use of MMR in international development, particularly in policy and program evaluation, has garnered support over the past decade based on a realization of the need for more contextualized and in-depth understanding of people's experiences of poverty, social inclusion, and development—which are hard to capture with more static quantitative instruments alone. Although there is great value in rigorously collected quantitative data to generate robust and more generalizable findings, there are levels of detail, nuance, and dynamism that are best captured by complementary qualitative data. Thus the complex and nuanced findings stemming from mixed methods evaluations, exploring not only whether there has been an impact but also how and why that impact has been achieved, are increasingly seen as important to inform development policy design. Still, a limited number of evaluations concerned with poverty and social exclusion engage in detail with the policy implications of the research findings, so there is considerable scope for further innovation in terms of developing stronger policy-relevant and policy-informed research and to engage decision-makers with the complex and rich evidence generated through mixed methods development evaluations.

Suggested Websites

http://www.trentu.ca/ids/qsquared.php

The Q2 Working Paper Series is hosted by the Department of International Development Studies at Trent University in Canada. With over 60 papers, largely focused on the Global South, the series not only provides a plethora of examples of how MMR can be used in development studies but also directly addresses the methodological debates most important to the field.

http://go.worldbank.org/UY6Q0BK4W0

The World Bank has developed Poverty and Social Impact Analysis as a way to combine the strengths of economic and social analysis to better understand the impact of policy reforms on the well-being of a variety of stakeholders, particularly the poor and vulnerable. MMR is key to this analysis, as it is aimed at the "whys" of surprising results.

http://dmeforpeace.org/learn/subject/data/methods/mixed

The Learning Portal for Design, Monitoring & Evaluation for Peacebuilding hosts a collaborative site dedicated to, among other things, evaluation and research methodologies and tools. While the site is broader than mixed methods, it also has a strong subsection on mixed methods approaches, focused on peace building within the broader field of development studies.

Discussion Questions

1. How and why is MMR used differently in development studies compared to other disciplines? Is there a specific value in using it in development studies?

2. How have MMR evaluations helped changed the discourse and discussions around key development challenges such as poverty and social exclusion?

3. How can a better balance be achieved between the strong push for quantitative evaluations—RCTs in particular—as the "gold standard" of evaluations and a growing body of evidence on the value added of mixed methods?

Notes

1. See http://www.ifpri.org/dataset/mexico-evaluation-progresa

2. See http://www.arts.cornell.edu/poverty/kanbur/QQZ.pdf

3. See http://www.trentu.ca/ids/qsquared.php. Several peer-reviewed journal special issues, including the *Journal of Mixed Methods Research* and the *International Journal of Multiple Research Approaches*, both first published in 2007, are also available.

References

Adato, M. (2008). *Integrating survey and ethnographic methods to evaluate conditional cash transfer programs* (Discussion Paper 00810). Washington, DC: International Food Policy Research Institute.

Bamberger, M. (2012). *Introduction to mixed methods in impact evaluation*. Impact Evaluation Notes 3. Retrieved from http://www.interaction.org/document/guidance-note-3-introduction-mixed-methods-impact-evaluation

Bamberger, M., Rao, V., & Woolcock, M. (2010). Using mixed methods in monitoring and evaluation: Experiences from international development. In A. Tashakkori & C. Teddlie (Eds.), *SAGE handbook of mixed methods in social & behavioral research* (2nd ed., pp. 613–642). Thousand Oaks, CA: Sage.

Barahona, C., & Levy, S. (2007). The best of both worlds: Producing national statistics using participatory methods. *World Development, 35*(2), 326–341.

Bevan, P. (2005). *Studying multi-dimensional poverty in Ethiopia: Towards a Q-integrated approach* (Q-Squared Working Paper 15). Toronto, ON: Centre for International Studies, University of Toronto.

Bicchieri, C. (2006). *The grammar of society: The nature and dynamics of social norms*. New York, NY: Cambridge University Press.

Boudet, A. M. M., Petesch, P., Turk, C., & Thumala, A. (2013). *On norms and agency: Conversations about gender equality with women and men in 20 countries*. Washington, DC: World Bank.

Buch-Hansen, M., & Lauridsen, L. (2012). The past, present and future of development studies. *Forum for Development Studies, 39*(3), 293–300.

Burawoy, M. (1998). The extended case method. *Sociological Theory, 16*(1), 4–33.

Carvalho, S., & White, H. (1997). *Combining the quantitative and qualitative approaches to poverty measurement and analysis* (Technical Paper 366). Washington, DC: World Bank.

Cash, D. W., Clark, W., Alcock, F., Dickson, N., Eckley, N., Guston, D., Jager, J., & Mitchell, R. (2003) Knowledge systems for sustainable development. *Proceedings of the National Academy of Science of the United States of America, 100*(14), 8086–8091.

Chronic Poverty Research Centre. (2009). *Chronic poverty research report 2008–09: Escaping poverty traps*. Manchester, UK: Author.

Corbridge, S. (2007). The (im)possibility of development studies. *Economy and Society, 36*(2), 179–211.

Creswell, J., Plano Clark, V., Guttmann, M., & Hanson, W. (2003). Advanced mixed methods research design. In A. Tashakkori & C. Teddlie (Eds.), *Handbook of mixed methods in social & behavioral research* (pp. 209–240). Thousand Oaks, CA: Sage.

Department for International Development. (2011). *DFID's approach to value for money (VfM)*. London, England: Author.

Dhaliwal, I., Duflo, E., Glennerster, R., Tulloch, C., & Latif, A. (2012). *Comparative cost-effectiveness analysis to inform policy in developing countries: A general framework with applications for education*. Chicago, IL: University of Chicago Press.

Dodson, E., Brownson, R., & Weiss, S. (2012). Policy dissemination research. In R. Brownson, G. Colditz, & E. Proctor (Eds.), *Dissemination and implementation research in health: Translating science to practice* (pp. 437–458). Oxford, UK: Oxford University Press.

Escobar, A. (1995). *Encountering development: The making and unmaking of the third world*. Princeton, NJ: Princeton University Press.

Fairhead, J., Leach, M., & Small, M. (2006). Public engagement with science? Local understandings of a vaccine trial in the Gambia. *Journal of Biosocial Sciences, 38*(1), 1–16.

Fielding, N. (2012). Triangulation and mixed methods designs: Data integration with new research technologies. *Journal of Mixed Methods Research, 6*(2), 124–136.

Greene, J. (2008). Is mixed methods social inquiry a distinctive methodology? *Journal of Mixed Methods Research, 2*(1), 7–22.

Hickey, S. (2010). *The government of chronic poverty: From exclusion to citizenship?* (Working Paper 151). Manchester, UK: Chronic Poverty Research Centre.

Holmes, R., & Jones, N. (2013). *Gender and social protection in the developing world: Beyond mothers and safety nets*. London, England: Zed Books.

Johnson, R. B., & Onwuegbuzie, A. (2004). Mixed methods research: A research paradigm whose time has come. *Educational Researcher, 33*, 14–26.

Jones, H., Jones, N., Shaxson, L., & Walker, D. (2012a). *Knowledge, policy and power in international development: A practical guide*. Bristol, UK: Policy Press.

Jones, N., Jones, H., & Walsh, C. (2008). *Political science? Strengthening science–policy dialogue in developing countries* (Working Paper 294). London, England: Overseas Development Institute.

Jones, N., & Sumner, A. (2009). Does mixed methods research matter to understanding childhood well-being? *Social Indicators Research, 90*(1), 35–50.

Jones, N., Van Anh, T. T., & Malachowska, A. (2012b). *The politics of gender and social protection in Viet Nam: Opportunities and challenges for a transformative approach*. London, England: Overseas Development Institute.

Kanbur, R. (2002). Economics, social science and development. *World Development, 30*(3), 477–486.

Kanbur, R. (2003). Q-squared? A commentary on qualitative and quantitative poverty appraisal. In R.

Kanbur (Ed.), *Q-squared: Qualitative and quantitative methods of poverty appraisal* (pp. 1–21). Delhi, India: Permanent Black.

Leech, N., & Onwuegbuzie, A. (2009). A typology of mixed methods research designs. *Quality & Quantity, 43*(2), 265–275.

Mallett, R., Hagen-Zanker, J., Slater, R., & Duvendack, M. (2012). The benefits and challenges of using systematic reviews in international development research. *Journal of Development Effectiveness, 4*(3), 445–455.

Maluccio, J. A., & Rafael, F. (2005). *Impact evaluation of a conditional cash transfer program: The Nicaraguan Red de Protección Social* (Research Report 141). Washington, DC: International Food Policy Research Institute.

Miguel, E., & Kremer, M. (2001). *Worms: Education and health externalities in Kenya* (Working Paper 8481). Cambridge, MA: National Bureau of Economic Research.

Moser, C. (2003). "Apt illustration" or "anecdotal information?" Can qualitative data be robust or representative? In R. Kanbur (Ed.), *Q-squared: Qualitative and quantitative methods of poverty appraisal* (pp. 79–89). Delhi, India: Permanent Black.

Pawson, R. (2001). *Evidence-based policy: I. In search of a method* (Centre for Evidence-Based Policy and Practice Working Paper 3). London, England: Economic and Social Research Council.

Pereznieto, P., Jones, N., Abu-Hammad, B., & Shaheen, M. (2014). *Effects of the Palestinian National Cash Transfer Programme on children and adolescents: A mixed methods analysis* (Report for UNICEF Occupied Palestinian Territories). London, England: Overseas Development Institute.

Sen, A. (1999). *Development as freedom.* Oxford: Oxford University Press.

Shaffer, P., Kanbur, R., Thu Hang, N., & Bortei-Doku Aryeetey, E. (2008). *Introduction to Q-squared in policy: The use of qualitative and quantitative methods of poverty analysis in decision-making* (Q-Squared Working Paper 60). Maleny, Australia: EContent Management.

Snilstveit, B., Oliver, S., & Vojtkova, M. (2012). Narrative approaches to systematic review and synthesis of evidence for international development policy and practice. *Journal of Development Effectiveness, 4*(3), 409–429.

Taylor, G., & Pereznieto, P. (2014). *Review of evaluation approaches and methods used by interventions on women and girls' economic empowerment.* London, England: Overseas Development Institute.

Teddlie, C., & Tashakkori, A. (2006). A general typology of research designs featuring mixed methods. *Research in the Schools, 13*(1), 12–28.

Terrell, S. (2012). Mixed-methods research methodologies. *The Qualitative Report, 17*(1), 254–280.

The Lancet. The World Bank is finally embracing science. (2004). *The Lancet, 364*(9436), 731–732.

Waddington, H., White, H., Snilstveit, B., Garcia Hombrados, J., Vojtkova, M., Davies, . . . Tugwell, P. (2012). How to do a good systematic review of effects in international development: A tool kit. *Journal of Development Effectiveness, 4*(3), 359–387.

White, H. (2009). *Theory-based impact evaluation: Principles and practice* (Working Paper 3). London, England: International Initiative for Impact Evaluation.

White, H., & Waddington, H. (2012). Why do we care about evidence synthesis? An introduction to the special issue on systematic reviews. *Journal of Development Effectiveness, 4*(3), 351–358.

PART 4

Incorporating New Technologies into Multimethod and Mixed Methods Research

Mixed Methods and Multimodal Research and Internet Technologies

Christine M. Hine

Abstract

This chapter explores the varied ways in which qualitative and quantitative, large-scale and small-scale research designs have been combined in the study of the Internet. The chapter also considers multimodal and online/offline studies, which explore a research object by combining diverse forms of data drawn by crossing the offline/online boundary or combining digital and analogue data. The focus of the chapter is on exploring the motivations for these combinations and outlining the distinctive issues that heterogeneous research designs in these domains encounter. Internet research has occasioned many innovative research designs, as the sheer quantity of data available online often prompts even those overtly committed to a qualitative paradigm to explore techniques for visualizing data, and exploring patterns on a larger scale through social network analysis or sentiment analysis. The spatial complexities entailed in networked communication often, however, introduce a challenge for researchers seeking to combine perspectives.

Key Words: internet, online, visualizing data, multimodal, social network analysis, sentiment analysis, digital

Introduction

The Internet is still a relatively young phenomenon, but in a short and lively history it has stirred up debate and questioned assumptions in many fields of endeavor, including social science research. The Internet has occasioned the development of new social science research methods and the rearticulation of traditional methods, and it has also stimulated researchers to come up with many examples of novel combinations of method. The history of Internet research contains numerous studies that, whether overtly claiming to use a mixed methods approach or not, are heterogeneous in their designs, combining approaches derived from different methodological traditions. Within the scope of this chapter are many different forms of mixed method and mixed mode study, including the combination of qualitative and quantitative techniques or an amalgamation of data derived from online and offline settings. Some such studies

aim for integration at the outset or adopt contrasting approaches synchronously, while others implement a sequential approach or leave integration to a final stage where the contribution of different approaches to understanding an overall research question is compared or synthesized. The studies discussed in this chapter fall within the broad definition offered by Johnson et al. (2007) of method combination as an "intellectual and practical synthesis" (p. 129), in which the mixing of methods is a choice in its own right made according to the demands of a particular research question.

As Creswell (2011) notes, the field of possible ways in which to combine methods is both baffling and complex, and the variety of practice defies attempts to produce a straightforward typology. This is certainly true in the case of Internet research. When I appealed to the mailing list maintained by the Association of Internet Researchers (http://aoir.org/email-list/) for suggestions of current mixed methods studies in Internet research, I was overwhelmed by responses describing published studies, ongoing dissertation research, and major funded projects (full list of responses available at http://christinehine.wordpress.com/). It became clear that the combining of methods, and of methodological traditions, was proving extremely fruitful within Internet research. Many Internet researchers were able to identify themselves with the practice of mixing methods even if they had not overtly set out to do a mixed methods study, or to describe it in terms of triangulation, sequencing of methods, and the like. It was also apparent that it would be challenging to provide a taxonomy of different approaches according to a systematic typology such as that mapped out by Creswell and Plano Clark (2007), and indeed, as Creswell (2011) acknowledged, it often proves to be the case that such a typology turns out to be insufficient to capture the complexity of actual practice. This chapter does not, therefore, review current practice in the mixing of modes and methods in Internet research in a systematic way intended to map differing approaches to design, although it aims to capture some of the diversity of approaches.

The field of Internet research does indeed provide examples of many of the forms of a mixed method study identified elsewhere across the social sciences by Creswell and Plano Clark (2007), including studies where concurrent methods are intended to provide triangulation, those where one method succeeds another in explanatory mode and studies where one method is embedded in another, such as a small quantitative component within a largely qualitative ethnographic study of an online environment. Many of these designs have arisen in somewhat ad hoc fashion within Internet studies rather than as a concerted program of methodological development, as researchers explore the affordances of the data available to them and progressively formulate research questions that morph over time, with research projects sometimes employing unanticipated methods over the lifetime of the project in the face of the development of the Internet itself. To enforce a structure on this emergent diversity of experience would possibly not be the most helpful thing to do. Instead, I have chosen to focus on what the experience of Internet research reveals about mixed and multimodal approaches to research more broadly, focusing on the opportunities and challenges that Internet researchers have experienced in their attempts to build research designs appropriate for the job at hand. The chapter

therefore focuses on why Internet researchers combine methods and explores the distinctive twist that a focus on the Internet confers on attempts to mix research modes and methods.

Instead of systematically assigning studies to a typology of mixed methods approaches, this chapter therefore instead begins with a focus on the motivations for mixed method studies in Internet research, attempting to understand why these approaches seem to flourish particularly well in this field. The first section of the chapter explores these motivations by considering the emergence of Internet research as a relatively recent phenomenon not colonized from the outset by any particular methodological stance but also characterized by a certain anxiety about the capacity of any one method to capture the situation. The following section then focuses on Internet ethnography, which has been a particularly rich source of mixed research designs. The next sections then move on to consider some of the distinctive qualities of Internet data that have encouraged mixed methods research, dwelling first on the notion of "big data" and considering the opportunities and challenges offered by the advent of large amounts of digital data emanating from social interactions online. This luxurious abundance of data has notably stimulated the methodological imagination and prompted a wide array of studies that explore both the small-scale qualitative understanding of experience and the larger scale notions of pattern and emergence. The chapter then explores the research opportunities offered by combining studies of different sites in the research of Internet-mediated phenomena, and it concludes by looking specifically at the benefits and challenges of combining data derived from both online and offline sites within a single study.

Are There Separate Methodological Paradigms in Internet Research?

I have argued previously (Hine, 2005) that Internet research was characterized, almost from the outset, by a mood of methodological innovation: simply because the Internet seemed so new and because it appeared to occasion new ways of being present in the world and interacting with one another, it appeared almost self-evident that new approaches would be required in order to grasp these new phenomena. Discussions of the challenges of researching Internet phenomena at this time were thus not focused simply on the development of some new techniques or the emergence of new methods, but they touched on a methodological level of debate too. This methodological level of debate involved considering what the conditions for production of robust knowledge about Internet phenomena might be, given the apparently fundamental uncertainties about such issues as the identity and location of research subjects and the appropriate units of analysis to use for the phenomena that researchers were encountering. In fact, as social science research progressively came to grips with the Internet this mood of self-evident novelty gradually dissipated, and many more continuities with previous modes of existence than had been anticipated came to light. However, a legacy of interest in the Internet as a ripe field for discussions about methods and methodology remains.

One characteristic of Internet research that has endured from the earlier days is a consciousness of the limitations of relying on single approaches and a willingness to explore various combinations of methods appropriate to the job at hand. It may be that the relatively recent emergence of the Internet as a mainstream phenomenon of interest to social science means that it was not, from the outset, locked into one particular methodological paradigm (where a methodological paradigm implies a particular set of views on the nature of the phenomenon to be studied, how questions should be formulated, and what methods should be used for collecting and analyzing data). In contrast to some other fields, where distinct methodological paradigms have come into sharp contrast and even competition with one another, in Internet research the distinctions have been less starkly drawn. Internet research is young enough to have largely avoided the "paradigm wars" experienced in other substantive domains (Bryman, 2006). As a field, Internet research has also tended to be multidisciplinary rather than constituting itself as a single discipline with an agreed set of central theoretical premises or common discourse (Sterne, 2005). That there is a common meeting ground for scholars interested in the Internet at all is due in no small part to the Association of Internet Researchers, which held its inaugural meeting in 2000 and has met annually since, continuing throughout to welcome researchers from diverse disciplines. These Internet researchers come from departments of sociology, anthropology, information science, library studies, communications, psychology, geography, politics, and many more (Baym, 2005), and this disciplinary diversity may have contributed to intervisibility and mutual respect among researchers espousing different methodological approaches

to understanding the Internet. At early conferences of the Association of Internet Researchers there was, for example, no clear distinction made between Internet researchers who espoused qualitative approaches and those who sought quantitative understandings of online phenomena.

This methodological diversity also means, however, that different communities of scholars come into contact around studies of the Internet but are not necessarily talking about precisely the same object. There have been some fundamental ontological complexities in determining what the Internet is, which affect how we define it as an object of research. These complexities arise, for example, when deciding whether to separate out the online sphere from other aspects of everyday life for research purposes, and whether it is appropriate to focus on "the Internet" as an object as opposed to a specific site such as Facebook, or even a particular user's experience of Facebook. In addition, because the Internet has been identified as the territory of many different disciplines at once, there is a corresponding complexity in methodological approaches. One researcher might see the Internet as a site for ethnographic exploration, while another might view it not as a location in its own right but as a source of documents for textual analysis (Hine, 2000).

The diversity in definitions of the Internet as a research object has not, however, necessarily led researchers to see different methodological approaches as incommensurable paradigms. Schneider and Foot (2004), for example, pointed out that the World Wide Web as an object of research had been constituted in multiple ways. Among researchers who shared a belief that there are phenomena of social interest to study on the web, they distinguished those who took a discursive or rhetorical approach to understanding website content, those who undertook analysis of the structures and features of individual websites, or mapped patterns of linkage between sites, and those who undertook what they described as sociocultural analysis of the web, exploring the circumstances of production and maintenance of websites as a context for understanding website content and linking. Having identified these three quite different formulations of the web as a research object, Schneider and Foot (2004) positioned their own approach as an overtly multimethod approach, which encompassed aspects of all three. Their "web sphere analysis" involved saving a collection of websites related to a chosen topic or theme, capturing not only the sites themselves but also the patterns of linkage between the sites. Changes in sites over time might also be captured in this archive. The analysis then deploys a combination of computer-assisted and manual annotation of features of the web sphere, which is triangulated with accounts given by producers and users of the sites.

Scolari (2009) describes a field of cybercultural[1] studies that has, over time, encompassed empirical research, philosophical speculations, journalistic analysis, apocalyptic visions, optimistic forecasts, literary criticism, and cyberpunk literature. As Schneider and Foot (2004) exemplify, Internet research represents an area in which researchers from diverse disciplines are exposed to one another's theoretical and methodological resources and become conscious of different ways of constituting the Internet as a research object. It seems little surprise then that the field has been methodologically diverse and disposed toward mixed method research designs. As Peng, Zhang, Zhong, and Zhu (2012) describe it: "Internet studies are a melting pot that attracts researchers from different disciplines to transcend their disciplinary boundaries to develop new theoretical, methodological, and practical concerns" (p. 15). Peng et al. (2012) based their claims about the nature of the field of Internet research on analysis of a corpus of journal articles published in English between 2000 and 2009, retrieved for their use of a set of indicative keywords: *Internet, web, cyberspace, cyber-space, online*, and *on-line*. The resulting corpus was subjected to cluster analysis and text-mining for keywords. The cluster analysis demonstrated that the field spanned the social sciences and clustered most readily into substantive themes such as e-health, e-business, e-society, and human–technology interactions. The methods used in these areas of research were explored by manually coding a sample according to the type of method. Peng et al. found that Internet research in the broadest sense had been dominated by quantitative methods in the time period they studied. They did not specifically look for mixed methods, but they found that the research cluster of e-society was particularly methodologically heterogeneous, suggesting a mutual visibility of different methodological approaches at the very least. Internet studies appear to be an area within which commonality of substantive concerns coupled with an inherent multidisciplinarity may promote awareness of, and respect for, different methodological traditions.

This mutual visibility of different disciplinary perspectives and different methodological traditions, clustered through their mutual concern with substantive areas focused on the Internet, has produced fields of literature, which form a methodological mosaic of studies looking at related research objects through different methodological traditions. Each method is seen as having its own strengths and weaknesses and focuses the object of research in a different way: Table 28.1 outlines some of the key methods that have become established in Internet studies, outlining the insights they offer and the potential limitations associated with each. The awareness of overlapping and related if not identical research objects does not in itself, of course, guarantee that individual studies will contain a mixing of methods, even though it potentially encourages learning about methods across disciplinary divides and might position researchers to experiment with approaches not usually within the methodological remit of their home disciplines. Combining of methods within individual studies was, however, also an early phenomenon, as researchers struggled to find effective ways of grasping the Internet as a social phenomenon. These mixed methods approaches particularly flourished within Internet ethnographies. The next section looks specifically at the mixed methods tradition in Internet ethnography, exploring the factors that drew ethnographers toward combinations of qualitative and quantitative analysis.

Internet Ethnography as a Mixed Method Approach

The claim that the Internet provided a field site for the study of culture using ethnographic techniques was made relatively early on in the mainstreaming of the Internet (Hine, 2005). Baym's (1995, 2000) work on a rec.arts.tv.soaps newsgroup[2] was highly significant for the field in demonstrating that the Internet could be a place where rich social formations emerged and, as a corollary, that it was appropriate to set out to understand these social formations through the combination of participation, observation, and systematic exploration that characterizes ethnography. Subsequently, the notion of Internet ethnography has expanded and diversified (for discussions see Boellstorff, 2008; Hine, 2000; Markham, 1998; Miller & Slater, 2000; Hine, 2008b; Murthy, 2008; Garcia, Standlee, Bechkoff, & Cui, 2009; Kozinets, 2009; Nardi, 2010). Authors vary on the extent to which they see the online domain as a discrete field amenable to ethnographic study in its own right (Boellstorff, 2010), with Miller and Slater having

Table 28.1 Commonly Used Internet Research Methods That May Feature in Mixed Methods Research Designs

Method	Data Source	Typical Research Questions/Insights	Potential Limitations
Participant observation in an online setting	Field notes based on direct observation and participation by the researcher in group activities. In an online ethnography, field notes based on participant observation are often supplemented by interviews, surveys, etc. to provide descriptive statistics and to corroborate the researcher's emerging interpretations.	What are the group norms and behaviors? What is the social hierarchy? How is social order maintained within the group? Participant observation allows the researcher to develop an in-depth experiential understanding.	Focusing on the online group as a bounded social space may limit understanding of how people move between and combine different online and offline spaces in their everyday lives.
Online interviews	Online interviews can be conducted in real time, using chat and messaging services, or asynchronously, for example by e-mail. Interviews may be very structured or may involve use of a more flexible interview guide adapted for each individual encounter. Data will be in the form of text files recording the messages exchanged during the interview.	How do interviewees experience and understand the topic of interest? Online interviews allow the researcher to focus in on areas of specific concern and can allow for uninhibited discussion of sensitive topics.	Interviewers can find that reliance on online interviews alone limits their ability to understand interviewees' offline worlds. Interviews provide an artificial interactional context. There is little possibility of cross-checking between what interviewees say they do and what they actually do.
Online surveys	Online surveys involve collecting answers to a structured set of questions, often presented on a website. Invitations to take part in the survey may be posted to a known population, for example via a mailing list, or may be publicized more widely, for example via social networking sites, to an undetermined population of potential participants.	How does the population of interest experience and understand the topic of interest? What sociodemographic factors account for differences? Surveys allow a structured approach to exploring participants' experiences and understandings and lend themselves to quantitative analysis.	Generalizability can be problematic for online surveys where the underlying population is unknown: it can be unclear who saw the survey invitation, and response biases are thus hard to determine. Surveys provide an artificial context for expression of attitudes.
Face-to-face interviews	Interviews with Internet users can be conducted face-to-face, in either structured, semistructured or open formats, resulting in audio or video recordings for transcription into text files, accompanied by field notes.	How do interviewees experience and understand the topic of interest? A face-to-face interview can be a powerful way to build rapport with an interviewee.	Face-to-face interviews can be limited as a tool for understanding people's Internet activities if not cross-checked with what people actually do online.

(continued)

Table 28.1 Continued

Method	Data Source	Typical Research Questions/Insights	Potential Limitations
Structured activity sessions	Internet users are asked to complete a set task while being observed by the researcher.	How do people retrieve information from the Internet, and how do they interpret what they find? By asking people to focus on a task of interest researchers generate a data set directly targeted on their topic of interest and avoid the distortions of retrospective accounts.	These task-based sessions can be somewhat artificial, in that they do not represent the way that people ordinarily go about using the Internet in their everyday lives.
Surveys using offline media	Surveys can be completed on paper, by telephone, or through various forms of computer-assisted interviewing. A structured set of questions is answered by a population, which may be systematically sampled.	How does the population of interest experience and understand the topic of interest? What sociodemographic factors account for differences? A survey using offline media to explore aspects of people's Internet use can use representative sampling techniques and can avoid response bias in favor of intensive Internet users.	Surveys about what people do online can fail to pick up on the nuances of the meaning they place on these behaviours. Recall about online activities in survey responses can be inaccurate.
Content analysis on a corpus of data found online	Structured analyses can be conducted on the content of a corpus of data such as blogs or messages sent to an online forum	What different kinds of contribution can be identified in this content? How do different online settings differ? A topic of interest can be explored in naturally occurring data, avoiding the need to ask people questions.	Analysis may be restricted to taking what people say at face value, and the ability to understand nuances can be limited. Content analysis may neglect the very different meanings which people may be giving to overtly similar online interactions.
Online experiments	Experiments can be conducted online via websites, allowing for people who are not geographically co-located to undertake an experimental task aimed at exploring some aspect of their behavior, attitudes, cognitive function, etc.	Online experiments can provide large pools of participants and allow for a structured analysis of the effects of varying the conditions in relation to the focus of the research.	Some data collected may be unusable since the commitment of participants to sensible completion of the task cannot be guaranteed. The experimental conditions may not mirror more complex real-life circumstances.

Social network analysis	Network analysis can be carried out on any data set, which can be used as a proxy for different forms of relationship. For example, log files of interactions, comments on blog posts, or hyperlinks between websites can all be used to conduct network analysis.	What is the pattern of connections between nodes (e.g., people, organizations) in this network? How do patterns of connection change over time? Which entities are more central to the network, and which are peripheral?	The assumptions made by the network analysis about the relationships depicted by the dataset may not be valid—numerous hyperlinks between two websites may not always, for example, mean that the two organizations producing them are ideologically close in some way.
Sentiment analysis	Sentiment analysis uses machine learning, deploying techniques from natural language processing to determine the emotional mood of communications. It is often latterly used on large data sets from social networking sites and Twitter.	What are the large-scale patterns of positive and negative sentiments expressed by users in relation to the topic? How does opinion change over time?	Sentiment analysis relies on the ability to develop stable means of determining the mood of a message. This is inevitably error prone and may miss out on specific nuances. It is particularly difficult to reliably identify sentiment in very short messages.
Semiotic analysis of individual online artifacts	Semiotic analysis looks at the composition of an artifact, such as a website, as a set of signifying elements chosen by the creator. Semiotic analysis looks at the consequences of the choices of signs and their arrangement, looking beyond overt meanings to the connotations of the various choices.	Who are the audience addressed by this text, and what meanings does it convey to them?	Semiotic analysis depends on the cultural competencies of the analyst. The analyst must be able confidently to identify the repertoire of signs available to the author and the connotations of the different choices. This may differ from the way that diverse actual readers may interpret the text in their own local circumstances.

early on questioned the extent to which the "virtual" should be taken to be an objectively existing discrete domain of experience. Hine stressed that the Internet could be construed as both culture and cultural artifact and noted the significance of offline circuits of interpretation for shaping online experiences. Markham noted the multiplicity of the Internet experience, specifically arguing that it could be encountered as a tool, place, or a way of being and that each entailed a different orientation from the ethnographer. Both across and within ethnographic studies of the Internet from the outset there has been recognition of its ontological multiplicity (Mol, 2002), such that it is experienced and defined quite differently from different perspectives. Since ethnographers tend to strive for a rich and multifaceted understanding of the phenomenon they study, it is therefore not surprising that multiple methods were employed to develop an ethnographic understanding of the Internet and that in many instances researchers have combined these multiple approaches within a single study.

Baym's pioneering Internet ethnography (1995, 2000), which has acted as a model for many subsequent studies, employed a combined methodological approach. Baym (2000) recognized three senses in which the group that she studied was a community: as a discrete Internet newsgroup, as an audience community oriented to a specific soap opera, and as a community of practice. Her understanding of these multiple community formations was itself developed through multiple forms of engagement with the group. She was a long-standing member of the group (and viewer of the television program that they discussed), and much of her initial insight was developed through a deep understanding of how participation was structured and how it felt to participate. She deployed a variety of data collection techniques, including archiving of messages themselves, interviewing participants, attending offline events when they occurred, and surveying members to collect background demographic information. She conducted a variety of modes of analysis on samples of messages, including structured coding of message genres and a content analysis of agreements and disagreements. Baym (2000) was thus able to combine an impressionistic, rich, and situated account of participation with a structured account of patterns emergent across the group. Just as many qualitative researchers recognize the necessity of providing quantification as a mode of description (Maxwell, 2010), Internet ethnographers have found that they can quantify

and that developing structured, content analytic descriptions can complement more impressionistic approaches.

The urge to quantify, for an Internet ethnographer, can arise because so much data presents itself quite readily in a form that the researcher can search, copy, and manipulate. Conversely, if one does not carry out some form of quantitative analysis or data visualization as an online ethnographer, the sheer amount of data that is available can come to seem overwhelming. For example, Boellstorff (2008) describes his ethnography of Second Life[3] as producing over 10,000 pages of field notes based on participant observation, interviews, and focus groups together with another 10,000 pages of documents such as websites, blogs, and newsletters. He explains that for an ethnographer in an offline setting, producing field notes and collecting data are often hard work, and a lot of filtering therefore happens at the stage of deciding what to write down and which data to focus on acquiring. Online data can be much more ready-to-hand. Traditionally an ethnographer in an offline setting might have to laboriously conduct a house-to-house survey in order to be able to describe a population and to formulate quantitative statements about the nature of relationships there to complement qualitative descriptions based on participant observation. In an online world surveys can still be conducted (by sending messages rather than trudging from house to house), but the ethnographer can also develop an overview of the participants and their activities by analyzing ready-to-hand data in archives of messages, membership lists, or log files recording details of interaction.

Many forms of online interaction are already archived for the use of participants themselves quite independently of the activities of the ethnographer, so ethnographers can not only experience real-time interactions as a participant observer but also explore the precedents and antecedents of the activities they are experiencing now through the archives that record the history of the group. For example, while studying an online discussion group of biologists, I found that it seemed a quite natural step to combine insights based on participant observation and interviews with participants with a quantitative analysis of the group membership using membership records given to me by the list owner and an analysis of the temporal patterning of participation using data taken directly from the archive of messages (Hine, 2008a). These descriptive statistics gave me a context in which to situate my own impressions of the dynamics of the group and the accounts of other participants. I also found that looking at the archives gave me the opportunity to rapidly develop a sense of the history of the group and to situate activities I was observing in the present against the past of the group. It was possible to travel back and forth in time through the archive, finding that activities currently taken for granted as normal, such as asking for identification of a plant by sharing an image of it with other participants in the group, were once deemed remarkable, even risible. The archive makes certain forms of temporal mobility possible for ethnographers, as well as encouraging use of descriptive statistics to complement insights from participant observation.

Ethnography is often an inherently mixed method in its attempts to capture multiple dimensions of its substantive focus, and Internet ethnography has continued and developed this tradition, with extra fervor thanks to the particular qualities of the phenomenon being studied. In particular, so much of the data that Internet ethnographers encounter is "born digital," and thus relatively readily rendered as a corpus for structured analysis, that quantitative forms of inquiry become accessible even for single researchers or small teams. Ethnography online thus builds on the existing mixed methods tradition of ethnography and raises it to a new level:

> As a form of ethnography, netnography encompasses multiple methods, approaches and analytic techniques. Experienced ethnographers are inevitably bricoleurs, and I would fully expect netnographers to deploy any of a number of techniques as they approach the rich lived worlds of cultural experience that people share and experience online. These techniques would include projective techniques, historical analysis, semiotic analysis, visual analysis, musical analysis, survey work, content analysis, kinesics and any of a world of specialities, as well as the more obvious observational, participative and interview techniques. (Kozinets, 2007, p. 132)

Ethnography has been used here as an example of an approach that is already predisposed to being adaptive in its choice of methods and where mixed methods research has particularly flourished in Internet research. However, the mixing of modes and methods is of course not confined to Internet ethnography. The experimental tradition has also thrived in Internet contexts, and here again combining of approaches has been found beneficial. Reips and Buffardi (2012), for example, discuss various web-based approaches for studying migrants using psychological techniques and explore the purchase offered by combining different approaches. These approaches include Internet-based interviews and surveys, nonreactive data collection of existing documents, and traces of interaction such as from social networking sites, Internet-based tests, and online experiments. Each approach carries its own challenges, affordances, and limitations, but each is seen to offer a form of knowledge that remains unavailable from other perspectives.

Ess and Dutton (2013) talk about mixed methods designs in Internet research as a response to the weakness of particular methods, and to some extent this is apparent in the motivation of Internet researchers toward mixed methods designs, but this formulation possibly underplays the extent to which the methodological imagination has been stimulated in a positive sense by the particular complexities of the Internet as a research object, the interdisciplinary nature of Internet research as a field, and the kind of data brought into being by use of the Internet. It is not entirely accurate to describe the mixing of methods in Internet research as wholly a response to the perceived inadequacies of singular approaches. Mixing of methods in Internet research has been as much occasioned by a mood of exploring new possibilities and accepting the opportunities offered by the wealth of data the Internet makes available, as it has by a sense of weakness or lack in any particular method. The next section illustrates this sense of the opportunities of mixed methods designs in Internet research by focusing further on some of the unusual qualities of the Internet as a source of data for doing social science. This section looks particularly at the affordances of born digital data for large-scale analysis and explores in more detail some of the methodological responses this kind of data has prompted.

Combining Large-Scale and Small-Scale Approaches to Internet Research

While discussing mixed methods research designs within Internet studies, it is crucial to recognize that this is not simply a question of mixing together preexisting methods and approaches. The distinctive qualities of the Internet, as a vast, interconnected searchable territory, generated through the activities of myriad uniquely situated participants, offers up possibilities for study not anticipated within previous methods. Rogers (2013) argues that the advent of this born digital data requires not only the transfer of traditional methods to the new domain but also the development of digital methods, which offer a new way of conceptualizing what society is and are particularly attuned to the qualities of this new domain. For example, analysis of the links between websites offers new possibilities for exploring the emergence of issues and the development of political debates (see, e.g., Rogers & Marres, 2000). The patterns of hyperlinking,[4] in this approach, are taken to constitute a form of novel social connection in their own right—the issue network, rather than simply being artifacts reflective of an underlying social structure that could be uncovered by conventional techniques. The study of the issue network is thus construed as offering a distinctive window on contemporary social existence. Given its claims to offer such a distinctive perspective, it is perhaps no surprise that this kind of technique has been employed within mixed methods designs. For example, this technique was used in a study of political party organization and activism, which explored political blogs through a combination of interviews, content analysis, surveys of users and data on usage, and hyperlink analysis to explore the emergent networks of connection (Gibson, Gillan, Greffet, Lee, & Ward, 2013).

While the Internet has occasioned some altogether new methods, such as issue network analysis, it has also reinvigorated some preexisting methods. Social network analysis, and related techniques for visualizing social structure on a large scale, have thrived in the face of the visibility of social connections, which the Internet offers (Garton, Haythornthwaite, & Wellman, 1997; Hogan, 2008). A social network analysis aims to understand the social world as a network of connected entities, for example treating individual people as nodes in a network and various forms of relationship, such as friendship, kinship, or working relations as the ties between the nodes. This form of analysis long predates the Internet, but data collection was often very laborious because people had to be asked to recount in exhaustive detail the relevant relationships in which they were engaged. The advent of the Internet, with persistent data on many forms of relationship and interaction, has made large-scale approaches such as social network analysis a much easier prospect. Provided that the relationship one wishes to study is reflected in some way in online interactions, archived data from those interactions can be used as a proxy to portray the nature and strength of those relationships and enable the social network to be visualized.

One form of large-scale analysis fostered by the Internet focuses on depicting relationships by using the patterns of connection between websites or the amount of online interactions between individuals as a proxy for the strength of the relationship. Initially websites were often produced by organizations, and researchers were able to study the various forms of connection between them depicted by the patterns of linking in cyberspace.[5] Subsequently, the advent of large-scale user-generated content (the participatory web, or Web 2.0; Blank & Reisdorf, 2012), offered up for analysis a dramatic increased array of traces of the daily activities and connections of large swathes of the population. Blogging, social networking sites such as Facebook, and micro-blogging (e.g., Twitter) allow people to express their thoughts on a public stage and as a by-product make those thoughts available for social researchers to mine for patterns. The visibility and persistence of digital data makes it possible to map out networks and explore structure on a grand scale, removing the previously often insurmountable barrier to large-scale analysis presented by the lack of resources to collect the necessary data.

In Internet studies it is clear that many novel research approaches have been occasioned by the distinctive qualities of the data, particularly its persistence, searchability, and ready accessibility. The possibility of generating large data sets for relatively little cost, whether through collection of publicly available traces such as hyperlinks or social networking site activities or via negotiation of access to institutionally held log files and message corpora, makes large-scale quantitative analysis more feasible than it was before. Small teams of researchers, with relatively little resources, can now access large data sets and, with appropriate computational support, make sense of them. The advent of publicly available tools specifically designed to make sense of these large corpora, such as the Issue Crawler (http://www.govcom.org/),[6] SocSciBot (http://socscibot.wlv.ac.uk/),[7] and SentiStrength (http://sentistrength.wlv.ac.uk/),[8] means that researchers do not necessarily have to design their own analytic tools.

While this form of large-scale analysis is undoubtedly powerful in its sheer scale and ability to see a "big picture," it has also been subject to criticism for the lack of fine detail and ability to interpret findings for what they mean to participants. Large-scale analysis of "found data" from the Internet has often, therefore, featured in mixed methods research designs that exploit the ready availability of large-scale data but also seek other means to assist in interpreting the resulting patterns. In the rest of this section I outline some different examples of mixed method designs that combine a large-scale analysis of publicly available data with other forms of contextualizing data. First I outline the conditions under which digital data becomes available for research purposes and offer some diverse examples of large- and small-scale approaches to analysis of found data from social networking sites, blogs, and Twitter, before turning to a more in-depth exploration of the motivations for combining methods and the methodological assumptions behind different forms of combination.

The most obvious motivation for conducting large-scale analysis based on born digital data is prompted by the simple fact that this kind of data is readily available. Almost every conceivable facet of human activity is reflected in some way on the Internet (albeit often in a somewhat selective or partial way). Hyperlinks on the web are generally publicly available data, as are blogs by their nature, and as such can be accessible for use by researchers without the need to negotiate additional access. Social networking sites offer up a rich array of found data for quantitative analysis, provided the individual users' privacy settings render the data visible to researchers. For example, Thelwall (2008) inventively deployed public MySpace comments to conduct a study of contemporary swearing and cursing practices. The study utilized the tendency of many users to allow access to their profiles to others besides their known friends. Some forms of data, by contrast, are amenable to large-scale analysis but can be harder to come by. For example, access to institutional intranets, or log files of internal communications such as used by Dirksen, Huizing, and Smit (2010), requires negotiation with stakeholders. While the Internet, in general, promotes the use of big data approaches as a complement to qualitative studies, it depends on the individual research object whether big data is in practice readily accessible or not. However, in many cases, the research imagination is piqued by the actual or potential availability of a set of data that, before the Internet, could not have existed on such a scale.

Provided that the data is publicly available, the same kind of data can often in fact be viewed both as fodder for a large-scale analysis and as a potential site for a detailed qualitative inquiry. Blogs offer up data that can be subjected to both large-scale qualitative and more in-depth quantitative approaches: Herring (2010) discusses the challenge that blogging poses to conventional forms of content analysis and suggests that researchers can usefully combine different approaches in order to attend to the various qualities of blogs as meaningful contexts in their own right and as part of structured and interconnected fields of discourse. For example, Herring et al. (2005) carried out a study of blogging that combined a qualitative analysis of the comments made on interconnected blogs with a social network analysis and visualization that allowed the researchers to explore the emergent patterns in the blogosphere. Efimova (2009) completed a qualitative study of blogging practices, in which she complemented her ethnographic observations with a systematic visualization of blog conversations as they emerged over time. The temporal dimension can be particularly significant in analysis of blogs: Park and Kluver (2009), for example, conducted a longitudinal analysis of the blogs of politicians in South Korea, involving analysis of hyperlinking over time together with interviews.

Twitter also offers up rich data for both large-scale approaches and more targeted studies. Murthy (2013) presents a commentary on Twitter that combines both qualitative and quantitative approaches to understanding its role in mediating disasters, promoting activism, and enacting health concerns. Bruns (see, e.g., Bruns 2011; Bruns & Burgess, 2011; Bruns & Liang, 2012; Bruns & Stieglitz, 2012) has developed quantitative approaches to characterizing and comparing the emergence of debates on Twitter as a complement to case study and anecdotal approaches. Bruns and Liang discuss the methodological diversity within quantitative Twitter studies, which can deploy a mixture of repurposing of existing tools and custom-designed analytic approaches. Procter, Vis, and Voss (2013) discuss the mixed method design, which they developed to analyze the corpus of tweets relating to the riots that took place in England in 2011, provided directly to the research team by the Twitter organization. Here the large-scale computational analysis of the substantial corpus of tweets (2.6 million tweets from 700,000 distinct user accounts) was used to direct the researchers' attention to potentially interesting sections of the corpus for an in-depth qualitative exploration. This combination of methods allowed the researchers to handle the corpus on a range of different scales: as a corpus, as information flows, and as individual communicative events.

Various forms of network analysis and visualization described here have been deployed by researchers interested in online phenomena to orient their studies and add different perspectives, conscious of the affordances that different methods offer. The research designs within which these methods are combined can, however, differ widely, as can the understanding of their affordances. Designs can be built on a very specific notion of how methods complement one another. For example, like Proctor et al. (2013), Howard (2002) used a sequential design, deploying social network analysis of the patterns of communication across a distributed organization to orient his choice of case study sites for an in-depth exploration. As Howard describes it, social network analysis can act as a guide to conducting the kind of purposive sampling that an ethnographer will often deploy to home in on a potentially interesting site to study. It is, however, overly limited as the sole portrayal of a field, particularly with regard to temporal dimensions:

> On its own, social network analysis misses much of the rich information that the researcher can obtain by participating in the hypermedia organization and observing small-group interaction. As a method it can bring perspective to complex-layered social networks, sometimes artificially making employment, peer, and personal networks congruent. More importantly, social network analysis has limited use in revealing stories of mobility within communities. Narratives about how people enter and leave a network, or about how people move from periphery to core and back, are difficult to reduce to comparative values. (p. 560)

As he points out, most social network analysis involves some form of on-the-ground verification. However, the combination of a formal social network analysis followed by a full ethnographic exploration of selected field sites informed by the social network analysis that Howard uses is distinct in the more equal weight it gives to both methods as different modes of understanding. As he portrays it, the network analysis gave him a comprehensive overview of the territory but in a rather static format, while the subsequent participant observation offered a more processual understanding.

In similar vein, De Maeyer (2013) conducts a critical analysis of hyperlink studies and finds that many authors combine an automated or large-scale link analysis with some form of contextualization or qualitative exploration to allow the meaning of the links being analyzed to be inferred. In itself, a hyperlink, or a Twitter "hashtag," or a "like" on a social networking site does not tell us what meaningful social connection is being forged. De Maeyer stresses the importance of supplementing link analysis with other methods to allow for both patterns and meanings to be explored. Such combinations of link analysis to study structure and qualitative methods to explore process, depth, and meaning have been powerful approaches in Internet studies. Vasileiadou and van den Besselaer (2006) discuss a mixed method design for studying collaborations between organizations in the field of communication motivated by these concerns, combining an analysis of web links with qualitative interviews. Brügger (2013) discusses similar issues in the context of historical analysis of web archives. He argues that "a hyperlink is always a semantic, a formal, and a physically performative entity," and while it might be informative, a network analysis of hyperlinks explores only the physically performative entity (p. 308). He argues that alternative approaches based on textual analysis are needed in order to explore other aspects of the hyperlink. For a historian, Brügger explains, the challenge of working out just what a hyperlink might signify is compounded by the imperfect and selective rendering of the web in archived form and the multiple ways of rendering the web as an object of study, such that a singular methodological approach is often insufficient.

To some extent, then, researchers combining large-scale quantitative analysis with smaller scale qualitative approaches to online phenomena have done so because one or other approach on its own seems to lack explanatory power, or, to put it more positively, because the different methods offer complementary and distinctive ways of understanding the phenomenon. These researchers combining large-scale analysis with qualitative methods tend to see the qualitative method in general as adding depth or meaning, but not all necessarily see the combination as a process of triangulation on a singular research object. Howard's (2002) sequential understanding of the mixing of methods in online ethnographic work with social network analysis as the preliminary step is only one of the possible models for understanding how the different methods combine. Dirksen et al. (2010) describe a somewhat different model in their study, which used social network analysis of log files from a company intranet to enable them both to interpret qualitative data and to target their detailed attention to various online and offline sites. Dirksen et al. describe their approach as "piling on layers of understanding" (p. 1045), positioning the different methodological approaches as layers that contribute to development of a picture of the overall phenomenon of the dynamics of online social practices within the organization. Dirksen et al. describe their approach as a connective one, moving between sites to explore meaning-making as linked by various discourses and forms of technologically mediated practice. Their approach to combining methods in this way is inspired by Strathern's (2002) comment that different methods add "layers of understanding" (p. 303), not necessarily triangulating with one another or providing a straightforward contextualization, since each method offers up a new viewpoint and a new version of what a context might be, effectively creating a new research object. A researcher might therefore make use of network analysis or visualizations alongside qualitative analysis in order to provide distinctive perspectives on a field without necessarily accepting that one straightforwardly contextualized the other.

Researchers even vary in the extent to which they see different forms of analysis as separable and distinct. Markham (2012) folds the role of network analysis into ethnographic research, describing network analysis as a means of developing "network sensibilities," explaining "the reflexive, ethical power of using network analysis to help shift our perspective constantly and radically, by attending to different senses we might use to locate, interpret, and represent that which we might call 'data'" (p. 48). She describes network analysis as an enhancement to ethnographic work, neither necessarily preceding qualitative and participatory work nor depending on it, but both become part of the ways in which the researcher senses and moves through the field. Geiger and Ribes (2011) take a related stance in their discussion of "trace ethnography," which takes seriously the role of various forms of document and trace in rendering participants present to one another, as well as to the researcher. Their aim is to integrate techniques, taking in both the richness of participant observation and the decoding of various documentary traces: an approach that they demonstrate

using the example of the log file traces of edits to Wikipedia pages. They stress that the analysis of traces does not precede or inform the ethnography but to a large extent is the ethnography, since this is the means through which participants are visible to one another.

As these latter examples from Dirksen et al. (2010), Markham (2012), and Geiger and Ribes (2011) show, some Internet researchers from largely qualitative traditions may thus have adopted larger scale approaches, but they have done so because these are seen as appropriate adaptations to the circumstances they find, rather than because these large-scale approaches are seen as somehow inherently better than small-scale qualitative research. boyd and Crawford (2011) argue that there are concerns that big-data approaches may come to dominate the research landscape as appearing inherently more informative, and this "scaling up" may instead entail loss as well as gain in terms of our understanding of social phenomena. They stress that different forms of data are not necessarily interchangeable; for example, a social network analysis based on people's use of social networking sites does not necessarily tell us about their social networks as they would be represented by other forms of data. They formulate a distinction between the articulated networks that people specify through their use of social networking sites, the behavioral networks of the connections people forge through the various forms of communication available to them, and the personal networks that entail a more subtle understanding of the value people place on their relationships with other people. In their caveats about the use of big data, boyd and Crawford (2011) remind us that data that tells us about one of these forms of network may well not tell us about the others. They offer a principled argument for a form of mixing that remains attentive to the different claims that different forms of data make about the significant phenomena for our research attention. This stance appears consistent with the line taken by ethnographers such as Markham, Geiger and Ribes, and Dirksen et al.

Thus even while many researchers have combined various forms of quantitative and network analysis with qualitative approaches to the Internet, then, their conceptions of the necessary link between the components of the study afforded by different methods can differ dramatically. This section has included designs that deploy methods in sequential fashion as one orients and directs the next, designs that use different methods to offer different perspectives on a phenomenon without claiming that either explains or contextualizes the other, and designs that use multiple methods precisely in order to provide contextualization. Internet researchers are very conscious of being overwhelmed by the sheer quantity of data available, and in this context the possibility of new ways of exploring and visualizing patterns holds considerable promise. These new approaches do not necessarily displace other forms of analysis, nor do large-scale big-data approaches make small-scale qualitative research redundant. Instead, many researchers are discovering the explanatory power of combined approaches, which look both for patterns and for meanings. Rather than triangulating on a singular object, however, many researchers in this domain are highly conscious of the complex and multiple nature of the Internet as a research object and see different methodological approaches as complementary but not necessarily cumulative in the understanding that they offer.

Multimodal Research On and Off the Internet and the Challenges of Triangulation

A further aspect of the complex and multiple nature of the Internet as a research object that has troubled researchers and influenced research designs concerns the extent to which the Internet is seen to be understandable through data collected solely online. Because the Internet is as much a component of everyday life offline as it is a discrete online space, many studies of Internet phenomena do not collect their data solely through the medium of the Internet itself. These studies often mix both methods and modes in their attempts to gain a rounded perspective on a phenomenon, which both understands the Internet for its own qualities and explores its embedding in diverse circumstances offline (Wellman & Haythornthwaite, 2002). Baym (2009) argues for multimodal approaches to understanding new media, stressing that these new technologies are not experienced in isolation and that our practices connect them in complex and unpredictable fashion. This has serious implications for the design of adequate research approaches for understanding new media:

> We cannot bank our research future on the technological forms. Instead we need to interrogate the underlying dynamics through which technology use is patterned across media, relationships, and communicative purposes and with what effects for

how we understand and conduct our relations, our communities, and ourselves. (p. 721)

Where our concern is to find out what the Internet means to people, it is often difficult to render a study that focuses only on the online as adequate to describe the phenomenon. At the same time, a study of what the Internet means to people, which focuses only on face-to-face interviews and ignores what they actually do when they are online, despite the multiple traces that these activities leave, would seem somewhat perverse. Researchers conducting studies of the embedding of the Internet in everyday life thus find themselves almost inevitably deploying a mixture of methods and modes to explore their key concern with understanding the way that online and offline are entwined. There are, indeed, many studies that could be cited here, so the following represent only a very selective sample for illustrative purposes, focusing on studies in which the combination of methods notably allows for an expansion in the scope of the explanatory or descriptive possibility of the study.

One such example of a mixed mode, mixed method study is boyd's (2007, 2008) exploration of teenage use of social networking sites. Her work combined online fieldwork in social networking sites themselves, offline interviews, and observation in less structured and less predictable environments where teenagers hang out. Through this combination of modes and methods, boyd was able to position her study as an exploration of how teenagers lived their lives in and through social networking sites and at the same time how this activity was rendered salient in various other aspects of their lives. In another example of research aimed at finding out what people make of the Internet, Hargittai (2002) has conducted studies of the ways in which people find and interpret online materials, deploying mixed modes and methods, including structured observation sessions based on participants completing an online task together with more open interviews and larger scale surveys, often conducted on a longitudinal basis. Vittadini et al. (2012) argue that researching the practices of digital learners requires a multitool and multimodal approach that treats boundaries between online and offline as blurred. Hampton (e.g., 2007) has conducted various studies of the embedding of the Internet in everyday life, focusing on multimethod and multimode data collection to explore such issues as the role of Internet communications in neighborhood community relations. One notable study combined a national telephone survey of Facebook users with analysis of their Facebook profiles and log files of their activity on the site, to allow for a triangulation between what people said about the site and what they did (Hampton, Goulet, Marlow, & Rainie, 2012). These mixed mode, mixed method studies have in common that they seek both to understand in detail what people do online but also to explore what those online activities mean within people's everyday lives. This kind of study must, perforce, move around and adopt different perspectives in order to capture these different aspects of Internet activity. Similarly, connective and multisited approaches to ethnography have developed through the ethnographer's urge to "follow the thing" as it is manifested in diverse locations (Marcus, 1995), and increasingly this includes both online and offline locations (Hine, 2007; Burrell, 2009).

A different kind of mixed mode study is a rather more pragmatic response to the affordances of the Internet for conducting research interactions with participants. For example, the mixing of modes in interview-based studies is now relatively commonplace, in part due to pressure from research participants, some of whom will feel comfortable with one or other form of online interview and others of whom will strongly prefer face-to-face interviews. The qualitative researcher's interest in finding the medium for interviews that will put participants most at ease provides an impetus toward the combination of different modes of interview in the same study, as does the urge to maximize participation (Kazmer & Xie, 2008). This set of concerns provided the impetus for a methodologically plural study of the role of the Internet in gay men's sexual practice, which recruited from online and offline sites and used both face-to-face and online interviews (Elford, Bolding, Davis, Sherr, & Hart, 2004). Similarly, Malta (2012) studied the online dating experiences of older adults and deployed interviews conducted face-to-face, by e-mail, by instant messaging, and by telephone, according to the choice of the participant.

Another set of pragmatic motivations for mixing modes in Internet research occurs among survey-based studies. According to Dillman (2011), survey approaches mix modes for a variety of reasons, including collecting the same data from different members of a sample, collecting panel data from the same respondent at a different time, collecting different data from a respondent at one time, collecting comparison data from different populations, and using one mode to prompt a respondent to complete a survey in another mode. Each occurs for different pragmatic motivations and introduces distinctive concerns for the interpretation of measurement differences across modes. There are therefore quite different motivations for mixing modes in Internet research studies, some of which are based in quite fundamental ways on a particular conception of the research object and others that are rather more pragmatic in their orientation to the most effective or efficient ways to collect interview or survey data.

In some methodologically plural and mixed mode studies, it appears relatively straightforward to view different approaches as triangulating on the same research object. One might study an online community for example, through a mixture of approaches including observation, interviews online or offline, and online surveys (as in the studies by Williams et al., 2006, and Nip, 2004b, 2004a, described by Hesse-Biber & Griffin, 2013) and still be relatively straightforwardly able to claim that one was studying the same community. Temporal fluctuations in the membership of the community and sampling issues can, however, mean that the research object is not completely the same as viewed through each approach. Even in the case of a single context study, it is not necessarily straightforward to determine a single research object, since participants may come and go over the course of a study, or different approaches draw in different subsections of the membership, such as active posters or lurkers. In some mixed mode studies that combine online and offline but do not follow a distinct sample from one site to another, it is markedly less straightforward to identify a single research object on which different methods triangulate. For example, boyd's (2007, 2008) study of teenage use of social networking sites used a variety of methods, but unlike the study by Hampton et al. (2012) described earlier, it did not follow the same teenagers between online and offline because of ethical concerns. Thus boyd could be said to have studied teenage use of social networking sites but not as experienced by a specific sample of teenagers across online and offline. Mixed mode studies that combine interviews online and offline can also have difficulties in aligning the two forms of data. Orgad's (2005b, 2005a) study of the use of online forums by women experiencing breast cancer moved between online and offline but found that the two modes of interviewing did not necessarily straightforwardly align: the two modes provided two different views of the phenomenon, even where the same woman was encountered both online and offline. Orgad found that online and offline interviews were not straightforwardly windows on the same phenomenon, nor was either inherently more informative.

Conclusion

It appears that mixed methods research designs are occurring relatively easily to the methodological imagination of Internet researchers. These designs have flourished in part due to the prevailing interdisciplinary tradition within Internet research and the relatively recent emergence of the Internet itself, within an era more accepting of mixed methods research than may be the case for more established disciplines. Adaptive approaches such as ethnography have readily embraced the possibilities for combining qualitative and quantitative designs on the Internet. Even where there is a preexisting commitment to qualitative research and its related philosophical paradigms, the sheer amount of data that comes readily to hand thanks to Internet search tools, log files, and the like often prompts the adoption of a quantitative stance, or at least some means of aggregating, visualizing, and exploring patterns. In adopting this stance, indeed, Internet researchers are aligned with developments in the world around them, which is increasingly oriented to the potential offered by big data (Savage & Burrows, 2007).

Internet researchers are often in the position described by Johnson et al. (2007) "when the nexus of contingencies in a situation, in relation to one's research question(s), suggests that mixed methods research is likely to provide superior research findings and outcomes" (p. 129). Particularly, the complex, fragmented, and embedded nature of the contemporary Internet means that it often feels inadequate to rely on a single source of data, and instead methods are combined and data from different sources examined in order to shed alternative sources of light on facets of a problem (Mason, 2011) if not to triangulate on a singular answer. Different methods and modes intersect in the illumination of a phenomenon but not necessarily in an additive sense in which each simply contributes "more" to understanding. Sometimes different forms of data and different modes of inquiry will align to add to certainty, but such is the complexity, interpretive flexibility, and multiple embedding of the Internet that this is rarely the case. More often the combination of modes and methods in the study of the Internet adds another form of understanding to our grasp of a complex phenomenon without triangulating on a singular solution.

Working against the methodological innovation and mixing promoted by a culture accepting of methodological innovation, a ready availability of data and an emergent set of tools, however, is the volatility of the Internet itself. The rapid development of Internet technologies and the constant emergence of new forms of data that has been experienced in recent years make it a considerable challenge for researchers to maintain the necessary skills to access and make sense of online phenomena and for developers of tools to maintain the currency of their technologies for the contemporary situation. Mixing of methods in Internet studies brings with it challenges as well as promises, and not least of these is accessing the range of skills and tools needed to combine qualitative and quantitative perspectives on an ever-shifting array of phenomena.

Discussion Questions

1. How is a large-scale social network analysis of an online community compatible with an ethnographic approach? How and when might the ethnographer best make use of the network analysis?

2. Why might a researcher choose to conduct both online and face-to-face interviews? What problems of interpretation might arise when the researcher tries to analyze the two sets of interviews side by side?

3. Is it appropriate to talk about mixing methods in Internet research as a form of triangulation? What other motivations do Internet researchers have for mixing methods?

Suggested Websites

http://aoir.org/

The Association of Internet Researchers is an interdisciplinary scholarly network and membership organization that organizes regular conferences, hosts a lively discussion list, and publishes ethical guidelines for Internet research.

https://www.digitalmethods.net/Digitalmethods/

This site, originating from Richard Roger's research group at University of Amsterdam, contains training materials on a range of approaches to social analysis of digital data.

http://webometrics.wlv.ac.uk/

Introduction to Webometrics by Mike Thelwall contains material related to his work on methods for quantitative analysis of the web and social media.

http://mappingonlinepublics.net/

Mapping Online Publics describes an interlinked series of research projects conducted by a research team led by Axel Bruns, focusing on the use and impact of social networking tools in Australia and beyond.

Notes

1. *Cyberculture* is a term used to denote cultural formations occasioned by use of computer networks.

2. A newsgroup was a publicly available asynchronous discussion group, focused on a specific topic. The rec.arts.tv.soaps newsgroup was focused on discussion of television soap operas; Baym (1995, 2000) focused in particular on threads related to one US soap opera, studying the social norms, hierarchies, and practices of the group of contributors to threads of discussion.

3. Second Life is a graphical virtual world in which the user is visually represented by an avatar. Users can socialize, conduct business, and create objects within the virtual world.

4. A hyperlink on the World Wide Web is way of connecting two websites, or two parts of a site, so that the user can navigate between them. Patterns of hyperlinking on the web can therefore potentially tell us something about patterns of affiliation or affinity between websites, as conceptualized by the creators of the links.

5. Thelwall (2004, 2009) provides an overview of techniques for subjecting the patterns of hyperlinks between websites to quantitative analysis, which can, he argues, inform social science questions and can be combined with qualitative approaches.

6. The Issue Crawler collects data from a set of websites specified by the researcher and visualizes the links between them, based on the pages that they link to. It allows the researcher to explore the patterns of affiliation and connection between sites.

7. SocSciBot collects data on the links between a specified set of websites and also allows researchers to carry out textual analysis on word frequencies and concordance for basic corpus linguistics approaches.

8. SentiStrength analyzes positive and negative sentiment in short texts such as Twitter data, allowing researchers to explore emotional content and trends.

References

Baym, N. (1995). The emergence of community in computer-mediated communication. In S. Jones (Ed.), *Cybersociety* (pp. 138–163). Thousand Oaks, CA: Sage.

Baym, N. K. (2000). *Tune in, log on: Soaps, fandom and online community*. Thousand Oaks, CA: Sage.

Baym, N. K. (2005). Introduction: Internet research as it isn't, is, could be, and should be. *The Information Society*, *21*(4), 229–232. Retrieved from http://dx.doi.org/10.1080/01972240591007535

Baym, N. K. (2009). A call for grounding in the face of blurred boundaries. *Journal of Computer-Mediated Communication*, *14*(3), 720–723. Retrieved from http://dx.doi.org/10.1111/j.1083-6101.2009.01461.x

Blank, G., & Reisdorf, B. C. (2012). The participatory web. *Information, Communication & Society*, *15*(4), 537–554. Retrieved from http://dx.doi.org/10.1080/1369118X.2012.665935

Boellstorff, T. (2008). *Coming of age in Second Life: An anthropologist explores the virtually human*. Princeton, NJ: Princeton University Press.

Boellstorff, T. (2010). A typology of ethnographic scales for virtual worlds. In W. S. Bainbridge (Ed.), *Online worlds: convergence of the real and the virtual* (pp. 123–133). London, England: Springer.

boyd, d. (2007). Why youth ♥ social network sites: The role of networked publics in teenage social life. In D. Buckingham (Ed.), *Youth, identity and digital media* (pp. 119–142). Cambridge, MA: MIT Press.

boyd, d., & Crawford, K. (2011, September). *Six provocations for big data*. Paper presented at A Decade in Internet Time: Symposium on the Dynamics of the Internet and Society, Oxford Internet Institute.

boyd, d. m. (2008). *Taken out of context: American teen sociality in networked publics* (Doctoral dissertation). University of California, Berkeley. Retrieved from http://www.danah.org/papers/TakenOutOfContext.pdf

Brügger, N. (2013). Historical network analysis of the web. *Social Science Computer Review*, *31*(3), 306–321. Retrieved from http://dx.doi.org/10.1177/0894439312454267

Bruns, A. (2011). How long is a tweet? Mapping dynamic conversation networks on Twitter using gawk and gephi. *Information, Communication & Society*, *15*(9), 1323–1351. Retrieved from http://dx.doi.org/10.1080/1369118X.2011.635214

Bruns, A., & Burgess, J. (2011). #Ausvotes: How twitter covered the 2010 Australian federal election. *Communication, Politics & Culture*, *44*(2), 37–56.

Bruns, A., & Liang, Y. E. (2012). Tools and methods for capturing Twitter data during natural disasters, *First Monday*, *17*(4). Retrieved from http://pear.accc.uic.edu/ojs/index.php/fm/article/view/3937/3193

Bruns, A., & Stieglitz, S. (2012). Quantitative approaches to comparing communication patterns on Twitter. *Journal of Technology in Human Services*, *30*(3–4), 160–185. Retrieved from http://dx.doi.org/10.1080/15228835.2012.744249

Bryman, A. (2006). Paradigm peace and the implications for quality. *International Journal of Social Research Methodology*, *9*(2), 111–126.

Burrell, J. (2009). The field site as a network: A strategy for locating ethnographic research. *Field Methods*, *21*(2), 181–199.

Creswell, J. W. (2011). Controversies in mixed methods research. In N. K. Denzin & Y. S. Lincoln (Eds.), *The SAGE handbook of qualitative research* (pp. 269–283). Thousand Oaks, CA: Sage.

Creswell, J. W., & Plano Clark, V. L. (2007). *Designing and conducting mixed methods research*. Thousand Oaks, CA: Sage.

De Maeyer, J. (2013). Towards a hyperlinked society: A critical review of link studies. *New Media & Society*, *15*(5), 737–751. Retrieved from http://dx.doi.org/10.1177/1461444812462851

Dillman, D. A. (2011). *Mail and Internet surveys: The tailored design method—2007 update with new Internet, visual, and mixed-mode guide*. Hoboken, NJ: Wiley.

Dirksen, V., Huizing, A. & Smit, B. (2010). "Piling on layers of understanding": the use of connective ethnography for the study of (online) work practices. *New Media & Society*, *12*(7), 1045–1063. Retrieved from http://dx.doi.org/10.1177/1461444809341437

Efimova, L. A. (2009). Passion at work: Blogging practices of knowledge workers (Doctoral disseration). *Novay PhD Research Series*: *Vol. 24*. Retrieved from http://igitur-archive.library.uu.nl/dissertations/2009-0626-200434/UUindex.html

Elford, J., Bolding, G., Davis, M., Sherr, L., & Hart, G. (2004). The Internet and HIV study: Design and methods. *BMC Public Health*, *1*, 39. Retrieved from http://www.biomedcentral.com/1471-2458/4/39

Ess, C. M., & Dutton, W. H. (2013). Internet studies: Perspectives on a rapidly developing field. *New Media & Society*, *15*(5), 633–643. Retrieved from http://dx.doi.org/10.1177/1461444812462845.

Garcia, A. C., Standlee, A. I., Bechkoff, J., & Cui, Y. (2009). Ethnographic approaches to the Internet and computer-mediated communication. *Journal of Contemporary Ethnography*, *38*(1), 52–84. Retrieved from http://dx.doi.org/10.1177/0891241607310839.

Garton, L., Haythornthwaite, C., & Wellman, B. (1997). Studying online social networks. *Journal of Computer Mediated Communication*, *3*(1). Retrieved from http://jcmc.indiana.edu/vol3/issue1/garton.html

Geiger, R. S., & Ribes, D. (2011). Trace ethnography: Following coordination through documentary practices. In *Proceedings of the 2011 44th Hawaii International Conference on System Sciences* (pp. 1–10). Los Alamitos, CA: IEEE Computer Society. Retrieved from http://doi.ieeecomputersociety.org/10.1109/HICSS.2011.455

Gibson, R. K., Gillan, K., Greffet, F., Lee, B. J., & Ward, S. (2013). Party organizational change and ICTs: The growth of a virtual grassroots? *New Media & Society*, *15*(1), 31–51. Retrieved from http://dx.doi.org/10.1177/1461444812457329

Hampton, K. (2007). Neighborhoods in the network society: The e-neighbors study. *Information, Communication & Society*, *10*(5), 714–748.

Hampton, K. N., Goulet, L. S., Marlow, C., & Rainie, L. (2012). *Why most Facebook users get more than they give*. Washington, DC: Pew Research Center. Retrieved from http://pewinternet.org/Reports/2012/Facebook-users.aspx

Hargittai, E. (2002). Beyond logs and surveys: In-depth measures of people's online skills. *Journal of the American Society for Information Science and Technology*, *53*(14), 1239–1244.

Herring, S. C. (2010). Web content analysis: Expanding the paradigm. In J. Hunsinger, L. Klastrup, & M. Allen (Eds.), *International handbook of Internet research* (pp. 233–249). Amsterdam, The Netherlands: Springer Netherlands.

Herring, S. C., Kouper, I., Paolillo, J. C., Scheidt, L. A., Tyworth, M., Welsch, P., Wright, E., & Yu, N. (2005). Conversations in the blogosphere: An analysis "from the bottom up." In *Proceedings of the Thirty-Eighth Hawaii International Conference on System Sciences* (p. 107b). Los Alamitos, CA: IEEE. Retrieved from http://dx.doi.org/10.1109/HICSS.2005.167

Hesse-Biber, S., & Griffin, A. J. (2013). Internet-mediated technologies and mixed methods research: Problems and prospects. *Journal of Mixed Methods Research*, *7*(1), 43–61. Retrieved from http://dx.doi.org/10.1177/1558689812451791

Hine, C. (2000). *Virtual ethnography*. London, England: Sage.

Hine, C. (2005). Internet research and the sociology of cyber-social-scientific knowledge. *The Information Society*, *21*(4), 239–248.

Hine, C. (2007). Connective ethnography for the exploration of e-science. *Journal of Computer Mediated Communication*, *12*(2). Retrieved from http://jcmc.indiana.edu/vol12/issue2/hine.html

Hine, C. (2008a). *Systematics as cyberscience: Computers, change and continuity in science*. Cambridge, MA: MIT Press.

Hine, C. (2008b). Virtual ethnography: Modes, varieties, affordances. In R. M. Lee, N. Fielding, & G. Blank (Eds.), *The SAGE handbook of online research methods* (pp. 257–270). London, England: Sage.

Hogan, B. (2008). Analyzing social networks via the Internet. In N. Fielding, R. M. Lee & G. Blank (Eds.), *The SAGE handbook of online research methods* (pp. 141–160). London, England: Sage.

Howard, P. N. (2002). Network ethnography and the hypermedia organization: New media, new organizations, new methods. *New Media & Society*, *4*(4), 550–574. Retrieved from http://dx.doi.org/10.1177/146144402321466813

Johnson, R. B., Onwuegbuzie, A. J., & Turner, L. A. (2007). Toward a definition of mixed methods research. *Journal of Mixed Methods Research*, *1*(2), 112–133. Retrieved from http://dx.doi.org/10.1177/1558689806298224

Kazmer, M. M., & Xie, B. (2008). Qualitative interviewing in Internet studies: Playing with the media, playing with the method. *Information, Communication & Society*, *11*(2), 257–278. Retrieved from http://www.informaworld.com/10.1080/13691180801946333

Kozinets, R. (2007). Netnography 2.0. In R. W. Belk (Ed.), *Handbook of qualitative research methods in marketing* (pp. 129–142). Cheltenham, UK: Edward Elgar.

Kozinets, R. V. (2009). *Netnography: Doing ethnographic research online*. London, England: Sage.

Malta, S. (2012). Using online methods to interview older adults about their romantic and sexual relationships. In M. Leontowisch (Ed.), *Researching later life and ageing: Expanding qualitative research horizons* (pp. 146–172). Basingstoke, UK: Palgrave Macmillan.

Marcus, G. (1995). Ethnography in/of the world system: the emergence of multi-sited ethnography. *Annual Review of Anthropology*, *24*, 95–117.

Markham, A. N. (1998). *Life online: Researching real experience in virtual space*. Walnut Creek, CA: AltaMira Press.

Markham, A. N. (2012). Moving into the flow: Using a network perspective to explore complexity in Internet contexts. In S. Lonborg (Ed.), *Network analysis: Methodological challenges* (pp. 47–58). Aarhus, Denmark: University of Aarhus Center for Internet Research.

Mason, J. (2011). Facet methodology: The case for an inventive research orientation. *Methodological Innovations Online*, *6*(3), 75–92. Retrieved from http://www.pbs.plym.ac.uk/mi/pdf/8-02-12/MIO63Paper31.pdf

Maxwell, J. A. (2010). Using numbers in qualitative research. *Qualitative Inquiry*, *16*(6), 475–482. Retrieved from http://dx.doi.org/10.1177/1077800410364740

Miller, D., & Slater, D. (2000). *The Internet: An ethnographic approach*. Oxford: Berg.

Mol, A. (2002). *The body multiple: Ontology in medical practice*. Durham, NC: Duke University Press.

Murthy, D. (2008). Digital ethnography. *Sociology*, 42(5), 837–855. Retrieved from http://dx.doi.org/10.1177/0038038508094565

Murthy, D. (2013). *Twitter: Social communication in the Twitter age*. Cambridge, UK: Polity.

Nardi, B. A. (2010). *My life as a Night Elf Priest: An anthropological account of World of Warcraft*: Ann Arbor: University of Michigan Press.

Nip, J. Y. M. (2004a). The Queer Sisters and its electronic bulletin board. *Information, Communication & Society*, 7(1), 23–49. Retrieved from http://dx.doi.org/10.1080/1369118042000208889

Nip, J. Y. M. (2004b). The relationship between online and offline communities: The case of the Queer Sisters. *Media, Culture & Society*, 26(3), 409–428. Retrieved from http://dx.doi.org/10.1177/0163443704042262

Orgad, S. S. (2005a). From online to offline and back: Moving from online to offline relationships with research informants. In C. Hine (Ed.), *Virtual methods: Issues in social research on the Internet* (pp. 51-65). Oxford, UK: Berg.

Orgad, S. S. (2005b). *Storytelling online: Talking breast cancer on the Internet*. New York, NY: Peter Lang.

Park, H. W., & Kluver, R. (2009). Trends in online networking among South Korean politicians: A mixed-method approach. *Government Information Quarterly*, 26(3), 505–515.

Peng, T.-Q., Zhang, L., Zhong, Z.-J., & Zhu, J. J. (2012). Mapping the landscape of Internet studies: Text mining of social science journal articles 2000–2009. *New Media & Society*, 15(5), 644–664. Retrieved from http://dx/doi.org/10.1177/1461444812462846

Procter, R., Vis, F., & Voss, A. (2013). Reading the riots on Twitter: Methodological innovation for the analysis of big data. *International Journal of Social Research Methodology*, 16(3), 197–214. Retrieved from http://dx.doi.org/10.1080/13645579.2013.774172

Reips, U.-D., & Buffardi, L. E. (2012). Studying migrants with the help of the Internet: Methods from psychology. *Journal of Ethnic and Migration Studies*, 38(9), 1405–1424. Retrieved from http://dx.doi.org/10.1080/1369183X.2012.698208

Rogers, R. (2013). *Digital methods*. Cambridge, MA: MIT Press.

Rogers, R., & Marres, N. (2000). Landscaping climate change: A mapping technique for understanding science and technology debates on the World Wide Web. *Public*

Understanding of Science, 9(2), 141–163. Retrieved from http://dx.doi.org/10.1088/0963-6625/9/2/304

Savage, M., & Burrows, R. (2007). The coming crisis of empirical sociology. *Sociology*, 41(5), 885–899. Retrieved from http://dx.doi.org/10.1177/0038038507080443

Schneider, S. M., & Foot, K. A. (2004). The web as an object of study. *New Media & Society*, 6(1), 114–122.

Scolari, C. A. (2009). Mapping conversations about new media: The theoretical field of digital communication. *New Media & Society*, 11(6), 943–964. Retrieved from http://dx.doi.org/10.1177/1461444809336513

Sterne, J. (2005). Digital media and disciplinarity. *The Information Society*, 21(4), 249–256. Retrieved from http://dx.doi.org/10.1080/01972240591007562

Strathern, M. (2002). Abstraction and decontextualization: An anthropological comment. In S. Woolgar (Ed.), *Virtual society? Technology, cyberbole, reality* (pp. 303–313). Oxford, UK: Oxford University Press.

Thelwall, M. (2004). *Link analysis: An information science approach*. Amsterdam, The Netherlands: Elsevier.

Thelwall, M. (2008). Fk yea I swear: Cursing and gender in MySpace. *Corpora*, 3(1), 83–107. Retrieved from http://www.euppublishing.com/doi/abs/10.3366/E1749503208000087

Thelwall, M. (2009). *Introduction to webometrics: Quantitative web research for the social sciences*. San Rafael, CA: Morgan and Claypool.

Vasileiadou, E., & van den Besselaar, P. (2006). Linking shallow, linking deep: How scientific intermediaries use the web for their network of collaborators. *Cybermetrics: International Journal of Scientometrics, Informetrics and Bibliometrics*, 10(1). Retrieved from http://cybermetrics.cindoc.csic.es/articles/v10i1p4.html

Vittadini, N., Carlo, S., Gilje, Ø., Laursen, D., Murru, M. F., & Schrøder, K. C. (2012). Multi-method and innovative approaches to researching the learning and social practices of young digital users. *International Journal of Learning*, 4(2), 33–45.

Wellman, B., & Haythornthwaite, C. (Eds.). (2002). *The Internet in everyday life*. Oxford, UK: Blackwell.

Williams, D., Ducheneaut, N., Xiong, L., Zhang, Y., Yee, N., & Nickell, E. (2006). From tree house to barracks: The social life of guilds in World of Warcraft. *Games and Culture*, 1(4), 338–361. Retrieved from http://dx.doi.org/10.1177/1555412006292616

Conducting Multimethod and Mixed Methods Research Online

Janet E. Salmons

Abstract

This chapter discusses uses of technology in collection of data for multimethods research designs (i.e., research using more than one approach within a qualitative or quantitative paradigm) or mixed methods studies (i.e., research designs that use both qualitative and quantitative approaches). As selected exemplars show, researchers use a wide range of information and communications technologies such as web and videoconferencing conferencing, e-mail, social media, and mapping tools in studies that may occur in a local community or across the globe. Through an analysis of a set of exemplars and a meta-synthesis of the collection, This chapter examines ways that the unique characteristics of 2 influence the experiences of researchers and participants and the phenomena being investigated.

Key Words: qualitative methods, multimethods, mixed methods, online research

Introduction

We need mixed modes and methods to study a mixed-reality world. Personal and social, reading and study, creative and cultural, professional and organizational, governmental and economic activities in the lives of the people we study have changed profoundly with the advent of information and communications technologies (ICTs). At first, new computer users experienced a sense of awe at the immediacy of e-mail as compared to the paper letter and the intriguing possibility of global exchange by user groups and emerging online communities. But as the *computer* left the office desk and started to live in our pockets, Internet technologies began to permeate all areas of our lives. For many people, it is no longer possible to fully separate online and offline aspects of life. Boundaries are seemingly permeable between the physical world and cyberspace; between and across them we navigate our various identities, cultures, friends, and communities.

Some yet unnamed form of liminality is emerging at the threshold between these identities and realities, an augmented reality, which encompasses electronic and physical presence. Elwell (2013) describes self-identity in this space as the "transmediated self" that is developed narratively with audience response and ongoing interactions (p. 11). The perspective that relationships occur over the Internet "in juxtaposition to, and competition with, a world of strong, deep, rewarding face-to-face relationships" has been replaced by an understanding that "relationships are maintained through multiple media" (Baym, Zhang, & Lin, 2004, p. 303). DeLyser and Sui (2013) draw on de Freitas' (2010) work to describe how

> users can sit publicly while engaging in private work or conversation, or sit privately while engaging in public work or conversation. . . . The transformation leaves physical space fixed, and digital space fluid, while both kinds of spaces fundamentally overlap and coexist, each shaped by the other—and their users. (pp. 300–301)

In this overlapping physical/online space we can no longer distinguish these dimensions as "face-to-face" versus "online" now that our devices contain still and video cameras with the capability of instant sharing or videoconferencing allowing us to see one another's faces and hear each other's voices, wherever we might be.

When we access the Internet, we now receive information through a mix of formats. Developments in electronic communication have increased a shift not only from page to screen but also from the written word to communication and representation through verbal, aural, and visual modes (Dicks, Soyinka, & Coffey, 2006; Kress, 1997, 2003; Skains, 2010). What started as online communication known as *text chat* due to its reliance on the written word has evolved into multimedia messaging services with the ability to share images and audio (Lillie, 2012) or replace words with emoticons (Laflen & Fiorenza, 2012) or emoji (Baron & Ling, 2011; Ueda & Nojima, 2011; Wortham, 2013), the digital images that convey emotions through a symbolic shorthand. In addition to a shift from purely written to a hybrid form of text and visual elements in online dialogue, we now access information differently. We may learn about an event by reading text, viewing images or video clips, listening to audio comments, or even interacting with others in a virtual environment. Such highly visual, multimedia forms of representation and communication are more effective for transmitting large amounts of certain kinds of information (Kress, 1997) and reducing information overload caused by excessive reliance on written communications (Jerejian, Reid, & Rees, 2013; Sumecki, Chipulu, & Ojiako, 2011).

Online communication options and representations are inherently multimodal, and with these varied choices the modes of meaning-making multiply (Kress & Selander, 2012, p. 267). This being the case, the contemporary researcher is "challenged to find multimodal ways to expand our methodological toolbox to better capture this social reality" (Beneito-Montagut, 2011, p. 717). To expand the methodological toolbox, researchers may need to creatively expand the ways they use technology and the Internet. Richard Rogers (2009, 2010) distinguishes between what he calls *virtual* approaches, those that import traditional data collection methods online, and *digital* approaches that take advantage of the unique characteristics and capabilities of the Internet for research. While trying to distinguish between virtual and digital may seem a semantic exercise, the methodological distinction is relevant. Digital approaches require the researcher

to do more than simply repurpose real-world data collection techniques to collect data electronically. We need to rethink the meaning and practices associated with research paradigms and methods—just as we have rethought the ways we take and share pictures, listen to music, go to the library or bank, or the many other activities of everyday life that are different in the digital age.

Quantitative and qualitative researchers view this challenge differently. The ever-growing use of online communication and social media—and the resulting big data—excites quantitative researchers who can scrape and download secondary data rich with potential relationships and correlations. Similarly, the ability to use online communication and social media to create deep exchanges with research participants across the globe—the humans on the other side of the monitor or device—excites qualitative researchers. While quantitative researchers typically collect data or track movements posted at a previous time, qualitative researchers can use synchronous approaches to gain insights in the moment.

Longstanding boundaries are blurring. As Yoshikawa, Weisner, Kalil, and Way (2008) observe:

> The world is not inherently qualitative or quantitative; it is the act of human representation through numbers or non-numeric signifiers like words that make aspects of the scientific enterprise qualitative or quantitative. Behaviors or contexts relevant to human development are not inherently qualitative or quantitative, but the methods of representation through which behaviors or contexts are recorded in research are. (p. 345)

New methods of representing, recording, and understanding behaviors or contexts do not necessarily fit within existing molds. Types of qualitative data collection are not neatly differentiated online, since computer-mediated communications often blend text and video chat, posted images, comments, and/or links to documents. Online interviews will most likely include some observations and/or review of user-posted material from the participants. Online observations may involve some review of users' dialogue with other users or with the researcher. Both quantitative and qualitative approaches are being used to analyze large bodies of content (Lindgren, 2012). Meanwhile quantitative researchers are realizing that "experts with deep knowledge of a subject are needed to ask the right questions and to recognize the shortcomings of statistical models" (Lohr, 2013). Sometimes in the midst of a sea of data, the quantitative researcher needs to stop and ask individual participants, "why?"

When researchers mix modes and methods, virtual, digital, and in-person approaches, drawing from both qualitative and quantitative traditions, they may discover a unique potential for research that is both big in scope and deep in meaning.

Ways to Think About the Mix

This chapter focuses on emerging ways to use technology with qualitative and quantitative methods. For the purpose of this chapter, research activities occurring in the same physical location are referred to as *in-person*. Research activities that use the Internet are referred to as *online*, and activities using non-Internet technologies are referred to as *technology enabled*. While these varied approaches require thinking and rethinking about all aspects of research from initial formulation of questions through discussion of findings, this chapter centers attention primarily on data collection.

Researchers in the field have interpreted the term *mixed methods* many ways (Johnson, Onwuegbuzie, & Turner, 2007) to address different stages of the research process (Bryman, 2006). A simple, broad definition is used here: mixed methods studies are those that include at least one qualitative and one quantitative method at so3me stage of the study. Some studies included in this chapter use sequential designs, meaning more or less ordered steps from one method to another. Standard notations are used to display the elements and modes for joining them for each respective study (Creswell & Clark, 2011; Johnson et al., 2007). QUAL → QUAN indicates the sequence of qualitative or quantitative approaches. Other studies use multiple methods concurrently, shown as QUAL + QUAL. Capital letters indicate a dominant method, and lowercase show a supportive approach. In diagrams that map elements of each exemplar, circles are used for qualitative approaches, squares are used for quantitative approaches, and arrows are used to distinguish between stages of the study. The vertical axis signifies parts of the study conducted concurrently, and the horizontal access shows sequential steps.

The value of "mixing" also exists within qualitative or quantitative research paradigms, a point reflected in the terms *integral research* (Sean, 2006) or *combined research* (Vogt, Gardner, & Haeffele, 2012), *multimodal research* (Dicks et al.,

2006; Rall, 2009) or *multimethod research* (Brewer & Hunter, 2006). Brewer and Hunter observe that

> a mix of qualitative and quantitative methods in each project. . . may sometimes be the case, but some research problems might be better served by combining two different types of quantitative methods (e.g., a survey and an experiment), or of qualitative methods (e.g., a field study and textual analysis of archival documents). In short, the multimethod strategy focuses more on the particular problem's demands than on some particular set or combination of methods. (p. 64)

For the purposes of this chapter, the term *multimethod research* is used to describe studies drawing from more than one method; in this chapter multimethod studies use multiple ways to collect data within qualitative studies.

This chapter begins with an examination of the multiple modes and mixed methods used in 13 research exemplars. Next, a cross-case analysis allows for further critique and discussion of the implications for researchers. Finally, some practical recommendations are offered to researchers interested in designing mixed or multimodal research.

Mix-and-Match Research Exemplars

A purposeful sampling strategy was used to select 13 diverse studies. The exploratory review included a broad search of peer-reviewed journals and academic databases as well as conference proceedings and working papers. Rather than picking a set of exemplars that employed the same kinds of technologies or methods, studies were chosen on the basis of "maximum variation sampling," to purposefully locate a "wide range of cases that represent a variation on the dimensions of interest" (Patton, 2002, p. 243). The "dimensions of interest" were defined generally to encompass research use of some type of ICT to with multimethod and mixed methods. Exemplars for this chapter were chosen primarily because each one represented a different way to collect and mix data.

With selection criteria articulated without regard to the research topic or purpose, the selected exemplars span disciplines including urban planning, music, sociology, education, health, geography, technology, gaming, marketing, and business. They variously mix in-person or online interviews, in-person or online observations, online surveys (quantitative) or questionnaires (qualitative), secondary datasets, maps, or content analysis of user-generated online content. Of 13 exemplars, 6 are mixed methods (quantitative and qualitative) while 7 are multimethod qualitative studies.

Mixing In-Person Interviews With Technology-Enabled Data Collection in Qualitative Multimethod Studies

Researchers studying local issues have the option to meet in-person to discuss or observe phenomena of interest. At the same time, researchers may find ways to enhance those immediate exchanges with technologies that allow them to collect additional data. The studies by Jones, Bunce, Evans, Gibbs, and Hein (2008), Jones, Evans, and Burwood (2008), Kwan (2008), Kwan and Ding (2008), Evans and Jones (2011), and Dowling (2012) variously explored the lived experiences of participants with interviews conducted in-person and online through e-mail, photographs, diaries, and other narrative records. Two of these exemplars utilize data from in-person interviews in conjunction with location-specific data generated using the mapping capabilities of geographic information system (GIS) and/or global positioning system (GPS) technologies.

The neighborhood, the sense of place, home, and local civic life are important, even in our Internet-connected world. Technology-enabled narrative and visual studies can be used to understand community members' views about local planning and development projects, neighborhood health and safety, or potential impacts of public policies (Jones et al., 2008; Kwan, 2008; Kwan & Ding, 2008).

To collect location-specific data for the studies discussed in several articles, Jones et al. used a multimethod qualitative approach to technology-enhanced in-person interviews (Evans & Jones, 2011; Jones et al., 2008, 2012). In what are called *walking interviews*, the interviewer and participant observe and talk about the phenomena of interest while they walk together. This is an unstructured, life history style of interview. Researchers use walking interviews to explore issues around people's relationship with physical space or the environment as a way to "link words and location" and directly connect "*what* people say with *where* they say it" (Jones et al., 2008, pp. 2, 6). As a result walking interviews produce a "spatial and locational discourse of place" (Evans & Jones, 2011, p. 856).

Jones et al. (2008) added an important update to this research approach by connecting walking

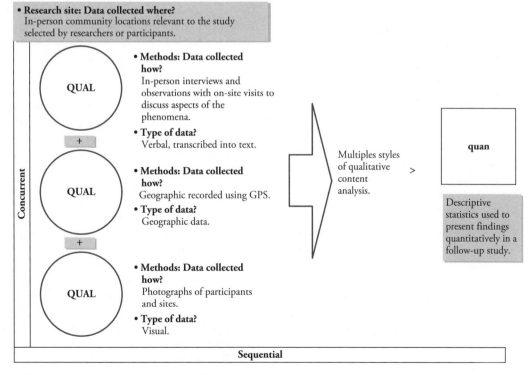

Fig. 29.1 An overview of walking interview research.
Jones et al. (2008, 2012); Evans and Jones (2011).

interviews precisely with locations by using GPS. As such the researchers were able to collect two complementary streams of data simultaneously: the responses participants made to interview questions and the geographic information about the location in which comments were made.

Jones et al. (2008) described three cases where walking interviews allowed researchers to study (a) perceptions of "café culture" in public spaces in newly regenerated areas of a postindustrial city, (b) perceptions of urban design and distinctive types of buildings and spaces in a redeveloped area, and (c) "local understandings and memories" of a community prior to a major redevelopment project for an effort called "Rescue Geography" (p. 6). A fixed route for the walk was used for the first case; in the second and third cases, participants were asked to determine the route and to choose the places where they wanted to share their perspectives.

Using GPS researchers were able to record the routes walked by interviewers and participants. Interview logs were combined with the GPS data. These streams of data collected from walking interviews were integrated, analyzed, and displayed using GIS or other mapping software. In the three research cases described, researchers generated multilayered maps "creating a kind of spatialised transcript" (Jones et al., 2008, p. 6). Jones et al. describe their approach to mixing data and analysis:

> As the chronology of people's experience and the sequence of events are central elements in narrative analysis, we use time geography as the representational framework for our approach of GIS-based narrative analysis. . . creating visual narratives that tell stories about people's experience or unfolding events over space and time. . . . With this analytical approach, the user can step back to read the linked text passages or memos, listen to voice clips, and view photos. These materials together provide a rich and vivid account of a participant's experience. (pp. 449, 459)

Jones et al. considered using video as an additional stream, referencing Sarah Pink's (2007) thinking about visual ethnography, but rejected it because they felt it would be cumbersome and intrusive to film, walk, and talk at the same time. The GPS provided a simple way to track specific locations; images could be added later. For example, the Rescue Geography project followed up the interviews with a photographic project that included portraits of participants and the locations they felt were meaningful. These photographs

were meshed with quotes from the interviews and the maps of the study area (Evans & Jones, 2011). Researchers exhibited these photographs and also made them available online, together with the maps, interview transcripts, and a link to a site that meshed study findings with Google Earth (Jones et al., 2012).

Jones et al. (2008) expressed concerns about a possible dampening of participants' uncensored sharing if they perceive the use of recording with GPS tracking as a type of surveillance. Researchers observed that they could have conducted the study without using the GPS technology by creating fixed routes for the walking interviews and inserting their own verbal notations of the location for each interview segment. However, this option would have changed the power dynamic from participant-generated to researcher-generated selection and prioritization of the interview settings—a change that would not allow the researchers to achieve the purpose of the study.

While the initial study used a multimethod qualitative approach (shown as QUAL + QUAL + QUAL) in a follow-up study, the same researchers mixed qualitative and quantitative methods (Evans & Jones, 2011). They analyzed qualitative data from the conversations with participants and quantitative data concerning the routes taken. They used descriptive statistics to show differences in data collection between walking and sedentary interviews (QUAL → QUAN). Using descriptive statistics they were able to quantitatively show that walking interviews resulted in longer interviews and more spontaneous data generated with a larger number of relevant comments made by participants without interviewer prompts and greater degree of specificity (Evans & Jones, 2011) (see Figure 29.1).

Another group of researchers similarly looked at mixing interview and narrative data with mapping capabilities of a GIS in what they termed "geo-narratives" (Kwan & Ding, 2008). Kwan and Ding argue that GIS is a valuable technology for qualitative researchers since it can incorporate qualitative materials (e.g., photos, videos, and written accounts) and generate visual narratives and maps. This inherently multimethod style is appropriate to study questions where it is important to understand what Daniels and Nash (2004) described as "the intersection of the geographical and the biographical" (p. 450).

Kwan (2008) used the geo-narrative approach to explore American Muslim women's experiences of fear, harassment, and concerns about potential hate

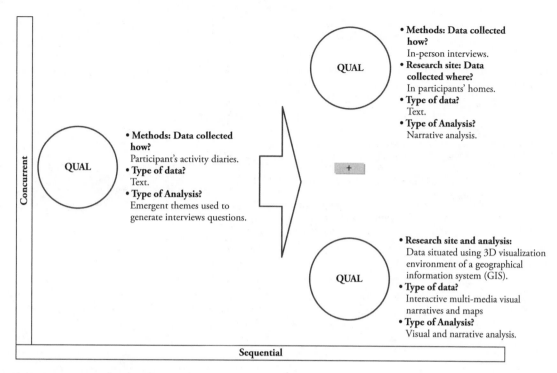

Fig. 29.2 Overview of "From Oral Histories to Visual Narratives: Re-presenting the Post-September 11 Experiences of the Muslim Women in the United States."
Kwan (2008).

crimes as they moved about their community to take children to school or to shop. The study is discussed in an article, "From Oral Histories to Visual Narratives: Re-Presenting the Post-September 11 Experiences of the Muslim Women in the United States" (Kwan, 2008). Mixed data collected from participants included activity diaries and in-depth oral history interviews. This data was mapped using the Trajectory Generator of 3D-VQGIS, a tool that allows for creation of a to visual space-time display of the participant's reported activities.

The geonarrative approach enabled Kwan (2008) to identify relationships between temporal patterns in the chronology of the participant's experience and the sites where they occurred such as the airport, school, or grocery store. This study follows a QUAL → QUAL + QUAL approach (see Figure 29.2).

Location was a critical element in the studies by Kwan (2008) and Jones et al. (2008, 2012). In the next exemplar, place has a different significance, since researcher Sally Dowling (2012) turned to online interviews when local participants were not able to meet in the same place.

Dowling (2012), in a public health-focused study of women who breastfeed long term,

originally designed her multimethod grounded theory study to complement participant observation in breastfeeding support groups with face-to-face interviews. She continued with the original plan for in-person interviews; however, when some participants could not attend meetings, she started to communicate with them through e-mail. What started as a solution to a logistical barrier evolved into a systematic approach using e-mail-based online interviews with about half of the study participants. This mid-course research design adjustment that resulted in a multimethod mix of interviews. This study follows a QUAL → qual + QUAL approach (see Figure 29.3).

Dowling (2012) adapted the approach to e-mail interviews introduced by Kralik, Koch, and Brady (2000), including establishment of clear expectations with participants and a planned serial approach to questioning. She paid attention to timeliness of her response to participants, aiming to balance the need for a steady communication flow with recognition that participants needed time to think about the question and formulate a response. By judiciously sharing her own experiences, Dowling tried to honor what Kralik et al.

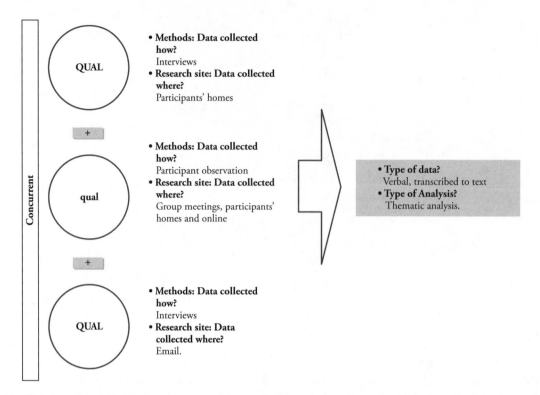

Fig. 29.3 Overview of "Online Asynchronous and Face-To-Face Interviewing: Comparing Methods for Exploring Women's Experiences of Breast-Feeding Long Term." Dowling (2012).

call the "reciprocal and reflexive nature of data generation" by monitoring her own inputs to ensure that that her story did not dominate or influence the directions of the exchange. Dowling said of the process of learning how to conduct interviews by e-mail as she conducted this study:

> There were other times when I, perhaps naively, was surprised by aspects of the process. Intending to correspond with my participants in an open-ended and reciprocal way, with ideas about the co-creation of data, I thought that participants would see it in the same way—and, of course, this was not always so. One participant fully entered into the relationship in the way I anticipated, with long e-mails reflecting honestly and openly on her experience, raising issues as well as responding to points that I had made. Two others responded at times like this but sometimes as if they were taking part in a more structured interview than was intended, responding to a question and then waiting for another to be posed. (p. 289)

The study also included in-person interviews that were conducted in participants' homes. These were semistructured, based on an interview guide. Prior to the in-person interview, Dowling used

e-mail for introductions and to establish rapport with participants. In reflectively comparing the two sets of interviews, Dowling commented:

> While the F2F interviewees were often distracted (as was I) by the presence of their children and others, online interviewees could respond at suitable times and at their own pace (and often commented on how they were writing late at night, or while a child napped). The use of e-mail rather than F2F interaction allowed for more thoughtful and considered responses than were possible in the sometimes distracting interview settings. In the same way, I was also able to consider my questions and comments differently as well as being able to fit my participation more comfortably into a busy life. (pp. 283–284)

In Dowling's case, even with local participants, the e-mail option allowed her to proceed with the study and collect rich data from those who otherwise would have withdrawn from the study.

Mixing Forms of Observation in Qualitative Multimethod Studies

Qualitative researchers have long collected data by recording their observations in field notes, photography, or film. The Internet has extended the concept of observation to include data collection for cultures and events occurring or discussed online. The following set of exemplars demonstrates the potential for mixing online observations with other types of qualitative data.

Scaraboto, Rossi, and Costa (2012) mixed forms of online observation in a study described in the article titled "How Consumers Persuade Each Other: Rhetorical Strategies of Interpersonal Influence in Online Communities." This study mixed online ethnography with computer-mediated discourse analysis to answer the main research question: "How do consumers exert, verify, and respond to interpersonal influence in online communities?" (p. 248). The researchers preferred observation to interviews "to preserve as much as possible the non-intrusive character of the method" (p. 253).

Drawing on the work of Kozinets (2010) and Herring (2007), Scaraboto et al. (2012) organized the study in four QUAL → QUAL → QUAL → QUAL stages: (a) defining the field, (b) entering the field, (c) collecting data, and (d) analyzing data (p. 252) (see Figure 29.4). To define the field they conducted what they termed *unobtrusive observation* on a number of online communities that fit the study's criteria and identified one to use as the research site. Next, to enter the field, they spent three months doing "nonparticipant observation" to gain an in-depth understanding of the community's norms, functions, and styles of participation before

obtaining consent from the community owner. Once a consent agreement was signed, Scraboto et al. posted a note on the discussion board describing the research project and requesting the consent of all members to collect data and use the information from the community for academic purposes (pp. 252–253). This thread was left open throughout the period of observation on the site.

Observation of current discussions, retrieval of archived discussions, as well as content from consenting members' profile pages generated a large body of material, all in the form of text narratives. Since Scaraboto et al. (2012) wanted to utilize qualitative approach to analysis, they sampled the collected data to select messages to use for discourse analysis. Five years later the researchers returned to the same community and conducted another round of observations "in order to update the dataset and verify if any changes had occurred to the interactions unfolding in the community" (p. 253). Throughout the data collection and analysis, members of the research team recorded their insights and observations directly into the data files. In the data analysis stage the dataset was "manually and independently coded by each of the three authors, who then conferred, debated, and identified a set of conditions and practices that were pertinent to the research questions" (p. 253). This collaborative approach allowed for intercoder reliability. Subsequently they conducted member checks with participants for further verification

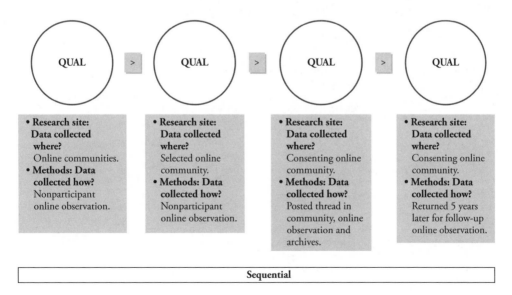

Fig. 29.4 Overview of "How Consumers Persuade Each Other: Rhetorical Strategies of Interpersonal Influence in Online Communities."
Scaraboto et al. (2012).

and "to capture their perspectives on our research findings and interpretation" (p. 253).

Observation is a systematic process of collecting data that one "see[s] with your own eyes and perceive[s] with your own senses" (Yin, 2011, p. 143). The use of the word *see* in this fairly typical definition signals a usual foregrounding of concern for the visual attributes of the phenomenon. In Scaraboto et al.'s (2012) study, for example, text narratives were collected and no mention was made of visual content or other media. However, as noted earlier in the chapter, the evolution from text-based to multimedia communications offers new challenges and opportunities for researchers. A multimethod qualitative QUAL + QUAL exploratory study utilizing both visual and aural observations for data collection was described by Fiore and Kelly (2007) in the article "Surveying the Use of Sound in Online Stores: Practices, Possibilities and Pitfalls" (see Figure 29.5). The purpose of this exploratory study was "not to confirm or disprove predetermined hypotheses, but instead provide a basis for discussion around current trends in the use of sound by online retailers and explore possible directions for the use of (auditory) multimedia online" (p. 605).

Fiore and Kelly (2007) explored the integration of auditory features at online stores. Methods included visually oriented observations of characteristics exhibited in a sample of 70 online stores

and direct selling websites. In the first stage of the observation, researchers surveyed selected sites to determine the sales and marketing activities and to identify the types of interface used. They noted whether or not auditory features were present and, if so, in what form (p. 605). The researchers then recorded audio data from each site and classified the use of sound into three main categories: sound used to display products, sound present within multimedia features, or atmospheric sound used within the site (p. 606). In their discussion of the study's findings, the researchers observe that "the audio-visual format helps to bring people closer to the actual product by making the experience more physically rich and incorporating the expressiveness of spoken language" (p. 608). At the same time they consider social and experiential ramifications from a "noisy" World Wide Web (p. 607). Fiore and Kelly see the need for more research, particularly from the users' perspectives, but they make no methodological recommendations for how future researchers might collect or use aural data.

Implicit in the articles is an understanding that the researchers conducted online observations from external, "outsider" positions. Fiore and Kelly (2007) observed publicly accessible information on the open web. These researchers did not interact with or identify any specific participants. In their recommendations for future research Fiore and

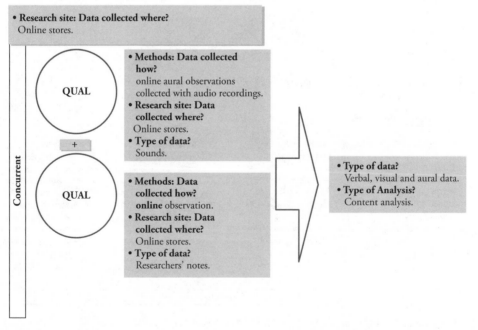

Fig. 29.5 Overview of "Surveying the Use of Sound in Online Stores: Practices, POSSIBILITIES and pitfalls." Fiore and Kelly (2007).

Kelly suggested that future researchers could use interviews to learn about user experiences of online shopping, rather than simply assume an understanding of attitudes or preferences based on purchase histories. The following set of exemplars did just that with studies that combined various styles of observation with in-depth interviews.

Mixing Interviews With Online Observations in Qualitative Multimethod and Mixed Methods Studies

Consumer researchers are interested in ways that individual preferences influence responses to marketing and ultimately purchasing decisions. In the article "Taste Regimes and Market-Mediated Practice," Arsel and Bean (2013) describe a mixed methods study: quan + QUAL → QUAL → (see Figure 29.6). It included qualitative and quantitative analysis of a blog, interviews with blog participants, and participant observations conducted online and in-person. Qualitative methods were dominant in this study. The researchers aimed to inductively develop a theory that explains "how taste is performed as a practice with effects on the material" based on their conceptualization of a construct of the *taste regime*, as a discursive system that links aesthetics to practice" (p. 899).

The research site was a home design blog called Apartment Therapy (AT), a site that includes design services, sale of products, opinions, and advice, as well as users' posts, questions, and comments.

A quantitative content analysis was the first stage of the study; Arsel and Bean (2013) extracted the textual content of all AT posts from January 2004 to August 2011 to form a 145 million-word database (p. 904). The researchers tagged and coded this data, then invited another person to code the data for comparison and verification. This stage on analysis allowed Arsel and Bean to "catalog the configuration of objects, doings, and meanings that the AT regime regulates and solidify our theoretical framework" (p. 904) which became the basis for qualitative observations.

The next stage of the study was a qualitative narrative analysis of the blog's RSS feed (an e-mail digest of new posts to the site) and three subsamples of blog material written by AT bloggers with related comments written by community members. This material was openly coded using key terms until the researchers reached theoretical saturation. Semistructured, in-person qualitative interviews and observations related to décor were then conducted with 12 community members in their homes. Finally, the researchers used participant observation to not only experience the site as users and contributors but also to "subjectively experience activities endorsed by AT" (p. 905).

The researchers were able to tie these step-wise analyses back into their theoretical framework and "provide a practice-based approach to taste" that updates previous consumer theories (Arsel & Bean,

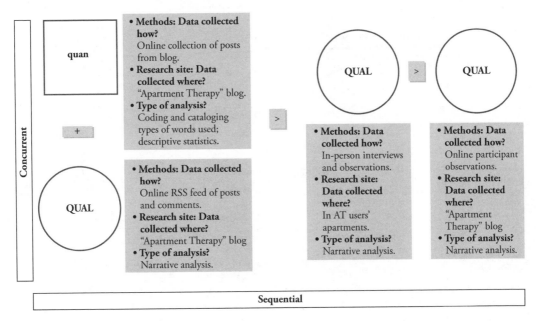

Fig. 29.6 Overview of "Taste Regimes and Market-Mediated Practice."
Arsel and Bean (2013).

2013, p. 912). One of the contributions the study makes to the field of marketing and brand management is an acknowledgement of the influence of online sites like AT on consumer identity and actions.

Online observations in ethnographic studies offer a methodological approach for studying interactions within defined Internet user groups or communities. Waldron (2011, 2013) used a mix of qualitative approaches she called a "cyber ethnographic narrative field study" that led her to "carry out research in a virtually defined space instead of a geographically based physical setting" (p. 32). Her QUAL + QUAL + QUAL study was designed to explore ways people interact for the purpose of informal music learning and teaching in a community named the Banjo Hangout (BH) (see Figure 29.7). Her study explored an online community in which people informally interact in order to learn from and teach each other about music. She found BH a rich environment for research about exchange among music enthusiasts since the community members maintain an online learning and teaching library, media and forum archive, chat room, links to related sites, online store, member blogs, and home pages (Waldron, 2011). Waldron sought to examine "the BH online music community through the words of its members" (p. 33).

Waldron (2011) referenced Hine's (2005) writings about online ethnography to support her decision to conduct some observations as a lurker, that is, to remain hidden as a participant observer while reading and recording discussions in the online community. She received permission from her research ethics board, the community, and interviewees but not from members she observed, who remain unidentified in reports of the research findings (Waldron, 2013). Waldron was careful to note that her approach did not "violate the BH's forum guidelines, rules, or regulations" (p. 37).

After a six-month period of naturalistic observation and collection of written narrative texts posted in the community, she posted an advertisement on the site to recruit interview participants. She offered volunteers the choice: either participate in a videoconference interview via Skype or fill in an open-ended questionnaire consisting of the interview questions. Nine participants completed the interview while 17 completed the questionnaire.

Waldron (2011) was able to cross-check data collected from her multiple sources. Since the community maintains a complete time-stamped archive, "forum threads and hyperlinks functioned as observation data obtained through researcher 'lurking' and also served to triangulate data gathered from interviews and email questionnaires" (p. 39).

Waldron (2011) also collected audio data from site files and audiovisual data from interviews in Skype; however, she transcribed those sources and

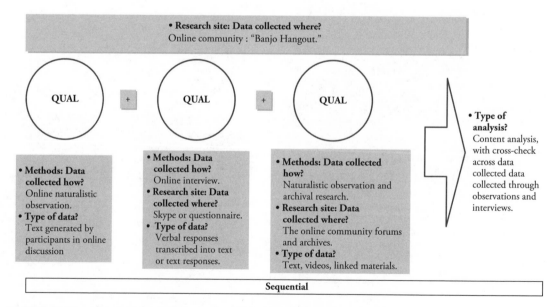

Fig. 29.7 Overview of a cyber-ethnographic narrative field study in the Banjo Hangout. Waldron (2011, 2013).

worked in a text format. Unlike earlier researchers' studies of audio in online environments, Waldron was interested not in the music or sounds per se but in the informal learning experiences fostered by the BH site.

While Waldron (2011, 2013) used an existing online community as a research setting, another type of exemplar is found in a study by Castaños and Percy (2010) where an online wiki community was formed for the purpose of creating a research setting.

Castaños and Percy conducted a qualitative multimethod Delphi study in order to identify the model course content most useful for family therapists who wish to learn about how to consult on family business issues (p. 949). Using a QUAL + QUAL + QUAL multistage process common to Delphi studies, the researchers collected data from telephone interviews, an online questionnaire, and online observations of the participants in a wiki constructed for this purpose (see Figure 29.8). First, exploratory, semistructured interviews allowed the researchers to identify various perspectives on core content areas for the proposed course. These perspectives were brought together in the form of an online questionnaire. The questionnaire contained nine general questions participants could answer with a Likert-type scale as well as with narrative comments. With this approach, researchers hoped to elicit more details on the themes that emerged from the interview and to gauge the degree to which participants agreed or disagreed about the direction for course content.

Finally, the researchers created a wiki where they could observe participants' interactions. The researchers did not discuss other options for collecting data on participant interactions, such as group interviews, focus groups, or observations conducted in an existing community. The researchers described their rationale for using a wiki:

> Unlike other electronic means such as e-mails or forums, [the wiki] allowed us to design a more complex instrument for collecting our data. Our wiki had several pages and links which let us gather information about different topics in a way that was friendly to the participants. . . . In essence, we asked the group to discuss specific findings of particular interest to us. We believed that such discussions would provide richer information and a deeper understanding of controversies than interviewing participants one by one. . . Also, in Delphi studies there is typically a phase that allows participants to reflect on and possibly modify their own opinion based on the responses of other participants. The wiki structure was ideal for this purpose. (Castaños & Percy, 2010, p. 950)

The researchers provided 10 topics for discussion but did not post comments. They maintained observer, not participant observer, roles. However, they note that a wiki offers a mechanism for researchers who do want to participate and either

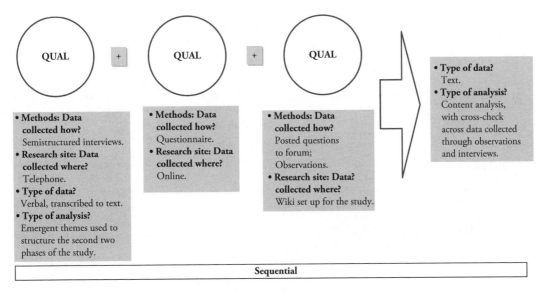

Fig. 29.8 Overview of "The Wiki as a Virtual Space for Qualitative Data Collection."
Castaños and Piercy (2010).

add their perspectives or comments they feel will enhance or stimulate participants' discussions.

Like Waldron (2011, 2013) and the other multimethod qualitative research exemplars discussed previously, Castaños and Percy (2010) used the various forms of qualitative data collected to cross- and member-check and to triangulate the data. The following exemplars mix qualitative and quantitative approaches to collect and analyze data in mixed methods studies.

Mixing Interviews and Observations With Online Surveys in Mixed Methods Studies

In "Achievements, Motivations And Rewards in Faunasphere," Begy and Consalvo (2011) explored motivations and characteristics of gamers in a qual+ QUAL → quan → QUAN mixed methods study (see Figure 29.9). They used online observations and an online survey as well as usage data and an expert interview.

The game Faunasphere is a massive multiplayer online game played synchronously, using graphic avatars controlled by players (Begy & Consalvo, 2011). Unlike other massive multiplayer online games, Faunasphere is played predominantly by women over the age of 35 (Begy & Consalvo, 2011).

Begy and Consalvo (2011) began preparing for the research by playing the game and by reading Faunasphere forums. They did not identify themselves as researchers at this observation stage, nor did they post to the forums or interact with others. They simply lurked in order to understand more about the players, issues and priorities, and ways players and the community manager communicated. The researchers took two more steps to learn about the game and community of players at this stage: they conducted an interview with a community manager and they requested usage data. They used this exploratory qualitative and quantitative data to develop the next stage of the study: a survey. The survey used closed- and open-ended questions to solicit players' responses about their past and present gameplay experiences, feelings about other players, and their use of the forums (Begy & Consalvo, 2011).

Begy and Consalvo (2011) used descriptive statistics and correlational analysis of the data to develop their findings about gamers and their motivations. They looked at identity and use patterns as compared with usage statistics provided by the company and from other studies of massive multiplayer online games. They also drew from open-ended responses using textual analysis to identify themes. They made an effort to use this qualitative data to make sure it "best represented the words of participants" while cross-checking their analyses to verify reliability. They did not include observations from the initial stage of the study in the textual analysis.

The next exemplar also mixed qualitative observations and interviews with statistical analyses of

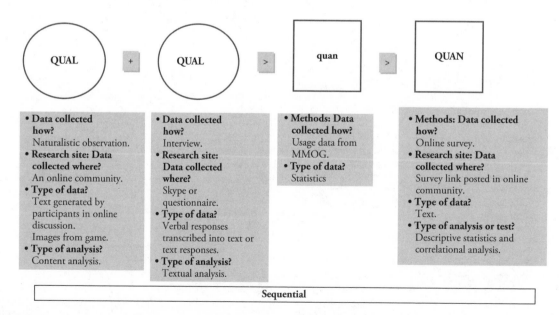

Fig. 29.9 Overview of "Achievements, Motivations and Rewards in Faunasphere."
Begy and Consalvo (2011).

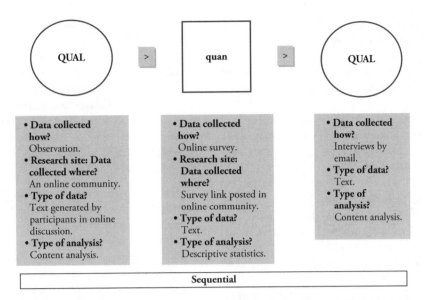

Fig. 29.10 Overview of "Youth on the Virtual Edge: Researching Marginalized Sexualities and Genders Online." McDermott and Roen (2012).

questionnaires in a mixed methods study: QUAL → quan → QUAL. McDermott and Roen's (2012) research is discussed in the article "Youth on the Virtual Edge: Researching Marginalized Sexualities and Genders Online" (see Figure 29.10). Based on the assumption that lesbian, gay, bisexual, and transgender youth would be more likely to communicate honestly with researchers online, the researchers chose to use online approaches to address "twin methodological dilemmas of sampling a 'hidden' population and generating in-depth data on a sensitive subject" (p. 561).

In the first stage of the study, three researchers used Google to locate sites where young people from the United Kingdom discuss issues related to sexual and gender identity. This step served as a "short ethnographic (scoping) exploration of online activity" conducted to "record key observations while spending time in virtual spaces that might be inhabited by prospective research participants" (McDermott and Roen, 2012, p. 563). McDermott and Roen looked at the organization, management, and moderation of each site, and they also followed chat or threads on deliberate self-harm and mental health issues (p. 563). Based on these observations, the researchers selected three potential sites for participant recruitment and received permission from one site administrator who was willing to post a notice about the study.

Respondents to the notice were linked to a study website where they could learn about the study,

take the questionnaire, and, if interested, respond to a further request and consent to participate in an interview. Researchers took several steps, in line with guidelines from British Psychological Society and the National Centre for Social Research, to ensure respect for ethical practices and protection of participants.

Interviews were conducted via e-mail with questions the researchers constructed based on what they learned in the observation and questionnaire stages of the study. McDermott and Roen (2012) used the responses by participants to gauge which question(s) to pose next.

> We were also careful to use easy and less-intrusive questions first to give the participants time to think and ourselves time to judge whether the participant was unhappy or distressed by the line of questioning. If at any point we believed the questions might be causing distress, we halted the line of questioning and moved on to a less-intrusive question. Over the duration of the interview, we sent 10 emails to each respondent, but any single email might have included one to four questions. Often the replies from respondents were lengthy. (pp. 565, 567)

In this exemplar, the qualitative observations and interviews generated most of the results related directly to the study's central purpose—understanding risks for deliberate self-harm in lesbian, gay, bisexual, and transgender youth. The survey provided contextual background on participants' social class and education. The researchers pointed to the usefulness of this information for understanding the effectiveness of recruitment approaches of participants for future research.

The next exemplar mixed existing health services utilization data, national online survey data, and local in-person qualitative interview data in a mixed methods study: QUAN → QUAN → QUAL (see Figure 29.11). The study is discussed in the article titled "Canadian Rural-Urban Differences in End-of-Life Care Setting Transitions" (Wilson et al., 2012). This study explored sensitive decisions that occur in the last year of life in order to provide needed information for agencies and healthcare providers in the area.

In the preliminary stage of the study, Wilson et al. (2012) wanted to determine the nature and scope of the phenomena. Several statistical analyses were conducted on three data sets drawn from provincial inpatient hospital and ambulatory databases. Researchers first wanted to determine the number of healthcare setting transitions for each person within the timeframe of the study, to classify each one as having resided in an urban or rural area, and to compare the rural and urban residents based on a number of variables such as the number of inpatient discharges or procedures. Following that analysis, researchers devised, pilot-tested, and posted an online survey to collect information from a more diverse geographic area, rural or urban, across Canada. Descriptive statistics were used to summarize data collected from 108 participants.

Finally, in-person interviews were conducted. Wilson et al. (2012) discussed why and how these interviews contributed to the study:

> Qualitative interviews were chosen as the most appropriate method for gathering in-depth insight into the implications and practical impacts of care setting transitions that occur in the last year of life. . . . One taped 50–75 minute semi-structured interview was conducted with each participant. Field notes were taken prior to, during, and after each interview to capture additional information of relevance that was seen, heard, or otherwise gained by the researcher. (pp. 4–5)

While researchers did not intend to develop a theory, Wilson et al. used grounded theory approaches for ongoing constant-comparative data analysis that allowed them to identify additional questions or probes needed to be asked in subsequent interviews (p. 5).

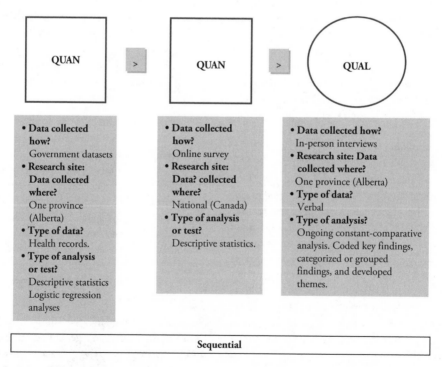

Fig. 29.11 Overview of "Canadian Rural–Urban Differences in End-of-Life Care Setting Transitions." Wilson et al. (2012).

This mix of quantitative and qualitative, national and local, online and in-person approaches allowed the researchers not only to identify usage differences in rural versus urban end-of-life healthcare services but also to gain insights about the challenges for dying rural populations when multiple moves are required.

Mixing Qualitative and Quantitative Content Analysis in Mixed Methods Studies

The studies by Begy and Consalvo (2011) and McDermott and Roen (2012) both included observations in online communities and discussion forums as an exploratory first step. In both cases researchers were lurkers, meaning they observed discussions without participating and without announcing their presence as researchers. User-generated posts to discussions, online communities, or social media sites offer the researcher a type of data collection that melds observation with document analysis. The next two exemplars mixed qualitative and quantitative analysis of posted content in their mixed methods studies.

Hussain (2012) used analysis of both content and web metrics to explore the uses and influences of video content in political campaigns that is distributed primarily by users through social media sites. This was a mixed methods study: qual → QUAN, described in the article titled "Journalism's Digital Disconnect: The Growth of campaign Content and Entertainment Gatekeepers in Viral Political Information" (Hussain, 2012) (see Figure 29.12). Hussain used the 2008 presidential election as the basis for a mixed methods case study to explore three research questions about genres of civic content introduced in election viral videos, categories of blogs, and categories of blogs that preferred specific genres of content. Hussain described the multistep process used to collect data:

> [An] Election 2008 metadata archive [was] constructed through relational datasets combining a sample of the top viral election videos ($n = 120$) and the known-universe of blogs ($n = 9556$). Additionally, I constructed a separate dataset tracking all known blogs linking to these 120 videos. The most popular YouTube URL for each of the 120 viral videos was identified to track blog links because the most popular links to all videos originated from YouTube.com. Technorati and Google Blog Search were used to reverse-crawl videos being linked by blogs. . . . Lastly, because blog data and video data were stored in separate datasets, I connected them using a relational database to construct the Election 2008 metadata archive. (p. 1030)

The initial qualitative stage of this study entailed observations conducted with a selected set of blogs and videos. Hussain used an inductive process to identify definitions and categories. These categories became the basis for a set of codes that six trained coders used to categorize all viral videos ($n = 120$) and 10% of the blogs ($n = 1,000$). Hussain used descriptive statistics and Mann–Whitney U tests to explain the study's findings.

Hussain's (2012) research utilized mixed methods to offer an analysis of groundbreaking trends that have great potential ramifications for the field of journalism. Since his study focused on changing "gatekeepers" and growth of news from outside professional journalism, he needed the exploratory dimension of the qualitative review process. Otherwise critical omissions may have ensued had existing, accepted frameworks or categories been used to order the analysis.

In a different discipline, higher education, the Internet is similarly forcing new thinking about how information is conveyed—in the next case, within class discussions. Similar to Hussain (2012), the study by Yang, Richardson, French, and Lehman (2011) described in the article "The Development of

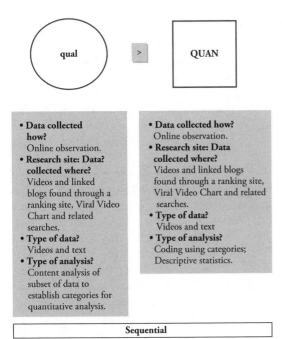

Fig. 29.12 Overview of "Journalism's Digital Disconnect: The Growth of Campaign Content and Entertainment Gatekeepers in Viral Political Information."

Hussain (2012).

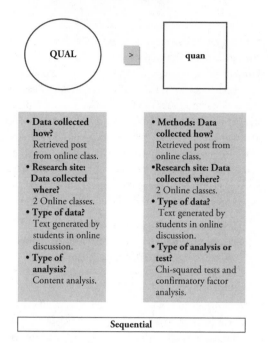

QUAL	>	quan
• **Data collected how?** Retrieved post from online class. • **Research site: Data collected where?** 2 Online classes. • **Type of data?** Text generated by students in online discussion. • **Type of analysis?** Content analysis.		• **Methods: Data collected how?** Retrieved post from online class. • **Research site: Data collected where?** 2 Online classes. • **Type of data?** Text generated by students in online discussion. • **Type of analysis or test?** Chi-squared tests and confirmatory factor analysis.

Sequential

Fig. 29.13 Overview of "The Development of a Content Analysis Model for Assessing Students' Cognitive Learning in Asynchronous Online Discussions."
Yang et al. (2011).

a Content Analysis Model for Assessing Students' Cognitive Learning in Asynchronous Online Discussions," uses a sequential methods design with qualitative stages followed by a quantitative analysis: QUAL → quan (see Figure 29.13).

Asynchronous online discussions are central to most online classes, yet assessment of students' participation and learning has challenged educators. Approaches common to assessment of participation in an on-ground, live discussion do not translate into the online classroom milieu (Yang et al., 2011). The researchers note that while a number of models have been used and studied, none are comprehensive. To address this need, Yang et al. endeavored to develop a new model that assesses learning according to criteria from the revised Bloom's Taxonomy (Anderson, Bloom, Krathwohl, & Airasian, 2000). To do so they needed to understand "the components, in terms of knowledge acquisition and cognitive skills, of a content analysis model that can help an instructor assess students' cognitive learning in asynchronous online discussions" (Yang et al., 2011, p. 47). The researchers also used a qualitative approach when soliciting initial expert feedback on the descriptive model. At the next stage, they used statistical methods, such as confirmatory factor analysis, to

test the descriptive models and examine whether the constructs accounted for or predict responses on the identified indicators.

Yang et al. (2011) collected data from two online courses that included weekly asynchronous online discussions assignments. The discussion questions were intentionally articulated to elicit responses needed to meet the needs of the study:

> The qualitative data consisted of 800 online postings generated by discussion topics selected in weeks 2, 4, 6, 8, 10, 12, and 14. The quantitative data consisted of 803 online postings generated by discussion topics selected from weeks 3, 5, 7, 9, 11, 13, and 15 from both courses. . . . Since the two sets of data were generated from different weeks and from different discussion questions, they were considered to be different but similar allowing for the use of one sample for development of the model and a second sample as a way to test it. (p. 49)

The qualitative stage of the study used grounded theory. Researchers collected 800 discussion posts for the first qualitative phase. They worked through the stages of open, axial, and selective coding to develop a coding scheme. The scheme was checked for intercoder reliability and comparison with codes used in other models the authors had identified in the literature review. An expert review stage welcomed input from experienced online instructors about usability of the model for assessing students' cognitive learning to check the content validity of the new model regarding whether the categories and subcategories were representative of the constructs (Yang et al., 2011, p. 51).

In the quantitative stage of the study, each online posting ($N = 803$) was coded "1" if a subcategory of learning in the initial model was revealed and "0" if it was not. The frequency count and proportion of each subcategory for every posting were calculated, and chi-squared tests were conducted to compare the frequency counts of both sets of data. Researchers then excluded or regrouped subcategories if they did not appear in the quantitative data as often as they did in the qualitative data. A confirmative factor analysis was then used to determine "the ability of the initial model to fit a new sample of online postings, the quantitative data" (Yang et al., 2011, p. 51).

In their conclusions, Yang et al. (2011) point to the strengths of their study: by using an entire semester of two classes' discussion as "cases or observations" they were able to track students' development of skills more substantially and contextually than prior researchers who have typically drawn on a few weeks of postings. But they believed that the real contribution the study made was attributed to the use of mixed methods to generate a reliable and valid content analysis model.

Learning From the Exemplars Through Meta-Synthesis

This meta-synthesis of 13 studies highlights some of the more intriguing aspects of these studies and raises questions for consideration by those who might design their own mixed or multimethod studies. A maximum variation sampling strategy used for selection of these multimethod and mixed methods exemplars allows for an exploration of "common patterns that cut across the variations" (Patton, 2002, p. 243). The patterns of interest in this multidisciplinary set of studies are associated with the ways researchers used ICTs to accomplish some steps involved with qualitative or quantitative data collection.

The term *meta-synthesis*, coined by Stern and Harris (1985), refers to a qualitative examination of a body of research. Unlike a *meta-analysis*, which usually entails reanalysis of original data or findings from multiple studies (Cooper, 2010), a meta-synthesis allows for a critical rereading of a selection of studies. Another distinction of the quantitative meta-analysis is a more inclusive scope that can include both quantitative and qualitative, scholarly and practitioner, working papers and conference proceedings (Denyer & Tranfield, 2009). Walsh (2005) suggests that looking at "studies in a related area enables the nuances, taken-for-granted assumptions, and textured milieu of varying accounts to be exposed, described, and explained in ways that bring fresh insights" (. 205). Weed (2005) uses the term *meta-interpretation* to describe an "interpretive synthesis" that contributes value "determined by the extent to which it is synergistic, the extent to which it produces insights that are more than the sum of the parts"(p. 21).

This is not an analysis/reanalysis of the data from the 13 exemplars. Such an action would not be possible given that the original data—especially the raw qualitative data—is not available in the published articles profiled in this chapter. Instead, we use the recommendation for "appraisal of studies according to predetermined criteria" (Weed, 2005).

The E-Interview Research Framework (Salmons, 2012) criteria are adapted for this purpose and serve as the basis of this meta-synthesis. The E-Interview

Research Framework (see Figure 29.14) was devised as a schema for qualitative studies that include data collected online with interviews as well as observations and documents (Salmons, 2012). It is displayed as a circle to represent the systems-thinking approach needed to consider how choices made in one area of the research design create implications for other aspects of the study. As a multi-dimensional conceptual model, the E-Interview Research Framework offers a lens through which this selection of multi-mode or mixed methods studies may be reviewed individually and understood collectively.

As adapted for this multimethod and mixed methods meta-synthesis, interrelated categories and key questions from the E-Interview Research Framework are

- **Aligning purpose and design:** Are research purpose, theories and epistemologies, methodologies and methods clearly aligned? Does the researcher offer a compelling rationale for using the designated methods to achieve the research purpose? Do the qualitative and quantitative aspects of the study fit in a complementary way?
- **Choosing online or technology-enabled data collection:** Are online or technology-enabled methods chosen in order to investigate real-world phenomena? Or are online methods chosen in order to investigate online phenomena?
- **Selecting the ICT and milieu:** Does the study use text-based, audio, and/or visual communication data?
- **Determining the research approach and collecting the data:** How does the researcher ensure that choices made in regard to technology use are appropriate to the particular study? How does the researcher align ICT functions, features, and/or limitations with the selected methods for collecting and analyzing data?

A Meta-Synthesis of Exemplars
Aligning Purpose and Design

Mixed methods studies are broadly defined as sequential, concurrent, or embedded (Bryman, 2006). The designs used by the exemplars discussed in this chapter were primarily sequential, either exploratory (QUAL → QUAN) or explanatory (QUAN → QUAL). Qualitative approaches were mostly dominant, and inductive reasoning was used throughout their analyses. See Table 29.1 for an overview of the study designs.

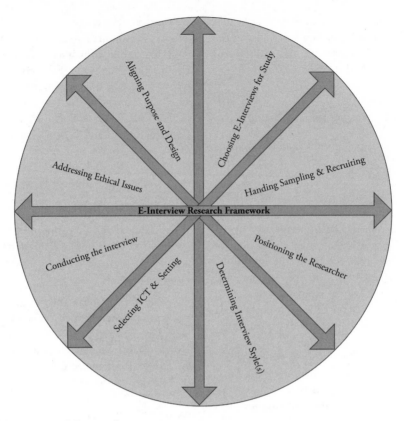

Fig. 29.14 E-Interview Research Framework.
Salmons (2012). © 2012 Vision2Lead, Inc.

The choice of methodology is important to the organization of the study and to choices made in other areas of the research design. How does the respective methodology align with the research questions and purpose? What is the population the researcher wants to understand? When we look at our research questions and purpose, does the researcher want to know about or hear the perspectives of individuals, groups, communities, crowds, or the entire society (including non-computer users)? Some methodologies are more aligned to the study of the individual's lived experiences. This is particularly true of qualitative methodologies such as autoethnography or phenomenology. Other methodologies are suitable for studying groups, organizations, or communities, such as grounded theory or case methods, experimental studies, or quasi-experimental studies. Grounded theory or case methods could be designed as qualitative, quantitative, or mixed methods research. At the large group or societal level, ethnography, netnography, or Delphi methodologies, as well as survey studies, can be used.

Overall, this group of researchers did not focus deeply on methodology in the published articles reviewed for this chapter. It is possible that they were simply more concerned with the research topic area and findings of their respective studies; it is also possible that the formats followed the journals' editorial preferences. For the most part, methodological choices were discussed in passing, with little depth of discussion or rationale for selection. While methods were explicated in detail by the respective authors, in most of the exemplars methodologies and theoretical frameworks were not. In three cases, no specific methodology was named. As a result, it is difficult to fully assess the extent to which the studies' research designs were appropriate and whether or how the approaches used aligned with the methodologies. An exception is the ethnographic studies where the approaches to online ethnography were discussed with reference to the work of Hine (2000, 2005) and Kozinets (2010). This overall weakness makes it difficult for readers to ascertain whether or how the methodologies and methods align. As well, it is unclear

Table 29.1 Research Paradigms and Methods

Exemplars	Research Paradigms	Data Collection Methods
1. Walking Interview Research (Evans & Jones, 2011; Jones et al., 2008, 2012)	Narrative and visual research; follow-up study used quantitative methods in analysis QUAL + QUAL + QUAL and QUAL → QUAN	• Interviews in-person • Observations in-person • Photographs • Aligned GPS- or GIS-identified location and narratives
2. "Geo-Narratives" (Kwan & Ding, 2008) and "From Oral Histories to Visual Narratives" (Kwan, 2008)	Narrative and visual research QUAL → QUAL + QUAL	• Interviews in-person • Participant-generated narratives • Aligned GPS- or GIS-identified location and narratives
3. "Online Asynchronous and Face-to-Face Interviewing: Comparing Methods for Exploring Women's Experiences of Breast-Feeding Long Term" (Dowling, 2012)	Grounded theory QUAL → qual + QUAL	• Interviews in-person • Interview online
4. "How Consumers Persuade Each Other: Rhetorical Strategies of Interpersonal Influence in Online Communities" (Scaraboto et al., 2012)	Netnographic research QUAL → → →	• Observations online • User-posted content
5. "Surveying the Use of Sound in Online Stores" (Fiore & Kelly, 2007)	Methodology not identified QUAL + QUAL	• Interview online • User-posted content
6. "Taste Regimes and Market-Mediated Practice" (Arsel & Bean, 2013)	Methodology not identified Quan + QUAL → QUAL	• User-posted content • Interviews and observations in-person • Observations online
7. "Cyber Ethnographic Narrative Field Study in the Banjo Hangout" (Waldron, 2011, 2013)	Cyber-ethnographic research QUAL + QUAL + QUAL	• Observations online • Interview online • Observations online and user-posted content
8. "The Wiki as a Virtual Space for Qualitative Data Collection" (Castaños & Piercy, 2010)	Delphi QUAL + QUAL + QUAL	• Interview online • Questionnaire online • Observations online and user-posted content
9. "Achievements, Motivations and Rewards in Faunasphere" (Begy & Consalvo, 2011)	Cyber-ethnographic research qual + QUAL → quan → QUAN	• Observations online • Interview online • Site usage data • Survey online
10. "Youth on the Virtual Edge" (McDermott & Roen, 2012)	Cyber-ethnographic research QUAL → quan → QUAL	• Observations online and user-posted content • Survey online • Interview online
11. "Canadian Rural-Urban in End-of-Life Care Setting Transitions" (Wilson et al., 2012)	Methodology not identified QUAN → → QUAL	• Government datasets • Survey online • Interviews in-person

(continued)

Table 29.1 Continued

Exemplars	Research Paradigms	Data Collection Methods
12. "Journalism's Digital Disconnect: The Growth of Campaign Content and Entertainment Gatekeepers in Viral Political Information" (Hussain, 2012)	Methodology not identified qual → QUAN	• Observations online • User-posted content
13. "The Development of a Content Analysis Model for Assessing Students' "Cognitive Learning in Asynchronous Online Discussions" (Yang et al., 2011)	Grounded theory, sequential exploratory study QUAL → quan	• User-posted content

whether the extant methodologies are adequate for such technology-infused research or whether new methodological thinking is called for.

Choosing Online or Technology-Enabled Data Collection

Is the Internet or other ICT part of the research phenomena, or is it the research setting? Some researchers chose to collect data online because they want to study behaviors, patterns of usage, or activities that take place online. For these researchers, the technology is intrinsic to the research problem; it is part of the phenomenon being investigated. For other researchers, the ICT is the research setting, a convenient place to collect data or means for communicating with participants about research problems unrelated to technology.

For example, a social media platform may serve as a means for communication that allows us to understand a real-world research phenomenon. For such studies, the social media community serves as the research setting. Alternatively, the social media community could itself be part of the phenomenon being investigated. Given our mixed-reality world, researchers may conduct studies to explore overlapping or interrelated online and real-world events or behaviors. This researcher might use a mix of online and in-person approaches to collect data.

This fundamental choice about the research purpose and researcher's motivation for using ICTs influences the entire research design, sampling, and mode of data collection: what data to collect from whom and how to collect it, using synchronous or asynchronous communications. The exemplars selected for this chapter illustrate varied options for choosing how, where, and why technology fits the purpose research. Seven studies used online methods to study lived experiences in an online setting (Begy & Consalvo, 2011; Castaños & Piercy, 2010; Fiore & Kelly, 2007; Hussain, 2012; Scaraboto et al., 2012; Waldron, 2011, 2013; Yang et al., 2011). In these studies, the Internet is both phenomenon and research setting. Four studies used technology to assist in either locating or better understanding in-person local phenomena (Dowling, 2012; Jones et al., 2008; Kwan & Ding, 2008; Wilson et al., 2012), and two studies looked at experiences that mesh in-person and online life (Arsel & Bean, 2013; McDermott & Roen, 2012).

As noted previously, methodology aligns with methods in quality research designs. Similarly, methods—qualitative and/or quantitative—should align with the population, sample, data collection, and analysis. Sampling approaches and data analysis are not included in the present discussion. However, we can look broadly at the exemplars' respective interests in individuals, small groups, or large groups and explore alignment with choices for data collection approach and ICT choice.

Several studies were designed in order to understand individual experiences (Dowling, 2012; Kwan, 2008; McDermott & Roen, 2012) or perceptions of community issues or policies (Evans & Jones, 2011; Jones et al., 2008, 2012; Wilson et al., 2012). The studies with an interest in individual views included data collection through interviews and written narratives.

Another group of studies looked at ways individuals and small groups play together (Begy & Consalvo, 2011), influence one another (Arsel & Bean, 2013; Scaraboto et al., 2012), or learn from each other (Waldron, 2011, 2013). These studies used online communities or online classes as the research setting and collected data from observations, questionnaires or surveys, and qualitative or quantitative analysis of posted content.

A third group of studies were designed with the intention of creating a model or theory based on views of group members (Castaños & Piercy, 2010; Yang et al., 2011), and a fourth group was designed to explore emerging technologies from observations and qualitative or quantitative analysis of posted content (Fiore & Kelly, 2007; Hussain, 2012). Data collected through these approaches came primarily in the form of text or verbal interviews transcribed into text. Some studies included visually oriented approaches but simply presented the visual materials without detailed analysis of their framing, composition, or perspectives. For example, this group of studies used photographs or screen shots to represent or describe phenomena central to the respective study subjects: walking interviews (Evans & Jones, 2011; Jones et al., 2008, 2012), geo-narratives (Kwan & Ding, 2008), Faunasphere (Begy & Consalvo, 2011), and taste regimes (Arsel & Bean, 2013). Waldron (2011, 2013) used video-conferencing for interviews but did not discuss any visual elements (i.e., facial expressions of participants or other nonverbal signals.)

Determining the Research Approach and Collecting the Data

All of the exemplars were designed to answer research questions using data collected with more than one method. Some of the reviewed studies were truly exploratory, with few prior examples for the researchers to build upon. With or without other empirical foundations, this group of researchers made conscious choices to mesh online and/or in-person, qualitative, and/or quantitative approaches. By doing so they were able to create meaning in ways not possible with data collected from a single online approach or with in-person only research. By using quantitative surveys or qualitative questionnaires in the same study as interviews, researchers could aim for both breadth and depth (Castaños & Piercy, 2010; McDermott & Roen, 2012; Wilson et al., 2012). They could also encompass a range of questioning styles, from structured to semistructured to conversational. Similarly, some studies mixed collection of user-generated online posts (which were analyzed with either statistical or content analysis) and interviews, which allowed researchers to gain participants' own unprompted views, then to ask key questions (Arsel & Bean, 2013; Begy & Consalvo, 2011; Castaños & Piercy, 2010; Fiore & Kelly, 2007; McDermott & Roen, 2012). In all of the exemplars, technology facilitated a more

expanded range of possibilities than would have been available with a single method or in-person only research. Some of the reviewed studies were truly exploratory, with few prior examples for the researchers to build upon. As more literature is published and critically discussed, it will become clearer what specific theoretical and methodological approaches or choices improve the quality of the technology-enhanced mixed and multimode research.

Conclusions

Technologies continue to develop and become more widely accessible. The Internet, now portable and ever-present, allows people to conflate online and face-to-face life in a mixed-reality world. "Connectivity has become the material and metaphorical wiring of our culture, a culture in which technologies shape and are shaped not only by economic and legal frames, but also by users and content" (van Dijck, 2013, p. 142). This connected culture pervades social, cultural, entertainment and education, political and economic life. We might go so far to say that the imperative to develop a credible understandings and create new knowledge about the lived experience in this evolving, connected, multiple reality calls for new research approaches.

There are many yet unexplored ways to think about research conducted with and about the Internet and other emerging technologies, and there are also many unanswered questions and challenges. While alignment of diverse theoretical, methodological, and practical research approaches has always used critical and creative thinking, multimethod and mixed methods e-researchers have numerous additional considerations.

The nature of online mixed or multimethod research is inherently multidisciplinary, which means researchers use a range of philosophical and disciplinary perspectives and approaches in their research designs. Yet when Peng, Zhang, Zhong, and Zhu (2013) conducted an analysis of social sciences Internet studies articles from 2000 to 2009 they found that "only about 30% of Internet studies cite one or more theoretical references, suggesting that Internet studies in the past decade were modestly theorized" (p. 655). Perhaps this trend explains why established, accepted research or disciplinary theories are minimally discussed in the studies that were explored in this chapter. While six of the exemplars used a variation of grounded theory with the intention to generate theory (Arsel

& Bean, 2013; Dowling, 2012; Jones et al., 2008; Kwan & Ding, 2008; Wilson et al., 2012; Yang et al., 2011), the findings were generally not presented in terms of new theoretical frameworks or constructs. Four exemplars made no mention of guiding or developing theories (Fiore & Kelly, 2007; Hussain, 2012). For this kind of research to merit serious academic respect, attention to multidisciplinary thinking and theory development is apparently needed—and offers an opportunity for the emergence of new theorists who can help to explain the complex multiple-reality connected world and the use of technology to study it in multimethod and mixed methods research (MMMR).

In addition to the need for advances in theory, the new types of data call for new approaches for collection, analysis, and interpretation. Not only do mixed methods e-researchers look for and analyze words and numbers, they may also collect messy, eclectic data types given the communications montage of the online world. Data collected may include visual, verbal and text-based discourses, materials, and artifacts. Researchers need to be able to make design choices appropriate to the research purpose and intentionally determine which types to use. They need to think about what they want to grasp from the images or media and how those visual representations relate to the research problem at hand. Of course they must think about how to analyze visually rich data qualitatively and/or quantitatively—besides simply transcribing them into text. The literacies needed to understand and interpret the multimedia, multiple platform, mobile, augmented reality world are not yet adequately defined. Learning to access and use emerging technologies is an ongoing educational process, creating an additional hurdle for researchers.

Online interaction between individuals and online communities increasingly occurs on social media sites. Kaplan and Haenlein (2010) define social media as "a group of Internet-based applications that build on the ideological and technological foundations of Web 2.0, and that allow the creation and exchange creation and exchange of User Generated Content" (p. 61). However free and welcoming these platforms may seem, they are mostly commercially owned. They are designed to generate revenue, not simply for a social good. They are not neutral; features are designed to encourage users to navigate and participate in certain ways. This means participants—unless they program their own online sites or interactive spaces—are not functioning and communicating online independent of technical and other constraints. Such limitations may proscribe word or character length in messages, the number or type of images or media that can be posted, or the visibility of messages that are quickly replaced by new posts. These parameters must also be considered. As well, scholars who want to access archives, download or scrape raw data, or use social media as modes of communication with participants may encounter community use or other restrictions.

How can scholars navigate these issues in order to collect important data about contemporary technology-infused life? They would tread very carefully, from the perspective of those concerned with potential ethical dilemmas. Qualitative researchers always need informed consent for interviews and direct exchanges with research participants. Protecting human subjects is a given, but the situation is fuzzier when it comes to protecting multiple identities and avatars in cyberspace. There are also many gray areas about what behavior is ethical when the researcher is conducting observations, drawing content from posted materials, or downloading whole threads of conversation in online settings where it may be hard to distinguish public from private. Furthermore, researchers need to consider intellectual property rights of materials posted by users or pictures that include other people who have not given permission for their use.

In order to design and conduct research that the academy will deem acceptable, it is essential to determine when and why is it appropriate and ethical to use what technology and method to answer what questions. But in this new area of research the traditional resources such as methods books and even research faculty are often inadequate guides, leaving researchers to experiment with methodology and methods in situ. A review of several Tellingly, responses to a questionnaire distributed to the network of researchers involved in a New Social Media, New Social Sciences project, indicated that while 59% said they would go by their own values and instincts, only 39% said they would turn to published research methods books or articles for guidance on appropriate, ethical online research approaches (Salmons, 2013). Explanations for these choices included comments such as

> Technology is moving so fast that by the time guidance is in place the technology has moved on and the guidance is out of date. There is

a lack of guidance from both institution and discipline—they are too far behind the changes in technology and the changing expectations of both the researchers and the researched. (p. 2)

Qualitative approaches have long been recognized as appropriate for exploring new questions that may stretch methodological and theoretical traditions, which may be a reason for the presence of those approaches in the exemplars examined in this chapter. These researchers included some quantitative methods that allow researchers to reveal and follow patterns and analyze a larger context. These exemplars contrast with so called "big data" research that focuses primarily, if not entirely, on quantitative analysis of massive databases (DeLyser & Sui, 2013). DeLyser and Sui and others are concerned that this "tide. . . could submerge traditional interpretative scholarship with superficial number crunching" (p. 295). These opportunities and risks again point to the need for attention to mixed methods.

The researchers whose work is profiled in this chapter offer some signposts for future directions in regard to both topics and innovative approaches for research. Their work, taken together, also signals some areas where methodological and theoretical development are still needed.

The exemplars in this chapter show how researchers were able to conduct interviews, observations, questionnaires, and surveys without leaving their offices. They variously combined quantitative and qualitative paradigms to develop understandings of collective and individual experiences. Profiled researchers tapped into the rich, multiple ways groups of people experience an event by collecting large numbers of posts or archived comments on social media sites. Then they shifted attention to the individual by conducting a personal interview to ask each person about his or her singularly unique experience. Researchers reached across the globe or collected important local perspectives about the experience of a specific place using locative and mapping tools.

The use of GPS and mapping, combined with participant-generated narrative accounts and pictures described by Jones et al. (2008, 2012, 2013) and Kwan (2008) could be applied in other studies where research problems have a geographic component. The audio data collection approaches described by Fiore and Kelly (2007) may be applied in studies of participants who, in a world where every device includes a digital recorder, post verbal comments instead of text ones. The use of restricted-access research wikis demonstrated by Castaños and Piercy (2010) may be attractive to those who prefer more private exchanges and more control of the data than is possible on commercial social media sites. Other researchers may find that the use of online and face-to-face interviews and observations in the same study, as Dowling (2012) and Arsel and Bean (2013) demonstrated, allows for exploration of online-offline realities. As well, others may find value the complementary approaches used by Wilson et al. (2012): mining large-scale data to locate trends and conducting personal interviews to apprehend the stories behind the numbers.

New approaches were used in exploratory ways in this set of exemplars. Hopefully they will inspire other researchers to continue the developmental process in multimethod and mixed methods online research methods, theories, and approaches.

Discussion Questions

1. "Digital literacy" or "tech literacy" is more than a set of skills needed to contribute or access information online. What new literacies and competencies do emerging researchers need to be capable of designing for digital research? How can you develop your own literacies?

2. Do you tend to communicate ideas with numbers, words, sounds, and/or pictures? If you plan to conduct interviews, how can you determine what kinds of communication fit your proposed study? How will you develop skills that allow you to collect data in ways that vary from your own typical style?

3. Knowing how to build trust and rapport with participants and obtain agreement from research sites are all somewhat different online. What steps or approaches would you use in order to convey a credible and trustworthy identity as an online researcher?

4. Much of today's online life occurs on commercial networks that may or may not welcome researchers. What are the most important issues for qualitative researchers and/or quantitative researchers who want to recruit participants or collect data in these online communities?

5. Most of us still need someone's approval—faculty, dissertation supervisors, peer reviewers, editors, or funders—for research

designs or completed studies. How can you develop a coherent rationale that someone unfamiliar with multimethod and mixed methods e-research will understand?

6. How do we assess the quality for research design, conduct, and results when one or more methods involve an e-research approach? What should we look for as indicators of a well-designed study?

7. This chapter dissected a number of exemplars. Can you use the same approaches to closely examine mixed or multimethod studies relevant to your areas of interest?

Suggested Websites

http://aoir.org/documents/ethics-guide/
Association of Internet Researchers: Ethics Guide

www.vision2lead.com
More on the E-Interview Research Framework and online research.

www.methodspace.org
Discussion of emerging research methods

References

Anderson, L., Bloom, B. S., Krathwohl, D., & Airasian, P. (2000). *Taxonomy for learning, teaching and assessing: A revision of Bloom's Taxonomy of Educational Objectives* (2nd ed.). New York, NY: Allyn & Bacon.

Arsel, Z., & Bean, J. (2013). Taste regimes and market-mediated practice. *Journal of Consumer Research*, *39*(5), 899–917. doi:10.1086/666595

Baron, N. S., & Ling, R. (2011). Necessary smileys & useless periods. *Visible Language*, *45*(1–2), 45–67.

Baym, N. K., Zhang, Y. B., & Lin, M.-C. (2004). Social interactions across media: Interpersonal communication on the internet, telephone and face-to-face. *New Media & Society*, *6*(3), 299–318. doi:10.1177/1461444804041438

Begy, J., & Consalvo, M. (2011). Achievements, motivations and rewards in Faunasphere. *Game Studies: The International Journal of Game Research*, *11*(1).

Beneito-Montagut, R. (2011). Ethnography goes online: Towards a user-centred methodology to research interpersonal communication on the internet. *Qualitative Research*, *11*(6), 716–735. doi:10.1177/1468794111413368

Brewer, J., & Hunter, A. (2006). Collecting data with multiple methods. In J. Brewer & A. Hunter (Eds.), *Foundations of multimethod research* (pp. 58–78). Thousand Oaks, CA: Sage.

Bryman, A. (2006). Integrating quantitative and qualitative research: How is it done? *Qualitative Research*, *6*(1), 97–113.

Castaños, C., & Piercy, F. P. (2010). The wiki as a virtual space for qualitative data collection. *The Qualitative Report*, *15*(4), 948–955.

Cooper, H. (2010). *Research synthesis and meta-analysis*. Thousand Oaks, CA: Sage.

Creswell, J. W., & Clark, V. L. P. (2011). *Designing and conducting mixed methods research* (2nd ed.). Thousand Oaks, CA: Sage.

Daniels, S., & Nash, C. (2004). Lifepaths: Geography and biography. *Journal of Historical Geography*, *30*, 449–458.

DeLyser, D., & Sui, D. (2013). Crossing the qualitative-quantitative divide: II. Inventive approaches to big data, mobile methods, and rhythmanalysis. *Progress in Human Geography*, *37*(2), 293–305. doi:10.1177/0309132511423349. Retrieved from http://dx.doi.org/10.1177/0309132512444063

Denyer, D., & Tranfield, D. (2009). Producing a systematic review. In D. A. Buchana & A. Bryman (Eds.), *The SAGE handbook of organizational research methods* (pp. 671–689). Thousand Oaks, CA: Sage.

Dicks, B., Soyinka, B., & Coffey, A. (2006). Multimodal ethnography. *Qualitative Research*, *6*(1), 77–96. doi:10.1177/1468794106058876

Dowling, S. (2012). Online asynchronous and face-to-face interviewing: Comparing methods for exploring women's experiences of breast-feeding long term. In J. Salmons (Ed.), *Cases in online interview research* (pp. 277–296). Thousand Oaks, CA: Sage.

Elwell, J. S. (2013). The transmediated self: Life between the digital and the analog. *Convergence: The International Journal of Research into New Media Technologies*, *20*(2), 233–249. doi: 10.1177/1354856513501423

Evans, J., & Jones, P. (2011). The walking interview: Methodology, mobility and place. *Applied Geography*, *31*(2), 849–858. doi:http://dx.doi.org/10.1016/j.apgeog.2010.09.005

Fiore, S. G., & Kelly, S. (2007). Surveying the use of sound in online stores. *International Journal of Retail & Distribution Management*, *35*(7), 600–611.

Herring, S. (2007). A faceted classification scheme for computer-mediated discourse. *Language@Internet*, *4*(1), 1–37.

Hine, C. (Ed.). (2000). *Virtual ethnography*. Oxford: Berg.

Hine, C. (2005). *Virtual methods: Issues in social research on the internet*. New York, NY: Berg.

Hussain, M. M. (2012). Journalism's digital disconnect: The growth of campaign content and entertainment gatekeepers in viral political information. *Journalism*, *13*(8), 1024–1040. doi:10.1177/1464884911433253

Jerejian, A. C. M., Reid, C., & Rees, C. S. (2013). The contribution of email volume, email management strategies and propensity to worry in predicting email stress among academics. *Computers in Human Behavior*, *29*(3), 991–996. doi:http://dx.doi.org/10.1016/j.chb.2012.12.037

Johnson, R. B., Onwuegbuzie, A. J., & Turner, L. A. (2007). Toward a definition of mixed methods research. *Journal of Mixed Methods Research*, *1*(2), 112–133. doi:10.1177/1558689806298224

Jones, P., Bunce, G., Evans, J., Gibbs, H., & Hein, J. R. (2008). Exploring space and place with walking interviews. *Journal of Research Practice*, *4*(2), 1–9.

Jones, P., & Evan, J. (2013). Rescue Geography. Retrieved from http://www.rescuegeography.org.uk

Jones, P., Evans, J., & Burwood, D. (2012). Rescue Geography: Place making, affect and regeneration. *Urban Studies*, *49*(11), 2315–2330. doi:10.1177/0042098011428177

Kaplan, A. M., & Haenlein, M. (2010). Users of the world, unite! The challenges and opportunities of social media. *Business Horizons*, *53*(1), 59–68. doi:http://dx.doi.org/10.1016/j.bushor.2009.09.003

Kozinets, R. V. (2010). *Netnography: Doing ethnographic research online*. Thousand Oaks, CA: Sage.

Kralik, D., Koch, T., & Brady, B. M. (2000). Pen pals: Correspondence as a method for data generation in qualitative research. *Journal of Advanced Nursing, 31*(4), 909–917. doi:http://dx.doi.org/10.1046/j.1365-2648.2000. 01358.x

Kress, G. (1997). Visual and verbal modes of representation in electronically mediated communication: The potentials of new forms of text. In I. Snyder (Ed.), *Page to screen: Taking literacy into the electronic era* (pp. 53–80). New York, NY: Routledge.

Kress, G. (2003). *Literacy in the new media age.* London, England: Routledge.

Kress, G., & Selander, S. (2012). Multimodal design, learning and cultures of recognition. *The Internet and Higher Education, 15*(4), 265–268. doi:http://dx.doi.org/10.1016/j.iheduc.2011.12.003

Kwan, M.-P. (2008). From oral histories to visual narratives: Re-presenting the post-September 11 experiences of the Muslim women in the United States. *Social and Cultural Geography, 9*(6), 653–669.

Kwan, M.-P., & Ding, G. (2008). Geo-narrative: Extending geographic information systems for narrative analysis in qualitative and mixed-method research. *Professional Geographer, 60*(4), 443–465. doi:10.1080/00330120802211752

Laflen, A., & Fiorenza, B. (2012). "Okay, My Rant is Over": The language of emotion in computer-mediated communication. *Computers and Composition, 29*(4), 296–308. doi:http://dx.doi.org/10.1016/j.compcom.2012.09.005

Lillie, J. (2012). Nokia's MMS: A cultural analysis of mobile picture messaging. *New Media & Society, 14*(1), 80–97. doi:10.1177/1461444811410400

Lindgren, S. (2012, September 20–21). *Introducing connected concept analysis: Confronting the challenge of large online texts through a qualitative approach to quantity.* Paper presented at the IPP2012: Big Data, Big Challenges, University of Oxford. Retrieved from http://www.academia.edu/6582142/Introducing_Connected_Concept_Analysis_Confronting_the_challenge_of_large_online_texts_through_a_qualitative_approach_to_quantity_The_challenge_of_large_online_texts

Lohr, S. (2013, January 27). Dickens, Austen and Twain, through a digital lens, *New York Times.*

McDermott, E., & Roen, K. (2012). Youth on the virtual edge: Researching marginalized sexualities and genders online. *Qualitative Health Research, 22*(4), 560–570. doi:10.1177/1049732311425052

Patton, M. Q. (2002). *Qualitative research & evaluation methods* (3rd ed.). Thousand Oaks, CA: Sage.

Peng, T.-Q., Zhang, L., Zhong, Z.-J., & Zhu, J. J. (2013). Mapping the landscape of Internet studies: Text mining of social science journal articles 2000–2009. *New Media & Society, 15*(5), 644–664. doi:10.1177/1461444812462846

Pink, S. (2007). *Doing visual ethnography* (2nd ed.). London, England: Sage.

Rall, M. (2009). A multimodal social semiotic analysis of a museum rock art display. *International Journal of Learning, 16*(9), 323–330.

Rogers, R. (2009). *The end of the virtual: Digital methods.* Amsterdam, The Netherlands: Vossiuspers.

Rogers, R. (2010). Internet research: The question of method. *Journal of Information Technology and Politics, 7*(2), 241–260.

Salmons, J. (2013). *New social media, new social science: Research ethics findings.* New Social Media, New Social Science Project Report, London. Retrieved from https://drive.google.com/file/d/0B1-gmLw9jo6fLTQ5X0oyeE1aRjQ/edit

Salmons, J. (Ed.). (2012). *Cases in online interview research.* Thousand Oaks, CA: Sage.

Scaraboto, D., Rossi, C. A. V., & Costa, D. (2012). How consumers persuade each other: Rhetorical strategies of interpersonal influence in online communities. *Brazilian Administration Review, 9*(3), 246–267.

Sean, E.-H. (2006). Integral research: A multi-method approach to investigating phenomena. *Constructivism in the Human Sciences, 11*(1–2), 88–116. doi:10.1177/135050769 202300302

Skains, R. L. (2010). The shifting author–reader dynamic: Online novel communities as a bridge from print to digital literature. *Convergence: The International Journal of Research into New Media Technologies, 16*(1), 95–111. doi:10.1177/1354856509347713

Stern, P., & Harris, C. (1985). Women's health and the self-care paradox: A model to guide self-care readiness—clash between the client and nurse *Health Care for Women International, 6,* 151–163.

Sumecki, D., Chipulu, M., & Ojiako, U. (2011). Email overload: Exploring the moderating role of the perception of email as a "business critical" tool. *International Journal of Information Management, 31*(5), 407–414. doi:http://dx.doi.org/10.1016/j.ijinfomgt.2010.12.008

Ueda, Y., & Nojima, M. (2011). Effect of dispositional factors on perception of text messaging by cell phone. *Interdisciplinary Journal of Contemporary Research in Business, 3*(6), 606–614.

van Dijck, J. (2013). Facebook and the engineering of connectivity: A multi-layered approach to social media platforms. *Convergence: The International Journal of Research into New Media Technologies, 19*(2), 141–155. doi:10.1177/1354856512457548

Vogt, W. P., Gardner, D. C., & Haeffele, L. M. (2012). *When to use what research design.* New York, NY: Guilford Press.

Waldron, J. (2011). Locating narratives in postmodern spaces: A cyber ethnographic field study of informal music learning in online community. *Action, Criticism & Theory for Music Education, 10*(2), 32–60.

Waldron, J. (2013). YouTube, fanvids, forums, vlogs and blogs: Informal music learning in a convergent on- and offline music community. *International Journal of Music Education, 31*(1), 91–105. doi:10.1177/0255761411434861

Walsh, D. (2005). Meta-synthesis method for qualitative research: A literature review. *Journal of Advanced Nursing, 50*(2), 204–211.

Weed, M. (2005). "Meta interpretation": A method for the interpretive synthesis of qualitative research. *Forum: Qualitative Social Research, 6*(1, Art. 37).

Wilson, D. M., Thomas, R., Burns, K. K., Hewitt, J. A., Osei-Waree, J., & Robertson, S. (2012). Canadian rural–urban differences in end-of-life care setting transitions. *Global Journal of Health Science, 4*(5), 1–13. doi:10.1177/1525822X05279903

Wortham, J. (2013, March 10). Online emotions, in hundreds of new flavors. *The New York Times.*

Yang, D., Richardson, J., French, B., & Lehman, J. (2011). The development of a content analysis model for assessing students' cognitive learning in asynchronous online discussions. *Educational Technology Research & Development, 59*(1), 43–70. doi:10.1007/s11423-010-9166-1

Yin, R. K. (2011). *Qualitative research from start to finish.* New York, NY: Guilford Press.

Yoshikawa, H., Weisner, T. S., Kalil, A., & Way, N. (2008). Mixing qualitative and quantitative research in developmental science: Uses and methodological choices. *Developmental Psychology, 44*(2), 344–354.

Emergent Technologies in Multimethod and Mixed Methods Research: Incorporating Mobile Technologies

Leo Remijn, Nathalie Stembert, Ingrid J. Mulder, *and* Sunil Choenni

Abstract

This chapter presents an overview of the developments and potentials of mobile technologies and their major impact on society and the daily activities of individuals. The increase of sensors embedded in everyday objects enable these objects to sense the environment and communicate. This creates new possibilities to gather and process large amounts of data. We show how these opportunities can trigger a paradigm shift in the social sciences. Social scientists no longer collect data but use data that is available and collected for other reasons. These data will vary in validity and quality. It can come from sensors in personal mobile devices, smart environments, or social infrastructures. This asks a strong interpretive approach from multimethod- and mixed methods researches to harness these data.

Key Words: mobile technologies, sensors, data, mixed method research, smart environments, mobile devices, social infrastructure

Introduction: Technology and the Research Process

Imagine a mobility panel that aims to explore the relationship between changes in travel behavior, personal and household characteristics, and other factors influencing mobility. For such a study on mobility patterns, changes in travel behavior of a fixed group of people and households over a longer period are required. Here we reflect on experiences of participants in the introduced example. Participants were asked to keep a diary for three days and list all their movement. Before that, participants had to register online; once they had a profile they could continue with the study. For example, participants were asked to enter the complete addresses they expected to visit in the days under study. Each day participants were reminded by e-mail that they had to complete the online questionnaire at the end of the day, which actually meant right after midnight. Consequently,

participants had to type the same information into the website, which they already had written down in the dairy. Interestingly, additional questions were asked about distance and transport means. Our experiences showed it is hard to estimate what distance one walks or takes the tram. People have to come up with creative ways to calculate the distance, for example, by typing the addresses in Google maps to check distances. After that, participants must confirm each movement after a pop-up question. Without highlighting every detail, it is clear that such a setup is more efficient for the research team than it is for the research participant, as it increases the work for them.

This type of mobility study can benefit greatly from using a range of multimethod and multimethods. Why ask a participant to complete a survey right after midnight if it is already in a diary? Why ask for the exact distance if the system already knows both addresses? Why ask participants to write down the exact time of arrival on paper while current mobile phones already have apps installed that capture peoples' moves and distances? Moreover, apps are more accurate than people's estimations, as participants can sometimes forget to note the time upon arrival due to delay, phone calls, or simply meeting colleagues or friends.

In this chapter, we elaborate on the role of emerging technologies with a focus on how mobile technologies can contribute to the field of multi-method and mixed methods research (MMMR) by offering new avenues of data collection as well as opening up a set of newly emergent research questions. We begin with an overview of challenging emerging technologies made possible through the increasing functionality of mobile devices and discuss their characteristics.

In the second part, we explain how these emergent technologies create new possibilities to gather, process, and interpret mixed and multiple data. We discuss the ways in which new technologies allow for the incorporation of mixed and multilevel data that links macro-level patterns with micro-level processes. More specifically, we look at how emerging mobile technologies can show dynamic behavior patterns in the city, and on the other hand how mobile devices can also be linked in order to provide insight into personal behavior. In the discussion, we address some drawbacks and issues to be solved.

What Are Emerging Technologies?

Although it is hard to give a precise definition of emergent technologies, they refer to contemporary and significant advances and innovation in various fields of technology, which may have a major impact on the society and the daily activities of individuals. *Mobile technology* is considered an emergent technology and is a generic term to refer to a variety of concepts, ranging from very technical to oversimplistic. In general it allows people to access data and information from wherever they

are. This is often narrowed to mobile devices like smartphones. We prefer a broader concept, keeping the emphasis on mobile, wireless, personal, and wearable. We define access to data broadly, so it can store, create, allow to modify, organize, and manipulate the data. We do not elaborate on the technical infrastructure of mobile technologies but assume that wireless connections are available for the required service.

The recent acceleration in mobile devices is caused by progressively smaller and more powerful computing devices. This is often referred to as the third wave of computing technologies to emerge since computers first appeared (Sargunam, 2007). The first wave is the mainframe computing era, whereby one computer is shared by many people via workstations. The second wave is the PC era, where one computer is used by one person, requiring a conscious interaction and the user is largely bound to the desktop. The third and most recent wave of computing technologies is the pervasive computing era: one person uses many computers (Figure 30.1). Millions of small computing devices are embedded in the environment, allowing technology to recede into the background. The computing devices include everything from mobile phones, smart watches, smart glasses, GPS, tablets, heart rate sensors, blood pressure sensors, and pollution meters.

In 2012 the Association for Computing Machinery (2013), the world's largest educational and scientific computing society, updated its computing classification system. In the new taxonomy, the cluster we focus on is human-centered computing. This has become a discipline in its own right since the last iteration of the classification because of its increasing importance in the literature. It is an emerging interdisciplinary academic field concerned with computing in relation to the human condition. In this discipline, upcoming research areas like human computing interaction, interaction

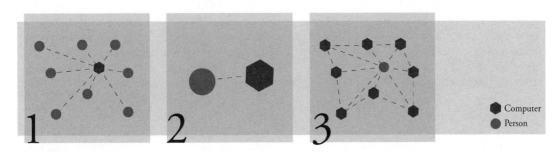

Fig. 30.1 Three waves of computing technologies.

design, collaborative and social computing, ubiquitous and mobile computing, visualization, and accessibility are clustered. The area we focus on is ubiquitous computing and mobile computing. This is the cluster where the interaction between people and computers is very important and where computer science meets behavioral science and design.

Human–computer interaction (HCI) evolved in the past decades through three major intellectual waves that have formed the field, each building on the previous one and resulting in an in-depth understanding of the interwoven activity of humans and nonhumans (Harrison, Tatar, & Sengers, 2007). The first wave started in the early 1980s and oriented from engineering/human factors with its focus on optimizing man–machine fit, inspired by industrial engineering and ergonomics. It focused on identifying problems in coupling and developing pragmatic solutions to them. The assumption was that users can be analyzed in the same manner as the information processing of technology. The second wave started in the late 1980s, when graphical user interfaces succeeded. The focus was on optimizing accuracy and efficiency of information transfer, increasing emphasis on theory and on what is happening not only in the computer but, simultaneously, in the human mind. The third and most recent wave of HCI is a consequence of the ever-increasing penetration of computers around us, at work, at home, and following us from context to context. The focus of the third wave is more on support for situated action in the world. Questions of interest are: How can we support interaction without being constrained by what a computer can do? How do users appropriate technologies, and how can we support those appropriations? What are the values of the interaction, and how can we support those in design?

Around 1988, Mark Weiser (1991) introduced the phrase *ubiquitous computing* as a refinement of HCI, hoping to create a world in which people interacted with and used computers without thinking about them. His first thoughts on ubiquitous computing were very futuristic; the necessary hardware was very expensive and physically quite large in those days. He stated

> The most profound technologies are those that disappear. They weave themselves into the fabric of our everyday lives until they are indistinguishable from it. . . . Such a disappearance is a fundamental consequence not of technology but of human psychology. Whenever people learn something

sufficiently well, they cease to be aware of it. . . in this way are we freed to use technology without thinking. (p. 94)

Ubiquitous computing (also called ubicomp), ambient computing, and pervasive computing are synonyms for this trend toward embedding computing devices in the form of microprocessors and wireless communication in everyday objects and activities. Related emerging research areas are sensitive environments and context-aware computing, where the computing device knows where the user is, what he or she is doing, and what his or her mental state is. Depending on this context, the computing device can act differently. For example if a person is driving a car, sleeping, or in a noisy place he or she may not want to accept a phone call. Lately the term the *Internet of Things* has been used to describe this phenomenon. We discuss its main characteristics later in this chapter.

Besides the progressively smaller and more powerful computing devices, the recent acceleration in mobile devices is caused by the growth of sensor technology. A sensor is a device that measures a physical quantity and converts it into a signal, which can be read by an observer or by an instrument (Lane et al., 2010). The latest smartphones have more than 20 sensors. To give insight into their potential, we briefly discuss some recent sensor technologies in smartphones:

• proximity, to measure how close the screen of the phone is to a person's body. This allows the phone to sense when someone has brought it to his or her ear. It can then turn off the display and also stop detecting touches to avoid unwanted input.

• ambient light, to extend battery life and enable easy-to-view displays that are optimized to the amount of light in the environment.

• global positioning system (GPS), to allow navigation tracking and location detection. For indoor location detection it can be extended with assisted GPS.

• accelerometer, to detect the orientation and motion of a phone. It can adapt the screen accordingly. Applications like games and the camera can use this information.

• compass, to sense orientation and direction, for better indoor location.

• gyros, to measure very accurate position, orientation, and motion of the phone.

• back-illumination, to increase the amount of light captured and thereby improving low-light camera performance.

Increasingly sensors are becoming available in inexpensive and miniature form. They can be integrated in various mobile devices. Possible physical quantities sensors can measure include distance, image, motion, bending, pressure, gas, heart rate, angular turn, height, identity (e.g., radio-frequency identification), orientation, acceleration, compass, infrared, tilt, color, force, light, air pressure, magnetism, object detection, position, rotation, voltage, current, temperature, time, oscillation, ultrasound, humidity, and solar radiation. An example of such availability is Sensordrone (http://sensorcon.com/products/sensordrone-multisensor-tool), a sensor-filled wireless dongle for use with a smartphone or other computer-like device. It is a new mobile device that expands the number of sensors a smartphone or other device can accommodate in a very user-friendly way. It can measure, for example, air quality, breath alcohol, weather, crowd sourced sensor data, and gas sensors. It is like a Swiss army knife for environmental input: users can leave it outside to measure air quality and receive updates on their smartphone or warnings when the air quality drops below a self-adjusted threshold.

Google Glass is another example of the growing power of recently available sensor technology. It is a wearable computer with an optical head-mounted-display (see Figure 30.2). It displays information in a smartphone-like, hands-free format and can communicate with the Internet via natural language voice commands. It contains sensors like a camera, touchpad, gyroscope, accelerometer, magnetometer, ambient light sensing, proximity sensors, and bone conduction transducer. The glass senses one's orientation, motion, voice, and vision. It is the first conceptualization of a mainstream, augmented-reality, wearable eye display and in this way an instigator for the adoption of a new paradigm in HCI (Pendersen & Trueman, 2013). The device is expected to generate new ideas about wearable computing, collecting data and interfaces for technology, which are designed to be available when one needs them and absent when one does not. With face recognition software, for example, the glass will provide information about individuals in the wearer's vicinity. Complementary techniques exploit the intuition that such factors as clothing color, decorations, and even human motion patterns can together make it feasible to recognize individuals without seeing their faces.

The increase of sensors embedded in various devices also opens new directions for data processing. A sensor can be regarded as a device that measures physical quantities or signals in an environment and converts it into meaningful figures for an observer. For example, to track the position of an aircraft, sensors submit signals to and receive signals from an aircraft with a high frequency. On the basis of these signals, the location of an aircraft may be estimated quite accurately. Today, sensors are used in applications in which nonspecialists are involved. For example, with the Copenhagen Wheel, sensors can be attached to city bicycles to submit data about pollution, road conditions, and congestion. These data may be used to determine the condition of the environment. A typical characteristic of sensor data is that it is generated at a high frequency. In the case of the Copenhagen Wheel project, many bicycles continuously submit data to a processing unit. When tracking an aircraft, many sensors are involved in submitting signals to and receiving signals from a single aircraft.

To process such a large volume of data in a timely manner and to integrate it with different types of data, such as data from social media, new

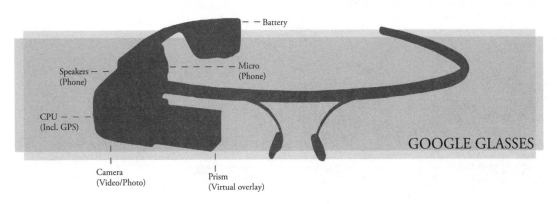

Fig. 30.2 Google glasses, an optical head-mounted-display.

architectures and techniques are required. This is the research field of big data. This field may have an enormous impact for social research, especially for behavioral sciences. In social sciences, a well-known method to collect data is via questionnaires, where the researcher asks a respondent a series of questions. It remains a tough task to determine whether or not a respondent gives a socially accepted answer. By equipping a respondent with sensors, many questions may be answered by processing the information from a sensor. For example, one may ask a respondent which shops he or she has visited in the last 10 days. But this question may also be answered by tracking that person's mobile phone during that time. Another example might be that one may ask a person how he or she feels at the moment. But this question could also be answered by using sensors to measure a number of body variables such as blood pressure, heart rate, perspiration level, and so on.

Using sensors to reveal answers to questions has two advantages over using questionnaires. First, the chance that a respondent may give a socially acceptable answer rather than the full truth is minimized. Second, respondents may be burdened by the many questions that are involved in a questionnaire. Key characteristics of the big data field are volume (various data sets with sizes beyond the ability of commonly used software tools), velocity (data coming in and going out), and variety (range of data types and sources; see Figure 30.3). The sensors generate a vast amount of data that can hardly be processed by existing data processing systems in a reasonable amount of time. Furthermore, sensor data can be regarded in some sense as agile (i.e., the validity of the data is limited). For example, suppose your car is equipped with a set of sensors that determines your location on time and is connected to a database that records your eating behavior. Suppose now that you tell your system that you are hungry and that your favorite restaurant is within two miles of your current location. Furthermore, you are driving 70 miles per hour on the highway. The system in your car should be able to process all data within 1.5 seconds in order to recommend a nearby restaurant. If the system requires more computational time, you may pass the desired restaurant without being notified about it in time.

In the field of social research, the dimension of time may have an impact on the nature of decision-making. Due to big data architectures and techniques, decision-makers may have a more actual and complete "picture" of a situation (e.g., an emergency situation). To what extent this will have an impact on the decision-making is an interesting question.

Handling vast amounts of data generated by sensors in an adequate manner gives rise to the development of alternative architectures for data processing such as Hadoop. Instead of a central node that processes data, contemporary processing architectures are based on a distributed concept, also called cloud computing. Data junks are assigned to different processors to be processed in a parallel way. Big data architectures and techniques embrace the distributed concept to handle, among others, sensor data. Actually the field of big data focuses on an effective and efficient processing of vast amounts of data without putting any restrictions on the type of data. Furthermore, these techniques and architectures take the agile character of the data into account. The field of big data faces challenges, such as how best to process semistructured and unstructured data combined with sensor data quickly (i.e., almost real-time).

These emerging technologies are the enablers for a whole new area of (social) research. They make it possible for objects to sense the environment and to communicate, to become powerful tools for understanding complexity and respond

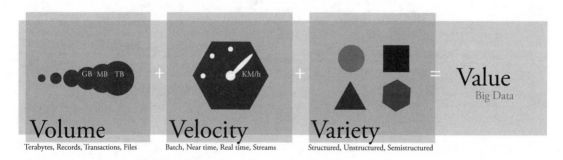

Fig. 30.3 Key characteristics of big data: volume, velocity, and variety of data.

to it effectively. These smart objects can interact with humans, as well as with each other, automatically, without human intervention, updating themselves on a periodic schedule (Figure 30.4). This evolution marks a technological disruption and is a prelude to a new paradigm for the relationship between human beings and objects. This emerging field of research is called the Internet of Things Kevin Ashton (2009) first used the term as the title of a presentation to give expression to this new insight. In those days, radio-frequency identification was seen as a prerequisite for the Internet of Things, whereby all objects and people in daily life were equipped with radio tags, to be identified and inventoried by computers. Nowadays, the unique identification of things can easily be achieved by Internet-like wireless equipment. The Internet of Things evolves in various directions, which are not necessarily divergent.

The Internet of Things can be studied as a technology, facilitating connectivity between objects and humans, with complex distributed data stores and flexible infrastructures. The Internet of Things can also be studied as a concept using everyday people and objects as sources of information. Finally, it can be studied as a practice, an instrument to empower people in a do-it-yourself philosophy to design their own interactive environment.

Although emerging technologies present potential and opportunities, they also make it necessary to revise or to overthink some concepts in our society. For example, what impact might these technologies have on the privacy of individuals? The combination of data that are collected by different organizations and shared (e.g., through the Internet) may expose too much of an individual, such as privacy-identifying information. Suppose a university publishes the average grade of an exam on the Internet split along the dimension of sex. Suppose that only one female student took part in the exam. Then the grade of the woman is exposed, and therefore her privacy is violated. In addition, equipping people with a lot of sensors may give a (more) integral view of a person, such as preferences, travel destinations, favorite stores, and so on. This may expose too much of a person and might be undesired. Suppose someone has an online sports tracking app, such as Runkeeper or SportsTracker, on his or her mobile device, which records his or her running speed on a map. With GPS techniques, the physical location of a runner can be determined, and, therefore the route of the runner can be established. This information might be shared with others via social media. If this is the case, it may disclose personal routine activities, such as under which weather conditions the person runs, his or her favorite day and time for running, favorite routes, and so on. If the information also reveals someone's home address (which is not unlikely), then a burglar can easily plan a burglary at this address.

What impact do these technologies have on the rule of laws? For example, cloud computing

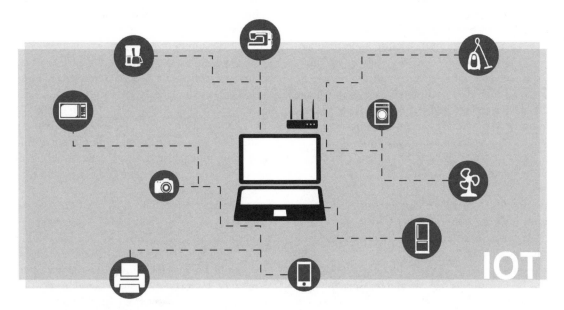

Fig. 30.4 Internet of Things technology to facilitate connectivity between objects.

is an underpinning technology for implementing the concept of Internet of Things. Cloud computing entails the "loss of location," since data/information is stored within the cloud. However, it is unclear where the server of the cloud is located and what data/information is stored on which servers. The loss of location may become an important issue for security and judicial institutes if cloud computing becomes a widespread reality. For example, today the police are allowed (under certain circumstances and conditions) to investigate the computer of a suspect. They take the hard disk with them and can relatively easily search for the information they are looking for. If everything is stored in the cloud, new working procedures and techniques should be developed to search for the same information. Furthermore, since evidence with regard to a person may be scattered across the cloud and the servers of the cloud may be located in different countries, this could cause problems in using the information in a court from a legal perspective. For example, adultery is illegal in some countries. Suppose that someone in such a country has an extramarital relation with someone in a country where adultery is legal. Evidences of this relation are stored on a server (e.g., loggings of chat sessions on social media) in the country where adultery is not illegal. Can these evidences be used as proof in a court if the person of the country where adultery is illegal is prosecuted?

Emergent Technologies and Their Impact on Social Research

The emerging technologies we have discussed so far create new opportunities for the research enterprise that were previously almost impossible and beyond imagination. There are also great challenges to be resolved. In this section, we provide a range of ways in which these technologies are already being used by researchers, and we highlight their implications for MMMR. We discuss some in-depth case studies that have successfully deployed these technologies and also discuss the ongoing challenges encountered in their deployment.

Gathering New Data Formations at the Macro Level: Smart Cities

As mentioned earlier, emerging technologies and corresponding mobile sensing are rapidly becoming a part of everyday life. The proliferation of sensor platforms (e.g., wearables, smartphones) at city level enables the opportunity to collect and analyze rich, large-scale mobile-sensor data. David

Barnes (2011) spoke on the Web 2.0 Summit 2011 about IBM's future plans for developing smart cities and a smarter planet—actually more a literal notion of big data, one that involves sensors everywhere to measure the living, breathing planet. IBM wants to build a web of sensors producing massive amounts of big data for governments, healthcare providers, first responders, and businesses. It wants to measure the weather, the sewers, the vehicles, the buildings, and the people.

IBM's Smarter Planet team has created a five-minute video explaining the emerging trend of the Internet of Things (IBM, 2010). The Internet of Things is about the coming future when there are more "things" on the Internet (sensors especially) than there are people. The result will be "a kind of global data field," the video says. "If we can actually begin to see the patterns in the data, then we have a much better chance of getting our arms around this. That's where societies become more efficient, that's where more innovation is sparked." A person's alarm clock goes off, for example, at the right time because it knows from that individual's diary when his or her first meeting is for the day and at what time the ferry leaves. The bathroom heater will kick on a half an hour before time to get up so the bathroom will be warm. During the drive to work, the person may get an audio notification, based on his or her geolocation and the calculated delay of the ferry, that the ferry is running five minutes late, so no need to rush. All of this is taken care of by autonomic agents looking out for people based on the things they "know." This is possible by linking all systems with each other and making them accessible for the autonomic agents.

If we collect massive amount of data with a web of sensors, we make the city instrumented, interconnected, and intelligent (Presser, 2011). The intelligence could include, for example, self-control of street lights: turning off to save energy and turning on depending on traffic or to highlight something dangerous. It enables detailed data gathering of information on a much higher granularity and with much better precision than ever before. Imagine, for example, a Smart Urban Waste Management application scenario, where garbage collection can be optimized (e.g., in terms of route optimization based on fill levels of the bins). In addition, incentives can be brought forward to encourage citizens to produce less waste and recycle more. In the past, the encouragement came from financial incentives, preferable as instant feedback to have impact. If one could give instant feedback in the form of credits, like in a computer game, other incentives can be tested, like tax return or social rewards, whereby citizens can compare themselves to each other.

Imagine gathering data about a city with sensors on every lamppost. The sensors measure data about, for example, noise, traffic, environment, crowds, and temperature. This data is transmitted and processed, and information is presented through dynamic data visualization, showing interesting details about the city as a living organism, for example, how it is used by people, flow of traffic, and impact on the environment in a map illustrating real-time and historic data of pollution. TED and YouTube include many videos that show the beauty and richness of data visualization created by combining various data sources and presenting them as dynamic historic data (see, e.g., McCandless, 2010, and Rosling, 2010).

Recently government data in many industrialized countries is made available to the public. This concept of open data denotes data that is reusable and distributed without cost. Data sets that are available include, for example, location of trees, buildings, stairs, slopes, traffic signs, benches, roads, and street robberies. Combining these data sets makes various applications possible. From the street information, a route planner can be made for wheelchairs, to avoid stairs and steep slopes. The position of sun shadows can be calculated from the height of buildings. Combining these and other sensor information generates new possibilities.

Traditionally, government-generated data that is used for planning is relatively stable and is sourced with well-established methods. Imagine if this is supplemented with much more detailed dynamic data coming from public as well as private sources, such as crowdsourced data from citizens about potholes in the road they want to have fixed in the form of a picture with geolocation. Environment data from sensors placed all over the city might be owned by private or public organizations and need to be combined to form a complete picture.

All of these types of data forms are accessible to researchers and allow them to ask a range of new questions at the macro level that can be linked to micro-level processes. Such new technologically generated data forms can provide the researcher with a wealth of multimethod and mixed methods qualitative, quantitative, and newly emergent data forms that are derived from sensors and a variety of user-generated data forms.

Understanding the Social Fabric—Infrastructure for Joint Fact Finding

Having a unique mobile and wireless infrastructure, enhanced with public screens and open data, the foundations for a smart city are there. Public-sector information is released and available in the city's open data store. Currently, initiatives are being launched to add crowdsourced citizen-generated data for public-sector reuse. Simultaneously, the city's infrastructure has become much smarter, aiming to facilitate the social fabric and with that the possibilities to share information. However, to benefit from the opportunities offered by the smart-city concept, citizens need to be able to participate fully in an Internet-enabled society, through adequate skills and the ability to generate credible, comparable, and complete data (Gouveia, Fonseca, Câmara, & Ferreira, 2004).

Mobile devices seamlessly connect and integrate people with the smart-city infrastructure. These personal devices enable people to gather data in and about the public domain. In the case of the Pothole Patrol (Eriksson et al., 2008), sensor data are collected and submitted by smartphones carried by people and are analyzed by municipalities to assess road quality. The Copenhagen Wheel project (Savage, 2010) uses sensor-enhanced city bicycles that collect and submit air pollution, road conditions, and congestion data, which can be submitted not only to the municipality but also to the data collectors themselves. In these examples, people are involved as carriers of such mobile devices and, with that, are carriers of numerous sensors. By carrying their mobile devices every moment of the day, they passively gather and send data, forming a network of billions of sensors, making them part of the smart-city infrastructure (Goodchild, 2007).

While making use of mobile and sensor technologies has its advantages (i.e., ensuring data credibility, comparability of data, data completeness, and overcoming logistical issues), it ignores the capability of the human senses and intelligence of the carriers of these devices. In traditional data gathering initiatives, human senses and intelligence are utilized to observe and interpret local events, such as crime prevention initiatives, where people walk inspection rounds to map neighborhood safety (Levine & Fisher, 1984). These approaches still offer certain advantages, such as making better use of qualitative knowledge embedded in communities (Corburn, 2007).

Qualitative knowledge embedded in communities can provide us with valuable understanding about the social world, giving us a reading of individuals' sense of their surroundings. However, generally adding and making use of qualitative knowledge is not evident, since data submitted is often subjective, asking for a more interpretive approach from multimethod- and mixed methods researchers to harness these data. FixMyStreet, a platform to log problems in the public domain, such as broken lanterns or trashcans, proves that it is possible to make good use of subjective qualitative data gathered by citizens (King & Brown, 2007). Empowered by the advantages of mobile devices, people are invited to gather data in the form of a photograph and apply contextual knowledge on what is being submitted. The automatically attached quantitative information in the form of a time stamp and GPS location also makes it possible to facilitate processing, analysis, and comparison of the qualitative data.

Qualitative subjective data can be incorporated in its own right into more quantitatively driven measures, providing mixed method researchers with a range of new data to collect and analyze from which new questions can be derived. It can raise a set of questions at the policy level, such as how do we integrate individually gathered qualitative data with more quantitative, macro-level data gathered from sensors in order to draw valuable conclusions about the urban environment? These conclusions, based on data collected by social collaboration, could possibly contribute to the ongoing transformation from controlling to regulating government.

Score Ze: Emergent Analytics, Ways to Analyze Mixed and Multilevel Data

In contrast with applications (i.e., FixMyStreet, which mostly reports incidents), Score Ze (Creating010, 2013) is an application that measures location-based quality of life to inform city maintenance about people's long-term feelings concerning how clean, intact, and safe the city is (Figure 30.5). Supported by mobile devices, Score Ze is based on a traditional data gathering model consisting of six key elements, attempting to capture what is important to people in their process of gathering data to influence public policy.

Based on a case study research on three traditional data gathering initiatives, the six elements forming this model can be utilized to inform the design of new digital data gathering applications. The first element that distinguishes the model is the importance of a *mother organization,* which supports the data gathering initiative logistically, communally, and financially. The second element, *internal and external motivational triggers,* originates often from a sense of dissatisfaction and is not always easy to trace back. The third element describes the initiatives needed to collaborate with authority and other trusted third parties to warrant the *legitimacy* of the initiative. The fourth element, the agreed-on *standardization and methodology* of the data gathering process, warrants the credibility, comparability, and completeness of data. The fifth element is iterative

Fig. 30.5 "Score Ze," an application to score the city on the parameters clean, intact, and safe.

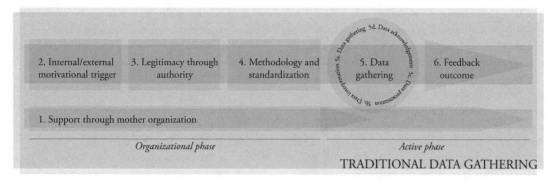

Fig. 30.6 Model to describe the process of traditional data gathering initiatives.

and consists of the actual action of *data gathering* by citizens, *data interpretation* and *presentation* by an objective third party, and *data acknowledgement* by the local authorities. Finally, the sixth element emphasizes the importance of the provision of *feedback about short, mid-, and long-term outcomes* to the data gatherers (Stembert, Conradie, Mulder, & Choenni, 2013). Figure 30.6 illustrates these data gathering processes.

Supported by mobile devices, Score Ze can potentially be used by multimethod and mixed methods researchers who seek innovative ways to analyze a range of complex multilevel, multimode qualitative and quantitative data gathering forms. Score Ze is not only based on citizen-led traditional data gathering initiatives but also on a standardized data gathering method designed according to the well-established methods of City Works. Consequentially, the data gathered can be used to determine, for example, city maintenance budgets based on the maintenance norm set as acceptable by citizens themselves. Moreover, standardizing the data gathering method stimulates coproduction of data, an approach whereby all stakeholders are accepted as potential contributors and hard distinctions between expert and novice are rejected (Susskind & Elliott, 1983). An overview of the data gathered by several stakeholders (i.e., the individual data gatherer, data gathering community, and authority) is presented in an overview where the scores are compared and insight in the norm set by the authority is given. In turn, this form of joint fact-finding similarly assists in increasing data credibility while also contributing to more cohesive relationships among stakeholders and a better understanding of differing views, thus supporting the social fabric (Ehrmann & Stinson, 1999).

Receiving crowdsourced citizen-generated qualitative data is not self-evident. An incentive is often lacking for people to actively add information. Therefore, supplying people with an engaging user experience over time is important to keep people interested and motivated to gather and submit data (Karapanos, Zimmerman, Forlizzi, & Martens, 2009). Taking Score Ze as an example, a short-term incentive can be seen as legitimacy of the application. It is important for people to know that their efforts are useful, and an application therefore derives legitimacy from the fact that the authority supports the initiative and acknowledges the data gathered (Stembert et al., 2013). As mentioned earlier, Score Ze provides an overview, norm, and comparison of data gathered by several stakeholders. This overview stimulates the experience of joint fact-finding and can be seen as a midterm incentive. As longer term incentive, it is important to give feedback on how the gathered data is put to use and the effect it caused on the public domain. The current application does not provide long-term feedback on, for example, cleaning schedules, action points, building plans, or improved locations. The system and data of authority is currently not computed to be implemented in an application, since data is not organized, is saved in a different format, has a different turnaround, or is not real-time available.

The data generated with the Score Ze application can be plotted on a map to inform City Works about critical locations in the city. Based on the geo-coordinates and the timestamp of the data submitted, other data sets (i.e., meteorological, traffic density, road work, refuse collection, event agendas) could be combined to gain insight in the context in which the data was submitted. Combining governmental, formal, and social data (Kalampokis, Tambouris, & Tarabanis, 2011) adds great value to the smart city infrastructure.

These new forms of big data can be used to inform policy- and decision-making procedures of private or public organizations. Yet combining this overwhelming amount of data also adds great complexity to the equation, a pitfall that cannot be ignored. Besides complexity, ethical issues like privacy must also be taken into account. By consequentially monitoring the environment, citizens imperceptibly submit large amounts of data. Data that itself seem harmless, combined with other data sets, can lead to direct (name, date of birth, address), indirect (income or value of property), or sensitive personal information (race, religion or belief, political opinion, health, criminal record, sexual orientation, union membership) that in a certain context or situation can be very harmful. Communicating integrity is extremely important to build and gain trust of data gatherers, and data handling MMMR should therefore always be treated with great care.

Discussion and Future Directions

The rise of emerging technologies is transforming data forms and how quickly these data forms can be collected and stored. Data are everywhere—data from the sensors in our personal mobile devices to smart environments and social infrastructures. The amount of data is very large. It is distributed and stored, it can have agile characteristics, and it can be unstructured. To process such types of data in a timely manner, new architectures and techniques are required. At this moment data is growing too quickly for data analysis to keep up.

The emerging technologies make it possible for all objects to sense the environment and communicate. But what impact might these technologies have on the privacy of individuals? In particular, combining data from various sources can violate a person's privacy. The information of an online sports tracking app, for example, combined with social media can reveal when a person is not at home, and a burglary can be planned. Social media combined with detailed location information can reveal someone's sexual orientation. Furthermore, the data may be stored within the cloud, scattered over the world on various servers. It is unclear, then, who the legal owner of the data is and what the quality of the data is. Thus other than privacy, security is another issue to be resolved.

Researchers have the possibility of mining this vast field of qualitative and quantitative data forms, but how can multimethod and mixed methods researchers gather these data in a meaningful way? How can we collect and act on these data? How can these data be used in a way that informs our understanding of social life? Although these emerging technologies open a wealth of opportunities, for the moment they leave us with many questions as to how to deal with these data in a safe and secure way.

The growth of sensor technology in mobile devices increases day by day. This is caused by the progressively smaller and more powerful computing devices and the increasing availability of inexpensive and miniature forms of sensors. HCI focuses research on understanding the interwoven activity of humans and nonhumans. Recently the research area has been refined to ubiquitous computing and the Internet of Things, caused by the trend toward embedding computing devices and wireless communication into everyday objects and activities. A computing device can detect where a person is, what he or she is doing, and how he or she is feeling and, depending on this context, it can act differently.

The increase in embedded sensors and wireless communication generates huge amounts of data. This is the research field of big data. Key characteristics of the big data field are the enormous volume of data, the high velocity of data coming in, and the variety of data types. This trend gave rise to new architectures for data processing and data storage in a distributed way (cloud computing). It enables a whole new area of (social) research previously almost impossible and beyond imagination.

One might speculate that we are in fact moving toward a paradigm shift in the social sciences triggered by Internet of Things opportunities. The Smart City concept, for example, whereby the city becomes instrumented, interconnected, and intelligent through the massive collection of data with a web of sensors, gives citizens instant feedback and control. In the example of the social fabric we show how citizens can participate fully in an Internet-enabled society through adequate skills and the ability to generate credible, comparable, and complete data. By carrying their mobile devices they passively gather and send data, forming a network of billions of sensors, making them part of the smart city infrastructure. Such massive changes are moving the social research enterprise in new directions. Participants no longer have to be asked to complete a survey when information is already gathered through sensors. Qualitative subjective data can be mixed with more quantitative measures for valuable information.

With the case description of Score Ze, an analysis application is shown that measures location-based quality of life to inform city maintenance on people's long-term feelings concerning how clean, intact, and safe the city is. The method of citizen-led traditional data gathering initiatives, combined with a standardized data gathering method like City Works, is explained. An incentive is needed for people to actively add information. Instead of a financial incentive, instant feedback can be given, like social rewards where people can compare themselves to others. Therefore, supplying people with an engaging user experience over time is important to keep people interested and motivated to gather and submit data.

Emerging technologies have expanded the role of participants in social research. Instead of social scientists, participants are generating the overwhelming amount of data by using the emerging technologies. These data are no longer the outcome of data collected by social scientists but are available and collected for other reasons. These data are of various types: stable or dynamic, from public or private sources, sensor data or submitted by humans, and so on. The validity and quality of the data can vary greatly. This asks for a strong interpretive approach from multimethod- and mixed methods researchers to harness these data.

Discussion Questions

1. In social research we are increasingly dealing with structured and unstructured data from multiple sources. How can we cope with such complex data?

2. Data is increasingly real-time available. How might this change social research?

3. Data in itself seems harmless but when combined with other data sets, it can sometimes become very harmful. How can we avoid this?

Suggested Websites

http://www.internet-of-things.eu/
This hub serves as access point to the activities around the Internet of Things in Europe and worldwide.

http://www.oii.ox.ac.uk/research/projects/? id=98
Site from Oxford Internet Institute about the use of big data in social science.

http://www.gartner.com/technology/research/hype-cycles/
The hype cycle is a graphical tool from IT research and advisory firm Gartner for representing the maturity, adoption, and social application of specific technologies.

References

Ashton, K. (2009, June 22). That 'Internet of things' thing. *RFID Journal*. Retrieved from http://www.rfidjournal.com/articles/view?4986

Association for Computing Machinery. (2013). ACM Computing Classification System. (2013). New York, NY: Author. Retrieved from http://dl.acm.org/ccs.cfm?CFID=185239034&CFTOKEN=67637699

Barnes, D. (2011). Five innovations that will change cities in the next five years. Web 2.0 Summit 2011. Retrieved from http://www.ibm.com/smarterplanet/us/en/overview/ideas/index.html

Corburn, J. (2007). Community knowledge in environmental health science: Co-producing policy expertise. *Environmental Science & Policy, 10*, 150–161.

Creating 010. (2013). Rotterdam University of Applied Sciences. Professionals Supported—Rotterdam Open Data. Retrieved from http://project.cmi.hr.nl/misc/rdamopendata/score-ze

Ehrmann, J., & Stinson, B. (1999). Joint fact-finding and the use of technical experts. In L. Susskind, S. McKearnan, & J. Thomas-Larmer (Eds.), *The consensus building handbook: A comprehensive guide to reaching agreement* (pp. 375–400). Thousand Oaks, CA: Sage.

Eriksson, J., Girod, L., Hull, B., Newton, R., Madden, S., & Balakrishnan, H. (2008). The pothole patrol: Using a mobile sensor network for road surface monitoring. In *Proceedings of the Sixth International Conference / Mobile Systems* (pp. 29–39). New York, NY: Association for Computing Machinery.

Goodchild, M. F. (2007). Citizens as sensors: The world of volunteered geography. *GeoJournal, 69*(4), 211–221. doi:10.1007/s10708-007-9111-y

Gouveia, C., Fonseca, A., Câmara, A., & Ferreira, F. (2004). Promoting the use of environmental data collected by concerned citizens through information and communication technologies. *Journal of Environmental Management, 71*, 135–154.

Harrison, S., Tatar, D., & Sengers, P. (2007, April–May). *The three paradigms of HCI*. Paper presented at the ACM SIGCHI Conference on Human Factors in Computing Systems, San Jose, CA.

IBM. (2010). The Internet of Things [Video file]. http://www.youtube.com/watch?v=sfEbMV295Kk&feature=player_embedded

Kalampokis, E., Tambouris, E., & Tarabanis, K. (2011). Open government data : A stage model. *Lecture Notes in Computer Science, 6846*, 235–246.

Karapanos, E., Zimmerman, J., Forlizzi, J., & Martens, J. (2009). User experience over time : An initial framework. In *Proceedings of the SIGCHI Conference on Human Factors in Computing Systems* (pp. 729–738). New York, NY: Association for Computing Machinery.

King, S. F. S., & Brown, P. (2007). Fix my street or else: Using the Internet to voice local public service concerns. In *Proceedings of the International Conference on Theory and Practice of Electronic Governance* (pp. 72–80). New York: Springer.

Lane, N., Miluzzo, E., Lu, H., Peebles, D., Choudhury, T., & Campbell, A. (2010). A survey of mobile phone sensing. *IEEE Communications* (September), 140–150.

Levine, C., & Fisher, G. (1984). Citizenship and service delivery: The promise of coproduction. *Public Administration Review, 44*, 178–189.

McCandless, D. (2010). The beauty of data visualization [Video file]. Retrieved from http://ed.ted.com/lessons/david-mccandless-the-beauty-of-data-visualization.

Pendersen, S., & Trueman, D. (2013, April–May). *"Sergey Brin is Batman": Google's Project Glass & the instigation of computer adoption in popular culture.* Paper presented at the ACM SIGCHI Conference on Human Factors in Computing Systems, Paris.

Presser, M. (2011). IoT comic book. Retrieved from http://iot-comicbook.org/

Rosling, H. (2010). The joy of stats [Video file]. Retrieved from http://www.youtube.com/watch?v=jbkSRLYSojo&list=PL694E7411BD18F280

Sargunam, V. (2007). Pervasive computing. Retrieved from http://ezinearticles.com/?Pervasive-Computing&id=547376

Savage, N. (2010). Cycling through data. *Communications of the ACM, 53*, 16.

Stembert, N., Conradie, P. D. Mulder, I., & Choenni, S. (2013). Participatory data gathering for public sector reuse: Learning from traditional data gathering initiatives. *Lecture Notes in Computer Science, 8074*, 87–98. Retrieved from http://dx.doi.org/10.1007/978-3-642- 40358-3_8

Susskind, L., & Elliott, M. (1983). *Paternalism, conflict, and coproduction: Learning from citizen action and citizen participation in Western Europe.* New York, NY: Plenum Press.

Weiser, M. (1991). The computer for the 21st century. *Scientific American, 265*(3), 94–104.

Emergent Technologies in Multimethod and Mixed Methods Research: Incorporating GIS and CAQDAS

Jane L. Fielding *and* Nigel G. Fielding

Abstract

This chapter provides an introduction to spatial analysis in mixed methods research (MMR), which is part of the "spatial turn" in social research. As more and more data are being "geo-referenced," opportunities arise for the inclusion of such data in MMR. For example, survey respondents' postcodes (zipcodes), or geo-referenced police crime data, can be mapped and related to other data in a multimethod project. Even qualitative data can be "mapped"—the global positioning system tracks of mobile, go-along interviews and their accompanying transcripts may be geo-coded or geo-linked and analyzed in relation to the spatial location of the talk. Freely available maps and geo-referenced data together with developments in computer software (ARCGIS, CAQDAS) have greatly increased the opportunity to represent and analyze spatial data. This chapter describes the use of emergent technologies for spatial data collection and analysis, providing extended examples of spatially oriented strategies in MMR.

Key Words: spatial turn, go-along interview, geo-referenced data, CAQDAS, geo-coded, geo-linked, qualitative data, ARCGIS

Introduction: The Spatial Turn in Social Science

The purpose of this chapter is to engage with new methodological practices and technological resources that have recently gained prominence in social science research and that are intrinsically sympathetic to mixed methods research (MMR) designs. We first need to understand these practices and tools as part of what has been termed "the spatial turn in social science."

The 20th century was largely the arena for contest between theoretical positions flowing from the founding figures of social theory: Marx, Weber, and Durkheim. Toward the end of the century, the reach of such theoretical positions came to seem limited and to have neglected dimensions of the social world that shaped human experience in society in ways at least as fundamental as the analytic preoccupations of the founding figures. One recent innovative perspective was the "discovery" of time as an organizing theoretical construct, which brought generations into sharper focus and inspired new fields, such as death studies (Bergmann, 1992). Another was the "discovery" of the body, which spawned new interest in cultural forms relating to corporeality long disregarded as inconsequential (Howson & Inglis, 2001). The present chapter reflects another fresh theoretical construct, that of the "spatial turn" in social science. The chapter will focus on the practical application of newly emergent methods, techniques, and technologies with which to incorporate the spatial dimension into multimethod and mixed methods research. We start by considering what kinds of analytic benefits the spatial perspective can provide for the research questions engaged with by social science.

Adding the Spatial Dimension to Research Questions

Social science came late to the spatial turn, and there are whole disciplines already formed around it, namely human geography, social geography, and qualitative geography. These fields, especially the last, are also pursuing their own fuller engagement with social science (Fielding & Cisneros-Puebla, 2009). Qualitative geography challenges mainstream human geography, and its emergence has sparked much debate, but in exploring the canon of qualitative social science, qualitative geographers have consistently emphasized the idea that geography is an inherently mixed methods discipline. We are enthusiastic about that kind of convergence around the spatial dimension between different disciplines, but we should also consider exactly what the spatial turn offers sociology that our established theoretical, conceptual, and analytic tools cannot provide. In a historical moment so preoccupied with the global, it is perhaps unnecessary to labor the theoretical significance accorded to globalization. A rich analytic vein flows from exploring the contemporary global reach of product innovations, technology, and cultural forms and practices. Likewise, from the equally valuable explorations of how apparently homogenizing influences are reshaped in local contexts, the local comes to represent a mix of the global and the local that is distinctive to the specific region.

Robertson's founding concept of *globalization*—an import from marketing—contained an explicit concern to explore *glocalization*, the way that an original innovation then plays in different corners of the social globe, in processes always more complex than the marketing origin of the idea, where glocalization simply meant adding more sugar to cola drink syrups in regions with a sweeter tooth (Robertson, 1992). If the spatial turn is, in sociologically analytical terms, about the currents and counter-currents in the extension of, and resistance to, corporate and state hegemonies, one could regard its essential knowledge base as studies that document sameness and difference across a span of regions, forms of human settlement, and social strata. Much of this work has a subtext about the steady extension of the sway of Western institutions and multinational corporations headquartered in the developed West. That is important work, but for the purposes of this chapter, the spatial turn cannot be read as being simply in the service of any *single* analytic agenda.

Our take on the spatial turn is more fundamental. We see its place in a mixed methods toolkit as a means to extend the generalizability of social science analyses. Sociology is often criticized as a discipline whose findings are not cumulative. We think that attention to location helps researchers build "contextualized generalizations" and thus to address the problem of cumulative explanation. The mixed methods tools and techniques we profile in this chapter enable researchers to identify the features of social phenomena that are invariant—they occur in every setting where the phenomenon occurs—and the dimensions around which innovation occurs as social phenomena are performed and adopted in local settings remote from the context of their origin—that is, the features of social phenomena around which variation occurs.

To take an example, research on obstacles to social mobility conventionally examined the proportion of people in an occupation who had particular socioeconomic and educational backgrounds. The "temporal turn" in social science led to a longer term, more holistic view, as people moved between jobs and developed a career history. Social mobility could be understood against a fuller context of the opportunities that related to developments in the economy over time. A *spatial analysis* directs attention to variation in economic opportunities by region; social mobility is not solely related to education and skills but to the distance people are prepared to travel to work, the physical features of the region (its ecology, its natural resources), its accessibility, and so on. Understanding specific career decisions may then be a matter of understanding the interaction between the spatial and the temporal, whose dimensions need a mix of methods to capture. Transport links may be poor in a given region, such that a journey of 20 miles takes two hours. What appears to be an unreasonable unwillingness to "get on one's bike" and take a job in a nearby region becomes understandable if the journey to and from work takes half the working day.

As well as assisting generalization, by providing insights into the scale and reach of a social phenomenon the spatial perspective also contributes to our understanding of causality. Critics of social science as lacking cumulativeness note that causal explanation has proved elusive in sociological inquiry. When people ask, "what are the causes of poverty?" or "why do people commit crime?" they assume that social science will have the answers. Yet often, the answer is contradictory (camp A says poverty is caused by poor educational opportunities, camp B says it is caused by fecklessness, and so on) or, worse, met by another question ("just what do you mean by poverty?"). Social scientists do not do this to be perverse but because the big issues with which they engage are complex, and the "answer" often lies in a multifactor chain that is intricately related to specific empirical cases from which it has been derived. Capturing multiple factors and understanding how they relate requires a heavy effort involving comparative multisite research with coordinated and consistent delivery of methods, definitions, fieldwork procedures, and analytic techniques. A smart mix of methods attentive to the spatial dimension can meet this challenge. The issue with social science causality is that social scientists, policymakers, and the general public alike are fixated on a positivist theory of causation whereas the social issues we study require a process-based or "realist" theory of causation attentive to situational context. Mixed methods research designs with a spatial element are uniquely suited to the development and application of a realist approach to the causation of social phenomena and so will help the social sciences produce adequate causal explanations of significant social issues.

WHAT KINDS OF DATA?

The previous example relating to job mobility is couched in the variable-centered terms of survey research but also alludes to the importance of personal perspectives that motivate behavior. Like other research questions, capturing motivations and perspectives requires qualitative methods. The social science engagement with mixed methods has evolved and developed, and MMR designs are not solely employed on the basis that "triangulation" will enable convergent validation, although it remains a significant perspective. However, mixed designs are nowadays often adopted with a view to gaining a fuller, more rounded picture, the aspiration being an account that displays "analytic density" (Fielding, 2009). While there is no logical reason that methods of the same type (e.g., two qualitative methods) cannot be regarded as a MMR design, the majority of mixed methods designs combine a quantitative and a qualitative method (Fielding & Fielding, 1986).

A spatial representation such as a map can be regarded as "qualitative" since the only numbers that appear on many maps represent the scale to which they have been drawn. However, maps and other spatial representations (but not photographs such as Google Earth [GE] Street View images) are better regarded as mixing qualitative and quantitative data, because the images such as streets or land surface contours are based on measurements and projections. Thus it is possible to argue that work with spatial representations is, implicitly, a MMR practice. However, things get more interesting where a map not only figuratively represents the space in question but also contains additional layers of information. Often the information will be quantitatively based (e.g., proportions of dwellings held under different kinds of housing tenure), but a graphical device (e.g., cross-hatching) or coloring will be used to represent the different proportions, groups, types, and so on. How the nonspatial data (such as statistical data or textual data) in a spatially oriented mixed methods project is linked to spatial coordinates is a topic to which we now turn.

FROM NONSPATIAL DATA TO SPATIAL DATA

Spatial data may be "point" data, linking one point in space (e.g., the location of a town in a large-scale map or a crime incident at smaller scale), or the data may be defined by lines—such as roads or global positioning system (GPS) tracks. Or it may be defined by areas—for example, areas of deprivation or high crime. Figure 31.1 illustrates a UK local government ("Local Authority") map containing two layers of information. First we see a layer of area classifications derived from the UK Census 2001 data and depicted by a "chloropleth" map (a thematic map using graded symbols, colors, or lines to indicate the presence or magnitude of various characteristics). In this case the chloropleth map is a layer of different shades and is labelled according to the values of the variables from which each classification has been derived (Vickers & Rees, 2007). Thus areas with higher proportions of minority ethnic groups have been labelled "multicultural" and areas with higher levels of multiple deprivation have been labelled "constrained by circumstances" (terms relating to a social classification system published by Vickers & Rees, 2007). Second, the map has a layer of points locating reported violent crime events in 2009 (specifically Surrey Police data). To "contain" such information in a manageable form, it is usual to employ geographic information system (GIS) software tools (such as the ESRI ArcMap discussed later), which allow researchers to switch the layers on and off in many combinations in order to search for patterns, interesting coincidences, or juxtapositions of information. The content underpinning the layers is data derived from mixed methods. Thus a GIS

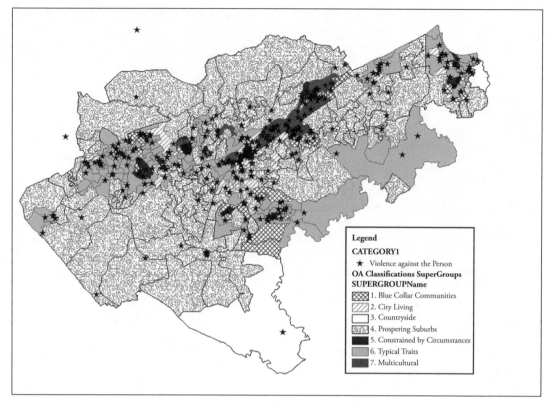

Fig. 31.1 A map with two layers (violent crime against the person and 2001 Census Output Area Classifications)

is a sophisticated database of layers of spatially related data, which may be manipulated, either statistically or qualitatively, to reveal patterns or display relationships using the cartographic aesthetic of map symbology. Increasingly, researchers explore and visualize in geographic space using not only statistical data (such as that derived from Census returns or the incidence and count of crime events) but also qualitative data derived from and about the people who live in or move through such geographic space.

In order to fully understand how we might integrate qualitative data and spatial analysis we need to distinguish between the terms *geo-referencing, geo-linking,* and *geo-coding.*

In cartography, geo-referencing means aligning geographic data (which has no explicit coordinate system[1]) to a coordinate system (i.e., a paper map). This may also be called geo-linking. Thus we have interpreted geo-referencing or geo-linking as the process that links data, such as a segment of an interview transcript, to locations in Cartesian space where the data is produced or referred to (see Figure 31.2). The data is located in 2D space via hyperlinks to the qualitative data. Figure 31.2 depicts a

segment of an interview with a local resident and is hyperlinked to a location ("Community Centre") in GE. Such hyperlinks to GE can be saved and coded within various CAQDAS software packages (including MAXQDA, ATLAS-ti, NVivo, and QDA Miner) and returned to at any point during the analysis.

In the geography disciplines, *geo-coding* is generally the term used to indicate the process that assigns coordinates to postal addresses so that point locations can be added to maps. However, within the social science approach to spatial analysis, geo-coding has taken on a different meaning to do with "reading" and coding spatial information. Here the landscape is treated as "text"—as data that can be codified (Verd & Porcel, 2012). Thus points, lines, or areas of the visual landscape are coded by the researcher, and these coded points, lines, or areas are linked to documents such as verbatim transcripts or policy documents dealing with area transactions—things that occur in the area.

Thus in Figure 31.3, the mapped Census classification data describes an area as "constrained by circumstances." The area is linked to the qualitative

RESP - The Community Centre, everybody has a sneaky feeling, and this is purely supposition, because the Community Centre is built on land that belongs to the council, and the little bit of grass next to it also belongs to the council, and they've got a 100 year lease, but the building belongs to the community. Everyone's got a sneaky feeling that the council is waiting for the Community Centre to get to the point where it becomes too dangerous to keep there, and they can knock it down and build housing on the site. Because whenever they apply for a grant for money to repair the roof or whatever, they are denied, whereas people in M** and S**r get millions. Umm, and our Community Centre is gently falling to pieces.

INT- It's a surprisingly large building.

Fig. 31.2 Geo-linking data to a geographic location
©Google Earth 2012 Infoterra Ltd and Bluesky

data through coding points in the landscape to coded segments of text in the transcript data. The latter refers to the high level of social housing in the area and instances of incivilities (e.g., litter in the streets), which may explain the area's poor reputation. However, photo images, also linked to a point adjacent to the area, identify a signifier of strong community cohesion, namely, a residents' association noticeboard.

Another relevant term with a mixed method nuance is *geo-tagging*, which is the attachment, or tagging, of geographic information, such as longitude and latitude or geographical coordinates to other media such as photographs or video. This represents meta-data (i.e., data about data).

Inclusion of Spatial Data: Conceptual Uses and Presentation of Information

Before we explore practical examples of how we can geo-reference or geo-code our data to include a spatial dimension in a mixed methods project, we first need to consider three questions: (a) Why are we doing this, and what are we hoping to be the end result? (b) What audience are we doing this for? and (c) How might our spatial presentation be used in our ongoing work and that of others?

The first question speaks to the need to have a clear analytic purpose behind including a spatial dimension in our MMR. Without a rationale for using spatial data, and particularly a strategy for

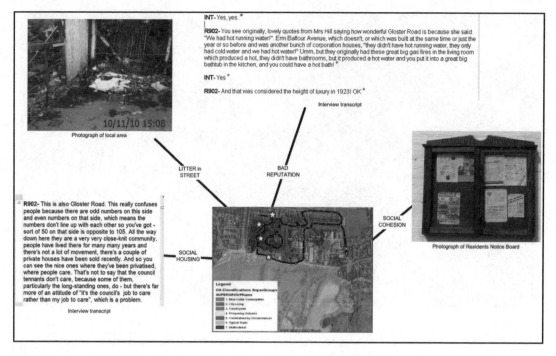

Fig. 31.3 Geo-coding: Qualitative data in spatial context
©Google Earth 2011 Infoterra Ltd and Bluesky

integrating such data with that from other methods in our research design, we may produce a trivial or superficial analysis. Maps are attractive objects, but we should use them because they are the right tool for the job rather than simply because they provide a pretty illustration. Just because it is possible to "map the tracks," we still need to ensure that the additional layer of analysis furthers our knowledge of the issue we are investigating and is integrated within the project as an essential component. Concerns over the purpose of spatial representation were first identified by the cartographer, Alan MacEachren (1994, 2004). For example, the purpose of the spatial display might be to present known information purely as a means of communication—such as a road map identifying the route from A to B or a weather map displaying the forecast. Or it might be to visualize data displays to reveal previously unknown relationships (i.e., to act as an analytic tool). Subsequent research (Holland, Burgess, Grogan-Kaylor, & Delva, 2011) using spatial techniques in an action research project confirmed that mapping results are visually appealing and "capture the imagination of the participants" (p. 703), leading to greater community dialogue. However, there was still the danger that the findings of the project may be seen as trivial by

the participants. Both participants and researchers gain the most when the spatial dimension adds to, rather than simply illustrates, the analysis. The purpose of MMR is often to extend or deepen understanding, so the spatial dimension is best justified where it aids analysis.

Our second preliminary question concerned the intended audience for the spatial display. For example, was it for the researcher's background use in pursuit of analytic purposes, or to emphasize a point in a publication, or both? One issue to bear in mind is that of the pact between the researcher and the respondent to safeguard their anonymity. Clearly, private use by the researcher of a map that may identify the home location of respondents is not generally an issue if used for analytic purposes to help the researcher visualize relationships between interview utterances and place, but it may present serious ethical consequences if it was to be published. Another consideration is that maps used for presentation purposes for a public audience need to be simplified and clear of "map clutter" to make a strong point to nonspecialists. This is especially important where spatial representations are used in research relating to public controversies, such as planning decisions or inquiries into public health issues such as disease hotspots.

This links to the final question about presentation and whether the final display will be static, where the viewer has little or no input to change the display (as in a publication) with the display being used toward a multimedia presentation where viewers are able to manipulate the display for their own purposes. These dimensions of use (known in the geographical literature as MacEachren's cube; MacEachren, 1994) have been developed and debated by subsequent geographers and cartographers (Kraak & Ormerling, 2010) but equally lend themselves to any application of geo-visualization within social research, especially the inclusion of different kinds of data in a mixed methods project. Knowing how we wish to use spatial techniques and analyses within MMR is a first step to effective communication of our results.

Relationship Between Social/ Human Geography and Other Social Science: Technological Change, Innovation, and Social Transformation

Social geography as a discipline has had a fruitful engagement with social science in recent years. As noted earlier, a particular growth point has been around qualitative geography (Doel, 2001; Jung, 2009; Jung & Elwood, 2010; Kwan & Ding, 2008; Pavlovskaya, 2002; Sheppard, 2005) and the role of social geography in MMR. Qualitative geography has an associated technical practice of "qualitative GIS," using existing GIS technologies in new ways or using new features and functionalities in customized GIS databases (Jung, 2009). Qualitative GIS, and qualitative geography more generally, are strongly oriented to mixed methods work. A pioneering example was work on the post-Soviet economy (Pavlovskaya, 2002). Pavlovskaya used census data to profile the official economy and interview data to capture the "black" (informal) economy. She mixed data from both sources in maps created by using GIS. To enable the qualitative data to be integrated in this way, she quantified features of the interview data. More recent approaches, such as CAQ-GIS (Jung, 2009), employs a "hybrid relational database" that allows qualitative data to be held directly as an additional layer in the GIS package where other layers in the "stack" are quantitative data or maps. Such techniques are further discussed in the exemplar in a later section, but for now the important point is that qualitative geography is an avowedly mixed methods approach. Qualitative geographers such as Knigge and Cope (2006) advocate a convergence of quantitative and qualitative methods in GIS representations; as Skinner, Matthews, and Burton (2005) put it, the objective is to enable research to capture "both 'context' and 'content' in a spatial dimension" (p. 230), and technology plays a vital role in achieving this. For mixed methods researchers, the developments in qualitative geography open up new technological resources and intellectual resources to bring the spatial dimension into mixed methods inquiry.

Use of Technologies

In this section, we profile spatially oriented research technologies for data collection, discuss the role of the resulting information in data analysis, and explain how spatial information has a metaphorical function in data visualization. We go on to consider two principal technologies relevant to work with spatial data: mapping software and geo-enabled qualitative software. In both the profiles of software and the exemplars illustrating their use, we highlight the ways that the technologies enable spatial data to contribute to MMR projects.

Using Technologies for Data Collection

Many textbooks on data collection techniques discuss using technologies like digital recorders and cameras to collect visual data, both still and video, but here we wish to concentrate on technologies that enable spatial data to be collected alongside other forms of data. A common technology to use to capture such data is the GPS device. In recent years these have become common for personal use and in cars. Not only are there many forms of specific standalone GPS devices on the market, many cameras and mobile phones are now GPS-enabled, allowing photographs to be "tagged" and the tracks of routes to be recorded with ease. Here we explore the social research use of such devices to provide a spatial dimension to a mixed methods study using a standard field-work technique, the qualitative interview.

A data collection technique that is becoming increasingly popular is the mobile interview. The technique involves interviewing in a spatial context—interviewing a participant while travelling, either by car but usually on foot, around a locale, generally on a route chosen by the participant and one that is familiar to them. These are also called "go-along" or "walkabout" interviews (Anderson, 2004; Anderson, Adey, & Bevan, 2010; Brown & Durrheim, 2009; Murray, 2009; Ross, Renold, Holland, & Hillman, 2009). Methods such as these go back to the systematic social observation studies of urban neighborhoods and police patrols by Reiss (1971) and more recently by Sampson and Raudenbush (1999) and carry through to socioenvironmental audit studies such as those carried out by Fielding, Innes, and Fielding (2002). In other disciplines, such as tourism studies and in research on the built environment and policy strategies, especially relating to public health and well-being, there are many walkability studies that employ similar techniques. These include the Active Living Research studies employing the Irvine-Minnesota Inventory, developed and tested at the University of California, Irvine, and at the University of Minnesota and administered by researchers at the University of California, San Diego.[2]

In addition to capturing the GPS tracks of routes and conversations while walking or driving around a neighborhood or other locale, it is also possible to employ software (such as SurveyToGo[3]) on suitable devices (such as an Android or Windows mobile phone) that allows users to "survey" the areas of interest and record the occurrence or frequency of specific events or objects located in the area—effectively to carry out a quantitative "audit" of the area that can later be spatially integrated with all the other kinds of data in a mixed methods project. Exemplifying this technique, Fielding et al. (2002) used an "environmental scan" instrument to create an inventory of physical and social indicators of crime and disorder, providing a quantitative baseline enabling comparison of different inner-urban areas that was used in developing interview schedules attuned to the specific problems of each area. In turn, the interviews drew on the quantitative data to probe respondents' awareness and concerns about the specific indicators present in their area. Here, the environmental scan instrument underpinned further data collection methods. Another example of a spatial device being used for data elicitation is that of the "tag cloud."

Using Technologies for Data Analysis

Using spatial metaphors is one way to visualize qualitative data. One popular way of visualizing text is by producing a tag cloud, which presents the text such that those words occurring most frequently appear most prominently within a word diagram—either by size or by color. Such tag clouds are comparable to exploratory data analysis techniques used with numerical data such as stem and leaf diagrams or box plots. Such techniques are designed to give an initial indication of the content of the data before more in-depth analysis may be considered. This is often done using bespoke web applications. While many CAQDAS software packages (such as MAXQDA and NVivo) include tag cloud capability, web applications, such as "wordle"[4] are also very quick and easy to use.

In Figure 31.4, the nomination acceptance addresses of the Democratic (Barak Obama) and Republican (Mitt Romney) nominees for the 2012 US presidential election have been copied and pasted into the wordle web application and tag clouds produced. Clearly, *America, Americans*, and *American* featured strongly in Romney's speech while *new, future*, and *years* appeared more prominently in Obama's speech. Of course, these words are out of context and further analysis would be needed to understand their full significance, but the tag cloud gives us a first insight into what the candidates emphasized in their speeches. This provides a good way to begin the analysis. First impressions can be followed up more systematically using other data in a mixed methods design, such as the full transcripts in an interview-based study. Spatial metaphors such as "islands" of homely language surrounded by "seas" of threat words point to patterns that we can search for across a corpus of speeches by different politicians.

Thus tag clouds relate to extent of coverage, contributing a sense of dominant/subordinate themes to a mixed methods analysis where the primary data are text-based.

The access we now have to great amounts of data associated with the Internet has made the use of software to help us manage and explore it absolutely necessary. So to extend the spatial metaphor to visualizing textual and social data, we now want to profile not only the use of traditional mapping software as an enhancement to our mixed methods toolkit but also the newer web applications such as GE and other open source mapping applications. The following section explores both commercial mapping software and freeware available for social research.

Mapping Software: Mainstream and Open Source Applications
GOOGLE EARTH AND GOOGLE STREET VIEW

Many readers will be familiar with GE and Google Maps from their use in everyday life. Google Earth, developed by a CIA-funded company (Keyhole), was first released in 2005 and has been used by many research projects in the natural sciences, especially the environmental sciences, to visualize data such as historic natural hazards data,

Fig. 31.4 Tag Clouds: A: Obama B: Romney. Citation: Barack Obama: "Remarks Accepting the Presidential Nomination at the Democratic National Convention in Charlotte, North Carolina," September 6, 2012. Online by Gerhard Peters and John T. Woolley, The American Presidency Project. http://www.presidency.ucsb.edu/ws/?pid=101968 Citation: Mitt Romney: "Address Accepting the Presidential Nomination at the Republican National Convention in Tampa, Florida," August 30, 2012. Online by Gerhard Peters and John T. Woolley, The American Presidency Project. http://www.presidency.ucsb.edu/ws/?pid=101966

climate change models, and weather applications. But use of GE and Street View in social science research has taken longer.

Some express caution in the widespread use of these virtual globe applications that, by virtue of their hyper-reality, evoke "emotional and intuitive responses, with associated issues of uncertainty, credibility, and bias in interpreting the imagery" (Sheppard & Cizek, 2009 p. 1). Be that as it may, in the social sciences the reality of the images shows promise to support the mixed methods analysis of

real-life events by putting quantitative and qualitative data vividly in their spatial context. The virtual globe applications are also useful in a team-working context, such as a feature that enables one team member to track the route of another researcher in a neighborhood and a feature that allows one to go back in time to look at previous satellite images of an area. In one geo-referenced study (Matthews, Detwiler, & Burton, 2005), the "tracking" facility enabled the research team to decode some anomalous results that turned out to have come about when the fieldworker had inadvertently wandered out of the sample area. This speaks to the data integration element of MMR designs (Creswell, 2013), where bringing together quantitative and qualitative information requires that we have confidence in the robustness of each information source, to which anomalous results are an obvious threat. Mixed methods research also values context, not only in terms of the situational context that qualitative methods have long valued but in terms of the context that findings from different methods make for each other. The spatial dimension can add important context for findings from both quantitative and qualitative methods.

OPEN STREET MAP AND THE JAVA OPEN STREET MAP EDITOR

Google Earth and Google Maps are proprietorial software programs whose use is regulated by licensing restrictions. However, there are also open source applications that can be useful in spatially oriented mixed methods work. Two open source (free) mapping tools are Open Street Map (OSM, [5] The Free Wiki World Map) and Java Open Street Map editor (JOSM). OSM was founded in 2004 and developed in the UK to get around the large cost of the licenses to use government-owned map products (later the UK Ordnance Survey released OS OpenData,[6] a freely available mapping product). The maps in OSM were originally created by volunteers carrying out ground surveys with handheld GPS devices with the help of digital cameras and voice recorders. Over the years, several government maps and satellite images have become available in the public domain and have been incorporated into OSM. Further, OSM now has a multinational member base and is available to anyone with an Internet connection.

JOSM is an offline tool that allows anyone to download maps created by the OSM community, and, while JOSM was created as a tool to enable people to contribute to the mapping wiki, it also has useful features for social research such as the ability to synchronize audio with a GPS track. In addition, there are tools such as MapOSMatic,[7] a free software web service that enables one to download and print off city maps with street indices for one's own purposes, especially useful in a research environment where paper maps are needed. This can be particularly useful in team research where different team members take responsibility for fieldwork in particular areas in the research site. While such tools are useful in monomethod

research, they are particularly valuable in MMR because such work often involves team research. Also, insofar as MMR has several parts, it lends itself to "citizen science," where the visual appeal of work with maps encourages input from volunteers, an example being the work undertaken by Knigge and Cope (2006) on planning and urban redevelopment, where volunteers input experiences relating to the value of "community gardens" that had been ignored by town planners.

WEB MAPPING AND PARTICIPATORY MAPPING—WIKIMAPIA

In accord with such examples, wikimapia[8] is a collaborative project begun in 2006 and involving Internet volunteers tagging any kind of geographical content, creating layers on top of a Google Map satellite image.

Both OSM and wikimapia are tools contributing to the expanding phenomenon of involving "citizen scientists" in the collection of data, often through the practice of "crowdsourcing" using technologies such as 4G- and 5G-enabled mobile phones and public cloud computing. The engagement of citizen scientists can expand the scope and range of MMR in circumstances where budgets are limited and also provide a mixed methods project with a valuable element of feedback about interim findings and/or analysis as they develop. One example is a sociohistorical study of ancient Egyptian papyruses that is making thousands of these documents available in facsimile form for armchair archaeologists to help catalogue and translate (BBC News Oxford, 2011). Here, the amateur interpretations are being combined with the systematic text analysis techniques used by Egyptologists and feminist analysis to study the representation of women in ancient texts.

ARCGIS AND THE FREEWARE ARC EXPLORER

One of the mainstream mapping packages is ArcGIS, developed by Environmental Systems Research Institute, Inc. (Esri),[9] in Redlands, California, founded in 1969. Esri software includes a standalone desktop application (version ArcGIS 10.1 at the time of writing) and ArcGIS online. In 2010, a free tool, Arc Explorer (available in both desktop and online versions)[10] was released, enabling an even wider community of spatial analysts and citizen researchers to share and view spatial information. Again, mixed methods projects find this useful in the context of team research; annotation facilities enable the interactive shaping of the analysis, and dialogue about quality assurance matters.

The applications we have considered in this section are mainstream applications generated by programmers responding to the needs of researchers in human and social geography. However, another field of software development—qualitative software (or CAQDAS for "Computer Assisted Qualitative Data AnalysiS")—was also quick to respond to the spatial turn in social science. Several CAQDAS packages now offer support for work with geo-referenced data.

Mapping Software: CAQDAS Applications

From a mixed methods perspective, the vital thing about the elements of geo-coding or tagging provided by CAQDAS is that it facilitates the analytic combination of different data types. Such work is often around work with codes. The hypothesis test feature in the HyperRESEARCH[11] package is one example. The analytic focus moves from the relationship between data and code to the relationship between codes. This move to a more abstract level could render broad interim conclusions about, say, the relationship between street lighting and fear of crime that could then be compared to maps of crime hotspots and lighting levels in such places. Packages providing geo-coding or tagging support include ATLAS-ti, QDA Miner, MAXQDA, and NVivo, with ATLAS-ti actually embedding GE within the package, while QDA Miner is distinguished by not only allowing text to be hyperlinked to locations with GE, but offering the facility to attach time stamps. The fundamental benefit of the technology here is shared by all the packages—that of geo-linking text to places and the ability to "code" geographic images of place.

USING SPATIAL REFERENCES IN CAQDAS

The mixed methods researcher wanting to add a spatial dimension should start by opening GE and saving point locations of interest as either Keyhole Markup Language (.kml) files or Zipped .kml files (.kmz), or by saving GE images as .jpg files. Then, once the files have been saved and stored in appropriate folders set by the specific CAQDAS package, the CAQDAS software can be opened and geo-images can be imported and "coded," or the existing text within the project can be hyperlinked (geo-linked) with the locations of interest. These two types of geo-coding or geo-linking are described next.

Coding of geo-images. Figure 31.5 displays a GE image saved as an image file that has been coded in MAXQDA. Areas of the image have been defined and then codes attached to them, as indicated by the coding strips in the margins. The coding strip format, and the process of coding, is the same in application to the image as it is in application to textual data. The image provides an immediate idea of the context in which an interview respondent may, for example, express their feeling of being at risk in a particular location.

Geo-linking text. Figure 31.6 illustrates the other form of adding spatial referents within a CAQDAS package. In this figure, underlined text within MAXQDA has been geo-linked to a .kml file (the arrow points to the round geo-link icon), which, if selected, will open GE and "fly" to that location. The location in this example is actually a waypoint that was saved during a mobile interview using a GPS device. During these mobile interviews, the conversation was also recorded and then transcribed. Transcription was carried out using f4,[12] which put time stamps into the transcript, also indicated by an icon (⬤) in the margins. Note that these time stamps indicate the time elapsed since the start of the recorded interview rather than clock time. For the mixed methods researcher, geo-linked and time-stamped data adds contextual information that could be vital to interpreting a respondent's comments but that would not be evident from a simple transcript of an interview.

ATLAS-TI—AND "THE WORLD AS YOUR PRIMARY DOCUMENT"

In ATLAS-ti, GE images can be embedded into the program as primary documents or as GE snapshots (i.e., as image documents). An example presented by the developer is the use of photographs taken of the same area over time to show changes in the mix of residential and business use in a city, or to capture population growth. Because all primary documents can be linked, comment boxes including statistical data or interview accounts can be linked to the images, either as a stimulus to analysis or as a presentational device. To create a new GE primary document, one can either open GE from within ATLAS-ti or one can be created by importing existing .kmz or .kml files. Creating a GE snapshot involves first positioning GE so the chosen view is visible and then creating the GE snapshot from within the ATLAS-ti program. The following section describes both procedures in ATLAS-ti in more detail.

Fig. 31.5 Google Earth image coded in MAXQDA
©Google Earth 2010 Infoterra Ltd and Bluesky

Geo-tagging point locations in ATLAS-ti using GE primary documents. Geographic point locations that will be hyperlinked to text segments or images first need to be created as "quotations" in ATLAS-ti. The first step is to assign GE as a new primary document. One can then start to create

"quotations." Quotations are created by first locating the point of interest in GE and double-clicking on the map at the exact location. This has the effect of moving that location to the center of the map where new "free quotations" can be assigned. Figure 31.7 illustrates how GE has been embedded

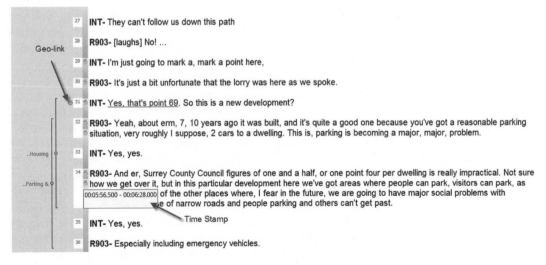

Fig. 31.6 Geo-linking in MAXQDA

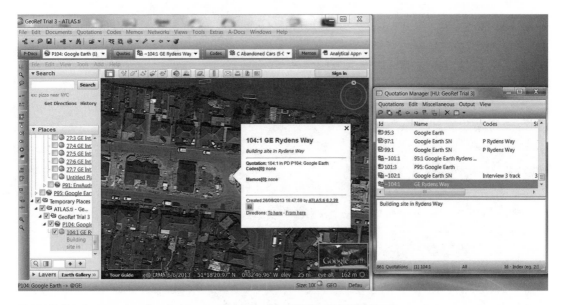

Fig. 31.7 Creating quotations from locations in Google Earth in ATLAS–ti © 2014 Google

within ATLAS-ti showing a new quotation created at a point for Rydens Way and the comment "Building site in Rydens Way" is visible in the pop-up under the title.

Once quotations have been created in GE primary documents, segments of text can be hyperlinked to them, inserting a geo-link code in the coding margins. Subsequent clicking on these geo-links will open GE within ATLAS-ti, and the image will be centered on that geographic point location.

Geo-coding GE snapshot images in ATLAS-ti. Google Earth snapshots in ATLAS-ti are static GE images assigned as primary documents. These are created from within ATLAS-ti by assigning a view of GE as a GE Snapshot. Note that the GE views are then frozen at the date of the GE imagery. Areas in these image documents can be coded as with any other image file. Thus, at the time of the research in our exemplar, a snapshot of GE (imagery date: May 24, 2009) was coded in ATLAS-ti, and this is seen in the middle of Figure 31.9. The rectangular boxes in this image are the areas to which codes have been assigned as displayed in the right-hand margin. This image displays a strip of open land in Rydens Way, mentioned by the respondents as a playground for children, a picnic area, or an overspill car park and described variously as an eye sore or a vital local community space (Figure 31.8). Five years later a GE snapshot captured more recently (imagery date: June 6, 2013) showed that the new development is now a building site (seen in Figure 31.7). At the time of the research between 2009 and 2011, this area was a center of dissent as residents lobbied for their preferred uses of the area.

Google Earth can be set to display a set of historical imagery in this area going back through all years that images were captured: from 1945, through 1999, 2002, 2004, 2005, 2009, and finally 2013. This can be useful in examples such as the population growth imagery mentioned earlier; in the developer's example, the technique was used to track population growth in districts of Tokyo.

Note that the only kind of geo-link hyperlink that can be created in ATLAS-ti (or MAXQDA, QDAMiner, or NVivo) that can be linked to transcript data is *point* data, that is, a single location in Cartesian space as opposed to "line" or "area" locations in space. If one wants to show a route (as we did with our mobile interviews), one must import the track data into GE (from the GPS device) and then create a GE Snapshot to assign as a primary document in ATLAS-ti.

Geotagging location and time with QDA Miner 4. QDA Miner not only allows the creation of hyperlinks in GE that can be attached to segments of text but also allows the coding of time stamps along with the geo-location. Such resources allow the mixed methods researcher to construct a sense of spatial change over time and, through coding and memoing features, to allow quantitative and qualitative information to be attached at each time point. Such affordances are particularly valuable

Fig. 31.8 Google Earth Snapshot in ATLAS-ti (imagery date May 24, 2009)
©Google Earth 2010 Infoterra Ltd and Bluesky

in longitudinal research, which is also especially receptive to a mixed methods approach as different information sources become available (or are lost due to normal attrition) over time. Longitudinal research in effect comprises an inherently MMR design, because it is driven by an interest in how attitudes or experiences change in human populations over time. Such work seeks to isolate key factors or variables by seeing which are present invariantly between different "sweeps."

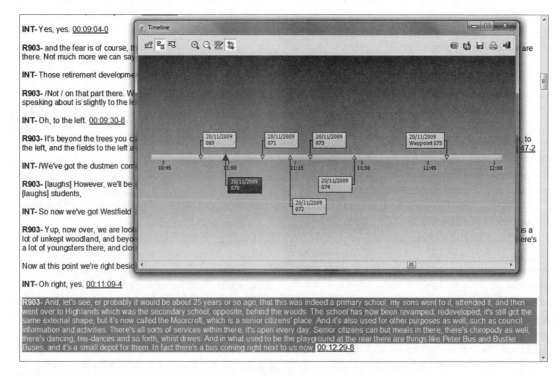

Fig. 31.9 A timeline in QDA Miner

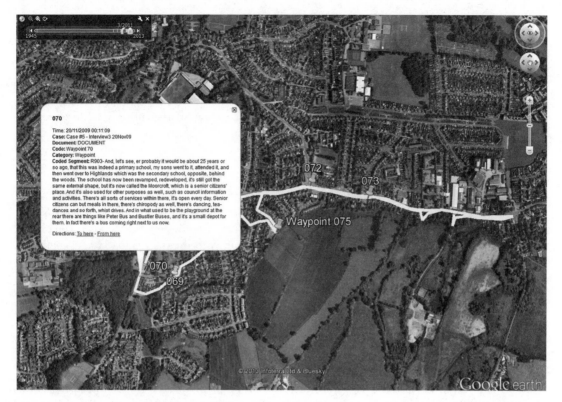

Fig. 31.10 Google Earth view of hyperlinked coded segments in QDA Miner
©Google Earth 2013 Infoterra Ltd and Bluesky

To keep a track of our mixed methods community crime-perception project, we found it useful to create a timeline indicating the dates on which we conducted mobile interviews, thus allowing the date spread of our data collection to be visualized. Time lines are especially useful when a specific event may affect the topic of interest, such as attitudes toward Muslims before and after 9/11 (Kwan & Ding, 2008). A longitudinal study mixing periodic surveys and interviews would capture broad change in the survey and the strength of feeling in subsample interviews.

In an individual interview, timelines, created from the time stamps in the original transcript, can be hyperlinked to coded segments of text. Thus in Figure 31.9, clicking on the timeline at "070" (Waypoint 070), the corresponding segment of coded text is seen highlighted in the mobile interview transcript.

In addition, these coded segments can be geo-linked to GE locations by hyperlinking to previously created .kml files. In Figure 31.10, coded segments appear in GE pop-ups by clicking on any geo-linked waypoint in the mobile interview track.

These facilities have a range of uses for MMR. The CAQDAS software can be used as a receptacle for all forms of data as the mixed methods project develops, enabling efficient and integrated data management. This approach also facilitates data integration during analysis, alerting the researcher to connections between different forms of data from the methods being mixed. Finally, these resources are informative and visually arresting when presenting findings. We now illustrate these techniques and features in a detailed exemplar from recent MMR.

Linking Data in Space/Place: Extended Exemplar Studying Vulnerability and Risk

The topic we explore in our example is whether residents of a community feel vulnerable to risk and what factors influence such feelings. Along with other fields, this is a major concern in contemporary criminology and socioenvironmental studies. The exemplar here is drawn from a spatially referenced mixed methods project in which we were concerned with risk from the natural environment and risk from the social environment. Our research question was whether there were common factors in the way that people relate to space that lay behind their feelings of vulnerability to environmental threats such as floods and social threats such as crime. A good way into this exemplar is to start by introducing a distinction—particularly important in a mixed methods context—between *emic* and *etic* approaches to a substantive topic. The *emic/etic* distinction is important in a mixed methods approach because MMR designs are fundamentally about integrating information from different methods that capture different dimensions of the same phenomena. To understand the relationship to mixed methods, we need to explain the *emic/etic* distinction.

Emic and Etic Approaches

The terms *emic* and *etic* originate in linguistics where phon*emic* was a unit of understanding and phon*etic* a unit of sound. Pike (1967) was the first to explicitly apply emic and etic concepts to social behavior. The emic approach is concerned with portraying a culture in terms of its internal elements and functions—an insider perspective—while the etic perspective draws on external structures and an outside position for its descriptions—an outsider perspective. An etic viewpoint defines vulnerable individuals as those at greater risk based on where they live. Risk is seen as a matter of living in vulnerable places, such as a flood plain, crime hot spot, or deprived neighborhood. Another etic approach defines people as vulnerable depending on their demographic characteristics. Risk is a matter of having a particular demographic profile. Characteristics that are seen to increase social dependency are often those that define vulnerable people, such as the very young or very old, the sick, or the poor. The orientation of an etic approach to external variables means that etic vulnerability is often aligned with quantitative data—that is, scientific measurements (e.g., using telemetry) of previous flood extents, from which flood risk maps are created, or census data, government surveys, and crime statistics that collect data on vulnerable people. Such an approach addresses questions such as

Are the deprived more likely to live within the flood plains?
Are high crime rates associated with neighborhood levels of deprivation?

Since the etic approach draws on apparent "facts" and external observable features, this view often informs public policy.

In contrast, an emic approach seeks to identify vulnerability on the basis of meanings held by individuals arising from their lived experience. This approach is often aligned with qualitative data—from interview/focus group transcripts, photographs taken by or about subjects of the research, diaries, and so on. The emic approach can address questions such as

Why are some areas seen as more risky than others?
Why do some people feel more vulnerable?

Much in accord with the principles of MMR, the value of the etic/emic distinction becomes most apparent when the two approaches are combined. For instance, individuals who may be defined as belonging to an at-risk group (etic vulnerability) may only *feel* vulnerable if they consider some threat to their self to exceed their capacity to adequately respond, despite "rationally" acknowledging their possession of vulnerable characteristics of the kind that register as externally observable indicators of vulnerability. From a policy perspective, a critical point is that it is only when people actually acknowledge their risk that they will engage in some kind of self-help behavior to respond to the risk. So policymakers who seek effective interventions need to acknowledge the emic dimension rather than rely on the "objective" etic dimension.

Spatial Emic and Etic Measures

To introduce a spatial element into an analysis of vulnerability, we need to provide the data collected with a spatial referent. Fortunately, individual survey data often contains postcodes or coordinates, and interview data may refer to geographic locations to act as prompts to enhance the flow of the interview or encourage the memory of the interviewee. Alternatively, the interview may be conducted while walking around a neighborhood, with GPS tracks being recorded during the walk as per our earlier discussion of mobile methods.

Once the data collected are "mapped," other spatial data can be added as layers to enhance the spatial evidence and to explore patterns of coincidence. Thus in an etic analysis, flood risk maps and various types of crime maps could be added, or small area statistics or derived statistics, such as deprivation indices or area classifications derived from census data. For an emic perspective, mobile interviews can be synchronized in time with GPS tracks to explore the coincidence of place and its connections elicited in the conversation. Another approach is where participants are asked to draw maps of their neighborhoods and indicate areas in which they feel safe/unsafe/confident.

Alternatively, and importantly for a mixed method project, the landscape itself could be coded (geo-coded) to inform, complement, or link to other data, both quantitative and qualitative (Verd & Porcel, 2012). For example, topographical features that affect journey times can be coded and visually represented to show parts of a city where the physical environment obstructs timely response to an incident by officers in patrol cars. To explore the various possibilities for MMR from including the spatial dimension, we next pursue examples concerning risk from the social environment. One of the most widely experienced forms of perceived risk in contemporary society is that of crime risk and fear of crime. While such risk has long been a public preoccupation, as measured by attitude survey data, new prominence has come from official websites that publish detailed information about crime in very exact local areas. Whether this heightens public fear and a sense of risk is debatable. Where crime rates are low, such information may actually reassure the public. We set out to pursue such issues in a study of fear of crime in residential and mixed residential/commercial areas in southern England.

We first defined "risky areas" using crime maps derived from police data (both area crime levels and individual crime event data) and from the 2001 UK Census area classifications data (Vickers & Rees, 2007). The "at-risk people" were seen as the local residents, employees in local business, and people visiting these groups—those that may pass through or live in those areas. Having identified risk-bearing people in terms of the etic approach by drawing on data sources external to their subjective or perceived experience, we followed this by collecting data from the at-risk people on their perception of their local area. This was spatially linked to the physical features and built environment of the area by conducting walking interviews in selected parts of the area with local people, police community support officers, neighborhood watch coordinators, and people who were active in the community.

Two kinds of mobile interview were carried out: mobile interviews with local residents and officials and researcher-led environmental audits of the area in which paired fieldworkers walked the area trading observations with each other. Prior to the interviews, respondents were asked to sketch their local areas and then take the researcher around their area. In the citizen interviews, we recorded the talk using a digital recorder (an Olympus DS-40) while walking around the area following a route of the interviewee's own choosing, which was recorded as a GPS track using a GPS device (a Garmin Etrex Vista C).

The environmental audits of the area were conducted by two researchers walking around the area defined by the extent of the citizen walks and recording their conversation about observations of the area. In addition, a survey instrument was deployed on a smartphone, which made it possible to record/count instances of various social and physical incivilities (such as people arguing, graffiti, signs of vandalism, or presence of rubbish), while at the same time recording the GPS location of the events. We also used the smartphone to take photographs, which were linked to the GPS location. The software used was SurveyToGo[13] on a supported Windows Mobile (Sony Ericsson Xperia X1) or Android smartphone (a Samsung Galaxy). To reduce the number of devices carried while on the environmental audit, the GPS tracks were recorded on the smartphone using Garmin Mobile XT on the Windows Smartphone (and Google My Tracks App[14] on the Android).

The interviews were transcribed (using f4,[15] which inserts time stamps allowing for synchronization with CAQDAS software) and the GPS tracks were downloaded—first into MapSource (the software that is shipped with Garmin GPS devices)—and then exported either into ArcMap (via a mapping utility called GPS Utility,[16] which will save the tracks and waypoints as Esri shapefiles) or into GE (either simply by clicking "view[ing] in Google Earth" from MapSource or by opening as a Global Positioning eXchange [.gpx] or Garmin DataBase [.gdb] file in GE; Figure 31.11). It is often useful to see the route map of a mobile interview and/or boundaries around participant or nonparticipant observation in the context of the physical features of the area, such as land contours, rivers, and other features. Equally, the route map can usefully be displayed in relation to the built environment.

Of the technical options mentioned previously, importing into ArcMap allowed a fuller and easier form of analysis—it is designed to allow overlay of several map layers for visualization and to print out professional-looking map output. Map calculations can also be performed—for instance, areas that coincide may be calculated (e.g., buffer zones can be created around areas of interest,

Fig. 31.11 Audit walk 2 gpx file opened in Google Earth including the time slider
© 2014 Google

for instance particular crime hot spots or deprived areas, and point data—respondents with particular characteristics—within those zones can be enumerated). Using ArcMap on a desktop computer also ensures secure storage of participant data to comply with confidentiality requirements. This was a consideration when using GE, since Google can, as a private company, potentially record and tracks all uses of their software.

While the superimposing of topographical features is helpful, things are taken a large step further when routes are contextualized by photographic images of the locale. In the case of the mobile interview, if the .gpx file is opened in GE (see Figure 31.11) then the track can be followed and sections of the interview can be listened to in relation to the route taken. Given that MMR often involves more than one researcher, this visualization within GE is also useful for co-researchers who may not have collected the original data but who wish to immerse themselves in the analysis. However, it is not possible to synchronize the GPS track animation within GE while listening to the interview audio file in real time—the animation is much too fast at its slowest speed. Fortunately, in several CAQDAS packages, including MAXQDA

and Transana,[17] one can synchronize the audio interview with the interview transcript (using the time stamps inserted by f4) for easier coding and retrieval.

Figure 31.12 shows the transcript of Audit Walk 2 in MAXQDA with a segment highlighted where the researcher mentions that the time is 2:40. The arrow in the diagram points to the time slider in GE, which also shows a time of 2:40. The actual track followed is marked 'track' with the arrowhead showing the direction (and position at 2:40) of the track.[18]

To get around the lack of synchronization between the mapping software and the CAQDAS software and to be able to follow the tracks and conversation in real time, the GPS tracks and the audio interview can be linked and synchronized in JOSM. In JOSM the conversation and the route can be followed in real time. However, in order to code the transcript with observations of the route in context, the CAQDAS software would also need to be opened alongside the map view in JOSM.

An idea of the value to a mixed methods project is given by the fact that observation data from the environmental audit walks revealed surprisingly little vandalism or other signs of crime and

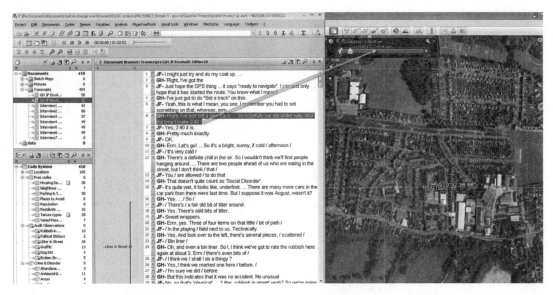

Fig. 31.12 The transcript in MAXQDA beside Google Earth showing the track position of mobile interview audit 2
©Google Earth 2013 Infoterra Ltd and Bluesky

disorder. Importantly, testimony from the mobile interview respondents indicated that where there were eyesores, there were also signs of efforts to deal with them. Moreover, mixing the mapping software and aerial view data allowed us to estimate the occurrence of the signs of poor physical environment in proportion to the overall area of housing and light business premises. Comparative analysis established that the area's principal problems were too little parking and too much dog mess, problems associated with more prosperous areas in the region. This gave us a lead in interpreting data from other sources in the project, as we discuss next.

Utility of the Spatial Turn

The procedures and techniques just discussed helped us develop a wider interpretation. Previous work in the area (Fielding & Fielding, 2013) had shown that people avoid certain parts—comprising just a few streets—because of their "bad reputation." Supporting this view was area classification data derived from the 2001 Census data that labelled residents in this area as "constrained by circumstances." Further support for this view, from an etic perspective, was the police crime data—which, when plotted in this area as individual crime events by postal sector, showed a cluster of events in this area.

Mixed methods projects often work in stages, with findings from one source informing work with the next. A common case is where interviews follow up a puzzling survey finding. In the case at hand, spatially plotting the police crime data helped focus mobile interviews and also prompted us to hone in on mobile interviews conducted in a particular place. The negative picture from the etic sources led us to concentrate the mobile interviews on how the respondents felt about this area: did they avoid taking us into this area? If they did take us through the area, did they talk about it, and what did they say? Using ArcMap we identified four interviews whose routes transversed this area of special interest (walks 2, 4, 5, and 6). Thus we were able to track the conversation transcripts in MAXQDA between the waypoints that were mapping in this area.

One interview extract appeared to confirm the impressions from the etic sources:

> And on the other side, as I've said, is the cul-de-sac that causes us no end of grief. Two houses at the end have huge big dogs, serious drug problems in at least four of the houses, and. . . lots of, dare I say, violence erupts without very much, very much to take it, to kick it off, if you know what I mean. . . . I really would avoid going into that cul-de-sac unless I have to, actually. . . . they keep getting new doors because they keep bashing them in. (Interview 2)

An unfavorable comparison is made with the area in earlier times: "You see originally, lovely quotes from Mrs. Hill saying how wonderful G**** Road is because she said 'We had hot running water'. . . And that was considered the height of luxury in 1923!" (Interview 2). However, another respondent offered a more balanced and nuanced evaluation, in which its bad reputation lingered among outsiders whereas residents with better local knowledge were aware that it no longer applied:

Well it has the worst reputation in this area, but actually it's not that bad. It's actually quite nice to live here. It's a good community'. (Interview 4)

Interviewer: hm hm. Why do you think it has a bad reputation?

R904: Oh! I mean we've had some bad trouble here over the years. I mean they used to put all the riff raff down here. Everybody that didn't pay their rent anywhere else, they used to dump them down here

. . .

I mean you'll find most people that are scared to come down G**** Road are people that don't live there. They've just heard about it, and they won't even walk down it. (Interview 4)

Similarly, another respondent saw the area as being one in transition. Rather than being disheartened by the act of vandalism referred to in the data extract, responding to it had drawn people together:

I got involved with trying to set a Residents Association up, and we decided we wanted to get

a bit of a community by getting a seat in the street and some more rubbish bins. . . . But then we had a young Traveller boy, who ended up in the prison in the end, he got a saw to it, and amazingly cut one of the planks. So, in fact, that rather galvanised everybody to realize that what we had achieved was being nibbled away immediately. So, although we didn't get a great amount of people coming to the Residents Association, we did start to get a bit of community building, realising what we were missing. (Interview 5)

There was further corroboration from Respondent 6:

Someone was saying to me the other day, we should change the name of the road, . . . That wouldn't make a whole difference, because . . . actually it's quite a nice road. I mean to look at and things it's not that bad.

In the next step in our mixed method data integration, we turned to the spatial dimension to develop a possible explanation of the rather differing responses. To contextualize them against the spatial dimension, we began by visually inspecting the area in GE (Figure 31.13).

Displaying crime events for just one of the postcode sector locations in the area of interest revealed that there were multiple crime events attributed to it (as shown by the star-burst display in Figure 31.13),

Fig. 31.13 GPS Tracks in Google Earth with crime events displayed for one location
©Google Earth 2013 Infoterra Ltd and Bluesky

but the neighborhood itself, seen in Google Street View, presented as a "normal" public housing area (Figure 31.14). Passing through the area the interviews had discussed, one sees a tidy streetscape with few if any indicators of crime/disorder risk. In fact when we conducted our audit walks, we were the ones perceived as suspicious and were asked what we were doing—regardless of the etic measures of high crime and deprivation, our obvious "outsider" status marked us as the "risk" factors to the local residents. This in itself was a sign that the area had what criminal ecology theory calls the "capable guardians" who help make communities resilient against crime and disorder.

To reconcile the emic and etic in this MMR, the spatial dimension helped us to understand that we had encountered an area in transition. From a place of bad reputation where local government public housing policy had previously created a sink estate, considerable investment of public funds in line with a new policy approach had visibly improved the built environment and engendered a measure of community spirit. The "constrained by circumstances" tag assigned by the 2001 Census analysts no longer adequately described the area (Fielding & Fielding, 2013). In our closing discussion we draw out more broadly some of the strengths and limitations in adding a technologically aided spatial dimension to mixed methods projects.

Conclusion: State of the Art and Future Prospects

Although social science theory came late to the spatial turn, the geographical dimension has a long, distinguished lineage in applied, empirical social science, including criminology, where social ecology theory emerged from studies of the relationship between crime patterns and place as far back as the 1920s. Having "arrived" more generally across social science in recent years, we do not expect interest in the spatial perspective to subside any time soon. The social problems that we study, such as the effects of advancing urbanization and overcrowding, and the resources available to us for such studies, such as mobile technologies, are dynamic and constantly changing. Environmental change is set to join longer established issues as a fundamental problematic for every social science discipline, and the environment is inescapably about place and space. Also, the field of research methods has further to go in working out the affordances, techniques, and value of "mobile methods." A good deal of the running in mobile methods in the next few years will be in keeping up with the advance of smart technologies, designing ways that research can benefit. For instance, the frequent, digitally persistent nature of Twitter messages is a largely untapped source of information about the hectic pace of modern life, but monitoring it may reveal spatial patterns and routine behind the

Fig. 31.14 Google Street View of one street in the sample area
© 2012 Google

seemingly shifting exterior, age, and gender differences that speak to enduring social divisions and so on.

But that is only to look at the convergence of CAQDAS and GIS in contemporary MMR from a Western-centric perspective. For instance, the norms of "private" and "public" that inform the ethical standards to which the examples in this chapter conform are not necessarily the same as those prevalent outside the established Western democracies. In a mixed methods context, what information may or may not be brought together could differ in, say, the Islamic world or in societies with a different relationship to the military. The horizons of social science are expanding, and new research communities are emerging (Liamputtong, 2010). Contemporary methodology captures this emergence in ideas and practices around "Indigenous knowledge" (Tuhiwai-Smith, 1999). Although there are certainly communities that have been closed to social research or that have only lately begun to generate their own research capacity, the change is more a matter of supplanting the dominance of external research traditions imported from (or imposed by) the West (Gobo, 2011). As we work through the implications of postcolonial social science in our own societies and in those that have previously understood social science through the Western-centric frame of reference, we can expect change in the purposes as well as the techniques of a geo-referenced practice of MMR. For example, people with non-Western sociocultural references may bring a quite different perspective on risk and security to their sense of public space, reflected in different patterns of interaction that can be captured by research technologies with a level of consent to surveillance not possible in the individualistic societies of North America and Western Europe.

We are already used to spatial representations like maps being sensitive documents because of the nervousness of governments about identifying military and other installations (Fielding & Fielding, 2013), but future researchers may need to negotiate other sensitivities, such as information about who visits particular kinds of establishments on journeys originating in residential areas associated with deeply religious communities. The glocal frame of reference is useful here, because it alerts us not only to the incursion into local areas of global trends but also to the way these are recast in the encounter. Mobile telephony gives us

an example. Innovative reuses of the technology range from guidance systems for mini-satellites—a low-cost alternative to purpose-designed optics (Moore & Highfield, 2005)—to their more prosaic but transformative use as receivers of web TV in remote rural Indian subcontinent villages with no local TV transmission (Frohlich, Robinson, Eglinton, Jones, & Vartiainen, 2012). The devices are donated by users when upgrading their handset. Villagers can use GPS-enabled devices to display their location in crop fields, information that also enables researchers to understand local farming practices and track the use of resources, such as water. This can then inform fieldwork using local informants, who train locals in the use of the devices. Here, mobile methods, allied with Indigenous knowledge, provide new opportunities for social science interventions in the action research tradition. The appeal of mixed methods has long been its promise to combine the analytic reach of quantitative methods with the analytic depth of qualitative methods. Its convergence with the spatial sciences, themselves inherently based on a mix of the qualitative and quantitative, adds a new dimension to our use of methods in combination.

Discussion Questions

1. What can mobile interview methods add to the collection of qualitative interview data in a mixed, quantitative, and qualitative study?

2. Think of all the different kinds of spatial data that can be used in evidence to answer your research question and then how you can bring it all together in a mixed methods project. Is the use of technology a help or a hindrance to the analysis of mixed data?

3. Describe your strategy for ethics using an empirical study. What are the ethical issues you need to consider in using spatially referenced data? Is there a privacy issue in using Google Earth in social research?

Suggested Websites
CAQDAS Software and Geo-Linking

http://www.atlasti.com/192.html
ATLAS-ti

http://www.maxqda.com/products/what-is-maxqda/geolinking
MAXQDA

http://provalisresearch.com/products/qualitative-data-analysis-software/qda-miner-whats-new/
QDA Miner

http://www.qsrinternational.com/support_resource-articles_detail.aspx?view=405

NVivo

More Help With Geo-Linking From the CAQDAS Networking Project Website

http://www.surrey.ac.uk/sociology/research/researchcentres/caqdas/support/integrating/index.htm

http://www.surrey.ac.uk/sociology/research/researchcentres/caqdas/support/integrating/georeferencing_and_caqdas_linking_to_google_earth_with_atlasti_6.htm

Notes

1. A coordinate system is a reference system that locates the position of items in space, enabling different geographic data sets to be matched within a common geographic framework. The most commonly known geographic coordinate system is longitude and latitude.

2. http://www.activelivingresearch.org/node/10634

3. http://www.dooblo.net/

4. http://www.wordle.net/

5. www.openstreetmap.org

6. http://www.ordnancesurvey.co.uk/oswebsite/products/os-opendata.html

7. http://maposmatic.org./

8. www.wikimapia.org

9. http://www.esri.com/

10. http://www.esri.com/software/arcgis/explorer

11. http://www.researchware.com/products/hyperresearch.html

12. http://www.audiotranskription.de/english/f4.htm

13. http://www.dooblo.net/stgi/surveytogo.aspx

14. http://www.google.com/mobile/mytracks/

15. http://www.audiotranskription.de/english/f4.htm

16. http://www.gpsu.co.uk/

17. http://www.transana.org/

18. However, it should be noted that the time recorded in the CAQDAS software is time elapsed from zero, while the time attached to the GE track is the real clock time.

References

Anderson, J. (2004). Talking whilst walking: A geographical archaeology of knowledge. *Area, 36*(3), 254–261. doi:10.1111/j.0004-0894.2004.00222.x

Anderson, J., Adey, P., & Bevan, P. (2010). Positioning place: Polylogic approaches to research methodology. *Qualitative Research, 10*(5), 589–604. doi:10.1177/1468794110375796

BBC News Oxford. (2011).Oxford University wants help decoding Egyptian papyri. Retrieved from http://www.bbc.co.uk/news/uk-england-oxfordshire-14289685

Bergmann, W. (1992). The problem of time in sociology: An overview of the literature on the state of theory and research on the "Sociology of time," 1900–82. *Time & Society, 1*(1), 81–134. doi:10.1177/0961463X92001001007

Brown, L., & Durrheim, K. (2009). Different kinds of knowing: Generating qualitative data through mobile interviewing. *Qualitative Inquiry, 15*(5), 911–930.

Creswell, J. W. (2013). *Research design: Qualitative, quantitative, and mixed methods approaches*. London, England: Sage.

Doel, M. A. (2001). 1a. Qualified quantitative geography. *Environment and Planning D: Society & Space, 19*(5), 555–572. doi:10.1068/d292

Fielding, J., & Fielding, N. (2013). Integrating information from multiple methods into the analysis of perceived risk of crime: The role of georeferenced field data and mobile methods. *Journal of Criminology.* Retrieved from http://dx.doi.org/10.1155/2013/284259

Fielding, N. G. (2009). Going out on a limb: Postmodernism and multiple method research. *Current Sociology, 57*(3), 427–447. doi:10.1177/0011392108101591

Fielding, N., & Cisneros-Puebla, C. (2009). CAQDAS–GIS convergence: Toward a new integrated mixed method research practice? *Journal of Mixed Methods Research, 3*(4), 349–370. doi:10.1177/1558689809344973

Fielding, N. G., & Fielding, J. L. (1986). *Linking data: The articulation of qualitative and quantitative methods in social research*. Beverly Hills, CA: Sage.

Fielding, N., Innes, M., & Fielding, J. (2002). *Reassurance policing and the visual environmental crime audit in surrey police: A report*. Guildford, UK: University of Surrey.

Frohlich, D., Robinson, S., Eglinton, K., Jones, M., & Vartiainen, E. (2012). Creative cameraphone use in rural developing regions. In *Proceedings of the 14th International Conference on Human-Computer Interaction with Mobile Devices and Services* (pp. 181–190). New York, NY: Association for Computing Machinery. doi:10.1145/2371574.2371603

Gobo, G. (2011). Glocalizing methodology? The encounter between local methodologies. *International Journal of Social Research Methodology, 14*(6), 417–437.

Holland, S., Burgess, S., Grogan-Kaylor, A., & Delva, J. (2011). Understanding neighbourhoods, communities and environments: New approaches for social work research. *British Journal of Social Work, 41*(4), 689–707. doi:10.1093/bjsw/bcq123

Howson, A., & Inglis, D. (2001). The body in sociology: Tensions inside and outside sociological thought. *The Sociological Review, 49*(3), 297–317. doi:10.1111/1467-954X.00333

Jung, J. (2009). Computer-aided qualitative GIS: A software-level integration of qualitative research and GIS. In S. Elwood & M. Cope (Eds.), *Qualitative GIS: A mixed methods approach* (pp. 115–136). London, England: Sage.

Jung, J., & Elwood, S. (2010). Extending the qualitative capabilities of GIS: Computer-aided qualitative GIS. *Transactions in GIS, 14*(1), 63–87. doi:10.1111/j.1467-9671.2009.01182.x

Knigge, L., & Cope, M. (2006). Grounded visualization: Integrating the analysis of qualitative and quantitative data through grounded theory and visualization. *Environment and Planning A, 38*(11), 2021–2037. doi:10.1068/a37327

Kraak, M. J., & Ormerling, F. J. (2010). *Cartography: Visualization of spatial data* (3rd ed.). New York, NY: Pearson Education.

Kwan, M., & Ding, G. (2008). Geo-narrative: Extending geographic information systems for narrativeanalysis in qualitative and mixed-method research. *Professional Geographer, 60*(4), 443–465. doi:10.1080/ 00330120802211752

Liamputtong, P. (2010). *Performing qualitative cross-cultural research*. Cambridge, UK: Cambridge University Press.

MacEachren, A. (1994). Visualization in modern cartography: Setting the agenda. In A. MacEachren & D. R. F. Taylor (Eds.), *Visualization in modern cartography* (pp. 1–12). New York, NY: Elsevier Science.

MacEachren, A. (2004). *How maps work: Representation, visualization, and design.* New York, NY: Guilford Press.

Matthews, S. A., Detwiler, J. E., & Burton, L. M. (2005). Geo-ethnography: Coupling geographic information analysis techniques with ethnographic methods in urban research. *Cartographica: The International Journal for Geographic Information and Geovisualization, 40*(4), 75–90.

Moore, M., & Highfield, R. (2005, December *29*). How to build space satellites out of iPods. *Daily Telegraph.*

Murray, L. (2009). Looking at and looking back: Visualization in mobile research. *Qualitative Research, 9*(4), 469–488. doi:10.1177/1468794109337879

Pavlovskaya, M. (2002). Mapping urban change and changing GIS: Other views of economic restructuring. *Gender, Place & Culture, 9*(3), 281–289. doi:10.1080/0966369022000003897

Pike, K. L. (1967). *Language in relation to a unified theory of human behavior.* The Hague, The Netherlands: Mouton.

Reiss, A. J. (1971). Systematic observation of natural social phenomena. *Sociological Methodology, 3*, 3–33.

Robertson, P. R. (1992). *Globalization: Social theory and global culture.* London, England: Sage.

Ross, N. J., Renold, E., Holland, S., & Hillman, A. (2009). Moving stories: Using mobile methods to explore the everyday lives of young people in public care. *Qualitative Research, 9*(5), 605–623. doi:10.1177/1468794109343629

Sampson, R. J., & Raudenbush, S. W. (1999). Systematic social observation of public spaces: A new look at disorder in urban neighborhoods. *American Journal of Sociology, 105*(3), 603–651.

Sheppard, E. (2005). Knowledge production through critical GIS: Genealogy and prospects. *Cartographica: The International Journal for Geographic Information and Geovisualization, 40*(4), 5–21. doi:10.3138/GH27-1847-QP71-7TP7

Sheppard, S. R. J., & Cizek, P. (2009). The ethics of google earth: Crossing thresholds from spatial data to landscape visualisation. *Journal of Environmental Management, 90*(6), 2102–2117. doi:10.1016/j.jenvman.2007.09.012

Skinner, D., Matthews, S. A., & Burton, L. M. (2005). Combining ethnography and GIS technology to examine constructions of developmental opportunities in contexts of poverty and disability. In T. S. Weisner (Ed.), *Discovering successful pathways in children's development: Mixed methods in the study of childhood and family life* (pp. 223–239). Chicago, IL: University of Chicago Press.

Tuhiwai-Smith, L. (1999). *Decolonizing methodologies: Research and indigenous peoples.* New York, NY: St. Martin's Press.

Verd, J., & Porcel, S. (2012). An application of qualitative geographic information systems (GIS) in the field of urban sociology using ATLAS.ti: Uses and reflections. *Forum Qualitative Sozialforschung / Forum: Qualitative Social Research, 13*(2). Retrieved from http://www.qualitative-research.net/index.php/fqs/article/view/1847

Vickers, D., & Rees, P. (2007). Creating the UK national statistics 2001 output area classification. *Journal of the Royal Statistical Society: Series A (Statistics in Society), 170*(2), 379–403. doi:10.1111/j.1467-985X.2007.00466.x

Commentaries: Dialoguing About Future Directions of Multimethod and Mixed Methods Research

What Problem Are We Trying to Solve?: Practical and Innovative Uses of Multimethod and Mixed Methods Research

Thomas A. Schwandt *and* Lauren Lichty

Abstract

This chapter claims that multimethod and mixed methods research (MMMR) can be justified in two matter-of-fact ways without appeals to paradigm arguments. One justification is a straightforward appeal to the practical utility of MMMR for generating a more complete understanding and explanation of social phenomena than can be obtained by using only one method. MMMR can also be justified on the grounds that it can be used as a heuristic to leverage innovations in communities of research practice. Of particular interest are innovations related to conducting interdisciplinary team science and employing systems thinking. ~~fosters innovation in scientific practice.~~ The chapter discusses both forms of justification and argues that the latter holds more promise and deserves more careful study.

Key Words: Practical utility, innovation, interdisciplinarity, heuristics, systems thinking, styles of reasoning

In recent years, multimethod and mixed methods research (MMMR) has become the new orthodoxy in several fields of research, including nursing, public health, and program evaluation. This is a consequence of a general trend in social science research to move beyond the purism advocated by some adherents of both experimental and narrative-interpretivist methodologies into what Klein (2007) calls a third methodological movement that seeks to blend the two.

In this brief commentary, we offer some observations on what MMMR can contribute to the conduct of social research. We take an avowedly practice-oriented, quotidian, and practical approach to this task. In so doing, we do not engage the debate over the definition of MMMR and the efforts to parse differences in related terms. Morse (2003), for example, makes the distinction between mixed and multimethod approaches as follows: *Mixed* design means incorporating quantitative or qualitative "strategies" in a single project

that "may have either a qualitative or quantitative theoretical drive. . . . The 'imported' strategies are supplemental to the major or core method and serve to enlighten or provide clues that are followed up within the core method." *Multimethod* design, on the other hand, is "the conduct of two or more research methods, each conducted rigorously, and complete in itself, in one project. The results are then triangulated to form a comprehensive whole" (p. 190). Nor do we seek to engage here the merits of different ways of combining methods into types of QUAL + QUAN or QUAN + QUAL research designs labeled sequential, concurrent, and so forth.

Finally, we are not interested in efforts to justify MMMR by explicating its alignment with one or more methodological paradigms (Creswell & Plano Clark, 2011; Denscombe, 2008; Harrits, 2011; Morgan, 2007). For example, pragmatism is the paradigmatic framework often used to warrant MMMR, although how this particular conceptual framework is read and understood varies considerably (Denscombe, 2008; Feilzer, 2010; Johnson & Onwuegbuzie, 2006; Morgan, 2007; Teddlie & Tashakkori, 2009). Creswell and Plano Clark argue that pragmatism is most often associated with MMMR because it focuses on "the consequences of research, on the primary importance of the questions asked rather than the methods, and on the use of multiple methods of data collection to inform the problems under study" (p. 41). Morgan claims that pragmatism "provides new options for addressing methodological issues in the social sciences" by moving beyond dualistic thinking (e.g., deduction vs. induction, subjectivity vs. objectivity, idiographic vs. nomothetic conclusions) toward more practical choices (p. 70). A "transformative" paradigm (Creswell & Plano Clark, 2011; Mertens, 2003) has also been put forward as the appropriate worldview justifying the use of MMMR. The argument here is that multiple methods can be (and should be?) deployed in ways that illuminate linking the results of social inquiry to practical action especially as that action relates to achieving social justice and equity for typically marginalized groups. No doubt there is much to be gained by careful explication of ideas central to several schools of thought within pragmatist philosophy and how they might serve as a conceptual framework for the use of MMMR: for example, that theories and models are instruments or tools to be judged in terms of their problem-solving capability and (following Dewey) that *warranted assertion* is a more proper term than *knowledge*. Likewise, exploring how feminist, critical, and/or racial and ethnic theory invigorate a transformative paradigm can potentially lead to a particular valuable justification for MMMR.

That said, we regard MMMR primarily as a way of actually *doing* scientific investigation. That way of working involves deploying multiple types of empirical methods and research designs in concert to generate knowledge of consequence for understanding and explaining social and behavioral phenomena. The phrase "in concert" is used deliberately to acknowledge that there are variety of ways in which different methods and different kinds of data can be brought together to address problems in the fields of education, health, and social services and to achieve the goals of explaining and understanding (Creswell & Plano Clark, 2011).

With that understanding of MMMR in mind, we offer two ways in which MMMR might be justified on rather more prosaic epistemological

grounds as a credible form of inquiry: (a) on the basis of its practical utility and (b) as facilitating innovation in scientific practice. The former is the most common form of justification and the latter less explored and potentially more promising.

The Practical Utility of Multimethod and Mixed Methods Research

Practical utility refers to the fact that MMMR is operable (i.e., implementable, practicable), and it has a real-world use for scientific investigators—that is, it "works" in the sense that it can be employed for useful purposes in a variety of research contexts. MMMR is *not* inherently a *new* method. Yet in the past two decades we have seen remarkable growth in adoption and discussion of MMMR reflecting an empirically driven desire to generate a more complete understanding or explanation of social phenomena than can be obtained via the use of a single method, type of data, or study design. As Small (2011) recently observed, MMMR has arisen because it has a particular kind of utility:

> Dissatisfaction breeds creativity. Empirical researchers have been unhappy with the natural limits of conventional methods, including experiments that do not uncover mechanisms, case studies that do not speak to distributions, interpretive techniques that lack formalization, and statistical techniques that lack contextualization. Their efforts have given rise to a large, diverse literature that combines or integrates either data collection techniques or analytical approaches from multiple perspectives. (p. 79)

Small argues that the two primary, practical uses of MMMR are confirmation and complementarity. *Confirmation* (most commonly referred to as *triangulation*) involves verifying the findings derived from one type of data or study design with those derived from another. This involves, for example, asking the same questions in surveys and interviews (with different respondents) and examining whether the same pattern of findings emerge across methods. *Complementarity* involves combining data or study designs in order to compensate for the weaknesses inherent in any one type of data or design. This would mean, for example, using experimental methods to measure outcomes while employing narrative/interpretive methods to understand process and context; using the latter kinds of methods to explore a phenomenon and generate a conceptual model and testable hypotheses while using statistical methods to test the hypotheses; or using one set of methods (e.g., in-depth interviews) to generate knowledge that complements what is known from the application of another set of methods (e.g., surveys; Curry, Nembhard & Bradley, 2009; Palinkas et al., 2011).

The practical utility of MMMR rests on the working assumption that different methods aim to do different things; as Abbott (2004) noted, "they envision different kinds of explanations" (p. 27). Abbott described three different explanatory programs (general styles of thinking about questions of explanation) evident in the social sciences: (a) a pragmatic view of explanation as an account that allows us to intervene (reflected in methods of standard causal analysis); (b) a semantic view of explanation that "explains the world of social particulars by assimilating it to more and more general patterns" (p. 28) (reflected in ethnography, for example); and (c) a syntactic view that explains the social world by modeling its action and interrelations (as, for example, takes place in historical narration and more formally in modeling and simulation).

Abbott (2004) points out that *within* each of these explanatory programs, some experimentation is likely to take place. Typically, a *heuristic of addition* is commonly employed to facilitate this experimentation—researchers add a new data set, investigate a new variable, examine more cases, examine previous cases in more depth, and even add a new method of analysis. This additive heuristic is characteristic of much social science practice and is one way of viewing the use of MMMR. A new set of methods is added to a given explanatory program—for example, the evaluator primarily interested in impact evaluation via counterfactual analysis adds interpretive methods to better understand context and anticipate heterogeneity in treatment implementation across sites (White, 2009). The school-community ethnographer adds a survey of the community to complement his or her in-depth interviews with key informants. These are no doubt profoundly useful ideas. Hence, MMMR has practical utility because it makes possible a heuristic of addition. In using MMMR in this way, social scientists are able to develop more complete, thorough, in-depth understandings of a social phenomenon or social problem that they could not otherwise generate.

The Innovative Promise of Multimethod and Mixed Methods Research

The practical utility of MMMR is not a particularly groundbreaking or novel idea in scientific

practice. Mixing methods (of in-depth interviewing, participation observation, surveys, questionnaires, document analysis, statistical analysis, etc.) or designs (ethnographies, experiments, etc.) in the examination of social-behavioral phenomena has been taking place for quite some time in cultural anthropology and fieldwork sociology (Hunter & Brewer, 2003; Johnson, Onwuegbuzie, & Turner, 2007).

However, MMMR *might* be linked to genuinely *innovative* social science practice. Innovation suggests some kind of breakthrough in the way we practice. For example, Abbott (2004) claims that innovation requires thinking of explanatory programs, the methods typically associated with them, and the great epistemological and ontological debates (e.g., positivism vs. interpretivism, analysis vs. narration, realism vs. constructionism) not as self-contained and clearly demarcated schools of thought (or paradigms) but as themselves heuristic tools that can produce new questions and new problems. He argues for the "heuristic fertility" of mutual methodological critique and takes the position (illustrated with numerous examples) that basic epistemological and ontological debates

> are not grand, fixed positions taken once and for all in one's choice of method. They arise as choices day in, day out. They pervade the process of research. And hardly anyone makes them the same way in all contexts and at all moments. . . . This complex. . . character of the basic debates makes them into a crucial heuristic resource for social science. (pp. 78–79)

Abbott's (2004) notion of treating the tools and methodologies of social science as heuristics that facilitate the invention of new ideas is one example of what might qualify as a genuine innovation in scientific practice. Ragin and Amoroso (2011) might call this an example of "looking. . . in unexpected places" (p. 116) for insights into a phenomenon.

What is thought provoking is whether MMMR has the potential to contribute to or foster innovation of this kind (versus simply having practical utility as an additive heuristic). To begin exploring this possibility, we might first consider Greene's (2007) effort to defend the use of MMMR as a process of "actively engaging with difference":

> The core meaning of mixing methods in social inquiry is to invite multiple mental models into the same inquiry space for purposes of respectful

conversation, dialogue, and learning from one another, toward a collective generation of better understanding of the phenomena being studied. (p. 13)

Achieving "active engagement with difference" is a key to the potential for MMMR to foster innovation in scientific practice; yet the notion requires further elaboration of two matters. The first is the problem of achieving interdisciplinary team science. The second is how to promote in the social scientific community greater awareness of and ability to address complexity and to engage in systems thinking.

Interdisciplinarity

To do MMMR well, it seems inevitable that studies must be conducted by a multidisciplinary, collaborative team of investigators each with particular ways of framing and studying a phenomenon. There are a variety of issues entailed in understanding the science of team science, and it is beyond the brief of this chapter to examine them carefully. Here we simply suggest several matters that must be explored.

Greene's (2007) idea of "inviting multiple mental models into the same inquiry space" inevitably raises the issue of ways of doing social inquiry characterized as an interdisciplinary approach to problem solving as opposed to the more familiar multidisciplinary approach. Klein (2007) distinguishes the two as follows:

Multidisciplinary approaches juxtapose separate disciplinary perspectives, adding breadth of knowledge, information, and methods. Individuals and groups work independently or sequentially in an encyclopedic alignment or ad hoc mix. They retain their separate perspectives. . . . Interdisciplinarity is conventionally defined as a more conscious and explicitly focused integration that creates a holistic view or common understanding of a complex issue, question or problem. (pp. 37–38)

The US National Academies (Committee on Facilitating Interdisciplinary Research, 2004) further adds that interdisciplinary research is

A mode of research by teams or individuals that integrates information, data, techniques, tools, perspectives, concepts, and/or theories from two or more disciplines or bodies of specialized knowledge to advance fundamental understanding or to solve problems whose solutions are beyond the scope of a single discipline or area of research practice. (p. 2)

Whether MMMR can be used as a heuristic that can leverage interdisciplinary innovation in communities of research practice is an empirical question. That question must be examined by assessing the nature of work, learning, and innovation in the context of actual communities of practice (Brown & Duguid, 1991). For example, we might examine whether the promotion of MMMR by the Office of Behavioral and Social Sciences Research of the National Institutes of Health (NIH) has actually resulted in interdisciplinary ways of addressing problems related to the sociocultural dimensions of health and the effectiveness of public health interventions.

There are, of course, cognitive, political, and sociological barriers to such innovation. As Hacking (1992) noted, communities of investigators and disciplines are characterized by styles of reasoning—not simply reasoning in private (mental models), but reasoning in public by talking, arguing, and showing—and a single investigator and a community of like-minded investigators are rarely at home in more than one style. This is perhaps not surprising given that, as Bruner (1990) once observed, researchers have a tendency to "seal themselves within their own rhetoric and within their own parish of authorities" (pp. ix–x). Hacking (p. 3) also made reference to Freeman Dyson's Gifford lectures of 1985 in which Dyson pointed out two general, contrasting styles of reasoning in the sciences—one welcoming diversity, the other deploring it; one trying to diversify, the other trying to unify. Embracing diversity seems quite central to interdisciplinarity and to thinking innovatively.

Styles of reasoning are also connected to the status hierarchy of the academic disciplines, and yielding on a preferred style of reasoning can be perceived as a threat to that status. The initial collaborative tenor of researchers from different disciplines and with different styles of reasoning working together on a problem can, in some instances, dissolve into sharp disagreements and power struggles as commitments to different ways of understanding tied to different explanatory programs become clearer to all involved (Lunde, Heggen, & Strand, 2013). Yet, even absent quarrels stemming from the politics of epistemology, working together in a research team across different explanatory programs involves challenges that all small groups seeking to work effectively together inevitably face—dealing with differences, trusting each other, creating a meaningful group, handling essential conflicts and tension, and enacting effective leadership roles (Curry et al., 2012). We cannot expect MMMR to be an all-encompassing framework in which all these issues are carefully and systematically addressed, but we can reasonably inquire into whether a justification for MMMR can be found in the notion that it supports interdisciplinary social science.

Systems Thinking and Complexity

In 2011, the Office of Behavioral and Social Sciences Research at the US NIH joined with 11 other NIH institutes to request research proposals to develop projects that used systems science methodologies relevant to understanding and explaining behavioral and social issues in health. In 2012, the NIH announced a funding opportunity to develop theory and methods to better understand complex social behavior through a systems perspective. The James S. McDonnell Foundation, as part of its 21st-century science initiative, called for research proposals to develop tools for the study of complex, adaptive, nonlinear systems in several fields, including demography, epidemiology, technological change, economic developments, and governance. The 2008 Global Science Forum of the Organisation for Economic Co-operation and Development focused on the importance of complexity science for public policy. These are few examples of how a systems perspective and ideas from complexity science are beginning to influence the ways in which we think about doing research useful in addressing social and behavioral problems.

There is a rapidly growing awareness in the community of social-behavioral researchers as well as among policymakers that longstanding reliance on reductive explanations, universal laws, and linear causal models as the apparatus for understanding and evaluating policy interventions is not a particularly useful kind of science for addressing complex systems and the uncertainty that attends them. Mitchell (2009), for example, argues that sole reliance on predict-and-act models of policymaking is mistaken; instead, both scientists and policymakers should emphasize robust adaptive planning—flexible management of the situation, continued investigation of alternative scientific solutions to problems, and close monitoring of both. A social science informed by a systems approach does not assume that policy interventions are neatly analyzable in terms of the success of their component parts. It holds that standard

intervention logic—namely, that participation in a social program leads to increased knowledge that leads to attitude change that leads to behavior change and that results in a desired outcome—is rarely an accurate description of how things work (Organisation for Economic Co-operation and Development, 2009). Hence, systems-based thinking suggests a shift away from the linear transfer project centered on establishing a reservoir of knowledge to be used "downstream" to solve social problems and toward a learning system that continuously draws on a variety of types of knowledge, in conjunction with experiential learning that occurs as policies are implemented in different contexts.

In discussing the relevance of systems thinking in the field of public health, Sterman (2006) argues that what he calls "policy resistance"—the fact that policies "often fail or worsen the problems they are intended to solve"—is in large part attributable to a "lack of a meaningful systems thinking capability" (p. 513). He adds,

> Where the world is dynamic, evolving, and interconnected, we tend to make decisions using mental models that are static, narrow, and reductionist. . . . Systems thinking is an iterative learning process in which we replace a reductionist, narrow, short-run, static view of the world with a holistic, broad, long-term dynamic view, reinventing our policies and institutions accordingly. (pp. 506, 509)

Mitchell (2009) notes that significant challenges to the tenets of traditional epistemology (universality, determinism, simplicity, and unification) arise from the "cutting edge science of complex systems" (p. 12). She argues for an expanded approach to epistemology that incorporates *pluralism,* integrating multiple explanations and models at many levels of analysis instead of always expecting a single bottom-level reductive explanation; *pragmatism,* in the place of absolutism, which recognizes there are many ways to accurately, if only partially, represent the nature of nature, including various degrees of generality and levels of abstraction and where which representation "works" best is dependent, in part, on our interests and abilities; and the *dynamic and evolving character of knowledge* in place of static universalism (p. 13, emphasis in original).

How MMMR fits with this evolving interest in a new social-behavioral science of complexity is yet another empirical question worthy of investigation in actual scientific practice. A quick search on the term *complexity* in issues of the *Journal of*

Mixed Methods Research reveals many instances of the appeal of MMMR for investigating and better understanding complexity of several kinds—the complexity of social and behavioral phenomena, the complexity of the effects of interventions (causal complexity), the complexity of processes, and the complexity of implementation of interventions. To the extent that this appeal resides in a well-articulated challenge to traditional epistemology, as Mitchell (2009) characterizes it, we might reasonably conclude that MMMR is one tool (or set of tools) that encourages an expanded approach to epistemology.

Thoughts for the Future of Multiple and Mixed Inquiry

One can defend the use of MMMR in scientific practice on epistemological grounds without recourse to complicated appeals to special definitions or paradigmatic justifications. On the one hand, there is a straightforward, practical argument that the combination of multiple methods yields more comprehensive understanding of a phenomenon. On the other hand, there is a more complicated argument that MMMR can potentially function as a catalyst of sorts facilitating both innovation in scientific practice and a new way of thinking about what knowledge of social phenomenon entails and how it is justified.

MMMR studies per se are not inherently innovative. Innovation is not necessarily a function of mixing methods, research designs, or paradigms. The promise of MMMR as supportive of innovation in scientific practice lies in the extent to which it can be demonstrated that it facilitates ways of researchers working together in interdisciplinary fashion to generate knowledge claims that display "critical reflection on the social roles and values of the research team, the social processes of generating evidence, the role of substantive theory in conceptualizing the evidence, and how the evidence fits with background theory" (Avis, 2003, p. 1003). Whether the deployment of MMMR strategies is consonant with the development of a new interdisciplinary social science that embraces complexity and an accompanying refinement to ways in which we conceptualize the world, investigate that world, and act in it (Mitchell, 2009, p. 18) remains to be seen.

Discussion Questions

1. How would one go about bolstering the argument for the practical utility of MMMR?

2. In what ways might MMMR be helpful in developing an expanded approach to epistemology?

3. What organizational arrangements, funding, and other kinds of supports need to be in place in order for scholars to adopt MMMR in ways that foster interdisciplinary team science?

Suggested Websites

https://ccrod.cancer.gov/confluence/display/NIHOMBUD/Home

http://sites.nationalacademies.org/DBASSE/BBCSS/CurrentProjects/DBASSE_080231#.UZFKaODirN4)

http://www.aaas.org/cspsp/interdisciplinary/guide/

http://www.teamsciencetoolkit.cancer.gov/Public/GetStarted.aspx

References

Abbott, A. (2004). *Methods of discovery: Heuristics for the social sciences.* New York, NY: W. W. Norton.

Avis, M. (2003). Do we need methodological theory to do qualitative research? *Qualitative Health Research, 13*(7), 995–1004.

Brown, J. S., & Duguid, P. (1991). Organizational learning and communities of practice: Toward a unified theory of working, learning and innovation. *Organizational Science, 2*(1), 40–57.

Bruner, J. (1990). *Acts of meaning.* Cambridge, MA: Harvard University Press.

Committee on Facilitating Interdisciplinary Research. (2004). *Facilitating interdisciplinary research.* Washington, DC: National Academies Press.

Creswell, J. W., & Plano Clark, V. I. (2011). *Designing and conducting mixed methods research* (2nd ed.). Los Angeles, CA: Sage.

Curry, L. A., Nembhard, I. M., & Bradley, E. H. (2009). Qualitative and mixed methods provide unique contributions to outcome research. *Circulation, 119,* 1442–1452.

Curry, L. A., O'Cathain, A., Plano Clark, V. L., Aroni, R., Fetters, M., & Berg, D. (2012). The role of group dynamics in mixed methods health sciences research teams. *Journal of Mixed Methods Research, 6*(1), 5–20.

Denscombe, M. (2008). Communities of practice: A research paradigm for the mixed methods approach. *Journal of Mixed Methods Research, 2*(3), 270–283.

Feilzer, M. Y. (2010). Doing mixed methods research pragmatically: Implications for the rediscovery of pragmatism as a research paradigm. *Journal of Mixed Methods Research, 4*(1), 6–16.

Greene, J. C. (2007). *Mixed methods in social inquiry.* San Francisco, CA: Wiley.

Hacking, I. (1992). "Style" for historians and philosophers. *Studies in the History and Philosophy of Science, 23*(1), 1–20.

Harrits, G. S. (2011). More than method? A discussion of paradigm differences within mixed methods research. *Journal of Mixed Methods Research, 5*(2), 150–166.

Hunter, A., & Brewer, J. (2003). Multimethod research in sociology. In A. Taskkori & C. Teddlie (Eds.), *Handbook of mixed methods in social & behavioral research* (pp. 577–594). Thousand Oaks, CA: Sage.

Johnson, R. B., & Onwuegbuzie, A. T. (2006). Mixed methods research: A research paradigm whose time has come. *Educational Researcher, 33*(7), 14–26.

Johnson, R. B., Onwuegbuzie, A. T., & Turner, L. A. (2007). Toward a definition of mixed method research. *Journal of Mixed Methods Research, 1*(2), 112–133.

Klein, J. T. (2007). Interdisciplinary approaches in social science research. In W. Outhwaite & S. P. Turner (Eds.), *Handbook of social science methodology* (pp. 32–49). Los Angeles, CA: Sage.

Lunde, Å., Heggen, K., & Strand, R. (2013). Knowledge and power: Exploring unproductive interplay between quantitative and qualitative researchers. *Journal of Mixed Methods Research.* doi:10.1177/1558689812471087

Mertens, D. M. (2003). Mixed methods and the politics of human research: The transformative-emancipatory perspective. In A. Tasakkori & C. Teddlie (Eds.), *Handbook of mixed methods in social & behavioral research* (pp. 135–2164). Thousand Oaks, CA: Sage.

Mitchell, S. D. (2009). *Unsimple truths: Science, complexity, and policy.* Chicago, IL: University of Chicago Press.

Morgan, D. L. (2007). Paradigms lost and pragmatism regained: Methodological implications of combining qualitative and quantitative methods. *Journal of Mixed Methods Research, 1*(1), 48–76.

Morse, J. M. (2003). Principles of mixed methods and multimethod research design. In A. Tasakkori & C. Teddlie (Eds.), *Handbook of mixed methods in social & behavioral research* (pp. 189–208). Thousand Oaks, CA: Sage.

Organisation for Economic Co-operation and Development. (2009). *Applications of complexity science for public policy: New tools for finding unanticipated consequences and unrealized opportunities.* Paris, France: Author.

Palinkas, L. A., Aarons, G. A., Horwitz, S., Chamberlain, P., Hurlburt, M., & Landsverk, J. (2011). Mixed methods designs in implementation research. *Administration and Policy in Mental Health, 38*(1), 44–53.

Ragin, C. C., & Amaroso, L. (2011). *Constructing social research: The unity and diversity of method.* Thousand Oaks, CA: Pine Forge Press.

Small, M. L. (2011). How to conduct a mixed methods study: Recent trends in a rapidly growing literature. *Annual Review of Sociology, 37*, 57–86.

Sterman, J. D. (2006). Learning from evidence in a complex world. *American Journal of Public Health, 96*(3), 505–514.

Teddlie, C., & Tashakkori, A. (2009). *Foundations of mixed methods research.* Los Angeles, CA: Sage.

White, H. (2009). Theory-based impact evaluation: Principles and practice. *Journal of Development Effectiveness, 1*(3), 271–284.

Mixed Methods and the Problems of Theory Building and Theory Testing in the Social Sciences

Udo Kelle

Abstract

This chapter shows how mixed methods can be used to deal with challenges of relating empirical data to theoretical concepts in empirical research. Three strategies of theory use (application, testing, and building of theories) and their problems are discussed: applying theory to empirical data may lead to arbitrary results, a deductive model of theory testing may fail due to a lack of auxiliary assumptions, and theory building will go astray if the role of previous theoretical knowledge is not acknowledged. The role of mixed methods designs in theory building and testing is also discussed: in designs focused on exploration, theoretical categories can be developed with qualitative methods and their generalizability can be examined with quantitative methods. In other forms of mixed methods designs, quantitative data can be used to identify empirical explananda and to construct sampling frames for a subsequent qualitative study in which quantitative findings are explained.

Key Words: theory building, theory testing, empirical research, theory use, empirical data, explanation, induction, deduction

Introduction

Regarding he relation between theory and data, "the link between observation and formulation is one of the most difficult and crucial of the scientific enterprises" (Scott Greer, 1969, p. 160). This holds especially true for the multi-paradigmatic social sciences where competing theories exist for almost every research field. This, however, is an issue frequently overlooked in methodological debates, in literature about research methods, and also in current discussions about mixed methods, which usually focus on questions of design structure, on the use of methods in the research process, and on philosophical and metatheoretical foundations of mixed methods research.

This chapter addresses problems of theory use that occur in qualitative and quantitative research (some of which have been discussed for a long time now) and discusses how these difficulties

can (at least partly) be overcome with the help of mixed methods designs and mixed methods research. Mixed methods can provide solutions for a perennial and often bemoaned problem of social research—the gap between theoretical concepts and empirical data.[1]

The strategies developed in the history of social science methodology to cope with that problem, namely the hypothetico-deductive approach (popular in quantitative research) and the idea of inductive theory generation from empirical data (that plays an important role in the qualitative research tradition) have clear limits, which will be discussed in the following. However, problems of theory building and testing arising in quantitative and qualitative research can be treated through a combination of methods from both traditions.

I start by describing the crucial challenge of theory use in empirical research—empirical data have to be related to networks of theoretical concepts. Thereafter, three basic strategies of theory use in research (the application, the testing, and the building of theories) are discussed and their problems examined: applying theory to empirical data may lead to arbitrary results, a strict hypothetico-deductive model of theory testing may fail due to a lack of necessary auxiliary assumptions, and theory building will go astray if the role of previous theoretical knowledge is not adequately taken into account.

These problems can be dealt with in mixed methods designs, and the functions of two different mixed methods designs for theory building and theory testing are discussed in the final part of the chapter. First, in a sequential qualitative-quantitative design focused on exploration, empirically grounded theoretical concepts can be developed with the help of qualitative methods, and their generalizability and transferability can be examined by using quantitative methods. Second, in a sequential quantitative-qualitative design, quantitative data are used to identify empirical phenomena that need to be explained (the "explananda") as well as to construct a sampling frame for a subsequent qualitative study that may provide deeper theoretical explanations for findings from the quantitative part of the design. This design could then be supplemented by a further quantitative study that allows for more formal testing of the mechanisms and theoretical explanations developed during the qualitative component.

The Crucial Task: Relating Empirical Observations and Theoretical Concepts to Each Other

"Empirical science has two major objectives: to describe particular phenomena in the world of our experience and to establish general principles by means of which they can be explained and predicted" (Hempel, 1952, p. 1). Such "particular phenomena in the world of our experience" mentioned by Carl Gustav Hempel in his classic concept of a "covering law model" of scientific research may be addressed as "empirical observations" or "data"; the "general principles"[2] are described by theoretical statements. However, the relation between theoretical statements and empirical data is a highly debated and contested issue in the social sciences. Different ideas and models have been developed to adequately understand and describe this relation— all of them having certain limitations and leading to specific problems in research practice. Therefore

it is of utmost importance that, when using concepts (of varying degrees of abstractness), it is possible to clarify their relevance for concrete research processes. For this purpose one may have a look at a famous metaphor Hempel invented: a theory may be compared to

> a complex spatial network: its terms are represented by the knots, while the threads connecting the latter correspond, in part to the definitions and, in part, to the fundamental and derivative hypotheses included in the theory. The whole system floats, as it were, above the plane of observation and is anchored to it by rules of interpretation." (p. 36)

With these remarks Hempel refers to the fact that theoretical terms and empirical observations cannot easily be related to each other. Empirical observations have to be interpreted in a certain way so that they can be understood in terms of certain theoretical concepts. These interpretations, however, must be governed by rules. These rules

> might be viewed as strings which are not part of the network but link certain points of the latter with specific places in the plane of observation. By virtue of those interpretative connections, the network can function as a scientific theory: From certain observational data, we may ascend, via an interpretive string, to some point in the theoretical network, thence proceed, via definitions and hypotheses to other points, from which another interpretive string permits a descent to the plane of observation. (Hempel, 1952, p. 36)

There are basically two ways to "descend" from the network of theoretical statements to the "plane of observation": theories can be *applied* to empirical observation and theories can be *tested* with the help of empirical data. To "ascend" from the plane of empirical observation would mean to construct or *build* theories on the basis of empirical data.

Let us now consider these three ways of connecting theory and data and the problems they may create in research practice: the application, the testing and the construction or building of theories.

Theory Application and the Problems of Ex Post Facto Explanations

The most common way to connect theory and data is the application of theoretical concepts to empirical observations—an exercise every student is called on to learn when starting his or her studies: a piece of theory (which may be a single concept or statement embedded in a more general network of other concepts and statements) is used to describe, understand, or explain an empirical fact. Thereby, in the social sciences the term *empirical fact* can be applied to a great variety of differing objects or events, ranging from single events to statistical facts describing a general state of a given society. A straightforward example of a single social encounter can serve as an example: a person is selling illegal drugs to someone else. Drawing on theoretical terms commonly used in sociology and criminology, one might see this as a typical instance of "deviant behavior." By this, one does not only apply a single concept ("deviance") to an empirical observation; one also relates this event to a more general network of sociological theories (ranging from most the abstract and general sociological concepts to middle range or even local theories). The observed act of drug selling can be regarded, for instance, as a transgression of the normative order of a given society. In this manner the application of the term *deviance* to the data can be viewed as a theoretical *description*; in the next step one can make an attempt to also *explain* this particular deviant behavior by drawing on theories of deviant behavior: one may, for instance, use structural strain theory for this purpose, thus making the assumption that the observed transgression is a consequence of the fact that the drug-selling person is not able to reach culturally accepted goals with the help of socially approved means. This strategy of ex post facto explanation (i.e., "after the fact" explanation) can be employed with statistical facts likewise—one can also use structural strain theory to account for a statistical correlation between unemployment and criminal behavior. However, it will be equally possible to explain a single instance of drug-selling behavior (or a statistical correlation between unemployment and crime) by applying another theoretical approach, for instance social control theory. In this case, one would see the deviant behavior as a result of a weakening of the perpetrator's social bonds to nondeviant groups. In his metaphor Hempel (1952) had used the term *interpretive string* to denote the links between theory and empirical observation—the relation between the "plane of observation" and the network of theoretical statements obviously involves acts of interpretation, as it can be easily seen from these examples.

A serious problem comes into play here: A specific empirical fact, be it a single event or a statistical figure, can frequently be explained by various (possibly mutually exclusive) theories. Thereby,

different theoretical explanations for the same empirical observation may easily contradict each other. This is a well-known philosophical problem of any kind of scientific research, described, for instance, by John Stuart Mill (1872) in his "System of Logic":

> most thinkers of any degree of sobriety allow, that an hypothesis. . . is not received as probably true because it accounts for all the known phenomena; since this is a condition sometimes fulfilled tolerably well by two conflicting hypotheses; while there are probably many others which are equally possible, but which, for want of anything analogous in our experience, our minds are unfitted to conceive. (Mill, 1872, p. 21)

In more current debates about the philosophical underpinnings of empirical research this problem has also been referred to as "underdetermination of theory by evidence" (cf. Phillips & Burbules, 2000, p. 17). To illuminate the problem with the help of an example: a comparably high crime rate among immigrants can be attributed to differing cultural norms between the immigrants' culture and the host society but can also be explained by the existence of discriminatory practices of legal authorities that treat foreigners unfairly. To make the situation even worse, a sociobiologist may explain differences between crime rates among different ethnic groups as a consequence of genetic differences between these groups.

As a consequence, the mere application of theoretical concepts to empirical observations can lead to the formulation of varying and even contradictory ex post facto explanations, especially since a great variety of different and even competing theoretical networks is available in the social sciences.

Theory Testing and the Problem of Insufficient Bridge Assumptions

One can try to avoid the arbitrariness of ex post facto descriptions and explanations by using another strategy to link theory and data: the evaluation of theoretical concepts with the help of empirical observations obtained after making a theory based prediction. The idea of a "rigorous" empirical testing of theories and hypotheses is most clearly described by the "hypothetico-deductive" (HD) approach, which is an influential philosophical model for quantitative research (although this model is often highly valued in course books but neglected in research practice). The application of the HD model requires that before collecting empirical data researchers had to precisely formulate theoretical hypotheses that consist of terms and propositions with high empirical content or high "falsifiability." In other words, theoretical statements have to be constructed, and the research process has to be designed in such a way that possible–counter-evidence (empirical data that may disprove the hypotheses) can emerge.

This methodological textbook model of scientific inquiry, inspired by the ideas of Karl Popper (1959) about falsifiability of theories as a basic precondition of scientific progress, is often extremely difficult to put into research practice—which is due to some deeper lying methodological problems of this approach: for several reasons the social sciences very rarely provide us with theoretical concepts on a high level of generality and abstraction that can easily be tested (or "disproved") with the help of empirical data. This problem has led to intensive debates among advocates of theoretical approaches with strong affiliations to HD research, namely theories of rational choice or rational action (Esser, 1998; Kelle & Lüdemann, 1998). It is usually conceded that the core assumptions of rational action theory (which may take the form "given a set of alternatives, actors will choose the action that to them seems the most appropriate for achieving desired goal[s]") do not allow for the deduction or empirically contentful (i.e., testable) statements on their own. To test such a statement it must be possible to derive clear-cut predictions of human behavior from it. But without specifying which goals an actor pursues and which actions he or she considers to be adequate, the previous sentence simply has no empirical content.

> Assumptions of value, expectation, and belief. . . have to be added to the models before they can yield predictions of behavior. Authors who use rational choice models are not always conscious of the extent to which their conclusions are independent of the assumptions of those models, but depend, instead, mainly upon auxiliary assumptions. (Simon, 1985, p. 300)

Such auxiliary assumptions have been called *bridge assumptions* or *bridge hypotheses* (cf. Kelle & Lüdemann, 1998; Lindenberg, 1992), statements and concepts that bridge a gap between highly abstract theoretical concepts (e.g., concepts of "rational action") and empirical data. Without specifying such bridge assumptions, rational action theory has a "(quite empty) core" (Lindenberg, 1992, p. 6) that means that it would

not be possible to derive empirically contentful (i.e., testable or "falsifiable") statements from the theoretical core alone. The same holds true for theoretical definitions and categories from other sociological "grand theories"—categories like "identity," "status," "roles," "systems," "structure," and the like—usually lack empirical content: their broadness and abstractness makes it difficult, if not impossible, to directly deduce empirically testable propositions from them. As an example one could take the statement, "A social role defines the expected behavior connected to a given social status." An empirical test providing counter-evidence to such a sentence is hard to imagine—a person who tries to find a counter-example (that means a social role *not* defining behavior connected to a certain status) would even demonstrate thereby that he or she does not understand this statement, which is not meant to be directly tested through empirical data but to define a particular category ("social role").

Each general theory in the social sciences entails or at least refers to categories and assumptions of that kind, of which the most important represent the basic axioms (or paradigmatic assumptions) of theoretical traditions. In order to follow a HD approach by deducing empirically testable statements from such basic assumptions one must invent bridge assumptions of various kinds. In the case of rational action theory, these would be assumptions about the expectations or beliefs of the actors in the investigated domain; in the case of the term *social role* one would need bridge assumptions that describe concrete expectations regarding a certain role in a specific organization; and so on.

Information needed to formulate bridge assumptions is often domain specific and context dependent—it is part of culturally or subculturally specific stocks of everyday knowledge of the actors in the field. Being themselves members of the investigated (or similar and comparable) life worlds, social researchers often use a "heuristic of common sense knowledge"—bridge hypotheses are formulated based on personal knowledge and own experiences. This often causes no major problems, especially if research takes place within the researcher's own culture or subculture where he or she has access to everyday knowledge. But since a great deal of this knowledge is self-evident or implicit, the application of this heuristic strategy is usually not discussed explicitly. This methodology of theory construction usually remains in the shadows—many (if not most) quantitative researchers employ it at least from time to time but often fail to systematically reflect on the use of such a strategy of theory building. However, the shortcomings of such a "shadow methodology" are obvious if foreign cultures or unfamiliar domestic subcultures are investigated—social researchers often do not possess sufficient knowledge to formulate hypotheses about the actors' preferences, about expectations connected to certain roles, and so on. Within the context of a HD approach, which requires that theoretical concepts and hypotheses are formulated before empirical data are collected, this problem cannot be solved. This is exactly the point where qualitative research and mixed methods come into play; one would need empirical methods to gain access to knowledge initially not available to researchers—methods, in other words, for the empirically grounded construction of bridge hypotheses.

Theory Building and Problems of Transferability and Generalization

Strategies for generating theoretical concepts with the help of empirical data have been developed mainly in the context of qualitative research. The most prominent among these approaches has become famous under the label *grounded theory methodology*. In their renowned monograph "The Discovery of Grounded Theory," Barney Glaser and Anselm Strauss (1967) provided a strategy of empirical research whereby empirical data are not used to test ready-made hypotheses—the authors opted instead for an "initial, systematic discovery of the theory from the data of social research" (p. 3) whereby categories and statements are considered to be empirically "grounded," if they "emerge" from the data. Since too much of previous theoretical knowledge could lead to a "forcing" of inappropriate theoretical concepts on the data, Glaser and Strauss recommended "literally to ignore the literature of theory and fact on the area under study, in order to assure that the emergence of categories will not be contaminated" (p. 37). Such remarks reflect an inductivist model of theory building that at least one of the two authors, Barney Glaser, strongly advocated until nowadays (for more details see Kelle 2007, 2013). The roots of this model can be traced back to the philosophy of early empiricism: empiricist philosophers in the 17th and 18th century proposed the idea that sound scientific theories are derived by a rigorous generalization from observables. According to the philosopher Francis Bacon, for instance, researchers must free

their minds from any theoretical preconceptions before entering their research field for that purpose. However, such an idea leads to unsolvable problems, as Immanuel Kant had already shown. Nowadays, it is one of the most widely accepted insights of epistemology and cognitive psychology that "there are and can be no sensations unimpregnated by expectations" (Lakatos, 1978, p. 15) and that the construction of theories cannot be based on data alone but must draw on already existing knowledge, since "the world is always perceived through the 'lenses' of some conceptual network or other and that such networks and the languages in which they are embedded may, for all we know, provide an ineliminable 'tint' to what we perceive" (Laudan, 1977, p. 15). The reason for that is "seeing is a 'theory-laden' undertaking. Observation of x is shaped by prior knowledge of x" (Hanson, 1965, p. 19). The term *theory-ladenness* coined by Hanson is now often used in epistemological debates to denote the fact that in research there is no such thing as a "mere observation" with no reference to any theoretical concept or idea whatsoever.

Glaser and Strauss (1967) did not fully overlook this problem, however: "Of course, the researcher does not approach reality as a tabula rasa. He (*sic*) must have a perspective that will help him see relevant data and abstract significant categories from his scrutiny of the data" (p. 3). This competence to reflect on empirical data in theoretical terms was named *theoretical sensitivity* by Glaser and Strauss, a faculty that builds up "in the sociologist an armamentarium of categories and hypotheses. . . . This theory that exists within a sociologist can be used in generating his specific theory" (p. 46). In their own empirical work, Glaser and Strauss employed a strategy of theory building that was very much in accordance with the already described procedure of constructing bridge hypotheses based on general, abstract theoretical notions on the one hand and empirical data on the other hand. In their well-known study about "Awareness of Dying" they write:

> Shortly after Glaser and Strauss joined forces, they systematically worked out the concepts (and types) of death experiences and awareness contexts, and the paradigm for the study of awareness contexts. Thus, a concern with death expectations and awareness guided the preliminary data collection. (Glaser & Strauss, 1965, p. 287)

Their theoretical concepts explaining interactions between doctors, hospital staff, and moribund patients thus did not "emerge from the data" alone: the idea that social interaction is structured by the actors' knowledge and expectations as well as by "mutual awareness" of such knowledge and expectations is one of the most important tenets of symbolic interactionism.

In later writings Glaser and Strauss described the role of grand theories for empirically grounded theory building in greater detail: Barney Glaser invented the terms *theoretical coding* and *theoretical codes* (Glaser, 1978) to denote terms that help in developing empirically grounded categories from the data. Glaser advises the researcher to draw thereby on an extended list of 14 "coding families"—theoretical codes stemming from different sociological and philosophical grand theories, such as the "degree family," which contains terms referring to the degree of an attribute or property, like *limit, range, extent, amount,* and so on or the "cultural family" encompassing terms relating to cultural phenomena like *social norms, social values, social beliefs,* and others.

Strauss (partly together with Juliet Corbin) proposed a similar and less complicated strategy to structure qualitative data with the help of general and abstract theoretical concepts: a model of action derived from pragmatist and interactionist social theory (cf. Corbin, 1991, p. 36) called the "coding paradigm" (Strauss, 1987, p. 18f.; Strauss & Corbin, 1990, p. 99ff.) should serve as the "axis" of the core category and the developing grounded theory.

With "theoretical" (Glaser, 1978) or "axial coding" (Strauss & Corbin, 1990), concepts from grand or (as Glaser and Strauss preferred to say) "formal" theories are used to develop empirically grounded "substantive theories," categories, and statements that help to describe, understand, and explain phenomena in a given research field. However, the research field in which the substantive theory is "grounded" may be very small, due to the usual limitations of qualitative field work and data analysis. Conducting and analyzing a small number of interviews can be a tedious and cumbersome task—qualitative research is typically "small-*N* research." One may now ask whether theories grounded in empirical data from such limited research fields can be considered "real" theories, at least if one refers to Hempel's (1952) already quoted definitions, which require that theoretical statements describing and explaining empirical observations be "general principles." According to Hempel, this term denotes universal laws valid regardless of time and space. It is exactly this point where Hempel's approach comes into trouble—such an understanding of the term *theory* would imply that social action and interaction is governed by stable and timeless ahistoric rules or laws, an idea that is highly controversial in the social sciences. Important and established theoretical schools of thought in the social sciences have disputed this claim. Adherents of symbolic interactionism (an approach that formulated basic theoretical tenets for qualitative research; see, e.g., Blumer, 1969) would argue, for instance, that social interaction always entails acts of interpretation and that this leads to a great complexity, variability, and uniqueness of social phenomena and to the fact that social rules are always context-bound and flexible. If one adopts such a perspective and simultaneously wants to retain the notion of *theory* in social research, one must use this term in a way that it refers to (spatio-temporally) limited domains. Robert Merton's (1949) concept of "theories of the middle range" points in that direction; these are theories that

> lie between the minor but necessary working hypotheses that evolve in abundance during day-to-day research and the all inclusive systematic efforts to develop a unified theory that will explain all the observed uniformities of social behavior, social organizations, and social change. (p. 38)

With respect to that concept, Mario Bunge (1996, p. 121ff.) has proposed a further differentiation: apart from grand theories and theories of the middle range, theories of "narrow range" play an important role the social sciences. However, even if one limits the confines of a given empirically grounded theory to the middle or narrow range, one still cannot bypass further questions about its concrete scope: Is the concerned theory only applicable to the field where the data of research were collected (be it a specific hospital, a school, a village, or the like), or does it also pertain to similar or comparable hospitals, schools, villages? Adherents of the qualitative research tradition who follow poststructuralist or postmodern approaches like Norman Denzin, Egon Guba, or Yvonna Lincoln have even argued that the principle of context-boundedness of social phenomena may us lead to a general renouncement of any attempt to generalize (cf., e.g., Lincoln & Guba, 1985, 2000).

However, in the social sciences there is an urgent need for a more limited form of generalization that falls between the extremes of lawlike generalizations valid regardless of time and space on the one hand and statements about concrete singular events on the other hand, since it is easier said than done to simply abandon the whole idea of generalization—the investigation of a single person, group, and organization can be, of course, a research goal justified in itself but poses the danger of focusing on marginal cases, whereby this marginality must remain unnoticed if one abandons any idea of generalization. This would cause even more problems if one adheres to the interpretivist postulate that social order is highly flexible and evolves through processes of interpretation in micro-social contexts. The resulting pluralization and heterogeneity of social structures and patterns of action poses serious challenges for any methodological approach that relies on the investigation of small numbers of cases. The question of whether one captures structural patterns relevant for a certain group, culture, or society with the investigated cases or whether one describes mere idiosyncrasies cannot be dismissed.

Thus it is difficult in social research to avoid questions like: To which kinds of people, groups, organizations, and so on does the knowledge derived from a certain study also apply? To address this question, the term *transferability* was proposed as an alternative to *generalizability* in the context of qualitative research (Lincoln & Guba, 2000). However, transferability and generalizability are notions closely related to each other, especially since the latter term does not necessarily imply generalization toward universal laws valid in all places at all times but can also refer to theoretical statements of the middle or narrow range. Any research project aiming at the investigation of groups, organizations, cultures, societies, and so on as limited wholes situated in concrete spatiotemporal contexts has to address such questions of limited context- and time-bound generalization (or *transferability,* if one prefers that term), for instance: Is a certain pattern of interaction that is occurring between dying patients, their relatives, and hospital staff prevalent only in one single hospital ward where the research took place? Or does it represent a more general pattern of dealing with death and dying in our society? Do certain problems experienced by teachers at a particular school reflect deeper lying problems of the whole organization or of schools in a certain state or country, or are these problems only an expression of the situation in that specific school? One needs not to cling to the idea of universal social laws to think about possible scopes and ranges of application of a given theory. The most feasible way to address these questions would certainly be to apply new theories of a limited range (developed, for instance, to study a certain kind of social action and interaction in a certain school) to closely related areas (e.g., another school of the same or a similar type). Since middle or narrow range concepts and statements stemming from qualitative research projects contain real empirical content (compared to abstract and general notions from grand theories), researchers can now apply a hypothetico-deductive approach and quantitative methods to examine whether patterns found in one domain also exist in related areas. Especially if organizations, groups, or other social life worlds are investigated, where heterogeneous norms and patterns of action exist, the use of quantitative methods can be extremely helpful in capturing such diversity. Interestingly enough, this point was made early by one of the founders of symbolic interactionism and advocate of qualitative methods, Herbert Blumer (1928), who maintained that statistical methods are important research tools, since they take into account the "complexity, variability or uniqueness" of social phenomena (p. 47f.). The interpretive tradition of social research itself thus provides arguments in favor of "the importance of statistical analysis" (Hammersley, 1989, p. 219): quantitative research can capture social heterogeneity by providing information about great numbers of persons or situations.

Especially mixed methods designs therefore offer possibilities to deal with the sometimes limited transferability of qualitative findings. However, the notion of "theory testing" may be misleading, since it can evoke the ideas that one tries to establish the truth or falsehood of universal statements instead of examining the boundaries of concepts with limited ranges.

Functions of Theory in Different Mixed Methods Designs

Up to now we have discussed basic strengths and limitations of quantitative and qualitative methods in dealing with the challenges of linking theory and data: the strengths of quantitative research based on a hypothetico-deductive approach lie in the possibility to apply and test empirically contentful categories and statements. But researchers will get in trouble with such an approach if empirically testable theoretical concepts are not available for the investigated field. In such cases, bridge assumptions have to be developed, drawing on specific information from the field that cannot be obtained with pure HD research.

Qualitative research allows for an empirically grounded construction of categories and thus represents a powerful tool to generate bridge assumptions, which transform abstract theoretical notions into empirically contentful descriptions and explanations of concrete phenomena. Empirically grounded concepts of that kind are (contrary to abstract concepts from grand theories) not context-free; they always pertain to a limited range of empirical fields (peoples, groups, organizations, and the like). Qualitative research thus inevitably raises questions about the (context-bound) generalizability or transferability of findings.

One of the strongest arguments in favor of mixed methods designs is that they offer "a strategy for overcoming each method's weaknesses and limitations by deliberately combining different types of methods" (Brewer & Hunter, 1989, p. 11; see also Hunter & Brewer, 2003). Johnson and Christensen (2014) elaborated this idea slightly as follows:

> [The fundamental principle of mixed research. . .] advises researchers to thoughtfully and strategically mix or combine qualitative and quantitative research methods, approaches, procedures, concepts, and other paradigm characteristics in a way that produces an overall design with multiple (convergent and divergent) and complementary strengths (broadly viewed) and nonoverlapping weaknesses. (p. 663)

The question now would be: How can qualitative and quantitative methods be combined to compensate for limitations that occur in both methodological traditions in dealing with the task of linking theory and data? It should have become clear from the preceding discussion that the qualitative and quantitative tradition each have certain difficulties in closing specific gaps between theory and empirical observations frequently occurring in social research: quantitative researchers who rely exclusively on the HD model often experience serious difficulties in finding useful bridge assumptions (and then resort to a "shadow methodology" of common sense knowledge; see previous discussion). Due to the very nature of qualitative inquiry, qualitative researchers must restrict themselves to a thorough analysis of small numbers of cases. On this basis they may develop excellent thick descriptions and even explanations about a rather limited domain of society without being able to provide any information about the scope and range of such findings. Qualitative research is usually embedded in a social science framework—it takes place in a context of academic disciplines that investigate structures and processes on a societal macro level. Qualitative research itself, however, focuses on the micro level of daily social action and interaction. Bridging the gap between empirical observations on the micro level and theoretical statements on the societal macro level through acts of epistemologically responsible generalizations is an ambitious and complex endeavor.

A complete and detailed overview of how problems of theory building and testing may be treated in mixed methods designs would go beyond the scope of this chapter—but the following considerations may show how some of the basic problems mentioned earlier are addressed by using sequential mixed methods designs.

In a sequential qualitative-quantitative design (QUAL→ QUAN) a qualitative study can be used to develop empirically grounded theoretical concepts and hypotheses with the help of a small number of cases, and a subsequent quantitative study may be carried out to examine the range of the already developed concepts (which means their applicability to other and similar domains). Such a strategy of mixing qualitative and quantitative methods has also been called an "exploratory design" in the literature (Creswell & Plano-Clark, 2007, p. 75ff.). However, the purpose of the design is not just exploration, since the "limited generalizability" of concepts and theories (developed in the first qualitative stage of the design) for other domains is examined during the second quantitative stage. One could call this an "exploratory-confirmatory design" (Johnson, personal communication) if one does not lose sight of the fact that quantitative methods are not used to "test" or "prove" theoretical concepts in the strict sense (used, e.g., in experimental research) but to assess the transferability and applicability of certain hypotheses or theoretical concepts to similar and comparable domains. Such a design can be employed to treat classical problems of qualitative and quantitative research with regard to theory testing and theory building the problem that the range (transferability and generalizability) of qualitative findings can be particularly doubtful if these findings are based on small numbers of cases and the problem that adequate bridge hypotheses can often not be formulated in quantitative research projects due to a lack of context-related, local, or culture-specific knowledge. In a sequential qualitative-quantitative design, researchers may obtain information from the field in the initial qualitative study that helps to develop empirically grounded and contentful theoretical concepts and hypotheses and that can be used to construct quantitative research instruments suited for the domain under study. The subsequent quantitative study then serves for the examination of the range and the limits of the theoretical concepts developed in the qualitative part of the design. Such an approach, already proposed by Paul Lazarsfeld and Allan Barton (1969) decades ago, is sometimes criticized for restricting qualitative research to unsystematic pilot studies. However, qualitative studies as part of mixed methods designs will provide valuable results only if they are carried out in a systematic way so that theoretical descriptions and explanations are really grounded in the (possibly small number of) investigated cases. This can hardly be accomplished with a casual pilot study but requires a considerable amount of resources.

The incomprehensibility of many statistical phenomena represents a classical problem for quantitative research. Quantitative researchers are often faced with the need to explain and understand unanticipated quantitative findings. This may either be the case if hypotheses are falsified by surprising empirical data or if quantitative research does not follow the HD model but is carried out for mere descriptive purposes. Theories that can explain such unexpected findings (and especially bridge assumptions that close the gap between general theoretical terms and statistical data) are often not available, and researchers would have to draw on additional context-related knowledge from the field.

This classical problem of quantitative research can be treated in a sequential quantitative-qualitative design (QUAN → QUAL) where "qualitative data helps explain or build upon initial quantitative results." Such a design is sometimes called an "explanatory design" (Creswell & Plano-Clark, 2007, p. 71). This label, however, may lead to misunderstandings: explanations also play an important role both in quantitative and qualitative monomethod design. In quantitative research, for instance, explanations for statistical facts are formulated by drawing on available theoretical concepts. The particular strength of a sequential quantitative-qualitative design comes into play if theories at hand are not sufficient to develop meaningful explanations—in this case a subsequent qualitative study may provide additional information that helps to construct bridge assumptions. In such a design, quantitative research helps to define

problem areas and research questions by empirically identifying "explananda," statistical social phenomena that need to be explained. These phenomena are further investigated during the qualitative part of the mixed methods study in order to develop empirically grounded explanations.

Furthermore, the quantitative part of such a design can help to solve problems of generalizability and transferability of qualitative findings: quantitative data can guide systematic case comparison in the subsequent qualitative study by helping to identify criteria for the selection of cases and by providing a "qualitative sampling frame." This mixed methods strategy of qualitative sampling can easily be combined with different forms of purposive selection of cases via maximization or minimization of differences that were developed in the qualitative research tradition to cope with problems of transferability, like "theoretical sampling" (Glaser & Strauss, 1967, p. 45ff.). Quantitative findings can also inform and support other types of purposeful qualitative sampling, for example, the search for extreme, deviant, or typical cases (Patton, 2002; cf. also Silverman, 2000, p. 102f; Gobo, 2004). The quantitative part of a mixed methods design may, for instance, give an overview about the distribution of certain problems, structures, or patterns of action relevant for the overall research question. Or, by employing a "participant selection model" (Creswell & Plano Clark, 2007, p. 74), the quantitative study may provide a sampling frame that allows for a comfortable selection of typical, deviant, or extreme cases. Thus a mixed methods design can be helpful to deal with an important threat for validity of qualitative research—a focus on remote and marginal cases.

A further problem often experienced in qualitative research can be also treated with this design: since a quantitative study can capture heterogeneity in the field by describing the distribution of predefined phenomena, quantitative data may help to avoid a qualitative study with an "oversized scope," which is a study with a research domain too heterogeneous to be captured by a small qualitative sample. To take an easy example: a qualitative study about the influence of family forms on the academic achievement of students nowadays must take into account more different forms of families than a similar study in a traditional rural community in the beginning of the 20th century. By drawing on statistical information about the distribution of different family forms, researchers can learn about minimal requirements for qualitative sampling and may downsize the research question and research domain (to a limited number of family forms with a certain social background) such that it can be covered by the planned investigation.

Conclusions and Suggestions for Future Directions

The relation between empirical knowledge and social theory is a perennial issue in theoretical and methodological debates in the social sciences. In this chapter some of the most crucial problems of theory building and theory testing in social research have been discussed. Some of these problems arise from the multiparadigmatic nature of the social sciences: for many social phenomena different and even contradictory theoretical descriptions and explanations are available. Furthermore, general social theories can often not be applied to empirical observations without making auxiliary assumptions that draw on information only available in the empirical field itself. This leads, on the one hand, to a variety of difficulties for the operationalization and construction of measurement instruments in quantitative research. Efforts to develop empirically grounded theories from the data, on the other hand, often fail to account for the real heterogeneity and diversity of patterns and structures in the research field since the problem of transferability and generalizability of findings is not adequately addressed. One reason for the difficulties in solving these problems of theory use, theory building, and theory testing is that the adherents of the quantitative and qualitative methodological tradition in social research never joined efforts to freely discuss and work on these difficulties. Nowadays, the mixed methods approach makes it possible to make practical progress in a field that was too often characterized by infertile debates in the past.

During the past decades a great expansion and differentiation of discourses and research communities in the field of social research has taken place. The scientific community did not only grow quantitatively, new issues and concerns also emerged, improved methods and techniques of research were developed, and discussions about certain topics were deepened. This came in tandem with a growing specialization of social scientists: in the first half of the 20th century it was quite common for sociologists to do profound work both in the fields of theory and methodology and to also combine this with empirical research. Take Max Weber as an example: Weber extensively worked about the foundations of social theory, made contributions to methodological debates—the so-called *Werturteilsstreit*" [Weber, 1904/1949] may serve as a good example for that—and discussed statistical distributions in his book about the "protestant ethic" (Weber 1904/1992). A further example would be Aaron Garfinkel, who combined thoughtful and sophisticated theoretical work with a great expertise in practical empirical research (e.g., Garfinkel 1967). Nowadays, social scientists are often either skilled experts in theory, specialists in methods and methodology, or devoted empirical researchers. While this specialization leads to an increase of knowledge and experience in many subdisciplines and to a growing elaboration and sophistication of theoretical and methodological discourses, it also carries certain risks. Subdisciplines and discourses begin to become independent from each other and develop their own terminologies and "logics" that only specialists are familiar with. As a consequence, discussants coming from different fields (e.g., from methodology and social theory) may gradually lose the ability to jointly discuss new developments and current problems of their fields and to relate these to each other. This situation has contributed (apart from other factors, of course) to the mutual alienation between qualitative and quantitative research since the 1920s; and a whole methodological movement (the mixed methods community) had to arise where strategies to overcome the speechlessness between both traditions could be developed. Nowadays the mixed methods community experiences a similar danger by developing an own terminology and vocabulary and an almost institutionalized focus on very specific questions and problems (concentrating, among others, on attempts to systematize types of different mixed methods designs).

We must keep in mind that the development of both quantitative and qualitative methods was inspired by debates in the field of social theory: the rise of statistics in social research, for instance, was accompanied by Durkheim's ideas (1895) about "social facts," and the growing interest in qualitative research in the 1960s and 1970s was stimulated by works about theoretical and epistemological foundations of qualitative research that argued from a social theory perspective: the necessity for an "interpretive paradigm" (Wilson, 1970) was justified and clarified with the help of theoretical considerations about the nature of social structure, social processes. and social action (see also

Giddens, 1992). From this viewpoint theoretical arguments regarding the investigated domain (i.e., social phenomena) may become far more important when deciding about the use of qualitative and quantitative methods than general epistemological and methodological ideas. When Grounded Theory became popular in the 1970s, many qualitative researchers started to emulate the inclination of their quantitative colleagues towards discussing technical and methodological issues independently from theoretical questions. What is necessary now in debates about mixed methods is the reestablishment and strengthening of the link between methods and methodology on the one hand and theory about the investigated domain on the other hand. The ongoing debates about different types of mixed methods designs would clearly benefit if questions like the following are posed more often: Which forms of (monomethod or mixed) designs are adequate given the theoretical perspective of the researchers? Which methods and combination of methods are required if certain theories are used in a given research projects?

Acknowledgments

I am especially grateful to Burke Johnson for his thoughtful comments on an earlier version of this chapter.

Discussion Questions

1. What are theory and data, and in which ways can these be related in the research process?

2. Why are bridge assumptions important and how are they used?

3. How can mixed methods research aid in our understanding of social theory?

4. What is the problem of labelling a sequential qualitative-quantitative design (QUAL→QUAN) an "exploratory design"?

5. What is the problem of labelling a sequential quantitative-qualitative design (QUAN→QUAL) an "explanatory design"?

6. How can one make generalizations in social science when using mixed methods research?

Suggested Websites

http://enposs.eu/
European Network for the Philosophy of the Social Sciences

http://pos.sagepub.com/
Philosophy of the Social Sciences

http://www.iep.utm.edu/soc-sci/
Internet Encyclopedia of Philosophy: The Philosophy of Social Science

Notes

1. With the shift in Anglo-American social research and especially in the mixed methods community toward pragmatism (Johnson & Onwuegbuzie, 2004), the link between theory and practice is often considered as similarly important as the relation between theory and empirical data. If one, however, attempts to judge theories according to their practical consequences it still remains the questions how such practical consequences can be identified—at this point the role of empirical observations comes into play again.

2. The idea that the most important task of the social sciences would be to identify "general principles" or "laws" has been subjected to severe criticism since the days of Hempel (see, e.g., Dray 1957)—nevertheless, Hempel's idea can also be applied to generalizations with a limited scope, "middle range theories," and the like (the problem is discussed in more detail later).

References

Barton, A. H., & Lazarsfeld, P. F. (1969). Some functions of qualitative analysis in social research. In G. C. McCall & J. L. Simmons (Eds.), *Issues in participant observation* (pp. 216–228). Reading, MA: Addison-Wesley.

Blumer, H. (1928). *Method in social psychology* (Unpublished doctoral dissertation). University of Chicago.

Blumer, H. (1969). *Symbolic interactionism: Perspective and method*. Englewood Cliffs, NJ: Prentice Hall.

Brewer, J., & Hunter, A. (1989). *Multimethod research: A synthesis of styles*. Newbury Park, CA: Sage.

Bunge, M. (1996). *Finding philosophy in the social sciences*. New Haven, CT: Yale University Press.

Corbin, J. (1991). Anselm Strauss: An intellectual biography. In D. R. Maines (Ed.), *Social organization and social process: Essays in honor of Anselm Strauss* (pp. 17–44). New York, NY: Aldine.

Creswell, J. W., & Plano-Clark, V. L. (2007). *Designing and conducting mixed methods research*. Thousand Oaks, CA: Sage.

Dray, W. (1957). *Laws and explanation in history*. London: Oxford University Press.

Durkheim, E. (1982). *The rules of sociological method*. Glencoe, IL: Free Press. (Original work published 1895)

Esser, H. (1998). Why are bridge hypotheses necessary? In H.-P. Blossfeld & G. Prein (Eds.), *Rational choice theory and large scale data analysis* (pp. 94–111). Boulder, CO: Westview Press.

Garfinkel, A. (1967). *Studies in ethnomethodology*. Englewood Cliffs, NJ: Prentice Hall.

Giddens, A. (1992). *New rules of sociological method: A positive critique of interpretative sociologies*. London, England: Hutchinson.

Glaser, B. (1978). *Theoretical sensitivity: Advances in the methodology of grounded theory*. Mill Valley, CA: Sociology Press.

Glaser, B., & Strauss, A. (1965). *Awareness of dying*. Chicago, IL: Aldine.

Glaser, B., & Strauss, A. (1967). *The discovery of grounded theory: Strategies for qualitative research*. Chicago, IL: Aldine.

Gobo, G. (2004). Sampling, representativeness and generalizability. In C. Seale, G. Gobo, F. Jaber, & D. Silverman (Eds.), *Qualitative research practice* (pp. 435–456). London, England: Sage.

Greer, S. A. (1969). *The logic of social inquiry*. Chicago, IL: Aldine.

Hanson, N. R. (1965). *Patterns of discovery: An inquiry into the conceptual foundations of science.* Cambridge, UK: Cambridge University Press.

Hammersley, M. (1989). *The dilemma of qualitative method: Herbert Blumer and the Chicago tradition.* London, England: Routledge.

Hempel, C. G. (1952). *Fundamentals of concept formation in empirical science.* Chicago, IL: University of Chicago Press.

Hunter, A., & Brewer, J. (2003). Multimethod research in sociology. In A. Tashakkori & C. Teddlie (Eds.), *Handbook of mixed methods in social and behavioral sciences* (pp. 577–594). Thousand Oaks, CA: Sage.

Johnson, R. B., & Christensen, L. B. (2014). *Educational research methods: Quantitative, qualitative, and mixed approaches* (5th ed.). Los Angeles, CA: Sage.

Johnson, R. B., & Onwuegbuzie, A. J. (2004). Mixed methods research: A research paradigm whose time has come. *Educational Researcher, 33*(7), 14–26.

Kelle, U. (2007). The development of categories—Different approaches in grounded theory. In A. Bryant & K. Charmaz (Eds.), *Grounded theory* (pp. 191–213). London, England: Sage.

Kelle, U. (2013). Theorization from data. In U. Flick (Ed.), *The SAGE handbook of qualitative data analysis* (pp. 554–568). London, England: Sage.

Kelle, U., & Lüdemann, C. (1998). Bridge assumptions in rational choice theory: Methodological problems and possible solutions. In H.-P. Blossfeld & G. Prein (Eds.), *Rational choice theory and large-scale data analysis* (pp. 112–125). Boulder, CO: Westview Press.

Lakatos, I. (1978). *The methodology of scientific research programmes.* Cambridge, UK: Cambridge University Press.

Laudan, L. (1977). *Progress and its problems: Towards a theory of scientific growth.* London, England: Routledge & Kegan Paul.

Lincoln, Y. S., & Guba, E. G. (1985). *Naturalistic inquiry.* Beverly Hills, CA: Sage.

Lincoln, Y. S., & Guba, E. G. (2000). The only generalization is: There is no generalization. In R. Gomm,

M. Hammersley, & P. Foster (Eds.), *Case study method: Key issues, key texts* (pp. 27–44). Thousand Oaks, CA: Sage.

Lindenberg, S. (1992). The method of decreasing abstraction. In J. S. Coleman & T. J. Fararo (Eds.), *Rational choice theory: Advocacy and critique* (pp. 3–20). Newbury Park, CA: Sage.

Merton, R. K. (1949). On sociological theories of the middle range. In R. K. Merton, *Social theory and social structure* (pp. 39–53). New York, NY: Simon and Schuster.

Mill, J. S. (1872). *A system of logic. Ratiocinative and Inductive. Being a connected view of the principles of evidence and the methods of scientific investigation.* London, England: Longmans, Green, Reader and Dyer.

Patton, M. Q. (2002). *Qualitative research & evaluation methods* (3rd ed.). Thousand Oaks, CA: Sage.

Phillips, D. C., & Burbules, N. C. (2000). *Postpositivism and educational research.* Lanham, MD: Rowman & Littlefield.

Popper, K. (1959). *The logic of scientific discovery.* New York, NY: Basic Books.

Silverman, D. (2000). *Doing qualitative research: A practical handbook.* London, England: Sage.

Simon, H. A. (1985). Human nature in politics: The dialogue of psychology with political science. *American Political Science Review, 79*(2), 293–304.

Strauss, A. L. (1987). *Qualitative analysis for social scientists.* Cambridge, UK: Cambridge University Press.

Strauss, A. L., & Corbin, J. (1990). *Basics of qualitative research: Grounded theory procedures and techniques.* Newbury Park, CA: Sage.

Weber, M. (1949). *The methodology of the social sciences* (E. A. Shils & H. A. Finch, trans.). Glencoe, IL: Free Press. (Original work published 1904)

Weber, M. (1992): *The protestant ethic and the spirit of capitalism.* London, England: Routledge. (Original work published 1904–1905)

Wilson, T. P. (1970). Conceptions of interaction and forms of sociological explanation. *American Sociological Review, 35*(4), 697–710.

Preserving Distinctions Within the Multimethod and Mixed Methods Research Merger

Jennifer C. Greene

Abstract

This chapter aims to underscore commonalities and differences between multiple and mixed methods approaches to social inquiry, and to argue for maintaining the distinctions between these two inquiry traditions. Compared to a multimethod approach, a mixed methods approach offers (a) opportunities to mix at a method, methodology, and paradigm level; (b) a valuing of both consonance and dissonance; and (c) key opportunities for respectful conversations among different ways of knowing and different ways of valuing. In these ways, a mixed methods approach to inquiry is considered to have a broader reach and potential than a multiple methods approach. An extended example is offered to illustrate and support the conceptual arguments made.

Key Words: mixed methods approaches, method, methodology, paradigm, consonance, dissonance, respectful conversations

Social science inquiry methodology continues to be a lively and dynamic domain of creative thinking and innovative development. From the comparatively drab days in the middle of the previous century, when becoming a social science inquirer was a matter of learning "the proper methods properly applied" (Smith, 1983), the contemporary social scientist is educated into a substantial diversity of ways of thinking about and doing social science (called inquiry "approaches" in this chapter). Unlike the old days, the contemporary social scientist faces a broad panoply of inquiry approaches and stances, from traditional "net effects" inquiry (Ragin, 2006) to autoethnography (Ellis, 2004) to postmodern critique of inquiry itself (Lather & St. Pierre, 2013). Also unlike the old days, the contemporary social scientist engages with the philosophical, theoretical, ethical, and political dimensions of methodology, in addition to mastering the technical tools of the craft. Responsible social inquiry today requires thoughtful consideration of methodology's multiple layers, well beyond the technical layer.

Amidst this busy contemporary landscape of varied and diverse approaches to social science, the borders and boundaries between various approaches, especially approaches in the same sector of the landscape, can readily be expected to be fuzzy in places and even porous in others. This is not inherently problematic, as social science will ever be an inexact practice. In fact, border contestations can generate internal critique and external dialogue, leading to clarifications and enhancements of inquiry approaches on both sides of the border, including the discovery of shared spaces and commitments.

This handbook joins two formerly distinct, albeit neighborly, social science approaches—the *use of multiple methods* and the *mixing of different methods* in a single study—into one "multiple and mixed methods research inquiry" genre.[1] Among the primary rationales for this merger is to shift the conversation away from a focus on methods and onto a reclamation of the inquiry question as the main driver of inquiry design and methodology *and* a reclamation of real-world problems or substantive theory as the primary drivers of meaningful inquiry questions. A second important rationale motivating this handbook is to emphasize—especially for mixed methods approaches to social inquiry—the possibilities of including not just more than one method in an inquiry study but also the possibilities of including more than one *methodology*, more than one *philosophical paradigm*, as well as more than one *discipline* and *substantive theory*.

I fully agree with both rationales guiding this handbook. Regarding the first, the fundamental purpose of social inquiry is to address substantive issues of importance in the world. One does not begin a study with a statement like, "I want to do a quasi-experimental study with propensity score matching," or "I want to do a critical ethnography." One begins with a substantive issue, problem, or concern of consequence in the social world; considers how well current knowledge, theory, and practice address this issue or problem; and formulates specific questions about it that warrant further empirical study. Only then does one begin to think about how best to study such questions—with what approach, design, and methods.

Regarding the second rationale, I would agree that labels of multiple and mixed *methods* misrepresent the reach and potential of mixed methods approaches to social inquiry and, to a lesser extent, multimethod approaches as well. From the beginning of explicit attention to the possibilities of methodological mixes (Greene & McClintock, 1985; Greene, Caracelli, & Graham, 1989; Kidder & Fine, 1987; Madey, 1982; Mathison, 1988; Reichardt & Cook, 1979; Rossman & Wilson, 1985), ideas about mixing included methodological mixing at all levels—methods, methodologies, and paradigms—as well as substantive mixing across disciplines and theories. In fact, I would argue that today, considerations regarding what levels will be mixed in a mixed methods inquiry study is a key design decision. Further, the inquirer's decision about levels to be mixed and the justification for this decision should be clearly articulated in the presentation of the study.

Within this handbook's proposed merger of multimethod and mixed methods approaches to social inquiry, I believe there are some distinctions worth preserving. In the remainder of this chapter, I underscore these distinctions through brief historical notes on each tradition and then an extended example.

Historical Notes

Multiple methods from the same family or inquiry tradition have been advocated in social science inquiry by diverse scholars and researchers for quite some time (Cook, 1985; Denzin, 1978; Morse & Niehaus, 2009). Broadly speaking, multiple methods have been advanced largely as a way to engage more fully with the scope and complexity of social phenomena. In traditional ethnography, for example, ethnographers have learned that they cannot just rely on what people say but must also observe and watch what they do. These *multiple* ethnographic methods are needed to fully and accurately understand the cultural dimensions of particular individual and community activities (Denzin, 1978). And, in program evaluation, evaluators have learned that meaningful understanding of social programs is best captured by the use of *multiple* theoretical and stakeholder perspectives and *multiple* analytic techniques, because evaluation contexts are multifaceted and complex (Cook, 1985). So the primary challenge or problem addressed by the use of multiple methods or multiple techniques for data collection and analysis is that of understanding more fully the inherent complexity of human phenomena.

In contrast, mixed approaches to social inquiry go beyond multimethod approaches in the opportunities they provide to *meaningfully engage with difference* precisely through the possibility of mixing at multiple levels. Mixed methods approaches arose largely as one "solution" to the relatively intense "paradigm wars" of the 1970s and 1980s—wars that continue with skirmishes still today.[2] A mixed methods approach to inquiry was generated as a political settlement to this decades-long dispute, a settlement that acknowledged the legitimacy of all sides (representing different philosophical traditions) and, moreover, emphasized the need for all sides to join together to respond well to the challenges of understanding the complexity and contextuality of human phenomena. That is, like multimethod approaches, mixed methods approaches to social inquiry also aim for better understanding of complex social phenomena, but the field of mixed methods embraces methods and methodologies from all social science families, and it has deep roots in paradigmatic debates. So the possibility of mixing is a possibility engaged not just at the technical level of method but also at the broader level of methodology and at the highest (most abstract) level of paradigm, which commonly also invokes mixing at additional levels of theory and discipline. This *possibility of mixing at multiple levels* is integral to the character of mixed methods approaches to social inquiry, even though not all mixed methods studies do or even should mix at multiple levels. That is, in some contexts a mix of methods alone is most justifiable, while in others a limited methods mix may represent a missed opportunity for deeper insights. But, with the possibility of mixing at all levels, mixed methods approaches to social inquiry can intentionally incorporate quite different perspectives and assumptions about the phenomena being studied and thus offer important potential to meaningfully engage with difference, dissonance, and diversity.

In summary, multimethod and mixed methods approaches to social inquiry share a common ambition to understand complex social phenomena more fully and with greater depth and breadth. More distinctively, mixed methods approaches to social inquiry further offer the possibility of meaningful engagement with and dialogue across not just different types of methods and data but also different logics of inquiry, different ways of knowing, and thus different perspectives on understanding important social phenomena.

I next turn to a practical example to further examine the commonalities, overlap, and differences between multimethod and mixed methods approaches to social inquiry. The example is drawn from my own field of practice, which is educational and social program evaluation. Areas of shared perspective and areas of difference between multimethod and mixed methods approaches are articulated and the distinctive character of mixed methods approaches highlighted, as this is what may be lost or overshadowed in the merger of multiple and mixed approaches to social inquiry. Ideas about ways forward conclude this commentary.

Evaluating an Obesity Prevention Program

Obesity remains a major threat to the health of people around the globe, and obesity prevention programs for both adults and children remain high policy priorities in many countries, including the United States. (See especially the recent set of reports on preventing childhood obesity from the US Institute of Medicine, http://iom.edu/Reports.aspx?Search=obesity%20prevention). A fairly typical school-based obesity prevention program is described next, followed by two plans for evaluating this program, illustrating a multimethod and a mixed methods approach to evaluating the same program. This example is used to underscore the commonalities and differences between these two social inquiry approaches, as concrete descriptions can more effectively accomplish this comparison than can abstract pronouncements.

Program Description and Evaluation Priorities

Eat Right! Be Fit! is a nutrition and exercise program for elementary school children, developed by faculty at a Midwestern university, that has three major components:

1. Children are encouraged to walk or bike to school with adult supervision (primarily parent volunteers) along well-traveled and safe routes.

2. The amount of physical activity children experience doing the school day is increased, through additional breaks in the day for classroom, playground, and gymnasium physical activity and play.

3. The cafeteria menu is completely revamped to feature fruits, vegetables, whole-grain carbohydrates, and other healthy food. All soda is banned from school grounds.

The program's intended short-term outputs are that all children in the school will have adequate exercise and a balanced, healthy diet during the school day. The intended longer term outcomes are a healthy student population in terms of obesity measures like body mass (BMI) index and other physiological measures related to such conditions as diabetes and in terms of children's attitudes and commitments to living a healthy life.

This program is relatively well established; the logic of the program's design has been supported by considerable research and prior evaluations in other communities. Adoption of *Eat Right! Be Fit!* in the eight elementary schools of the small urban community of Westlake, as well as the evaluation of the program, are being funded by a local philanthropic organization. Westlake inhabitants are quite diverse in terms of race, ethnicity, language, social class, and religious preference, and each elementary school has a unique demographic profile. In the evaluation, both implementation and outcome data are desired. Thus the key evaluation questions address (a) the quality of program implementation and participant experiences and (b) the character and magnitude of short-term outputs and longer term outcomes attained. The program is being implemented for four years, after which time the school district is expected to institutionalize successful program activities and practices. The evaluation design presented next is for the first year of the *Eat Right! Be Fit!* program implementation in Westlake. The results of the first-year evaluation, along with any changes made to the program or its implementation, would influence the evaluation designs in subsequent years.

Multimethod Approach to Evaluation

The philanthropic organization that is funding Westlake's adoption of the *Eat Right! Stay Fit!* program and its evaluation is a long-time advocate for children's health in the region. Staff in the organization are thus most accustomed to and familiar with traditional health intervention evaluation designs that feature standardized measurement and planned comparisons and that enable causal inference. The multimethod evaluation team was selected for their expertise in large-scale health program evaluation.

CRITERIA FOR JUDGING PROGRAM QUALITY

At the outset, the multimethod evaluation team works with the program and foundation staff to establish the criteria to be used for judging the quality of the *Eat Right! Stay Fit!* program as implemented in Westlake. For program implementation these are:

- The program is implemented as designed (with fidelity).
- Intended program outputs are reached for students on the average and for at least 75% of the children participants in each grade level. These outputs include adequate physical activity and a healthy diet during the school day, as per national guidelines for elementary school children.
- A significant majority of children, teachers, and parents perceive the program as relevant, useful, and important for the children's health.

For outcomes they are:

- Progress toward the intended program health outcomes (one year pre–post differences) are attained on the average and for at least 75% of the children participants in each grade level. These outcomes include changes in BMI and other standard indicators of child health.
- A majority of children participants report initial commitments to adopting a healthy lifestyle and striving to become and remain healthy.

EVALUATION DESIGN

The team then adopts a quasi-experimental design for this evaluation. Planned comparisons involve (a) pre- and postassessments for Westlake children, as well as (b) comparisons of Westlake children to children in similar sociodemographic areas on regional and national indicators of obesity-related health and fitness. Recognizing that these are not the strongest comparisons for establishing causal inferences and desiring additional data on key constructs in the evaluation, the evaluation team decides to use multiple methods for these key constructs, namely, the character and quality of program implementation and the priority health-related outcomes for children.

EVALUATION METHODS

Program implementation in this evaluation will be assessed with two methods.

1. The fidelity of program implementation (e.g., Is the program being implemented as designed?) will be assessed through structured observations of representative samples of all program activities, across all grade levels and program sites (walking/biking routes; playground, gym, and classrooms [for physical activity]; and the cafeteria). These observations will record what is happening, for example, how many children are walking or biking to school and what kinds of food are being served *and eaten* in the lunchroom,[3] to be followed by analyses of what happened compared to what should have happened, based on the program design. This analysis will also assess attainment of intended program outputs—adequate physical exercise and healthy food consumption during the school day.

2. The fidelity and quality of program implementation will also be assessed from the standpoint of participants. At the end of the year, semistructured group interviews will be conducted with samples of children, purposefully selected to represent the diversity of the Westlake school district. The interviews will ask the children to describe their experiences with physical activity and food over the past year and to share their viewpoints on these experiences.

This use of multiple methods is intended to garner a richer understanding of program implementation, an understanding that represents the intentions of program designers alongside the experiences of children, than would be possible with one method alone.

In parallel fashion, program outcomes will also be assessed with two methods, one that assesses intended outcomes using various standardized health measures and one that assesses outcomes again from the standpoint of key participants.

1. Attainment of intended program health outcomes will be assessed for all children using accepted standardized health measures. While

improvements are expected, they may be modest during this first year of *Eat Right! Be Fit!* in Westlake.

2. At the end of the year, age-appropriate structured questionnaires will be administered to all children in Grades 2 through 5. The questionnaire will include a section on children's attitudes toward staying healthy through eating well and getting adequate exercise. (In future years, parental attitudes will also likely be assessed, to determine any spillover effects of the program to children's life outside of school.)

SUMMARY OF THE MULTIMETHOD EVALUATION

In sum, this multimethod evaluation design for the first-year evaluation of the *Eat Right! Stay Fit!* program in Westlake will use a quasi-experimental design with two planned comparisons for outcomes and a set of multiple methods designed to assess the quality of program implementation and the magnitude of program outcomes more comprehensively than could a single method. The multiple methods in this evaluation are included specifically to capture the *children's* program experiences and perceived benefits, alongside those intended by the program designers. Understanding the children's experiences is considered the highest priority by the evaluation team. Further, general consonance of the results from the various methods is expected.

Mixed Methods Approach to Evaluation

The mixed methods approach to evaluation team is knowledgeable about the history and evaluation preferences of the philanthropic organization that is funding Westlake's adoption of the *Eat Right! Stay Fit!* program and its evaluation. The evaluation team selects a mixed methods approach with intentional mixing at all levels—methods, methodologies, and paradigms. This approach is expected to be responsive to the organization's expressed needs for structured and generalizable comparative evaluative information, while also enabling the team to understand how the program is experienced by participants,[4] including the connections of the program to the participants' daily lives both in and outside of school. Following the ecocultural theories of Thomas Weisner (2002), the team believes that events and activities that are important to people "show up" in a meaningful way in their daily lives. Further, the mixed methods approach enables the evaluation team to capture possible variation in program experiences and outcomes for the diverse population of elementary school children in Westlake, including differences among elementary schools, each of which is demographically distinctive. The mixed methods evaluation team is eager to engage these possible contextual differences because team members believe that context is a powerful influence on behavior and its meaningfulness.

CRITERIA FOR JUDGING PROGRAM QUALITY

Like the multimethod evaluation team, the mixed methods team initiates their work by collaborating with the program and foundation staff to establish the criteria to be used for judging the quality of the *Eat Right! Stay Fit!* program as implemented in Westlake. These are differentiated from those established in the multimethod evaluation primarily by their attention to (school) context and to disaggregation of data by relevant demographic subgroups. These subgroups include children from both traditional and more recent racial and ethnic groups in the United States, children from families living near or below poverty levels, girls and boys, language minority children, and children with disabilities.

Quality criteria for program implementation are:

• The program is implemented as designed (with fidelity) in each school, or with minor modifications appropriate to that school.

• Intended program outputs are reached for at least 75% of the children participants in each school, grade level, and demographic subgroup. These outputs include adequate physical activity and a healthy diet during the school day, as per national guidelines for elementary school children.

• A significant majority of children, teachers, and parents in each school, grade level, and demographic subgroup perceive the program as contextually meaningful, relevant, and of important consequence for the children's health.

Quality criteria for outcomes are:

• The intended program health outcomes are attained for at least 75% of the children participants in each school, grade level, and demographic subgroup. These outcomes include BMI and other standard indicators of child health.

• A majority of children participants in each school, grade level, and demographic subgroup report commitments to adopting a healthy lifestyle and striving to become and remain healthy in ways that connect to their daily lives.

EVALUATION APPROACH, PURPOSES FOR MIXING, AND MIXED DESIGN

This evaluation team selects a mixed methods approach because it fits well with the importance of assessing the *Eat Right! Stay Fit!* program, both as designed and as experienced.[5] The team envisions the evaluation ideally as a respectful conversation between the implementation and accomplishments of the program as intended by its developers on the one hand and the contextualized experiences of the program by the members of the Westlake elementary school community on the other. The primary purpose for mixing in this evaluation is *complementarity*, defined as developing broader, deeper, and more comprehensive social understandings of complex social phenomena by using methods that tap into different facets or dimensions of these phenomena (Greene, 2007, p. 101). Again, these facets include the program as designed and the program as experienced in diverse contexts by diverse people. A secondary purpose for mixing is *initiation*, defined as generating new and even unanticipated insights about key phenomena through the resolution of divergent or dissonant results from different methods and methodologies (Greene, 2007, pp. 102–103). Recognizing that it is difficult to plan for dissonant results, the initiation purpose offers a generative pathway to pursue the "empirical puzzle" (Cook, 1985) that such results present, rather than discard or reject them wholesale.

After identifying the key purposes for mixing in this study, the evaluation team then makes the following decisions about their mixed methods design. These decisions are fitting and appropriate for the mixed methods purposes of complementarity and initiation. First, like the multimethod team, the mixed methods evaluation team determines that the mixing will be conducted around the key constructs of importance in this evaluation—quality of program implementation and attainment of program outcomes. Second, the team determines the sensibility of mixing at all levels—method, methodology, and paradigm—and opts for such a mix in their assessments of these key constructs. Third, the team opts for a design in which the perspectives (methods/methodologies/paradigms) of the program and evaluation funder (the philanthropic organization) are the dominant framework for the study, and the perspectives of participants serve a secondary or supportive role. (The team would prefer a design in which both sets of perspectives have equal voice, but funding parameters limit this option.) Fourth, the team decides that the different

methods (representing the different perspectives) are to be implemented concurrently rather than sequentially. And finally, the mixed methods evaluation team plans for the integration of the data and results from the different perspectives as an ongoing process throughout the study and then also at the end of the evaluation in the development of final conclusions and inferences.

It is important to call attention to the specific and unique aspects of planning a mixed methods study just discussed—those of identifying appropriate purposes for mixing and then crafting a mixed methods design, using extant guidance on mixed methods design dimensions, that best addresses these purposes. Although a "theory" of mixed methodology is still under development (Greene, 2008), the concepts of distinctive purposes for mixing and distinctive dimensions of mixed designs are fairly well established. In fact, a number of mixed methods design typologies and frameworks have been developed and are readily available to inform the work of mixed inquiry practitioners (Teddlie & Tashakkori, 2006; Greene, 2007; Maxwell & Mittapalli, 2010). Furthermore, in mixed methods inquiry design, intentional attention is paid to the study's underlying paradigmatic and value assumptions, as decisions about mixing at this level are a requisite part of planning a mixed study.

EVALUATION PARADIGMS, METHODOLOGIES, AND METHODS

Now it is time to select the actual *sets* of paradigms, methodologies, and methods for the *Eat Right! Be Fit!* program evaluation and to plan the mixing to take place. The selection of paradigms, methodologies, and methods is not conducted independently, as in selecting paradigm A from column 1, methodology B from column 2, or method C from column 3. Rather, mixed methods inquirers identify the perspectives/paradigms of value and relevance to a given study and then, within those, the methodologies and methods that are most appropriate for the context. And, of course, this decision-making is fully iterative, as later decisions suggest changes to earlier ones.

For the *Eat Right! Be Fit!* program evaluation, the mixed methods evaluation team identifies the paradigms of postpositivism (Phillips & Burbules, 2000) and constructivism (Lincoln & Guba, 1985) as appropriate for this evaluation. With its realist assumptions and its aspirations for inferences that are generalizable, postpositivism generally calls for structured, quantitative methods and data that support the comparative causal inferences desired by the philanthropic funder of the program. With its interpretive assumptions and its aspirations for inferences that represent understanding of contextual meaningfulness, constructivism generally calls for unstructured, qualitative methods and data that represent the evaluation team's commitments to contextual understanding and honoring of the diversity of experience.

With respect to methodologies, the mixed methods evaluation team selects a quasi-experimental methodology for the postpositivist strand of the evaluation and mini-case studies for the constructivist strand. Again, the postpositivist framework and quasi-experimental methodology are intended to address the philanthropic organization's stated information needs and stances on what counts as credible evidence in evaluation. And the mini-case study framework represents the evaluation team's commitments to contextual understanding for the full diversity of program participants. The quasi-experimental component of the mixed methods evaluation emphasizes structured, quantitative assessments of program implementation and outcomes as *externally defined* by the *Eat Right! Be Fit!* program developers—as in the multimethod evaluation described earlier. However, in lieu of additional *methods* to assess children's program experiences (as featured in the multiple evaluation), the mixed methods evaluation design features a set of three mini-case studies[6] of the experiential character and consequence of *Eat Right! Be Fit!* program in three purposively selected classrooms. The classrooms are selected on the criteria of information richness and coverage of key dimensions of diversity in the Westlake district, such that each classroom affords rich and relevant information regarding the character and consequence of the *Eat Right! Be Fit!* program for the diversity of children in the Westlake elementary school communities.

Thus the methodologies and methods to be used in the mixed methods evaluation of the *Eat Right! Be Fit!* program in the Westlake elementary schools are the following.

For program implementation:

1. Just like the multimethod quasi-experimental evaluation design, the fidelity and quality of program implementation in the mixed evaluation will be partially assessed through structured observations of representative samples of all program activities, across all grade levels and program sites (walking/biking routes; playground, gym, and classrooms [for physical activity]; and the cafeteria). These observations will record what is happening, for example, how many children are walking or biking to school and what kinds of food are being served and eaten (and, again, possibly also thrown away) in the lunchroom, to be followed by analyses of what happened compared to what should have happened, based on the program design. These analyses will also assess attainment of intended program outputs—adequate physical exercise and healthy food consumption during the school day.

2. As part of the mixed methods mini-case study design, unstructured ethnographic observations will also be conducted of program activities in the three mini-case study classrooms. These observations will span the school year and will foreground the engagement of diverse students with the program curriculum—in the classroom, in the gym, in the lunchroom, and on the playground. These observations will endeavor to provide a portrait of varied student engagement with and sense-making of the *Eat Right! Be Fit!* program.

For program outcomes:

1. Again, like the multimethod design, in the quasi-experimental component of the mixed methods design, attainment of intended program health outcomes will be assessed for all children using accepted standardized health measures, with two planned comparisons: (a) comparisons of pre- to postassessments for Westlake children and (b) comparisons of Westlake children to children in similar sociodemographic areas on regional and national indicators of obesity-related health and fitness. And again, while improvements are expected, they may be modest during this first year of *Eat Right! Be Fit!* in Westlake.

2. As part of the mini-case study design, the salience and relevance of the *Eat Right! Be Fit!* program in the lives of the Westlake children will be captured in a series of group interviews to be conducted with samples of children in the three case-study classrooms (one in the autumn and two in the spring), group interviews with the teaching staff in these three classrooms, and the "testimony" of parents of children in these three classrooms who volunteer to attend a meeting at the end of the school year to share their experiences of their children's engagement in this program.

SAMPLE MIXES AND RESULTS

To illustrate more concretely the potential of a fully mixed methods design to yield results that well represent both the interests of funders and program developers and the on-the-ground experiences and meaningfulness of program participation for the Westlake school community, possible sample mixes and results are described next.

A method mix. This evaluation will mix at a methods level[7] to measure the key output of children's food consumption—using a structured, quantitative analysis of food eaten (and food thrown away) and an unstructured, qualitative collection (as part of the group interviews) of children's reports of how much they like and eat the new cafeteria fare. The method mix to assess children's food consumption could yield mostly congruent results, providing additional support for stronger inferences about this important program output.

A methodological mix. The quasi-experimental and mini-case study methodological mix will assess (among other constructs) the implementation quality of the classroom-based physical activity component of the program (which is the least well tested program component), using structured observations of classrooms and unstructured, ethnographic observations of the three classes that are part of the mini-case study. For the structured observations of this classroom-based physical activity component, the evaluators may first review classroom schedules for the frequency and amount of planned physical activity and then conduct a stratified sampling of physical activity times for a representative sample of classrooms to systematically document the nature and extent of activity actually happening. One focus of the mini-case studies may be the character and quality of the rhythms and integration of physical activity into the daily life of the children in these classrooms. This methodological mix around the in-classroom physical activity component of the program could generate rich portraits of how activity and action are integrated into, as well as disruptive of, classroom rhythms and learning, complemented by some insights into the contextual parameters that matter in such portraits.

A paradigm mix. Finally, the evaluation's mix at the paradigmatic level will assess the major outcome of children's understanding of, participation in, and perspectives on the diet and exercise facets of their school day introduced by the *Eat Right! Be Fit!* program. As discussed, this mix will employ different methods and methodologies that are intentionally linked to different assumptions about the social world and our knowledge of it—notably, the postpositivist realist view that seeks to understand the predictive power of various program components on observed outcomes and the constructivist view that seeks to understand children's own contextualized sense makings of the activity and food strands of their school day. The realist asks: What component of the program makes the most powerful difference in the outcomes observed? The constructivist asks: How do the program's components show up in a meaningful way in the children's school day?

This multilayered paradigmatic mix around children's understandings of this program could possibly offer a complex canvas with areas of patterned alignments, with some areas where children's sense makings are congruent with the intents of the program developers and other areas of discordance and even contradiction—areas of "empirical puzzles" that warrant further analysis and review, perhaps leading to unanticipated new insights and revelations. For instance, some children may report being wary of these new opportunities to run around the classroom three times or dance for five minutes to a popular hip-hop song and do not fully trust their teachers' requests to do so, as these requests are quite out of sync with the classroom norms and expectations previously established. Pursuit of understanding how this wariness affects program implementation and experiences in this classroom could yield a new insight into the importance of cultural congruence between the program activities and the children's life experiences.

SUMMARY OF THE MIXED METHODS APPROACH TO EVALUATION

In sum, this mixed methods evaluation of the first year of the *Eat Right! Stay Fit!* program in Westlake will mix a postpositivist, realist, quasi-experimental design with a constructivist, contextualized set of mini-case studies to assess the quality and contextual meanings of program implementation as well as the magnitude, character, and contextual consequentiality of program outcomes. The evaluation will attend intentionally to the ways in which diverse children engage with the program and make meaning from their program engagement. The evaluation will also describe and aspire to understand the ways in which context matters for the meaningfulness and effectiveness of the *Eat Right! Be Fit!* program. In these ways, the evaluation seeks to respect and value both the perspectives and expertise of the program developers and funders, as well as the lifeworlds and experiences of the children, teachers, and parents in Westlake. The combination (mix) of these diverse perspectives is intended to yield important and perhaps unanticipated insights into the program's potentialities and contextual limitations or even disconnects. Dissonance among evaluation results can well lead to these important insights. In these ways, the evaluation seeks to be educative and enlightening as well as instrumentally useful.

Reprise

Multimethod approaches to social inquiry are neighbors of mixed methods approaches to social inquiry. Like many neighbors, they have interests in common, including an interest in a better and more complete understanding of important and complex social phenomena and a valuing of multiple perspectives on the character and meanings of these phenomena. Multimethod and mixed methods approaches to social inquiry also share several important characteristics and stances. Notably, both types of studies are dynamically and often contextually crafted, rather than taken off the shelf or from a textbook.

As this extended example of both a multimethod and a mixed methods evaluation plan for an obesity prevention program has aspired to illustrate, there are also vital differences between these two approaches to social inquiry, differences that I believe are worth retaining. I consider three such differences especially important. First, multimethod approaches generally seek consonance and harmony in the results from multiple methods, while mixed methods approaches intentionally make space for dissonance and disharmony as a pathway to insights not foreseen. Second, mixed methods approaches to social inquiry have the potential to have a broader, deeper, and more inclusive reach than multimethod approaches. Because mixed methods approaches can mix across different ways of seeing, knowing, and understanding, the perspectives included in mixed methods studies can be more inclusive of these many different standpoints. While such inclusion can be valuable in and of itself, I further believe that incorporating different ways of knowing in the same study can yield deeper, broader, and more insightful and worthy insights than one way of knowing alone can. And third, because paradigms, methodologies, and methods from different traditions or families offer different standpoints on what is knowledge and what is worth knowing, they carry with them different values about social phenomena and how best to understand them. Standpoints that seek generalizable knowledge value average effects or "what works"

on the average. Standpoints that foreground feminist ways of knowing value the well-being of women and girls. Standpoints that engage in critique of societal structures that silently maintain inequities value social justice and equity in life chances for all groups and individuals. A mixed methods approach, especially when mixing at all levels of method *and* standpoint, offers key opportunities for respectful conversations among these different ways of knowing and different ways of valuing. In this world of frightening disharmony and strife, respectful conversations are one vital pathway out.

In the spirit of respectful conversations, my hope is these ideas will contribute to a continuance of this conversation between multimethod and mixed methods approaches to social inquiry.

Discussion Questions

1. In what ways do the distinctions between multimethod and mixed methods approaches to social inquiry presented in this chapter fit your own inquiry interests and contexts?

2. In what contexts might a multimethod approach to inquiry be the best fit? In what contexts might a mixed methods approach be the best fit? For what reasons?

3. What challenges can you generate to the conceptualizations of multimethod and mixed methods approaches to social inquiry presented in this chapter?

Suggested Websites

http://www.sagepub.com/journals/Journal201775
Journal of Mixed Methods Research

http://www.tashakkori.com/bridges.html
Abbas Taskakkori's website on mixed approaches to inquiry

http://mra.e-contentmanagement.com/
International Journal of Multiple Research Approaches

http://comm.eval.org/mixedmethodsevaluation/home
American Evaluation Association, Mixed Methods Topical Interest Group

http://www.aera.net/SIG158/MixedMethods
ResearchSIG158/tabid/12201/Default.aspx
American Educational Research Association, Mixed Methods Special Interest Group

http://mmira.wildapricot.org/
International Mixed Method Research Association

Notes

1. It must be acknowledged that different methodologists use the labels of *multimethod* and *mixed methods* approaches to social inquiry in very different ways. It is thus incumbent on each of us to clearly define these terms when using them. I offer my understandings of these traditions later in the chapter.

2. These skirmishes appear to be more about territory than outright negation of the other side. As one example, the current favoring of experimental impact evaluation in many policy circles, for example by the Center for Global Development (http://www.cgdev.org/section/publications) is a territorial victory for the "randomistas."

3. Resources permitting, analyses of *food thrown away* in the lunchroom will supplement these direct observations of program activities.

4. The desire to understand participant experiences is shared by the multimethod evaluation team.

5. Again, this ambition is shared by the multimethod team. The mixed methods team engages more fully with assessments of the program as experienced, as such engagement is explicitly invited by a mixed methods approach.

6. Fuller case studies would be conducted, resources permitting.

7. But, of course, methods do not stand alone but are rather embedded in their respective methodologies and paradigms.

References

Cook, T. D. (1985). Postpositivist critical multiplism. In R. L. Shotland & M. M. Mark (Eds.), *Social science and social policy* (pp. 21–62). Thousand Oaks, CA: Sage.

Denzin, N. K. (1978). *The research act: A theoretical introduction to sociological methods*. New York, NY: McGraw-Hill.

Ellis, C. (2004). *Ethnographic I: A methodological novel about autoethnography*. Walnut Creek, CA: Left Coast Press.

Greene, J. C. (2007). *Mixed methods in social inquiry*. San Francisco, CA: Wiley.

Greene, J. C. (2008). Is mixed methods social inquiry a distinctive methodology? *Journal of Mixed Methods Research*, *2*(1), 7–21.

Greene, J. C., Caracelli, V. J., & Graham, W. F. (1989). Toward a conceptual framework for mixed-method evaluation designs. *Educational Evaluation and Policy Analysis*, *11*, 255–274.

Greene, J. C., & McClintock, C. (1985). Triangulation in evaluation: Design and analysis issues. *Evaluation Review*, *9*, 523–545.

Kidder, L. H., & Fine, M. (1987). Qualitative and quantitative methods: When stories converge. In M. M. Mark & R. L. Shotland (Eds.), *Multiple methods in program evaluation* (pp. 57–75) (New Directions for Program Evaluation 35). San Francisco, CA: Jossey-Bass.

Lather, P. A. & St. Pierre, E. A. (Eds.) (2013). Post qualitative research. *International Journal of Qualitative Studies in Education*, *26*(6), 629–633.

Lincoln, Y. S., & Guba, E. G. (1985). *Naturalistic inquiry*. Thousand Oaks, CA: Sage.

Madey, D. L. (1982). Some benefits of integrating qualitative and quantitative methods in pro-gram evaluation, with illustrations. *Educational Evaluation and Policy Analysis*, *4*, 223–236.

Mathison, S. (1988). Why triangulate? *Educational Researcher*, *17*(2), 13–17.

Maxwell, J. A., & Mittapalli, K. (2010). Realism as a stance for mixed methods research. In A. Tashakkori & C. Teddlie (Eds.), *SAGE handbook of mixed methods research in social & behavioral research* (2nd ed., pp. 145–167). Thousand Oaks, CA: Sage.

Morse, J. M., & Niehaus, L. (2009). *Mixed methods design: Principles and procedures*. Walnut Creek, CA: Left Coast Press.

Phillips, D. C., & Burbules, N. (2000). *Postpositivism and educational research*. Lanham, MD: Rowman & Littlefield.

Ragin, C. C. (2006). The limitations of net effects thinking. In B. Rihoux & H. M. Grimm (Eds.), *Innovative comparative methods for policy analysis* (pp.13–41). New York, NY: Springer.

Reichardt, C. S., & Cook, T. D. (1979). Beyond qualitative versus quantitative methods. In T. D. Cook & C. S. Reichardt (Eds.), *Qualitative and quantitative methods in evaluation research* (pp. 7–32). Beverly Hills, CA: Sage.

Rossman, G. B., & Wilson, B. L. (1985). Numbers and words: Combining quantitative and qualitative methods in a single large-scale evaluation study. *Evaluation Review*, *9*, 627–643.

Smith, J. K. (1983). Quantitative versus qualitative research: An attempt to clarify the issue. *Educational Researcher*, *12*(3), 6–13.

Teddlie, C., & Tashakkori, A. (2006). A general typology of research designs featuring mixed methods. *Research in the Schools*, *13*(1), 12–28.

Weisner, T. S. (2002). Ecocultural understanding of children's developmental pathways. *Human Development*, *45*(4), 275–281.

CHAPTER
35

Conundrums of Multimethod Research

Albert Hunter *and* John Brewer

Abstract

The spirit of multimethod research embraces an openness to the use of more than one method in a research project and the possibility of convergent and divergent findings because both provide opportunities for greater knowledge. *Multimethod research*, as the term is used here, refers to the use of either multiple quantitative methods, multiple qualitative methods, or mixtures of these two types of methods. This chapter addresses questions and reflects on conundrums that have arisen about multimethods as a social science research strategy. Three categories are considered—first, conundrums about multimethods in relation to the social sciences as science, second conundrums about multimethods in relation to social theory, and third, conundrums raised about where multimethod research, as we understand and define it, fits in relation to other methodological approaches. The chapter begins with a brief historical account of the development of "methods" that have produced the conundrums surrounding multimethod research.

Key Words: multimethod research, multiple quantitative methods, multimethods, conundrums, theory

Once upon a time poetry and science were one,
and its name was magic.

    C. D. Lewis

We turn to this observation of C. D. Lewis (1957) in the spirit of attempting to restore the magic and majesty of science. Magic consists of the yet unexplained phenomena experienced in our world, and science attempts to transform that magic into elegant explanations and understanding—a type of poetry in numbers, words, and images. The use of multimethods in the social sciences as a particular strategy has arisen out of a set of concerns, questions, or conundrums about the current state and future directions of the social sciences themselves, and it is a strategy we think will work its magic.

Within the social sciences, the early dialogues between scientists and the real world consisted of a limited number of different methods and types of data focused on people in their collective endeavors—historical accounts and archives of various kinds from administrative accounts of economic transactions to state censuses—but perhaps most central were personal observations of participants themselves, whether observing their own social milieu or journeying to observe far-off lands and people. The later development of explicit methods and procedures of research evolved in response to skeptics who often questioned the veracity of a given account and/or submitted alternative data, observations, and interpretations (Brewer & Hunter, 2006, pp. 26–29). The process of publicly presenting, challenging, defending, and debating theoretical interpretations, research techniques, and concrete data continues to be the lifeblood of the scientific method writ large. The multimethod perspective has both grown out of and furthered these debates.

In this brief discussion we address questions and reflect on conundrums that have arisen about multimethods as a social science research strategy, and we break our consideration into three categories—first, conundrums about multimethods in relation to the social sciences as *science;* second, conundrums about multimethods in relation to social theory; and third, conundrums raised about where multimethod research, as we understand and define it, fits in relation to other methodological approaches. But first we give a brief historical account of the development of "methods" that have produced the conundrums surrounding multimethod research.

Historical Development—The Initial Conundrum

There is but one central scientific method, and it is based on "observations" of the world related to our "ideas" about what that real world is and how it operates. Modern science itself was born when Sir Francis Bacon took the questions that medieval rhetoricians posed to one another and instead suggested we pose them to nature itself and observe its responses (Hunter, 1990, p. 1). We begin from this premise with the central epistemological conundrum or question that sets up the entire discussion of methods and methodology: *How* do you know? (not *what* do you know?, while recognizing full well that what you know is intimately tied to the question of how you know). This simple question is the basis of all the processes and nature of observations that are relied on for knowledge of that real world.

A related central conundrum we pose is the relationship between what the methods of social inquiry are "in use" and what it is that social investigators think and write about their methods—between what they do and what they think about what they are doing—in short, between deeds and words. The question becomes how and why this *consciousness,* this reflexivity about methods, has arisen and resulted in our current concern with the multimethod perspective. Methodological consciousness need not be a precondition for research; as Max Weber (1949) noted,

> Methodology can only bring us reflective understanding of the means which have *demonstrated* their value in practice by raising them to the level of consciousness; it is no more the precondition of fruitful intellectual work than the knowledge of anatomy is the precondition for "correct" walking. (p. 115)

And as Jennifer Platt (1966) simply put it: "it need not be the case that all aspects of method actually practiced are written about, or conceptualized as distinct" (p. 32).

Within the social sciences and sociology in particular early methods of observation were eclectic and disparate such as the early "social survey" movement at the turn of the 20th century that included, among numerous others, Booth (1889) in London, Addams (2006) in Chicago, and duBois (1899/2006) in Philadelphia. Their "methods" ranged from interviews, census statistics, and especially mapping. The early definition of *field work* also included such eclectic methods, and numerous exemplars of the adumbration of what would later be defined as *multimethods* exist (see Brewer & Hunter, 2006, pp. xvi–xxiv). In short, from their beginnings, the newly emerging social sciences were multimethod.

As the social sciences grew and became specialized in substance and method, debates began to arise about distinctions among methods, and an early one was that between the case study and the use of interviews. This was soon followed by the most enduring distinction between quantitative and qualitative methods, though during this early period a genuflection in the direction of one method toward the value of the other in some combination was usually noted (Platt, 1996). The quan and qual distinction and debate continued for decades with a shadow chorus in the background always presenting the alternative to an "either/or" dichotomy with a simple "both." Out of this cacophony was eventually to emerge the current call for "mixed method" research in addition to the prior "multimethod" eclecticism. The multimethod call for an integration if not a return to a unity of science and knowledge (as in the case of "consilience" to be discussed later) has grown out of the increasing specialization and diversity of both methods and substance within scientific and social thought.

Multimethods and Social Science as Science

When we first introduced multimethod research in 1989, we did so within a positivist scientific framework with all the assumptions that would entail such as physicalism, patterned order, objectivity, and intersubjectivity. In our subsequent writings we have extended it to address other frameworks or perspectives such as constructivist and postpositive perspectives. Multimethods can include what some call "different paradigms" unless people are so wedded to one or another particular paradigm and are unwilling to relax or consider alternative assumptions of different paradigms, which is not in the overall open spirit of the multimethod perspective. The more constructivist perspective of science studies, for example, does not by definition nor of necessity negate the utility of narrow scientific research results but rather provides yet another layer of skepticism and questioning. Any given datum or observation of the real world is not inherently the province of one paradigm or another. For example, take the responses of a person to questions asked in an interview as a particular method; they can be treated as either qualitative or quantitative data and can be analyzed as a report of factual information (date of birth) or reports of behavior (whether or not one voted in the last election), statements of internal feelings, or attitudes or preferences (anxiety over job, stance on abortion); or, more directly, an interview may be seen as interaction with an interviewer and respondent (discourse analysis or power relations). The "facticity" or "constructivist" meaning of the data depends on the assumption one wishes to make about them. There is no qualitative nor quantitative mode of analysis determined by a given paradigm.

The question of where multimethod research fits in terms of social science research requires that we first have some degree of understanding of social science. Critical here is the question of whether or not the various so called social sciences—the traditional disciplines ranging from anthropology through communication to economics, history, political science, and sociology—should be defined as "sciences" at all. Some suggest that all of these could be more aptly encompassed in the more nebulous and broader noncommittal concept of "social studies." For example, *communication studies* is the more common label for the field, and only later did departments of "government" become relabeled "political science." We cannot review the depth and diversity of these debates fully here but touch on a few points in relation to a multimethod perspective that highlight the conundrum: Are the social sciences science?

One answer to this question has been offered using Thomas Kuhn's (1996) concept of "paradigm," which he introduced in his influential book *The Structure of Scientific Revolutions.* He defined a scientific paradigm as: "universally recognized scientific achievements that, for a time, provide model problems and solutions for a community of practitioners" (1996, p. 10). This would characterize "normal science" operating within a dominant

paradigm in contrast to "revolutionary science," which would involve competing paradigms and the eventual succession of one by another. The social sciences were exempt from this analysis and labelled "preparadigmatic" in that there was not a single consensually agreed-on paradigm operating to define research agendas but rather many different "perspectives," "orientations," or "frameworks." To refer to these as "multiple paradigms" is to vitiate the meaning of paradigm itself as a hegemonic framework and perhaps run the risk of creating an oxymoron. The social sciences were at best a "qualified science."

In our first formulation of the multimethod perspective we explicitly stressed the need to consider multimethods at various stages of the research process, from problem definition, to data collection and measurement, to analysis and theoretical framing and presentation. One could pose at each of these stages an additional set of more specific questions that would or could challenge a "scientific" set of answers or assumptions or caveats with an infinite regress of problematizing challenges. One specific case in point is that of causation—a philosophical assumption of claims to science challenged by David Hume and one that leads to such refined distinctions as necessary versus sufficient versus contingent causation. A narrow conception of the goal of scientific pursuits might hinge on whether or not one seeks in analysis "understanding" or "prediction," or ideographic versus nomothetic explanation. Another could be the very meaning of what constitutes "measurement." Are "facts" discovered or constructed? And by what physical and social process? Are qualitative distinctions sufficient for some purposes (the chemist's "flame test" matching compound to color) or are "numeric" equivalencies (metric scales of weights) required? Clearly the answer is not a uniform one or the other but rather the more qualified and contingent response that "it depends on the question asked" and "what do you want to use the answer for?" This is precisely where a multimethod perspective is of value. It forces one to confront the numerous decision points of research to bring assumptions to the fore and recognize the multiplicity of potential answers rather than sweeping them under the rug, through ignorance, mental laxness, habits, or narrowed competencies.

Some see the use of the word *research* itself as a loaded preformative concept privileging what they consider a "scientistic" orientation. Other concepts and words admit broader more inclusive interpretations that imply or connote alternative activities and modes of thought and analysis, such as *investigation, inquiry, study*. For example *the case study* or *science studies* are two joined terms that loosen the activities of such scholars from what they see as the more narrow connotations of "scientific research." The details of a narrative account of a case is a contribution to scholarship, but is it science? We might see it as a contribution to data and to science "writ large" as an ongoing collective social endeavor. A "piece" of research within science is an artificially bounded entity (a paper, a book, a report of an experiment) and makes sense in the larger context. Multimethod research can be seen as a property or characterization of science as a whole, or of a discipline, or a subdiscipline, or of a research program, or of a single piece of research undertaken by a research group or a single researcher. In general the use of the term today implies that it can occur at the level of the single piece of research, the study of a specific question, wherein researchers consciously employ different methods of inquiry or investigation.

Multimethods and the Conundrums of Theory

Theory is a central component of the social sciences, and multimethods have a significant relationship to theory. The specific conundrums posed here include: "What do we mean by *theory*?" and "What bearing might multimethods have with respect to theory?" In a now classic formulation, Robert Merton (1968) explored the relationship between research methods and theory, elucidating some of the contributions that each makes to the other. He explicitly formulated what the contributions of methods to theory might be. Drawing directly from Merton, there are four ways in which research methods are significant for theory: initiation, reformulation, refocusing, and clarification. Parallel to his argument, we can suggest how multimethods contribute to social theory.

Let us first note that theory itself is a complex concept with numerous definitions and connotations within the sciences in general and the social sciences in particular. Let us take the simplest approach that theory is a generalized set of statements offered as explanations to account for disparate set of distinct "facts" (Latour & Woolgar, 1986). This of course then raises the additional question of what constitutes a fact. The conundrum

posed here is whether one takes the scientific positivist view that facts about the real world are "discovered" through research or the more postmodernist view that facts are "socially constructed" and constitute or are constituted by a degree of collective consensus. This literature is too extensive to address in this brief discussion other than to note it is another of the conundrums raised by a multimethod perspective. Different methods may be seen on the one hand to create different facts that may or may not converge, or, on the other hand, the different methods may together be seen to produce different facets of a more general and perhaps nuanced conclusion, a different level and type of "facticity."

Another way of viewing theory is generalized abstraction that simplifies the complexities of the real world. One way we do this is by building models—facsimiles that simplify the real world by making various assumptions and ignoring some elements of that complexity such as invoking *ceterus paribus* while fully recognizing of course that in the real world it is rare to find "other things being equal." It is in this sense that "scientific" theories are by definition abstractions from the real world and are based on simplifying assumptions. The central scientific question to ask about theory, then, is not whether it is true or not but rather whether it is a model of reality that seems to "work" (i.e., is it congruent with and does it account for observed facts?). Multimethod research addresses different types of "modelling" from the statistical mathematical model, to the metaphoric modelling of rhetoricians recognizing the simplifying assumptions of each but also recognizing the different insights each may produce.

A related conundrum to this idea of theory as abstraction or generalization is the question of how broad or narrow the generalizations might be. All research is contingent (on the method used) and contextualized (to the specific observations made), and a good researcher acknowledges these "limitations." Note, however, that with the use of multimethods the limitations may be reduced in that different phenomena of observation may be available to different methods, and a diversity of contexts may broaden the potential generalization. This is readily apparent, for example, when addressing the "ethical" strictures that may be posed by the use of different methods (Humphreys, 1970)

We now briefly look at Merton's (1968) four types of method in relation to theory: initiation, reformulation, refocusing, and clarification.

The Serendipity Pattern: The Unanticipated, Anomalous, and Strategic Datum Exerts Pressure for Initiating Theory

Merton (1968) termed "serendipity . . . the discovery by chance or sagacity" of results unanticipated. (p. 103) Multimethods can generate theory as well as test it, and this goes far beyond the old dichotomous assertion that qualitative research generates post hoc theory to fit the observations while quantitative research tests hypotheses deductively derived from theory. Qualitative research can test theory (as in field researchers' use of the constant comparative method to test grounded theories or historical comparative case studies testing causal theories), and quantitative research can generate new theory as well, such as when new statistics are produced such as Facebook network data. As Merton succinctly states, "fruitful empirical research not only tests theoretically derived hypotheses; it also originates new hypotheses" (p. 103). With multimethod research, testing and generating theory are an ongoing cyclical and iterative process, and in Merton's felicitous phrase it is "fruitful" and multiples. The use of multiple different methods to explore propositions of a theory may therefore expand the breadth of a theory by allowing a variety of propositions to be explored.

The Recasting of Theory: New Data Exert Pressure for the Elaboration of a Conceptual Scheme

Merton (1968) elaborates this as theory "reformulation" that "centers in the hitherto neglected but relevant fact which presses for an extension of the conceptual scheme" (p. 108). Multimethods we suggest not only generate new facts but different kinds and types of facts that call for theoretical extension. Often subfields within a discipline rightly build on one another in research programs that in the sense of normal science lead to cumulative research and deeper understanding of a phenomenon. By using multimethods of data collection or analysis that may simultaneously be inside *and* outside, or different from those deemed "traditional" within such a subfield, new data and analyses may reformulate theory. An example is the way in which "victimization surveys" reformulated theories of varying "crime rates" apart from traditional officially reported crime statistics. (Ennis, 1967).

The Refocusing of Theoretic Interest: New Methods of Empirical Research Exert Pressure for New Foci of Theoretic Interest

Merton (1968) further clarifies this as "the invention of research procedures which tend to shift the foci of theoretic interest to the growing points of research. . . new centers of theoretic interest have followed upon the invention of research procedures" (p. 112). As an example, Merton discusses how new research procedures such as content-analysis, the panel technique, and the focused interview led to an accumulation of data that spawned a growing interest in the theory of propaganda as a state instrument of social control (p. 112). In today's world, the Internet and big-data technology are examples that have led to an explosive interest in "network theory" in the social sciences, and these have not displaced but been incorporated with other methods in a multimethod approach (Witte, 2004). As noted previously, multimethod research generates the application of methods developed in one area of research to different areas of theoretic interest that may have developed primarily on a body of facts generated by a singular set of data collection and modes of analysis. Here we are suggesting a further extension in that familiarity with multimethods can lead to the invention of hybridized forms such as quasi-experiments built into survey research and even into field research experiments. (Schuman & Presser, 1996)

The Clarification of Concepts: Empirical Research Exerts Pressure for Clear Concepts

Merton (1968) quotes Rebecca West who disparages "methodological empiricism" that reports a plethora of "causal findings" without understanding the concepts themselves, and she states "one might know that A and B and C were linked by certain causal connexions (*sic*), but he would never apprehend with any exactitude the nature of A or B or C" (p. 115). Merton himself notes that "Operationalism is one case of researchers demanding a clarification of concepts in terms of procedures of research" (p. 115). And we note that in this light, multimethods may be thought of in one sense as multioperationalism. Multimethods thus contribute to this refinement of the various nuanced meanings of concepts.

If people contend that multimethod research is only looking explicitly for confirmation or corroboration of results from the use of distinct methods, they are implying that multimethod research is restricted to ascertaining the validity of different methods with respect to the same concept and hypotheses or propositions. Now a given concept may have multiple real-world referents or "operational measurements," just as conversely a single measurement or operational definition may be logically linked to multiple concepts. Another way of viewing this is to understand there is always a concept—a measurement gap, or the "inferential leap" from observation to concept. This inferential leap is characteristic of all sciences—and is a singular moment of creativity difficult to teach and to learn. More prosaically it is a question of the validity of a given measurement and more specifically is assessed by "face validity," which precisely addresses the question of whether it makes sense on its surface. (This is apart from other forms of validity that have more technical procedures to establish their claims such as construct validity and predictive validity.) This conundrum then becomes a question of "meaning" and the degree to which a concept is embedded in a language community that can agree on the nuances and myriad connotations of a concept and its implications and referents for a given measurement. It is at this point that multimethods can offer not an ultimate solution to this conundrum of multiple meanings but a working solution that accepts the conundrum by offering multiple meanings inherent within the very idea of "the inferential leap" and that will speak to different different communities of inquiry both scientific and humanistic.

Merton (1968) acknowledges that these four ways in which research is important for theory are not exhaustive and readily concludes that "doubtless there are others" (p. 117) and that theory and research do not have a preferred sequence of one required before the other. We leave to the reader to consider additional ways in which multimethod research contributes to social theory.

Multimethods and Methods and Methodology

Many of the methodological questions of multimethods in relation to other methods within the social sciences come to focus on questions of measurement and the nature and meaning of those measurements. First, multimethods takes a broad view of the meaning of measurement itself. Measurement may be either quantitative or qualitative in nature. Multimethods can include multiple qualitative methods (e.g., interviews and ethnographic observations). Second, it can include multiple quantitative methods (e.g., survey Likert-type questions and archival data such as grades in school). Third, it can include a mix of quantitative and qualitative methods. That is, what is generally referred to as "mixed method" research (e.g., quantitative Likert survey questions and qualitative data such as a life history). Though qualitative and quantitative methods are clearly different and involve different types of data and modes of analysis, they are nonetheless also similar in that they share central concerns of all sciences such as discernment of patterns and reproducibility and falsifiability.

Validity, corroboration, and triangulation are not the same thing, and multimethods does not assume one answer to a research question. When different measures of phenomena do produce similar results in support of a proposition, that does produce a heightened sense of the validity of one's assertions, while still recognizing that all such assertions come with the *ceteris paribus* caveat "given the methods used and data available at this time." However, divergent results with different methods are also of significance in multimethod research, and this extends beyond the more narrow measurement question of triangulation. Divergent results from a multimethod piece of research may speak to different aspects of reality that the different methods are tapping into. This is not a problem in and of itself, but, on the contrary, where things get interesting and exciting! One must now seek to explain how and why it is that the very procedures of different methods may produce divergent research results. Triangulation may occur or it may not; triangulation is not the "goal" per se; if it occurs, well and good, but absence of "same results" is also knowledge. This was particularly the case in Janet Lever's (1978) research on children's play wherein she used three different methods of data collection comparing boys' and girls' play—diaries, observations, and interviews. Systematic differences of the size of play groups and the nature of the play were documented depending on the data from the different methods. For example, in-person interviews produced more gender-stereotypical normative results than did either observations or diaries.

Finally we turn to a set of methodological questions and conundrums that have been posed about multimethod research that go beyond the narrow question of measurement and triangulation. One is the question of the distinction between subjective/emic versus objective/etic stances or frames. The former includes exemplars from deep ethnography and the latter more mathematical statistical modelling. These concern the nature of data, units, and mode of analysis. Again, the beauty of a multimethod perspective is that it would not disparage one or the other but rather encourage both perspective and combine Weber's (1949) *verstehen* with Durkheim's "social facts" in the same piece of research. Multimethod also recognizes that the subjective versus objective distinction is not the same as the emic versus etic distinction and that one can in fact conceive of a four-fold table of objective emic and objective etic research, as well as subjective emic and subjective etic research.

A second conundrum posed of multimethod research methods is whether or not they have the ability to combine micro and macro levels of analysis—often framed as individual and interpersonal versus structural levels. We would suggest that from the multimethod perspective this addresses the question of units of observation and analysis. We have elsewhere shown that multimethod research is particularly adept at addressing "structural effects" and the way in which structural contexts (a more macro level) impact individuals' properties (a micro level). John Kasarda (1974), in a landmark piece of multimethod research, demonstrated how system size is related to ratios of administrative control at three different levels of analysis from organizations, to local communities, to nations.

Conclusion: The Conundrum of Consilience

The concept of *consilience*" has a narrow and a broader definition, both of which produce conundrums of different kinds for the multimethod perspective and constitute a summary conclusion to our discussion. The narrow definition first proposed by William Whewell (1870) in the mid-19th century asserts that agreement of inductions from different methods of measurement strengthens conclusions. In essence he was asserting a central conclusion of the multimethod perspective that divergent methods, when they concur, increase the credibility of research results. The broader conception of consilience most recently championed by Edward O. Wilson (1998) in his book of the eponymous title refers to the "unity of knowledge" more generally across disciplines, especially the "two cultures" of science and the humanities demarcated by C. P. Snow (1959). The narrow definition poses the conundrum of confirmation and corroboration, while the broader definition raises the conundrum

of multimethod's relation to science and to humanistic postmodern conceptions of knowledge. Both speak to a "coming together," one in the sense of more narrow method and measurement and the other in a sense of overarching patterns and order. They were both responding to the specialization and differentiation that have become prevalent over time in research, inquiry, or the search for knowledge, meaning, and understanding. Both are in the spirit of multimethod research.

Beginning and Concluding Assumptions

The only way we know what reality might be is through our observations and systematic research. We cannot compare the results of our research to reality, because we do not know what that reality might be; if we did know it we would not need to do the research in the first place. We may place an intuitive higher probability of having captured some aspect of reality from a given piece of research if we have followed procedures that attempt to address various threats to the validity of our assertions. But we recognize that all research methods have systematic biases and errors—known and unknown. All methods and measurement are flawed and have errors, and we strive to reduce these to the best of our ability, fully recognizing threats to validity will persist. We can only assess the validity of our research when we compare our research results to other observations and other research results, not directly to reality itself, but it is a reality always filtered through observation and measurement. Now one way of doing this is through replication research (Hunter, 1983). Replication is done to assess the "reproducibility" of research results, and it consists of using the same methods and measurements as the original research (monomethod) and seeing if one attains the same results. This may also be considered a form of "reliability"—assessing if repeated use of the same methods and measurements produce the same results. The more similar the results, the more likely one has faith in the reliability of the methods. Whether they are valid or not is a more stringent assessment, for one may have reliability without validity. That additional criterion is the degree to which it fits with additional research results from other studies or from a multimethod perspective with results from the same research that has used different methods and measurements. And if results are not reproducible, then one can question the validity of the original assertions because of an inconsistency in the method itself. Claims to cold fusion research in physics were ultimately discredited when other researchers using the same procedures could not achieve the same results. Also, true scientists, when reporting the results of their research, are hesitant in their assertions awaiting additional confirmation.

It is a misconception of science that it purports to state the universal truth about reality. It is much more modest in its claims and conclusions. In this day and age, when there are many critics of science and the social sciences specifically, it is important that we not oversell what science can and does do and acknowledge its limitations. But at the same time we should not sell it short nor accede any ground to those who purport to make claims to truth that do not acknowledge their own shortcomings and the provisional nature of their knowledge as well. Science rightly is skeptical of true believers proclaiming "truth," especially those internal to its own ranks. Science is not perfect, but to paraphrase what Winston Churchill said about democracy and the art of governance, it is an imperfect system but better than all the alternatives; so, too, science is an imperfect system of arriving at a conception of reality, but it is far better and more powerful than any others yet devised. And we should use all the weapons in our arsenal.

References

Addams, J. (2006). *Hull-house maps and papers.* Urbana: University of Illinois Press.

Brewer, J., & Hunter, A. (2006). *Foundations of multimethod research: Synthesizing styles.* Thousand Oaks, CA: Sage.

Booth, C. (1889). *Life and labour of the people of London.* London, England: Macmillan.

Du Bois, W. E. B. (1996). *Philadelphia Negro.* Philadelphia, PA: University of Pennsylvania Press. (Original work published in 1899)

Ennis, P. (1967). Crimes, victims and the police. *Trans-action, 4*(7), 36–37.

Humphreys, L. (1970). *Tearoom trade.* London, England: Duckworth

Hunter, A. (1983). The Gold Coast and the slum revisited: Paradoxes in replication research and the study of social change. *Urban Life, 11*(4), 461–476.

Hunter, A., ed. (1990). *The rhetoric of social research: Understood & believed.* New Brunswick, NJ: Rutgers University Press.

Latour, B., & Woolgar, S. (1986). *Laboratory life: The construction of scientific facts.* Princeton, NJ: Princeton University Press.

Lever, J. (1978). Sex differences in the complexity of children's play and games. *American Sociological Review, 4*(4), 471–483.

Lewis. C. D. (1957). *The Poet's Way of Knowledge.* Cambridge University Press, p. 3.

Kasarda, J. D. (1974). The structural implications of social system size: A three-level analysis. *American Sociological Review, 39*(1), 19–28.

Merton, R. (1968). The bearing of the empirical research on sociological theory. In *Social theory and social structure* (pp. 102–117). New York, NY: Free Press. (Original work published 1957)

Platt, J. (1966). *A history of sociological research methods in America 1920–1960.* Cambridge, UK: Cambridge University Press.

Schuman, H., & Presser, S. (1996). *Questions and answers in attitude surveys.* Thousand Oaks, CA: Sage.

Snow, C. P. (1998). *The two cultures.* Cambridge, UK: Cambridge University Press. (Original work published 1959)

Weber, M. (1949). *The methodology of the social sciences.* New York, NY: Free Press.

Whewell, W. (1870). *History of the inductive sciences.* New York, NY: Appleton.

Wilson, E. O. (1998). *Consilience: The unity of knowledge.* New York, NY: Random House.

Witte, J. C. (2004). Prologue: The case for multimethod research. In P. N. Howard & S. Jones (Eds.), *Society online: The Internet in context* (pp. xv–xxxiv). Thousand Oaks, CA: Sage.

It Depends: Possible Impacts of Moving the Field of Mixed Methods Research Toward Best Practice Guidelines

Julianne Cheek

Abstract

At first it may seem that the idea of moving the field of mixed methods research to best practice guidelines is unproblematic. It is assumed that identifying correct, effective, and best ways to do mixed methods research in the form of best practice guidelines is an admirable and desirable goal that can only enhance the development of the field. However this may not necessarily be so as it depends on how and why those guidelines are developed, as well what they are used for. Using examples drawn from contemporary best practice guideline development in mixed methods research such as those developed in the US for the National Institutes of Health (NIH), this chapter explores the impact any move to best practice guidelines could have on understandings of what can, and might, be *called* mixed methods research, as well as on how mixed methods research can, or might, be *done*. The conundrum is if, and if so how, such a move can retain the promise of a "mixed methods way of thinking" (Greene, 2007) and not sell out to new forms of methods-centric thinking (Hesse-Biber, 2010b).

Key Words: best practice guidelines, mixed methods research, mixed methods way of thinking, NIH, methods-centric thinking

An Invitation

This chapter is an invitation. Readers are invited to pull up a chair at the "dialogue table" alluded to by Hesse-Biber (Hesse-Biber 2010a, p. 417) and participate in a thoughtful "dialogue across differences" (Maxwell, 2004, p. 35) regarding possible impacts of moving the field of mixed methods research toward best practice guidelines. Joining this dialogue does not mean that at the end of it we will all necessarily agree about those differences. However, it does mean that we will have a deeper understanding of each other's points of view, appreciate that there are different ways of looking at issues in mixed methods research, and put our energy into how to work with and use these differences constructively. Such dialogue across differences is an important part of the

ongoing growth and development of an inclusive, respectful, vibrant, and consequently strong field of mixed methods research. It can contribute to new and different ways of looking at and addressing the conundrum that arises for mixed methods researchers from the interfaces of mixed methods, best practice, and guidelines. Cutting to the chase, this conundrum is how to make sure that the impact of any best practice guideline(s) for mixed methods research enables, rather than constrains, the thinking about and subsequent development of this emerging research field.

So what is this "dialogue table"? It is a table that has been around for a long time and that has had different groups of people sitting around it in various combinations at various points in time. Many scholars in the field of qualitative inquiry found themselves pulling up chairs at this table in the 1990s when interest in qualitative research was increasing and there were calls for the development of checklists, standards, and guidelines for qualitative research from funders, governments, journal editors, and others (e.g., Treloar, Champness, Simpson, & Higginbotham, 2000). To sit at this table is thus to join and build on a dialogue about the interfaces and intersections of research, research methods, best practice, and guidelines that has been in existence in research-related contexts for decades.

This dialogue is not just about talking, putting forth a point of view, and maybe even trying to score points in a discussion. Rather, it is about listening actively, deeply, and respectfully to others' points of view to locate where commonalities exist and how tensions and points of contention can be navigated and traversed. It is about exploring and understanding how to work together by recognizing and pooling collective knowledge and wisdom. It is about how to get through, and what happens as a result of, disagreements or different emphases in that dialogue and emerge the stronger for having done so. Dialogue is about learning to tolerate ambiguity and uncertainty and learning to work with it rather than seeking to eliminate it. Such dialogue is not about "anything goes" but rather what might go and why or why not. It opens up possibilities rather than shutting them down.

Consequently, at this table the dialogue is comprised of first and tentative words rather than last or definitive ones. Last-word positions that aim to bring about closure with respect to guidelines for best practices in mixed methods research are premature and unhelpful to a research approach that is still relatively fluid as it matures and develops. First and tentative word positions enable ongoing dialogue that offers the possibility of resisting simplistic and unhelpful dichotomies in relation to best practice and best practice guidelines *themselves*, such as best practice guidelines being good or bad, useful or not useful. Such resistance is important, as sustaining these dichotomies gives rise to polemic positions and last-word positions such as *the* way—or worse, the *only* way—to think about best practice in relation to the conduct of mixed methods research. The impact of these last-word positions is to stunt and skew the development of the field of mixed methods research by excluding other possibilities for the field's development.

To illustrate what I mean when talking about bringing first-word positions to the dialogue table,

Maxwell provides us with an example of how this might be done. When writing about the impact of the move by the Bush administration in the United States to narrow understandings of, and create last-word positions about, what could be called science and scientific inquiry in the field of education, Maxwell (2004) declared that he was speaking from his own standpoint rather than "asserting 'One Right Way' of addressing this issue" (p. 39)—a final word or absolute position. Acknowledging that any speaking done is done from a particular standpoint or view recognizes there are other views possible and leaves open the door for dialogue. This is the position from which I offer the ideas to follow. It is one that actively seeks to resist promoting the idea of "one right way" of looking at the complex issues we are exploring.

Thus readers will be disappointed if they expect the chapter to offer definitive answers to the conundrum posed by any move of the field of mixed methods research to best practice guidelines. Instead, they are urged to actively consider and reflect on the material presented here, thereby enabling the dialogue to continue well after the reading of the chapter.

And the Short Answer Is, "It Depends"

Any movement of the field of mixed methods research toward some form(s) of best practice guidelines is complex. There are cascading choices to be made at every stage of considering and enacting such a move. These choices are interrelated and interdependent in that each choice made affects the next series of choices that are, or even can be, made. For example, one possible choice that can be made is to decide to develop best practice guidelines for mixed methods research. Once this choice is made, there are further layers of choices to be navigated. These choices include what aspect(s) of mixed methods research the guidelines are for, what will be in those guidelines, who will make that decision, and what gives them the authority to do so. There are also choices to be made about the use of the guidelines once they have been developed. Thus best practice guidelines are built on layers of choices about choices about choices.

Because there are so many choices possible at each point of the thinking about and enactment of best practice guidelines, any move to best practice guidelines in the field of mixed methods research is likely to be contentious. There may be disagreement about any or all of the choices to be made in such a move and resultant turbulence in the wake of such debate (Hesse-Biber & Johnson, 2013). However as Hesse-Biber and Johnson point out, such turbulence is a necessary moment in, and part of, the healthy development of the field of mixed methods research, providing "spaces for innovation and productive dialogue across our methods and paradigmatic standpoints" (p. 104). It is from the turbulence that new knowledge and questions arise, resulting in more choices being available to mixed methods researchers in terms of developing a dynamic, robust, and exciting research field.

In many ways the impact of moving the field of mixed methods research toward best practice guidelines depends on how such turbulence is navigated and what emerges from it. Will the field of mixed methods research be able to engage with any move to best practice guidelines, rather than having that move engage it? This depends on whether the best practices are seen as means to an end and not an end in themselves, and if guidelines guide rather than prescribe. Put another way, it depends on whether the focus remains on using best practice guidelines to advance and develop the field of mixed methods research rather than shifting the focus to the best practice guidelines themselves, to which the field of mixed methods research is, and even must be, fitted.

We begin our exploration of these questions, and our contribution to a dialogue across differences about their possible answers, by taking a closer look at the idea of the term *best* itself. What does this term actually mean, and what are the assumptions that are embedded within it? Thinking about this will enable us to consider the effects that this meaning and those assumptions have when the ideas of *best* and *practice* are combined into *best practice(s)* and transported into fields such as mixed methods research.

Cutting and Pasting "Best" into "Best Practices" and "Best Practices" into Research—What Gets Lost Along the Way?

The *Oxford Online Dictionary* ("Best Practice," 2013) defines *best practice* as "commercial or professional procedures that are accepted or prescribed as being correct or most effective." Similarly, the *Cambridge Online Dictionary* ("Best Practice," 2013) offers this definition: "a working method or set of working methods that is officially accepted as being the best to use in a particular business or industry, usually described formally and in detail." From these definitions, we can glean that best

practice has to do with procedures or ways of doing things that are accepted or prescribed in some sort of authoritative way as being "correct," "most effective," or "the best to use." The procedures can then be captured and/or provided in guidelines and standards published by, for example, government organizations, professional associations, and quality groups (e.g., Cochrane Collaboration Methods Group [Hannes, 2011]; National Institutes of Health [Creswell, Klassen, Plano Clark, & Smith, 2011]).

These definitions of best practice carry within them the residual footprint of where the term came from in the first place. It originated in the areas of business and management where "best" was associated with a desire for improved business-related output. Best practice and understandings associated with it were therefore focused on the development of procedures designed to promote efficiency and effectiveness. Efficiency and effectiveness in turn were defined in relation to increasing output of specific products by, for example, reducing manufacturing time or production costs (Nadel, Shipley, & Elliott, 2004). In addition, stating that a product had been produced in line with accepted/prescribed best practices became an important marketing tool and ploy. The term *best practice*, along with the understandings and emphases within it, derived from business, has been transported to, imitated by, and adapted by areas as diverse as education, healthcare, service delivery, policy, project management, and research methods (Bardach, 2011). As a result, the idea of best practice has become entrenched in much of the rhetoric and writing in many varied fields, inevitably with a positive connotation.

Yet such definitions of best practice are partial. This is because within them there are terms that remain undefined. One of these is *best*. *Best* is a term that is so common in usage that its meaning is often taken for granted or assumed to be common sense. However, as Bardach (2011) points out, common-sense terms can be used in "special" ways, and the use of these terms in these special ways may strip them of certain connotations while importing others to them. Applying Bardach's contention to the use of the term *best* in relation to best practice, the "special" way that the term *best* is used relates to what is considered to work optimally in terms of producing a specific outcome or product. In turn, *optimal* is assumed to be what works most effectively and efficiently, terms that are also defined in relation to the production of that specific predetermined outcome or product. Thus, *best* in relation to best practice is transformed into a relative term. What is best or can be considered as best depends on the practices that it is best in relation to.

Yet not all products produced by best practice are necessarily "best" or even good products in themselves. For example, we can speak of best practices for the production of weapons of mass destruction, or conducting a political campaign for an extremist political party, but surely none of us would even remotely think of associating *best* with the products these best practices are defined in relation to. As Ambler (2012), reminds us, "Depending on the context, sometimes a practice is 'best' and sometimes it's not. Calling something a 'best practice' implies that it's a good idea all of the time, something we inherently know to be false." Being produced by best practices does not in itself make a product good, the only "good," or even the best product possible. The *best* in best practices is defined in terms of its connection to layers of other terms, all of which are focused on articulating how to develop or do "best practice" in a specific context for a specific predetermined product or outcome. One consequence of this is that the idea of best is stripped of associations or judgments about the product itself. Another is that over time it may be possible for someone to claim something to be best on the basis of an association with the term *best practice* alone.

Paramount in all this is holding on to the distinction between the question of what *best* in a given field actually means and signifies, and the question of what set of actions might be called *best* in relation to the production of a specific product in a given field or context. The first question gives emphasis to a much wider concept of *best* itself. For example, we might ask: What is the best way to think about answering or addressing a particular problem? Here, *best* emerges in relation to thinking about the problem. Possibilities for what is and can be considered as best are not bounded or confined to particular practices. The second question focuses on *best* in relation to practices that are best in terms of producing a specific product or outcome, for example, increasing compliance with specific occupational and safety regulations in a specific work setting. This is a much more bounded concept of best. *Best* in this instance relates to practices designed to get workers to comply with those regulations. It does not necessarily mean that those regulations are the best or only ones possible.

Distinguishing between what best in a given field actually means and signifies and what set of actions might be called best in relation to the production of a specific product in a given field or context is something that is often overlooked, ignored, or simply not thought about in the rush to develop guidelines and statements about best practice. It is the second question that is given mainframe in most discussions about and definitions of best practice. The first question is seldom asked. Consequently, in discussions of best practice, *best* is often defined by default and limited to an understanding of *best* in terms of ways of producing a specific product in a specific context. However, as we have seen, *best practice* and *best* are not synonymous terms. *Best* as it applies to best practices is always a bounded concept of best that applies to, and can only be understood in relation to, a specific context.

Thus, when considering any move within, or of, the field of mixed methods research to best practice guidelines, the concept of *best* itself must not get lost sight of along the way. There is a difference between best practice as a tool for identifying procedures that are "best" in the context of helping produce a specific form of mixed methods research product, and best practice as necessarily ensuring the production of "the best" of the many possible mixed methods products. In a developing and relatively fluid field such as mixed methods research, productive and continuing dialogue is needed about what desired and "best" products in this research field are and might be. This is a dialogue about what mixed methods are and are not, can and might be, as well as how they might and might not be done. It is one about reflecting on how to keep to the fore the possibility of plurality of approach to, and innovation in thinking about, mixed method research design that is its inherent strength. It is part of holding on to and protecting the possibility for dialogue about "multiple ways of hearing, multiple ways of making sense of the social world, and multiple standpoints on what is important and to be valued and cherished" (Greene, 2007, p. 20). It is a dialogue that avoids the danger of an "othering" (Maxwell, 2004, p. 39) or exclusion of a range of views as to what "best" in mixed methods research is and might be.

Without dialogue across these differences, any move of the field of mixed methods research toward best practice guidelines may well be premature and have the effect, intended or otherwise, of homogenizing or even shutting down dialogue about what "best" is in relation to mixed methods research. In the next section I use the US National Institutes of Health (NIH) report *Best Practices for Mixed Methods Research in the Health Sciences* (Creswell et al., 2011) to develop this point further.

Using One Thing to Say Something About Another?

The NIH report *Best Practices for Mixed Methods Research in the Health Sciences* (Creswell et al., 2011) provides us with an excellent vehicle for grounding and testing the ideas we have been exploring. We will do this by asking a cascading series of questions of the report. These include questions about what *best* is understood to be in the report, how these understandings about what *best* is have been translated or transformed into best practices, who can name this set of practices as "best practice," and the basis on which they can do so. In so doing we undertake a version of the armchair walkthrough advocated by Morse, which involves us "mentally walking through" the report and using a lot of "if" and/or "if. . . then" thinking when doing so (Morse & Niehaus, 2009, p. 78). This involves us, as it were, working backward from what is written in the report to explore the understandings and/or assumptions about best, practice, mixed methods research, and best practice on which this document is premised. It involves asking questions of the layers of decisions and choices upon which the impact of any move of the field of mixed methods research toward best practice guidelines depends.

The statement *Best Practices for Mixed Methods Research in the Health Sciences* (Creswell et al., 2011) is one of the most comprehensive statements developed to date specifically in response to a formal brief to identify and list best practices related to mixed method research. This brief came from a very powerful and influential US government funding body responsible for the allocation of millions of dollars of highly sought-after and prestigious health-related research funding: the Office of Behavioral and Social Sciences Research of the NIH. The NIH is part of the US Department of Health and Human Services and describes itself as "the primary federal agency conducting and supporting basic, clinical, and translational medical research investigating the causes, treatments, and cures for both common and rare diseases" (grants. nih.gov). In 1999 a taskforce of the NIH had released guidelines for conducting rigorous qualitative and multimethod investigations (National Institutes of Health, 1999). "In a brief section at the

end of the NIH document, the task force noted the 'broad appeal' of combining qualitative and quantitative methods in public health research, and it recommended that investigators be specific about how their methods will be combined and how the findings will be integrated" (Creswell, Fetters, & Ivankova, 2004, p. 8). Thus the 1999 report provided some of the impetus for the mixed methods specific guidelines produced by the NIH in 2011. In both the 1999 and 2011 NIH reports, the focus was on providing detail about how to do mixed methods research.

The 2011 document comprises an opening one-page section on the need for best practices and then some 37 pages about those best practices. Topics covered are comprehensive, ranging from when mixed methods should be used, how a mixed method study should be designed, teamwork, infrastructure, resources and training for mixed methods research, writing mixed methods applications for specific NIH funding schemes, and reviewing mixed methods applications for those schemes. The rationale given for the NIH commissioning a team of leading mixed method researchers (Creswell et al., 2011) to develop this statement was that "no recent guidelines for 'best practices' exist to assist scientists developing applications for funding or to aid reviewers assessing the quality of mixed methods investigations" (p. 2). In keeping with this rationale, the authors of the report were asked "to develop a resource that would provide guidance to NIH investigators on how to rigorously develop and evaluate mixed methods research applications" (p. 1).

There is no doubt that there are good reasons for responding positively to, and acting on, calls from the NIH for the identification of best practices about how to assess and develop applications for funding using mixed methods approaches. The very identification by the NIH of the need for some sort of guidance in this regard demonstrates an awareness of and interest in this research approach. There is a will to fund, and thereby enable, projects that use mixed methods approaches. It is important to the NIH that those projects are the best possible in terms of their use of mixed methods research. Thus not to participate in the development of best practices for writing and assessing NIH grant applications using mixed methods research seems inappropriate and somewhat self-defeating on the part of mixed methods researchers. Furthermore, it opens up the distinct possibility that such guidelines and statements of best practice will be developed anyway, perhaps from outside of the mixed methods field itself. The conundrum in all of this is therefore not so much whether to develop the best practices or not. Rather, it relates to how to be clear about what the best practices that are developed are about and can be used for—and equally important—what they are not about and cannot be used for.

To achieve such clarity involves thinking deeply about what these best practices are actually best practices for: What is the "best" that they relate to? Is it "best" in relation to doing mixed methods research in a specific context (NIH), for a specific audience (NIH investigators), and for a specific purpose (NIH funding applications), as the statements about the brief for and the purpose of the report suggest? Or is it "best" in terms of mixed methods research in health sciences generally, as the title of the report, *Best Practices for Mixed Methods Research in the Health Sciences,* suggests? As I discussed in the previous section of this chapter, it is crucial that a distinction is made between what is or might be "best" in a given field and what is best practice in relation to the production of a specific product in a given context in that field. If this distinction is not made then it is possible that a set of best practice guidelines developed for one purpose—in this case the writing and assessment of grant applications using mixed methods for one funding agency—might be applied to and used in other contexts for which they may not be appropriate.

The point here is that any understanding of best practices, or any statement of them, is a situated one. Best practices can only be understood in relation to the specific context from which they emerge and in which they are situated. Best practices developed in one context may not necessarily be best practices in another. This is an important point to keep to the fore in any move of the field of mixed methods research toward best practice guidelines. Applying a set of best practices developed about mixed methods research in relation to a specific context and understanding of *best* to other areas and aspects of the field may have the effect of privileging one way of viewing the field of mixed methods over another, or worse, excluding other ways of thinking about that field. The definition of mixed methods research that is given in the NIH report provides an example of how this might happen.

Asking Questions of Bullet Point 2: Best Practices as Partial

The definition of mixed methods given in the NIH report is in the form of five bullet points, each of which is about a different aspect of what mixed methods research does. The authors of the report acknowledge that "many definitions of mixed methods are available in the literature" (Creswell et al., 2011, p. 4). They then proceed to state, "For the purposes of this discussion mixed methods research will be defined as. . ." (p. 4), although they do not say why this particular definition was chosen from the many available definitions, nor do they say how or why this particular definition fits with the purposes of the discussion or why other possible definitions might not have. This omission is surprising, given the considerable debates about and variations in the way the terms *mixed* and *mixed methods* are defined and/or used (Denscombe, 2008; Hesse-Biber & Johnson, 2013; Johnson, Onwuegbuzie, & Turner, 2007; Onwuegbuzie, 2012). It is also surprising given that the definition of mixed methods research chosen profoundly affects the shape and possibilities for the best practices that can be developed. We use Bullet Point 2 in the definition to explore and develop this point.

The second of the 5 bullet points comprising the definition of mixed methods research in the NIH report states that it is a research approach or methodology "employing rigorous quantitative research assessing magnitude and frequency of constructs and rigorous qualitative research exploring the meaning and understanding of constructs" (Creswell et al., 2011, p. 4). The rest of the document, and all the best practices identified therein, are therefore premised on an understanding of mixed methods research as necessarily employing quantitative and qualitative research. However, it is not clear from the NIH statement of best practices why, if a research question is best answered using a research design employing a number of only qualitative or only quantitative methods, this is not considered best practice with respect to mixed methods research or possibly not even mixed methods at all.

Some leading scholars in the mixed methods field offer wider and more inclusive definitions of mixed methods research than the one in the NIH report. For example, Morse and Niehaus (2009) define mixed methods research as "a systematic way of using two or more research methods to answer a single research question. It includes using two (or more) qualitative or quantitative methods or it uses *both* (emphasis in original) qualitative and quantitative methods" (p. 9). Morse and Niehaus's definition allows for and enables the possibility of mixed methods research that uses two or more different qualitative methods or two or more different quantitative methods, the QUAL + *qual*, QUAN + *quan* research designs they explore in their key text about principles and procedures in mixed method design. Yet, according to the NIH statement, such research designs would not be considered best practices for mixed methods in the health sciences on the basis of the combination of methods they employ and would therefore be unlikely to attract funding from the NIH because they do not tick the box in terms of Bullet Point 2. Thus the impact of bullet points such as the second one in the definition of mixed methods research in the NIH report is to put the emphasis on how to do, rather than how to think about (Cheek, 2008; Kvale, 1996), mixed methods research.

An impact of this emphasis on how to do mixed methods research is that developments in the field, including best practice guidelines, are more and more narrowly focused on the development of ever-increasingly sophisticated systems of notations and technical terms and procedures. This places the methods used and their associated techniques at the center, with thinking about mixed methods research design positioned in relation to those methods and techniques. In so doing, a relatively simplistic methods-centric thinking is promoted about mixed methods *and* quantitative and qualitative research approaches. As Denscombe (2008) notes,

> The point has been made on many occasions that the distinction between the notions of quantitative and qualitative is not watertight and that any simple quantitative–qualitative distinction hardly does justice to the variety of epistemological and ontological assumptions that underpin the terms. (p. 273)

A result of such methods-centric thinking is that the relationship between the research question and the research design is inverted. In effect, the methods and techniques that must be used in the design (quantitative and qualitative in some form of combination) determine the questions that mixed methods research can answer—questions requiring both quantitative and qualitative data to answer them. This limits possibilities for the research questions that mixed methods researchers can ask on the basis of choice of method combination, running counter to the very idea of mixed methods research in the first place as "an intuitive way of doing research" (Creswell & Plano Clark, 2011, p. 1). It violates Morse and Niehaus's (2009) principle #n of mixed method design, namely that "the

possibilities are endless" (p. 155), and contributes to a very real danger of an impoverishment of the field of mixed methods research. And it ignores the observation made over 40 years ago by Moscovici (1972) during "the period of the so-called 'crisis' in social psychology. . . that no discipline can remain in good health if it prioritizes the way in which questions are investigated over the way in which questions are asked" (Reicher, 2000, p. 1).

None of this is to suggest that the NIH report does not make an important contribution to the field of mixed methods. It is a significant and influential document that is a serious and scholarly contribution to ongoing dialogue about mixed methods, best practices, and best practice guidelines. However, what our exploration has revealed is that the NIH report of best practices for mixed methods research in the health sciences is a partial one. This is in two senses. The first is that, like any statement of best practices, the NIH report is a context-bound statement about how best practices in mixed methods might be thought about in relation to a specific context-bound product—in this case how to develop and assess funding applications for NIH that use mixed methods. It is one of a range of possible statements of best practices about specific aspects of the field of mixed methods research. Others might include, for example, best practices in writing mixed methods journal articles, best practices in writing mixed methods doctoral dissertations, and so on. It is not a statement of best practices in mixed methods research per se. The second sense in which the NIH report is a partial statement of best practices in relation to the field of mixed methods is that it takes a partial view of what mixed methods as a field is and might be, as reflected in Bullet Point 2. Given this, perhaps the set of actions named best practices for mixed methods research in the health sciences in the NIH report might be more accurately called "best practices for the specific context of applying for, assessing, and being awarded funding from NIH using mixed methods research."

Recognizing this point, and not losing sight of it, is a key part of making sure that the impact of the move toward any form of best practice guideline(s) for mixed methods research enables rather than constrains the thinking about and subsequent development of this emerging research field. So is the issue of who can say that something is best practice and on what basis they are able to do that. In the next section of the chapter I explore why this is so.

It Depends on Who Says and What They Say

Earlier in the discussion exploring definitions of the term *best practice* itself, I concluded that despite some variation in the way the term is defined, what these definitions have in common is a concept of best practice as procedures or ways of doing things that are accepted or prescribed in some sort of authoritative way as being "correct," "most effective," or "the best to use." Thus for something to be able to be termed *best practice* it is not enough that the procedures or ways of doing things are actually best in some way. This must also be supported and confirmed in some sort of authoritative way. In effect this means that whether or not something can be designated as best practice depends on who has the authority to deem that something is "correct," the "most effective," or "the best to use" and consequently that something else is not. In addition, those determining this must also have the power in some way to ensure that these practices will be accepted and/or prescribed.

While some form of authoritative endorsement of any set of procedures termed *best practice* seems perfectly reasonable—indeed desirable—questions arise about who has the power to speak about any set of best practices in an authoritative way. In what context can they speak and on what basis? These central questions must be asked and thought about when considering possible impacts of any move of the field of mixed methods research to best practice guidelines. I develop this idea by asking these questions of two of the range of voices that are considered authoritative in some way in the field of mixed methods research, the NIH and the *Journal of Mixed Methods Research* (*JMMR*).

Like the term *best, authoritative* is a relative term. Institutions, journals, and individuals can only be authoritative in relation to something specific. In the case of best practice, to be authoritative relates to the production of something that is considered "best" in a specific context. For example, the NIH statement of best practices is authoritative with respect to the way to apply for, review, and think about doing mixed methods research in relation to its funding schemes. It is also authoritative because it is written for and published by one of the most powerful and influential funding bodies in the United States. However, as we have seen, this does not necessarily make either the NIH itself, or the NIH report, authoritative about the field of mixed methods research generally. What it does make the NIH authoritative about is the area of funding research and specifically best practices related to applying for and gaining funding from the NIH.

Similarly, the *JMMR*, a highly ranked and respected journal in its field, is widely considered authoritative in relation to the review and publication of articles about mixed methods research. Much of its status and authority resides in the fact that it employs rigorous processes of peer review. Peer review is widely accepted as best practice in scientific publishing in terms of ensuring the quality of the papers published and "has come to secure for itself, the legitimacy and authority of a taken-for-granted in scholarly life" (Walker, 2004, p. 136). Like the NIH report, the *JMMR* employs a definition of mixed methods research based on the combination of both qualitative and quantitative approaches or methods in a single study or program of study. Papers must "fit the definition of mixed methods research by collecting and analyzing data, integrating the findings, and drawing inferences using both qualitative and quantitative approaches or methods" (http://www.uk.sagepub.com/journalsProdDesc.nav?prodId=Journal201775&ct_p=manuscriptSubmission&crossRegion=antiPod). The *JMMR's* peer-review and editorial processes are very clear that manuscripts that do not fit this particular view or definition of mixed methods research will be rejected (Mertens, 2011). The authority afforded to the journal on the basis of its use of rigorous and accepted peer-review processes enables the *JMMR* to position itself as being able to speak about the definition of mixed methods research authoritatively and acts to sustain a specific definition of mixed methods research and exclude others.[1]

In addition, the positioning of both the NIH and the *JMMR* as authoritative and able to speak about best practices in relation to mixed methods research relates to the research marketplace that they are both part of (Cheek, 2011). Mixed method researchers, like all researchers, live and research in a world saturated by the language of the market and business. It is an environment where neoliberal-influenced politics, with its notions of competition, efficiency, performance measures, quality, and the marketplace, is paramount (Cheek, 2011; Kvale, 2008; Torres, 2002). The notion of a research marketplace is one outworking of such a politics. Here publications, especially those in peer-reviewed journals, become transformed to outputs, research funding to inputs, and research plans to throughputs (Cheek, 2011). Such research outputs and inputs are the hard currency of this research marketplace and can be used to "buy" tenure and promotion, for example. Thus in this marketplace, mixed methods researchers, like all researchers, face the imperative to gain funding and produce papers. The imperative of accruing currency in a research marketplace in effect makes gaining funding or publishing a paper ends in themselves.

The effect of this is to place funders of research, such as NIH, and editorial boards of refereed journals, such as the *JMMR*, in powerful and authoritative positions. This is because they offer products in the form of research funding and refereed journal articles that are highly sought after in this marketplace. Researchers seeking currency in the research marketplace will thus give much weight to any statements of best practices or guidelines emanating from them. Guidelines for best practices in mixed methods research put out by a potential funder will be followed, even if that means fitting the research question and design to those guidelines. Getting the funding is the goal. Similarly, if publishing an article in a particular journal is the goal, then the way that the journal says that research must be thought about and reported will be adhered to.

All of this acts to cement the authority of these funders and journals in the research marketplace. They are seen as authoritative and as able to act authoritatively in terms of what gets funded or published and what does not. This enables funders and journals to claim authority and authoritative positions in relation to their definitions of mixed methods, statements of best practices, and statements about how to publish mixed methods research. What is funded and published in relation to mixed methods research as a result of such authority being claimed in turn gives rise to more funding and papers in keeping with the original authoritative viewpoints.

Viewed in this way, funding and publishing guidelines and associated review systems act as a form of discourse that "provides a set of possible statements about a given area, and organizes and gives structure to the manner in which a particular topic, object, process is to be talked about" (Kress, 1985, p. 7). Not only do these understandings guide researchers about the way that "authoritatively" derived effective and/or correct practices are to be done in relation to NIH grants or *JMMR* articles, but they also guide researchers and others in how that effectiveness or correctness can be thought about. This is why the issue of who can

say something is best practice and on what basis is important to consider in any move of the field of mixed methods research to best practice guidelines. Who can speak authoritatively and how that authoritative position is claimed and maintained in relation to the field of mixed methods research affects what best practices can, and do, emerge for that field.

Considerations such as these provide us with another piece of the puzzle when trying to address the conundrum of how to make sure that the impact of any best practice guideline(s) for mixed methods research enables, rather than constrains, the thinking about and subsequent development of this emerging research field. This is a piece that highlights the importance of considering who is speaking authoritatively, about what, and from what position, with respect to any move of the field of mixed methods research to best practice guidelines. Reflecting on this will help ensure that authoritative positions in relation to one aspect of the field of mixed methods research—for example, how to do a particular type of funded mixed methods research or how to publish papers in a particular journal—are not assumed to confer authority in relation to speaking about other aspects, such as what understandings of *mixed* and *mixed methods* can or might be.

The Importance of Dialogue About Navigating the Tension Between How to Do and How to Think About Mixed Methods Research

So where does all this leave us in terms of the conundrum that lies at the heart of this chapter? There is no doubt that at first glance it may seem a simple matter of common sense for the field of mixed methods research to emulate many contemporary fields of practice, transport the concept of best practice into the field of mixed methods, identify best practices, and develop guidelines for them. Indeed, in some ways this may be viewed as reflecting the maturation, increasing interest in, and uptake of this research approach. However—and this is a big "however"—as we have seen it is not quite that simple. There are arguments both for and against the movement of the field to best practice guidelines, and this is where the crux of the conundrum lies.

Addressing this conundrum involves thinking deeply about how to navigate the tension between "how to do" mixed methods research and "how to think about" that research (Cheek, 2008; Kvale,

1996, p. xv). How to think about mixed methods research and how to do mixed methods research are inexorably linked. Such a linkage, and how to navigate the tensions it creates, must not be overlooked in any move to best practice guidelines in the field of mixed methods research. Research design from choice of question, to choice of method, to use of techniques and subsequent analysis involves a complex interaction between the research context, researcher, and research methods. No research exists or is conducted in a vacuum, removed from the messy and unpredictable reality of the context in which the research is enacted. Developing any research field and/or best practice guidelines for that field, therefore, must be as much about how to think about that field of research as it is about doing that research in terms of specified steps and procedures.

Kvale (2006, 2008) saliently reminds us that all aspects of research design have embedded within them three interdependent and related dimensions: the theoretical, the methodological, and the ethical. These dimensions can be overlooked in the scramble for ever more concrete and uniform details of "how to do" mixed methods. The effect of this is to deempathize "how to think about" mixed methods research, thereby potentially reducing the field of mixed methods research to one focused on context-free rules and procedures for,

> if the recipe or steps to be followed [the how to do] become thought of as synonymous with method or, in practice, with what method is reduced or stripped to, then the emphasis will be placed on establishing and following rules rather than developing an understanding of the principles that shape the way a particular method is thought about, the effect this might have on the research, and the purpose for which a method might be used [the how to think about]. (Cheek, 2008, p. 206)

Best practice guidelines are not, and must not become, simply a set of decontextualized instructions that can be rolled out and applied regardless of the research context. In addition, once any steps or procedures in terms of how to do mixed methods research are put forward, they too must be constantly thought about rather than congealing into rigid, immutable prescriptions of what must be done. A question that is not asked enough, or even at all, of best practice guidelines that are developed is: When and how can they change? Furthermore, what are the best practices in terms of evaluating any best practice guidelines that may have been developed?

There is a high price to be paid if the tension between how to do and how to think about mixed methods research is not navigated. This price is the loss of the original intent and promise of the development of mixed methods research. An emphasis on the how to do mixed methods, to the detriment of how to think about that mixed methods research, creates and sustains what Hesse-Biber (2010b) has referred to as the current "methods-centric" state of the field of mixed methods research (p. vi). A methods-centric focus runs the very real risk of creating forms of orthodoxy about mixed methods upon which all subsequent layers of development in mixed methods research are based. The impact of this could be to constrain the development of the field by shutting down or marginalizing some possibilities for forms of mixed methods research prematurely. Any methods-centric focus runs counter to the idea of a mixed methods way of thinking put forward by Greene (2007) and defined as

> a stance or an orientation. . . rooted in a multiplistic mental model and that actively invites to participate in dialogue—at the large table of empirical inquiry. . . . A mixed methods way of thinking rests on assumptions that there are multiple legitimate approaches to social inquiry and that any given approach to social inquiry is inevitably partial. . . . A mixed methods way of thinking is thus generative and open. (p. 20)

Losing sight of Greene's (2007) idea of a mixed methods way of thinking is fraught with danger in a field of research that is still trying to sort out its basic constructs and direction. It risks losing the creativity that mixed methods brings to research. This is a creativity that comes from "new problematics, concepts, hypotheses, and purposes of inquiry, not new methods themselves" (Emke, 1996, p. 85). Losing this creativity risks an "impoverishment" of the imagination (Emke, 1996) in relation to possibilities for the mixed methods field by creating a focus on research techniques, and specific techniques at that, as ends in themselves. In other words, the "how to do" takes priority over the "how to think about" mixed methods research. Best practice guidelines developed from any methods-centric premise, inadvertently or otherwise, can thus in effect contribute to the impoverishment of the field of mixed methods research.

Such an impoverishment must be resisted at all costs. This is because it devalues the field of mixed methods research by reducing it to a focus on techniques, it excludes possibilities for the contribution that the field of mixed methods research can make to solving important questions and problems by limiting the questions that can be asked in the first place, and it excludes research that does not conform to prescriptive and rigid definitions and guidelines. In addition it fails to take into account the messiness of the reality in which much research is conducted—the blood, sweat, and tears that sit behind the deceptively simple, abbreviated, and somewhat sanitized version of most research reports and papers (Morse, 2008). It is from this messiness that many innovations and creativity can and do arise.

Where to Go From Here? Pausing the Dialogue Rather Than Concluding It

At the outset of this chapter readers were invited to pull up a chair at a table of dialogue to explore possible impacts of moving the field of mixed methods research to best practice guidelines. At the heart of the dialogue was the conundrum facing mixed methods researchers of how to make sure that the impact of any best practice guideline(s) for mixed methods research enables rather than constrains the thinking about and subsequent development of this emerging research field. The critical question is: How can guidance be given about what mixed methods are, and what best practices in them might be, in a way that avoids prescription, dogmatism, and exclusion of other possibilities? Or, put another way, how can we achieve the endless possibilities in mixed method design (Morse & Niehaus, 2009) yet at the same time avoid an "anything goes" position in relation to mixed methods research?

Our dialogue has suggested that part of the answer may lie in a closer look at the ideas of best, best practice, and best practice guidelines *themselves*. They are not neutral and value-free terms, nor can their meaning be assumed. Best practices, and any guidelines developed about them, arise from specific understandings of what best is in a given context and are practices designed to ensure the production of that best. Thus, as we have seen, the NIH statement of best practices in mixed methods research (Creswell et al., 2011) relates to a specific understanding of what those methods are, in a specific context, for a specific purpose or product, as does the *JMMR* statement about publishing mixed methods research (Mertens, 2011). If the context specificity of any form of best practice guidelines developed in relation to aspects of mixed methods research is kept to the fore, then it is possible that moving to these sets of best practices and

guidelines can contribute to a vibrant, inclusive, diverse, and still rigorous field of mixed methods research. Conversely, if best practice guidelines are developed, are removed from, and are used without reference to the context in which they were developed and the product that they are best practices for, then it is doubtful that a move to them will enhance the development and vibrancy of the field of mixed methods research.

This is to refocus the dialogue away from polemic and ultimately destructive questions such as whether or not there should be guidelines for best practice at all in the field of mixed methods research. Instead, it is to put the concept of *best* at the center of the dialogue, thereby focusing on what the product is that any best practices are designed to produce. In other words, it is to focus on thinking about why these best practices were developed and therefore what they can and cannot be used for. It is to speak of best practices *for*, rather than best practices per se. *Best* is not an absolute term, nor is *best practice*. What is best depends on the context in which we are seeking that best. Thus what best practice is depends on what those practices are designed to produce. As our dialogue in this chapter has indicated, best practices might be best for doing a specific part of the field of mixed methods research but if used inappropriately outside of that context may not necessarily be best for the field of mixed methods research generally. Thus we cannot assume that something is best in every context. This takes us back to the central and critical distinction made by Ambler (2012) referred to earlier: "Depending on the context, sometimes a practice is 'best' and sometimes it's not. Calling something a 'best practice' implies that it's a good idea all of the time, something we inherently know to be false." This is why the answer to the question of what the possible impacts are of moving the field of mixed methods research to best practice guidelines is an equivocal one. In short, it depends.

So where does this leave us, and where might we go from here? Cutting to the chase, the take-home point that emerges from all this is that it is far too simplistic to talk of any moves to best practice guidelines in mixed methods research as good, bad, or somewhere in between. When writing about impacts of the move of many fields to evidence-based practice, Denzin (2009), building on the work of Morse (2006), pointed out that "it is not a question of evidence or no evidence" (p. 142). Rather, it is about what counts as evidence and who can say that it counts. In the same way the conundrum in all this is not a question of best practice guidelines or no best practice guidelines for the field of mixed methods research. Rather, it is about what counts as best practice and who can say that it counts. It is about recognizing and acknowledging the cascading choices to be made at every stage of considering and enacting any move of the field of mixed methods research to any form of best practice guidelines. It is about making sure that those who claim authority about a form of mixed methods research on the basis of a set of best practice guidelines pertaining to that specific form of mixed methods research, do not allow those guidelines by default to become guidelines for all forms of mixed methods research. It is about whether best practice guidelines can guide not prescribe, enable not constrain, and assist rather than impede how to think about and therefore how to do mixed methods research. In short, it is about all of the above, for as we have seen, every one of those decisions affects the impact that any move to best practice guidelines might have on the field of mixed methods research.

For all of these reasons, it is imperative that mixed methods researchers accept the invitation to take a chair at the table of dialogue and explore this conundrum as part of a healthy, positive, and ongoing dialogue across their differences. Then, and only then, can the answer to the questions we have been discussing be more than "it depends."

Note

1. Other journals are now publishing other types of mixed methods designs. For instance, *Qualitative Health Research* is publishing qualitatively driven mixed-method designs (Morse & Cheek, 2014).

References

Ambler, S. (2012). Questioning "best practices" for software development. Retrieved from www.ambysoft.com/essays/bestPractices.html

Bardach, E. (2011). *A practical guide for policy analysis: The eightfold path to more effective problem solving* (4th ed.). Thousand Oaks, CA: Sage.

Best practice. (2013). *Cambridge online dictionary*. Retrieved from http://dictionary.cambridge.org/dictionary/british/best-practice

Best practice. (2013). *Oxford online dictionary*. Retrieved from www.oxforddictionaries.com/definition/english/best-practice

Cheek, J. (2008). Beyond the "how to": The importance of thinking about, not simply doing, qualitative research. In K. Nielsen, S. Brinkmann, C. Elnholdt, L. Tanggaard, P. Musaeus, & G. Kraft (Eds.), *A qualitative stance: Essays in honour of Steinar Kvale* (pp. 203–214). Aarhus, Denmark: Aarhus University Press.

Cheek, J. (2011). The politics and practices of funding qualitative inquiry. In N. K. Denzin & Y. S. Lincoln (Eds.), *The SAGE handbook of qualitative research* (4th ed., pp. 251–268). Thousand Oaks, CA: Sage.

Creswell, J. W., Fetters, M. D., & Ivankova, N. V. (2004). Designing a mixed methods study in primary care. *Annals of Family Medicine, 2*(1), 7–12. doi:10.1370/afm.104

Creswell, J. W., Klassen, A. C., Plano Clark, V. L., & Smith, K. C. (2011). *Best practices for mixed methods research in the health sciences*. Bethesda, MD: National Institutes of Health.

Creswell, J. W., & Plano Clark, V. L. (2011). *Designing and conducting mixed methods research*. Thousand Oaks, CA: Sage.

Denscombe, M. (2008). Communities of practice: A research paradigm for the mixed methods approach. *Journal of Mixed Methods Research, 2*(3), 270–283. doi:10.1177/1558689808316807

Denzin, N. K. (2009). The elephant in the living room: Or extending the conversation about the politics of evidence. *Qualitative Research, 9*, 139–160. doi:10.1177/1468794108098034

Emke, I. (1996). Methodology and methodolatry: Creativity and the impoverishment of the imagination in sociology. *Canadian Journal of Sociology/Cahiers canadiens de sociologie, 21*(1), 77–90. doi:10.2307/3341433

Greene, J. C. (2007). *Mixed methods in social inquiry*. San Francisco, CA: Wiley.

Hannes, K. (2011). Critical appraisal of qualitative research. In J. Noyes, A. Booth, K. Hannes, A. Harden, J. Harris, S. Lewin, & C. Lockwood (Eds.), *Supplementary guidance for inclusion of qualitative research in Cochrane Systematic Reviews of interventions*. London, England: Cochrane Collaboration Qualitative Methods Group. Retrieved from http://cqrmg.cochrane.org/supplemental-handbook-guidance

Hesse-Biber, S. (2010a). Emerging methodologies and methods practices in the field of mixed methods research. *Qualitative Inquiry, 16*(6), 415–418. doi:10.1177/1077800410364607

Hesse-Biber, S. (2010b). *Mixed methods research: Merging theory with practice*. New York, NY: Guildford Press.

Hesse-Biber, S., & Johnson, R. B. (2013). Coming at things differently: Future directions of possible engagement with mixed methods research. *Journal of Mixed Methods Research, 7*(2), 103–109. doi:10.1177/1558689813483987

Johnson, R. B., Onwuegbuzie, A. J., & Turner, L. A. (2007). Toward a definition of mixed methods research. *Journal of Mixed Methods Research, 1*(2), 112–133. doi:10.1177/1558689806298224

Kress, G. (1985). *Linguistic processes in socio-cultural practice*. Melbourne, Australia: Deakin University Press.

Kvale, S. (1996). *InterViews: An introduction to qualitative research interviewing*. London, England: Sage.

Kvale, S. (2006). Dominance through interviews and dialogues. *Qualitative Inquiry, 12*(3), 480–500.

Kvale, S. (2008). Qualitative inquiry between scientistic evidentialism, ethical subjectivism and the free market. *International Review of Qualitative Research, 1*(1) 5–18.

Maxwell, J. A. (2004). Reemergent scientism, postmodernism, and dialogue across differences. *Qualitative Inquiry, 10*(1), 35–41. doi:10.1177/1077800403259492

Mertens, D. (2011). Publishing mixed methods research. *Journal of Mixed Methods Research, 5*(1), 3–6. doi:10.1177/1558689810390217

Morse, J. M. (2006). The politics of evidence. *Qualitative Health Research*, *16*(3), 395–404. doi:10.1177/1049732305285482

Morse, J. M. (2008). Deceptive simplicity. *Qualitative Health Research*, *18*, 1311. doi:10.1177/1049732308322486

Morse, J. M., & Cheek, J. (2014). Making room for qualitatively-driven mixed-method research [Editorial]. *Qualitative Health Research*, *24*(1), 3–5.

Morse, J. M., & Niehaus, L. (2009). *Mixed-method design: Principles and procedures.* Walnut Creek, CA: Left Coast Press.

Moscovici, S. (1972). Society and theory in social psychology. In J. Israel & H. Tajfel (Eds.), *The context of social psychology: A critical assessment* (pp. 17–68). London, England: Academic.

Nadel, S., Shipley, A., & Elliott, R. N. (2004). The technical, economic and achievable potential for energy-efficiency in the United States: A meta-analysis of recent studies. Retrieved from www.eceee.org/library/conference_proceedings/ACEEE_buildings/2004/Panel_8/p8_19

National Institutes of Health, Office of Behavioral and Social Science Research. (1999). *Qualitative methods in health research: Opportunities and considerations in application and review.* Washington, DC: Author.

Onwuegbuzie, A. J. (2012). Introduction: Putting the *MIXED* back into quantitative and qualitative research in educational research and beyond: Moving toward the *radical middle*. *International Journal of Multiple Research Approaches*, *6*, 192–219. doi:10.5172/mra.2012.6.3.192

Reicher, S. (2000). Against methodolatory: Some comments on Elliott, Fischer, and Rennie. *British Journal of Clinical Psychology*, *39*, 1–6. doi:10.1348/014466500163031

Torres, C. A. (2002). The state, privatization and educational policy: A critique of neo-liberalism in Latin America and some ethical and political considerations. *Comparative Education*, *38*(1) 19–36. doi:10.1080/0305006022000030766

Treloar, C., Champness, S., Simpson, P. L., & Higginbotham, N. (2000). Critical appraisal checklist for qualitative research studies. *Indian Journal of Pediatrics*, *67*(5), 347–351. doi:10.1007/BF02820685

Walker, K. (2004). Double b(l)ind: Peer review and the politics of scholarship. *Nursing Philosophy*, *5*(2), 135–146. doi:10.1111/j.1466-769X.2004.00173.x

Feminism, Causation, and Mixed Methods Research

Sharon Crasnow

Abstract

This chapter explores feminist approaches to social science research and how they use mixed methods to support causal claims. Investigating the relationship between mixed methods research and causality reveals two types of causal pluralism that give rise to two dimensions of causal space: ontological causal pluralism and conceptual causal pluralism. Ontological causal pluralism delineates causal space through reconceptualizing the objects of knowledge—different sorts of objects bear different causal relationships to one another. Conceptual causal pluralism is directly related to the concept of causation that is appropriate to research questions. The question of which concept of causation is appropriate is closely tied to the question of the goals of the research. If it is to advocate for change, the question of how to advocate for this change may require understanding the mechanism that prevents the change. Feminist research illustrates the value of methodological pluralism and suggests that such methodological pluralism supports a form of causal pluralism.

Key Words: feminist social science, causation, causal pluralism, mechanism, feminist research

Introduction

This chapter explores some ways in which feminist mixed methods approaches to social science research provide insight into causal reasoning. One result of this exploration is an argument for *methodological pluralism*—the view that multiple methodological approaches should be simultaneously pursued. Another is an argument for *causal pluralism*—the view that there is more than one form that causal explanation takes and more than one sense of causal inference appropriate to understanding the social world.

Examining feminist approaches to research provides insight into knowledge production for several reasons. First, there is no one methodology that is appropriately identified as feminist—feminist approaches are quantitative, qualitative, and mixed methods. What unites them under the "feminist" umbrella are their various liberatory aims. I say "*various* liberatory aims" because just as there is no one feminist method, there is no one feminist aim

but rather a family of aims and goals that might be considered feminist. These aims overlap and intersect in a variety of ways, and so I treat *feminist* and *feminism* as cluster concepts. By this I mean that they are akin to Wittgenstein's (2009) notion of a family resemblance term in that there are some shared or intersecting characteristics of feminist approaches but there is not a definition of *feminist* or *feminism* that can be given through specifying the necessary and sufficient conditions for the proper use of these terms.[1] Some key elements of feminist approaches relevant for this chapter are: they are critical—they question the status quo; they are liberatory and egalitarian—they seek to counter oppression, though precisely what that looks like may vary considerably as contexts vary; and, perhaps most important, they focus on sex/gender as a crucial element for understanding the social.

Another reason feminist approaches offer a useful perspective on knowledge production is that they share a critical stance. The cluster of feminist aims identified in the previous paragraph all require the examination of assumptions about the process of knowledge production. Two specific examples are the commitment to see gender/sex as salient and so to interrogate research using that lens and the commitment to "start from the lives of women."

Given that feminism provides the framework through which questions of mixed methods and causality are explored in this chapter, I begin with an overview of feminist approaches to questions of method, methodology, and epistemology in the next section. I argue that both the plurality of aims and the critical stance that feminists doing research take are particularly useful. I identify two ways that this has been the case with particular attention to causal claims and discuss them each in turn in the third and fourth sections of the chapter. First, the critical stance of feminist mixed methods research functions as an aid to uncovering assumptions about the social phenomena under investigation—the objects of inquiry. Conceptions of these objects are sometimes inadequate to the analysis of the social world needed for liberatory projects. The critical stance of feminist approaches to social science may lead to reconceptualizing the objects of inquiry and thus produce different ontologies and consequently different causal relations among the objects of inquiry. The plurality of goals motivates a review of alternate ontologies. Thus feminist approaches motivate what I call *ontological causal pluralism*. Different understandings of the objects of study—different ways of conceiving them—give rise to alternate and perhaps incompatible causal spaces.[2]

In the fourth section, I examine a second way that the critical stance of feminist mixed methods research has served feminist aims. Namely, it supports a second sort of causal pluralism that I call *conceptual causal pluralism*—the view that different understandings of causality require different approaches to evidence and support different causal inferences. Such differences in the concept of cause define a second dimension of the causal space in which knowledge production takes place. In the fifth and sixth sections, I examine how the use of feminist mixed methods in the social sciences can alter causal arguments and how tensions between different types of causal inference can improve feminist research. Causal pluralism in both of the forms discussed is more clearly visible through the use of mixed methods research, sometimes clarifying and sometimes complicating our understanding of the phenomena.

The seventh section explores the fit between type of causal inference and the goals of feminist research with the distinction between the varieties of causal pluralism in hand. Particularly, I consider how different forms of causal inference are suited to diverse feminist goals. I conclude by urging a further exploration of causality through feminist mixed methods research.

Feminist Approaches to Research: Methods, Methodology, and Epistemology

This chapter considers methods—quantitative, qualitative, and mixed methods (some combination of the two). In doing so it also addresses methodology and epistemology. It may be helpful here to use Sandra Harding's (1987) distinction between method, methodology, and epistemology. Methods are "techniques for gathering evidence," whereas methodology is "a theory and analysis of how research should proceed." Epistemology is the "theory of knowledge or justificatory strategy" that underlies the methodology (p. 2). The two methodologies that figure most prominently in the literature are, as Harding (1986) identifies them, feminist empiricist and feminist standpoint theory.[3]

Methodology and epistemology are closely entwined. Methodological claims presuppose epistemological arguments that explain how the evidence produced through various methods justifies knowledge claims and hence why a particular approach (methodology) to research is to be preferred. For example, Harding (1986) characterizes feminist empiricism through its adherence to empiricist methodology as the primary means of achieving good (feminist or other) science. Joey Sprague (2005) describes feminist empiricism as maintaining some of the core standards of positivism, and more recently Kristen Intemann (2010) suggests that "feminist empiricism is *empiricist* in the sense that empirical success is held to be a necessary condition for accepting scientific theories, models, or auxiliary hypotheses as justified" (p. 780). Each of these accounts appeals either explicitly or implicitly to epistemological principles to make the methodological claim.

While feminist empiricism is committed to better use of empirical method as the solution to sexist bias in science, standpoint theories challenge the view that empirical methodology is the cure. Standpoint theories generally endorse some version of the following three theses: the situated knowledge thesis, the thesis of epistemic privilege, and the achievement thesis (Crasnow, 2013; Intemann, 2010; Rolin, 2009; Wylie 2011). The thesis of situated knowledge is that knowledge is local in a profound way—knowledge is knowledge *for* and *by* a particular set of historically, culturally, politically, and socially situated knowers. The thesis can best be understood in contrast to the conception of knowledge that it is intended to oppose the modernist view that there is one viewpoint from which the truth about reality can be discerned. This is the idea of objective knowledge as a God's eye view of the world—"the view from nowhere," in Thomas Nagel's phrase (1986), or, as Donna Haraway (1988) says, "the god trick." The situated knowledge thesis denies that there can be any such knowledge and instead treats knowledge as relative to cultural/social/political location. Standpoint theories combine the thesis of situated knowledge with epistemic privilege—those in particular social locations (who are situated in specific ways) will have access to evidence and perhaps ways of knowing the social world that those who are not in those situations will not have. This is fundamentally different from feminist empiricism in that standard empiricist methods are thought not to be able to alter this access. The third thesis, the achievement thesis, clarifies that epistemic privilege is not automatic but rather must be achieved and so emphasizes the social nature of knowledge (Crasnow, 2013).

Feminism is at heart political—feminists seek knowledge that serves the political goals to which they are committed. It is thus not surprising that both feminist empiricist epistemology and feminist standpoint epistemologies have sought to respond to the criticism that feminist social science is illegitimate *because* it is political. Feminist empiricism originally addressed this worry through adhering to a value-free conception of science and arguing that proper use of scientific method would eliminate sexist science. But in the last 25 years a growing body of philosophy of science literature has challenged and offered alternatives to the conception of scientific objectivity that was based on the value-free ideal (e.g., Crasnow, 2013; Douglas, 2009; Harding, 2008; Intemann, 2010, Lacey, 1999; Longino, 1990, 2002; Wylie, 2011). The core feature of these challenges rests in an emphasis on the complexity of the social world. This complexity means that any account of it will necessarily focus on particular aspects and deemphasize or even ignore others. These alternative accounts vary in

their understanding of how these choices are made, but they agree that our interests play some role. But although our knowledge of the social world might be relative to those interests, that does not mean that those interests are the sole determinants of that knowledge.

There are disputes about exactly what roles social, cultural, and political values can legitimately play in social science, but most accounts reject extreme forms of relativism such as subjectivism (the view that knowledge is fully relative to the beliefs of an individual), and many reject epistemic relativism (the view that knowledge is relative to the epistemic norms of a culture or social group) as antithetical to the idea of universal scientific knowledge. A value-imbued science need not be a science that is at the whim of political commitments. Minimally, a shared goal of feminist social science is an interest in features of the social world that matter in women's lives—particularly aspects of that world that limit women's freedoms, including their freedom to conceptualize the world in which they find themselves and empirically test the efficacy of the social science that incorporates such conceptualization.

Both the modified feminist empiricism that has come out of these changes and interpretations of feminist standpoint theory that offer accounts of objectivity that are compatible with a role of values in science (Crasnow, 2013; Harding, 2004; Wylie, 2011) pose challenges to the idea that feminist empiricism and feminist standpoint theory should be seen as competing epistemologies. Intemann (2010) has thus argued for a blending of the views and suggests that perhaps a better term for this view is "feminist standpoint empiricism" (p. 794).

I agree with Intemann's (2010) analysis and in the exploration of feminist approaches, causality, and mixed methods that follows I do not specifically delineate epistemological positions using these characterizations. However, I have reviewed this background because the use of quantitative methods has sometimes been identified with feminist empiricism and feminist standpoint theorists often rely on qualitative methods. However, although there are examples of strong feminist approaches to research that conform to this alignment, one of the features of the exploration of causal reasoning in this chapter is that it is not locked into either a dichotomy of methods or of epistemologies. I turn now to causality. As an aid to the reader, Table 37.1 includes definitions to some of the key terms used in the remainder of the chapter.

Table 37.1 Explanation of Key Terms

Average effects causation	One way of thinking about causality is in terms of average effects—the increased probability of an effect occurring within a population given the presence of the purported cause. In this chapter, average effects causation is contrasted with processual causation.
Causal pluralism	There are varieties of causal pluralism and so causal pluralism is ambiguous. It can be characterized as the view that there is more than one sense of "causality" appropriate to understanding the (social) world. More precisely, it is the view that no one account of causality can sustain the various causal inferences that we make. To disambiguate, I distinguish: conceptual causal pluralism and ontological causal pluralism.
Causal spaces	A metaphorical way of talking about constraints on causal accounts that result from methodological, epistemological, or ontological commitments that are causally relevant.
Conceptual causal pluralism	The view that there are alternative concepts of cause suited for different purposes and that evidence for causal inference under one concept is not necessarily evidence for causal inference under another concept. "Conceptual" modifies "causal pluralism."
Epistemic relativism	The view that knowledge is always relative to the epistemic norms (standards) of a culture or social group.
Evidential pluralism	Taken from Reiss (2009)—the view that there are different paths to the discovery of causes, each producing different sorts of evidence, but the underlying concept of cause remains the same.
Methodological pluralism	The view that not only is it acceptable to use more than one method in the pursuit of knowledge but that multiple methodological approaches should be simultaneously pursued.
Object of inquiry	The objects of inquiry are the objects under investigation as they are conceptualized for the purpose of investigation.
Objectivism	Harding refers to the view of science as objective in the sense that it is disinterested, impartial, impersonal, and value-free as "objectivism."
Ontological causal pluralism	"Ontological" modifies "causal pluralism." Ontological causal pluralism is the view that different understandings of the objects of inquiry present different ontologies that may require different causal accounts.
Processual causation	Processual causation covers a range of causal relations that hold between individuals. Examples include mechanistic, manipulationist, necessary and sufficient, and counterfactual understandings of causation. The key idea is that this notion of causality focuses on the causal pathway.
Subjectivism	The view that knowledge is always relative to the beliefs of an individual.

Causality and the Objects of Inquiry: Ontological Causal Pluralism

Much contemporary social science is concerned with postulating and establishing causal relations through statistical analysis or experimental research (randomized controlled trials); however, feminists have not explicitly addressed the methodological issues surrounding causal claims. This is not to say that feminists doing research do not make causal claims. They do and support such claims through quantitative, qualitative, and mixed methods research.

For example, quantitative work clearly can provide excellent evidence of the effects of sex discrimination. The work by Amartya Sen (1990) on "missing" women and the documentation of and research on the wage gap provide two well-known examples.[4] Empirical generalizations such as these drive a search for explanations and remedies and stem from the feminist commitment to making gender relevant. However, making gender relevant may mean more than counting women. When research starts from the lives of women, the objects of the social world may need to be understood differently. This is not merely a matter of numbers. Thus the power of quantitative data and the need to critically examine the concepts through which the social world is understood and data are collected suggests one motivation for mixing qualitative with quantitative methods. And indeed there is considerable use of mixed methods by such researchers using the feminist lens.

Sprague (2005) notes some commonalities among research projects that feminist using mixed methods research engage in. Often such research progresses against the backdrop of previous non-feminist research. Feminist research takes a critical stance toward that work in a variety of ways. While quantitative work operates at a fairly high level of abstraction, the local and specific approaches in which feminism's qualitative traditions are rooted challenge inequalities that are apparent from "the downside of the social hierarchies" (p. 114). That is to say, awareness of inequality is often only revealed through the lived experience of those who occupy that downside. Sprague's description of such research thus incorporates elements of feminist standpoint analysis.

For example, Julie Brines (1994) engaged in a reevaluation of the distribution of housework in households with male and female partners and challenged the standard economic explanation (women earn lower wages and so have less bargaining power when it comes to housework)—an explanation given from a fairly high level of generality. In doing this research, she used quantitative methods to discover other factors that affect this distribution, but the research questions and the recognition that such factors needed to be considered emerged from the specific social context of the lives of women.

While feminists using quantitative methods in their research begin with standard measures, they examine and question the assumptions behind these measures. Pamela Paxton (2002) challenges measures of democracy, noting that they frequently depend on operationalizing universal suffrage—one of the standard indicators of democracy—as universal male suffrage (either explicitly or implicitly). When universal suffrage is operationalized as inclusive of women, the change poses a challenge to many of the standard accounts of the spread of democracy since the 18th century.

The research of Brines (1994) and Paxton (2000) are both examples that illustrate changes in how the objects of inquiry are conceived. The critical stance that feminism brings to social science can motivate reconceptualizations of the social objects, institutions, roles, and relations among them. The resulting altered ontology can shift the causal space both because what is thought to be in need of causal explanation and how that explanation can be given depends on how we conceive of and describe the objects of inquiry. The shift in ontology might be radical—there may be objects, events, or properties that emerge that were not part of the ontological landscape previously.

For example, sexual harassment did not exist as a category of social interaction prior to the late 1970s. It emerged in Lin Farley's analysis (1978), grounded in the lived experience of women, identified and described in consciousness-raising groups. Or a shift might be more subtle, as in the case of Paxton's (2000) critique of standard notions of democracy. Paxton does not advocate eliminating the category "democracy" or replacing it with a new category but revising it—"fixing" it to make it better fit the reality of a political world that does, in fact, include women. In such cases, the understanding of the object, category, or property may either affect the causal claims in which it figures or suggest new causal relations. These are changes in the causal space. Because the changes are changes in the way the objects are conceived and so changes in the object of inquiry, I refer to this as *ontological causal pluralism*.

Varieties of Causality: Conceptual Causal Pluralism

In addition to ontological causal pluralism, there is *conceptual causal pluralism*. This pluralism, as the name implies, has to do with the concept of cause or varieties of causation. In the literature on causality and social science, the different senses of "cause" have been closely connected with different methods. Methods produce different sorts of evidence, which in turn support different causal conclusions—in other words, they define different forms of causal inference.

Quantitative and experimental methods support conclusions about "average effects causation"—indications of the increased probability of an effect (dependent variable) occurring within a particular population given the presence of a causal factor (independent variable). We frequently see conclusions about average effects supported by experimental data in medicine. Drug studies are a paradigm case. The claim that taking birth control pills prevents unwanted pregnancy is a claim about a causal relationship, but it is clearly a claim that is probabilistic—that is, it tells us an average effect for women taking birth control pills. To return to the example of the wage gap, statistical evidence supports that gender is a causal factor in salary—also an average effect. Of course, a causal claim presented as an average effect in a population is not a claim that the effect will occur for every member of that population. One possible reason that the claim about the population does not translate into a claim about any particular individual in that population may be because such a claim gives us no information about the mechanism or process through which the effect comes about, and hence we cannot discern whether or to what extent the features of the mechanism are realized in any individual. Another reason is because of local/contextual conditions that might moderate a general relationship.

Experiments are thought to provide excellent evidence for average effects (if carried out correctly); however, it is not always possible to do experiments in the social sciences, for both practical and moral reasons. But even when experiments are possible, there is often a problem of external validity.[5] Statistical methods are sometimes treated as alternatives to experiments[6]—they are seen as ways of simulating experiments or as quasi-experiments. Although a nonexperimental research design that incorporates multiple regression or its variants does not have a control group and a treatment group, the statistical techniques that such methods employ aim at taking all of the potentially relevant variables into account and in this way "control" for all factors (variables) that might confound the causal argument—a strength of randomized controlled experiments that are often claimed to be the "gold standard" of evidence for establishing causality.

Experiments and statistical analyses are well suited to support conclusions about large populations in which researchers have a fairly high degree of confidence that relevant variables have been identified and that conditions support external validity. However, both the complexity and the nuance of social life suggest that social phenomena are not always best understood through such

analysis. Another way of putting this is that quantitative (statistical) research sometimes fails to pay sufficient attention to the contexts and particularities of human life.

Thus while questions about causality have mostly been understood as establishing average effects causal claims through quantitative research (and feminists doing quantitative research have used those methodologies in this way), using insights from qualitative research can enhance our understanding of causal inference. Given that feminism seeks to bring about social change—a task for which reasoning to causes is presumably useful—feminist philosophers and researchers would benefit from devoting more attention to these insights.

While average effects causation has dominated social science in recent decades, it is not the only way of thinking about causality. In fact, there are a wide variety of alternative approaches to causality—so much so that it is difficult to give an umbrella description of alternatives to average effects causation. Causation might be identified as necessary and sufficient conditions, manipulability, a process, through counterfactual conditionals, or, one of the more popular current approaches, through an analysis of mechanisms.[7] John Gerring (2010) elaborates on the popularity of the last approach:

> In recent years, the importance of mechanism-centered explanation and analysis has become an article of faith within the social sciences. The turn toward mechanisms unites researchers practicing a wide array of methodologies—quantitative and qualitative, experimental and nonexperimental, cross-case and case study, formal models and narrative prose. Indeed, perhaps the only thing that practitioners of these diverse approaches share is an appreciation for the value of causal mechanisms and a corresponding suspicion of "covariational" (aka "correlational" or "associational") arguments. (p. 1500)

It is worth noting that Gerring finishes this description of the interest in causal mechanisms by defining it negatively, as driven by an opposition to a covariational approach.

The description of a causal mechanism may be formulated in general terms, but establishing the presence or absence of a mechanism in a particular circumstance suggests an opportunity for mixed methods research. An average effects approach is grounded in the correlation between a dependent and independent variable, but qualitative research is local and focuses on the rich detail of the particular. For example, in-depth case studies may use qualitative methods to establish the intervening steps that constitute a causal mechanism. While establishing that there is an average effect of some putative causal factor may tell *that* there is a causal relationship between two variables, it does not tell us *what* the relationship is or *how* it operates. The appeal of examining particular instances is that it holds out the promise of being able to "see" the mechanism in operation. Political methodologists Alexander George and Andrew Bennett (2004) have described the method of tracing a causal pathway as "process tracing" and have explored the ways in which the use of multiple methods might sustain a more complex and detailed causal analysis, including establishing whether hypothesized causal mechanisms are operating in particular cases.

I refer to this second concept of cause as *processual causation* (which does not preclude there being multiple causes or complex causes).[8] Processual causation, in my usage, encompasses causes as mechanisms in the sense that I have been discussing them, but the key feature of this concept of cause is that it makes reference to causal relations between individuals—events, nations, social groups, persons—and it focuses on causal pathways between such individuals—which is partly why the idea of process tracing that George and Bennett (2004) describe is so evocative.

Because the analysis in this section puts the concept of "cause" under scrutiny, I call this *conceptual* causal pluralism. It is the sort of causal pluralism that philosophers have been most concerned with recently (Cartwright, 2007; Crasnow, 2010, 2012; Reiss, 2009). Answers to questions about the role of mixed methods research in supporting causal inference are complicated by conceptual causal pluralism, as well as ontological causal pluralism. The following sections of the chapter examine some of these complications and offer an analysis in the context of feminist approaches to research.

Insights from Feminist Research: Causal Spaces

While feminist research has benefited from a mixed methods approach, there is still some disagreement about how the qualitative and quantitative elements are best integrated. As Sharlene Hesse-Biber (2010) notes, qualitative methods are sometimes just "added in" to supplement or "humanize" research. If this is what is happening,

then there is some question as to whether it is appropriate to call such uses *mixed* methods research given that in such circumstances the methods are not doing epistemological work *together*. Hesse-Biber attributes this additive understanding of combining the two methods as partly due to presuppositions about the nature of reality that are made in such research designs: "contained in this mixed methods design is the assumption of a positivist view that social reality is objective" (p. 457). However, the examples offered previously (Brines, 1994; Paxton, 2000) are not examples of qualitative methods merely adding something to improve quantitative methods. It is not a matter of qualitative methods uncovering new variables that need to be considered quantitatively. Variables are not added in, but concepts are altered or even invented.

New research questions are often the result of reframing phenomena based on the inability of current descriptions to capture the lived experience of those who are researched. In the feminist contexts, Dorothy Smith (1987) calls such mismatches "lines of fault"—her metaphor for the tensions that occur when the lived experience of women does not conform to the standard concepts and categories used by the research discipline.[9] Such lines of fault often emerge when the results of different methods seem to be in conflict, and this is one way that the need to rethink concepts and categories becomes apparent.

An example is the need for a reconceptualization of women's work. Traditionally the analysis of labor counted only paid work in the public sphere, but much "women's work" is in the private, domestic domain. A consequence of understanding labor as paid work is that domestic labor remains invisible. The line of fault results since the lived experience of work is in conflict with the research category of labor. Reconceptualization of labor begins by including women as subjects of research, since without doing so it may not be possible to even notice domestic labor. But inclusion (adding in) does not accomplish the needed shift on its own since, though now visible, such work still needs to be recognized as labor. It is only at that point that the category is altered.

Many other examples of the use of qualitative research to identify missing factors or alternative hypotheses, as well as for offering alternative categorization of the phenomena, appear in feminist work. For example, Elizabeth Stanko (1997), in doing research on women and violence, found that when she asked women to describe "things that we do to keep safe," she elicited descriptions of a variety of strategies that function as self-defense: choosing a place to live, deciding when and where to walk, choosing a time to go to the laundromat or grocery shopping, deciding what to wear, and so on. She would not have uncovered these if she had asked specifically about self-defense.

In her research, the critical stance of Stanko's (1997) feminism was crucial, leading her to function as an insider and outsider. As a woman (insider), she was aware that there are many things women do that are associated with "keeping safe" and incorporated into the way they live. As a sociologist (outsider), she recognized both the role that such behaviors play in shaping the daily lives of women and the way these behaviors are in turn shaped by the societal structures in which women live. This insider/outsider double vision allowed her to identify different aspects of behavior as relevant and see them as part of a larger social structure. The feminist nature of her research led her to change the typology (different categories were seen to be relevant than those used in previous research) and thereby identify different factors as key to the research.

Marjorie DeVault's (1999) work offers an example in which qualitative methods aid in identifying missing factors. In interviewing for her research on housework, she came to see that the "messiness" in the everyday speech of her interview subjects frequently revealed emotional attitudes that were relevant to her project (pp. 77–78). Traditional interviewing and transcribing methods call for the interviewer to "smooth out" these features of speech and record only the content of the respondent's remarks as data. DeVault came to believe that the hesitations—the "you knows" and other such features of conversational speech—were evidence revealing the respondent's emotional attitudes toward the topics discussed. Her methods thus led to recognizing potential variables that would be hidden by conventional methodology—in this case, the frequency of hesitations and their conjunction with some subjects but not others.

These examples suggest ways in which qualitative methods lead to reconceptualizing phenomena but also to alternative understandings of the structures of social reality. The use of one method in informing another also can be seen when qualitative data result in new variables for use in quantitative analysis. Concepts are revised or developed and operationalized through new understandings of appropriate indicators. Such uses of mixed methods research have the effect of changing the research question and design. Increased frequency of hesitations while responding during interviews can be an indicator that there is something important going on. A quantitative analysis of things we do to stay safe may reveal patterns of behavior that are prevalent in some communities but not in others and can aid in the analysis of violence against women.

These examples of the use of mixed methods for the development of alternative hypotheses or the altering of categories through which phenomena and events are conceived might be thought of as contributing indirectly rather than directly to the production of evidence that supports causal conclusions. If we take the identification of causes or causal factors as a primary aim of social science, as so much mainstream social science does, this analysis of the use of qualitative methods may seem to delegate them to an auxiliary role in research—or, as Hesse-Biber (2010) puts it, to serve as a handmaiden to quantitative methods (p. 457).

However, these are not examples of qualitative methods merely uncovering new variables that need to be considered quantitatively, as valuable as that might be. Variables are not added in but concepts are invented, revised, or fundamentally altered.[10] A result may be that phenomena and properties of phenomena that were once thought to be irrelevant become relevant, but new objects of inquiry may emerge as well. When sexual harassment becomes a phenomenon to be investigated, that is not a matter of refining the description of a sociological object of inquiry or inserting missing factors previously left out of the account. It is a reordering of properties so that they are understood in relation to a new social object. The local and particular experience of women ground this new ontology.

The refinement of the concept of democracy that Paxton (2000) urges is a conceptual adjustment of a different sort. She argues that a problematic interpretation of a key indicator of democracy—suffrage—results in failure to code democracy adequately and consequently distorts many of the results in the field. Paxton's argument is best understood as claiming that the coding of democracy is not empirically adequate because it ignores women. But even in this case the effect on the key concepts under which the phenomena are understood is not simply an additive one.

Reconceptualizations result from an appreciation and incorporation of the subjective or interpretive nature of social reality—in effect, reshaping the causal space of that reality. This may happen in ways that preserve the subjective—as in the case of sexual harassment. Or it can point toward a better characterization of the objective as in the case of Paxton's (2000) point about democracy. But in both cases the phenomena are understood differently and that difference in understanding makes a difference in what causal conclusions we can draw.

To return to the example of domestic work, the work that (mostly) women do preparing meals, getting children ready for school, seeing that their homework is done, packing their lunches, and sending their husbands off to work in the visible economy is real work seen through the eyes of the (mostly) women who are engaged in it. However, it can be invisible, in part because it sustains and perpetuates an institutional structure that requires the invisibility of women's work and hence the invisibility of women. Beginning from the reality of the daily lives of women allows the work to be made visible (as work) and reveals the discrepancies that exist between women's experiences and the concepts of work, leisure time, individual choice, and other conceptual models of the social world that nonfeminist social scientists use. The critical attitude of the feminist researcher requires recognizing that the descriptions with which we begin research are interpretations, and hence that stage of research is deeply value-laden and has ramifications for whatever further research it serves as a basis for.

One way to think of these alternate characterizations of the objects of inquiry is as producing different causal spaces in which different types of causal inferences are warranted. The ontologies of these new causal spaces may include concepts, properties, and descriptions that previously developed accounts did not include. Such accounts may even be incommensurable with the ontologies to which prior descriptions were committed. In understanding "work" differently, we operationalized the relevant variables differently. While quantitative methods still might be used to make the causal arguments, the nature of both the phenomena and their relationships to each other can alter the causal conclusions that are drawn. Feminism's critical stance combined with the willingness to engage in mixed methods research supports the search for such alternate causal spaces.

Causal Spaces: The Conceptual Dimension

One argument for mixed methods research is that the use of two or more methods can provide a way for each method to compensate for the weaknesses of the others. In a similar vein, mixed methods research is sometimes thought to be valuable as a way of testing that results are not an artifact of method. Both claims depend on the idea that more than one method can aim at the same causal conclusion. How this might work is not always very clear, however. The "same" result is not always clearly defined across methods. Nonetheless, the idea seems plausible, and the following example seems to be an example of this sort.

In a recent study on violence against women (Htun & Weldon, 2012), the authors sought to establish a causal relationship between strong, autonomous women's movements and government adoption of social policies to address violence against women: "H1: Strong, autonomous feminist movements will be significant influences on policies on violence against women at all points in time" (p. 554). The research was mixed methods and took place in several stages, beginning with the collection of both qualitative and quantitative data from a variety of sources on 70 countries over 40 years. These data were then coded to produce two data sets—the first for the dependent variable (government adoption of social policies) and the second for the independent variable (presence of strong, autonomous women's movements). Once coded the data were analyzed (quantitatively) and showed a clear correlation between the dependent and independent variable consistent with the hypothesis.

The authors note, "Although correlational findings such as these do not establish that autonomous feminist movements precede government response, we know from case evidence and previous research that such movements usually predate government response by a long period of time" (Htun & Weldon, 2012, p. 560). In other words, although the statistical work supports a correlation, the causal connection is only established through "case evidence" (qualitative) and "previous research" (mixed methods).[11] The correlational findings are average effects, but the causal conclusion appears to depend on process tracing.[12] In this research qualitative elements are interwoven with quantitative both in the production of the data sets and in supporting the causal conclusions of the research.

Htun and Weldon's (2012) research appears to illustrate how two methods can work together to support the same causal conclusion. However, this idea depends on two assumptions—assumptions that are often made about the use of mixed methods research: (a) that the objects of study explored quantitatively are objects understood under the same concepts that are explored qualitatively—the assumption discussed in the previous section—and (b) that the concept of "cause" is used consistently. Considerations that are relevant to the first assumption have already been addressed in the discussion of ontological causal pluralism. In this particular case, the question of whether the objects of inquiry are the same would seem to depend on the coding and so could presumably be determined. The second assumption is specifically about conceptual causal pluralism.

Nancy Cartwright (2007) argues that no one, universal account of causality is adequate to all the different relations that we call "causal." "There are, I maintain, a variety of different kinds of causal relations that we might be pointing to with the label *cause*, and each different kind of relation needs to be matched to the right methods for finding out about it, as well as with the right inference rules for how to use our knowledge of it" (p. 9). This way of thinking about causality does not support a "one size fits all" or, as Cartwright refers to it, an "off the shelf" methodology to be applied in all contexts.

Similarly, Julian Reiss (2009) follows Cartwright (2007) in arguing that all current philosophical accounts of causality face unresolvable counterexamples when they are treated as universal accounts of causality. As Reiss notes, causal pluralism is ambiguous. He identifies two varieties of causal pluralism: "evidential pluralism" and "conceptual pluralism." Evidential pluralism is the view that there are different paths to discovery, each producing different sorts of evidence for one underlying conception of cause. Reiss contrasts evidential pluralism with conceptual pluralism—what I have been calling conceptual causal pluralism. If mixed methods researchers are evidential pluralists, then various methods are all worth pursuing because they are all various ways of confirming or disconfirming the single and seemingly straightforward causal hypothesis. Furthermore, presumably some of these straightforward causal hypotheses might require qualitative methods in addition to quantitative methods. This seems to be the argument that Htun and Weldon (2012) are making. Thus their line of reasoning appears to be a version of evidential pluralism.

But Reiss (2009) argues that not all differences between causal concepts can be resolved through evidential pluralism. Identifying a cause includes specifying a causal relation, and different causal relations result in different causal conclusions that are, in turn, supported by different patterns of inference. Establishing causal claims under one concept of causality does not always secure the sorts of inferences in which we are interested. Reiss argues that because different concepts of causality (conceptual pluralism) support different types of inference, this would mean that an analysis of mixed methods that focuses on using results of different methods to support the same causal conclusion can be misleading. Consequently, Reiss argues that we should be conceptual causal pluralists because methodologies, methods, and the evidence they produce are specific to different sorts of causes.[13] For example, process tracing using qualitative methods (such as we find in case study research) may reveal some types of causation—processual causation—that are not revealed through other methods (statistical quantitative reasoning, or average effects causation).

In the discussion of ontological causal pluralism in the previous section, I claimed that causal spaces were shaped by the ways in which the objects of study were conceived and how the properties of those objects give rise to the causal relations that are possible among them. In this way, I argued that what the objects of inquiry are taken to be constrains the causal space. Reiss's (2009) analysis of conceptual causal pluralism offers an additional dimension along which causal spaces may be constrained. As I have argued, they may vary along the ontological dimension (ontological causal pluralism)—where the conception of the objects of inquiry constrains the causal claims that can be sustained. But additionally causal spaces are shaped by the conceptual dimension (conceptual causal pluralism)—where the concern is about the appropriate sense of causality (e.g., average effects or processual).

The ability to make causal inferences is asymmetrical. We can draw conclusions about the populations from individuals fairly reliably, but we cannot draw conclusions about individuals from our conclusions about populations. This inferential asymmetry results from the use of different conceptions of causality and also illustrates how the different conceptions of causality are claiming causal relations between different levels of objects. Average effects causation claims causal relations within a large population or between populations, but processual causation is concerned with causal relations between individual events, nations, person, social groups, and so forth.

Such considerations might seem to indicate that mixed methods research could *never* be useful in producing evidence for establishing a causal conclusion, but this would follow only if the only goal of science was to converge on one causal account (under one causal description). But the goals of science are diverse. When average effects causation cannot sustain an inference to individual groups and cases, that failure calls for an explanation. The misfit between the general and the particular can be an indicator of missing factors and so can feed back into an improved average effects account through the identification of variables that had not been considered, or it can point to the need for a processual account that keeps attention on the particular.

Feminist Concerns

To return to feminist concerns, there are at least two circumstances where using different methods to establish one causal relation is not or should not be a goal of feminists using mixed methods research. The first is when the operationalization of the key concepts is not informed by feminist qualitative research. Paxton's (2000) critique of democracy research is one example of this. Stanko's (1997) rethinking of self-defense ("things we do to stay safe") is another. In such cases, feminist researchers should argue that the research is taking place in the wrong causal space and that the objects of study have not been appropriately conceived to reveal causes that are relevant to their goals. One way in which we can come to have better concepts with which to engage in social science is through paying attention to the tensions that arise when methods are mixed. The second circumstance is when the desired causal inferences cannot be sustained with the sort of evidence that the method can produce. Evidence for causal relations between populations may only be suggestive of where to seek additional evidence for causal mechanisms or of a causal pathway that should be traced. In the case of democracy, we may be looking in the wrong places for causes if we count as democracies polities that do not have universal suffrage. In the second, the causal connections between environments that are unsafe for women and crime against women may be invisible until the "ordinary" activities of women are redescribed as ways that they stay safe.

The considerations of the previous paragraphs are not merely caveats for feminist research of course, but for all good social science research, since either of these errors is symptomatic of *poor* research. The value of mixed methods research is, in part, that the tensions between the methods push

researchers to question research design, concepts, and the other presuppositions that they make in order to get research off the ground. Getting clearer about what factors are relevant in causal reasoning and why also keeps us sensitive to the diverse goals of research and the reality that methods may not all suit those goals equally.

Feminist research that uses mixed methods can be strengthened when it is informed with an awareness of conceptual causal pluralism—mixed methods research is one way to achieve this awareness. Htun and Weldon's (2012) research, with which I began this section, is ambiguous when it comes to the question of conceptual causal pluralism. They appear to claim that they have established causality through identification of mechanisms that connect strong, autonomous feminist movements with government responses to redress violence against women; however, their language is almost exclusively the language of average effects causality. Although they argue that the correlation they find between the dependent and independent variable is established as a causal relation through case evidence revealing the appropriate temporal relationship to sustain a causal claim, they find it necessary to turn to quantitative methods to garner further support. Hence they argue, "Perhaps most definitively, analysis of a lagged variable found that strong, autonomous feminist movements remained a strongly significant predictor of our index" (p. 560). But an overemphasis of the quantitative and average effects features of research can downplay the value of research supporting the knowledge of processual causality. The specifics of how strong, autonomous feminist movements are built locally, and differences among them are surely features that are hidden in the average effects account and perhaps even lost in the coding. And they may be crucial for knowing what actions will work *here*, as opposed to *in general*, to bring about a reduction in violence against women. Treating causality under one concept supports the invisibility of the particular, and it emphasizes the generalizing goals of research at the expense of other goals.

Mixed Methods for Feminism's Diverse Goals

Feminists doing social science provide examples of some ways in which mixed methods research integrates quantitative and the qualitative data and reconceptualizes social reality so that our understanding is more reflective of the lived experience of women. Such reconceptualizations affect the identification of the concepts and variables that might be used in quantitative work and may also result in a different understanding of the social concepts and structures that serve as the backdrop of the search for causal relations. Feminists have also used mixed methods to support causal conclusions and enhance understandings of average effects as we have seen in the example of Htun and Weldon's (2012) research. But I have argued that conceptual causal pluralism is at least plausible and that it may provide a reason to resist the idea that, when seeking evidence for causal relations, we always use evidence for causal claims as understood through the same concept of causality. Different methodological approaches may result in different types of evidence, each best suited for different purposes and consequently not suited to support the same causal inferences. In such cases, there is not an accumulation of evidence through mixed methods for one causal conclusion.

There are at least two dimensions across which causal spaces vary. I have characterized them through distinguishing ontological causal pluralism and conceptual causal pluralism. Good feminist mixed methods research concepts and their operationalizations are qualitatively informed and deeply dependent on what we want to do with the results of our research. We see this with the development of a new concept, such as sexual harassment, but also in the revisions of concepts currently in use, as illustrated in Paxton's (2000) critique of democracy. That dependence affects the causal conclusions that can be drawn from the research, and an ongoing awareness of how the concepts have been formulated is needed. This is a lesson that, while not solely apparent in feminist research, is well illustrated there.

The second dimension of causal space affects the inferences that can be sustained through different concepts of causality. When average effects are established, we are not easily and directly able to transform that knowledge into processual causal claims. Consequently, mixing methods to support causal claims without careful consideration of these issues may be problematic, since different types of causal claims may be useful for different purposes.

I close with one further thought on the rhetorical use of mixed methods research in feminist social science to serve the goal of advocating for social transformation. Sharlene Hesse-Biber (2010) remarks that

Along the way, there is also a movement in some of these case studies towards providing data grounded in individuals' lived experiences and situated in a macrocontext. Such data provide policy makers with a much-needed "dual perspective" on the social world that uses words and numbers to convey their findings to social policy makers and in addition seeks to uncover new knowledge that is critical to those who lives have been disempowered. (p. 467)

We know both that there is a strong push from policymakers for evidence-based policy and that quantitative research is valued in that sphere. We also know from social psychology findings that particular cases are often more effective for changing beliefs than statistical evidence.[14]

One goal of feminist social science is to produce knowledge that can be *used* to change the social and political status of women and/or alleviate effects of subordination. Attention to the particularities of women's experience is one method that contributes to the production of such knowledge. A strong motive for knowing causes is to intervene in causal processes and bring about change. Quantitative methods that provide evidence for average effects might be thought of as best suited for justification of general causal claims—for example, a feminist researcher could use such methods to establish a link between wages and gender, as Hesse-Biber (2010) notes that Louise Marie Roth does in her 2006 study of MBAs (p. 466). But without identifying processual causes—perhaps mechanisms—we do not know why there is such a gap, and consequently average effects provide little guidance for bringing about change.

Qualitative methods help to focus on specific features of the causal pathway and so provide better evidence for knowledge that is practice-oriented or "evidence for use" in Nancy Cartwright's (2006) phrase (Cartwright & Hardie, 2012; Cartwright & Stegenga, 2011).[15] When we aim at an abstract body of knowledge—what we ought to believe about the world—average effects will dominate our discourse, but if we are thinking about what we want to use our knowledge for, the particularity and contextuality of the "on the ground" knowledge that qualitative research provides may be more appropriate.

Another benefit of the understanding provided by feminist using mixed methods research is that such research provides a rhetorical framework from which to make arguments about such change. Human beings find causal stories compelling—we give sense to our experiences through understanding them causally in a way that more closely resembles processual causation than average effects causation. While average effects arguments support general and abstract conclusions by giving us statistical evidence about populations, it is the immediacy of the story—the qualitative case study—that has the rhetorical force to make people act for change. Feminist social science provides knowledge *for* women in order to support their autonomy in ways that will change society and their lives. Those goals require both an abstract understanding of the relations between causes and effects in populations and an understanding of how causes manifest themselves (or do not) in particular cases.

Conclusions

Feminists use mixed methods research in ways that aid in understanding and in turn support distinguishing two dimensions of causal spaces. This chapter outlines one way in which feminist approaches to research use mixed methods to explore the ontological dimension of causal space. In addition, it urges an awareness of how different conceptions of causality embedded in different methods may be used in mixed methods research. Different conceptions of cause can be in tension in ways that both motivate new areas of research and require a more careful consideration of the diverse goals that knowledge projects may have. Such tensions have been particularly productive for feminist approaches to research. Causal pluralism needs to be explored further. The uses of mixed methods research by feminists offers a particularly rich venue in which to do so.

Discussion Questions

1. What are some ways that mixed methods research might lead to extending research to different causal spaces? Consider this for both dimensions of causal spaces discussed in this chapter.

2. This chapter suggests that mixed methods research does not always make use of more than one method to produce evidence for the same causal claim. Are there times when different methods do produce evidence for the same causal claim? What factors would need to be considered to determine this?

3. This chapter argues that the critical stance of feminist research provides a particularly good site for investigating how mixed methods research might be used for establishing causal relationships. Are there examples of nonfeminist research that also seem to follow some of the patterns suggested here? For instance, are there examples of mixed methods research where the considerations that arise from one method lead to a reconceptualization of the objects of inquiry?

4. One aspect of conceptual causal pluralism as it appears in the philosophical literature is the idea that difference concepts of cause are suited to difference uses. This idea relies on distinguishing between evidence for use and evidence for belief (Cartwright & Hardie, 2012). Does this distinction seem like a reasonable one?

5. Two dimensions of causal space were identified in this chapter: an ontological dimension (how the objects of inquiry conceived, what properties they have, what properties are relevant) and a conceptual dimension (what concept of cause is in use). Are there other dimensions that might be of interest?

Suggested Websites

http://plato.stanford.edu/entries/feminism-epistemology/
This section of the *Stanford Encyclopedia of Philosophy* provides a good discussion of the key issues in feminist philosophy of science and addresses some of the concerns that were touched on in the introductory section of the chapter.

http://plato.stanford.edu/search/searcher.py?query=causation
The *Stanford Encyclopedia of Philosophy* provides an introduction into a variety of philosophical approaches to causation.

Notes

1. Wittgenstein's (2009) *Philosophical Investigations* (§66 and §67).

2. I borrow the idea of causal spaces from Helen Longino (2013) who uses it to discuss methodological pluralism in the research on human behavior.

3. "Feminist standpoint *theories*" is more accurate given that there are multiple versions of standpoint theory.

4. Gurr and Naples (2014) also mention the work of anthropologist Susan Greenlagh in demonstrating the missing girls in China resulting from that country's one-child policy (p. 34).

5. See Cartwright and Hardie (2012) on the many requirements that must be met in order for randomized controlled trials to be applicable in a realm outside of the experimental context.

6. Statistical methods are also used in conjunction with experiments, but here I am focusing on their use in place of experiments.

7. These approaches are not mutually exclusive, nor are they jointly exhaustive but rather just a sample of the many ways that causality might be thought of.

8. In the political science literature they are often distinguished by referring to average effects as *effects of causes* whereas *causes of effects* is used to refer to causation such as we see in mechanisms. This terminology does not seem particularly illuminating to me, and I mention it here only to indicate that I am referring to the same distinction.

9. Smith (1987) advocates using this tension between the lived experience of women (known through qualitative methods) and the "objective" descriptions of social science to discern "lines of fault" that call for alternative account.

10. To refer to these factors as "variables" is to adopt quantitative language. I do so for convenience sake here, but the question of whether a concept can be usually treated as a variable is an open question.

11. The previous research cited is Weldon's work (2002a, 2002b).

12. Htun and Weldon (2012) make theoretical arguments that support their hypothesized causal mechanism as well. The role that theory plays is not something I have addressed in this chapter, and it plays an important role in causal explanation in a number of ways that deserve exploration.

13. Cartwright (2007) makes the same point, noting that different methods are good for capturing causality in different sorts of systems but not useful in others.

14. For example, research shows that people will donate more when a single individual in need is identified than when they are presented with statistics about victims who would benefit from their charity (Loewenstein, Small, & Slovic, 2003).

15. This sort of causal pluralism bears some similarity to the distinction between idiographic and nomothetic explanations (Levy, 1997; Johnson & Gray, 2010) where idiographic accounts focus on single events and nomothetic accounts are concerned with events insofar as they fall under laws or lawlike generalizations. That way of making the distinction does not seem quite right for my purposes, however. Generally, the use of knowledge is linked to prediction, while the nomothetic/idiographic distinction is usually drawn in reference to explanation. Also, identifying correlations, even those thought to be causal, need not conclude with discovering laws, and so describing the claims supported by statistical evidence as nomothetic is not always accurate.

References

Brines, J. (1994). Economic dependency and the division of labor. *American Journal of Sociology*, *100*(3), 652–688.

Cartwright, N. (2006). Well-ordered science: Evidence for use. *Philosophy of Science*, *73*(5), 981–990.

Cartwright, N. (2007). *Hunting causes and using them.* New York, NY: Cambridge University Press.

Cartwright, N., & Hardie, J. (2012). *Evidence based policy: A practical guide to doing it better.* New York, NY: Oxford University Press.

Cartwright, N., & Stegenga, J. (2011). A theory of evidence for evidence-based policy. In P. Dawid, W. Twining, & M. Vasilaki (Eds.), *Evidence, inference and enquiry: Proceedings of the British Academy* (pp. 291–322). New York, NY: Oxford University Press.

Crasnow, S. (2010). Evidence for use: Causal pluralism and the role of case studies in political science. *Philosophy of Social Science*, *41*(1), 26–49.

Crasnow, S. (2012). The role of case study research in political science: Evidence for causal claims. *Philosophy of Science*, *79*(5), 655–666.

Crasnow, S. (2013). Feminist philosophy of science: Values and objectivity. *Philosophy Compass*, *8*(4), 413–423. Retrieved from http://onlinelibrary.wiley.com/doi/10.1111/phc3.12023/full

DeVault, M. L. (1999). *Liberating method: Feminism and social research*. Philadelphia, PA: Temple University Press.

Douglas, H. (2009). *Science, policy, and the value-free ideal.* Pittsburgh, PA: University of Pittsburgh Press.

Farley, L. (1978). *Sexual shakedown: The sexual harassment of women on the job.* New York, NY: McGraw-Hill.

George, A. L., & Bennett, A. (2004). *Case studies and theory development in the social sciences*. Cambridge, MA: MIT Press.

Gerring, J. (2010). Causal mechanisms: Yes, but... *Comparative Political Studies*, *43*(11), 1499–1526.

Haraway, D. (1988). Situated knowledge: The science question in feminism and the privilege of partial perspective. *Feminist Studies, 14*, 575–599.

Harding, S. (1986). *The science question in feminism*. Ithaca, NY: Cornell University Press.

Harding, S. (1987). Introduction: Is there a feminist method? In S. Harding (Ed.), *Feminism and methodology* (pp. 1–14). Bloomington: Indiana University Press.

Harding, S. (1998). *Is science multicultural? Postcolonialisms, feminisms, and epistemologies.* Bloomington: Indiana University Press.

Harding, S. (2004). Rethinking standpoint epistemology: What is "strong objectivity"? In S. Harding (Ed.), *The feminist standpoint theory reader* (pp. 127–140). New York, NY: Routledge.

Harding, S. (2008). *Sciences from below: Feminisms, postcolonialities, and modernities.* Durham, NC: Duke University Press.

Hesse-Biber, S. (2010). Qualitative approaches to mixed methods practice. *Qualitative Inquiry*, *16*(6), 455–468.

Htun, M. & Weldon, S. L. (2012). The civic origins of progressive policy change: Combating violence against women in global perspective, 1975–2005. *American Political Science Review*, *106*(3), 548–569.

Intemann, K. (2010). Twenty-five years of feminist empiricism and standpoint theory: Where are we now? *Hypatia: A Journal of Feminist Philosophy*, *25*(4), 778–796.

Johnson, R. B., & Gray, R. (2010). A history of philosophical and theoretical issues for mixed methods research. *SAGE handbook of mixed methods in social & behavioral research* (2nd ed., pp. 69–94). Thousand Oaks, CA: Sage.

Lacey, H. (1999). *Is science value free? Values and scientific understanding.* New York, NY: Routledge.

Levy, J. S. (1997). Too important to leave to the other: History and political science in the study of international relations. *International Security*, *22*(1), 22–33.

Longino, H. (1990). *Science as social knowledge: Values and objectivity in scientific inquiry.* Princeton, NJ: Princeton University Press.

Longino, H. (2002). *The fate of knowledge.* Princeton, NJ: Princeton University Press.

Longino, H. (2013). *Studying human behavior: How scientists investigate aggression and sexuality.* Chicago, IL: University of Chicago Press.

Nagel, T. (1986). *The view from nowhere.* New York, NY: Oxford University Press.

Paxton, P. (2000). Women's suffrage and the measurement of democracy: Problems of operationalization. *Studies in Comparative International Development*, *43*, 92–111.

Reiss, J. (2009). Causation in the social sciences: Evidence, inference, and purpose. *Philosophy of the Social Sciences*, *39*(1), 20–40.

Rolin, K. (2009). Standpoint theory as a methodology for the study of power relations. *Hypatia: A Journal of Feminist Philosophy, 24*(4), 218–226.

Sen, A. (1990). More than 100 million women are missing. *The New York Review of Books, 37*(20), 61–66.

Small, D. A., Loewenstein, G., & Slovic, P. (2007). Sympathy and callousness: The impact of deliberative thought on donations to identifiable and statistical victims. *Organizational Behavior and Human Decision Processes, 102*(2), 143–53.

Smith, D. (1987). *The everyday world as problematic*. Boston, MA: Northeastern University Press.

Sprague, J. (2005). *Feminist methodologies for critical researchers: Bridging differences*. Lanham, MD: AltaMira Press.

Stanko, E. A. (1997). Conceptualizing women's risk assessment as a "technology of the soul." *Theoretical Criminology, 1*(4), 479–499.

Weldon, S. L. (2002a). Beyond bodies: Institutional sources of representation for women. *Journal of Politics, 64*(4), 1153–74.

Weldon, S. L. (2002b). *Protest, policy and the problem of violence against women: A cross-national comparison*. Pittsburgh, PA: University of Pittsburgh Press.

Wittgenstein, L. (2009). *Philosophical investigations* (4th ed.). (G. E. M. Anscombe, P. M. S. Hacker, & Joachim Schulte, trans.). Chichester, UK: Blackwell.

Wylie, A. (2011). Standpoint (still) matters: Research on women, work, and the academy. In H. Grasswick (Ed.), *Feminist epistemology and philosophy of science: Power in knowledge* (pp. 157–179). Dordrecht, The Netherlands: Springer.

Causality, Generalizability, and the Future of Mixed Methods Research

Robert K. Yin

Abstract

Mixed methods research (MMR) has struggled to bridge paradigms that differ starkly on two central concepts—causality and generalizability. This chapter depicts the differences and the efforts made to bridge them. However, MMR can go beyond sheer bridging and strive to create an integrated craft. In particular, both the qualitative and quantitative camps have left four procedures underspecified: triangulating, examining plausible rival explanations, analyzing mixed methods data, and making analytic generalizations. For instance, no criteria exist to show whether a study has sufficiently triangulated or examined rivals. If MMR developed operational benchmarks, its studies could then use all four procedures in a compelling manner. In so doing, MMR might become a truly blended craft—not just one that bridges existing paradigms.

Key Words: causality, generalizability, paradigms, bridging, integrated, triangulation, plausible rival explanations, analytic generalizations

Introduction

The editors of this volume asked that this chapter address the following conundrum:

> Two of the primary differences between qualitatively driven and quantitatively driven research have been about how one should frame causation and generalizability. How might MMR contribute to the conversation? Specifically, how might MMR bridge qualitative and quantitative understandings of these concepts and bring new meanings to them?

The Setting for the Conundrum

Landmark work by Yvonne Lincoln and Egon Guba (Guba & Lincoln, 1989; Lincoln & Guba, 1985) sharply contrasted the differences between two paradigms underlying social science research and evaluation: *naturalistic inquiry* (later relabeled *constructivism*) and *positivism* (now referred to as *postpositivism*; Phillips & Burbules, 2000; Johnson, 2009). Within these two paradigms, the issues of causality and generalizability have assumed central places in characterizing the differences.

With regard to causality, whereas the postpositivist paradigm focuses on independent and dependent variables in attempts to establish lawful cause-and-effect relationships, the constructivist paradigm questions whether causality is a valid concept for the social sciences in the first place. Instead, the constructivist paradigm depicts a social world of "mutual simultaneous shaping" (Lincoln & Guba, 1985, pp. 150–157). In this world,

> Everything influences everything else. . . Many elements are implicated in any given action, and each element interacts with all of the others in ways that change them all while simultaneously resulting in something that we, as outside observers, label as outcomes or effects. But the interaction has *no directionality*, no *need* to produce *that particular outcome*. (Lincoln & Guba, 1985, p. 151, emphasis in the original).

With regard to generalizability, the post-positivist paradigm seeks to establish the representativeness—and even universality—of a study's findings (e.g., Campbell & Stanley, 1963, p. 5). As a result, the ideal generalizations have been presented as "assertions of enduring value that are context-free" (Lincoln & Guba, 1985, p. 110). As an alternative, constructivism points to the uniqueness of local conditions and the likelihood that, at most, generalizability only can take the form of the "transferability of a working hypothesis" (Lincoln & Guba, 1985, p. 297). The extent of transferability depends upon "the degree of similarity of the sending and receiving contexts" (Lincoln & Guba, 1985, p. 297.).

For many scholars, the basic incompatibility of the two paradigms means that no single research study can credibly embrace both. Guba and Lincoln (1994, p. 116) spoke of the *incommensurability* of the two paradigms. Later, the same authors recognized three additional paradigms and then suggested that the then-current trends had put social scientists on the threshold of "a history marked by multivocality, contested meanings, paradigmatic controversies, and new textual forms" (Guba & Lincoln, 2005, p. 212). Other strongly worded reservations have included researchers not being able to adopt both sets of assumptions "without contradiction" (Small, 2011, p. 78) and an incompatibility "if the qualitative paradigm assumes that there are no external referents for understanding reality" (Sale, Lohfeld, & Brazil, 2002, p. 47).

Within this milieu, exacerbated by the paradigm wars, emerged mixed methods research (MMR) "as we know it today" (Creswell, 2009, p. 101). Although the combining of qualitative and quantitative methods had occurred in earlier research (some studies now retrospectively considered MMR classics)—especially in such fields as evaluation and sociology (e.g., Jick, 1979; Lipset, Trow, & Coleman, 1956; Sieber, 1973; Trend, 1979)—the reenergized MMR community has continually challenged itself to address the "incommensurate" or "incompatible" point of view.

Introduction to the Chapter

This chapter first reviews ongoing conversations about causality and generalizability—especially in the context of the two paradigms. In addition, a short section of the chapter touches on related conversations in the field of history. Both sets of ongoing conversations then become the backdrop for speculating about what might be MMR's most helpful future contributions. The chapter concludes by suggesting that the Conundrum presents an unusual opportunity for MMR. Its future contributions can not only fill gaps in the ongoing conversations but also can establish MMR's identity as a uniquely integrated craft, augmenting preexisting qualitative and quantitative methods with its own set of practices.

The Ongoing Conversations

To date, the ongoing conversations about causality and generalizability have indeed reflected the two themes in the Conundrum:

1. *Bridging* qualitative and quantitative understandings by
   a. Trying to accommodate both paradigms within the same framework; and
   b. Focusing on methodological practices and downplaying paradigmatic differences
2. *Bringing new meaning* to causality and generalizability and creating a deeper understanding of them.

The contributions have been made by researchers doing MMR studies, as well as by researchers doing other forms of qualitative and quantitative research.

Bridging Qualitative and Quantitative Understandings

The first theme has two components, both representing ways in which MMR and other studies have tried to bridge the contrasting approaches to causality and generalization.

TRYING TO ACCOMMODATE BOTH PARADIGMS WITHIN THE SAME FRAMEWORK

Some of the dialogue has been aimed at smoothing over the paradigmatic differences. The dilemma has been that, if such differences cannot be overcome, studies based on both paradigms would be "neither possible nor sensible" (Greene, Caracelli, & Graham, 1989, p. 257). For example, although Guba and Lincoln (2005, pp. 195–196, Table 8.3) had eventually expanded their analysis to cover five, not just two, paradigms, the newly added paradigms did not alleviate the original tension between constructivism and postpositivism to any noticeable degree. In other words, truly paradigmatic differences, by definition, cannot be smoothed over.

Nevertheless, others have attempted conciliatory efforts. Partly in response to Guba and Lincoln's (2005) work, Teddlie and Tashakkori (2009, p. 88, Table 5.2) presented their own array of multiple paradigms. Key to Teddlie and Tashakkori's new array—with causality and generalizability considered two of the important contrasting dimensions across the paradigms—was the introduction of *pragmatism*, a paradigm based on the contributions of Creswell, Plano Clark, Gutmann, and Hanson (2003, p. 186), Howe (1988), Johnson and Onwuegbuzie (2004), and Morgan (2007), among others.

The pragmatic approach calls for proceeding to apply relevant methods and procedures—enabling a study to be completed—without trying to settle the paradigmatic differences. In this way, Teddlie and Tashakkori used pragmatism to argue that all the paradigms represent a continuum of options rather than an "either-or" condition (Tashakkori & Teddlie, 2010, p. 274; Teddlie & Tashakkori, 2009, pp. 87–90). The authors consider pragmatism as the "best paradigm for justifying the use of mixed methods research" (Teddlie & Tashakkori, 2009, p. 99). On causation, they claim that pragmatists believe "there may be causal relationships but. . . these relationships are transitory and hard to identify" (p. 93). As for generalizability, pragmatists "are concerned with issues of both the external validity and the transferability of results" (p. 93). Thus pragmatism enables a researcher to adapt selectively the features from postpositivism and constructivism.

In a similar way, other scholars have offered a more congenial view of the two paradigms, suggesting that they are complementary rather than competitive and can foster new qualitative-quantitative partnerships (e.g., Dellinger & Leech, 2007; Reichardt & Cook, 1979; Reichardt & Rallis, 1994). Mixed method research even can offer itself as a "third paradigm" choice—although the definition of the third paradigm appears to rest on a mechanistic combination of the first two, not necessarily the development of new concepts or methods or any true integration of the two (e.g., Johnson, Onwuegbuzie, & Turner, 2007, p. 129; Teddlie & Tashakkori, 2009, pp. 14–16).

Regardless of the convincing or nonconvincing nature of the conciliatory claims, they have permitted researchers to avoid being backed into purist stances about the original two paradigms. The result has been the ability to proceed with studies that draw from both paradigms—that is, by studying social phenomena "eclectically," by assuming "multiple perspectives" (Tashakkori & Creswell, 2008, p. 4), and by pursuing "multiple mental models" (Greene, 2007, p. 30).

FOCUSING ON METHODOLOGICAL PRACTICES AND DOWNPLAYING PARADIGMATIC DIFFERENCES

A second way of bridging the qualitative and quantitative paradigms has been to turn to the sheer mixture of methodological practices, apart from addressing any paradigmatic differences. As already noted, earlier studies had mixed methods before MMR emerged in its current form. In addition, Greene and colleagues (1989) had identified 57 mixed methods studies in the field of evaluation alone, based on a limited search of evaluations published from 1980 to 1988.

The mixing of practices can occur in different ways: the mixing of data, of design, and of analyses. The plainest approach involves the *mixing of data*. For instance, both qualitative (nonnumeric) and quantitative (numeric) data can be produced within the same study by having open-ended and closed-ended questions in the same survey. The two types of data can be analyzed in a number of ways (Caracelli & Greene, 1993), one of the variations being to code the nonnumeric data, to assign numeric values to the codes, and then to analyze the combined data, whether addressing causal relationships or not (e.g., Sandelowski, Voils, & Knafl, 2009).

Somewhat more complex mixing can occur with the *mixing of designs* and not just the mixing of data. MMR texts have devoted considerable attention to the various designs (e.g., Creswell, 1999; Creswell & Plano Clark, 2007; Creswell, Plano Clark, Gutmann, & Hanson, 2003; Greene, 2007; Steckler et al., 1992; Tashakkori & Teddlie, 1998). In general, the designs recognize many ways of combining the qualitative and quantitative components. The arrangements usually involve sequential, parallel, or nested combinations but can include more complicated relationships between the two components.

Much of the design mixing assumes that a study is interested in examining causal relationships. This interest has especially dominated evaluation studies, with some studies even juxtaposing a randomized control trial as the quantitative component with a field-based qualitative component (e.g., Hesse-Biber, 2010b; O'Cathain, 2009). Going beyond evaluation studies, Paluck (2010) contends that random assignment designs should become more central to future qualitative research—"to generate strong causal inferences while extracting new ideas at close range" (p. 64).

The attention to design choices also has addressed generalizability, especially raising awareness about the implications of different types of samples to generalize the findings beyond a particular study. For instance, random samples may be used when trying to generalize to a larger population or universe—befitting the postpositivist paradigm, but purposive samples may be selected to tighten the comparisons with different kinds of other cases not being studied and therefore to increase the transferability of findings to those other cases—befitting the constructivist paradigm (Teddlie & Yu, 2007, pp. 78–80). A single MMR study can include both types of samples, thereby creating "complementary" databases that include information having "both depth and breadth regarding the phenomenon under study" (Teddlie & Yu, 2007, p. 85).

Apart from the data and design options, the methodological practices can include the *mixing of analyses*—that is, using qualitative and quantitative methods during a study's analysis phase. One analytic technique consists of Charles Ragin's (1987, 2000, 2004, 2009) innovative *qualitative comparative analysis* or QCA, with enhancements and clarifications by other scholars (e.g., Bennett, 2004; Byrne, 2009; Fielding & Warnes, 2009; Rihoux & Lobe, 2009). Despite the appearance of the word *qualitative* in the label, QCA embraces both qualitative and quantitative procedures, calling for the assembly of both variable-based and case-based configurations as part of the same analysis. The practice "reject[s] any fundamental distinction between the quantitative and the qualitative" (Byrne, 2009, p. 4) and has drawn support in different fields—for example, sociology (Luker, 2008, pp. 203–209), political science (George & Bennett, 2004, pp. 161–162), and evaluation (Befani, 2013).

An upshot of these various forms of mixed methods—the mixing of data, the use of mixed designs, and the conduct of mixed analyses—has been the continued abundance of MMR studies. For instance, Bryman (2006) found 232 mixed methods studies published during the period from 1994 to 2003, and in 2009 an editor of the *Journal of Mixed Methods* said he had reviewed close to 300 manuscripts submitted to the journal during the preceding three years (Creswell, 2009).

Bringing New Meaning to Causality and Generalizability

The conversations also have included "bringing new meaning" to causality and generalizability.

CAUSALITY

As noted earlier, the two paradigms deal with causality in extremely different ways—either trying to establish lawful cause-and-effect relationships (postpositivism) or questioning the usefulness of the concept in the first place (constructivism). Nevertheless, between these extremes now exist other variants.

One variant that has brought new meaning to the constructivist and postpositivist extremes has been the study of *causal processes*—that is, using field-based methods to study directly the actual array of events and actions that lead to specific outcomes in local settings (Erickson, 2012, p. 688; Maxwell, 2004, 2012; Miles & Huberman, 1994, p. 132). The conventional postpositivist approach—relying on inferences based largely on a correlative (input–output) relationship between an independent and a dependent variable—has become a point of departure rather than being accepted as the overarching definition of causality (e.g., Donmoyer, 2012a).

Scholars in different fields have recognized the process variant as *process tracing* in political science (e.g., Bennett, 2010; George & Bennett, 2004; Harrits, 2011), *explanation building* when doing case studies (e.g., Yin, 2014, pp. 147–150), and *process analysis* more generally (e.g., Anderson & Scott, 2012). Desirably, such process inquiries also can embrace the real-life contextual conditions relevant to the local settings, and the inquiries even can highlight nonlinear and recursive flows of events (e.g., Maxwell, 2012). As a result, the process alternative appears to be suitably compatible with the constructivist paradigm (Maxwell, 2012, p. 658). Thus the correlational and process approaches to causality can have a complementary relationship within the same study, with the process inquiry producing additional (process) information that is absent from what is essentially an input–output analysis between the independent and dependent variables (Harrits, 2011, p. 153).

The attention given to studying actual causal processes has been especially important in the field of evaluation, where the complexity of interventions requires process inquiries based on field methods (e.g., Yin, 1994; Yin & Ridde, 2012). For instance, Howell and Yemane (2006) examined 12 evaluations of large, federally supported human services programs involving complex interventions as well as multiple sites within each program. The authors found that the evaluations drilled into the complexity of the interventions while trying to make causal connections with quantitative outcomes.

Studying causal processes directly also can offer at least two benefits. First, the inquiry can focus explicit attention on systematic ways of specifying the contextual conditions, which even qualitative research has usually left undifferentiated. For example, one suggestion usefully splits contextual conditions into three levels (Anderson & Scott, 2012): (a) a macro level that includes the political economy and market and cultural norms, (b) a meso level that includes institutions and organizations, and (c) a micro-level that includes the people in a given setting. The proper depiction of the context in the resulting process inquiry might then need to cover two or more of these levels (Anderson & Scott, 2012, p. 681).

Second, a process inquiry—especially when based on *thick description* (e.g., Geertz, 1973)—can provide an extensive body of evidence. Such an extensive body may then move toward creating a "preponderance of evidence" (e.g., Donmoyer, 2012b), serving as a contrast to the frequently over-estimated valuing of quantitative analyses when response rates are low and instruments are of questionable relevance (Donmoyer, 2012b).

Besides the correlation-based and the process-based variants, there is at least one other variant. It distinguishes between *mechanical causation* and *agential causation* (Howe, 2004, 2012). Whereas the former derives from the conventional postpositivist position that assumes a social world working like the physical world, the latter occurs in human settings, when people may intentionally take some causal action. For instance, Lincoln and Guba (1985) point to the paradoxical situation wherein humans, being anticipatory, can produce an effect in anticipation of its cause (p. 142). Thus agential causation can be considered a third type of causality. From an MMR perspective, although quantitative methods might tend to be used to study mechanical causation and qualitative methods to study agential causation, Howe (2011) shows how these pairings can be interchanged.

GENERALIZABILITY

As with causality, extreme positions also have marked the original depiction on generalizability.

At the same time, the earlier literature already had started to articulate an alternative to either the constructivist or postpositivist positions—what has become known as *analytic generalization* (Yin, 2013, 2014, pp. 68–69). Although not always using the exact same terminology, many researchers have contrasted this type of generalizability with *statistical generalization* (e.g., Bromley, 1986, pp. 290–291; Burawoy, 1991, pp. 271–280; Donmoyer, 1990; Halkier, 2011; Mitchell, 1983; Small, 2009). Whereas statistical generalization derives from the postpositivist notions about the representativeness of a sample in characterizing a larger universe or population, analytic generalization moves generalizability to a higher level of abstraction—not whether a study's findings pertains to a large number of like-venues but whether it has produced key ideas potentially applicable to a myriad of other situations.

Key to analytic generalization is the use of "theoretical concepts to enable a more general perspective on specific qualitative patterns" (Halkier, 2011, p. 787). For instance, in case study research, the aim is not to consider the case as a sample of a larger population of like-cases but to discover patterns and processes within the case and to use analytic generalization to extract the lessons learned (Erickson, 2012, p. 687). The lessons may later be limited to a single type of case but—as with some of the most famous single-case studies in political science (e.g., Allison, 1971) and sociology (e.g., Whyte, 1943)—may turn out to "apply to many different types of cases" (Bennett, 2004, p. 50). Similarly, an excellent example of a multiple-case study, covering vaccination programs in three countries in sub-Saharan Africa, shows how an empirically derived analytic framework (explaining the flow of preconditions, contextual conditions, and drivers) can form the basis for generalizing the findings to the rest of the region (Mookherji & LaFond, 2013). In fact, the framework appears to be relevant to immunization projects outside of the region and possibly to community health initiatives more broadly (Yin, 2013).

The dialogue about analytic generalization continues to create yet richer understandings. Halkier (2011) suggests three forms of analytic generalization and offers procedures for producing them from empirical studies: (a) ideal-typologizing, (b) category zooming (depth on a single point), and (c) positioning (the reflection of multiple voices and discourse). Small (2009, p. 18) highlights the critical relationship between the manner of choosing a study—that is, starting with a substantive proposition rather than a numeric or distributional one (e.g., electing to study an "average" community)—and the subsequent ability (or not) to arrive at an analytic generalization.

Observing these developments with analytic generalization, Collins, Onwuegbuzie, and Jiao (2007) have augmented the original constructivist–postpositivist dichotomy by suggesting that there may be three ways of generalizing: case-to-case transfers, statistical generalizations, and analytic generalizations. They reviewed 121 studies to determine the presence and frequency of each type, finding that most of the studies had tried to make statistical generalizations even though the samples were not necessarily random or of sufficient size. More relevant to MMR, the authors indicated that any given MMR study could involve all three types of generalizing.

In summary, scholars from different fields have been bringing new meaning to causality and generalizability. These ongoing conversations about alternative forms of causality (e.g., studying causal processes directly) or generalizability (e.g., striving for analytic generalizations) also create opportunities for future MMR contributions. The final portion of this chapter speculates about the nature of such contributions. However, before moving to the final portion, a brief diversion covers related developments in the field of history.

Parallel Conversations in the Field of History

For the social sciences, no discussion of causality, if not also of generalizability, would be complete without reference to the field of history. In fact, the field has been undergoing its own internal conversations that, in some manner, may be said to mimic those between constructivism and postpositivism.

Two Paradigms?

In history's case, the traditional or conventional view, as stated by one of the most authoritative scholars in the field, starts with the assumption that "the study of history is the study of causes" (Carr, 1961, p. 113). The role of the historian is then to extract those "historically significant" causes from the multiplicity of sequences of cause and effect (Carr, 1961, p. 138). Historians therefore struggle with establishing and confirming causal

relationships even when admitting that "everything depends upon everything else" (Gaddis, 2002, p. 92).

The challenge to this conventional view comes from latter day historians who—whether advocating the position or not—have recognized what have become known as *postmodernism* and a *linguistic turn* (e.g., Roberts, 2004). Somewhat like constructivism, this alternative view suggests that historical works rest on interpretation, in turn resting on a historian's language. Thus postmodernism claims that, although historians might believe they are presenting work based on objective methods and trustworthy sources, the ensuing historical narrative is in fact a hypothetical construct—created by a historian who may or may not be aware of the narrative's relativist and constructivist orientations (Howell & Prevenier, 2001, p. 149). In a similar manner, the language embedded in a historical source itself can lead to obscuring the classic distinction between a primary and a secondary source (Evans, 1999, p. 98).

The depth of the postmodernist view can pose a severe threat to all conventional history. Because "language constructs reality rather than referring to it" (Iggers, 1997, p. 9), historical "facts" and their portrayal of reality can be seen as "the reality that sources construct rather than 'reality' itself" (Howell & Prevenier, 2001, p. 149). As one possibility, fact and fiction can be seen as indistinguishable from each other (Evans, 1999, p. 82), and historical discourse even may be considered closer to literature than to science (Iggers, 1997, p. 9). The same linguistic turn can challenge the conventional, one-dimensional conception of time, in which later events follow earlier ones in a coherent sequence (Iggers, 1997, p. 3). Stated more boldly, postmodernism "obliterates the secure linear relation between present and past upon which conventional historical interpretation depends" (Roberts, 2004, p. 233).

The field of history has had to mediate between the conventional and postmodernist paradigms in a way that downplays their differences but potentially deepens understandings of causality and generalizability. A brief exploration of the ongoing conversations in history, therefore, can offer an additional context for understanding how MMR might bridge understandings of these concepts and bring new meanings to them, even though the conversations in history cannot be strictly interpreted as occurring between qualitatively driven and quantitatively driven research.

Bridging Historical Concepts and Bringing New Meaning to Them?

History has no equivalent to MMR in that historians have not tried to produce histories that combine both the conventional and postmodernist views. However, specific historiographic practices do, in a sense, occupy a middle ground.

For instance, historians readily accept that complex events have complex antecedents (Howell & Prevenier, 2001, p. 128). A common feature of the complexity is the presence of immediate and particular events—such as triggering events—in the face of broader and more general but no less important antecedents—such as political and economic conditions (e.g., Bloch, 1953). Although no single condition is necessarily central, causal analysis can still take place, as in Evans's (1999) well-regarded study of how and why a major cholera epidemic occurred in Hamburg in 1892 but nowhere else in Europe.

One way in which historians can narrow their causal attributions is to examine "the fit between theoretical ideas and their complex implications, on the one hand, and the best empirical evidence, on the other" (Rueschemeyer, 2003, p. 318). Such an approach has been referred to as *pattern-matching* in doing case studies (e.g., Yin, 2014, pp. 143–147) and as the *congruence method* in political science (e.g., George & Bennett, 2004, ch. 9). In pursuing the fit between theoretical ideas and empirical evidence, the historian faces similar conditions as in the other social sciences (e.g., in using theory to support the analysis of quasi-experiments—e.g., Rosenbaum, 2002): The goal is to overspecify rather than underspecify the original theory and its implications—that is, to provide more rather than less detail, thereby creating more elaborate and hence more stringent conditions for comparing the theoretical with the empirical (Rueschemeyer, 2003, p. 328).

In this type of analysis, a readily accepted procedure is to reject a pattern if any part of its does not fit the empirical data (Mahoney, 2004, p. 342). More difficult is deciding when to accept an approximate "fit." Here, acknowledging the impossibility of specifying any numeric threshold, historians have rightfully latched onto the importance of specifying *plausible, rival explanations* as part of an overall analysis (e.g., Gaddis, 2002, pp. 100–102; Mahoney, 2004, p. 339). Better "fits" are claimed the more that rivals can be considered but then rejected. As a result, much attention has been given to the need to specify alternative explanations—again making sure they are not underspecified—in analyzing historical patterns.

Regarding the role of generalizability, the methods for dealing with generalizability in history have not drawn as much attention as those given to causality. Historians generalize again by noting patterns—in this situation from one historic case to another—though the procedure is hardly precise and tolerates exceptions (Evans, 1999, pp. 49–50). The desired patterns appear to be one level more abstract than the particular events being studied, in a manner somewhat similar to analytic generalization. In this sense, although all events are acknowledged as being unique, "the historian is not really interested in the unique but in what is general in the unique" (Carr, 1961, p. 80). Although the methods for generalizing have not been spelled out with great clarity, single-case histories rank among the most influential works in the history field (Rueschemeyer, 2003, p. 307).

In summary, the field of history also has witnessed the emergence of a contrasting paradigm—postmodernism—that bears some resemblance to constructivism and that seriously challenges conventional methods of doing history. As in the MMR situation, the two paradigms differ sharply in their approaches to causality and generalizability. However, unlike the case with MMR, no overt bridging between the two paradigms has yet taken place in history. Nevertheless, history has contributed to the conversations about causality and generalization by articulating practices such as a pattern matching like procedure in interpreting causal relationships, as well as explicit attention to the importance of examining rival explanations. Although less has been said about generalizability, historical works, including single-case histories, may be following an analytic practice resembling the use of analytic generalization in the other social sciences.

Future Mixed Methods Research Contributions

All these ongoing conversations form a backdrop for speculating about MMR's potential future contributions. The ongoing conversations have left gaps and incomplete developments that deserve MMR's attention. In directing this attention, MMR studies can and should pursue both of two strategic choices. First, the studies can continue to provide an opportunity for *bridging* two or more methods in the same study—usually meaning that the methods coexist and yield findings and conclusions beyond those that the methods alone might have supported. In this arrangement, each method still follows its own procedures, and the MMR study more or less mechanically or additively combines the methods—albeit in some meaningful way (e.g., by using sequential, nested, or parallel designs).

Second, and more ambitiously, MMR can explore ways of developing hybrid practices—*integrating* or *blending* qualitative and quantitative features—that augment the preexisting methods. This second strategy could then lead to methodological advances, not just the mechanical combining of preexisting procedures. These two strategies are discussed in the remainder of this chapter.

Continuing to Bridge Qualitative and Quantitative Research

MMR has become a rich platform, with its own books, journals, and conferences bringing an impressive energy to the scene (Denzin, 2012). The platform supports studies that bridge qualitative and quantitative research, showing how they can be arranged within the same study. As a result, MMR studies are able to examine topics that can produce more comprehensive findings than either qualitative or quantitative research might do alone. Moreover, the MMR platform compares favorably with those in other fields, such as in history, where no such platform has yet emerged, and where historical studies combining both conventional and postmodernist paradigms are infrequent.

As part of the continued bridging, future MMR contributions could help to reduce the nagging dialogue over whether the qualitative or quantitative component tends to be more ascendant in MMR studies. An early perception was that MMR studies favored a hierarchical arrangement, with the "large-*n*" quantitative component "at the top" and the "small-*n*" qualitative component "relegated to a largely auxiliary role" (Denzin & Lincoln, 2005, p. 9). An alternative approach can reverse this hierarchy by invoking interpretivism, inclusion, and dialogue through stakeholder participation in the MMR study itself (Howe, 2004). However, regardless of which component is positioned to be ascendant, and even if the qualitative and quantitative components are thought to be part of the same continuum, an implicit hierarchical arrangement might appear to be unavoidable.

To relieve this situation, more empirical evidence would not hurt, and MMR's future contributions could solicit new data on this (and other) issue(s). The data could come from interviews of the lead authors of contemporary MMR studies, especially how the latest generation of MMR lead researchers accomplishes the mixing in their studies—as well as how the researchers think about the mixing, about the ascendancy problem, or about the salience of paradigms as opposed to practices—all would be worth knowing and could provide beneficial insights.

Along the same lines, such interviews might help to codify the researchers' skill sets—for example, whether more of them have both the qualitative and quantitative experiences as recommended by Creswell and Plano Clark (2007, p. 180), or whether MMR studies are more frequently being done by teams of co-leaders with contrasting perspectives and for whom "one person's anxieties are another's chance for self-fulfillment" (Weisner, 2005, p. 16). How MMR studies are conducted under these teaming conditions might then also provide more insights into the bridging process.

Integrating: Going Beyond Bridging

At the same time, a bridging strategy tends to favor arrangements that only juxtapose, in a side-by-side manner, preexisting qualitative and quantitative procedures—arrangements that have been called *additive* but not *conjoint* (Bazeley & Kemp, 2012). For instance, as previously noted, the common MMR designs cover sequential, nested, or parallel relationships between the quantitative and qualitative methods. Similarly, MMR data collection can involve complementary but still separate quantitative and qualitative methods. Yet, in neither the design nor the data collection example does any actual integration or blending take place between the methods.

As an opportunistic alternative strategy, a more ambitious aim for MMR's future contributions might be not only to search for other ways of bridging what already preexists but to encourage new inquiries into still-evolving practices and procedures. Over time, the contributions might lead to a truly integrated craft (Bazeley, 2012; Johnson et al., 2007, p. 125; Yin, 2006) that also brings new meanings to causality and generalizability. In this way, MMR would go beyond struggling with the visions of how to combine qualitative and quantitative methods—such as whether to embrace their differences and not impose a heterogeneous perspective (Herrits, 2011), or whether the use of both methods within the same study only can "serve as opportunities for respectful listening and understanding" (Greene, 2008, p. 20).

The payoff here is that the integrated craft might become distinctive—that is, more than just a bridging of two preexisting crafts. In this spirit, MMR's most relevant future contributions might cover such still-evolving methodological practices as (a) triangulation, (b) the use of plausible rival explanations, (c) mixed methods analyses, and (d) some form of distinctive generalizing from mixed method studies.

None of the topics would simply mimic the preexisting qualitative or quantitative procedures but would seek to develop hybrid practices distinctive to MMR. The distinctive practices might then be addressed in every subsequent MMR study, discussing their use (or absence) in the particular study, much as "sampling" appears as a topic in all quantitative studies. Together, the MMR practices would augment the continued use of the preexisting qualitative or quantitative methods, ultimately marking MMR as a truly special craft.

TRIANGULATION

As an example, take the challenge of triangulation. Over the years it has been repeatedly addressed as a principle (e.g., Denzin, 1978, 2012; Denzin & Lincoln, 2011; Greene et al., 1989; Jick, 1979; Patton, 2002, p. 247): The aim is to use triangulation as a way of combining multiple methods to study the same phenomenon (Denzin & Lincoln, 2011, p. 2).

Nevertheless, carrying out triangulation as an operational practice has not been spelled out in any systematic terms. No benchmarks exist to define when the triangulation in a given study might be considered "strong" or "weak" or "complete" or "incomplete," much less whether the triangulation has been done to enhance the validity of a study's findings or simply to make them more comprehensive. Moreover, the challenge might be more difficult than has been acknowledged to date, because proper triangulation may very well involve an intricate number of steps that need to be represented as formal designs. The designs would be central to a rigorous process of triangulating. Yet neither the qualitative nor the quantitative camp appears to be trying hard to clarify (or placing any priority on) any of these issues about triangulation. Thus triangulation could become one of MMR's own key practices.

PLAUSIBLE RIVAL EXPLANATIONS

As another example, the use of plausible rival explanations already has received some recognition in the ongoing conversations, with possibly more attention in history than outside of it. However, beyond being addressed as a principle, neither qualitative nor quantitative methods have given attention to any procedures involving plausible rival explanations, such as the benchmarks for deciding how and whether a rival is to be "rejected," "accepted," or "still equivocal," or even how to distinguish a strong, plausible rival from a mere red herring. As with triangulation, the procedures for examining and testing plausible rivals—especially substantive, not craft rivals or artifacts (Yin, 2000)—also might involve an intricate number of steps represented as formal designs.

Moreover, to date, the practice has largely been limited to its application in making causal inferences (e.g., Maxwell, 2004, pp. 257–260; Yin, 2000, 2012). Yet, the broader potential of this practice, possibly cast in terms of *rival thinking* rather than rival explanations, might be extended to every aspect of an MMR study. These aspects could include the data collection phase as well as a study's interpretative phase, where Maxwell (2004, p. 260) points to member checks—which might be taken as a multivocal opportunity that permits stakeholders to offer rival ideas. The procedures underlying various forms of rival thinking also have not been covered well by either the qualitative or the quantitative camps. Thus contributions covering how to undertake rival thinking could again become one of MMR's own distinctive practices.

MIXED METHODS ANALYSES

Carrying out mixed methods analyses serves as yet a third opportunity for defining practices pertinent to MMR studies. Whether MMR analyses might continue to be limited, as they now are, to a combination of commonly used qualitative or quantitative procedures (e.g., Caracelli & Greene, 1993)—or whether MMR might involve some integrated type of analyses—deserves to be another topic of new contributions. For example, Tashakkori and Teddlie (1998) identified *social network analysis* as an example of "an inherently mixed data analysis," where the same analysis relies on both qualitative and quantitative data (p. 272). This type of integrated analysis also might include other social applications or strategies when working visually with data (e.g., Bazeley, 2012, pp. 823–824). Along the same vein, discussed earlier was how QCA has both qualitative and quantitative features (e.g., Byrne, 2009, p. 4), thereby demonstrating a type of analysis that may have broad applicability to many different kinds of MMR studies. New MMR contributions might build on or modify the current QCA procedures, as well as the other alternatives such as social network analysis. The goal again would be to have the contributions lead to the identification of MMR's own key practices.

GENERALIZABILITY

As a final example, there is the issue of how to generalize from an MMR study. New MMR contributions might start afresh in this endeavor or try to build on and modify some variant of *analytic generalization*. The procedures for conducting analytic generalization, for instance, remain underspecified and are not readily found among either qualitative or quantitative methods. New contributions to formalizing analytic generalization as a procedure would help MMR to avoid its sole current reliance on the derivatives of qualitative and quantitative research—that is, case-to-case transfers and statistical generalizations. In other words, whether generalizing from an MMR study simply means using some mechanical arrangement between these two derivatives—or whether MMR also might augment these with its own integrated type of generalizing—deserves further inquiry.

MIXED METHODS RESEARCH AS AN INTEGRATING, NOT JUST BRIDGING CRAFT

In essence, MMR's long-term identity might be based on becoming a unique craft with a set of integrating practices, like the four just discussed. With adequate development, the integrating practices could become part of MMR's signature method and even transcend the qualitative and quantitative crafts being bridged. MMR could then achieve a new synthesis, moving away from a status limited to the acceptance of a "multiplism" of methods (e.g., Bazeley, 2012, p. 815; Greene, 2007, p. 24)—to a new status that includes but does not rely on the preexisting crafts.

Although some readers might not agree with or even appreciate the analogy, if MMR becomes an integrating craft, the accomplishment may be similar to the way that quasi-experimental research now has its own designs and methods and has distanced itself from either of its roots—laboratory-based experiments and fieldwork in natural settings. Because the unique blend has by now been so well documented, researchers conduct quasi-experimental research without referring directly to the root experimental or fieldwork designs or procedures, even though they may still be used in any given quasi-experimental study. The studies simply rely on "quasi-experimental" methods. By contributing to the ongoing conversations on causality and generalizability, MMR might eventually achieve an analogous status.

SUMMARY

The final section of this chapter has proposed that future MMR contributions to conversations on causality and generalizability can have a potentially significant impact on the advancement of MMR itself. First, the contributions can strengthen the ways that MMR studies can continue to serve as a rich platform, bridging qualitative and quantitative methods. Second, and more challenging but with greater ultimate payoffs, the contributions can enrich new meanings of causality and generalizability by attending to known but still underdeveloped methodological practices, currently not well covered by either qualitative or quantitative research, though germane to both. By pursuing the more challenging alternative, MMR stands to become its own distinct craft while still embracing preexisting qualitative and quantitative methods.

Acknowledgments

I would like to thank Pat Bazeley, Burke Johnson, and Sharlene Hesse-Biber for their extremely insightful and helpful comments on an earlier draft of this chapter.

Discussion Questions

1. How does causation and generalizability differ between the constructivist and postpositivist paradigms?

2. Discuss some of the different ways that an MMR study could mix data on a continuum from simple to more complex. Make sure you discuss how the mixing occurs and at what level (i.e. data level, design, or analysis phase)

3. The ways that constructivists and postpositivists deal with causality are quite different. Compare and contrast some of the other ways that people look at causality, such as correlational, input-output analyses; causal processes; and agential causation.

4. Compare and contrast statistical generalization and analytic generalization. Think of some of the ways that both could be used in MMR studies.

5. If you were planning to conduct a study using MMR, think of some ways you could use plausible rival explanations.

Suggested Websites

http://onlinelibrary.wiley.com/doi/10.1002/ev.v1997:76/ issuetoc

Special issue on theory, practice, and methods in *New Directions in Program Evaluation*.

http://onlinelibrary.wiley.com/doi/10.1002/ev.v2012.135/ issuetoc

Special issue on context in evaluation practice in *New Directions in Program Evaluation*:

References

Allison, G. T. (1971). *Essence of decision: Explaining the Cuban missile crisis*. Boston, MA: Little, Brown.

Anderson, G. L., & Scott, J. (2012). Toward an intersectional understanding of process causality and social context. *Qualitative Inquiry, 18,* 674–685.

Bazeley, P. (2012). Integrative analysis strategies for mixed data sources. *American Behavioral Scientist, 56,* 814–828.

Bazeley, P., & Kemp, L. (2012). Mosaics, triangles, and DNA: Metaphors for integrated analysis in mixed methods research. *Journal of Mixed Methods Research, 6,* 55–72.

Befani, B. (2013). Between complexity and generalization: Addressing evaluation challenges with QCA. *Evaluation, 19,* 269–283.

Bennett, A. (2004). Testing theories and explaining cases. In C. C. Ragin, J. Nagel, & P. White (Eds.), *Workshop on scientific foundations of qualitative research* (pp. 49–51). Arlington, VA: National Science Foundation.

Bennett, A. (2010). Process tracing and causal inference. In H. Brady & D. Collier (Eds.), *Rethinking social inquiry: Diverse tools, shared standards* (2nd ed., pp. 207–219). Lanham, MD: Rowman & Littlefield.

Bennett, A., & Elman, C. (2006a). Complex causal relations and case study methods: The example of path dependence. *Political Analysis, 14,* 250–267.

Bennett, A., & Elman, C. (2006b). Qualitative research: Recent developments in case study methods. *Annual Review of Political Science, 9,* 455–476.

Bloch, M. (1953). *The historian's craft*. New York, NY: Vintage Books. (Original work published 1941)

Bromley, D. B. (1986). *The case method in psychology and related disciplines*. Chichester, UK: Wiley.

Bryman, A. (2006). Integrating quantitative and qualitative research: How is it done? *Qualitative Research, 6,* 97–113.

Burawoy, M. (1991). The extended case method. In M. Burawoy, A. Burton, A. A. Ferguson, K. J. Fox, J. Gamson, L. Hurst, . . . S. Ui, *Ethnography unbound: Power and resistance in the modern metropolis* (pp. 271–287). Berkeley: University of California Press.

Byrne, D. (2009). Case-based methods: Why we need them; what they are; how to do them. In D. Byrne & C. C. Ragin (Eds.), *The SAGE handbook of case-based methods* (pp. 1–10). London, England: Sage.

Campbell, D. T., & Stanley, J. C. (1963). *Experimental and quasi-experimental designs for research*. Chicago, IL: Rand McNally.

Caracelli, V. J., & Greene, J. C. (1993). Data analysis strategies for mixed-method evaluation designs. *Educational Evaluation and Policy Analysis, 15,* 195–207.

Carr, E. H. (1961). *What is history?* New York, NY: Vintage Books.

Collins, K. M. T., Onwuegbuzie, A. J., & Jiao, Q. G. (2007). A mixed methods investigation of mixed methods sampling designs in social and health science research. *Journal of Mixed Methods Research, 1,* 267–294.

Creswell, J. W. (1999). Mixed method research: Introduction and application. In T. Cijek (Ed.), *Handbook of educational policy* (pp. 455–472). San Diego, CA: Academic Press.

Creswell, J. W. (2009). Mapping the field of mixed methods research. *Journal of Mixed Methods Research, 3,* 95–108.

Creswell, J. W., & Plano Clark, V. L. (2007). *Designing and conducting mixed methods research*. Thousand Oaks, CA: Sage.

Creswell, J. W., Plano Clark, V. L., Gutmann, M. L., & Hanson, W. E. (2003). Advanced mixed methods research designs. In A. Tashakkori & C. Teddlie (Eds.), *Handbook of mixed methods in social & behavioral research* (pp. 209–240). Thousand Oaks, CA: Sage.

Dellinger, A. B., & Leech, N. L. (2007). Toward a unified validation framework in mixed methods research. *Journal of Mixed Methods Research, 1,* 309–332.

Denzin, N. K. (1978). *The research act: A theoretical introduction to sociological methods* (2nd ed.). New York, NY: McGraw-Hill.

Denzin, N. K. (2012). Triangulation 2.0. *Journal of Mixed Methods Research, 6,* 80–88.

Denzin, N. K., & Lincoln, Y. S. (2005). Introduction: The discipline and practice of qualitative research. In N. K. Denzin & Y. S. Lincoln (Eds.), *The SAGE handbook of qualitative research* (3rd ed., pp. 1–32). Thousand Oaks, CA: Sage.

Denzin, N. K., & Lincoln, Y. S. (2011). The discipline and practice of qualitative research. In N. K. Denzin & Y. S. Lincoln (Eds.), *SAGE handbook of qualitative research* (4th ed., pp. 1–19). Thousand Oaks, CA: Sage.

Donmoyer, R. (1990). Generalizability and the single-case study. In E. W. Eisner & A. Peshkin (Eds.), *Qualitative inquiry in education: The continuing debate* (pp. 175–200). New York, NY: Teachers College Press.

Donmoyer, R. (2012a). Attributing causality in qualitative research: Viable option or inappropriate aspiration? *Qualitative Inquiry, 18,* 651–654.

Donmoyer, R. (2012b). Can qualitative researchers answer policymakers' what-works question? *Qualitative Inquiry, 18,* 662–673.

Erickson, F. (2012). Comments on causality in qualitative inquiry. *Qualitative Inquiry, 18,* 686–688.

Ertman, T. (1997). *Birth of the Leviathan: Building states and regimes in medieval and early modern Europe*. Cambridge, UK: Cambridge University Press.

Evans, R. J. (1999). *In defense of history*. New York, NY: W. W. Norton.

Fielding, N., & Warnes, R. (2009). Computer-based qualitative methods in case study research. In D. Byrne & C. C. Ragin (Eds.), *The SAGE handbook of case-based methods* (pp. 270–288). London, England: Sage.

Gaddis, J. L. (2002). *The landscape of history: How historians map the past*. New York, NY: Oxford University Press.

Geertz, C. (1973). *The interpretation of cultures*. New York, NY: Basic Books.

George, A. L., & Bennett, A. (2004). *Case studies and theory development in the social sciences*. Cambridge, MA: MIT Press.

Greene. J. C. (2007). *Mixed methods in social inquiry*. San Francisco, CA: Jossey-Bass.

Greene, J. C. (2008). Is mixed methods social inquiry a distinctive methodology? *Journal of Mixed Methods Research*, *2*, 7–22.

Greene, J. C., Caracelli, V. J., & Graham, W. F. (1989). Toward a conceptual framework for mixed-methods evaluation designs. *Educational Evaluation and Policy Analysis*, *11*, 255–274.

Guba, E. G., & Lincoln, Y. S. (1989). *Fourth generation evaluation*. Thousand Oaks, CA: Sage.

Guba, E. G., & Lincoln, Y. S. (1994). Competing paradigms in qualitative research. In N. K. Denzin & Y. S. Lincoln (Eds.), *Handbook of qualitative research* (pp. 105–117). Thousand Oaks, CA: Sage.

Guba, E. G., & Lincoln, Y. S. (2005). Paradigmatic controversies, contradictions, and emerging confluences. In N. K. Denzin & Y. S. Lincoln (Eds.), *The SAGE handbook of qualitative research* (3rd ed., pp. 191–215). Thousand Oaks, CA: Sage.

Halkier, B. (2011). Methodological practicalities in analytical generalization. *Qualitative Inquiry*, *17*, 787–797.

Harrits, G. S. (2011). More than method? A discussion of paradigm differences within mixed methods research. *Journal of Mixed Methods Research*, *5*, 150–166.

Hesse-Biber, S. N. (2010a). *Mixed methods research: Merging theory with practice*. New York, NY: Guilford Press.

Hesse-Biber, S. N. (2010b). Weaving a multimethodology and mixed methods praxis into randomized control trials to enhance credibility. *Qualitative Inquiry*, *18*, 876–889.

Howe, K. R. (1988). Against the quantitative-qualitative incompatibility thesis or dogmas die hard. *Educational Researcher*, *17*, 10–16.

Howe, K. R. (2004). A critique of experimentalism. *Qualitative Inquiry*, *10*, 42–61.

Howe, K. R. (2011). Mixed methods, mixed causes? *Qualitative Inquiry*, *17*, 166–171.

Howe, K. R. (2012). Mixed methods, triangulation, and causal explanation. *Journal of Mixed Methods Research*, *6*, 89–96.

Howell, E. M., & Yemane (2006). An assessment of evaluation designs: Case studies of 12 large federal evaluations. *American Journal of Evaluation*, *27*, 219–236.

Howell, M., & Prevenier, W. (2001). *From reliable sources: An introduction to historical methods*. Ithaca, NY: Cornell University Press.

Iggers, G. G. (1997). *Historiography in the twentieth century: From scientific objectivity to the postmodern challenge*. Middletown, CT: Wesleyan University Press.

Jick, T. D. (1979). Mixing qualitative and quantitative methods: Triangulation in action. *Administrative Science Quarterly*, *24*, 602–611.

Johnson, R. B. (2009). Toward a more inclusive "scientific research in education." *Educational Researcher*, *38*, 449–457.

Johnson, R. B., & Onwuegbuzie, A. J. (2004). Mixed methods research: A research paradigm whose time has come. *Educational Researcher*, *33*, 14–26.

Johnson, R. B., Onwuegbuzie, A. J., & Turner, L. A. (2007). Toward a definition of mixed methods research. *Journal of Mixed Methods Research*, *1*, 112–133.

Lincoln, Y. S., & Guba, E. G. (1985). *Naturalistic inquiry*. Thousand Oaks, CA: Sage.

Lipset, S. M., Trow, M., & Coleman, J. (1956). *Union democracy: The inside politics of the International Typographical Union*. New York, NY: Free Press.

Luker, K. (2008). *Salsa dancing in the social sciences: Research in an age of info-glut*. Cambridge, MA: Harvard University Press.

Mahoney, J. (2004). The distinctive contributions of qualitative data analysis. In C. C. Ragin, J. Nagel & P. White (Eds.), *Workshop on scientific foundations of qualitative research* (pp. 95–99). Arlington, VA: National Science Foundation.

Maxwell, J. A. (2004). Using qualitative methods for causal explanation. *Field Methods*, *16*, 243–264.

Maxwell, J. A. (2010). Using numbers in qualitative research. *Qualitative Inquiry*, *16*, 475–482.

Maxwell, J. A. (2012). The importance of qualitative research for causal explanation in education. *Qualitative Inquiry*, *18*, 655–661.

Maxwell, J. A., & Loomis, D. M. (2003). Mixed methods design: An alternative approach. In A. Tashakkori & C. Teddlie (Eds.), *Handbook of mixed methods in social & behavioral research* (pp. 209–240). Thousand Oaks, CA: Sage.

Miles, M., & Huberman, M. (1994). *Qualitative data analysis: A sourcebook for new methods*. Thousand Oaks, CA: Sage.

Mitchell, J. C. (1983). Case and situation analysis. *Sociological Review*, *31*, 187–211.

Mookherji, S., & LaFond, A. (2013). Strategies to maximize generalization from multiple case studies: Lessons from the Africa routine immunization system essentials (ARISE) project. *Evaluation*, *19*, 284–303.

Morgan, D. L. (2007). Paradigms lost and pragmatism regained: Methodological implications of combining qualitative and quantitative methods. *Journal of Mixed Methods Research*, *1*, 48–76.

O'Cathain, A. (2009). Mixed methods research in the health sciences: A quiet revolution. *Journal of Mixed Methods Research*, *3*, 3–6.

Onwuegbuzie, A. J., Johnson, R. B., & Collins, K. M. T. (2011). Assessing legitimation in mixed research: A new framework. *Qualitative-Quantitative*, *45*(6), 1253–1271.

Paluck, E. L. (2010). The promising integration of qualitative methods and field experiments. *The Annals of the American Academy of Political and Social Science*, *628*, 59–71.

Patton, M. Q. (2002). *Qualitative research and evaluation methods* (3rd ed.). Thousand Oaks, CA: Sage.

Phillips, D. C., & Burbules, N. C. (2000). *Postpositivism and educational research*. Lanham, MD: Rowman & Littlefield.

Ragin, C. C. (1987). *The comparative method: Moving beyond qualitative and quantitative strategies*. Berkeley: University of California Press.

Ragin, C. C. (2000). *Fuzzy set social science*. Chicago, IL: University of Chicago Press.

Ragin, C. C. (2004). Combining qualitative and quantitative research. In C. C. Ragin, J. Nagel & P. White (Eds.), *Workshop on scientific foundations of qualitative research* (pp. 109–115). Arlington, VA: National Science Foundation.

Ragin, C. C. (2009). Reflections on casing and case-oriented research. In D. Byrne & C. Ragin. (Eds.), *The SAGE handbook of case-based methods* (pp. 522–534). London, England: Sage.

Reichardt, C. S., & Cook, T. D. (1979). Beyond qualitative versus quantitative methods. In T. D. Cook & C. S. Reichardt (Eds.), *Qualitative and quantitative methods in evaluation research* (pp. 7–32). Beverly Hills, CA: Sage.

Reichardt, C. S., & Rallis, S. F. (1994). Qualitative and quantitative inquiries are not incompatible: A call for a new partnership. In C. S. Reichardt & S. F. Rallis (Eds.), *The qualitative-quantitative debate: New perspectives* (pp. 85–92). San Francisco, CA: Jossey-Bass.

Rihoux, B., & Lobe, B. (2009). The case for qualitative comparative analysis (QCA): Adding leverage for thick cross-case comparison. In D. Byrne & C. C. Ragin (Eds.), *The SAGE handbook of case-based methods* (pp. 222–242). London, England: Sage.

Roberts, M. (2004). Postmodernism and the linguistic turn. In P. Lambert & P. Schofield (Eds.), *Making history: An introduction to the history and practices of a discipline* (pp. 227–240). London, England: Routledge.

Rosenbaum, P. R. (2002). *Observational studies*. New York, NY: Springer.

Rueschemeyer, D. (2003). Can one or a few cases yield theoretical gains? In J. Mahoney & D. Rueschemeyer (Eds.), *Comparative historical analysis in the social sciences* (pp. 305–336). Cambridge, UK: Cambridge University Press.

Sale, J. E. M., Lohfeld, L. H., & Brazil, K. (2002). Revisiting the quantitative-qualitative debate: Implications for mixed-methods research. *Quality & Quantity, 36*, 43–53.

Sandelowski, M., Voils, C. L., & Knaft, G. (2009). On quantitizing. *Journal of Mixed Methods Research, 3*, 208–222.

Sieber, S. D. (1973). The integration of field work and survey methods. *American Journal of Sociology, 78*, 1335–1359.

Small, M. L. (2009). How many cases do I need? On science and the logic of case selection in field-based research. *Ethnography, 10*, 5–38.

Small, M. L. (2011). How to conduct a mixed methods study: Recent trends in a rapidly growing literature. *Annual Review of Sociology, 37*, 57–86.

Steckler, A., McLeroy, K. R., Goodman, R. M., Bird, S. T., & McCormick, L. (1992). Toward integrating qualitative and quantitative methods: An introduction. *Health Education Quarterly, 19*, 1–8.

Tashakkori, A., & Creswell, J. W. (2008). Mixed methodology across disciplines. *Journal of Mixed Methods Research, 2*, 3–6.

Tashakkori, A., & Teddlie, C. (1998). *Mixed methodology: Combining qualitative and quantitative approaches*. Thousand Oaks, CA: Sage.

Teddlie, C., & Tashakkori, A. (2009). *Foundations of mixed methods research: Integrating quantitative and qualitative approaches in the social and behavioral sciences*. Thousand Oaks, CA: Sage.

Tashakkori, A., & Teddlie, C. (2010). Putting the human back in "human research methodology": The researcher in mixed methods research. *Journal of Mixed Methods Research, 4*, 271–277.

Teddlie, C., & Yu, F. (2007). Mixed methods sampling: A typology with examples. *Journal of Mixed Methods Research, 1*, 77–100.

Trend, M. G. (1979). On the reconciliation of qualitative and quantitative analyses: A case study. In T. D. Cook & C. S. Reichardt (Eds.), *Qualitative and quantitative methods in evaluation research* (pp. 68–86). Thousand Oaks, CA: Sage.

Weisner, T. S. (2005). Introduction. In T. S. Weisner (Ed.), *Discovering successful pathways in children's development: Mixed methods in the study of childhood family and life* (pp. 1–18). Chicago, IL: University of Chicago Press.

Whyte, W. F. (1943). *Street corner society: The social structure of an Italian slum*. Chicago, IL: University of Chicago Press.

Wickham-Crowley, T. (1992). *Guerillas and revolutions in Latin America: A comparative study of insurgents and regimes since 1956*. Princeton, NJ: Princeton University Press.

Yin, R. K. (1994). Evaluation: A singular craft. In C. Reichardt & S. Rallis (Eds.), *New directions in program evaluation* (pp. 71–84). San Francisco, CA: Jossey-Bass.

Yin, R. K. (2000). Rival explanations as an alternative to "reforms as experiments." In L. Bickman (Ed.), *Validity & social experimentation: Donald Campbell's legacy* (pp. 239–266). Thousand Oaks, CA: Sage.

Yin, R. K. (2006). Mixed methods research: Are the methods genuinely integrated or merely parallel? *Research in the Schools, 13*, 41–47.

Yin, R. K. (2012). Case study methods. In H. Cooper (Ed.), *APA handbook of research methods in psychology* (Vol. 2, Chap. 9). Washington, DC: American Psychological Association.

Yin, R. K. (2013). Validity and generalization in future case study evaluations. *Evaluation, 19*, 321–332.

Yin, R. K. (2014). *Case study research: Design and method* (5th ed.). Thousand Oaks, CA: Sage.

Yin, R. K., & Ridde, V. (2012). Théorie et pratiques des études de cas en évaluation de programmes. In V. Ridde & C. Dagenais (Eds.), *Approches et practiques en évaluation de programmes* (2nd ed., Chap. 10). Montreal, QC: University of Montreal Press.

Mixed Methods: Dissonance and Values in Research With Marginalized Groups

Dawn Freshwater *and* Pamela Fisher

Abstract

This chapter critically addresses the preoccupation with the integration of data and findings in much mixed methods research (MMR). It argues that traditional modernist strivings must be considered in the specific context of knowledge production in the 21st century and that a preoccupation with integration in MMR may undermine social justice–related aspirations by erasing marginalized perspectives. This is identified as a particular feature of MMR research undertaken in the areas of medicine and the health sciences. The value of research conducted in the transformative-emancipatory paradigm is considered alongside the contribution of postmodern literature. The chapter concludes with a summary of how social justice–related MMR can contribute to new ideas.

Key Words: social justice, marginalized perspectives, transformative-emancipatory paradigm, mixed methods research, postmodern literature

Mixed Methods Research and the Promotion of Social Justice

Highly valued by funding organizations, mixed methods research (MMR) has been taken up and developed by many influential researchers; indeed MMR has become a field of study in its own right. The specific value of applying mixed methods is that researchers have access to a broader range of tools for the development of a more in-depth and extended understanding of the diversity of the social worlds (Somekh & Lewin, 2005). These benefits are often rationalized with recourse to the pragmatic paradigm, a standpoint from which mixed method studies appear to mark the welcome demise of the "paradigm wars" (Tashakkori & Teddlie, 2003; Bryman, 2006; Morgan, 2007). The underlying rationale suggests that researchers are free to select their methods (either quantitative or qualitative), thereby extending the range of approaches that can be used to address their specific research questions. Sometimes termed *complementarity*, the argument goes that the shortcomings of one method may be offset by the application of

other methods. However, for some researchers, MMR is not, in the first instance, about drawing on multiple methods but instead embraces a plurality of philosophical and theoretical paradigms. This, it is argued, facilitates fruitful dialogue that ultimately leads to the generation of a deeper and enhanced understanding of the social world. For Greene (2007), for example, the aim should be not primarily to seek commensurability of paradigms but to access "a better understanding of social phenomena" (p. 15). Greene (2008) writes of "a dynamic interplay" of methods and of paradigms, arguing that

> Better understanding of the multifaceted and complex character of social phenomena can be obtained from the use of multiple approaches and ways . . . knowing. . . of thinking [that] also generates questions, alongside possible answers; . . . both smooth and jagged, full of relative certainties alongside possibilities. (p. 20)

With her focus on "surprises" and "jagged results," Greene (2008) clearly associates mixed methods studies with opportunities for adding layers of richness to data without privileging convergence, consonance, or consensus. This is not an endorsement of relativism; instead Greene (2007, 2008) argues that the crisis and complexity of problems require an engagement with knowledge, insights, and artistry, which cannot be accessed via one discipline alone. Her position is equally a rejection of postpositivism, a paradigm that identifies objectivity and neutrality as values associated with science, while maintaining that all other values should be separated out from science. Similarly, Greene's conviction in the value of diversity and dissonance appears to be at variance with the emphasis that much MMR places on the value of integration. Integration in this context refers to a desire for commensurable findings and data. Bazeley (2006), for example, has discussed techniques for the integration of quantitative and qualitative data using data analysis software; Teddlie and Tashakkori (2006) have considered the processes involved in making meta-inferences; and Onwuegbuzie and Johnson (2006) have discussed integration from various perspectives. As Johnson, Onwuegbuzie, and Turner (2007) put it, "The key idea that mixed methods research requires some form of integration is clear" (p. 125).

What is perhaps less clear is the extent to which integration can be reconciled with an appreciation of marginalized perspectives. In using the term *marginalized perspectives*, we refer to all discordant voices that challenge "the common sense"; however, our shared interest in social justice means that we have a particular concern regarding the silencing of socially disadvantaged groups (often those that are labelled "vulnerable"), for instance those who are marginalized for reasons of social class, ethnicity, disability, health, and so forth. Members of these groups wield significantly less deliberative power in public debates than others. Whenever people's voices are muted, they are made vulnerable in a world that is likely to deny their human rights and dignity (Arendt, 2004, in Fisher, 2012). The reasons why the integration of findings and paradigms in some MMR may contribute to marginalization are discussed in this chapter. We consider the value of MMR conducted within the transformative-emancipatory paradigm and the emancipatory potential offered by postmodern critiques of pragmatism. The ideological and political barriers to emancipatory MMR are found to be particularly intractable in medicine and the health sciences.

First we turn to a discussion outlining the context for knowledge production in the 21st century, which at least partially explains why preoccupations with the integration of findings continue to occupy a central place in much MMR.

Why Integration?
The Rise of Mode 2 Knowledge Production

Any consideration of how MMR may contribute to social justice needs to take account of the reconfiguration of knowledge production that has taken place over recent decades (Gibbons et al., 1994; Nowotny, Scott, & Gibbons, 2001). In short, the academy has witnessed a retreat of independent scholarship in the face of growing demands for the production of knowledge suited to market-driven economies. Neoliberal forms of governance have led to the decline of the collegial system based on academic and intellectual authority toward management hierarchies. University leaders are no longer necessarily expected to deliberate on the intrinsic quality of research, but instead they are charged with applying systems of regulatory audit, which is reflected in the UK government's emphasis on "impact" measures (Holmwood, 2010). This constitutes a move from an era of *Mode 1 knowledge production* (knowledge that is disciplined based and instigated by the researcher) to one of *Mode 2 knowledge production* (problem based and interdisciplinary). We acknowledge that this definition constitutes a brief and somewhat unnuanced description; indeed, it has been contended that distinguishing between Mode 1 and Mode 2 production constitutes a false dichotomy and that knowledge production in the UK, for instance, has historically been (and remains) reliant on a hidden world of patronage (Bresnan & Burrell, 2013). Equally, the fact that academic disciplines no longer enjoy the privilege of defining what is counted as relevant knowledge can be regarded as a gain in democratic participation, although with the caveat that the scientific "agora" is highly structured by certain institutions (Nowotny et al., 2001). Beyond this, however, what strikes us as being of concern in relation to social justice is that Mode 2 knowledge prioritizes the solving of problems that may be predefined according to dominant understandings. Put differently, there can be an uncritical "taken-for-grantedness" about what the problems are and a concomitant failure to take into account the relations of power that act to define (and therefore to *construct*) the issues to be addressed. As a result, the focus may be deflected away from critical evaluation of how problems come to be identified (and by whom). To provide an example, if the starting point of a project is that a child with a disability is an unfortunate individual with a medical problem, the risk is that broader issues of human flourishing and social justice are missed (see Fisher, 2008). Our point is that in the interests of social justice, all assumptions should be constantly subject to critical evaluation. Drawing on the work of the moral philosopher Charles Taylor (see Fisher & Freshwater, 2014), we see critical evaluation as a process that requires an openness to alterity and the critical scrutiny of all assumptions, including one's own. Our point is that Mode 2 knowledge production, with its emphasis on pragmatic problem-solving, may encourage a form of pragmatism based on a tacit acceptance of the "common sense." In some sociological literature, Mode 2 knowledge has been associated with the shift toward interdisciplinarity (Cooper, 2013; Holmwood, 2010) but not necessarily a form of interdisciplinarity that is critical, but one that sometimes be directed toward addressing predefined problems. Arguably, both MMR and interdisciplinarity spring from a preoccupation with problem-solving. As Hadorn, Pohl, and Bammer (2010) have argued, "Problem solving in the real world is an important driver for integrative and collaborative research" (p. 431). Jagged and discordant findings may hinder the search for clear solutions.

The assumption is often made that mixed methods are preferable on the basis that they represent a more open, plural, and democratic approach to knowledge production, in either implicit or explicit contradiction to the supposed dogmatism and narrowness associated with studies applying single methods based on a single worldview. This largely optimistic support for MMR contrasts with the observations of some researchers on the intrinsically political nature of Mode 2 knowledge, namely that is most enthusiastically espoused by those who have the most to gain form it (Nowotny et al., 2001). For example, current government policy around science and innovation in the UK links funding and capital resources directly with significance of outcomes and impact on society. The Research Excellence Framework in the UK and the Excellence in Research Activity in Australia are both examples of how specific governments incentivize and integrate the quality and focus of research with direct public benefit and indirectly *votes*. In this context, interdisciplinary knowledge and MMR can be seen as a means of both collecting the evidence of the impact of research and justifying its outcomes as serving the public good. The story that is told, and which resonates with the electorate, is that research conducted in universities is strictly orientated toward the public good. Thus the proponents of mixed methods include, we argue, politicians and civil servants, who are obliged to develop mechanisms for linking knowledge with innovation, and researchers in professional disciplines, such as management, who are seeking to improve the status vis-à-vis of their field-established "academic" disciplines'. Similarly as arts, humanities, and social sciences lose status, funds and capital resources are "ring-fenced" to support the advancement of "strategically important subjects," such as biological sciences, physics, and chemistry (BIS, 2013). Consequently, knowledge production in the early 21st century can be seen as involving a quest for knowledge products that have market value and that bestow funding, prestige, and power (Cooper, 2013). In other words, the knowledge that is produced by MMR and through MMR is now more widely legitimated by a broader range of disciplines and as such has gained more credibility with the public, who are critical of public spending on research, and consumers, who are keen to feel the benefit and impact of the outcomes of publicly funded interests. This means that MMR has a utilitarian value, which is open to exploitation in the market.

As discussed, the context of knowledge production in the 21st century offers its own challenges that support the desirability of producing findings that are integrated that is findings that triangulate to reinforce a particular perspective rather than point to areas of dissonance. Nevertheless, this tendency toward integration can be viewed at a more profound level as a *by-product of modernist thinking*, which is manifest in the belief that there is always one preferred way of achieving an objective. This is not surprising when research is constructed as furthering positive social change; integrated findings after all encourage unified action in the interests of a common cause.

Rise of a Pragmatic Approach to Mixed Methods Research

For this reason, the end of the paradigm wars can be greeted as a pragmatic approach that assists the production of goal-orientated research. Johnson and Onwuegbuzie (2004) have expressly argued for the use of pragmatism in MMR, suggesting that it constitutes a middle ground in which workable solutions can be found. Pragmatism, as it is generally articulated in MMR, is based on the assumption that all methods and, indeed, differing research paradigms—whether realist, postpositivist, constructionist, or interpretative—have their respective virtues and limitations. What matters from a pragmatist viewpoint is that methods, quantitative and qualitative, and the paradigms in which they are located, should be selected judiciously in order to best answer the research questions (Morgan, 2007). From this perspective, answering the research questions is the priority, and philosophical debates are seen as less important than the adoption of a tolerant and practical approach orientated toward the production of knowledge. Philosophical arguments should yield to practicality. While such a stance is to be welcomed in relation to the production of Mode 2 knowledge, this ostensibly neutral stance toward differing philosophical traditions is problematic. To adopt "a fairness to all approach," which encourages the integration of findings, is to ignore the lack of parity that differs between research methods and paradigms. While this may rarely constitute an issue in the social sciences in the UK, it is nevertheless clear that quantitative methods embedded in the postpositivist paradigm are privileged over other approaches in the fields of medicine and healthcare. A further concern with pragmatism is that the drive for integrated findings, often one of its hallmarks, can result in a neglect of nuanced understandings and peripheral perspectives. As we all know, one voice does not and cannot represent the slightly different tones, dialect, inflections, and language use of all voices. In any unified approach to knowledge creation or representation, decisions have to be taken around what is left out and what is not viewed as central. The process by which these decisions are reached are very often driven by the research process, and indeed the loudest voices, as we have already noted, may be reinforced by political rhetoric. Seen this way, the pragmatic paradigm that so often underpins MMR, offering an ostensibly nonideological stance, can be viewed as nefariously shoring up the interests of the powerful. House and Howe (1999), for example, prompt us to ask that if a particular approach is viewed as being practical, for whom it is practical? Studies "may serve whatever ends clients or policy makers endorse" (p. 36). For this reason, the widespread adoption of pragmatism among mixed methods researchers has raised concerns that question-led pragmatic approaches may lead to a neglect of power inequalities (Creswell,

2010; Creswell & Plano Clark, 2007; Denzin & Lincoln, 2005). A key point is that when research is driven by predefined questions, which themselves are not the object of critical evaluation, the interest of subordinate groups will necessarily be neglected.

Thus already marginalized populations (and discourses), for example the mentally ill, the disabled, and the elderly, are less likely to be involved in the setting of research priorities and in identifying the foci of study and research questions. Mode 2 knowledge may be developed through the collaboration of academic, public, and private institutions, but these are institutions that are based on societal or dominant forms of reasoning (Bresnan & Burrell, 2013).

Transformative-Emancipatory Perspectives

Mode 1 knowledge production is, as mentioned earlier, associated with disciplinary knowledge rather than problem-solving. While this may arguably facilitate the *potential* for greater criticality, it is nevertheless important to note that Mode 1 knowledge production traditionally took place in hierarchical and stable institutions that regularly exercised exclusionary policies and practices toward women and minorities. For this reason, the interests of social justice would not necessarily be served by a return to the days before academic freedom and privileges were constrained. While there might have been more scope for criticality, the reality was that it was exercised selectively. Nevertheless, there may be something to be said in favor of salvaging some aspects of Mode 1 knowledge. Forty-nine years after Peter Higgs identified the Higgs boson particle (for which he won the 2013 Nobel Prize), he revealed in an interview with *The Guardian* (Higgs, 2013) that his idiosyncratic approach and lack of productivity (in terms of papers and grants) would mean that he would not be tolerated in academia nowadays. Work of outstanding originality cannot be easily combined with an impressive record of measurable research outputs. This point aside, while we generally endorse research conducted in the transformative-emancipatory perspective, we are not contending that researchers pursuing social justice aims should seek a return to the production of Mode 1 knowledge, although there may be instances when the freedom for criticality associated with it would be helpful. Our point is that what we perceive as being of particular value in the emancipatory perspective is that it involves an explicit recognition of power inequalities and an acknowledgment that values cannot be disaggregated from knowledge production. This means that criticality is aspired to *through collaboration with marginalized communities*. When we refer to the emancipatory-transformative paradigm, we include, alongside feminist studies, others in this category, for example, disability (Fisher, 2008), queer studies (Tucker, 2009), and other studies that aspire toward democratic collaboration with disadvantaged communities (MacLean, Warr, & Pyett, 2009). What all these have in common is that criticality is sought through democratic relationships of parity with the communities investigated.

In considering the transformative-emancipatory paradigm it is helpful to refer first to Guba and Lincoln's (2005) work, which provides a useful explication of how research paradigms function by identifying four fundamental belief systems that underpin them. These are (a) the axiological, which is related to ethics; (b) the ontological, which is concerned with beliefs about the nature of reality; (c) the epistemological, which concerns the relationships between the knower and what is known; and (d) the methodological, which focuses on how knowledge, viewed as valid or warrantable, may be discovered. In transformative-emancipatory studies, the axiological dimension is prioritized and beneficence is defined in terms of the promotion of human rights and the improvement of social justice. The transformative-emancipatory research distinguishes itself from the positivist/postpositivist paradigm, which is associated with the view that "the truth" can be accessed through scientific methods.

The transformative-emancipatory approaches share with constructivist perspectives the view that many meanings are socially derived and that some constructs are more privileged than others (Mertens, 2003). However, the specific focus within the transformative-emancipatory paradigm is on asymmetrical power relations and on revealing the perspectives of marginalized groups, for example those oppressed for reasons of gender, disability, ethnicity, or social class. Unlike some constructivist approaches, which may neglect politics in favor of cultural relativism, the transformative-emancipatory paradigm places the relationship between researchers and members of marginalized groups at the center; the political aims of the study are identified in collaboration. In this respect, the transformative-emancipatory approaches are derived largely from feminist theories, for example Sandra Harding, Dorothy Smith, and Patricia Hill Collins, in that they emphasize

the relational dimensions of research, locating these as inextricably linked to a political commitment to social justice. As Creswell (2003) puts it, transformative researchers "believe that inquiry needs to be intertwined with politics and a political agenda" and that they should incorporate an agenda for social change "that may change the lives of the participants, the institutions in which individuals work or live, and the researcher's life" (pp. 9–10). While *versions* of reality are regarded as constructed and *opinions* on truths as relative, this does not necessarily mean that "truths" themselves are viewed as relative (Mertens et al., 2010). Within the transformative-emancipatory paradigm, objectivity is possible, but through the direct involvement of the communities concerned.

Specific criteria for transformative-emancipatory research have been identified (Mertens, 2003; Sweetman, Badiee, & Creswell, 2010). Mertens, for example, has developed a framework that links the steps to be taken in the research process, starting with the formulation of questions through to the drawing of conclusions from the results. This involves directing the attention of researchers to whether the communities being investigated have participated in the development of the research questions, whether an emancipatory theoretical lens has been applied, the extent to which the literature review directly relates to issues of oppression and diversity, and whether the findings benefit the community concerned. Ideally the community should be involved in all aspects of the study, but the extent to which this happens in practice varies considerably (see Sweetman et al., 2010). Perhaps the crucially defining feature of transformative-emancipatory MMR should be the application of a theoretical lens. In direct contradistinction to the "apolitical" stance of pragmatism, there is a growing body of MMR that applies critical standpoint theories relating to gender, ethnicity, and the social model of disability (see, e.g. Buck, Cook, Quigley, Eastwood, & Luca, 2009; Hesse-Biber, 2012; Mertens, Farley, Madison, & Singleton, 1994).

Within this critical tradition of MMR, researchers are more likely to embrace dissonant findings that, instead of being viewed as obstacles to be overcome, are seen as opening up new conceptual vistas. Hesse-Biber (2012), for example, discusses studies in which methodological innovation entails reconfiguring triangulation. Whereas classical triangulation requires that two or more methods are applied for the purposes of validation and ensuring accuracy of results, some feminist studies have reinvented it as a means of seeking out conflicting findings. This diminishes the risk that some marginalized perspectives may be highlighted at the expense of others, although there may be an implicit hierarchy of discourses even within marginalized groups. Even within marginalization communities, some perspectives may have less legitimacy than others. Nevertheless, the feminist reworking of triangulation, discussed earlier, appears to be close to Lather's (1993) concept of "transgressive validity" whereby the validity of research stems from its capacity to transgress or challenge dominant understandings. Some may counter that the lack of closure that this entails risks undermining or diluting the transformative aims of the research. While this may constitute a valid criticism, validity within transgressive research is enacted when researchers reflect critically on their own stance. This is key to maintaining an open-endedness, which, in our view, is more likely to serve social justice than closure (Fisher & Freshwater, 2014). Definitions of research objectives and the methods applied to investigate them should be under constant critical scrutiny as limits to be transgressed in themselves.

We view the questioning of all approaches to research as a critical dimension of studies with transformative aims, particularly when challenging "common sense" enables the legitimization of voices that are normally silenced. This has an importance in relation to social justice that often remains unacknowledged. However, numerous historical and contemporary examples teach us that whenever those on the margins of society are denied opportunities to exercise civil rights, including the right to a voice and the right to seek social justice, much more than even democratic participation and human dignity is at stake. Human life itself is in peril (see Fisher, 2012), a point that can be poignantly illustrated by numerous historical and contemporary examples. To take one example, in 2009, Martin Ryan, a patient with learning difficulties, starved to death in a British hospital after 26 days without proper nourishment. This could happen because Martin Ryan had ceased to be a person with a voice—or at least a voice that was worth listening to. To use Arendt's (2004, p. xviii, cited in Fisher, 2012) chilling word, Martin Ryan had become "superfluous" and was abandoned to the mercy of an institution that excluded him. This is just one example among many possible ones that powerfully illustrates the importance of research conducted from the perspective of the excluded. Transformative-emancipatory research is important precisely because it renders visible suffering, which is unacknowledged and therefore invisible.

While our fundamental endorsement of MMR in the transformative-emancipatory must be evident, the question remains whether its emancipatory goals can be achieved with MMR. Our response is cautiously affirmative in relation to studies that apply an emancipatory theoretical lens. However, this is not the same as saying that MMR with transformative aims necessarily avoids reproducing exclusionary discourses. So much depends on the types of questions that are asked and those that remain unasked—and of course who is doing the asking. Paradoxically, this is always a danger whenever people pursue a principled decision to bring about a more equal and just society: history reminds us that strivings for utopia are often beset by "collateral damage" that tends to negate the original idealistic. To provide one example, we can consider a study relating to ex-members of the former leading Socialist Unity Party in the German Democratic Republic, in particular how they justified their support for the regime after its demise. Fisher (2002) observed that many had been idealistically motivated and had aspired toward "a better socialist Germany." On this basis, many of the ex-Party members had rationalized the abuses of human rights on the basis that "the end sometimes justify the means." Put differently, injustices to specific individuals were viewed as a price worth paying in the interest of achieving a "higher good." While at first sight this may at appear unconnected to MMR, we suggest that it may in fact be highly relevant insofar as MMR, which seeks the integration of findings and data, can be similarly regarded as promoting a unified worldview. The production of a unified view—whether in state ideology or in research studies—necessarily means that there is little space for dissonance. It *requires* the silencing or neglect of marginalized voices. This is an insight that prompts us to defend the value of research that permits competing data and findings to coexist in a dynamic disequilibrium. Further, we would argue that the urge to integrate runs the risk of achieving premature closure on unending and imaginative possibilities, which may create uncertainty but offer new ways and as yet unrevealed ways of conceptualizing the world.

Ideological Barriers to Transformative-Emancipatory Mixed Method Research in the Health Sciences

Integration is likely to be associated to a general tendency within MMR that favors postpositivism (Creswell, 2007). As Howe (2004) puts it, MMR "elevates quantitative–experimental methods to the top of the methodological hierarchy and constrains qualitative methods to a largely auxiliary role in pursuit of the *technocratic* aim of accumulating knowledge of what works" (pp. 53–54).

If this applies to MMR research in behavioral and social sciences, it constitutes a yet more significant issue in areas of policy developed through the application of evidence-based practice (EBP), for example, medicine, education, and social welfare. In making disciplinary distinctions, we refer to Rao (2007, cited in Tashakkori & Creswell, 2008, p. 3) who has noted the "disciplinarization" of mixed methods, by pointing out that MMR is significantly shaped by its disciplinary location. In the following discussion we address why the political and ideological obstacles impeding social justice are particularly trenchant in medicine and the health sciences.

Understanding how urges for scientific certainty are enacted within medicine and healthcare requires an understanding of EBP or what can be termed the ideology of EBP. Originally developed from a methodology associated with clinical epidemiology, EBP was conceptualized as a judicious blending of research evidence in order to provide the best care for individual patients (Sackett, Rosenberg, Muir Gray, Haynes, & Richardson, 1996). The reality has generally been somewhat different, with EBP largely driven by the work of Archie Cochrane, who argued that randomized control trials constituted the highest level of evidence, with other forms of evidence, including qualitative inquiry, professional knowledge, and experiential knowledge being viewed as less legitimate (Freshwater & Rolfe, 2004; Rolfe, 2006). This is based on the assumption that practice within medicine and the health sciences should be based on rationality and objectivity, with randomized control trials being viewed as an ideologically neutral method. Put differently, medicine and the health sciences remain embedded within a postpositivist paradigm in which the truth is accessed by a single correct approach. Other types of evidence, including qualitative studies and practitioner, are relegated to the margins. As Holmes, Murray, Perron, and Rail (2006) put it, "we are currently witnessing the health sciences engaged in a strange process of eliminating some ways of knowing" (p. 181). In short, EBP has become a "regime of truth" that closes off possibilities for pluralism or the acceptance of multiple viewpoints.

While EBP was initially viewed as a leveller of hierarchy, the exaltation of randomized control trials has served the interests of the positivist/postpositivist paradigm, which sustains the preeminence of medical expertise while devaluing the professional and experiential forms of knowledge associated with allied health professionals. The message is that health professionals (and teachers and social workers) should base their practice on guidelines established through EBP rather than drawing on their own experience or professional training. This is one form of social injustice associated with EBP. Yet another is that those who benefit most from its dominance are those who shape the research landscape, including the research funding mechanisms (Freshwater & Rolfe, 2004).

While "lip service" may be paid to MMR by politicians and policymakers, by funding bodies, and by powerful groups within the academy, qualitative methods are generally restricted to those that can be reconciled with and support the postpositive's paradigm. Giddings (2006) has suggested that MMR acts to neutralize attempts by qualitative researchers to challenge the dominance of quantitative research designs. What is clear is that virtually no space is provided within EBP for those in transformative-emancipatory and interpretive/constructionist frameworks and that, as a consequence, EBP silences marginalized perspectives. Indeed, systematic reviewing and meta-analyses are conceptualized as methods *intended to exclude the peripheral*, in order to ensure validity and generalizability.

Ideology is most powerful when invisible, meaning when it constitutes part of the "common sense" of the everyday. One example might be the near consensus within medical and health sciences research regarding the desirability of consigning the paradigm wars to history. This is manifest in the dominant view that MMR offers a wealth of possibilities to address human disorders, which overcomes the prejudices that have hampered studies in the past. As would be expected, the pragmatic paradigm dominates in medicine and health sciences. To take one example, Glogowska (2011) acknowledges that while some people maintain entrenched positions, with some quantitative researchers continuing to devalue qualitative research and some qualitative researchers resisting the adoption of postpositivism, the paradigms wars have nevertheless been consigned to the past. The view that reconciliation is an unproblematic good can be challenged on several counts. First it assumes parity between quantitative and qualitative studies, a fiction within medicine and the health sciences; second, we would suggest that it could be contended that some qualitative researchers are justified in refusing to yield to the postpositivist paradigm. The desire for pragmatism and consensus supported by Glogowska may be conducive to the production of Mode 2 knowledge, but it is harder to reconcile with a position that accords equal respect to marginalized perspectives, especially in a context as inherently political as medicine or health.

The imperative to protect the status quo is liable to arise in areas of research associated with professionals with "official" policy where powerful stakeholder groups jealously guard their privileges and seek to uphold the worldviews that support these. This is nowhere more the case than in medicine and the health sciences, fields in which MMR has been taken up with particular enthusiasm. The prevailing wisdom in medicine and in the health sciences is that MMR is most suited to address the multidimensional factors influencing and affecting health and illness (Ivankova & Kawamura, 2010). The drive for the integration of data and findings, often through triangulation, is particularly strong in research conducted in the field of health sciences (see Freshwater, 2007; Ivankova & Kawamura, 2010).

As has been previously discussed, a focus on the integration of findings is associated with the marketability of knowledge—Mode 2 knowledge—which has an inbuilt aversion to ambivalence. Ambivalence does not lend itself to the production of marketable knowledge. However, beyond contemporary preoccupations with commodified knowledge, it is fairly safe to assume that people generally prefer certainty to uncertainty and that yearnings for the former can prompt a reliance on external authority that provides a soothing narrative. It is precisely this desire for predictability, which can be regarded as a cornerstone of modernist thinking, that produces the vantage point from which the world can be regarded as amenable to control though scientific progress. In many areas of life, this type of optimism has yielded to a postmodern recognition that the world is complex, ambivalent, and, above all, unpredictable. For example, postmodern/queer theorists have challenged gender and sexuality binaries, suggesting that identities are more fluid and unpredictable than is often acknowledged (McPhail, 2006). Indeed, the postmodern world is one in which the pursuit of constant and unchanging "truths" can be viewed with relative cynicism. This said, it is equally one that offers liberating opportunities for breaking meta-narratives, which may have provided security for some at the cost of exclusion of others. Exclusion in the modern world is related to the relentless construction of "scientific" categories associated with normality and deviancy; in other words, it is related to the construction of groups, which are located both geographically and metaphorically at the margins (see Fisher, 2008, 2012; Fisher & Owen, 2008).

Medicine and the health sciences constitute something of an exception in an increasingly postmodern terrain in the sense that they remain attached to the hope and to the expectation that the accumulation of objectively established interventions arrived at through scientific procedures can create a better world (Rose, 2013). What is particularly remarkable, and perhaps ironic, is that the fluid identities that are a hallmark of postmodernity are often constructed with (sometimes misplaced) confidence in modernist medical and scientific progress. Individuals may draw on reproductive technologies that enable them to have children later in life, or they may replace body parts that have worn out; alternatively, they may attempt to reduce their risk of disease through the manipulation of diet and exercise, and growing numbers are having to redress to surgery to halt the signs of aging. The apparent endless flexibility of the self-determining subject of the postmodern era is therefore often ready to overlook the reality that medical and scientific certainty is itself a myth. Truth discourses pertaining to health and the body are now disseminated through a tightly woven network that incorporates schools, work, leisure, and the media. Within the academy, the grip of the truth discourses has been further reinforced by "the translational imperative"—a feature of Mode 2 knowledge. Our view of the oppressive consequences of certainties is discussed later, in which we contend that while a vision of social justice is important, it should not nevertheless to lead to closure. While convictions and identifications provide a frame of reference, and it is important to have one, a frame of reference should be seen as a point on a journey rather than a final resting place (Fisher & Freshwater, 2014).

Deconstructing Integration

While our focus so far has been directed on the contributions of MMR embedded in what is commonly termed the *transformative-emancipatory* tradition, we do not regard this as a discrete category that stands alone in its orientation toward the furtherance of social justice. To a certain extent, we are inescapably limited by conventional discursive categories (pragmatic, transformative-emancipatory) that shape the social world and our ability to think about it. At the same time we strive to maintain a stance of critical evaluation in order to seek ways to think beyond our current limitations (Fisher & Freshwater, 2014). In this spirit we see a closure of perspective as inimical to the interests of social justice, and we recognize that the emancipatory-transformative tradition, while often associated with a particular type of political allegiance, should not be regarded as a unique path to social progress. Indeed, as discussed earlier, striving for a utopia can lead to blinkered vision with oppressive consequences. For this reason, we turn our attention to the analytical techniques associated with postmodernism, for example, deconstructionism (Derrida, 2004) and poststructuralism (Foucault, 1972), which have revealed the inherently political nature of the totalizing narratives associated with EBP (Freshwater, 2007; Freshwater & Rolfe, 2004; Holmes et al., 2006; Mantzoukas, 2007; Rolfe, 2006). Challenging the tendency to search for unifying or "heroic" narratives Freshwater argues that texts arise as co-constructions between the producers and the readers/audience. Texts, therefore, should not be fixed by their producers but should instead be constantly reinvented through different readings. The interpretations of readers/audience do not, of course, appear in a cultural vacuum but are shaped by the conventions in which the readers/audience have been socialized.

In relation specifically to nursing, Freshwater (2007) argues that reading is associated with "being faithful to the text through an act of subservience" (p. 135). This, she argues, is a requirement of the prevailing culture of technical rationalism, which is characteristic of institutions in health and social care. Thus, for a nurse, the point of departure in responding to a text tends to be orientated toward uncritical absorption rather than toward developing the type of creative interplay described by Greene (2007). This results in an ossification or reification of meaning, which undermines the putative openness and vitality that MMR was originally

conceptualized as generating. As Freshwater puts it, "The Text [in this case MMR] [should] draw its energy from the reader/audience. Otherness is crucial to its survival [and yet] it struggles with the very notion of otherness" (p. 138). Therefore, MMR, originally conceptualized as freeing up the imagination and extending thinking, has become absorbed into the constraining institutional structures it was originally intended to challenge. The same argument has been made in relation to interdisciplinarity (Derrida, 2004), a natural "bedfellow" of MMR, which is equally associated with the ascendancy of Mode 2 knowledge. With researchers trapped in the material and social relations of knowledge production, opportunities for the discovery of new research objects, particularly in the health sciences, are stifled.

Heidegger (2002) argued that science is premised on the idea of "a bounded object domain" (p. 63). Foucault (1972) claimed that discourses bring into being the very objects they describe (p. 49). Medicine and the health sciences are associated with therapeutic regimes that are strongly attached to notions of normality and deviance; categories are constructed and sustained through institutional expertise, which is deemed competent to speak the truth. Termed "biopower" by Foucault, this is a form of power that is necessarily based on constructing exclusion; it involves the identification of subgroups, particularly those that supposedly pose some form of risk to the wider populace, for example, the disabled, the mentally ill, the obese, the vulnerable, and so on. This is a postpositivist strategy that relies on investigatory foundationalism, meaning that there is a real world out there that can be objectively investigated.

What does all this mean for MMR in health and health sciences? It might seem a little late to be asking this question, but actually we believe that it needs to be asked continuously and reflexively. Perhaps MMR could be deployed in ways that ward off assaults that could topple the postpositivist paradigm on which medical expertise and other forms of institutional power depend. We remind the reader of Rolfe's (2002, p. 4) contention that multidisciplinarity constitutes a shrewd tactic by the proponents of biomedical power. While appearing to cede some ground to the arguments put forward by qualitative researchers, this constitutes a highly strategic retreat, which ultimately ensures that the dominance of biomedicine and of foundational enquiry is maintained. In short, the field of medicine and the health sciences remain rooted within the postpositivist paradigm and are therefore essentially inimical to the promotion of MMR research, which seeks to put forward the perspectives of the marginalized.

Conclusion

Research that supports social justice must necessarily challenge dominant postpositivist understandings embedded in the view that the role of research is to discover "the truth." We have argued that this is inimical to the aims of social justice, particularly as it is a worldview tenaciously held on to by those with power: witness the reprivileging of quantification and standardization to support governments' wholesale adoption of accountability orientated policies. To adopt pragmatism is to miss the point that ideological neutrality is impossible—one that can only lend weight to the status quo. Pragmatism appears to remain largely based on foundationalism—the view that there is a "real" world "out there" waiting to be discovered. This is manifest in continuing preoccupations with integration. However, concerns for integration can quickly merge into a focus on validity and generalizability, which avoids, represses, or delegitimizes marginalized perspectives.

Beyond embracing diversity, mixed methods researchers need to acknowledge that the world is not merely discovered through research, and research is a part of social production. MMR that produces researchers and the social world in differing ways is needed in the interests of social justice. Research does not merely reveal a world waiting to be discovered but is instead active in constructing the world by reconfiguring it in ways previously not thought of. Research is therefore not necessarily about investigating predefined objects but considers new objects that emerge from the research process. This does not involve a whole-scale endorsement of postmodern relativity. If there is really no such thing as reality, then there is also no such thing as discrimination or injustice. At its most extreme, postmodernism "drives the enforced injustices of social inequality into the personal cupboard of privately experienced suffering" (Oakley, 2000, p. 209). This being said, deconstruction is a useful tool in challenging entrenched and oppressive forms of power. Above all, it shows us that research is not necessarily about changing the world through investigation; research can be about attempting to shape ourselves and others in ways that differ from past and current representations, particularly those based on oppressive classifications. While

the techniques of deconstruction offer a good starting place for social justice, we learn from the transformative-emancipatory tradition that social justice requires democratic relationships, an emancipatory social lens, and power-sharing. This is based on an appreciation that while understandings of the social world differ, oppression is not merely a social construct—it is a lived experience. Crucially, emancipatory aims cannot be furthered by experts who conduct research on communities. It requires researchers who undertake research in equal partnership with communities. The challenge is not easy: it involves a principled adherence to a political vision and to a specific community while continuing to welcome "jagged" findings and dissonances that potentially lead to stories not yet told.

Discussion Questions

1. In this chapter, why have we have challenged the supposed value-neutrality of MMR within the pragmatic tradition?

2. What are the relative merits of the transformative-emancipatory paradigm of MMR?

3. At the same, what are some of the problems with the utopian visions?

4. Why should researchers (and others) strive to combine political commitment with an openness that recognizes partiality?

References

Bazeley, P. (2006). The contribution of computer software to integrating qualitative and quantitative data analyses. *Research in the Schools, 13*(1), 64–74.

Bresnan, M., & Burrell, G. (2013). Journal à la mode? Twenty years of living alongside Mode 2 and the new production of knowledge. *Organization, 20*(1), 25–37.

Bryman, A. (2006). Paradigm peace and the implication for quality. *International Journal of Social Research Methodology, 9*(3), 111–126.

Buck, G., Cook, K., Quigley, C., Eastwood, J., & Luca, Y. (2009). Profiles of urban, low SES African-American girls' attitudes towards science: A sequential explanatory mixed methods study. *Journal of Mixed Methods Research, 3*(4), 386–410.

Cooper, G. (2013). A disciplinary matter: Critical sociology, academic governance and interdisciplinarity. *Sociology, 47*(1), 74–89.

Creswell, J. W. (2003). *Research design: Qualitative, quantitative, and mixed methods approaches* (2nd ed.). Thousand Oaks, CA: Sage.

Creswell, J. W. (2007). Controversies in mixed methods research. In N. K. Denzin & Y. S. Lincoln (Eds.), *The SAGE handbook of qualitative research* (4th ed., pp. 269–285). London, England: Sage.

Creswell, J. W., & Plano Clark, V. L. (2007). *Designing and conducting mixed methods research.* Thousand Oaks, CA: Sage.

Creswell, J. W. (2010). Mapping the developing landscape of mixed methods research. In A. Tashakkori & C. Teddlie

(Eds.), *SAGE handbook of mixed methods in social & behavioral research* (2nd ed., pp. 45–68). London, England: Sage.

Denzin, N. K., & Lincoln, Y. S. (Eds.). (2005). *The SAGE handbook of qualitative research* (3rd ed.). Thousand Oaks, CA: Sage.

Department for business innovation and skills (BIS). (March 2013). *Investing in research, development and innovation.* London: HMSO.

Derrida, J. (2004). *Eyes of the university: The right to philosophy.* Stanford, CA: Stanford University Press.

Fisher, P. (2002). Creating a Marxist-Leninist cultural identity: Women's memories of the German Democratic Republic's Friedensfahrt. *Culture, Sport and Society, 5*(1), 39–52.

Fisher, P. (2008). Wellbeing and empowerment: The importance of recognition. *Sociology of Health and Illness, 30*(4), 583–598.

Fisher, P., & Owen, J. (2008). Empowering interventions in health and social care: Recognition through "ecologies of practice." *Social Science & Medicine, 67*(12), 2063–2071.

Fisher, P. (2012). Questioning the ethics of vulnerability and informed consent in qualitative studies from a citizenship and human rights perspective. *Ethics and Social Welfare, 6*(1), 2–17.

Fisher, P., & Freshwater, D. (2014). An emancipatory approach to practice and qualitative inquiry in mental health: Finding "voice" in Charles Taylor's *Ethic of Identity. Ethics and Social Welfare.* doi:org/10.1080/17496535.2014.884611

Foucault, M. (1972). *The archaeology of knowledge.* London, England: Tavistock.

Freshwater, D., & Rolfe, G. (2004). *Deconstructing evidence-based practice.* London, England: Routledge.

Freshwater, D. (2007). Reading mixed methods research: Contexts for criticism. *Journal of Mixed Methods Research, 1*(2), 134–146.

Gibbons, M., Limosges, C., Nowotny, H., Schwartman, H., Scott, P., & Trow, M. (1994). *The new production of knowledge.* London, England: Sage.

Giddings, L. S. (2006). Mixed methods research: Positivism dressed in drag? *Journal of Research in Nursing, 11*(3), 195–203.

Glogowska, M. (2011). Paradigms, pragmatism and possibilities: Mixed methods research in speech and language therapy. *International Journal of Language & Communication Disorders, 46*(3), 251–260.

Greene, J. C. (2007). *Mixed methods in social inquiry.* San Francisco, CA: Jossey-Bass.

Greene, J. C. (2008). Is mixed methods social inquiry a distinctive methodology? *Journal of Mixed Methods Research, 2*(1), 7–22.

Hesse-Biber, S. (2010). Feminist approaches to mixed methods research: Linking theory and praxis. In A. Tashakkori & C. Teddlie (Eds.). *SAGE Handbook of mixed methods in social & behavioral research* (2nd ed., pp. 169–192). Thousand Oaks, CA: Sage.

Hesse-Biber, S. (2012). Feminist approaches to triangulation: Uncovering subjugated knowledge and fostering social change in mixed methods research. *Journal of Mixed Methods Research, 6*(2), 137–146.

Holmes, D., Murray, S. J., Perron, A., & Rail, G. (2006). Deconstructing the evidence-based discourse in health sciences: Truth, power and fascism. *International Journal of Evidence-Based Health Care, 4*, 180–186.

Hadorn, G. H., Pohl, C., & Bammer, G. (2010). Solving problems through transdisciplinary research. In R. Frodeman (Ed.), *The Oxford handbook of interdisciplinarity* (pp. 496–525). Oxford, UK: Oxford University Press.

Heidegger, M. (2002). *Off the beaten track.* Cambridge, UK: Cambridge University Press.

Higgs, P. (2013, December 6). Peter Higgs interview: "I have this kind of underlying incompetence." *The Guardian.* Retrieved from http://www.theguardian.com/science/higgs-boson/

Holmwood, J. (2010). Sociology's misfortunes: Disciplines, interdisciplinarity and the impact of the audit culture. *The British Journal of Sociology, 61*(4), 639–665.

House, E. R., & Howe, K. R. (1999). *Values in evaluation and social research.* Thousand Oaks, CA: Sage.

Ivankova, N., & Kawamura, Y. (2010). Emerging trends in the utilization of integrated designs in the social, behavioral and health sciences. In A. Tashakkori & C. Teddlie (Eds.), *SAGE Handbook of mixed methods in social & behavioral research* (2nd ed., p. 581–612). London, England: Sage.

Johnson, R. B., & Onwuegbuzie, A. J. (2004). Mixed methods research: A research paradigm whose time has come. *Educational Researcher, 33*(7), 14–26.

Johnson, R. B., Onwuegbuzie, A. J., & Turner, L. A. (2007). Towards a definition of mixed methods research: A research paradigm whose time has come. *Journal of Mixed Methods Research, 1*(2), 112–133.

Lather, P. (1993). Validity after post structuralism. *The Sociological Quarterly, 34*(4), 673–693.

MacLean, S., Warr, D., & Pyett, P. (2009). Was it good for you too? Impediments to conducting university-based collaborative research with communities experiencing disadvantage. *Australian and New Zealand Journal of Public Health, 33*(4), 407–412.

Mantzoukas, S. (2007). The evidence-based practice ideologies. *Nursing Philosophy, 8*, 244–255.

McPhail, B. A. (2006). Questioning gender and sexuality binaries: What queer theorists, transgendered individuals, and sex researchers can teach social work. *Journal of Gay & Lesbian Social Services, 17*(1), 3–21.

Mertens, D. M., Farley, J., Madison, A. M., & Singleton, P. (1994). Diverse voices in evaluation practice: Feminists, minorities and persons with disabilities. *Evaluation Practice, 15*(2), 123–129.

Mertens, D. (2003). Mixed methods and the politics of human research: The transformatory-emancipatory perspective. In A. Tashakkori & C. Teddlie (Eds.), *Handbook of mixed methods in social & behavioral research* (pp. 135–167). London, England: Sage.

Mertens, D. M., Bledsoe, K. L., Sullivan, M., & Wilson, A. (2010). Utilization of mixed methods for transformative purposes. In A. Tashakkori & C. Teddlie (Eds.), *SAGE handbook of mixed methods in social & behavioral research* (2nd ed., pp. 193–214). London, England: Sage.

Morgan, D. L. (2007). Paradigms lost and pragmatism regained: Methodological implications of combining qualitative and quantitative methods. *Journal of Mixed Methods Research, 1*(1), 48–76.

Nowotny, H., Scott, P., & Gibbons, M. (2001). *Rethinking science: Knowledge and the public in an age of uncertainty.* Cambridge, UK: Polity Press.

Oakley, A. (2000). *Experiments in knowing.* Cambridge, UK: Polity Press.

Onwuegbuzie, A. J., & Johnson, R. B. (2006). The validity issue in mixed methods. *Research in Schools, 13*(1), 48–63.

Rolfe G. (2002). Reflexive research and the use of self. In D. Freshwater (Ed.), *Therapeutic nursing* (pp. 175–194). London, England: Sage.

Rolfe, G. (2006). Judgements without rules: Towards a postmodern concept of research validity. *Nursing Inquiry*, *13*, 7–15

Rose, N. (2013). The human sciences in a biological age. *Theory, Culture and Society*, *30*(1), 3–34.

Sackett, D. L., Rosenberg, W. M. C., Muir Gray, J. A., Haynes, R. B., & Richardson, W. S. (1996). Evidence based medicine: What it is and what it isn't. *British Medical Journal*, *312*, 71–2.

Somekh, B., & Lewin, C. (2005). *Research methods in the social sciences*. Thousand Oaks, CA: Sage.

Sweetman, D., Badiee, M., & Creswell, J. W. (2010). Use of the transformative framework in mixed methods. *Qualitative Inquiry*, *16*(6), 441–454.

Tashakkori, A., & Creswell, J. W. (2008). Editorial: Mixed methodology across disciplines. *Journal of Mixed Methods Research*, *2*(3), 3–6.

Tashakkori, A., & Teddlie, C. (Eds.). (2003). *Handbook of mixed methods in social & behavioral research*. London, England: Sage.

Teddlie, C., & Tashakkori, A. (2006). A general typology of research designs featuring mixed methods. *Research in Schools*, *13*(1), 12–28.

Tucker, A. (2009). *Queer visibilities: Space, identity and interaction in Cape Town*. Malden, MA: Wiley-Blackwell.

Harnessing Global Social Justice and Social Change With Multimethod and Mixed Methods Research

Fiona Cram

Abstract

Multimethod and mixed methods research (MMMR) based on principles of equity, social justice, and decolonization has a role to play in enabling people to see, to understand, and to take action in support of those who are on the margins of society. As an endeavor undertaken collaboratively with those whose circumstances researchers seek to improve, MMMR can speak to hearts and to minds, instilling motivation and harnessing resources needed for social change. This chapter examines the role of MMMR in changing personal deficit understandings of social exclusion to multilayered explanations that examine historical, cultural, socioeconomic, and political influences operating within a society. Intervening then requires the moderation of structural impediments in order to respond effectively to people's needs, priorities, and aspirations for inclusion. The scene is also set for mixed method, equity-focused evaluations of the success or otherwise of interventions to promote social justice and inclusion around the globe.

Key Words: equity, social justice, decolonization, social inclusion, multilayered explanations

Introduction

It's sunset and the end of a working day for many people in the city. An old man moves to a space on the footpath in front on an abandoned and derelict theatre and unpacks his wares. He doesn't have his hand out for change; rather he sets up shop and offers goods for sale. He has a variety of reasonably priced shells, some decorated with religious texts, and some adorning framed religious pictures that are more expensive. A young man pauses to talk with him. While he doesn't buy anything he offers the old man a wrapped supermarket sandwich, which the old man accepts and sets aside for later. A woman stands on the footpath waiting for a bus or some other ride. Gradually she moves backward to get out of the way of pedestrian traffic and ends up close to the old man, with her back to him. She holds herself as if she doesn't see him, hasn't noticed what he sells or that she has actually entered his shop. I watch from a distance and wonder where

his family is and what brought him to this place, but I know I have little right to ask even if I were to linger and make a selection for purchase. I should not even make any assumptions about whether he is there by choice or design. Still I want to ask someone what this place is; this country that doesn't feel shame that those with meager means are spending nights on our footpaths—some with their hands out, some busking with meager or time-improved musical talent, and still others offering wares for sale.

My travels have shown me that this scene from my hometown is replayed in towns and cities around the world, with the people on footpaths coming in many colors. The connection I make between them is that many have ended up as beggars, buskers, and stall keepers through no fault of their own. They are often just trying to get enough coins so they and their family might eat and possibly find some shelter for the night.

However, I am not naïve. I know some will be caught up in beggar gangs that roam cities, like the young women and their babies in Mumbai. Others will be spending their takings on alcohol or drugs, but who am I to put conditions on the small amounts I give? My actions are not a long-term solution, and they possibly do not even contribute to short-term relief. Their value is mostly in making me feel less invisible, as this is what I become when I look away and refuse to see people on the margins of society.

More than this, I want to be able influence change that re-includes people, brings them in from the margins, and re-members them within their society. Marginalization and social exclusion are issues the world over, and they have negative repercussions for health and longevity (Graham, 2007). Social exclusion is a multidimensional, dynamic, and often intergenerational process (Hunter, 2009; Muras, 2006). Individuals who belong to two or more of the groups who experience marginalization within society may find that their experiences of discrimination are amplified (e.g., belonging to a minority group and being disabled). This amplification can result in further exclusion from their already marginalized groups. For example, Indigenous women who take a stand over the rights of Indigenous women often find themselves ostracized by Indigenous movements as well as women's movements (Richards, 2005). The problems that cause social exclusion (e.g., discrimination, oppression, economic conditions) "are linked and mutually reinforcing, and can combine to create a complex and fast-moving vicious cycle. Only when this process is properly understood and addressed will policies really be effective" (UK Social Exclusion Unit, 2001, cited in Toye & Infanti, 2004, p. 10).

The skills I bring to issues of inequality and social exclusion are those of a researcher and evaluator, largely within *Māori* (Indigenous New Zealanders) health, social services, and education. With this expertise, I work on understandings and solutions that aim to make my society more just and equitable. I have found that knowledge is not power; rather, being able to define what is acceptable knowledge is power. For example, the Indigenous peoples of the Pacific Ocean have extensive knowledge of ocean navigation. It was this knowledge that enabled Māori migration to Aotearoa New Zealand many hundreds of years prior to the country's "discovery" by a Dutch explorer (Salmond, 1991; Te Rangi Hiroa [Sir Peter Buck], 1982). A 1898 painting in the Auckland Art Gallery by C. F. Goldie and L. J. Steele, however, defied this knowledge. Called "The Arrival of the Maoris (*sic*) in New Zealand" it depicts those who journeyed across the Pacific as emaciated, near death, and "mad-eyed" with relief upon sighting land. The knowledge embodied in this painting is of Māori as uncivilized, haphazard travellers, and accidental settlers in Aotearoa. Such knowledge made it easier for the British to justify colonization, including the redistribution of Māori resources to British settlers. This process would have been more difficult if the colonial discourse had been of actual Māori strengths and knowledge traditions (Reid & Cram, 2004). The lesson for researchers interested in social justice or decolonization is to be attentive to whose knowledge is being privileged within their research context (e.g., family, community, society). Initiatives developed from widely accepted knowledge may reinforce rather than mitigate inequalities if the knowledge of those who are marginalized is not well represented.

The multimethod and mixed methods research (MMMR) methodology advocated in this chapter therefore draws on principles of equity (World Health Organization, 2010), social justice (International Forum for Social Development, 2006), and decolonization (Smith, 2012). The MMMR being discussed is therefore about speaking the truths of those on the margins of our societies, in ways that are recognized as knowledge and therefore acceptable to those in positions of power. Put simply, some people will find truth within stories, while for others it is within numbers. For example, politicians are often swayed by narratives whereas policy writers prefer quantitative, population data. To dismiss research findings simply because the data is either qualitative or quantitative is to commit an error of using the wrong quality criteria to assess that research (Dixon-Woods et al.,2006). It is also about misjudging potential research users and what will speak to their minds, their hearts, and, as Māori say, their *puku* (stomach) and thereby stir them to action. The transformative potential of MMMR also lies in the credibility that the convergence (i.e., triangulation) of research findings from different methods brings to understanding an issue. It is their confidence that an issue has been fully understood, gained from the complementarity of findings, that will prompt some people to act. It is also in the initiation of further research in response to contradictory findings, to answer questions that may not have arisen in a single method study (Hesse-Biber, 2010).

Mill and colleagues (2008), for example, conducted community-based MMMR about HIV testing among Canadian Aboriginal young people (15- to 30-year-olds). Their survey of 413 young people provided them with information about the prevalence of HIV testing behavior and young people's attitudes. Qualitative interviews with 28 young people, 26 of whom had been tested for HIV and 9 of whom were positive, allowed more in-depth exploration of HIV test decision-making. The researchers report on the complementarity of quantitative and qualitative data. They also take a methodological stance, acknowledging the multiple determinants of young people's circumstances, including colonization, and interpreting their findings within the context of these young people's risk environment rather than as their more individualized risk behavior. The convergence of findings of delayed care-seeking among those diagnosed as HIV-positive then highlighted access issues that needed to be addressed. This may not have arisen if risk had been individualized and young people blamed for not attending to their own health needs.

Within this chapter the first task of MMMR is seen as understanding and representing the context of people's everyday lives. The methodological task is to move people's understanding away from notions of victim-blaming and individual deficits to more nuanced knowledge and wisdom about the complexities of how societies exclude certain groups of people. Once understanding is acquired, the next task of MMMR is to question and inform the mechanisms for intervening for equity and social justice. The third part of the chapter then examines the evaluation of whether interventions are successful. Stories and examples of MMMR illustrate the points being made.

Understanding

When people are presented with a complex problem, they will probably try and find a solution. A "problem" of graffiti vandalism, for example, will lead to a discussion of what to do about it. However, the first step should be developing an understanding of the problem: whether graffiti vandalism is criminal behavior or the action of bored teenagers. Explanations are important as they have implications for the solutions that are designed: a criminal justice solution or a community design solution.

Camara Jones (2000) tells a story about flower seeds growing in different types of flower boxes.

The red flower seeds are planted in a flower box that has rich soil, full of nutrients. The pink flower seeds are planted in a flower box that has poor soil, full of rocks and clay. The red flower seeds flourish in their soil; they germinate, grow, and bloom. The pink flower seeds do not fare so well; fewer of them germinate, they grow spindly, and the blooms are few and far between. A person looking at just the mature plants might easily come to the conclusion that the red flower seeds are so much better than the pink flower seeds. However, an examination of the soil would soon show them that something else was affecting the "success" of the seeds. Camara uses the soil as a metaphor for understanding racism; that is ,"behavior that stems from a belief that people can be differentiated mainly or entirely on the basis of their ancestral lineage" (Cochrane, 1991, p. 127). This belief is embedded within societal norms and institutions that maintain the socioeconomic, political, and cultural privilege of the group(s) presumed to be superior. Philomena Essad (1990) writes

> Institutions are government agencies, businesses, and organisations that are responsible for legislation and for maintaining labour policy, political policy, health care, education, housing, social and commercial services, and other frameworks of society. When these institutions function in such a way as to limit certain racial/ethnic groups in their opportunities for growth, granting them fewer rights or limiting their opportunities to make use of these rights, then institutional racism exists. (pp. 18–19)

Failure to recognize the determinants of how people are positioned within societies (i.e., that the soil determines how well the flower seeds fare) is an act of omission that is often supported by institutionalized policies and practices, including research practices that fail to look beyond surface explanations for people's circumstances. Mixed method research can bring a commitment to understanding what lies beneath "common-sense" explanations of research findings. For example, Robson and Harris (2007) bring an Indigenous lens to the interpretation of Māori health disparities. They therefore raise questions about the unfulfilled responsibilities of government and the inaccessibility of healthcare for Māori, rather than accepting that Māori are somehow sicker and dying earlier than non-Māori through some fault of their own. The same lens can be applied to qualitative interviews with Māori women about their access to healthcare

(Walker, et al., 2008). When extended to MMMR, the value of this lens is, as described earlier, the convergence, consistency, and contradictions that emerge when findings from different methods are integrated.

Loring Jones (2008), for example, writes that despite at least three decades of attention by policy-makers and social service and health provider organizations, there is very little literature on domestic violence among Native Americans and virtually nothing on how to intervene. Even then the research highlights alcohol and drugs as key risk factors for domestic violence; however, the "full stop" does not belong there in terms of seeking an explanation. Jones stresses the importance of historical and current reasons for domestic violence in Indian communities:

> Trauma has been transmitted across generations as a result of the historic mistreatment and oppression of Indian people by the dominant culture. Genocide, racism, forcible expulsion from ancestral lands, and removal of children from Indian homes was all part of this legacy. This history left most Native Americans clustered in economically marginal rural areas of the country. . . abuse of alcohol and drugs is at least partially a response to this trauma. (p. 114)

From this methodological understanding, Jones (2008) conducted a MMMR study of domestic violence in Native American communities, identifying service needs and barriers to service access for those experiencing domestic violence. Methods included participant observation of service planning group meetings, a focus group interview with service providers, and versions of a structured survey instrument to assess service needs that were completed by professionals and service users, including elders. From the findings, he described the community as "an impoverished rural community" (p. 115), with the high level of domestic violence able to be understood as "anger turned inward as a result of historical trauma" (participant quote, p. 115). The participants described cultural factors that were both barriers to and facilitators of help seeking by those in the community for domestic violence. They also made suggestions about service needs (e.g., community education, 24-hour services). Overall, Jones found that domestic violence in the community was distinct and multifaceted, concluding that "family violence occurs within a cultural context" (p. 117) and that "interventions must be selected that can be incorporated into the everyday

experience of Native Americans" (p. 117). The suggestions made for intervening involved a collaborative, multimodal approach involving a range of professionals who could deliver services related to, for example, domestic violence, drug and alcohol problems, housing, training, child care, and transportation. The application of an Indigenous lens in the interpretation and integration of findings from the methods used strengthens confidence in Jones's findings and, in turn, the potential efficacy of his recommended actions.

Important research questions and tools explicitly call on us to recognize and explain inequalities such as American Indian women's increased risk of domestic violence compared to White women. The first three questions of one such tool, the Health Equity Assessment Tool (HEAT), designed to assist health practitioners develop interventions that improve public health and reduce health disparities, focus on understanding health inequalities (Signal, Martin, Cram, & Robson, 2008):

1. What inequalities exist in relation to the health sector issue under consideration?
2. Who is most advantaged and why?
3. How did these inequalities occur? What are the mechanisms by which the inequalities were created, maintained, or increased?

These questions, especially question 2, remind us that those who are socially included are privileged by greater access to economic, educational, social, political, and cultural resources (Shaw, Dorling, & Davey Smith, 2005). The tool also encourages the consideration of the ways in which inequalities might be "doubled-up" for those who belong to more than one vulnerable group (e.g., elderly people with disabilities). The principles of the HEAT methodology include equity, social democracy, and sustainability. Practitioners are encouraged to draw on multiple sources, as well as conduct new research, to answer the HEAT questions. While the researchers whose work informs the answers may not have necessarily used mixed methods, the drawing together of multiple strands of evidence requires HEAT users to integrate research findings in similar ways to those in MMMR studies. This requires practitioners to interrogate research findings for the insights they provide to understanding the multiple determinants of societal inequalities. "Some determinants are close to the individual (such as biological or lifestyle factors), while others are more distant (social, cultural and economic factors) and their effect is mediated through closer factors" (Public Health Advisory Committee, 2005, p. 15). For example, there is a higher risk of respiratory infections when people live in cold and damp houses; roads can create or disrupt community linkages, affecting access to social support and, in turn, people's health and well-being; and job security affects mental health (Public Health Advisory Committe, 2007).

In summary, it can be argued that MMMR is essential to research that seeks to document and understand the determinants of inequality and social injustice. Quantitative population data highlights inequities in the distribution of a society's resources (Graham, 2007). This is complemented by research into the intimacies of people's lives and how these are shaped by historical and contemporary experiences, institutions, and systems. Borrowing from disability advocates, such research should say "nothing about us without us" (Charlton, 1998). In other words, equity and social inclusion must be embedded within research practices as axiological assumptions.

Intervening

Intervening to eliminate or even reduce inequality can be difficult because privilege usually goes unnamed. Roland Barthes coined the term *ex-nomination* to describe how the economic determinants of a society remain anonymous. Just as Barthes talked of the bourgeoisie as not wanting to be named, "whiteness is constructed as natural, innocent and omnipresent. . . in our common-sense reality" (Spencer, 2006, p. 16). In an international development context, ex-nomination can operate to leave outsider donor nations and agencies unnamed and therefore naturalize their privileged status and worldview (Hopson, Kirkhart, & Bledsloe, 2012). The first step in addressing inequality is naming those who might otherwise go unnamed, so that their worldview becomes "a" worldview rather than "the" worldview (Cram, Ormond, & Carter, 2006). The next step is the recognition of inequality, social justice, and/or colonization.

Missy Titus (2013) writes in response to those who complain (incorrectly) that in order for women to get ahead in technology fields, men have to be pulled down. In her metaphor, all tech jobs are on the second floor, and, because of limited room space, jobs go to those who get there fastest (read "fast" as "most skilled"). An ascending escalator to the second floor is packed with men. When women realize there is no room on it for them, many give up; however, other women attempt to ascend using

the descending escalator between floors, and the fastest of these women make it before the room fills up. The fastest men, along with the ones who walk and a few of those who simply stand on the ascending escalator, also make it into the room. When some of the men ask about the low numbers of women in the room, the women explain the situation and suggest turning off both escalators so there is a level playing field. This draws an outraged response from the men that slowing them down is not the solution. The women then suggest building a women-only elevator that will move at the same speed as the ascending escalator but will carry only a small number of women. Again the men are outraged that women might get special treatment. "The point here is that women are not asking for a lot. We are simply asking that everyone start from an equal place and with an equal amount of upward force" (Titus, 2013).

The women in Titus's (2013) metaphor came up with interventions that they thought would help combat the systemic disadvantage they were experiencing. In real-life contexts, MMMR can support the building of qualitative and quantitative understandings and interventions that help systems to change so that people can remain themselves and experience social inclusion. Garcia, Melgar, and Sordé, in conversation with Cortés, Santiago, and Santiago (2013, p. 368) write about the reaction of Romani families in Spain to research projects about Roma social exclusion from quality education. Two research studies described "the problems" faced by Romani families but did not address structural issues such as exclusion and racism. These first two studies offered what Labonte (2004, p. 117) called "remedial" social inclusion solutions; that is, making people a better fit while ignoring their structural disadvantage within that society. A third study focused on problem-solving through the tranformation of the social context and thereby attended to issues of social and cultural justice (O'Halloran, 2004). Only this third study was acceptable to the Romani.

The endorsement of this third study's approach led to a transformative, longitudinal MMMR study of the La Milgrosa neighborhood using a communicative methodology that engaged the people in the neighborhood in finding answers to the main research question: "In what ways does community involvement in education contribute to strengthen connections between education and diverse areas of society?" (Garcia et al., 2013, p. 377). The communicative methods used evolved from dialogue with the community and included interviews, focus groups, life-stories, observations, and questionnaires. In the first year, the research focused on identifying educational strategies that would facilitate educational achievement and community cohesion. The second year focused on community participation models that would facilitate student educational success. The following two years took this analysis deeper.

As a result of the team's collaborative research with the community, including building the research capabilities of community members, the local school was redesigned. The result is a school that is a community hub, offering education that children, young people, and their families want to participate in. "The principal is really good and. . . the teachers really care about the students. Mothers and other community members can freely enter the school" (Luisa, Romani researcher, speaking to Garcia et al., 2013, p. 376). The research team (of Roma and non-Roma researchers) demonstrated the transformative power of their mixed methods communicative methodology. They worked with the Romani neighborhood to identify culturally responsive intervention strategies and used their research findings to inform a more inclusive educational solution. Their research transformed the school from one that excluded Romani children and young people to an institution where they could succeed as Roma.

Garcia et al.'s (2013) research began with building understandings of what was happening for the Romani community. When this ground-up process is lacking in the development of policies, plans, and projects, MMMR impact assessment tools can be used to assess the potential impact of planned initiatives on the environment and people.

Health impact assessment (HIA) considers the public health and equity implications of initiatives (Public Health Advisory Committee, 2005). Central to the HIA methodology is the consideration of equity, the determinants of health and wellness, and the role that sectors other than health (e.g., housing, education) play in the reduction of health disparities.

The MMMR approach in HIA examines and integrates "available scientific data, public testimony, and modeling to predict potential impacts" of planned initiatives on health (Powder River Basin Counsil, 2008, p. 11). In addition to this strong scientific foundation, the focus on equity often means that there is a strong political dimension to HIA. HIA practitioners, therefore, anticipate having to negotiate political viewpoints and ideologies (Taylor, Gowman, & Quigley, 2003). Key benefits of HIA for decision-makers are the provision of more information to inform decisions, more open decisions due to the involvement of more stakeholders, and an improved understanding of health issues (Kemm, 2007).

In 2008 Apatu, Rohleder, and the Hastings District Council in New Zealand undertook an HIA on the Council's Graffiti Vandalism Strategy. Evidence for the four stages of the HIA (screening, scoping, appraisal and reporting, evaluation) was drawn from the Council, community organizations, the police, taggers/graffiti artists, community representatives, and the social science literature (see Figure 40.1). A community profile was developed, interviews held with stakeholder groups, and relevant policy and strategy documents were scanned. The equity issues for Māori, youth, and males in the Graffiti Vandalism Strategy were explicitly

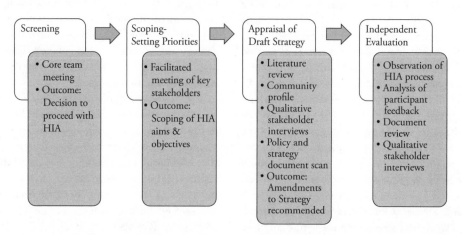

Fig. 40.1 Overview of stages and methods used in Graffiti Strategy HIA

considered. The data enabled the well-being and health pathways that the strategy would promote to be critiqued for positive and negative outcomes; that is, the identification of those pathways that would facilitate equity and that would promote disparities or negative outcomes. The following is the conclusion drawn from mapping these pathways according to Apatu et al. (2008):

> Interventions such as [the Strategy] have the potential to address the needs of rangatahi [young people], particularly those "at risk," by shifting resource allocation to prevent graffiti vandalism leading to a string of negative consequences for the rangatahi and wider community. (p. 20)

In summary, MMMR implemented within methodologies that are about equity, social justice, decolonization, and social inclusion enables the examination of institutional factors and pathways that lead to unequal outcomes for some groups of people within our societies, compared with other, privileged groups. Rather than expecting those who are disadvantaged to change, the representation of their realities and the structural impediments to their educational, health, and other advancement provide a rationale and direction for institutional change. This change, in turn, is not imposed on them because they are recognized and involved as key stakeholders in the MMMR project.

Evaluating

The use of MMMR to identify a community's needs and aspirations, along with structural constraints that maintain deprivation, marginalization, and inequality, can lay the foundation for not only intervening in appropriate ways but also evaluating whether an intervention is successful. The evaluator's role includes recognizing the wider context in which a program is operating, capturing the likely meandering journey of a program, and creating new knowledge (LaFrance & Nichols, 2009). "The evaluation must be responsive to the history, needs, and dreams of the people participating in and being affected by the program being evaluated" (LaFrance & Nichols, 2009, p. 9). In thinking about multicultural validity within evaluation, Karen Kirkhart (2005) argues that culture shapes evaluation theory and is also impacted by it. Cultural bias arises within evaluation because White social history dominates current evaluation theory. Such theory has the potential to magnify some aspects of evaluation and minimize others. Linking this to Barthes' concept of ex-nomination

highlights the potential of evaluation to leave White privilege unnamed and inequities, if observed, attributed to personal deficits.

Kildea, Stapleton, Murphy, Low, and Gibbons (2012) describe their process and impact evaluation of an Aboriginal and Torres Strait Islander specialist antenatal clinic (Murri clinic) as a participatory, triangulated mixed method approach. Using retrospective clinic data about mothers and babies, mother and infant audit data, survey data (from the women and staff), and interviews, they compared the clinical outcomes of women (Indigenous and also the partners of Indigenous men) attending the Murri clinic with those who received standard care. Individual and focus group interviews were conducted with a range of stakeholders, including the women themselves. Two Indigenous women were employed and trained as researchers, one of whom was a co-author. A reference group of Indigenous and non-Indigenous health stakeholders that met fortnightly during the evaluation provided feedback and advice, including cultural guidance and advice about stakeholders to interview.

The evaluation was able to identify those elements of the Murri clinic that underpinned its success as a culturally appropriate service where Indigenous women and their babies experienced better outcomes. These included it being community based, having Indigenous and other specialist staff (including an Indigenous midwife), and offering culturally responsive practices. The researchers also reported, "due to the participatory nature of the evaluation, changes to service provision intended to decrease delays in referral processes, and inaccurate or incomplete recording of data, have commenced" (Kildea et al., 2012, p. 10).

In the development world, the United Nations Children's Fund (UNICEF) has strengthened its evaluation approach to address equity issues in recognition that population progress in realizing the Millennium Development Goals might well conceal widening within-country disparities (Bamberger & Segone, 2011). Hopson and colleagues (2012, p. 61) also call upon Western evaluators to consider the issues that arise in international, cross-cultural evaluation work, even when it has an equity focus. The need to understand and develop participatory interventions described earlier is extended to draw out the "unstated assumptions about development, its processes, goals, and expected outcomes" (Hopson et al., 2012, p. 61). Questions that might not be within scope are therefore asked; for example, "what do development initiatives actually promote; or what type of development is to be carried out?" (Hopson et al., 2012, p. 60). The participation and capability building of "worst-off groups," including co-leadership of evaluations, are an important part of equity evaluation practice (Bamberger & Segone, 2011). The inclusion and empowerment of these people to speak and advocate for their own people during an equity evaluation may raise important questions that highlight the ideological conflicts between those practicing development and nations who face development (Ferguson, 1994). In this way equity evaluation is seeking an answer to question 10 of the HEAT: How will you know if inequalities have been reduced? (Signal et al., 2008), as well as a larger question of how we will know development has taken place and for whom.

Mixed methods equity evaluations combine population information with the lived reality of people within excluded groups, including those factors that affect service demand and access (Bamberger & Segone, 2011). An example is the evaluation of community-led total sanitation (CLTS) in Cambodia that used MMMR to ensure the participation of all stakeholders, including those who were most vulnerable (Kunthy & Catalla, 2009). The evaluation objectives were to review the achievements of the CLTS, and assess the sustainability, equity, access, and effectiveness of CLTS compared to other sanitation options. The methods employed included interviews, observations in villages, field surveys, and discussions with CLTS facilitators, project staff, and stakeholders. Initial evaluation findings were also discussed at a national workshop. The evaluation found that all the poor village households had participated in meetings about CLTS, but there was little evidence of the poor taking positions of responsibility within the initiative, and there was no special emphasis on the poor or vulnerable when latrines were built. The absence of the poor and vulnerable from focal person selections by local chiefs or councils was attributed to their lack of time or education.

> While poor and vulnerable households were more often visited by focal persons (because this group generally lags in latrine construction), visits were for the purpose of verbal encouragement/push rather than actual physical or material assistance in building their latrines. However, there were reports by some (for example, Kok Sangkea village in Otdar Meanchay province) village focal persons that vulnerable households (elderly, female-headed)

were assisted by village focal persons in constructing latrines especially in digging the pit. (Kunthy & Catalla, 2009, p. 81)

Some additional assistance was therefore provided to those who were poor or vulnerable to ensure equitable outcomes from the CLTS initiative. In other villages, however, the poor were unable to prioritize this program. This suggests that additional equity considerations in the implementation of the CLTS were needed to promote social inclusion and equity.

In summary, mixed methods, equity-focused evaluation of initiatives (hopefully) designed to reduce inequalities and promote social inclusion must understand and incorporate the voices of those targeted by the initiatives. This occurs when data (especially qualitative data) are collected about their lives. Quantitative measurement data and qualitative experience data will show whether those who are most vulnerable experience equitable outcomes as a result of an initiative.

Conclusions and Vision for Future Multimethod and Mixed Methods Research

> My friend in Alaska only gives to native people and once, when I was with her, told a white man to ask his own people for help. Her choice to be visible to her own people and take no responsibility for the plight of the "other" was an act of resistance that conjured up a predictably angry reaction from the white man with his hand out. I laughed with joy at her small defiance of white privilege and entitlement.

Wilson's (2008 p. 34) axiological questions provide a framework for concluding this chapter. His questions are: "What part of reality is worth finding out?" and "What is it ethical to do in order to gain this knowledge, and what will this knowledge be used for?"

The answer to the first question is that it is worth finding out the reality experienced by those who are least privileged and marginalized in our societies, that is, those who experience social exclusion and the unequal lives that accompany this. Colonization and other exercises in exclusion and displacement rely on the ability of those in positions of power to dehumanize others (Smith, 2012). This creates the artificial and inequitable prestige that impacts negatively on the lives of those seen as less deserving. In order to support these people to become fully human again, we need quantitative methods that identify the inequities they experience and the determinants of these inequities based on population data. We also need quantitative and qualitative methods that allow us to represent the lived realities of these people within our research and evaluations. A key factor in this is the inclusion of members of these groups on our research teams, as leaders and advocates, so that our research and evaluation does not reinforce the status quo.

Toye and Infanti (2004) provide an answer to Wilson's (2009) second question with their call for research to be owned by communities if it is to be useful for a social inclusion agenda. They also write that the "methods for gaining understanding of community contexts are varied and may include both quantitative and qualitative forms" (p. 39). A critique of some equity-focused evaluations in the development context is that they fall short of integrating the qualitative and quantitative data they collect (UNICEF, 2012). This integration and triangulation can also rest in the hands of communities as researchers and evaluators work to facilitate the epistemological privilege that the most marginalized in our communities should have to make sense of and give meaning to the impact of inequities on their lives.

There should be no point at which analysis becomes a "desk job," undertaken as an insular task by outsiders. At the same time, we should be aware of internalized racism and other "-isms" whereby people take on board the messages they receive about how they are positioned in the status and power hierarchy of society (Jones, 2000). Marginalized people may think their lack of money, education, or success is solely their own fault. Likewise, those who are privileged may think that their success is solely through their own effort. Our capability-building efforts with research teams and communities may include developing with them a structural analysis of the determinants of inequality. This occurs as part of the process of implementing tools such as HEAT and HIA, and we should not underestimate the value and transformative power of a process that applies research evidence collected through a range of methods to developing an understanding of the pathways that lead to, or away from, equity.

This chapter began with a discussion of how MMMR can speak to the hearts, minds, and *puku* of those in positions of power, to prompt them to take action for social justice. This conclusion has come back to grassroots, to community ownership of MMMR. It is timely to now connect the two with a future vision for MMMR that is about strengthening the sharing of knowledge and understanding between those with privilege and those who are vulnerable. There has been a lot of researching "down" that has highlighted the social and economic position and day-to-day realities of those who are vulnerable. Gains have been made in easing this downward gaze by building the capacity of marginalized groups to document their own circumstances. In MMMR this capacity building has been easier to achieve for qualitative methods, but gains have also been made in sharing skills and expertise about quantitative research methods. This effort should continue. In addition, we should encourage "upward gazing" whereby MMMR is put to more use to name, critique, and challenge privilege and what counts as knowledge. The best collaborators in this endeavor may well be those who have to strain their necks the hardest to gaze up.

Finally, it is imperative that the current unequal social order is contested and that "inclusion" is not about the chaotic "others" being brought back into the fold of an unchanged society (Humpage, 2006). Our MMMR and mixed method evaluation work should promote "a transformative agenda that aims to eliminate the barriers to full social and economic participation and create a more just and equitable world" (Toye & Infanti, 2004, p. 17). There are still conversations to be had about what this world looks like, and tensions will no doubt arise between different agendas (e.g., social justice and decolonization). However, if I was evaluating this tranformation, I would want to celebrate that these conversations had begun.

Discussion Questions

1. What methodology is needed for MMMR to fulfill the aspirations for it expressed in this chapter?

2. What MMMR strategies and tools are available to researchers to understand the inequality of different groups within a society or country?

3. What is the relationship between understanding a "problem" and knowing how to intervene to resolve it?

4. What role can MMMR play in evaluating whether an intervention is effective?

Suggested Websites

http://www.ub.edu/includ-ed/

The INCLUD-ED project (2006–2011) is described on the website as being about "Strategies for inclusion and social cohesion from education in Europe." The researchers used MMMR to include those who have often been silenced in research and marginalized with their societies. The focus on education provided a community-focused action component. The website contains a wealth of information about the methodology, methods, and findings from the project.

www.rangahau.co.nz

Rangahau is a research resource website aimed at Māori researchers. It also provides an introduction to those wanting to know more about Māori or Indigenous research. Information is provided to guide researchers from the development of a research idea to a proposal to sharing the findings of their research. While not explicitly about MMMR, the site provides a methodological context for the conduct of MMMR within Māori communities.

http://mymande.org

My M&E is an open website developed to encourage the sharing of information on how countries around the world are undertaking monitoring and evaluation. It contains numerous resources in its library and toolkits, as well as opportunities for e-learning. Users create a log-in and can then access information. The website also links to partner organizations.

References

Apatu, A., Rohleder, M., & Hastings District Council. (2008). *Health impact assessment on the draft Hastings District Council Graffiti Vandalism Strategy*. Hastings, New Zealand: Hawkes Bay District Health Board.

Bamberger, M., & Segone, M. (2011). *How to design and manage equity-focused evaluations*. New York, NY: UNICEF.

Charlton, J. I. (1998). *Nothing about us without us: Disability oppression and empowerment*. Berkeley: University of California Press.

Cochrane, R. (1991). Racial prejudice. In R. Cochrane & D. Carroll (Eds.), *Psychology and social issues: A tutorial text*. London, England: Falmer Press.

Cram, F., Ormond, A., & Carter, L. (2006). Researching our relations: Reflections on ethics. *Alternative: An International Journal of Indigenous Scholarship*, Special Supplement 2006—Marginalisation, 280–198.

Dixon-Woods, M., Cavers, D., Agarwal, S., Annandale, E., Arthur, A., Harvey, J., . . . Sutton, A. J. (2006). Conducting a critical interpretive synthesis of the literature on access to healthcare by vulnerable groups. *BMC Medical Research Methodology*, 6, 35.

Essad, P. (1990). *Everyday racism*. Claremont, CA: Hunter House.

Ferguson, J. (1994). *The anti-politics machine: "Development," depoliticization, and bureaucractic power in Lesotho*. Cambridge, MA: Cambridge University Press.

Garcia, R., Melgar, P., & Sordé, T. (2013). From refusal to getting involved in Romani research. In D. Mertens, F. Cram, & B. Chilisa (Eds.), *Indigenous pathways into social research: Voices of a new generation* (pp. 367–380). Walnut Creek, CA: Left Coast Press.

Graham, H. (2007). *Unequal lives: Health and socioeconomic inequalities*. New York, NY: Open University Press.

Hesse-Biber, S. N. (2010). *Mixed methods research: Merging theory with practice*. New York, NY: Guilford Press.

Hopson, R., Kirkhart, K. E., & Bledsloe, K. L. (2012). Decolonizing evaluation in a developing world: Implications and cautions for equity-focused evaluations. In M. Segone (Ed.), *Evaluation for equitable development results* (pp. 59–82). New York, NY: UNICEF.

Humpage, L. (2006). An "inclusive" society: A "leap forward" for Māori in New Zealand? *Critical Social Policy*, 26, 220–242.

Hunter, B. H. (2009). Indigenous social exclusion: Insights and challenges for the concept of social inclusion. *Family Matters*, 82, 52–61.

International Forum for Social Development. (2006). *Social justice in an open world: The role of the United Nations*. New York, NY: United Nations.

Jones, C. P. (2000). Levels of racism: A theoretic framework and a gardner's tale. *American Journal of Public Health*, 90(8), 1212–1215.

Jones, L. (2008). The distinctive characteristics and needs of domestic violence victims in a Native American community. *Journal of Family Violence*, 23, 113–118.

Kemm, J. (2007). *More than a statement of the crushingly obvious: A critical guide to HIA*. Birmingham, UK: West Midlands Pubic Health Observatory.

Kildea, S., Stapleton, H., Murphy, R., Low, N. B., & Gibbons, K. (2012). The Murri clinic: A comparative retrospective study of an antenatal clinic developed for Aboriginal and Torres Strait Islander women. *BMC Pregnancy & Childbirth*, 12, 159.

Kirkhart, K. L. (2005). Through a cultural lens: Reflections on validity and theory in evaluation. In S. Hood, R. K. Hopson, & H. T. Frierson (Eds.), *The role of culture and cultural context: A mandate for inclusion, the discovery of truth, and understanding in evaluative theory and practice* (pp. 21–39). Greenwich, CT: Information Age Publishing.

Kunthy, S., & Catalla, R. N. (2009). *Community-Led Total Sanitation (CLTS) in Cambodia: Evaluation report*. New York, NY: UNICEF.

Labonte, R. (2004). Social inclusion/exclusion: Dancing the dialect. *Health Promotion International*, 19(1), 115–121.

LaFrance, J., & Nichols, R. (2009). *Indigenous evaluation framework: Telling our story in our place and time*. Alexandria, VA: American Indian Higher Education Consortium.

Mill, J. E., Jackson, R. C., Worthington, C. A., Archibald, C. P., Wong, T., Myers, T., . . . Sommerfeldt, S. (2008). HIV testing and care in Canadian Aboriginal youth: A community based mixed methods study. *BMC Infectious Diseases*, 8, 132. Retrieved from http://www.biomedcentral.com/1471-2334/8/132

Muras, M. (2006). Social exclusion, social inclusion and sustainable development. In A. Ivanov & M. Mura (Eds.), *Social exclusion and integration in Poland. An indicators-based approach* (pp. 11–26). Warsaw, Poland: Ministry of Labour and Social Policy.

O'Halloran, K. (2004). Social inclusion and the Indigenous people of Australia: Achieving a better fit between social need and the charity law framework. *The International Journal of Not-For-Profit Law*, 6(2). Retrieved from http://www.icnl.org/research/journal/vol6iss2/special_1.htm

Powder River Basin Council. (2008, September-October). Resolutions to be considered at Powder River's Annual Meeting. *Powder River Breaks*, 36(5), 10–11.

Public Health Advisory Committee. (2007). *An idea whose time has come: New opportunities for health impact assessment in New Zealand public policy and planning*. Wellington, New Zealand: Author.

Public Health Advisory Committee. (2005). *A guide to health impact assessment: A policy tool for New Zealand* (2nd ed.). Wellington, New Zealand: Author.

Reid, P., & Cram, F. (2004). Connecting health, people and country in Aotearoa/New Zealand. In K. Dew & P. Davis (Eds.), *Health and society in Aotearoa New Zealand* (2nd ed., pp. 33–48). Auckland, New Zealand: Oxford University Press.

Richards, P. (2005). The politics of gender, human rights, and being Indigenous in Chile. *Gender and Society, 19*(2), 199–220.

Robson, B., & Harris, R. (Eds.). (2007). *Hauora: Māori standards of health IV: A study of the years 2000–2005.* Wellington, New Zealand: Te Rōpū Hauora a Eru Pōmare.

Salmond, A. (1991). *Two worlds: First meeting between Māori and Europeans 1642–1772.* Auckland, New Zealand: Viking.

Shaw, M., Dorling, D., & Davey Smith, G. (2005). Poverty, social exclusion, and minorities. In M. Marmot & R. G. Wilkinson (Eds.), *Social determinants of health* (2nd ed. pp. 196–223). Oxford, UK: Oxford University Press.

Signal, L., Martin, J., Cram, F., & Robson, B. (2008). *The Health Equity Assessment Tool: A user's guide.* Wellington, New Zealand: Ministry of Health.

Smith, L. T. (2012). *Decolonizing methodologies—Research and Indigenous peoples* (2nd ed.). London, England: Zed Books.

Spencer, S. (2006). *Race and ethnicity: Culture, identity and representation.* New York, NY: Routledge.

Taylor, L., Gowman, N., & Quigley, R. (2003). Yorkshire, England: Health Development Agency.

Te Rangi Hiroa (Sir Peter Buck). (1982). *The coming of the Māori.* Wellington, New Zealand: Māori Purposes Fund Board.

Titus, M. (2013, April 23). Why do women try to get ahead by pulling men down? [Web log post] Retrieved from https://medium.com/thoughts-on-society/a1345b36b91b

Toye, M., & Infanti, J. (2004). *Social inclusion and community economic development: Literature review.* Victoria, BC: Pan-Canadian Community Development Learning Network Project Framework.

United Nations Children's Fund. (2012). UNICEF supported evaluations with elements of equity-focused evaluations. In M. Segone (Ed.), *Evaluation for equitable development results* (pp. 258–262). New York, NY: Author.

Walker, T., Signal, L., Russell, M., Smiler, K., Tuhiwai-Ruru, R., & Tuhiwai-Ruru, R. (2008). The road we travel: Māori experience of cancer. *New Zealand Medical Journal, 121*(1279), 27–35.

Wilson, S. (2008). *Research is ceremony: Indigenous research methods.* Black Point, Nova Scotia: Fernwood.

World Health Organization. (2010). *Glossary of terms used.* Retrieved from http://www.who.int/hia/about/glos/en/print.html

Conclusions: Toward an Inclusive and Defensible Multimethod and Mixed Methods Science

R. Burke Johnson

Every chapter in this handbook makes an important new contribution to the literature. I offer my thanks and cheers (and cin cin, gānbēi, Le'tenachin!, Prost, Şerefe, Skål., etc.) to each of the authors of this handbook! They have provided a wealth of new knowledge. I am humbled by their work, which will, without question, continue the growth of mixed methods research (MMR).[1] I am certainly more informed about mixed methods research and its brothers and sisters and other relatives (e.g., multimethod research, interdisciplinary research, multiple level research, multiple paradigm research, multiple nation and people research). The authors provide new shoulders for all of us to build on.

In this epilogue I do not attempt to summarize the 40 chapters in this handbook. One reason is because I do not think it can be done briefly. Instead, I offer a few observations, some personal insights, a quote or two from each chapter, and then end with a continued call for all of us, *together*, to become part of a large and inclusive and dynamic social/behavioral/human science, that is, a basic and applied science that uses all of our skills and the knowledge we generate. We are different, but at a macro level we are one. We are part of this movement we call MMR. And we should continue to grow and become better at producing knowledge and improving our one world. That's what the MMR attitude or mindset is about. There is strength in differences *and* similarities, especially when we know how to put them together.

What Is Mixed Methods Research Today?

Addressing the issue of what MMR actually is, Jennifer Greene (Chapter 34) has provided an enlightening and important chapter that helps us to continue to reflect about mixed methods research.

Jennifer Greene is, as many readers know, one of the "founders" of MMR, back in the 1980s. There is no single founder, of course, because MMR has always been around in some form and it was founded "again" in the 1980s and 1990s in multiple places (e.g., Brannen, 1992; Brewer & Hunter, 1989; Bryman, 1988; Creswell, 1994; Greene, Caracelli, & Graham, 1989; Fielding & Fielding, 1986; Jick, 1979; Kelle & Erzberger, 1999; Morse, 1991; Rossman & Wilson, 1985; Tashakkori & Teddlie, 1998). I am sure my list of founders is woefully inexhaustive, but it's a start.

Greene continues to take the lead in mapping the legitimate terrain of mixed methods research. Greene points out that she believes MMR is and has always been about more than just the use of at least one qualitative and one quantitative method of data collection in a research study. To clarify her vision, Greene conceptualizes MMR as operating at three levels. She calls the first or lowest or most concrete level *method*, where method mixes can occur. I call this *method of data collection* (Christensen, Johnson, & Turner, 2014; Johnson & Christensen, 2014). Some major methods (of data collection) are tests, questionnaires, interviews, observations, focus groups, existing and secondary data, and constructed data. Each of these major methods has a quantitative, qualitative, and mixed form or instantiation. A mixed questionnaire including multiple open-ended and closed-ended items would be an example of *intramethod* mixing. One also can engage in *intermethod* mixing by using a combination of different methods of data collection. Some authors seem to suggest that MMR is just the mixing of methods of data collection. I agree that that is a sufficient condition, but I do not think it is a necessary condition and, more important, if that is all we discuss, then we are missing much of what MMR has to offer. Greene points out that the label *mixed methods* seems to suggest that one starts research inquiry with the assumption that mixed methods will be used, and that it seems to miss, prima facie, the possibilities of also including "more than one methodology, more than one philosophical paradigm, as well as multiple disciplines and substantive theories" (p. 607). Greene is asking for a thicker and fuller mixed methods research, one that embraces diverse methods, paradigms, methodologies, disciplines, and theories.

Extending MMR, Greene's second, slightly more abstract level is that of *methodology*, where methodology mixes can occur. This allows the use of two or more methodologies or a mixed version of a methodology. Examples of some well-known methodologies are experimental and quasi-experimental research, survey research, grounded theory, case study research, ethnography, and so forth. Methodologies help to structure research studies, and they come with their own logics and assumptions (Greene, 2007). Methodologies often have their own popular research designs (especially in experimental research, as well as in popular mixed methods research books). Methodologies have preferred methods and styles of data collection and cannot operate without the lower or concrete level of methods to obtain data.

In MMR, one can (a) have a primary and a secondary methodology (in addition to methods), (b) rely on two equally important methodologies in a research study, and/or (c) rely on new, creative mixed forms of methodologies. For an example of the last, I have argued for the use of a mixed methods grounded theory (MMGT) approach that focuses on exploration *and* confirmation or theory generation *and* theory testing (Johnson, McGowan, & Turner, 2010). I contend that an excellent area for advancement in MMR is for researchers and methodologists to construct new hybrid methodologies (i.e., *intramethodological* mixing). In addition to grounded theory, a recent example of expanding a methodology is seen in Mayoh and Onwuegbuzie's (2013) attempt to expand phenomenology into a mixed phenomenological methodology. I recommend others engage in this creative activity with grounded theory, phenomenology, quasi-experimental design, ethnography, and every other methodology that can help us to better understand our world. Greene gives an example of *intermethodological* mixing with a combination of a quasi-experiment (to measure changes

in outcome variables) and case studies (to study difference and local meaning and understanding).

The third and most abstract level for MMR provided by Greene is that of *paradigm*, where paradigm mixes can occur. In addition to paradigms, this also includes additional mixing of disciplines and theories. This third level is the level that the "paradigm dialog/war" focused on (not methods) and is still at the heart of most philosophical disagreements among purist research groups. Researchers are asked: Are you a postpositivist or are you a constructivist? Are you a realist, a pragmatist, or an interpretivist? Are you someone who emphasizes the importance of value neutrality during the conduct of research, or do you emphasize critical/transformative and participatory research? Researchers and graduate students are sometimes told that they must select one side of each dichotomy or trichotomy. They may be told, categorically, that one must be an A or B type because the conjoint of A and B is "impossible." That opinion often makes me wonder how one can make such an a priori claim of incompatibility rather than relying on creative and empirical observation and evidence. For example, I see mixes of philosophical poles frequently in heterogeneous research teams where the researchers dialogue and still "do their own thing" to produce a better whole. My own philosophy/theory of *dialectical pluralism* (Johnson, 2012; Johnson, Onwuegbuzie, Tucker, & Icenogle, 2014; Johnson & Stefurak, 2013) rejects simplistic categorical and either/or arguments. Instead, it builds on the dialectical approach long advocated by Greene or what some authors in this handbook call "both/and" statements. Paradigm incompatibility statements are based on a priori arguments (deductive logic), and ignore the radically real world (James, 1912/2012) that we continually construct and reconstruct (Dewey, 1920/2012) and live in. It is in the flow of the world in which we live and experience moment-to-moment and day-to-day consciousness that paradigmatic mixing is readily achievable through practice.

Sometimes I wonder how incompatibilist or purist or a priori thinking overlooks the millions of people across the world who have multiple cultural allegiances and people who move back and forth between two or even three or more languages. Moving from language to language is not especially dissimilar to moving across worldviews/paradigms, at least not according to those holding a strong or weak version of the linguistic relativity hypothesis. Even the father of "paradigms," Thomas Kuhn

(1962), thought that some researchers could learn how to make Gestalt switches. Making Gestalt switches is at the heart of mixed methods research, when a single researcher hopes to conduct MMR at the paradigm level. If a single researcher has not obtained competence at this, it is readily obtained with a heterogeneous research team composed of reasonable, open-minded researchers whose primary paradigms are different. On a heterogeneous research team, the mixed researcher needs to facilitate, and emphasize, good communication and translation, listening, empathy, process, and openness to larger and more complex wholes than what is obtained via a single paradigm.

Working in a single paradigm is easier, but it is not always best, and a sizable number of researchers today are interested in interacting and dialoging with more than one paradigm. In short, I believe Greene includes this highest level of paradigm in her defining of MMR to point out that the mixing or interaction or dialogue of paradigms is one legitimate style of MMR for some people. Greene points out that she believes mixed methods research was born in the late 1980s because many researchers wanted to listen to more than one paradigm. It was a rejection of either/or paradigmatic thinking. Welcome to the new world of "both/and"!

Greene's latest contribution to our field provides a large, medium, and small definition of mixed methods research, and the one a researcher uses will rightfully depend on his or her dispositions and practical needs. One is free to select the definition and style used to frame and answer the research questions. MMR can focus on two or more methods of data collection, two or more methodologies, or two or more paradigms. Frequently, MMR will rely on more complex combinations within and across Greene's three levels. I hope that multiple groups will be happy with this rendering of MMR. Ultimately we need to focus on conducting defensible empirical research. The history of research and science shows that we need to use multiple approaches to studying our world.

This last point suggests the importance of a close relative and friend of mixed methods research that is traditionally called *multimethod research*. Because of its inclusion of a version of mixed methods research and its use for answering many research questions, we decided to include *multimethod* in the title of this handbook. Part of the initial reasoning was that in order to mix, one has to have two or more (i.e., multiple) of something, typically two or more methods or methodologies but also paradigms, philosophies, theories, perspectives, disciplines, conceptual languages, and so forth. *Multiple is a necessary but not sufficient condition for mixed.* As Greene (Chapter 34) and Hunter and Brewer (Chapter 35) point out, multimethod research likes to follow research questions with appropriate multiple qualitative methods, or multiple quantitative methods, or multiple methods where at least one is qualitative and one is quantitative.

The Hunter and Brewer style of multimethod research is explained in Chapters 11 and 35 in this handbook (also see Brewer & Hunter, 1989, 2006). In Chapter 35, Hunter and Brewer point out that the spirit of multimethod research can help researchers deal with a number of conundrums that they face as they attempt to produce knowledge about humans and the world in which they live (i.e., behavioral and social science). First, an epistemological conundrum is "How do we know?" and one answer is through the use of multiple ways of knowing (using all of our senses and minds to learn) and logically speaking using both/and rather than either/or thinking. Second, sometimes there is a disconnect between what researchers think and say they do and what they actually do. A solution is better reflexivity in practice and transparency in writing. A third conundrum is: "Are the social sciences science?" A multimethod perspective says mostly yes, even though Kuhn (1962/1996) viewed social sciences as preparadigmatic. The multimethod perspective (and especially the mixed methods perspective) is comfortable with multiple paradigms and attempts to strategically capitalize on learning in multiple ways.

Hunter and Brewer also provide a set of theory-related conundrums that multimethod (and mixed methods) researchers are well equipped to navigate. The theory-related conundrums we are well prepared for are (a) identifying the unanticipated, and focusing on both theory generation and theory testing; (b) using multiple and mixed methods to help identify new foci of theoretic interest; (c) using our new methods to provide new foci of theoretic interest (e.g., network theory and analysis); and (d) clarifying concepts to reduce confusion, elucidate meaning, and increase the ontological space of study. Sharon Crasnow's chapter in this handbook (Chapter 37) provides elaboration on conceptual clarity, and she discusses causal spaces, causal pluralism, evidential pluralism, and related ideas and assumptions that usually exist in the background of research but lead to many communication confusions in science, especially between researchers operating in different paradigms. The use of different disciplines and conceptual schemes can lead to new and exciting understandings that we were not previously able to "see." As an aside, Hunter and Brewer also point out that both quantitative approaches and qualitative approaches can be used for both theory generation and testing, which is not how they are often typified in our books, which might limit their potential.

Hunter and Brewer remind readers that multimethod (and mixed methods) research can provide better answers to research questions. They remind us that we learn about reality through both converging and diverging findings, and both of these results are important in their own right. They remind us that mixed and multimethod research is helpful in enabling us to study levels of reality including the macro and the micro (and their connections), providing greater scientific knowledge and understanding. They remind us that multimethod research is strong for studying both the emic and the etic and the subjective and the objective, and they note again that both qualitative and quantitative research can address each of these. Last, Hunter and Brewer remind us how the use of multiple methods can, together, produce much stronger and better wholes.

Greene characterizes multimethod research as one of two "formally distinct, albeit neighborly, social science approaches" that has multiple strengths. One can argue that the use of qualitative and quantitative methods is a special case of multimethod research. However, that would miss what is special about mixed methods research. In the late 1980s, in its first rendition, multimethod research was situated mostly in positivism and postpositivism. In contrast, Greene tells us that mixed methods was born out of the paradigm debates and provided a solution to be worked out over ensuing years. Multimethod research today has an increased paradigmatic openness, but, as explained by Greene, mixed methods thrives on building different standpoints into its research and often includes deep contextual and multi-stakeholder standpoints so that we understand our world more deeply and fully. The goal is not just knowledge for the sake of knowledge but descriptive, predictive, and explanatory knowledge and understanding of the world through multiple voices. The idea is to add the human part to natural science, because both are better than just one. My concluding point here is that we do not need a universal and essentialist definition of mixed methods research, but working definitions are very useful to think about who we are. I like having both a narrow definition and a broad definition, with the former providing practical direction and the latter providing room for flexibility, creativity, openness, and continual growth. I am a holist, and I take an "and" approach to some definitions, where more than one can be "right" and allow study-to-study and context-to-context definitional tailoring and flexibility. Readers will find some different kinds of MMR definitions/uses by comparing the chapters of this handbook. Next I briefly look at the content of the handbook.

What Do the Authors Address in This Handbook?

One quick way to answer this question is to browse the table of contents to see some big topics and ideas and browse the index to see smaller concepts and ideas. In addition, I did some content analysis to see what words were used by our authors. Table C.1 shows the words of interest to the authors, including the word frequencies and rankings. Also see the word-cloud graphic (Figure C.1). Do you notice anything interesting? I hope this exercise will motivate readers to examine in detail some of the ideas and many concepts discussed in the handbook!

In a nutshell, most of the authors in this handbook embrace the benefits of MMR and multiple or multimethod research (i.e., they embrace the words *multiple* and especially the word *mixed*). The authors focus on data, ethics, causation, knowledge, theory, understanding, and the many benefits of "both" (and there are many "boths," as seen in the many dualisms and tensions we face in research practice). The authors take a flexible approach to mixed design, allowing many different and creative designs in MMR because of the nearly infinite number of research questions and the complex and domain-specific needs facing particular research studies.

I studied the text surrounding the word *both* in the various chapters to see what authors wanted to combine in research practice. The results of this examination are shown in Box C.1. Could you imagine if we were to examine additional words, for example, *knowledge, theory, science, combine, integrate, generalize, ethics,* and so forth? I leave that as an exercise for the reader to complete.

Table C.1 Frequencies and Ranks of Keywords in This Handbook

Word	Freq	Rank	Word	Freq	Rank
Method	4,330	1	Diversity	65	49
Mixed	2,149	2	Shared	63	50
Multiple/Multi	1,628	3	Dominant	58	51
Qualitative	1,557	4	Discover	55	52
Data	1,510	5	Language	51	53
Quantitative	1,054	6	Rigor	50	54
Design	914	7	Truth	47	55
Science	637	8	Tension	46	T57
Understand	555	9	Inductive	46	T57
Causation	485	10	Embedded	46	T57
Knowledge	462	11	Justify	44	59
Theory	442	12	Divergence	41	T60.5
Paradigm	372	13	Conflict	41	T60.5
Both	363	14	Epistemology	39	T62.5
MMR	338	15	Credibility	39	T62.5
Experiment	316	16	Feminism	37	64
Perspective	312	17	Progress	34	T65.5
Survey	267	18	Advantage	34	T65.5
Complex	266	19	Micro	33	67
Ethics	265	20	Growth	32	68
Level	247	21	Integrate	31	69
Internet	242	22	Prediction	29	T70.5
Experiment	230	23	Mono	29	T70.5
Explore	220	24	Macro	28	T72.5
Combine	211	25	Creative	28	T72.5
Measurement	202	26	Agreement	27	74
Merge	199	27	Deductive	26	75
Power	195	28	Iterative	25	T76.5
Team	190	29	Balance	25	T76.5
Transformative	170	30	Concurrent	24	78
Qual	167	31	MM	22	79
Triangulation	164	32	Longitudinal	21	T80.5

(continued)

Table C.1 Continued

Word	Freq	Rank	Word	Freq	Rank
Explain	156	33	Disadvantage	21	T80.5
Generalize	155	34	Ontology	19	T82.5
Validity	148	35	Dialectic	19	T82.5
Theory	144	36	Contradiction	17	84
Quality	135	37	Postpositivism	14	85
Network	126	38	Postmodernism	13	T87
Objective	94	39	Positivism	13	T87
Sampling	92	40	Constructivism	13	T87
Dialogue	90	41	Parallel	12	88
Meta	87	42	Sequential explanatory	11	89
Sequential	84	43	Sequential exploratory	10	T91
Pluralism	81	44	Disagreement	10	T91
Convergence	80	45	Axiology	10	T91
Pragmatism	78	46	Relativism	7	T93.5
Quan	76	47	Convergent	7	T93.5
Values	72	T48.5	Realism	6	95
Future	72	T48.5			

Note: In the ranking columns, T = tie.

Fig. C.1 Word cloud graph of keywords in this handbook.

Box C.1 Some Ideas Surrounding the Word *Both* in This Handbook

Who and what MMR should help us understand

Theory building and theory testing; macro and micro; breadth and depth of understanding; individuals and groups; material and nonmaterial culture, process and outcomes, nomothetic explanation and idiographic understanding; both (multiple)sets of experiences; Weber's *verstehen* and Durkheim's social facts in one study; emic and etic; economic and social factors; listen to researchers/practitioners both in the United States and in every country; research and policy; additive and interaction effects; objective context and qualitative experiences; both ends of the socioeconomic spectrum; doctors and patients; program effectiveness and implementation processes; women and men; both Gaza and the West Bank; individual and collective processes; evaluand and the reality that surrounds it; both sides of each border (including discovery of shared spaces and commitments); children and adults; children's lives inside and outside of the school; barriers and facilitators; subjective and objective data; factual and spiritual.

Skills needed

Need to be well versed in both qual and quan in order to conduct MMR.

Epistemology/logic

Both scientific and humanistic conceptions of knowledge are important; both mixed and multi-method studies are helpful in science; an important position is both/and such as insider and outsider perspectives; there can be a kernel of truth in conflicting truth claims; integrate inductive and deductive approaches; draw on the strengths of both qualitative and quantitative data; study both research-tested and practice-tested interventions; knowledge can be obtained from both the mixed methods literature review and the study level; both sides on issues have strengths and weaknesses; average effects and case-level effects; reject either/or and advocate both/and/multiple; center standpoint includes qual and quan thinking; every discipline has both strengths and weaknesses; there are differences both within and between quantitative and qualitative methods and perspectives; social science is social in both form and substance; trend in social science research to move beyond the purism advocated by some adherents of both experimental and narrative-interpretivist methodologies; there are arguments both for and against the movement for universal best practices; both MMR and interdisciplinarity research spring from a preoccupation with problem-solving; both small-N and large-N research have a place in scientific research.

Teams

Teams need both quantitative and qualitative methods expertise; learn from both successful and unsuccessful team efforts.

Purposes of mixing

Both triangulation and bracketing (showing difference) can be helpful; qualitative and quantitative data for the same purpose, such as development and designing the next stage of a study; qualitative and quantitative data can be used to address mediation; understand both mediation and moderation; triangulation across methods and complementarity by examining overlapping and different facets of a phenomenon.

Literature review

Mixing exists at both the study level and the literature level; need mediation and moderation mixed methods literature reviews.

Measurement

One should use both qualitative and quantitative measures.

Sampling

Frequently need to incorporate techniques from both quantitative and qualitative sampling methods; both probability and purposive sampling can be useful.

Methods

We need both qualitative and quantitative methods; both open and semistructured questions; both closed-ended and open-ended questions; structured and in-depth interviews; methods and modes (e.g., face-to-face and Internet interviews); study both physical and virtual space.

Design

We need to both generate and test hypotheses; both qual and quan can be used for discovery/exploration as well as for explanation; a mixed methods study can have both concurrent and longitudinal elements; study process and outcome and both proximal and distal impacts of programs; design can consciously occur before starting the research, or the process can occur as the research unfolds in an organic, opportunistic, and serendipitous fashion; need to explore both the small-scale qualitative understanding of experience and the larger scale notions of pattern and emergence; experimental research outcomes can be studied with both quantitative and qualitative data; explore both patterns and meanings; listen to perspectives on both sides of borders; give equal voice to different perspectives.

Values and ethical matters

We need to value both traditional scientific criteria and practice-based realities; intersectionality is both a normative and a research paradigm; we need to represent *both* the interests of funders and program developers *and* the on-the-ground experiences and meaningfulness of program participation; we should respect and value both the perspectives and expertise of the program developers and funders, as well as the lifeworlds and experiences of the children, teachers, and parents.

Research process

Both formal and informal power relations operate in research; researchers are affected by both the content of the research and their disciplinary perspectives and language; one can be both a participant and an observer; participants can react both positively and negatively to the content of research; communication needs to go in both/multiple directions among researchers, participants, audiences.

Analysis

Both qual and quan analyses can be used for exploration; analyze both data sets separately and then put them in conversation (sometimes by merging the data sets); we need to conduct both historical analyses and comparative analyses; both variable-based and case-based analysis are useful.

Quality/validity

We need to use both visibility and credibility in our research; we need both internal validity and external/transferability validity; both statistical generalization and analytic generalization are important.

Results

Integration allows for both consistencies and contradictions; both qualitative and quantitative findings are important; findings from qual and quan will sometimes both converge and diverge; both qualitative and quantitative methods are required to produce a full and complete portrait; conclusions made in evaluation encompass both an empirical aspect and a normative aspect.

Research use

Both academic and practical implications of studies are important; practical advice and scholarly insights are important; research is important in both the academy and policy; evidence bases are needed for both research and practice.

Quotes From the Handbook to Pique the Reader's Interest

In this section I provide at least one quote from each chapter that I found interesting and hope will entice readers to explore more chapters in the handbook. The quotes show some fascinating, challenging, and sometimes conflicting points, as well as creative diversity in what we believe, who we are, what we care about, and where we want to go. Together they fit my mantra for this chapter: "We are different *and* we are one."

• [Qualitatively driven] approaches have the common core assumption that social reality is constructed and that subjective meaning is a critical component of knowledge-building. (Hesse-Biber, Rodriguez, & Frost, Chapter 1)

• For many quantitatively oriented researchers, studying mediation [or causal explanation] will entail multiple rather than mixed methods, with the addition of another quantitative method. . . . Qualitative methods can also be employed to test mediation. (Mark, Chapter 2)

• Qualitative mediational tests [in explanatory research] can be conducted before, during, or after an experimental or quasi-experimental test of treatment effects. It appears that most often in practice, these two components will be implemented concurrently. (Mark, Chapter 2)

• There are probably thousands of experiments and quasi-experiments in various substantive literatures in which qualitative data are collected, coded, and analyzed quantitatively. (Mark, Chapter 2)

• A qualitative procedure can be used to measure the outcome of interest within the framework of a randomized experiment [also called a qualitative experiment]. (Mark, Chapter 2)

• Skilled researchers have long been mixing qualitative and quantitative methods. (Mark, Chapter 2)

• A new lexicon that takes us outside the boxes labeled "qualitative" and "quantitative" to explicitly as well as implicitly cross the boundaries insinuated will increase the possibilities for research and clarify our understanding and evaluation of various projects. It will hopefully also squelch the unproductive accusations of one type of research being better than another or one type of research being handmaiden to the other (Pearce, Chapter 3).

• In mixed methods, both quantitative and qualitative approaches are highly and equally valued. (Creswell, Chapter 4)

• We need to continue to provide evidence of the add-on value of mixed methods. (Creswell, Chapter 4)

• To engage in feminist research means to challenge knowledge that excludes while seeking to include—assuming that what is true for dominant groups must also be true for women and other oppressed groups. Feminists ask "new" questions. (Hesse-Biber & Griffin, Chapter 5)

• The transformative paradigm has space within it for many worlds and tolerance of the complexity of subjectivities and identities of inhabitants. (Mertens & Cram, Chapter 6)

• Many intersectionality scholars emphasize the need to explore how multiple and interacting social locations position individuals and groups in asymmetrical relation to one another, affecting their perceptions, experiences, and outcomes (Grace, 2013a; Hankivsky et al., 2012). Rather than *additive*, these are often operationalized as *multiplicative* approaches in intersectionality research. Explicit attention to interactions ensures an understanding of how constructs such as race, gender, and class are the result of social processes rather than primarily characteristics of individuals. (Hankivsky & Grace, Chapter 7)

• Intersectionality brings to the fore that differences among women and among men are often as significant, if not more so, than those between women and men (Crashaw & Smith, 2009; Varcoe, Hankivsky, & Morrow, 2007). Furthermore, intersectionality research has highlighted the contexts in which some groups of women exercise power over some groups of men (Pease, 2006), illustrating the complexity of power dynamics and the multiple, shifting social locations individuals occupy across time and space. (Hankivsky & Grace, Chapter 7)

• One way to handle the expertise challenge of MMR is to engage in team research. (Szostak, Chapter 8)

• The interdisciplinarian can ask whether the disciplinary analysis has ignored critical variables studied by other disciplines (or perhaps ignored by all) and analyze how the discipline's conclusions would change if these were included. (Szostak, Chapter 8)

• Four techniques for creating common ground [are]. . . *redefinition* [which] involves altering the way a concept is employed by different authors to achieve a common meaning. . . . *extension* [which] involves extending a theory, or the assumptions underlying a theory, so that it includes elements identified by other authors. . . . *organization* [which] involves using a map to show how different insights are related. . . . [and] *transformation* [which] is a technique for addressing opposites by placing these on a continuum. (Szostak, Chapter 8)

• Transdisciplinarians (and interdisciplinarians) also often stress the critical importance of ensuring that the voices of small and or powerless groups are heard and their insights integrated. (Szostak, Chapter 8)

• MMR researchers often refer to the existence of quantitative and qualitative paradigms. Indeed, the *methods* in *mixed methods* really means—at least for most practitioners—a much broader *mixed methodologies.* Scholars of interdisciplinarity stress instead the existence of multiple *disciplinary perspectives.* . . . But the disciplinary perspective also embraces theory to a much greater extent than this is stressed in the MMR literature. (Szostak, Chapter 8)

• Interdisciplinarians expect that there will be some kernel of truth in opposing points of view. (Szostak, Chapter 8)

• MMR designs may provide a greater flexibility and range of tools for ameliorating ethical dilemmas as they arise. (Preissle, Glover-Kudon, Rohan, Boehm, & DeGroff, Chapter 9)

• Because MMLRs [mixed methods literature reviews] include methodologically diverse findings and multiple methods, they are well suited to the goal of capturing and analyzing the breadth of evidence needed to incorporate users' contexts and perspectives into the understanding and use of interventions. (Leeman, Voils, & Sandelowski, Chapter 10)

• Multimethods can generate theory as well as test it. . . . Qualitative research can test theory. . . and quantitative research can generate new theory as well. (Hunter & Brewer, Chapter 35)

• If one has a *qual* supplementary component, it may be used simultaneously to develop case studies, exemplars, and examples in order to answer questions that are beyond the reach of the core method or for sequentially clarifying questions that have arisen from the core. (Morse, Chapter 12)

• We discuss "integration" from an alternative understanding of, and approach to, design

(Maxwell, 2012; Maxwell & Loomis, 2003). This understanding is of design as the actual relationships among all of the components of a study, not just a categorization of the study as a particular type of design. (Maxwell, Chmiel, & Rogers, Chapter 13)

• Construction of strong validity designs requires researchers to consider thoughtfully the particular criteria that are relevant and important for each study. (Collins, Chapter 14)

• In the analysis phase of MMR, the framing of the research questions becomes critical, affecting when, to what extent, and in what ways data from different methods are integrated. (Brannen & O'Connell, Chapter 15)

• [Paraphrased]: Some advanced qualitative-dominant crossover mixed analyses include correspondence analysis, qualitative comparative analysis, and micro-interlocutor analysis; some advanced quantitative-dominant crossover mixed analyses include hierarchical linear modeling, social network analysis, and Bayesian analysis; an equal-status crossover mixed analysis is spatial analyses. (Onwuegbuzie & Hitchcock, Chapter 16)

• "[Connecting analysis and presentation,] You know what you display" (Bazeley, Chapter 17, quoting Miles and Huberman, 1994)

• Despite attempts to classify them, mixed methods studies are infinitely variable in their design. Equally variable are strategies used to integrate the data, methods, analyses, and conclusions in a study. (Bazeley, Chapter 17).

• At the US NIH, general review criteria include significance, innovation, investigators, approach, and environment. The US National Science Foundation includes general review criteria of intellectual merit and broader impacts. With private funding agencies, details about the process may be less clear. (Wisdom & Fetters, Chapter 18)

• When an experienced research scholar takes the lead to establish a safe and empathic environment by *letting go* and being open to discussing his or her own limitations with respect to perspective, knowledge, and skills, the result can be a dynamic, flexible mentoring relationship with limitless imagination. (Frels, Newman, & Newman, Chapter 19)

• The methods of data selection, collection, and analysis are multiple and mixed, but the actual conduct of research is informal in the sense that anthropologists do not customarily use design recipes. (Hall & Preissle, Chapter 20)

• One solution to the problem of retaining the value of the qualitative approach without its subjugation to quantitative scientific design is to combine qualitative approaches with each other. (Frost & Shaw, Chapter 21)

• We advocate moving a step beyond the mixed methods approach to one of *participatory* mixed methods. The method we are presenting here, PMMR [participatory mixed methods research], might be seen as bringing the best of participatory action research (PAR) into the mixed methods community in the form of PMMR. (Olson & Jason, Chapter 22)

• An industry has grown up around RCTs of drugs. Yet much of what is evaluated in health is more complex than a drug and is known as a *complex intervention*. (Drabble & O'Cathain, Chapter 23)

• We have considered two frameworks [the temporal framework and the process outcome framework] for thinking about mixed methods intervention evaluations. A third and final framework is offered by ourselves and detailed in O'Cathain et al. (2013), where we considered how qualitative research was actually used in practice with RCTs rather than how it *might* be used. (Drabble & O'Cathain, Chapter 23)

• A dialectical approach places assumptions, practices, understandings, standpoints, and findings from one or more studies emanating from different paradigmatic positions in conversation with each other (Greene & Hall, 2010; Johnson, 2011). (Mertens & Tarsilla, Chapter 24)

• Commonly mentioned critiques of the Best Practices [for Mixed Methods Research in the Health Sciences] reflect broader concerns about the efforts to formalize and spread mixed methods research methods and include (a) design type is privileged above theory; (b) qualitative methods are demoted to an inferior position; (c) the discovery phase of research, where problems, questions, and hypotheses are formulated, is given short shrift; (d) designs are insufficiently chosen on the basis of research questions and instead are picked from a finite list of design types; and (e) inadequate consideration is given to incorporating new technologies, such as geosampling. . . that render multiple and mixed methods decidedly more complex than simply qualitative plus quantitative methods. (Weine, Chapter 25)

• Mixed methods studies should be encouraged because they can yield richer insights regarding both process and outcomes. (Molina-Azorin & Cameron, Chapter 26)

• [Business research is learning about the] contributions mixed methods can make to both theory building and testing and by exploring innovative ways in which to investigate business phenomena in increasingly complex contexts and environments. (Molina-Azorin & Cameron, Chapter 26)

• While it is true that development studies are characterized by considerable diversity, development evaluations have been dominated by mainstream paradigms and research questions, with methodological approaches reflecting these underlying foci. (Jones, Pereznieto, & Presler-Marshall, Chapter 27)

• The complex and nuanced findings stemming from mixed methods evaluations, exploring not only whether there has been an impact but also how and why that impact has been achieved, are increasingly seen as important to inform development policy design. (Jones, Perznieto, & Presler-Marshall, Chapter 27)

• Internet studies appear to be an area within which commonality of substantive concerns coupled with an inherent multidisciplinarity may promote awareness of, and respect for, different methodological traditions. . . . . Ethnography online thus builds on the existing mixed methods tradition of ethnography and raises it to a new level. (Hine, Chapter 28)

• We need mixed modes and methods to study a mixed-reality world. . . . .Researchers in the field have interpreted the term *mixed methods* many ways (Salmons, Chapter 29)

• The rise of emerging technologies is transforming data forms and how quickly these data forms can be collected and stored. Data are everywhere. (Remijn, Stembert, Mulder, & Choenni, Chapter 30)

• Our take on the spatial turn is more fundamental. We see its place in a mixed methods toolkit as a means to extend the generalizability of social science analyses. . . . We think that attention to location helps researchers to build "contextualized generalizations." (Fielding & Fielding, Chapter 31)

• Thus a GIS is a sophisticated database of layers of spatially related data, which may be manipulated, either statistically or qualitatively, to reveal patterns or display relationships using the cartographic aesthetic of map symbology. (Fielding & Fielding, Chapter 31)

• [Mixed methods research] lends itself to "citizen science," where the visual appeal of work with maps encourages input from volunteers. (Fielding & Fielding, Chapter 31)

• We offer two ways in which MMR might be justified on rather more prosaic epistemological grounds as a credible form of inquiry: (a) on the basis of its practical utility and (b) as facilitating innovation in scientific practice. (Schwandt & Lichty, Chapter 32)

• A *heuristic of addition* is commonly employed to facilitate this experimentation [or exploration within explanatory research]—researchers add a new data set, investigate a new variable, examine more cases, examine previous cases in more depth, and even add a new method of analysis. (Schwandt & Lichty, Chapter 32)

• Qualitative research allows for an empirically grounded construction of categories and thus represents a powerful tool to generate bridge assumptions, which transform abstract theoretical notions into empirically contentful descriptions and explanations of concrete phenomena. (Kelle, Chapter 33)

• In a sequential quantitative-qualitative design (QUAN ◊ QUAL) where "qualitative data helps explain or build upon initial quantitative results". . . Such a design is sometimes called an "explanatory design" (Creswell & Plano-Clark 2007, p. 71). This label, however, may lead to misunderstandings: explanations also play an important role both in quantitative [e.g., path analysis, structural equation modeling, experiments] and qualitative [e.g., grounded theory, ethnography] monomethod design. (Kelle, Chapter 33) [In other words, explanation is more than just research participants' reasons and awareness of causative factors in their places and lives.]

• I would argue that today, considerations regarding what levels will be mixed in a mixed inquiry study is a key design decision. (Greene, Chapter 34)

• Like multiple approaches, mixed approaches to social inquiry also aim for better understanding of complex social phenomena, but the field of mixed approaches embraces methods and methodologies from all social science families, and it has deep roots in paradigmatic debates. (Greene, Chapter 34)

• Among the primary rationales for this merger [of multiple and mixed research inquiry] is to shift the conversation away from a focus on methods and onto a reclamation of the inquiry question as the main driver of inquiry design and methodology *and* a reclamation of real-world problems or substantive theory as the primary drivers of meaningful inquiry questions. A second important rationale. . . is to emphasize—especially for mixed approaches to social inquiry—the possibilities of including not just more than one *method* in an inquiry study but also the possibilities of including more than one *methodology*, more than one *philosophical paradigm*, as well as multiple *disciplines* and *substantive theories*. (Greene, Chapter 34; italics in original)

• Mixed approaches to social inquiry go beyond multiple approaches in the opportunities they provide to *meaningfully engage with difference* precisely through the possibility of mixing at multiple levels. Mixed approaches arose largely as one "solution" to the relative intense "paradigm wars" of the 1970s and 1980s. (Greene, Chapter 34)

• Although a "theory" of mixed methodology is still under development (Greene, 2008), the concepts of distinctive purposes for mixing and distinctive dimensions of mixed designs are fairly well established. (Greene, Chapter 34)

• Incorporating different ways of knowing in the same study can yield deeper, broader, and more insightful and worthy insights than one way of knowing alone can. (Greene, Chapter 34)

• Multimethods can lead to the invention of hybridized forms such as quasi-experiments built into survey research and [much more]. Hunter & Brewer, Chapter 35)

• The multimethod spirit is one that is open to new, innovative, and at times unanticipated techniques. (Hunter & Brewer, Chapter 11)

• Unlike mixed method research, it [multimethod research] is not restricted to combining qualitative and quantitative methods but rather is open to the full variety of possible methodological combinations. (Hunter & Brewer, Chapter 11)

• Again, the beauty of a multimethod perspective is that it would not disparage one or the other but rather encourage both perspectives and combine Weber's (1949) *verstehen* with Durkheim's "social facts" in the same piece of research. (Hunter & Brewer, Chapter 35)

• The multimethod perspective. . . extends beyond different types of data and data collection to include different analytic frameworks and strategies. (Hunter & Brewer, Chapter 11)

• This conundrum is how to make sure that the impact of any best practice guideline(s) for mixed methods research enables, rather than constrains, the thinking about and subsequent development of this emerging research field. (Cheek, Chapter 36)

• If the context specificity of any form of best practice guidelines developed in relation to aspects of mixed methods research is kept to the fore, then it is possible that moving to these sets of best practices and guidelines can contribute to a vibrant, inclusive, diverse, and still rigorous field of mixed methods research. (Cheek, Chapter 36)

• A values-imbued science need not be a science that is at the whim of political commitments. (Crasnow, Chapter 37)

• *Conceptual causal pluralism* [is] the view that different understandings of causality require different approaches to evidence and support different causal inferences. (Crasnow, Chapter 37)

• Given that feminism seeks to bring about social change—a task for which reasoning to causes is presumably useful—feminist philosophers and researchers would benefit from devoting more attention to these insights. (Crasnow, Chapter 37)

• The conventional postpositivist approach—relying on inferences based largely on a correlative (input–output) relationship between an independent and a dependent variable—has become a point of departure rather than being accepted as the overarching definition of causality. (Yin, Chapter 38)

• Second, and more ambitiously, MMR can explore ways of developing hybrid practices—*integrating* or *blending* qualitative and quantitative features—that augment the preexisting methods. This second strategy could then lead to methodological advances, not just the mechanical combining of preexisting procedures. (Yin, Chapter 38)

• A preoccupation with integration in MMR may undermine social justice–related aspirations by erasing marginalized perspectives. (Freshwater & Fisher, Chapter 39)

• I want to be able influence change that re-includes people, brings them in from the margins, and re-members them within their society. Marginalization and social exclusion are issues the world over, and they have negative repercussions for health and longevity. (Cram, Chapter 40)

• The multimethod and mixed methods research (MMMR) methodology advocated in this chapter therefore draws on principles of equity (World Health Organization, 2010), social justice (International Forum for Social Development, 2006), and decolonization (Smith, 2012). (Cram, Chapter 40)

• MMMR can help us understand general patterns, but it also can help us understand a world characterized by equifinality (an outcome or end can be reached in multiple and different ways) and multifinality (the same starting point or cause can lead to different outcomes. (Burke Johnson theoretical memo)

Reflection: What Did I Learn About Myself While Coediting this Handbook?

(Please skip to "Where Do We Go Now?" if you are not interested my admittedly idiosyncratic reflections in this section.) My first insight from editing half the chapters and reading the rest is that MMR researchers are developing significant and diverse new knowledge. Second, MMR within-group heterogeneity exists, including differences in goals, values, languages, and concepts. At the same time, we have much in common, such as a commitment to data and the use of multiple sources of evidence for our claims, and improving, through research and practice, our "spaceship earth" on which we all live. Respectful and constructive difference is good; it leads to creativity and innovation, but our differences need to be balanced with some common goals and shared identity. Paradoxically, we need to be both similar and different.

I realized that I have multiple conceptual and practical identities. I have always viewed myself as a contingency theorist, believing that I want to select methods, methodologies, and paradigms based on my research questions and goals (that can change from project to project), and I take pride in rejecting reductionisms. I found my home in MMR because I am an interdisciplinarian and appreciate multiple methods, methodologies, paradigms, and conceptual systems from several disciplines. I choose to be an "equal-status or interactive" mixed methods researcher rather than qualitatively driven or quantitatively driven. The "driven approaches" are important and have their place, and the pluralist part in me respects them and sees the advantages they offer for particular groups. However, I prefer to be multiple and mixed, and nonaligned to a single approach. I have realized that I am a quantitative researcher, a qualitative researcher, *and* a mixed methods researcher.

I have learned that I am a constructivist, a post-positivist, a pragmatist, *and* a realist. I believe in complexity and context but also hope for some relatively general findings that might operate at a national level without major modification. I want researchers to learn from practitioners, rather than just pushing a top-down knowledge pipeline. I am an advocate of critical race theory, feminism, and social justice, and I am, concurrently, a believer in rigorous traditional quantitative research. I am a numbers person, a stories-and-narrative person, a pictures/visual person, and an empiricist capitalizing on multiple preceptual senses for data. I like all of the methods of data collection (and hope to see new ones developed). I like all of the methodologies (and hope to see new ones developed). I like all of the paradigms (and hope to see new ones developed). Rather than relying on a single discipline, I thrive on dialoging with concepts and voices from multiple disciplines, such as psychology, sociology, political science, history, and the natural sciences. I thrive in the phenomenological space where different ideas interact and intersect and spur new understandings. I believe in listening to what peoples and researchers in the United States say, but I am especially interested in what peoples and researchers in other nations, across each continent, have to say and contribute to world knowledge. I am biased in that I am not fond of ethnocentrism or egocentrism in researchers. I want to see knowledge developed in every country and place in the world, not just my own. I believe top-down (deductive) and bottom-up (inductive) research are both important, as well as abduction, retroduction, dialecticalism, dialogism, and fuzzy logic (i.e., I like *multiple* logics). I think participatory research is excellent, as well as traditional structured experiments and surveys. I am multiple. I am not any *one* thing or type, despite some writers' belief that they can categorize me and others—they didn't engage in member checking before making their claims. *I wish all writers would engage in member checking before making a claim about what someone else is said to believe*—this would help produce much better dialogue and growth. I hope that I cannot be labeled, unless the label is I am multiple. I strive not to be reducible to any monism, and I intellectually reject all essentialisms. I am a pluralist. *But, I know good research when I see it, and I can*

give strong reasons for my claims! I am a stickler for quantitative validities, qualitative "validities," and mixed methods validities. Tony Onwuegbuzie and I call this important idea *multiple validities,* and we wish all mixed methods writers would recognize its importance. The following is a definition from Johnson and Christensen (2014) (the concept was coined in Onwuegbuzie & Johnson, 2006):

> The last type of validity or legitimation in mixed research is **multiple validities**.
>
> This term refers to the extent to which the mixed methods researcher successfully addresses and resolves all relevant validity types, including the quantitative and qualitative validity types discussed earlier in this chapter as well as the mixed validity dimensions. In other words, *the researcher must identify and address all of the relevant validity issues facing a particular research study.* Successfully addressing the pertinent validity issues will help researchers produce the kinds of inferences and meta-inferences that should be made in mixed research. (p. 311)

I am on a mission to make sure MMR does not forget or ignore the kinds of validity that are required for good quantitative research and for good qualitative research. Mel Mark (Chapter 2) also expresses a concern that mixed methods researchers too often ignore the threats to internal validity when they make causal claims about the relationships between variables. The same concern goes for qualitative validities (see Johnson & Christensen, 2014, or, for a lecture on validity in quantitative, qualitative, and MMR, see https://www.dropbox.com/s/82gzvbg9c7u2de6/44402_11ln.doc).[2] In sum, I am multiple; I aim to be both creative and rigorous. Both are important to a defensible science.

Where Do We Go Now?

In this last section of the chapter I go into some philosophy of social science that I hope to see in the future. I start by calling for a science where all can contribute and foreshadow my strategy to identify this science. Next, I explain the political philosophy of John Rawls because it provides an analogy we can use for developing an inclusive science. Last, I end with a working list of action characteristics of an inclusive science.

Mixing and the Enterprise of Science

I want us to work together to produce an inclusive science that has a place for all of our contributions, a science that thrives on quantitative, qualitative, and mixed methods concepts, ideas, and practice. To work my way through this idea, I draw on some political/social philosophy. Using, by analogy, a strategy taken from John Rawls, I engage in a thought experiment. I specifically attempt to identify the position that most or all *reasonable* researchers/scientists/practitioners would agree to *if they did not know where they would end up*. My goal is to ponder, and motivate the reader to think about, what an inclusive science could look like. My ideas are neither comprehensive nor final but suggestive and a beginning. Please bear with me as I go through a little political philosophy to provide the background for my analogy and strategy.

John Rawls, Realistic Utopias, and My Realistic Utopia for Social/Behavioral Science

Perhaps the most prominent American political philosopher of the second half of the 20th century was John Rawls. That is because he offered a new theory of justice and liberal social contract theory for the contemporary world. Rawls's initial political theory was outlined in his 1971 book *A Theory of Justice,* where he positioned his theory as superior to classical utilitarianism. Rawls used the strategy of starting from an *original position* behind a *veil of ignorance* to determine the ideal basic structure of society and its principles of justice. When one is behind a veil of ignorance, one must act without knowing where one would end up and then determine the basic structure of society that would be just/fair to all. In this situation, each person would act *rationally*, selecting the political rules and structure of society that would give the best opportunity to all people and all groups. In his initial book, two principles of justice were constructed to regulate or underlie a structure that would be fair/just for all people and would reduce inequality that was due to lack of full economic opportunity.[3] In a shorter book titled *Justice as Fairness*, Rawls (2001) provided his final revision of his theory of justice.

In *Political Liberalism* (1993), Rawls focused on the fact of *reasonable pluralism* in democratic societies (i.e., that society is composed of people with different traditions of thought and different cultures), and he argued that these peoples can interact *reasonably* toward one another, through public reasoning. Rawls argued that it is good and fine for different peoples to have different comprehensive doctrines and that this was a fact of democracies where people have freedom of thought. He argued

that these different peoples need to have a place, a *public sphere*, where public reasoning and public justification occur. Reasonable comprehensive doctrines will respect the need for this shared sphere of reasonable discussion using public reasoning.

Rawls applied the original position and veil of ignorance to society in *Political Liberalism* to find the political conception of justice that will fit all citizens with their many differences. Comprehensive (including irreconcilable) doctrines (e.g., different religions and secular doctrines), if they are reasonable, will include a public sphere and public reasoning for the good of the society. This is called an *overlapping consensus*, but people still follow their primary or first doctrines in the larger part of their lives. Comprehensive doctrines can enter the public sphere, but public reasoning must be used in the public sphere (i.e., reasons that focus on the agreed-upon political conception of justice). Ultimately, the majority principle determines the outcome, but minority rights are always respected (i.e., groups can and should do what they value in their own lives).

In Rawls's system, public decisions will be accepted as fair and just because of the process, even if it goes against one's personal beliefs and interests. Ideas found in comprehensive doctrines can be adopted for the whole, but this would result from public reasons and would have to be logical and helpful to the whole and not just the group holding the comprehensive doctrine. *Reasonable* comprehensive doctrines will include reasons why everyone should support the public political conception of justice. Some reasons might be that the adopted position treats other peoples and their comprehensive doctrines fairly, it is democratic, and it does not impose any comprehensive doctrine on people such as in a theocracy or a dictatorship. A politically just system, Rawls believes, *is possible* and is approximated in some democracies in the world today. Rawls envisions a deliberative democracy where citizens carefully think about and discuss issues and then vote for representatives that will support their positions.

Perhaps Rawls's most relevant book for the present purpose is his *The Law of Peoples* (1999). It is here that he applied his vision (of a just political system operating in the public sphere using public reasoning) to the peoples of the world (i.e., international rather than domestic groups of people). He applies his idea to peoples and not directly to individuals at the international level. *By analogy, we can view the peoples as qualitative, quantitative, and mixed researchers operating in their respective communities of practice.* As a thought experiment, Rawls applied the strategy of the original position a second time (called the *second original position*) for representatives of peoples from across the world to produce a law of peoples that would be fair and just for all peoples (i.e., groups) in a society of peoples. The resulting principles, for the interested reader, are provided (without discussion) in footnote.[4] I provide the analogous principles (or aspects) of an inclusive science resulting from my thought experiment in the section below titled "Characteristics of an Inclusive Social/Behavioral Science: A Realistic Utopia?"

In the Law of Peoples, Rawls presents his "society of peoples" as a *realistic utopia* because it is a reasonable relationship among peoples and it is empirically possible in the world in which we live. For the purposes of this chapter, I urge the reader to start envisioning and articulating the kind of social/behavioral science that will capture our different strengths, produce basic and applied knowledge, and improve our world, with outcomes that we all desire (e.g., better health, students that learn and later contribute to society, reduction in mental illness, freedom and equal opportunity for all people, etc.). In short, I ask: *What is your vision for an inclusive and effective social/behavioral science?* Your vision will be what you believe we should work toward, and you should articulate, discuss, and share it with others. In doing so, please follow what Rawls calls the *norm of reciprocity*, which means you must truly believe that your vision is just and will be acceptable to other *reasonable* social/behavioral scientists and will be good for social/behavioral science as a practice, social institution, and system of knowledge.

Characteristics of an Inclusive Social/Behavioral Science: A Realistic Utopia?

I used Rawls's philosophical strategy of the original position to identify what a just/justifiable and inclusive scientific enterprise (capitalizing on all our strengths) might look like to reasonable people.[5] It closely fits the spirit of mixed methods research and multimethod research. I believe that most of us will agree that it is a realistic utopia (with continual revision/improvement of course) *if we did not know where we would end up in today's enterprise of science* (i.e., if you did not know you would end up being a realist, a constructivist, a postpositivist, and/or a qualitative, quantitative, and/or mixed researcher, and/or a sociologist, a psychologist, a

political scientist, a health researcher, or rich or poor, etc.). Similar to Rawls, I have constructed my initial vision through careful thinking about different scholars and practitioners and interests in social/behavioral science. It is your task to improve this list, share it with others, and revise it based on reasonable ideas that they provide.

I initially had this idea several years ago (Johnson, 2009), after spending many years listening to the arguments between qualitative and quantitative researchers (and their related paradigm and interdisciplinary debates). Everyone seemed to think that they were "right." I used to wonder why so many highly qualified scholars were arguing, and I came to believe that all of these intelligent people and scholars have an important point to make and that we should work toward a science where all could contribute.

I have dialoged with differences and used the mixed methods principles of comparison, combination, dynamic interaction of different concepts, and complementarity (along with the original position), and I have tried to describe an inclusive, big science that also is more than the sum of its parts. Although the word *science* is a contested word in some circles, I use the term expansively, somewhat similar to its original use in ancient Greece (where it meant knowledge and philosophy, and at that time philosophy included all of today's sciences). Given this broad definition, it is easy to see that there are multiple kinds of knowledge (e.g., biological, psychological, sociological, theoretical, practical) that can add to scientific knowledge and practice.

It is important to recognize that science includes values (Putnam, 2002). Sometimes we forget that epistemological goals and standards (e.g., description, explanation, prediction, generalization, parsimony, discovery, open-mindedness, neutrality, coherence, correspondence, plausibility, verstehen, understanding, authenticity, practical theory, perspicaciousness, interest in divergent standpoints) *are values*—they are epistemological values. The practice of science is based on additional moral values (e.g., conduct research ethically, nonmaleficence, beneficence). Some researchers like to recognize and emphasize, explicitly, the social/political importance and impact of their research, to improve the lives of people in their communities and our world. It is good that science has values, and heterogeneity in what we value can make us a better whole and enable us to solve more problems. It gives us a bigger and better science. I hope we will stop being "ethnocentric" with arguments that our personal view of science is the one "true" view. A defensible science includes many activities and has many purposes. I have argued in many places against reductionisms and one-way-isms (Johnson & Gray, 2010). We can be a large and inclusive extended *family*, and if we did not know where we would end up in this family, we would be more open to the many possibilities for an inclusive science.

In my use of Rawls's original position and veil of ignorance, I have identified 17 characteristics, stated with action verbs, of a science that builds on our strengths. The following is my working set that I hope is defensible to multiple social/behavioral/human science stakeholders:

1. Identify important research problems and positive possibilities and pose questions that can be investigated through any potentially useful research approach that can add to human knowledge (e.g., empirically, philosophically, historically, artistically). This attitude provides an important place for the natural sciences, social sciences, behavioral sciences, and humanistic sciences.

2. Carve conceptual and empirical reality in multiple ways that are beneficial. One way of carving reality is through what the disciplines show us (disciplinary based knowledge). Reality also can be carved into it into its subjective, intersubjective, and objective/physical/material components, and each of these is worthy of study.

3. Study humans in multiple ways through the lens of multiple academic and research disciplines *and* through the collaboration of these via interdisciplinary and transdisciplinary research.

4. Continually generate, discover, describe, and construct new knowledge, *and* test/evaluate knowledge claims.

5. Separately and interconnectively explore, reflect upon, describe, predict, and explain the natural world *and* the meaningful social and personal "worlds" and experiences of humans.

6. Explicate researcher and research values, purposes, commitments, and key background assumptions.

7. Use different methods and strategies that, separately or in combination, can produce warranted investigation of particular research questions.

8. Obtain understanding and knowledge of human processes in laboratory and in natural settings.

9. Rely on multiple sources of evidence.

10. Link explanatory research to relevant theories through theory generation and theory testing, and ongoing theory modification.

11. Describe the nomological/nomothetic (i.e., general, law-like) knowledge domain, *and* describe the idiographic, local, and contextual knowledge domains, and interconnect these to continually produce meaningful and "practical theories."

12. Study the micro, meso, and macro and interconnect these to produce a fuller and interconnected understanding of our world.

13. Replicate, translate, transfer, and document mediating and moderating processes, delineate conditions of generalization, and identify broad generalizations when possible, *and* identify complex contextual, cultural, and ecological interactions to aid in particular understanding and practical application and adaptation of social/behavioral theory.

14. Articulate, explicate, develop, and test "manualized models," practice-based models, middle-level theoretical models, meta-models (i.e., models of models), and transtheoretical and transdisciplinary models of human phenomena and interconnect these continually for scientific learning.

15. Explicate creative and formal reasoning processes (e.g., deductive, inductive, abductive, dialectical, critical theory) to help situate and warrant findings and value choices.

16. Study the world through traditional and transformative methodologies.

17. Fully disclose research activities and findings to facilitate professional, societal, and local scrutiny.

18. Continually encourage self-examination and critique and ongoing improvement of the social/behavioral/human scientific enterprise.

This social/behavioral/human science does not reduce to any single action characteristic, and it certainly does not reduce to physics (as in philosophical physicalism) even though physics, perhaps, is the most basic discipline. The full set of actions will not be relevant in a single research study but should be selected strategically, reconstructed as needed, and instantiated well from study to study. Thoughtful and defensible combinations of these ideas will be needed for each community of practice and, more specifically, each research study, to address the research purpose and research questions. Furthermore, additional action statements will need to be constructed by *you*, continually, and articulated for the projects you face. These ideas should be open and shared as we, together, develop our inclusive and interdisciplinary social/behavioral science that continually learns and includes diverse, multicultural, and constructively disputatious interactions that will result in continual development and improvement of knowledge and practice in our world.

Notes

1. I believe this handbook also builds on the epochal handbook edited by my respected colleagues Abbas Tashakkori and Charles Teddlie (2003, 2010).

2. See this link for 22 lectures on multiple research topics: http://www.sagepub.com/bjohnson5e/study/default.htm

3. There are two principles of justice that Rawls (1999) thinks would be agreed upon by rational actors in the original position behind the veil of ignorance: "the first requires equality in the assignment of basic rights and duties, while the second holds that social and economic inequalities. . . are just only if they result in compensating benefits for everyone, and in particular for the least advantaged members of society" (p. 13).

4. The principles of justice for free and democratic peoples operating in a society of peoples are: "(1) Peoples are free and independent, and their freedom and independence are to be respected by other peoples. (2) Peoples are to observe treaties and undertakings. (3) Peoples are equal and are parties to the agreements that bind them. (4) Peoples are to observe a duty of non-intervention. (5) Peoples have the right of self-defense, but no right to instigate war for reasons other than self-defense. (6) Peoples are to honor human rights. (7) Peoples are to observe certain specified restrictions in the conduct of war. (8) Peoples have a duty to assist other peoples living under unfavorable conditions that prevent their having a just or decent political social regime" (Rawls, 1999, p. 37).

5. The version presented here is a revision of the version I provided in an *Educational Researcher* article (Johnson, 2009). I have discussed and shared it with multiple audiences. I am interested in your thoughts and suggestions. Please send your improvements to me at bjohnson@southalabama.edu.

References

Brannen, J. (1992). *Mixing methods: Quantitative and qualitative research*. Aldershot, UK: Avebury.

Brewer, J., & Hunter, A. (1989). *Multimethod research: A synthesis of styles*. Newbury Park, CA: Sage.

Brewer, J., & Hunter, A. (2006). *Foundations of multimethod research: Synthesizing styles*. Newbury Park, CA: Sage.

Bryman, A. (1988). *Quantity and quality in social research*. London, England: Unwin Hyman.

Christensen, L. B., Johnson, R. B., & Turner, L. A. (2014). *Research methods, design, and analysis* (12th ed.). Boston, MA: Pearson.

Creswell, J. W. (1994). *Research design: Qualitative and quantitative approaches*. Thousand Oaks, CA: Sage.

Dewey, J. (2012). *Reconstruction in philosophy*. London, England: Forgotten Books. (Original work published in 1920)

Fielding, N. G., & Fielding, J. L. (1986). *Linking data* (Qualitative Research Methods 4). London, England: Sage.

Greene, J. C. (2007). Mixed methods in social inquiry. San Francisco, CA: Wiley.

Greene, J. C., Caracelli, V. J., & Graham, W. F. (1989). Toward a conceptual framework for mixed-method evaluation designs. *Educational Evaluation and Policy Analysis, 11*, 255–274.

James, W. (2013). *Essays in radical empiricism*. London, England: Forgotten Books. (Original work published in 1912)

Jick, T. D. (1979). Mixing qualitative and quantitative methods: Triangulation in action. *Administrative Science Quarterly, 24*, 602–611.

Johnson, R. B. (2009). Toward a more inclusive "scientific research in education." *Educational Researcher, 38*, 449–457.

Johnson, R. B. (2012). Guest editor's editorial: Dialectical pluralism and mixed research. *American Behavioral Scientist, 56*, 751–754

Johnson, R. B., & Christensen, L. B. (2014). *Educational research methods: Quantitative, qualitative, and mixed approaches* (5th ed.). Los Angeles, CA: Sage.

Johnson, R. B., & Gray, R. (2010). A history of philosophical and theoretical issues for mixed methods research. In A. Tashakkori & C. Teddlie (Eds.), *SAGE handbook of mixed methods in social & behavioral research* (2nd ed., pp. 69–94). Thousand Oaks, CA: Sage.

Johnson, R. B., McGowan, M. W., & Turner, L. A. (2010). Grounded theory in practice: Is it inherently a mixed method? *Research in the Schools, 17*(2), 65–78.

Johnson, R. B., Onwuegbuzie, A. J., Tucker, S., & Icenogle, M. L. (2014). Conducting mixed methods research using dialectical pluralism and social psychological strategies. In P. Leavy (Ed.), *The Oxford handbook of qualitative research* (pp. 557–578). New York, NY: Oxford.

Johnson, R. B., & Stefurak, T. (2013). Considering the evidence-and-credibility discussion in evaluation through the lens of dialectical pluralism. In D. Mertens & S. Hesse-Biber (Eds.), *Mixed methods and credibility of evidence in evaluation* (pp. 103–109) (New Directions for Evaluation 138). Hoboken, NJ: Wiley.

Kelle, U., & Erzberger, C. (1999). Integration qualitativer und quantitativer Methoden: me-thodologische Modelle und ihre Bedeutung für die Forschungspraxis. *Kölner Zeitschrift für Soziologie und Sozialpsychologie, 51*(3), 509–531.

Mayoh, J., & Onwuegbuzie, A. J. (2013). Toward a conceptualization of mixed methods phenomenological research. *Journal of Mixed Methods Research, 26*. doi:10.1177/1558689813505358

Morse, J. M. (1991). Approaches to qualitative-quantitative methodological triangulation. *Nursing Research, 40*, 120–123.

Onwuegbuzie, A. J., & Johnson, R. B. (2006). The "validity" issue in mixed methods research. *Research in the Schools, 13*(1), 48–63.

Putnam, H. (2002). *The collapse of the fact/value dichotomy and other essays*. Cambridge, MA: Harvard University Press.

Rawls, J. (1971). *A theory of justice*. Cambridge, MA: Belknap.

Rawls, J. (1993). *Political liberalism*. New York, NY: Columbia University Press.

Rawls, J. (1999). *The law of peoples*. Cambridge, MA: Harvard University Press.

Rawls, J. (2001). *Justice as fairness: A restatement*. Cambridge, MA: Belknap.

Rossman, G. B., & Wilson, B. (1985). Numbers and words: Combining quantitative and qualitative methods in a single large scale evaluation study. *Evaluation Review, 9,* 627–643.

Tashakkori, A., & Teddlie, C. (1998). *Mixed methodology: Combining qualitative and quantitative approaches.* Thousand Oaks, CA: Sage.

Tashakkori, A., & Teddlie, C. (Eds.). (2003). *Handbook of mixed methods in social & behavioral research.* Thousand Oaks, CA: Sage.

Tashakkori, A., & Teddlie, C. (Eds.). (2010). *SAGE handbook of mixed methods in social & behavioral research* (2nd ed.). Thousand Oaks, CA: Sage.

INDEX

Primary research reports, 176–177
Prince, S. H., 197
Principles of Geology (Lyell), 229
PRISMA guidelines, 179
Privilege and penalty, simultaneous
    experience of, 111
Probability sampling, 148–149
Problem-solving way of being, in SRM,
    338–339
Process analysis, 655
Process-outcome framework, 412–414
Process theory, 227
Process tracing, in political
    science, 655
Processual causation, 640, 643
Professional organization ethical
    guidelines, 163
Program evaluation design, threats to
    validity of, 65
Progresa-Oportunidades cash transfer
    program (Mexico), 487–488
Progressive focusing, 310
Proposals. *See* Funding for MMMR
*Protestant Ethic and Spirit of
    Capitalism, The* (Weber), 196
Psychology, MMMR in, 375–392
    combining methods within and
        across paradigms, 376–377
    development of, 382–386
    future directions for, 386–387
    importance of method in, 377–379
    mixing paradigms in, 379–382
    researcher in, 388–389
    "turn to language" in, 375–376
Publications, limitations of, 301–302
Purposeful way of being, in SRM,
    339–340
Purposive selection, 148
Putnam, R., 196

Q
Qatar National Research Fund, 316
QDA Miner software, 571, 573–575
Q Methodology, 385–386
Q2 Poverty Appraisal Conference, 489
Qualitative analyses
    common, 278–279
    comparative, 287–288, 655
    in mixing positions, 47–48
    nomothetic uses of, 50–51
    in participatory MMR, 394–395
    reflexivity in, 51–52
    thematic, 18
Qualitative data, convergent design to
    collect, 62–63
Qualitative-dominant crossover mixed
    analysis, 285–287
Qualitative Inquiry (journal), 378
Qualitatively driven approach to
    MMMR, 3–20
    case studies, 11–18
        depression discussion with
            doctors, 15–17

draw-and-tell conversations with
    children about fear, 17–18
gender inequality in the
    workplace, 14–15
rape culture, 12–13
uncovering subjugated
    knowledge, 13–14
description of, 5–6
design of, 9–11
future directions, 18–19
qualitatively driven inquiry, 4–5
reasons for, 6
selecting, 6–9
websites on, 19
Qualitatively driven mixed method
    designs, 206–222
    aim identification, 208–209
    armchair walkthrough, 210–213
    deviations and other pitfalls,
        217–220
    diagramming, 215–217
    future directions, 220–221
    literature review, 209
    overview, 206–208
    question refining, 209–210
    reflexivity and proposal diagram in
        research, 214–215
    study diagramming, 213–214
    theoretical perspective, 209
Qualitative Psychology (journal), 378
Qualitative research
    bridge assumptions generated by, 601
    difference and intersectionality in
        MMMR and, 114–117
    idiographic knowledge from, 395
    quantitative understanding bridge
        to, 653–655, 659
    representation in, 246
    with trials at different stages,
        409–414
*Qualitative Research in Accounting and
    Management*, 475
Qualitative Research in Psychology
    (journal), 378
Quality-of-life theories, 61
Quality of research, report writing
    affected by, 300
Quality & Quantity Journal, 302
Quantitative analyses
    in effectiveness reviews, 168
    measurement techniques in, 280–284
    in mixing positions, 49–50
    in participatory MMR, 394–395
Quantitative data, convergent design to
    collect, 62–63
Quantitative-dominant crossover
    mixed analysis, 285
Quantitative research
    design-related validity in, 245–246
    difference and intersectionality in
        MMMR and, 117–119
    group assignment used in, 397
    measurement validity in, 246

qualitatively driven approaches
    versus, 4–5
qualitative research bridge to,
    653–655, 659
statistical phenomena
    comprehension in, 602
Quantity and Quality in Social Research
    (Bryman), 468–469

R
Racialized students, education and,
    120–123
Ragin, C., 194, 655
Randomized experiments. *See also*
        Interventions
    assessing compliance with, 35
    for data analysis, 33–34
    for hypothesis generation, 31–32
    for interpretation and reporting, 34
    mediation piggybacked on, 35–36
    moderation study added to, 36
    overview, 30–31
    for variable conceptualization, 32–33
Rape culture, case study on, 12–13
Rashomon effect, 308
Rawls, J., 702–703
Reactions to Crime Project, Center
        for Urban Affairs and Policy
        Research, Northwestern
        University, 187
Realistic utopia for social/behavioral
        science, 702–705
Redefinition, in interdisciplinarity, 135
Reflexivity
    as axis of inquiry, 46
    importance of, xlix
    as practice challenge, xliii
    in qualitative data uses, 51–52
    in qualitatively driven mixed method
        designs, 214–215
    in qualitative research validity, 247
    in research relationships, 151–152
Reiss, J., 646
Reliability, of qualitative findings, 7
Remijn, L., 548
Renaissance mindset in SRM, 341
Reporting, ethics of, 155–157
Representation
    alternate modes of, 308
    ethics of, 155–157
    in qualitative research, 246
    scientific developments in, 66–67
Rescue Geography project, 526
Research agendas, xxxv
*Research Design: Qualitative,
    Quantitative, and Mixed Methods
    Approaches* (Creswell), 467
Research purpose and design, ethics of,
    147–149
Research quality framework examples,
    249–251
Research relationships, ethics of, 151–153
Research tensions in MMMR, xlv–xlvi